British Literature 1640–1789

Wiley Blackwell Anthologies

Editorial Advisers

Wiley Blackwell Anthologies are a series of extensive and comprehensive volumes designed to address the numerous issues raised by recent debates regarding the literary canon, value, text, context, gender, genre, and period. While providing the reader with key canonical writings in their entirety, the series is also ambitious in its coverage of hitherto marginalized texts, and flexible in the overall variety of its approaches to periods and movements. Each volume has been thoroughly researched to meet the current needs of teachers and students.

Old and Middle English *c.*890–*c.*1450: An Anthology. Third edition
edited by Elaine Treharne

Medieval Drama: An Anthology
edited by Greg Walker

Chaucer to Spenser: An Anthology of English Writing 1375–1575
edited by Derek Pearsall

Renaissance Literature: An Anthology of Poetry and Prose. Second edition
edited by John C. Hunter

Renaissance Drama: An Anthology of Plays and Entertainments. Second edition
edited by Arthur F. Kinney

Restoration Drama: An Anthology
edited by David Womersley

British Literature 1640–1789: An Anthology. Fourth edition
edited by Robert DeMaria, Jr

Romanticism: An Anthology. Fourth edition
edited by Duncan Wu

Irish Literature 1750–1900: An Anthology
edited by Julia Wright

Children's Literature: An Anthology 1801–1902
edited by Peter Hunt

Victorian Women Poets: An Anthology
edited by Angela Leighton and Margaret Reynolds

Victorian Literature: An Anthology
edited by Victor Shea and William Whitla

Modernism: An Anthology
edited by Lawrence Rainey

The Literatures of Colonial America: An Anthology
edited by Susan Castillo and Ivy T. Schweitzer

African American Literature: Volume 1, 1746–1920
edited by Gene Andrew Jarrett

African American Literature: Volume 2, 1920 to the Present
edited by Gene Andrew Jarrett

American Gothic: An Anthology from Salem Witchcraft to H. P. Lovecraft. Second edition.
edited by Charles L. Crow

Nineteenth-Century American Women Writers: An Anthology
edited by Karen L. Kilcup

Nineteenth-Century American Women Poets: An Anthology
edited by Paula Bernat Bennett

Native American Women's Writing: An Anthology of Works *c.*1800–1924
edited by Karen L. Kilcup

British Literature 1640–1789

AN ANTHOLOGY

Fourth Edition

EDITED BY ROBERT DEMARIA, JR

WILEY Blackwell

This fourth edition first published 2016

Edition history: Blackwell Publishers Ltd (1e, 1996); Blackwell Publishing Ltd (2e, 2001 and 3e, 2008)

Registered Office
John Wiley & Sons, Ltd, The Atrium, Southern Gate, Chichester, West Sussex, PO19 8SQ, UK

Editorial Offices
350 Main Street, Malden, MA 02148-5020, USA
9600 Garsington Road, Oxford, OX4 2DQ, UK
The Atrium, Southern Gate, Chichester, West Sussex, PO19 8SQ, UK

For details of our global editorial offices, for customer services, and for information about how to apply for permission to reuse the copyright material in this book please see our website at www.wiley.com/wiley-blackwell.

Library of Congress Cataloging-in-Publication data is available for this title

Paperback 9781118952481

A catalogue record for this book is available from the British Library.

Cover image: Woman Reading a Book, by Jean-Frédéric Schall / Private Collection / Photo © Rafael Valls Gallery, London / Bridgeman Images

Set in 10.5/12pt Dante by SPi Global, Pondicherry, India

Contents

List of Authors

Chronology

Date	Literary event	Historical event
1638	John Milton, *Lycidas*	
1640	John Donne, *LXXX Sermons*	Long Parliament assembled Archbishop Laud and the Earl of Strafford impeached
1641	Milton, *Of Reformation*	Strafford executed
1642		First English Civil War begins London theaters closed
1643	Milton, *The Doctrine and Discipline of Divorce*	
1644	Milton, *Areopagitica*	
1645		Archbishop Laud executed
1646	Milton, *Poems* (dated 1645)	Charles I surrenders at Southwell after falling out of favor End of the first English Civil War
1647	Abraham Cowley, *The Mistress*	
1648	Robert Herrick, *Hesperides*	Second English Civil War begins Oliver Cromwell defeats Scots at Preston End of the Thirty Years' War
1649	Charles I, *Eikon Basilike* Richard Lovelace, *Lucasta* Milton, *Eikonoklastes*	Charles I tried and executed Commonwealth proclaimed Monarchy and the House of Lords abolished Cromwell invades Ireland
1650	Anne Bradstreet, *The Tenth Muse* Abiezer Coppe, *A Fiery Flying Roll* Andrew Marvell, *An Horatian Ode upon Cromwell's Return from Ireland* composed	Cromwell defeats Scots at Dunbar

Date	Literary event	Historical event
1651	Thomas Hobbes, *Leviathan*	Charles II crowned king of the Scots Charles II invades England, is defeated at Worcester, and flees to France
1652	Correspondence between Dorothy Osborne and her future husband William Temple begins	
1653	Margaret Cavendish, *Poems and Fancies*	A new parliament is nominated Protectorate established Cromwell becomes Lord Protector
1654	Isaac Walton, *The Compleat Angler*	
1655	Henry Vaughan, *Silex Scintillans* (second edition)	Parliament is dissolved after attempting to reduce the army English capture Jamaica
1656	John Reeve and Lodowicke Muggleton, *A Divine Looking Glass*	
1657		Cromwell is offered and declines the crown
1658	Richard Allestree, *The Whole Duty of Man* Edward Phillips, *The New World of English Words*	Death of Oliver Cromwell Richard Cromwell succeeds as Lord Protector
1659		Collapse of the Protectorate
1660	Samuel Pepys begins his diary Robert Boyle, *New Experiments* John Dryden, *Astraea Redux* Milton, *Readie and Easy Way*	End of the Commonwealth Charles II begins his reign
1662		Act of Uniformity requires English to accept the book of Common Prayer
1663	William Shakespeare, Third Folio	
1664	Katherine Philips, *Poems*	
1665		The Great Plague
1666	John Bunyan, *Grace Abounding*	The Great Fire of London
1667	Milton, *Paradise Lost* Dryden, *Annus Mirabilis*	
1668	Dryden, *Of Dramatic Poesy*	England takes control of Bombay, India
1671	Milton, *Paradise Regained*	
1672	George Villiers, *The Rehearsal*	Declaration of Indulgence proffers religious freedom
1673		Parliament passes the Test Act, precluding Roman Catholics from holding public office
1674	Milton, *Paradise Lost* (second edition)	
1675	William Wycherley, *The Country-Wife*	

Date	Literary event	Historical event
1676	Dryden, *Aureng-Zebe*	Charles II signs secret treaty with Louis XIV
1677	Aphra Behn, *The Rover*	
1678	Bunyan, *Pilgrim's Progress*	Popish Plot to kill Charles II and crown the Duke of York is exposed
1679	Dryden, *All for Love* "Ephelia," *Female Poems* John Wilmot, Second Earl of Rochester, *Satyr against Reason and Mankind* Lucy Hutchinson, *Order and Disorder*	Parliament passes the Habeas Corpus Act
1680	Robert Filmer, *Patriarcha* Rochester, *Poems*	
1681	Dryden, *Absalom and Achitophel*	Exclusion Bill defeated
1682	Dryden, *Mac Flecknoe* published	
1684	Behn, *Poems*	
1685		Death of Charles II Execution of Duke of Monmouth James II begins his reign
1686	Sarah Fyge Egerton, *The Female Advocate*	Isaac Newton proposes his laws of motion and theory of gravity
1687	Dryden, *The Hind and the Panther*	James II issues Declaration of Indulgence, suspending the Test Act and allowing freedom of worship
1688	Behn, *Oroonoko: or, the Royal Slave. A True History* Jane Barker, *Poetical Recreations*	William of Orange marches on London, causing James II to flee Beginning of the Glorious Revolution
1689	Anne Wharton, *Christian Love*	Parliament formulates Declaration of Rights William and Mary accept the Declaration and the crown William III and Mary II begin their reign
1690	John Locke, *An Essay Concerning Human Understanding* and *Two Treatises of Government*	Battle of the Boyne
1691	John Dunton, *Athenian Gazette*	
1694	Mary Astell, *A Serious Proposal* George Fox, *Journal*	
1695	William Congreve, *Love for Love* Richard Blackmore, *Prince Arthur*	
1696	Thomas Southerne, *Oroonoko*	

Date	Literary event	Historical event
1697	Daniel Defoe, *An Essay upon Projects*	Treaty of Ryswick
	Dryden, *The Works of Virgil*	
1698	Edward Ward, *London Spy*	
	Mary Pix, *Queen Catharine*	
1700	Congreve, *The Way of the World*	
	Dryden, *Fables Ancient and Modern*	
1701	Mary Chudleigh, *The Ladies Defence*	Grand Alliance formed
1702	Defoe, *The Shortest-Way with the Dissenters*	Death of William III
		Queen Anne begins her reign
		England declares war on France
1703	Nicholas Rowe, *The Fair Penitent*	
1704	Jonathan Swift, *A Tale of a Tub*	Duke of Marlborough victorious at Blenheim
	John Dennis, *The Grounds of Criticism in Poetry*	
1705	Susanna Centlivre, *The Gamester*	
1706	George Farquhar, *The Recruiting Officer*	Marlborough defeats French at Ramillies
1707	Farquhar, *The Beaux Stratagem*	Act of Union joining England and Scotland
1708	Isaac Watts, *Hymns*	Abortive invasion by Pretender
1709	Delarivier Manley, *New Atalantis* and *The Female Tatler*	
	Richard Steele et al., *The Tatler*	
1710	Swift, *The Examiner*	Tories win general election
1711	Alexander Pope, *An Essay on Criticism*	Inception of South Sea Company
1712	Pope, *The Rape of the Lock* in two cantos	
1713	Joseph Addison, *Cato*	Treaty of Utrecht
	Anne Kingsmill Finch, *Miscellany Poems*	
1714	Pope, *The Rape of the Lock* in five cantos	Death of Queen Anne
	Bernard Mandeville, *The Fable of the Bees*	George I begins his reign
1715	Pope, Homer's *Iliad*, vol. 1	Jacobite Rebellion in Scotland
1716	John Gay, *Trivia*	Whigs win general election
	Lady Mary Wortley Montagu, *Court Poems*	
	Mary Molesworth Monck, *Marinda*	
1718	Centlivre, *A Bold Stroke for a Wife*	Quadruple Alliance
	Allan Ramsay, *Scots Songs*	
1719	Defoe, *Robinson Crusoe*	
	Matthew Prior, *Poems on Several Occasions*	
1720		South Sea Bubble
1721	Nathan Bailey, *Universal Etymological Dictionary*	

Date	Literary event	Historical event
1722	Defoe, *Moll Flanders* and *Journal of the Plague Year*	
1723		George I visits Hanover
1724	Swift, *Drapier's Letters* Eliza Fowler Haywood, *Fantomina*	
1725	Pope's edition of *The Works of Shakespeare*	George I in Hanover for seven months
1726	Swift, *Gulliver's Travels*	
1727	James Thomson, *Winter* Gay, *Fables*	Death of George I George II begins his reign
1728	Ephraim Chambers, *Cyclopaedia* John Gay, *The Beggar's Opera*	
1729	Pope, *The Dunciad* Swift, *A Modest Proposal*	
1730	Pope, *The Dunciad Variorum* Stephen Duck, *Poems on Several Subjects*	
1731	*Gentleman's Magazine*, vol. 1	
1732		Georgia founded
1733	Pope, *An Essay on Man*	Excise crisis
1734	Mary Barber, *Poems on Several Occasions* George Sale (trans.), *Koran*	
1735	Pope, Epistle to *Arbuthnot* and *Epistle to a Lady*	
1737		Death of Queen Caroline
1738	Elizabeth Carter, *Poems Upon Particular Occasions* Samuel Johnson, *London*	
1739	Mary Collier, *The Woman's Labour*	War of Jenkins' Ear
1740	Samuel Richardson, *Pamela*	War of Austrian Succession
1741	David Hume, *Essays Moral and Political*	
1742	Pope, *The New Dunciad* Henry Fielding, *Joseph Andrews* Edward Young, *Night-Thoughts*	Robert Walpole resigns as prime minister
1744	John Armstrong, *The Art of Preserving Health*	Declaration of war with France
1745	Johnson, *Shakespeare Proposals*	Second Jacobite Rebellion
1746	William Collins, *Odes on Several Descriptive and Allegoric Subjects*	Battle of Culloden
1747	Johnson, *The Plan of a Dictionary* Richardson, *Clarissa*	
1748	Hume, *An Enquiry Concerning Human Understanding* Mary Leapor, *Poems on Several Occasions*	Treaty of Aix-la-Chapelle

Date	Literary event	Historical event
1749	Johnson, *The Vanity of Human Wishes* Fielding, *Tom Jones*	
1750	Johnson, *The Rambler* Mary Jones, *Miscellanies in Prose and Verse*	London earthquake
1751	Thomas Gray, *An Elegy Wrote in a Country Church Yard*	Death of Prince Frederick
1752	Charlotte Lennox, *The Female Quixote*	
1753	Jane Collier, *The Art of Tormenting*	British Museum founded
1755	Richardson, *Charles Grandison* Johnson, *A Dictionary of the English Language*	
1756		Seven Years' War begins
1757	Edmund Burke, *A Philosophical Inquiry into the Origin of our Ideas of the Sublime and the Beautiful*	
1759	Oliver Goldsmith, *The Bee* Johnson, *Rasselas*	Capture of Quebec
1760		Death of George II George III begins his reign
1761	Laurence Sterne, *Tristram Shandy*, vol. 1	Resignation of William Pitt as prime minister
1762	James Macpherson, *Fingal*	British capture Grenada and West Indies from France, and Cuba and Manila from Spain
1763	Montagu, *Travels* Christopher Smart, *A Song to David*	Peace of Paris
1764	Horace Walpole, *The Castle of Otranto*	
1765	Johnson (ed.), *The Plays of Shakespeare*	
1766	Goldsmith, *The Vicar of Wakefield*	
1768	*Encyclopaedia Britannica* James Boswell, *An Account of Corsica*	Royal Academy founded
1769	Joshua Reynolds, first *Discourse*	Shakespeare Jubilee
1770	Goldsmith, *The Deserted Village*	Boston Massacre James Hargreaves's spinning jenny patented
1772	Henry Mackenzie, *The Man of Feeling*	Financial crash
1773	Anna Laetitia Aiken Barbauld, *Poems*	Boston Tea Party
1774	Lord Chesterfield, *Letters to his Son* Thomas Warton, *History of English Poetry*	Copyright law settled by Lords
1775	Richard Brinsley Sheridan, *The Rivals*	American War of Independence begins
1776	Thomas Paine, *Common Sense* Charles Burney, *History of Music* Edward Gibbon, *Decline and Fall*, vol. 1	American Declaration of Independence
1777	Burke, *Letter on America*	

Date	Literary event	Historical event
1778	Thomas Chatterton, *Miscellanies* Frances Burney (later d'Arblay), *Evelina*	War with France
1779	*Olney Hymns*	War with Spain
1780	Sheridan, *School for Scandal* published	Gordon riots in London
1781	Gibbon, *Decline and Fall*, vols. 2–3	
1782	Ignatius Sancho, *Letters*	
1783	William Blake, *Poetical Sketches* George Crabbe, *The Village*	Peace of Versailles
1784	James Cook, *Voyage to the Pacific Ocean*	
1785	William Cowper, *The Task* Ann Cromartie Yearsley, *Poems*	
1786	Hester Lynch Thrale Piozzi, *Anecdotes of the Late Samuel Johnson* Robert Burns, *Poems, Chiefly in the Scottish Dialect*	
1787	Mary Wollstonecraft, *Thoughts on the Education of Daughters*	United States Constitution is ratified Committee for the Abolition of the Slave Trade is founded in England
1788	Hannah More, *Slavery* Charlotte Smith, *Emmeline*	First English settlers arrive in Australia
1789	Blake, *Songs of Innocence* Olaudah Equiano, *The Interesting Narrative of the Life of Olaudah Equiano*	French Revolution begins with the fall of the Bastille
1790	Burke, *Reflections on the Revolution in France* Wollstonecraft, *A Vindication of the Rights of Men*	
1791	Paine, *The Rights of Man*	

Thematic Table of Contents

Authorship

Ballads and Songs

Biography and Autobiography

Children

City Life (see London)

Country Life

The Devil

Elegy

Friendship and Same-Sex Love

Gender and Domesticity (see also Friendship and Same-Sex Love)

Literary Criticism (see also Aesthetics; Authorship)

London

Nation-Building see Affairs of State

Orientalism

Paradise and the Golden Age

Pastoral (see also Country Life; Paradise and the Golden Age)

Race and Slavery

Sex and Erotic Literature

Work and Workers

Introduction

One of the most instructive facts about the period of British literature often referred to as "the eighteenth century" is that it is hard to name and impossible to confine to settled boundaries. It is not only that the period contains such a variety of works, some of them built on principles entirely antagonistic to each other; it is also that many of the great writers of the period were engaged in exploding myths or revealing the specious falsehood hidden under a popular name or tag. One of the most enduring exhortations of the eighteenth century is, as Samuel Johnson put it: "Clear your mind of cant!" By "cant" he meant primarily the jargon of any school of thought or any trade or profession, but, by extension, he also meant the language of uncritically received assumptions. Cant about the eighteenth century abounds: it was a period in which reason dominated the imagination; men dominated women in literature as well as in all other aspects of life; the upper class dominated all the other classes and kept them out of sight; didacticism was the predominant literary mode; and so on. These are very partial truths, and the diversity and variety of the present anthology should do something to clear out such cant, but the problem begins with naming the period itself.

The period of literary history in Britain from 1660 to 1798 used to be called the "long eighteenth century." In pushing the earlier date back twenty years, while curtailing the later by nine, the present anthology seems to suggest an even longer eighteenth century, one that illogically occupies only twenty-nine years less of the seventeenth than of the eighteenth century. It must be confessed from the outset, then, that this is not an anthology of eighteenth-century British literature; instead, it covers a broader period in which there is some semblance of coherence in literary sensibility, though within that period there are several identifiable shifts and many changes in literary thinking, as well as in the overall economy of writers, publishers, and readers. The period 1640–1789 is bounded at either end by a political event of great importance: the beginning (arguably) of the Civil War in England and the start of the French Revolution. Each of these events had wide-ranging effects on British culture, including, of course, its literary culture. Although this way of bounding the period runs roughshod over the traditional division of history into centuries, it has several advantages over that illogical division and over the old "long eighteenth century."

No epoch-making event occurred in 1700 or 1800 that inaugurated a new century. On the other hand, 1660 did contain such an epoch-making event, the restoration of the Stuart monarchy in the person of Charles II, who had been in exile on the Continent since shortly after his "miraculous" escape from the Battle of Worcester in 1651. When he returned everything changed – the court, foreign policy, the religion, and the situation of writers in London and the rest of Britain. The year 1798 contained an epoch-making event of an entirely different kind – the publication of a book of poetry by William Wordsworth and Samuel Taylor Coleridge called *Lyrical Ballads*. Not only is this a different sort of event than the restoration, its epoch-making value has repeatedly been challenged in the last forty or fifty years. The year 1798 is no longer seen as the beginning of the Romantic period; its boundaries have been pushed back well into the eighteenth century. Burke's essay *A Philosophical Inquiry into the Origin of our Ideas of the Sublime and the Beautiful* (1757) is often seen as a Romantic statement, for example, and some theorists of Romanticism would like to put at its head James Thomson, who was born in 1700 and published his very important poem *Winter* in 1726. Hence, the date 1798 as a bookend to 1660 is illogical, because it celebrates not only a different sort of event but one that unfolded on a different scale of time.

Recent anthologies of British Romantics, including Duncan Wu's excellent volume in the Blackwell series, have escaped the problem of dating by being about Romanticism, rather than the Romantic Period. Although the old rubric continues to exert an effect in fact, if not in name, the new one gives the anthologist scope to search both before and after the old dates of, say, 1798–1830. Characteristically, no such easy, nominal solution is as available and as defensible for the eighteenth century – short, long, or longer. The inadequacy of the old tags for the eighteenth century – Classicism or the Age of Reason – has been known for a long time. The present anthology, in fact, rides a tide of discoveries about the eighteenth century that has overwhelmed such categories. A third possibility is the "Age of Experience." This tag is also inadequate, of course, but in my view it offers us a better "stay against confusion" (in Robert Frost's phrase) than the others. As the important late-eighteenth-century writer William Blake suggested in his *Songs of Innocence and of Experience*, there is an antagonism between the untested, innocent ideal and the lived experience, though both are essential to humanity. The period represented in the present anthology is bounded by a pair of political events in which untested political ideals won out, dramatically though temporarily, against the authority of the ages. The "Long Parliament" convened in 1640 was strong enough by 1641 to execute one of King Charles I's closest advisors and friends; in 1649 it was able to order the execution of the monarch himself. The dramatic happenings of July 1789 in France culminated more rapidly in the execution of the king and many of his supporters. Both events influenced literature, as well as every other aspect of culture. The Civil War divided the country into Puritans, or Roundheads, and Royalists, and each group had literary as well as political and personal habits that distinguished it. The French Revolution was naturally not as important in Britain as the Civil War, but it was felt deeply, pondered, discussed, and written about. It too tended to divide the country into cultural and social camps, much as the Civil War had. For some it confirmed the fears aroused by the civic disorder of the Gordon riots of 1780, which led to the establishment for the first time of a regular police force in London. For others, it was a continuation of the spirit of democracy that had inspired the Revolution in England in 1688–9, the "Glorious" or "Bloodless" Revolution in which Parliament removed King James II from the throne and replaced him with a daughter of his first marriage, Mary, and her husband William of Orange. As in the Civil War, it seemed for a while as though there were two kinds of people in Britain – those for and those against the insurgents. Those who were against them, I wish to argue, were in the mainstream of literary life in Britain in the period between the two wars, and they were advocates of *experience* rather than *ideas*.

Why should the advocates of the status quo, and the age itself, be classed under the rubric of *experience*? Monarchy, it will be argued, is based on ideals every bit as much as

Democracy is. This is true, but by the seventeenth century monarchy was an ideal that had endured centuries of negotiation and compromise, inadequate as the result may have seemed to many people living under the rule of kings at that time. Some of the writing of the period obviously reflects that sense of dissatisfaction. However, the majority of the writing in the period reflects a skeptical attitude to new ideas and, in general, to untested, speculative ideals. Many of the writers of the eighteenth century are better known for their critiques of existing ideas than for presenting new ideas of their own. The great targets of attack throughout this contentious age were innovators of various kinds, and they were invariably seen as people who confuse ideas and reality. Jonathan Swift's satires on scientific and social inventors (or projectors) are perhaps the most famous attacks of this kind, but Samuel Johnson was equally hard on the "aeronautical projector" and the many unrealistic philosophers who offer solutions to the great questions of life in *Rasselas*. At the very end of the period, Burke attacked British apologists for the French Revolution and the "rights of man" as people who were willing to put their abstract ideas ahead of the real state of real people in the world. Burke's most trenchant opponent, Mary Wollstonecraft, objects to Burke's own fictionalizing and his own willingness to ignore the real state of suffering endured by the millions of real people oppressed by the kings, queens, and bishops, whose reality Burke glorified. In defending the Revolution by attacking Burke's idealism, however, Wollstonecraft shows her affinity with eighteenth-century mainstream thinking even as she sets herself up in opposition to one of its heroes.

The same might be said of the most important writer in the first part of the period covered in this anthology. Although Milton had been a "rebel" himself in the Civil War, his villains in *Paradise Lost* (1667) are also innovators with big ideas. The fact is that Milton did not see himself as a rebel. Milton's God and the status quo he upholds are images of the world seen from the point of view of the Puritans' brief period of empowerment (c.1640–60). Milton's rebel angels are the Royalists and High Churchmen of the Stuart monarchy, whom he saw as departing from the true, God-given, Puritan path. For many readers, this is so counterintuitive, and Milton's connection with Cromwell makes him so unmistakably a rebel, that they see the rebel angels as the true heroes of *Paradise Lost*. But, however we feel about Milton's God or his Satan, the poem undeniably delivers us into a world of experience and bars the way to the ideal, pastoral world of Eden. Moreover, Milton tells us that this new world of experience is ultimately better than Eden, even though living in it is a lot more work. Here men and women must work out the details of marriage and family life; men must labor; and everyone has to work out his or her own salvation. In addition, speech is more complicated in the world of experience; there is, for example, much more irony in language. The perfect two people of Eden become the much more numerous but much more imperfect people of history. It is an oversimplification, of course, but in a way *Paradise Lost* is the epic of experience, and it ushers in an age devoted to working out the ramifications of a preference for experience. Novels, examples of a fledgling genre in the eighteenth century, and many plays are devoted to the task. Innocence and romantic ideals are turned aside, for example, in works as diverse as Eliza Haywood's novel of masquerade, *Fantomina*, and Congreve's urbane and witty comedy of experience, *The Way of the World*. A wonderful marriage between two beautiful people comes about in this play, but it is decidedly contrived in a postlapsarian world, in which knowledge and experience are the keys to success. Appropriately, the plot turns finally on one character's knowledge of a prior document involved in complex legal machinations.

Most literary constructions of the Commonwealth rule did not achieve the prominence of *Paradise Lost*; Marvell's excellent "Horatian Ode upon Cromwell's Return from Ireland," for example, was expunged from the books and was not circulated in print until after the next revolution, the Glorious Revolution of 1688–9. *Paradise Lost*, however, was immediately felt to be great literature, so great that it transcended political commitments and quickly became the most frequently cited poem in English for writers of almost all political persuasions. Partly out of helplessness before its grandeur, partly in reaction to its splendor, and partly in obedience to its message, poets began writing more about history, more about experience, and more than ever before about the ironies inherent in the difference between the old ideals and the new real world in which they lived. The best of epic poetry was ironic; the historical mode was as high as poets dared to soar, and even then they rarely did so without irony; and there was a renewed awareness that the best of art had been discovered by giants before the flood: ancients – especially Homer, Virgil, Horace, and Juvenal – and giant Englishmen – especially Shakespeare and Milton.

But if the modern writers lacked greatness, they enjoyed numerical superiority. In addition to releasing a flood of new ideas, the English Civil War engendered new races of authors and new genres of writing. The increased volume of pamphlets, newsbooks, and other ephemera eclipsed the relatively small production of such works in earlier times. A hunger for news expanded the reading public, especially among the middle class and, later, among workers. The social range of those doing the writing also increased vastly, and print was resoundingly confirmed as the supreme medium for the dissemination of literature. Earlier in the seventeenth century manuscript circulation of poetry was still very highly respected, and publication was regarded as somewhat vulgar. Ben Jonson carefully shepherded his works through the press, but he was unusual for his time. Such famous writers as Donne and Herbert favored manuscript circulation, and this preference lived on well into the seventeenth century. Rochester authorized the publication of only a few of his poems, for example, and many, many poets claimed that they submitted to publication only because they learned that manuscripts of their work had been obtained by piratical booksellers about to make a profit on their efforts. The percentage of such claims that were disingenuous steadily increased, however, and by the eighteenth century proper more writers were willing to be frank about their wish to appear in print. Still, it was not common for writers to put their names on the title pages of their works, and part of the reason for this was fidelity to the older idea of authorship in which the writer was separate from the vulgar world of publication. Even Samuel Johnson, who was frank about the fact that he published for a living, did not put his name on a published work until 1749, when he was forty years old.

By mid-century the author's passion for publication had survived so many lampoons that it was almost universally accepted. Partly because the medium of print sought broader avenues of circulation than the coteries that exchanged manuscripts among themselves, new parts of society were heard from in the new medium: women published in much greater numbers in the eighteenth century than ever before, and some inroads were made by working people. Subscription publication, which began in the mid-seventeenth century, had something to do with this: the capital for the publication of these projects was supplied by the public, who bought books before the first printing and enjoyed the privilege of seeing their names on the list of subscribers in the preliminary matter of the book. Such lists replaced, or at least competed with, dedications to wealthy individuals who supported publication in the old regime of literary production. Like readers and writers, the patrons of literature grew numerically and became more widely distributed across the social spectrum.

The democratization of literature did not occur without resistance, however. A great deal of the most famous literature in the early eighteenth century satirizes writers, new modes of writing, and print itself. Highly successful writers like Dryden and Pope were constantly at war with the lesser writers who, in their view, tended to lessen the prestige of the guild or bring down the dignity of the new print-world class of authors. (Of course, there were counterattacks, and Dryden in particular had to defend himself both against new-world hacks and old-world, aristocratic writers.) Many authors made anxious attempts to link themselves with classical and earlier English writers and to distinguish themselves from the "common herd" of their contemporaries. Pope's grandest and most laborious work, *The Dunciad*, is designed largely to distance himself from what he describes as the countless and culturally unwashed mass of writers emerging in his time. For Pope, as for Dryden, there had to be an aristocracy of writers based on skill rather than class. Swift carried his version of elitism even further than Pope and found that all modern writing, most writing of any age, and nearly all of what passes for thought is a stupendous waste of time. Swift's *Tale of a Tub* should have done more than any book in history to discourage publication, but Swift was wise, or cynical, enough to know that not even his *Tub* could long distract the Leviathan of society from its follies.

* * *

Though they may never have kept a single author from publishing, writers like Pope and Swift seem to have had an immense influence on the critics and scholars who specialize in the eighteenth century. Perhaps this is, ironically, because they are particularly critical of scholars and critics and make even more fun of them than of other poets and prose writers. Whatever the reason, and nineteenth-century attitudes may have more to do with it than Pope and Swift, the canon of eighteenth-century works was for a long time intensively focused on a few writers selected as supreme. Arguably, students of the eighteenth century imbibed the period's high standards for elegance and other forms of aesthetic excellence in writing, and they could be satisfied with nothing much less than the best. This is a specious fiction, and there may be some truth in it, but it is also true that elements of class awareness, snobbery, and politics played into the construction of these aesthetic standards. Moreover, whatever the validity of the aesthetic standards, the feeling that they had to be upheld through the exclusion and derision of many writers was as much an expression of anxiety as of taste or judgment.

In the past four decades the focus on the central figures of the eighteenth century has diminished somewhat, and attention has shifted to the so-called margins. For quite some time now there has been a desire, as well as a demand, to hear other voices than those that have traditionally spoken for the century and a half represented in this anthology. The strongest, most welcome, and most productive desire has been to hear the voices of women: the reappearance of women writers on the scene has made for the greatest change in eighteenth-century studies over the last forty years. In 1969, a fine new anthology of the literature of the "long eighteenth century" appeared, edited by three excellent scholars. But of the three thousand columns in this large book, with a wide, double-column page format, a total of four were occupied by the writings of women. What's more, as far as I know, few people objected or were even surprised. That book is a monument to a certain kind of fine taste and mature judgment, with very large selections from Dryden, Pope, Swift, and Johnson, but also with selections from numerous lesser figures. There are over ninety in the supporting cast, but their inferior position is carefully marked. The majority of writers, including the three women, do not get introductions and so are clearly relegated to a farther circle of literary society. In the present anthology over a third of the writers present are women; they contribute about twenty percent of the writing, and they are all introduced. The difference by no means represents an innovation of my own; it merely reflects important and very welcome changes in the study and teaching of this period that have occurred over the last forty years and are continuing as new editions of women's writing and new biographies of women writers continue to appear. In revising the headnotes for the successive editions of this anthology, I most often had to make changes because new scholarly work about women writers had made my earlier information obsolete.

The rediscovery of the women writers of the period is the most important development in eighteenth-century studies in the last forty years, but it is not the only one. The literature of the English Civil War has undergone long-overdue reconsideration and become a period of study in its own right. At the other end of the chronology, the roots of Romanticism have been very widely explored and found to lie deep in the eighteenth century, as early as the poems of William Collins, or James Thomson, or even those of Richard Savage, who was born in the seventeenth century. Along with a recognition of Romantic elements in eighteenth-century writing has come a richer understanding of related movements, such as the cult of sensibility, or sensitivity, which grew throughout the eighteenth century proper. Furthermore, although it was once considered immune to theory and a bastion of old-fashioned literary history, the eighteenth century has recently become a focal point for various kinds of theorists: feminist literary critics, new historicists, sociologists of the text, Bakhtinian analysts of culture, and queer theorists, to name just a few. The study of the eighteenth century has provided interesting material for all of these approaches, and, in turn, it has become essential to their full development as methods of studying British literature.

With all of these changes few things have remained exactly as they were. Milton is still the most important poet in the seventeenth century (and perhaps any century), but he is no longer located among the Elizabethans, as he was in the old days of E. M. W. Tillyard's *Elizabethan World Picture* (1943). Instead, Milton has been resituated in the time period in which he wrote his most important work, *Paradise Lost* (1667), and the thematic emphases of his work have been revised. Scholars have known for a long time that the importance of Milton to the eighteenth century can hardly be overestimated. A renewed respect for chronology reveals that the obvious reason for this is that Milton is part of the eighteenth century: he wrote his most important literary works after the Restoration, within the bounds of the long century. The presence of *Paradise Lost* makes almost everything that comes after it in the anthology more intelligible, even though I have reduced the poem to four of the twelve books that appeared in the second edition of 1674. With advice from Miltonists, I selected books I–II, IV and IX. I–II are obvious choices as they include the somewhat separate story of the devils in Hell and the most famous statement of the poem's theme. Book IX includes the climax of the poem and also stands alone, to a degree, making a short classical tragedy in itself. Book IV was chosen for more interesting reasons; it shows Adam and Eve in Eden and provides the fullest expression of the domestic themes in the poem. Its importance in contemporary appreciation of the poem reflects the work of feminist critics and others interested in the history of family life. These critics and historians have revealed the strength of Milton's interest in domestic, sexual economy. He is therefore as important to Samuel Richardson, a novelist of domestic life, as he is to votaries of the sublime like Thomson and Collins.

Although it is always more desirable to read any literary work in its entirety, including all of *Paradise Lost* in the first edition of this anthology meant that some other writers were even more severely squeezed for space than they are now. Most important among them was Dryden, who in the mid-1990s seemed to be shrinking on college curricula all over America, if not in Britain. The undeniably conscious artifice of his verse, as well as its responsiveness to political occasions no longer well understood, had long made Dryden a tough sell among American students. Lately, however, there has been a reaction in favor of Dryden. The single work that teachers most often asked for in the second edition of this anthology was Dryden's *Absalom and Achitophel*. By reducing *Paradise Lost* to four of its twelve books, I made space for Dryden's important poem about a crisis in the reign of Charles II. Thanks in part to changing critical perspectives, the provocative sensuality of Dryden's verse is now more visible than it has been for years and an engagement in contemporary politics now seems more commonplace among authors of all periods.

Dryden is still not as conspicuous in this anthology as he was in the great anthologies of the twentieth century. He has had to compete with Milton (twenty-three years his senior) in the older generation and in his own with Aphra Behn (about nine years his junior). Behn is well represented here by her novel *Oroonoko*, her popular play *The Rover*, and a selection of her poetry. In real life, Behn competed with Dryden for the Royalist theater audiences of their time, but was successfully lampooned into disrepute by Pope and his allies in the following generation. Recent scholarship by Janet Todd and others has restored her to her place in the historical scene alongside Dryden and her other competitors for fame. It is a pleasure to reflect that restoration herewith because the quality of Behn's writing is answerable to its topical interest for students of feminism and cultural studies.

As Milton is of his, Pope is still the most prominent poet of his century. The anthology reflects this, but, like Dryden's, Pope's customary proportions are diminished in order to admit other voices. *The Rape of the Lock* has become even better and more interesting to students; in an age of extreme sexual explicitness, the eroticism is more evidently brilliant than ever. *The Dunciad* has become harder to understand, but it is still crucial to an understanding of the period. Some of the great occasional poems and philosophical poems have become harder still, and with great regret I did not find room for *Windsor Forest* or *An Essay on Man*. *An Essay on Criticism* is essential for students of criticism and theory. I added *Eloisa and Abelard* in the third edition of the anthology. This work about love and sensitivity shows Pope's range and virtuosity. I added it at the expense of Book Four of *The Dunciad*. I regret the loss, of course, but the change reflects an evolution in the reception of Pope.

Another change that has been registered in the last forty years of study of the eighteenth century is a growing interest in the prose and drama and a decreased interest in the poetry. I discovered one indication of this when I selected articles for the *Critical Reader* that serves as a companion to this volume (Blackwell, 1999). A great majority of the critical writing on the eighteenth century in the last forty years has been primarily directed to the prose, especially the fictional prose, the novels, and the "protonovelistic" writings of the period. To a degree, the anthology also reflects this change in interest, despite the aesthetic sacrifice sometimes entailed. There is no question that much of the poetry of Pope excluded from the anthology is, line for line, linguistically richer than the prose stories for the sake of which, in part, it was sacrificed. But verbal beauty is only one of the attractions of literature, and it seemed more important to have Eliza Haywood, who mainly wrote prose, represented than to have all the Pope I wanted. A number of the longest works included in full in the anthology are works of prose: *Oroonoko, A Tale of a Tub*, and *Rasselas*. This partly reflects the increased interest in prose over the last forty years, but it also serves the very practical purpose of providing teachers with some complete texts between two covers, so they can reduce the number of books they require students to buy. The anthology aims to provide a complete syllabus for a variety of courses on the period. It failed to do so most glaringly in the first edition by not including a play. The reduction in the extent of *Paradise Lost* made it possible to address that failing by including William Congreve's final play

The Way of the World. In the third edition I added *The School for Scandal* by Richard Brinsley Sheridan, but teachers indicated that they wanted still more drama. So, I have added Gay's *Beggar's Opera* and Behn's *Rover*. These additions mitigate the oddity of representing the period's varied dramatic output with one great play. The three additional plays are also great works, but they are not as tightly wound as Congreve's masterpiece. *The School for Scandal*, for example, is easier to understand than *The Way of the World*; its comedy is broader and its plot not as complex. The comedy of *The Rover* is broader still, though its elaborate masquerading presents complexities of its own. Like *The Way of the World*, *The Beggar's Opera* is perfect in its kind, but this musical farce further diversifies the anthology's offerings in drama.

The Way of the World is so terse and elegant that it is hard to remember sometimes that it too is a work of prose. This is not the case with all of the prose works included in the anthology; some are pieces that a generation ago would have belonged, at best, to the background of literature. Journal entries and letters, as well as most historical and philosophical works, used to seem infra-literary to the highest critics. But this was very much not the case in the eighteenth century itself because the word "literature" still meant almost everything in a written form – certainly everything learned appearing in that form. The eighteenth century had a great deal to do with creating the specialized nineteenth-century meaning of the term "literature," but it resisted it even as it created the word "literary" and glided toward a more restricted sense of the phrase "literary history." I have taken advantage of the old meaning of "literature" to include a few works that some might think of as primarily documentary (such as the reports on trials at the Old Bailey), or political (such as the excerpts from Locke's *Two Treatises of Government*), or philosophical (such as the excerpts from Hobbes's *Leviathan*). These inclusions are completely justifiable in terms of literary understanding at the time, and recent tendencies in literary criticism have led to some reacceptance of the older sense of the term "literature."

In restoring some of the old meaning of "literature," recent trends have been true to the outlook of the period itself. This is also so when it comes to the reintroduction of women onto the scene. There were plenty of places in the eighteenth-century world where women were not seen – for example, the polling places, the universities, and the ecclesiastical benefices. They may not have been prominent in the literary scene, but they were more present than we used to think. Several of Samuel Johnson's closest associates were women writers: Hester Thrale, his best friend; Elizabeth Carter, who was already working for the *Gentleman's Magazine* when Johnson arrived in London; Charlotte Lennox; and Frances Burney, to name a few. He much preferred the novels of Sarah Fielding to those of her brother Henry. Four of the five *Ramblers* written wholly by others are by women; Johnson subscribed to the publication of several volumes of poetry by women, and he participated in the mixed company of Samuel Richardson's literary circle. Women worked under numerous disadvantages as writers in the eighteenth century, and they did not produce as much as men, but they were present in publications of the period, and they deserve to be restored to something like the prominence they once struggled to enjoy. Several anthologies of the time were more receptive to women than most anthologies in the twentieth century; indeed, the proportion of women represented in Robert Dodsley's *Collection of Poems by Several Hands* (1748) is probably higher than what I present here.

Despite all the changes I have made in relation to the best anthology of the last generation, I have followed tradition in many respects. Moreover, I found my willingness to do so strengthened in revising the work for the second, third, and fourth editions. For example, the total number of authors is now somewhat smaller than it was at first, which means that there is a greater concentration on the major figures in the anthology and less representation of the full variety of writing known to contemporary readers. Many of the writers I cut were too scantily represented to be teachable; several of these were women poets in whose complete known works there was not a wide choice for the editor to begin with. Others whom I cut are major, male writers, like Richardson, Fielding, and Gibbon, whose most important works could not easily be included, even in excerpts. On the whole, therefore, the balance between men and women writers has remained about the same.

The revised editions of the anthology are also more traditional in offering fewer works that are less notable for their literary art than for their social or historical significance. In the end I was more willing to cut medical writers, like George Cheyne, than to subtract anything more from poets and writers of prose fiction. A final way in which the book has become more traditional is by moving the chronological median a little forward. The subtraction of so much Milton and the addition of Congreve and Sheridan moved the focal point of the work closer to the eighteenth century proper. The fourth edition has continued to move in that direction by excluding some minor seventeenth-century authors, such as Henry Vaughan and Dorothy Osborne Temple. The reasons for these changes, however, are much more a matter of practice than of theory. Having fifty-eight authors instead of the original ninety-three has some theoretical implications, but the fact is that many teachers found the selections from several of the ninety-three too slender, or too marginal with respect to the author's main body of work, to be useful.

Anyone who has edited an anthology knows that the most difficult problem is exclusion. When a writer is excised, not only the selection disappears from the book, so do the biography and the cross-references in headnotes and footnotes to the remaining authors. Admission and exclusion are editorial responsibilities, just as much as the selection of copy-texts and the composition of footnotes. In this age of electronic texts, a truly revolutionary editor might soon be able to reject this responsibility, and present a program that allows readers to have every text and every version of every text published in the period. However, the work of editing would not then disappear; it would become the work of each and every student and teacher who wanted to learn the literature of this period.

The same could be said for the editorial responsibility of arranging the texts in some order. In traditional fashion, I have chosen to arrange the texts by author (rather than theme or genre, for example) and to arrange the authors according to their dates of birth (rather than, say, their political or thematic affinities with one another). Despite reports toward the end of the last century that the author was dead, and despite some challenges to the importance of chronology in literary relationships, both of these basic principles of literary study have survived and ought to survive. The authorship of a work is, at least, one of its defining characteristics, and an author is defined, in large part, by his or her place in history and his or her chronological relationship to other authors. That being said, no reader of any book ever signs a contract to read it entirely in order from front to back. There is certainly no responsibility to do so for the present book. Readers of all political and theoretical persuasions may make their own designs as they peruse the contents of this anthology; the book humbly offers itself to be read according to each reader's discretion and imagination. A chronology and a thematic table of contents are included to facilitate but not to limit imaginative navigation of this very large text.

Editorial Principles

One of the many difficult decisions about how to present the following material was whether or not to retain the spelling and punctuation of the original texts. Texts are not fully separable from their material manifestations: capitalization, italicization, spelling, punctuation, even paper and ink contribute to making a text what it is, or what it was when it first appeared. On the other hand, a certain amount can be changed without significantly altering the text. The question is, how much? This is a good question for a philosopher because it cannot be answered without revealing commitments about the definition of "the text," but it is also a practical question because the likely readers of this book must be taken into account. I wanted to make the book as accessible as possible to students, while retaining as much of the original text as possible. My solution in these circumstances was: (1) I modernized the representation of letters completely: no long *s* (*ſ*), no representation of *th* by *y*, and no unusual abbreviations; (2) I modernized spelling where it could be done without changing the sound that readers would gather from it; for example, there did not seem to be any reason to use most of the old *'d* spellings meant to prevent readers from making a syllable out of the past-participial ending *-ed* because, as a rule, we do not hear that *-ed* as a syllable today; where it was meant to be heard, I added an accent over the *e* (thus, *è*). Such cases are relatively rare and it seemed worth adding a few accent marks to accommodate a lot of harmless modernization; (3) in poetry it seemed impossible to change punctuation without changing sound, so I left it, except in a few very rare cases where a slight change seemed absolutely necessary for sense; in prose, I was just slightly bolder in making changes; (4) I introduced quotation marks, opening and closing in the modern way, to indicate direct speech in both prose and poetry; in some cases I used these in place of the italicization used to indicate quotation in the original texts; furthermore, I used commas in place of parentheses indicating a break in the direct quotation: "Begone," he said, instead of "Begone" (he said), to make up an extreme case; (5) except in rare cases (mainly in the dramatic works), I did not represent reverse italicization (common in the titles of some works), but I retained regular italicization used for emphasis (and often for proper names) as well as all forms of capitalization. The end result of all these decisions is a text that retains a good deal of the typographical diversity of the original but poses less of an obstacle for students, especially those reading extensively in this period for the first time.

One goal of modernization in this book was to reduce the number of footnotes. As Samuel Johnson said, "Notes are often necessary, but they are necessary evils." Footnotes distract readers from the consecutive progress of the text; they interrupt the thoughts and ideas that one has in reading and diminish the force of the experience. As Johnson put it, "The mind is refrigerated by interruption." On the other hand, reference to a dictionary or an encyclopedia would be even more distracting than glancing to the foot of the page, and a failure to investigate the meaning of some phrases can completely disrupt understanding. Most of my notes explain the meanings of words no longer current or proper names no longer familiar to college and university students. I have very frequently cited Johnson's *Dictionary* (1755), and in this way made the notes part of the literature of the period. There are also very numerous citations of the *Oxford English Dictionary* (*OED*). I also widely used a variety of dictionaries and atlases of the Bible, the *Oxford Classical Dictionary*, the *Encyclopaedia Britannica* (especially the eleventh edition and the new electronic version), the *Oxford Dictionary of National Biography*, and *A Dictionary of British and American Women Writers 1660–1800*, edited by Janet Todd. In later editions I also used Wikipedia, which is getting better all the time, and I used Google. Both of these web resources often led me to more reliable digital or printed sources of information. But perhaps most of all I relied on the notes already compiled in the many great editions of the works I reprint here. Works such as the *Twickenham Pope* and the *Yale Johnson*, to name only two, saved me months of work, even though I double-checked their information in nearly every case. I have acknowledged these scholarly editions and their editors separately in the introductions to my authors and sometimes in the individual notes where they helped most.

In headnotes and footnotes I have noted which editions I used for copy-texts. For much the most part I have preferred first editions, and I have given the dates of these editions along with the titles of the works. (However, in those few cases where publication lagged far behind composition, I have given an approximate date of composition with the title.) Where there is a choice, I have used New Style dates, in which the year begins on January 1 rather than on March 25, as it did in the Julian calendar, which Great Britain did not abandon until 1752.

Preface to the Fourth Edition

Our knowledge of eighteenth-century literary works has advanced since 2008 when the third edition of this anthology appeared. Among the achievements directly related to works included herewith are the appearance of: the late D. F. McKenzie's magnificent edition of *The Works of William Congreve* (2011); several volumes of *The Cambridge Edition of the Works of Jonathan Swift*; several volumes of the Oxford edition of *The Complete Works of John Milton*; six volumes in *The Yale Edition of the Works of Samuel Johnson*; two volumes in the Research Editions segment of the Yale Boswell Editions; four volumes of Frances Burney's *Court Journals and Letters*; an edition of Behn's *The Rover and Other Plays* (Oxford University Press, 2008); a significantly revised Blackwell edition of Rochester (2010); Gordon Campbell and Thomas N. Corns's *John Milton: Life, Work, and Thought* (Oxford University Press, 2008); Leopold Damrosch's *Jonathan Swift: His Life and His World* (Yale University Press, 2013); and the first volume of David Bromwich's *Intellectual Life of Edmund Burke* (Harvard University Press, 2014). Several important works also became available digitally in these past seven years: the *Yale Edition of Horace Walpole's Correspondence*; the *Yale Edition of the Works of Samuel Johnson*; and (for a price) the vast resources of the *Oxford Scholarly Editions*, which includes the Oxford English Texts as well as excellent editions, such as the California Dryden, from other university presses.

Many other printed and digital titles could be added to this list, but these alone surely make it evident that work on eighteenth-century British literature is active, and scholars are steadily increasing our knowledge of the period. Shifts in the interpretive winds of academia are harder for me to detect. Much of the interpretive work and perhaps the largest portion of innovative interpretive work focuses on the prose fiction of the period, which is only slightly represented in this anthology. The general interest in private life, in race, gender, and class, however, has certainly been applied to all aspects of the eighteenth century. Precisely how this interest alters the reception of eighteenth-century writers, however, is clearer to me in my teaching than in my reading of my colleagues' work. My students are ever more alert to various kinds of gender politics in the writing of this period, as they are to evidence of rigidity in this domain. Their minds are simultaneously more open to plural attitudes toward sexual identity and more sensitive to intolerance. As a result, I have found Milton's divorce tracts easier to teach in recent years than in the past, and I have learned more than ever from my students about how to read them. On the other hand I find Pope's *Epistle to a Lady* harder than ever to teach and have dropped it from the anthology in favor of his *Essay on Criticism*. This is not because my students are politically correct; it's because they are better prepared than ever before to discuss gender, and even when they are inclined to read genially (as they usually are) this particular poem is hard for them to like. I considered including the *Epistle to Arbuthnot*, a much greater poem, but I am not sure how avidly my students could greet Pope's nasty derision of Sporus – either Nero's castrated boy or the bisexual lord for whom he stands. On the other hand, I knew my students and many of my colleagues would enthusiastically greet the inclusion of *The Rover*. My students like talking about its gender politics, and they read the play this year with greater interest and attention than ever.

Students at Vassar in recent years also have more skill than those in the past have had in discussing racial politics. This is one of the reasons that I included this time the sermon of Samson Occom. *Oronooko* has become almost too easy for them at this point, and I sometimes struggle to keep up. On state politics, however, I find my students less prepared than they are on the politics of gender or race. The hatred of war that appears in many writings of the period seems surprising to them. When so much cruelty is reported in various media and often displayed on line, the time seems ripe for teaching again such works as Johnson's *Idlers* 22 and 81, and I think Burke's *Reflections* is more interesting than ever. Of course, the answers to Burke from Wollstonecraft and Paine are also important, and I have amplified Paine by adding the American *Declaration of Independence*. It is difficult to avoid the question of whether this document, drafted by Thomas Jefferson, is American or British, but I think that is becoming an antiquated worry. Such worries have been replaced in some respects by the greater awareness in recent years of the "Atlantic" location of the American colonies as well as the "archipelagic" nature of the British Isles. The four nations of these islands surely were no less separate historically and culturally than the American colonies were in 1776. Since the literature of Britain in this period must include Robert Burns as well as Swift, Goldsmith, and Sheridan, why should it not include Paine, Occom, and Jefferson? American literature has been persuasively invited in recent years to join the Atlantic world and even the greater globe (by Wai Chee Dimock and others). Surely its forays outside its national boundaries should begin with Britain. Many of us teach to audiences that are racially and nationally diverse, and it makes sense to them that the literatures they study should be as globally oriented as themselves. In many ways, the concept of a national literature was just coming into view in the seventeenth and eighteenth centuries, as British writers distinguished their traditions from those of their continental counterparts, despite all their common heritage. If we are now prepared to denaturalize the concept of national literature, that can only bring into sharper focus the special properties, protocols, and proclivities of the writing we most love to read and teach.

Acknowledgments

Although I am responsible for the contents of this book, I had a great deal of help. My editor for the first two editions, Andrew McNeillie, was my constant correspondent during the long process of building, expanding, contracting, and shaping the table of contents. Like me, he solicited and read contributions on the subject from scores of teachers and scholars. I am grateful to everyone who contributed, and I am sorry it was impossible to construct a book that satisfied every reasonable request. The following scholars made thoughtful suggestions or supplied me with expert opinions on the works of particular authors: Carol Barash, John Bender, O M Brack, Jr., Bliss Carnochan, Caryn Chaden, Brian Connery, Patricia Craddock, Marlies Danziger, Lennard Davis, D. N. DeLuna, Margaret Doody, Aileen Douglas, David Duff, Gordon Fulton, Richard Greene, Robert Griffin, Achsah Guibbory, Patrick Harrison, Nelson Hilton, J. Paul Hunter, Ann Imbrie, Felix Irwin, Roxanne Kent-Drury, Deborah Knuth Klenck, Gwin Kolb, Anne Krook, Joanne Long, Jack Lynch, Robert Markley, Carey McIntosh, Jeslyn Medoff, James Merrell, Wendy Motooka, David Oakleaf, John O'Neill, Michael Payne, David Radcliffe, Claude Rawson, John Richetti, George Rousseau, Ted Ruml, Jonathan Sawday, John Scanlan, John Shawcross, Stuart Sherman, David Shields, John Sitter, Chloe Wigston Smith, Nigel Smith, Lars Troide, Eleanor Ty, Cynthia Wall, and Richard Wendorf. I owe a greater debt to Terry Castle, who advised me at the very outset and later became an official advisory editor of the volume. She helped me appreciate the importance of many writers in the period whose work I did not know. I owe a similar debt to my former colleague in eighteenth-century studies at Vassar, Donna Heiland. David Norbrook, the volume's other advisory editor, supplied much information I lacked concerning writers of the earliest period in the book. Robert Brown and Rachel Kitzinger assisted me, as ever, with numerous notes concerning Latin and Greek works.

The bulk of this volume, great as it is, indicates less than half of the volume of text that had to be processed in the course of its compilation and frequent revision. Stephanie Harzewski, my regular student assistant for three years, gave me indispensable assistance with the enormous tasks of typing and collating. She was joined by an equally diligent student, Jennifer Simpson, for our frantic summer of assembling the first draft of the book. Lindsey Briggs helped me throughout the preparation of the second edition. In revising the book again I had help from Per Henningsgrad and Shaina Brassard. For assistance in the preparation of the fourth edition I am grateful to Grace Sparapani and Allison Pearl. All of these excellent students were supported, like me, by Vassar College. Some also had the support of the Ford Foundation. Part of the earliest work on this project was done in the friendly confines of the Center for Advanced Study in the Behavioral Sciences with the support of the Mellon Foundation.

In pursuit of early editions of eighteenth-century texts I had the pleasure of working in numerous fine libraries. I wish to thank the librarians at Stanford University, Vassar College, the New York Public Library, the Beinecke Rare Books and Manuscript Library, the British Library, the Yale Center for British Art, the London Library, and the Bodleian Library.

I am also indebted to the following publishers and editors for granting me permission to publish parts of editions to which they hold the copyright: HarperCollins Publishers for material from *The Diary of Samuel Pepys*, ed. Robert Latham and William Matthews, G. Bell & Sons, 1970; John Wiley & Sons, Ltd and Nicholas Fisher for "A Letter from Artemiza in the Towne to Chloe in the Countrey," "Lampoone ['Too longe the Wise Commons have been in debate']," "Seigneur Dildoe," "Satyr ['In the Isle of Brittain long since famous growne']," "The Imperfect Enjoyment," "A Ramble in St. James's Parke," "A Satyre against Reason and Mankind," and "The Disabled Debauchee," from *John Wilmot, Earl of Rochester: The Poems and Lucina's Rape*, ed. Keith Walker and Nicholas Fisher, 2013; Oxford University Press for: "Letter to Lady Wortley Montagu 1 September 1718" from *The Correspondence of Alexander Pope*, ed. George Sherburn, 5 vols., Clarendon Press, 1956; letter from Samuel Johnson to Mrs. Thrale, Saturday 29 May '73 and Mrs. Thrale to Samuel Johnson, no date, Streatham, from *The Letters of Samuel Johnson with Mrs. Thrale's Genuine Letters to Him*, ed. by R. W. Chapman, vol. 1, Clarendon Press, 1952; letter from Mrs. Thrale to Samuel Johnson, 8 July 1775 from *The Letters of Samuel Johnson with Mrs. Thrale's Genuine Letters to Him*, ed. R.W. Chapman, vol. 2, Clarendon Press, 1952; "Letter to Esther Burney 30 September 1811" from *Journals and Letters of Frances Burney d'Arblay*, ed. Joyce Hemlow, vol. 6, 1975; and "Letter to Mrs. and Miss Thrale 27/8 March 1777" from *The Early Journals and Letters of Frances Burney d'Arblay*, ed. Lars E. Troide, vol. 2, 1990. Every effort has been made to trace all the copyright holders, but if any have been inadvertently overlooked the publishers will be pleased to make the necessary arrangement at the first opportunity.

Partly because of its size, partly because of its frequent revision, and partly because of the varied constituency it tries to please, this book has required even more patience than usual from my family. I am grateful to Alex, Davy, and especially Joanne for their unfailing support and good humor.

Ballads and Newsbooks from the Civil War (1640–1649)

One of the dramatic effects of the revolution in England was a change in the character and in the amount of publication. The popular appetite for news was stimulated by the political upheaval, which also disturbed and suspended the usual forms of government censorship and control. From about 1641 the many and various factions in the kingdom were freer to express their views than they ever had been before or were to be for many years after the restoration of conventional government in 1660. This period did not give birth to the newspaper and the political editorial (Ben Jonson satirized the industry of newsmaking in the 1620s in *The Staple of News*), but the revolution fostered unprecedented coverage of domestic news and changed the nature of periodical publication for good.[1] Along with the newsbooks came an increased production of pamphlets and broadsides, the cheapest and most ephemeral kinds of publication. One of the most consciously literary forms appearing in such publications was the ballad. Long an oral vehicle of news and commentary, the ballad came more often to take printed form during the interregnum. Herewith are two pieces from newsbooks and three ballads. Four of the five focus on the execution of Charles I, which was the most frequently mentioned event in English writing from 1649 until well into the eighteenth century.

Hyder Rollins edited a collection of ballads called *Cavalier and Puritan* (New York University Press, 1923); his careful transcriptions of the original texts in the Thomason collection at the British Library provide the basis of the ballads I present here. The newsbooks were selected from *Making the News*, edited by Joad Raymond (St. Martin's Press, 1993).

The World is Turned Upside Down (1646)

To the tune of, When the King enjoys his own again[1]

Listen to me and you shall hear,
News hath not been this thousand year:
Since *Herod, Caesar,* and many more,[2]
You never heard the like before.
    Holy-days are despised.
    New fashions are devised.

Notes

Ballads and Newsbooks from the Civil War

1 I am paraphrasing the introduction of *Making the News: An Anthology of the Newsbooks of Revolutionary England, 1641–1660*, ed. Joad Raymond (St. Martin's Press, 1993); on the effects of the war on literature, see Nigel Smith, *Literature and Revolution in England, 1640–1660* (Yale University Press, 1994). For a full discussion of early newsbooks, see Joad Raymond, *The Invention of the Newspaper: English Newsbooks, 1641–1649* (Clarendon Press, 1996).

The World is Turned Upside Down

1 This royalist ballad has been dated April 8, 1646.

2 *Herod* ruler in Judea who condemned John the Baptist and returned Christ to his subordinate Pontius Pilate, having set him at nought (Luke 23.11); he was subject to Augustus Caesar.

British Literature 1640–1789: An Anthology, Fourth Edition. Edited by Robert DeMaria, Jr.

Old Christmas is kicked out of Town.[3]
Yet let's be content, and the times lament,
You see the world turned upside down.

The wise men did rejoice to see
Our Saviour Christ's Nativity:
The Angels did good tidings bring,
The Shepherds did rejoice and sing.
Let all honest men,
Take example by them.
Why should we from good Laws be bound?[4]
Yet let's be content, &c.

Command is given, we must obey,
And quite forget old Christmas day:
Kill a thousand men, or a Town regain,[5]
We will give thanks and praise amain.[6]
The wine pot shall clink,
We will feast and drink.
And then strange motions will abound.[7]
Yet let's be content, &c.

Our Lords and Knights, and Gentry too,
Do mean old fashions to forgo:
They set a porter at the gate,
That none must enter in thereat.
They count it a sin,
When poor people come in.

Hospitality itself is drowned.
Yet let's be content, &c.

The serving men do sit and whine,
And think it long ere dinner time:
The Butler's still out of the way,
Or else my Lady keeps the key,
The poor old cook,
In the larder doth look,
Where is no goodness to be found,
Yet let's be content, &c.

To conclude, I'll tell you news that's right,
Christmas was killed at *Naseby* fight:[8]
Charity was slain at that same time,

Notes

[3] *Old Christmas is kicked out* The Puritans banned Christmas festivities and other holidays as idolatrous.

[4] *bound* "gone away from" (*OED*, s.v. *boun*).

[5] *Kill … regain* Puritan victories in the Civil War.

[6] *amain* with vigor.

[7] *motions* legal motions, like the one banning Christmas festivities.

[8] *Naseby* the decisive battle of the Civil War, June 14, 1645.

Jack Tell Troth too, a friend of mine,
Likewise then did die,
Roast beef and shred pie,[9]
Pig, Goose and Capon no quarter found.
Yet let's be content, and the times lament,
You see the world is quite turned round.

The King's Last farewell to the World, or The Dead King's Living Meditations, at the approach of Death denounced against Him[1] (1649)

Through fear of sharp and bitter pain,
by cutting off my days,
No pleasure in my Crown I take,
nor in my Royal Rays.[2]
I shall descend with grievèd heart,
(for none my life can save)
Unto the dismal gates of death,
to moulder in the Grave.

Farewell my Wife, and Children all,
wipe off my brinish teares.
I am deprivèd of my Throne,
and from my future years.
Farewell my people every one,
for I no more shall see
The wonders of the Lord on earth,
nor with you shall I be.

Mine eyes do fail, and to the earth
to worms I must be hurled:
Henceforth no more shall I behold
the people of the world.
My Crown and Sceptre I must leave,
my glory, and my Throne:
Adieu my fellow Princes all,
I from the earth am gone.

Mine Age (which did approach to me)
departed is away;
And as a Shepherd's tent removed,
and I returned to clay;

Notes

[9] *shred pie* mince pie.

The King's Last farewell to the World

[1] This Puritan ballad appeared on January 31, 1649, the day after the execution of King Charles I; *denounce* "To threaten by proclamation" (Johnson).

[2] *Rays* "Any lustre corporeal or intellectual" (Johnson).

And as a Weaver doth cut off
his thrum,[3] even so my life,
Must be cut off, from people and
from Children, and from Wife.

In sighs by day, and groans by night
with bitterness I moan,
And do consume away[4] with grief,
my end to think upon.
Fear in the morning me assails,
Death Lion-like I see,
Even all the day (till night) to roar
to make an end of me.

I chattered as the shrieking Crane,
or Swallow that doth fly:
As Dove forlorn, in pensiveness,
doth mourn, even so do I.
I lookèd up to thee, O Lord,
but now mine eyes do fail.
Oh ease my sad oppressèd soul,
for death doth now prevail.

What shall I say, to God's Decree,
if he would speak, I then
should live; it is a work for God,
I find no help from men.
Yet if my life prolongèd was,
my sins for to repent,
Then softly I would go and mourn,
until my life was spent.

And all my years, that I should live,
for mine offences foul,
I would pass o'er in bitterness,
of my distressèd soul.
O Lord, thou hast discoverèd
to me, that by these things
Men live; through thee, Princes do Reign,
thou swayest over Kings.

In all things here God's Providence,
and will alone commands,
The life of my poor spirit sad,
is only in his hands,
Oh, that the Lord would me restore.
My strength then I would give,
To serve my God in humbleness
whilst he would let me live.

Notes

[3] *thrum* "The ends of weavers' threads" (Johnson).

[4] *consume away* "burn away" (*OED*, 6c).

Behold, O Lord, when I in peace,
did look to be restored,
Then was my soul in bitterness,
cast off, and I abhorred,
Yet in the love of God most good,
his righteousness most just
Hath thrown me down into the pit,
and to corrupted dust,

Because that I have gone astray,
And cherished war and strife,
My days are now cut off, and I
am quite bereft of life,
Oh cast my sins behind thy back,
good God, I humbly pray,
And my offences with the blood
of Christ wash clean away.

When my dead body is interred,
I cannot praise thee there,
Death cannot celebrate the Lord,
my God, most good, most dear;
They that go down into the pit
destructions them devour:
For in thy truth they cannot hope,
but perish by thy power.

The living, Lord, the living, they
shall praise thy holy name.
With all the glorious host above,
and I shall do the same,
The father to his children here,
that are of tender youth,
Shall them forewarn, and unto them
make known thy glorious truth.

Forgive my sins, and save my soul
O Lord, I thee entreat,
And blot out mine offences all,
for they are very great:
Receive my soul for Christ his sake,[5]
my Prophet, Priest, and King,
That I with Saints and Angels may
eternal praises sing.

FINIS

Notes

[5] *Christ his* Christ's.

The Royal Health to the Rising Sun (1649)

To the tune of, *O my pretty little winking, &c.*[1]

As I was walking forth one day,
I heard distressèd people say,
Our Peace and Plenty now is gone,
And we poor people quite undone:
A Royal Health I then begun[2]
Unto the rising of the Sun,
Gallant English Spirits
do not thus complain;
The Sun that sets
may after rise again.

The Tempest hath endurèd long,
We must not say, we suffer wrong,
The Queen of Love sits all alone.[3]
No man is Master of his own.

We over-whelmèd are with grief,
And harbour many [a] private Thief,
Poor House-keepers can hardly live,
Who used in former times to give:[4]

The Thistle chokes the Royal Rose,
And all our bosom friends turned foes,
The Irish Harp is out of tune,[5]
And we, God knows, undone too soon.

The second Part, to the same tune.
True love and friendship doth now decay,
Poor People's almost starved they say,
Our Trading's spoiled, and all things dear
We may complain, and ne'er the near:[6]

Though all be true that here is said,
Kind Country-men be not dismayed,
For when the worst of harms is past,
We shall have better times at last.

When Rulers cast off self-respects,[7]
Then shall our Yokes fall from our Necks,

Notes

THE ROYAL HEALTH TO THE RISING SUN

1 This bravely optimistic royalist ballad laments the state of the kingdom after the execution of Charles I on January 30, 1649 and predicts a happy turn of events. The tune is unknown.

2 The six-line refrain follows every stanza.

3 *Queen of Love* Henrietta Maria, daughter of Henry IV of France, wife to Charles I.

4 *to give* to give to the poor.

5 *Thistle ... Harp* the thistle is symbolic of the Scots, whose Presbyterian forces contributed importantly to the defeat of Charles; the Royal Rose is England (and Charles); the Irish were nearly in rebellion against Charles, but suffered most terribly under Cromwell.

6 *near* nearer; *nar* (see *OED*).

7 *self-respects* selfish aims.

Our safeties shall not then depend
On promise of a Faithless Friend:

When as the Cloud of War is down,
The Royal Sun enjoys the Crown,
The Lamb shall with the Lion feed,
'Twill be a happy time indeed:

Let us cheer up each other then,
And show ourselves true English-men,
And not like bloody wolves and Bears,
As we have been these many years.

The Father of our Kingdom's dead,
His Royal Sun from *England's* fled,
God send all well that Wars may cease,
And we enjoy a happy peace.
A Royal Health I then begun
Unto the rising of the Sun,
Gallant English Spirits,
do not thus complain;
The Sun that sets
may after rise again.

from *A Perfect Diurnal of Some Passages in Parliament* (1649)

Number 288
29 January–5 February 1649

Tuesday, January 30

This day the King was beheaded, over against the Banqueting house by White-Hall. The manner of Execution, and what passed before his death take thus.

He was brought from Saint *James* about ten in the morning, walking on foot through the Park, with a Regiment of Foot for his guard, with Colours flying, Drums beating, his private Guard of Partisans, with some of his Gentlemen before, and some behind bareheaded, Doctor Juxon late Bishop of London next behind him, and Colonel Thomlinson (who had charge of him) to the Gallery in Whitehall, and so into the Cabinet Chamber, where he used to lie, where he continued at his Devotion. … The Scaffold was hung round with black, and the floor covered with black, and the Axe and Block laid in the middle of the Scaffold. There were divers companies of Foot and Horse, on every side the Scaffold, and the multitudes of people that came to be Spectators, very great. The King making a Pass upon the Scaffold, looked very earnestly on the Block, and asked Colonel *Hacker* if there were no higher; and then spake thus, directing his speech to the Gentlemen upon the Scaffold. King. 'I shall be very little heard of anybody here, I shall therefore speak a word unto you here;[1] indeed I could

Notes

FROM *A PERFECT DIURNAL*

[1] *here* on the scaffold; ranks of soldiers separated King Charles from the large crowd.

hold my peace very well, if I did not think that holding my peace, would make some men think that I did submit to the guilt, as well as to the punishment; but I think it is my duty to God first, and to my Country, for to clear myself both as an honest man, and a good king, and a good Christian. I shall begin first with my Innocency. In troth I think it not very needful for me to insist long upon this, for all the world knows that I never did begin a war with the two houses of Parliament, and I call God to witness, to whom I must shortly make an account, that I never did intend for to encroach upon their Privileges; they began upon me; it is the Militia they began upon; they confessed that the Militia was mine, but they thought it fit to have it from me; and to be short, if anybody will look to the dates of Commissions, theirs and mine, and likewise to the Declarations, will see clearly that they began these unhappy troubles, not I; so that as the guilt of these Enormous crimes that are laid against me, I hope in God that God will clear me of it. ... yet for all this, God forbid that I should be so ill a Christian, as not to say that God's Judgements are just upon me: Many times he does pay Justice by an unjust Sentence, that is ordinary; I only say this, That an unjust sentence [meaning Strafford[2]] that I suffered for to take effect, is punished now, by an unjust sentence upon me; that is, so far I have said, to show you that I am an innocent man. Now for to show you that I am a good Christian: I hope there is [pointing to Dr. Juxon] a good man that will bear me witness, That I have forgiven all the world, and those in particular that have been the chief causers of my death; who they are, God knows; I do not desire to know; I pray God forgive them. But this is not all, my Charity must go further; I wish that they may repent, for indeed they have committed a great sin in particular. I pray God with St. *Stephen*,[3] That this be not laid to their charge; nay, not only so but that they may take the right way to the Peace of the Kingdom, for Charity commands me not only to forgive particular men, but to endeavour to the last gasp the Peace of the Kingdom: so (sirs) I do wish with all my soul, and I do hope (there is some here will carry it further) that they may endeavour the Peace of the Kingdom'.

from *Mercurius Pragmaticus* (1649)

Number 43
30 January–6 February 1649

Nay, you may e'en go to rest now, your *Great* and *Acceptable* WORK is done; the *Fatal Blow* is given, the Kingdom is translated to the Saints – Oh Horror! Blood! Death! Had you none else to wreak your cursed *malice* on, but the sacred Person of the King? *cursed be your* rage *for it is fierce, and your* malice *for it is implacable.*

Good God, how every day adds fresh supplies of Miseries to poor dying England; enough of Care, but little enough of Cure; though years and months end, yet your sorrows are still beginning, and our Calamities cease not. ...

Beware the building, for the *Foundation* is taken away, the winds begin to blow, and the waves to beat, the Restless *Ark* is tossed; none but unclean Beasts are

Notes

[2] *Strafford* Privy councillor to Charles I, executed May 12, 1641 for treason.

[3] *St. Stephen* A martyr, who, before he died, 'kneeled down, and cried with a loud voice, Lord, lay not this sin to their charge' Acts 7.60.

entered into her, the *Dove* will not return, neither will the *Olive Branch* appear.[1] The Axe is laid to the Root,[2] even of the Royal Cedar, then what can the Inferior Tree expect but to be crushed and bruised in His fall, and afterwards hewn down and cast into the fire. …

Notes

FROM *MERCURIUS PRAGMATICUS*

1 Genesis 8.11; the olive branch is the sign that the waters of the great flood have subsided, and there is peace on earth.

2 The apocalyptic prophecy of John the Baptist, reported in all four gospels (e.g., Matthew 3.10).

Thomas Hobbes (1588–1679)

Hobbes says that his mother, frightened by the impending attack of the Spanish Armada, gave premature birth to twins – himself and fear. Commentators have cherished this anecdote because Hobbes's twin, fear, plays such an important role in his philosophy. He describes human life in its natural state as a horrible field of contestation in which people are driven to sociability by their passions, especially fear, rather than by an innate sense of charity or love of community. Hobbes's conception of natural life as "nasty, brutish, and short" and his complex views on liberty and determinism, which he saw as compatible, made him the most controversial philosopher of the period. Long after his death in 1679, writers were still reacting to Hobbes's disturbing views. Swift's *Tale of a Tub* (1704) is an attempt to keep Hobbes at bay, and Samuel Johnson's *Dictionary* is another: Johnson consciously excluded Hobbes from his illustrative quotations and inserted numerous sentences from John Bramhall, one of his chief antagonists. But both Johnson and Swift felt the validity of Hobbes's views and paraphrased them on occasion, as did practically all philosophical writers in the period.

First published in 1651, *Leviathan* consists of four parts: "Of Man"; "Of Commonwealth"; "Of a Christian Commonwealth"; and "Of the Kingdom of Darkness." The following chapter, one of Hobbes's most famous and infamous pieces of writing, comes towards the end of part one and provides part of the transition to part two. Despite his royalist background and his defense of monarchy in most of *Leviathan*, Hobbes made concessions in his conclusion and took a pledge of loyalty to the Commonwealth government in 1652. Nevertheless Charles II, his former tutee, pensioned Hobbes at the Restoration (1660), although the restored episcopal church found Hobbes's defense of independency heretical. Hobbes's work is complex and his personality was evidently rebarbative as well. He is satirized in numerous poems of the period as well as attacked in serious treatises. He was certainly one of the most accomplished, least understood, most frequently attacked, and most influential writers of the whole period.

The standard edition of *Leviathan*, which includes Hobbes's Latin translation (1668), is Noel Malcolm's, 3 vols. (Clarendon Press, 2012). Malcolm's introduction and notes are definitive, but all modern texts, including the one presented below, derive from the first edition of 1651. *Aspects of Hobbes* (Clarendon Press, 2002), also by Malcolm, provides biographical and intellectual context. Also see *A Hobbes Dictionary*, ed. A. P. Martinich (Blackwell, 1995) and his handy introduction, *Hobbes* (Routledge, 2005).

from *Leviathan* (1651)

Chapter XIII: Of the NATURAL CONDITION of Mankind, as concerning their Felicity, and Misery

Men by nature equal. Nature hath made men so equal, in the faculties of the body, and mind; as that though there be found one man sometimes manifestly stronger in body, or of quicker mind than another; yet when all is reckoned together, the difference

British Literature 1640–1789: An Anthology, Fourth Edition. Edited by Robert DeMaria, Jr.

between man, and man, is not so considerable, as that one man can thereupon claim to himself any benefit, to which another may not pretend, as well as he. For as to the strength of body, the weakest has strength enough to kill the strongest, either by secret machination, or by confederacy with others, that are in the same danger with himself.

And as to the faculties of the mind (setting aside the arts grounded upon words, and especially that skill of proceeding upon general, and infallible rules, called Science; which very few have, and but in few things; as being not a native faculty, born with us; nor attained – as Prudence – while we look after somewhat else) I find yet a greater equality amongst men, than that of strength. For Prudence, is but Experience; which equal time, equally bestows on all men, in those things they equally apply themselves unto. That which may perhaps make such equality incredible, is but a vain conceit of one's own wisdom, which almost all men think they have in a greater degree than the Vulgar;[1] that is, than all men but themselves, and a few others, whom by Fame, or for concurring with themselves, they approve. For such is the nature of men, that howsoever they may acknowledge many others to be more witty, or more eloquent, or more learned; yet they will hardly believe there be many so wise as themselves: for they see their own wit at hand, and other men's at a distance. But this proveth rather that men are in that point equal, than unequal. For there is not ordinarily a greater sign of the equal distribution of any thing, than that every man is contented with his share.

From Equality proceeds Diffidence.[2] From this equality of ability, ariseth equality of hope in the attaining of our Ends. And therefore if any two men desire the same things, which nevertheless they cannot both enjoy, they become enemies; and in the way to their End (which is principally their own conservation, and sometimes their delectation[3] only) endeavour to destroy, or subdue one another. And from hence it comes to pass, that where an invader hath no more to fear, than another man's single power; if one plant, sow, build, or possess[4] a convenient Seat, others may probably be expected to come prepared with forces united, to dispossess, and deprive him, not only of the fruit of his labour, but also of his life, or liberty. And the Invader again is in the like danger of another.

From Diffidence War. And from this diffidence of one another, there is no way for any man to secure himself, so reasonable, as Anticipation; that is, by force, or wiles, to master the persons of all men he can, so long, till he see no other power great enough to endanger him: And this is no more than his own conservation requireth, and is generally allowed. Also because there be some, that taking pleasure in contemplating their own power in the acts of conquest, which they pursue farther than their security requires; if others, that otherwise would be glad to be at ease within modest bounds, should not by invasion increase their power, they would not be able, long time, by standing only on their defence, to subsist. And by consequence, such augmentation of dominion over men being necessary to a man's conservation, it ought to be allowed him.

Again, men have no pleasure (but on the contrary a great deal of grief) in keeping company, where there is no power able to over-awe them all. For every man looketh that his companion should value him, at the same rate he sets upon himself: And upon all signs of contempt, or undervaluing, naturally endeavours, as far as he dares (which amongst them that have no common power to keep them in quiet, is far enough to

Notes

FROM *LEVIATHAN*

1 *Vulgar* "The common people" (Johnson).

2 *Diffidence* mistrust.

3 *delectation* pleasure of any kind.

4 *possess* obtain, seize (Malcolm)

make them destroy each other) to extort a greater value from his contemners, by dommage;[5] and from others, by the example.

So that in the nature of man, we find three principal causes of quarrel. First, Competition; Secondly, Diffidence; thirdly, Glory.

The first, maketh men invade for Gain; the second, for Safety; and the third, for Reputation. The first use Violence, to make themselves Masters of other men's persons, wives, children, and cattle; the second, to defend them; the third, for trifles, as a word, a smile, a different opinion, and any other sign of undervalue, either direct in their Persons, or by reflection in their Kindred, their Friends, their Nation, their Profession,[6] or their Name.

Out of Civil States, there is always War of every one against every one. Hereby it is manifest, that during the time men live without a common Power to keep them all in awe, they are in that condition which is called War; and such a war, as is of every man, against every man. For WAR, consisteth not in Battle only, or the act of fighting; but in a tract of time, wherein the Will to contend by Battle is sufficiently known: and therefore the notion of *Time*, is to be considered in the nature of War; as it is in the nature of Weather. For as the nature of Foul weather, lieth not in a shower or two of rain; but in an inclination thereto of many days together: So the nature of War, consisteth not in actual fighting; but in the known disposition thereto, during all the time there is no assurance to the contrary. All other time is PEACE.

The Incommodities of such a War. Whatsoever therefore is consequent to a time of War, where every man is Enemy to every man; the same is consequent to the time, wherein men live without other security, than what their own strength, and their own invention shall furnish them withal. In such condition, there is no place for Industry; because the fruit thereof is uncertain: and consequently no Culture of the Earth; no Navigation, nor use of the commodities that may be imported by Sea; no commodious Building; no Instruments of moving, and removing, such things as require much force; no Knowledge of the face of the Earth; no account of Time; no Arts; no Letters; no Society; and which is worst of all, continual fear, and danger of violent death; And the life of man, solitary, poor, nasty, brutish, and short.

It may seem very strange to some man, that has not well weighed these things; that Nature should thus dissociate, and render men apt to invade, and destroy one another: and he may therefore, not trusting to this Inference, made from the Passions,[7] desire perhaps to have the same confirmed by Experience. Let him therefore consider with himself, when taking a journey, he arms himself, and seeks to go well accompanied; when going to sleep, he locks his doors; when even in his house he locks his chests; and this when he knows there be Laws, and public Officers, armed, to revenge all injuries shall be done him; what opinion he has of his fellow subjects, when he rides armed; of his fellow Citizens, when he locks his doors; and of his children, and servants, when he locks his chests. Does he not there as much accuse mankind by his actions, as I do by my words? But neither of us accuse man's nature in it. The Desires, and other Passions of man, are in themselves no Sin. No more are the Actions, that proceed from those Passions, till they know a Law that forbids them: which till Laws be made they cannot know: nor can any Law be made, till they have agreed upon the Person that shall make it.

Notes

[5] *dommage* damage.

[6] *Profession* religious or political commitments.

[7] *the Passions* principles in the psychology of Hobbes and other writers of the period.

It may peradventure be thought, there was never such a time, nor condition of war as this; and I believe it was never generally so, over all the world: but there are many places, where they live so now. For the savage people in many places of *America*, except the government of small Families, the concord whereof dependeth on natural lust, have no government at all; and live at this day in that brutish manner, as I said before. Howsoever, it may be perceived what manner of life there would be, where there were no common Power to fear, by the manner of life, which men that have formerly lived under a peaceful government, use[8] to degenerate into, in a civil War.

But though there had never been any time, wherein particular men were in a condition of war one against another; yet in all times, Kings, and Persons of Sovereign authority, because of their Independency, are in continual jealousies, and in the state and posture of Gladiators; having their weapons pointing, and their eyes fixed on one another; that is, their Forts, Garrisons, and Guns upon the Frontiers of their Kingdoms; and continual Spies upon their neighbours; which is a posture of War. But because they uphold thereby, the Industry of their Subjects; there does not follow from it, that misery, which accompanies the Liberty of particular men.

In such a War nothing is Unjust. To this war of every man against every man, this also is consequent, that nothing can be Unjust. The notions of Right and Wrong, Justice and Injustice have there no place. Where there is no common Power, there is no Law: no Injustice. Force, and Fraud, are in war the two Cardinal virtues. Justice, and injustice are none of the Faculties neither of the Body, nor Mind. If they were, they might be in a man that were alone in the world, as well as his Senses, and Passions. They are Qualities, that relate to men in Society, not in Solitude. It is consequent also to the same condition, that there be no Propriety,[9] no Dominion, no *Mine* and *Thine* distinct; but only that to be every man's that he can get; and for so long, as he can keep it. And thus much for the ill condition, which man by mere Nature is actually placed in; though with a possibility to come out of it, consisting partly in the Passions, partly in his Reason.

The Passions that incline men to Peace. The Passions that incline men to Peace, are Fear of Death; Desire of such things as are necessary to commodious living; and a Hope by their Industry to obtain them. And Reason suggesteth convenient Articles of Peace, upon which men may be drawn to agreement. These Articles, are they, which otherwise are called the Laws of Nature: whereof I shall speak more particularly, in the two following Chapters.

Notes

[8] *use* "To be customarily in any manner; to be wont" (Johnson).

[9] *Propriety* "Peculiarity of possession; exclusive right" (Johnson).

Robert Herrick (1591–1674)

Hesperides: or, the Works both Humane & Divine of Robert Herrick Esq. was published in 1648. The title contains the first use of *Works* to describe a collection of English poetry, as the new standard edition points out. The volume's 1,402 poems, almost all that Herrick would produce, celebrate aspects of the country life that he experienced, or witnessed, as a vicar in Devonshire in the late 1630s and 1640s. As a loyal royalist, he lost his living in 1646 and returned to his beloved London. After being restored to his living in 1660, however, Herrick returned to the country for good.

Herrick's delight in country things is evident in poems like "The Hock-Cart," and his pleasure in other kinds of sensual life comes out in his poems to Julia. Yet Herrick is also evidently pleased by the composition of his own verse. His poetic sportiveness and his awareness of classical and renaissance genres give his verse a fine tone of cultivation which blends brilliantly with his sensual impulses. Eager to sound like a real poet and yet to write about his personal experience, the juvenile Samuel Johnson chose Herrick's "Daffodils" as the pattern for his first attempt at formal verse. Like almost every attempt to emulate Herrick, Johnson's was both less energetic and less polished than his model. Because of their clear rhythms and easy style, many of Herrick's poems have been set to music. His melodious poem "To the Virgins, to make much of Time" is one of the most famous in all of British literature. Although earlier twentieth-century criticism branded Herrick as a minor poet, recent studies have elevated him, partly by paying attention to the political elements of his verse, and partly by discussing the latent integrity of his collection of heterogeneous poems.

The texts presented here are based on the first edition of *Hesperides*. The standard edition is now *The Complete Poetry of Robert Herrick*, ed. Tom Cain and Ruth Connolly, 2 vols. (Oxford University Press, 2013). This excellent edition includes a documentary biography and thorough annotation, to both of which I am indebted.

from *Hesperides* (1648)

The Argument of His Book

I sing of *Brooks*, of *Blossoms*, *Birds*, and *Bowers*:
Of *April*, *May*, of *June*, and *July*-Flowers.
I sing of May-poles, Hock-carts, Wassails, Wakes,[1]
Of Bride-grooms, Brides, and of their Bridal-cakes.
I write of *Youth*, of *Love*, and have Access
By these to sing of cleanly-*Wantonness*.
I sing of *Dews*, of *Rains*, and piece by piece

Notes

THE ARGUMENT OF HIS BOOK

[1] *Hock-carts* decorated carts carrying the last load of the harvest; *wassails* liquors used for celebratory drinks of health; *Wakes* "The local annual festival of an English (now chiefly rural) parish" (*OED*, 4.b).

British Literature 1640–1789: An Anthology, Fourth Edition. Edited by Robert DeMaria, Jr.

Of *Balm*, of *Oil*, of *Spice*, and *Amber-Greece*.[2]
I sing of *Times trans-shifting*; and I write
How *Roses* first came *Red*, and *Lilies White*.
I write of *Groves*, of *Twilights*, and I sing
The Court of *Mab*, and of the *Fairy-King*.[3]
I write of *Hell*; I sing (and ever shall)
Of *Heaven*, and hope to have it after all.

To Daffodils

Fair Daffodils, we weep to see
You haste away so soon:
As yet the early-rising Sun
Has not attained his Noon.
Stay, stay,
Until the hasting day
Has run
But to the Even-song;
And, having prayed together, we
Will go with you along.
We have short time to stay, as you,
We have as short a Spring;
As quick a growth to meet Decay,
As you, or any thing.
We die,
As your hours do, and dry
Away,
Like to the Summer's rain;
Or as the pearls of Morning's dew
Ne'er to be found again.

The Night-piece, to Julia

Her Eyes the Glow-worm lend thee,
The Shooting Stars attend thee;
And the Elves also,
Whose little eyes glow,
Like the sparks of fire, befriend thee.

No *Will-o'-th'-Wisp* mis-light thee;[1]
Snake, or Slow-worm bite thee:
But on, on thy way
Not making a stay,
Since Ghost there's none to affright thee.

Notes

2 *Amber-Greece* Ambergris; "A fragrant drug … used both as a perfume and a cordial" (Johnson).
3 *Mab* Queen Mab of the fairies (a mab is also a slattern or loose woman); *Fairy-King* Oberon.

The Night-piece, to Julia
1 *Will-o'-th'-Wisp* false beacon of marsh gas.

Let not the dark thee cumber;
What though the Moon does slumber?
    The Stars of the night
    Will lend thee their light,
Like Tapers clear without number.

Then *Julia* let me woo thee,
Thus, thus to come unto me:
    And when I shall meet
    Thy silv'ry feet,
My soul I'll pour into thee.

The Hock-Cart, or Harvest Home[1]

To the Right Honourable Mildmay, Earl of Westmorland[2]

Come Sons of Summer, by whose toil
We are the Lords of Wine and Oil:
By whose tough labours, and rough hands,
We rip up first, then reap our lands.
Crowned with the ears of corn, now come,
And, to the Pipe, sing Harvest home.
Come forth, my Lord, and see the Cart
Dressed up with all the Country Art.
See, here a *Maukin*, there a sheet,[3]
As spotless pure as it is sweet:
The Horses, Mares, and frisking Fillies
(Clad, all, in Linen, white as Lillies).
The Harvest Swains and Wenches bound
For joy, to see the *Hock-cart* crowned.
About the Cart, hear how the Rout
Of Rural Younglings raise the shout;
Pressing before, some coming after,
Those with a shout, and these with laughter.
Some bless the Cart; some kiss the sheaves;
Some prank them up with Oaken leaves:
Some cross the Fill-horse; some with great[4]
Devotion stroke the home-borne wheat;
While other Rustics, less attent
To Prayers than to Merriment,
Run after with their breeches rent.
Well, on, brave boys, to your Lord's Hearth,

Notes

The Hock-Cart, or Harvest Home

[1] *Hock-Cart* the decorated last wagon of the harvest.

[2] *Earl of Westmorland* Mildmay Fane (1600?–66).

[3] *Maukin* "A kind of mop made of clouts [rags] for sweeping ovens; thence a frightful figure of clouts dressed up; thence a dirty wench" (Johnson, quoting Hanmer); a *sheet* could be used as an instrument of punishment for fornication, or simply for decoration (see *OED*).

[4] *cross the Fill-horse* bless the horse positioned between the fills (thills or shafts) of the cart.

Glitt'ring with fire; where, for your mirth,
Ye shall see first the large and chief
Foundation of your Feast, Fat Beef,
With Upper Stories, Mutton, Veal[5]
And Bacon (which makes full the meal)
With several dishes standing by,
As here a Custard, there a Pie,
And here all tempting Frumenty,[6]
And for to make the merry cheer,
If smirking Wine be wanting here,[7]
There's that which drowns all care, stout Beer;
Which freely drink, to your Lord's health,
Then to the Plough (the Common-wealth)
Next to your Flails, your Fans, your Fats[8]
Then to the Maids with Wheaten Hats:
To the rough Sickle, and crook'd Scythe,
Drink, frolic boys, till all be blithe.
Feed, and grow fat; and as ye eat
Be mindful that the lab'ring Neat[9]
(As you) may have their fill of meat.[10]
And know, besides, ye must revoke[11]
The patient Ox unto the Yoke,
And all go back unto the Plough
And Harrow (though they're hanged up now).
And, you must know, your Lord's word's true,
Feed him ye must, whose food fills you;
And that this pleasure is like rain,
Not sent ye for to drown your pain,
But for to make it spring again.

Upon Julia's Clothes

Whenas in silks my *Julia* goes,
Then, then (methinks) how sweetly flows
That liquefaction of her clothes.

Next, when I cast mine eyes and see
That brave Vibration each way free;[1]
O how that glittering taketh me!

Notes

[5] *Upper Stories* additional courses.

[6] *Frumenty* "Food made of wheat boiled in milk" (Johnson).

[7] *smirking* "Nice; smart; jaunty" (Johnson, s.v. "to smerk").

[8] *Fans* winnowing fans; *Fats* large tubs used in making beer.

[9] *neat* "Black cattle; oxen" (Johnson).

[10] *meat* nourishment, food in general.

[11] *revoke* call back.

Upon Julia's Clothes

[1] *Vibration* "The act of moving or being moved with quick reciprocations, or returns; the act of quivering" (Johnson).

When he would have his verses read

In sober mornings, do not thou rehearse[1]
The holy incantation of a verse;
But when that men have both well drunk, and fed,
Let my Enchantments then be sung, or read.
When Laurel spirts i' th' fire, and when the Hearth
Smiles to itself, and gilds the roof with mirth;
When up the *Thyrse* is raised, and when the sound[2]
Of sacred *Orgies* flies, A round, A round.[3]
When the *Rose* reigns, and locks with ointments shine,
Let rigid *Cato* read these Lines of mine.[4]

Delight in Disorder

A sweet disorder in the dress
Kindles in clothes a wantonness:
A Lawn about the shoulders thrown[1]
Into a fine distraction:
An erring Lace, which here and there
Enthrals the Crimson Stomacher:[2]
A Cuff neglectful, and thereby
Ribbands to flow confusedly:
A winning wave (deserving Note)
In the tempestuous petticoat:
A careless shoe-string, in whose tie
I see a wild civility:
Do more bewitch me, than when Art
Is too precise in every part.

To the Virgins, to make much of Time

Gather ye Rose-buds while ye may,
    Old Time is still a flying:
And this same flower that smiles to day
    Tomorrow will be dying.

The glorious Lamp of Heaven, the Sun,
    The higher he's a getting;
The sooner will his Race be run,
    And nearer he's to Setting.

Notes

When he would have his verses read

1 *rehearse* recite.
2 *Thyrse* the scepter of Bacchus, god of revelry.
3 *Orgies* "Mad rites of Bacchus, frantic revels" (Johnson).
4 *Cato* M. Porcius Cato the elder, a strict Roman moralist. Lines 9–10 translate Martial, *Epigrams*, X, 20. Roses and oiled locks signify luxurious festivities.

Delight in Disorder

1 *A Lawn* a scarf or shawl made of lawn, fine linen.
2 *Stomacher* "An ornamental covering worn by women on the breast" (Johnson).

That Age is best, which is the first,
When Youth and Blood are warmer;
But being spent, the worse, and worst
Times, still succeed the former.

Then be not coy, but use your time;
And while ye may, go marry:
For having lost but once your prime,
You may forever tarry.

His Return to London

From the dull confines of the drooping West,
To see the day spring from the pregnant East,
Ravished in spirit, I come, nay more, I fly
To thee, blest place of my Nativity!
Thus, thus with hallowed foot I touch the ground,
With thousand blessings by thy Fortune crowned.
O fruitful Genius! that bestowest here
An everlasting plenty, year by year.
O *Place*! O *People*! Manners! framed to please
All *Nations, Customs, Kindreds, Languages*!
I am a free-born *Roman*; suffer then,
That I amongst you live a Citizen.
London my home is: though by hard fate sent
Into a long and irksome banishment;
Yet since called back; henceforward let me be,
O native country, repossessed by thee!
For, rather than I'll to the West return,
I'll beg of thee first here to have mine Urn.
Weak I am grown, and must in short time fall;
Give thou my sacred Relics Burial.[1]

The Bad Season Makes the Poet Sad

Dull to myself, and almost dead to these
My many fresh and fragrant Mistresses:
Lost to all Music now; since every thing
Puts on the semblance here of sorrowing.
Sick is the Land to th' heart; and doth endure
More dangerous faintings by her desperate cure.
But if that golden Age would come again,
And *Charles* here Rule, as he before did Reign;
If smooth and unperplexed the Seasons were,

Notes

His Return to London

[1] *Relics* physical remains, sometimes those of a saint.

As when the *Sweet Maria* livèd here:[1]
I should delight to have my Curls half drowned
In *Tyrian Dews*, and Head with Roses crowned;[2]
And once more yet (ere I am laid out dead)
Knock at a Star with my exalted Head.

The Pillar of Fame[1]

Fame's pillar here, at last, we set,
Out-during *Marble*, *Brass*, or *Jet*,
Charmed and enchanted so,
As to withstand the blow
Of overthrow:
Nor shall the seas
Or Outrages
Of storms o'erbear
What we up-rear
Tho' Kingdoms fall,
This pillar never shall
Decline or waste at all;
But stand for ever by his owne
Firm and well fixed foundatiòn.

Notes

The Bad Season Makes the Poet Sad

1 *Maria* Henrietta Maria (1609–69), Queen Consort of Charles I.

2 *Tyrian Dews* oil, used, like roses, in luxurious festivities.

The Pillar of Fame

1 Except for a two-line envoy, this is the last poem in the volume.

John Milton (1608–1674)

John Milton believed, with much justification, that he was gifted and that only a very great work would vindicate his special, God-given talents. He regarded his early life as preparation for his high promise and never doubted that he had the ability to write a work that the world, in his words, "would not willingly let die."[1] He contemplated an epic about King Arthur, feeling that such a poem (like the *Aeneid* or the *Iliad*) must have national implications. Although *Paradise Lost* reflects Milton's view of English politics, its canvas is biblical and therefore, for Milton, universal history. Although he explores the full scope of biblical history in the last two books, Milton concentrates mainly on the portion of it described in brief in Genesis 1–3. Drawing on his encyclopedic knowledge of classical and biblical learning, Milton makes this crystal grow to embrace a vision of all human life – domestic, political, religious, social, and artistic.

For all its universality, however, Milton's vision is tinged with his own views: the polity between the sexes is his idealized vision of marriage formed partly through the experience of his first, difficult marriage, for example, while his devils are frequently made to resemble Roman Catholics or Episcopal figures who, in Milton's view, had revolted or rebelled from the true religion of the Protestants. Because Milton saw the established monarchy in England and the Catholic Church as usurpers, it is probably misleading to imagine, with William Blake and some great critics, that he sides with the Devil's party, despite the exciting poetry he created to describe them. In fact, the language of Satan and the devils is filled with irony and innuendo that redounds against them. God and Christ can also be ironic, but the joke is always on the devils who imagine they can outwit God, whose enduring nature is ever to work good out of whatever evil they contrive.

Partly because of its tinges of contemporary satire and its ironies, *Paradise Lost* has some affinities with the world of mock-heroic, satirical, and ironic poetry that was prevalent throughout the main part of the period covered in this anthology. Most subsequent writers of the period recognized its greatness and immediately incorporated it into their literary backgrounds: because it provided an example of truly heroic English poetry on a grand scale, *Paradise Lost* made mock-heroic poetry in English much more possible. Like Milton himself, succeeding generations of poets continued to refer to Spenser's more pastoral epic, and the language of Shakespearian tragedy provided a standard of high seriousness, but Milton became the most important model of grandeur and sublimity in English writing.

Paradise Lost was not published until 1667, when Milton was fifty-eight and seven years from his death. It might never have been finished if the collapse of Cromwell's government had not freed Milton from his duties as Latin secretary to the lord protector and disengaged him from his life as a polemicist. It also would not have been finished if Charles II's government had decided to prosecute Milton for the views he espoused during the interregnum,

Notes

John Milton

1 *The Reason of Church Government* (1642).

British Literature 1640–1789: An Anthology, Fourth Edition. Edited by Robert DeMaria, Jr.

which included justifications for the execution of Charles I. He boldly reaffirmed the Commonwealth's most drastic single measure, among other places, in *Eikonoklastes* (1649), his attack on Charles's popular, posthumously published *Eikon Basilike*. As it was, partly through the intervention of Andrew Marvell, the government allowed Milton to live a private life in which he completed his life's work. I include two selections from Milton's prose: a small part of *The Doctrine and Discipline of Divorce* (1643); and most of *Areopagitica* (1644), an attack on licensing, or censorship. Both works were written partly in response to personal experience. Milton expounded the scriptural justification for divorce shortly after his wife of one month, Mary Powell, returned to her father's house because she found life with her husband too difficult. *Areopagitica* is partly Milton's response to complaints about his unlicensed publication of the divorce tracts. In both cases, however, as in all of his works, Milton combines universal with personal considerations. Despite the various roles that Milton played in society, he was always a consummate artist who brilliantly and egotistically transmuted the stuff of his own experience into works that are important and inspiring for readers whom he never imagined, and about whose lives he certainly would not have cared to learn.

In the first edition of this anthology all of *Paradise Lost* was included. Although this made even Milton disproportionately conspicuous in the representation of the period, having the poem whole seemed best. In many ways that still seems the best course, and there is something almost sacrilegious about trimming *Paradise Lost*. However, by printing only four of the twelve books, room has been made for other selections, and Milton no longer occupies a quarter of the contents of the book. The books of *Paradise Lost* that I have chosen to include are I, II, IV, and IX. The first two have long been the choice of editors forced to make a selection, and for very good reasons: they provide the crucial opening of the epic, including Milton's most important statement of his purpose; in containing the most continuous treatment of Satan and his crew, they are essential to any understanding of the politics of the poem and its place in civil history; and they are, happily, a fairly integral and complete unit of poetry in themselves. Book IX is also an obvious choice because it contains the climax of the poem, the fall of man, and it too is a fairly integral unit, resembling in length as well as structure a classical tragedy. Book IV has more recently become indispensable as readers have learned to be fully conscious of the domestic concerns in the poem. Here we learn most about the relationship between Adam and Eve in the Garden and hence about the primeval polity between the sexes as Milton saw it. Old hands at teaching *Paradise Lost* may not agree with Samuel Johnson that "no man ever wished it longer," but I think most would concede that there is enough in even these four books to give Milton his share of the stage in a study of literature produced in Britain from 1640 to 1789. The "arguments," Milton's summaries, of the excluded books have been retained for obvious reasons.

In addition to the pieces of prose and the four books of Paradise Lost, I include three of Milton's sonnets. I follow the text of *Poems* (1673) in Sonnets 18 and 19, but take the numbering of all three sonnets from the *Columbia Edition of the Works of John Milton*. The text of sonnet 16 is based on a Trinity College (Cambridge) manuscript. My texts of Milton are based on first editions, except in the case of *Paradise Lost*, where the second edition of 1674 is the copytext. There have been many fine editors of Milton and I am indebted to several of them, particularly Douglas Bush and Merrit Hughes, from whose texts I was taught and have taught for many years. *The Yale Edition of the Complete Prose Works of John Milton* (1953–82) is a magnificent achievement, and I am also indebted to its editors. The Columbia Edition of the complete works, 18 vols. (1931–8) is being superseded by the Oxford Edition, ed. Thomas N. Corns and Gordon Campbell, 9 vols. (2008–).

Important biographies of Milton include William Riley Parker's definitive *Milton: Biography* (1968; 2nd edition, revised version edited by Gordon Campbell, Clarendon Press, 1996), Barbara Lewalski's *The Life of John Milton: A Critical Biography* (Blackwell, 2000) and Gordon Campbell and Thomas N. Corns's *John Milton: Life, Work, and Thought* (Oxford University Press, 2008).

from *The Doctrine and Discipline of Divorce; Restored to the Good of Both Sexes, From the bondage of Canon Law, and other mistakes, to Christian freedom, guided by the Rule of Charity. Wherein also many places of Scripture, have recovered their long-lost meaning. Seasonable to be now thought on in the Reformation intended.* (1643)

Matthew. 13.52.

Every Scribe instructed to the Kingdom of Heaven, is like the Master of a house which bringeth out of his treasury things old and new.

Book I
The Preface

Many men, whether it be their fate, or fond opinion, easily persuade themselves, if GOD would be pleased a while to withdraw his just punishments from us, and to restrain what power either the devil, or any earthly enemy hath to work us woe, that then man's nature would find immediate rest and releasement from all evils. But verily they who think so, if they be such as have a mind large enough to take into their thoughts a general survey of human things, would soon prove themselves in that opinion far deceived. For though it were granted us by divine indulgence to be exempt from all that can be harmful to us from without, yet the perverseness of our folly is so bent, that we should never lin[1] hammering out of our own hearts, as it were out of a flint, the seeds and sparkles of new miseries to our selves, till all were in a blaze again. And no marvel if out of our own hearts, for they are evil; but even out of those things which God meant us, either for a principal good, or a pure contentment, we are still hatching and contriving upon our selves matter of continual sorrow and perplexity. What greater good to man than that revealed rule, whereby God vouchsafes to show us how he would be worshipped? and yet that not rightly understood, became the cause that once a famous man in *Israel*[2] could not but oblige his conscience to be the sacrificer, or if not, the jailer of his innocent and only daughter. And was the cause ofttimes that Armies of valiant men have given up their throats to a heathenish enemy on the Sabbath day: fondly[3] thinking their defensive resistance to be as then a work unlawful. What thing more instituted to the solace and delight of man than marriage, and yet the misinterpreting of some Scripture[4] directed mainly against the abusers of

Notes

FROM *THE DOCTRINE AND DISCIPLINE OF DIVORCE*

1 *lin* "stop; give over" (Johnson).

2 *famous man in Israel* Jephthah the Gileadite vowed to make a sacrifice to God of whatever walked first through his door to greet him upon his return from successful battle with the children of Ammon. His daughter greeted him and he kept his vow, though commentators disagree on whether or not this entailed human sacrifice (Judges 11.30–40).

3 *fondly* foolishly.

4 *Scripture* Matthew 5.31–2, where Christ says only adultery is cause for a man to divorce his wife; Mosaic law cited any kind of "uncleanness" as an adequate cause for divorce (Deuteronomy 24.1).

the Law for divorce given them by *Moses*, hath changed the blessing of matrimony not seldom into a familiar and co-inhabiting mischief; at least into a drooping and disconsolate household captivity, without refuge or redemption. So ungoverned and so wild a race doth superstition run us from one extreme of abused liberty into the other of unmerciful restraint. For although God in the first ordaining of marriage, taught us to what end he did it, in words expressly implying the apt and cheerful conversation of man with woman, to comfort and refresh him against the evil of solitary life, not mentioning the purpose of generation till afterwards, as being but a secondary end in dignity, though not in necessity; yet now, if any two be but once handed[5] in the Church, and have tasted in any sort of the nuptial bed, let them find themselves never so mistaken in their dispositions through any error, concealment, or misadventure, that through their different tempers, thought, and constitutions, they can neither be to one another a remedy against loneliness, nor live in any union or contentment all their days, yet they shall, so they be but found suitably weaponed to the least possibility of sensual enjoyment, be made, [in] spite of *antipathy* to fadge[6] together, and combine as they may to their unspeakable wearisomeness & despair of all sociable delight in the ordinance which God established to that very end. What a calamity is this, and as the Wise-man, if he were alive, would sigh out in his own phrase, what a *sore evil is this under the Sun!*[7] All which we can refer justly to no other author than the Canon Law[8] and her adherents, not consulting with charity, the interpreter and guide of our faith, but resting in the mere element of the Text; doubtless by the policy of the devil to make that gracious ordinance become unsupportable, that what with men not daring to venture upon wedlock, and what with men wearied out of it, all inordinate licence might abound. It was for many ages that marriage lay in disgrace with most of the ancient Doctors,[9] as a work of the flesh, almost a defilement, wholly denied to Priests, and the second time dissuaded to all, as he that reads *Tertullian* or *Jerome* may see at large. Afterwards it was thought so Sacramental, that no adultery or desertion could dissolve it; and this is the sense of our Canon Courts in *England* to this day, but in no other reformed Church else; yet there remains in them also a burden on it as heavy as the other two were disgraceful or superstitious, and of as much iniquity, crossing a Law not only written by *Moses*, but charactered[10] in us by nature, of more antiquity and deeper ground than marriage itself; which Law is to force nothing against the faultless proprieties of nature: yet that this may be colourably[11] done, our Saviour's words touching divorce, are as it were congealed into a stony rigour, inconsistent both with his doctrine and his office, and that which he preached only to the conscience, is by canonical tyranny snatched into the compulsive censure of a judicial Court; where Laws are imposed even against the venerable & secret power of nature's impression, to love, whatever cause be found to loathe. Which is a heinous barbarism both against the honour of marriage, the dignity of man and his soul, the goodness of Christianity, and all the humane respects of civility. Notwithstanding that some of the wisest and gravest among the Christian Emperors, who had about them, to consult with, those of

Notes

5 *handed* joined, hand in hand.

6 *fadge* "To do with, put up with" (*OED*, 2).

7 *sore evil is this under the Sun* Ecclesiastes 5.13, where the evil is "riches kept for the owners thereof to their hurt."

8 *Canon Law* "that law which is made and ordained in general council, or provincial synod of the church" (Johnson, quoting John Ayliffe).

9 *ancient Doctors* early interpreters of the Bible, church fathers like Tertullian (c.160–c.240) and Jerome (c.342–420).

10 *charactered* written.

11 *colourably* plausibly.

the fathers then living, who for their learning & holiness of life are still with us in great renown, have made their statutes & edicts concerning this debate, far more easy and relenting in many necessary cases, wherein the Canon is inflexible. And *Hugo Grotius*,[12] a man of these times, one of the best learned, seems not obscurely to adhere in his persuasion to the equity of those imperial decrees, in his notes upon the *Evangelists*, much allaying the outward roughness of the Text, which hath for the most part been too immoderately expounded; and excites the diligence of others to enquire further into this question, as containing many points which have not yet been explained. By which, and by mine own apprehension of what public duty each man owes, I conceive myself exhorted among the rest to communicate such thoughts as I have, and offer them now in this general labour of reformation, to the candid view both of Church and Magistrate; especially because I see it the hope of good men, that those irregular and unspiritual Courts have spun their utmost date in this Land; and some better course must now be constituted. He therefore that by adventuring shall be so happy as with success to ease & set free the minds of ingenuous and apprehensive men[13] from this needless thraldom, he that can prove it lawful and just to claim the performance of a fit and matchable conversation, no less essential to the prime scope of marriage than the gift of bodily conjunction, or else to have an equal plea of divorce as well as for that corporal deficiency; he that can but lend us the clue that winds out this labyrinth[14] of servitude to such a reasonable and expedient liberty as this, deserves to be reckoned among the public benefactors of civil and humane[15] life; above the inventors of wine and oil; for this is a far dearer, far nobler, and more desirable cherishing to man's life, unworthily exposed to sadness and mistake, which he shall vindicate. Not that licence and levity and unconsented breach of faith should herein be countenanced, but that some conscionable, and tender pity might be had of those who have unwarily in a thing they never practised before, made themselves the bondmen of a luckless and helpless matrimony. In which Argument he whose courage can serve him to give the first onset, must look for two several oppositions; the one from those who having sworn themselves to long custom and the letter of the Text, will not out of the road: the other from those whose gross and vulgar apprehensions conceit[16] but low of matrimonial purposes, and in the work of male and female think they have all. Nevertheless, it shall be here sought by due ways to be made appear, that those words of God in the institution, promising a meet help against loneliness;[17] and those words of Christ, *That his yoke is easy and his burden light*,[18] were not spoken in vain; for if the knot of marriage may in no case be dissolved but for adultery, all the burdens and services of the Law are not so intolerable. This only is desired of them who are minded to judge hardly of thus maintaining, that they would be still and hear all out, nor think it equal to answer deliberate reason with sudden heat and noise; remembering this, that many truths now of reverend esteem and credit, had their birth and beginning once from singular and private thoughts; while the most of men were otherwise possessed; and had the fate at first to be generally exploded[19] and exclaimed on by many violent opposers;

Notes

12 *Hugo Grotius* (1585–1645), Dutch scholar who excelled especially in theology and law.

13 *ingenuous and apprehensive* intelligent and perceptive.

14 *clue that winds out this labyrinth* Ariadne gave Theseus the clue of thread that helped him out of the labyrinth in which her father kept the minotaur; Theseus promised to marry her, but (in the most popular account) abandoned her on Naxos where she became the wife of Dionysus.

15 *humane* polite

16 *conceit* conceive.

17 *a meet help against loneliness* Genesis 2.18; *meet* "Fit; proper; qualified" (Johnson).

18 *his yoke is easy and his burden light* Matthew 11.30, where the yoke symbolizes devotion to Christ.

19 *exploded* driven "out disgracefully with some noise of contempt" (Johnson).

yet I may err perhaps in soothing myself that this present truth revived, will deserve to be not ungently received on all hands; in that it undertakes the cure of an inveterate disease crept into the best part of humane society: and to do this with no smarting corrosive, but with a smooth and pleasing lesson, which received hath the virtue to soften and dispel rooted and knotty sorrows; and without enchantment or spell used hath regard at once both to serious pity, and upright honesty; that tends to the redeeming and restoring of none but such as are the object of compassion; having in an ill hour hampered[20] themselves to the utter dispatch of all their most beloved comforts & repose for this life's term. But if we shall obstinately dislike this new overture of unexpected ease and recovery, what remains but to deplore the frowardness[21] of our hopeless condition, which neither can endure the estate we are in, nor admit of remedy either sharp or sweet. Sharp we ourselves distaste; and sweet, under whose hands we are, is scrupled and suspected as too luscious.[22] In such a posture Christ found the *Jews*, who were neither won with the austerity of *John the Baptist*, and thought it too much licence to follow freely the charming pipe of him[23] who sounded and proclaimed liberty and relief to all distress: yet Truth in some age or other will find her witness, and shall be justified at last by her own children.

from Chapter I

To remove therefore, if it be possible, this great and sad oppression which through the strictness of a literal interpreting hath invaded and disturbed the dearest and most peaceable estate of household society, to the over-burdening, if not the overwhelming of many Christians better worth than to be so deserted of the Church's considerate care, this position shall be laid down; first proving, then answering what may be objected either from Scripture or light of reason.

That indisposition, unfitness, or contrariety of mind, arising from a cause in nature unchangeable, hindering and ever likely to hinder the main benefits of conjugal society, which are solace and peace, is a greater reason of divorce than natural frigidity, especially if there be no children, and that there be mutual consent....

from Chapter VI

... Fourthly, Marriage is a covenant the very being whereof consists, not in a forced cohabitation, and counterfeit performance of duties, but in unfeigned love and peace. Thence, saith *Solomon* in *Ecclesiastes*, "Live joyfully with the wife whom thou lovest, all thy days, for that is thy portion."[24] How then, where we find it impossible to rejoice or to love, can we obey this precept? how miserably do we defraud ourselves of that comfortable portion which God and nature will not join, adding but more vexation and violence to that blissful society by our importunate superstition, that will not hearken to St. *Paul*, 1 *Corinthians* 7 [15] who speaking of marriage and divorce, determines plain enough in general that God therein "hath called us to peace" and not "to

Notes

[20] *hampered* shackled.

[21] *frowardness* advanced state.

[22] *luscious* "Sweet, so as to nauseate" (Johnson).

[23] *him* Jesus (Matthew 11.16–19).

[24] Ecclesiastes 9.9.

bondage". Yet God himself commands in his Law more than once, and by his Prophet *Malachi*, as *Calvin* and the best translations read, that "he who hates let him divorce"; that is, he who cannot love, or delight.[25] I cannot therefore be so diffident, as not securely to conclude, that he who can receive nothing of the most important helps in marriage, being thereby disenabled to return that duty which is his, with a clear and hearty countenance; and thus continues to grieve whom he would not [be married to], and is no less grieved, that man ought even for love's sake and peace to move divorce upon good and liberal conditions to the divorced. And it is less breach of wedlock to part with wise and quiet consent betimes, than still to soil and profane that mystery of joy and union with a polluting sadness and perpetual distemper; for it is not the outward continuing of marriage that keeps whole that covenant, but whosoever does most according to peace and love, whether in marriage, or in divorce, he it is that breaks marriage least; it being so often written, that "love only is the fulfilling of every Commandment."[26]

from *Areopagitica*; A Speech of Mr. *John Milton* for the Liberty of Unlicensed Printing, to the Parliament of England[1] (1644)

They who to States and Governors of the Commonwealth direct their Speech, High Court of Parliament, or wanting such access in a private condition, write that which they foresee may advance the public good; I suppose them as at the beginning of no mean endeavour, not a little altered and moved inwardly in their minds: Some with doubt of what will be the success, others with fear of what will be the censure; some with hope, others with confidence of what they have to speak. And me perhaps each of these dispositions, as the subject was whereon I entered, may have at other times variously affected; and likely might in these foremost expressions now also disclose which of them swayed most, but that the very attempt of this address thus made, and the thought of whom it hath recourse to, hath got the power within me to a passion, far more welcome than incidental to a Preface. Which though I stay not to confess ere any ask, I shall be blameless, if it be no other, than the joy and gratulation which it brings to all who wish and promote their Country's liberty; whereof this whole Discourse proposed will be a certain testimony, if not a Trophy. For this is not the liberty which we can hope, that no grievance ever should arise in the Commonwealth, that let no man in this World expect; but when complaints are freely heard, deeply considered, and speedily reformed, then is the utmost bound of civil liberty attained, that wise men look for. To which if I now manifest by the very sound of this which I shall utter, that we are already in good part arrived, and yet from such a steep disadvantage of tyranny and superstition grounded into our principles as was beyond the manhood of a *Roman* recovery, it will be attributed first, as if most due, to the strong assistance of God our deliverer, next to your faithful guidance and undaunted Wisdom, Lords and Commons of *England*. Neither is it in God's esteem the diminution of his glory, when honourable things are spoken of good men and worthy Magistrates; which if I now first should begin to do, after so fair a progress of your laudable deeds,

Notes

[25] *Calvin and the best ... delight* Malachi 2.16; Milton adopts a very doubtful reading.

[26] "love only is the fulfilling of every Commandment" Romans 13.10, "love is the fulfilling of the law."

FROM *AREOPAGITICA*

[1] Milton derives his title from an oration by Isocrates called *Areopagiticus*, which concerned a legal institution called the Court of the Areopagus.

and such a long obligement upon the whole Realm to your indefatigable virtues,[2] I might be justly reckoned among the tardiest, and the unwillingest of them that praise ye. Nevertheless there being three principal things, without which all praising is but Courtship and flattery, First, when that only is praised which is solidly worth praise: next, when greatest likelihoods are brought that such things are truly and really in those persons to whom they are ascribed, the other, when he who praises, by showing that such his actual persuasion is of whom he writes, can demonstrate that he flatters not; the former two of these I have heretofore endeavoured, rescuing the employment from him[3] who went about to impair your merits with a trivial and malignant *Encomium*; the latter as belonging chiefly to mine own acquittal, that whom I so extolled I did not flatter, hath been reserved opportunely to this occasion. For he who freely magnifies what hath been nobly done, and fears not to declare as freely what might be done better, gives ye the best covenant of his fidelity; and that his loyallest affection and his hope waits on your proceedings. His highest praising is not flattery, and his plainest advice is a kind of praising; for though I should affirm and hold by argument, that it would fare better with truth, with learning, and the Commonwealth, if one of your published Orders which I should name, were called in, yet at the same time it could not much redound to the lustre of your mild and equal Government, whenas private persons are hereby animated to think ye better pleased with public advice, than other statists[4] have been delighted heretofore with public flattery. And men will then see what difference there is between the magnanimity of a triennial Parliament,[5] and that jealous haughtiness of Prelates and cabin Counsellors that usurped of late,[6] whenas they shall observe ye in the midst of your Victories and successes more gently brooking written exceptions against a voted Order, than other Courts, which had produced nothing worth memory but the weak ostentation of wealth, would have endured the least signified dislike at any sudden Proclamation. If I should thus far presume upon the meek demeanour of your civil and gentle greatness, Lords and Commons, as what your published Order hath directly said, that to gainsay, I might defend myself with ease, if any should accuse me of being new or insolent, did they but know how much better I find ye esteem it to imitate the old and elegant humanity of Greece, than the barbaric pride of a *Hunnish* and *Norwegian* stateliness. And out of those ages, to whose polite wisdom and letters we owe that we are not yet *Goths* and *Jutlanders*, I could name him who from his private house wrote that discourse to the Parliament of *Athens*,[7] that persuades them to change the form of *Democracy* which was then established. Such honour was done in those days to men who professed the study of wisdom and eloquence, not only in their own Country, but in other Lands, that Cities and Seigniories[8] heard them gladly, and with great respect, if they had ought in public to admonish the State. Thus did *Dion Prusaeus*[9] a stranger and a private Orator counsel the *Rhodians* against a former Edict: and I abound with other like examples, which to

Notes

2 *your indefatigable virtues* the Long Parliament that Milton praises had been meeting since 1640, about four years.

3 *him* Joseph Hall, bishop of Norwich (1574–1656).

4 *statists* statesmen; politicians.

5 *triennial Parliament* a Parliament that would meet only every three years; Charles I had agreed to such a minimum in an act of February 16, 1641.

6 *usurped of late* Parliamentary supporters regarded the king's refusal to convene Parliament as a usurpation of authority.

7 *him who from ... Athens* Isocrates (436–338 BCE) addressed the assembled citizens of Athens, whom Milton styles the Parliament; like *Areopagitica*, Isocrates' oration was written to be read rather than for him to perform.

8 *Seigniories* territories under the control of a feudal lord.

9 *Dion Prusaeus* Greek orator of the first century CE.

set here would be superfluous. But if from the industry of a life wholly dedicated to studious labours, and those natural endowments haply not the worst for two and fifty degrees of northern latitude,[10] so much must be derogated, as to count me not equal to any of those who had this privilege, I would obtain to be thought not so inferior, as yourselves are superior to the most of them who received their counsel: and how far you excel them, be assured, Lords and Commons, there can no greater testimony appear, than when your prudent spirit acknowledges and obeys the voice of reason from what quarter soever it be heard speaking; and renders ye as willing to repeal any Act of your own setting forth, as any set forth by your Predecessors.

If ye be thus resolved, as it were injury to think ye were not, I know not what should withhold me from presenting ye with a fit instance wherein to show both that love of truth which ye eminently profess, and that uprightness of your judgement which is not wont to be partial to yourselves; by judging over again that Order which ye have ordained "to regulate Printing. That no Book, pamphlet, or paper shall be henceforth Printed, unless the same be first approved and licensed by such", or at least one of such as shall be thereto appointed.[11] For that part which preserves justly every man's Copy to himself,[12] or provides for the poor,[13] I touch not, only wish they be not made pretences to abuse and persecute honest and painful[14] Men, who offend not in either of these particulars. But that other clause of Licensing Books,[15] which we thought had died with his brother *quadragesimal* and *matrimonial*[16] when the Prelates expired, I shall now attend with such a Homily, as shall lay before ye, first the inventors of it to be those whom ye will be loath to own; next what is to be thought in general of reading, whatever sort the Books be; and that this Order avails nothing to the suppressing of scandalous, seditious, and libellous Books, which were mainly intended to be suppressed. Last, that it will be primely to the discouragement of all learning, and the stop of Truth, not only by the disexercising and blunting our abilities in what we know already, but by hindering and cropping the discovery that might be yet further made both in religious and civil Wisdom.

I deny not, but that it is of greatest concernment in the Church and Commonwealth, to have a vigilant eye how Books demean[17] themselves as well as men; and thereafter to confine, imprison, and do sharpest justice on them as malefactors: For Books are not absolutely dead things, but do contain a potency of life in them to be as active as that soul was whose progeny they are; nay they do preserve as in a vial the purest efficacy and extraction of that living intellect that bred them. I know they are as lively, and as vigorously productive, as those fabulous Dragon's teeth; and being sown up and down, may chance to spring up armed men.[18] And yet on the other hand unless

Notes

[10] Milton seems to believe that northern climates dampen intellectual vigor; cf. *Paradise Lost* 9.44–5.

[11] This order of Parliament was passed on June 14, 1643 and effectively reinstituted the procedures for controlling the press decreed by the Star Chamber in 1637. Milton's eloquence did not impel Parliament to rescind its order.

[12] The order forbade republication of licensed books without the consent of the owner; *Copy* means "The autograph; the original" (Johnson).

[13] The order protected books granted to the Stationers' Company for the maintenance of their poor.

[14] *painful* painstaking.

[15] The principal clause of the order banned publication of books, pamphlets, or papers unless they were licensed by a committee of Parliamentary appointees and entered in the rollbooks of the Stationers' Company.

[16] *quadragesimal and matrimonial* dispensations concerning Lent and marriage in the Episcopal Church; its Prelates', or bishops', power expired in a bill passed in 1642.

[17] *demean* "To behave; to carry one's self" (Johnson).

[18] Cadmus killed the fabulous dragon on his way to founding Thebes; following a god's advice he planted the dragon's teeth, which sprang up as the belligerent Sparti, the fore-fathers of the city.

wariness be used, as good almost kill a Man as kill a good Book; who kills a Man kills a reasonable creature, God's Image; but he who destroys a good Book, kills reason itself, kills the Image of God, as it were in the eye. Many a man lives a burden to the Earth; but a good Book is the precious life-blood of a master spirit, embalmed and treasured up on purpose to a life beyond life. 'Tis true, no age can restore a life, whereof perhaps there is no great loss; and revolutions of ages do not oft recover the loss of a rejected truth, for the want of which whole Nations fare the worse. We should be wary therefore what persecution we raise against the living labours of public men, how we spill that seasoned life of man preserved and stored up in Books; since we see a kind of massacre, whereof the execution ends not in the slaying of an elemental life, but strikes at that ethereal and fifth essence,[19] the breath of reason itself, slays an immortality rather than a life. But lest I should be condemned of introducing licence, while I oppose Licensing, I refuse not the pains to be so much Historical, as will serve to show what hath been done by ancient and famous Commonwealths, against this disorder, till the very time that this project of licensing crept out of the *Inquisition*,[20] was catched up by our Prelates, and hath caught some of our Presbyters.[21]

In *Athens* where Books and Wits were even busier then in any other part of *Greece*, I find but only two sorts of writings which the Magistrate cared to take notice of; those either blasphemous and Atheistical, or Libellous. Thus the Books of *Protagorus* were by Judges of *Areopagus* commanded to be burnt, and himself banished the territory for a discourse begun with his confessing not to know *whether there were gods, or whether not*: And against defaming, it was decreed that none should be traduced by name, as was the manner of *Vetus Comœdia*,[22] whereby we may guess how they censured libelling: And this course was quick enough, as *Cicero* writes,[23] to quell both the desperate wits of other Atheists, and the open way of defaming, as the event shewed. Of other sects and opinions though tending to voluptuousness, and the denying of divine providence they took no heed.... [24]

And thus ye have the Inventors and the original of Book-licensing ripped up, and drawn as lineally as any pedigree. We have it not, that can be heard of, from any ancient State, or polity, or Church, nor by any Statute left us by our Ancestors, elder or later; nor from the modern custom of any reformed City, or Church abroad; but from the most Antichristian Council, and the most tyrannous Inquisition that ever inquired. Till then Books were ever as freely admitted into the World as any other birth; the issue of the brain was no more stifled than the issue of the womb: no envious *Juno* sat cross-legged over the nativity of any man's intellectual offspring;[25] but if it proved a Monster, who denies, but that it was justly burnt, or sunk in the Sea. But that a Book in worse condition than a peccant soul, should be to stand before a Jury ere it be born to the

Notes

[19] *fifth essence* quintessence; a mystical substance above the four elements of nature.

[20] *Inquisition* a Roman Catholic institution for suppressing heresy, especially strong in Spain after 1478.

[21] *Presbyters* representative officers in the reformed but censorious Presbyterian organization of the church which was officially accepted by the British Parliament in 1646 but swiftly rejected in the same year because of objections by Independents in the House of Commons.

[22] *Vetus Comœdia* the old comedy, which was more direct and personal in its satire than the comedy that flourished in mid-fifth-century BCE Athens and later.

[23] *Cicero writes* in *De Natura Deorum*.

[24] I omit several pages in which Milton continues to find the Athenian and Roman governments free of licensing and traces its origins in the popes and its perfection to the Council of Trent (1545–63) and the Spanish Inquisition.

[25] Juno caused one of the guardian deities of birth to sit cross-legged on the threshold of Alcmena when she was trying to give birth to Hercules, son of Juno's husband Zeus (Ovid, *Metamorphoses* 9.281–313).

World, and undergo yet in darkness the judgement of *Radamanth* and his Colleagues,[26] ere it can pass the ferry backward into light, was never heard before, till that mysterious iniquity provoked and troubled at the first entrance of Reformation, sought out new limbos and new hells wherein they might include our Books also within the number of their damned. And this was the rare morsel so officiously snatched up, and so ill-favouredly imitated by our inquisiturient Bishops, and the attendant minorities their Chaplains. That ye like not now these most certain Authors of this licensing order, and that all sinister intention was far distant from your thoughts, when ye were importuned the passing it, all men who know the integrity of your actions, and how ye honour Truth, will clear ye readily.

But some will say, what though the Inventors were bad, the thing for all that may be good? It may so: yet if that thing be no such deep invention, but obvious, and easy for any man to light on, and yet best and wisest Commonwealths through all ages, and occasions have forborn to use it, and falsest seducers, and oppressors of men were the first who took it up, and to no other purpose but to obstruct and hinder the first approach of a Reformation; I am of those who believe, it will be a harder alchemy than *Lullius*[27] ever knew, to sublimate[28] any good use out of such an invention. Yet this only is what I request to gain from this reason, that it may be held a dangerous and suspicious fruit, as certainly it deserves, for the tree that bore it, until I can dissect one by one the properties it has. But I have first to finish as was propounded, what is to be thought in general of reading Books, whatever sort they be, and whether be more the benefit, or the harm that thence proceeds?

Not to insist upon the examples of *Moses, Daniel* and *Paul*, who were skilful in all the learning of the Egyptians, Chaldeans, and Greeks, which could not probably be without reading their Books of all sorts, in *Paul* especially, who thought it no defilement to insert into holy Scripture the sentences of three Greek Poets, and one of them a Tragedian, the question was, notwithstanding sometimes controverted among the Primitive Doctors,[29] but with great odds on that side which affirmed it both lawful and profitable, as was then evidently perceived, when *Julian* the Apostate,[30] and subtlest enemy to our faith, made a decree forbidding Christians the study of heathen learning: for, said he, they wound us with our own weapons, and with our own arts and sciences they overcome us. And indeed the Christians were put so to their shifts by this crafty means, that the two *Apollinarii*[31] were fain as a man may say, to coin all the seven liberal Sciences out of the Bible, reducing it into divers forms of Orations, Poems, Dialogues, even to the calculating of a new Christian Grammar. But saith the Historian *Socrates* [Scholasticus], The providence of God provided better than the industry of *Apollinarius* and his son, by taking away that illiterate law with the life of him who devised it. So great an injury they then held it to be deprived of *Hellenic* learning; and thought it a perfection more undermining, and secretly decaying the Church than the open cruelty of *Decius* or *Dioclesian*.[32] And perhaps it was the same politic drift that the Devil whipped

Notes

26 *Radamanth and his Colleagues* judges of Hades supervising the embarcation of souls on Charon's ferry across the River Styx into the land of darkness.

27 *Lullius* Ramon Llull, thirteenth-century Catalan mystic.

28 *sublimate* "To raise by the force of chemical fire" (Johnson).

29 *Primitive Doctors* early commentators on the Bible, or church fathers.

30 *Julian the Apostate* Flavius Claudius Julianus (331–63), emperor of Rome from 361 CE, reverted from Christianity to worship of natural but also symbolic entities like the sun.

31 *the two Apollinarii* father and son, Christian scholars in the fourth century.

32 *Decius or Dioclesian* Decius and Diocletian, Roman emperors infamous for their persecution of Christians.

St. *Jerome*[33] in a lenten dream, for reading *Cicero*; or else it was a phantasm bred by the fever which had then seized him. For had an Angel been his discipliner, unless it were for dwelling too much upon Ciceronianisms,[34] and had chastised the reading, not the vanity, it had been plainly partial; first to correct him for grave *Cicero*, and not for scurril[ous] *Plautus*[35] whom he confesses to have been reading not long before; next to correct him only, and let so many more ancient Fathers[36] wax old in those pleasant and florid studies without the lash of such a tutoring apparition; insomuch that *Basil*[37] teaches how some good use may be made of *Margites*[38] a sportful Poem, not now extant, writ by *Homer*; and why not then of *Morgante* an Italian Romance[39] much to the same purpose. But if it be agreed we shall be tried by visions, there is a vision recorded by *Eusebius*[40] far ancienter than this tale of *Jerome* to the nun *Eustochium*, and besides has nothing of a fever in it. *Dionysius Alexandrinus* was about the year 240, a person of great name in the Church for piety and learning, who had wont to avail himself much against heretics by being conversant in their Books; until a certain Presbyter laid it scrupulously among those defiling volumes. The worthy man loath to give offence fell into a new debate with himself what was to be thought; when suddenly a vision sent from God, it is his own Epistle that so avers it, confirmed him in these words: Read any books what ever come to thy hands, for thou art sufficient both to judge aright, and to examine each matter. To this revelation he assented the sooner, as he confesses, because it was answerable to that of the Apostle to the Thessalonians, Prove all things, hold fast that which is good.[41] And he might have added another remarkable saying of the same Author; To the pure all things are pure,[42] not only meats and drinks, but all kind of knowledge, whether of good and evil; the knowledge cannot defile, nor consequently the books, if the will and conscience be not defiled. For books are as meats and viands are; some of good, some of evil substance; and yet God in that unapocryphal vision, said without exception, Rise *Peter*, kill and eat, leaving the choice to each man's discretion.[43] Wholesome meats to a vitiated stomach differ little or nothing from unwholesome; and best books to a naughty mind are not unappliable to occasions of evil. Bad meats will scarce breed good nourishment in the healthiest concoction; but herein the difference is of bad books, that they to a discreet and judicious Reader serve in many respects to discover, to confute, to forewarn, and to illustrate. Whereof what better witness can ye expect I should produce, than one of your own now sitting in Parliament, the chief of learned men reputed in this Land, Mr. *Selden*,[44] whose volume of natural and national laws proves, not only by great authorities brought together, but by exquisite reasons and theorems almost mathematically demonstrative, that all opinions, yea errors, known, read, and collated, are of main service and assistance toward the speedy attainment of what is truest. I conceive therefore, that when God did enlarge the universal diet of man's body, saving ever the rules of temperance, he

Notes

33 *St. Jerome* fourth-century Christian scholar and translator of the Bible into Latin.

34 *Ciceronianisms* imitations of Cicero's Latin prose style.

35 *Plautus* Roman comic dramatist of the second century BCE.

36 *ancient Fathers* early Christian commentators.

37 *Basil* fourth-century bishop who wrote on the proper use of pagan writing.

38 *Margites* a mock-heroic poem traditionally ascribed to Homer.

39 *Romance* "A military fable of the middle ages; a tale of wild adventures in war and love" (Johnson).

40 *Eusebius* fourth-century bishop and author of a most important history of the church; the story comes from Book 7.

41 Prove all things … 1 Thessalonians 5.21.

42 *To the pure* … Titus 1.15.

43 *Rise Peter* … Acts 10.13.

44 *Selden* John Selden (1584–1654), learned lawyer and historian, author of *De Jure Naturali et Gentium juxta Disciplinam Ebraeorum* (1640), to which Milton refers.

then also, as before, left arbitrary the dieting and repasting of our minds; as wherein every mature man might have to exercise his own leading capacity. How great a virtue is temperance, how much of moment through the whole life of man? yet God commits the managing so great a trust, without particular Law or prescription, wholly to the demeanour[45] of every grown man. And therefore when he himself tabled[46] the Jews from heaven, that Omer[47] which was every man's daily portion of Manna, is computed to have been more than might have well sufficed the heartiest feeder thrice as many meals. For those actions which enter into a man, rather than issue out of him, and therefore defile not, God uses not to captivate under a perpetual childhood of prescription, but trusts him with the gift of reason to be his own chooser; there were but little work left for preaching, if law and compulsion should grow so fast upon those things which heretofore were governed only by exhortation. *Solomon* informs us that much reading is a weariness to the flesh;[48] but neither he, nor other inspired author tells us that such, or such reading is unlawful: yet certainly had God thought good to limit us herein, it had been much more expedient to have told us what was unlawful, than what was wearisome. As for the burning of those Ephesian books by St. *Paul's* converts,[49] 'tis replied the books were magic, the Syriac[50] so renders them. It was a private act, a voluntary act, and leaves us to a voluntary imitation: the men in remorse burnt those books which were their own; the Magistrate by this example is not appointed: these men practised the books, another might perhaps have read them in some sort usefully. Good and evil we know in the field of this World grow up together almost inseparably; and the knowledge of good is so involved and interwoven with the knowledge of evil, and in so many cunning resemblances hardly to be discerned, that those confused seeds which were imposed on *Psyche* as an incessant labour to cull out, and sort asunder, were not more intermixed.[51] It was from out the rind of one apple tasted, that the knowledge of good and evil as two twins cleaving together leapt forth into the World. And perhaps this is that doom which *Adam* fell into of knowing good and evil, that is to say of knowing good by evil. As therefore the state of man now is; what wisdom can there be to choose, what continence to forbear without the knowledge of evil? He that can apprehend and consider vice with all her baits and seeming pleasures, and yet abstain, and yet distinguish, and yet prefer that which is truly better, he is the true warfaring Christian. I cannot praise a fugitive and cloistered virtue, unexercised and unbreathed,[52] that never sallies out and sees her adversary, but slinks out of the race, where that immortal garland is to be run for, not without dust and heat. Assuredly we bring not innocence into the world, we bring impurity much rather: that which purifies us is trial, and trial is by what is contrary. That virtue therefore which is but a youngling in the contemplation of evil, and knows not the utmost that vice promises to her followers, and rejects it, is but a blank virtue, not a pure; her whiteness is but an excremental[53] whiteness; Which was the reason why our sage and serious Poet *Spenser*, whom I dare be known to think a better teacher then *Scotus* or *Aquinas*,[54]

Notes

45 *demeanour* behavior.

46 *tabled* banqueted, fed; see Exodus 16.

47 *Omer* a Hebrew measure equal to approximately 5 pints; see Exodus 16.33.

48 *much reading is a weariness* Ecclesiastes 12.12, where he also says, "Of making many books there is no end."

49 *the burning of those Ephesian books* Acts 19.19.

50 *Syriac* a Semitic language used in ancient Syria.

51 *Psyche* in her attempts to win back Eros and appease his mother Aphrodite the beautiful Psyche had to undergo many trials; sorting the seeds tested her industry.

52 *unbreathed* not made to breathe hard with exertion.

53 *excremental* useless.

54 *Scotus or Aquinas* scholastic philosophers, less entertaining and therefore less successful in their teaching than Spenser.

describing true temperance under the person of *Guyon*,[55] brings him in with his palmer through the cave of Mammon, and the bower of earthly bliss that he might see and know, and yet abstain. Since therefore the knowledge and survey of vice is in this world so necessary to the constituting of human virtue, and the scanning of error to the confirmation of truth, how can we more safely, and with less danger scout into the regions of sin and falsity than by reading all manner of tractates, and hearing all manner of reason? And this is the benefit which may be had of books promiscuously read. But of the harm that may result hence three kinds are usually reckoned. First, is feared the infection that may spread; but then all human learning and controversy in religious points must remove out of the world, yea the Bible itself; for that oft-times relates blasphemy not nicely, it describes the carnal sense of wicked men not unelegantly, it brings in holiest men passionately murmuring against providence through all the arguments of *Epicurus*: in other great disputes it answers dubiously and darkly to the common reader.... Seeing therefore that those books, and those in great abundance which are likeliest to taint both life and doctrine, cannot be suppressed without the fall of learning, and of all ability in disputation, and that these books of either sort are most and soonest catching to the learned, from whom to the common people whatever is heretical or dissolute may quickly be conveyed, and that evil manners are as perfectly learnt without books a thousand other ways which cannot be stopped, and evil doctrine not with books can propagate, except a teacher guide, which he might also do without writing, and so beyond prohibiting, I am not able to unfold, how this cautelous[56] enterprise of licensing can be exempted from the number of vain and impossible attempts. And he who were pleasantly disposed, could not well avoid to liken it to the exploit of that gallant man who thought to pound up the crows by shutting his Parkgate. Besides another inconvenience, if learned men be the first receivers of books and dispreaders both of vice and error, how shall the licensers themselves be confided in, unless we can confer upon them, or they assume to themselves above all others in the Land, the grace of infallibility, and uncorruptedness? And again if it be true, that a wise man like a good refiner can gather gold out of the drossiest[57] volume, and that a fool will be a fool with the best book, yea or without book, there is no reason that we should deprive a wise man of any advantage to his wisdom, while we seek to restrain from a fool, that which being restrained will be no hindrance to his folly. For if there should be so much exactness always used to keep that from him which is unfit for his reading, we should in the judgement of *Aristotle* not only, but of *Solomon*, and of our Saviour, not vouchsafe him good precepts, and by consequence not willingly admit him to good books, as being certain that a wise man will make better use of an idle pamphlet, than a fool will do of sacred Scripture. 'Tis next alleged we must not expose ourselves to temptations without necessity, and next to that, not employ our time in vain things. To both these objections one answer will serve, out of the grounds already laid, that to all men such books are not temptations, nor vanities; but useful drugs and materials wherewith to temper and compose effective and strong medicines, which man's life cannot want. The rest, as children and childish men, who have not the art to qualify and prepare these working minerals, well may be exhorted to forbear, but hindered forcibly they cannot be by all the licensing that Sainted Inquisition could ever yet

Notes

[55] *Guyon* the hero of Book II of Spenser's *Faerie Queene* (1590) passes the Cave of Mammon, symbolic of luxury (his spiritual guide, the Palmer (i.e. pilgrim), does not accompany him here), and the Bower of Bliss on his way to holiness.

[56] *cautelous* treacherous.

[57] *drossiest* most impure and worthless.

contrive; which is what I promised to deliver next, That this order of licensing conduces nothing to the end for which it was framed; and hath almost prevented[58] me by being clear already while thus much hath been explaining. See the ingenuity of Truth, who when she gets a free and willing hand, opens herself faster, than the pace of method and discourse can overtake her. It was the talk of which I began with, To shew that no Nation, or well instituted State, if they valued books at all, did ever use this way of licensing; and it might be answered, that this is a piece of prudence lately discovered. To which I return, that as it was a thing slight and obvious to think on, for if it had been difficult to find out, there wanted not among them long since, who suggested such a course; which they not following, leave us a pattern of their judgement, that it was not the not knowing, but the not approving, which was the cause of their not using it. *Plato*, a man of high authority indeed, but least of all for his Commonwealth, in the book of his laws, which no City ever yet received, fed his fancy with making many edicts to his airy Burgomasters, which they who otherwise admire him, wish had been rather buried and excused in the *genial* cups of an *Academic* night-sitting.[59] By which laws he seems to tolerate no kind of learning, but by unalterable decree, consisting most of practical traditions, to the attainment whereof a Library of smaller bulk than his own dialogues would be abundant. And there also enacts that no Poet should so much as read to any private man, what he had written, until the Judges and Law-keepers had seen it, and allowed it: But that *Plato* meant this Law peculiarly to that Commonwealth which he had imagined, and to no other, is evident. Why was he not else a Law-giver to himself, but a transgressor, and to be expelled by his own Magistrates both for the wanton epigrams and dialogues which he made, and his perpetual reading of *Sophron Mimus*,[60] and *Aristophanes*,[61] books of grossest infamy, and also for commending the latter of them though he were the malicious libeller of his chief friends,[62] to be read by the Tyrant *Dionysius*, who had little need of such trash to spend his time on? But that he knew this licensing of Poems had reference and dependence to many other provisos here set down in his fancied republic, which in this world could have no place: and so neither he himself, nor any Magistrate, or City ever imitated that course, which taken apart from those other collateral injunctions must needs be vain and fruitless. For if they fell upon one kind of strictness, unless their care were equal to regulate all other things of like aptness to corrupt the mind, that single endeavour they knew would be but a fond labour; to shut and fortify one gate against corruption, and be necessitated to leave others round about wide open. If we think to regulate Printing, thereby to rectify manners, we must regulate all recreations and pastimes, all that is delightful to man. No music must be heard, no song be set or sung, but what is grave and *Doric*. There must be licensing dancers, that no gesture, motion, or deportment be taught our youth but what by their allowance shall be thought honest; for such *Plato* was provided of. It will ask more than the work of twenty licensers to examine all the lutes, the violins, and the guitars in every house; they must not be suffered to prattle as they do, but must be licensed what they may say. And who shall silence all the airs and madrigals, that whisper softness in chambers? The Windows also, and the *Balconies* must be thought on; there are shrewd books, with dangerous Frontispieces set to sale; who shall prohibit them, shall twenty licensers? The villages

Notes

58 *prevented* precluded.

59 *Academic night-sitting* an evening meeting of Plato's school in the house of Academus.

60 *Sophron Mimus* a popular writer of Plato's time.

61 *Aristophanes* the greatest Greek writer of comedy.

62 *his chief friends* philosophers, especially Socrates, whom Aristophanes derides in *Clouds*.

also must have their visitors to enquire what lectures the bagpipe and the rebec[63] reads even to the balladry, and the gammuth[64] of every *municipal* fiddler, for these are the Countryman's *Arcadias*[65] and his *Monte Mayors*.[66] Next, what more National corruption, for which England hears ill abroad, than household gluttony; who shall be the rectors of our daily rioting? and what shall be done to inhibit the multitudes that frequent those houses where drunkenness is sold and harboured? Our garments also should be referred to the licensing of some more sober work-masters to see them cut into a less wanton garb. Who shall regulate all the mixed conversation of our youth, male and female together, as is the fashion of this Country, who shall still appoint what shall be discoursed, what presumed, and no further? Lastly, who shall forbid and separate all idle resort, all evil company? These things will be, and must be; but how they shall be least hurtful, how least enticing, herein consists the grave and governing wisdom of a State. To sequester out of the world into *Atlantic*[67] and *Utopian* polities, which never can be drawn into use, will not mend our condition; but to ordain wisely as in this world of evil, in the midst whereof God hath placed us unavoidably. Nor is it *Plato*'s licensing of books will do this, which necessarily pulls along with it so many other kinds of licensing, as will make us all both ridiculous and weary, and yet frustrate; but those unwritten, or at least unconstraining laws of virtuous education, religious and civil nurture, which *Plato* there mentions, as the bonds and ligaments of the Commonwealth, the pillars and the sustainers of every written Statute; these they be which will bear chief sway in such matters as these, when all licensing will be easily eluded. Impunity and remissness, for certain are the bane of a Commonwealth, but here the great art lies to discern in what the law is to bid restraint and punishment, and in what things the persuasion only is to work. If every action which is good, or evil in man at ripe years, were to be under pittance,[68] and prescription, and compulsion, what were virtue but a name, what praise could be then due to well-doing, what gramercy[69] to be sober, just, or continent? many there be that complain of divine Providence for suffering *Adam* to transgress, foolish tongues! when God gave him reason, he gave him freedom to choose, for reason is but choosing; he had been else a mere artificial *Adam*, such an *Adam* as he is in the motions.[70] We ourselves esteem not of that obedience, or love, or gift, which is of force: God therefore left him free, set before him a provoking object, ever almost in his eyes; herein consisted his merit, herein the right of his reward, the praise of his abstinence. Wherefore did he create passions within us, pleasures round about us, but that these rightly tempered are the very ingredients of virtue? They are not skilful considerers of human things, who imagine to remove sin by removing the matter of sin; for, besides that it is a huge heap increasing under the very act of diminishing though some part of it may for a time be withdrawn from some persons, it cannot from all, in such a universal thing as books are; and when this is done, yet the sin remains entire. Though ye take from a covetous man all his treasure, he has yet one jewel left; ye cannot bereave him of his covetousness. Banish all objects of lust, shut up all youth into the severest discipline that can be exercised in any hermitage, ye cannot make them chaste, that came not thither so; such great care and

Notes

63 *rebeck* a kind of fiddle.

64 *gammuth* gamut, the whole series of notes used by a musician.

65 *Arcadia* a prose romance by Sir Philip Sidney (1590).

66 *Monte Mayor* Jorge de Montemayor, author of the romance *Diana* (c.1559).

67 *Atlantic* Atlantis-like, belonging to a fanciful utopia.

68 *pittance* "An allowance of meat in a monastery" (Johnson).

69 *gramercy* thanks.

70 *motions* puppet shows.

wisdom is required to the right managing of this point. Suppose we could expel sin by this means; look how much we thus expel of sin, so much we expel of virtue: for the matter of them both is the same; remove that, and ye remove them both alike. This justifies the high providence of God, who though he command us temperance, justice, continence, yet pours out before us even to a profuseness all desirable things, and gives us minds that can wander beyond all limit and satiety. Why should we then affect a rigour contrary to the manner of God and of nature, by abridging or scanting those means, which books freely permitted are, both to the trial of virtue, and the exercise of truth. It would be better done to learn that the law must needs be frivolous which goes to restrain things, uncertainly and yet equally working to good, and to evil. And were I the chooser, a dram of well-doing should be preferred before many times as much the forcible hindrance of evil-doing. For God sure esteems the growth and completing of one virtuous person, more than the restraint of ten vicious. And albeit whatever thing we hear or see, sitting, walking, travelling, or conversing may be fitly called our book, and is of the same effect that writings are, yet grant the thing to be prohibited were only books, it appears that this order hitherto is far insufficient to the end which it intends. Do we not see, not once or oftener, but weekly that continued Court-libel against the Parliament and City,[71] Printed, as the wet sheets can witness, and dispersed among us for all that licensing can do? yet this is the prime service a man would think, wherein this order should give proof of itself....

Another reason, whereby to make it plain that this order will miss the end it seeks, consider by the quality which ought to be in every licenser. It cannot be denied but that he who is made judge to sit upon the birth, or death of books whether they may be wafted into this world, or not, had need to be a man above the common measure, both studious, learned, and judicious; there may be else no mean mistakes in the censure of what is passable or not; which is also no mean injury. If he be of such worth as behooves him, there cannot be a more tedious and unpleasing journey-work, a greater loss of time levied upon his head, than to be made the perpetual reader of unchosen books and pamphlets, oft-times huge volumes. There is no book that is acceptable unless at certain seasons; but to be enjoined the reading of that at all times, and in a hand scarce legible, whereof three pages would not down at any time in the fairest Print, is an imposition which I cannot believe how he that values time, and his own studies, or is but of a sensible nostril should be able to endure....

I lastly proceed from the no good it can do, to the manifest hurt it causes, in being first the greatest discouragement and affront that can be offered to learning and to learned men. It was the complaint and lamentation of Prelates, upon every least breath of a motion to remove pluralities, and distribute more equally Church revenues, that then all learning would be forever dashed and discouraged. But as for that opinion, I never found cause to think that the tenth part of learning stood or fell with the Clergy: nor could I ever but hold it for a sordid and unworthy speech of any Churchman who had a competency left him. If therefore ye be loath to dishearten utterly and discontent, not the mercenary crew of false pretenders to learning, but the free and ingenuous sort for itself, not for lucre, or any other end, but the service of God and of truth, and perhaps that lasting fame and perpetuity of praise which God and good men have consented shall be the reward of those whose published labours advance the good of

Notes

[71] *Court-libel against the Parliament and City Mercurius Aulicus*, a Royalist newsbook.

mankind, then know, that so far to distrust the judgement and the honesty of one who hath but a common repute in learning, and never yet offended, as not to count him fit to print his mind without a tutor and examiner, lest he should drop a schism,[72] or something of a corruption, is the greatest displeasure and indignity to a free and knowing spirit that can be put upon him. What advantage is it to be a man over it is to be a boy at school, if we have only escaped the ferular,[73] to come under the fescu[74] of an *Imprimatur*?[75] if serious and elaborate writings, as if they were no more than the theme of a Grammar lad under his Pedagogue must not be uttered without the cursory eyes of a temporizing and extemporizing licenser. He who is not trusted with his own actions, his drift not being known to be evil, and standing to the hazard of law and penalty, has no great argument to think himself reputed in the Commonwealth wherein he was born, for other than a fool or a foreigner. When a man writes to the world, he summons up all his reason and deliberation to assist him; he searches, meditates, is industrious, and likely consults and confers with his judicious friends; after all which done he takes himself to be informed in what he writes, as well as any that writ before him; if in this the most consummate act of his fidelity and ripeness, no years, no industry, no former proof of his abilities can bring him to that state of maturity, as not to be still mistrusted and suspected, unless he carry all his considerate diligence, all his midnight watching, and expense of *Palladian*[76] oil, to the hasty view of an unleasured licenser, perhaps much his younger, perhaps far his inferior in judgement, perhaps one who never knew the labour of book-writing, and if he be not repulsed, or slighted, must appear in Print like a puny[77] with his guardian, and his censor's hand on the back of his title to be his bail and surety, that he is no idiot, or seducer, it cannot be but a dishonour and derogation to the author, to the book, to the privilege and dignity of Learning. And what if the author shall be one so copious of fancy, as to have many things well worth the adding, come into his mind after licensing, while the book is yet under the Press, which not seldom happens to the best and diligentest writers; and that perhaps a dozen times in one book. The Printer dares not go beyond his licensed copy; so often then must the author trudge to his leave-giver, that those his new insertions may be viewed; and many a jaunt will be made, ere that licenser, for it must be the same man, can either be found, or found at leisure; meanwhile either the Press must stand still, which is no small damage, or the author lose his accuratest thought, and send the book forth worse than he had made it, which to a diligent writer is the greatest melancholy and vexation that can befall....

And lest some should persuade ye, Lords and Commons, that these arguments of learned men's discouragement at this your order, are mere flourishes, and not real, I could recount what I have seen and heard in other Countries, where this kind of inquisition tyrannizes; when I have sat among their learned men, for that honour I had, and been counted happy to be born in such a place of *Philosophic* freedom, as they supposed England was, while themselves did nothing but bemoan the servile condition into which learning amongst them was brought; that this was it which had damped the glory of Italian wits; that nothing had been there written now these many years but flattery and fustian. There it was that I found and visited the famous *Galileo* grown

Notes

72 *schism* an opinion that causes disunity in the church.

73 *ferular* "An instrument of correction with which young scholars are beaten on the hand" (Johnson).

74 *fescu* "A small wire by which those who teach to read point out the letters" (Johnson).

75 *Imprimatur* "let it be printed," the seal of approval from the pope and then from any body of licensers.

76 *Palladian* belonging to Pallas Athena, the goddess of wisdom.

77 *puny* "A young unexperienced, unseasoned wretch" (Johnson).

old, a prisoner to the Inquisition, for thinking in astronomy otherwise than the Franciscan and Dominican licensers thought. And though I knew that England then was groaning loudest under the Prelatical yoke, nevertheless I took it as a pledge of future happiness, that other Nations were so persuaded of her liberty. Yet was it beyond my hope that those Worthies were then breathing in her air, who should be her leaders to such a deliverance, as shall never be forgotten by any revolution of time that this world hath to finish. When that was once begun, it was as little in my fear, that what words of complaint I heard among learned men of other parts uttered against the Inquisition, the same I should hear by as learned men at home uttered in time of Parliament against an order of licensing; and that so generally, that when I disclosed myself a companion of their discontent, I might say, if without envy, that he[78] whom an honest *quæstorship* had endeared to the *Sicilians*, was not more by them importuned against *Verres*, than the favourable opinion which I had among many who honour ye, and are known and respected by ye, loaded me with entreaties and persuasions, that I would not despair to lay together that which just reason should bring into my mind, toward the removal of an undeserved thraldom upon learning. That this is not therefore the disburdening of a particular fancy, but the common grievance of all those who had prepared their minds and studies above the vulgar pitch to advance truth in others, and from others to entertain it, thus much may satisfy. And in their name I shall for neither friend nor foe conceal what the general murmur is; that if it come to inquisitioning again, and licensing, and that we are so timorous of ourselves, and so suspicious of all men, as to fear each book, and the shaking of every leaf, before we know what the contents are, if some who but of late were little better than silenced from preaching, shall come now to silence us from reading, except what they please, it cannot be guessed what is intended by some but a second tyranny over learning: and will soon put it out of controversy that Bishops and Presbyters are the same to us both name and thing....

There is yet behind of what I purposed to lay open, the incredible loss, and detriment that this plot of licensing puts us to, more than if some enemy at sea should stop up all our havens and ports, and creeks, it hinders and retards the importation of our richest Merchandise Truth; nay it was first established and put in practice by Antichristian malice and mystery on set purpose to extinguish, if it were possible, the light of Reformation, and to settle falsehood; little differing from that policy wherewith the Turk upholds his *Alcoran*, by the prohibition of Printing. 'Tis not denied, but gladly confessed, we are to send our thanks and vows to heaven, louder than most Nations, for that great measure of truth which we enjoy, especially in those main points between us and the Pope, with his appurtenances the Prelates: but he who thinks we are to pitch our tent here, and have attained the utmost prospect of reformation, that the mortal glass wherein we contemplate, can show us, till we come to *beatific* vision, that man by this very opinion declares, that he is yet far short of Truth.

Truth indeed came once into the world with her divine Master, and was a perfect shape most glorious to look on: but when he ascended, and his Apostles after him were laid asleep, then straight arose a wicked race of deceivers, who as that story goes of the *Egyptian Typhon* with his conspirators, how they dealt with the good *Osiris*, took the virgin Truth, hewed her lovely form into a thousand pieces, and scattered them to the

Notes

[78] *he* Cicero, who indicted Verres in two famous orations which forced the corrupt official into exile.

four winds. From that time ever since, the sad friends of Truth, such as durst appear, imitating the careful search that *Isis* made for the mangled body of *Osiris*, went up and down gathering up limb by limb still as they could find them. We have not yet found them all, Lords and Commons, nor ever shall do, till her Master's second coming; he shall bring together every joint and member, and shall mould them into an immortal feature of loveliness and perfection. Suffer not these licensing prohibitions to stand at every place of opportunity forbidding and disturbing them that continue seeking, that continue to do our obsequies to the torn body of our martyred Saint. We boast our light; but if we look not wisely on the Sun itself, it smites us into darkness. Who can discern those planets that are oft *Combust*,[79] and those stars of brightest magnitude that rise and set with the Sun, until the opposite motion of their orbs bring them to such a place in the firmament, where they may be seen evening or morning. The light which we have gained, was given us, not to be ever staring on, but by it to discover onward things more remote from our knowledge. It is not the unfrocking of a Priest, the unmitring of a Bishop, and the removing him from off the *Presbyterian* shoulders that will make us a happy Nation, no, if other things as great in the Church, and in the rule of life both economical and political be not looked into and reformed, we have looked so long upon the blaze that *Zuinglius* and *Calvin*[80] hath beaconed up to us, that we are stark blind. There be who perpetually complain of schisms and sects, and make it such a calamity that any man dissents from their maxims. 'Tis their own pride and ignorance which causes the disturbing, who neither will hear with meekness, nor can convince, yet all must be suppressed which is not found in their *Syntagma*.[81] They are the troublers, they are the dividers of unity, who neglect and permit not others to unite those dissevered pieces which are yet wanting to the body of Truth. To be still searching what we know not, by what we know, still closing up truth to truth as we find it (for all her body is *homogeneal*, and proportional) this is the golden rule in *Theology* as well as in Arithmetic, and makes up the best harmony in a Church; not the forced and outward union of cold, and neutral, and inwardly divided minds.

Lords and Commons of England, consider what Nation it is whereof ye are, and whereof ye are the governors: a Nation not slow and dull, but of a quick, ingenious, and piercing spirit, acute to invent, subtle and sinewy to discourse, not beneath the reach of any point the highest that human capacity can soar to. Therefore the studies of learning in her deepest Sciences have been so ancient, and so eminent among us, that Writers of good antiquity, and ablest judgement have been persuaded that even the school of *Pythagoras*, and the *Persian* wisdom took beginning from the old Philosophy of this Island.[82] And that wise and civil Roman, *Julius Agricola*,[83] who governed once here for *Cæsar*, preferred the natural wits of Britain, before the laboured studies of the French. Nor is it for nothing that the grave and frugal *Transylvanian*[84] sends out yearly from as far as the mountainous borders of *Russia*, and beyond the *Hercynian* wilderness,[85] not their youth, but their staid men, to learn our language, and our *theologic* arts. Yet that which is above all this, the favour and the love of heaven we

Notes

[79] *Combust* 8.5 degrees in elevation from the sun.

[80] *Zuinglius and Calvin* Ulrich Zwingli and John Calvin, famous Protestant reformers.

[81] *Syntagma* systematic treatise.

[82] *the old Philosophy of this Island* the teachings of druids, perhaps; Milton's sources for this opinion are obscure or shaky, or both.

[83] *Julius Agricola* proconsul in Britain 78–85 CE, subject of a biography by his son-in-law Tacitus.

[84] *Transylvanian* ruler of a then independent Protestant country with an elective government, near present-day Romania.

[85] *Hercynian wilderness* Hercynia Silva, Roman name of a forested area in Germany.

have great argument to think in a peculiar manner propitious and propending towards us. Why else was this Nation chosen before any other, that out of her as out of *Zion*[86] should be proclaimed and founded forth the first tidings and trumpet of Reformation to all *Europe*. And had it not been the obstinate perverseness of our Prelates against the divine and admirable spirit of *Wicklef*,[87] to suppress him as a schismatic and *innovator*, perhaps neither the *Bohemian Husse* and *Jerom*,[88] no nor the name of *Luther*, or of *Calvin* had been ever known: the glory of reforming all our neighbours had been completely ours. But now, as our obdurate Clergy have with violence demeaned the matter, we are become hitherto the latest and the backwardest Scholars,[89] of whom God offered to have made us the teachers. Now once again by all concurrence of signs, and by the general instinct of holy and devout men, as they daily and solemnly express their thoughts, God is decreeing to begin some new and great period in his Church, even to the reforming of Reformation itself: what does he then but reveal Himself to his servants, and as his manner is, first to his English-men; I say as his manner is, first to us, though we mark not the method of his counsels, and are unworthy. Behold now this vast City; a City of refuge, the mansion house of liberty, encompassed and surrounded with his protection; the shop of war hath not there more anvils and hammers waking, to fashion out the plates and instruments of armed Justice in defence of beleaguered Truth, than there be pens and heads there, sitting by their studious lamps, musing, searching, revolving new notions and ideas wherewith to present, as with their homage and their fealty the approaching Reformation: others as fast reading, trying all things, assenting to the force of reason and convincement. What could a man require more from a Nation so pliant and so prone to seek after knowledge. What wants there to such a towardly and pregnant soil, but wise and faithful labourers, to make a knowing people, a Nation of Prophets, of Sages, and of Worthies. We reckon more than five months yet to harvest; there need not be five weeks, had we but eyes to lift up, the fields are white already.[90] Where there is much desire to learn, there of necessity will be much arguing, much writing, many opinions; for opinion in good men is but knowledge in the making. Under these fantastic terrors of sect and schism, we wrong the earnest and zealous thirst after knowledge and understanding which God hath stirred up in this City. What some lament of, we rather should rejoice at, should rather praise this pious forwardness among men, to reassume the ill-deputed care of their Religion into their own hands again. A little generous prudence, a little forbearance of one another, and some grain of charity might win all these diligences to join, and unite in one general and brotherly search after Truth; could we but forgo this Prelatical tradition of crowding free consciences and Christian liberties into canons and precepts of men. I doubt not, if some great and worthy stranger should come among us, wise to discern the mould and temper of a people, and how to govern it, observing the high hopes and aims, the diligent alacrity of our extended thought and reasoning in the pursuance of truth and freedom, but that he would cry out as *Pyrrhus*[91] did, admiring the Roman docility[92] and courage, if such were my *Epirots*, I would not despair the

Notes

86 *Zion* Jerusalem and the mount of the Temple in particular.

87 *Wicklef* John Wyclif (c.1320–84), English church reformer and translator of the Bible.

88 *Husse and Jerom* John Huss and Jerome of Prague, church reformers, contemporaries of Wyclif.

89 *Scholars* students.

90 *the fields are white already* John 4.35.

91 *Pyrrhus* (c.318–272 BCE), king of Epirus (land of the Epirots), a country in northwestern Greece, one of the greatest generals in history.

92 *docility* "Aptness to be taught; readiness to learn" (Johnson).

greatest design that could be attempted to make a Church or Kingdom happy. Yet these are the men cried out against for schismatics and sectaries; as if, while the Temple of the Lord was building, some cutting, some squaring the marble, others hewing the cedars, there should be a sort of irrational men who could not consider there must be many schisms and many dissections made in the quarry and in the timber, ere the house of God can be built. And when every stone is laid artful together, it cannot be united into a continuity, it can but be contiguous in this world; neither can every piece of the building be of one form; nay rather the perfection consists in this, that out of many moderate varieties and brotherly dissimilitudes that are not vastly disproportional arise the goodly and the graceful symmetry that commends the whole pile[93] and structure. Let us therefore be more considerate builders, more wise in spiritual architecture, when great reformation is expected. For now the time seems come, wherein *Moses* the great Prophet may sit in heaven rejoicing to see that memorable and glorious wish of his fulfilled, when not only our seventy Elders, but all the Lord's people are become Prophets.... [94]

Methinks I see in my mind a noble and puissant Nation rousing herself like a strong man after sleep, and shaking her invincible locks: Methinks I see her as an Eagle mewing[95] her mighty youth, and kindling her undazzled eyes at the full midday beam; purging and unscaling her long abused sight at the fountain itself of heavenly radiance, while the whole noise of timorous and flocking birds, with those also that love the twilight, flutter about, amazed at what she means, and in their envious gabble would prognosticate a year of sects and schisms.

What should ye do then, should ye suppress all this flowery crop of knowledge and new light sprung up and yet springing daily in this City, should ye set an *Oligarchy* of twenty engrossers[96] over it, to bring a famine upon our minds again, when we shall know nothing but what is measured to us by their bushel? Believe it, Lords and Commons, they who counsel ye to such a suppressing, do as good as bid ye suppress yourselves; and I will soon show how. If it be desired to know the immediate cause of all this free writing and free speaking, there cannot be assigned a truer than your own mild, and free, and human government; it is the liberty, Lords and Commons, which your own valorous and happy counsels have purchased us, liberty which is the nurse of all great wits; this is that which hath rarefied and enlightened our spirits like the influence of heaven; this is that which hath enfranchised, enlarged and lifted up our apprehensions degrees above themselves. Ye cannot make us now less capable, less knowing, less eagerly pursuing of the truth, unless ye first make yourselves, that made us so, less the lovers, less the founders of our true liberty. We can grow ignorant again, brutish, formal, and slavish, as ye found us; but you then must first become that which ye cannot be, oppressive, arbitrary, and tyrannous, as they were from whom ye have freed us. That our hearts are now more capacious, our thoughts more erected to the search and expectation of greatest and exactest things, is the issue of your own virtue[97] propagated in us; ye cannot suppress that unless ye reinforce an abrogated and merciless law, that fathers may dispatch at will their own children. And who shall then stick closest to ye, and excite others? not he who takes up arms for coat and conduct,[98] and

Notes

[93] *pile* "An edifice; a building" (Johnson).

[94] *not only our seventy Elders* ... Numbers 12.24–9.

[95] *mewing* "confining in a mew or cage at moulting time" (*OED*).

[96] *engrossers* copyists; i.e., licencers.

[97] *virtue* strength, influence.

[98] *coat and conduct* a tax exacted by Charles I to support the military (*OED, coat, sb* 12).

his four nobles of Danegelt.[99] Although I dispraise not the defence of just immunities, yet love my peace better, if that were all. Give me the liberty to know, to utter, and to argue freely according to conscience, above all liberties.

... if all cannot be of one mind, as who looks they should be? this doubtless is more wholesome, more prudent, and more Christian that many be tolerated, rather then all compelled. I mean not tolerated Popery, and open superstition, which as it extirpates all religions and civil supremacies, so itself should be extirpate, provided first that all charitable and compassionate means be used to win and regain the weak and misled: that also which is impious or evil absolutely either against faith or manners no law can possibly permit, that intends not to unlaw itself: but those neighbouring distances, or rather indifferences, are what I speak of, whether in some point of doctrine or of discipline, which though they may be many, yet need not interrupt "the unity of Spirit," if we could but find among us "the bond of peace."[100] In the meanwhile if any one would write, and bring his helpful hand to the slow-moving Reformation we labour under, if Truth have spoken to him before others, or but seemed at least to speak, who hath so bejesuited us that we should trouble that man with asking licence to do so worthy a deed? and not consider this, that if it come to prohibiting, there is not aught more likely to be prohibited than truth itself; whose first appearance to our eyes bleared and dimmed with prejudice and custom, is more unsightly and unplausible than many errors, even as the person is of many a great man slight and contemptible to see to....

And as for regulating the Press, let no man think to have the honour of advising ye better than yourselves have done in that Order published next before this, that no book be Printed, unless the Printer's and the Author's name, or at least the Printer's be registered.[101] Those which otherwise come forth, if they be found mischievous and libellous, the fire and the executioner[102] will be the timeliest and the most effectual remedy, that man's prevention can use. For this *authentic* Spanish policy of licensing books, if I have said aught, will prove the most unlicensed book itself within a short while; and was the immediate image of a Star-chamber decree[103] to that purpose made in those very times when that Court did the rest of those her pious works, for which she is now fallen from the Stars with *Lucifer*. Whereby ye may guess what kind of State prudence, what love of the people, what care of Religion, or good manners there was at the contriving, although with singular hypocrisy it pretended to bind books to their good behaviour. And how it got the upper hand of your precedent Order so well constituted before, if we may believe those men whose profession gives them cause to enquire most, it may be doubted[104] there was in it the fraud of some old *patentees* and *monopolizers* in the trade of book-selling; who under pretence of the poor in their Company not to be defrauded, and the just retaining of each man his several copy, which God forbid should be gainsaid, brought divers glozing colours[105] to the House, which were indeed but colours, and serving to no end except it be to exercise a superiority over their neighbours, men who do not therefore labour in an honest profession to which learning is indebted, that they should be made other men's vassals. Another end is thought

Notes

99 *Danegelt* another kind of tax to support the military (originally tribute to the Danes) levied by Charles.

100 *unity of spirit ... bond of peace* Ephesians 4.3.

101 Milton refers to the order of January 29, 1642.

102 *the fire and the executioner* condemned books were burned by the hangman.

103 *Star-chamber* a royal court that was proverbial for arbitrary and tyrannical rule in the hands of James I and Charles I; it was abolished by the Long Parliament in 1641 (*OED*).

104 *doubted* suspected.

105 *glozing colours* false, rhetorical arguments.

was aimed at by some of them in procuring by petition this Order, that having power in their hands, malignant books might the easier escape abroad, as the event shows. But of these *Sophisms* and *Elenchs*[106] of merchandise I skill not: This I know, that errors in a good government and in a bad are equally almost incident; for what Magistrate may not be misinformed, and much the sooner, if liberty of Printing be reduced into the power of a few; but to redress willingly and speedily what hath been erred, and in highest authority to esteem a plain advertisement[107] more than others have done a sumptuous bribe, is a virtue, honoured Lords and Commons, answerable to Your highest actions, and whereof none can participate but greatest and wisest men.

from *Poems* (1673)

Sonnet 18[1] (1655)
On the Late Massacre in Piemont

Avenge O Lord thy slaughtered Saints, whose bones
 Lie scattered on the Alpine mountains cold,
 Ev'n them who kept thy truth so pure of old
 When all our fathers worshipped Stocks and Stones,[2]
Forget not: in thy book record their groans
 Who were thy Sheep, and in their ancient Fold
 Slain by the bloody *Piemontese* that rolled
 Mother with Infant down the Rocks. Their moans
The Vales redoubled to the Hills, and they
 To Heav'n. Their martyred blood and ashes sow
 O'er all th' *Italian* fields where still doth sway
The triple Tyrant, that from these may grow[3]
 A hundred-fold, who having learnt thy way,
 Early may fly the *Babylonian* woe.[4]

Sonnet 19[5] (1652?)
'When I Consider how my Light is Spent'

When I consider how my light is spent,
 Ere half my days, in this dark world and wide,

Notes

[106] *Elench* "An argument; a sophism" (Johnson).

[107] *advertisement* "Instruction; admonition" (Johnson).

FROM *POEMS* (1673)

[1] This poem responds to the slaughter of Waldensians (a sect of reformed Christians) on April 24, 1655 by Catholic troops billeted in Piedmont, now the northwestern region of Italy but then part of Savoy.

[2] *all our fathers* the imagery of superstitious worship comes from the Old Testament (Jeremiah 2.27), but Milton applies it to pre-Reformation England; the Waldensian sect arose in the twelfth century but claimed earlier origins.

[3] *triple Tyrant* the Pope with his triple crown.

[4] *Babylonian* a common epithet for the papacy among Protestants, recalling Revelation 17.1–6.

[5] The date of this poem is uncertain, but the theme strongly suggests that it was composed close to the winter of 1651–2, when Milton's blindness became complete, and before he began the great work of his life, *Paradise Lost*, in 1657 or 1658.

And that one Talent which is death to hide,[6]
Lodged with me useless, though my soul more bent
To serve therewith my Maker, and present
My true account, lest he returning chide,
'Doth God exact day labour, light denied?'[7]
I fondly ask; But patience to prevent[8]
That murmur, soon replies: 'God doth not need
Either man's work or his own gifts; who best
Bear his mild yoke, they serve him best. His State
Is Kingly. Thousands at his bidding speed,
And post o'er Land and Ocean without rest:
They also serve who only stand and wait'.

Sonnet 16[9]
[To the Lord General Cromwell, 1652]

Cromwell, our chief of men, who through a cloud
Not of war only, but detractions wide,
Guided by faith & matchless Fortitude
To peace & truth thy glorious way hast ploughed
And on the neck of crownèd Fortune proud
Hast reared God's Trophies & his work pursued[10]
While Darwen stream with blood of Scots imbrued,[11]
And Dunbar field resounds thy praises loud,[12]
And Worcester's laureate wreath; yet much remains[13]
To conquer still; peace hath her victories
No less renowned than war, new foes arise
Threat'ning to bind our souls with secular chains;
Help us to save free Conscience from the paw
Of hireling wolves whose Gospel is their maw.[14]

from *Paradise Lost* (1667)

The following text of *Paradise Lost*, books I, II, IV, and IX, is based on the second edition (1674); like other editors of the poem I have admitted a few substitutions from the manuscript of Book I and the first edition of 1667. In a very few cases

Notes

6 *Talent* in the parable of the talents (Matthew 25.14–30) the servant who hides money (the one talent) given him by the lord, rather than using it to earn more, is cast into "outer darkness."

7 *day labour* labor paid in daily wages; Milton jests about his blindness: he has not daylight so would not expect to do day labor.

8 *Fondly* foolishly.

9 The title on the manuscript is crossed out but reads, "To the Lord General Cromwell, May 1652, on the proposals of certain ministers at the Committee for Propagation of the Gospel." The proposals that alarmed Milton concerned the institution of a clerical hierarchy that reminded Milton of the Catholic Church. The poem was not printed until 1694.

10 *Crowned Fortune ... Trophies* Milton refers to the beheading of Charles I.

11 *Darwen stream* ... at the battle of Preston in which the Royalist Scots were defeated, August 17, 1648.

12 *Dunbar field* scene of Cromwell's victory over the Scots, September 3, 1650.

13 *Worcester* the battle in which Charles II was defeated and narrowly escaped capture, September 3, 1651.

14 *hireling wolves* corrupt clergy (John 10.11–16; Matthew 7.15).

I have accepted emendations of other editors. The textual problems of *Paradise Lost* are numerous and have been the subject of much controversy, but on the whole the problems are not crucial; they have mainly to do with spelling and, less often, with punctuation.

I have modernized the spelling in this edition only where I was confident I could do so without significantly changing the sound or the prosody of the poem. I have retained the original capitalization, italicization, and punctuation. How much Milton cared about capitalization and italicization is unclear; sometimes it matters, but rather than attempting to judge each instance, I have left that part of the text, despite its inconsistencies, intact; at the least, these features provide a sense of what the text looked like to contemporary readers, without adding to the difficulty of the poem. Milton cared about spelling and punctuation; he used them to direct readers of his poem to hear it correctly. His punctuation is not grammatical in the modern sense but an indication of tempo: comma, semicolon, colon, and period (full stop) represent incrementally longer pauses. Despite his interesting ideas about spelling and punctuation, Milton was not completely consistent in his efforts to regulate his text (his blindness was certainly an obstacle), and, in addition, there are aspects of the spelling and typography that seem needlessly distracting to students. These have been silently modernized. Hence, Milton's "tast" appears as "taste" and "Rhime" as "Rhyme." Spellings that seem to direct pronunciation, such as "Heav'n," are retained, except where the modern spelling indicates the pronunciation just as well. Weak verbs in the past tense and past participles, for example, are given a modern "-ed" ending in preference to Milton's " 'd" as long as the modern ending does not add a syllable. Hence "flam'd" is rendered "flamed." Milton's spellings of some participles with " 't" or "-t" (ravish't, mixt) are changed to "-ed" (ravished, mixed) because, after much deliberation and consultation, I find that there is little or no difference in sound between the original and the modernized forms, as we realize them in speech today. Also modernized are the variant spelling of "thir" and "their," and "mee" and "me." Milton used the added "e" to indicate that the word was stressed, but the text is very inconsistent, and, usually, the added "e" is not needed to hear the stress. I have retained Milton's spelling of words that we think of as contractions, such as "adventrous," although in potentially confusing cases I have added an apostrophe in place of the "missing" letter.

Of course, there are many instances in which it was hard to decide about the effects of modernization, and overall I must confess to falling short of scientific regularity or even complete consistency. My text is a compromise between what is there in 1674 and what I thought would be most intelligible. There is thus plenty of work left for the reader. I must ask British readers, for example, usually to pronounce "been" with a short sound because I have not retained Milton's "bin." Grave accent marks are added to indicate the presence of an unusual syllable, and acute accents are added to indicate surprising stress: it must be "obdúrate pride," for example, and "fixèd anchor." Most abnormalities of pronunciation, however, could not be marked, and the reader must be highly conscious of Milton's tendency to use pronunciations (normal, variant, and abnormal) that fit within the pentametric "Heroic" measure. Hence, for example, American readers must recognize that "Disobedience" (I.1) has four syllables, not five, and all readers must hear that "Spirit" (I.17) and "Power" (I.44) can be pronounced as one syllable rather than two, "aspiring" as two syllables rather than three, and "dire Arms," "many a" or "to incur" as two syllables, to give just a few examples. As a further aid to readers, quotation marks and apostrophes indicating the possessive form are also added, although Milton never used either.

In myriad ways that this edition cannot begin to chronicle, Milton believed there was a strong connection between the form and the meaning of his poetry. For him, spelling, punctuation, and prosody were all of a piece not only with his aesthetic life but also with his political and religious convictions. The strength of Milton's feelings about the importance of his prosody is clearly evident in the paragraph on "The Verse" that he added in 1668 in order to defend what some readers saw as his failure to use rhyme.

The Verse

The Measure is *English* Heroic Verse without Rhyme, as that of *Homer* in Greek, and of *Virgil* in *Latin*; Rhyme being no necessary Adjunct or true Ornament of Poem or good Verse, in longer Works especially, but the Invention of a barbarous Age, to set off wretched matter and lame Meter; graced indeed since by the use of some famous modern Poets, carried away by Custom, but much to their own vexation, hindrance, and constraint to express many things otherwise, and for the most part worse than else they would have expressed them. Not without cause therefore some both *Italian* and *Spanish* Poets of prime note have rejected Rhyme both in longer and shorter Works, as have also long since our best *English* Tragedies, as a thing of itself, to all judicious ears, trivial and of no true musical delight; which consists only in apt Numbers,[1] fit quantity[2] of Syllables, and the sense variously drawn out from one Verse into another, not in the jingling sound of like endings, a fault avoided by the learned Ancients both in Poetry and all good Oratory. This neglect then of Rhyme so little is to be taken for a defect, though it may seem so perhaps to vulgar[3] Readers, that it rather is to be esteemed an example set, the first in *English*, of ancient liberty recovered to Heroic Poem from the troublesome and modern[4] bondage of Rhyming.

Book I
The Argument

This first Book proposes, first in brief, the whole Subject, Man's disobedience, and the loss thereupon of Paradise wherein he was placed: Then touches the prime cause of his fall, the Serpent, or rather Satan in the Serpent; who revolting from God, and drawing to his side many Legions of Angels, was by the command of God driven out of Heaven with all his Crew into the great Deep. Which action passed over, the Poem hastes into the midst of things, presenting Satan with his Angels now fallen into Hell, described here, not in the Centre (for Heaven and Earth may be supposed as yet not made, certainly not yet accursed) but in a place of utter darkness, fitliest called Chaos: Here Satan with his Angels lying on the burning Lake, thunder-struck and astonished, after a certain space recovers, as from confusion, calls up him who next in Order and Dignity lay by him; they confer of their miserable fall. Satan awakens all his Legions, who lay till then in the same manner confounded; They rise, their Numbers, array of Battle, their chief Leaders named, according to the Idols known afterwards in Canaan[1]

Notes

The Verse

1 *Numbers* prosodical meter, with some sense of musical harmony and proportion.

2 *quantity* in classical prosody, refers to the length or duration of syllables, but English prosody usually "measures" syllables only as stressed or unstressed.

3 *vulgar* unlearned.

4 *modern* both recent and "vulgar; mean; common" (Johnson).

Book I

1 *Canaan* Palestine, the biblical Holy Land.

and the Countries adjoining. To these Satan directs his Speech, comforts them with hope yet of regaining Heaven, but tells them lastly of a new World and new kind of Creature to be created, according to an ancient Prophecy or report in Heaven; for that Angels were long before this visible Creation, was the opinion of many ancient Fathers.[2] To find out the truth of this Prophecy, and what to determine thereon he refers to a full Council. What his Associates thence attempt. Pandemonium the Palace of Satan rises, suddenly built out of the Deep: The infernal Peers there sit in Council.

Of Man's First Disobedience, and the Fruit
Of that Forbidden Tree whose mortal taste
Brought Death into the World, and all our woe,
With loss of *Eden*, till one greater Man
Restore us, and regain the blissful Seat,
Sing, Heav'nly Muse, that on the secret top[3]
Of *Oreb*, or of *Sinai*, didst inspire
That Shepherd, who first taught the chosen Seed,
In the Beginning how the Heav'ns and Earth
Rose out of *Chaos*: or, if *Sion* hill[4]
Delight thee more, and *Siloa*'s Brook that flowed[5]
Fast by the Oracle of God; I thence
Invoke thy aid to my adventrous Song,
That with no middle flight intends to soar
Above th' *Aonian* Mount, while it pursues[6]
Things unattempted yet in Prose or Rhyme.
And chiefly Thou, O Spirit, that dost prefer
Before all Temples th' upright heart and pure,
Instruct me, for Thou know'st; Thou from the first
Wast present, and with mighty wings outspread
Dove-like sat'st brooding on the vast Abyss,
And mad'st it pregnant: What in me is dark
Illumine, what is low raise and support;
That to the highth of this great Argument,
I may assert Eternal Providence,
And justify the ways of God to men.
  Say first, for Heav'n hides nothing from thy view,
Nor the deep tract of Hell, say first what cause
Moved our Grand Parents, in that happy State,
Favoured of Heav'n so highly, to fall off
From their Creator, and transgress his Will
For one restraint, Lords of the World besides?
Who first seduced them to that foul revolt?
Th' infernal Serpent; he it was, whose guile,

Notes

[2] *Fathers* church fathers, early Christian commentators on the Bible.

[3] *Oreb ... Sinai* mounts where Moses ("That Shepherd") may have received the word of God.

[4] *Sion* or Zion, one of the hills of Jerusalem, where David brought the ark of the covenant.

[5] *Siloa's Brook* a pool in Jerusalem, used by Jesus for healing (John 9.7), but perhaps Shiloh is meant, a town where there was an annual feast of Jehovah and where the ark resided for some time.

[6] *Aonian Mount* located in Boetia, a district in central Greece famous for ancient poets and musicians.

Stirred up with Envy and Revenge, deceived
The Mother of Mankind, what time his Pride
Had cast him out from Heav'n, with all his Host
Of Rebel Angels, by whose aid aspiring
To set himself in Glory above his Peers,
He trusted to have equalled the Most High,
If he opposed; and with ambitious aim
Against the Throne and Monarchy of God
Raised impious War in Heav'n and Battle proud
With vain attempt. Him the Almighty Power
Hurled headlong flaming from th' Ethereal Sky,
With hideous ruin and combustion down
To bottomless perdition, there to dwell
In Adamantine Chains and penal Fire,
Who durst defy th' Omnipotent to Arms.
Nine times the Space that measures Day and Night
To mortal men, he with his horrid crew
Lay vanquished, rolling in the fiery Gulf,
Confounded though immortal: But his doom
Reserved him to more wrath; for now the thought
Both of lost happiness and lasting pain
Torments him; round he throws his baleful eyes,
That witnessed huge affliction and dismay,
Mixed with obdúrate pride and steadfast hate:
At once as far as Angels' ken he views
The dismal Situation waste and wild,
A Dungeon horrible, on all sides round
As one great Furnace flamed; yet from those flames
No light, but rather darkness visible
Served only to discover sights of woe,
Regions of sorrow, doleful shades, where peace
And rest can never dwell, hope never comes
That comes to all; but torture without end
Still urges, and a fiery Deluge, fed
With ever-burning Sulphur unconsumed.
Such place Eternal Justice has prepared
For those rebellious, here their Prison ordained
In utter darkness, and their portion set
As far removed from God and light of Heav'n
As from the Centre thrice to th' utmost Pole.
O how unlike the place from whence they fell!
There the companions of his fall, o'erwhelmed
With Floods and Whirlwinds of tempestuous fire,
He soon discerns, and weltering by his side
One next himself in power, and next in crime,
Long after known in *Palestine*, and named
Beëlzebub. To whom th' Arch-Enemy,
And thence in Heav'n called Satan, with bold words
Breaking the horrid silence, thus began.
'If thou beest he; But O how fall'n! how changed
From him, who in the happy Realms of Light

Clothed with transcendent brightness didst out-shine
Myriads though bright: If he whom mutual league,
United thoughts and counsels, equal hope
And hazard in the Glorious Enterprise,
Joined with me once, now misery hath joined
In equal ruin: into what Pit thou seest
From what highth fall'n, so much the stronger proved
He with his Thunder: and till then who knew
The force of those dire Arms? yet not for those,
Nor what the Potent Victor in his rage
Can else inflict, do I repent or change,
Though changed in outward lustre; that fixed mind
And high disdain, from sense of injured merit,
That with the mightiest raised me to contend,
And to the fierce contention brought along
Innumerable force of Spirits armed
That durst dislike his reign, and, me preferring,
His utmost power with adverse power opposed
In dubious Battle on the Plains of Heav'n,
And shook his throne. What though the field be lost?
All is not lost; the unconquerable Will,
And study of revenge, immortal hate,
And courage never to submit or yield:
And what is else not to be overcome?
That Glory never shall his wrath or might
Extort from me. To bow and sue for grace
With suppliant knee, and deify his power,
Who from the terror of this Arm so late
Doubted his Empire, that were low indeed,
That were an ignominy and shame beneath
This downfall; since by Fate the strength of Gods
And this Empyreal Substance cannot fail,
Since through experience of this great event
In Arms not worse, in foresight much advanced,
We may with more successful hope resolve
To wage by force or guile eternal War
Irreconcilable, to our grand Foe,
Who now triúmphs, and in th' excéss of joy
Sole reigning holds the Tyranny of Heav'n'.
  So spake th' Apostate Angel, though in pain,
Vaunting aloud, but racked with deep despair:
And him thus answered soon his bold Compeer.
  'O Prince, O Chief of many Thronèd Powers,
That led th' embattled Seraphim to War
Under thy conduct, and in dreadful deeds
Fearless, endangered Heaven's perpetual King;
And put to proof his high Supremacy,
Whether upheld by strength, or Chance, or Fate,
Too well I see and rue the dire event,
That with sad overthrow and foul defeat
Hath lost us Heav'n, and all this mighty Host

In horrible destruction laid thus low,
As far as Gods and Heav'nly Essences
Can perish: for the mind and spirit remains
Invincible, and vigour soon returns,
Though all our Glory extinct, and happy state
Here swallowed up in endless misery.
But what if he our Conqueror, (whom I now
Of force believe Almighty, since no less
Than such could have o'erpow'red such force as ours)
Have left us this our spirit and strength entire,
Strongly to suffer and support our pains,
That we may so suffice his vengeful ire,
Or do him mightier service as his thralls
By right of War, what e'er his business be
Here in the heart of Hell to work in Fire,
Or do his Errands in the gloomy Deep;
What can it then avail though yet we feel
Strength undiminished, or eternal being
To undergo eternal punishment?'
Whereto with speedy words th' Arch-fiend replied.
'Fall'n Cherub, to be weak is miserable
Doing or Suffering: but of this be sure,
To do aught good never will be our task,
But ever to do ill our sole delight,
As being the contrary to his high will
Whom we resist. If then his Providence
Out of our evil seek to bring forth good,
Our labour must be to pervert that end,
And out of good still to find means of evil;
Which oft times may succeed, so as perhaps
Shall grieve him, if I fail not, and disturb
His inmost counsels from their destined aim.
But see the angry Victor hath recalled
His Ministers of vengeance and pursuit
Back to the Gates of Heav'n: the Sulphurous Hail
Shot after us in storm, o'erblown hath laid
The fiery Surge, that from the Precipice
Of Heav'n received us falling, and the Thunder,
Winged with red Lightning and impetuous rage,
Perhaps hath spent his shafts, and ceases now
To bellow through the vast and boundless Deep.
Let us not slip th' occasion, whether scorn,
Or satiate fury yield it from our Foe.
Seest thou yon dreary plain, forlorn and wild,
The seat of desolation, void of light,
Save what the glimmering of these livid flames[7]

Notes

[7] *livid* "of a bluish leaden colour" (*OED*).

Casts pale and dreadful? Thither let us tend
From off the tossing of these fiery waves,
There rest, if any rest can harbour there,
And reassembling our afflicted Powers,
Consult how we may henceforth most offend[8]
Our Enemy, our own loss how repair,
How overcome this dire Calamity,
What reinforcement we may gain from Hope,
If not what resolution from despair'.
  Thus Satan, talking to his nearest Mate
With head up-lift above the wave, and eyes
That sparkling blazed, his other Parts besides
Prone on the Flood, extended long and large
Lay floating many a rood, in bulk as huge[9]
As whom the Fables name of monstrous size,
Titanian or *Earth-born*, that warred on *Jove*,
Briareos or *Typhon*, whom the Den[10]
By ancient *Tarsus* held, or that Sea-beast
Leviathan, which God of all his works[11]
Created hugest that swim th' Ocean stream:
Him, haply slumbering on the *Norway* foam
The Pilot of some small night-foundered Skiff,
Deeming some Island, oft, as Sea-men tell,
With fixèd anchor in his scaly rind
Moors by his side under the Lee, while Night
Invests the Sea, and wishèd Morn delays:
So stretched out huge in length the Arch-fiend lay
Chained on the burning Lake, nor ever thence
Had ris'n, or heaved his head, but that the will
And high permission of all-ruling Heaven
Left him at large to his own dark designs,
That with reiterated crimes he might
Heap on himself damnation, while he sought
Evil to others, and enraged might see
How all his malice served but to bring forth
Infinite goodness, grace, and mercy shewn
On Man by him seduced, but on himself
Treble confusion, wrath and vengeance poured.
Forthwith upright he rears from off the Pool
His mighty Stature; on each hand the flames
Driv'n backward slope their pointing spires, and rolled
In billows, leave i' th' midst a horrid Vale.
Then with expanded wings he steers his flight

Notes

[8] *offend* "To strike so as to hurt" (*OED*).

[9] *rood* a rough measure of land.

[10] *Briareos and Typhon* Titans or older gods, sons of Gaia (earth); three-hundred-headed Briareos fought with Zeus, against his brethren; Zeus (Jove) killed Typhon with his hundred serpent heads and buried him under Mount Aetna, near Tarsus (mod. Terassus), Sicily.

[11] *Leviathan* a sea-dragon in the Bible (see Isaiah 27.1; Psalm 74.13–14).

Aloft, incumbent on the dusky Air[12]
That felt unusual weight, till on dry Land
He lights, if it were Land that ever burned
With solid, as the Lake with liquid fire;
And such appeared in hue, as when the force
Of subterranean wind transports a Hill
Torn from *Pelorus*, or the shattered side[13]
Of thundering *Ætna*, whose combustible
And fuellèd entrails thence conceiving fire,
Sublimed with Mineral fury, aid the Winds,
And leave a singèd bottom all involved
With stench and smoke: Such resting found the sole
Of unblessed feet. Him followed his next Mate,
Both glorying to have 'scaped the *Stygian* flood[14]
As Gods, and by their own recovered strength,
Not by the sufferance of supernal Power.
'Is this the Region, this the Soil, the Clime,'
Said then the lost Arch-angel, 'this the seat
That we must change for Heav'n?, this mournful gloom
For that celestial light? Be it so, since he
Who now is Sovereign can dispose and bid
What shall be right: farthest from him is best
Whom reason hath equalled, force hath made supreme
Above his equals. Farewell happy Fields
Where Joy for ever dwells: Hail horrors, hail,
Infernal world, and thou profoundest Hell
Receive thy new Possessor: One who brings
A mind not to be changed by Place or Time.
The mind is its own place, and in itself
Can make a Heav'n of Hell, a Hell of Heav'n.
What matter where, if I be still the same,
And what I should be, all but less than he
Whom Thunder hath made greater? Here at least
We shall be free; th' Almighty hath not built
Here for his envy, will not drive us hence:
Here we may reign secure; and, in my choice
To reign is worth ambition though in Hell:
Better to reign in Hell, than serve in Heav'n.
But wherefore let we then our faithful friends,
Th' associates and copartners of our loss
Lie thus astonished on th' oblivious Pool,[15]
And call them not to share with us their part
In this unhappy Mansion, or once more
With rallied Arms to try what may be yet
Regained in Heav'n, or what more lost in Hell?'

Notes

12 *incumbent* pressing.

13 *Pelorus* a sandy promontory in Sicily (mod. Capo di Faro).

14 *Stygian* into Hell. from Styx, the poisonous, cold river said to flow

15 *astonished* stunned, stupefied; *oblivious* causing forgetfulness.

So *Satan* spake; and him *Beëlzebub*
Thus answered. 'Leader of those Armies bright,
Which but th' Omnipotent none could have foiled,
If once they hear that voice, their liveliest pledge
Of hope in fears and dangers, heard so oft
In worst extremes, and on the perilous edge
Of battle, when it raged, in all assaults
Their surest signal, they will soon resume
New courage and revive, though now they lie
Grovelling and prostrate on yon Lake of Fire,
As we erewhile, astounded and amazed,
No wonder, fall'n such a pernicious highth'.
He scarce had ceased when the superior Fiend
Was moving toward the shore; his ponderous shield,
Ethereal temper, massy, large and round,
Behind him cast; the broad circumference
Hung on his shoulders like the Moon, whose Orb
Through Optic Glass the *Tuscan* Artist views[16]
At Evening, from the top of *Fésole*,
Or in *Valdarno*, to descry new Lands,
Rivers or Mountains in her spotty Globe.
His Spear, to equal which the tallest Pine
Hewn on *Norwegian* hills, to be the Mast
Of some great Ammiral, were but a wand,[17]
He walked with to support uneasy steps
Over the burning Marl, not like those steps
On Heaven's Azure, and the torrid Clime
Smote on him sore besides, vaulted with Fire,
Nathless he so endured, till on the Beach
Of that inflamèd sea, he stood, and called
His Legions, Angel Forms, who lay entranced
Thick as Autumnal Leaves that strow the Brooks
In *Vallombrosa*, where th' *Etrurian* shades[18]
High overarched imbow'r; or scattered sedge
Afloat, when with fierce Winds *Orion* armed[19]
Hath vexed the Red-Sea Coast, whose waves o'erthrew
Busiris and his *Memphian* Chivalry,[20]
While with perfidious hatred they pursued
The sojourners of Goshen, who beheld[21]

Notes

[16] *the Tuscan artist* Galileo, the astronomer and maker of telescopes; Milton visited him in Fiesole or the nearby valley of the Arno (*Valdarno*).

[17] *Ammiral* "the ship which carries the admiral or commander of the fleet" (Johnson).

[18] *Vallombrosa* (literally "shady valley") a place in Etruria (mod. Tuscany).

[19] *Orion* the rising of this constellation, named after the mythical hunter, was said to be accompanied by storms.

[20] *Busiris* a most cruel tyrant of Egypt, commander of cavalry ("Chivalry") from Memphis, whom Milton associates with the Pharaoh in Exodus 14 whose troops are engulfed by the Red Sea.

[21] *Sojourners of Goshen* the Jews passing through a place in Egypt in search of the Promised Land.

From the safe shore their floating carcases
And broken Chariot Wheels, so thick bestrown
Abject and lost lay these, covering the Flood,
Under amazement of their hideous change.
He called so loud, that all the hollow Deep
Of Hell resounded. 'Princes, Potentates,
Warriors, the Flow'r of Heav'n, once yours, now lost,
If such astonishment as this can seize
Eternal Spirits, or have ye chos'n this place
After the toil of Battle to repose
Your wearied virtue, for the ease you find
To slumber here, as in the Vales of Heav'n?
Or in this abject posture have ye sworn
To adore the Conqueror? who now beholds
Cherub and Seraph rolling in the flood
With scattered Arms and Ensigns, till anon
His swift pursuers from Heav'n Gates discern
Th' advantage, and descending tread us down
Thus drooping, or with linkèd Thunderbolts
Transfix us to the bottom of this Gulf.
Awake, arise, or be for ever fall'n'.
    They heard, and were abashed, and up they sprung
Upon the wing, as when men wont to watch
On duty, sleeping found by whom they dread,
Rouse and bestir themselves ere well awake.
Nor did they not perceive the evil plight
In which they were, or the fierce pains not feel;
Yet to their General's voice they soon obeyed
Innumerable. As when the potent Rod
Of *Amram*'s Son in *Egypt*'s evil day[22]
Waved round the Coast, upcalled a pitchy cloud
Of *Locusts*, warping on the Eastern Wind,[23]
That o'er the Realm of impious *Pharaoh* hung
Like Night, and darkened all the Land of *Nile*:
So numberless were those bad Angels seen
Hovering on wing under the Cope of Hell[24]
'Twixt upper, nether, and surrounding Fires;
Till, as a signal giv'n, th' uplifted Spear
Of their great Sultan waving to direct
Their course, in even balance down they light
On the firm brimstone, and fill all the Plain:
A multitude, like which the populous North
Poured never from her frozen loins, to pass
Rhene or the *Danaw*, when her barbarous Sons[25]
Came like a Deluge on the South, and spread

Notes

[22] *Amram's Son* Moses (see Exodus 10.12–15).

[23] *warping* swarming, as bees (*OED* 7b).

[24] *Cope* canopy, vault.

[25] *Rhene or the Danaw* Rhine and Danube, homelands of Goths.

Beneath *Gibraltar* to the *Libyan* sands.
Forthwith, from every Squadron and each Band
The Heads and Leaders thither haste where stood
Their great Commander; Godlike shapes, and forms
Excelling human, Princely Dignities,
And Powers that erst in Heaven sat on Thrones,
Though of their Names in heav'nly Records now
Be no memorial, blotted out and razed
By their Rebellion from the Books of Life.
Nor had they yet among the Sons of *Eve*
Got them new Names, till wandring o'er the Earth,
Through God's high sufferance, for the trial of man,
By falsities and lies the greatest part
Of Mankind they corrupted to forsake
God their Creator, and th' invisible
Glory of him that made them, to transform
Oft to the Image of a Brute, adorned
With gay Religions full of Pomp and Gold,
And Devils to adore for Deities:
Then were they known to men by various Names,
And various Idols through the Heathen World.
Say, Muse, their Names then known, who first, who last,
Roused from the slumber, on that fiery Couch,
At their great Emperor's call, as next in worth
Came singly where he stood on the bare strand,
While the promiscuous crowd stood yet aloof?
The chief were those who from the Pit of Hell
Roaming to seek their prey on earth, durst fix
Their Seats long after next the Seat of God,
Their Altars by his Altar, Gods adored
Among the Nations round, and durst abide
Jehovah thundering out of *Sion*, throned
Between the Cherubim; yea, often placed
Within his Sanctuary itself their Shrines,
Abominations; and with cursèd things
His holy Rites, and solemn Feasts profaned,
And with their darkness durst affront his light.
First *Moloch*, horrid King besmeared with blood[26]
Of human sacrifice, and parents' tears,
Though for the noise of Drums and Timbrels loud,[27]
Their children's cries unheard, that passed through fire
To his grim Idol. Him the *Ammonite*[28]
Worshipped in *Rabba* and her wat'ry Plain,
In *Argob* and in *Basan*, to the stream
Of utmost *Arnon*. Nor content with such

Notes

[26] *Moloch* a Caananite god of fire to whom children were sacrificed.

[27] *Timbrels* tambourines.

[28] *the Ammonite* a tribe hostile to the Israelites, inhabiting a land of giants.

Audacious neighbourhood, the wisest heart
Of *Solomon* he led by fraud to build
His Temple right against the Temple of God
On that opprobrious Hill, and made his Grove[29]
The Pleasant valley of *Hinnom*, *Tophet* thence[30]
And black *Gehenna* called, the Type of Hell.[31]
Next *Chemos*, th' óbscene dread of *Moab*'s sons,[32]
From *Aroar* to *Nebo*, and the wild
Of Southmost *Abarim*; in *Hesebon*
And *Horonaim*, *Seon*'s realm, beyond
The flowry Dale of *Sibma* clad with Vines,
And *Eleale* to th' *Asphaltic* Pool.[33]
Peor his other name, when he enticed
Israel in *Sittim*, on their march from Nile,
To do him wanton rites, which cost them woe.[34]
Yet thence his lustful Orgies he enlarged
Even to that Hill of scandal, by the Grove
Of *Moloch* homicide, lust hard by hate;[35]
Till good *Josiah* drove them thence to Hell.[36]
With these came they, who, from the bord'ring flood
Of old *Euphrates* to the Brook that parts
Egypt from *Syrian* ground, had general Names
Of *Baalim* and *Ashtaroth*, those male,[37]
These Feminine. For Spirits when they please
Can either Sex assume, or both; so soft
And uncompounded is their Essence pure,
Not tied or manacled with joint or limb,
Nor founded on the brittle strength of bones,
Like cumbrous flesh; but in what shape they choose
Dilated or condensed, bright or obscure,
Can execute their airy purposes,
And works of love or enmity fulfil.
For those the Race of *Israel* oft forsook
Their living strength, and unfrequented left
His righteous Altar, bowing lowly down
To bestial gods; for which their heads as low
Bowed down in Battle, sunk before the Spear
Of despicable foes. With these in troop
Came *Astoreth*, whom the *Phoenicians* called[38]
Astarte, Queen of Heav'n, with crescent Horns;

Notes

29 *that opprobrious Hill* the Mount of Olives near Jerusalem (I Kings 11.7).

30 *Tophet* literally, place of fire (Isaiah 30.33).

31 *Type* "That by which something future is prefigured" (Johnson).

32 *Chemos* a false god worshiped in Moab; equated with *Peor*.

33 *th' Asphaltic Pool* the Dead Sea, north and east of which lie the other places in the passage.

34 See Numbers 25.1–3, where the Israelites are seduced by the daughters of Moab.

35 *Hill of Scandal and the Grove of Moloch* see l. 403 above.

36 II Kings 23.1–14.

37 *Baal* is a Semitic word for lord or owner.

38 *Astoreth* II Kings 23.13; as Astarte, identified with Venus and associated with sexual rites.

To whose bright Image nightly by the Moon
Sidonian Virgins paid their Vows and Songs;
In *Sion* also not unsung, where stood
Her Temple on th' offensive Mountain, built
By that uxorious King, whose heart though large,[39]
Beguil'd by fair Idolatresses, fell
To Idols foul. *Thammuz* came next behind,[40]
Whose annual wound in *Lebanon* allured
The *Syrian* Damsels to lament his fate
In amorous ditties all a Summer's day,
While smooth *Adonis* from his native Rock[41]
Ran purple to the Sea, supposed with blood
Of *Thammuz* yearly wounded: the Love-tale
Infected *Sion*'s daughters with like heat,
Whose wanton passions in the sacred Porch[42]
Ezekiel saw, when by the Vision led
His eye surveyed the dark Idolatries
Of alienated *Judah*. Next came one
Who mourned in earnest, when the Captive Ark
Maimed his brute Image, head and hands lopped off
In his own Temple, on the grunsel edge,[43]
Where he fell flat, and shamed his Worshippers:
Dagon his Name, Sea Monster, upward Man[44]
And downward Fish; yet had his Temple high
Reared in *Azotus*, dreaded, through the Coast
Of *Palestine*, in *Gath* and *Ascalon*,
And *Accaron* and *Gaza*'s frontier bounds.
Him followed *Rimmon*, whose delightful Seat[45]
Was fair *Damascus*, on the fertile Banks
Of Abbana and Pharphar, lucid streams.
He also against the house of God was bold:
A Leper once he lost and gained a King,[46]
Ahaz his sottish Conqueror, whom he drew[47]
God's Altar to disparage and displace
For one of *Syrian* mode, whereon to burn
His odious offrings, and adore the Gods
Whom he had vanquished. After these appeared
A crew who under Names of old Renown,
Osiris, *Isis*, *Orus*, and their Train[48]

Notes

[39] *that uxorious King* Solomon; see l. 401 above.

[40] *Thammuz* Phoenician Adonis, in love with Astarte and killed by a wild boar; the cult of Adonis celebrated his death annually in a festival of regeneration.

[41] *Adonis* the river Adonis; *his* its

[42] *sacred Porch* scene of pagan worship in Ezekiel 8.13–18.

[43] *grunsel* variant of groundsel, "the lower part of the building" (Johnson).

[44] *Dagon* national god of the Philistines, who occupied the places named in the passage.

[45] *Rimmon* a Syrian god identical with Hadad.

[46] *Leper* Naaman, saved by Elijah, renounced Rimmon (II Kings 5.1–18).

[47] *Ahaz* II Kings 16.10–18; *sottish* "Dull; stupid … doltish" (Johnson).

[48] *Osiris, Isis, Orus* father, mother, and son, gods of ancient Egypt.

With monstrous shapes and sorceries abused
Fanatic *Egypt* and her Priests, to seek
Their wand'ring Gods disguised in brutish forms
Rather than human. Nor did *Israel* 'scape
Th' infection when their borrowed Gold composed
The Calf in *Oreb*: and the Rebel King[49]
Doubled that sin in *Bethel* and in *Dan*,
Lik'ning his Maker to the Grazèd Ox,
Jehovah, who in one Night, when he passed[50]
From *Egypt* marching, equalled with one stroke
Both her firstborn and all her bleating Gods.
Belial came last, than whom a Spirit more lewd
Fell not from Heav'n, or more gross to love
Vice for itself: To him no Temple stood
Or Altar smoked; yet who more oft than he
In Temples and at Altars, when the Priest
Turns Atheist, as did *Eli*'s Sons, who filled[51]
With lust and violence the house of God.
In Courts and Palaces he also Reigns
And in luxurious Cities, where the noise
Of riot ascends above their loftiest Tow'rs,
And injury and outrage: And, when Night
Darkens the Streets, then wander forth the Sons
Of *Belial*, flown with insolence and wine.[52]
Witness the Streets of *Sodom*, and that night[53]
In *Gibeah*, when the hospitable door
Exposed a Matron to avoid worse rape.
These were the prime in order and in might;
The rest were long to tell, though far renowned
Th' *Ionian* Gods – of Javan's issue held[54]
Gods, yet confessed later than Heav'n and Earth,
Their boasted Parents; *Titan*, Heav'n's first-born,
With his enormous brood, and birthright seized
By younger *Saturn*, he from mightier *Jove*,[55]
His own and *Rhea*'s Son, like measure found;
So *Jove* usurping reigned: these, first in *Crete*

Notes

49 *The Calf* Aaron commanded the forging and worship of the golden calf (Exodus 32.1–6); *the Rebel King* Jeroboam, an idolater (1 Kings 12.25–33).

50 The event celebrated in Passover, when the Israelites were delivered from Egypt (Exodus 12.29–36), and Jehovah killed all Egyptian first-borns, man and beast.

51 *Eli* a high priest who did not sufficiently correct his sons (1 Samuel 2.22–5).

52 *flown* "puffed; inflated; elate" (Johnson).

53 *the Streets of Sodom* Lot protected two angels from the carousing men of Sodom, even offering his daughters to distract them (Genesis 19.4–14); *that night in Gibeah* a man gave up his daughter and his concubine to gang rape in order to protect a sojourning Levite (Judges 19.16–30).

54 *Javan* son of Japhet (Genesis 10.2), reputed sire of Greek gods, though Heaven and Earth, parents of the Titans, are said to be older.

55 *Saturn* the youngest Titan, who seized the throne from his elders and was likewise displaced by his son *Jove* (Jupiter, Zeus), fled over the Adriatic sea (*Adria*), then west to the edge of the Atlantic (*Hesperides*), and north to the British Isles "*utmost Isles*."

And *Ida* known, thence on the Snowy top[56]
Of cold *Olympus* ruled the middle Air,
Their highest Heav'n; or on the *Delphian* Cliff,
Or in *Dodona*, and through all the bounds
Of *Doric* Land; or who with *Saturn* old
Fled over *Adria* to th' *Hesperian* Fields,
And o'er the *Celtic* roamed the utmost Isles.
All these and more came flocking; but with looks
Downcast and damp; yet such wherein appeared[57]
Obscure some glimpse of joy, to have found their chief
Not in despair, to have found themselves not lost
In loss itself; which on his count'nance cast
Like doubtful hue: but he his wonted pride
Soon recollecting, with high words, that bore
Semblance of worth, not substance, gently raised
Their fainting courage, and dispelled their fears.
Then straight commands that at the warlike sound
Of Trumpets loud and Clarions be upreared
His mighty Standard; that proud honour claimed
Azazel as his right, a Cherub tall:
Who forthwith from the glittering Staff unfurled
Th' Imperial Ensign, which full high advanced,
Shone like a Meteor streaming to the Wind,[58]
With Gems and Golden lustre rich emblazed,
Seraphic arms and Trophies: all the while
Sonórous metal blowing Martial sounds:
At which the universal Host upsent
A shout that tore Hell's Concave, and beyond
Frighted the Reign of *Chaos* and old Night.
All in a moment through the gloom were seen
Ten thousand Banners rise into the Air
With Orient Colours waving: with them rose[59]
A Forest huge of Spears: and thronging Helms
Appeared, and serried Shields in thick array
Of depth immeasurable: Anon they move
In perfect *Phalanx* to the *Dorian* mood[60]
Of Flutes and soft Recorders; such as raised
To height of noblest temper Heroes old
Arming to Battle, and instead of rage
Deliberate valour breathed, firm and unmoved
With dread of death to flight or foul retreat,
Nor wanting power to mitigate and swage[61]
With solemn touches, troubled thoughts, and chase

Notes

[56] *Ida* mountain in Crete, birthplace of Zeus and the gods who occupied *Olympus*, *Delphi*, *Dodona*, and other Greek (*Doric*) places.

[57] *damp* "Dejected; sunk; depressed" (Johnson).

[58] *Meteor* any shooting star or comet.

[59] *Orient* "Bright; shining … sparkling" (Johnson).

[60] *Phalanx* square formation; *Dorian mood* the most stately and dignified of the scales, or modes, of classical music.

[61] *swage* assuage.

Anguish and doubt and fear and sorrow and pain
From mortal or immortal minds. Thus they
Breathing united force with fixèd thought
Moved on in silence to soft Pipes that charmed
Their painful steps o'er the burnt soil; and now
Advanced in view, they stand, a horrid Front
Of dreadful length and dazzling Arms, in guise
Of Warriors old with ordered Spear and Shield,
Awaiting what command their mighty Chief
Had to impose: He through the armèd Files
Darts his experienced eye, and soon traverse
The whole Battalion views, their order due,
Their visages and stature as of Gods,
Their number last he sums. And now his heart
Distends with pride, and hard'ning in his strength
Glories: For never since created man,
Met such embodied force, as named with these
Could merit more than that small infantry[62]
Warred on by Cranes: though all the Giant brood
Of *Phlegra* with th' Heroic Race were joined[63]
That fought at *Thebes* and *Ilium*, on each side
Mixed with auxiliar Gods; and what resounds
In Fable or *Romance* of *Uther*'s Son,[64]
Begirt with *British* and *Armoric* Knights;[65]
And all who since, Baptized or Infidel,
Jousted in *Aspramont* or *Montalban*,[66]
Damasco, or *Marocco*, or *Trebisond*,
Or whom *Biserta* sent from *Afric* shore[67]
When *Charlemain* with all his Peerage fell
By *Fontarabbia*. Thus far these beyond
Compare of mortal prowess, yet observed
Their dread commander: he above the rest
In shape and gesture proudly eminent,
Stood like a Tower; his form had yet not lost
All her Original brightness, nor appeared
Less than Arch Angel ruined, and th' excess
Of Glory obscured: As when the Sun new ris'n
Looks through the Horizontal misty Air
Shorn of his Beams, or from behind the Moon,
In dim Eclipse disastrous twilight sheds
On half the Nations, and with fear of change
Perplexes Monarchs. Darkened so, yet shone

Notes

62 *that small infantry* Pygmies, thought to have been destroyed by cranes.

63 *Phlegra* a town in Thessaly on the plains near which giants were said to have fought against the gods.

64 *Uther's Son* King Arthur.

65 *Armoric Knights* Arthur's comrades from Brittany.

66 *Aspramont ... Trebisond* scenes of battles between Christian and Islamic warriors, from France to Turkey.

67 *Biserta* African town under the control of Islamic Tunis, across the sea from Spanish *Fontarabbia*, supposed site of Charlemagne's defeat at Roncevaux (Spain) and the death of his nephew Roland.

Above them all th' Arch Angel: but his face
Deep scars of Thunder had entrenched, and care
Sat on his faded cheek, but under Brows
Of dauntless courage, and considerate Pride
Waiting revenge: cruel his eye, but cast
Signs of remorse and passion to behold
The fellows of his crime, the followers rather
(Far other once beheld in bliss), condemned
Forever now to have their lot in pain,
Millions of Spirits for his fault amerced[68]
Of Heav'n, and from Eternal Splendours flung
For his revolt, yet faithful how they stood,
Their Glory withered. As, when Heaven's fire
Hath scathed the Forest Oaks, or Mountain Pines,
With singèd top their stately growth though bare
Stands on the blasted Heath. He now prepared
To speak; whereat their doubled Ranks they bend
From wing to wing, and half enclose him round
With all his Peers: attention held them mute.
Thrice he assayed, and thrice in spite of scorn,
Tears such as Angels weep, burst forth: at last
Words interwove with sighs found out their way:
'O Myriads of immortal Spirits, O Powers
Matchless, but with th' Almighty, and that strife
Was not inglorious, though th' event was dire,[69]
As this place testifies, and this dire change,
Hateful to utter: but what power of mind
Foreseeing or presaging, from the Depth
Of knowledge past or present, could have feared
How such united force of Gods, how such
As stood like these, could ever know repulse?
For who can yet believe, though after loss,
That all these puissant Legions, whose exile
Hath emptied Heav'n, shall fail to re-ascend
Self-raised, and repossess their native seat?
For me be witness all the Host of Heav'n,
If counsels different, or danger shunned
By me, have lost our hopes. But he who reigns
Monarch in Heav'n till then as one secure
Sat on his Throne, upheld by old repute,
Consent or custom, and his Regal State
Put forth at full, but still his strength concealed,
Which tempted our attempt, and wrought our fall.
Henceforth his might we know, and know our own

Notes

[68] *amerced* from *amerce*, "To punish with a pecuniary penalty; to exact a fine; to inflict a forfeiture" (Johnson).

[69] *event* result, outcome.

So as not either to provoke, or dread
New war, provoked; our better part remains
To work in close design, by fraud or guile
What force effected not: that he no less
At length from us may find, who overcomes
By force, hath overcome but half his foe.
Space may produce new Worlds; whereof so rife
There went a fame in Heav'n that he ere long
Intended to create, and therein plant
A generation, whom his choice regard
Should favour equal to the Sons of Heav'n:
Thither, if but to pry, shall be perhaps
Our first eruption, thither, or elsewhere:
For this Infernal Pit shall never hold
Celestial Spirits in Bondage, nor th' Abyss
Long under darkness cover. But these thoughts
Full Counsel must mature: Peace is despaired,
For who can think Submission? War then, War
Open or understood must be resolved'.
He spake: and, to confirm his words, out-flew
Millions of flaming swords, drawn from the thighs
Of mighty Cherubim; the sudden blaze
Far round illumined hell: highly they raged
Against the Highest, and fierce with graspèd Arms
Clashed on their sounding Shields the din of war,
Hurling defiance toward the Vault of Heav'n.
    There stood a Hill not far whose grisly top
Belched fire and rolling smoke; the rest entire
Shone with a glossy scurf, undoubted sign[70]
That in his womb was hid metallic Ore,
The work of Sulphur. Thither winged with speed
A numerous Brigade hastened. As when Bands
Of Pioneers with Spade and Pickaxe armed[71]
Forerun the Royal Camp, to trench a Field,
Or cast a Rampart. *Mammon* led them on,
Mammon, the least erected Spirit that fell
From heav'n; for ev'n in heav'n his looks and thoughts
Were always downward bent, admiring more
The riches of Heav'n's pavement, trodd'n Gold,
Than aught divine or holy else enjoyed
In vision beatific: by him first
Men also, and by his suggestion taught,
Ransacked the Centre, and with impious hands
Rifled the bowels of their mother Earth

Notes

[70] *scurf* "Any incrustation on the surface of a body" (*OED*, 3).

[71] *Pioneers* "One whose business is to level the road, throw up works, or sink mines in military operations" (Johnson).

For Treasures better hid. Soon had his crew
Opened into the Hill a spacious wound
And digged out ribs of Gold. Let none admire[72]
That riches grow in Hell; that soil may best
Deserve the precious bane. And here let those
Who boast in mortal things, and wond'ring tell
Of *Babel*, and the works of *Memphian* Kings,[73]
Learn how their greatest Monuments of Fame,
And Strength and Art are easily out-done
By Spirits reprobate, and in an hour
What in an age they with incessant toil
And hands innumerable scarce perform.
Nigh on the Plain in many cells prepared,
That underneath had veins of liquid fire
Sluiced from the Lake, a second multitude
With wondrous Art founded the massy Ore,[74]
Severing each kind, and scummed the Bullion dross:
A third as soon had formed within the ground
A various mould, and from the boiling cells
By strange conveyance filled each hollow nook,
As in an Organ from one blast of wind
To many a row of Pipes the sound-board breathes.
Anon out of the earth a Fabric huge[75]
Rose like an Exhalation, with the sound
Of Dulcet Symphonies and voices sweet,
Built like a Temple, where *Pilasters* round[76]
Were set, and Doric pillars overlaid
With Golden Architrave; nor did there want
Cornice or Frieze, with bossy Sculptures grav'n;
The Roof was fretted Gold. Not *Babylon*
Nor great *Alcairo* such magnificence[77]
Equalled in all their glories, to enshrine
Belus or *Sarapis* their Gods, or seat
Their Kings, when *Egypt* with *Assyria* strove
In wealth and luxury. Th' ascending pile
Stood fixed her stately highth, and straight the doors,
Op'ning their brazen folds discover wide
Within, her ample spaces, o'er the smooth
And level pavement: from the archèd roof
Pendant by subtle Magic many a row
Of Starry Lamps and blazing Cressets fed[78]

Notes

[72] *admire* "to regard with wonder" (Johnson).

[73] *Babel* the tower built by Nimrod that was supposed to reach heaven; *works of Memphian Kings* pyramids or other Egyptian monuments.

[74] *founded* melted.

[75] *Fabric* building.

[76] *Pilasters* square columns set within a wall; like the rest of the architectural terms in the passage, it suggests ornamental excess.

[77] *Alcairo* "the" Cairo, ancient Memphis.

[78] *Cressets* beacons, from "*croissette*, Fr. because beacons had crosses anciently on their tops" (Johnson).

With Naphtha and Asphaltus yielded light[79]
As from a sky. The hasty multitude
Admiring entered, and the work some praise
And some the Architect: his hand was known
In Heav'n by many a Towered structure high,
Where Sceptred Angels held their residence,
And sat as Princes, whom the súpreme King
Exalted to such power, and gave to rule,
Each in his Hierarchy, the Orders bright.
Nor was his name unheard or unadored
In ancient *Greece*; and in *Ausonian* land[80]
Men called him *Mulciber*; and how he fell[81]
From Heav'n, they fabled, thrown by angry *Jove*
Sheer o'er the Crystal Battlements; from Morn
To Noon he fell, from Noon to dewy Eve,
A Summer's day; and with the setting Sun
Dropped from the Zenith like a falling Star,
On *Lemnos*, th' Ægean Isle: thus they relate,
Erring; for he with this rebellious rout
Fell long before; nor aught availed him now
To have built in Heav'n high Towers; nor did he 'scape
By all his Engines, but was headlong sent,
With his industrious crew to build in hell.
Meanwhile the wingèd Heralds by command
Of Sovereign power, with awful Ceremony
And Trumpet's sound, throughout the Host proclaim
A solemn Council forthwith to be held
At *Pandæmonium*, the high Capital[82]
Of Satan and his Peers: their summons called
From every Band and squarèd Regiment
By place or choice the worthiest; they anon
With hundreds and with thousands trooping came
Attended: all access was thronged, the Gates
And Porches wide, but chief the spacious Hall
(Though like a covered field, where Champions bold
Wont ride in armed, and at the Soldan's chair[83]
Defied the best of *Paynim* chivalry
To mortal combat, or career with Lance)
Thick swarmed, both on the ground and in the air,
Brushed with the hiss of rustling wings. As Bees
In spring time, when the Sun with *Taurus* rides,[84]
Pour forth their populous youth about the Hive

Notes

[79] *Naphtha and Asphaltus* bituminous minerals.

[80] *Ausonian land* Italy in general, but especially an early culture established in the volcanic Aeolian Islands near Sicily and trading in volcanic minerals such as sulfur.

[81] *Mulciber* Hephaestus, god of fire and metalworking.

[82] *Pandæmonium* a place (literally) "of all demons."

[83] *Soldan* "[for sultan] The emperor of the Turks" (Johnson), considered *Paynims*, or pagans, by the Christian warriors in the Crusades.

[84] *when the Sun with Taurus rides* from April 19 to May 20 the sun appears to be in this constellation.

In clusters; they among fresh dews and flow'rs
Fly to and fro, or on the smoothèd Plank,
The suburb of their Straw-built Citadel,
New rubbed with Balm, expatiate and confer[85]
Their State affairs. So thick the airy crowd
Swarmed and were straitened; till the Signal giv'n,
Behold a wonder! they but now who seemed
In bigness to surpass Earth's Giant Sons
Now less than smallest Dwarfs, in narrow room
Throng numberless, like that Pygméan Race
Beyond the *Indian* Mount; or Faerie Elves,[86]
Whose midnight Revels, by a Forest side
Or Fountain some belated Peasant sees,
Or dreams he sees, while over-head the Moon
Sits Arbitress, and nearer to the Earth
Wheels her pale course, they on their mirth and dance
Intent, with jocund Music charm his ear;
At once with joy and fear his heart rebounds.
Thus incorporeal Spirits to smallest forms
Reduced their shapes immense, and were at large,
Though without number still amidst the hall
Of that infernal Court. But far within,
And in their own dimensions like themselves,
The great Seraphic Lords and Cherubim
In close recess and secret conclave sat,[87]
A thousand Demi-Gods on golden seats,
Frequent and full. After short silence then[88]
And summons read, the great consult began.

Book II
The Argument

The Consultation begun, Satan debates whether another Battle be to be hazarded for the recovery of Heaven: some advise it, others dissuade: A third proposal is preferred, mentioned before by Satan, to search the truth of that Prophecy or Tradition in Heaven concerning another world, and another kind of creature equal or not much inferior to themselves, about this time to be created: Their doubt who shall be sent on this difficult search: Satan their chief undertakes alone the voyage, is honoured and applauded. The Council thus ended, the rest betake them several ways and to several employments, as their inclinations lead them, to entertain the time till Satan return. He passes on his Journey to Hell Gates, finds them shut, and who sat there to guard them, by whom at length they are opened, and discover to him the great Gulf between

Notes

[85] *balm* pollen, perhaps, but also oil used in rites such as Roman Catholic confirmation and part of the implicit similarity between *Pandæmonium* and St. Peter's Cathedral, Rome; *expatiate* "To range at large; to rove without any prescribed limits" (Johnson).

[86] *Indian Mount* the Himalayas.

[87] *recess* "departure into privacy" (Johnson); conclave "the assembly of the cardinals" (Johnson).

[88] *Frequent* crowded (*OED*, 1).

Hell and Heaven; with what difficulty he passes through, directed by Chaos, the Power of that place, to the sight of this new World which he sought.

High on a Throne of Royal State, which far
Outshone the wealth of *Ormus* and of *Ind*,[1]
Or where the gorgeous East with richest hand
Show'rs on her Kings *Barbaric* Pearl and Gold,[2]
Satan exalted sat, by merit raised
To that bad eminence; and from despair
Thus high uplifted beyond hope, aspires
Beyond thus high, insatiate to pursue
Vain War with Heav'n, and by success untaught
His proud imaginations thus displayed.
'Powers and Dominions, Deities of Heav'n,
For since no deep within her gulf can hold
Immortal vigour, though oppressed and fall'n,
I give not Heav'n for lost. From this descent
Celestial virtues rising, will appear[3]
More glorious and more dread than from no fall,
And trust themselves to fear no second fate:
Me though just right, and the fixed Laws of Heav'n
Did first create your Leader, next free choice,
With what besides, in Counsel or in Fight,
Hath been achieved of merit, yet this loss
Thus far at least recovered, hath much more
Established in a safe unenvied Throne
Yielded with full consent. The happier state
In Heav'n, which follows dignity, might draw
Envy from each inferior; but who here
Will envy whom the highest place exposes
Foremost to stand against the Thunderer's aim
Your bulwark, and condemns to greatest share
Of endless pain? where there is then no good
For which to strive, no strife can grow up there
From Faction; for none sure will claim in Hell
Precedence, none, whose portion is so small
Of present pain, that with ambitious mind
Will covet more. With this advantage then
To union, and firm Faith, and firm accord,
More than can be in Heav'n, we now return
To claim our just inheritance of old,
Surer to prosper than prosperity
Could have assured us; and by what best way,
Whether of open War or covert guile,
We now debate; who can advise may speak'.

Notes

Book II

1 *Ormus* an island at the mouth of the Persian Gulf.

2 *Barbaric* "foreign; far-fetched" (Johnson).

3 *Celestial virtues* a high order of angels.

He ceased, and next him *Moloch*, Sceptred King
Stood up, the strongest and the fiercest Spirit
That fought in Heav'n; now fiercer by despair:
His trust was with th' Eternal to be deemed
Equal in strength, and rather than be less
Cared not to be at all; with that care lost
Went all his fear: of God, or Hell, or worse
He recked not, and these words thereafter spake.
'My sentence is for open War: Of Wiles,[4]
More unexpert, I boast not: them let those
Contrive who need, or when they need, not now.
For while they sit contriving, shall the rest,
Millions that stand in arms, and longing wait
The Signal to ascend, sit lingering here
Heav'n's fugitives, and for their dwelling place
Accept this dark opprobrious Den of shame,
The Prison of his Tyranny who Reigns
By our delay? no, let us rather choose
Armed with Hell flames and fury all at once
O'er Heav'n's high Towers to force resistless way,
Turning our tortures into horrid arms
Against the Torturer; when, to meet the noise
Of his Almighty Engine, he shall hear[5]
Infernal Thunder, and for Lightning see
Black fire and horror shot with equal rage
Among his Angels; and his Throne itself
Mixed with *Tartárean* Sulphur, and strange fire,[6]
His own invented Torments. But perhaps
The way seems difficult and steep to scale
With upright wing against a higher foe.
Let such bethink them, if the sleepy drench[7]
Of that forgetful Lake benumb not still,[8]
That in our proper motion we ascend
Up to our native seat: descent and fall
To us is adverse. Who but felt of late
When the fierce Foe hung on our broken Rear[9]
Insulting, and pursued us through the Deep,[10]
With what compulsion and laborious flight
We sunk thus low? Th' ascent is easy then;
Th' event is feared; should we again provoke
Our stronger, some worse way his wrath may find

Notes

[4] *sentence* "Determination or decision, as of a judge civil or criminal" (Johnson).

[5] *Engine* "A military machine" (Johnson); God's thunder.

[6] *Tartarean* of Tartarus, that part of the underworld where the wicked are punished.

[7] *drench* potion.

[8] *forgetful Lake* the River Lethe, which means forgetfulness, one of the five rivers of the underworld; see the "oblivious Pool" (ll.576–86 below).

[9] *Rear* "The hinder troop of an army" (Johnson).

[10] *Insulting* from *insult*, "To trample upon; to triumph over" (Johnson).

To our destruction: if there be in Hell
Fear to be worse destroyed: what can be worse
Than to dwell here, driv'n out from bliss, condemned
In this abhorrèd deep to utter woe;
Where pain of unextinguishable fire
Must exercise us without hope of end
The Vassals of his anger, when the Scourge
Inexorably, and the torturing hour
Calls us to Penance? More destroyed than thus
We should be quite abolished, and expire.
What fear we then? what doubt we to incense
His utmost ire? which to the highth enraged,
Will either quite consume us, and reduce
To nothing this essential, happier far[11]
Than miserable to have eternal being:
Or if our substance be indeed Divine,
And cannot cease to be, we are at worst
On this side nothing; and by proof we feel[12]
Our power sufficient to disturb his Heav'n,
And with perpetual inroads to Alarm,
Though inaccessible, his fatal Throne:
Which if not Victory is yet Revenge'.
He ended frowning, and his look denounced[13]
Desperate revenge, and Battle dangerous
To less than Gods. On th' other side up rose
Belial, in act more graceful and humane;
A fairer person lost not Heav'n; he seemed
For dignity composed and high exploit:
But all was false and hollow; though his Tongue
Dropped Manna, and could make the worse appear[14]
The better reason, to perplex and dash
Maturest Counsels: for his thoughts were low;
To vice industrious, but to Nobler deeds
Timorous and slothful: yet he pleased the ear,
And with persuasive accent thus began.
'I should be much for open War, O Peers,
As not behind in hate; if what was urged
Main reason to persuade immediate War,
Did not dissuade me most, and seem to cast
Ominous conjecture on the whole success:
When he who most excels in fact of Arms,
In what he counsels and in what excels
Mistrustful, grounds his courage on despair
And utter dissolution, as the scope

Notes

[11] *essential* being.
[12] *we ... nothing* we are at the lowest point of existence.
[13] *denounced* declared.
[14] *Manna* a mysterious gum with honey-like juice which was miraculously supplied to the Israelites to sustain them on their forty-day sojourn in the wilderness (Exodus 16).

Of all his aim, after some dire revenge.
First, what Revenge? the Tow'rs of Heav'n are filled
With Armèd watch, that render all access
Impregnable; oft on the bordering Deep
Encamp their Legions, or with óbscure wing
Scout far and wide into the Realm of night,
Scorning surprise. Or could we break our way
By force, and at our heels all Hell should rise
With blackest Insurrection, to confound
Heav'n's purest Light, yet our great Enemy,
All incorruptible would on his Throne
Sit unpolluted, and th' Ethereal mould[15]
Incapable of stain would soon expel
Her mischief, and purge off the baser fire
Victorious. Thus repulsed, our final hope
Is flat despair: we must exasperate
Th' Almighty Victor to spend all his rage,
And that must end us, that must be our cure,
To be no more; sad cure; for who would lose,
Though full of pain, this intellectual being,
Those thoughts that wander through Eternity,
To perish rather, swallowed up and lost
In the wide womb of uncreated night,
Devoid of sense and motion? and who knows,
Let this be good, whether our angry Foe
Can give it, or will ever? how he can
Is doubtful; that he never will is sure.
Will he, so wise, let loose at once his ire,
Belike through impotence, or unaware,[16]
To give his Enemies their wish, and end
Them in his anger, whom his anger saves
To punish endless? "wherefore cease we then?"
Say they who counsel War, "we are decreed,
Reserved and destined to Eternal woe;
Whatever doing, what can we suffer more,
What can we suffer worse?" is this then worst,
Thus sitting, thus consulting, thus in Arms?
What when we fled amain, pursued and strook
With Heav'n's afflicting Thunder, and besought
The Deep to shelter us? this Hell then seemed
A refuge from those wounds: or when we lay
Chained on the burning Lake? that sure was worse.
What if the breath that kindled those grim fires
Awaked should blow them into sevenfold rage

Notes

[15] *mould* "cast; form" (Johnson), with a suggestion of the heat-resistant matrix in which molten metal is poured when something is cast.

[16] *Belike* perhaps.

And plunge us in the flames? or from above
Should intermitted vengeance arm again
His red right hand to plague us? what if all
Her stores were opened, and this Firmament
Of Hell should spout her Cataracts of Fire,
Impendent horrors, threatning hideous fall[17]
One day upon our heads; while we perhaps
Designing or exhorting glorious war,
Caught in a fiery Tempest shall be hurled
Each on his rock transfixed, the sport and prey
Of racking whirlwinds, or forever sunk
Under yon boiling Ocean, wrapped in Chains;
There to converse with everlasting groans,
Unrespited, unpitied, unreprieved,
Ages of hopeless end; this would be worse.
War therefore, open or concealed, alike
My voice dissuades; for what can force or guile[18]
With him, or who deceive his mind, whose eye
Views all things at one view? he from Heav'n's highth
All these our motions vain, sees and derides;
Not more Almighty to resist our might
Than wise to frustrate all our plots and wiles.
Shall we then live thus vile, the race of Heav'n
Thus trampled, thus expelled, to suffer here
Chains and these Torments? Better these than worse,
By my advice; since fate inevitable
Subdues us, and Omnipotent Decree,
The Victor's will. To suffer, as to do,
Our strength is equal, nor the Law unjust
That so ordains: this was at first resolved,
If we were wise, against so great a foe
Contending, and so doubtful what might fall.[19]
I laugh when those who at the Spear are bold
And vent'rous, if that fail them, shrink and fear
What yet they know must follow, to endure
Exile, or ignominy, or bonds, or pain,
The sentence of their Conqueror: This is now
Our doom; which if we can sustain and bear,
Our Súpreme Foe in time may much remit
His anger, and perhaps thus far removed
Not mind us not offending, satisfied
With what is punished; whence these raging fires
Will slacken, if his breath stir not their flames.
Our purer essence then will overcome
Their noxious vapour, or inured not feel,

Notes

[17] *Impendent* "Imminent; hanging over" (Johnson).

[18] *can* avails.

[19] *fall* fall out, happen.

Or changed at length, and to the place conformed
In temper and in nature, will receive
Familiar the fierce heat, and void of pain;
This horror will grow mild, this darkness light,
Besides what hope the never-ending flight
Of future days may bring, what chance, what change
Worth waiting, since our present lot appears
For happy though but ill, for ill not worst,
If we procure not to ourselves more woe'.
  Thus *Belial*, with words clothed in reason's garb
Counselled ignoble ease, and peaceful sloth,
Not peace: and after him thus *Mammon* spake.
  'Either to disenthrone the King of Heav'n
We war, if war be best, or to regain
Our own right lost: him to unthrone we then
May hope when everlasting Fate shall yield
To fickle Chance, and *Chaos* judge the strife:
The former vain to hope argues as vain
The latter: for what place can be for us
Within Heav'n's bound, unless Heav'n's Lord supreme
We overpower? Suppose he should relent
And publish Grace to all, on promise made
Of new Subjection; with what eyes could we
Stand in his presence humble, and receive
Strict Laws imposed, to celebrate his Throne
With warbled Hymns, and to his Godhead sing
Forced Hallelujahs; while he Lordly sits
Our envied Sovereign, and his Altar breathes
Ambrosial Odours and Ambrosial Flow'rs,
Our servile offerings. This must be our task
In Heav'n this our delight; how wearisome
Eternity so spent in worship paid
To whom we hate. Let us not then pursue
By force impossible, by leave obtained
Unacceptable, though in Heav'n, our state
Of splendid vassalage, but rather seek
Our own good from ourselves, and from our own
Live to ourselves, though in this vast recess,
Free, and to none accountable, preferring
Hard liberty before the easy yoke
Of servile Pomp. Our greatness will appear
Then most conspicuous, when great things of small,
Useful of hurtful, prosperous of adverse
We can create, and in what place soe'er
Thrive under evil, and work ease out of pain
Through labour and endurance. This deep world
Of darkness do we dread? How oft amidst
Thick clouds and dark doth Heav'n's all-ruling Sire
Choose to reside, his Glory unobscured,
And with the Majesty of darkness round
Covers his Throne; from whence deep thunders roar

Must'ring their rage, and Heav'n resembles Hell?
As he our darkness, cannot we his Light
Imitate when we please? This Desert soil
Wants not her hidden lustre, Gems and Gold;
Nor want we skill or Art, from whence to raise
Magnificence; and what can Heav'n show more?
Our torments also may in length of time
Become our Elements, these piercing Fires[20]
As soft as now severe, our temper changed
Into their temper; which must needs remove
The sensible of pain. All things invite[21]
To peaceful Counsels, and the settled State
Of order, how in safety best we may
Compose our present evils, with regard
Of what we are and where, dismissing quite
All thoughts of War: ye have what I advise'.
He scarce had finished, when such murmur filled
Th' Assembly, as when hollow Rocks retain
The sound of blustering winds, which all night long
Had roused the Sea, now with hoarse cadence lull
Sea-faring men o'erwatched, whose Bark by chance[22]
Or Pinnace anchors in a craggy Bay[23]
After the Tempest: Such applause was heard
As *Mammon* ended, and his Sentence pleased,
Advising peace: for such another Field
They dreaded worse than Hell; so much the fear
Of Thunder and the Sword of *Michaël*
Wrought still within them; and no less desire
To found this nether Empire, which might rise
By policy and long process of time,
In emulation opposite to Heav'n.
Which when *Beëlzebub* perceived, than whom,
Satan except, none higher sat, with grave
Aspect he rose, and in his rising seemed
A Pillar of State; deep on his Front engraven[24]
Deliberation sat and public care;
And Princely counsel in his face yet shone,
Majestic though in ruin: *Sage* he stood
With *Atlantean* shoulders fit to bear[25]
The weight of mightiest Monarchies; his look
Drew audience and attention still as Night
Or summer's Noon-tide air, while thus he spake.

Notes

20 *Elements* the components of life: fire, air, earth, and water.

21 *The sensible of pain* the feeling of pain.

22 *o'erwatched* strained by too long a watch, or stretch of duty; *Bark* "a small ship" (Johnson).

23 *Pinnace* "a small sloop or bark attending a larger ship" (Johnson).

24 *Front* brow, face.

25 *Atlantean* having the strength of Atlas, the Titan who was said to support the sky.

'Thrones and Imperial Powers, off-spring of Heav'n
Ethereal Virtues; or these Titles now[26]
Must we renounce, and changing style be called
Princes of Hell? for so the popular vote
Inclines, here to continue, and build up here
A growing Empire; doubtless; while we dream,
And know not that the King of Heav'n hath doomed
This place our dungeon, not our safe retreat
Beyond his Potent arm, to live exempt
From Heav'n's high jurisdiction, in new League
Banded against his Throne, but to remain
In strictest bondage, though thus far removed,
Under th' inevitable curb, reserved
His captive multitude: For he, be sure
In highth or depth, still first and last will Reign
Sole King, and of his Kingdom lose no part
By our revolt, but over Hell extend
His Empire, and with Iron Sceptre rule[27]
Us here, as with his Golden those in Heav'n.
What sit we then projecting peace and War?
War hath determined us and foiled with loss
Irreparable; terms of peace yet none
Vouchsafed or sought; for what peace will be giv'n
To us enslaved, but custody severe,
And stripes, and arbitrary punishment
Inflicted? and what peace can we return,
But to our power hostility and hate,
Untamed reluctance, and revenge though slow,
Yet ever plotting how the Conqueror least
May reap his conquest, and may least rejoice
In doing what we most in suffering feel?
Nor will occasion want, nor shall we need
With dangerous expedition to invade
Heav'n, whose high walls fear no assault or Siege,
Or ambush from the Deep. What if we find
Some easier enterprise? There is a place
(if ancient and prophetic fame in Heav'n
Err not) another World, the happy seat
Of some new Race called *Man*, about this time
To be created like to us, though less
In power and excellence, but favoured more
Of him who rules above; so was his will
Pronounced among the Gods, and by an Oath,
That shook Heav'n's whole circumference, confirmed.
Thither let us bend all our thoughts, to learn
What creatures there inhabit, of what mould,
Or substance, how endued, and what their Power,

Notes

[26] *Virtues* angels (l.15 above).

[27] *Iron Sceptre* see Psalms 2.9 for this image of stern justice.

And where their weakness, how attempted best,
By force or subtlety: Though Heav'n be shut,
And Heav'n's high Arbitrator sit secure
In his own strength, this place may lie exposed
The utmost border of his Kingdom, left
To their defence who hold it: here perhaps
Some advantageous act may be achieved
By sudden onset, either with Hell fire
To waste his whole Creation, or possess
All as our own, and drive as we were driven,
The puny habitants, or if not drive,[28]
Seduce them to our Party, that their God
May prove their foe, and with repenting hand
Abolish his own works. This would surpass
Common revenge, and interrupt his joy
In our Confusion, and our Joy upraise
In his disturbance; when his darling Sons,
Hurled headlong to partake with us, shall curse
Their frail original, and faded bliss,
Faded so soon. Advise if this be worth
Attempting, or to sit in darkness here
Hatching vain Empires'. Thus *Beëlzebub*
Pleaded his devilish Counsel, first devised
By *Satan*, and in part proposed: for whence,
But from the Author of all ill could Spring
So deep a malice, to confound the race
Of mankind in one root, and Earth with Hell
To mingle and involve, done all to spite
The great Creator? But their spite still serves
His glory to augment. The bold design
Pleased highly those infernal States, and joy
Sparkled in all their eyes; with full assent
They vote: whereat his speech he thus renews.
'Well have ye judged, well ended long debate,
Synod of Gods, and like to what ye are,
Great things resolved, which from the lowest deep
Will once more lift us up, in spite of Fate,
Nearer our ancient Seat; perhaps in view
Of those bright confines, whence with neighbouring Arms
And opportune excursion we may chance
Re-enter Heav'n; or else in some mild Zone
Dwell not unvisited of Heav'n's fair Light
Secure, and at the brightning Orient beam
Purge off this gloom; the soft delicious Air,
To heal the scar of these corrosive Fires
Shall breathe her balm. But first whom shall we send

Notes

[28] *puny* "(puis né, Fr.) 1. Young. 2. Inferior" (Johnson).

In search of this new world? whom shall we find
Sufficient? who shall tempt with wandring feet[29]
The dark unbottomed infinite Abyss
And through the palpable obscure find out
His uncouth way, or spread his airy flight
Upborne with indefatigable wings
Over the vast abrupt, ere he arrive[30]
The happy Isle; what strength, what art can then
Suffice, or what evasion bear him safe
Through the strict Senteries and Stations thick[31]
Of Angels watching round? Here he had need
All circumspection, and we now no less
Choice in our suffrage; for on whom we send,
The weight of all and our last hope relies'.
   This said, he sat; and expectation held
His look suspense, awaiting who appeared
To second, or oppose, or undertake
The perilous attempt: but all sat mute,
Pondering the danger with deep thoughts; and each
In other's count'nance read his own dismay
Astonished: none among the choice and prime
Of those Heav'n-warring Champions could be found
So hardy as to proffer or accept
Alone the dreadful voyage; till at last
Satan, whom now transcendent glory raised
Above his fellows, with Monarchal pride
Conscious of highest worth, unmoved thus spake.
   'O Progeny of Heav'n! Empyreal Thrones,
With reason hath deep silence and demur
Seized us, though undismayed: long is the way
And hard, that out of Hell leads up to light;[32]
Our prison strong, this huge convex of Fire,
Outrageous to devour, immures us round
Ninefold, and gates of burning Adamant
Barred over us prohibit all egress.
These passed, if any pass, the void profound
Of unessential Night receives him next[33]
Wide gaping, and with utter loss of being
Threatens him, plunged in that abortive gulf.
If thence he 'scape into whatever world,
Or unknown Region, what remains him less
Than unknown dangers and as hard escape.
But I should ill become this Throne, O Peers,
And this Imperial sovereignty, adorned

Notes

[29] *tempt* "to try; to attempt" (Johnson).

[30] *abrupt* a noun from Latin *abruptus* (precipitous, sheer).

[31] *Senteries* sentries; *stations* "post[s] assigned" (Johnson).

[32] *long is the way … light* recalls the words of the Sibyl to Aeneas before his descent into Hades (VI.126–9).

[33] *unessential* unliving.

With splendour, armed with power, if aught proposed
And judged of public moment, in the shape
Of difficulty or danger could deter
Me from attempting. Wherefore do I assume
These Royalties, and not refuse to Reign,
Refusing to accept as great a share
Of hazard as of honour, due alike
To him who Reigns, and so much to him due
Of hazard more, as he above the rest
High honoured sits? Go therefore mighty Powers,
Terror of Heav'n, though fall'n; intend at home,[34]
While here shall be our home, what best may ease
The present misery, and render Hell
More tolerable; if there be cure or charm
To respite or deceive, or slack the pain
Of this ill Mansion: intermit no watch
Against a wakeful Foe, while I abroad
Through all the Coasts of dark destruction seek
Deliverance for us all: this enterprise
None shall partake with me'. Thus saying rose
The Monarch, and prevented all reply,
Prudent, lest from his resolution raised
Others among the chief might offer now
(Certain to be refused) what erst they feared;
And so refused might in opinion stand
His Rivals, winning cheap the high repute
Which he through hazard huge must earn. But they
Dreaded not more th' adventure than his voice
Forbidding; and at once with him they rose;
Their rising all at once was as the sound
Of Thunder heard remote. Towards him they bend
With awful reverence prone; and as a God
Extol him equal to the highest in Heav'n:
Nor failed they to express how much they praised,
That for the general safety he despised
His own: for neither do the Spirits damned
Lose all their virtue; lest bad men should boast
Their specious deeds on earth, which glory excites,
Or close ambition varnished o'er with zeal.[35]
Thus they their doubtful consultations dark
Ended rejoicing in their matchless Chief:
As when from mountain tops the dusky clouds
Ascending, while the North wind sleeps, o'erspread
Heav'n's cheerful face, the louring Element
Scowls o'er the darkened lantskip Snow or shower;[36]

Notes

[34] *intend* "To pay regard or attention to" (Johnson).

[35] *close* concealed.

[36] *lantskip* landscape.

If chance the radiant Sun with farewell sweet
Extend his ev'ning beam, the fields revive,
The birds their notes renew, and bleating herds
Attest their joy, that hill and valley rings.
O shame to men! Devil with Devil damned
Firm concord holds, men only disagree
Of Creatures rational, though under hope
Of heavenly Grace: and God proclaiming peace,
Yet live in hatred, enmity, and strife
Among themselves, and levy cruel wars
Wasting the Earth, each other to destroy:
As if (which might induce us to accord)
Man had not hellish foes enow besides,
That day and night for his destruction wait.
　The *Stygian* Counsel thus dissolved; and forth[37]
In order came the grand infernal Peers,
Midst came their mighty Paramount, and seemed
Alone th' Antagonist of Heav'n, nor less
Than Hell's dread Emperor with pomp Supreme,
And God-like imitated State; him round
A Globe of fiery Seraphim enclosed
With bright emblazonry, and horrent Arms.[38]
Then of their Session ended they bid cry
With Trumpet's regal sound the great result:
Toward the four winds four speedy Cherubim
Put to their mouths the sounding Alchemy[39]
By Herald's voice explained: the hollow Abyss
Heard far and wide, and all the host of Hell
With deaf'ning shout, returned them loud acclaim.
Thence more at ease their minds and somewhat raised
By false presumptuous hope, the rangèd powers
Disband, and wand'ring, each his several way
Pursues, as inclination or sad choice
Leads him perplexed, where he may likeliest find
Truce to his restless thoughts, and entertain
The irksome hours, till his great Chief return.
Part on the Plain, or in the Air sublime[40]
Upon the wing, or in swift Race contend,
As at th' *Olympian* Games or *Pythian* fields;[41]
Part curb their fiery Steeds, or shun the Goal[42]
With rapid wheels, or fronted Brígades form.[43]
As when to warn proud Cities war appears

Notes

[37] *Stygian* "Hellish; infernal; pertaining to Styx, one of the poetical rivers of hell" (Johnson).

[38] *horrent* Latinate English, from *horrens*, dreadful, awful and *horrere*, to bristle.

[39] *sounding Alchemy* sound-producing gold, i.e., the trumpets.

[40] *sublime* "raised aloft" (*OED*, 1).

[41] *Olympian … Pythian* the first and second most important contests in the ancient world.

[42] *shun the Goal* cut in close to the turning post on the oval racetrack, without hitting it.

[43] *fronted* opposing.

Waged in the troubled Sky, and Armies rush
To Battle in the Clouds, before each Van[44]
Prick forth the Airy Knights, and couch their spears
Till thickest Legions close; with feats of Arms
From either end of Heav'n the welkin burns.
Others with vast *Typhœan* rage, more fell[45]
Rend up both Rocks and Hills, and ride the Air
In whirlwind; Hell scarce holds the wild uproar.
As when *Alcides* from *Oechalia* Crowned
With conquest, felt th' envenomed robe, and tore
Through pain up by the roots *Thessalian* Pines,
And *Lichas* from the top of *Oeta* threw[46]
Into th' *Euboic* Sea. Others more mild,
Retreated in a silent valley, sing
With notes Angelical to many a Harp
Their own Heroic deeds and hapless fall
By doom of battle; and complain that Fate
Free Virtue should enthral to Force or Chance.
Their Song was partial, but the harmony
(What could it less when Spirits immortal sing?)
Suspended Hell, and took with ravishment
The thronging audience. In discourse more sweet
(For Eloquence the Soul, Song charms the Sense)
Others apart sat on a Hill retired,
In thoughts more elevate, and reasoned high
Of Providence, Foreknowledge, Will and Fate,
Fixed Fate, free will, foreknowledge absolute,
And found no end, in wandring mazes lost.
Of good and evil much they argued then,
Of happiness and final misery,
Passion and Apathy, and glory and shame,[47]
Vain wisdom all, and false Philosophy:
Yet with a pleasing sorcery could charm
Pain for a while or anguish, and excite
Fallacious hope, or arm th' obdurèd breast[48]
With stubborn patience as with triple steel.[49]
Another part in Squadrons and gross Bands,[50]
On bold adventure to discover wide

Notes

44 *Van* "the front of an army; the first line" (Johnson).

45 *Typhœan* like Typhon, a terrible monster with a hundred heads, driven into Tartarus by Zeus or buried under volcanic Mount Aetna; *fell* "Cruel; barbarous, inhuman" (Johnson).

46 *Alcides … Euboic Sea* an allusion to the story of Hercules' (Alcides') death: he returns from sacking *Oechalia* with a girl; his wife Deianira sends *Lichas* to him with the burning shirt of Nessus, which she believes to carry a love potion; Hercules goes mad with pain, tears up the landscape, and destroys his friend Lichas. In most stories the action occurs in Euboea, an island in the Aegean close to central Greece, but Ovid places it on the nearby mainland of southern Thessaly, the location of Mount Oeta (*Metamorphoses* 9.134–272). There were cities named Oechalia in both places.

47 *Apathy* "The quality of not feeling; exemption from passion; freedom from mental perturbation" (Johnson).

48 *obdurèd* obdurate, hardened.

49 *patience* "The power of suffering; endurance" (Johnson).

50 *Squadron* "A body of men drawn up square" (Johnson); *gross* "Thick; bulky" (Johnson).

That dismal world, if any Clime perhaps
Might yield them easier habitation, bend
Four ways their flying March, along the Banks
Of four infernal Rivers that disgorge
Into the burning Lake their baleful streams;
Abhorrèd *Styx* the flood of deadly hate,[51]
Sad *Acheron* of sorrow, black and deep;
Cocytus, named of lamentation loud
Heard on the rueful stream; fierce *Phlegeton*
Whose waves of torrent fire inflame with rage.
Far off from these a slow and silent stream,
Lethe the River of Oblivion, rolls
Her wat'ry Labyrinth, whereof who drinks,
Forthwith his former state and being forgets,
Forgets both joy and grief, pleasure and pain.
Beyond this flood a frozen Continent
Lies dark and wild, beat with perpetual storms
Of Whirlwind and dire Hail, which on firm land
Thaws not, but gathers heap, and ruin seems
Of ancient pile; all else deep snow and ice,
A gulf profound as that *Serbonian* bog[52]
Betwixt *Damiata* and mount *Casius* old,
Where Armies whole have sunk: the parching Air
Burns frore, and cold performs th' effect of Fire.[53]
Thither by harpy-footed Furies hailed,[54]
At certain revolutions all the damned
Are brought: and feel by turns the bitter change
Of fierce extremes, extremes by change more fierce,
From Beds of raging Fire to starve in Ice[55]
Their soft Ethereal warmth, and there to pine
Immovable, infixed, and frozen round,
Periods of time, thence hurried back to fire.
They ferry over this *Lethean* Sound
Both to and fro, their sorrow to augment,
And wish and struggle, as they pass, to reach
The tempting stream, with one small drop to lose
In sweet forgetfulness all pain and woe,
All in one moment, and so near the brink;
But Fate withstands, and to oppose th' attempt
Medusa with *Gorgonian* terror guards[56]
The Ford, and of itself the water flies

Notes

51 *Styx ... Phlegeton* the four rivers of Hell, with the literal meanings of their names.

52 *Serbonian bog* a region east of the Nile delta where the Persian army was supposed to have sunk as it advanced on Egypt in 350 BCE.

53 *frore* "Frozen. This word is not used since the time of Milton" (Johnson).

54 *harpy-footed Furies* harpies are winged beings with talons for snatching, sometimes described as servants to the Furies or Erinyes, avenging spirits.

55 *starve* "To kill with cold" (Johnson).

56 *Medusa ... Gorgonian* Medusa, also called Gorgo, was a monster with snakes for hair and eyes that turned the beholder to stone; her sisters were also gorgons.

All taste of living wight, as once it fled
The lip of *Tantalus*. Thus roving on[57]
In confused march forlorn, th' adventrous Bands
With shuddring horror pale, and eyes aghast
Viewed first their lámentable lot, and found
No rest: through many a dark and dreary Vale
They passed, and many a Region dolorous,
O'er many a Frozen, many a fiery Alp,
Rocks, Caves, Lakes, Fens, Bogs, Dens, and shades of death,
A Universe of death, which God by curse
Created evil, for evil only good,
Where all life dies, death lives, and Nature breeds,
Perverse, all monstrous, all prodigious things,
Abominable, inutterable, and worse
Than Fables yet have feigned, or fear conceived,
Gorgons and *Hydras*, and *Chimeras* dire.[58]
Meanwhile the Adversary of God and Man,
Satan with thoughts inflamed of highest design,
Puts on swift wings, and towards the Gates of Hell
Explores his solitary flight; sometimes
He scours the right hand coast, sometimes the left,[59]
Now shaves with level wing the Deep, then soars
Up to the fiery Concave tow'ring high.
As when far off at Sea a Fleet descried
Hangs in the Clouds, by Equinoctial Winds
Close sailing from *Bengala*, or the Isles[60]
Of *Ternate* and *Tidore*, whence Merchants bring
Their spicy Drugs: they on the Trading Flood
Through the wide *Ethiopian* to the Cape[61]
Ply stemming nightly toward the Pole. So seemed
Far off the flying Fiend: at last appear
Hell bounds high reaching to the horrid Roof,
And thrice threefold the Gates; three folds were Brass,
Three Iron, three of Adamantine Rock,
Impenetrable, impaled with circling fire,
Yet unconsumed. Before the Gates there sat
On either side a formidable shape;
The one seemed Woman to the waist, and fair,
But ended foul in many a scaly fold
Voluminous and vast, a Serpent armed
With mortal sting: about her middle round

Notes

57 *Tantalus* punished eternally for stealing the food of the gods, he stands in water up to his chin but cannot drink because the water disappears when he tries to bring his lips to it.

58 *Gorgons and Hydras, and Chimeras* three kinds of monster: respectively, snake-haired; many-headed; and compounded of a lion's head, goat's belly, and dragon's tail.

59 *scour* "To rove; to range" (Johnson).

60 *Bengala … Ternate* and *Tidore* trading ports in India (Bengala) and Indonesia.

61 *the wide Ethiopian to the Cape* from the Indian Ocean to the Cape of Good Hope, on their way back to Europe from Bengala or Ternate.

A cry of Hell Hounds never ceasing barked
With wide *Cerberian* mouths full loud, and rung[62]
A hideous Peal: yet, when they list, would creep,
If aught disturbed their noise, into her womb,
And kennel there, yet there still barked and howled,
Within unseen. Far less abhorred than these
Vexed *Scylla* bathing in the Sea that parts[63]
Calabria from the hoarse *Trinacrian* shore:
Nor uglier follow the Night-Hag, when called[64]
In secret, riding through the Air she comes
Lured with the smell of infant blood, to dance
With *Lapland* Witches, while the labouring Moon[65]
Eclipses at their charms. The other shape,
If shape it might be called that shape had none
Distinguishable in member, joint, or limb,
Or substance might be called that shadow seemed,[66]
For each seemed either; black it stood as Night,
Fierce as ten Furies, terrible as Hell,
And shook a dreadful Dart: what seemed his head
The likeness of a Kingly Crown had on.
Satan was now at hand, and from his seat
The Monster moving onward came as fast
With horrid strides; Hell trembled as he strode.
Th' undaunted Fiend what this might be admired,[67]
Admired, not feared; God and his Son except,
Created thing naught valued he nor shunned;
And with disdainful look thus first began.
　'Whence and what art thou, execrable shape,
That dar'st, though grim and terrible, advance
Thy miscreated Front athwart my way
To yonder Gates? through them I mean to pass,
That be assured, without leave asked of thee.
Retire, or taste thy folly, and learn by proof,
Hell-born, not to contend with Spirits of Heav'n'.
　To whom the Goblin full of wrath, replied,
'Art thou that Traitor Angel, art thou he,
Who first broke peace in Heav'n and Faith, till then
Unbroken, and in proud rebellious Arms
Drew after him the third part of Heav'n's Sons
Conjured against the Highest, for which both Thou
And they outcast from God, are here condemned

Notes

[62] *Cerberian* like Cerberus, the three-headed dog assigned to guard the entrance to Hades.

[63] *Scylla* a six-headed monster inhabiting a cave in the Straits of Messina between the toe of Italy (part of *Calabria*) and Sicily (*Trinacria*).

[64] *Night-Hag* Hecate, a goddess of the underworld who deploys ghosts and whose approach is signaled by howling dogs.

[65] *labouring* "To be in distress; to be pressed" (Johnson) by the forces causing the eclipse.

[66] *shadow* "An imperfect or faint representation; opposed to substance" (Johnson).

[67] *admired* wondered.

To waste Eternal days in woe and pain?
And reckonst thou thyself with Spirits of Heav'n,
Hell-doomed, and breath'st defiance here and scorn
Where I reign King, and to enrage thee more,
Thy King and Lord? Back to thy punishment,
False fugitive, and to thy speed add wings,
Lest with a whip of Scorpions I pursue
Thy lingring, or with one stroke of this Dart
Strange horror seize thee, and pangs unfelt before'.
So spake the grisly terror, and in shape,
So speaking and so threatning, grew tenfold
More dreadful and deform: on th' other side
Incensed with indignation *Satan* stood
Unterrified, and like a Comet burned,
That fires the length of *Ophiucus* huge[68]
In th' Arctic sky, and from his horrid hair
Shakes Pestilence and War. Each at the head
Levelled his deadly aim; their fatal hands
No second stroke intend, and such a frown
Each cast at th' other, as when two black Clouds
With Heav'n's Artillery fraught, come rattling on
Over the *Caspian*, then stand front to front
Hov'ring a space, till winds the signal blow
To join their dark encounter in mid air:
So frowned the mighty Combatants, that Hell
Grew darker at their frown, so matched they stood;
For never but once more was either like
To meet so great a foe: and now great deeds
Had been achieved, whereof all Hell had rung,
Had not the Snaky Sorceress that sat
Fast by Hell Gate and kept the fatal key,
Ris'n, and with hideous outcry rushed between:
'O Father, what intends thy hand', she cried,
'Against thy only Son? What fury O Son,
Possesses thee to bend that mortal Dart
Against thy Father's head? and know'st for whom:
For him who sits above and laughs the while
At thee ordained his drudge, to execute
What e'er his wrath, which he calls Justice, bids,
His wrath which one day will destroy ye both'.
She spake, and at her words the hellish Pest
Forbore, then these to her *Satan* returned:
'So strange thy outcry, and thy words so strange
Thou interposest, that my sudden hand[69]

Notes

[68] *Ophiucus* (Gk., "serpent-bearer"), a constellation.

[69] *sudden* "Hasty; violent; rash; passionate, precipitous; not in use" (Johnson).

Prevented spares to tell thee yet by deeds
What it intends; till first I know of thee,
What thing thou art, thus double-formed, and why
In this infernal Vale first met thou call'st
Me Father, and that Phantasm call'st my Son?
I know thee not, nor ever saw till now
Sight more detestable than him and thee'.
T' whom thus the Portress of Hell Gate replied;
'Hast thou forgot me then, and do I seem
Now in thine eye so foul, once deemed so fair
In Heav'n, when at th' Assembly, and in sight
Of all the Seraphim with thee combined
In bold conspiracy against Heav'n's King,
All on a sudden miserable pain
Surprised thee, dim thine eyes, and dizzy swum
In darkness, while thy head flames thick and fast
Threw forth, till on the left side op'ning wide,
Likest to thee in shape and count'nance bright,
Then shining heav'nly fair, a Goddess armed
Out of thy head I sprung: amazement seized[70]
All th' Host of Heav'n; back they recoiled afraid
At first, and called me *Sin*, and for a Sign
Portentous held me; but familiar grown,
I pleased, and with attractive graces won
The most averse, thee chiefly, who full oft
Thyself in me thy perfect image viewing
Becam'st enamoured, and such joy thou took'st
With me in secret, that my womb conceived
A growing burden. Meanwhile War arose,
And fields were fought in Heav'n; wherein remained
(For what could else) to our Almighty Foe
Clear Victory, to our part loss and rout
Through all the Empyrean: down they fell
Driv'n headlong from the Pitch of Heav'n, down
Into this Deep, and in the general fall
I also; at which time this powerful Key
Into my hands was giv'n, with charge to keep
These Gates forever shut, which none can pass
Without my op'ning. Pensive here I sat
Alone, but long I sat not, till my womb,
Pregnant by thee, and now excessive grown
Prodigious motion felt and rueful throes.
At last this odious offspring whom thou seest
Thine own begotten, breaking violent way
Tore through my entrails, that with fear and pain

Notes

[70] *Out of thy head I sprung* the birth of *Sin* imitates the birth of Athena, goddess of wisdom, from the head of Zeus, but the connection between lust, sin, and death comes from James 1.15.

Distorted, all my nether shape thus grew
Transformed: but he my inbred enemy
Forth issued, brandishing his fatal Dart
Made to destroy: I fled, and cried out "Death";
Hell trembled at the hideous Name, and sighed
From all her Caves, and back resounded "Death";
I fled, but he pursued (though more, it seems,
Inflamed with lust than rage) and swifter far,
Me overtook his mother all dismayed,
And in embraces forcible and foul
Engend'ring with me, of that rape begot
These yelling Monsters that with ceaseless cry
Surround me, as thou sawst, hourly conceived
And hourly born, with sorrow infinite
To me, for when they list into the womb
That bred them they return, and howl and gnaw
My Bowels, their repast; then bursting forth
Afresh with conscious terrors vex me round,
That rest or intermission none I find.
Before mine eyes in opposition sits
Grim *Death* my Son and foe who sets them on,
And me his Parent would full soon devour
For want of other prey, but that he knows
His end with mine involved; and knows that I
Should prove a bitter Morsel, and his bane,
Whenever that shall be; so Fate pronounced.
But thou O Father, I forewarn thee, shun
His deadly arrow; neither vainly hope
To be invulnerable in those bright Arms,
Though tempered Heav'nly, for that mortal dint,[71]
Save he who reigns above, none can resist'.
She finished, and the subtle Fiend his lore
Soon learned, now milder, and thus answered smooth.
'Dear Daughter, since thou claim'st me for thy Sire,
And my fair Son here showst me, the dear pledge
Of dalliance had with thee in Heav'n, and joys
Then sweet, now sad to mention, through dire change
Befall'n us unforeseen, unthought of, know
I come no enemy, but to set free
From out this dark and dismal house of pain,
Both him and thee, and all the heav'nly Host
Of Spirits that in our just pretences armed
Fell with us from on high: from them I go
This uncouth errand sole, and one for all
Myself expose, with lonely steps to tread
Th' unfounded deep, and through the void immense

Notes

[71] *dint* "stroke or blow" (*OED*, 1).

To search with wandring quest, a place foretold
Should be, and, by concurring signs, ere now
Created vast and round, a place of bliss
In the Purlieus of Heav'n, and therein placed
A race of upstart Creatures, to supply
Perhaps our vacant room, though more removed,
Lest Heav'n, surcharged with potent multitude
Might hap to move new broils: Be this or aught
Than this more secret now designed, I haste
To know, and this once known, shall soon return,
And bring ye to the place where Thou and Death
Shall dwell at ease, and up and down unseen
Wing silently the buxom Air, embalmed[72]
With odours; there ye shall be fed and filled
Immeasurably, all things shall be your prey'.
He ceased, for both seemed highly pleased, and Death
Grinned horrible a ghastly smile, to hear
His famine should be filled, and blessed his maw
Destined to that good hour: no less rejoiced
His mother bad, and thus bespake her Sire.
'The key of this infernal Pit by due,
And by command of Heav'n's all-powerful King
I keep, by him forbidden to unlock
These Adamantine Gates; against all force
Death ready stands to interpose his dart,
Fearless to be o'ermatched by living might.
But what owe I to his commands above
Who hates me, and hath hither thrust me down
Into this gloom of *Tartarus* profound,
To sit in hateful Office here confined,
Inhabitant of Heav'n, and heav'nly-born,
Here in perpetual agony and pain,
With terrors and with clamours compassed round
Of mine own brood, that on my bowels feed:
Thou art my Father, thou my Author, thou
My being gav'st me; whom should I obey
But thee, whom follow? thou wilt bring me soon
To that new world of light and bliss, among
The Gods who live at ease, where I shall Reign
At thy right hand voluptuous, as beseems
Thy daughter and thy darling, without end'.
Thus saying, from her side the fatal Key,
Sad instrument of all our woe, she took;
And towards the Gate rolling her bestial train,
Forthwith the huge Portcullis high up drew,
Which but herself, not all the *Stygian* powers

Notes

[72] *buxom* obedient.

Could once have moved; then in the key-hole turns
Th' intricate wards, and every Bolt and Bar
Of massy Iron or solid Rock with ease
Unfastens: on a sudden open fly
With impetuous recoil and jarring sound
Th' infernal doors, and on their hinges grate
Harsh Thunder, that the lowest bottom shook
Of *Erebus*. She opened, but to shut[73]
Excelled her power; the Gates wide op'n stood,
That with extended wings a Bannered Host
Under spread Ensigns marching might pass through
With Horse and Chariots ranked in loose array;
So wide they stood, and like a Furnace mouth
Cast forth redounding smoke and ruddy flame.
Before their eyes in sudden view appear
The secrets of the hoary deep, a dark
Illimitable Ocean without bound,
Without dimension; where length, breadth, & highth,
And time and place are lost; where eldest Night
And *Chaos*, ancestors of Nature, hold
Eternal *Anarchy*, amidst the noise
Of endless Wars, and by confusion stand.
For hot, cold, moist, and dry, four Champions fierce[74]
Strive here for Mast'ry, and to Battle bring
Their embryon Atoms; they around the flag[75]
Of each his Faction, in their several Clans,
Light-armed or heavy, sharp, smooth, swift, or slow,
Swarm populous, unnumbered as the Sands
Of *Barca* or *Cyrene's* torrid soil,[76]
Levied to side with warring Winds, and poise
Their lighter wings. To whom these most adhere,
He rules a moment; *Chaos* Umpire sits,
And by decision more embroils the fray
By which he Reigns: next him high Arbiter
Chance governs all. Into this wild Abyss,
The Womb of nature and perhaps her Grave,
Of neither Sea, nor Shore, nor Air, nor Fire,
But all these in their pregnant causes mixed
Confus'dly, and which thus must ever fight,
Unless th' Almighty Maker them ordain
His dark materials to create more Worlds,
Into this wild Abyss the wary fiend
Stood on the brink of Hell and looked a while,

Notes

[73] *Erebus* a place of darkness making a passage between earth and Hades.

[74] *hot, cold, moist, and dry* the four elements in the old physics: fire, earth, water, air (cf. l. 912 below).

[75] *embryon Atoms* embryonic constituent elements of matter, as described by Lucretius in *De Rerum Natura*.

[76] *Barca, Cyrene* cities of Cyrenaica, the land west of Egypt on the North African coast.

Pondering his Voyage; for no narrow frith[77]
He had to cross. Nor was his ear less pealed[78]
With noises loud and ruinous (to compare
Great things with small) than when *Bellona* storms,[79]
With all her battering Engines bent to raze
Some Capital City; or less than if this frame
Of Heav'n were falling, and these Elements
In mutiny had from her Axle torn
The steadfast Earth. At last his Sail-broad vans[80]
He spreads for flight, and in the surging smoke
Uplifted spurns the ground, thence many a League
As in a cloudy Chair ascending rides
Audacious, but that seat soon failing, meets
A vast vacuity: all unawares
Flutt'ring his pennons vain plumb down he drops[81]
Ten thousand fadom deep, and to this hour[82]
Down had been falling, had not by ill chance
The strong rebuff of some tumultuous cloud
Instinct with Fire and Nitre, hurried him
As many miles aloft: that fury stayed,
Quenched in a Boggy *Syrtis*, neither Sea,[83]
Nor good dry Land: nigh foundered on he fares,
Treading the crude consistence, half on foot,
Half flying; behoves him now both Oar and Sail.
As when a Gryphon through the Wilderness[84]
With winged course o'er Hill or moory Dale,
Pursues the *Arimaspian*, who by stealth
Had from his wakeful custody purloined
The guarded Gold: So eagerly the Fiend
O'er bog or steep, through strait, rough, dense, or rare,
With head, hands, wings or feet pursues his way,
And swims, or sinks, or wades, or creeps, or flies:
At length a universal hubbub wild
Of stunning sounds, and voices all confused
Borne through the hollow dark assaults his ear
With loudest vehemence: thither he plies,
Undaunted to meet there what ever power
Or Spirit of the nethermost Abyss
Might in that noise reside, of whom to ask
Which way the nearest coast of darkness lies

Notes

[77] *frith* firth, arm of the sea.

[78] *peal* "To assail with noise" (Johnson).

[79] *Bellona* Roman goddess of war.

[80] *van* "A wing with which the air is beaten" (Johnson).

[81] *pennon* poetic for *pinion*, wing.

[82] *fadom* fathoms.

[83] *Syrtis* according to old dictionaries, two quicksands on the African shore; more properly, the name of two bays, famous for treacherous navigation and dangerous, sandy shores.

[84] *Gryphon* a beast with the head of a lion and the wings and talons of an eagle, guardian of the gold of the north, enemy of the one-eyed Arimaspians who dwelt in Scythia, north of the Black Sea.

Bordering on light; when straight behold the Throne
Of *Chaos*, and his dark Pavilion spread
Wide on the wasteful Deep; with him enthroned
Sat Sable-vested *Night*, eldest of things,
The consort of his reign; and by them stood
Orcus and *Ades*, and the dreaded name[85]
Of *Demogorgon*; *Rumour* next, and *Chance*,[86]
And *Tumult* and *Confusion* all embroiled,
And *Discord* with a thousand various mouths.
T' whom *Satan*, turning boldly, thus. 'Ye Powers
And Spirits of this nethermost Abyss,
Chaos and *ancient Night*, I come no Spy,
With purpose to explore or to disturb
The secrets of your Realm, but by constraint
Wandring this darksome Desert, as my way,
Lies through your spacious Empire up to light,
Alone, and without guide, half lost, I seek
What readiest path leads where your gloomy bounds
Confine with Heav'n; or if some other place
From your Dominion won, th' Ethereal King
Possesses lately, thither to arrive
I travel this profound, direct my course;
Directed no mean recompense it brings
To your behoof, if I that Region lost,
All usurpation thence expelled, reduce
To her original darkness and your sway
(Which is my present journey) and once more
Erect the Standard there of *ancient Night*;
Yours be th' advantage all, mine the revenge'.
Thus *Satan*; and him thus the Anarch old
With faltring speech and visage incomposed
Answered. 'I know thee, stranger, who thou art,
That mighty leading Angel, who of late
Made head against Heav'n's King, though overthrown.
I saw and heard, for such a numerous Host
Fled not in silence through the frighted deep
With ruin upon ruin, rout on rout,
Confusion worse confounded; and Heav'n Gates
Poured out by millions her victorious Bands
Pursuing. I upon my Frontiers here
Keep residence; if all I can will serve,
That little which is left so to defend,
Encroached on still through our intestine broils[87]

Notes

[85] *Orcus and Ades* (Hades) both names for the god of the underworld.

[86] *Demogorgon* a renaissance name for the primaeval god, corrupted from *demiurge*, and dreaded because it sounds like *gorgon* (see Spenser, *Faerie Queene* 4.2.47).

[87] *intestine* domestic, internal; cf. *Henry IV Part 1*, I.i.12.

Weak'ning the Sceptre of old *Night*: first Hell
Your dungeon stretching far and wide beneath;
Now lately Heav'n and Earth, another World
Hung o'er my Realm, linked in a golden Chain[88]
To that side Heav'n from whence your Legions fell:
If that way be your walk, you have not far;
So much the nearer danger; go and speed;
Havoc and spoil and ruin are my gain'.
He ceased; and *Satan* stayed not to reply,
But glad that now his Sea should find a shore,
With fresh alacrity and force renewed
Springs upward like a Pyramid of fire
Into the wild expanse, and through the shock
Of fighting Elements, on all sides round
Environed wins his way; harder beset
And more endangered, than when *Argo* passed[89]
Through *Bosporus* betwixt the justling Rocks:
Or when *Ulysses* on the Larboard shunned[90]
Charybdis, and by th' other whirlpool steered.
So he with difficulty and labour hard
Moved on, with difficulty and labour he;
But he once past, soon after when man fell,
Strange alteration! Sin and Death amain
Following his track, such was the will of Heav'n,
Paved after him a broad and beaten way
Over the dark Abyss, whose boiling Gulf
Tamely endured a Bridge of wondrous length
From Hell continued reaching th' utmost Orb
Of this frail World; by which the Spirits perverse
With easy intercourse pass to and fro
To tempt or punish mortals, except whom
God and good Angels guard by special grace.
But now at last the sacred influence
Of light appears, and from the walls of Heav'n
Shoots far into the bosom of dim Night
A glimmering dawn; here Nature first begins
Her farthest verge, and *Chaos* to retire
As from her outmost works a broken foe
With tumult less and with less hostile din;
That *Satan* with less toil, and now with ease,
Wafts on the calmer wave by dubious light
And like a weather-beaten Vessel holds

Notes

[88] *golden Chain* an image of divine order from Homer (*Iliad* 8.18–27) to the eighteenth century, when it becomes known as the great chain of being (cf. l. 1051 below).

[89] *Argo* the ship used by Jason and his Argonauts; on their quest for the golden fleece, they had to pass through the dangerous *Bosporus*, a strait leading to the Black Sea.

[90] *Ulysses ... steered Charybdis* is the whirlpool in the Strait of Messina, on the *Larboard*, or Sicilian side as Ulysses sailed west; he preferred the rocks on the starboard, Italian side where Scylla snatched six of his men (*Odyssey* 12.234–59).

Gladly the Port, though Shrouds and Tackle torn;
Or in the emptier waste, resembling Air,
Weighs his spread wings, at leisure to behold
Far off th' Empyreal Heav'n, extended wide
In circuit, undetermined square or round,
With Opal Towers and Battlements adorned
Of living Sapphire, once his native Seat;
And fast by hanging in a golden Chain
This pendant world, in bigness as a Star
Of smallest Magnitude close by the Moon.
Thither full fraught with mischievous revenge,
Accursed, and in a cursèd hour he hies.

Book III
The Argument

God sitting on his Throne sees Satan *flying towards this world, then newly created; shows him to the Son who sat at his right hand; foretells the success of* Satan *in perverting mankind; clears his own Justice and Wisdom from all imputation, having created Man free and able enough to have withstood his Tempter; yet declares his purpose of Grace towards him, in regard he fell not of his own malice, as did* Satan, *but by him seduced. The Son of God renders praises to his Father for the manifestation of his gracious purpose towards Man; but God again declares, that Grace cannot be extended towards Man without the satisfaction of Divine Justice; Man hath offended the majesty of God by aspiring to God-head, and therefore with all his Progeny devoted to death must die, unless some one can be found sufficient to answer for his offence, and undergo his Punishment. The Son of God freely offers himself a Ransom for Man: the Father accepts him, ordains his incarnation, pronounces his exaltation above all Nations in Heaven and Earth; commands all the Angels to adore him, they obey, and hymning to their Harps in full Choir, celebrate the Father and the Son. Meanwhile* Satan *alights upon the bare Convex of this World's outermost Orb; where wandering he first finds a place since called The Limbo of Vanity; what persons and things fly up thither; thence comes to the Gate of Heaven, described ascending by stairs, and the waters above the Firmament that flow about it: His passage thence to the Orb of the Sun; he finds there* Uriel *the Regent of that Orb, but first changes himself into the shape of a meaner Angel; and pretending a zealous desire to behold the new Creation and Man whom God had placed here, inquires of him the place of his habitation, and is directed; alights first on Mount* Niphates.

Book IV
The Argument

Satan *now in prospect of* Eden, *and nigh the place where he must now attempt the bold enterprise which he undertook alone against God and Man, falls into many doubts with himself, and many passions, fear, envy, and despair; but at length confirms himself in evil, journeys on to Paradise, whose outward prospect and situation is described, overleaps the bounds, sits in the shape of a Cormorant on the Tree of life, as highest in the Garden, to look about him. The Garden described;* Satan's *first sight of* Adam *and* Eve; *his wonder at their excellent form and happy state, but with resolution to work their fall; overhears their discourse, thence gathers that the Tree of knowledge was forbidden them to eat of, under penalty of death; and thereon intends to found his Temptation, by seducing them to transgress: then leaves them a while, to know further of their state by some other means. Meanwhile* Uriel *descending on a Sun-beam warns* Gabriel, *who had in his charge the Gate of Paradise, that some evil spirit had escaped the Deep, and passed at Noon by his Sphere in the shape of a good Angel down to Paradise, discovered after by his furious gestures in the Mount.* Gabriel *promises to find him ere morning. Night coming on,* Adam *and* Eve, *discourse of going to their rest: their Bower described; their Evening worship.* Gabriel *drawing forth his Bands of Night-watch to walk the round of Paradise, appoints two strong Angels to* Adam's *Bower, lest the evil spirit should be there doing some harm to* Adam *or* Eve *sleeping; there they find him at the ear of* Eve, *tempting her in a dream, and bring him, though unwilling, to* Gabriel; *by whom questioned, he scornfully answers, prepares resistance, but hindered by a Sign from Heaven, flies out of Paradise.*

O For that warning voice, which he who saw[1]
Th' *Apocalypse*, heard cry in Heav'n aloud,
Then when the Dragon, put to second rout,
Came furious down to be revenged on men,
'Woe to the inhabitants on earth!' that now,[2]
While time was, our first-Parents had been warned
The coming of their secret foe, and 'scaped,
Haply so 'scaped his mortal snare; for now
Satan, now first inflamed with rage, came down,
The Tempter ere th' Accuser of man-kind,
To wreak on innocent frail man his loss
Of that first Battle, and his flight to Hell:
Yet not rejoicing in his speed, though bold,
Far off and fearless, nor with cause to boast,
Begins his dire attempt, which nigh the birth
Now rolling, boils in his tumultuous breast,
And like a devilish Engine back recoils[3]
Upon himself; horror and doubt distract
His troubled thoughts, and from the bottom stir
The Hell within him for within him Hell
He brings, and round about him, nor from Hell
One step no more than from himself can fly
By change of place: Now conscience wakes despair
That slumbered, wakes the bitter memory
Of what he was, what is, and what must be
Worse; of worse deeds worse sufferings must ensue.
Sometimes towards *Eden* which now in his view
Lay pleasant, his grieved look he fixes sad,
Sometimes towards Heav'n and the full-blazing Sun,
Which now sat high in his Meridian Tower:
Then much revolving, thus in sighs began.
'O thou that with surpassing Glory crowned,
Look'st from thy sole Dominion like the God

Notes

BOOK IV

[1] *he who saw Th' Apocalypse* St. John (Revelation 12.10).

[2] *Woe ... earth!* Revelation 12.12.

[3] *devilish Engine* cannon, invented by Milton's devils in their war with heaven (cf. 6.518).

Of this new World; at whose sight all the Stars
Hide their diminished heads; to thee I call,
But with no friendly voice, and add thy name
O Sun, to tell thee how I hate thy beams
That bring to my remembrance from what state
I fell, how glorious once above thy Sphere;
Till Pride and worse Ambition threw me down
Warring in Heav'n against Heav'n's matchless King:
Ah wherefore! he deserved no such return
From me, whom he created what I was
In that bright eminence, and with his good
Upbraided none; nor was his service hard.
What could be less than to afford him praise,
The easiest recompense, and pay him thanks,
How due! yet all his good proved ill in me,
And wrought but malice; lifted up so high
I sdeined subjection, and thought one step higher[4]
Would set me highest, and in a moment quit[5]
The debt immense of endless gratitude,
So burthensome still paying, still to owe;
Forgetful what from him I still received,
And understood not that a grateful mind
By owing owes not, but still pays, at once
Indebted and discharged; what burden then?
O had his powerful Destiny ordained
Me some inferior Angel, I had stood
Then happy; no unbounded hope had raised
Ambition. Yet why not? some other Power
As great might have aspired, and me though mean
Drawn to his part; but other Powers as great
Fell not, but stand unshaken, from within
Or from without, to all temptations armed.
Hadst thou the same free Will and Power to stand?[6]
Thou hadst: whom hast thou then or what to accuse,[7]
But Heav'n's free Love dealt equally to all?
Be then his Love accurst, since love or hate,
To me alike, it deals eternal woe.
Nay cursed be thou; since against his thy will
Chose freely what it now so justly rues.
Me miserable! which way shall I fly
Infinite wrath, and infinite despair?
Which way I fly is Hell; myself am Hell;
And in the lowest deep a lower deep
Still threat'ning to devour me opens wide,
To which the Hell I suffer seems a Heav'n.
O then at last relent: is there no place

Notes

[4] *sdeined* disdained.
[5] *quit* repay.
[6] *thou* Satan addresses himself in the second person (cf. l. 71).
[7] *to accuse* vowel coalescence.

Left for Repentance, none for Pardon left?
None left but by submission; and that word
Disdain forbids me, and my dread of shame
Among the *Spirits* beneath, whom I seduced
With other promises and other vaunts
Than to submit, boasting I could subdue
Th' Omnipotent. Ay me, they little know
How dearly I abide that boast so vain,
Under what torments inwardly I groan,
While they adore me on the Throne of Hell.
With Diadem and Sceptre high advanced
The lower still I fall, only Supreme
In misery; such joy Ambition finds.
But say I could repent and could obtain,
By Act of Grace my former state; how soon
Would highth recall high thoughts, how soon unsay
What feigned submission swore: ease would recant
Vows made in pain, as violent and void.
For never can true reconcilement grow
Where wounds of deadly hate have pierced so deep:
Which would but lead me to a worse relapse,
And heavier fall: so should I purchase dear
Short intermission bought with double smart.
This knows my punisher; therefore as far
From granting he, as I from begging peace:
All hope excluded thus, behold instead
Of us out-cast, exiled, his new delight,
Mankind created, and for him this World.
So farewell Hope, and with hope farewell fear,
Farewell Remorse: all Good to me is lost;
Evil be thou my Good; by thee at least
Divided Empire with Heav'n's King I hold
By thee, and more than half perhaps will reign;[8]
As Man ere long, and this new World shall know'.
    Thus while he spake, each passion dimmed his face
Thrice changed with pale, ire, envy, and despair,[9]
Which marred his borrowed visage, and betrayed[10]
Him counterfeit, if any eye beheld.
For heav'nly minds from such distempers foul
Are ever clear. Whereof he soon aware,
Each perturbation smoothed with outward calm,
Artificer of fraud; and was the first
That practised falsehood under saintly show,
Deep malice to conceal, couched with revenge:

Notes

[8] *reign* probably reign over, govern; but possibly a variant spelling of *rein* or *arraign*.

[9] *pale* paleness, pallor; *ire, envy, and despair* make the three changes of pallor.

[10] *borrowed visage* the likeness of the "stripling Cherub," which he had assumed (3.636).

Yet not enough had practised to deceive
Uriel once warned; whose eye pursued him down
The way he went, and on th' *Assyrian* mount[11]
Saw him disfigured, more than could befall
Spirit of happy sort: his gestures fierce
He marked and mad demeanour, then alone,
As he supposed, all unobserved, unseen.
So on he fares, and to the border comes,
Of *Eden*, where delicious Paradise,
Now nearer, Crowns with her enclosure green,
As with a rural mound, the champaign head[12]
Of a steep wilderness, whose hairy sides
With thicket overgrown, grotesque and wild,[13]
Access denied; and overhead up grew
Insuperable highth of loftiest shade,
Cedar, and Pine, and Fir, and branching Palm,
A Sylvan Scene, and as the ranks ascend
Shade above shade, a woody Theatre[14]
Of stateliest view. Yet higher than their tops
The verdurous wall of Paradise upsprung:
Which to our general Sire gave prospect large
Into his nether Empire neighbouring round.
And Higher than that Wall a circling row
Of goodliest Trees loaden with fairest Fruit,
Blossoms and Fruits at once of golden hue
Appeared, with gay enamelled colours mixed:[15]
On which the Sun more glad impressed his beams
Than in fair Evening Cloud, or humid Bow,[16]
When God hath showered the earth; so lovely seemed
That Lantskip: And of pure now purer air
Meets his approach, and to the heart inspires[17]
Vernal delight and joy, able to drive
All sadness but despair: now gentle gales,[18]
Fanning their odoriferous wings dispense
Native perfumes, and whisper whence they stole
Those balmy spoils. As when to them who sail
Beyond the *Cape of Hope*, and now are past[19]
Mozambic, off at Sea North-East winds blow
Sabean Odours from the spicy shore

Notes

11 *Assyrian mount* Niphates, the first place Satan lands on earth (3.742), an eastern part of the Taurus Mountains, in Armenia, near old Assyria, now Iran.

12 *champaign* "A flat open country" (Johnson).

13 *grotesque* grotto-like, as well as "distorted ... wildly formed" (Johnson).

14 *Theatre* (literally "a place for viewing") "A place rising by steps like a theatre" (Johnson).

15 *enamelled* glossy.

16 *humid Bow* rainbow.

17 *inspires* "To breathe into; to infuse into the mind; to impress upon the fancy" (Johnson).

18 *gales* "A wind not tempestuous, yet stronger than a breeze" (Johnson).

19 *Cape of Hope ... Araby the blest* past the southern tip of Africa, sailing north, up the east coast, beyond Mozambique and smelling the frankincense and myrrh produced in Saba (modern Yemen), to the northeast, in the southern part of Arabia, formerly called *Arabia Felix* (blessed, fortunate).

Of *Araby* the blest, with such delay
Well pleased they slack their course, and many a League
Cheered with the grateful smell old Ocean smiles.
So entertained those odorous sweets the Fiend,
Who came their bane, though with them better pleased
Than *Asmodeus* with the fishy fume,[20]
That drove him, though enamoured, from the Spouse
Of *Tobit's* Son, and with a vengeance sent
From *Media* post to *Ægypt*, there fast bound.[21]
  Now to th' ascent of that steep savage Hill
Satan had journeyed on, pensive and slow;
But further way found none, so thick entwined,
As one continued brake, the undergrowth
Of shrubs and tangling bushes had perplexed
All path of Man or Beast that passed that way:
One Gate there only was, and that looked East
On th' other side: which when th' arch-felon saw
Due entrance he disdained, and in contempt,
At one slight bound high overleaped all bound
Of Hill or highest Wall, and sheer within
Lights on his feet. As when a prowling Wolf,
Whom hunger drives to seek new haunt for prey,
Watching where Shepherds pen their Flocks at eve
In hurdled Cotes amid the field secure,[22]
Leaps o'er the fence with ease into the Fold:
Or as a Thief bent to unhoard the cash
Of some rich Burgher, whose substantial doors,
Cross-barred and bolted fast, fear no assault,
In at the window climbs, or o'er the tiles:[23]
So clomb this first grand Thief into God's Fold:
So since into his Church lewd Hirelings climb.[24]
Thence up he flew, and on the Tree of Life
The middle Tree and highest there that grew,
Sat like a Cormorant; yet not true Life
Thereby regained, but sat devising Death
To them who lived; nor on the virtue thought[25]
Of that life-giving Plant, but only used
For prospect, what well used had been the pledge
Of immortality. So little knows

Notes

[20] *Asmodeus* the demon in the Book of Tobit (part of the *Apocrypha*) who haunts Sarah and kills her first seven husbands on their wedding nights. Acting on instructions from the angel Raphael, Tobias, the son of Tobit, burns the heart and liver of a fish on the ashes of incense as he enters Sarah's chamber on his wedding night; the demon flees from Media (the kingdom of the Medes in Asia, south of the Caspian Sea) into uppermost Egypt, where he is bound by the angel (Tobit 8).

[21] *post* posthaste; with great speed.

[22] *hurdled Cotes* heepfolds made of a "texture of sticks woven together" (Johnson).

[23] *tiles* the tiled roof.

[24] *lewd* "1. Lay; not clerical … 2. Wicked, bad, naughty" (Johnson).

[25] *virtue* power.

Any, but God alone, to value right
The good before him, but perverts best things
To worst abuse, or to their meanest use.
Beneath him with new wonder now he views
To all delight of human sense exposed
In narrow room Nature's whole wealth, yea more,
A Heav'n on Earth, for blissful Paradise
Of God the Garden was, by him in the East
Of *Eden* planted; *Eden* stretched her Line[26]
From *Auran* Eastward to the Royal Towers
Of great *Seleucia*, built by *Grecian* Kings,
Or where the Sons of Eden long before
Dwelt in *Telassar*: in this pleasant soil
His far more pleasant Garden God ordained;
Out of the fertile ground he caused to grow
All Trees of noblest kind for sight, smell, taste;
And all amid them stood the Tree of Life,
High eminent, blooming Ambrosial Fruit
Of vegetable Gold; and next to Life
Our Death the Tree of Knowledge grew fast by,
Knowledge of Good bought dear by knowing ill.
Southward through *Eden* went a River large,
Nor changed his course, but through the shaggy hill
Passed underneath engulfed, for God had thrown
That Mountain as his Garden mould high raised[27]
Upon the rapid current, which, through veins
Of porous Earth with kindly thirst up drawn,
Rose a fresh Fountain, and with many a rill
Watered the Garden; thence united fell
Down the steep glade, and met the nether Flood,
Which from his darksome passage now appears,
And now divided into four main Streams,
Runs diverse, wand'ring many a famous Realm
And Country whereof here needs no account,
But rather to tell how, if Art could tell,
How from that Sapphire Fount the crispèd[28] Brooks,
Rolling on orient Pearl and sands of Gold,
With mazy error under pendant shades[29]
Ran Nectar, visiting each plant, and fed
Flow'rs worthy of Paradise which not nice Art[30]
In Beds and curious Knots, but Nature boon[31]

Notes

26 *Eden* is located near the northern end of the Persian Gulf, west of Haran (*Auran*), Abraham's chosen home, near *Telassar*; *Seleucia*, founded by Seleucus (one of five kings of the Greek dominion of Syria), was on the coast of northern Palestine, near Antioch.

27 *Garden mould* topsoil.

28 *crispèd* "having a surface curled into minute waves" (OED).

29 *error* wandering, in the etymological sense (Latin, *error*).

30 *worthy of* vowel coalescence; *nice* fastidious; overly careful.

31 *Knots* a feature of formal gardens; *boon* bounteous (*OED*) but also jovial, convivial.

Poured forth profuse on Hill and Dale and Plain,
Both where the morning Sun first warmly smote
The open field, and where the unpierced shade
Imbrowned the noontide Bow'rs: Thus was this place
A happy rural seat of various view;
Groves whose rich Trees wept odorous Gums and Balm,
Others whose fruit burnished with Golden Rind
Hung amiable, *Hesperian* Fables true,[32]
If true, here only, and of delicious taste:
Betwixt them Lawns, or level Downs, and Flocks
Grazing the tender herb, were interposed,
Or palmy hillock, or the flowry lap
Of some irriguous Valley spread her store,[33]
Flowers of all hue, and without Thorn the Rose:
Another side, umbrageous Grots and Caves[34]
Of cool recess, o'er which the mantling vine
Lays forth her purple Grape, and gently creeps
Luxuriant; meanwhile murmuring waters fall
Down the slope hills, dispersed, or in a Lake,
That to the fringèd Bank with Myrtle crowned,
Her crystal mirror holds, unite their streams.
The Birds their quire apply; airs, vernal airs,
Breathing the smell of field and grove, attune
The trembling leaves, while Universal *Pan*,[35]
Knit with the *Graces* and the *Hours* in dance,
Led on th' Eternal Spring. Not that fair field
Of *Enna*, where *Proserpine* gath'ring flowers,[36]
Herself a fairer Flower by gloomy *Dis*
Was gathered, which cost *Ceres* all that pain
To seek her through the world; nor that sweet Grove[37]
Of *Daphne* by *Orontes*, and th' inspired
Castalian Spring, might with this Paradise
Of *Eden* strive; nor that *Nyseian* Isle[38]
Girt with the River *Triton*, where old *Cham*,
Whom Gentiles *Ammon* call and *Libyan Jove*,
Hid *Amalthea* and her Florid Son

Notes

32 *Hesperian Fables* the Hesperides, daughters of Night and Erebus, were guardians of a tree of golden apples.

33 *irriguous* "Watery; watered" (Johnson).

34 *umbrageous Grots* shady grottoes.

35 *Universal Pan … Graces … Hours* nature (Greek *τὸ πάν*), with the three Graces and the four Hours, goddesses of giving, receiving and returning favors, and of the seasons.

36 *Enna* city in the center of Sicily from which Pluto (*Dis*) carried *Proserpina* off to Hades (Ovid, *Metamorphoses* 5.385–408); her mother Ceres sought her all over the earth; Zeus' adjudication of the matter put an end to the primordial eternal spring. The story suggests the seduction of Eve by Satan.

37 *Grove of Daphne* a park near Antioch where Apollo was worshipped and celebrations were held remembering his pursuit of the nymph Daphne, daughter of a river god, which ended with her transformation into the tree of her name (laurel).

38 *that Nyseian Isle* an island in the *Triton* river, North Africa, conflated with an Arabian place called Nysa; there *Cham* (Hammon, son of Noah), conflated with *Ammon* (an Egyptian Jupiter), sent his son *Bacchus* (Dionysius, literally, "god of Nysa") by *Amalthea* (in some myths, though usually Semele) to escape *Rhea*, his jealous wife (though she is usually his mother).

Young *Bacchus* from his Stepdame *Rhea's* eye;
Nor where *Abassin* Kings their issue Guard,
Mount *Amara*, though this by some supposed[39]
True Paradise under the *Ethiop* Line
By *Nilus* head, enclosed with shining Rock,
A whole day's journey high, but wide remote
From this *Assyrian* Garden, where the Fiend
Saw undelighted all delight, all kind
Of living Creatures new to sight and strange:
Two of far nobler shape erect and tall,
Godlike erect, with native Honour clad
In naked Majesty seemed Lords of all,
And worthy seemed, for in their looks Divine
The image of their glorious Maker shone,
Truth, wisdom, Sanctitude severe and pure,
Severe but in true filial freedom placed;
Whence true authority in men; though both
Not equal, as their sex not equal seemed;
For contemplation he and valour formed,
For softness she and sweet attractive Grace,
He for God only, she for God in him:
His fair large Front and Eye sublime declared[40]
Absolute rule; and Hyacinthine Locks[41]
Round from his parted forelock manly hung
Clustring, but not beneath his shoulders broad:[42]
She as a veil down to the slender waist
Her unadornèd golden tresses wore
Dishevelled, but in wanton ringlets waved
As the Vine curls her tendrils, which implied
Subjection, but required with gentle sway,
And by her yielded, by him best received,
Yielded with coy submission, modest pride,[43]
And sweet reluctant amorous delay.
Nor those mysterious parts were then concealed,
Then was not guilty shame, dishonest shame[44]
Of nature's works, honour dishonourable,
Sin-bred, how have ye troubled all mankind
With shows instead, mere shows of seeming pure,

Notes

39 *Amara* (Amhara) a place near the supposed head of the Nile where Abyssinian (*Abassin*) kings raised their princes (see Samuel Johnson, *Rasselas*, p. 845 below); it is above the equator, not *under the Ethiop Line*.

40 *Front* forehead.

41 *Hyacinthine* Homer uses the epithet of hair and says it resembles a craftsman's mixture of gold with silver (*Odyssey* 6.231–2).

42 *but not beneath* ... the long hair styles worn by Cavaliers are forbidden in Milton's Eden.

43 *coy* "Modest; decent" (Johnson).

44 *dishonest* "Disgraceful; ignominious" (Johnson).

And banished from man's life his happiest life,
Simplicity and spotless innocence.
So passed they naked on, nor shunned the sight
Of God or Angel, for they thought no ill:
So hand in hand they passed, the loveliest pair
That ever since in love's embraces met,
Adam the goodliest man of men since born
His Sons, the fairest of her Daughters *Eve*.
Under a tuft of shade that on a green
Stood whispering soft, by a fresh Fountain side
They sat them down; and, after no more toil
Of their sweet Gardening labour than sufficed
To recommend cool *Zephyr*, and made ease[45]
More easy, wholesome thirst and appetite
More grateful, to their Supper Fruits they fell,[46]
Nectarine Fruits which the compliant boughs
Yielded them, side-long as they sat recline
On the soft downy Bank damasked with flowers:
The savoury pulp they chew, and in the rind
Still as they thirsted scoop the brimming stream;
Nor gentle purpose, nor endearing smiles
Wanted, nor youthful dalliance as beseems
Fair couple, linked in happy nuptial League,
Alone as they. About them frisking played
All Beasts of th' Earth, since wild, and of all chase[47]
In Wood or Wilderness, Forest or Den;
Sporting the Lion ramped, and in his paw
Dandled the Kid; Bears, Tigers, Ounces, Pards,
Gambolled before them, th' unwieldy Elephant
To make them mirth used all his might, and wreathed
His Lithe Proboscis; close the Serpent sly
Insinuating, wove with Gordian twine[48]
His braided train, and of his fatal guile
Gave proof unheeded; others on the grass
Couched, and now filled with pasture gazing sat,
Or Bedward ruminating: for the Sun[49]
Declined was hasting now with prone career
To th' Ocean Isles, and in th' ascending Scale
Of Heav'n the Stars that usher Evening rose:
When *Satan* still in gaze, as first he stood,
Scarce thus at length failed speech recovered sad.

Notes

[45] *Zephyr* "The west wind; and poetically any calm soft wind" (Johnson).

[46] *grateful* pleasing.

[47] *chase* "Open ground stored with such beasts as are hunted" (Johnson) (plural).

[48] *Insinuating* from *to insinuate*: "to enfold; to wreathe; to wind" (Johnson); *Gordian twine* a famous knot in Gordium, cut by Alexander the Great.

[49] *ruminating* chewing the cud.

'O Hell! what do mine eyes with grief behold,
Into our room of bliss thus high advanced
Creatures of other mould, earth-born perhaps,
Not Spirits, yet to heav'nly Spirits bright
Little inferior; whom my thoughts pursue
With wonder, and could love, so lively shines
In them Divine resemblance, and such grace
The hand that formed them on their shape hath poured.
Ah gentle pair, ye little think how nigh
Your change approaches, when all these delights
Will vanish and deliver ye to woe;
More woe, the more your taste is now of joy;
Happy, but for so happy ill secured
Long to continue, and this high seat your Heav'n
Ill fenced for Heav'n to keep out such a foe
As now is entered; yet no purposed foe
To you whom I could pity thus forlorn
Though I unpitied: League with you I seek,
And mutual amity so straight, so close,
That I with you must dwell, or you with me
Henceforth; my dwelling haply may not please
Like this fair Paradise, your sense, yet such
Accept your Maker's work; he gave it me,
Which I as freely give; Hell shall unfold,
To entertain you two, her widest Gates,
And send forth all her Kings; there will be room,
Not like these narrow limits, to receive
Your numerous offspring; if no better place,
Thank him who puts me loath to this revenge
On you who wrong me not for him who wronged.
And should I at your harmless innocence
Melt, as I do, yet public reason just,
Honour and Empire with revenge enlarged,
By conquering this new World, compels me now
To do what else though damned I should abhor'.
So spake the Fiend, and with necessity,
The Tyrant's plea, excused his devilish deeds.
Then from his lofty stand on that high Tree
Down he alights among the sportful Herd
Of those four-footed kinds, himself now one,
Now other, as their shape served best his end
Nearer to view his prey, and unespied
To mark what of their state he more might learn
By word or action marked: about them round
A Lion now he stalks with fiery glare,
Then as a Tiger, who by chance hath spied
In some Purlieu two gentle Fawns at play,
Straight couches close, then rising changes oft
His couchant watch, as one who chose his ground
Whence rushing he might surest seize them both

Gripped in each paw: When *Adam* first of men
To first of women *Eve* thus moving speech,
Turned him all ear to hear new utterance flow.[50]
'Sole partner and sole part of all these joys,
Dearer thyself than all; needs must the power
That made us, and for us this ample World
Be infinitely good, and of his good
As liberal and free as infinite,
That raised us from the dust and placed us here
In all this happiness, who at his hand
Have nothing merited, nor can perform
Aught whereof he hath need, he who requires
From us no other service than to keep
This one, this easy charge, of all the Trees
In Paradise that bear delicious fruit
So various, not to taste that only Tree
Of knowledge, planted by the Tree of Life,
So near grows Death to Life, whate'er Death is,
Some dreadful thing no doubt; for well thou knowst
God hath pronounced it death to taste that Tree,
The only sign of our obedience left
Among so many signs of power and rule
Conferred upon us, and Dominion giv'n
Over all other Creatures that possess
Earth, Air, and Sea. Then let us not think hard
One easy prohibition, who enjoy
Free leave so large to all things else, and choice
Unlimited of manifold delights:
But let us ever praise him, and extol
His bounty, following our delightful task
To prune these growing Plants, and tend these Flowers,
Which were it toilsome, yet with thee were sweet'.
To whom thus *Eve* replied. 'O thou for whom
And from whom I was formed flesh of thy flesh,
And without whom am to no end, my Guide
And Head, what thou hast said is just and right.
For we to him indeed all praises owe,
And daily thanks, I chiefly who enjoy
So far the happier Lot, enjoying thee
Pre-eminent by so much odds, while thou
Like consort to thyself canst nowhere find.
That day I oft remember, when from sleep
I first awaked, and found myself reposed
Under a shade of flowers, much wond'ring where
And what I was, whence thither brought, and how.
Not distant far from thence a murmuring sound
Of waters issued from a Cave and spread

Notes

[50] *him* himself; Eve is all *ear*.

Into a liquid Plain, then stood unmoved
Pure as th' expanse of Heav'n; I thither went
With unexperienced thought, and laid me down
On the green bank, to look into the clear
Smooth Lake, that to me seemed another Sky.
As I bent down to look, just opposite,[51]
A Shape within the watry gleam appeared
Bending to look on me, I started back,
It started back, but pleased I soon returned,
Pleased it returned as soon with answering looks
Of sympathy and love; there I had fixed
Mine eyes till now, and pined with vain desire,
Had not a voice thus warned me, "What thou seest,
What there thou seest fair Creature is thyself
With thee it came and goes: but follow me,
And I will bring thee where no shadow stays[52]
Thy coming, and thy soft embraces, he
Whose image thou art, him thou shalt enjoy
Inseparably thine, to him shalt bear
Multitudes like thyself, and thence be called
Mother of human Race": what could I do,
But follow straight, invisibly thus led?
Till I espied thee, fair indeed and tall,
Under a Platan; yet methought less fair,[53]
Less winning soft, less amiably mild,
Than that smooth watry image; back I turned,
Thou following cryd'st aloud, "Return fair *Eve*,
Whom fli'st thou? whom thou fli'st, of him thou art,
His flesh, his bone; to give thee being I lent
Out of my side to thee, nearest my heart
Substantial Life, to have thee by my side
Henceforth an individual solace dear;[54]
Part of my Soul I seek thee, and thee claim
My other half": with that thy gentle hand
Seized mine, I yielded, and from that time see
How beauty is excelled by manly grace,
And wisdom, which alone is truly fair'.
So spake our general Mother, and with eyes
Of conjugal attraction unreproved,
And meek surrender, half embracing leaned
On our first Father, half her swelling Breast
Naked met his under the flowing Gold
Of her loose tresses hid: he in delight
Both of her Beauty and submissive Charms

Notes

[51] The story recalls the myth of Narcissus, who loves only his own reflection (Ovid, *Metamorphoses* 3).

[52] *stays* awaits.

[53] *Platan* plane tree.

[54] *individual* "Undivided; not to be parted or disjoined" (Johnson).

Smiled with superior Love, as *Jupiter*[55]
On *Juno* smiles, when he impregns the Clouds
That shed *May* Flowers; and pressed her Matron lip
With kisses pure: aside the Devil turned
For envy, yet with jealous leer malign
Eyed them askance, and to himself thus plained.
'Sight hateful, sight tormenting! thus these two,
Imparadised in one another's arms
The happier *Eden*, shall enjoy their fill
Of bliss on bliss, while I to Hell am thrust,
Where neither joy nor love, but fierce desire,
Among our other torments not the least,
Still unfulfilled with pain of longing pines;
Yet let me not forget what I have gained
From their own mouths; all is not theirs it seems:
One fatal Tree there stands of Knowledge called,
Forbidden them to taste: Knowledge forbidd'n?
Suspicious, reasonless. Why should their Lord
Envy them that? can it be sin to know,
Can it be death? and do they only stand
By Ignorance, is that their happy state,
The proof of their obedience and their faith?
O fair foundation laid whereon to build
Their ruin! Hence I will excite their minds
With more desire to know, and to reject
Envious commands, invented with design
To keep them low, whom knowledge might exalt
Equal with Gods; aspiring to be such,
They taste and die: what likelier can ensue?
But first with narrow search I must walk round
This Garden, and no corner leave unspied;
A chance but chance may lead where I may meet
Some wand'ring Spirit of Heav'n by Fountain side,
Or in thick shade retired, from him to draw
What further would be learnt. Live while ye may,
Yet happy pair; enjoy, till I return,
Short pleasures, for long woes are to succeed'.
So saying, his proud step he scornful turned,
But with sly circumspection, and began
Through wood, through waste, o'er hill, o'er dale, his roam.
Meanwhile in utmost Longitude, where Heav'n
With Earth and Ocean meets, the setting Sun
Slowly descended, and with right aspéct
Against the eastern Gate of Paradise

Notes

[55] *Jupiter/On Juno smiles* recalling *Iliad* 14.346–51, a somewhat rough but glittery scene in which the gods are momentarily equated with the elements of the heavens.

Levelled his evening Rays: it was a Rock
Of Alabaster, piled up to the Clouds,
Conspicuous far, winding with one ascent
Accessible from Earth, one entrance high;
The rest was craggy cliff, that overhung
Still as it rose, impossible to climb.
Betwixt these rocky pillars *Gabriel* sat
Chief of th' Angelic Guards, awaiting night;
About him exercised Heroic games
Th' unarmed youth of Heav'n, but nigh at hand
Celestial Armoury, Shields, Helms, and Spears,
Hung high with Diamond flaming, and with Gold.
Thither came *Uriel*, gliding through the Even
On a Sunbeam, swift as a shooting Star
In *Autumn* thwarts the night, when vapours fired[56]
Impress the Air, and shows the Mariner
From what point of his Compass to beware
Impetuous winds: he thus began in haste.
'*Gabriel*, to thee thy course by Lot hath giv'n
Charge and strict watch that to this happy Place
No evil thing approach or enter in;
This day at highth of Noon came to my Sphere
A Spirit, zealous, as he seemed, to know
More of th' Almighty's works, and chiefly Man
God's latest Image: I described his way
Bent all on speed, and marked his Airy Gate;[57]
But in the Mount that lies from *Eden* North,
Where he first lighted, soon discerned his looks
Alien from Heav'n, with passions foul obscured:
Mine eye pursued him still, but under shade
Lost sight of him; one of the banished crew
I fear, hath ventured from the deep, to raise
New troubles; him thy care must be to find'.
To whom the wingèd Warrior thus returned:
'*Uriel*, no wonder if thy perfect sight,
Amid the Sun's bright circle where thou sitst,
See far and wide: in at this Gate none pass
The vigilance here placed, but such as come
Well known from Heav'n; and since Meridian hour
No Creature thence: if Spirit of other sort,
So minded, have o'erleapt these earthy bounds
On purpose, hard thou knowst it to exclude
Spiritual substance with corporeal bar.
But if within the circuit of these walks

Notes

[56] *thwarts* crosses; *vapours fired* probably lightning; Johnson mentions "electrical vapours" (s.v. *electricity*).

[57] *Gate* way, path.

In whatsoever shape he lurk, of whom
Thou tellst, by morrow dawning I shall know'.
    So promised he; and *Uriel* to his charge
Returned on that bright beam, whose point now raised
Bore him slope downward to the Sun now fall'n[58]
Beneath th' *Azores*; whither the prime Orb,[59]
Incredible how swift, had thither rolled
Diurnal, or this less volúble Earth[60]
By shorter flight to th' East, had left him there
Arraying with reflected Purple and Gold
The Clouds that on his Western Throne attend:
Now came still Evening on, and Twilight grey
Had in her sober Livery all things clad;
Silence accompanied, for Beast and Bird,
They to their grassy Couch, these to their Nests
Were slunk, all but the wakeful Nightingale;
She all night long her amorous descant sung;
Silence was pleased: now glowed the Firmament
With living Sapphires: *Hesperus* that led
The starry Host, rode brightest, till the Moon
Rising in clouded Majesty, at length
Apparent Queen unveiled her peerless light,
And o'er the dark her Silver Mantle threw.
    When *Adam* thus to *Eve*: 'Fair Consort, th' hour
Of night, and all things now retired to rest
Mind us of like repose, since God hath set
Labour and rest, as day and night to men
Successive, and the timely dew of sleep
Now falling with soft slumbrous weight inclines
Our eye-lids; other Creatures all day long
Rove idle, unemployed, and less need rest;
Man hath his daily work of body or mind
Appointed, which declares his Dignity,
And the regard of Heav'n on all his ways;
While other Animals unactive range,
And of their doings God takes no account.
Tomorrow ere fresh Morning streak the East
With first approach of light, we must be ris'n,
And at our pleasant labour, to reform
Yon flow'ry Arbors, yonder Alleys green,
Our walks at noon, with branches overgrown,
That mock our scant manuring, and require[61]
More hands than ours to lop their wanton growth:
Those Blossoms also, and those dropping Gums,
That lie bestrown, unsightly and unsmooth,

Notes

[58] *slope* slantwise; obliquely.

[59] *whither* a seventeenth-century spelling of *whether* (see OED, A, γ); *prime Orb* the sun.

[60] *voluble* "Rolling; having quick motion" (Johnson).

[61] *manuring* from *manure*, "To cultivate by manual labour" (Johnson).

Ask riddance, if we mean to tread with ease;
Meanwhile, as Nature wills, Night bids us rest'.
  To whom thus *Eve* with perfect beauty adorned.[62]
'My Author and Disposer, what thou bidst
Unargued I obey; so God ordains,
God is thy Law, thou mine: to know no more
Is woman's happiest knowledge and her praise.
With thee conversing I forget all time,
All seasons and their change, all please alike.
Sweet is the breath of morn, her rising sweet,
With charm of earliest Birds; pleasant the Sun[63]
When first on this delightful Land he spreads
His orient Beams, on herb, tree, fruit, and flower,
Glist'ring with dew; fragrant the fertile earth
After soft showers; and sweet the coming on
Of grateful Evening mild; then silent Night
With this her solemn Bird and this fair Moon,
And these the Gems of Heav'n, her starry train:
But neither breath of Morn when she ascends
With charm of earliest Birds, nor rising Sun
On this delightful land, nor herb, fruit, flower,
Glist'ring with dew, nor fragrance after showers,
Nor grateful Evening mild, nor silent Night
With this her solemn Bird, nor walk by Moon,
Or glittering Star-light without thee is sweet.
But wherefore all night long shine these, for whom
This glorious sight, when sleep hath shut all eyes?'
  To whom our general Ancestor replied.
'Daughter of God and Man, accomplished *Eve*,
Those have their course to finish, round the Earth,
By morrow Evening, and from Land to Land
In order, though to Nations yet unborn,
Minist'ring light prepared, they set and rise;
Lest total darkness should by Night regain
Her old possession, and extinguish life
In Nature and all things, which these soft fires
Not only enlighten, but with kindly heat
Of various influence foment and warm,
Temper or nourish, or in part shed down
Their stellar virtue on all kinds that grow[64]
On Earth, made hereby apter to receive
Perfection from the Sun's more potent Ray.
These then, though unbeheld in deep of night,
Shine not in vain, nor think, though men were none,

Notes

[62] *beauty adorned* vowel coalescence.

[63] *charm* variant of *chirm*, "The blended singing or noise of many birds" (*OED*, *charm*, 2).

[64] *virtue* power, influence.

That heav'n would want spectators, God want praise:
Millions of spiritual Creatures walk the Earth
Unseen, both when we wake, and when we sleep:
All these with ceaseless praise his works behold
Both day and night: how often from the steep
Of echoing Hill or Thicket have we heard
Celestial voices to the midnight air,
Sole, or responsive each to other's note
Singing their great Creator: oft in bands
While they keep watch, or nightly rounding walk
With Heav'nly touch of instrumental sounds
In full harmonic number joined, their songs
Divide the night, and lift our thoughts to Heaven'.[65]
Thus talking hand in hand alone they passed
On to their blissful Bower; it was a place
Chos'n by the sovereign Planter, when he framed
All things to man's delightful use; the roof
Of thickest covert was inwoven shade
Laurel and Myrtle, and what higher grew
Of firm and fragrant leaf; on either side
Acanthus, and each odorous bushy shrub
Fenced up the verdant wall; each beauteous flower,
Iris all hues, Roses, and Jessamine
Reared high their flourished heads between, and wrought
Mosaic; underfoot the Violet,
Crocus, and Hyacinth with rich inlay
Broidered the ground, more coloured than with stone
Of costliest Emblem: other Creature here[66]
Beast, Bird, Insect, or Worm durst enter none;
Such was their awe of Man. In shadier Bower
More sacred and sequestered, though but feigned,
Pan or *Sylvanus* never slept, nor Nymph,[67]
Nor *Faunus* haunted. Here in close recess
With Flowers, Garlands, and sweet-smelling Herbs
Espousèd *Eve* decked first her nuptial Bed,
And Heav'nly Choirs the Hymenaean sung,[68]
What day the genial Angel to our Sire[69]
Brought her in naked beauty more adorned,
More lovely than *Pandora*, whom the Gods[70]
Endowed with all their gifts, and O too like
In sad event, when to the unwiser Son

Notes

[65] *Divide the night* into watches, or portions, as bells once did.

[66] *Emblem* "Inlay; enamel; anything inserted into the body of another" (Johnson).

[67] *Pan ... Sylvanus ... Faunus* woodland gods.

[68] *Hymenaean* bridal song.

[69] *genial* "That which contributes to propagation" (Johnson).

[70] *Pandora* ("all gifts"), the first woman in Greek mythology; she received gifts from all the gods, but Hermes taught her flattery and brought her, at Zeus' command, to Prometheus' *unwiser* brother Epimetheus, son of the Titan Iapetos (traditionally associated with *Japhet*, son of Noah); she released the contents of a jar containing all the ills of mankind; see Hesiod, *Works and Days*, 80.

Of *Japhet* brought by *Hermes*, she ensnared
Mankind with her fair looks, to be avenged
On him who had stole *Jove's* authentic fire.
Thus at their shady Lodge arrived, both stood
Both turned, and under op'n Sky adored
The God that made both Sky, Air, Earth and Heav'n
Which they beheld, the Moon's resplendent Globe
And starry Pole: 'Thou also mad'st the Night,[71]
Maker Omnipotent, and thou the Day,
Which we in our appointed work employed
Have finished happy in our mutual help
And mutual love, the Crown of all our bliss
Ordained by thee, and this delicious place
For us too large, where thy abundance wants
Partakers, and uncropped falls to the ground.
But thou hast promised from us two a Race
To fill the Earth, who shall with us extol
Thy goodness infinite, both when we wake,
And when we seek, as now, thy gift of sleep'.
This said unanimous, and other Rites
Observing none, but adoration pure
Which God likes best, into their inmost bower
Handed they went; and eased the putting off [72]
These troublesome disguises which we wear,
Straight side by side were laid, nor turned I ween,
Adam from his fair Spouse, nor *Eve* the Rites
Mysterious of connubial Love refused:
Whatever Hypocrites austerely talk
Of purity and place and innocence,
Defaming as impure what God declares
Pure, and commands to some, leaves free to all.
Our Maker bids increase, who bids abstain[73]
But our destroyer, foe to God and Man?
Hail wedded Love, mysterious Law, true source
Of human offspring, sole propriety,[74]
In Paradise of all things common else,
By thee adulterous lust was driv'n from men
Among the bestial herds to range, by thee
Founded in Reason, Loyal, Just, and Pure,
Relations dear, and all the Charities[75]
Of Father, Son, and Brother, first were known.
Far be it, that I should write thee sin or blame,
Or think thee unbefitting holiest place,
Perpetual Fountain of Domestic sweets,

Notes

71 *Pole* sky, heavens.

72 *Handed* hand in hand.

73 *Our Maker bids increase* Genesis 1.28.

74 *propriety* "Peculiarity of possession; exclusive right" (Johnson).

75 *Charities* "Tenderness; kindness; love" (Johnson).

Whose bed is undefiled and chaste pronounced,
Present, or past, as Saints and Patriarchs used.
Here Love his golden shafts employs, here lights
His constant Lamp, and waves his purple wings,
Reigns here and revels; not in the bought smile
Of Harlots, loveless, joyless, unendeared,
Casual fruition, nor in Court Amours
Mixed Dance, or wanton Mask, or Midnight Ball,
Or Serenate, which the starved Lover sings[76]
To his proud fair, best quitted with disdain.[77]
These lulled by Nightingales embracing slept,
And on their naked limbs the flowry roof
Showered Roses, which the Morn repaired. Sleep on
Blest pair; and O yet happiest if ye seek
No happier state, and know to know no more.
  Now had night measured with her shadowy Cone
Half way up Hill this vast Sublunar Vault,[78]
And from their Ivory Port the Cherubim
Forth issuing at th' accustomed hour stood armed
To their night watches in warlike Parade,
When *Gabriel* to his next in power thus spake.
  '*Uzziel*, half these draw off, and coast the South
With strictest watch; these other wheel the North,
Our circuit meets full West. As flame they part
Half wheeling to the Shield, half to the Spear'.[79]
From these, two strong and subtle Spirits he called
That near him stood, and gave them thus in charge.
  '*Ithuriel* and *Zephon*, with winged speed
Search through this Garden, leave unsearched no nook,
But chiefly where those two fair Creatures Lodge,
Now laid perhaps asleep secure of harm.
This Evening from the Sun's decline arrived
Who tells of some infernal Spirit seen[80]
Hitherward bent (who could have thought?) escaped
The bars of Hell, on errand bad no doubt:
Such where ye find, seize fast, and hither bring'.
  So saying, on he led his radiant Files,
Dazzling the Moon; these to the Bower direct
In search of whom they sought: him there they found
Squat like a Toad, close at the ear of *Eve*;
Assaying by his Devilish art to reach[81]
The Organs of her Fancy, and with them forge
Illusions as he list, Phantasms and Dreams,[82]

Notes

[76] *Serenate* serenade, "Music or songs with which ladies are entertained by their lovers in the night" (Johnson).

[77] *quitted* requited; responded to.

[78] It is 9:00 P.M.; the point of the cone of the earth's shadow, if visible, would be seen at the zenith at midnight.

[79] *Shield* ... *Spear* left hand ... right hand.

[80] *Who* one who.

[81] *Assaying* trying.

[82] *list* wished; chose.

Or if, inspiring venom, he might taint
Th' animal Spirits, that from pure blood arise[83]
Like gentle breaths from Rivers pure, thence raise
At least distempered, discontented thoughts,
Vain hopes, vain aims, inordinate desires
Blown up with high conceits engend'ring pride.
Him thus intent *Ithuriel* with his Spear
Touched lightly; for no falsehood can endure
Touch of Celestial temper, but returns
Of force to its own likeness: up he starts
Discovered and surprised. As when a spark
Lights on a heap of nitrous Powder, laid[84]
Fit for the Tun some Magazine to store
Against a rumoured War, the Smutty grain
With sudden blaze diffused, inflames the Air:
So started up in his own shape the Fiend.
Back stepped those two fair Angels half amazed
So sudden to behold the grisly King;
Yet thus, unmoved with fear, accost him soon.
'Which of those rebel Spirits adjudged to Hell
Com'st thou, escaped thy prison, and transformed,
Why sat'st thou like an enemy in wait
Here watching at the head of these that sleep?'
'Know ye not then' said *Satan*, filled with scorn,
'Know ye not me? ye knew me once no mate
For you, there sitting where ye durst not soar;
Not to know me argues yourselves unknown,
The lowest of your throng; or if ye know,
Why ask ye, and superfluous begin
Your message, like to end as much in vain?'
To whom thus *Zephon*, answering scorn with scorn.
'Think not, revolted Spirit, thy shape the same,
Or undiminished brightness, to be known
As when thou stoodst in Heav'n upright and pure;
That Glory then, when thou no more wast good,
Departed from thee, and thou resembl'st now
Thy sin and place of doom obscure and foul.
But come, for thou, be sure, shalt give account
To him who sent us, whose charge is to keep
This place inviolable, and these from harm'.[85]
So spake the Cherub, and his grave rebuke
Severe in youthful beauty, added grace
Invincible: abashed the Devil stood,
And felt how awful goodness is, and saw[86]

Notes

[83] *animal Spirits* those governing the *anima* (mind).
[84] *nitrous Powder, laid Fit for the Tun* gunpowder ready to be barreled.
[85] *these* Adam and Eve.
[86] *awful* inspiring awe.

Virtue in her shape how lovely, saw, and pined
His loss; but chiefly to find here observed
His lustre visibly impaired; yet seemed
Undaunted. 'If I must contend', said he,
'Best with the best, the Sender not the sent,
Or all at once; more glory will be won,
Or less be lost'. 'Thy fear', said *Zephon* bold,
'Will save us trial what the least can do
Single against thee wicked, and thence weak'.
    The Fiend replied not, overcome with rage;
But like a proud Steed reined, went haughty on,
Champing his iron curb: to strive or fly[87]
He held it vain; awe from above had quelled
His heart, not else dismayed. Now drew they nigh
The western Point, where those half-rounding guards[88]
Just met, and closing stood in squadron joined
Awaiting next command. To whom their Chief
Gabriël, from the Front thus called aloud.
    'O friends, I hear the tread of nimble feet
Hasting this way, and now by glimpse discern
Ithuriël and *Zephon* through the shade,
And with them comes a third of Regal port,
But faded splendour wan; who by his gait
And fierce demeanour seems the Prince of Hell,
Not likely to part hence without contest;
Stand firm, for in his look defiance lours'.
    He scarce had ended, when those two approached
And brief related whom they brought, where found,
How busied, in what form and posture couched.
    To whom with stern regard thus *Gabriel* spake.
'Why hast thou, *Satan*, broke the bounds prescribed
To thy transgressions, and disturbed the charge
Of others, who approve not to transgress
By thy example, but have power and right
To question thy bold entrance on this place;
Employed it seems to violate sleep, and those
Whose dwelling God hath planted here in bliss?'
    To whom thus *Satan* with contemptuous brow.
'*Gabriel*, thou hadst in Heav'n th' esteem of wise,
And such I held thee; but this question asked
Puts me in doubt. Lives there who loves his pain?
Who would not, finding way, break loose from Hell,
Though thither doomed? Thou wouldst thyself, no doubt,
And boldly venture to whatever place
Farthest from pain, where thou mightst hope to change
Torment with ease, and soonest recompense

Notes

[87] *iron curb* a horse's bit.

[88] *half-rounding* "forming a semicircle" (*OED*).

Dole with delight, which in this place I sought;[89]
To thee no reason; who knowst only good,
But evil hast not tried: and wilt object[90]
His will who bounds us? Let him surer bar
His Iron gates, if he intends our stay
In that dark durance: thus much what was asked.[91]
The rest is true, they found me where they say;
But that implies not violence or harm'.
    Thus he in scorn. The warlike Angel moved,
Disdainfully half smiling thus replied.
'O loss of one in Heav'n to judge of wise,[92]
Since *Satan* fell, whom folly overthrew,
And now returns him from his prison 'scaped,
Gravely in doubt whether to hold them wise
Or not, who ask what boldness brought him hither
Unlicensed from his bounds in Hell prescribed;
So wise he judges it to fly from pain
However, and to 'scape his punishment.
So judge thou still, presumptuous, till the wrath,
Which thou incurr'st by flying, meet thy flight
Sev'nfold, and scourge that wisdom back to Hell,
Which taught thee yet no better, that no pain
Can equal anger infinite provoked.
But wherefore thou alone? wherefore with thee
Came not all Hell broke loose? is pain to them
Less pain, less to be fled, or thou than they
Less hardy to endure? courageous Chief,
The first in flight from pain, hadst thou alleged
To thy deserted host this cause of flight,
Thou surely hadst not come sole fugitive'.
    To which the Fiend thus answered frowning stern.
'Not that I less endure, or shrink from pain,
Insulting Angel, well thou knowst I stood
Thy fiercest, when in Battle to thy aid
The blasting volleyed Thunder made all speed
And seconded thy else not dreaded Spear.
But still thy words at random, as before,
Argue thy inexperience what behooves
From hard assays and ill successes past
A faithful Leader, not to hazard all
Through ways of danger by himself untried.
I therefore, I alone first undertook
To wing the desolate Abyss, and spy
This new created World, whereof in Hell
Fame is not silent, here in hope to find

Notes

[89] *Dole* "Grief, sorrow, mental distress" (*OED*).
[90] *wilt object* will you cite?
[91] *durance* imprisonment.
[92] *to judge of wise* to determine what is wise.

Better abode, and my afflicted Powers
To settle here on Earth, or in mid Air;[93]
Though for possession put to try once more[94]
What thou and thy gay Legions dare against;
Whose easier business were to serve their Lord
High up in Heav'n, with songs to hymn his Throne,
And practised distances to cringe, not fight'.
To whom the warrior Angel soon replied.
'To say and straight unsay, pretending first
Wise to fly pain, professing next the Spy,
Argues no Leader but a liar traced,
Satan, and couldst thou faithful add? O name,
O sacred name of faithfulness profaned!
Faithful to whom? to thy rebellious crew?
Army of Fiends, fit body to fit head;
Was this your discipline and faith engaged,
Your military obedience, to dissolve
Allegiance to th' acknowledged Power supreme?
And thou sly hypocrite, who now wouldst seem
Patron of liberty, who more than thou
Once fawned, and cringed, and servily adored
Heav'n's awful Monarch? wherefore but in hope
To dispossess him, and thyself to reign?
But mark what I areed thee now, avaunt;[95]
Fly thither whence thou fledst; if from this hour
Within these hallowed limits thou appear,
Back to th' infernal pit I drag thee chained,
And Seal thee so, as henceforth not to scorn
The facile gates of Hell too slightly barred'.[96]
So threatened he, but *Satan* to no threats
Gave heed, but waxing more in rage replied.
'Then when I am thy captive talk of chains,
Proud limitary Cherub, but ere then[97]
Far heavier load thyself expect to feel
From my prevailing arm, though Heav'n's King
Ride on thy wings, and thou with thy Compeers,
Used to the yoke, draw'st his triumphant wheels
In progress through the road of Heav'n Star-paved'.
While thus he spake, th' Angelic Squadron bright
Turned fiery red, sharp'ning in moonèd horns
Their Phalanx, and began to hem him round
With ported Spears, as thick as when a field[98]
Of *Ceres* ripe for harvest waving bends
Her bearded Grove of ears, which way the wind

Notes

[93] *mid Air* the middle air, between heaven and earth.

[94] *Though ... against* even if I must fight against your opposition.

[95] *areed* advise; *avaunt* depart.

[96] *facile* "contemptibly easy" (*OED*).

[97] *limitary* in charge of the limit or boundary, a border guard.

[98] *ported* carried diagonally in military form.

Sways them; the careful Ploughman doubting stands
Lest on the threshing floor his hopeless sheaves
Prove chaff. On th' other side, *Satan*, alarmed
Collecting all his might dilated stood,
Like *Teneriff* or *Atlas*, unremoved:[99]
His stature reached the Sky, and on his Crest
Sat horror Plumed; nor wanted in his grasp
What seemed both Spear and Shield: now dreadful deeds
Might have ensued, nor only Paradise
In this commotion, but the Starry Cope[100]
Of Heav'n perhaps, or all the Elements[101]
At least had gone to wrack, disturbed and torn
With violence of this conflict, had not soon
Th' Eternal to prevent such horrid fray
Hung forth in Heav'n his golden Scales, yet seen[102]
Betwixt *Astrea* and the *Scorpion* sign,
Wherein all things created first he weighed,
The pendulous round Earth with balanced Air
In counterpoise, now ponders all events,
Battles and Realms: in these he put two weights
The sequel each of parting and of fight,[103]
The latter quick up flew, and kicked the beam;
Which *Gabriel* spying, thus bespake the Fiend.
'*Satan*, I know thy strength, and thou knowest mine,
Neither our own but giv'n; what folly then
To boast what Arms can do, since thine no more
Than Heav'n permits, nor mine, though doubled now
To trample thee as mire: for proof look up,
And read thy Lot in yon celestial Sign
Where thou art weighed, and shown how light, how weak,
If thou resist'. The Fiend looked up, and knew
His mounted scale aloft: nor more; but fled
Murmuring, and with him fled the shades of night.

Book V
The Argument

Morning approached, Eve *relates to* Adam *her troublesome dream; he likes it not, yet comforts her: They come forth to their day labours: Their Morning Hymn at the Door of their Bower.* God *to render Man inexcusable sends* Raphael *to admonish him of his obedience, of his free estate, of his enemy near at hand; who he is, and why his enemy, and whatever else may avail* Adam *to know.* Raphael *comes down to Paradise, his appearance described, his coming*

Notes

99 *Teneriff or Atlas* mountain peaks off the coast of North Africa and in Morocco, respectively.

100 *Cope* "Anything which is spread over the head; as the concave of the skies" (Johnson).

101 *Elements* earth, air, fire, and water.

102 *golden Scales* the balance beam of the constellation Libra, on the zodiac between Virgo, or *Astrea*, and *Scorpio*; God's action resembles Zeus' judgement on the Trojan War (*Iliad* 8.69–72).

103 *sequel* outcome.

discerned by Adam *afar off sitting at the door of his Bower; he goes out to meet him, brings him to his lodge, entertains him with the choicest fruits of Paradise got together by* Eve; *their discourse at Table:* Raphael *performs his message, minds* Adam *of his state and of his enemy; relates at* Adam*'s request who that enemy is, and how he came to be so, beginning from his first revolt in Heaven, and the occasion thereof; how he drew his Legions after him to the parts of the* North, *and there incited them to rebel with him, persuading all but only* Abdiel *a Seraph, who in Argument dissuades and opposes him, then forsakes him.*

Book VI
The Argument

Raphael *continues to relate how* Michael *and* Gabriel *were sent forth to battle against* Satan *and his Angels. The first fight described:* Satan *and his Powers retire under Night: He calls a Council, invents devilish Engines, which in the second day's Fight put* Michael *and his Angels to some disorder; but they at length pulling up Mountains overwhelmed both the force and Machines of* Satan: *Yet the Tumult not so ending, God on the third day sends* Messiah *his Son, for whom he had reserved the glory of that Victory: He in the Power of his Father coming to the place, and causing all his Legions to stand still on either side, with his Chariot and Thunder driving into the midst of his Enemies, pursues them unable to resist towards the Wall of Heaven; which opening, they leap down with horror and confusion into the place of punishment prepared for them in the Deep:* Messiah *returns with triumph to his Father.*

Book VII
The Argument

Raphael *at the request of* Adam *relates how and wherefore this world was first created; that God, after the expelling of* Satan *and his Angels out of Heaven, declared his pleasure to create another World and other Creatures to dwell therein; sends his Son with Glory and attendance of Angels to perform the work of Creation in six days: the Angels celebrate with Hymns the performance thereof, and his reascension into Heaven.*

Book VIII
The Argument

Adam *inquires concerning celestial Motions, is doubtfully answered, and exhorted to search rather things more worthy of knowledge:* Adam *assents, and still desirous to detain* Raphael, *relates to him what he remembered since his own Creation, his placing in Paradise, his talk with God concerning solitude and fit society, his first meeting and Nuptials with* Eve, *his discourse with the Angel thereupon; who after admonitions repeated departs.*

Book IX
The Argument

Satan *having compassed the Earth, with meditated guile returns as a mist by Night into Paradise, enters into the Serpent sleeping.* Adam *and* Eve *in the Morning go forth to their labours, which* Eve *proposes to divide in several places, each labouring apart:* Adam *consents not, alleging the danger, lest that Enemy, of whom they were forewarned, should attempt her found alone:* Eve *loath to be thought not circumspect or firm enough, urges her going apart, the rather desirous to make trial of her strength;* Adam *at last yields: The Serpent finds her alone;*

his subtle approach, first gazing, then speaking, with much flattery extolling Eve *above all other Creatures.* Eve *wond'ring to hear the Serpent speak, asks how he attained to human speech and such understanding not till now; the Serpent answers, that by tasting of a certain Tree in the Garden he attained both to Speech and Reason, till then void of both:* Eve *requires him to bring her to that Tree, and finds it to be the Tree of Knowledge forbidden: The Serpent now grown bolder, with many wiles and arguments induces her at length to eat; she pleased with the taste deliberates a while whether to impart thereof to* Adam *or not, at last brings him of the Fruit, relates what persuaded her to eat thereof:* Adam *at first amazed, but perceiving her lost, resolves through vehemence of love to perish with her; and extenuating the trespass, eats also of the Fruit: The Effects thereof in them both; they seek to cover their nakedness; then fall to variance and accusation of one another.*

No more of talk where God or Angel Guest
With Man, as with his Friend, familiar used
To sit indulgent, and with him partake
Rural repast, permitting him the while
Venial discourse unblamed: I now must change[1]
Those Notes to Tragic; foul distrust, and breach
Disloyal on the part of Man, revolt,
And disobedience: On the part of Heav'n
Now alienated, distance and distaste,
Anger and just rebuke, and judgement giv'n,
That brought into this World a world of woe,
Sin and her shadow Death, and Misery
Death's Harbinger: Sad task, yet argument
Not less but more Heroic than the wrath[2]
Of stern *Achilles* on his Foe pursued
Thrice Fugitive about *Troy* Wall; or rage[3]
Of *Turnus* for *Lavinia* disespoused,
Or *Neptune*'s ire, or *Juno*'s, that so long[4]
Perplexed the *Greek* and *Cytherea*'s Son;
If answerable style I can obtain
Of my Celestial Patroness, who deigns[5]
Her nightly visitation unimplored,
And dictates to me slumbring, or inspires
Easy my unpremeditated Verse:
Since first this Subject for Heroic Song
Pleased me long choosing, and beginning late;
Not sedulous by Nature to indite
Wars, hitherto the only Argument
Heroic deemed, chief mast'ry to dissect

Notes

Book IX

1 *Venial* "Permitted; allowed" (Johnson).

2 *the wrath of ... Achilles* the theme, or argument, of the *Iliad*, which reaches its conclusion after Achilles pursues and kills Hector, the hero of high-walled Troy.

3 *rage/Of Turnus for Lavinia* a major theme in the second half of the *Aeneid*, which ends with the single combat between Turnus, the Italian suitor of Lavinia, and Trojan Aeneas.

4 *Neptune's ire, or Juno's* Neptune tormented *the Greek*, Odysseus, as Juno did Aeneas, *Cytherea's Son*, throughout their travels, which are described in the *Odyssey* and in the first six books of the *Aeneid*, respectively.

5 *Celestial Patroness* the muse of epic poetry (cf. 1.6 and 7.1).

With long and tedious havoc fabled Knights
In Battles feigned; the better fortitude
Of Patience and Heroic Martyrdom
Unsung; or to describe Races and Games,
Or tilting Furniture, emblazoned Shields,[6]
Impresses quaint, Caparisons and Steeds;[7]
Bases and tinsel Trappings, gorgeous Knights[8]
At Joust and Tournament; then marshalled Feast
Served up in Hall with Sewers and Seneschals;[9]
The skill of Artifice or Office mean,
Not that which justly gives Heroic name
To Person or to Poem. Me of these
Nor skilled nor studious, higher Argument
Remains, sufficient of itself to raise
That name, unless an age too late, or cold
Climate, or Years damp my intended wing
Depressed, and much they may, if all be mine,
Not Hers who brings it nightly to my Ear.
The Sun was sunk, and after him the Star
Of *Hesperus*, whose Office is to bring
Twilight upon the Earth, short Arbiter
Twixt Day and Night, and now from end to end
Night's Hemisphere had veiled the Horizon round:
When *Satan* who late fled before the threats
Of *Gabriel* out of *Eden*, now improved
In meditated fraud and malice, bent
On man's destruction, maugre what might hap
Of heavier on himself, fearless returned.
By Night he fled, and at Midnight returned
From compassing the Earth, cautious of day,
Since *Uriel* Regent of the Sun descried
His entrance, and forewarned the Cherubim
That kept their watch; thence full of anguish driv'n,
The space of seven continued Nights he rode
With darkness; thrice the Equinoctial Line
He circled, four times crossed the Car of Night[10]
From Pole to Pole, traversing each Colure;[11]
On the eighth returned, and on the Coast averse
From entrance or Cherubic Watch, by stealth
Found unsuspected way. There was a place,
Now not, though Sin, not Time, first wrought the change,
Where *Tigris* at the foot of Paradise

Notes

6 *tilting Furniture* "Equipage" (Johnson) for jousting.

7 *Impresses quaint* neat, subtle, or fine mottoes; *Caparisons* horse armor.

8 *Bases* those "part[s] of any ornament that hang down, as housings" (Johnson).

9 *Sewers and Seneschals* feudal names for waiters and managers of ceremonial feasts.

10 *Car of Night* Night's chariot, which brings darkness, as Apollo's brings daylight.

11 *each Colure* "Two great circles supposed to pass through the poles of the world, one through the equinoctial … the other through the solstitial points [of the ecliptic of the Sun]" (Johnson, quoting Harris, *Lexicon Technicum*).

Into a Gulf shot under ground, till part
Rose up a Fountain by the Tree of Life;
In with the River sunk, and with it rose
Satan involved in rising Mist, then sought
Where to lie hid; Sea he had searched and Land
From *Eden* over *Pontus*, and the Pool[12]
Mæotis, up beyond the River *Ob*;[13]
Downward as far Antarctic; and in length
West from *Orontes* to the Ocean barred[14]
At *Darien*, thence to the Land where flows[15]
Ganges and *Indus*: thus the Orb he roamed
With narrow search; and with inspection deep
Considered every Creature, which of all
Most opportune might serve his Wiles, and found
The Serpent subtlest Beast of all the Field.[16]
Him after long debate, irresolute
Of thoughts revolved, his final sentence chose[17]
Fit Vessel, fittest Imp of fraud, in whom
To enter, and his dark suggestions hide
From sharpest sight: for in the wily Snake,
Whatever sleights none would suspicious mark,
As from his wit and native subtlety
Proceeding, which in other Beasts observed
Doubt might beget of Diabolic power[18]
Active within beyond the sense of brute.
Thus he resolved, but first from inward grief
His bursting passion into plaints thus poured:
　'O Earth, how like to Heav'n, if not preferred
More justly, Seat worthier of Gods, as built
With second thoughts, reforming what was old!
For what God after better worse would build?
Terrestrial Heav'n, danced round by other Heav'ns
That shine, yet bear their bright officious Lamps,[19]
Light above Light, for thee alone, as seems,
In thee concentring all their precious beams
Of sacred influence: As God in Heav'n
Is Centre, yet extends to all, so thou,
Centring, receiv'st from all those Orbs; in thee,
Not in themselves, all their known virtue appears
Productive in Herb, Plant, and nobler birth
Of Creatures animate with gradual life
Of Growth, Sense, Reason, all summed up in Man.
With what delight could I have walked thee round,

Notes

12 *Pontus* the Black Sea, connected to which is the *Maeotis* (now the Sea of Azov).

13 *Ob* it flows into the Kara Sea north of Siberia.

14 *Orontes* a river in western Syria; *the Ocean* the Atlantic.

15 *Darien* the old name for Panama.

16 The line repeats Genesis 3.1.

17 *sentence* judgment.

18 *Doubt* suspicion.

19 *officious* kind.

If I could joy in aught, sweet interchange
Of Hill, and Valley, Rivers, Woods, and Plains,
Now Land, now Sea and Shores with Forest crowned,
Rocks, Dens, and Caves; but I in none of these
Find place or refuge; and the more I see
Pleasures about me, so much more I feel
Torment within me, as from the hateful siege
Of contraries; all good to me becomes
Bane, and in Heav'n much worse would be my state.
But neither here seek I, no nor in Heav'n
To dwell, unless by mast'ring Heav'n's Supreme;
Nor hope to be myself less miserable
By what I seek, but others to make such
As I, though thereby worse to me redound:
For only in destroying I find ease
To my relentless thoughts; and him destroyed,
Or won to what may work his utter loss,
For whom all this was made, all this will soon
Follow, as to him linked in weal or woe,
In woe then; that destruction wide may range:
To me shall be the glory sole among
The infernal Powers, in one day to have marred
What he *Almighty* styled, six Nights and Days
Continued making, and who knows how long
Before had been contriving, though perhaps
Not longer than since I in one Night freed
From servitude inglorious well nigh half
Th' Angelic Name, and thinner left the throng
Of his adorers: he to be avenged,
And to repair his numbers thus impaired,
Whether such virtue spent of old now failed
More Angels to Create, if they at least
Are his Created, or to spite us more,
Determined to advance into our room
A Creature formed of Earth, and him endow,
Exalted from so base original,
With Heav'nly spoils, our spoils: What he decreed
He effected; Man he made, and for him built
Magnificent this World, and Earth his seat,
Him Lord pronounced, and, O indignity!
Subjected to his service Angel wings,
And flaming Ministers to watch and tend
Their earthly Charge: Of these the vigilance
I dread, and to elude, thus wrapped in mist
Of midnight vapour glide obscure, and pry
In every Bush and Brake, where hap may find
The Serpent sleeping, in whose mazy folds
To hide me, and the dark intent I bring.
O foul descent! that I who erst contended
With Gods to sit the highest, am now constrained
Into a Beast, and mixed with bestial slime,
This essence to incarnate and imbrute,

That to the height of Deity aspired;
But what will not Ambition and Revenge
Descend to? who aspires, must down as low
As high he soared, obnoxious first or last[20]
To basest things. Revenge, at first though sweet,
Bitter ere long back on itself recoils;
Let it; I reck not, so it light well aimed,
Since higher I fall short, on him who next
Provokes my envy, this new Favourite[21]
Of Heav'n, this Man of Clay, Son of despite,
Whom, us the more to spite his Maker raised
From dust: spite then with spite is best repaid'.
So saying, through each Thicket Dank or Dry,
Like a black mist low creeping, he held on
His midnight search, where soonest he might find
The Serpent: him fast-sleeping soon he found
In Labyrinth of many a round self-rolled,
His head the midst, well stored with subtle wiles:
Not yet in horrid Shade or dismal Den,
Nor nocent yet, but on the grassy Herb[22]
Fearless unfeared he slept: in at his Mouth
The Devil entered, and his brutal sense,
In heart or head, possessing, soon inspir'd
With act intelligential; but his sleep
Disturbed not, waiting close th' approach of Morn.
Now whenas sacred Light began to dawn
In *Eden* on the humid Flowers, that breathed
Their morning incense, when all things that breathe
From th' Earth's great Altar send up silent praise
To the Creator, and his Nostrils fill
With grateful Smell, forth came the human pair
And joined their vocal worship to the quire
Of Creatures wanting voice, that done, partake
The season, prime for sweetest Scents and Airs:
Then commune how that day they best may ply
Their growing work: for much their work outgrew
The hands' dispatch of two Gard'ning so wide,
And *Eve* first to her Husband thus began.
'*Adam*, well may we labour still to dress
This Garden, still to tend Plant, Herb and Flower,
Our pleasant task enjoined, but till more hands
Aid us, the work under our labour grows,
Luxurious by restraint; what we by day[23]

Notes

[20] *obnoxious* "Liable; exposed" (Johnson).

[21] *Favourite* "One chosen as a companion by his superior; a mean wretch whose whole business is by any means to please" (Johnson); cf. Thomas Gray, "Ode on the Death of a Favourite Cat," l. 36, p. 935, below.

[22] *nocent* "Hurtful; mischievous" (Johnson).

[23] *Luxurious* luxuriant; excessive.

Lop overgrown, or prune, or prop, or bind,
One night or two with wanton growth derides
Tending to wild. Thou therefore now advise,
Or hear what to my mind first thoughts present.
Let us divide our labours, thou, where choice
Leads thee, or where most needs, whether to wind
The Woodbine round this Arbour, or direct
The clasping Ivy where to climb, while I
In yonder Spring of Roses intermixed
With Myrtle, find what to redress till Noon:
For while so near each other thus all day
Our task we choose, what wonder if so near
Looks intervene and smiles, or object new
Casual discourse draw on, which intermits
Our day's work, brought to little, though begun
Early, and th' hour of Supper comes unearned'.
   To whom mild answer *Adam* thus returned.
'Sole *Eve*, Associate sole, to me beyond
Compare above all living Creatures dear;
Well hast thou motioned, well thy thoughts employed
How we might best fulfil the work which here
God hath assigned us, nor of me shalt pass
Unpraised: for nothing lovelier can be found
In Woman, than to study household good,
And good works in her Husband to promote.
Yet not so strictly hath our Lord imposed
Labour, as to debar us when we need
Refreshment, whether food, or talk between,
Food of the mind, or this sweet intercourse
Of looks and smiles, for smiles from Reason flow,
To brute denied, and are of Love the food,
Love not the lowest end of human life.
For not to irksome toil, but to delight
He made us, and delight to Reason joined.
These paths & Bowers doubt not but our joint hands
Will keep from Wilderness with ease, as wide
As we need walk, till younger hands ere long
Assist us: But if much convérse perhaps
Thee satiate, to short absence I could yield.
For solitude sometimes is best society,
And short retirement urges sweet return.
But other doubt possesses me, lest harm
Befall thee severed from me; for thou knowst
What hath been warned us, what malicious Foe
Envying our happiness, and of his own
Despairing, seeks to work us woe and shame
By sly assault; and somewhere nigh at hand
Watches, no doubt, with greedy hope to find
His wish and best advantage, us asunder,
Hopeless to circumvent us joined, where each
To other speedy aid might lend at need;

Whether his first design be to withdraw
Our fealty from God, or to disturb
Conjugal Love, than which perhaps no bliss
Enjoyed by us excites his envy more;
Or this, or worse, leave not the faithful side[24]
That gave thee being, still shades thee and protects.
The Wife, where danger or dishonour lurks,
Safest and seemliest by her Husband stays,
Who guards her, or with her the worst endures'.
  To whom the Virgin Majesty of *Eve*,
As one who loves, and some unkindness meets,
With sweet austere composure thus replied,
  'Offspring of Heav'n and Earth, and all Earth's Lord,
That such an Enemy we have, who seeks
Our ruin, both by thee informed I learn,
And from the parting Angel over-heard
As in a shady nook I stood behind,
Just then returned at shut of Evening Flowrs.
But that thou shouldst my firmness therefore doubt
To God or thee, because we have a foe
May tempt it, I expected not to hear.
His violence thou fearst not, being such
As we, not capable of death or pain,
Can either not receive, or can repel.
His fraud is then thy fear, which plain infers
Thy equal fear that my firm Faith and Love
Can by his fraud be shaken or seduced;
Thoughts, which how found they harbour in thy breast
Adam, misthought of her to thee so dear?'
  To whom with healing words *Adam* replied.
'Daughter of God and Man, immortal *Eve*,
For such thou art, from sin and blame entire:
Not diffident of thee do I dissuade
Thy absence from my sight, but to avoid
The attempt itself, intended by our Foe.
For he who tempts, though in vain, at least asperses
The tempted with dishonour foul, supposed
Not incorruptible of Faith, not proof
Against temptation: thou thyself with scorn
And anger wouldst resent the offered wrong,
Though ineffectual found: misdeem not then,
If such affront I labour to avert
From thee alone, which on us both at once
The Enemy, though bold, will hardly dare,
Or daring, first on me the assault shall light.

Notes

[24] *Or … or* whether … or … is the case.

Nor thou his malice and false guile contemn;
Subtle he needs must be, who could seduce
Angels, nor think superfluous others' aid.
I from the influence of thy looks receive
Accéss in every Virtue, in thy sight[25]
More wise, more watchful, stronger, if need were
Of outward strength; while shame, thou looking on,
Shame to be overcome or over-reached,
Would utmost vigour raise, and raised unite.
Why shouldst not thou like sense within thee feel
When I am present, and thy trial choose
With me, best witness of thy Virtue tried'.
So spake domestic *Adam* in his care
And Matrimonial Love; but *Eve*, who thought
Less attribúted to her Faith sincere,
Thus her reply with accent sweet renewed.[26]
'If this be our condition, thus to dwell
In narrow circuit straitened by a Foe,
Subtle or violent, we not endued
Single with like defence, wherever met,
How are we happy, still in fear of harm?
But harm precedes not sin: only our Foe
Tempting affronts us with his foul esteem[27]
Of our integrity: his foul esteem
Sticks no dishonour on our Front, but turns[28]
Foul on himself; then wherefore shunned or feared
By us? who rather double honour gain
From his surmise proved false, find peace within,
Favour from Heav'n, our witness from th' event.
And what is Faith, Love, Virtue unassayed
Alone, without exterior help sustained?
Let us not then suspect our happy State
Left so imperfect by the Maker wise,
As not secure to single or combined.
Frail is our happiness, if this be so,
And *Eden* were no *Eden* thus exposed'.
To whom thus *Adam* fervently replied.
'O Woman, best are all things as the will
Of God ordained them, his creating hand
Nothing imperfet or deficient left
Of all that he Created, much less Man,
Or aught that might his happy State secure,
Secure from outward force; within himself
The danger lies, yet lies within his power:

Notes

[25] *Accéss* "Increase; enlargement; addition" (Johnson).
[26] *accent* "A modification of the voice, expressive of the passions or sentiments" (Johnson).
[27] *esteem* estimate.
[28] *Front* "The face" (Johnson).

Against his will he can receive no harm.
But God left free the Will, for what obeys
Reason, is free, and Reason he made right,
But bid her well beware, and still erect,[29]
Lest by some fair appearing good surprised
She dictate false, and misinform the Will
To do what God expressly hath forbid.
Not then mistrust, but tender love enjoins,
That I should mind thee oft, and mind thou me.
Firm we subsist, yet possible to swerve,
Since Reason not impossibly may meet
Some specious object by the Foe suborned,
And fall into deception unaware,
Not keeping strictest watch, as she was warned.
Seek not temptation then, which to avoid
Were better, and most likely if from me
Thou sever not: Trial will come unsought.
Wouldst thou approve thy constancy, approve[30]
First thy obedience; th' other who can know,
Not seeing thee attempted, who attest?
But if thou think, trial unsought may find[31]
Us both securer than thus warned thou seemst,
Go; for thy stay, not free, absents thee more;
Go in thy native innocence, rely
On what thou hast of virtue, summon all,
For God towards thee hath done his part, do thine'.
    So spake the Patriarch of Mankind, but *Eve*
Persisted, yet submiss, though last, replied.[32]
    'With thy permission then, and thus forewarned
Chiefly by what thy own last reasoning words
Touched only, that our trial, when least sought,
May find us both perhaps far less prepared,
The willinger I go, nor much expect
A Foe so proud will first the weaker seek;
So bent, the more shall shame him his repulse'.
Thus saying, from her Husband's hand her hand
Soft she withdrew, and like a Wood-Nymph light
Oread or *Dryad*, or of *Delia's* Train,[33]
Betook her to the Groves, but *Delia's* self
In gait surpassed, and Goddess-like deport,
Though not as she with Bow and Quiver armed,
But with such Gard'ning Tools as Art yet rude,
Guiltless of fire had formed, or Angels brought.

Notes

[29] *erect* "Vigorous; not depressed" (Johnson).

[30] *approve* prove.

[31] *find* determine that (we are stronger than you seem), as a finding of the trial.

[32] *last* last to speak, which is not indicative of submission.

[33] *Oread or Dryad* mountain or tree nymph, follower of Artemis of Delos (hence *Delia*).

To *Pales*, or *Pomona*, thus adorned,[34]
Likest she seemed, *Pomona* when she fled
Vertumnus, or to *Ceres* in her Prime,[35]
Yet Virgin of *Proserpina* from *Jove*.
Her long with ardent look his Eye pursued
Delighted, but desiring more her stay.
Oft he to her his charge of quick return
Repeated, she to him as oft engaged
To be returned by Noon amid the Bower,
And all things in best order to invite
Noontide repast, or Afternoon's repose.
O much deceived, much failing, hapless *Eve*,
Of thy presumed return! event perverse!
Thou never from that hour in Paradise
Foundst either sweet repast, or sound repose;
Such ambush hid among sweet Flowers and Shades
Waited with hellish rancour imminent
To intercept thy way, or send thee back
Despoiled of Innocence, of Faith, of Bliss.
For now, and since first break of dawn the Fiend,
Mere Serpent in appearance, forth was come,
And on his Quest, where likeliest he might find
The only two of Mankind, but in them
The whole included Race, his purposed prey.
In Bower and Field he sought, where any tuft
Of Grove or Garden-Plot more pleasant lay,
Their tendance or Plantation for delight,
By Fountain or by shady Rivulet
He sought them both, but wished his hap might find
Eve separáte, he wished, but not with hope
Of what so seldom chanced, when to his wish,
Beyond his hope, *Eve* separáte he spies,
Veiled in a Cloud of Fragrance, where she stood,
Half spied, so thick the Roses blushing round
About her glowed, oft stooping to support
Each Flower of slender stalk, whose head though gay
Carnation, Purple, Azure, or specked with Gold,
Hung drooping unsustained, them she upstays
Gently with Myrtle band, mindless the while,[36]
Herself, though fairest unsupported Flower,
From her best prop so far, and storm so nigh.
Nearer he drew, and many a walk traversed
Of stateliest Covert, Cedar, Pine, or Palm,
Then voluble and bold, now hid, now seen[37]

Notes

[34] *Pales* a Roman goddess of flocks and shepherds, whose festival of purification was associated with the founding of Rome; *Pomona* goddess of fruit, wife to Vertumnus, a god of seasonal change.

[35] *Ceres* mother of *Proserpina*, whose abduction by Pluto put an end to perpetual spring on earth.

[36] *mindless* inattentive to.

[37] *voluble* "Rolling; having quick motion" (Johnson).

Among thick-woven Arborets, and Flowers
Imbordered on each Bank, the hand of *Eve*:
Spot more delicious than those Gardens feigned
Or of revived *Adonis*, or renowned[38]
Alcinous, host of old *Laertes'* Son,[39]
Or that, not Mystic, where the Sapient King[40]
Held dalliance with his fair *Egyptian* Spouse.
Much he the Place admired, the Person more.
As one who long in populous City pent,
Where Houses thick and Sewers annoy the Air,
Forth issuing on a Summer's Morn to breathe
Among the pleasant Villages and Farms
Adjoined, from each thing met conceives delight;
The smell of Grain, or tedded Grass, or Kine,[41]
Or Dairy, each rural sight, each rural sound;
If chance with Nymphlike step fair Virgin pass,
What pleasing seemed, for her now pleases more,
She most, and in her look sums all Delight.
Such Pleasure took the Serpent to behold
This Flowry Plat, the sweet recess of *Eve*[42]
Thus early, thus alone; her Heav'nly form
Angelic, but more soft, and Feminine,
Her graceful Innocence, her every Air
Of gesture or least action overawed
His Malice, and with rapine sweet bereaved
His fierceness of the fierce intent it brought:
That space the Evil one abstracted stood
From his own evil, and for the time remained
Stupidly good, of enmity disarmed,
Of guile, of hate, of envy, of revenge;
But the hot Hell that always in him burns,
Though in mid Heav'n, soon ended his delight,
And tortures him now more, the more he sees
Of pleasure not for him ordained: then soon
Fierce hate he recollects, and all his thoughts
Of mischief, gratulating, thus excites.[43]
'Thoughts, whither have ye led me, with what sweet
Compulsion thus transported to forget
What hither brought us, hate, not love, nor hope
Of Paradise for Hell, hope here to taste[44]

Notes

38 *Adonis* a divinity of vegetation and fertility; Spenser gave full allegorical and allusive life to his garden (*Faerie Queene* 3.6.29–51).

39 *Alcinous* a king whose gardens are described when he offers hospitality to Odysseus, *Laertes' Son* (*Odyssey* 6).

40 *Mystic* "pertaining to ancient religious mysteries" (*OED*), like the festival of Adonis; *Sapient King* Solomon, whose garden appears in the Song of Solomon, took an *Egyptian Spouse* (1 Kings 3.1).

41 *tedded* from *to ted*, "To lay grass newly mown in rows" (Johnson); *kine* archaic plural of *cow*.

42 *Plat* place, plot of ground.

43 *gratulating* expressing joy at the coming of someone or something; greeting.

44 *for* in exchange for.

Of pleasure, but all pleasure to destroy,
Save what is in destroying, other joy
To me is lost. Then let me not let pass
Occasion which now smiles: behold alone
The Woman, opportune to all attempts,
Her Husband, for I view far round, not nigh,
Whose higher intellectual more I shun,
And strength, of courage haughty, and of limb
Heroic built, though of terrestrial mould,
Foe not informidable, exempt from wound,
I not; so much hath Hell debased, and pain
Enfeebled me, to what I was in Heav'n.
She fair, divinely fair, fit Love for Gods,
Not terrible, though terror be in Love
And beauty, not approached by stronger hate,
Hate stronger, under show of Love well feigned,
The way which to her ruin now I tend'.
So spake the Enemy of Mankind, enclosed
In Serpent, Inmate bad, and toward *Eve*
Addressed his way, not with indented wave,
Prone on the ground, as since, but on his rear,
Circular base of rising folds, that tower'd
Fold above fold a surging Maze, his Head
Crested aloft, and Carbuncle his Eyes;
With burnished Neck of verdant Gold, erect
Amidst his circling Spires, that on the grass
Floated redundant: pleasing was his shape,[45]
And lovely, never since of Serpent kind
Lovelier, not those that in *Illyria* changed
Hermione and *Cadmus*, or the God[46]
In *Epidaurus*; nor to which transformed[47]
Ammonian Jove, or *Capitoline* was seen,[48]
He with *Olympias*, this with her who bore
Scipio the highth of *Rome*. With tract oblique[49]
At first, as one who sought accéss, but feared
To interrupt, side-long he works his way.
As when a Ship by skilful Steersmen wrought
Nigh River's mouth or Foreland, where the Wind
Veers oft, as oft so steers, and shifts her Sail;

Notes

[45] *redundant* "Superabundant; exuberant" (Johnson), but also Latinate, "wave on wave."

[46] *Hermione and Cadmus* having fled from Thebes, the city he founded in central Greece, to the Balkan wilds of Illyria, Cadmus in despair prayed to be turned into a serpent; his wife embraced him and successfully wished herself a serpent too (Ovid, *Metamorphoses* 4.562–603).

[47] *Epidaurus* a Greek city on the Peloponnese renowned for its sanctuary to the healing god Aesculapius, who took the form of a serpent while triumphantly proceeding to Rome to stop a plague (*Metamorphoses* 15.622–744).

[48] *Ammonian Jove* Egyptian Zeus (cf. 4.277), who took the form of a serpent when he conceived Alexander the Great with *Olympias*; when the legend was transferred to the great Roman general and ruler *Scipio* Africanus (236–184), Jove was given his local designation.

[49] *tract* course, path.

So varied he, and of his tortuous Train
Curled many a wanton wreath in sight of *Eve*,
To lure her Eye; she busied heard the sound
Of rustling Leaves, but minded not, as used
To such disport before her through the Field,
From every Beast, more duteous at her call,
Than at *Circean* call the Herd disguised.[50]
He bolder now, uncalled before her stood;
But as in gaze admiring: Oft he bowed
His turret Crest, and sleek enamelled Neck,
Fawning, and licked the ground whereon she trod.
His gentle dumb expression turned at length
The Eye of *Eve* to mark his play; he glad
Of her attention gained, with Serpent Tongue
Organic, or impulse of vocal Air,[51]
His fraudulent temptation thus began.
'Wonder not, sovereign Mistress, if perhaps
Thou canst, who art sole Wonder, much less arm
Thy looks, the Heav'n of mildness, with disdain,
Displeased that I approach thee thus, and gaze
Insatiate, I thus single, nor have feared
Thy awful brow, more awful thus retired.
Fairest resemblance of thy Maker fair,
Thee all things living gaze on, all things thine
By gift, and thy Celestial Beauty adore
With ravishment beheld, there best beheld
Where universally admired; but here
In this enclosure wild, these Beasts among,
Beholders rude, and shallow to discern
Half what in thee is fair, one man except,
Who sees thee? (and what is one?) who shouldst be seen
A Goddess among Gods, adored and served
By Angels numberless, thy daily Train'.
So glozed the Tempter, and his Proem tuned;[52]
Into the Heart of *Eve* his words made way,
Though at the voice much marvelling; at length
Not unamazed she thus in answer spake.
'What may this mean? Language of Man pronounced
By Tongue of Brute, and human sense expressed?
The first at least of these I thought denied
To Beasts, whom God on their Creation-Day
Created mute to all articulate sound;
The latter I demur, for in their looks[53]

Notes

[50] *Circean call* Circe transformed or disguised men as beasts and controlled them, but wily Odysseus eluded her charms (*Odyssey* 10.210–574).

[51] *Organic* "Consisting of various parts co-operating with each other" (Johnson); the two parts of the forked tongue cannot "co-operate" in Ovid's stories of those transformed to snakes (l. 507 above and l. 749 below).

[52] *glozed* from *gloze*, "To flatter; to wheedle; to insinuate; to fawn" (Johnson).

[53] *demur* "To doubt of" (Johnson).

Much reason, and in their actions, oft appears.
Thee, Serpent, subtlest beast of all the field
I knew, but not with human voice endued;
Redouble then this miracle, and say,
How cam'st thou speakable of mute, and how
To me so friendly grown above the rest
Of brutal kind, that daily are in sight?
Say, for such wonder claims attention due'.
 To whom the guileful Tempter thus replied.
'Empress of this fair World, resplendent *Eve*,
Easy to me it is to tell thee all
What thou commandst, and right thou shouldst be obeyed:
I was at first as other Beasts that graze
The trodden Herb, of abject thoughts and low,
As was my food, nor aught but food discerned
Or Sex, and apprehended nothing high:
Till on a day roving the field, I chanced
A goodly Tree far distant to behold
Loaden with fruit of fairest colours mixed,
Ruddy and Gold: I nearer drew to gaze;
When from the boughs a savoury odour blown,
Grateful to appetite, more pleased my sense
Than smell of sweetest Fennel or the Teats[54]
Of Ewe or Goat dropping with Milk at Ev'n,
Unsucked of Lamb or Kid, that tend their play.
To satisfy the sharp desire I had
Of tasting those fair Apples, I resolved
Not to defer; hunger and thirst at once,
Powerful persuaders, quickened at the scent
Of that alluring fruit, urged me so keen.
About the mossy Trunk I wound me soon,
For high from ground the branches would require
Thy utmost reach or *Adam's*: Round the Tree
All other Beasts that saw, with like desire
Longing and envying stood, but could not reach.
Amid the Tree now got, where plenty hung
Tempting so nigh, to pluck and eat my fill
I spared not, for such pleasure till that hour
At Feed or Fountain never had I found.
Sated at length, ere long I might perceive
Strange alteration in me, to degree
Of Reason in my inward Powers, and Speech
Wanted not long, though to this shape retained.
Thenceforth to Speculations high or deep
I turned my thoughts, and with capacious mind
Considered all things visible in Heav'n,

Notes

[54] *Fennel or the Teats/Of Ewe* folkloric favorites of snakes.

Or Earth, or Middle, all things fair and good;
But all that fair and good in thy Divine
Semblance, and in thy Beauty's heav'nly Ray
United I beheld; no Fair to thine
Equivalent or second, which compelled
Me thus, though importune perhaps, to come
And gaze, and worship thee of right declared
Sovereign of Creatures, universal Dame'.[55]
So talked the spirited sly Snake; and *Eve*
Yet more amazed unwary thus replied.
'Serpent, thy overpraising leaves in doubt
The virtue of that Fruit, in thee first proved:
But say, where grows the Tree, from hence how far?
For many are the Trees of God that grow
In Paradise, and various, yet unknown
To us, in such abundance lies our choice,
As leaves a greater store of Fruit untouched,
Still hanging incorruptible, till men
Grow up to their provision, and more hands
Help to disburden Nature of her Birth'.
To whom the wily Adder, blithe and glad.
'Empress, the way is ready, and not long,
Beyond a row of Myrtles, on a Flat,
Fast by a Fountain, one small Thicket past
Of blowing Myrrh and Balm; if thou accept
My conduct, I can bring thee thither soon'.
'Lead then', said Eve. He leading swiftly rolled
In tangles, and made intricate seem straight,
To mischief swift. Hope elevates, and joy
Brightens his Crest, as when a wand'ring Fire,[56]
Compact of unctuous vapour, which the Night
Condenses, and the cold environs round,
Kindled through agitation to a Flame,
Which oft, they say, some evil Spirit attends
Hovering and blazing with delusive Light,
Misleads th' amazed Night-wanderer from his way
To Bogs and Mires, and oft through Pond or Pool,
There swallowed up and lost, from succour far.
So glistered the dire Snake, and into fraud
Led *Eve* our credulous Mother, to the Tree
Of prohibition, root of all our woe;
Which when she saw, thus to her guide she spake.
'Serpent, we might have spared our coming hither,
Fruitless to me, though fruit be here to excess,
The credit of whose virtue rest with thee,

Notes

55 *Dame* one who controls, feminine (Latin, *domina*); mistress.

56 *wand'ring Fire* will-o'-the-wisp, *ignis fatuus*, deceptive marsh gas.

Wondrous indeed, if cause of such effects.
But of this Tree we may not taste nor touch;
God so commanded, and left that Command
Sole Daughter of his voice; the rest, we live
Law to ourselves, our Reason is our Law'.
　To whom the Tempter guilefully replied.
'Indeed? hath God then said that of the Fruit
Of all these Garden Trees ye shall not eat,
Yet Lords declared of all in Earth or Air?'
　To whom thus *Eve* yet sinless. 'Of the Fruit
Of each Tree in the Garden we may eat,
But of the Fruit of this fair Tree amidst
The Garden, God hath said, "Ye shall not eat
Thereof, nor shall ye touch it, lest ye die" '.
　She scarce had said, though brief, when now more bold
The Tempter, but with show of Zeal and Love
To Man, and indignation at his wrong,
New part puts on, and as to passion moved,
Fluctuates disturbed, yet comely and in act
Raised, as of some great matter to begin.
As when of old some Orator renowned
In *Athens* or free *Rome*, where Eloquence
Flourished, since mute, to some great cause addressed,
Stood in himself collected, while each part,
Motion, each act won audience ere the tongue,
Sometimes in highth began, as no delay
Of Preface brooking, through his Zeal of Right.
So standing, moving, or to highth upgrown
The Tempter all impassioned thus began.
　'O Sacred, Wise, and Wisdom-giving Plant,
Mother of Science, Now I feel thy Power [57]
Within me clear, not only to discern
Things in their Causes, but to trace the ways
Of highest Agents, deemed however wise.
Queen of this Universe, do not believe
Those rigid threats of Death; ye shall not Die:
How should ye? by the Fruit? it gives you Life
To Knowledge? by the Threatner, look on me,
Me who have touched and tasted, yet both live,
And life more perfet have attained than Fate
Meant me, by vent'ring higher than my Lot.
Shall that be shut to Man, which to the Beast
Is open? or will God incense his ire
For such a petty Trespass, and not praise
Rather your dauntless virtue, whom the pain
Of Death denounced, whatever thing Death be,

Notes

[57] *Science* "Knowledge" (Johnson).

Deterred not from achieving what might lead
To happier life, knowledge of Good and Evil;
Of good, how just? of evil, if what is evil
Be real, why not known, since easier shunned?
God therefore cannot hurt ye, and be just;
Not just, not God; not feared then, nor obeyed:
Your fear itself of Death removes the fear.
Why then was this forbid? Why but to awe,
Why but to keep ye low and ignorant,
His worshippers; he knows that in the day
Ye Eat thereof, your Eyes that seem so clear,
Yet are but dim, shall perfetly be then
Opened and cleared, and ye shall be as Gods,
Knowing both Good and Evil, as they know.
That ye shall be as Gods, since I as Man,
Internal Man, is but proportion meet,
I of brute human, ye of human Gods.
So ye shall die perhaps, by putting off[58]
Human, to put on Gods, death to be wished,
Though threatened, which no worse than this can bring.
And what are Gods that Man may not become
As they, participating God-like food?
The Gods are first, and that advantage use
On our belief, that all from them proceeds;
I question it, for this fair Earth I see,
Warmed by the Sun, producing every kind,
Them nothing: If they all things, who enclosed
Knowledge of Good and Evil in this Tree,
That whoso eats thereof, forthwith attains
Wisdom without their leave? and wherein lies
Th' offence, that Man should thus attain to know?
What can your knowledge hurt him, or this Tree
Impart against his will if all be his?
Or is it envy, and can envy dwell
In heav'nly breasts? these, these and many more
Causes import your need of this fair Fruit.
Goddess humane, reach then, and freely taste'.
He ended, and his words replete with guile
Into her heart too easy entrance won:
Fixed on the Fruit she gazed, which to behold
Might tempt alone, and in her ears the sound
Yet rung of his persuasive words, impregned
With Reason, to her seeming, and with Truth;
Meanwhile the hour of Noon drew on, and waked
An eager appetite, raised by the smell

Notes

58 *ye shall die* … a perverse version of the New Testament teaching (e.g., 1 Corinthians 15.51–8).

So savoury of that Fruit, which with desire,
Inclinable now grown to touch or taste,
Solicited her longing eye; yet first
Pausing a while, thus to herself she mused.
'Great are thy Virtues, doubtless, best of Fruits,
Though kept from Man, and worthy to be admired,
Whose taste, too long forborne, at first assay
Gave elocution to the mute, and taught
The Tongue not made for Speech to speak thy praise:
Thy praise he also, who forbids thy use,
Conceals not from us, naming thee the Tree
Of Knowledge, knowledge both of good and evil;
Forbids us then to taste, but his forbidding
Commends thee more, while it infers the good
By thee communicated, and our want:
For good unknown sure is not had, or had
And yet unknown, is as not had at all.
In plain then, what forbids he but to know,
Forbids us good, forbids us to be wise?
Such prohibitions bind not. But if Death
Bind us with after-bands, what profits then
Our inward freedom? In the day we eat
Of this fair Fruit, our doom is, we shall die.
How dies the Serpent? he hath eat'n and lives,
And knows, and speaks, and reasons, and discerns,
Irrational till then. For us alone
Was death invented? or to us denied
This intellectual food, for beasts reserved?
For Beasts it seems: yet that one Beast which first
Hath tasted, envies not, but brings with joy
The good befall'n him, Author unsuspect,[59]
Friendly to man, far from deceit or guile.
What fear I then, rather what know to fear
Under this ignorance of good and Evil,
Of God or Death, of Law or Penalty?
Here grows the Cure of all, this Fruit Divine,
Fair to the Eye, inviting to the Taste,
Of virtue to make wise: what hinders then
To reach, and feed at once both Body and Mind?'[60]
So saying, her rash hand in evil hour
Forth reaching to the Fruit, she plucked, she eat:[61]
Earth felt the wound, and Nature from her seat[62]
Sighing through all her Works gave signs of woe,
That all was lost. Back to the Thicket slunk

Notes

[59] *Author unsuspect* "The first beginner or mover of any-thing ... Not considered as likely to do or mean ill" (Johnson).

[60] *Body and* two syllables, as often with *y* and following *a*.

[61] *eat* variant past tense, pronounced et.

[62] The description links Eve with Dido in her loss of honor (*Aeneid* 4.166–70). Cf. Romans 8.22.

The guilty Serpent, and well might, for *Eve*
Intent now wholly on her taste, nought else
Regarded, such delight till then, as seemed,
In Fruit she never tasted, whether true
Or fancied so, through expectation high
Of knowledge, nor was God-head from her thought.
Greedily she engorged without restraint,
And knew not eating Death: Satiate at length,
And heightened as with Wine, jocund and boon,[63]
Thus to herself she pleasingly began.
'O Sovereign, virtuous, precious of all Trees
In Paradise, of operation blessed
To Sapience, hitherto obscured, infamed.
And thy fair Fruit let hang, as to no end
Created; but henceforth my early care,
Not without Song, each Morning, and due praise
Shall tend thee, and the fertile burden ease
Of thy full branches offered free to all;
Till dieted by thee I grow mature
In knowledge, as the Gods who all things know;
Though others envy what they cannot give;
For had the gift been theirs, it had not here
Thus grown. Experience, next, to thee I owe,
Best guide; not following thee, I had remained
In ignorance, thou op'nest Wisdom's way,
And giv'st accéss, though secret she retire.
And I perhaps am secret; Heav'n is high,
High and remote to see from thence distinct
Each thing on Earth; and other care perhaps
May have diverted from continual watch
Our great Forbidder, safe with all his Spies[64]
About him. But to *Adam* in what sort
Shall I appear? shall I to him make known
As yet my change, and give him to partake
Full happiness with me, or rather not,
But keep the odds of Knowledge in my power
Without Copartner? so to add what wants
In Female Sex, the more to draw his Love,
And render me more equal, and perhaps,
A thing not undesirable, sometime
Superior; for inferior who is free?
This may be well: but what if God have seen,
And Death ensue? then I shall be no more,
And *Adam* wedded to another *Eve*,

Notes

[63] *boon* "Gay, merry; as a *boon* companion" (Johnson).

[64] *safe* "No longer dangerous; reposited out of the power of doing harm" (Johnson).

Shall live with her enjoying, I extinct;
A death to think. Confirmed then I resolve,
Adam shall share with me in bliss or woe:
So dear I love him, that with him all deaths
I could endure, without him live no life'.
So saying, from the Tree her step she turned,
But first low Reverence done, as to the power
That dwelt within, whose presence had infused
Into the plant sciential sap, derived[65]
From Nectar, drink of Gods. *Adam* the while
Waiting desirous her return, had wove
Of choicest Flowers a Garland to adorn
Her Tresses, and her rural labours crown,
As Reapers oft are wont their Harvest Queen.
Great joy he promised to his thoughts, and new
Solace in her return, so long delayed;
Yet oft his heart, divine of something ill,[66]
Misgave him; he the falt'ring measure felt;
And forth to meet her went, the way she took
That Morn when first they parted; by the Tree
Of Knowledge he must pass, there he her met,
Scarce from the Tree returning; in her hand
A bough of fairest fruit that downy smil'd,
New gathered, and ambrosial smell diffused.
To him she hasted, in her face excuse
Came Prologue, and Apology to prompt,
Which with bland words at will she thus addressed.
'Hast thou not wondered, *Adam*, at my stay?
Thee I have missed, and thought it long, deprived
Thy presence, agony of love till now
Not felt, nor shall be twice, for never more
Mean I to try, what rash untried I sought,
The pain of absence from thy sight. But strange
Hath been the cause, and wonderful to hear:
This Tree is not as we are told, a Tree
Of danger tasted, nor to evil unknown
Op'ning the way, but of Divine effect
To open Eyes, and make them Gods who taste;
And hath been tasted such: the Serpent wise,
Or not restrained as we, or not obeying,[67]
Hath eaten of the fruit, and is become,
Not dead, as we are threatened, but thenceforth
Endued with human voice and human sense,
Reasoning to admiration, and with me[68]
Persuasively hath so prevailed, that I

Notes

[65] *sciential* producing knowledge.
[66] *divine* "Presageful; divining; prescient" (Johnson).
[67] *Or ... or* either...or.
[68] *to admiration* admirably.

Have also tasted, and have also found
Th' effects to correspond, op'ner mine Eyes,
Dim erst, dilated Spirits, ampler Heart,
And growing up to Godhead; which for thee
Chiefly I sought, without thee can despise.
For bliss, as thou hast part, to me is bliss,
Tedious, unshared with thee, and odious soon.[69]
Thou therefore also taste, that equal Lot
May join us, equal Joy, as equal Love;
Lest thou not tasting, different degree
Disjoin us, and I then too late renounce
Deity for thee, when Fate will not permit'.
  Thus *Eve* with Count'nance blithe her story told;
But in her Cheek distemper flushing glowed.
On the other side, *Adam*, soon as he heard
The fatal Trespass done by *Eve*, amazed,
Astonied stood and Blank, while horror chill[70]
Ran through his veins, and all his joints relaxed;
From his slack hand the Garland wreathed for *Eve*
Down dropped, and all the faded Roses shed:
Speechless he stood and pale, till thus at length
First to himself he inward silence broke.
  'O fairest of Creation, last and best
Of all God's works, Creature in whom excelled
Whatever can to sight or thought be formed,
Holy, divine, good, amiable, or sweet!
How art thou lost, how on a sudden lost,
Defaced, deflowered, and now to Death devote?
Rather how hast thou yielded to transgress
The strict forbiddance, how to violate
The sacred Fruit forbidd'n! some cursèd fraud
Of Enemy hath beguil'd thee, yet unknown,
And me with thee hath ruined, for with thee
Certain my resolution is to Die;
How can I live without thee, how forgo
Thy sweet Convérse and Love so dearly joined,
To live again in these wild Woods forlorn?
Should God create another *Eve*, and I
Another Rib afford, yet loss of thee
Would never from my heart; no no, I feel
The Link of Nature draw me: Flesh of Flesh,
Bone of my Bone thou art, and from thy State
Mine never shall be parted, bliss or woe'.

Notes

69 *Tedious* echoes Latin *taedet*, the description of Dido's state of mind when she prays for death after Aeneas leaves her (*Aeneid* 4.451).

70 *Astonied* momentarily dazed or paralysed (*OED*).

So having said, as one from sad dismay
Recomforted, and after thoughts disturbed
Submitting to what seemed remediless,
Thus in calm mood his Words to *Eve* he turned.
'Bold deed thou hast presumed, advent'rous *Eve*,
And peril great provoked, who thus hath dared,
Had it been only coveting to Eye
That sacred Fruit, sacred to abstinence,
Much more to taste it under ban to touch.
But past who can recall, or done undo?
Not God Omnipotent, nor Fate, yet so
Perhaps thou shalt not Die, perhaps the Fact
Is not so heinous now, foretasted Fruit,
Profaned first by the Serpent, by him first
Made common and unhallowed ere our taste;
Nor yet on him found deadly, he yet lives;
Lives, as thou saidst, and gains to live as Man
Higher degree of Life, inducement strong
To us, as likely tasting to attain
Proportional ascent, which cannot be
But to be Gods, or Angels, Demi-gods.
Nor can I think that God, Creator wise,
Though threat'ning, will in earnest so destroy
Us his prime Creatures, dignified so high,
Set over all his Works, which in our Fall,
For us created, needs with us must fail,
Dependent made; so God shall uncreate,
Be frustrate, do, undo, and labour lose,
Not well conceived of God, who though his Power
Creation could repeat, yet would be loath
Us to abolish, lest the Adversary
Triumph and say; "Fickle their state whom God
Most Favours, who can please him long? Me first
He ruined, now Mankind; whom will he next?"
Matter of scorn, not to be giv'n the Foe,
However I with thee have fixed my Lot,
Certain to undergo like doom, if Death
Consort with thee, Death is to me as Life;
So forcible within my heart I feel
The Bond of Nature draw me to my own,
My own in thee, for what thou art is mine;
Our State cannot be severed, we are one,
One Flesh; to lose thee were to lose myself'.
So *Adam*, and thus *Eve* to him replied.
'O glorious trial of exceeding Love,
Illustrious evidence, example high!
Engaging me to emulate, but short
Of thy perfection, how shall I attain,
Adam, from whose dear side I boast me sprung,
And gladly of our Union hear thee speak,
One Heart, one Soul in both; whereof good proof

This day affords, declaring thee resolved,
Rather than Death or aught than Death more dread
Shall separate us, linked in Love so dear,
To undergo with me one Guilt, one Crime,
If any be, of tasting this fair Fruit,
Whose virtue, for of good still good proceeds,
Direct, or by occasion, hath presented[71]
This happy trial of thy Love, which else
So eminently never had been known.
Were it I thought Death menaced would ensue[72]
This my attempt, I would sustain alone
The worst, and not persuade thee, rather die
Deserted, than oblige thee with a fact
Pernicious to thy Peace, chiefly assured
Remarkably so late of thy so true,
So faithful Love unequalled; but I feel
Far otherwise th' event, not Death, but Life[73]
Augmented, opened Eyes, new Hopes, new Joys,
Taste so Divine, that what of sweet before
Hath touched my sense, flat seems to this, and harsh.
On my experience, *Adam*, freely taste,
And fear of Death deliver to the Winds'.
  So saying, she embraced him, and for joy
Tenderly wept, much won that he his Love
Had so ennobled, as of choice to incur
Divine displeasure for her sake, or Death.
In recompense (for such compliance bad
Such recompense best merits) from the bough
She gave him of that fair enticing Fruit
With liberal hand: he scrupled not to eat
Against his better knowledge, not deceived,
But fondly overcome with Female charm.
Earth trembled from her entrails, as again
In pangs, and Nature gave a second groan,
Sky loured and muttering Thunder, some sad drops
Wept at completing of the mortal Sin
Original; while *Adam* took no thought,
Eating his fill, nor *Eve* to iterate
Her former trespass feared, the more to soothe
Him with her loved society, that now
As with new Wine intoxicated both
They swim in mirth, and fancy that they feel
Divinity within them breeding wings
Wherewith to scorn the Earth: but that false Fruit
Far other operation first displayed,
Carnal desire inflaming, he on *Eve*

Notes

[71] *by occasion* fortuitously.
[72] *Were it* if it were the case that.
[73] *event* outcome; result.

Began to cast lascivious Eyes, she him
As wantonly repaid; in Lust they burn:
Till *Adam* thus 'gan *Eve* to dalliance move.
'Eve, now I see thou art exact of taste,
And elegant, of Sapience no small part,
Since to each meaning savour we apply,[74]
And Palate call judicious; I the praise
Yield thee, so well this day thou hast purveyed.[75]
Much pleasure we have lost, while we abstained
From this delightful Fruit, nor known till now
True relish, tasting; if such pleasure be
In things to us forbidd'n, it might be wished,
For this one Tree had been forbidden ten.
But come, so well refreshed, now let us play,
As meet is, after such delicious Fare;
For never did thy Beauty since the day
I saw thee first and wedded thee, adorned
With all perfections, so inflame my sense
With ardour to enjoy thee, fairer now
Than ever, bounty of this virtuous Tree'.
So said he, and forbore not glance or toy[76]
Of amorous intent, well understood
Of *Eve*, whose Eye darted contagious Fire.
Her hand he seized, and to a shady bank,
Thick overhead with verdant roof embowered
He led her nothing loath; Flowers were the Couch,
Pansies, and Violets, and Asphodel,
And Hyacinth, Earth's freshest softest lap.
There they their fill of Love and Love's disport
Took largely, of their mutual guilt the Seal,
The solace of their sin, till dewy sleep
Oppressed them, wearied with their amorous play.
Soon as the force of that fallacious Fruit,
That with exhilarating vapour bland
About their spirits had played, and inmost powers
Made err, was now exhaled, and grosser sleep
Bred of unkindly fumes, with conscious dreams
Encumbered, now had left them, up they rose
As from unrest, and each the other viewing,
Soon found their Eyes how opened, and their minds
How darkened; innocence, that as a veil
Had shadowed them from knowing ill, was gone,
Just confidence, and native righteousness
And honour from about them, naked left
To guilty shame he covered, but his Robe

Notes

[74] *savour* "Flavour, taste" (*OED*, 3); "Knowledge, understanding" (*OED*, 6).

[75] *purveyed* "made provision for" (*OED*, 3).

[76] *toy* "Play; sport; amorous dalliance" (Johnson).

Uncovered more. So rose the *Danite* strong
Herculean Samson from the Harlot-lap
Of *Philistean Dalilah*, and waked
Shorn of his strength, They destitute and bare
Of all their virtue: silent, and in face
Confounded long they sat, as strucken mute,
Till *Adam*, though not less than *Eve* abashed,
At length gave utterance to these words constrained.
'O *Eve*, in evil hour thou didst give ear
To that false Worm, of whomsoever taught
To counterfeit Man's voice, true in our Fall,
False in our promised Rising; since our Eyes
Opened we find indeed, and find we know
Both Good and Evil, Good lost, and Evil got,
Bad Fruit of Knowledge, if this be to know,
Which leaves us naked thus, of Honour void,
Of Innocence, of Faith, of Purity,
Our wonted Ornaments now soil'd and stained,
And in our Faces evident the signs
Of foul concupiscence; whence evil store;
Even shame, the last of evils; of the first
Be sure then. How shall I behold the face
Henceforth of God or Angel, erst with joy
And rapture so oft beheld? those Heav'nly shapes
Will dazzle now this earthly with their blaze
Insufferably bright. O might I here
In solitude live savage, in some glade
Obscured, where highest Woods impenetrable
To Star or Sunlight, spread their umbrage broad
And brown as Evening: Cover me ye Pines,
Ye Cedars, with innumerable boughs
Hide me, where I may never see them more.
But let us now, as in bad plight, devise
What best may for the present serve to hide
The Parts of each from other, that seem most
To shame obnoxious, and unseemliest seen,[77]
Some Tree whose broad smooth Leaves together sewed
And girded on our loins, may cover round
Those middle parts; that this new comer, Shame,
There sit not, and reproach us as unclean'.
So counselled he, and both together went
Into the thickest Wood; there soon they chose
The Figtree, not that kind for Fruit renowned,
But such as at this day, to *Indians* known,
In *Malabar* or *Decan* spreads her Arms[78]
Branching so broad and long, that in the ground

Notes

[77] *obnoxious* exposed.

[78] *Malabar or Decan* places in India.

The bended Twigs take root, and Daughters grow
About the Mother Tree, a Pillared shade
High overarched, and echoing Walks between;
There oft the *Indian* Herdsman, shunning heat
Shelters in cool, and tends his pasturing Herds
At Loopholes cut through thickest shade: Those Leaves
They gathered, broad as *Amazonian* Targe,[79]
And with what skill they had, together sewed,
To gird their waist, vain Covering if to hide
Their guilt and dreaded shame; O how unlike
To that first naked Glory. Such of late
Columbus found the *American* so girt
With feathered Cincture, naked else and wild[80]
Among the Trees on Isles and woody Shores.
Thus fenced, and as they thought, their shame in part
Covered, but not at rest or ease of Mind,
They sat them down to weep, nor only Tears
Rained at their Eyes, but high Winds worse within
Began to rise, high Passions, Anger, Hate,
Mistrust, Suspicion, Discord, and shook sore
Their inward State of Mind, calm Region once
And full of Peace, now tossed and turbulent:
For Understanding ruled not, and the Will
Heard not her lore, both in subjection now
To sensual Appetite, who from beneath
Usurping over sovereign Reason claimed
Superior sway: from thus distempered breast,
Adam, estranged in look and altered style,
Speech intermitted thus to *Eve* renewed.
'Would thou hadst hearkened to my words, and stayed
With me, as I besought thee, when that strange
Desire of wand'ring, this unhappy Morn,
I know not whence possessed thee; we had then
Remained still happy, not as now, despoiled
Of all our good, shamed, naked, miserable.
Let none henceforth seek needless cause to approve[81]
The Faith they owe; when earnestly they seek
Such proof, conclude, they then begin to fail'.
To whom soon moved with touch of blame thus *Eve*.
'What words have passed thy Lips, *Adam* severe,
Imput'st thou that to my default, or will
Of wand'ring, as thou call'st it, which who knows
But might as ill have happened thou being by,
Or to thyself perhaps: hadst thou been there,

Notes

[79] *Targe* "A kind of buckler or shield borne on the left arm. It seems to be commonly used for a defensive weapon less in circumference than a shield" (Johnson).

[80] *cincture* belt.

[81] *approve* prove.

Or here th' attempt, thou couldst not have discerned
Fraud in the Serpent, speaking as he spake;
No ground of enmity between us known,
Why he should mean me ill, or seek to harm.
Was I to have never parted from thy side?
As good have grown there still a lifeless Rib.
Being as I am, why didst not thou the Head
Command me absolutely not to go,
Going into such danger, as thou saidst?
Too facile then thou didst not much gainsay,
Nay didst permit, approve, and fair dismiss.
Hadst thou been firm and fixed in thy dissent,
Neither had I transgressed, nor thou with me'.
To whom then first incensed, *Adam* replied.
'Is this the Love, is this the recompense
Of mine to thee, ingrateful *Eve*, expressed
Immutable when thou wert lost, not I,
Who might have lived and joyed immortal bliss,
Yet willingly chose rather Death with thee:
And am I now upbraided, as the cause
Of thy transgressing? not enough severe,
It seems, in thy restraint: what could I more?
I warned thee, I admonished thee, foretold
The danger, and the lurking Enemy
That lay in wait; beyond this had been force,
And force upon free will hath here no place.
But confidence then bore thee on, secure
Either to meet no danger, or to find
Matter of glorious trial; and perhaps
I also erred in overmuch admiring
What seemed in thee so perfet, that I thought
No evil durst attempt thee, but I rue
That error now, which is become my crime,
And thou th' accuser. Thus it shall befall
Him who to worth in Women overtrusting,
Lets her will rule; restraint she will not brook,
And left to herself, if evil thence ensue,
She first his weak indulgence will accuse'.
Thus they in mutual accusation spent
The fruitless hours, but neither self-condemning,
And of their vain contést appeared no end.

Book X
The Argument

Man's transgression known, the Guardian Angels forsake Paradise, and return up to Heaven to approve their vigilance, and are approved, God declaring that The entrance of Satan *could not by them be prevented. He sends his Son to judge the Transgressors, who descends and gives Sentence accordingly; then in pity clothes them both, and reascends.* Sin *and* Death *sitting till then at the Gates of Hell, by wondrous sympathy feeling the success of* Satan *in this new World, and the sin by Man there committed, resolve to sit no longer confined in Hell, but to follow* Satan *their Sire up to the place of Man: To make the way easier from Hell to this World to and fro, they pave a broad Highway or Bridge over* Chaos, *according to the Track that* Satan *first made; then preparing for Earth, they meet him proud of his success returning to Hell; their mutual gratulation.* Satan *arrives at* Pandemonium, *in full assembly relates with boasting his success against Man; instead of applause is entertained with a general hiss by all his audience, transformed with himself also suddenly into Serpents, according to his doom given in Paradise; then deluded with a show of the forbidden Tree springing up before them, they greedily reaching to take of the Fruit, chew dust and bitter ashes. The proceedings of* Sin *and* Death; *God foretells the final Victory of his Son over them, and the renewing of all things; but for the present commands his Angels to make several alterations in the Heavens and Elements.* Adam *more and more perceiving his fallen condition heavily bewails, rejects the condolement of* Eve; *she persists and at length appeases him: then to evade the Curse likely to fall on their Offspring, proposes to* Adam *violent ways which he approves not, but conceiving better hope, puts her in mind of the late Promise made them, that her Seed should be revenged on the Serpent, and exhorts her with him to seek Peace of the offended Deity, by repentance and supplication.*

Book XI
The Argument

The Son of God presents to his Father the Prayers of our first Parents now repenting, and intercedes for them: God accepts them, but declares that they must no longer abide in Paradise; sends Michael *with a Band of Cherubim to dispossess them; but first to reveal to* Adam *future things:* Michael's *coming down.* Adam *shows to* Eve *certain ominous signs; he discerns* Michael's *approach, goes out to meet him: the Angel denounces*[1] *their departure.* Eve's *Lamentation.* Adam *pleads, but submits: The Angel leads him up to a high Hill, sets before him in vision what shall happen till the Flood.*

Book XII
The Argument

The Angel Michael *continues from the Flood to relate what shall succeed; then, in the mention of* Abraham, *comes by degrees to explain, who that Seed of the Woman shall be, which was promised* Adam *and* Eve *in the Fall; his Incarnation, Death, Resurrection, and Ascension; the state of the Church till his second Coming.* Adam *greatly satisfied and recomforted by these Relations and Promises descends the Hill with* Michael; *wakens* Eve, *who all this while had slept, but with gentle dreams composed to quietness of mind and submission.* Michael *in either hand leads them out of Paradise, the fiery Sword waving behind them, and the Cherubim taking their Stations to guard the Place.*

Notes

Book XI

[1] *denounces* proclaims or sentences them with.

Abraham Cowley (1618–1667)

Cowley began publishing poetry at the age of fifteen and had three editions of a youthful collection in print by age nineteen. The Parliamentary government forced him out of Cambridge in 1643, and he soon migrated from Oxford to Paris, where he served Charles I's queen. In 1654 Cowley went on a mission to England, was arrested, and saw the publication in 1656 of his most important collection of poems. After the Restoration he pursued scientific interests and willed his literary remains to Thomas Sprat, the Royal Society's first historian. Cowley wrote all kinds of verse; he achieved fame for love poetry, for his strenuous Pindaric odes, for his epic *Davideis* and his long historical poem on the Civil War. Within a generation of his death, however, Cowley's reputation sank, as his name became synonymous with extravagantly witty, linguistically contorted poetry that Samuel Johnson permanently labeled "Metaphysical." He remained important but became old-fashioned.

The texts are based on the edition of Cowley's works published by Sprat in 1668. The *Collected Works of Abraham Cowley* in six volumes is in progress (University of Delaware Press, 1989–).

Anacreontiques: Or, Some Copies of Verses Translated Paraphrastically out of Anacreon[1]

I. Love[2]

I'll sing of *Heroes,* and of *Kings;*
In mighty Numbers, mighty things,
Begin, my *Muse;* but lo, the strings
To my great *Song* rebellious prove;
The strings will sound of nought but *Love.*
I broke them all, and put on new;
'Tis this or nothing sure will do.
'These sure', said I, 'will me obey;
These sure *Heroick Notes* will play'.
Straight I began with thund'ring *Jove,*
And all th' immortal Pow'rs but *Love.*
Love smiled, and from my enfeebled *Lyre*
Came gentle airs, such as inspire
Melting love, soft desire.

Notes

Anacreontiques

1 *Anacreontiques* This is the first recorded usage of the term in English (1656), but the great publisher Henri Estienne produced a collection of imitations of Anacreon called *Anacreontea* in 1554. Although Anacreon (6th century BCE) composed some poems on politics, he is mainly remembered for his celebrations of wine, erotic love, and song.

2 A loose translation of Anacreon's Ode 1, "To his Lyre." (The numbering of Anacreon's odes has varied over time; I have used the old numbering, familiar to Cowley.)

British Literature 1640–1789: An Anthology, Fourth Edition. Edited by Robert DeMaria, Jr.

Farewell then *Heroes*, farewell *Kings*,
And mighty *Numbers*, mighty *Things;*
Love tunes my *Heart* just to my *strings.*

II. Drinking[3]
The thirsty *Earth* soaks up the *Rain*,
And drinks, and gapes for drink again.
The *Plants* suck in the *Earth*, and are
With constant drinking fresh and fair.
The *Sea* itself, which one would think
Should have but little need of *Drink*,
Drinks ten thousand *Rivers* up,
So filled that they o'erflow the *Cup*.
The busy *Sun* (and one would guess
By 'is drunken fiery face no less)
Drinks up the *Sea*, and when h 'as done,
The *Moon* and *Stars* drink up the *Sun*.
They drink and dance by their own light,
They drink and revel all the night.
Nothing in *Nature*'s *Sober* found,
But an eternal *Health* goes round.
Fill up the *Bowl* then, fill it high,
Fill all the *Glasses* there, for why
Should every creature drink but *I*,
Why, *Man* of *Morals*, tell me why?

III. Beauty[4]
Liberal *Nature* did dispense
To all things *Arms* for their defense;
And some she arms with sinewy force,
And some with swiftness in the course;
Some with hard Hoofs, or forkèd claws,
And some with Horns, or tuskèd jaws.
And some with Scales, and some with Wings,
And some with Teeth, and some with Stings.
Wisdom to *Man* she did afford,
Wisdom for *Shield*, and *Wit* for *Sword*.
What to beauteous *Woman-kind*,
What *Arms*, what *Armour* has sh' assigned?
Beauty is both; for with the *Fair*
What *Arms*, what *Armour* can compare?
What *Steel*, what *Gold*, or *Diamond*,
More *Impassible* is found?
And yet what *Flame*, what *Lightning* e'er
So great an *Active* force did bear?

Notes

[3] An imitation of Anacreon's much briefer Ode 19, "That We Ought to Drink."

[4] An imitation of Ode 2, "On Women."

They are *all weapon*, and they dart
Like *Porcupines* from every part.
Who can, alas, their strength express,
Armed, when they themselves undress,
Cap-à-pie[5] with *Nakedness?*

IV. The Duel[6]
Yes, I will love then, I will love,
I will not now *Love's Rebel* prove,
Though I was once his *Enemy;*
Though ill-advised and stubborn I,
Did to the Combat him defy,
An Helmet, Spear, and mighty shield,
Like some new *Ajax* I did wield.[7]
Love in one hand his *Bow* did take,
In th'other hand a *Dart* did shake.
But yet in vain the *Dart* did throw,
In vain he often drew the *Bow.*
So well my *Armour* did resist,
So oft by flight the blow I missed.
But when I thought all danger passed,
His *Quiver* emptied quite at last,
Instead of *Arrow*, or of *Dart*,
He shot *Himself* into my Heart.
The *Living* and the *Killing Arrow*
Ran through the skin, the Flesh, the *Blood*,
And broke the Bones, and scorched the Marrow,
No *Trench* or *Work* of *Life* withstood.[8]
In vain I now the *Walls* maintain,
I set out *Guards* and *Scouts* in vain,
Since th' *En'my* does within remain.
In vain a *Breastplate* now I wear,
Since in my *Breast* the Foe I bear.
In vain my *Feet* their swiftness try;
For from the *Body* can they fly?

V. Age[9]
Oft am I by the Women told,
Poor *Anacreon* thou grow'st old.
Look how thy Hairs are falling all;
Poor *Anacreon* how they fall?
Whether I grow old or no,

Notes

5 *Cap-à-pie* head to toe.
6 An imitation of Ode 14, one of several called "To Eros," the god of love.
7 *Ajax Telamon* a mighty Greek warrior who goes mad when he loses a contest to Odysseus. Anacreon used Achilles, a nobler hero, in this place.
8 *Work* a defensive structure.
9 An imitation of Ode 11, one of several called "On Himself."

By th' effects I do not know.
This I know without being told,
'Tis Time to *Live* if I grow *Old*,
'Tis time short pleasures now to take,
Of little *Life* the best to make,
And manage *wisely* the *last stake.*[10]

VI. The Account[11]
When all the *Stars* are by thee told,
(The endless Sums of heavenly Gold)
Or when the *Hairs* are reckoned all,
From sickly *Autumn's Head* that fall,
Or when the drops that make the *Sea*,
Whilst all her *Sands* thy *Counters* be.
Thou then, and Thou alone may'st prove
Th' *Arithmetician* of my *Love.*
An hundred Loves at *Athens* score,
At *Corinth* write an hundred more.
Fair *Corinth* does such Beauties bear,[12]
So few is an *Escaping* there.[13]
Write then at *Chios* seventy three;
Write then at *Lesbos* (let me see)
Write me at *Lesbos* ninety down,
Full ninety *Loves*, and half a One.
And next to these let me present,
The fair *Ionian Regiment.*
And next the *Carian Company*,
Five hundred both *Effectively.*[14]
Three hundred more at *Rhodes* and *Crete;*
Three hundred 'tis I'm sure *Complete.*
For arms at *Crete* each *Face* does bear,
And every *Eye's* an *Archer* there.
Go on; this stop why dost thou make?
Thou thinkst, perhaps, that I mistake.
Seems this to thee too great a *Sum?*
Why many *Thousands* are to come;
The mighty *Xerxes* could not boast
Such different *Nations* in his Host.[15]
On; for my Love, if thou be'st weary,
Must find some better *Secretary.*
I have not yet my *Persian* told.
Nor yet my *Syrian Loves* enrolled,[16]

Notes

[10] *Stake* "A sum of money earned or stored" (*OED*, 4); Cowley's usage predates the *OED*'s first quotation.

[11] An imitation of Ode 32, "On His Loves."

[12] *Corinth, Chios, Lesbos, Ionia, Caria, Rhodes*, and *Crete* were all places in the classical Greek world.

[13] *Escaping* an underestimate in which something has escaped notice.

[14] *Effectively* "Actually, in fact" (*OED*, 4a).

[15] Xerxes is said to have had Assyrians, Babylonians, Phoenicians, Egyptians, and Jews in his army (his *Host*).

[16] *Enrolled* written on a list.

Nor *Indian*, nor *Arabian;*
Nor *Cyprian* Loves, nor *African;*
Nor *Scythian*, nor *Italian* flames;
There's a whole *Map* behind of *Names.*
Of gentle Love i' th' *temperate Zone,*
And cold ones in the *Frigid One,*
Cold frozen *Loves* with which I pine,
And parched *Loves* beneath the *Line.*[17]

VII. Gold[18]
A Mighty pain *to Love* it is,
And 'tis a pain that pain to *miss.*
But of all pains the greatest pain
It is to love, but love in vain.
Virtue now nor noble *Blood,*
Nor *Wit* by *Love* is understood,
Gold alone does passion move,
Gold Monopolizes love!
A *curse* on her, and on the Man,
Who this traffic first began!
A *curse* on him who found the Ore!
A *curse* on him who digged the store!
A *curse* on him who did refine it!
A *curse* on him who first did coin it!
A *curse* all curses else above
On him, who used it first in *Love!*
Gold begets in Brethren hate,
Gold in *Families* debate;
Gold does Friendships separate,
Gold does Civil Wars create.
These the smallest harms of it!
Gold, alas, does *Love beget.*

VIII. The Epicure[19]
Fill the *Bowl* with rosy Wine,
Around our temples *Roses* twine,
And let us cheerfully awhile,
Like the *Wine* and *Roses* smile.
Crowned with Roses we contemn
Gyges' wealthy *Diadem.*[20]
To day is *Ours;* what do we fear?
To day is *Ours;* we have it here.
Let's treat it kindly, that it may
Wish, at least, with us to stay.
Let's banish *Business,* banish *Sorrow;*
To the *Gods* belongs *Tomorrow.*

Notes

[17] *Line* the Tropic of Cancer, or the equator (see *OED*, 10.b.).

[18] A very loose imitation of Ode 61, "To Gold."

[19] An imitation of Ode 15, another of those called "On Himself."

[20] *Gyges* according to Herodotus, he slew King Candules at the suggestion of the queen whom the boastful king allowed Gyges to see naked.

IX. Another[21]
Underneath this Myrtle shade,
On flow'ry beds supinely laid,
With odorous Oils my head o'er-flowing,
And around it Roses growing,
What should I do but drink away
The *Heat,* and *troubles* of the Day?
In this more than *Kingly* state,
Love himself shall on me wait.
Fill to me, *Love,* nay fill it up;
And mingled cast into the Cup,
Wit, and *Mirth,* and noble *Fires,*
Vigorous *Health,* and gay *Desires.*
The *Wheel* of Life no less will stay
In a *smooth* than *Rugged* way.
Since it equally does flee,
Let the *Motion* pleasant be.
Why do we precious *Ointments* shower,
Nobler *wines* why do we pour,
Beauteous *Flowers* why do we spread,
Upon the Monuments of the *Dead?*
Nothing they but *Dust* can show,
Or *Bones* that hasten to be so.
Crown me with *Roses* whilst I *Live,*
Now your *Wines* and *Ointments* give.
After *Death* I nothing crave,
Let me *Alive* my pleasures have,
All are *Stoics* in the *Grave.*

X. The Grasshopper[22]
Happy *Insect,* what can be
In happiness compared to Thee?
Fed with nourishment divine,
The dewy *Morning's* gentle *Wine!*
Nature waits upon thee still,
And thy verdant Cup does fill,
'Tis filled wherever thou dost tread,
Nature self's *thy Ganymed.*[23]
Thou dost drink, and dance, and sing;
Happier than the happiest *King!*
All the *Fields* which thou dost see,
All the *Plants* belong to *Thee,*
All that *Summer Hours* produce,
Fertile made with early juice.
Man for thee does sow and plow;
Farmer He, and *Land-Lord Thou*!
Thou dost innocently joy;

Notes

[21] An imitation of Ode 4, "To Himself."
[22] An imitation of Ode 43.
[23] *Ganymed* the beautiful Trojan boy abducted by Zeus to be cupbearer to the gods.

Nor does thy *Luxury* destroy;
The *Shepherd* gladly heareth thee,
More *Harmonious* than *He.*
Thee Country Hinds with gladness hear,[24]
Prophet of the ripened year!
Thee *Phoebus* loves, and does inspire;
Phoebus is himself thy *Sire.*[25]
To thee of all things upon earth,
Life is no longer than thy *Mirth.*
Happy *Insect,* happy Thou,
Dost neither *Age,* nor *Winter* know.
But when thou 'ast drunk, and danced, and sung,
Thy fill, the flow'ry Leaves among
(Voluptuous, and *Wise* with all,
Epicurean Animal!)[26]
Sated with thy *Summer Feast,*
Thou retirest to endless *Rest.*

XI. The Swallow[27]
Foolish *Prater,* what do'st thou
So early at my window do
With thy tuneless *Serenade?*
Well 't had been had *Tereus* made[28]
Thee as *Dumb* as *Philomel;*
There his Knife had done but well.
In thy undiscovered Nest
Thou dost all the winter rest,
And dream'st o'er thy summer joys
Free from the stormy season's noise:
Free from th' Ill thou 'ast done to me;
Who disturbs, or seeks out *Thee?*
Had'st thou all the charming notes
Of all the wood's *Poetic Throats,*
All thy art could never pay
What thou 'ast ta'en from me away;
Cruel *Bird,* thou 'ast ta'en away
A *Dream* out of my arms to day,
A *Dream* that ne'er must equalled be
By all that *waking Eyes* may see.
Thou this damage to repair,
Nothing half so sweet or faire,
Nothing half so good can'st bring,
Though men say, *Thou bring'st the Spring.*

Notes

24 *Hinds* deer.
25 Phoebus Apollo, god of the sun.
26 *Epicurean* pleasure-loving, as the philosopher Epicurus was supposed to be.
27 An imitation of Ode 12, "To a Swallow."
28 *Tereus* raped his sister-in-law Philomela and cut out her tongue to prevent her from telling; she is transformed into the nightingale in Ovid's *Metamorphoses* (cf. p. 792, n. 8 below).

To the *Royal Society*

1.

Philosophy the great and only Heir[1]
Of all that Human Knowledge which has been
Unforfeited by Man's rebellious Sin,
Though full of years He do appear,
(Philosophy, I say, and call it, He,
For whatsoe'er the Painter's Fancy be,[2]
It a Male-virtue seems to me)
Has still been kept in Nonage till of late,[3]
Nor managed or enjoyed his vast Estate:
Three or four thousand years one would have thought,
To ripeness and perfection might have brought
A Science so well bred and nursed,[4]
And of such hopeful parts too at the first.[5]
But, oh, the Guardians and the Tutors then,
(Some negligent, and some ambitious men)
Would ne'er consent to set him Free,
Or his own Natural Powers to let him see,
Lest that should put an end to their Authority.

2.

That his own business he might quite forget,
They amused him with the sports of wanton Wit,
With the Desserts of Poetry they fed him,
Instead of solid meats t'encrease his force;
Instead of vigorous exercise they led him
Into the pleasant Labyrinths of ever-fresh Discourse:
Instead of carrying him to see
The Riches which do hoarded for him lie
In Nature's endless Treasury,
They chose his Eye to entertain
(His curious but not covetous Eye)
With painted Scenes, and Pageants of the Brain.
Some few exalted Spirits this latter Age has shown,
That laboured to assert the Liberty
(From Guardians, who were now Usurpers grown)
Of this old *Minor* still, Captived Philosophy;
But 'twas Rebellion called to fight
For such a long-oppressed Right.
Bacon at last, a mighty Man, arose[6]

Notes

TO THE *ROYAL SOCIETY*

[1] *Philosophy* natural science, the branch of knowledge with which the Royal Society was most concerned.

[2] Cowley perhaps refers to a specific allegorical painting, but it is untraced.

[3] *Nonage* the state of being under age or a minor.

[4] *Science* branch of knowledge.

[5] *At the first* in ancient Greece.

[6] Sir Francis Bacon (1561–1626), statesman and philosopher, author of *Novum Organon* (1620), which established experimental principles in the natural sciences.

Whom a wise King and Nature chose[7]
Lord Chancellor of both their Laws,
And boldly undertook the injured Pupil's cause.

3.

Authority, which did a Body boast,
Though 'twas but Air condensed, and stalked about,
Like some old Giant's more Gigantic Ghost,
To terrify the Learned Rout
With the plain Magic of true Reason's Light,[8]
He chased out of our sight,
Nor suffered Living *Men* to be misled
By the vain shadows of the Dead:
To Graves, from whence it rose, the conquered Phantom fled;
He broke that Monstrous God which stood
In midst of th' Orchard, and the whole did claim,
Which with a useless Scythe of Wood,
And something else not worth a name,
(Both vast for show, yet neither fit
Or to Defend, or to Beget;
Ridiculous and senseless Terrors!) made
Children and superstitious Men afraid.
The Orchard's open now, and free;
Bacon has broke that Scarecrow Deity;
Come, enter, all that will,
Behold the ripened Fruit, come gather now your Fill.
Yet still, methinks, we fain would be
Catching at the Forbidden Tree,[9]
We would be like the Deity,
When Truth and Falsehood, Good and Evil, we
Without the Sense's aid within ourselves would see;
For 'tis God only who can find
All Nature in his Mind.

4.

From Words, which are but Pictures of the Thought,
(Though we our Thoughts from them perversely drew)
To things, the Mind's right Object, he it brought,
Like foolish Birds to painted Grapes we flew;[10]
He sought and gathered for our use the True;
And when on heaps the chosen Bunches lay,

Notes

[7] *King* James I made Bacon Lord Chancellor in 1618.
[8] *True Reason's light* a priori reasoning, such as Aristotle used in works on nature.
[9] *Catching at* snatching at; making a quick attempt to attain. *Forbidden Tree* the tree of knowledge, of which God forbade Adam and Eve to eat in Genesis.
[10] A reference to the paintings of the ancient Greek Apelles, so realistic that they deceived birds into trying to eat the grapes he depicted.

He pressed them wisely the Mechanic way,
Till all their juice did in one Vessel join,
Ferment into a Nourishment Divine,
    The thirsty Soul's refreshing Wine.
Who to the life an exact Piece would make,
Must not from others Work a Copy take;
    No, not from *Rubens* or *Van Dyke*;[11]
Much less content himself to make it like
Th' Ideas and the Images which lie
In his own Fancy, or his Memory.
    No, he before his sight must place
    The Natural and Living Face;
    The real object must command
Each Judgment of his Eye, and Motion of his Hand.

5.

From these and all long Errors of the way,
In which our wand'ring Predecessors went,
And like th' old *Hebrews* many years did stray
    In Deserts but of small extent,
Bacon, like *Moses*, led us forth at last,
    The barren Wilderness he passed,
    Did on the very Border stand
    Of the blessed promised Land,
And from the Mountains Top of his Exalted Wit,
    Saw it himself, and showed us it.[12]
But Life did never to one Man allow
Time to Discover Worlds, and Conquer too;
Nor can so short a Line sufficient be
To fathom the vast depths of Nature's Sea;
    The work he did we ought t' admire,
And were unjust if we should more require
From his few years, divided 'twixt th' Excess
Of low Affliction, and high Happiness.
For who on things remote can fix his sight,
That's always in a Triumph, or a Fight?[13]

6.

From you, great Champions, we expect to get
These spacious Countries but discovered yet;[14]
Countries where yet instead of Nature, we
Her Images and Idols worshipped see:
These large and wealthy Regions to subdue,

Notes

[11] Peter Paul Rubens (1577–1640) and Anthony Van Dyke (1599–1641), baroque painters.

[12] Exodus recounts Moses' attempts to lead the Israelites out of the desert and into the promised land, which he sees before his death from the top of Mount Pisgah.

[13] Bacon was impeached and imprisoned in 1621.

[14] *But discovered* barely discovered.

Though Learning has whole Armies at command,
Quartered about in every Land,
A better Troop she ne'er together drew.
Methinks, like *Gideon*'s little Band,[15]
God with Design has picked out you,
To do these noble Wonders by a Few:
When the whole Host he saw, "They are," said he,
"Too many to O'ercome for Me";
And now he chooses out his Men,
Much in the way that he did then:
Not those many whom he found
Idly extended on the ground,
To drink with their dejected head
The Stream just so as by their Mouths it fled:
No, but those Few who took the waters up,
And made of their laborious Hands the Cup.

7.

Thus you prepared; and in the glorious Fight
Their wondrous pattern too you take:
Their old and empty Pitchers first they brake,
And with their Hands then lifted up the Light.
Io! Sound too the Trumpets here!
Already your victorious Lights appear;
New Scenes of Heaven already we espy,
And Crowds of golden Worlds on high;
Which from the spacious Plains of Earth and Sea;
Could never yet discovered be
By Sailors' or *Chaldæans'* watchful Eye.[16]
Nature's great Works no distance can obscure,
No smallness her near Objects can secure:
Y' have taught the curious Sight to press
Into the privatest recess
Of her imperceptible Littleness.
Y' have learned to Read her smallest Hand,
And well begun her deepest Sense to Understand.

8.

Mischief and true Dishonour fall on those
Who would to laughter or to scorn expose
So Virtuous and so Noble a Design,
So Human for its Use, for Knowledge so Divine.
The things which these proud men despise, and call
Impertinent, and vain, and small,

Notes

[15] On God's instruction Gideon defeated the Midianites with a tiny band of 300 men (Judges, 6–7), selected for the way they drank water from a pool.

[16] *Chaldaeans* Babylonians, especially those practicing occult sciences, such as astrology (*OED*, B).

Those smallest things of Nature let me know,
Rather than all their greatest Actions Do.
Whoever would Deposèd Truth advance
Into the Throne usurped from it,
Must feel at first the Blows of Ignorance,
And the sharp Points of Envious Wit.
So when by various turns of the Celestial Dance,
In many thousand years
A Star, so long unknown, appears,
Though Heaven itself more beauteous by it grow,
It troubles and alarms the World below,
Does to the Wise a Star, to Fools a Meteor show.[17]

9.

With Courage and Success you the bold work begin;
Your Cradle has not Idle been:
None e'er but *Hercules* and you could be
At five years' Age worthy a History.[18]
And ne'er did Fortune better yet
Th' Historian to the Story fit:[19]
As you from all Old Errors free
And purge the Body of Philosophy;
So from all Modern Follies He
Has vindicated Eloquence and Wit.
His candid Style like a clean Stream does slide,
And his bright Fancy all the way
Does like the Sunshine in it play;
It does like *Thames*, the best of Rivers, glide,
Where the God does not rudely overturn,
But gently pour the Crystal Urn,
And with judicious hand does the whole Current Guide.
'T has all the Beauties Nature can impart,
And all the comely Dress without the paint of Art.

Notes

[17] *Meteor* a transient heavenly body, like a comet, portending evil.

[18] Hercules performed feats of strength while still an infant.

[19] *Historian* Thomas Sprat (1635–1713), who advocated a plain writing style, unadorned with metaphors and other figures of speech. This poem first appeared in Sprat's *History of the Royal Society* (1667).

Andrew Marvell (1621–1678)

In 1657, one year before Oliver Cromwell's death, Marvell became Milton's associate "secretary for foreign tongues." Unlike his elder colleague, Marvell remained in government service after the Restoration, being thrice elected the MP for his home district of Hull. He had influence enough to defend Milton from the possibility of prosecution for aiding and abetting regicide, and he served as secretary on several diplomatic missions abroad. Gradually, however, he became deeply disaffected: he composed satirical poems about Charles II, his government, and its defenders (including John Dryden); and he published anti-government pamphlets, including the anonymous and sensational *An Account of the Growth of Popery and Arbitrary Government in England* (1677). Most of Marvell's poetry did not appear until after his death. *Miscellaneous Poems* came out in 1681, but in every known copy of this edition but two Marvell's "Horatian Ode upon Cromwell's Return from Ireland" was canceled during the process of publication, and the poem did not reappear in print until 1776. Some of Marvell's other Cromwell poems suffered a similar fate, and his satires on the monarchy circulated only in manuscript form until after the Glorious Revolution of 1688–9. Although it does not lampoon anyone, Marvell's "Horatian Ode" is a powerful endorsement of Cromwell's most militant posture; it glorifies the execution of Charles; and it is excellent poetry that tends to recommend its opinions by the strength of its expression; it is dangerous literature at its best.

However, some readers will prefer Marvell's less political verse (practically no verse could be apolitical at this time). The poems are metaphysical, perhaps definitively so in the case of "On a Drop of Dew," or "The Coronet," yet they elude the kind of solutions and closure found in the similar verse of the previous generation. "The Garden," and "Bermudas," for example, are poems without answers or settled meanings. This may be true of all great poems, but these verses seem at first to invite us into a world of theorems and proofs,. But we soon find we have been misled; there is an enameled, artificial quality to the world we enter, and we may expect iconic or allegorical symbolism, as in "Little T.C.," but we can neither penetrate the surface to understand the experience below nor become satisfied that the poem is mere artifice. States of mind are expressed in Marvell's verse, sometimes several states in a single poem, but the furniture of these states of mind is so elegantly turned that we feel we have entered a society that may be too sophisticated for us to comprehend. There is some sense of this even when lust is the state of mind, as in "To his Coy Mistress." The speaker has such total command over the commonplaces of seduction verse and is able to deliver them with such poise that it seems reasonable to doubt he is ever, like mere mortals, subject to his passions.

The Poems of Andrew Marvell, ed. Nigel Smith (Longman, 2003) is the most thorough edition. Smith has also written an excellent biography (Yale University Press, 2010). The prose has been expertly edited by Annabel Patterson et al. (Yale University Press, 2003). The British Library copy of *Miscellaneous Poems* (1681) is the copy-text for the poems presented here.

British Literature 1640–1789: An Anthology, Fourth Edition. Edited by Robert DeMaria, Jr.

from *Miscellaneous Poems* (1681)

The Coronet

When for the Thorns with which I long, too long
With many a piercing wound,
My Saviour's head have crowned,
I seek with Garlands to redress that Wrong:
Through every Garden, every Mead,
I gather flowers (my fruits are only flowers)
Dismantling all the fragrant Towers
That once adorned my Shepherdess's head.
And now when I have summed up all my store,
Thinking (so I my self deceive)
So rich a Chaplet thence to weave
As never yet the king of Glory wore:
Alas I find the Serpent old
That, twining in his speckled breast,
About the flowers disguised does fold,
With wreaths of Fame and Interest.
Ah, foolish Man, that would'st debase with them,
And mortal Glory, Heaven's Diadem!
But thou who only could'st the Serpent tame,
Either his slippery knots at once untie,
And disintangle all his winding Snare:
Or shatter too with him my curious frame:
And let these wither, so that he may die,
Though set with Skill and chosen out with Care.
That they, while Thou on both their Spoils dost tread,
May crown thy Feet, that could not crown thy Head.

The Picture of Little *T.C.* in a Prospect of Flowers[1]

I.

See with what simplicity
This Nymph begins her golden days!
In the green Grass she loves to lie,
And there with her fair Aspect tames
The Wilder flowers, and gives them names;
But only with the Roses plays;
And them does tell
What Colour best becomes them, and what Smell.

Notes

THE PICTURE OF LITTLE *T. C.*

[1] *T. C.* possibly Theophilia Cornewall (Margoliouth).

II.

Who can foretell for what high cause
This Darling of the Gods was born!
Yet this is She whose chaster Laws
The wanton Love shall one day fear,[2]
And, under her command severe,
See his Bow broke and Ensigns torn.
Happy, who can
Appease this virtuous Enemy of Man!

III.

O then let me in time compound,
And parley with those conquering Eyes;
Ere they have tried their force to wound,
Ere, with their glancing wheels, they drive
In Triumph over Hearts that strive,
And them that yield but more despise.
Let me be laid,
Where I may see thy Glories from some Shade.

IV.

Meantime, whilst every verdant thing
Itself does at thy Beauty charm,
Reform the errors of the Spring;
Make that the Tulips may have share
Of sweetness, seeing they are fair;
And Roses of their thorns disarm:
But most procure
That Violets may a longer Age endure.

V.

But O young beauty of the Woods,
Whom Nature courts with fruits and flowers,
Gather the Flowers, but spare the Buds;
Lest *Flora* angry at thy crime,
To kill her Infants in their prime,
Do quickly make th' Example Yours;
And, ere we see,
Nip in the blossom all our hopes and Thee.

Bermudas (1653?)

Where the remote *Bermudas* ride
In th' Ocean's bosom unespied,

Notes

[2] *Love* Cupid.

From a small Boat, that rowed along,
The listening Winds received this Song.
'What should we do but sing his Praise
That led us through the wat'ry Maze,
Unto an Isle so long unknown,
And yet far kinder than our own?
Where He the huge Sea-Monsters wracks,
That lift the Deep upon their Backs.
He lands us on a grassy Stage;
Safe from the Storms, and Prelates' rage.[1]
He gave us this eternal Spring,
Which here enamels every thing;
And sends the Fowls to us in care,
On daily Visits through the Air,
He hangs in shades the Orange bright,
Like golden Lamps in a green Night.
And does in the Pom'granates close,
Jewels more rich than *Ormus* shows.[2]
He makes the Figs our mouths to meet;
And throws the Melons at our feet.
But Apples plants of such a price,[3]
No Tree could ever bear them twice.
With Cedars, chosen by his hand,[4]
From *Lebanon*, he stores the Land.
And makes the hollow Seas, that roar,
Proclaim the Ambergris on shore.[5]
He cast (of which we rather boast)
The Gospel's Pearl upon our Coast.[6]
And in these Rocks for us did frame
A Temple, where to sound his Name.
Oh let our voice his Praise exalt,
Till it arrive at Heaven's Vault:
Which thence (perhaps) rebounding, may
Echo beyond the *Mexique Bay*.'
Thus sung they, in the *English* boat,
An holy and a cheerful Note,
And all the way, to guide their Chime,
With falling Oars they kept the time.

Notes

BERMUDAS

[1] *Prelates* bishops or other high officers of the established church, from whom these Protestant singers have fled.

[2] *Ormus* Hormuz, a fabulously wealthy city on the Persian Gulf.

[3] *Apples* pineapples, which must be replanted each year.

[4] *Cedars* Lebanon cedars are symbolic of great stature and power in biblical writings (e.g., Ezekiel 31.3).

[5] *Ambergris* "A fragrant drug ... found on the seacoasts of several warm countries" (Johnson, quoting Ephraim Chambers's *Cyclopaedia*); the origin of the substance was then obscure, but many connected it correctly with whales.

[6] *Gospel's Pearl* perhaps the pearl of great price symbolic of Heaven (Matthew 14.46).

The Mower to the Glo-Worms[1] (1651–2?)

1

Ye living Lamps, by whose dear light
The Nightingale does sit so late,
And studying all the Summer-night,
Her matchless Songs does meditate;

2

Ye Country Comets, that portend[2]
No War, nor Prince's funeral,
Shining unto no higher end
Than to presage the Grass's fall;

3

Ye Glo-worms, whose officious Flame[3]
To wand'ring Mowers shows the way,
That in the Night have lost their aim,
And after foolish Fires do stray,[4]

4

Your courteous Lights in vain you waste,
Since *Juliana* here is come,
For She my Mind hath so displaced
That I shall never find my home.

An *Horatian* Ode upon *Cromwell's* Return from *Ireland*[1] (1650)

The forward Youth that would appear[2]
Must now forsake his *Muses* dear,
    Nor in the Shadows sing
    His Numbers languishing.[3]
'Tis time to leave the Books in dust,
And oil th' unused Armour's rust:
    Removing from the Wall
    The Corslet of the Hall.[4]

Notes

The Mower to the Glo-Worms

[1] *Glo-Worm* glow-worm, an insect that emits light, like a firefly.

[2] *Comets* were thought to be signs of dire events.

[3] *officious* kind.

[4] *foolish fires ignis fatuus*, delusive lights caused by marsh gases, will-o'-the-wisp.

An Horatian *Ode upon* Cromwell's *Return*

[1] Oliver Cromwell put down an Irish royalist rebellion against Parliamentary rule in 1649; he returned in 1650 to launch a similar campaign against the Scots, becoming at that time commander-in-chief of the Parliamentary army.

[2] *forward* "Warm; earnest" (Johnson); *appear* "to display oneself on the stage of action" (*OED*).

[3] *Numbers* verses.

So restless *Cromwell* could not cease
In the inglorious Art of Peace,
But through advent'rous War
Urgèd his active Star.[5]
And, like the three-forked Lightning, first
Breaking the Clouds where it was nursed,
Did thorough his own Side[6]
His fiery way divide.
For 'tis all one to Courage high
The Emulous or Enemy;
And with such to enclose[7]
Is more than to oppose.
Then burning through the Air he went,
And Palaces and Temples rent:
And *Cæsar's* head at last[8]
Did through his Laurels blast.[9]
'Tis Madness to resist or blame
The force of angry Heaven's flame:
And, if we would speak true,
Much to the Man is due.
Who, from his private Gardens, where
He lived reservèd and austere,
As if his highest plot
To plant the Bergamot,[10]
Could by industrious Valour climb
To ruin the great Work of Time,
And cast the Kingdom old
Into another Mould.
Though Justice against Fate complain,
And plead the ancient Rights in vain:
But those do hold or break
As Men are strong or weak.
Nature that hateth emptiness,[11]
Allows of penetration less:[12]
And therefore must make room
Where greater Spirits come.
What Field of all the Civil Wars,
Where his were not the deepest Scars?
And *Hampton* shows what part[13]
He had of wiser Art.

Notes

[4] *Corslet* "A light armour for the forepart of the body" (Johnson).

[5] *Star* "Configuration of the planets supposed to influence fortune" (Johnson).

[6] *thorough* through; *Side* "Party; interest; faction; sect" (Johnson). The metaphor describes Cromwell breaking out to lead his party.

[7] *enclose* limit (the rise or career).

[8] *Caesar* the monarch, Charles I.

[9] *Laurels* bay laurel was associated with kings and supposed to prevent lightning strikes (Pliny, *Natural History* 2.56).

[10] *Bergamot* a kind of pear.

[11] *Nature … hateth emptiness* nature abhors a vacuum, proverbial axiom of classical physics.

[12] *penetration* "a supposed or conceived occupation of the same space by two bodies at the same time" (*OED*).

[13] *Hampton* the palace where Charles I was under arrest in 1647 until his escape to Carisbrooke on the Isle of Wight, where he was recaptured. Marvell represents the events as part of Cromwell's plan to eliminate the king.

Where, twining subtle fears with hope,[14]
He wove a Net of such a scope,
That *Charles* himself might chase
To *Caresbrook*'s narrow case.
That thence the *Royal Actor* born
The *Tragic Scaffold* might adorn:
While round the armèd Bands
Did clap their bloody hands.
He nothing common did or mean
Upon that memorable Scene:
But with his keener Eye
The Axe's edge did try:[15]
Nor called the *Gods* with vulgar spite
To vindicate his helpless Right,
But bowed his comely Head,
Down as upon a Bed.
This was that memorable Hour
Which first assured the forcèd Pow'r.
So when they did design
The *Capitol's* first Line,[16]
A bleeding Head where they begun,
Did fright the Architects to run;
And yet in that the *State*
Foresaw its happy Fate.
And now the *Irish* are ashamed
To see themselves in one Year tamed:
So much one Man can do,
That does both act and know.
They can affirm his Praises best,
And have, though overcome, confessed
How good he is, how just,
And fit for highest Trust:
Nor yet grown stiffer with Command,
But still in the *Republic*'s hand:
How fit he is to sway
That can so well obey.
He to the *Common Feet* presents[17]
A *Kingdom*, for his first year's rents:
And, what he may, forbears
His Fame to make it theirs:
And has his Sword and Spoils ungirt,
To lay them at the *Public*'s skirt.
So when the Falcon high
Falls heavy from the Sky,

Notes

[14] *subtle* "Nice; fine; delicate; not coarse" (Johnson).

[15] *try* "To act on as a test" (Johnson), but also to experience.

[16] *Capitol* the Roman building of state, begun around 500 BCE and associated with the rise of the Roman republic; a bloody head found during the excavation was interpreted by soothsayers to foretell that Rome would be head of the world (Livy 1.55.6; Pliny, *Natural History* 28.15).

[17] *Common Feet* sometimes emended to *Common's Feet*.

She, having killed, no more does search,
But on the next green Bough to perch;
Where, when he first does lure,[18]
The Falc'ner has her sure.
What may not then our *Isle* presume
While Victory his Crest does plume?
What may not others fear
If thus he crown each year?
A *Cæsar* he ere long to *Gaul*,[19]
To *Italy* an *Hannibal*,[20]
And to all States not free
Shall *Climacteric* be.[21]
The *Pict* no shelter now shall find[22]
Within his party-coloured Mind;
But from this Valour sad
Shrink underneath the Plaid:
Happy if in the tufted brake[23]
The *English Hunter* him mistake;
Nor lay his Hounds in near
The *Caledonian* Deer.[24]
But thou the War's and Fortune's Son
March indefatigably on;
And for the last effect
Still keep thy Sword erect:
Besides the force it has to fright[25]
The Spirits of the shady Night,
The same *Arts* that did *gain*
A *Pow'r* must it *maintain*.

The Garden (1651–2?)

I

How vainly men themselves amaze
To win the Palm, the Oak, or Bays;[1]
And their uncessant Labours see
Crowned from some single Herb or Tree,
Whose short and narrow vergèd Shade
Does prudently their Toils upbraid;

Notes

[18] *lure* "To call hawks" (Johnson).

[19] *Gaul* France, conquered by Julius Caesar.

[20] *Hannibal* the Carthaginian general who conquered much of the Italian peninsula.

[21] *Climacteric* from *climacter*, "A certain space of time or progression of years, which is supposed to end in a critical or dangerous time" (Johnson).

[22] *Pict* British ancestors of the Scots; the Roman name means "painted" or "parti-colored"; Marvell puns on "party."

[23] *brake* "A thicket of brambles or of thorns" (Johnson).

[24] *Caledonian* Scottish.

[25] *the force it has to fright* because of the cross on the hilt.

The Garden

[1] *Palm, Oak, Bays* leaves used in crowns given for excellence in various spheres of activity: military, civic, and literary.

While all Flow'rs and all Trees do close
To weave the Garlands of repose.

2

Fair Quiet, have I found thee here,
And Innocence thy Sister dear!
Mistaken long, I sought you then
In busy Companies of Men.
Your sacred Plants, if here below,
Only among the Plants will grow.
Society is all but rude,
To this delicious Solitude.[2]

3

No white nor red was ever seen[3]
So am'rous as this lovely green.
Fond Lovers, cruel as their Flame,
Cut in these Trees their Mistress' name.
Little, Alas, they know, or heed,
How far these Beauties Hers exceed!
Fair Trees! wheres'e'er your barks I wound,
No Name shall but your own be found.

4

When we have run our Passion's heat,
Love hither makes his best retreat.
The *Gods*, that mortal Beauty chase,
Still in a Tree did end their race.
Apollo hunted *Daphne* so,[4]
Only that She might Laurel grow.
And *Pan* did after *Syrinx* speed,[5]
Not as a Nymph, but for a Reed.

5

What wond'rous Life is this I lead!
Ripe Apples drop about my head;
The Luscious Clusters of the Vine
Upon my Mouth do crush their Wine;
The Nectarine, and curious Peach,
Into my hands themselves do reach;

Notes

2 *To* compared with.

3 *white nor red* the colors of a lady's face in the traditional blazon, or laudatory description.

4 *Daphne* escaped being ravished by Apollo by being changed into a laurel, which the god adopted as his sacred tree (Ovid, *Metamorphoses* 1.452–567).

5 *Syrinx* escaped Pan by metamorphosis into marsh reeds, of which the god made his famous pipes (Ovid, *Metamorphoses* 1.689–712).

Stumbling on Melons, as I pass,
Ensnared with Flow'rs, I fall on Grass.

6

Meanwhile the Mind, from pleasure less,
Withdraws into its happiness:
The Mind, that Ocean where each kind
Does straight its own resemblance find;[6]
Yet it creates, transcending these,
Far other Worlds, and other Seas;
Annihilating all that's made[7]
To a green Thought in a green Shade.

7

Here at the Fountain's sliding foot,
Or at some Fruit-tree's mossy root,
Casting the Body's Vest aside,[8]
My Soul into the boughs does glide:
There like a Bird it sits, and sings,
Then whets, and combs its silver Wings;
And, till prepared for longer flight,
Waves in its Plumes the various Light.

8

Such was that happy Garden-state,
While Man there walked without a Mate:
After a Place so pure, and sweet,
What other Help could yet be meet![9]
But 'twas beyond a Mortal's share
To wander solitary there:
Two Paradises 'twere in one
To live in Paradise alone.

9

How well the skilful Gard'ner drew
Of flow'rs and herbs this Dial new;[10]
Where from above the milder Sun
Does through a fragrant Zodiac run;
And, as it works, th' industrious Bee[11]
Computes its time as well as we.
How could such sweet and wholesome Hours
Be reckoned but with herbs and flow'rs!

Notes

[6] In his *Pseudodoxia Epidemica* Sir Thomas Browne exploded the myth that "all Animals in the land are in their kind in the Sea" (3.24).

[7] *Annihilate* "To destroy, so as to make the thing otherwise than it was" (Johnson), but the lines are marvelously ambiguous.

[8] *Body's vest* corporeality as clothing.

[9] *Help... meet* plays on the description of Eve as "help meet [appropriate] for him" (Genesis 2.20).

[10] *Dial* sundial.

[11] *Bee Computes its time* a reference to the punctual behavior of bees, as described by Virgil, for example (*Georgics* 4.185–90).

On a Drop of Dew (1651–2?)

See how the Orient Dew,
Shed from the Bosom of the Morn
Into the blowing Roses,
Yet careless of its Mansion new;
For the clear Region where 'twas born
Round in its self incloses:
And in its little Globe's Extent,
Frames as it can its native Element.
How it the purple flow'r does slight,
Scarce touching where it lies,
But gazing back upon the Skies,
Shines with a mournful Light;
Like its own Tear,
Because so long divided from the Sphere.
Restless it rolls and unsecure,
Trembling lest it grow impure:
Till the warm Sun pity its Pain,
And to the Skies exhale it back again.
So the Soul, that Drop, that Ray
Of the clear Fountain of Eternal Day,
Could it within the human flow'r be seen,
Rememb'ring still its former height,
Shuns the swart leaves and blossoms green;
And, recollecting its own Light,
Does, in its pure and circling thoughts, express
The greater Heaven in an Heaven less.
In how coy a Figure wound,
Every way it turns away:
So the World excluding round,
Yet receiving in the Day.
Dark beneath, but bright above:
Here disdaining, there in Love.
How loose and easy hence to go:
How girt and ready to ascend.
Moving but on a point below,
It all about does upwards bend.
Such did the Manna's sacred Dew distil;[1]
White, and entire, though congealèd and chill.
Congealed on Earth: but does, dissolving, run
Into the Glories of th' Almighty Sun.

Notes

On a Drop of Dew

[1] *Manna's sacred Dew* the food that fell miraculously from the heavens to feed the Israelites during their sojourn in the desert (Exodus 16.13–15).

To *his* Coy Mistress (c.1645)

Had we but World enough, and Time,
This coyness Lady were no crime.
We would sit down, and think which way
To walk, and pass our long Love's Day.
Thou by the *Indian Ganges'* side
Should'st Rubies find: I by the Tide
Of *Humber* would complain. I would[1]
Love you ten years before the Flood:[2]
And you should if you please refuse
Till the Conversion of the *Jews*.
My vegetable Love should grow
Vaster than Empires, and more slow.
An hundred years should go to praise
Thine Eyes, and on thy Forehead Gaze.
Two hundred to adore each Breast:
But thirty thousand to the rest.
An Age at least to every part,
And the last Age should show your Heart.
For Lady you deserve this State;
Nor would I love at lower rate.
　But at my back I always hear
Time's wingèd Chariot hurrying near:
And yonder all before us lie
Deserts of vast Eternity.
Thy Beauty shall no more be found;
Nor, in thy marble Vault, shall sound
My echoing Song: then Worms shall try
That long preserved Virginity:
And your quaint Honour turn to dust;
And into ashes all my Lust.
The Grave's a fine and private place,
But none I think do there embrace.
　Now therefore, while the youthful glew[3]
Sits on thy skin like morning dew,
And while thy willing Soul transpires[4]
At every pore with instant Fires,
Now let us sport us while we may;
And now, like am'rous birds of prey,
Rather at once our Time devour,
Than languish in his slow-chapped pow'r.[5]

Notes

To *his* Coy Mistress

[1] *Humber* a river in Yorkshire, England, on the northern bank of which is Marvell's native city of Hull; from the Ganges to the Humber was reckoned about the extent of the classical world.

[2] *ten years before the Flood ... Conversion of the Jews* virtually all of biblical time, from Genesis to Revelation.

[3] *glew* an old form of *glow*.

[4] *transpire* "To be emitted by insensible vapour" (Johnson).

[5] *slow-chapped* (eating) with slowly moving jaws.

Let us roll all our Strength, and all
Our sweetness, up into one Ball:
And tear our Pleasures with rough strife,
Thorough the Iron gates of Life.
Thus, though we cannot make our Sun
Stand still, yet we will make him run.

Margaret Cavendish, Duchess of Newcastle (1623–1673)

Cavendish was one of the most prolific women writers in the seventeenth century, and for a long time she was one of the very few given any substantial recognition. However, she has been condemned at least as often as praised, and Virginia Woolf's characterization of her as a "giant cucumber," filling and crowding the literary garden, has stuck. More recent commentators have perceived that Cavendish self-protectively portrayed herself as an impulsive, distracted wit. Her productivity is incontrovertible. In addition to poems and plays, she published *Orations of Divers Sorts* (1662), *The Description of a New World, called The Blazing World* (1666), *Observations upon Experimental Philosophy* (1666), *The Life of William Cavendish* (1667), and several other books of literature, philosophy, and science.

The text of "Poets have most Pleasure in this Life" is based on Cavendish's first publication, *Poems and Fancies* (1653), which has recently been reprinted by the Brown University Women Writers Project. The extract from *The Blazing World* is based on the second edition (1668). Kate Lilley has edited a selection of Cavendish's prose, *The Blazing World and Other Writings* (Penguin, 1994). Anna Battigelli's *Margaret Cavendish and the Exiles of the Mind* (University of Kentucky Press, 1998), Lisa T. Sarasohn's *The Natural Philosophy of Margaret Cavendish* (Johns Hopkins University Press, 2010), and Lisa Walters's *Margaret Cavendish: Gender, Science and Politics* (Cambridge University Press, 2014) are three of the many recent studies that have revised traditional views of Cavendish.

from *Poems and Fancies* (1653)

Poets have most Pleasure in this Life

Nature most *Pleasure* doth to *Poets* give;
If *Pleasures* in *Variety* do live.
There every *Sense* by *Fancy* new is fed,
Which *Fancy* in a *Torrent Brain* is bred.
Contrary is to all that's born on *Earth*,
For Fancy is delighted most at's *Birth*.
Whatever else is born, with *Pain* comes forth,
But *Fancy* needs not time to make it grow,
Hath neither *Beauty*, *Strength* nor perfect *Growth* –
Those *Brain*-like *Gods*, from whence all things do flow.

Where *Gardens* are, them *Paradise* we call,
Forbidden Fruits, which tempt *young Lovers* all,
Grow on the *Trees*, which in the midst is placed
Beauty, on the other *Desire* vast.
The *Devil self-conceit* full craftily
Did take the *Serpent's* shape of *Flattery*,
For to deceive the *Female Sex* thereby;

Which made was only of *Inconstancy*.
The *Male high Credence*, which doth relax[1]
To any thing, the *Female Sex* will ask.
Two *Rivers* round this *Garden* run about,
The one is *Confidence*, the other *Doubt*.
Every *Bank* is set with *Fancy's Flowers*,
Wit rains upon them fine refreshing *Showers*.
Truth was the *Owner* of this place,
But *Ignorance* this *Garden* out did raze.
Then from this *Garden*, to a *Forest* goes,
Where many *Cedars* of high *Knowledge* grows;
Oaks of strong *Judgement*, *Hazel Wits*, which *Tree*
Bears *Nuts* full of *Conceits*,[2] when cracked they be.
And smooth-Tongued *Beech*, kind-hearted *Willow* bows,
And yields to all that *Honesty* allows.
Here *Birds* of *Eloquence* do sit, and sing,
Build *Nests*, *Logic* to lay *Reasons* in.
Some *Birds* of *Sophistry* till hatched there lie.
Winged with false *Principles* away they fly.
Here doth the *Poet* hawk, hunt, run a Race,
Until he weary grows, then leaves this *Place*.

Then goes a *Fishing* to a *River's* side,
Whose *Waters* clear, where *Fancy* flows high *Tide*:
Angles with *Wit*, to catch the *Fish* of *Fame*,
To feed his *Memory*, and preserve his *Name*:
And of *Ambition* builds *Ships* swift, and strong,
Sails of *Imaginations* drive her on.
With *Winds* of several *Praises* fills them full,
Swims on the salt *Sea Brain*, round the *World's Skull*,
Mariners' Thoughts labour both day, and night,
For to avoid a *Ship-wrack* of *dislike*.
These *Ships* are often cast upon the *Sands* of *Spite*,
And *Rocks* of Malice sometimes split them quite.
But *Merchant Poets*, and *Ship-Master Mind*,
Do compass take some unknown *Land* to find.

from *The Description of a New World, called The Blazing World* (1666)

A Merchant travelling into a foreign Country, fell extremely in Love with a young Lady; but being a stranger in that Nation, and beneath her both in Birth and Wealth, he could have but little hopes of obtaining his desire; however his Love growing more and more vehement upon him, even to the slighting of all difficulties, he resolved at last to Steal her away; which he had the better opportunity to do, because her Father's house was not far from the Sea, and she often using to gather shells upon the shore, accompanied not with above two or three of her servants, it encouraged him the more

Notes

Poets have most Pleasure in this Life

[1] *Credence* trust, faith; *relax* remit; bend.

[2] *Conceits* metaphors and similes.

to execute his design. Thus coming one time with a little light Vessel, not unlike a Packet-boat, manned with some few Seamen, and well victualled, for fear of some accidents, which might perhaps retard their journey, to the place where she used to repair; he forced her away: But when he fancied himself the happiest man of the World, he proved to be the most unfortunate; for Heaven frowning at his Theft, raised such a Tempest, as they knew not what to do, or whither to steer their course; so that the Vessel, both by its own lightness, and the violent motion of the Wind, was carried as swift as an Arrow out of a Bow, towards the North-pole, and in a short time reached the Icy Sea, where the wind forced it amongst huge pieces of Ice; but being little, and light, it did by the assistance and favour of the gods to this virtuous Lady, so turn and wind through those precipices, as if it had been guided by some experienced Pilot, and skilful Mariner: But alas! Those few men which were in it, not knowing whither they went, nor what was to be done in so strange an Adventure, and not being provided for so cold a Voyage, were all frozen to death; the young Lady only, by the light of her Beauty, the heat of her Youth, and Protection of the Gods, remaining alive: Neither was it a wonder that the men did freeze to death; for they were not only driven to the very end or point of the Pole of that World, but even to another Pole of another World, which joined close to it; so that the cold having a double strength at the conjunction of those two Poles, was insupportable: At last, the Boat still passing on, was forced into another World; for it is impossible to round this World's Globe from Pole to Pole, so as we do from East to West; because the Poles of the other World, joining to the Poles of this, do not allow any further passage to surround[1] the World that way; but if anyone arrives to either of these Poles, he is either forced to return, or to enter into another World: and lest you should scruple at it,[2] and think, if it were thus, those that live at the Poles would either see two Suns at one time, or else they would never want the Sun's light for six months together, as it is commonly believed: You must know that each of these Worlds having its own Sun to enlighten it, they move each one in their peculiar Circles; which motion is so just and exact, that neither can hinder or obstruct the other; for they do not exceed their Tropics:[3] and although they should meet, yet we in this World cannot so well perceive them, by reason of the brightness of our Sun, which being nearer to us, obstructs the splendor of the Sun of the other world, they being too far off to be discerned by our optic perception, except we use very good telescopes; by which, skilful Astronomers have often observed two or three Suns at once.

But to return to the wandering Boat, and the distressed Lady; she seeing all the men dead, found small comfort in life; their Bodies which were preserved all that while from putrefaction and stench, by the extremity of cold, began now to thaw, and corrupt; whereupon she having not strength enough to fling them overboard, was forced to remove out of her small Cabin, upon the deck, to avoid that nauseous smell; and finding the Boat swim between two plains of Ice, as a stream that runs betwixt two shores, at last perceived land, but covered all with Snow: from which came, walking upon the Ice, strange Creatures, in shape like Bears, only they went upright as men; those Creatures coming near the Boat, catched hold of it with their Paws, that served them instead of hands; some two or three of them entered first; and when they came out, the rest went in one after another; at last having viewed and observed all that was in the Boat, they spake to each other in a language which the Lady did not understand; and having carried her out of the Boat, sunk it, together with the dead men.

Notes

FROM *THE DESCRIPTION OF A NEW WORLD*

[1] *surround* circumnavigate.

[2] *scruple at it* doubt it.

[3] *they do not exceed their Tropics* the suns' sidereal paths run close to the poles of their respective planets.

The Lady now finding herself in so strange a place, and amongst such wonderful[4] kind of Creatures, was extremely strucken with fear, and could entertain no other Thoughts, but that every moment her life was to be a sacrifice to their cruelty; but those Bear like Creatures, how terrible soever they appeared to her sight, yet were they so far from exercising any cruelty upon her, that rather they showed her all civility and kindness imaginable; for she being not able to go upon the Ice, by reason of its slipperiness, they took her up in their rough arms, and carried her into their City, where instead of Houses, they had Caves underground; and as soon as they entered the City, both Males and Females, young and old, flocked together to see this Lady, holding up their Paws in admiration; at last having brought her into a certain large and spacious Cave, which they intended for her reception, they left her to the custody of the Females, who entertained her with all kindness and respect, and gave her such victuals as they used to eat; but seeing her Constitution neither agreed with the temper of that Climate, nor their Diet, they were resolved to carry her into another Island of a warmer temper; in which were men like Foxes, only walking in an upright shape, who received their neighbours the Bear-men with great civility and Courtship, very much admiring this beauteous Lady; and having discoursed some while together, agreed at last to make her a Present to the Emperor of their World; to which end, after she had made some short stay in the same place, they brought her cross that Island to a large River, whose stream runs smooth and clear, like Crystal; in which were numerous Boats, much like our Fox-traps; in one whereof she was carried, some of the Bear- and Fox-men waiting on her; and as soon as they had crossed the River, they came into an Island where there were Men which had heads, beaks, and feathers, like wild-Geese, only they went in an upright shape, like the Bear-men and Fox-men: their rumps they carried between their legs; their wings were of the same length with their bodies, and their tails of an indifferent size, trailing after them like a Lady's Garment; and after the Bear- and Fox-men had declared their intention and design to their Neighbours, the Geese- or Bird-men, some of them joined to the rest, and attended the Lady through that Island, till they came to another great and large River; where there was a preparation made of many Boats, much like Birds' nests, only of a bigger size; and having crossed that River, they arrived into another Island, which was of a pleasant and mild temper, full of Woods and the Inhabitants thereof were *Satyrs*, who received both the Bear- Fox- and Bird-men, with all respect and civility; and after some conferences (for they all understood each other's language) some chief of the *Satyrs* joining to them, accompanied the lady out of that Island to another River, wherein were many handsome and commodious Barges; and having crossed that River, they entered into a large and spacious Kingdom, the men whereof were of a Grass-Green Complexion, who entertained them very kindly, and provided all conveniences for their further voyage: hitherto they had only crossed Rivers, but now they could not avoid the open Seas any longer; wherefore they made their Ships and tacklings ready to sail over into the Island, where the Emperor of the Blazing-world (for so it was called) kept his residence. Very good Navigators they were; and though they had no knowledge of the Loadstone, or Needle, or pendulous Watches[5] yet (which was as serviceable to them) they had subtle observations, and great practice; in so much that they could not only tell the depth of the Sea in every place, but where there were shelves of Sand, Rocks, and other obstructions

Notes

[4] *wonderful* strange.

[5] *Loadstone, or Needle, or pendulous Watches* navigational devices; the first two for determining direction, the last for finding longitude.

to be avoided by skilful and experienced Seamen: Besides, they were excellent Augurers, which skill they counted more necessary and beneficial than the use of Compasses, Cards,[6] Watches, and the like; but, above the rest, they had an extraordinary Art, much to be taken notice of by Experimental Philosophers, and that was a certain Engine, which would draw in a great quantity of Air, and shoot forth Wind with a great force; this Engine in a calm, they placed behind their Ships, and in a storm, before; for it served against the raging waves, like Cannons against an hostile Army, or besieged Town; it would batter and beat the waves in pieces, were they as high as Steeples; and as soon as a breach was made, they forced their passage through, in spite even of the most furious wind, using two of those Engines at every Ship, one before, to beat off the waves, and another behind to drive it on; so that the artificial wind had the better of the natural; for, it had a greater advantage of the waves, than the natural of the Ships: the natural being above the face of the Water, could not without a downright motion enter or press into the Ships; whereas the artificial with a sideward-motion, did pierce into the bowels of the Waves: Moreover, it is to be observed, that in a great Tempest they would join their Ships in battle-array: and when they feared Wind and Waves would be too strong for them, if they divided their Ships; they joined as many together as the compass or advantage of the places of the Liquid Element would give them leave. For, their Ships were so ingeniously contrived, that they could fasten them together as close as a Honey-comb, without waste of place; and being thus united, no Wind nor Waves were able to separate them. The Emperor's Ships, were all of Gold; but the Merchants' and Skippers', of Leather; the Golden Ships were not much heavier than ours of Wood, by reason they were neatly made, and required not such thickness: neither were they troubled with Pitch, Tar, Pumps, Guns, and the like, which make our Wooden Ships very heavy; for though they were not all of a piece, yet they were so well soldered, that there was no fear of Leaks, Chinks, or Clefts; and as for Guns, there was no use of them, because they had no other enemies but the Winds: But the Leather Ships were not altogether so sure, although much lighter; besides, they were pitched to keep out Water.

Having thus prepared, and ordered their Navy, they went on in despite of Calm or Storm: And though the Lady at first fancied herself in a very sad condition, and her mind was much tormented with doubts and fears, not knowing whether this strange Adventure would tend to her safety or destruction; yet she being withal of a generous spirit, and ready wit, considering what dangers she had passed, and finding those sorts of men civil and diligent attendants to her, took courage, and endeavoured to learn their language; which after she had obtained so far, that partly by some words and signs she was able to apprehend their meaning, she was so far from being afraid of them, that she thought herself not only safe, but very happy in their company: By which we may see, that Novelty discomposes the mind, but acquaintance settles it in peace and tranquillity. At last, having passed by several rich Islands and Kingdoms, they went towards *Paradise*, which was the seat of the Emperor; and coming in sight of it, rejoiced very much; the Lady at first could perceive nothing but high Rocks, which seemed to touch the Skies; and although they appeared not of an equal higth, yet they seemed to be all one piece, without partitions: but at last drawing nearer, she perceived a cleft, which was a part of those Rocks, out of which she spied coming forth a great

Notes

[6] *Cards* "The circular piece of stiff paper on which the 32 points are marked in the mariner's compass" (*OED*).

number of Boats, which afar off showed like a company of Ants, marching one after another; the Boats appeared like the holes or partitions in a Honeycomb, and when joined together, stood as close; the men were of several Complexions but none like any of our World; and when both the Boats and Ships met, they saluted and spake to each other very courteously; for there was but one language in all that World: nor no more but one Emperor, to whom they all submitted with the greatest duty and obedience, which made them live in a continued Peace and Happiness; not acquainted with Foreign Wars, or Home-bred Insurrections. The Lady now being arrived at this place, was carried out of her Ship into one of those Boats, and conveyed through the same passage (for there was no other) into that part of the World where the Emperor did reside; which part was very pleasant, and of a mild temper: Within itself it was divided by a great number of vast and large Rivers, all ebbing and flowing, into several Islands of unequal distance from each other, which in most parts were as pleasant, healthful, rich, and fruitful, as Nature could make them; and, as I mentioned before, secure from all Foreign Invasions, by reason there was but one way to enter, and that like a Labyrinth, so winding and turning among the Rocks, that no other Vessels but small Boats, could pass, carrying not above three passengers at a time: On each side all along this narrow and winding River, there were several Cities, some of Marble, some of Alabaster, some of Agate, some of Amber, some of Coral, and some of other precious materials not known in our world; all which after the Lady had passed, she came to the Imperial City, named *Paradise*, which appeared in form like several Islands; for, Rivers did run betwixt every street, which together with the Bridges, whereof there was a great number, were all paved. The City itself was built of Gold; and their Architectures were noble, stately, and magnificent, not like our Modern, but like those in the *Romans'* time; for our Modern Buildings are like those Houses which Children use to make of Cards, one story above another, fitter for Birds, than Men; but theirs were more Large, and Broad, than high; the highest of them did not exceed two stories, besides those rooms that were underground, as Cellars, and other Offices. The Emperor's Palace stood upon an indifferent ascent[7] from the Imperial City; at the top of which ascent was a broad Arch, supported by several Pillars, which went round the Palace, and contained four of our English miles in compass: within the Arch stood the Emperor's Guard, which consisted of several sorts of Men; at every half mile, was a Gate to enter, and every Gate was of a different fashion; the first, which allowed a passage from the Imperial City into the Palace, had on either hand a Cloister, the outward part whereof stood upon Arches sustained by Pillars, but the inner part was close:[8] Being entered through the Gate, the Palace itself appeared in its middle like the Aisle of a Church, a mile and a half long, and half a mile broad; the roof of it was all Arched, and rested upon Pillars, so artificially[9] placed that a stranger would lose himself therein without a Guide; at the extreme sides, that is, between the outward and inward part of the Cloister, were Lodgings for Attendants; and in the midst of the Palace, the Emperor's own Rooms; whose Lights[10] were placed at the top of every one, because of the heat of the Sun: the Emperor's apartment for State was no more enclosed than the rest; only an Imperial Throne was in every apartment, of which the several adornments could not be perceived until one entered, because the Pillars were so just opposite to one another, that all the adornments could not be seen at once. The first part of the Palace was, as the Imperial City, all of Gold; and when it came to the Emperor's

Notes

7 *indifferent* "Of medium or moderate extent" (*OED*).

8 *close* enclosed.

9 *artificially* artfully.

10 *Lights* openings or windows.

apartment, it was so rich with Diamonds, Pearls, Rubies, and the like precious Stones, that it surpasses my skill to enumerate them all. Amongst the rest, the Imperial Room of State appeared most magnificent; it was paved with green Diamonds (for there are in that World Diamonds of all Colours) so artificially, as it seemed but of one piece; the Pillars were set with Diamonds so close, and in such a manner, that they appeared most Glorious to the sight; between every Pillar was a Bow or Arch of a certain sort of Diamonds, the like whereof our World does not afford; which being placed in every one of the Arches in several rows, seemed just like so many Rainbows of several different colours. The roof of the Arches was of blue diamonds, and in the midst thereof was a Carbuncle,[11] which represented the Sun; and the Rising and Setting-Sun at the East and West-side of the Room were made of Rubies. Out of this Room there was a passage into the Emperor's Bed-Chamber the Walls whereof were of Jet, and the Floor of black Marble; the Roof was of Mother of pearl, where the Moon and Blazing-Stars were represented by white Diamonds, and his Bed was made of Diamonds and Carbuncles.

No sooner was the lady brought before the Emperor, but he conceived her to be some Goddess, and offered to worship her; which she refused, telling him (for by that time she had pretty well learned their Language) that although she came out of another world, yet was she but a mortal. At which the Emperor rejoicing, made her his Wife, and gave her an absolute power to rule and govern all that World as she pleased. But her subjects, who could hardly be persuaded to believe her mortal, tendered her all the Veneration and Worship due to a Deity.

Her Accoutrement after she was made Empress, was as followeth: On her head she wore a Cap of Pearl, and a Half-moon of Diamonds just before it; on the top of her Crown came spreading over a broad Carbuncle, cut in the form of the Sun; her Coat was of Pearl, mixed with blue Diamonds, and fringed with red ones; her Buskins and Sandals were of green Diamonds: In her left hand she held a Buckler, to signify the Defence of her Dominions; which Buckler was made of that sort of Diamond as had several different Colours; and being cut and made in the form of an Arch, showed like a Rainbow; In her right hand she carried a Spear made of white Diamond, cut like the tail of a Blazing-Star, which signified that she was ready to assault those that proved her Enemies.

None was allowed to use or wear Gold but those of the Imperial Race, which were the only Nobles of the State; nor durst any one wear Jewels but the Emperor, the Empress, and their Eldest Son; notwithstanding that they had an infinite quantity both of Gold and precious Stones in that World; for they had larger extents of Gold, than our *Arabian* Sands; their precious Stones were rocks, and their Diamonds of several Colours; they used no Coin, but all their Traffic was by exchange of several Commodities.

Their Priests and Governors were Princes of the Imperial Blood, and made Eunuchs for that purpose; and as for the ordinary sort of men in that part of the World where the Emperor resided, they were of several Complexions; not white, black, tawny, olive- or ash-coloured; but some appeared of an Azure, some of a deep Purple, some of Grass-green, some of a Scarlet, some of an Orange-colour, &c. Which Colours and Complexions, whether they were made by the bare reflection of light, without the assistance of small particles; or by the help of well-ranged and

Notes

11 *Carbuncle* "A jewel shining in the dark, like a lighted coal or candle" (Johnson).

ordered Atoms; or by a continual agitation of little Globules, or some pressing and reacting motion, I am not able to determine. The rest of the Inhabitants of that World, were men of several different sorts, shapes, figures, dispositions, and humours, as I have already made mention, heretofore; some were Bear-men, some Worm-men, some Fish- or Mer-men; otherwise called Sirens, some Bird-men, some Fly-men, some Ant-men, some Geese-men, some Spider-men, some Lice-men, some Fox-men, some Ape-men, some Jackdaw-men, some Magpie-men, some Parrot-men, some Satyrs, some Giants, and many more, which I cannot all remember; and of these several sorts of men, each followed such a profession as was most proper for the nature of their Species, which the Empress encouraged them in, especially those that had applied themselves to the study of several Arts and Sciences; for they were as ingenious and witty in the invention of profitable and useful Arts, as we are in our world, nay, more; and to that end she erected Schools, and founded several Societies. The Bear-men were to be her Experimental Philosophers, the Bird-men her Astronomers, the Fly- Worm- and Fish-men her Natural Philosophers, the Ape-men her Chemists, the Satyrs her Galenical Physicians,[12] the Fox-men her Politicians, the Spider- and Lice-men her mathematicians, the Jackdaw Magpie- and Parrot-men her Orators and Logicians, the Giants her Architects, &c. But before all things, she having got a Sovereign power from the Emperor over all the World, desired to be informed both of the manner of their Religion and Government; and to that end, she called the Priests and Statesmen, to give her an account of either. Of the Statesmen she enquired, first, Why had they so few Laws? To which they answered, That many Laws made many Divisions, which most commonly did breed Factions, and at last break out into open Wars. Next, she asked, Why they preferred the Monarchical form of Government before any other? They answered, That as it was natural for one Body to have but one Head, so it was also natural for a Politic body to have but one Governor; and that a Commonwealth, which had many Governors was like a Monster with many Heads. Besides, said they, Monarchy is a divine form of Government, and agrees most with our Religion: For as there is but one God, whom we all unanimously worship and adore with one Faith; so we are resolved to have but one Emperor, to whom we all submit with one obedience.

Then the Empress seeing that the several sorts of her Subjects had each their Churches apart, asked the Priests, whether they were of several Religions? They answered her Majesty, That there was no more but one Religion in all that World, nor no diversity of opinions in that same Religion; for though there were several sorts of men, yet had they all but one opinion concerning the Worship and Adoration of God. The Empress asked them, Whether they were Jews, Turks, or Christians? We do not know, said they, what Religions those are; but we do all unanimously acknowledge, worship, and adore the Only, Omnipotent, and Eternal God, with all reverence, submission, and duty. Again, the Empress enquired, Whether they had several Forms of Worship? They answered, No: For our Devotion and Worship consists only in Prayers, which we frame according to our several Necessities, in Petitions, Humiliations, Thanksgiving, &c. Truly, replied the Empress, I thought you had been either Jews, or Turks, because I never perceived any Women in your Congregations: But what is the reason, you bar them from your religious Assemblies? It is not fit, said they, that Men

Notes

[12] *Galenical Physicians* doctors skilled in the adjustment of the four "humours" – blood, yellow bile, black bile, and phlegm.

and Women should be promiscuously together in time of Religious Worship; for their company hinders Devotion, and makes many, instead of praying to God, direct their Devotion to their Mistresses. But, asked the Empress, Have they no Congregation of their own, to perform the duties of Divine Worship, as well as Men? No, answered they; but they stay at home, and say their Prayers by themselves in their Closets. Then the Empress desired to know the reason why the Priests and Governors of their World were made Eunuchs? They answered, To keep them from Marriage: For Women and Children most commonly make disturbance both in Church and State. But, said she, Women and Children have no Employment in the Church or State. 'Tis true, answered they; but, although they are not admitted to public Employments, yet are they so prevalent with their Husbands and Parents, that many times by their importunate persuasions, they cause as much, nay, more mischief secretly, than if they had the management of public Affairs.

John Bunyan (1628–1688)

Bunyan's first child was born blind in 1650, and with his first wife he had three more children before her death in 1658. He remarried in 1659. During this emotional decade Bunyan underwent a period of spiritual doubt and conversion remarkable for its vicissitudes. *Grace Abounding* is the record of his tumultuous inner life during this period. It displays a concentration on the state of an individual soul and a striving for improvement that are startlingly intense. The pattern of achievement and temporary satisfaction followed by renewed awareness of inadequacy and corruption recurs with the frequency of waves in a tropical storm. Indeed, Bunyan's spiritual life is so tangible, that it seems to require the spiritual landscape of *Pilgrim's Progress* (1678). That later creation is Bunyan's most famous book and one of the most widely read and reprinted books in history.

Although Bunyan began publishing tracts in 1656, he prepared his longer works during his twelve or thirteen years of frequent imprisonment for illegal preaching. He was arrested shortly after the Restoration and refused to swear that he would not repeat his offense. *Grace Abounding* was first published in 1666; I follow this edition, ignoring the additions that Bunyan made in later printings. The late Roger Sharrock prepared an excellent edition of this work (Clarendon Press, 1962), and served as general editor of Bunyan's *Miscellaneous works*, 13 vols. (Clarendon Press, 1975–94).

from *Grace Abounding to the Chief of Sinners* (1666)

28. But upon a day, the good Providence of God did cast me to *Bedford*, to work on my calling; and in one of the streets of that town, I came where there was three or four poor women sitting at a door in the Sun, and talking about the things of God; and being now willing to hear them discourse, I drew near to hear what they said; for I was now a brisk talker also myself in the matters of Religion: but now *I* may say, *I heard, but I understood not*; for they were far above out of my reach, for their talk was about a new birth, the work of God on their hearts, also how they were convinced of their miserable state by nature: they talked how God had visited their souls with his love in the Lord Jesus, and with what words and promises they had been refreshed, comforted, and supported against the temptations of the Devil; moreover, they reasoned of the suggestions and temptations of Satan in particular, and told to each other by which they had been afflicted, and how they were borne up under his assaults: they also discoursed of their own wretchedness of heart, of their unbelief, and did contemn, slight, and abhor their own righteousness, as filthy, and insufficient to do them any good.

29. And methought they spake as if joy did make them speak: they spake with such pleasantness of Scripture language, and with such appearance of grace in all they said, that they were to me as if they had found a new world, as if they were people that dwelt alone, and were not to be reckoned amongst their Neighbours [Numbers 23.9].

30. At this I felt my own heart began to shake, as mistrusting my condition to be naught; for I saw that in all my thoughts about Religion and Salvation, the New birth

British Literature 1640–1789: An Anthology, Fourth Edition. Edited by Robert DeMaria, Jr.

did never enter into my mind, neither knew I the comfort of Word and Promise, nor the deceitfulness and treachery of my own wicked heart. As for secret thoughts, I took no notice of them; neither did I understand what Satan's temptations were, nor how they were to be withstood and resisted, *&c.*

31. Thus therefore when I had heard and considered what they said, I left them, and went about my employment again: but their talk and discourse went with me, also my heart would tarry with them, for I was greatly afflicted with their words, both because by them I was convinced that I wanted the true tokens of a truly godly man, and also because by them I was convinced of the happy and blessed condition of him that was such a one.

32. Therefore I should often make it my business to be going again and again into the company of these poor people; for I could not stay away; and the more I went amongst them, the more I did question my condition; and as I still do remember, presently I found two things within me, at which I did sometimes marvel (especially considering what a blind, ignorant, sordid, and ungodly Wretch but just before I was); the one was, a very great softness and tenderness of heart, which caused me to fall under the conviction of what by Scripture they asserted; and the other was, a great bending in my mind to a continual meditating on them, and on all other good things which at any time I heard or read of.

33. By these things my mind was now so turned, that it lay like a Horse-leech[1] at the vein, still crying out, 'Give, give' [Proverbs 30.15]. Yea, it was so fixed on Eternity, and on the things about the Kingdom of Heaven, that is, as far as I knew, though as yet God knows, I knew but little, that neither pleasures nor profits, nor persuasions, nor threats, could loosen it, or make it let go its hold; and though I may speak it with shame, yet it is in very deed a certain truth, it would then have been as difficult for me to have taken my mind from heaven to earth, as I have found it often since to get it again from earth to heaven. …

71. And now I was sorry that God had made me a man, for I feared I was a reprobate: I counted man, as unconverted, the most doleful of all the Creatures: Thus being afflicted and tossed about by my sad condition, I counted myself alone, and above the most of men unblessed. In this condition I went a great while, but when comforting time was come, I heard one preach a sermon upon those words in the *Song* (Song [of Solomon] 4.1), 'Behold thou art fair, My Love, behold, thou art fair'; but at that time he made these two words, 'My Love,' his chief and subject matter; from which after he had a little opened the text, he observed these several conclusions: 1. 'That the Church, and so every saved Soul, is Christ's Love, when loveless:' 2. 'Christ's Love without a cause:' 3. 'Christ's Love when hated of the world:' 4. 'Christ's Love when under temptation, and under desertion:' 5. 'Christ's Love from first to last.'

72. But *I* got nothing by what he said at present, only when he came to the application of the fourth particular, this was the word he said, 'If it be so, that the saved soul is Christ's love when under temptation and desertion; then poor tempted Soul, when thou art assaulted and afflicted with temptation, and the hidings of God's Face, yet think on these two words, MY LOVE, still.'

Notes

FROM *GRACE ABOUNDING TO THE CHIEF OF SINNERS*

[1] *Horse-leech* "A great leech that bites horses" (Johnson), applied for bloodletting, a common medical procedure of the time.

73. So as I was going home, these words came into my thoughts, and I well remember as they came in, I said thus in my heart, What shall I get by thinking on these two words? this thought had no sooner passed through my heart, but the words began to kindle in my Spirit, 'Thou art my Love, thou art my Love', twenty times together; and still as they ran thus in my mind, they waxed stronger and warmer, and began to make me look up; but being as yet between hope and fear, I still replied in my heart, 'But is it true too? but is it true?' at which, that sentence fell in upon me, 'He wist[2] not that it was true which was done unto him of the angel', Acts 12.9.

74. Then I began to give place to the Word, which with my power, did over and over make this joyful sound within my Soul, 'Thou art my Love, thou art my Love; and nothing shall separate thee from my love'; and with that Rom[ans] 8.39 came into my mind. Now was my heart filled full of comfort and hope, and now I could believe that my sins should be forgiven me; wherefore I said in my Soul with much gladness, 'Well, I would I had a pen and ink here; I would write this down before I go any further, for surely, I will not forget *this* forty years hence'; but alas! within less than forty days I began to question this all again. ...

214. At another time, though just before I was pretty well and savoury[3] in my spirit, yet suddenly there fell upon me a great cloud of darkness, which did so hide from me the things of God and Christ, that I was as if I had never seen or known them in my life; I was also so overrun in my Soul, with a senseless heartless frame of spirit, that I could not feel my soul to move or stir after grace and life by Christ; I was as if my loins were broken, or as if my hands and feet had been tied or bound with chains. At this time also I felt some weakness to seize my outward man,[4] which made still the other affliction the more heavy and uncomfortable.

215. After I had been in this condition some three or four days, as I was sitting by the fire, I suddenly felt this word to sound in my heart, 'I must go to Jesus'; at this my former darkness and atheism fled away, and the blessed things of heaven were set within my view; while I was on this sudden thus overtaken with surprise, 'Wife,' said I, 'is there ever such a Scripture, "I must go to Jesus"?' She said she could not tell; therefore I sat musing still to see if I could remember such a place, I had not sat above two or three minutes but that came bolting in upon me, 'And to an innumerable company of Angels', and withal, Hebrews the twelfth, about the mount of Zion, was set before mine eyes. Heb[rews] 12.22, 23, 24.

216. Then with joy I told my Wife, 'O now I know, I know!' but that night was a good night to me; I never had but few better; I longed for the company of some of God's people, that I might have imparted unto them what God hath showed me: Christ was a precious Christ to my Soul last night; I could scarce lie in Bed for joy, and peace, and triumph, through Christ; this great glory did not continue upon me until morning, yet that twelfth of the Author to the *Hebrews*, Heb[rews] 12.21, 22, 23. was a blessed Scripture to me for many days together after this.

217. The words are these, 'Ye are come to mount Zion, to the City of the living God, to the heavenly Jerusalem, and to an innumerable company of Angels, to the general assembly and Church of the first-born, which are written in heaven, and to God the

Notes

2 *wist* knew; understood.

3 *savoury* "Pleasing to the smell" (Johnson).

4 *outward man* the body, as opposed to the soul.

Judge of all, and to the spirits of just men made perfect, and to Jesus the Mediator of the New Testament, and to the blood of sprinkling, that speaketh better things than that of Abel'.[5] Through this blessed Sentence the Lord led me over and over, first to this word, and then to that, and showed me wonderful glory in every one of them. These words also have oft since this time been great refreshment to my Spirit. Blessed be God for having mercy on me.

Notes

[5] *Abel* the second son of Adam, slain by his brother Cain; his "blood cried unto [God] from the ground" and Cain was "cursed from the earth" (Genesis 4.10–11).

John Dryden (1631–1700)

Dryden stood beside Milton and Marvell at the funeral of Oliver Cromwell in 1658 and published *Heroic Stanzas* on the death of the Protector. Two years later, like most other poets, he shifted his loyalties and welcomed King Charles with poems of praise. Dryden adapted himself to the political changes of his day and became poet laureate and historiographer royal under Charles II and James II. Some of his greatest poetry was written in response to political events and tended both to exalt the king and to shed a comfortable and flattering light on his foibles as well as on the trials and tribulations of the nation. Perhaps the most famous of his political poems is *Absalom and Achitophel* (1681), which glorifies and fictionalizes the conflict between the king and his illegitimate son, the duke of Monmouth. Throughout the reigns of Charles and James, however, Dryden also cultivated a life as a professional writer who appealed to the public as well as to wealthy or lordly patrons: he made his living at his craft, and in the end he was better and more consistently supported by his publishers and the reading public than by royal patronage. He was thrown completely on his devices as a professional writer after the Glorious Revolution of 1688–9 when he made no attempt to shift party or religion again; he had become a Catholic out of loyalty to James, and that left him on the outside of King William's Protestant court.

The most lucrative part of Dryden's career may have been playwriting. He became one of the most popular dramatists of the Restoration supplying both comedies and tragedies to theaters, which had been closed for close to twenty years during the interregnum because of Puritan restrictions. *All for Love*, his version of Shakespeare's *Antony and Cleopatra*, and *Marriage à la Mode* are two of his most famous plays. In the prefaces to his plays and in the longer *Essay of Dramatic Poesy*, which he wrote after plague closed the theaters in 1665, Dryden also produced a great deal of influential dramatic criticism. Added to these works, his prefaces to some of his later translations, particularly the *Aeneid* (1697) and the *Fables Ancient and Modern* (1700), clearly justify Samuel Johnson's characterization of Dryden as "the father of English criticism."

The poems offered here, in addition to *Absalom and Achitophel*, display Dryden in only some of his very many literary modes. Like many poems of the time, "To My Honoured Friend, Dr Charleton" was written in order to win favor; Charleton was pleased, and Dryden was elected to the Royal Society. The poem shows how skilfully Dryden can flatter but also how adept he is at mastering an unusual subject well enough to draw it into the realm of poetry. "Mac Flecknoe" exhibits Dryden's powers of satire and shows him in the midst of the kind of Grubstreet controversy in which he was embroiled throughout his professional life. Many of the poets with whom Dryden was forever breaking lances are only remembered now because he immortalized them in his satires. Like so much of Dryden's poetry, the elegies for Oldham and Killigrew are occasional pieces that should not be taken as expressions of personal grief, as modern elegies might be, but rather as performances that celebrate and decorate the dead. Dryden's deftness at performances of this kind is sometimes difficult for readers used to expressiveness in verse to appreciate. But such poems, like funeral services or civil ceremonies of various kinds, give an enduring decency to the raw, disturbing, and moving events of life, especially when they are as brilliantly composed as

British Literature 1640–1789: An Anthology, Fourth Edition. Edited by Robert DeMaria, Jr.

Dryden's poems. The desirability of occasional verse is probably easiest to appreciate in Dryden's "Song for St. Cecilia's Day" and "Alexander's Feast," both of which celebrate music in musical verse.

Dryden's last major work was *Fables Ancient and Modern*. At this stage in his life Dryden was writing, mostly translating, full time for a living. He achieved such a facility in writing verse that it came as naturally to him as what he called "the other Harmony of prose." His retelling of the Ovidian story of Pygmalion heightens the sensuality of the original and takes a pleasure in the subject that is correspondent to the easiness Dryden achieved with his medium. In his translations of this period – in his *Aeneid*, his Juvenal, and Ovid above all – as in his prose, Dryden had an undeniable effect on English. He pushed the language much closer to its modern form both in diction and in syntax. He is only a scant generation younger than Milton, whom he deeply admired, but his language seems as close to ours as the English written in the late eighteenth century, almost a hundred years after his death. The last selection is the "Secular Masque," which Dryden composed for a new version of John Fletcher's *The Pilgrim* (1700). It's urbane and world-weary pose provides a fitting end to a career spend riding and observing several revolutions of the political wheel of fortune.

The texts are based on first editions, except in the case of "Mac Flecknoe." This great comic poem was probably composed in 1676 and circulated in manuscript for six years before it was pirated and badly printed in 1682; the preferred copy-text, which I follow, is the authorized edition in *Miscellany Poems ... By the most Eminent Hands* (1684). The standard edition of Dryden's works is *The California Dryden* (20 vols., University of California Press, 1956–2000); I am deeply indebted to this magnificent project. Another fine edition of the poems is that edited by Paul Hammond (Longman, 1995–2005). James Winn is the author of the standard biography, *John Dryden and his World* (Yale University Press, 1987).

To My Honoured Friend, Dr Charleton, on his learned and useful Works; and more particularly this of STONE-HENGE, by him Restored to the true Founders[1] (1663)

The longest Tyranny that ever swayed
Was that wherein our Ancestors betrayed
Their free-born *Reason* to the *Stagirite*,[2]
And made his Torch their universal Light.
So *Truth*, while only one supplied the State,
Grew scarce and dear, and yet sophisticate;[3]
Until 'twas bought, like Emp'ric Wares or Charms,[4]

Notes

TO MY HONOURED FRIEND

[1] Walter Charleton (1620–1707), author of *Chorea Gigantum; or the most famous antiquity of Great-Britain, vulgarly called Stone-Henge, standing on the Salisbury plain, restored to the Danes* (1663), a work which opposed the theory that they were the ruins of a Roman temple. Dryden's poem appears as a preliminary, commendatory poem in the book (which provides my copy-text). Charleton returned the favor by proposing Dryden for admission to the Royal Society.

[2] *Stagirite* Aristotle, who was born in the town of Stagirus in Macedonia; Dryden refers to the Aristotelian approach to science, which was formal rather than empirical, especially as elaborated by the scholastic philosophers of the middle ages.

[3] *sophisticate* "Adulterate; not genuine" (Johnson).

[4] *Emp'ric* an uneducated practitioner of medicine; a quack.

Hard words sealed up with *Aristotle*'s Arms.[5]
Columbus was the first that shook his Throne
And found a *Temp'rate* in a *Torrid* Zone:[6]
The fev'rish air fanned by a cooling breeze,
The fruitful Vales set round with shady Trees;
And guiltless *Men*, that danced away their time,
Fresh as their *Groves*, and *Happy* as their *Clime*.
Had we still paid homage to a *Name*,
Which only *God* and *Nature* justly claim;
The *western Seas* had been our utmost bound,[7]
Where *Poets* still might dream the *Sun* was drowned:
And all the *Stars* that shine in *Southern* Skies
Had been admired by none but *Salvage* Eyes[8]
Among th'*Assertors* of free Reason's claim,
The *English* are not the least in Worth, or Fame.
The World to *Bacon* does not only owe[9]
Its *present* Knowledge, but its *future* too.
Gilbert shall live, till *Loadstones* cease to draw,[10]
Or *British* Fleets the boundless Ocean awe;
And noble *Boyle*, not less in *Nature* seen,[11]
Than his great *Brother*, read in *States* and *Men*.[12]
The *Circling* streams, once thought but pools, of blood
(Whether Life's fuel, or the Body's food)
From dark Oblivion *Harvey*'s name shall save;[13]
While *Ent* keeps all the honour that he gave.[14]
Nor are *You*, Learned Friend, the least renowned;
Whose Fame, not circumscribed with *English* ground,
Flies like the nimble journeys of the Light,
And is, like that, unspent too in its flight.
Whatever *Truths* have been, by *Art* or *Chance*,
Redeemed from *Error*, or from *Ignorance*,
Thin in their *Authors* (like rich veins in Ore),
Your Works unite, and still discover more.
Such is the healing virtue of Your Pen,
To perfect Cures on *Books*, as well as *Men*.
Nor is This Work the least: You well may give
To *Men* new vigour, who make *Stones* to live.[15]

Notes

5 *Hard words* philosophic words; Latinate terms or jargon.

6 Aristotle assumed that the equatorial regions of the earth were all uninhabitably hot.

7 *western Seas* the Atlantic Ocean.

8 *Salvage* old spelling of savage, "Uncivilised; barbarous; untaught" (Johnson).

9 *Bacon* Sir Francis Bacon's *New Organon* provided a blueprint for the organization of knowledge.

10 *Gilbert* William Gilbert (1540–1603), author of a treatise on magnets, of which the loadstone (an iron ore) used in nautical compasses was the prime example.

11 *Boyle* Robert Boyle (1627–91), chemist and physicist, calculated barometric pressure.

12 *Brother* Roger Boyle, Lord Broghill, author of the romance *Parthenissa*.

13 *Harvey* William Harvey (1578–1657) correctly described the circulation of the blood.

14 *Ent* Sir George Ent (1604–89) defended Harvey's theory.

15 *Men ... who make Stones to live* apostles of the truth (I Peter 2.4–5).

Through You, the DANES (their short Dominion lost)[16]
A longer Conquest than the *Saxons* boast.
STONE-HENGE, once thought a *Temple*, You have found
A *Throne* where Kings, our Earthly Gods, were Crowned;
Where by their wond'ring Subjects They were seen,
Chose by their Stature, and their Princely mien.
Our *Sovereign* here above the rest might stand;[17]
And here be chose again to sway the Land.
These ruins sheltered once *His* Sacred Head,
Then when from *Worcester*'s fatal Field *He* fled,[18]
Watched by the Genius of this Kingly place,[19]
And mighty Visions of the Danish Race.
His *Refuge* then was for a *Temple* shown:
But, *He* Restored, 'tis now become a *Throne*.

Mac Flecknoe (1676?)

All human things are subject to decay,
And when Fate summons, Monarchs must obey:
This *Fleckno* found, who, like *Augustus*, young[1]
Was called to Empire, and had governed long;
In Prose and Verse, was owned, without dispute
Through all the Realms of *Nonsense*, absolute.
This agèd Prince now flourishing in Peace,
And blessed with issue of a large increase,
Worn out with business, did at length debate
To settle the succession of the State:
And pond'ring which of all his Sons was fit
To Reign, and wage immortal War with Wit,
Cried, ' 'Tis resolved; for Nature pleads that He
Should only rule, who most resembles me:
Sh——— alone my perfect image bears,[2]
Mature in dullness from his tender years.
Sh——— alone, of all my Sons, is he
Who stands confirmed in full stupidity.
The rest to some faint meaning make pretence,
But *Sh*——— never deviates into sense.

Notes

[16] *Danes* Danish vikings ruled parts of England under the Danelaw from about 870 to 920; Charleton proposed that Danes raised Stonehenge as a place to crown their kings centuries before the Danelaw.

[17] *Our Sovereign* Charles II was very tall.

[18] *Worcester's fatal field* the battle of Worcester, September 3, 1651, the end of Charles II's abortive attempt to establish himself on the throne; he eventually passed through Salisbury Plain on his flight to the Continent, where he remained until the restoration of the monarchy in 1660.

[19] *Genius* guardian spirit.

MAC FLECKNOE

[1] *Fleckno* Richard Flecknoe (c.1605–c.1677), a poor English poet and playwright lampooned about thirty-five years earlier in a hilarious poem by Andrew Marvell, "Flecknoe, an English Priest at Rome." *Augustus* he was nineteen when his great-uncle Julius Caesar was assassinated in 44 BCE; he gradually consolidated his rule and was emperor until his death in 14 CE.

[2] *Sh*——— stands for Shadwell, as contemporary readers knew; Thomas Shadwell was a poet and rival playwright with whom Dryden had skirmished for several years over questions of literary decorum.

Some Beams of Wit on other souls may fall,
Strike through and make a lucid interval;
But *Sh*———'s genuine night admits no ray,
His rising Fogs prevail upon the Day:
Besides his goodly Fabric fills the eye,[3]
And seems designed for thoughtless Majesty:
Thoughtless as Monarch Oaks, that shade the plain,
And, spread in solemn state, supinely reign.[4]
Heywood and *Shirley* were but Types of thee,[5]
Thou last great Prophet of Tautology:
Even I, a dunce of more renown than they,
Was sent before but to prepare thy way;
And coarsely clad in *Norwich* Drugget came[6]
To teach the Nations in thy greater name.
My warbling Lute, the Lute I whilom strung[7]
When to King *John* of *Portugal* I sung,
Was but the prelude to that glorious day,
When thou on silver *Thames* did'st cut thy way,
With well timed Oars before the Royal Barge,
Swelled with the Pride of thy Celestial charge;
And big with Hymn, Commander of an Host,
The like was ne'er in *Epsom* Blankets tossed.[8]
Methinks I see the new *Arion* Sail,[9]
The Lute still trembling underneath thy nail.
At thy well sharpened thumb from Shore to Shore[10]
The Treble squeaks for fear, the Basses roar:
Echoes from *Pissing-Alley*, "*Sh*———" call,[11]
And "*Sh*———" they resound from *A*——— *Hall*.[12]
About thy boat the little Fishes throng,
As at the Morning Toast, that Floats along.
Sometimes as Prince of thy Harmonious band
Thou wield'st thy Papers in thy threshing hand.[13]
St. *Andre*'s feet ne'er kept more equal time,[14]
Not even the feet of thy own *Psyche*'s rhyme:[15]
Though they in number as in sense excel;

Notes

3 *goodly Fabric* ample or large body.

4 *supinely* "1. With the face upward; 2. Drowsily; thoughtlessly; indolently" (Johnson).

5 *Heywood and Shirley* Thomas Heywood and James Shirley, popular, unsophisticated dramatists of the earlier seventeenth century; *Type* "That by which something future is prefigured" (Johnson).

6 *Norwich Drugget* a coarse cloth, in keeping with the representation of Flecknoe as John the Baptist (who wore coarse clothing), the herald of Shadwell's coming.

7 *Lute* Flecknoe actually played for King John, although the instrument is often a metaphor for poetry; *whilom* formerly.

8 *in Epsom Blankets tossed* this was an act of punishment or contempt (Johnson, s.v. *blanket*); Epsom probably refers to Shadwell's play *Epsom Wells*.

9 *Arion* a Greek musician and poet of the seventh century BCE, reputed to have been rescued on the back of a charmed dolphin when thrown overboard by thieves; he was also associated with the origins of drama.

10 *Shore* also means sewer.

11 *Pissing-Alley* a nasty little street near the river.

12 *A———Hall* Aston Hall in the first edition, but the place is unlocated and A———Hall may make a pair with Pissing-Alley.

13 *threshing* from thrash "To labour; to drudge" (Johnson).

14 *St. Andre* a French choreographer who worked on the opera *Psyche*.

15 *Psyche* Shadwell wrote the libretto.

So just, so like tautology they fell,
That, pale with envy, *Singleton* forswore[16]
The Lute and Sword which he in Triumph bore,
And vowed he ne'er would act *Villerius*[17] more.'
Here stopped the good old Sire; and wept for joy
In silent raptures of the hopeful boy.
All arguments, but most his Plays, persuade,
That for anointed dullness he was made.
  Close to the Walls which fair *Augusta* bind,[18]
(The fair *Augusta* much to fears inclined)[19]
An ancient fabric, raised t' inform the sight,[20]
There stood of yore, and *Barbican* it hight:[21]
A watch tower once; but now, so Fate ordains,
Of all the Pile an empty name remains.
From its old Ruins Brothel houses rise,
Scenes of lewd loves, and of polluted joys,
Where their vast Courts the Mother-Strumpets keep,
And undisturbed by Watch, in silence sleep.
Near these a Nursery erects its head,[22]
Where Queens are formed, and future Heroes bred;[23]
Where unfledged Actors learn to laugh and cry,
Where infant Punks their tender Voices try,[24]
And little *Maximins* the Gods defy.[25]
Great *Fletcher* never treads in Buskins here,[26]
Nor greater *Jonson* dares in Socks appear.
But gentle *Simkin* just reception finds[27]
Admist this Monument of vanished minds:
Pure Clinches, the suburban Muse affords;[28]
And *Panton* waging harmless War with words.[29]
Here *Fleckno*, as a place to Fame well known,
Ambitiously designed his *Sh*———'s Throne.
For ancient *Dekker* prophesied long since,[30]
That in this Pile should Reign a mighty Prince,[31]

Notes

16 *Singleton* an undistinguished actor and musician.

17 *Villerius* a character in *The Siege of Rhodes*, a bombastic play by John Davenant.

18 *Augusta* an old name for London.

19 *fears* Dryden alludes to the contemporary panic about the "Popish Plot" to overthrow the English government, considered folly by the high-church royalists (including Charles and his brother James, who actually was Roman Catholic), but fanned into a frenzy with the machinations of radicals like Titus Oates and Israel Tongue.

20 *inform* "To animate; to actuate by vital powers" (Johnson).

21 *Barbican* Burgh-kenning, Old English for "city-watching," a defensive wall or tower; *hight* archaic, was called.

22 *Nursery* "The place or state where any thing is fostered or brought up" (Johnson).

23 *Queen* with a pun on *quean*, a harlot.

24 *Punk* prostitute.

25 *Maximin* an emperor in one of Dryden's own plays, *Tyrannic Love*.

26 *Fletcher* John Fletcher, Elizabethan playwright whom Dryden admired; *Buskins* the elevated shoes worn by actors in Greek tragedy to make them taller and therefore more heroic in stature; comic actors wore socks to lower their stature.

27 *Simkin* clown in a popular farce of the day.

28 *Clinch* a pun. The suburbs were then considered low-class and dirty.

29 *Panton* perhaps Edward Panton, who hoped to found a school in the suburbs for royalty (Hammond).

30 *Dekker* Thomas Dekker (1572–1632), a playwright of relatively low city life.

31 *Pile* "An edifice; a building" (Johnson).

Born for a scourge of Wit, and flail of Sense:
To whom true dullness should some *Psyches* owe,
But Worlds of *Misers* from his Pen should flow:
Humorists and *Hypocrites* it should also produce,[32]
Whole *Raymond* families, and Tribes of *Bruce*;[33]
  Now Empress *Fame* had published the renown,
Of *Sh*———'s Coronation through the Town.
Roused by report of Fame, the Nations meet,
From near *Bun-Hill*, and distant *Watling-street*.[34]
No *Persian* Carpets spread th' Imperial way,
But scattered Limbs of mangled Poets lay:
From dusty shops neglected Authors come
Martyrs of Pies, and Relics of the Bum.[35]
Much *Heywood, Shirley, Ogleby* there lay,[36]
But loads of *Sh*——— almost choked the way.
Bilked *Stationers* for Yeomen stood prepared,[37]
And *H*——— was Captain of the Guard.[38]
The hoary Prince in Majesty appeared,
High on a Throne of his own Labours reared.[39]
At his right hand our young *Ascanius* sat[40]
Rome's other hope, and pillar of the State.
His Brows thick fogs, instead of glories, grace,
And lambent dullness played around his face.
As *Hannibal* did to the Altars come,[41]
Sworn by his *Sire* a mortal Foe to *Rome*;
So *Sh*———swore, nor should his Vow be vain,
That he till Death true dullness would maintain;
And in his father's Right, and Realm's defence,
Ne'er to have peace with Wit, nor truce with Sense.
The King himself the sacred Unction made,
As King by Office, and as Priest by Trade:
In his sinister hand, instead of Ball,[42]
He placed a mighty Mug of Potent Ale;
Love's Kingdom to his right he did convey,[43]
At once his Sceptre and his rule of Sway;
Whose righteous Lore the Prince had practised young,
And from whose Loins recorded *Psyche* sprung.[44]

Notes

32 *Psyche, Miser, Humorist, Hypocrite* plays by Shadwell.

33 *Raymond, Bruce* characters in Shadwell's plays.

34 *Bun-Hill, Watling-street* two places in the City of London less than a mile apart.

35 *Martyrs … Relics* remaindered, unbound pages of poetry sometimes ended up as wrapping or toilet paper.

36 *Ogleby* John Ogilby, a recently deceased translator of Virgil and Homer.

37 *Bilk* "To cheat; to defraud, by running into debt, and avoiding payment" (Johnson); *Stationers* booksellers or publishers, who sometimes gave authors advances on work to be completed.

38 *Herringman* Henry Herringman (1628–1704), a stationer.

39 *High on a Throne* cf. *Paradise Lost* 2. 1.

40 *Ascanius* son of Aeneas, whom Virgil describes in similar terms (*Aeneid*, 2.682–4).

41 *Hannibal* Carthaginian general whose father swore him at the altar to eternal enmity with Rome.

42 *sinister* Latin or heraldic, left; *Ball* a globe symbolizing power in regal portraits.

43 *Love's Kingdom* a play by Flecknoe.

44 *record* "To celebrate; to cause to be remembered solemnly" (Johnson).

His Temples last with Poppies were o'erspread,[45]
That nodding seemed to consecrate his head:
Just at that point of time, if Fame not lie,
On his left hand twelve reverend Owls did fly.[46]
So *Romulus*, 'tis sung, by *Tiber's Brook*,[47]
Presage of Sway from twice six Vultures took.
Th' admiring throng loud acclamations make,
And Omens of his future Empire take.
The *Sire* then shook the honours of his head,[48]
And from his brows damps of oblivion shed
Full on the filial dullness: long he stood,
Repelling from his Breast the raging God;[49]
At length burst out in this prophetic mood:
'Heavens bless my Son, from *Ireland* let him reign
To far *Barbadoes* on the Western main;
Of his Dominion may no end be known,
And greater than his Father's be his Throne.
Beyond love's Kingdom let him stretch his Pen';
He paused, and all the people cried '*Amen*'.
Then thus, continued he, 'My Son advance
Still in new Impudence, new Ignorance.
Success let others teach, learn thou from me
Pangs without birth, and fruitless Industry.
Let *Virtuoso's* in five years be Writ;
Yet not one thought accuse thy toil of Wit;
Let gentle *George* in triumph tread the Stage,[50]
Make *Dorimant* betray, and *Loveit* rage;
Let *Cully, Cockwood, Fopling* charm the Pit,
And in their folly show the Writer's wit.
Yet still thy fools shall stand in thy defence,
And justify their Author's want of sense.
Let 'em be all by thy own model made
Of dullness, and desire no foreign aid:
That they to future ages may be known,
Not Copies drawn, but Issue of thy own.
Nay let thy men of wit too be the same,
All full of thee, and differing but in name;
But let no Alien *S-dl-y* interpose,[51]
To lard with wit thy hungry *Epsom* prose.
And when false flowers of *Rhetoric* thou would'st cull,
Trust Nature, do not labour to be dull;

Notes

45 *Poppies* source of sleep-inducing opiates, to which Shadwell was known to be addicted.

46 *Owls* birds of night and therefore sleep.

47 *Romulus* with his brother Remus, the fabled founder of Rome, through which runs the Tiber river.

48 *honour* "ornament; decoration" (Johnson).

49 *Repelling ... the raging God* recalling the sibyl struggling as Apollo possesses and inspires her (*Aeneid* 6.78–9).

50 *George* Etherege (1636–92), comic playwright whose characters include *Dorimant*, *Loveit*, *Cully*, *Cockwood*, and *Fopling*.

51 *S-dl-y* Sir Charles Sedley, a playwright who helped Shadwell on *Epsom Wells*.

But write thy best, and top; and in each line,[52]
Sir *Formal*'s oratory will be thine.[53]
Sir *Formal*, though unsought, attends thy quill,
And does thy *Northern Dedications* fill.[54]
Nor let false friends seduce thy mind to fame,
By Arrogating *Jonson*'s Hostile Name;
Let Father *Flecknoe* Fire thy Mind with Praise,
And Uncle *Ogleby* thy envy raise.
Thou art my blood, where *Jonson* has no part;
What share have we in Nature or in Art?
Where did his wit on learning fix a brand,
Or rail at Arts he did not understand?
Where made he love in Prince *Nicander's* vein,[55]
Or swept the dust in *Psyche*'s humble strain?
Where sold he Bargains, "Whip-stitch, kiss my Arse,"[56]
Promised a Play and dwindled to a Farce?
When did his Muse from *Fletcher* scenes purloin,
As thou whole *Eth'rege* dost transfuse to thine?
But so transfused as Oil on Waters flow,
His always floats above, thine sinks below.
This is thy Province, this thy wondrous way,
New Humours to invent for each new Play:[57]
This is that boasted Bias of thy mind,
By which one way, to dullness, 'tis inclined.
Which makes thy writings lean on one side still,
And in all changes that way bends thy will.
Nor let thy mountain belly make pretence
Of likeness; thine's a tympany of sense.[58]
A Tun of Man in thy Large bulk is writ,[59]
But sure thou'rt but a Kilderkin of wit.
Like mine thy gentle numbers feebly creep,[60]
Thy Tragic Muse gives smiles, thy Comic sleep.
With whate'er gall thou sett'st thyself to write,
Thy inoffensive Satires never bite.
In thy felonious heart, though Venom lies,
It doth but touch thy *Irish* pen, and dies.
Thy Genius calls thee not to purchase fame
In keen Iambics, but mild Anagram:[61]
Leave writing Plays, and choose for thy command

Notes

52 *top* "To perform eminently ... This word, in this sense, is seldom used but on light or ludicrous occasions" (Johnson).

53 *Sir Formal* Sir Formal Trifle, one of Shadwell's characters.

54 *Northern Dedications* because directed to the duke and duchess of Newcastle, in northern England.

55 *Prince Nicander* a character in *Psyche*.

56 *sold ... Bargains* made sharp retorts; the examples that follow paraphrase Shadwell's *The Virtuoso* II.i.27–30.

57 *Humour* "General turn or temper of mind" (Johnson), exemplified in a flat, comic character.

58 *Tympany* "A kind of obstructed flatulence that swells the body like a drum" (Johnson).

59 *Tun* a large barrel, as opposed to a *kilderkin*, a small one.

60 *numbers* verses.

61 *Iambics* the classical measure for satire.

Some peaceful Province in *Acrostic* Land
There thou mayst wings display and Altars raise,[62]
And torture one poor word Ten thousand ways.[63]
Or if thou would'st thy different talent suit,
Set thy own Songs, and sing them to thy lute.'
He said, but his last words were scarcely heard,
For *Bruce* and *Longvil* had a *Trap* prepared,[64]
And down they sent the yet declaiming *Bard*.
Sinking he left the Drugget robe behind,
Borne upwards by a subterranean wind,
The Mantle fell to the young Prophet's part,[65]
With double portion of his Father's Art.

Absalom and Achitophel: A Poem (1681)

In pious times, ere Priest-craft did begin,[1]
Before *Polygamy* was made a sin;
When man, on many, multiplied his kind,
Ere one to one was, cursedly, confined:
When Nature prompted, and no law denied
Promiscuous use of Concubine and Bride;
Then, *Israel*'s Monarch, after Heav'n's own heart,
His vigorous warmth did, variously, impart
To Wives and Slaves: And, wide as his Command,
Scattered his Maker's Image through the Land.
Michal, of Royal blood, the Crown did wear,[2]
A Soil ungrateful to the Tiller's care:
Not so the rest; for several Mothers bore
To Godlike *David*, several Sons before.
But since like slaves his bed they did ascend,
No True Succession could their seed attend.

Notes

[62] *wings ... Altars* a reference to poems in which the lines are arranged to look like their subject, such as George Herbert's "Easter Wings" (about angels and the Ascension) and "The Altar"; Dryden and his age considered such poems mere gimmickry or false wit.

[63] *torture one poor word* the metaphysical practice of "catachresis," or using words in new and varied senses.

[64] *Bruce and Longvil* characters in *The Virtuoso*; *Trap* trapdoor.

[65] *the young Prophet* the scene imitates the prophet Elijah's reception of his father's mantle (II Kings 2).

Absalom and Achitophel

[1] *pious times* the days of the biblical King David; the story comes from II Samuel 13–19. In Dryden's allegory David represents King Charles II, and the biblical story as a whole is made to figure forth the Exclusion Crisis of 1678–81 as seen by political loyalists. Leading up to this period, Charles's strong Roman Catholic associations, along with his high-handed treatment of Parliament, engendered a climate of fear and paranoia concerning a "Popish Plot" to overthrow the government of England. As an avowed Catholic by 1673, Charles's brother, the duke of York (later James II), figured prominently in the imagined "Plot"; opponents of the king, led by Anthony Ashley Cooper, earl of Shaftesbury, sought to exclude James from the succession by means of the so-called "Exclusion Bill." In his place, they proposed to install James Scott, the popular duke of Monmouth, one of Charles's illegitimate children. In March 1681 Charles dissolved the contentious meeting of Parliament in Oxford before there could be a vote on the Exclusion Bill and proceeded to prosecute its proponents. Shaftesbury himself was arrested for treason on July 1, 1681 and was nearing his trial date when Dryden published *Absalom and Achitophel* in November.

[2] *Michal* a childless daughter of Saul (II Samuel 6. 16–23), representing Charles's childless wife, Catherine of Braganza (1638–1705).

Of all this Numerous Progeny was none
So Beautiful so brave as *Absalom:*[3]
Whether, inspired with some diviner Lust,
His Father got him with a greater Gust;
Or that his Conscious destiny made way
By manly beauty to Imperial sway.
Early in Foreign fields he won Renown,[4]
With Kings and States allied to *Israel*'s Crown:
In Peace the thoughts of War he could remove,
And seemed as he were only born for love.
What e'er he did was done with so much ease,
In him alone, 'twas Natural to please.
His motions all accompanied with grace;
And *Paradise* was opened in his face.
With secret Joy, indulgent *David* viewed
His Youthful Image in his Son renewed:
To all his wishes Nothing he denied,
And made the Charming *Annabel* his Bride.[5]
What faults he had (for who from faults is free?)
His Father could not, or he would not see.
Some warm excesses, which the Law forbore,
Were cónstrued Youth that purged by boiling o'er:
And *Amnon*'s Murther, by a specious Name,[6]
Was called a Just Revenge for injured Fame.
Thus Praised, and Loved, the Noble Youth remained,
While *David*, undisturbed, in *Sion* reigned.[7]
But Life can never be sincerely blessed:
Heav'n punishes the bad, and proves the best.[8]
The *Jews*, a Headstrong, Moody, Murmuring race,
As ever tried th'extent and stretch of grace;
God's pampered people whom, debauched with ease,
No King could govern, nor no God could please;
(Gods they had tried of every shape and size
That God-smiths could produce, or Priests devise.)
These *Adam*-wits, too fortunately free,[9]
Began to dream they wanted liberty;
And when no rule, no precedent was found
Of men, by Laws less circumscribed and bound,
They led their wild desires to Woods and Caves,
And thought that all but Savages were Slaves.

Notes

3 *Absalom* beautiful, popular, and beloved son of David (II Samuel 14.25) who rebelled against him, representing James, duke of Monmouth (1649–85), son of Charles and a mistress, who sided with the Exclusionists and was eventually executed for treason.

4 *in Foreign fields he won Renown* Monmouth fought alongside the French against the Dutch in 1672–3.

5 *Annabel* a non-biblical figure representing Anne, countess of Buccleuch (1651–1732), Monmouth's wife.

6 *Amnon* a son of David and half-brother of Absalom, who had him killed because he raped Absalom's sister; David forgave Absalom for this crime because of his great love of him. Amnon may represent either of two men with whose deaths Monmouth was associated.

7 *Sion* the city of David in the Bible; here, London.

8 *proves* tests.

9 *Adam-wits* the revolutionaries in the English Civil War; the appellation suggests their innocence and fallibility. *Jews* are Englishmen in the allegory.

They who when *Saul* was dead, without a blow,[10]
Made foolish *Isbosheth* the Crown forgo;[11]
Who banished *David* did from *Hebron* bring,[12]
And, with a General Shout, proclaimed him King:
Those very *Jews*, who, at their very best,
Their Humour more than Loyalty expressed,[13]
Now, wondered why, so long, they had obeyed
An Idol Monarch which their hands had made;
Thought they might ruin him they could create;
Or melt him to that Golden Calf, a State.[14]
But these were random bolts: No formed Design,
Nor Interest made the Factious Crowd to join:
The sober part of *Israel*, free from stain,
Well knew the value of a peaceful reign:
And, looking backward with a wise afright,
Saw Seams of wounds, dishonest to the sight;[15]
In contemplation of whose ugly Scars,
They Cursed the memory of Civil Wars.
The moderate sort of Men, thus qualified,
Inclined the Balance to the better side:
And *David*'s mildness managed it so well,
The Bad found no occasion to Rebel.
But, when to Sin our biased Nature leans,
The careful Devil is still at hand with means;
And providently Pimps for ill desires:
The Good old Cause revived, a Plot requires.[16]
Plots, true or false, are necessary things,
To raise up Commonwealths, and ruin Kings.
  Th'inhabitants of old *Jerusalem*
Were *Jebusites*: the Town so called from them;[17]
And theirs the Native right –
But when the chosen people grew more strong,[18]
The rightful cause at length became the wrong:
And every loss the men of *Jebus* bore,
They still were thought God's enemies the more.
Thus, worn and weakened, well or ill content,

Notes

[10] *Saul* the elected king of Israel before David (I Samuel 10); Oliver Cromwell (1599–1658).

[11] *Isbosheth* son of Saul, succeeded his father to the throne, but was soon murdered (II Samuel 4); he represents Richard Cromwell (1626–1712), who followed his father as Protector of England, but was forced to step down in 1660.

[12] *Hebron* In Hebron David was made king of Judah (II Samuel 2), and after the death of Isbosheth he was proclaimed king of Israel (II Samuel 5); in Scotland Charles was crowned king on January 1, 1651 and, after the rejection of Richard Cromwell in 1660, he was brought back to England from France and crowned king on April 23, 1661.

[13] *Humour* "Caprice; whim; predominant inclination" (Johnson, sense 9).

[14] *Golden Calf* an idol or false god; see the "molten calf" in Exodus 32:4; *State* "A republic; a government not monarchical" (Johnson, sense 7).

[15] *dishonest* "Disgraceful; ignominious" (Johnson, sense 3).

[16] *Good old Cause* the side of the Puritans or commonwealth's-men in the Civil War; *Plot* the "Popish Plot" (see n. 1 above).

[17] *Jebusites* the old inhabitants of Jerusalem, once called Jebus (II Samuel 5.6); in the allegory, Jerusalem is London, which was Roman Catholic before the Reformation in England (c.1535), and Jebusites are Catholics.

[18] *chosen people* Israelites; Protestants.

Submit they must to *David*'s Government:
Impoverished, and deprived of all Command,
Their Taxes doubled as they lost their Land,
And, what was harder yet to flesh and blood,
Their Gods disgraced, and burnt like common wood.
This set the Heathen Priesthood on a flame;[19]
For Priests of all Religions are the same:
Of whatsoe'er descent their Godhead be,
Stock, Stone, or other homely pedigree,
In his defence his Servants are as bold
As if he had been born of beaten gold.
The *Jewish Rabbins* though their Enemies,[20]
In this conclude them honest men and wise:
For 'twas their duty, all the Learned think,
T'espouse his Cause by whom they eat and drink.
From hence began that Plot, the Nation's Curse,[21]
Bad in itself, but represented worse.
Raised in extremes, and in extremes decried;
With Oaths affirmed, with dying Vows denied.
Not weighed, or winnowed by the Multitude;
But swallowed in the Mass, unchewed and Crude.
Some Truth there was, but dashed and brewed with Lies;
To please the Fools, and puzzle all the Wise.
Succeeding times did equal folly call,
Believing nothing, or believing all,
Th'*Egyptian* Rites the *Jebusites* embraced;[22]
Where Gods were recommended by their Taste.
Such savoury Deities must needs be good,
And served at once for Worship and for Food.
By force they could not Introduce these Gods;
For Ten to One, in former days was odds.
So Fraud was used (the Sacrificers' trade),[23]
Fools are more hard to Conquer than Persuade.
Their busy Teachers mingled with the *Jews*;
And raked, for Converts, even the Courts and Stews:[24]
Which *Hebrew* Priests the more unkindly took,
Because the Fleece accompanies the Flock.[25]
Some thought they God's Anointed meant to Slay[26]
By Guns, invented since full many a day:
Our Author swears it not; but who can know[27]
How far the Devil and *Jebusites* may go?

Notes

[19] *Heathen Priesthood* Roman Catholic priests, with a glance at the putative idolatry of saints in their churches.

[20] *Jewish Rabbins* Church of England priests.

[21] The Popish plot; see n. 1 above.

[22] *Egyptian Rites* Roman Catholic communion practices, in which the host given to communicants is the transubstantiated body of Christ and not, as in the reformed churches, merely symbolic of it.

[23] *Sacrificers* mass priests.

[24] *Stews* whorehouses.

[25] *Fleece* money that the priests get from their followers or *flock*.

[26] *God's Anointed* King Charles II.

[27] *Our Authour* Dryden's, or the speaker's, supposed authority for his version of the story.

This Plot, which failed for want of common Sense,
Had yet a deep and dangerous Consequence:
For, as when raging Fevers boil the Blood,
The standing Lake soon floats into a Flood;
And every hostile Humour, which before
Slept quiet in its Channels, bubbles o'er:
So, several Factions from this first Ferment,
Work up to Foam, and threat the Government.
Some by their Friends, more by themselves thought wise,
Opposed the Power, to which they could not rise.
Some had in Courts been Great, and thrown from thence,
Like Fiends, were hardened in Impenitence.
Some by their Monarch's fatal mercy grown,
From Pardoned Rebels, Kinsmen to the Throne;
Were raised in Power and public Office high:
Strong Bands, if Bands ungrateful men could tie.
Of these the false *Achitophel* was first:[28]
A Name to all succeeding Ages Cursed.
For close Designs, and crooked Counsel fit;
Sagacious, Bold, and Turbulent of wit:
Restless, unfixed in Principle and Place;
In Power unpleased, impatient of Disgrace.
A fiery Soul, which working out its way,
Fretted the Pigmy Body to decay:[29]
And o'er informed the Tenement of Clay.
A daring Pilot in extremity;[30]
Pleased with the Danger, when the Waves went high
He sought the Storms; but for a Calm unfit,
Would Steer too nigh the Sands, to boast his Wit.
Great Wits are sure to Madness near allied;
And thin Partitions do their Bounds divide:
Else, why should he, with Wealth and Honour blessed,
Refuse his Age the needful hours of Rest?
Punish a Body which he could not please;
Bankrupt of Life, yet Prodigal of Ease?
And all to leave, what with his Toil he won,
To that unfeathered, two Legg'd thing, a Son:[31]
Got, while his Soul did huddled Notions try;
And born a shapeless Lump, like Anarchy.
In Friendship False, Implacable in Hate:
Resolved to Ruin or to Rule the State.

Notes

[28] *Achitophel* senior counselor to Absalom (II Samuel 15–17), a name synonymous with untrustworthy advice. He represents Anthony Ashley Cooper, first earl of Shaftesbury (1621–83), who served in Cromwell's government and then became a leader in the movement to restore Charles; he favored the Exclusion Bill and became the leading supporter of Monmouth.

[29] *Fretted* corroded; ate away (Johnson, sense 4); *Pigmy Body* Shaftesbury was short and, by this point in his life, bent over with arthritis or some such affliction.

[30] *Pilot* one who steers a ship.

[31] *unfeathered ... thing* a reference to an unflattering definition of man attributed to Plato. Shaftesbury's son was sickly.

To Compass this the Triple Bond he broke;[32]
The Pillars of the public Safety shook:
And fitted *Israel* for a Foreign Yoke.
Then, seized with Fear, yet still affecting Fame,
Assumed a Patriot's All-atoning Name.[33]
So easy still it proves in Factious Times,[34]
With public Zeal to cancel private Crimes:
How safe is Treason, and how sacred ill,
Where none can sin against the People's Will:
Where Crowds can wink; and no offence be known,
Since in another's guilt they find their own.
Yet, Fame deserved, no Enemy can grudge;
The Statesman we abhor, but praise the Judge.
In *Israel*'s Courts ne'er sat an *Abbethdin*[35]
With more discerning Eyes, or Hands more clean:
Unbribed, unsought, the Wretched to redress;
Swift of Dispatch, and easy of Access.
Oh, had he been content to serve the Crown,
With virtues only proper to the Gown;[36]
Or, had the rankness of the Soil been freed
From Cockle, that oppressed the Noble seed:[37]
David, for him his tuneful Harp had strung,
And Heaven had wanted one Immortal song.[38]
But wild Ambition loves to slide, not stand;
And Fortune's Ice prefers to Virtue's Land:
Achitophel, grown weary to possess
A lawful Fame, and lazy Happiness;
Disdained the Golden fruit to gather free,
And lent the Crowd his Arm to shake the Tree.
Now, manifest of Crimes, contrived long since,[39]
He stood at bold Defiance with his Prince:
Held up the Buckler of the People's Cause,
Against the Crown; and skulked behind the Laws.
The wished occasion of the Plot he takes,
Some Circumstances finds, but more he makes.
By buzzing Emissaries, fills the ears
Of list'ning Crowds, with Jealousies and Fears[40]
Of Arbitrary Counsels brought to light,
And proves the King himself a *Jebusite*:
Weak Arguments! which yet he knew full well,

Notes

32 *Triple Bond* the Triple Alliance of England, Holland, and Sweden, of which, in fact, Charles II was the principal opponent because he favored an alliance with France.

33 *Patriot* a politically charged word; a name for the opposition; "a factious disturber of government" (Johnson, 1773, sense 2); in some versions, *Patron* appears instead of *Patriot*.

34 *So … Access* Lines 180–91 were added in the third London edition.

35 *Abbethdin* rabbinical term for a judge. Shaftesbury was, as Lord Chancellor, accounted a good judge.

36 *Gown* the profession of law (or divinity).

37 *Cockle* "A weed that grows in corn: 'Good seed degenerates, and oft' obeys/The soil's disease, and into cockle strays.' *Donne*" (Johnson).

38 *wanted one Immortal song* lacked Psalm 109, which was interpreted as a precative attack on Absalom and David's other enemies, who "have rewarded me evil for good, and hatred for my love" (verse 5; see *California Dryden* 2:251).

39 *manifest* "Detected; with *of* (Johnson, sense 2).

40 *Jealousies* "Suspicious fears" (Johnson, sense 2).

Were strong with People easy to Rebel.
For, governed by the *Moon*, the giddy *Jews*
Tread the same track when she the Prime renews:[41]
And once in twenty Years, their Scribes Record,
By natural Instinct they change their Lord.
Achitophel still wants a Chief, and none
Was found so fit as Warlike *Absalom*:
Not, that he wished his Greatness to create,
(For Politicians neither love nor hate):
But, for he knew, his Title not allowed,[42]
Would keep him still depending on the Crowd:
That Kingly power, thus ebbing out, might be
Drawn to the dregs of a Democracy.
Him he attempts, with studied Arts to please,
And sheds his Venom, in such words as these.
'Auspicious Prince! at whose Nativity
Some Royal Planet ruled the Southern sky;
Thy longing Country's Darling and Desire;
Their cloudy Pillar, and their guardian Fire:[43]
Their second *Moses*, whose extended Wand[44]
Shuts up the Seas, and shows the promised Land:
Whose dawning Day, in every distant age,
Has exercised the Sacred Prophet's rage:
The People's Prayer, the glad Diviner's Theme,
The Young men's Vision, and the Old men's Dream!
Thee, *Saviour*, Thee, the Nation's Vows confess;
And, never satisfied with seeing, bless:
Swift, unbespoken Pomps, thy steps proclaim,
And stammering Babes are taught to lisp thy Name.
How long wilt thou the general Joy detain;
Starve, and defraud the People of thy Reign?
Content ingloriously to pass thy days
Like one of Virtue's Fools that feed on Praise;
Till thy fresh Glories, which now shine so bright,
Grow Stale and Tarnish with our daily sight.
Believe me, Royal Youth, thy Fruit must be,
Or gathered Ripe, or rot upon the Tree.[45]
Heav'n has to all allotted, soon or late,
Some lucky Revolution of their Fate:
Whose Motions, if we watch and guide with Skill,
(For human Good depends on human Will),
Our Fortune rolls, as from a smooth Descent,
And, from the first Impression, takes the Bent:

Notes

[41] *Prime* the beginning of a new cycle, which, according to one popular system, was every nineteen years (or twenty, as Dryden suggests); hence 1680 might have followed 1640 and 1660 as a year of political revolution.

[42] *his Title* Absalom's (i.e., Monmouth's) claim to the throne.

[43] *cloudy Pillar ... Fire* the forms taken by God when he led the Israelites through the wilderness (Exodus 13.21).

[44] *Moses* leader of the Jews in their flight through the desert; God allowed him to part the waters of the Red Sea so that his people could pass into the Promised Land.

[45] *Or ... or* Either ... or.

But, if unseized, she glides away like wind;
And leaves repenting Folly far behind.
Now, now she meets you, with a glorious prize,
And spreads her Locks before her as she flies.
Had thus Old *David*, from whose Loins you spring
Not dared, when Fortune called him, to be King,
At *Gath* an Exile he might still remain,[46]
And heaven's Anointing Oil had been in vain.
Let his successful Youth your hopes engage,
But shun th'example of Declining Age:
Behold him setting in his Western Skies,
The Shadows lengthening as the Vapours rise.
He is not now, as when on *Jordan*'s Sand[47]
The Joyful People thronged to see him Land,
Cov'ring the *Beach*, and black'ning all the *Strand*:
But, like the Prince of Angels from his height,
Comes tumbling downward with diminished light;
Betrayed by one poor Plot to public Scorn,
(Our only blessing since his Cursed Return):
Those heaps of People which one Sheaf did bind,
Blown off and scattered by a puff of Wind.
What strength can he to your Designs oppose,
Naked of Friends, and round beset with Foes?
If *Pharaoh*'s doubtful Succour he should use,[48]
A Foreign Aid would more Incense the *Jews*:
Proud *Egypt* would dissembled Friendship bring;
Foment the War, but not support the King:
Nor would the Royal Party e'er unite
With *Pharaoh*'s Arms, t'assist the *Jebusite*;
Or if they should, their Interest soon would break,
And with such odious Aid make *David* weak.
All sorts of men by my successful Arts,
Abhorring Kings, estrange their altered Hearts
From *David*'s Rule: And 'tis the general Cry,
Religion, Commonwealth, and Liberty.
If you as Champion of the public Good,
Add to their Arms a Chief of Royal Blood;
What may not *Israel* hope, and what Applause
Might such a General gain by such a Cause?
Not barren Praise alone, that Gaudy Flower,
Fair only to the sight, but solid Power:
And Nobler is a limited Command,
Giv'n by the Love of all your Native Land,
Than a Successive Title, Long, and Dark,[49]
Drawn from the Mouldy Rolls of *Noah*'s Ark'.

Notes

[46] *Gath* place of refuge for David when he fled King Saul (I Samuel 27.4); for Charles II, Brussels.

[47] *Jordan's Sand* David was greeted there by his people after the death of Absalom (II Samuel 19); Charles II was met by his supporters at Dover when he returned to assume the throne.

[48] *Pharaoh* King of France, Louis XIV.

[49] *Successive Title* a proof of right to succeed to the throne.

What cannot Praise effect in Mighty Minds,
When Flattery Soothes, and when Ambition Blinds!
Desire of Power, on Earth a Vicious Weed,
Yet, sprung from High, is of Celestial Seed:
In God 'tis Glory: And when men Aspire,
'Tis but a Spark too much of Heavenly Fire.
Th' Ambitious Youth, too Covetous of Fame,
Too full of Angel's Metal in his Frame;[50]
Unwarily was led from Virtue's ways;
Made Drunk with Honour, and Debauched with Praise.
Half loath, and half consenting to the Ill,
(For Loyal Blood within him struggled still)
He thus replied – 'And what Pretence have I
To take up Arms for Public Liberty?
My Father Governs with unquestioned Right;
The Faith's Defender, and Mankind's Delight:
Good, Gracious, Just, observant of the Laws;
And Heav'n by Wonders has Espoused his Cause.
Whom has he Wronged in all his Peaceful Reign?
Who sues for Justice to his Throne in Vain?
What Millions has he Pardoned of his Foes,
Whom Just Revenge did to his Wrath expose?
Mild, Easy, Humble, Studious of our Good;
Inclined to Mercy, and averse from Blood.
If Mildness Ill with Stubborn *Israel* Suit,
His Crime is God's beloved Attribute.
What could he gain, his People to Betray,
Or change his Right, for Arbitrary Sway?
Let Haughty *Pharaoh* Curse with such a Reign,
His Fruitful *Nile*, and Yoke a Servile Train.
If *David's* Rule *Jerusalem* Displease,
The *Dog-star* heats their Brains to this Disease.[51]
Why then should I, Encouraging the Bad,
Turn Rebel, and run Popularly Mad?
Were he a Tyrant who, by Lawless Might,
Oppressed the *Jews*, and Raised the *Jebusite*,
Well might I Mourn; but Nature's Holy Bands
Would Curb my Spirits, and Restrain my Hands:
The People might assert their Liberty;
But what was Right in them, were Crime in me.
His Favour leaves me nothing to require;
Prevents my Wishes, and outruns Desire.[52]
What more can I expect while *David* lives,
All but his Kingly Diadem he gives;
And that': But there he Paused; then Sighing, said,

Notes

[50] *Angel's Metal* high ambition, with a double pun on angel (*angel-noble*, a gold coin) and *mettle* (temper or spirit).

[51] *Dog-star* Sirius, which is brightest in late summer, during the "dog-days," was thought to cause madness.

[52] *Prevents* goes before; anticipates (Johnson, sense 2).

'Is Justly Destined for a Worthier Head.
For when my Father from his Toils shall Rest,[53]
And late Augment the Number of the Blessed:
His Lawful Issue shall the Throne ascend,
Or the *Collateral* Line where that shall end.[54]
His Brother, though Oppressed with Vulgar Spite,[55]
Yet Dauntless and Secure of Native Right,
Of every Royal Virtue stands possessed;
Still Dear to all the Bravest, and the Best.
His Courage Foes, his Friends his Truth Proclaim;
His Loyalty the King, the World his Fame.
His Mercy even th' Offending Crowd will find,
For sure he comes of a Forgiving Kind.
Why should I then Repine at Heaven's Decree;
Which gives me no Pretence to Royalty?
Yet oh that Fate Propitiously Inclined,
Had raised my Birth, or had debased my Mind;
To my large Soul, not all her Treasure lent,
And then Betrayed it to a mean Descent.
I find, I find my mounting Spirits Bold,
And *David*'s Part disdains my Mother's Mould.
Why am I Scanted by a Niggard Birth,
My Soul Disclaims the Kindred of her Earth:
And made for Empire, Whispers me within;
Desire of Greatness is a Godlike Sin'.
Him Staggering so when Hell's dire Agent found,
While fainting Virtue scarce maintained her Ground,
He pours fresh Forces in, and thus Replies:
'Th' Eternal God Supremely Good and Wise,
Imparts not these Prodigious Gifts in vain;
What Wonders are Reserved to bless your Reign?
Against your will your Arguments have shown,
Such Virtue's only given to guide a Throne.
Not that your Father's mildness I condemn;
But Manly Force becomes the Diadem.
'Tis true, he grants the People all they crave;
And more perhaps than Subjects ought to have:
For Lavish grants suppose a Monarch tame,
And more his Goodness than his Wit proclaim.
But when should People strive their Bonds to break,
If not when Kings are Negligent or Weak?
Let him give on till he can give no more,
The Thrifty Sanhedrin shall keep him poor:[56]
And every Shekel which he can receive,
Shall cost a Limb of his Prerogative.
To ply him with new Plots, shall be my care,

Notes

[53] *Toils* with a pun on sexual endeavors.
[54] *Collateral* "those that stand in equal relation to some common ancestor" (Johnson, sense 4); Charles's brother James was his *collateral* heir to the throne.
[55] *Vulgar Spite* unpopularity.
[56] *Sanhedrin* supreme court of the Jews; Parliament.

Or plunge him deep in some Expensive War;
Which when his Treasure can no more Supply,
He must, with the Remains of Kingship, buy.
His faithful Friends, our Jealousies and Fears,
Call *Jebusites*, and *Pharaoh's* Pensioners:
Whom, when our Fury from his Aid has torn,
He shall be Naked left to public Scorn.
The next Successor, whom I fear and hate,
My Arts have made Obnoxious to the State;
Turned all his Virtues to his Overthrow,
And gained our Elders to pronounce a Foe.
His Right, for Sums of necessary Gold,
Shall first be Pawned, and afterwards be Sold:
Till time shall Ever-wanting *David* draw,
To pass your doubtful Title into Law:
If not; the People have a Right Supreme
To make their Kings; for Kings are made for them.
All Empire is no more than Power in Trust,
Which when resumed, can be no longer Just.
Succession, for the general Good designed,
In its own wrong a Nation cannot bind:
If altering that, the People can relieve,
Better one Suffer, than a Million grieve.
The *Jews* well know their power: ere *Saul* they Chose,
God was their King, and God they durst Depose.[57]
Urge now your Piety, your Filial Name,
A Father's Right, and fear of Future Fame;
The public Good, that Universal Call,
To which even Heav'n Submitted, and answers all.[58]
Nor let his Love Enchant your generous Mind;
'Tis Nature's trick to Propagate her Kind.
Our fond Begetters, who would never die,
Love but themselves in their Posterity.
Or let his Kindness by th' Effects be tried,
Or let him lay his vain Pretence aside.
God said he loved your Father; could he bring
A better Proof, than to Anoint him King?
It surely showed he loved the Shepherd well,
Who gave so fair a Flock as *Israel*.[59]
Would *David* have you thought his Darling Son?
What means he then, to Alienate the Crown?[60]
The name of Godly he may blush to bear:
'Tis after God's own heart to Cheat his Heir.[61]
He to his Brother gives Supreme Command;

Notes

[57] *Saul* Oliver Cromwell, who, as Lord Protector, had monarchical powers. Saul was the first king of Israel, so, in a way, replaced God.

[58] The couplet alludes to a Republican maxim, "Public good is the highest law."

[59] David was born a shepherd.

[60] *Alienate* "To transfer the property of anything to another" (Johnson).

[61] *after God's own heart* David is so described (1 Samuel 13.14); he resembles God in cheating his heirs because God can have no heirs.

To you a Legacy of Barren Land:
Perhaps th' old Harp, on which he thrums his Lays:
Or some dull *Hebrew* Ballad in your Praise.
Then the next Heir, a Prince, Severe and Wise,
Already looks on you with Jealous Eyes;
Sees through the thin Disguises of your Arts,
And marks your Progress in the People's Hearts.
Though now his mighty Soul its Grief contains;
He meditates Revenge who least Complains.
And like a Lion, Slumbering in the way,
Or Sleep-dissembling, while he waits his Prey,
His fearless Foes within his Distance draws;
Constrains his Roaring, and Contracts his Paws;
Till at the last, his time for Fury found,
He shoots with sudden Vengeance from the Ground:
The Prostrate Vulgar, passes o'er, and Spares;
But with a Lordly Rage, his Hunters tears.
Your Case no tame Expedients will afford;
Resolve on Death, or Conquest by the Sword,
Which for no less a Stake than Life, you Draw;
And Self-defence is Nature's Eldest Law.
Leave the warm People no Considering time;
For then Rebellion may be thought a Crime.
Prevail yourself of what Occasion gives,
But try your Title while your Father lives:
And that your Arms may have a fair Pretence,
Proclaim, you take them in the King's Defence:
Whose Sacred life each minute would Expose,
To Plots, from seeming Friends, and secret Foes.
And who can sound the depth of *David*'s Soul?
Perhaps his fear, his kindness may Control.
He fears his Brother, though he loves his Son,
For plighted Vows too late to be undone.
If so, by Force he wishes to be gained,
Like women's Lechery, to seem Constrained:
Doubt not, but when he most affects the Frown,
Commit a pleasing Rape upon the Crown.
Secure his Person to secure your Cause;
They who possess the Prince, possess the Laws'.
  He said, And this Advice above the rest,
With *Absalom*'s Mild nature suited best;
Unblamed of Life (Ambition set aside),
Not stained with Cruelty, nor puffed with Pride;
How happy had he been, if Destiny
Had higher placed his Birth, or not so high?
His Kingly Virtues might have claimed a Throne,
And blessed all other Countries but his own:
But charming Greatness, since so few refuse;
'Tis Juster to Lament him, than Accuse.
Strong were his hopes a Rival to remove,
With blandishments to gain the public Love;
To Head the Faction while their Zeal was hot,

And Popularly prosecute the Plot.
To farther this, *Achitophel* Unites
The Malcontents of all the *Israelites*,
Whose differing Parties he could widely Join,
For several Ends, to serve the same Design.
The Best, and of the Princes some were such,
Who thought the power of Monarchy too much:
Mistaken Men, and Patriots in their Hearts;
Not Wicked, but Seduced by Impious Arts.
By these the Springs of Property were bent,
And wound so high, they Cracked the Government.[62]
The next for Interest sought t'embroil the State,
To sell their Duty at a dearer rate;
And make their *Jewish* Markets of the Throne,
Pretending public Good, to serve their own.
Others thought Kings an useless heavy Load,
Who Cost too much, and did too little Good.
These were for laying Honest *David* by,
On Principles of pure good Husbandry.
With them Joined all th' Haranguers of the Throng,
That thought to get Preferment by the Tongue.
Who follow next, a double Danger bring,
Not only hating *David*, but the King,
The *Solymaean* Rout; well Versed of old,[63]
In Godly Faction, and in Treason bold;
Cow'ring and Quaking at a Conqueror's Sword,
But Lofty to a Lawful Prince Restored;
Saw with Disdain an *Ethnic* Plot begun,[64]
And Scorned by *Jebusites* to be Outdone.
Hot *Levites* Headed these; who pulled before[65]
From th' *Ark*, which in the Judges days they bore,
Resumed their Cant, and with a Zealous Cry,
Pursued their old beloved Theocracy;
Where Sanhedrin and Priest enslaved the Nation,
And justified their Spoils by Inspiration;
For who so fit for Reign as *Aaron*'s Race,[66]
If once Dominion they could found in Grace?
These led the Pack; though not of surest scent,
Yet deepest mouthed against the Government.
A numerous Host of dreaming Saints succeed;
Of the true old Enthusiastic breed:[67]

Notes

[62] Property rights were of paramount importance to some Whigs.

[63] *Solymaean Rout* London rabble; Solyma is a name for Jerusalem, after Salem (Genesis 14.18).

[64] *Ethnic* "Heathen; pagan; not Jewish" (Johnson); in the allegory, Roman Catholic.

[65] *Levites* Old Testament priests; in the allegory, dissenting ministers, deprived in 1662 of the clerical positions (tending *th' Ark* of the covenant with God) they held under the Commonwealth (*in the Judge's days*).

[66] *Aaron's Race* priests.

[67] *dreaming Saints ... Of the true old Enthusiastic breed* dissenting ministers with a "vain belief of private revelation" (Johnson, s.v. *enthusiasm*).

'Gainst Form and Order they their Power employ;
Nothing to Build and all things to Destroy.
But far more numerous was the herd of such,
Who think too little, and talk too much.
These, out of mere instinct, they knew not why,
Adored their fathers' God, and Property:
And, by the same blind benefit of Fate,
The Devil and the Jebusite did hate:
Born to be saved, even in their own despite;
Because they could not help believing right.
Such were the tools; but a whole Hydra more[68]
Remains, of sprouting heads too long, to score.
Some of their Chiefs were Princes of the Land:
In the first Rank of these did *Zimri* stand:[69]
A man so various, that he seemed to be
Not one, but all Mankind's Epitome.
Stiff in Opinions, always in the wrong;
Was everything by starts, and nothing long:
But, in the course of one revolving Moon,
Was Chemist, Fiddler, Statesman, and Buffoon:[70]
Then all for Women, Painting, Rhyming, Drinking;
Besides ten thousand freaks that died in thinking.
Blessed Madman, who could every hour employ,
With something new to wish, or to enjoy!
Railing and praising were his usual Themes;
And both (to show his Judgement) in Extremes:
So over-Violent, or over-Civil,
That every man, with him, was God or Devil.
In squand'ring Wealth was his peculiar Art:
Nothing went unrewarded, but Desert.
Beggared by Fools, whom still he found too late:
He had his Jest, and they had his Estate.
He laughed himself from Court, then sought Relief
By forming Parties, but could ne'er be Chief:
For, spite of him, the weight of Business fell
On *Absalom* and wise *Achitophel*:
Thus, wicked but in will, of means bereft,
He left not Faction, but of that was left.
Titles and Names 'twere tedious to Rehearse
Of Lords, below the Dignity of Verse.
Wits, warriors, Commonwealth's-men, were the best:
Kind Husbands and mere Nobles all the rest.

Notes

68 *Hydra* many-headed monster slain by Hercules.

69 *Zimri* the name of a lecherous murderer in Numbers 25 and a murderous usurper in 1 Kings 16; here he is George Villiers (1628–87), second duke of Buckingham, a minister in Charles's government until 1674 when he was impeached and went over to the opposition; he was also Dryden's literary adversary and had, in collaboration with others, ridiculed him in *The Rehearsal* (1671).

70 *Chemist* The meaning "alchemist" was still present in the word at this time. Buckingham was accomplished in chemistry, music, and politics, and he was a madcap rake who squandered a fortune, had open affairs at court, and killed a man in a duel.

And, therefore in the name of Dullness, be
The well-hung *Balaam* and cold *Caleb* free.[71]
And Canting *Nadab* let Oblivion damn,[72]
Who made new porridge for the Paschal Lamb.[73]
Let Friendship's holy band some Names assure:
Some their own Worth, and some let Scorn secure.
Nor shall the Rascal Rabble here have Place,
Whom Kings no Titles gave, and God no Grace:
Not Bull-faced *Jonas*, who could Statutes draw[74]
To mean Rebellion, and make Treason Law.
But he, though bad, is followed by a worse,
The wretch, who Heaven's Anointed dared to Curse.
Shimei, whose early Youth did Promise bring[75]
Of Zeal to God, and Hatred to his King;
Did wisely from Expensive Sins refrain,
And never broke the Sabbath, but for Gain:
Nor ever was known an Oath to vent,
Or Curse unless against the Government.
Thus, heaping Wealth, by the most ready way
Among the Jews, which was to Cheat and Pray;
The City, to reward his pious Hate
Against his Master, chose him Magistrate:
His Hand a Vare of Justice did uphold;[76]
His Neck was loaded with a Chain of Gold.
During his Office, Treason was no Crime.
The Sons of *Belial* had a glorious Time:[77]
For *Shimei*, though not prodigal of pelf,
Yet loved his wicked Neighbour as himself:
When two or three were gathered to declaim
Against the Monarch of *Jerusalem*,
Shimei was always in the midst of them.
And, if they Cursed the King when he was by,
Would rather Curse, than break good Company.
If any durst his Factious Friends accuse,
He packed a Jury of dissenting Jews:

Notes

71 *Balaam* a prophet or diviner who tried to ignore the word of God in order to serve the politically powerful (Numbers 22–4); probably Theophilus Hastings, who evidently fit the coarser meaning of "well-hung," which also means glib or well-spoken; *Caleb* a faithful servant of Moses (Numbers 13–14) who at an advanced age enters the Promised Land with Joshua (Joshua 14); enigmatically, he represents Arthur Capel, earl of Essex (1631–83), a strong advocate of the Exclusion Bill, eventually imprisoned in the Tower, where he died violently.

72 *Nadab* an idolatrous priest in Leviticus (10.1–2), he represents William, Lord Howard of Esrick (1626–94), a dissenting minister; *canting* preaching derisively.

73 *porridge* a slang term for the Church of England's Book of Common Prayer, but the line also refers to Lord Howard's innovative method of taking communion in a lumpy mixture of ale and apples.

74 *Jonas* Sir William Jones (1631–82), attorney general from 1675 to 1679 when he joined the opposition; the biblical character in the Book of Jonah offers only very rough parallels to Jones.

75 *Shimei* a man of the House of Saul who curses David and throws stones at him (II Samuel 16); he represents Slingsby Bethel (1617–97), an old commonwealth's-man and a sheriff of London in 1680–1.

76 *Vare* staff.

77 *Sons of Belial* proverbial for debauched and rebellious men; cf. Milton, *Paradise Lost* 1:500–2.

Whose fellow-feeling, in the godly Cause,
Would free the suff'ring Saint from Human Laws.
For Laws are only made to Punish those,
Who serve the King, and to protect his Foes.
If any leisure time he had from Power
(Because 'tis Sin to misimploy an hour),
His business was, by Writing, to Persuade,
That Kings were Useless, and a Clog to Trade:
And, that his noble Style he might refine,
No *Rechabite* more shunned the fumes of Wine.[78]
Chaste were his Cellars, and his Shrieval Board[79]
The Grossness of a City Feast abhorred:
His Cooks, with long disuse, their Trade forgot;
Cool was his Kitchen, though his Brains were hot.
Such frugal Virtue Malice may accuse,
But sure 'twas necessary to the Jews:
For Towns once burnt, such Magistrates require[80]
As dare not tempt God's Providence by fire.
With Spiritual food he fed his Servants well,
But free from flesh, that made the Jews Rebel:
And *Moses*'s Laws he held in more account,
For forty days of Fasting in the Mount.
To speak the rest, who better are forgot,
Would tire a well-breathed Witness of the Plot:
Yet, *Corah*, thou shalt from Oblivion pass;[81]
Erect thyself thou Monumental Brass:[82]
High as the Serpent of thy metal made,[83]
While Nations stand secure beneath thy shade.
What though this Bird were base, yet Comets rise
From Earthly Vapours ere they shine in Skies.
Prodigious Actions may as well be done
By Weaver's issue, as by Prince's Son.[84]
This Arch-Attestor for the Public Good,
By that one Deed Ennobles all his Blood.[85]
Who ever asked the Witnesses' high race,
Whose Oath with Martyrdom did *Stephen* grace?[86]
Ours was a *Levite*, and as times went then,
His Tribe was God Almighty's Gentlemen.
Sunk were his Eyes, his Voice was harsh and loud,

Notes

78 *Rechabite* a son of Rechab, sworn to abstinence from alcohol (Jeremiah 35).

79 *Shrieval Board* Sheriff's dinner table, which was traditionally a site of civic feasting.

80 *Towns once burnt* as London was in 1666.

81 *Corah* leader of a short-lived rebellion against the authority of Moses, recounted in Numbers 16; here, Titus Oates (1649–1705), a perjurious inventor of the "Popish Plot" (see n. 1 above) and, for three years, a prosecutor of alleged conspirators.

82 *Brass* also meaning "Impudence" (Johnson, sense 2).

83 *Serpent of thy metal made* God instructs Moses to make a serpent of brass to protect his people in the wilderness (Numbers 21.9).

84 *Weaver's issue* Oates's father was a weaver.

85 *Ennobles all his Blood* In his glory days, Oates commissioned a coat of arms to be found for his family.

86 *Stephen* St. Stephen, the first Christian martyr and a victim of false witnesses (Acts 6–7).

Sure signs he neither Choleric was, nor Proud:[87]
His long Chin proved his Wit; his Saintlike Grace
A Church Vermilion, and a *Moses*'s Face;[88]
His Memory, miraculously great,
Could Plots, exceeding man's belief, repeat;
Which, therefore cannot be accounted Lies,
For human Wit could never such devise.
Some future Truths are mingled in his Book;
But, where the witness failed, the Prophet Spoke:
Some things like Visionary flights appear;
The Spirit caught him up, the Lord knows where:
And gave him his *Rabbinical* degree[89]
Unknown to Foreign University.
His Judgement yet his Memory did excel;
Which pieced his wondrous Evidence so well:
And suited to the temper of the times;
Then groaning under Jebusitic Crimes.
Let *Israel*'s foes suspect his heav'nly call,
And rashly judge his wit Apocryphal;
Our Laws for such affronts have forfeits made:
He takes his life, who takes away his trade.
Were I myself in witness *Corah*'s place,
The wretch who did me such a dire disgrace,
Should whet my memory, though once forgot,
To make him an Appendix of my Plot.[90]
His Zeal to Heav'n, made him his Prince despise,
And load his person with indignities:
But Zeal peculiar privilege affords;
Indulging latitude to deeds and words.
And *Corah* might for *Agag*'s murder call,[91]
In terms as coarse as *Samuel* used to *Saul*.
What others in his Evidence did Join,
(The best that could be had for love of coin),
In *Corah*'s own predicament will fall:
For *witness* is a Common Name to all.
   Surrounded thus with Friends of every sort,
Deluded *Absalom*, forsakes the Court:
Impatient of high hopes, urged with renown,
And Fired with near possession of a Crown,
Th' admiring Crowd are dazzled with surprise,
And on his goodly person feed their eyes:

Notes

[87] These are the surest signs of choleric (hot) temper and pride.

[88] *Church Vermilion* the ruddy complexion of a well-fed parson; *Moses's Face* a face glowing with inspiration; both are ironic proofs of Oates's Saintlike Grace.

[89] *Rabbinical degree* Oates claimed to have a Doctor of Divinity degree from Salamanca.

[90] To his *True Narrative of the Horrid Plot* (1679) Oates appended a list of "conspirators."

[91] *Agag* king of the Amalekites, whom God, according to Samuel, wished Saul to annihilate; when Saul took Agag prisoner, Samuel told him he had incurred God's disfavor, and His anger was not entirely assuaged by Saul's penitent slaughter of his captive (1 Samuel 15). In the poem, Agag could be taken as James, though it is not clear.

Dissembling Joy, he sets himself to show;
On each side bowing popularly low:
His looks, his gestures, and his words he frames,
And with familiar ease repeats their Names.
Thus, formed by Nature, furnished out with Arts,
He glides unfelt into their secret hearts:
Then with a kind compassionate look,
And sighs, bespeaking pity ere he spoke,
Few words he said; but easy those and fit:
More slow than Hybla drops, and far more sweet.[92]
'I mourn, my Countrymen, your lost Estates;
Though far unable to prevent your fate:
Behold a Banished man, for your dear cause[93]
Exposed a prey to Arbitrary laws!
Yet oh! that I alone could be undone,
Cut off from Empire, and no more a Son!
Now all your Liberties a spoil are made;
Egypt and *Tyrus* intercept your Trade,[94]
And Jebusites your Sacred Rites invade.
My Father, whom with reverence yet I name,
Charmed into Ease, is careless of his Fame:
And, bribed with petty sums of Foreign Gold,
Is grown in *Bathsheba*'s Embraces old:[95]
Exalts his Enemies, his Friends destroys:
And all his power against himself employs.
He gives, and let him give my right away:
But why should he his own, and yours betray?
He only, he can make the Nation bleed,
And he alone from my revenge is freed.
Take then my tears (with that he wiped his Eyes)
'Tis all the Aid my present power supplies:
No Court Informer can these Arms accuse,
These Arms may Sons against their Fathers use,
And, 'tis my wish, the next Successor's Reign
May make no other Israelite complain'.
Youth, Beauty, Graceful Action, seldom fail:
But Common Interest always will prevail:
And pity never Ceases to be shown
To him, who makes the people's wrongs his own.
The Crowd (that still believes their Kings oppress)
With lifted hands their young *Messiah* bless:
Who now begins his Progress to ordain;[96]

Notes

92 *Hybla drops* honey, so called after a Greek town in Sicily renowned in Latin poetry for producing it.

93 *Banished man* Recovering from an illness that had galvanized both the exclusionists and the loyalists, Charles decommissioned Monmouth and ordered both him and York (later James II) to leave the country in September 1679, but by November 27, Monmouth was back in London.

94 *Egypt and Tyrus* France and Holland.

95 *Bathsheba* a beautiful married woman with whom David conceived a child before sending her husband off to die in battle and marrying her himself (II Samuel 11); in the poem, Louise de Kéroualle, duchess of Portsmouth (see Rochester's "A Satire on Charles II," l. 21, p. 391).

96 *Progress* "A journey of State" (Johnson, sense 5); Monmouth made such a *progress* in the summer of 1680.

With Chariots, Horsemen, and a numerous train:
From East to West his Glories he displays:
And, like the Sun, the promised land surveys.
Fame runs before him, as the morning Star;
And shouts of Joy salute him from afar:
Each house receives him as a Guardian God;
And Consecrates the Place of his abode:
But hospitable treats did most Commend
Wise *Issachar*, his wealthy western friend.[97]
This moving Court, that caught the people's Eyes
And seemed but Pomp, did other ends disguise:
Achitophel had formed it, with intent
To sound the depth, and fathom where it went:
The People's hearts, distinguish Friends from Foes;
And try their strength, before they came to blows:
Yet all was coloured with a smooth pretence
Of specious love, and duty to their Prince.
Religion, and Redress of Grievances,
Two names, that always cheat and always please,
Are often urged; and good King *David*'s life
Endangered by a Brother and a Wife.[98]
Thus, in a Pageant Show, a Plot is made;
And Peace itself is War in Masquerade.
Oh foolish *Israel*! never warned by ill,
Still the same bait, and circumvented still![99]
Did ever men forsake their present ease,
In midst of health Imagine a disease;
Take pains Contingent mischiefs to foresee,
Make Heirs for Monarchs, and for God decree?
What shall we think! can People give away
Both for themselves and Sons, their Native sway?
Then they are left Defenceless, to the Sword
Of each unbounded Arbitrary Lord:
And Laws are vain, by which we Right enjoy,
If Kings unquestioned can those laws destroy.
Yet, if the Crowd be Judge of fit and Just,
And Kings are only Officers in trust,
Then this resuming Cov'nant was declared[100]
When Kings were made, or is for ever barred:
If those who gave the Sceptre, could not tie
By their own deed their own Posterity,
How then could *Adam* bind his future Race?

Notes

[97] *Issachar* literally, "my hire"; a son of Jacob and Leah, so named because Leah had hired Jacob for the night of his conception with a portion of game given to Rachel (Genesis 30.14–18); when grown, Issachar is described as fat and lazy (Genesis 49.14–15); in the poem, Thomas Thynne (1648–82), a wealthy supporter of Monmouth from Wiltshire.

[98] *Brother and a Wife* Oates implicated both Charles's brother James and Queen Catherine.

[99] *circumvented* "deceived; cheated; deluded" (Johnson).

[100] *resuming* "To resume … To take back what has been given" (Johnson).

How could his forfeit on mankind take place?
Or how could heavenly Justice damn us all,
Who ne'er consented to our Father's fall?
Then Kings are slaves to those whom they Command,
And Tenants to their People's pleasure stand.
That Power, which is for Property allowed,
Is mischievously seated in the Crowd:
For who can be secure of private Right,
If Sovereign sway may be dissolved by might?
Nor is the People's Judgement always true:
The most may err as grossly as the few,
And faultless Kings run down, by Common Cry,
For Vice, Oppression, and for Tyranny.
What Standard is there in a fickle rout,[101]
Which flowing to the mark, runs faster out?[102]
Nor only Crowds, but Sanhedrins may be
Infected with this public Lunacy:
And Share the madness of Rebellious times,
To Murder Monarchs for Imagined crimes.
If they may Give and Take when e'er they please,
Not Kings alone (the Godhead's Images),
But Government itself at length must fall
To Nature's state; where all have Right to all.
Yet, grant our Lords the People Kings can make,
What Prudent men a settled Throne would shake?
For whatso'er their Sufferings were before,
That Change they Covet makes them suffer more.
All other Errors but disturb a State;
But Innovation is the Blow of Fate.
If ancient Fabrics nod, and threat to fall,[103]
To Patch the Flaws, and Buttress up the Wall,
Thus far 'tis Duty; but here fix the Mark:
For all beyond is to touch our Ark.[104]
To change Foundations, cast the Frame anew,
Is work for Rebels who base Ends pursue:
At once Divine and Human Laws control;
And mend the Parts by ruin of the Whole.
The Tampering World is subject to this Curse,
To Physic their Disease into a worse.[105]
 Now what Relief can Righteous *David* bring?
How Fatal 'tis to be too good a King!
Friends he has few, so high the Madness grows;
Who dare be such, must be the People's Foes:
Yet some there were, ev'n in the worst of days;

Notes

[101] *rout* "A clamorous multitude; a rabble; a tumultuous crowd" (Johnson).

[102] mark high tide or high water mark.

[103] *Fabrics* buildings.

[104] *Ark* the biblical ark of the covenant, to disturb which is sacrilege.

[105] *Physic* medicate, especially with purgatives.

Some let me name, and Naming is to praise.
In this short File *Barzillai* first appears;[106]
Barzillai crowned with Honour and with Years:
Long since, the rising Rebels he withstood
In Regions Waste, beyond the *Jordan's* Flood:[107]
Unfortunately Brave to buoy the State;
But sinking underneath his Master's Fate:
In Exile with his Godlike Prince he Mourned;
For him he Suffered, and with him Returned.
The Court he practised, not the Courtier's art:
Large was his Wealth, but larger was his Heart:
Which, well the Noblest Objects knew to choose,
The Fighting Warrior, and Recording Muse.
His Bed could once a Fruitful Issue boast:
Now more than half a Father's Name is lost.
His Eldest Hope, with every Grace adorned,[108]
By me (so Heav'n will have it) always Mourned,
And always honoured, snatched in Manhood's prime
By unequal Fates, and Providence's crime:
Yet not before the Goal of Honour won,
All parts fulfilled of Subject and of Son;
Swift was the Race, but short the Time to run.
Oh Narrow Circle, but of Power Divine,
Scanted in Space, but perfect in thy Line!
By Sea, by Land, thy Matchless Worth was known;
Arms thy Delight, and War was all thy Own:
Thy force, Infused, the fainting *Tyrians* propped:
And Haughty *Pharaoh* found his Fortune stopped.[109]
Oh Ancient Honour, Oh Unconquered Hand,
Whom Foes unpunished never could withstand!
But *Israel* was unworthy of thy Birth;
Short is the date of all Immoderate Worth.
It looks as Heaven our Ruin had designed,
And durst not trust thy Fortune and thy Mind.
Now, free from Earth, thy disencumbered Soul
Mounts up, and leaves behind the Clouds and Starry Pole:[110]
From thence thy kindred legions mayst thou bring
To aid the guardian Angel of thy King.
Here stop my Muse, here cease thy painful flight;
No Pinions can pursue Immortal height:
Tell good *Barzillai* thou canst sing no more,
And tell thy Soul she should have fled before;

Notes

[106] *Barzillai* a humble old man who was loyal to King David during Absalom's rebellion (II Samuel 19.31–9); here, James Butler, duke of Ormonde, lord lieutenant of Ireland under Charles I and Charles II; he joined Charles II in exile and with him returned.

[107] *Regions Waste* desert places; here Ireland.

[108] *His Eldest Hope* Thomas Butler, earl of Ossory, died at age 46, in the year before the publication of *Absalom and Achitophel*.

[109] The Duke of Ormonde's eldest son helped the Dutch (Tyrians) fight the French.

[110] *Pole* sky.

Or fled she with his life, and left this Verse
To hang on her departed Patron's Hearse?[111]
Now take thy steepy flight from heaven, and see
If thou canst find on earth another *He*,
Another he would be too hard to find,
See then whom thou canst see not far behind.
Zadok the Priest, whom, shunning Power and Place,[112]
His lowly mind advanced to *David*'s Grace:
With him the *Sagan* of *Jerusalem*,[113]
Of hospitable Soul and noble Stem;
Him of the Western dome, whose weighty sense[114]
Flows in fit words and heavenly eloquence.
The Prophets' Sons by such example led,[115]
To Learning and to Loyalty were bred:
For *Colleges* on bounteous Kings depend,
And never Rebel was to Arts a friend.
To these succeed the Pillars of the Laws,
Who best could plead and best can judge a Cause.
Next them a train of Loyal Peers ascend:
Sharp judging *Adriel* the Muses' friend,[116]
Himself a Muse – In Sanhedrin's debate
True to his Prince; but not a Slave of State,
Whom *David*'s love with Honours did adorn,
That from his disobedient Son were torn.
Jotham of ready wit and pregnant thought,[117]
Endued by nature, and by learning taught
To move Assemblies, who but only tried
The worse awhile, then chose the better side;
Nor chose alone, but turned the balance too;
So much the weight of one brave man can do.
Hushai the friend of *David* in distress,[118]
In public storms of manly steadfastness;
By foreign treaties he informed his Youth;
And joined experience to his native truth.
His frugal care supplied the wanting Throne,

Notes

111 *Hearse* "A temporary monument set over a grave" (Johnson, sense 2).

112 *Zadok* He follows King David into the wilderness, bringing with him the ark of the covenant, but David sends him with the ark to await God's judgment in Jerusalem (II Samuel 16.24–9). In the poem, he is William Sancroft (1617–93), archbishop of Canterbury.

113 *Sagan* a high Jewish clerical officer, representing Henry Compton (1632–1713), bishop of London.

114 *Him of the Western dome* John Dolben, Dean of Westminster Abbey.

115 *Prophets' Sons* the students of Westminster School, Dryden's old school.

116 *Adriel* son of Barzillai (II Samuel 21.8; see n. 101 above); he represents John Sheffield, third earl of Mulgrave (1647– 1721), one of Dryden's patrons, an enemy to Monmouth, friend to James, and poet.

117 *Jotham* the only son of Jerubaal to survive the murderous conspiracy of Abimelech, he delivers an oracular speech against usurpation (Judges 9.1–21); in the poem, George Savile (1633–95), marquess of Halifax, who, though he was a longtime ally of Shaftesbury, spoke effectively against the Exclusion Bill.

118 *Hushai* "David's friend" (II Samuel 15.37) and ally working covertly in Absalom's court; in the poem, Lawrence Hyde (1642–1711), earl of Rochester, first lord of the treasury under Charles, a stern opponent of Exclusion, and another of Dryden's patrons.

Frugal for that, but bounteous of his own:
'Tis easy conduct when Exchequers flow,
But hard the task to manage well the low:
For Sovereign power is too depressed or high,
When Kings are forced to sell, or Crowds to buy.
Indulge one labour more my weary Muse,
For *Amiel*, who can *Amiel*'s praise refuse?[119]
Of ancient race by birth, but nobler yet
In his own worth, and without Title great:
The Sanhedrin long time as chief he ruled,
Their Reason guided and their Passion cooled;
So dexterous was he in the Crown's defence,
So formed to speak a Loyal Nation's Sense,
That as their band was *Israel*'s Tribes in small,
So fit was he to represent them all.
Now rasher Charioteers the Seat ascend,
Whose loose Careers his steady Skill commend:
They like th' unequal Ruler of the Day,[120]
Misguide the Seasons and Mistake the Way;
While he withdrawn at their mad Labour smiles,
And safe enjoys the Sabbath of his Toils.
  These were the chief, a small but faithful Band
Of Worthies, in the Breach who dared to stand,
And tempt th' united Fury of the Land.[121]
With grief they viewed such powerful Engines bent,
To batter down the lawful Government.
A numerous Faction with pretended frights,
In Sanhedrins to plume the Regal Rights:[122]
The true Successor from the Court removed;
The Plot, by hireling Witnesses improved.
These Ills they saw, and, as their Duty bound,
They showed the King the danger of the Wound:
That no Concessions from the Throne would please,
But Lenitives fomented the Disease:
That *Absalom*, ambitious of the Crown,
Was made the Lure to draw the People down:[123]
That false *Achitophel*'s pernicious Hate,
Had turned the Plot to Ruin Church and State:
The Council violent, the Rabble worse:
That *Shimei* taught *Jerusalem* to Curse.
  With all these loads of Injuries oppressed,
And long revolving, in his careful Breast,
Th' event of things; at last his patience tired,[124]

Notes

[119] *Amiel* In the story of Absalom's rebellion, Machir, son of Amiel, accompanies Barzillai on a mission to supply David in the wilderness (II Samuel 17.27); in the poem, he is Edward Seymour, speaker of the House of Commons from 1673 to 1678 and treasurer of the Navy until 1681.

[120] *th' unequal Ruler of the Day* Phaeton, who lost control of the chariot of the sun and scorched the earth (Ovid, *Metamorphoses* 2.1–328).

[121] *tempt* to try, test, or attempt (to withstand).

[122] *plume* "To strip; to pill" (Johnson, sense 3).

[123] *Lure* an artificial bird used to attract hawks.

[124] *event* outcome.

Thus from his Royal Throne by Heav'n inspired,
The God-like *David* spoke: with awful fear
His Train their Maker in their Master hear.
'Thus long have I by native mercy swayed,
My wrongs dissembled, my revenge delayed:
So willing to forgive th' Offending Age,
So much the Father did the King assuage.
But now so far my Clemency they slight,
Th' Offenders question my Forgiving Right.
That one was made for many, they contend:
But 'tis to Rule, for that's a Monarch's End.
They call my tenderness of Blood, my Fear:
Though Manly tempers can the longest bear.
Yet, since they will divert my Native course,
'Tis time to show I am not Good by Force.
Those heaped Affronts that haughty Subjects bring,
Are burdens for a Camel, not a King:
Kings are the public Pillars of the State,
Born to sustain and prop the Nation's weight:
If my Young *Samson* will pretend a Call[125]
To shake the Column, let him share the Fall:
But oh that yet he would repent and live![126]
How easy 'tis for Parents to forgive!
With how few Tears a Pardon might be won
From Nature, pleading for a Darling Son!
Poor pitied Youth by my Paternal care,
Raised up to all the Height his Frame could bear:
Had God ordained his fate for Empire born,
He would have given his Soul another turn:
Gulled with a Patriot's name, whose Modern sense
Is one that would by Law destroy his Prince:
The People's Brave, the Politician's Tool;[127]
Never was Patriot yet, but was a Fool.
Whence comes it that Religion and the Laws
Should more be *Absalom*'s than *David*'s Cause?
His old Instructor, ere he lost his Place,
Was never thought endued with so much Grace.
Good Heav'ns, how Faction can a Patriot Paint!
My Rebel ever proves my People's Saint:
Would *They* impose an Heir upon the Throne?
Let Sanhedrins be taught to give their Own.
A King's at least a part of Government,
And mine as requisite as their Consent:
Without my Leave a future King to choose,

Notes

[125] *Samson* Called out of his cell by his reveling captors, Samson dislodges a supporting pillar and topples over the house, killing himself and many of his enemies (Judges 16.25–31).

[126] *But oh … Darling Son!* added in the third London edition (1681).

[127] *Brave* "A hector; a man daring beyond decency or discretion" (Johnson).

Infers a Right the Present to Depose:
True, they Petition me t' approve their Choice,
But *Esau*'s Hands suit ill with *Jacob*'s Voice.[128]
My Pious Subjects for my Safety pray,
Which to Secure they take my Power away.
From Plots and Treasons Heaven preserve my years,
But Save me most from my Petitioners.
Unsatiate as the barren Womb or Grave;[129]
God cannot Grant so much as they can Crave.
What then is left but with a Jealous Eye
To guard the Small remains of Royalty?
The Law shall still direct my peaceful Sway,
And the same Law teach Rebels to Obey:
Votes shall no more Established Power control,
Such Votes as make a Part exceed the Whole:
No groundless Clamours shall my Friends remove,
Nor Crowds have power to Punish ere they Prove:
For Gods, and Godlike Kings their care express,
Still to Defend their Servants in distress.
Oh that my Power to Saving were confined:
Why am I forced, like Heaven, against my mind,
To make Examples of another Kind?
Must I at length the Sword of Justice draw?
Oh cursed Effects of necessary Law!
How ill my Fear they by my Mercy scan,[130]
Beware the Fury of a Patient Man.
Law they require, let Law then show her Face;
They could not be content to look on Grace,
Her hinder parts, but with a daring Eye
To tempt the terror of her Front, and Die.[131]
By their own arts 'tis Righteously decreed,
Those dire Artificers of Death shall bleed.
Against themselves their Witnesses will Swear,
Till Viper-like their Mother Plot they tear:[132]
And suck for nutriment that bloody gore
Which was their Principle of Life before.
Their *Belial* with their *Belzebub* will fight;[133]
Thus on my Foes, my Foes shall do me Right:
Nor doubt th' event: for Factious crowds engage
In their first Onset, all their Brutal Rage;
Then, let 'em take an unresisted Course,
Retire and Traverse, and Delude their Force:[134]

Notes

128 *Esau's Hands ... Jacob's Voice* Jacob pretended to be his brother Esau, covering his hairless arms and neck with goat hair, and usurped the blessing of his father Isaac (Genesis 27).

129 See Proverbs 30.15–16.

130 *scan* "to judge by a certain rule" (*OED*, 2).

131 *Law... Front, and Die* The hinder part of law is grace, in this analogy between the king's law and God's glory, as it is described in Exodus: Moses cannot look upon God's face without death, but he is permitted to see God's "back parts" as He passes (33.19–23).

132 Snakes were thought to tear their mothers' bellies to be born.

133 *Belial ... Belzebub* fallen angels and leaders of the satanic crew in *Paradise Lost* 1–2.

134 *Retire ... Traverse ... Delude* take evasive action.

But when they stand all Breathless, urge the fight,
And rise upon 'em with redoubled might:
For Lawful Power is still Superior found,
When long driven back, at length it stands the ground'.
He said. Th' Almighty, nodding, gave Consent;
And Peals of Thunder shook the Firmament.
Henceforth a Series of new time began,
The mighty Years in long Procession ran:
Once more the Godlike *David* was Restored,
And willing Nations knew their Lawful Lord.

To the Memory of Mr. *Oldham*[1] (1684)

Farewell, too little and too lately known,
Whom I began to think and call my own;
For sure our Souls were near allied; and thine
Cast in the same Poetic mould with mine.
One common Note on either Lyre did strike,
And Knaves and Fools were both abhorred alike:
To the same Goal did both our Studies drive,
The last set out the soonest did arrive.
Thus *Nisus* fell upon the slippery place,[2]
While his young Friend performed and won the Race.
O early ripe! to thy abundant store
What could advancing Age have added more?
It might (what Nature never gives the young)
Have taught the numbers of thy native Tongue.[3]
But Satire needs not those, and Wit will shine
Through the harsh cadence of a rugged line.[4]
A noble Error, and but seldom made,
When Poets are by too much force betrayed,
Thy generous fruits, though gathered ere their prime
Still showed a quickness; and maturing time[5]
But mellows what we write to the dull sweets of Rhyme.
Once more, hail and farewell; farewell thou young[6]
But ah too short, *Marcellus* of our Tongue;[7]
Thy Brows with Ivy, and with Laurels bound;
But Fate and gloomy Night encompass thee around.

Notes

To the Memory of Mr. *Oldham*

1 John Oldham (1653–83) was a poet best known for his *Satyrs upon the Jesuits* (1681); he probably met Dryden in London shortly after the publication of that work, but allusions in his earlier work show that he had admired Dryden for years. The poem first appeared in *Remains of Mr. John Oldham in Verse and Prose* (1684).

2 *Nisus* having fallen near the finish line, he tripped the next runner and gave the victory to his close friend Euryalus (*Aeneid* 5.315–39).

3 *numbers* harmony, correct prosody.

4 The rugged harmony of this line exemplifies the kind of verse it praises.

5 *quickness* "Sharpness; pungency" (Johnson) as well as aliveness.

6 *hail and farewell* echoing a famous poem by Catullus (101) to his brother.

7 *Marcellus* adoptive son of Augustus Caesar, destined to rule, who died at the age of twenty and was memorialized in a famous passage of the *Aeneid* (6.860–6).

To the Pious Memory of the Accomplished Young LADY Mrs. Anne Killigrew[1], Excellent in the Two Sister-Arts of Poesy, and Painting. An Ode (1686)

I

Thou Youngest Virgin-Daughter of the Skies,
Made in the last Promotion of the Blessed;
Whose Palms, new plucked from Paradise,[2]
In spreading Branches more sublimely rise,
Rich with Immortal Green above the rest:
Whether, adopted to some Neighbouring Star,[3]
Thou roll'st above us, in thy wand'ring Race,
Or, in Procession fixed and regular,[4]
Moved with the Heaven's Majestic Pace;
Or, called to more Superior Bliss,
Thou tread'st, with Seraphims, the vast Abyss:
Whatever happy region be thy place,
Cease thy Celestial Song a little space;
(Thou wilt have time enough for Hymns Divine,
Since Heav'n's Eternal Year is thine.)
Hear then a Mortal Muse thy Praise rehearse,[5]
In no ignoble Verse;
But such as thy own voice did practise here,
When thy first Fruits of Poesy were giv'n,[6]
To make thyself a welcome Inmate there:
While yet a young Probationer,[7]
And Candidate of Heav'n.

2

If by Traduction[8] came thy Mind,
Our Wonder is the less to find
A Soul so charming from a Stock so good;
Thy Father was transfused into thy Blood:
So wert thou born into the tuneful strain,
(An early, rich, and inexhausted Vein.)
But if thy Pre-existing Soul
Was formed, at first, with Myriads more,
It did through all the Mighty Poets roll,

Notes

AN ODE

1 Anne Killigrew (1660–85), a talented noblewoman who died of smallpox at age twenty-five. Dryden's poem first appeared in the slender volume of Killigrew's poetry published shortly after her death. She was also a painter. "Mrs." in the title stands for "mistress," which was at the time usually prefixed to the names of upper-class women like Anne, whether married or not. Anne was unmarried.

2 *Palms* in the Book of Revelation the blessed are described as carrying *palms* (7.9), which were classical and Hebrew tokens of victory.

3 *Star* planet or, etymologically, wanderer.

4 *Procession fixed* the Ptolemaic fixed sphere of the stars.

5 *a Mortal Muse* a living poet.

6 *first Fruits* "entire revenue of one year" (*OED*, s.v. *annates*).

7 *Probationer* novice.

8 *Traduction* a process by which the *Mind*, or soul, destined for a mortal is transmitted through the medium of related souls.

Who *Greek* or *Latin* Laurels wore,
And was that *Sappho* last, which once it was before.[9]
If so, then cease thy flight, O Heav'n-born Mind!
Thou hast no Dross to purge from thy Rich Ore:[10]
Nor can thy Soul a fairer Mansion find,
Than was the Beauteous Frame she left behind:
Return, to fill or mend the Quire, of thy Celestial kind.

3

May we presume to say, that at thy Birth,
New joy was sprung in Heav'n, as well as here on Earth.
For sure the Milder Planets did combine
On thy Auspicious Horoscope to shine,
And ev'n the most Malicious were in Trine.[11]
Thy Brother-Angels at thy Birth
Strung each his Lyre, and tuned it high,
That all the People of the Sky
Might know a Poetess was born on Earth.
And then, if ever, Mortal Ears
Had heard the Music of the Spheres![12]
And if no clust'ring Swarm of Bees[13]
On thy sweet Mouth distilled their golden Dew,
'Twas that, such vulgar Miracles
Heav'n had not Leisure to renew:
For all the Blessed Fraternity of Love
Solemnised there thy Birth, and kept thy Holiday above.

4

O Gracious God! How far have we
Profaned thy Heav'nly Gift of Poesy!
Made prostitute and profligate the Muse,
Debased to each obscene and impious use,
Whose Harmony was first ordained Above
For Tongues of Angels, and for Hymns of Love!
O wretched We! why were we hurried down
This lubric and adult'rate age,[14]
(Nay added fat Pollutions of our own)[15]
T' increase the steaming Ordures of the stage?
What can we say t' excuse our *Second Fall*?
Let this thy *Vestal*, Heav'n, atone for all!
Her *Arethusian* Stream remains unsoiled,[16]
Unmixed with Foreign Filth, and undefiled;
Her Wit was more than Man, her Innocence a Child!

Notes

9 *Sappho* Greek lyric poet (fl. 600 BCE).
10 *no Dross to purge* in Plato's *Phaedrus*, the soul seeks to perfect itself through its successive reincarnations.
11 *Trine* a benign configuration of planets in astrology.
12 *Music of the Spheres* the harmonious sound thought to be generated by the synchronous movement of the spheres in the Ptolemaic universe, but inaudible after the fall of man.
13 *Bees* said to have buzzed round the lips of the infant Plato, an omen that he would have the gift of sweet speech.
14 *lubric* "Wanton; lewd" (Johnson).
15 *fat* "Coarse; gross; dull" (Johnson).
16 *Arethusian* chaste, pure, like Arethusa, a nymph changed by Diana into a stream to escape rape by Alpheus.

5

Art she had none, yet wanted none:[17]
For Nature did that Want supply:
So rich in Treasures of her Own,
She might our boasted Stores defy:
Such Noble Vigour did her Verse adorn,
That it seemed borrowed, where 'twas only born.
Her Morals too were in her Bosom bred,
By great Examples daily fed,
What in the best of Books, her Father's Life, she read:
And to be read herself she need not fear;
Each Test, and every Light, her Muse will bear,
Though *Epictetus* with his Lamp were there.[18]
Even Love (for Love sometimes her Muse expressed)
Was but a *Lambent-flame* which played about her Breast,
Light as the Vapours of a Morning Dream,
So cold herself, whilst she such Warmth expressed,
'Twas *Cupid* bathing in *Diana*'s Stream.

6

Born to the spacious Empire of the *Nine*,[19]
One would have thought, she should have been content
To manage well that Mighty Government;
But what can young ambitious Souls confine?
To the next Realm she stretched her Sway,
For *Painture* near adjoining lay,[20]
A plenteous Province, and alluring Prey.
A *Chamber of Dependences* was framed,[21]
(As Conquerors will never want Pretence,
When armed, to justify the offence)
And the whole Fief, in right of Poetry she claimed.
The Country open lay without Defence;
For Poets frequent inroads there had made,
And perfectly could represent
The Shape, the Face, with every Lineament,
And all the large Domains which the *Dumb-sister* swayed;
All bowed beneath her Government,
Received in Triumph wheresoe'er she went.
Her Pencil drew, whate'er her Soul designed,
And oft the happy Draught surpassed the Image in her Mind.[22]
The *Sylvan* Scenes of Herds and Flocks,

Notes

17 *wanted* lacked.

18 *Epictetus* Stoic philosopher of the first century CE who lived an exemplary, simple life, with no furniture except a bed and a lamp.

19 *Nine* the nine muses, none of them devoted to painting.

20 *Painture* the art of painting; painting and poetry were called the sister arts and their age-old affinity was made permanently memorable in Horace's famous dictum *ut pictura poesis* (*Ars Poetica*, l.361).

21 *Chamber of Dependences* an office devised by Louis XIV of France to justify his imperial designs.

22 *happy* lucky.

And fruitful Plains and barren Rocks,
Of shallow Brooks that flowed so clear,
The Bottom did the Top appear;
Of deeper too and ampler Floods,
Which, as in Mirrors, showed the Woods;
Of lofty Trees, with Sacred Shades,
And Perspectives of pleasant Glades,[23]
Where Nymphs of brightest Form appear,
And shaggy Satyrs standing near,
Which them at once admire and fear.
The Ruins too of some Majestic Piece,
Boasting the Pow'r of ancient *Rome* or *Greece*,
Whose Statues, Friezes, Columns broken lie,
And, though defaced, the Wonder of the Eye;
What Nature, Art, bold Fiction, e'er durst frame,
Her forming Hand gave Shape unto the Name.
So strange a Concourse ne'er was seen before,
But when the peopled Ark the whole Creation bore.

7

The Scene then changed, with bold Erected Look
Our Martial King the sight with Reverence strook:[24]
For not content to express his Outward Part,
Her hand called out the Image of his Heart,
His Warlike Mind, his Soul devoid of Fear,
His High-designing Thoughts, were figured there,
As when, by Magic, Ghosts are made appear.
Our Phoenix Queen was portrayed too so bright,[25]
Beauty alone could Beauty take so right:[26]
Her Dress, her Shape, her matchless Grace,
Were all observed, as well as heav'nly Face.
With such a Peerless Majesty she stands,
As in that Day she took from Sacred hands[27]
The Crown; 'mong num'rous Heroines was seen,
More yet in Beauty, than in rank, the Queen!
Thus nothing to her *Genius* was denied,
But like a Ball of Fire the further thrown,
Still with a greater Blaze she shone,
And her bright Soul broke out on every side.
What next she had designed, Heaven only knows,
To such Immod'rate Growth her Conquest rose,
That Fate alone its Progress could oppose.

Notes

23 *Perspective* "View; vista" (Johnson). The scenes suggest the paintings of Claude Lorrain (Hammond).

24 *Martial King* James II as he appears in Killigrew's portrait.

25 *Phoenix Queen* Mary of Modena (1658–1718); *phoenix* meant matchless (*OED*, 2).

26 *take* "To copy" (Johnson).

27 *Sacred hands* those of the Archbishop of Canterbury at the coronation of her husband, James II, in 1685.

8

Now all those Charms, that blooming Grace,
The well-proportioned Shape, and beauteous Face,
Shall never more be seen by Mortal Eyes;
In Earth the much lamented Virgin lies.
Not Wit, nor Piety could Fate prevent;
Nor was the cruèl *Destiny* content
To finish all the Murder at a Blow,
To sweep at once her Life, and Beauty too;
But, like a hardened Felon, took a pride
To work more Mischievously slow,
And plundered first, and then destroyed.[28]
O double Sacrilege on things Divine,
To rob the Relic, and deface the Shrine!
But thus *Orinda* died;[29]
Heaven, by the same Disease, did both translate,[30]
As equal were their Souls, so equal was their Fate.

9

Meantime her Warlike Brother on the Seas
His waving Streamers to the Winds displays,
And vows for his Return, with vain Devotion, pays.
Ah, Generous Youth! that Wish forbear,
The Winds too soon will waft thee here!
Slack all thy Sails, and fear to come,
Alas, thou know'st not, Thou art wrecked at home!
No more shalt thou behold thy Sister's Face,
Thou hast already had her last Embrace.
But look aloft, and if thou ken'st from far,[31]
Among the *Pleiads* a New-kindled Star,[32]
If any sparkles, than the rest, more bright,
'Tis she that shines in that propitious Light.

10

When in mid-Air, the Golden Trump shall sound,[33]
To raise the Nations under ground;
When in the Valley of *Jehoshaphat*,
The Judging God shall close the Book of Fate;
And there the last Assizes keep,[34]
For those who Wake, and those who Sleep;
When rattling Bones together fly,[35]

Notes

28 *plundered* smallpox robbed her of her beauty.

29 *Orinda* the much more accomplished poet Katherine Philips (see pp. 237–46 below).

30 *translate* transport to another plane of existence.

31 *ken'st* from *ken*, to know or see.

32 *Pleiads* Pleiades, the seven sisters or seven poets, a constellation.

33 *When* ... at the apocalypse, when God shall pass final judgment on the living and the dead (1 Corinthians 15.52; Joel 3.2).

34 *Assizes* "Any court of justice" (Johnson).

35 *When rattling Bones* the resurrection of the body at judgment day was a common Christian belief in the seventeenth century.

From the four Corners of the Sky;
When Sinews o'er the Skeletons are spread,
Those clothed with Flesh, and Life inspires the Dead;[36]
The sacred Poets first shall hear the Sound,
  And foremost from the Tomb shall bound,
For they are covered with the lightest Ground
And straight, with inborn Vigour, on the Wing,
Like mounting Larks, to the New Morning sing.
There *Thou*, Sweet Saint, before the Quire shalt go,
As Harbinger of Heav'n, the Way to show,
The Way which thou so well hast learned below.

Song for St. Cecilia's Day (1687)[1]

1

From Harmony, from heav'nly Harmony
  This Universal Frame began.[2]
  When Nature underneath a heap[3]
    Of jarring Atoms lay,
  And could not heave her Head,
The tuneful Voice was heard from high,
  Arise ye more than dead.
Then cold, and hot, and moist, and dry,
In order to their stations leap,
  And Music's Pow'r obey.
From Harmony, from Heav'nly Harmony
  This universal Frame began:
  From Harmony to Harmony
Through all the compass of the Notes it ran,
The Diapason closing full in Man.[4]

2

What Passion cannot Music raise and quell!
    When Jubal struck the corded Shell,[5]
  His list'ning Brethren stood around
  And wond'ring, on their Faces fell
  To worship that Celestial Sound.
Less than a God they thought there could not dwell
  Within the hollow of that Shell

Notes

[36] *inspires* breathes life into.

A Song for St. Cecilia's Day

[1] First published as a broadside to celebrate the day of St. Cecilia (November 22), the patron saint of music, and set to music by Giovanni Battista Draghi. This text comes from *Examen Poeticum* (1693).

[2] This *Universal Frame* the world.

[3] Cf. Milton's description of Chaos in *Paradise Lost* 2.898–900. The image is Lucretian.

[4] *Diapason* the full range of a voice or instrument, or a burst of harmony.

[5] *Jubal* biblical inventor of music (Genesis 4.21).

That spoke so sweetly and so well.
What Passion cannot MUSIC raise and quell!

3

The TRUMPET's loud Clangour
Excites us to Arms
With shrill Notes of Anger
And mortal Alarms.
The double double double beat
Of the thund'ring DRUM
Cries, hark the Foes come;
Charge, Charge, 'tis too late to retreat.

4

The soft complaining FLUTE
In dying Notes discovers
The Woes of hopeless Lovers,
Whose Dirge is whispered by the warbling LUTE.

5

Sharp VIOLINS proclaim
Their jealous Pangs, and Desperation,
Fury, frantic Indignation,
Depth of Pains, and height of Passion,
For the fair, disdainful Dame.

6

But oh! what Art can teach,
What human Voice can reach
The sacred Organ's praise?
Notes inspiring holy Love,
Notes that wing their heav'nly ways
To mend the Choirs above.[6]

7

Orpheus could lead the savage race;[7]
And Trees unrooted left their place;
Sequacious of the Lyre:[8]
But bright *CECILIA* raised the wonder high'r;
When to her ORGAN, vocal Breath was giv'n
An Angel heard, and straight appeared
Mistaking Earth for Heaven.

Notes

[6] *mend* "To improve; to increase" (Johnson).

[7] *Orpheus* mythical poet and musician who sailed with the Argonauts and could charm beasts (*the savage race*) and even move inanimate objects.

[8] *Sequacious* "Following; attendant" (Johnson).

Grand Chorus

As from the pow'r of sacred Lays
The Spheres began to move,
And sung the great Creator's praise
To all the blessed above;
So when the last and dreadful hour[9]
This crumbling Pageant shall devour,
The Trumpet *shall be heard on high,*
The Dead shall live, the Living die,
And Music *shall untune the Sky.*

Alexander's Feast; or The Power of Music. An Ode, In Honour of St. *Cecilia's* Day.[1]

I.

'Twas at the Royal Feast, for *Persia* won,
By *Philip*'s Warlike Son:[2]
Aloft in awful State
The God-like Hero sate
On his Imperial Throne:
His valiant Peers were placed around;
Their Brows with Roses and with Myrtles bound.
(So should Desert in Arms be Crowned:)[3]
The Lovely *Thais* by his side,[4]
Sat like a blooming *Eastern* Bride
In Flower of Youth and Beauty's Pride.
Happy, happy, happy Pair!
None but the Brave
None but the Brave
None but the Brave deserves the Fair.

CHORUS.
Happy, happy, happy Pair!
None but the Brave
None but the Brave
None but the Brave deserves the Fair.

Notes

9 *the last and dreadful hour* the day of final judgment (e.g., 1 Corinthians 15.52).

Alexander's Feast; or The Power of Music

1 *Alexander's Feast* this song was first performed on St. Cecilia's Day (November 22), 1697. The original music by Jeremiah Clarke is lost, but the arrangement by Handel (1736) is justly famous. The text is from the first edition (1697). *St. Cecilia* is the patron saint of musicians, martyred in the second century CE.

2 *Philip* of Macedonia, father of Alexander the Great.

3 *Desert* excellence.

4 *Thaïs* the Athenian mistress of Ptolemy who accompanied Alexander on his military missions and urged him, according to some reports, to burn Persepolis during a night of Dionysian revelry (Plutarch, *Life of Alexander*, ch. 38).

II.

Timotheus placed on high[5]
Amid the tuneful Choir,
With flying Fingers touched the Lyre:
The trembling Notes ascend the Sky,
And Heavenly Joys inspire.
The Song began from *Jove*;
Who left his blissful Seats above,
(Such is the Power of mighty Love.)
A Dragon's fiery Form belied the God:
Sublime on Radiant Spires He rode,[6]
When He to fair *Olympia* pressed:[7]
And while He sought her snowy Breast:
Then, round her slender Waist he curled,
And stamped an Image of himself, a Sovereign of the World.
The listening Crowd admire the lofty Sound,
'A present Deity', they shout around:
'A present Deity', the vaulted Roofs rebound.
With ravished Ears
The Monarch hears,
Assumes the God,
Affects to nod,[8]
And seems to shake the Spheres.

CHORUS.
With ravished Ears
The Monarch hears,
Assumes the God,
Affects to Nod,
And seems to shake the Spheres.

III.

The Praise of *Bacchus* then, the sweet Musician sung;
Of *Bacchus* ever Fair, and ever Young:
The jolly God in Triumph comes;
Sound the Trumpets; beat the Drums;
Flushed with a purple Grace[9]
He shows his honest Face,
Now give the Hautboys breath; He comes, He comes.[10]
Bacchus ever Fair and Young,
Drinking Joys did first ordain:
Bacchus' Blessings are a Treasure;

Notes

[5] Timotheus is the name of a famous flautist favored by Alexander and of an earlier Macedonian singer and lyre player.

[6] *Spires* the coils of his serpent form.

[7] *Olympia* Alexander's mother, wife of Philip.

[8] *Nod* "'To direct (a person) by a nod… . 1684 … 'God can speak or nod you to hell in a moment.'"

[9] *purple Grace* a wine-stained grace, or "mark of divine favour" (*OED*, 2d).

[10] *Hautboys* oboes; *He comes, He comes* Psalms 96.13.

Drinking is the Soldier's Pleasure;
Rich the Treasure,
Sweet the Pleasure;
Sweet is Pleasure after Pain.

CHORUS.
Bacchus *Blessings are a Treasure,*
Drinking is the Soldier's Pleasure;
Rich the Treasure,
Sweet the Pleasure;
Sweet is Pleasure after Pain.

IV.

Soothed with the Sound the King grew vain;
Fought all his Battles o'er again;
And thrice He routed all his Foes; and thrice He slew the slain.
The Master saw the Madness rise;[11]
His glowing Cheeks, his ardent Eyes;
And while He Heaven and Earth defied,
Changed his hand, and checked his Pride.[12]
He chose a Mournful Muse
Soft Pity to infuse:
He sung *Darius* Great and Good,[13]
By too severe a Fate,
Fallen, fallen, fallen, fallen,
Fallen from his high Estate
And welt'ring in his Blood:
Deserted at his utmost Need,
By those his former Bounty fed:
On the bare Earth exposed He lies,
With not a Friend to close his Eyes.
With downcast Looks the joyless Victor sat,
Revolving in his altered Soul
The various Turns of Chance below;
And now and then, a Sigh he stole;
And Tears began to flow.

CHORUS.
Revolving in his altered Soul
The various Turns of Chance below;
And now and then, a Sigh he stole;
And Tears began to flow.

Notes

[11] *Master* Timotheus, the music master.
[12] *Changed his hand* played in a different key.
[13] *Darius* Darius III, ruler of Persia, defeated by Alexander, but also mourned by him when he was killed by rebels.

V.

The Mighty Master smiled to see
That Love was in the next Degree:
'Twas but a Kindred Sound to move;
For Pity melts the Mind to Love.
Softly sweet, in *Lydian* Measures,[14]
Soon He soothed his Soul to Pleasures.
'War', he sung, 'is Toil and Trouble;
Honour but an empty Bubble.
Never ending, still beginning,
Fighting still, and still destroying,
If the World be worth thy Winning,
Think, O think, it worth Enjoying.
Lovely *Thais* sits beside thee,
Take the Good the Gods provide thee'.

The Many rend the Skies, with loud Applause;
So Love was Crowned, but Music won the Cause.
The Prince, unable to conceal his Pain,
Gazed on the Fair
Who caused his Care,
And sighed and looked, sighed and looked,
Sighed and looked, and sighed again:
At length, with Love and Wine at once oppressed,
The vanquished Victor sunk upon her Breast.

CHORUS.

The Prince, unable to conceal his Pain,
Gazed on the Fair
Who caused his Care,
And sighed and looked, sighed and looked,
Sighed and looked, and sighed again:
At length, with Love and Wine at once oppressed,
The vanquished Victor sunk upon her Breast.

VI.

Now strike the Golden Lyre again:
A louder yet, and yet a louder Strain.
Break his Bands of Sleep asunder,
And rouse him, like a rattling Peal of Thunder.
Hark, hark, the horrid Sound
Has raised up his Head,
As awaked from the Dead,
And amazed, he stares around.
'Revenge, Revenge', *Timotheus* cries,

Notes

[14] *Lydian measure* an ancient Greek mode of music known for its softness.

'See the Furies arise!
See the Snakes that they rear,
How they hiss in their Hair,
And the Sparkles that flash from their Eyes!
Behold a ghastly Band,
Each a Torch in his Hand!
Those are the Grecian Ghosts that in Battle were slain,
And unburied remain
Inglorious on the Plain.
Give the Vengeance due
To the Valiant Crew.
Behold how they toss their Torches on high,
How they point to the *Persian* Abodes,
And glitt'ring Temples of their Hostile Gods!'
The Princes applaud, with a furious Joy;
And the King seized a Flambeau, with Zeal to destroy;[15]
Thais led the Way,
To light him to his Prey,
And like another *Helen*, sired another *Troy*.

CHORUS.
And the King seized a Flambeau, with Zeal to destroy;
Thais *led the Way,*
To light him to his Prey,
And, like another Helen, *sired another* Troy.

VII.

Thus, long ago
Ere heaving Bellows learned to blow,[16]
While Organs yet were mute;
Timotheus, to his breathing Flute,
And sounding Lyre,
Could swell the Soul to rage, or kindle lost Desire.
At last Divine *Cecilia* came,
Inventress of the Vocal Frame;[17]
The sweet Enthusiast, from her Sacred Store,[18]
Enlarged the former narrow Bounds,
And added Length to solemn Sounds,
With Nature's Mother-Wit, and Arts unknown before.[19]
Let old *Timotheus* yield the Prize,
Or both divide the Crown;
He raised a Mortal to the Skies;
She drew an Angel down.[20]

Notes

15 *Flambeau* torch
16 *Bellows* the device that blows air into an organ.
17 *Vocal Frame* the organ.
18 *Enthusiast* one who is inspired by God.
19 *Mother-Wit* native intelligence.
20 Cecilia was said to have an angel watching over her; c.f. "A Song for St. Cecilia's Day," ll. 53–4 above.

Grand CHORUS.

At last Divine Cecilia came,
Inventress of the Vocal Frame;
The sweet Enthusiast, from her Sacred Store,
Enlarged the former narrow Bounds,
And added Length to solemn Sounds,
With Nature's Mother-Wit, and Arts unknown before.
Let old Timotheus yield the Prize,
Or both divide the Crown;
He raised a Mortal to the Skies;
She drew an Angel down.

from *Fables Ancient and Modern* (1700)

Pygmalion and the Statue[1]

Pygmalion loathing their lascivious Life,[2]
Abhorred all Womankind, but most a Wife:
So single chose to live, and shunned to wed,
Well pleased to want a Consort of his Bed.[3]
Yet fearing Idleness, the Nurse of Ill,
In Sculpture exercised his happy Skill;
And carved in Ivory such a Maid, so fair,
As Nature could not with his Art compare,
Were she to work; but in her own Defence
Must take her pattern here, and copy hence.
Pleased with his Idol, he commends, admires,
Adores; and last, the Thing adored, desires.
A very Virgin in her Face was seen,
And had she moved, a living Maid had been:
One would have thought she could have stirred, but strove
With Modesty, and was ashamed to move.
Art hid with Art, so well performed the Cheat,
It caught the Carver with his own Deceit:
He knows 'tis Madness, yet he must adore,
And still the more he knows it, loves the more:
The Flesh, or what so seems, he touches oft,
Which feels so smooth, that he believes it soft.
Fired with this Thought, at once he strained the Breast,[4]
And on the Lips a burning Kiss impressed.
'Tis true, the hardened Breast resists the Grip,

Notes

Pygmalion and the Statue

[1] The poem is a loose translation of Ovid, *Metamorphoses* 10.243–97.

[2] *their* the Propaetides, Cyprian girls who denied the divinity of Venus and were in consequence forced into prostitution by the goddess and later turned to stones (*Metamorphoses* 10.238–42). Dryden explains this in a note.

[3] *want* lack.

[4] *strain* "To squeeze in an embrace" (Johnson).

And the cold Lips return a Kiss unripe:
But when, retiring back, he looked again,
To think it Ivory, was a Thought too mean:
So would believe she kissed, and courting more,
Again embraced her naked Body o'er;
And straining hard the Statue, was afraid
His Hands had made a Dent, and hurt his Maid:
Explored her, Limb by Limb, and feared to find
So rude a Grip had left a livid Mark behind:
With Flatt'ry now, he seeks her Mind to move,
And now with Gifts (the pow'rful Bribes of Love)
He furnishes her Closet first; and fills
The crowded Shelves with Rarities of Shells;
Adds Orient Pearls, which from the Conchs he drew,[5]
And all the sparkling Stones of various Hue:
And Parrots, imitating Human Tongue,
And Singing-birds in Silver Cages hung;
And every fragrant Flower, and od'rous Green,
Were sorted well, with Lumps of Amber laid between:
Rich, fashionable Robes her Person deck,
Pendants her Ears, and Pearls adorn her Neck:
Her tapered Fingers too with Rings are graced,
And an embroidered Zone surrounds her slender Waist.[6]
Thus like a Queen arrayed, so richly dressed,
Beauteous she showed, but naked showed the best.
Then, from the Floor, he raised a Royal Bed,
With Cov'rings of *Sidonian* Purple spread:[7]
The Solemn Rites performed, he calls her Bride,
With Blandishments invites her to his Side,
And as she were with Vital Sense possessed,
Her Head did on a plumy Pillow rest.
    The Feast of *Venus* came, a Solemn Day,
To which the *Cypriots* due Devotion pay:[8]
With gilded Horns, the Milk-white Heifers led,
Slaughtered before the sacred Altars, bled:
Pygmalion off'ring, first, approached the Shrine,
And then with Prayers implored the Pow'rs Divine,
'Almighty Gods, if all we Mortals want,
If all we can require, be yours to grant;
Make this fair Statue mine', he would have said,
But changed his Words, for shame; and only prayed,
'Give me the Likeness of my Ivory Maid'.
    The Golden Goddess, present at the Prayer
Well knew he meant th' inanimated Fair,
And gave the Sign of granting his Desire;

Notes

5 *Orient* "Bright; shining; glittering; gaudy; sparkling" (Johnson).

6 *zone* girdle or belt.

7 *Sidonian* from Sidon, ancient Tyre, famous for purple dye.

8 *Cypriots* because Cyprus is the birthplace of Venus and one of her names.

For thrice in cheerful Flames ascends the Fire.
The Youth, returning to his Mistress, hies,
And impudent in Hope, with ardent Eyes,
And beating Breast, by the dear Statue lies.
He kisses her white Lips, renews the Bliss,
And looks, and thinks they redden at the Kiss;
He thought them warm before: Nor longer stays,
But next his Hand on her hard Bosom lays:
Hard as it was, beginning to relent,
It seemed, the Breast beneath his Fingers bent;
He felt again, his Fingers made a Print,
'Twas Flesh, but Flesh so firm, it rose against the Dent:
The pleasing Task he fails not to renew;
Soft, and more soft at every Touch it grew;
Like pliant Wax, when chafing Hands reduce[9]
The former Mass to Form, and frame for Use.
He would believe, but yet is still in pain,
And tries his Argument of Sense again,
Presses the Pulse, and feels the leaping Vein.
Convinced, o'erjoyed, his studied Thanks and Praise,
To her who made the Miracle, he pays:
Then Lips to Lips he joined; now freed from Fear,
He found the Savour of the Kiss sincere:
At this the wakened Image op'd her Eyes,
And viewed at once the Light and Lover, with surprise.
The Goddess present at the Match she made,
So blessed the Bed, such Fruitfulness conveyed,
That ere ten Moons had sharpened either Horn,[10]
To crown their Bliss, a lovely Boy was born;
Paphos his Name, who grown to Manhood, walled
The City Paphos, from the Founder called.[11]

Secular Masque[1]

Janus[2]
Chronos, Chronos, mend thy Pace,[3]
An hundred times the rolling Sun
Around the Radiant Belt has run[4]
In his revolving Race.

Notes

[9] *chafe* "To warm with rubbing" (Johnson).
[10] *either Horn* the points of the crescent moon.
[11] *Paphos* a Cyprian city and site of a famous temple of Venus, her chief resort according to Homer.

Secular Masque

[1] *Secular Masque* Dryden wrote this piece for a production of *The Pilgrim*, a play by John Fletcher (1579–1625), revised by John Vanbrugh (1664–1726), on April 29, 1700. Dryden died on the third day of the performance (*London Stage 1600–1800*, I.527). The first edition of Vanbrugh's *Pilgrim* (1700) is the source of the text. *Secular* (Latin *saeculum*) pertaining to an age or epoch, or the century ending in 1700.
[2] *Janus* the Roman god of beginnings or endings; he looks both ways.
[3] *Chronos* god of time or Father Time.
[4] *Radiant Belt* the zodiac.

Behold, behold, the Goal in sight,
Spread thy Fans, and wing thy flight,

Enter Chronos, with a Scythe in his hand, and a great Globe on his Back, which he sets down at his entrance.

Chronos.
Weary, weary of my weight,
Let me, let me drop my Freight,
And leave the World behind.
I could not bear
Another Year
The Load of Human kind.

Enter Momus Laughing.

Momus.[5]
Ha! ha! ha! Ha! ha! ha! well hast thou done,
To lay down thy Pack,
And lighten thy Back,
The World was a Fool, e'er since it begun,
And since neither *Janus*, nor *Chronos*, nor I,
Can hinder the Crimes,
Or mend the Bad Times,
'Tis better to Laugh than to Cry.

Chorus of all three.
'Tis better to Laugh than to Cry.

Janus.
Since *Momus* comes to laugh below,
Old Time begin the Show,
That he may see, in every Scene,
What Changes in this Age have been.

Chronos.
Then Goddess of the Silver Bow begin.[6]

Horns, or Hunting-Musique within. Enter Diana.

Diana.
With Horns and with Hounds I waken the Day.
And hie to my Woodland walks away;
I tuck up my Robe, and am buskined soon,[7]
And tie to my Forehead a waxing Moon.
I course the fleet Stag, unkennel the Fox,[8]

Notes

[5] *Momus* the personification of satire and criticism.
[6] *Diana* goddess of the hunt, the moon, and childbirth.
[7] *Buskined* fitted with boots.
[8] *Course* pursue; *unkennel* drive out into the open.

And chase the wild Goats o'er summits of Rocks,
With shouting and hooting we pierce through the Sky;
And Echo turns Hunter, and doubles the Cry.

Chorus of all.

With shouting and hooting, we pierce through the Sky,
And Echo turns Hunter, and doubles the Cry.

Janus.
Then our Age was in its Prime,

Chronos.
Free from Rage.

Diana.
— And free from Crime.

Momus.
A very Merry, Dancing, Drinking,
Laughing, Quaffing, and unthinking Time.

Chorus of all.
Then our Age was in its Prime,
Free from Rage, and free from Crime,
A very Merry, Dancing, Drinking,
Laughing, Quaffing, and unthinking Time.

Dance of Diana's Attendants.
Enter Mars.

Mars.[9]
Inspire the Vocal Brass, Inspire;
The World is past its Infant Age:
Arms and Honour,
Arms and Honour,
Set the Martial Mind on Fire,
And kindle Manly Rage.
Mars has looked the Sky to Red;[10]
And Peace, the Lazy Good, is fled.
Plenty, Peace, and Pleasure fly;
The Sprightly Green
In *Woodland*-Walks, no more is seen;
The Sprightly Green, has drunk the *Tyrian* Dye.[11]

Notes

[9] *Mars* god of War, representing the wars of the seventeenth century.

[10] *Look* "To cause (person or thing) to turn into a certain … state" (*OED*, 2c).

[11] *Tyrian* purple, royal.

Chorus of all.
Plenty, Peace, *&c.*

Mars.
Sound the Trumpet, Beat the Drum,
Through all the World around;
Sound a Reveille, Sound, Sound,
The Warrior God is come.

Chorus of all.
Sound the Trumpet, *&c.*

Momus.
Thy Sword within the Scabbard keep,
And let Mankind agree;
Better the World were fast asleep,
Than kept awake by Thee.
The Fools are only thinner,
With all our Cost and Care;
But neither side a winner,
For Things are as they were.

Chorus of all.
The Fools are only, *&c.*

Enter Venus.

Venus.[12]
Calms appear, when Storms are past;
Love will have his Hour at last:
Nature is my kindly Care;
Mars destroys, and I repair;
Take me, take me, while you may,
Venus comes not every Day.

Chorus of all.

Take her, take her, *&c.*

Chronos.

The World was then so light,
I scarcely felt the Weight;
Joy ruled the Day, and Love the Night.
But since the Queen of Pleasure left the Ground,
I faint, I lag,
And feebly drag
The pond'rous Orb around.

Notes

[12] *Venus* goddess of love, representing the amorous reign of Charles II.

Momus.

All, all, of a piece throughout;
Pointing to Diana.
Thy Chase had a Beast in View;

to *Mars.*
Thy Wars brought nothing about;

to *Venus.*
Thy Lovers were all untrue.
Janus.
'Tis well an Old Age is out,

Chronos.

And time to begin a New.

Chorus of all.

All, all, of a piece throughout;
Thy Chase had a Beast in View;
Thy Wars brought nothing about;
Thy Lovers were all untrue.
'Tis well an Old Age is out,
And time to begin a New.

Dance of Huntsmen, Nymphs, Warriors and Lovers.

Katherine Philips (1632–1664)

The "matchless Orinda," as Philips became known, was one of the most respected poets of her time. She and the ancient Greek Sappho (p. 219 above) were the great models to whom Dryden very flatteringly compared Anne Killigrew in his ode on that lesser poet's death. Although her connections were largely Puritan and her much older husband was an official of the Commonwealth, Philips was Royalist in her sympathies and published her first poems in the prefatory matter of an edition of Henry Vaughan's poetry. For the most part, her reputation was built on the circulation of her poetry in manuscript, and a responsibly published edition of her work did not come out until 1667. (That edition provides the basis for the selections that follow.) Philips's poems, letters, and translations have recently been edited by Patrick Thomas and others in three separate volumes (Stump Cross Books, 1990–3). Selected poems have been edited by Paula Loscocco (Ashgate, 2005).

Using code names for her friends – chiefly Lucasia (Anne Owen), Rosania (Mary Aubrey) – and Antenor (her husband), Philips is a coterie writer who wrote about and for a small circle of friends. She is rarely so private that she is obscure, however, and she touches on general themes even when relating private experience. Elizabeth Scott-Baumann has shown the important connections between Philips's poetry and Cowley's as well as her apparent influence on Andrew Marvell in *Forms of Engagement: Women, Poetry, and Culture 1640–1680* (Oxford University Press, 2013).

from *Poems by the most deservedly Admired Mrs. Katherine Philips, the matchless Orinda* (1667)

Friendship

Let the dull brutish World that know not Love
Continue Heretics, and disapprove
That noble Flame; but the refined know
'Tis all the Heaven we have here below.
Nature subsists by Love, and they do tie
Things to their Causes but by Sympathy.
Love chains the different Elements in one
Great Harmony, linked to th' Heavenly Throne.
And as on Earth, so the blessed Quire above
Of Saints and Angels are maintained by Love;
That is their Business and Felicity,
And will be so to all Eternity.
That is the Ocean, our Affections here
Are but streams borrowed from the Fountain there.
And 'tis the noblest Argument to prove
A Beauteous mind, that it knows how to Love:
Those kind Impressions which Fate can't control,
Are Heaven's mintage on a worthy Soul.
For Love is all the Arts' Epitome,
And is the Sum of all Divinity.

British Literature 1640–1789: An Anthology, Fourth Edition. Edited by Robert DeMaria, Jr.

He's worse than Beast that cannot Love, and yet
It is not bought for Money, Pains or Wit;
For no chance or design can Spirits move,
But the Eternal destiny of Love:
And when Two Souls are changed and mixèd so,
It is what they and none but they can do.
This, this is Friendship, that abstracted flame
Which grovelling Mortals know not how to name.
All Love is sacred, and the Marriage-tie
Hath much of Honour and Divinity.
But Lust, Design, or some unworthy ends
May mingle there, which are despised by Friends.
Passion hath violent extremes, and thus
All oppositions are contiguous.
So when the end is served their Love will bate,
If Friendship make it not more fortunate:
Friendship, that Love's Elixir, that pure fire
Which burns the clearer 'cause it burns the higher;
For Love, like earthly fires (which will decay
If the material fuel be away),
Is with offensive smoke accompanied,
And by resistance only is supplied:
But Friendship, like the fiery Element,
With its own Heat and Nourishment content,
Where neither hurt, nor smoke, nor noise is made,
Scorns the assistance of a foreign aid.
Friendship (like Heraldry) is hereby known,[1]
Richest when plainest, bravest when alone;[2]
Calm as a Virgin, and more Innocent
Than sleeping doves are, and as much content
As Saints in Visions; quiet as the Night,
But clear and open as the Summer's light;
United more than Spirits' Faculties,
Higher in thoughts than are the Eagle's eyes;
What shall I say? when we true friends are grown,
W'are – Alas, w'are like ourselves alone.

Friendship's Mystery, To my dearest Lucasia[1]

I

Come, my *Lucasia*, since we see
That Miracles Men's faith do move,

Notes

FRIENDSHIP

[1] *Heraldry* heraldic device or badge.
[2] *brave* worthy; excellent.

FRIENDSHIP'S MYSTERY

[1] *Lucasia* (Latin, *Lucas*, "light-giving") Philips's poetic name for her friend Anne Owen; the poem was set to music by Henry Lawes.

By wonder and by prodigy,
To the dull angry world let's prove
There's a Religion in our Love.

2

For though we were designed t' agree,
That Fate no liberty destroys,
But our Election is as free
As Angels, who with greedy choice
Are yet determined to their joys.[2]

3

Our hearts are doubled by the loss,
Here Mixture is Addition grown;
We both diffuse, and both engross:[3]
And we whose minds are so much one,
Never, yet ever are alone.

4

We court our own Captivity
Than Thrones more great and innocent:
'Twere banishment to be set free,
Since we wear fetters whose intent
Not bondage is, but Ornament.

5

Divided joys are tedious found,
And griefs united easier grow:
We are selves but by rebound,
And all our Titles shuffled so,
Both Princes, and both Subjects too.

6

Our Hearts are mutual Victims laid,
While they (such power in Friendship lies)
Are Altars, Priests, and Off'rings made:
And each Heart which thus kindly dies,
Grows deathless by the Sacrifice.

Notes

[2] *Angels … determined* Church doctrine was that angels were created with free will but gave it up a moment after they were formed and turned toward God, thus becoming fixed in goodness.

[3] *engross* thicken.

Epitaph On her Son *H. P.* at St. Syth's Church where her body also lies Interred[1]

What on Earth deserves our Trust?
Youth and Beauty both are dust.
Long we gathering are with pain,
What one Moment calls again.
Seven years Childless, Marriage passed,
A Son, a Son is born at last:
So exactly limbed and Fair,
Full of good Spirits, Mien, and Air,
As a long life promisèd;
Yet, in less than six weeks, dead.
Too promising, too great a Mind[2]
In so small room to be confined:
Therefore, as fit in Heav'n to dwell,
He quickly broke the Prison shell.
So the subtle Alchemist,
Can't with *Hermes'* Seal resist[3]
The Powerful Spirit's subtler flight,[4]
But 'twill bid him long good night.
So the Sun, if it arise
Half so glorious as his Eyes,
Like this Infant, takes a shroud,
Buried in a morning Cloud.

The Virgin

The things that make a Virgin please,
She that seeks, will find them these;
A Beauty, not to Art in debt,
Rather agreeable than great;
An Eye, wherein at once do meet,
The beams of kindness, and of wit;
And undissembled Innocence,
Apt not to give, nor take offence:
A Conversation, at once, free
From Passion, and from Subtlety;
A Face that's modest, yet serene,
A sober, and yet lively Mien;
The virtue which does her adorn,
By honour guarded, not by scorn;

Notes

EPITAPH

1 *H. P.* Hector Philips, born and died in 1655.

2 *Mind* soul.

3 *Hermes' Seal* hermetic, airtight closure on a bottle or test tube.

4 *Spirit* a volatile, distilled liquid, in alchemical language; *subtler* from *subtlety*, "Thinness; fineness; exility of particles" (Johnson).

With such wise lowliness indued,[1]
As never can be mean, or rude;
That prudent negligence enrich,
And Time's her silence and her speech;
Whose equal mind, does always move,
Neither a foe, nor slave to Love;
And whose Religion's strong and plain,
Not superstitious, nor profane.

Upon the graving of her Name upon a Tree in Barnelmes Walks

Alas how barbarous are we,
Thus to reward the courteous Tree,
Who its broad shade affording us,
Deserves not to be wounded thus;
See how the Yielding Bark complies
With our ungrateful injuries.
And feeling this, say how much then
Trees are more generous than Men,
Who by a Nobleness so pure
Can first oblige and then endure.

To the truly competent Judge of Honour, Lucasia, upon a scandalous Libel made by J. J.

Honour, which differs Man from Man much more
Than Reason differed him from Beasts before,
Suffers this common Fate of all things good,
By the blind World to be misunderstood.
For as some Heathens did their Gods confine,
While in a Bird or Beast they made their shrine;
Deposed their Deities to Earth, and then
Offered them Rites that were too low for Men;
So those who most to Honour sacrifice,
Prescribe to her a mean and weak disguise;
Imprison her to others' false Applause,
And from Opinion do receive their Laws,
While that inconstant Idol they implore,
Which in one breath can murther and adore.
From hence it is that those who Honour court
(And place her in a popular report)

Notes

THE VIRGIN

[1] *indue* "It seems sometimes to be, even by good writers, confounded with endow or indow, to furnish or enrich with any quality or excellence" (Johnson).

Do prostitute themselves to sordid Fate,
And from their Being oft degenerate.
And thus their Tenets too are low and bad,
As if 'twere honourable to be mad:
Or that their Honour had concernèd been
But to conceal, not to forbear, a sin.
But Honour is more great and more sublime,
Above the battery of Fate or Time.
We see in Beauty certain airs are found,
Which not one Grace can make, but all compound.
Honour's to th' Mind as Beauty to the Sense,
The fair result of mixèd Excellence.
As many Diamonds together lie,
And dart one lustre to amaze the Eye:
So Honour is that bright Ætherial Ray
Which many stars doth in one light display.
But as that Beauty were as truly sweet,
Were there no Tongue to praise, no Eye to see 't;
And 'tis the Privilege of a native Spark,[1]
To shed a constant Splendour in the dark:
So Honour is its own Reward and End,
And satisfied within, cannot descend
To beg the suffrage of a vulgar Tongue,[2]
Which by commending Virtue doth it wrong.
It is the Charter of a noble Action,
That the performance giveth satisfaction.
Other things are below 't; for from a Clown[3]
Would any Conqueror receive his Crown?
'Tis restless Cowardice to be a drudge
To an uncertain and unworthy Judge.
So the *Chameleon*, who lives on air,[4]
Is of all Creatures most inclined to fear.
But peaceable reflections on the Mind
Will in a silent shade Contentment find.
Honour keeps Court at home, and doth not fear
To be condemned abroad, if quitted there.[5]
While I have this retreat, 'tis not the noise
Of Slander, though believed, can wrong my Joys.
There is advantage in't: for Gold uncoined
Had been unuseful, nor with glory shined:
This stamped my Innocency in the Ore,
Which was as much, but not so bright, before.
Till an *Alembic* wakes and outward draws,[6]

Notes

To the truly competent Judge of Honour

[1] *native* "Produced by nature; natural, not artificial" (Johnson).

[2] *vulgar* "Plebeian; suiting to the common people; practised among the common people" (Johnson).

[3] *Clown* "A coarse, ill-bred man" (Johnson).

[4] *the Chameleon … lives on air* a popular belief (Browne, *Pseudodoxia Epidemica* 3.21).

[5] *quitted* acquitted, absolved.

[6] *Alembic* "A vessel used in distilling" (Johnson); *wake* boil, produce steam.

The strength of Sweets lies sleeping in their cause:
So this gave me an opportunity
To feed upon my own Integrity.
And though their Judgement I must still disclaim,
Who can nor give nor take away a fame:
Yet I'll appeal unto the knowing few,
Who dare be just, and rip my heart to you.[7]

To Mrs. Wogan, my Honoured Friend, on the Death of her Husband

Dry up your tears, there's enough shed by you,
And we must pay our share of Sorrows too.
It is not private loss when such men fall,
The World's concerned, and Grief is general.
But though of our Misfortune we complain,
To him it is injurious and vain.
For since we know his rich Integrity,
His real Sweetness, and full Harmony;
How free his heart and house were to his Friends,
Whom he obliged without Design or Ends;
How universal was his courtesy,
How clear a Soul, how even, and how high;
How much he scorned disguise or meaner Arts,
But with a native Honour conquered Hearts;
We must conclude he was a Treasure lent,
Soon weary of this sordid Tenement.[1]
The Age and World deserved him not, and he
Was kindly snatched from future Misery.
We can scarce say he's Dead, but gone to rest,
And left a Monument in every breast.
For you to grieve then in this sad excess,
Is not to speak your Love, but make it less.
A noble Soul no Friendship will admit,
But what's Eternal and Divine as it.
The Soul is hid in mortal flesh we know,
And all its weaknesses must undergo,
Till by degrees it does shine forth at length,
And gathers Beauty, Purity, and Strength:
But never yet doth this Immortal Ray
Put on full splendour till it put off Clay:
So Infant Love is in the worthiest breast

Notes

[7] *rip* disclose.

To Mrs. Wogan

[1] *Tenement* "Any thing held by a tenant" (Johnson); a common metaphor for the body, which is tenanted by the soul.

By Sense and Passion fettered and oppressed;
But by degrees it grows still more refined,
And scorning clogs, only concerns the mind.
Now as the Soul you loved is here set free
From its material gross capacity;
Your Love should follow him now he is gone,
And quitting Passion, put Perfection on.
Such Love as this will its own good deny,
If its dear Object have Felicity.
And since we cannot his great Loss Reprieve,
Let's not lose you in whom he still doth Live.
For while you are by Grief secluded thus,
It doth appear your Funeral to us.

Orinda to Lucasia

I

Observe the weary birds ere night be done,
How they would fain call up the tardy Sun,
    With feathers hung with dew,
    And trembling voices too.
They court their glorious Planet to appear,[1]
That they may find recruits of spirits there.[2]
    The drooping Flowers hang their heads,
    And languish down into their beds:
While Brooks more bold and fierce than they,
    Wanting those beams, from whence
    All things drink influence,
Openly murmur and demand the day.

2

Thou my Lucasia art far more to me,
Than he to all the underworld can be;[3]
    From thee I've heat and light,
    Thy absence makes my night.
But ah! my Friend, it now grows very long,
The sadness weighty, and the darkness strong:
    My tears (its dew) dwell on my cheeks,
    And still my heart thy dawning seeks,
And to thee mournfully it cries,
    That if too long I wait,
    Even thou may'st come too late,
And not restore my life, but close my eyes.

Notes

Orinda to Lucasia

[1] *Planet* literally "a wanderer"; any heavenly body that appears to move; here, the sun.

[2] *recruit* "Supply of any thing wanted" (Johnson).

[3] *underworld* the sublunary world; earth.

Parting with Lucasia, A Song

1

Well, we will do that rigid thing[1]
Which makes Spectators think we part;
Though Absence hath for none a sting
But those who keep each other's heart.

2

And when our Sense is dispossessed,
Our labouring Souls will heave and pant,
And gasp for one another's breast,
Since their Conveyances they want.

3

Nay, we have felt the tedious smart
Of absent Friendship, and do know
That when we die we can but part;
And who knows what we shall do now?

4

Yet I must go: we will submit,
And so our own Disposers be;
For while we nobly suffer it,
We triumph o'er Necessity.

5

By this we shall be truly great,
If having other things o'ercome,
To make our victory complete
We can be Conquerors at home.

6

Nay then to meet we may conclude,
And all Obstructions overthrow,
Since we our Passion have subdued,
Which is the strongest thing I know.

Notes

PARTING WITH LUCASIA
1 *rigid* "Sharp; cruel" (Johnson).

To Antenor, on a Paper of mine which J. J. threatens to publish to prejudice him[1]

Must then my Crimes become thy Scandal too?
Why, sure the Devil hath not much to do.
The weakness of the other Charge is clear,
When such a trifle must bring up the Rear.
But this is mad design, for who before
Lost his repute upon another's score?
My Love and Life I must confess are thine,
But not my Errors, they are only mine.
And if my Faults must be for thine allowed,
It will be hard to dissipate the Cloud:
For *Eve*'s Rebellion did not *Adam* blast,
Until himself forbidden Fruit did taste.
'Tis possible this Magazine of Hell
(Whose name would turn a verse into a spell,
Whose mischief is congenial to his life)
May yet enjoy an honourable Wife.
Nor let his ill be reckoned as her blame,
Nor yet my Follies blast *Antenor*'s name.
But if those lines a Punishment could call
Lasting and great as this dark Lanthorn's gall;[2]
Alone I'd court the Torments with content,
To testify that thou art Innocent.
So if my Ink through malice proved a stain,
My Blood should justly wash it off again.
But since that Mint of slander could invent
To make so dull a Rhyme his Instrument,
Let Verse revenge the quarrel. But he's worse
Than wishes, and below a Poet's curse;
And more than this Wit knows not how to give,
Let him be still himself, and let him live.

Notes

To Antenor
[1] *prejudice* injure.

[2] *dark lanthorn* lamp used in intrigue; hence an intriguer; *gall* poison; ill.

John Locke (1632–1704)

Although he published nothing until he reached the age of fifty-five, in the last ten years of his life Locke produced the most influential philosophical and political works of the age. His *Essay concerning Human Understanding* (1690) provided the basis for the durable school of British empiricism. Even more importantly, it expounded an epistemology so persuasive and commonsensical that it provided the language in which many succeeding generations would discuss their perceptions, and very probably, therefore, affected the mode of perception itself. His convictions about language were influential in the formation of Johnson's *Dictionary*, and he is quoted over and over in later philological works. His influence extended into all sorts of basic areas of understanding, but in none was his influence quite as dramatic and as unforeseen as in the realm of politics.

As the personal physician and advisor of Anthony Ashley Cooper, first earl of Shaftesbury, Locke was embroiled in the major national political disputes of his time. Like Cooper, Locke favored assignment of the throne to the duke of Monmouth, Charles II's illegitimate son, and the exclusion of James II, who was next in the royal line. After the so-called Exclusion Crisis came to a head in 1682, Locke and Shaftesbury fled the country. Recent evidence suggests that Locke continued to favor the appointment of Monmouth and may have contributed to the infamous Rye House Plot to kill the king. In 1685 James became king, but he was ousted in 1689 by the Glorious or Bloodless Revolution in which Parliament brought in William of Orange and Queen Mary (his daughter by his first wife Anne Hyde). The Revolution showed where the true power now lay, and put a final end to divine right as a principle of rule in England. In many respects Locke's *Two Treatises of Government* was written to defend and to elaborate the principles of the Revolution. The first treatise demolishes the theory of divine right, as expounded in Robert Filmer's posthumously published *Patriarcha* (1680). The second treatise, however, achieves a kind of universality that goes far beyond Filmer and the particular circumstances of the Revolution. It became a central document not only in the growth of liberal thinking in England but also in the formation of both the American and French republics in the following century. Locke could not possibly have agreed with the many disparate groups that adopted his political thinking in succeeding generations, nor could he have imagined that his particular, historically bound position could have become so thoroughly a part of the mainstream of political thought in the West.

The Clarendon Press edition of Locke's *Works* is setting the standard as each volume appears, but there is already a fine edition of the *Two Treatises* by Peter Laslett (2nd edn.; Cambridge University Press, 1967). I follow the text of the first edition of 1690, but I am indebted to Laslett's commentary.

British Literature 1640–1789: An Anthology, Fourth Edition. Edited by Robert DeMaria, Jr.

from *An Essay concerning the True Original, Extent and End of Civil Government* (1690)

from Chapter 1

I. It having been shown in the foregoing Discourse,[1]

1. That *Adam* had not, either by natural Right of Fatherhood, or by positive Donation from God, any such Authority over his Children, or Dominion over the World as is pretended.
2. That if he had, his Heirs, yet, had no right to it.
3. That if his Heirs had, there being no Law of Nature nor positive Law of God that determines, which is the Right Heir in all cases that may arise, the Right of Succession, and consequently of bearing Rule, could not have been certainly determined.
4. That if even that had been determined, yet the knowledge of which is the Eldest Line of *Adam's* Posterity, being so long since utterly lost, that in the Races of Mankind and Families of the World, there remains not to one above another, the least pretence to be the Eldest House, and to have the Right of Inheritance.

All these premises having, as I think, been clearly made out, it is impossible that the Rulers now on Earth, should make any benefit, or derive any the least shadow of Authority from that, which is held to be the Fountain of all Power, *Adam's Private Dominion and Paternal Jurisdiction*; so that, he that will not give just occasion, to think that all Government in the World is the product only of Force and Violence, and that Men live together by no other Rules but that of Beasts, where the strongest carries it, and so lay a Foundation for perpetual Disorder and Mischief, Tumult, Sedition, and Rebellion[2] (things that the followers of that Hypothesis so loudly cry out against) must of necessity find out another rise of Government, another Original of Political Power, and another way of designing and knowing the Persons that have it, than what Sir *Robert F*[ilmer] hath taught us.

2. To this purpose, I think it may not be amiss, to set down what I take to be Political Power. That the Power of a Magistrate over a Subject, may be distinguished from that of a Father over his Children, a Master over his Servant, a Husband over his Wife, and a Lord over his Slave. All which distinct Powers happening sometimes together in the same Man, if he be considered under these different Relations, it may help us to distinguish these Powers one from another, and show the difference betwixt a Ruler of a Commonwealth, a Father of a Family, and a Captain of a Galley.

3. Political Power, then, I take to be a Right of making Laws with Penalties of Death, and consequently all less Penalties, for the Regulating and Preserving of Property, and of employing the force of the Community, in the Execution of such Laws, and in the defence of the Commonwealth from Foreign Injury, and all this only for the Public Good. …

from Chapter 2 Of the State of Nature

4. To understand Political Power aright, and derive it from its Original, we must consider what Estate all Men are naturally in, and that is, a *State of perfect Freedom* to order their Actions, and dispose of their Possessions and Persons as they think

Notes

FROM *AN ESSAY CONCERNING THE TRUE ORIGINAL*

1 *foregoing Discourse* the first treatise, which is largely a refutation of Robert Filmer's *Patriarcha*.

2 … *Rebellion* a description of the Hobbesian state of nature (above, pp. 11–15), as also criticized by Filmer.

fit, within the bounds of the Law of Nature, without asking leave or depending upon the Will of any other Man.

A *State also of Equality*, wherein all the Power and Jurisdiction is reciprocal, no one having more than another, there being nothing more evident, than that Creatures of the same species and rank promiscuously born to all the same advantages of Nature, and the use of the same faculties, should also be equal one amongst another without Subordination or Subjection, unless the Lord and Master of them all should by any manifest Declaration of his Will set one above another, and confer on him by an evident and clear appointment an undoubted Right to Dominion and Sovereignty.

5. This *equality* of Men by Nature, the Judicious *Hooker*[3] looks upon as so evident in itself, and beyond all question, that he makes it the Foundation of that Obligation to mutual Love amongst Men, on which he Builds the Duties they owe one another, and from whence he derives the great Maxims *of Justice* and *Charity*. …

6. But though this be a *State of Liberty*, yet it is not a *State of Licence*, though Man in that State have an uncontrollable Liberty, to dispose of his Person or Possessions, yet he has not Liberty to destroy himself, or so much as any Creature in his Possession, but where some nobler use, than its bare Preservation calls for it. The State of Nature, has a Law of Nature to govern it, which obliges every one, and reason, which is that Law, teaches all Mankind, who will but consult it: That being all equal and independent, no one ought to harm another in his Life, Health, Liberty or Possessions; for Men being all the Workmanship of one Omnipotent, and infinitely wise maker – All the Servants of one Sovereign Master, sent into the World by his order and about his business – they are his Property, whose Workmanship they are, made to last during his, not one another's Pleasure. And being Furnished with like Faculties, sharing all in one Community of Nature, there cannot be supposed any such *Subordination* among us, that may Authorize us to destroy one another, as if we were made for one another's uses, as the inferior ranks of Creatures are for ours. Every one as he is *bound to preserve himself*, and not to quit his Station wilfully; so by the like reason when his own Preservation comes not in competition, ought he, as much as he can, *to preserve the rest of Mankind*, and may not, unless it be to do Justice on an Offender, take away, or impair the life, or what tends to the Preservation of the Life, the Liberty, Health, Limb or Goods of another.

7. And that all Men may be restrained from invading others' Rights, and from doing hurt to one another, and the Law of Nature be observed, which willeth the *Peace and Preservation of all Mankind*, the *Execution* of the Law of Nature is in that State, put into every Man's hands, whereby every one has a right to punish the transgressors of that Law to such a Degree, as may hinder its Violation. For the *Law of Nature* would, as all other Laws that concern Men in this World, be in vain, if there were nobody that in the State of Nature, had a *Power to Execute* that Law, and thereby preserve the innocent and restrain offenders, and if any one in the State of Nature may punish another, for any evil he has done, every one may do so. For in that *State of perfect Equality*, where naturally there is no superiority or jurisdiction of one over another, what any may do in Prosecution of that Law, every one must needs have a Right to do.

8. And thus in the State of Nature, one Man comes by a Power over another; but yet no Absolute or Arbitrary Power, to use a Criminal when he has got him in his hands,

Notes

[3] *Hooker* Richard Hooker (1554–1600), theologian, author of *Of the Laws of Ecclesiastical Polity* (1593); Locke cites a passage from *Laws* 1.8.7, which I omit.

according to the passionate heats, or boundless extravagancy of his own Will, but only to retribute to him, so far as calm reason and conscience dictates, what is proportionate to his Transgression, which is so much as may serve for Reparation and Restraint. For these two are the only reasons, why one Man may lawfully do harm to another, which is that we call *punishment*. In transgressing the Law of Nature, the Offender declares himself to live by another Rule, than that of *reason* and common equity, which is that measure God has set to the actions of Men, for their mutual security, and so he becomes dangerous to Mankind, the tie, which is to secure them from injury and violence, being slighted and broken by him, which being a trespass against the whole Species, and the Peace and Safety of it, provided for by the Law of Nature, every Man upon this score, by the Right he hath to preserve Mankind in general, may restrain, or where it is necessary, destroy things noxious to them, and so may bring such evil on any one, who hath transgressed that Law, as may make him repent the doing of it, and thereby deter him, and by his Example others, from doing the like mischief. And in this case, and upon this ground, *every Man hath a Right to punish the Offender, and be Executioner of the Law of Nature.*

from Chapter 4 Of Slavery

22. The *Natural Liberty* of Man is to be free from any Superior Power on Earth, and not to be under the Will or Legislative Authority of Man, but to have only the Law of Nature for his Rule. The *Liberty of Man, in Society*, is to be under no other Legislative Power, but that established, by consent, in the Commonwealth; nor under the Dominion of any Will, or Restraint of any Law, but what the Legislative shall enact, according to the Trust put in it. Freedom then is not what Sir R[obert] F[ilmer] tells us, *O[bservations on] A[ristotle]* 55. *A Liberty for every one to do what he lists,*[4] *to live as he pleases, and not to be tied by any Laws*: but *Freedom of Men, under Government*, is, to have a standing Rule to live by, common to everyone of that Society, and made by the Legislative Power erected in it; a Liberty to follow my own Will in all things, where that Rule prescribes not; not to be subject to the inconstant, uncertain, unknown, Arbitrary Will of another Man, as *Freedom of Nature* is to be under no other restraint but the Law of Nature.

23. This *Freedom* from Absolute, Arbitrary Power, is so necessary to, and closely joined with a Man's Preservation, that he cannot part with it, but by what forfeits his Preservation and Life together. For a Man, not having the Power of his own Life, *cannot*, by Compact, or his own Consent, *enslave himself* to any one, nor put himself under the Absolute, Arbitrary Power of another, to take away his Life, when he pleases. Nobody can give more Power than he has himself; and he that cannot take away his own Life, cannot give another power over it. Indeed having, by his fault, forfeited his own Life, by some Act that deserves Death, he, to whom he has forfeited it, may (when he has him in his Power) delay to take it, and make use of him to his own Service, and he does him no injury by it. For, whenever he finds the hardship of his Slavery outweigh the value of his Life, 'tis in his Power, by resisting the Will of his Master, to draw on himself the Death he desires.

24. This is the perfect condition of *Slavery*, which is nothing else, but the *State of War*[5] *continued, between a lawful Conqueror, and a Captive.* For, if once *Compact* enter

Notes

[4] *lists* wishes.

[5] *State of War* "a State of Enmity and Destruction," the subject of Locke's chapter 3.

between them, and make an agreement for a limited Power on the one side, and Obedience, on the other, the State of War and *Slavery* ceases, as long as the Compact endures. For, as has been said, no Man can, by agreement, pass over to another that which he hath not in himself, a Power over his own Life.

I confess, we find among the *Jews*, as well as other Nations, that Men did sell themselves; but, 'tis plain, this was only to *Drudgery*, not to *Slavery*.[6] For, it is evident, the Person sold was not under an Absolute, Arbitrary, Despotical Power. For the Master could not have Power to kill him, at any time, whom, at a certain time, he was obliged to let go free out of his Service: And the Master of such a Servant was so far from having an Arbitrary Power over his Life, that he could not, at pleasure, so much as maim him, but the loss of an Eye, or Tooth, set him free.

from Chapter 5 Of Property

25. Whether we consider natural *Reason*, which tells us, that Men, being once born, have a right to their Preservation, and consequently to Meat and Drink, and such other things, as Nature affords for their Subsistence: Or *Revelation*, which gives us an account of those Grants God made of the World to *Adam*, and to *Noah*, and his Sons; 'tis very clear, that God, as K[ing] *David* says, *Psalm* 115.16. 'has given the earth to the Children of men', given it to Mankind in common. But this being supposed, it seems to some a very great difficulty how any one should ever come to have a Property in anything; I will not content myself to answer, 'That if it be difficult to make out *Property*, upon a supposition, that God gave the world to *Adam* and his Posterity in common; it is impossible that any Man, but one universal Monarch, should have any *Property* upon a supposition, that God gave the World to *Adam*, and his Heirs in Succession, exclusive of all the rest of his Posterity'. But I shall endeavour to show, how Men might come to have a Property in several parts of that which God gave to Mankind in common, and that without any express Compact of all the Commoners.

26. God, who hath given the World to Men in common, hath also given them reason to make use of it to the best advantage of life, and convenience. The Earth, and all that is therein, is given to Men for the Support and Comfort of their being. And though all the Fruits it naturally produces, and Beasts it feeds, belong to Mankind in common, as they are produced by the spontaneous hand of Nature; and nobody has originally a private Dominion, exclusive of the rest of Mankind, in any of them, as they are thus in their natural state: yet being given for the use of Men, there must, of necessity, be a means *to appropriate* them some way or other before they can be of any use, or at all beneficial to any particular Men. The Fruit, or Venison which nourishes the wild Indian, who knows no Inclosure, and is still a Tenant in common, must be his, and so his, i.e. a part of him, that another can no longer have any right to it, before it can do him any good for the support of his Life.

27. Though the Earth, and all inferior Creatures be common to all Men, yet every Man has a *Property* in his own *Person*. This nobody has any Right to but himself. The Labour of his Body, and the Work of his Hands, we may say, are properly his. Whatsoever then he removes out of the State that Nature hath provided, and left it in, he hath mixed his *Labour* with, and joined to it something that is his own, and thereby makes it his *Property*. It being by him removed from the common state Nature placed

Notes

[6] *Jews ... Slavery* the Mosaic law with respect to servitude is laid out in Exodus 21.1–11, 20–1, 26–7; it provides for six years of service only, with freedom granted in the seventh.

it in, it hath by this *labour* something annexed to it, that excludes the common right of other Men. For this labour being the unquestionable Property of the Labourer, no Man but he can have a right to what that is once joined to, at least where there is enough, and as good left in common for others.

28. He that is nourished by the Acorns he picked up under an Oak, or the Apples he gathered from the Trees in the Wood, has certainly appropriated them to himself. Nobody can deny but the nourishment is his. I ask then, 'when did they begin to be his? When he digested? Or when he eat? Or when he boiled? Or when he brought them home? Or when he picked them up?' And 'tis plain, if the first gathering made them not his, nothing else could. That *labour* put a distinction between them and common. That added something to them more than Nature, the common Mother of all, had done; and so they became his private right. And will any one say he had no right to those Acorns or Apples he thus appropriated, because he had not the consent of all Mankind to make them his? Was it a Robbery thus to assume to himself what belonged to all in Common? If such a consent as that was necessary, Man had starved, notwithstanding the Plenty God had given him. We see in *Commons*,[7] which remain so by Compact, that 'tis the taking any part of what is common, and removing it out of the state Nature leaves it in, which *begins the Property*; without which the Common is of no use. And the taking of this or that part, does not depend on the express consent of all the Commoners. Thus the Grass my Horse has bit; the Turfs my Servant has cut; and the Ore I have digged in any place where I have a right to them in common with others, become my Property, without the assignation[8] or consent of anybody. The labour that was mine, removing them out of that common state they were in, hath *fixed* my *Property* in them.

Notes

[7] *Common* "An open ground equally used by many persons" (Johnson).

[8] *assignation* assigning.

Samuel Pepys (1633–1703)

With the possible exception of Boswell's *London Journal*, the diary kept by Samuel Pepys from 1660 to 1669 is the most famous work of its kind in English. Part of Pepys's motivation for beginning the work on January 1 of a momentous year was his interest in politics. As a household official in the service of Edward Mountagu (a staunch Cromwellian and a naval commander), Pepys found himself at the center of the events that led to the restoration of the Stuart monarchy in 1660, two years after the death of Oliver Cromwell and about a year after the failure of Richard Cromwell to maintain control over the revolutionary government. Pepys rose with Mountagu and became a member of the Navy Board, under the direction of the duke of York, later King James II. He had been schooled at St. Paul's and Cambridge, but as the son of a London tailor, Pepys knew little about naval affairs. Through diligence and a devotion to systematic methods, however, he mastered the difficulties of the job and enacted many reforms, especially in the area of purchasing. He streamlined costs and reduced corruption, though he did not puritanically reject all of the gifts presented by merchants and tradesmen looking for contractual favors. By 1669, when he ended his diary, he was known as the "right hand of the Navy." As he gratefully and lovingly records, his esteem and his finances grew vastly throughout the period of his diary, and by the end of it he was a made man with a large household and a private coach.

Political events may have prompted Pepys to begin his diary, but he gives at least equal attention to his rich private life. Especially interesting is his unsteady relationship with his Anglo-French wife, Elizabeth St. Michel, whom he had married in 1655 when he was twenty-two and she was fifteen. The two were separated for a time in 1668 when Elizabeth discovered that Pepys was conducting one of his many secret extramarital affairs with her companion, Deborah Willet. Pepys's self-examination in his personal crises leaves something to be desired, but his buoyancy, his range of feelings, and the scope of his interests make him an attractive personality nevertheless. The diary conveys Pepys's personal outlook on every subject, whether public or private, and he gives readers the distinct sense that the diary is not only an extension of his experience but a sign of being alive that gradually became for him inseparable from living. At the end of May 1669, Pepys was suffering so much eye-strain that he feared he was going blind and gave up his diary-keeping to preserve his sight. He writes that the sacrifice was "almost as much as to see myself go into my grave." It is hard not to view this attitude as a prototype or forerunner of a characteristically modern (or even postmodern) view of reality as something defined by language. In fact, the philosophical basis of this modern notion can be traced to the work of Pepys's nearly exact coeval, John Locke.

Although his eyesight returned and he kept some diaries after 1669, Pepys never again wrote anything on the scale of his famous work. We therefore know less than we might about his reactions to the death of his wife Elizabeth in late 1669 or the sort of domestic tranquility he evidently enjoyed in late middle age (without marriage) with Mary Skinner. We do know that after the diary years Pepys's professional success continued, although it was linked with the rise and fall of the duke of York. Pepys held positions in Parliament and rose to secretary for admiralty affairs in 1684. In that year he also became the president of the Royal Society. But in 1689, with the fall of James II, the former duke of York, and

British Literature 1640–1789: An Anthology, Fourth Edition. Edited by Robert DeMaria, Jr.

the Glorious Revolution that brought William of Orange to the English throne, Pepys was forced into retirement, as he had been temporarily so forced during five years (1679–84) when the duke and his supporters were thought to be complicitous in the so-called "Popish Plot" to sell the government of England to France and Roman Catholicism. In retirement Pepys pursued his interests in collecting books, manuscripts, ballads, prints, and drawings. His collections, especially the ballads, were among the greatest in England, and he enjoyed the company of other learned gentlemen, including Sir Isaac Newton and John Evelyn, who lived to write an admiring, elegiac note in his own diary about Pepys's death in 1703.

Pepys bequeathed the unique manuscript of his diary to Magdalene College, Cambridge, where it remains in six elegantly bound, gold-stamped volumes. Pepys had many of his books richly bound, and a codicil in his will makes it clear that he took pride in passing his private journals, and the rest of his library, on to succeeding generations. The manuscript is remarkably neatly written, and there is evidence that the Magdalene College volumes represent a fair copy of more haphazardly jotted notes. In fact, at least in many instances, Pepys probably engaged in an arduous process of composition. Assembling notes from his "pocket-books" and the backs of slips of paper, ephemera picked up at plays, receipts, and so on, Pepys compiled a rough draft of sorts. At the same time, he seems to have distributed some of his collections into other manuscript books (account books, and "by books," all now lost) which he kept simultaneously. Using notes, drafts for the diary and parts of his other books, Pepys then slowly and neatly composed the diary as we have it. It was once thought that Pepys's book represents an immediate expression of his experience rather than a careful composition involving several stages of writing. This view would make Pepys attractively romantic and spontaneous, but it does not account for the varying styles of composition in the work nor for its extraordinarily neat physical presentation. Nor would it sort with everything we know about the compulsively orderly and diligent habits of the diarist. The greatest oddity of the diary from a modern standpoint is also readily subject to misinterpretation. Although it is almost all written in shorthand, Pepys did not mean the work to be indecipherable – at least not to the learned people to whom he bequeathed it. Shorthand was a dignified, philosophical kind of writing in the seventeenth century, and it was the subject of many learned works in what now might be called communication theory. Pepys did not invent his shorthand but adopted (and in small ways adapted) one of the many methods invented in the seventeenth century. He obviously intended the work to frustrate casual inspection (most probably by members of his household), and he further obscured passages concerning his sexual adventures by using a macaronic vocabulary of French, Spanish, and Latin. However, although the work looks dauntingly cryptic, the deception was not meant to be lasting, and, though Pepys destroyed some personal papers, he carefully preserved his diary.

Visitors and residents of Magdalene College noticed Pepys's diary from time to time in the eighteenth century, but not a single line was quoted in print before 1812, and the first edition, abridged and bowdlerized, did not appear until 1825. Although there were several popular editions in the nineteenth century, the work has only recently been properly edited and published in its entirety, including Pepys's accounts of his sexual affairs, which Victorian editors had omitted as inappropriate for print. The following excerpts are from the standard edition, edited by Robert Latham and William Matthews, 9 vols. (G. Bell and Sons Ltd., 1970–83). The prefaces to these volumes and the accompanying *Pepys Handbook* provide excellent introductions to the life and works, and I rely on them here. The standard biography is by Sir Arthur Bryant, 3 vols. (London, 1933–47). There is a good short biography by Claire Tomalin (Viking, 2002).

The small extract from the diary presented here records Pepys's experience during a six-week period when the so-called Great Plague was devastating London. Plague was a disease transmitted by flea bites and peaked in the summer when fleas, infesting rats, thrived. Estimates put the death toll for London in 1665 at 100,000, one-quarter of the population of the city. Believing that the disease was airborne, wealthy people left the city in droves at this time. Pepys stayed, though he moved his delicate wife to Woolwich. He records his horror and his fears of the plague, but he does not neglect his other experiences. Fear does not prevent him from continuing his social and sometimes profligate ways, nor does it entirely dampen his wonderful and memorable good cheer.

from *Diary*

July 1665

1. Called up betimes, though weary and sleepy, by appointment by Mr. Povey and Colonel Norwood, to discourse about some payments of Tangier.[1] They gone, I to the office and there sat all morning. At noon dined at home, and then to the Duke of Albemarle's[2] by appointment to give him an account of some disorder in the yard at Portsmouth, by workmen's going away of their own accord for lack of money, to get work of haymaking or anything else to earn themselves bread.

Thence I to Westminster, where I hear the sickness increases greatly. And to the Harp and Ball[3] with Mary, talking, who tells me simply of losing her first love in the country in Wales and coming up hither unknown to her friends. And it seems Dr. Williams[4] doth pretend to love her, and I have found him there several times.

Thence by coach, and late at the office and so to bed – sad at the news that seven or eight houses in Bazing-hall street are shut up of the plague.

2. *Sunday.* Up, and all the morning dressing my closet[5] at the office with my plat[6] very neatly, and a fine place now it is and will be a pleasure to sit in – though I thank God I needed none before. At noon dined at home, and after dinner to my accounts and cast them up, and find that though I have spent above £90 this month yet I have saved £17 and am worth in all above £1450, for which the Lord be praised.

In the evening my Lady Penn[7] and daughter came to see and supped with us. Then a messenger about business of the office from Sir G. Carteret[8] at Chatham[9] – and by word of mouth did send me word that the business between my Lord[10] and him is fully agreed on and is mightily liked of by the King and the Duke of York, and that he sent me this word with great joy. They gone, we to bed.

I hear this night that Sir J. Lawson[11] was buried late last night at St. Dunstans by us, without any company at all – and that the condition of his family is but very poor,

Notes

FROM *DIARY*

1 *Povey ... Tangier* In 1665 Pepys succeeded Thomas Povey (c.1613–1705) as treasurer of the Privy Council's Committee for Tangier, a besieged, highly strategic and wealthy city acquired by England in 1661; Henry Norwood (c.1614–89) became the deputy governor of the colony in 1665.

2 *Duke of Albemarle* George Monck (1608–70), an important military leader under Cromwell but instrumental in restoring the monarchy.

3 *the Harp and Ball* a large tavern near Charing Cross.

4 *Dr. Williams* a physician who treated Pepys's wife.

5 *closet* "A small room of privacy and retirement" (Johnson).

6 *plat* an engraved plan or map, which Pepys had framed.

7 *Lady Penn* Margaret Jasper, wife of Sir William and mother of William, the Quaker leader.

8 *Sir G[eorge] Carteret* (c.1610–80), Navy Treasurer 1660–7.

9 *Chatham* site of the most important royal dockyard of the time.

10 *my Lord* Edward Mountagu, earl of Sandwich (1625–72), naval commander, father-in-law of Lady Mary Wortley Montagu (see below, p. 690).

11 *Sir J[ohn] Lawson* naval officer, died of wounds received at the Battle of Lowestoft.

which I could be contented to be sorry for, though he never was the man that ever obliged me by word or deed.

3. Up, and by water with Sir W. Batten[12] and Sir J. Mennes[13] by water to Whitehall to the Duke of Albemarle's, where, after a little business – we parted, and I to the Harp and Ball and there stayed a while talking with Mary, and so home to dinner; after dinner to the Duke of Albemarle's again, and so to the Swan[14] and there demeurais un peu de temps con la fille.[15] And so to the Harp and Ball and alone demeurais un peu de temps besándola;[16] and so away home and late at the office about letters; and so home resolving from this night forward to close all my letters if possible and end all my business at the office by daylight, and I shall go near to do it and put all my affairs in the world in good order, the season growing so sickly that it is much to be feared how a man can 'scape having a share with others in it – for which the good Lord God bless me or to be fitted to receive it.

So after supper to bed, and mightily troubled in my sleep all night with dreams of Jacke Cole my old school-fellow, lately dead, who was born at the same time with me, and we reckoned our fortunes pretty equal. God fit me for his condition.

5. Up, and advised about sending of my wife's bedding and things today to Woolwich,[17] in order to her removal thither. So to the office, where all the morning till noon; and so to the Change[18] and thence home to dinner. In the afternoon I abroad to St. James, and there with Mr. Coventry[19] a good while and understand how matters are ordered in the fleet. …

Being come to Deptford, my Lady[20] not being within, we parted; and I by water to Woolwich, where I found my wife come and her two maids, and very prettily accommodated they will be. And I left them going to supper, grieved in my heart to part with my wife, being worse by much without her, though some trouble there is in having the care of the family at home in this plague time. And so took leave, and I in one boat and W. Hewer[21] in another, home very late, first against tide – we having walked in the dark to Greenwich.

Late home and to bed – very alonely [*sic*].

24. … by appointment to Deptford to Sir G. Carteret between 6 and 7 a-clock, where I found him and my Lady[22] almost ready; and by and by went over to the Ferry and took coach and six horses nobly for Dagenhams,[23] himself and Lady and their little daughter Louisonne and myself in the coach – where when we came, we were bravely entertained and spent the day most pleasantly with the young ladies, and I so merry as never more. Only, for want of sleep, and drinking of strange beer, had a rheum[24] in one of my eyes which troubled me much. Here with great content all the day, as I think I ever passed a day in my life, because of the contentfulness of our errand – and the nobleness of the company and our manner of going. But I find Mr. Carteret[25] yet as

Notes

12 *Sir W[illiam] Batten* (c.1601–67), surveyor of the Navy 1660–7.

13 *Sir J[ohn] Mennes* (1599–1671), comptroller of the Navy 1660–71.

14 *Swan* one of several taverns by that name.

15 *demeurais … fille* "tarried a little while with the girl"; even though the whole diary is written in code, Pepys obscures his dalliances further by breaking into French or, elsewhere, a kind of Spanish or quasi-Latin.

16 *besándola* "kissing her."

17 *Woolwich* site of a shipyard, outside of London and so safer from the plague.

18 *Change* the Royal Exchange, a center for merchants.

19 *Mr. Coventry* Henry, younger brother of Sir William, Pepys's mentor and colleague.

20 *my Lady* Lady Sandwich, wife of Edward Mountagu.

21 *W[ill] Hewer* (1642–1715), naval official and close friend of Pepys.

22 *my Lady* Elizabeth Carteret, George's cousin and wife.

23 *Dagenhams* the home of Lady Wright (a relative of the Mountagus) in Essex.

24 *rheum* "A thin watery matter oozing through the glands" (Johnson, quoting Quincy).

25 *Mr. Carteret* Philip, who married Mountagu's daughter Jemima in this month.

backward almost in his caress as he was the first day. At night, about 7 a-clock, took coach again; but Lord, to see in what pleasant humour Sir G. Carteret hath been, both coming and going; so light, so fond, so merry, so boyish (so much content he takes in this business), it is one of the greatest wonders I ever saw in my mind. But once in serious discourse, he did say that if he knew his son to be a debauch, as many and most are nowadays about the Court, he would tell it, and my Lady Jem should not have him. And so enlarged, both he and she, about the baseness and looseness of the Court, and told several stories of the Duke of Monmouth[26] and Richmond.[27] And some great person married to a lady of extraordinary Quality (fit and that might have made a wife for the King himself) about six months since, that this great person hath given the pox[28] to. And discoursed how much this would oblige the Kingdom if the King would banish some of these great persons publicly from the Court – and wished it with all their hearts.

We set out so late that it grew dark, so as we doubted the losing of our way; and a long time it was or seemed before we could get to the waterside, and that about 11 at night; where when we come, all merry (only, my eye troubled me as I said), we find no ferry-boat was there nor no Oars[29] to carry us to Deptford. However, afterward oars was called from the other side at Greenwich; but when it came, a frolic, being mighty merry, took us, and there we would sleep all night in the Coach in the Isle of Dogs;[30] so we did, there being now with us my Lady Scott[31] – and with great pleasure drew up the glasses and slept till daylight; and then some victuals and wine being brought us we eat a bit, and so up and took boat, merry as might be; and when come to Sir G. Carteret, there all to bed – our good humour in everybody continuing;

25. and there I slept till 7 a-clock, then up, and to the office well refreshed, my eye only troubling me, which by keeping a little covered with my hankercher and washing now and then with cold water grew better by night. At noon to the Change, which was very thin; and thence homeward and was called in by Mr. Rawlinson,[32] with whom I dined, and some good company, very harmlessly merry. But sad the story of the plague in the City, it growing mightily. This day my Lord Brouncker[33] did give me Mr. Graunt's book upon the Bills of Mortality,[34] new-printed and enlarged.

26. Up; and after doing a little business, down to Deptford with Sir W. Batten – and there left him, and I to Greenwich to the park, where I hear the King and Duke are come by water this morn from Hampton Court.[35] They asked me several Questions. … Great variety of talk – and was often led to speak to the King and Duke. By and by they to dinner; and all to dinner and sat down to the King saving myself, which though I could not in modesty expect, yet God forgive my pride, I was sorry I was there, that Sir W. Batten should say that he could sit down where I could not – though he had twenty times more reason than I. But this was my pride and folly. …

[Mr. Castle][36] and I by and by to dinner, mighty nobly; and the King having dined, he came down, and I went in the barge with him, I sitting at the door – down to Woolwich

Notes

26 *Monmouth* James Scott, duke of Monmouth (1649–85), illegitimate son of Charles II.

27 *Richmond* Charles Stuart, third duke of Richmond.

28 *pox* "The venereal disease. This is the sense when it has no epithet" (Johnson).

29 *Oars* a large ferry operated by two men.

30 *Isle of Dogs* a marshy peninsula in the Thames.

31 *Lady Scott* wife of the soldier Sir Edward Scott.

32 *Mr. Rawlinson* landlord of the Mitre tavern.

33 *Lord Brouncker* William, second viscount (1620–84), Navy Commissioner.

34 *Bills of Mortality Natural and Political Observations … upon the Bills of Mortality* by John Graunt (1662), a pioneering work of demography registering deaths in London during the plague years.

35 *Hampton Court* a palace west of London used by Charles mainly during the plague.

36 *[Mr. Castle]* William Castle, a private shipbuilder.

(and there I just saw and kissed my wife, and saw some of her painting, which is very curious, and away again to the King) and back again with him in the barge, hearing him and the Duke talk and seeing and observing their manner of discourse; and God forgive me, though I adore them with all the duty possible, yet the more a man considers and observes them, the less he finds of difference between them and other men, though (blessed be God) they are both princes of great nobleness and spirits.

The Barge put me into another boat that came to our side, Mr. Holder[37] with a bag of gold to the Duke; and so they away, and I home to the office. The Duke of Monmouth is the most skittish, leaping gallant that ever I saw, always in action, vaulting or leaping or clambering.[38]

Thence, mighty full of the honour of this day – took coach and to Kate Joyce,[39] but she not within; but spoke with Anth,[40] who tells me he likes well of my proposal for Pall to Harman;[41] but I fear that less than £500 will not be taken, and that I shall not be able to give – though I did not say so to him. After a little other discourse, and the sad news of the death of so many in the parish of the plague, 40 last night – the bell always going – I back to the Exchange, where I went up and sat talking with my beauty, Mrs. Batelier,[42] a great while, who is indeed one of the finest women I ever saw in my life. After buying some small matter, I home, and there to the office and saw Sir J. Mennes, now come from Portsmouth; I home to set my Journal for these four days in order, they being four days of as great content and honour and pleasure to me as ever I hope to live or desire or think anybody else can live. For methinks if a man could but reflect upon this, and think that all these things are ordered by God Almighty to make me contented, and even this very marriage now on foot is one of the things intended to find me content in my life and matter of mirth, methinks it should make one mightily more satisfied in the world than he is. This day poor Robin Shaw at Backwell's[43] died – and Backwell himself now in Flanders. The King himself asked about Shaw; and being told he was dead, said he was very sorry for it.

The Sickness is got into our parish this week; and is got indeed everywhere, so that I begin to think of setting things in order, which I pray God enable me to put, both as to soul and body.

August 1665

8. Up, and to the office, where all the morning we sat. At noon I home to dinner alone. And after dinner Bagwell's wife[44] waited at the door, and went with me to my office, en lequel jo haze todo which I had a corasón a hazer con ella.[45] So parted, and I to Sir W. Batten's and there sat the most of the afternoon, talking and drinking too much with my Lord Brouncker, Sir G. Smith, G. Cocke,[46] and others, very merry. I drunk a little, mixed, but yet more than I should do. So to my office a little, and then to the

Notes

[37] *Mr. Holder* an accountant for the duke.

[38] *Vaulting ... clambering* the duke was then sixteen years old.

[39] *Kate Joyce* Pepys's cousin.

[40] *Anth[ony Joyce]* a candle-maker, brother-in-law of Kate.

[41] *Harman* Philip, Pepys's cousin by marriage, recently widowed.

[42] *Mrs. Batelier* a relative of Pepys's neighbours; Mrs. means mistress and does not indicate marriage.

[43] *Robin Shaw at Backwell's* a former colleague of Pepys's who had become managing clerk for Edward Backwell, a banker.

[44] *Bagwell's wife* one of Pepys's mistresses, wife of William, a ship's carpenter.

[45] *en lequel ... con ella* "where I did what I wished with her."

[46] *Sir G. Smith, G. Cocke* both George, a pair of well-to-do, hard-drinking merchants.

Duke of Albemarle's about some business. The streets mighty empty all the way now, even in London, which is a sad sight. And to Westminster Hall, where talking, hearing very sad stories from Mrs. Mumford[47] among others, of Mrs. Mitchell's son's family.[48] And poor Will that used to sell us ale at the Hall[49] door – his wife and three children dead, all I think in a day. So home through the City again, wishing I may have taken no ill in going; but I will go, I think, no more hither.

12. Coming back to Deptford, old Bagwell walked a little way with me and would have me in to his daughter's; and there, he being gone dehors, ego had my volunté de su hija.[50] Eat and drank, and away home; and after a little at the office, to my chamber to put more things still in order, and late to bed.

The people die so, that now it seems they are fain to carry the dead to be buried by daylight, the nights not sufficing to do it in. And my Lord Mayor commands people to be within 9 at night, all (as they say) that the sick may have liberty to go abroad for air. There is one also dead out of one of our ships at Deptford, which troubles us mightily – the *Providence* fire-ship, which was just fitted to go to sea. But they tell me today, no more sick on board. And this day W. Bodham[51] tell me that one is dead at Woolwich, not far from the Ropeyard. I am told too, that a wife of one of the grooms at Court is dead at Salisbury, so that the King and Queen are speedily to be all gone to Wilton.[52] God preserve us.

15. Up by 4 a-clock and walked to Greenwich, where called at captain Cocke's and to his chamber, he being in bed – where something put my last night's dream into my head, which I think is the best that ever was dreamed – which was, that I had my Lady Castlemaine[53] in my arms and was admitted to use all the dalliance I desired with her, and then dreamed that this could not be awake but that it was only a dream. But that since it was a dream and that I took so much real pleasure in it, what a happy thing it would be, if when we are in our graves (as Shakespeare resembles it), we could dream, and dream but such dreams as this that then we should not need to be so fearful of death as we are this plague-time?

Notes

47 *Mrs. Mumford* a shopkeeper.

48 *Mrs. Mitchell* a bookseller and old friend of Pepys.

49 *Hall* the great room in Westminster Palace, which accommodated many shops and stalls, as well as several government offices.

50 *dehors … hija* "[he] gone away, I had my pleasure on her."

51 *W[illiam] Bodham* clerk of the Ropeyard.

52 *Wilton* the earl of Pembroke's house in the country south-west of London.

53 *Lady Castlemaine* Barbara Palmer, countess of Castlemaine (1641–1709), a promiscuous beauty, a mistress of Charles II and other notables.

Aphra Behn (1640?–1689)

Poet, playwright, novelist, and translator, Aphra Behn was among the most versatile writers of her time. She is probably the first woman ever to make a living as a writer, and she was the first woman to be memorialized as a writer in Westminster Abbey. In surveying the history of English literature from her vantage point as a woman in the early twentieth century, Virginia Woolf would find in Behn a most important early advocate for the place of women in the world of letters.

Although the facts of Behn's early life are uncertain, she seems to have been born Eaffrey Johnson, and it is likely that as a young woman she travelled to Surinam or British Guiana. She places herself there amidst the scene of much of the action of her most famous novel, *Oroonoko*. On her return to England she probably married a merchant named Behn, whose family was Dutch. Shortly thereafter, from 1666 to 1667, Behn was in Antwerp as a spy for the English government under the code name "Astrea," which she later used as her literary name. At some point early on her husband died or abandoned her, for she was briefly in debtors' prison in 1667. Not long after this, Behn began writing for a living: remarkably, she published over thirty separate volumes or pamphlets between 1676 and 1689, including an enormous epistolary novel that presents a recent scandal in a thinly veiled fiction. Her work as a playwright began before this period of massive publication and continued deep into it. Behn wrote at least nineteen plays, the first of which to be published was *The Forced Marriage* (1670). *The Rover*, perhaps Behn's best play, was popular enough to support a sequel. *The Rover* is a romantic comedy about temporarily disenfranchised English cavaliers and their escapades in the masquerade world of Naples at carnival time. Like some of Behn's poetry, *The Rover* displays a mastery of sexual innuendo and bawdiness that is much more common in male writers and conventionally thought of as inappropriate in women. Contemporary satirical writings, like that of Thomas Brown, and later accounts, including the article in the first *Dictionary of National Biography*, express dismay about Behn's morals. Happily, times have changed and interest has returned to her diverse literary output, and most of all to her novel *Oroonoko, or, the Royal Slave*.

There is an obvious temptation to read *Oroonoko* as a manifesto of anti-slavery, anti-colonialist, egalitarian, and perhaps even proto-feminist values, but the novel is interesting in many different ways. Although Behn draws on her knowledge of some historical incidents and persons, in genre the work is a romance, a popular fictional form designed to appeal to women and to members of the recently educated middle class. *Oroonoko* was certainly meant to be popular; but in a startling reversal of stereotypes, Behn substitutes Africans for the European nobles that traditionally take the lead roles in seventeenth-century romances. Yet, in many respects, Prince Oroonoko and his bride are nobler and more traditional than their European counterparts, and the work can be read as profoundly conservative, even though it is concerned with the injustices of the colonial system. Behn's politics always revolved around her extremely loyal royalism, which was not in conflict, for her, with her obvious hatred of slavery, or her wishes for the empowerment of women in the public as well as the private sphere. In short, when one tries to interpret *Oroonoko*, it resists easy solutions

British Literature 1640–1789: An Anthology, Fourth Edition. Edited by Robert DeMaria, Jr.

and displays some of the complexity and difficulty that many critics think of as one of the defining qualities of art. Such complexity is not always evident in the language or the plot of the novel, but the book has all kinds of value for students of literature. In addition to its other virtues, *Oroonoko* shows the old, largely upper-class genre of the romance, in the process of transforming itself into a work with a broader social horizon and less parochial interests.

The text of *Oroonoko* is based on the first edition (1688). The text of *The Rover* is based on the first edition of 1677 but includes a few changes from later editions. The Oxford edition by Jane Spencer (1995), to which I am indebted, records significant variants. The Works have been edited by Janet Todd (Ohio State University Press, 1992–6). I am indebted to Todd's notes on the poetry and on *Oroonoko. The Secret Life of Aphra Behn* (A. Deutsch, 1996) is Todd's authoritative biography.

from *Poems upon Several Occasions* (1684)

The Golden Age
A Paraphrase on a Translation out of French[1]

I.

Blest Age! when every Purling Stream
Ran undisturbed and clear,
When no scorned Shepherds on your Banks were seen,
Tortured by Love, by Jealousy, or Fear;
When an Eternal Spring dressed every Bough,
And Blossoms fell, by new ones dispossessed;
These their kind Shade affording all below;
And those a Bed where all below might rest.
The Groves appeared all dressed with Wreaths of Flowers,
And from their Leaves dropped Aromatic Showers,
Whose fragrant Heads in Mystic Twines above,
Exchanged their Sweets, and mixed with thousand Kisses,
    As if the willing Branches strove
    To beautify and shade the Grove.
    Where the young wanton Gods of Love
Offer their Noblest Sacrifice of Blisses.

II.

Calm was the Air, no Winds blew fierce and loud,
The Sky was darkened with no sullen Cloud;
But all the Heav'ns laughed with continued Light,
And scattered round their Rays serenely bright.

Notes

The Golden Age

1 *A Paraphrase on a Translation out of French* As Janet Todd notes, Behn's poem derives from the opening chorus of Torquato Tasso's *Aminta* (1573); no intermediary French translation has been identified.

No other Murmurs filled the Ear
But what the Streams and Rivers purled,
When Silver Waves o'er Shining Pebbles curled;
Or when young *Zephyrs* fanned the Gentle Breeze,
Gath'ring fresh Sweets from Balmy Flow'rs and Trees,
Then bore 'em on their Wings to perfume all the Air:
While to their soft and tender Play,
The Gray-Plumed Natives of the Shades
Unwearied sing till Love invades,
Then Bill, then sing again, while Love and Music
makes the Day.

III.

The stubborn Plough had then,
Made no rude Rapes upon the Virgin Earth;
Who yielded of her own accord her plenteous Birth,
Without the Aids of men;
As if within her Teeming Womb,
All Nature, and all Sexes lay,
Whence new Creations every day
Into the happy World did come:
The Roses filled with Morning Dew,
Bent down their loaded heads,
T'Adorn the careless shepherds' Grassy Beds
While still young opening Buds each moment grew,
And as those withered, dressed his shaded Couch anew;
Beneath whose boughs the Snakes securely dwelt,
Not doing harm, nor harm from others felt;
With whom the Nymphs did Innocently play,
No spiteful Venom in the wantons lay;
But to the touch were Soft, and to the sight were Gay.

IV.

Then no rough sound of Wars' Alarms,
Had taught the World the needless use of Arms:
Monarchs were uncreated then,
Those Arbitrary Rulers over men;
Kings that made Laws, first broke 'em, and the Gods
By teaching us Religion first, first set the World at Odds:
Till then Ambition was not known,
That Poison to Content, Bane to Repose;
Each Swain was Lord o'er his own will alone,
His Innocence Religion was, and Laws.
Nor needed any troublesome defence
Against his Neighbours' Insolence.
Flocks, Herds, and every necessary good
Which bounteous Nature had designed for Food,
Whose kind increase o'er-spread the Meads and Plains,
Was then a common Sacrifice to all th'agreeing Swains.

V.

Right and Property were words since made,
When Power taught Mankind to invade:
When Pride and Avarice became a Trade;
Carried on by discord, noise and wars,
For which they bartered wounds and scars;
And to Enhance the Merchandise, miscalled it Fame,
And Rapes, Invasions, Tyrannies,
Was gaining of a Glorious Name:
Styling their savage slaughters, Victories;
Honour, the Error and the Cheat
Of the Ill-natured Busy Great,
Nonsense, invented by the Proud,
Fond Idol of the slavish Crowd,
Thou wert not known in those blessed days
Thy Poison was not mixed with our unbounded Joys;
Then it was glory to pursue delight,
And that was lawful all, that Pleasure did invite,
Then 'twas the Amorous world enjoyed its Reign;
And Tyrant Honour strove t'usurp in Vain.

VI.

The flow'ry Meads, the Rivers and the Groves,
Were filled with little Gay-winged Loves:
That ever smiled and danced and Played,
And now the woods, and the streams invade,
And where they came all things were gay and glad:
When in the Myrtle Groves the Lovers sat
Oppressed with a too fervent heat;
A Thousand Cupids fanned their wings aloft,
And through the Boughs the yielded Air would wait:
Whose parting Leaves discovered all below,
And every God his own soft power admired,
And smiled and fanned, and sometimes bent his Bow;
Where'er he saw a Shepherd uninspired.
The Nymphs were free, no nice, no coy disdain,
Denied their Joys, or gave the Lover pain;
The yielding Maid but kind Resistance makes;
Trembling and blushing are not marks of shame,
But the Effect of kindling Flame:
Which from the sighing burning Swain she takes,
While she with tears all soft, and downcast eyes,
Permits the Charming Conqueror to win the prize.

VII.

The Lovers thus, thus uncontrolled did meet,
Thus all their Joys and Vows of Love repeat:
Joys which were everlasting, ever new
And every Vow inviolably true:

Not kept in fear of Gods, no fond Religious cause,
Nor in Obedience to the duller Laws.
Those Fopperies of the Gown were then not known,[2]
Those vain those Politic Curbs to keep man in,[3]
Who by a fond mistake Created that a Sin;
Which freeborn we, by right of Nature claim our own.
Who but the Learnèd and dull moral Fool
Could gravely have foreseen, man ought to live by Rule?

VIII.

Oh cursèd Honour! thou who first didst damn,
A Woman to the Sin of shame;
Honour! that robb'st us of our Gust,[4]
Honour! that hindered mankind first,
At Love's Eternal Spring to squench his amorous thirst.
Honour! who first taught lovely Eyes the art,
To wound, and not to cure the heart:
With Love to invite, but to forbid with Awe,
And to themselves prescribe a Cruèl Law;
To Veil 'em from the Lookers on,
When they are sure the slave's undone,
And all the Charming'st part of Beauty hid;
Soft Looks, consenting Wishes, all denied.
It gathers up the flowing Hair,
That loosely played with wanton Air.
The Envious Net, and stinted order hold,
The lovely Curls of Jet and shining Gold,
No more neglected on the Shoulders hurled:
Now dressed to Tempt, not gratify the World,
Thou Miser Honour hoard'st the sacred store,
And starv'st thyself to keep thy Votaries poor.

IX.

Honour! that putt'st our words that should be free
Into a set Formality.
Thou base Debaucher of the generous heart,
That teachest all our Looks and Actions Art;
What Love designed a sacred Gift,
What Nature made to be possessed,
Mistaken Honour, made a Theft,
For Glorious Love should be confessed:
For when confined, all the poor Lover gains,
Is broken Sighs, pale Looks, Complaints & Pains.
Thou Foe to Pleasure, Nature's worst Disease,

Notes

[2] *Fopperies of the Gown* academic terms created by doctors of divinity or law.

[3] *Politic* "Prudent" (Johnson, sense 2).

[4] *Gust* "Height of perception; height of sensual enjoyment" (Johnson, sense 2).

Thou Tyrant over mighty Kings,
What mak'st thou here in Shepherds' Cottages;
Why troublest thou, the quiet Shades & Springs;
Be gone, and make thy Famed resort
To Princes' Palaces;
Go Deal and Chaffer in the Trading Court,[5]
That busy Market for fantastic Things;
Be gone and interrupt the short Retreat,
Of the illustrious and the Great;
Go break the Politician's sleep,
Disturb the Gay Ambitious Fool,
That longs for Sceptres, Crowns, and Rule,
Which not his Title, nor his Wit can keep;
But let the humble honest *Swain* go on,
In the blessed Paths of the first rate of man;[6]
That nearest were to Gods Allied,
And formed for love alone, disdained all other Pride.

X.

Be gone! and let the Golden age again,
Assume its Glorious Reign;
Let the young wishing Maid confess,
What all your Arts would keep concealed:
The Mystery will be revealed,
And she in vain denies, whilst we can guess,
She only shows the Jilt to teach man how,[7]
To turn the false Artillery on the Cunning Foe.
Thou empty Vision hence, be gone,
And let the peaceful *Swain* love on;
The swift paced hours of life soon steal away;
Stint not ye Gods his short lived Joy.
The Spring decays, but when the Winter's gone,
The Trees and Flowers anew come on;
The Sun may set, but when the night is fled,
And gloomy darkness does retire,
He rises from his Wat'ry Bed:
All Glorious, Gay, all dressed in Amorous Fire.
But *Sylvia* when your Beauties fade,
When the fresh Roses on your cheeks shall die,
Like Flowers that wither in the Shade,
Eternally they will forgotten lie,
And no kind Spring their sweetness will supply.
When Snow shall on those lovely Tresses lie
And your fair Eyes no more shall give us pain,
But shoot their pointless Darts in vain,

Notes

5 *Chaffer* buy or barter.
6 *rate* "Degree; comparative height or valour" (Johnson, sense 3).
7 *shows the Jilt* plays the part of "A woman who gives her lover hopes, and deceives him" (Johnson).

What will your duller honour signify?
Go boast it then! and see what numerous Store
Of Lovers, will your Ruined Shrine Adore.
Then let us *Sylvia* yet be wise,
And the Gay hasty minutes prize:
The Sun and Spring receive but our short Light,
Once set, a sleep brings an Eternal Night.

The Disappointment[1]

I

One day the Amorous *Lysander*,
By an impatient Passion swayed,
Surprised fair *Cloris*, that loved Maid,
Who could defend herself no longer.
All things did with his Love conspire;
That gilded Planet of the Day,
In his gay Chariot drawn by Fire,
Was now descending to the Sea,
And left no Light to guide the World,
But what from *Cloris'* Brighter Eyes was hurled.

2

In a lone Thicket made for Love,
Silent as yielding Maid's Consent,
She with a Charming Languishment,
Permits his Force, yet gently strove;
Her Hands his Bosom softly meet,
But not to put him back designed,
Rather to draw 'em on inclined:
Whilst he lay trembling at her Feet,
Resistance 'tis in vain to show;
She wants the power to say, 'Ah! What d'ye do?'

3

Her Bright Eyes sweet, and yet severe,
Where Love and Shame confus'dly strive,
Fresh Vigour to *Lysander* give;
And breathing faintly in his Ear,
She cried, 'Cease, Cease – your vain Desire,

Notes

The Disappointment

[1] This poem was long thought to be by John Wilmot (see selections below, pp. 376–98) and was first published, with many differences, in a poorly edited collection of his verse, *Poems on Several Occasions* (1680). It begins as a translation of a French poem called "Sur une Impuissance" by Jean Benech de Cantenac, first published in 1661, which in turn is based on Ovid, *Amores* 3.7.

Or I'll call out – What would you do?
My Dearer Honour ev'n to You
I cannot, must not give – Retire,
Or take this Life, whose chiefest part
I gave you with the Conquest of my Heart'.

4

But he as much unused to Fear,
As he was capable of Love,
The blessèd minutes to improve,
Kisses her Mouth, her Neck, her Hair;
Each Touch her new Desire Alarms,
His burning trembling Hand he pressed
Upon her swelling Snowy Breast,
While she lay panting in his Arms.
All her Unguarded Beauties lie
The Spoils and Trophies of the Enemy.

5

And now without Respect or Fear,
He seeks the Object of his Vows,
(His Love no Modesty allows)
By swift degrees advancing – where
His daring Hand that Altar seized,
Where Gods of Love do sacrifice:
That Awful Throne, that Paradise
Where Rage is calmed, and Anger pleased;
That Fountain where Delight still flows,
And gives the Universal World Repose.

6

Her Balmy Lips encount'ring his,
Their Bodies, as their Souls, are joined;
Where both in Transports Unconfined
Extend themselves upon the Moss.
Cloris half dead and breathless lay;
Her soft Eyes cast a Humid Light,
Such as divides the Day and Night;
Or falling Stars, whose Fires decay:
And now no signs of Life she shows,
But what in short-breathed Sighs returns & goes.

7

He saw how at her Length she lay;
He saw her rising Bosom bare;
Her loose thin *Robes*, through which appear
A Shape designed for Love and Play;
Abandoned by her Pride and Shame.

She does her softest Joys dispense,
Off'ring her Virgin-Innocence
A Victim to Love's Sacred Flame;
While the o'er-Ravished Shepherd lies
Unable to perform the Sacrifice.

8

Ready to taste a thousand Joys,
The too transported hapless Swain
Found the vast Pleasure turned to Pain;
Pleasure which too much Love destroys:
The willing Garments by he laid,
And Heaven all opened to his view,
Mad to possess, himself he threw
On the Defenceless Lovely Maid.
But Oh what envying God conspires
To snatch his Power, yet leave him the Desire!

9

Nature's Support (without whose Aid
She can no Human Being give)
Itself now wants the Art to live;
Faintness its slackened Nerves invade:
In vain th' enragèd Youth essayed[2]
To call its fleeting Vigour back,
No motion 'twill from Motion take;
Excess of Love his Love betrayed:
In vain he Toils, in vain Commands;
The Insensible fell weeping in his Hand.

10

In this so Amorous Cruel Strife,
Where Love and Fate were too severe,
The poor *Lysander* in despair
Renounced his Reason with his Life:
Now all the brisk and active Fire
That should the Nobler Part inflame,
Served to increase his Rage and Shame,
And left no Spark for New Desire:
Not all her Naked Charms could move
Or calm that Rage that had debauched his Love.

11

Cloris returning from the Trance
Which Love and soft Desire had bred,
Her timorous Hand she gently laid

Notes

[2] *essayed* tried.

(Or guided by Design or Chance)
Upon that Fabulous *Priapus*,[3]
That Potent God, as Poets feign;
But never did young *Shepherdess*,
Gath'ring of Fern upon the Plain,
More nimbly draw her Fingers back,
Finding beneath the verdant Leaves a Snake:

12

Than *Cloris* her fair Hand withdrew,
Finding that God of her Desires
Disarmed of all his Awful Fires,
And Cold as Flow'rs bathed in the Morning-Dew.
Who can the *Nymph*'s Confusion guess?
The Blood forsook the hinder Place,
And strewed with Blushes all her Face,
Which both Disdain and Shame expressed:
And from *Lysander*'s Arms she fled,
Leaving him fainting on the Gloomy Bed.

13

Like Lightning through the Grove she hies,
Or *Daphne* from the *Delphic God*,[4]
No Print upon the grassy Road
She leaves, t' instruct Pursuing Eyes.
The Wind that wantoned in her Hair,
And with her Ruffled Garments played,
Discovered in the Flying Maid
All that the Gods e'er made, if Fair.
So *Venus*, when her *Love* was slain,
With Fear and Haste flew o'er the Fatal Plain.[5]

14

The *Nymph*'s Resentments none but I
Can well Imagine or Condole:
But none can guess *Lysander*'s Soul,
But those who swayed his Destiny.
His silent Griefs swell up to Storms,
And not one God his Fury spares;
He cursed his Birth, his Fate, his Stars;
But more the *Shepherdess*'s Charms,
Whose soft bewitching Influence
Had Damned him to the *Hell* of Impotence.

Notes

[3] *Priapus* Greek fertility god whose symbol is a phallus; hence his name is synonymous with phallus.

[4] *Daphne ... Delphic God* the nymph's lengthy flight from Apollo ends with her transformation into a laurel tree (Ovid, *Metamorphoses* 1.502–52).

[5] *Venus ... o'er the Fatal Plain* the goddess, seeing Adonis slain, turns her swan-borne chariot and jumps down from the sky (Ovid, *Metamorphoses* 10.720–2).

from *Lycidus: or the Lover in Fashion* (1688)

To the Fair Clarinda, Who Made Love to Me, Imagined More than Woman

Fair lovely Maid, or if that Title be
Too weak, too Feminine for Nobler thee,
Permit a Name that more Approaches Truth:
And let me call thee, Lovely Charming Youth.
This last will justify my soft complaint,
While that may serve to lessen my constraint;
And without Blushes I the Youth pursue,
When so much beauteous Woman is in view.
Against thy Charms we struggle but in vain
With thy deluding Form thou giv'st us pain,
While the bright Nymph betrays us to the Swain.
In pity to our Sex sure thou wert sent,
That we might Love, and yet be Innocent:
For sure no Crime with thee we can commit;
Of if we should – thy Form excuses it.
For who, that gathers fairest Flowers believes
A Snake lies hid beneath the Fragrant Leaves.
  Thou beauteous Wonder of a different kind,
Soft *Cloris* with the dear *Alexis* joined;
Whene'er the Manly part of thee would plead,
Thou tempts us with the Image of the Maid,
While we the noblest Passions do extend
The Love to *Hermes*, *Aphrodite* the Friend.[1]

The Rover: Or, The Banished Cavaliers (1677)

The Actors' Names

Mr. *Jevorne, Don Antonio*, The Viceroy's Son.
Mr. *Medburne, Don Pedro*, A Noble *Spaniard*, his Friend.
Mr. *Betterton, Belvile*, An *English* Colonel in Love with *Florinda*.
Mr. *Smith, Willmore*, The ROVER.
Mr. *Crosbie, Frederick*, An *English* Gentleman, and Friend to *Bel*. and *Blunt*.
Mr. *Underhill, Blunt*, An *English* Country Gentleman.
Mr. *Richards, Stephano*, Servant to *Don Pedro*.
Mr. *Percivall, Philippo, Lucetta's* Gallant.
Mr. *John Lee, Sancho*, Pimp to *Lucetta*.
Biskey, and *Sebastian*, *Two Bravoes to* Angellica.
Officers and Soldiers.
Page To *Don Antonio*.

Notes

To the Fair Clarinda

[1] *Hermes, Aphrodite* the father and mother of Hermaphroditus, who became a mixture of man and woman when joined to Salmacis, the nymph whose love he spurned (Ovid, *Metamorphoses* 4.285–389).

Women.

Mrs. *Betterton, Florinda*, Sister to *Don Pedro*.
Mrs. *Barrer, Hellena*, A gay Young Woman designed for a Nun, and Sister to *Florinda*.
Mrs. *Hughs, Valeria*, A Kinswoman to *Florinda*.
Mrs. *Gwin, Angellica Bianca*, A Famous Courtesan.
Mrs. *Leigh, Moretta*, Her Woman.
Mrs. *Norris, Callis*, Governess to *Florinda* and *Hellena*.
Mrs. *Gillo, Lucetta*, A Jilting Wench.
Servants, Other *Masqueraders* Men and Women.

The Scene NAPLES, in Carnival time.

Prologue

Wits, like Physicians, never can agree,
When of a different Society;
And Rabel's *Drops were never more cried down*[1]
By all the Learned Doctors of the Town,
Than a new Play, whose Author is unknown:
Nor can those Doctors with more Malice sue
(And powerful Purses) the dissenting Few,
Than those with an Insulting Pride do rail
At all who are not of their own Cabal.[2]
If a Young Poet hit your Humour right,
You judge him then out of Revenge and Spite;
So amongst men there are Ridiculous Elves,
Who Monkeys hate for being too like themselves:
So that the reason of the grand debate,
Why Wit so oft is damned, when good Plays take,
Is, that you Censure as you love or hate.
Thus, like a Learned Conclave, Poets sit,[3]
Catholic Judges both of Sense and Wit,
And damn or save, as they themselves think fit.
Yet those who to others' Faults are so severe,
Are not so perfect, but themselves may err.
Some write correct indeed, but then the whole
(Bating their own Dull stuff i'th' Play) is stole:
As Bees do suck from Flowers their Honey-dew,
So they rob others, striving to please you.
Some write their Characters Genteel and fine,
But then they do so Toil for every Line,
That what to you does Easy seem, and Plain,
Is the hard Issue of their labouring Brain.
And some th' Effects of all their pains we see,
Is but to Mimic good Extempore.
Others by long Converse about the Town,

Notes

THE ROVER
1 *Rabel's drops* a patent medicine; "Rabell's styptic powder" continued to be advertised into the eighteenth century.
2 *Cabal* faction.
3 *Conclave* an assembly of Roman Catholic cardinals.

Have Wit enough to write a Lewd Lampoon,[4]
But their chief skill lies in a Bawdy Song.
In short, the only Wit that's now in Fashion,
Is but the gleanings of good Conversation.
As for the Author of this Coming Play,
I asked him what he thought fit I should say
In thanks for your good Company today:
He called me Fool, and said it was well known,
You came not here for our sakes, but your own.
New Plays are stuffed with Wits, and with Debauches,
That crowd and sweat like Cits in May-day *Coaches.*[5]

Written by a Person of Quality.

ACT the First

Scene the First. *A Chamber.*

Enter Florinda *and* Hellena.

FLOR: What an Impertinent thing is a Young Girl bred in a Nunnery! How full of Questions! Prithee no more, *Hellena*; I have told thee more than thou understand'st already.

HELL: The more's my grief; I would fain know as much as you, which makes me so Inquisitive; nor is't enough I know you're a Lover, unless you tell me too, who 'tis you sigh for.

FLOR: When you're a Lover, I'll think you fit for a Secret of that Nature.

HELL: 'Tis true, I never was a Lover yet – but I begin to have a shrewd guess, what 'tis to be so, and fancy it very pretty to sigh, and sing, and blush, and wish, and dream and wish, and long and wish to see the Man; and when I do, look pale and tremble; just as you did when my Brother brought home the fine English Colonel to see you – what do you call him? *Don Belvile.*

FLOR: Fye, *Hellena.*

HELL: That blush betrays you – I am sure 'tis so – or is it *Don Antonio* the Viceroy's Son? – or perhaps the Rich Old *Don Vincentio,* whom my father designs you for a Husband? – Why do you blush again?

FLOR: With Indignation; and how near soever my Father thinks I am to Marrying that hated Object, I shall let him see I understand better what's due to my Beauty, Birth and Fortune, and more to my Soul, than to obey those unjust Commands.

HELL: Now hang me, if I don't love thee for that dear disobedience. I love mischief strangely, as most of our Sex do, who are come to Love nothing else – but tell me, dear *Florinda,* don't you love that fine *Anglese?* – for I vow next to loving him myself, 'twill please me most that you do so, for he is so gay and so handsome.

FLOR: *Hellena,* a Maid designed for a Nun ought not to be so Curious in a discourse of Love.

Notes

[4] *Lampoon* "A personal satire; abuse; censure written not to reform but to vex" (Johnson).

[5] *Cit* "An inhabitant of a city in a low sense; a pert low townsman; a pragmatical trader" (Johnson); *May-day coaches* decorated, ostentatious vehicles for use in holiday parades.

HELL: And dost thou think that ever I'll be a Nun? or at least till I'm so Old, I'm fit for nothing else – Faith no, Sister; and that which makes me long to know whether you love *Belvile*, is because I hope he has some mad Companion or other, that will spoil my devotion; nay I'm resolved to provide myself this Carnival, if there be e'er a handsome proper fellow of my humour above ground, though I ask first.

FLOR: Prithee be not so wild.

HELL: Now you have provided yourself of a Man, you take no care for poor me – prithee tell me, what dost thou see about me that is unfit for Love – have I not a World of Youth? a humour gay? a Beauty passable? a Vigour desirable? well shaped? clean limbed?[6] sweet breathed? and sense enough to know how all these ought to be employed to the best advantage; yes I do and will. Therefore lay aside your hopes of my Fortune, by my being a Devote,[7] and tell me how you came acquainted with this *Belvile*; for I perceive you knew him before he came to *Naples*.

FLOR: Yes, I knew him at the Siege of *Pamplona*;[8] he was then a Colonel of *French* Horse, who when the Town was ransacked, Nobly treated my Brother and myself, preserving us from all Insolences; and I must own (besides great Obligations), I have I know not what, that pleads kindly for him about my Heart, and will suffer no other to enter. – But see my Brother.

Enter Don Pedro, Stephano, *with a Masquing Habit, and* Callis.

PEDRO: Good morrow Sister. – – Pray, when saw you your Lover *Don Vincentio*?

FLOR: I know not, Sir – *Callis*, when was he here? for I consider it so little, I know not when it was.

PEDRO: I have a Command from my Father here to tell you, you ought not to despise him, a Man of so vast a Fortune, and such a Passion for you – *Stephano*, my things –

Puts on his Masquing Habit.

FLOR: A Passion for me. 'Tis more than e'er I saw, or he had a desire should be known – I hate *Vincentio*, Sir, and I would not have a Man so dear to me as my Brother follow the ill Customs of our Country, and make a slave of his Sister – and Sir, my Father's Will, I'm sure, you may divert.[9]

PEDRO: I know not how dear I am to you, but I wish only to be ranked in your esteem, equal with the *English* Col. *Belvile* – Why do you frown and blush? Is there any guilt belongs to the Name of that Cavalier?

FLOR: I'll not deny I value *Belvile*: when I was exposed to such dangers as the Licensed Lust of common Soldiers threatened, when Rage and Conquest flew through the City – then *Belvile*, this Criminal for my sake, threw himself into all dangers to save my Honour, and will you not allow him my esteem?

PEDRO: Yes, pay him what you will in Honour – but you must consider *Don Vincentio's* Fortune, and the Jointure he'll make you.[10]

FLOR: Let him consider my Youth, Beauty and Fortune; which ought not to be thrown away on his Age and Jointure.

PEDRO: 'Tis true, he's not so young and fine a Gentleman as that *Belvile* – but what Jewels will that Cavalier present you with? those of his Eyes and Heart?

Notes

6 *Clean limbed* "well proportioned" (*OED*).

7 *Devote* one devoted to religion.

8 A battle between the French and Spanish in 1521, and therefore an anachronism.

9 *Divert* change; alter.

10 *Jointure* a bequest of income specifically for a wife on the death of her husband.

HELL: And are not those better than any *Don Vincentio* has brought from the *Indies*?

PEDRO: Why how now! Has your Nunnery-breeding taught you to understand the value of Hearts and Eyes?

HELL: Better than to believe *Vincentio* deserves Value from any Woman – He may perhaps increase her Bags,[11] but not her Family.

PEDRO: This is fine – go – up to your Devotion, you are not designed for the conversation of Lovers.

HELL: Nor Saints, yet a while I hope. [*Aside*.

Is't not enough you make a Nun of me, but you must cast my Sister away too, exposing her to a worse confinement than a Religious life?

PEDRO: The Girl's mad – Is it a confinement to be carried into the Country, to an Ancient Villa belonging to the Family of the *Vincentio's* these five hundred Years, and have no other Prospect than that pleasing one of seeing all her own that meets her Eyes – a fine Air, large Fields and Gardens, where she may walk and gather Flowers?

HELL: When? By Moonlight? For I am sure she dares not encounter with the heat of the Sun; that were a task only for *Don Vincentio* and his Indian breeding, who loves it in the Dog days[12] – And if these be her daily divertisements, what are those of the Night? to lie in a wide Moth-eaten Bed Chamber, with furniture in Fashion in the Reign of King *Sancho* the First;[13] the Bed that which his Forefathers lived and died in.

PEDRO: Very well.

HELL: This Apartment (new furbished and fitted out for the young Wife) he (out of freedom) makes his dressing Room, and being a Frugal and a Jealous Coxcomb, instead of a Valet to uncase his feeble Carcass, he desires you to do that Office – signs of favour, I'll assure you, and such as you must not hope for, unless your Woman be out of the way.

PEDRO: Have you done yet?

HELL: That Honour being past, the Giant stretches itself; yawns and sighs a Belch or two, loud as a Musket, throws himself into Bed, and expects you in his foul sheets, and ere you can get yourself undressed, calls you with a snore or Two – and are not these fine Blessings to a young Lady?

PEDRO: Have you done yet?

HELL: And this Man you must kiss, nay, you must kiss none but him too – and nuzzle through his Beard to find his Lips. – And this you must submit to for Threescore years, and all for a Jointure.

PEDRO: For all your Character of *Don Vincentio*, she is as like to Marry him as she was before.

HELL: Marry *Don Vincentio*! hang me, such a Wedlock would be worse than Adultery with another Man. I had rather see her in the *Hostel de Dieu*,[14] to waste her Youth there in Vows, and be a Handmaid to Lazars[15] and Cripples, than to lose it in such a Marriage.

PEDRO: You have considered, Sister, that *Belvile* has no Fortune to bring you to, banished his Country, despised at home, and pitied abroad.

HELL: What then? the Viceroy's Son is better than that Old Sir Fisty,[16] *Don Vincentio*! *Don Indian*! he thinks he's trading to *Gambo* still,[17] and would *Barter* himself (that Bell and Bauble)[18] for your Youth and Fortune.

Notes

11 *Bags* purse, money-bags.

12 *Dog days* late summer; when Sirius, the dog star, is prominent.

13 *Sancho the First* ruler of the Spanish state of Leon, 956–66.

14 *Hostel de Dieu* a church-run house for the poor and infirm.

15 *Lazar* a person afflicted with a horrible disease, particularly leprosy.

16 *Fisty* from *fist*, a fart, stink, or foul smell.

17 *Gambo* Gambia in West Africa.

18 *Bell and Bauble* worthless trinkets; perhaps suggesting his useless sexual organs.

PEDRO: *Callis*, take her hence, and lock her up all this Carnival, and at Lent she shall begin her everlasting Penance in a Monastery.

HELL: I care not; I had rather be a Nun, than be obliged to Marry as you would have me, if I were designed for't.

PEDRO: Do not fear the blessing of that choice – you shall be a Nun.

HELL: Shall I so? you may chance to be mistaken in my way of devotion: – A Nun! yes I am like to make a fine Nun! I have an excellent humour for a Grate:[19] No, I'll have a *Saint* of my own to pray to shortly, if I like any that dares venture on me. [*Aside*.

PEDRO: *Callis*, make it your business to watch this Wild Cat. As for you, *Florinda*, I've only tried you all this while and urged my Father's Will; but mine is, that you would love *Antonio*; he is brave and young, and all that can complete the happiness of a Gallant Maid – this absence of my Father will give us opportunity, to free you from *Vincentio*, by Marrying here, which you must do tomorrow.

FLOR: Tomorrow!

PEDRO: Tomorrow, or 'twill be too late – 'tis not my Friendship to *Antonio*, which makes me urge this, but Love to thee, and hatred to *Vincentio* – therefore resolve upon tomorrow.

FLOR: Sir, I shall strive to do, as shall become your Sister.

PEDRO: I'll both believe and trust you – Adieu. [*Ex.* Ped. *and* Steph.

HELL: As becomes his Sister! – that is, to be as resolved your way, as he is his –

Hell. *goes to* Callis

FLOR: I ne'er till now perceived my Ruin near,
I've no Defence against *Antonio*'s Love,
For he has all the Advantages of Nature,
The moving Arguments of Youth and Fortune.

HELL: But hark you, *Callis*, you will not be so cruel to lock me up indeed: will you?

CALL: I must obey the Commands I have – besides, do you consider what a life you are going to lead?

HELL: Yes, *Callis*, that of a Nun: and till then I'll be indebted a world of Prayers to you, if you'll let me now see, what I never did, the Divertisements of a *Carnival*.

CALL: What, go in Masquerade? 'twill be a fine farewell to the World I take it – pray what would you do there?

HELL: That which all the World does, as I am told, be as mad as the rest, and take all Innocent freedoms – Sister, you'll go too, will you not? come prithee be not sad – We'll outwit Twenty Brothers, if you'll be ruled by me – come put off this dull humour with your Clothes, and Assume one as gay, and as fantastic as the Dress my Cousin *Valeria* and I have provided, and let's Ramble.[20]

FLOR: *Callis*, will you give us leave to go?

CALL: I have a Youthful itch of going myself. [*Aside*.
– Madam, if I thought your Brother might not know it, and I might wait on you, for by my troth I'll not trust Young Girls alone.

FLOR: Thou see'st my Brother's gone already, and thou shalt attend, and watch us.

Notes

[19] *Grate* a window with security bars, such as were used in convents.

[20] *Ramble* from "*rammelen*, Dutch, to rove loosely in lust" (Johnson).

Enter Stephano.

STEPH: Madam, the Habits are come, and your Cousin Valeria is dressed, and stays for you.

FLOR: 'Tis well – I'll write a Note, and if I chance to see *Belvile*, and want an opportunity to speak to him, that shall let him know, what I've resolved in favour of him.

HELL: Come, let's in and dress us. [*Exeunt*.

Scene II. *A Long Street.*

Enter Belvile, *Melancholy*, Blunt *and* Frederick.

FRED: Whe,[21] what the Devil ails the Col., in a time when all the World is gay, to look like mere *Lent* thus? Hadst thou been long enough in *Naples* to have been in Love, I should have sworn some such Judgment had befall'n thee.

BELV: No, I have made no new Amours since I came to Naples.

FRED: You have left none behind you in *Paris*?

BELV: Neither.

FRED: I cannot divine the Cause then; unless the Old Cause, the want of Money.

BLUNT: And another Old Cause, the want of a Wench – Would not that revive you?

BELV: You are mistaken, *Ned*.

BLUNT Nay, 'Sheartlikins,[22] then thou'rt past Cure.

FRED: I have found it out; thou hast renewed thy acquaintance with the Lady that cost thee so many sighs at the Siege of *Pamplona* – pox on't, what d'you call her – her Brother's a Noble *Spaniard* – Nephew to the Dead General – *Florinda* – ay, *Florinda* – and will nothing serve thy turn but that damned virtuous Woman? whom on my Conscience thou lovest in spite too, because thou seest little or no possibility of gaining her?

BELV: Thou art mistaken, I have Interest enough in that lovely Virgin's heart, to make me proud and vain, were it not abated by the severity of a Brother, who perceiving my happiness –

FRED: Has civilly forbid thee the House?

BELV: 'Tis so, to make way for a Pow'rful Rival, the Viceroy's Son, who has the advantage of me, in being a Man of Fortune, a *Spaniard*, and her Brother's Friend, which gives him Liberty to make his Court, whilst I have recourse only to Letters, and distant looks from her Window, which are as soft and kind as those which Heaven sends down on Penitents.

BLUNT: Hey day! 'Sheartlikins, simile! by this Light the Man is quite spoiled – *Frederick*. What the Devil are we made of, that we cannot be thus concern'd for a Wench? – 'Sheartlikins, our Cupids are like the Cooks of the Camp, they can Roast or Boil a Woman, but they have none of the fine tricks to set 'em off, no Hogoes[23] to make the Sauce pleasant, and the Stomach sharp.

FRED: I dare swear I have had a hundred as young, kind and handsome as this *Florinda*; and Dogs eat me, if they were not as troublesome to me i' th' Morning as they were welcome o'er Night.

BLUNT: And yet I warrant, he would not touch another Woman, if he might have her for nothing.

BELV: That's thy joy, a cheap Whore.

Notes

21 *Whe* an interjection used for emphasis.

22 *'Sheartlikins By God's sweet heart*! A mild oath.

23 *Hogoes* strong seasonings.

BLUNT: Whe I, 'Sheartlikins, I love a Frank Soul – When did you ever hear of an honest Woman that took a Man's Money? I warrant 'em good ones – but, Gentlemen, You may be free, you have been kept so poor with Parliaments and Protectors,[24] that the little Stock you have is not worth preserving – but I thank my Stars, I have more Grace than to forfeit my Estate by Cavaliering.[25]

BELV: Methinks only following the Court[26] should be sufficient to entitle 'em to that.

BLUNT: 'Sheartlikins, they know I follow it to do it no good, unless they pick a hole in my Coat for lending you Money now and then, which is a greater Crime to my Conscience, Gentlemen, than to the Commonwealth.[27]

Enter Willmore.

WILL: Ha! dear *Belvile*! noble Colonel!

BELV: *Willmore!* welcome ashore, my dear Rover! – what happy wind blew us this good Fortune?

WILL: Let me salute you my dear *Fred*, and then Command me. – How is't honest Lad?

FRED: Faith, Sir, the old Complement, infinitely the better to see my dear mad *Willmore* again. – Prithee why camest thou ashore? and where's the Prince?[28]

WILL: He's well, and Reigns still Lord of the watery Element. – I must aboard again within a Day or two, and my business ashore was only to enjoy myself a little this Carnival.

BELV: Pray know our new Friend, Sir, he's but bashful, a raw Traveller, but honest, stout, and one of us. [*Embraces* Blunt.

WILL: That you esteem him, gives him an Interest here.

BLUNT: Your Servant, Sir.

WILL: But well, – Faith I'm glad to meet you again in a warm Climate, where the kind Sun has its Godlike Power still over the Wine and Woman. – Love and Mirth! are my business in *Naples*, and if I mistake not the place, here's an Excellent Market for Chapmen[29] of my humour.

BELV: See, here be those kind Merchants of Love you look for.

Enter several Men in Masquing Habits, some playing on Music, others dancing after, Women dressed like Courtesans, with Papers pinned on their Breasts, and Baskets of Flowers in their Hands.

BLUNT: 'Sheartlikins, what have we here?

FRED: Now the Game begins.

WILL: Fine pretty Creatures! may a stranger have leave to look and love? – What's here – "Roses for every Month?" [*Reads the Paper.*

BLUNT: Roses for every Month? what means that?

BELV: They are, or would have you think they're Courtesans, who here in *Naples* are to be hired by the Month.

WILL: Kind and obliging to inform us – Pray where do these Roses grow? I would fain plant some of 'em in a Bed of mine.

WOM: Beware such Roses, Sir.

Notes

24 *Parliaments and Protectors* the rulers during the interregnum (1640–1660): the Long Parliament; the Rump Parliament; Oliver and Richard Cromwell, Lord Protectors.

25 *Cavaliering* playing the chivalrous escort, but also suggesting the name for those who fought on the king's side in the Civil War.

26 *following the Court* siding with the king or living with the court in exile in France.

27 *Commonwealth* the parliamentary government of the interregnum.

28 *Prince* Charles II.

29 *Chapmen* buyers.

WILL: A Pox of fear: I'll be baked with thee between a pair of Sheets, and that's thy proper Still,[30] so I might but strew such Roses over me and under me – Fair one, Would you give me leave to gather at your Bush this idle Month, I would go near to make some Body smell of it all the year after.

BELV: And thou hast need of such a Remedy, for thou stink'st of Tar and Ropes Ends, like a Dock or Pest-house.[31]

The Woman puts herself into the Hands of a Man, and Exeunt.

WILL: Nay, nay, you shall not leave me so.

BELV: By all means use no violence here.

WILL: Death! Just as I was going to be damnably in Love, to have her led off! I could pluck that Rose out of his Hand, and even kiss the Bed, the Bush grew in.

FRED: No Friend to Love like a long Voyage at Sea.

BLUNT: Except a Nunnery, *Fred.*

WILL: Death! But will they not be kind, quickly be kind? Thou know'st I'm no tame sigher, but a Rampant Lion of the Forest.

Advances from the farther end of the Scenes, two Men dressed all over with Horns of several sorts, making Grimaces at one another, with Papers pinned on their Backs.

BELV: Oh the fantastical Rogues, how they're dressed! 'Tis a Satire against the whole Sex.

WILL: Is this a Fruit that grows in this warm Country?

BELV: Yes: 'Tis pretty to see these *Italians* start, swell, and stab at the word *Cuckold*, and yet stumble at Horns on every Threshold.[32]

WILL: See what's on their Back – "Flowers of every Night." [*Reads.* – Ah Rogue! and more sweet than Roses of every Month! This is a Gardener of *Adam's* own breeding.[33] [*They dance.*

BELV: What think you of those grave People? – is a Wake in *Essex* half so mad or Extravagant?[34]

WILL: I like their sober grave way, 'tis a kind of Legal Authorized Fornication, where the Men are not chid for't, nor the Women despised, as amongst our dull *English*; even the Monsieurs want that part of good Manners.

BELV: But here in *Italy*, a Monsieur is the humblest best-bred Gentleman – Duels are so baffled by Bravoes[35] that an Age shows not one, but between a *Frenchman* and a hangman,[36] who is as much too hard for him on the *Piazza*, as they are for a *Dutchman* on the New Bridge[37] – but see another Crew.

Enter Florinda, Hellena, *and* Valeria, *dressed like Gipsies;* Callis *and* Stephano, Lucetta, Philippo *and* Sancho *in Masquerade.*

HELL: Sister, there's your *Englishman*, and with him a handsome proper Fellow – I'll to him, and instead of telling him his Fortune, try my own.

Notes

30 A still was commonly used to heat rose petals and make the distillate rose-water, which was used as a perfume and a medicine.

31 *Pest-house* a hospital for sufferers of pestilential diseases, like plague.

32 *Horns* cuckolds are said to grow horns.

33 *A Gardener of Adam's own breeding* Like Adam, he brings forth women.

34 *Essex* a county in Southeast England sometimes derided as a country place where there is no decorum.

35 *Bravo* "A man who murders for hire" (Johnson).

36 *hangman* a term of derision.

37 The French beat the Dutch at the battle of Nieuwerbrug (New Bridge) in 1672 (Todd); William III arrived too late with reinforcements.

WILL: *Gipsies*, on my Life – sure these will prattle if a Man cross their hands.[38]

Goes to Hellena

– dear pretty (and I hope) young Devil, will you tell an Amorous stranger what luck he's like to have?

HELL: Have a care how you venture with me Sir, lest I pick your Pocket, which will more vex your *English* humour, than an *Italian* Fortune will please you.

WILL: How the Devil cam'st thou to know my Country and Humour?

HELL: The First I guess by a certain forward Impudence, which does not displease me at this time; and the loss of your Money will vex you, because I hope you have but very little to lose.

WILL: Egad Child, thou'rt i' th' right; it is so little, I dare not offer it thee for a kindness – but cannot you divine what other things of more value I have about me, that I would more willingly part with?

HELL: Indeed no, that's the business of a Witch, and I am but a Gipsy yet. – Yet, without looking in your hand, I have a parlous guess, 'tis some Foolish heart you mean, an Inconstant *English* heart, as little worth stealing as your Purse.

WILL: Nay, then thou dost deal with the Devil, that's certain. – thou hast guessed as right as if thou hadst been one of that number it has languished for. – I find you'll be better acquainted with it; nor can you take it in a better time, for I am come from Sea, Child, and *Venus* not being propitious to me in her own Element:[39] I have a world of Love in store – would you would be good-natured, and take some on't off my Hands.

HELL: Why – I could be inclined that way – but for a Foolish Vow I am going to make – to die a Maid.

WILL: Then thou art damned without redemption, and as I am a good Christian, I ought in Charity to divert so wicked a design – therefore prithee dear Creature let me know quickly when and where I shall begin to set a helping hand to so good a Work.

HELL: If you should prevail with my tender heart (as I begin to fear you will, for you have horrible loving Eyes) there will be difficulty in't that you'll hardly undergo for my sake.

WILL: Faith Child, I have been bred in dangers, and wear a Sword that has been employed in a worse Cause, than for a handsome kind Woman – name the danger – let it be anything but a long Siege – and I'll undertake it.

HELL: Can you storm?

WILL: Oh most furiously.

HELL: What think you of a Nunnery Wall? for he that wins me, must gain that first.

WILL: A Nun! Oh how I love thee for't! there's no sinner like a young Saint – nay now there's no denying me, the Old Law[40] had no Curse (to a Woman) like dying a Maid; witness *Jephtha's* Daughter.[41]

HELL: A very good Text this, if well handled; and I perceive, Father Captain, you would impose no severe penance on her who were inclined to Console herself before she took Orders.

WILL: If she be Young and Handsome.

Notes

[38] *Cross their hands* give them money.

[39] Venus, goddess of love, was born of sea-foam and associated with the watery element of the sea.

[40] *Old Law* Old Testament.

[41] *Jephtha's daughter* Jephtha sacrificed his virgin daughter in return for victories given him by the Lord. He allowed her, however, two months to roam the fields and weep with her friends because she would never marry (Judges 11.37–40).

HELL: Ay, there's it – but if she be not –

WILL: By this hand, Child, I have an Implicit Faith, and dare venture on thee with all Faults – besides, 'tis more meritorious to leave the World when thou hast tasted and proved the pleasure on't. Then 'twill be a virtue in thee, which now will be pure Ignorance.

HELL: I perceive, good Father Captain, you design only to make me fit for Heaven – but if on the contrary you should quite divert me from it, and bring me back to the World again, I should have a new Man to seek I find; and what a grief that will be – for when I begin, I fancy I shall love like anything, I never tried yet.

WILL: Egad, and that's kind – prithee dear Creature, give me credit for a Heart, for faith, I'm a very honest Fellow – Oh, I long to come first to the Banquet of Love! and such a swinging Appetite I bring – Oh, I'm impatient. – thy Lodging, sweetheart, thy Lodging! or I'm a dead man!

HELL: Why must we be either guilty of Fornication or Murder if we converse with you Men? – and is there no difference between leave to love me, and leave to lie with me?

WILL: Faith, Child, they were made to go together.

LUCET: Are you sure this is the Man? [*Pointing to* Blunt.

SANCHO: When did I mistake your Game?

LUCET: This is a Stranger, I know by his gazing; if he be brisk, he'll venture to follow me; and then, if I understand my Trade, he's mine: he's *English* too, and they say that's a sort of good-natured loving People, and have generally so kind an opinion of themselves, that a Woman with any Wit may Flatter 'em into any sort of Fool she pleases.

BLUNT: 'Tis so – she is taken – I have Beauties which my false Glass at home did not discover.

She often passes by Blunt *and gazes on him; he struts, and Cocks, and walks, and gazes on her.*

FLOR: This Woman watches me so, I shall get no opportunity to discover myself to him, and so miss the intent of my coming – but as I was saying, Sir, – by this Line you should be a Lover. [*Looking in his Hand.*

BELV: I thought how right you guessed, all Men are in Love, or pretend to be so – come, let me go, I'm weary of this fooling. [*Walks away.*

FLOR: I will not, till you have confessed whether the Passion that you have vowed *Florinda* be true or false. [*She holds him, he strives to get from her.*

BELV: *Florinda!* [*Turns quick towards her.*

FLOR: Softly.

BELV: Thou hast named one will fix me here for ever.

FLOR: She'll be disappointed then, who expects you this Night at the Garden-gate, and if you'll fail not – as let me see the other hand – you will go near to do – she vows to die or make you happy. [*Looks on Callis, who observes 'em.*

BELV: What canst thou mean?

FLOR: That which I say – Farewell. [*Offers to go.*

BELV: Oh charming Sybil, stay, complete that joy which, as it is, will turn into distraction! – where must I be? at the Garden-gate? I know it – at Night you say? – I'll sooner forfeit Heaven than disobey.

Enter Don Pedro *and other Masquers, and pass over the Stage.*

CALL: Madam, your Brother's here.

FLOR: Take this to instruct you farther. [*Gives him a Letter, and goes off.*

FRED: Have a care, Sir, what you promise; this may be a Trap laid by her Brother to ruin you.

BELV: Do not disturb my happiness with doubts. [*Opens the Letter.*

WILL: My dear pretty Creature, a Thousand Blessings on thee! still in this habit, you say, and after Dinner at this place.

HELL: Yes, if you will swear to keep your heart, and not bestow it between this and that.

WILL: By all the little Gods of Love I swear, I'll leave it with you, and if you run away with it, those Deities of Justice will revenge me. [*Ex. all the Women except Lucetta.*

FRED: Do you know the hand?

BELV: 'Tis *Florinda's*. All Blessings fall upon the virtuous Maid.

FRED: Nay, no Idolatry, a sober Sacrifice I'll allow you.

BELV: Oh Friends, the welcom'st News! the softest Letter! – nay, you shall see it; and could you now be serious, I might be made the happiest Man the Sun shines on!

WILL: The reason of this mighty joy?

BELV: See how kindly she invites me to deliver her from the threatened violence of her Brother – will you not assist me?

WILL: I know not what thou mean'st, but I'll make one at any mischief where a Woman's concerned – but she'll be grateful to us for the favour, will she not?

BELV: How mean you?

WILL: How should I mean? Thou know'st there's but one way for a Woman to oblige me.

BELV: Do not profane – the Maid is nicely[42] virtuous.

WILL: Who Pox, then she's fit for nothing but a husband; let her e'en go, Colonel.

FRED: Peace, she's the Colonel's Mistress, Sir.

WILL: Let her be the Devil; if she be thy Mistress, I'll serve her – name the way.

BELV: Read here this Postscript. [*Gives him a Letter.*

WILL: [*Reads.*] *At Ten at night – at the Garden-Gate – of which, if I cannot get the Key, I will contrive a way over the Wall – come attended with a Friend or Two.* – Kind heart, if we Three cannot weave a string to let her down a Garden-Wall, 'twere pity but the Hangman wove one for us all.

FRED: Let her alone for that: your Woman's wit, your fair kind Woman, will out-trick a Broker or a Jew, and contrive like a Jesuit in Chains – but see, *Ned Blunt* is stolen out after the Lure of a Damsel. [*Ex.* Blunt *and* Lucet.

BELV: So he'll scarce find his way home again, unless we get him cried[43] by the Bell-man in the Market-place, and 'twould sound prettily – a lost *English* Boy of Thirty.

FRED: I hope 'tis some Common crafty Sinner, one that will fit him; it may be she'll sell him for *Peru*, the Rogue's sturdy and would work well in a Mine; at least I hope she'll dress him for our Mirth; cheat him of all, then have him well-favouredly banged,[44] and turned out naked at Midnight.

WILL: Prithee what humour is he of, that you wish him so well?

BELV: Why, of an *English* Elder Brother's humour, Educated in a Nursery, with a Maid to tend him till Fifteen, and lies with his Grandmother till he's of Age; one that knows no pleasure beyond riding to the next Fair, or going up to *London* with his right Worshipful Father in Parliament-time; wearing gay Clothes, or making honourable Love to his Lady Mother's Laundry-Maid; gets drunk at a Hunting-Match, and ten to one then gives some proofs of his Prowess – A Pox upon him, he's our Banker, and has all our Cash about him, and if he fail, we are all Broke.

Notes

42 *nicely* carefully, scrupulously.

43 *cried* given "public oral notice of (things lost or found)" (*OED*, 5c).

44 *banged* beaten up.

FRED: Oh let him alone for that matter, he's of a damned stingy quality, that will secure our stock. I know not in what danger it were indeed, if the Jilt[45] should pretend she's in Love with him, for 'tis a kind believing Coxcomb; otherwise if he part with more than a piece of Eight[46] – geld him: for which offer he may chance to be beaten, if she be a Whore of the First Rank.

BELV: Nay the Rogue will not be easily beaten, he's stout enough; perhaps if they talk beyond his capacity, he may chance to exercise his Courage upon some of them, else I'm sure they'll find it as difficult to beat as to please him.

WILL: 'Tis a lucky Devil to light upon so kind a Wench!

FRED: Thou hadst a great deal of talk with thy little Gipsy, could'st thou do no good upon her? for mine was hard-hearted.

WILL: Hang her, she was some damned honest Person of Quality, I'm sure; she was so very free and witty. If her face be but answerable to her Wit and Humour, I would be bound to Constancy this Month to gain her – in the mean time, have you made no kind acquaintance since you came to Town? – you do not use to be honest so long, Gentlemen.

FRED: Faith Love has kept us honest, we have been all fired with a Beauty newly come to Town, the Famous *Paduana Angellica Bianca*.

WILL: What, the Mistress of the dead *Spanish* General?

BELV: Yes, she's now the only adored Beauty of all the Youth in *Naples*, who put on all their Charms to appear lovely in her sight, their Coaches, Liveries, and themselves, all gay, as on a Monarch's Birthday, to attract the Eyes of this fair Charmer, while she has the pleasure to behold all languish for her that see her.

FRED: 'Tis pretty to see with how much Love the Men regard her, and how much Envy the Women.

WILL: What Gallant has she?

BELV: None, she's exposed to Sale, and Four days in the Week she's yours – for so much a Month.

WILL: The very thought of it quenches all manner of Fire in me – yet prithee let's see her.

BELV: Let's first to Dinner, and after that we'll pass the day as you please – but at Night ye must all be at my Devotion.[47]

WILL: I will not fail you. [*Exeunt.*

ACT II.

Scene I. *The Long Street.*

Enter Belvile *and* Frederick *in Masquing Habits, and* Willmore *in his own Clothes, with a Vizard*[48] *in his Hand.*

WILL. But why thus disguised and muzzled?

BELV: Because whatever Extravagances we commit in these Faces, our own may not be obliged to answer 'em.

WILL: I should have changed my Eternal Buff[49] too: but no matter, my little Gipsy would not have found me out then: for if she should change hers, it is impossible

Notes

[45] *Jilt* whore.

[46] *Piece of Eight* Spanish silver dollar or peso.

[47] *Devotion* disposal.

[48] *Vizard* mask.

[49] *Buff* "A military coat made of thick leather" (Johnson).

I should know her, unless I should hear her prattle – A Pox on't, I cannot get her out of my Head: Pray Heaven, if ever I do see her again, she prove damnably ugly, that I may fortify myself against her Tongue.

BELV: Have a care of Love, for o' my conscience she was not of a quality to give thee any hopes.

WILL: Pox on 'em, why do they draw a Man in then? She has played with my Heart so, that 'twill never lie still till I have met with some kind Wench, that will play the Game out with me – Oh for my Arms full of soft, white, kind – Woman! such as I fancy *Angellica*.

BELV: This is her House, if you were but in stock to get admittance; they have not dined yet; I perceive the Picture is not out.

Enter Blunt.

WILL: I long to see the Shadow of the fair Substance,[50] a Man may gaze on that for nothing.

BLUNT: Colonel, thy Hand – and thine, *Fred*. I have been an Ass, a deluded Fool, a very Coxcomb from my Birth till this hour, and heartily repent my little Faith.

BELV: What the Devil's the matter with thee *Ned?*

BLUNT: Oh such a Mistress, *Fred*, such a Girl!

WILL: Ha! where?

FRED: Ay where!

BLUNT: So fond, so amorous, so toying and so fine! and all for sheer Love ye Rogue! Oh how she looked and kissed! and soothed my Heart from my Bosom – I cannot think I was awake, and yet methinks I see and feel her Charms still – *Fred*. – Try if she have not left the taste of her Balmy Kisses upon my Lips –

Kisses him.

BELV: Ha! Ha! Ha!

WILL: Death Man, where is she?

BLUNT: What a Dog was I to stay in dull *England* so long, – How have I laughed at the Colonel When he sighed for Love! but now the little Archer[51] has revenged him! and by his own Dart, I can guess at all his joys, which then I took for Fancies, mere Dreams and Fables – Well, I'm resolved to sell all in *Essex*, and plant here for ever.

BELV: What a Blessing 'tis, thou hast a Mistress thou dar'st boast of; for I know thy Humour is rather to have a proclaimed Clap, than a secret Amour.

WILL: Dost know her Name?

BLUNT: Her Name? No,'sheartlikins: what care I for Names? – She's fair! young! brisk and kind! even to ravishment! and what a Pox care I for knowing her by another Title?

WILL: Didst give her anything?

BLUNT: Give her! – Ha, ha, ha! whe she's a Person of Quality – that's a good one, give her! 'sheartlikins dost think such Creatures are to be bought? Or are we provided for such a Purchase? Give her, quoth ye? Why she presented me with this Bracelet, for the Toy of a Diamond I used to wear: No, Gentlemen, *Ned Blunt* is not Everybody – She expects me again Tonight.

Notes

[50] *Shadow* "An imperfect and faint representation; opposed to *substance*" (Johnson).

[51] *little Archer* Cupid.

WILL: Egad that's well; we'll all go.

BLUNT: Not a Soul: No, Gentlemen, you are Wits; I am a dull Country Rogue, I.

FRED: Well, Sir, for all your Person of Quality, I shall be very glad to understand your Purse be secure; 'tis our whole Estate at present, which we are loath to hazard in one Bottom:[52] come, Sir, unload.

BLUNT: Take the necessary Trifle, useless now to me, that am beloved by such a Gentlewoman – 'sheartlikins Money! Here take mine too.

FRED: No, keep that to be cozened, that we may laugh.

WILL: Cozened! – Death! would I could meet with one, that would cozen me of all the Love I could spare Tonight.

FRED: Pox 'tis some common Whore upon my Life.

BLUNT: A Whore! yes with such Clothes! such Jewels! such a House! such Furniture, and so Attended! a Whore!

BELV: Why yes, Sir, they are Whores, though they'll neither entertain you with Drinking, Swearing, or Bawdry; are Whores in all those gay Clothes, and right Jewels; are Whores with great Houses richly furnished with Velvet Beds, Store of Plate, handsome Attendance, and fine Coaches, are Whores and Errant ones.

WILL: Pox on't, where do these fine Whores live?

BELV: Where no Rogues in Office Ycleped[53] Constables dare give 'em Laws, nor the Wine-inspired Bullies of the Town break their Windows; yet they are Whores, though this *Essex* Calf believe 'em Persons of Quality.

BLUNT: 'Sheartlikins, y'are all Fools, there are things about this *Essex* Calf, that shall take with the Ladies, beyond all your Wit and Parts – this Shape and Size, Gentlemen, are not to be despised; my Waist too tolerably long, with other inviting signs, that shall be nameless.

WILL: Egad I believe he may have met with some Person of Quality that may be kind to him.

BELV: Dost thou perceive any such tempting things about him, that should make a fine Woman, and of Quality, pick him out from all Mankind, to throw away her Youth and Beauty upon, nay, and her dear heart too? – no, no, *Angellica* has raised the Price too high.

WILL: May she languish for Mankind till she die, and be damned for that one sin alone.

Enter Two Bravoes, and hang up a great Picture of Angellica's, *against the Balcony, and Two little ones at each side of the Door.*

BELV: See there the fair Sign to the Inn where a Man may lodge that's Fool enough to give her price. [Will. *gazes on the Picture.*

BLUNT: 'Sheartlikins, Gentlemen, what's this?

BELV: A famous Courtesan that's to be sold.

BLUNT: How? to be sold? nay then I have nothing to say to her – sold! what Impudence is practised in this Country? – With Order and decency Whoring's Established here by Virtue of the Inquisition – come let's be gone, I'm sure we're no Chapmen for this Commodity.

FRED: Thou art none I'm sure, unless thou could'st have her in thy Bed at the price of a Coach in the Street.

Notes

[52] *Bottom* "A chance; an adventure; state of hazard" (Johnson).

[53] *ycleped* named.

WILL: How wondrous fair she is – a Thousand Crowns a Month – by Heaven as many Kingdoms were too little, a plague of this Poverty – of which I ne'er complain, but when it hinders my approach to Beauty, which Virtue ne'er could purchase. [*Turns from the Picture.*

BLUNT: What's this? –[*Reads*] *A Thousand Crowns a Month!* – 'Sheartlikins, here's a Sum! sure 'tis a mistake. – Hark you, Friend, does she take or give so much by the Month?

FRED: A Thousand Crowns! why, 'tis a Portion for the *Infanta*.[54]

BLUNT: Hark ye, Friends, won't she trust?

BRAV: This is a Trade, Sir, that cannot live by Credit.

Enter Don Pedro *in Masquerade, followed by* Stephano.

BELV: See, here's more Company, let's walk off a while. [*Exeunt* English.

[Pedro *Reads.*

Enter Angellica *and* Moretta *in the Balcony, and draw a Silk Curtain.*

PED: Fetch me a thousand Crowns, I never wished to buy this Beauty at an easier rate. [*Passes off.*

ANG: Prithee what said those Fellows to thee?

BRAV: Madam, the first were admirers of Beauty only, but no purchasers; they were merry with your Price and Picture, laughed at the Sum, and so passed off.

ANG: No Matter, I'm not displeased with their rallying; their wonder feeds my Vanity, and he that wishes to buy, gives me more Pride, than he that gives my Price can make me Pleasure.

BRAV: Madam, the last I knew through all his disguises to be *Don Pedro*, Nephew to the General, and who was with him in *Pamplona*.

ANG: *Don Pedro!* my old Gallant's Nephew! when his Uncle died, he left him a vast Sum of Money; it is he who was so in love with me at *Padua*, and who used to make the General so Jealous.

MORET: Is this he that used to prance before our Window and take such care to show himself an Amorous Ass? If I am not mistaken, he is the likeliest Man to give your price.

ANG: The Man is brave and generous, but of an humour so uneasy and inconstant, that the victory over his heart is as soon lost as won; a Slave that can add little to the Triumph of the Conqueror: but Inconstancy's the sin of all Mankind, therefore I'm resolved that nothing but Gold shall charm my Heart.

MORET: I'm glad on't; 'tis only Interest that Women of our Profession ought to consider: though I wonder what has kept you from that general Disease of our Sex so long, I mean that of being in Love.

ANG: A kind, but sullen Star, under which I had the Happiness to be born; yet I have had no time for Love; the bravest and noblest of Mankind have purchased my favours at so dear a rate, as if no Coin but Gold were current with our Trade – but here's *Don Pedro* again, fetch me my Lute – for 'tis for him or *Don Antonio* the Viceroy's Son, that I have spread my Nets.

Notes

54 *the Infanta* Catherine of Braganza (1638–1705) who married Charles II in 1662.

Enter at one Door Don Pedro, Stephano; Don Antonio *and* Diego *[his page], at the other Door, with People following him in Masquerade, anticly*[55] *attired, some with Music: they both go up to the Picture.*

ANT: A Thousand Crowns! had not the Painter flattered her, I should not think it dear.

PEDRO: Flattered her! by Heaven he cannot. I have seen the Original, nor is there one Charm here more than Adorns her Face and Eyes; all this soft and sweet, with a certain languishing Air, that no Artist can represent.

ANT: What I heard of her Beauty before had fired my Soul, but this confirmation of it has blown it into a flame.

PEDRO: Ha!

PAG: Sir, I have known you throw away a Thousand Crowns on a worse face, and though y'are near your Marriage, you may venture a little Love here; *Florinda* will not miss it.

PEDRO: Ha! *Florinda!* – sure 'tis *Antonio*. [*Aside.*

ANT: *Florinda!* name not those distant joys, there's not one thought of her will check my Passion here.

PEDRO: *Florinda* scorned! and all my hopes defeated of the Possession of *Angellica!* [*A noise of a Lute above.* Ant. *gazes up.*] Her Injuries by Heaven he shall not boast of. [*Song to a Lute above.*

Song.

When Damon *first began to Love,*
He languished in a soft desire,
And knew not how the Gods to move,
To lessen or increase his Fire,
For Cælia *in her charming Eyes*
Wore all Love's sweets, and all his cruelties.

II.

But as beneath a Shade he lay,
Weaving of Flowers for Cælia's *hair,*
She chanced to lead her Flock that way,
And saw the Am'rous Shepherd there.
She gazed around upon the place,
And saw the Grove (resembling Night)
To all the joys of Love invite,
Whilst guilty smiles and blushes dressed her Face.
At this the bashful Youth all Transport grew,
And with kind force he taught the Virgin how
To yield what all his sighs could never do.

ANT: By Heaven she's charming fair!

Notes

55 *anticly* oddly, wildly.

Angellica throws open the Curtains, and bows to Antonio, who pulls off his Vizard and bows and blows up Kisses. Pedro unseen looks in his face.

PEDRO: 'Tis he, the false *Antonio!*

ANT: Friend, where must I pay my Offering of Love? [*To the* Bravo.] My Thousand Crowns I mean.

PEDRO: That Offering I have designed to make,
And yours will come too late.

ANT: Prithee be gone, I shall grow angry else,
And then thou art not safe.

PEDRO: My Anger may be fatal, Sir, as yours;
And he that enters here may prove this truth.

ANT: I know not who thou art, but I am sure thou'rt worth my killing, for aiming at *Angellica*.

They draw and fight.

Enter Willmore *and* Blunt, *who draw and part 'em.*

BLUNT: 'Sheartlikins, here's fine doings.

WILL: Tilting for the Wench I'm sure – nay gad, if that would win her, I have as good a Sword as the best of ye. – Put up, – put up, and take another time and place, for this is designed for Lovers only. [*They all put up.*

PEDRO: We are prevented; dare you meet me Tomorrow on the *Molo?*[56]
For I've a Title to a better quarrel,
That of *Florinda*, in whose credulous Heart
Thou'st made an Interest, and destroyed my hopes.

ANT: Dare?
I'll meet thee there as early as the day.

PEDRO: We will come thus disguised, that whosoever chance to get the better, he may escape unknown.

ANT: It shall be so. [*Ex.* Pedro *and* Stephano.] Who should this Rival be? unless the *English* Colonel, of whom I've often heard *Don Pedro* speak; it must be he, and time he were removed, who lays a claim to all my happiness.

Willmore *having gazed all this while on the Picture, pulls down a little one.*

WILL: This Posture's loose and negligent,
The sight on't would beget a warm desire
In Souls whom Impotence and Age had chilled.
– This must along with me.

BRAV: What means this rudeness, Sir? – restore the Picture.

ANT: Ha! Rudeness committed to the fair *Angellica*! – Restore the Picture, Sir.

WILL: Indeed I will not, Sir.

ANT: By Heaven but you shall.

WILL: Nay, do not show your Sword; if you do, by this dear Beauty – I will show mine too.

ANT: What right can you pretend to't?

WILL: That of Possession which I will maintain – you perhaps have 1000 Crowns to give for the Original.

Notes

[56] *Molo* a large dock or quay, but the Molo is in Venice.

ANT: No matter, Sir, you shall restore the Picture.
ANG: Oh, *Moretta!* what's the matter? [Ang. *and* Moret. *above.*
ANT: Or leave your life behind.
WILL: Death! you lie – I will do neither.
ANG: Hold, I command you, if for me you Fight.

They Fight, the Spaniards join with Ant., Blunt *laying on like mad. They leave off and bow.*

WILL: How heavenly fair she is! – ah Plague of her price.
ANG: You Sir in Buff, you that appear a Soldier, that first began this Insolence.
WILL: 'Tis true, I did so, if you call it Insolence for a Man to preserve himself; I saw your Charming Picture, and was wounded: quite through my Soul each pointed Beauty ran; and wanting a Thousand Crowns to procure my remedy, – I laid this little Picture to my Bosom – which if you cannot allow me, I'll resign.
ANG: No, you may keep the Trifle.
ANT: You shall first ask my leave, and this. [*Fight again as before.*

Enter Belv. *and* Fred. *who join with the* English.

ANG: Hold! will you ruin me? – *Biskey* – *Sebastian* – part'em. –

The Spaniards *are beaten off.*

MORET: Oh Madam, we're undone, a pox upon that rude Fellow, he's set on to ruin us: we shall never see good days, till all these fighting poor Rogues are sent to the Gallies.[57]

Enter Belvile, Blunt, Fred. *and* Willmore, *with his shirt bloody.*

BLUNT: 'Sheartlikins, beat me at this sport, and I'll ne'er wear Sword more.
BELV: The Devil's in thee for a mad Fellow, thou art always one at an unlucky Adventure. – come, let's be gone whilst we're safe, and remember these are *Spaniards*, a sort of People that know how to revenge an Affront.
FRED: You bleed! I hope you are not wounded. [*To* Will.
WILL: Not much: – a plague upon your *Dons*, if they fight no better they'll ne'er recover *Flanders*. – what the Devil was't to them that I took down the Picture?
BLUNT: Took it! 'Sheartlikins, we'll have the great one too; 'tis ours by Conquest. – prithee, help me up and I'll pull it down –
ANG: Stay Sir, and ere you Affront me farther, let me know how you durst commit this outrage – to you I speak, Sir, for you appear like a Gentleman.
WILL: To me, Madam? – Gentlemen, your Servant. [Belv. *stays him.*
BELV: Is the Devil in thee? do'st know the danger of entering the house of an incensed Courtesan?
WILL: I thank you for your care – but there are other matters in hand, there are, though we have no great Temptation. – Death! let me go.
FRED: Yes, to your Lodging, if you will, but not in here. – Damn these gay Harlots – by this hand I'll have as sound and handsome a Whore for a Patacoone.[58] – death, Man, she'll Murder thee.
WILL: Oh! fear me not, shall I not venture where a Beauty calls? a lovely Charming Beauty? for fear of danger! when by Heaven there's none so great as to long for her, whilst I want Money to purchase her.

Notes

[57] *Gallies* gallows.

[58] *Patacoone* any of various Spanish silver coins

FRED: Therefore 'tis loss of time, unless you had the Thousand Crowns to pay.

WILL: It may be she may give a Favour, at least I shall have the pleasure of Saluting her[59] when I enter, and when I depart.

BELV: Pox, she'll as soon lie with thee, as kiss thee, and sooner stab than do either – you shall not go.

ANG: Fear not Sir, all I have to wound with is my Eyes.

BLUNT: Let him go, 'Sheartlikins, I believe the Gentlewoman means well.

BELV: Well, take thy Fortune, we'll expect you in the next Street – farewell Fool – Farewell –

WILL: Bye Colonel – [*Goes in.*

FRED: The Rogue's stark mad for a Wench. [*Exeunt.*

Scene II. *A Fine Chamber.*

Enter Willmore, Angellica, *and* Moretta.

ANG: Insolent Sir, how durst you pull down my Picture?

WILL: Rather, how durst you set it up, to tempt poor Amorous Mortals with so much excellence? which I find you have but too well consulted by the unmerciful price you set upon't. – Is all this Heaven of Beauty shown to move despair in those that cannot buy? and can you think the effects of that despair should be less extravagant than I have shown?

ANG: I sent for you to ask my Pardon, Sir, not to Aggravate your Crime – I thought I should have seen you at my Feet imploring it.

WILL: You are deceived, I came to rail at you, and rail such truths too, as shall let you see the vanity of that Pride, which taught you how to set such a Price on Sin. For such it is, whilst that which is Love's due is meanly bartered for.

ANG: Ha! ha! ha! alas, good Captain, what pity 'tis your edifying Doctrine will do no good upon me – *Moretta!* fetch the Gentleman a Glass, and let him survey himself, to see what Charms he has – and guess my Business. [*Aside in a soft tone.*

MORET: He knows himself of Old, I believe those Breeches and he have been acquainted ever since he was beaten at *Worcester.*[60]

ANG: Nay, do not abuse the poor Creature –

MORET: Good Weather-beaten Corporal, will you march off? we have no need of your Doctrine, though you have of our Charity; but at present we have no scraps, we can afford no kindness for God's sake; in fine,[61] Sirrah, the price is too high i'th' Mouth[62] for you, therefore Troop, I say.

WILL: Here, good Forewoman of the Shop, serve me, and I'll be gone.

MORET: Keep it to pay your Laundress, your Linen stinks of the Gun-Room; for here's no selling by Retail.

WILL: Thou hast sold plenty of thy Stale Ware at a Cheap rate.

MORET: Ay, the more Silly kind Heart I, but this is an Age wherein Beauty is at higher rates – In fine, you know the price of this.

WILL: I grant you 'tis here – set down a Thousand Crowns a Month – pray how much may come to my Share for a Pistole.[63] – Bawd, take your black Lead and Sum it up, that I may have a Pistole-worth of these vain gay things, and I'll trouble you no more.

Notes

59 *saluting her* kissing her.
60 *Worcester* the last battle of the Civil War, 3 September 1651.
61 *in fine* in sum; in conclusion.
62 *high i' th' mouth* expensive; luxurious.
63 *Pistole* about one pound in Spanish money.

MORET: Pox on him, he'll fret me to death: – abominable Fellow, I tell thee, we only sell by the whole piece.

WILL: 'Tis very hard, the whole Cargo or nothing – Faith, Madam, my Stock will not reach it, I cannot be your Chapman. – Yet I have Countrymen, in Town, Merchants of Love, like me; I'll see if they'll put in for a share, we cannot lose much by it, and what we have no use for, we'll sell upon the *Friday's* Mart, at – "Who gives more?" I am studying, Madam, how to purchase you, though at present I am unprovided of Money.

ANG: Sure, this from any other Man would anger me – nor shall he know the Conquest he has made [*Aside*] – Poor angry Man, how I despise this railing.

WILL: Yes, I am poor – but I'm a Gentleman,
And one that Scorns this baseness which you practise.
Poor as I am, I would not sell myself,
No, not to gain your Charming high-prized Person.
Though I admire you strangely for your Beauty,
Yet I contemn your mind.
– And yet I would at any rate enjoy you,
At your own rate – but cannot – see here
The only Sum I can command on Earth;
I know not where to eat when this is gone:
Yet such a Slave I am to Love and Beauty,
This last reserve I'll sacrifice to enjoy you.
– Nay, do not frown, I know you're to be bought,
And would be bought by me, by me,
For a mean trifling Sum, if I could pay it down.
Which happy knowledge I will still repeat,
And lay it to my Heart, it has a Virtue in't,
And soon will cure those Wounds your Eyes have made.
– And yet – there's something so Divinely powerful there –
Nay, I will gaze – to let you see my strength.

Holds her, looks on her, and pauses and sighs.

– By Heaven, bright Creature – I would not for the World
Thy Fame were half so fair as is thy Face.

Turns her away from him.

ANG: His words go through me to the very Soul. [*Aside.*] – If you have nothing else to say to me –

WILL: Yes, you shall hear how Infamous you are –
For which I do not hate thee –
But that secures my heart, and all the Flames it feels
Are but so many Lusts –
I know it by their sudden bold Intrusion.
The Fire's impatient and betrays, 'tis false –
For had it been the purer flame of Love,
I should have pined and languished at your feet,
Ere found the impudence to have discovered it.
I now dare stand your scorn, and your denial.

MORET: Sure she's bewitched, that she can stand thus tamely, and hear his saucy railing – Sirrah, will you be gone?

ANG: How dare you take this liberty? – withdraw. [*To* Moret.]

– Pray tell me, Sir, are not you guilty of the same Mercenary Crime? When a Lady is proposed to you for a Wife, you never ask, how fair, discreet, or virtuous she is; but what's her Fortune – which if but small, you cry, 'She will not do my business', and basely leave her, though she languish for you – say, is not this as poor?

WILL: It is a Barbarous Custom, which I will scorn to defend in our Sex, and do despise in yours.

ANG: Thou'rt a brave Fellow! put up thy Gold, and know,
That were thy Fortune large as is thy Soul,
Thou shouldst not buy my Love,
Couldst thou forget those mean effects of vanity
Which set me out to sale, and as a Lover, prize my yielding joys.
Canst thou believe they'll be entirely thine,
Without considering they were Mercenary?

WILL: I cannot tell, I must bethink me first – ha – death, I'm going to believe her. [*Aside.*

ANG: Prithee, confirm that faith – or if thou canst not – flatter me a little, 'twill please me from thy mouth.

WILL: Curse on thy charming Tongue! dost thou return
My feigned contempt with so much subtlety? [*Aside.*
Thou'st found the easiest way into my heart,
Though I yet know that all thou say'st is false. [*Turning from her in a Rage.*

ANG: By all that's good 'tis real,
I never loved before, though oft a Mistress.
– Shall my first Vows be slighted?

WILL: What can she mean? [*Aside.*

ANG: I find you cannot credit me. – [*In an angry tone.*

WILL: I know you take me for an errant Ass,
An Ass that may be soothed into belief,
And then be used at pleasure;
– But, Madam, I have been so often cheated
By perjured, soft, deluding Hypocrites,
That I've no faith left for the cozening Sex,
Especially for Women of your Trade.

ANG: The low esteem you have of me, perhaps
May bring my heart again:
For I have pride that yet surmounts my Love. [*She turns with Pride, he holds her.*

WILL: Throw off this Pride, this Enemy to Bliss,
And show the Power of Love: 'tis with those Arms
I can be only vanquished, made a Slave.

ANG: Is all my mighty Expectation vanished?
– No, I will not hear thee talk – thou hast a Charm
In every word that draws my heart away.
And all the Thousand Trophies I designed[64]
Thou hast undone – Why art thou soft?
Thy Looks are bravely rough, and meant for War.
Couldst thou not storm on still?
I then perhaps had been as free as thou.

Notes

64 *Trophies* "Something shown or treasured up as a proof of victory" (Johnson).

WILL: Death! how she throws her Fire about my Soul! [*Aside.*
– Take heed, fair Creature, how you raise my hopes,
Which once assumed pretends to all dominion[65]
There's not a joy thou hast in store
I shall not then Command:
– For which I'll pay thee back my Soul! my Life!
– Come, let's begin th' account this happy minute.

ANG: And will you pay me then the price I ask?

WILL: Oh, why dost thou draw me from an awful Worship,[66]
By showing thou art no Divinity?
Conceal the Fiend, and show me all the Angel;
Keep me but ignorant, and I'll be devout,
And pay my Vows forever at this shrine. [*Kneels and kisses her hand.*

ANG: The pay I mean is but thy Love for mine. – Can you give that?

WILL: Entirely – come, let's withdraw! where I'll renew my Vows – and breathe 'em with such Ardour, thou shalt not doubt my zeal.

ANG: Thou hast a Power too strong to be resisted.[*Exeunt* Will. *and* Angellica.

MORET: Now my Curse go with you – is all our Project fallen to this? to love the only Enemy to our Trade? nay, to love such a Shameroon,[67] a very Beggar; nay, a Pirate-Beggar, whose business is to rifle and be gone, a No-Purchase, No-Pay Tatterdemalion,[68] an *English* Piccaroon;[69] a Rogue that fights for daily drink, and takes a Pride in being Loyally Lousy – Oh, I could curse now, if I durst. – This is the Fate of most Whores.

Trophies, which from believing Fops we win,
Are Spoils to those who cozen us again.

ACT III.

Scene I. *A Street.*

Enter Florinda, Valeria, Hellena, *in Antic different Dresses from what they were in before,* Callis *attending.*

FLOR: I Wonder what should make my Brother in so ill a humour: I hope he has not found out our Ramble this Morning.

HELL: No, if he had, we should have heard on't at both Ears, and have been Mewed up[70] this Afternoon; which I would not for the World should have happened – hey ho, I'm sad as a Lover's Lute. –

VAL: Well, methinks we have learnt this Trade of Gipsies as readily as if we had been bred upon the Road to *Loreto*:[71] and yet I did so fumble, when I told the stranger his Fortune, that I was afraid I should have told my own and yours by mistake – but, methinks *Hellena* has been very serious ever since.

Notes

65 *pretend to* claim.
66 *awful* awe-inspiring.
67 *shameroon* a made-up noun, meaning, apparently, a cheater.
68 *tatterdemalion* ragamuffin
69 *piccaroon* pirate; scoundrel.
70 *mewed up* confined.
71 *Loreto* site of a holy Catholic shrine on the Adriatic coast of Italy—a common destination for pilgrims.

FLOR: I would give my Garters she were in Love, to be revenged upon her, for abusing me – how is't, *Hellena*?

HELL: Ah – would I had never seen my mad Monsieur – and yet for all your laughing, I am not in Love – and yet this small acquaintance, o' my Conscience, will never out of my head.

VAL: Ha, ha, ha – I laugh to think how thou art fitted with a Lover, a fellow that, I warrant, loves every new Face he sees.

HELL: Hum – he has not kept his word with me here – and may be taken up – that thought is not very pleasant to me – what the Deuce[72] should this be now that I feel?

VAL: What is't like?

HELL: Nay, the Lord knows – but if I should be hanged, I cannot choose but be angry and afraid, when I think that mad Fellow should be in Love with Anybody but me – what to think of myself I know not – would I could meet with some true damned Gipsy, that I might know my Fortune.

VAL: Know it! why there's nothing so easy; thou wilt love this wandering Inconstant till thou find'st thyself hanged about his Neck, and then be as mad to get free again.

FLOR: Yes, *Valeria*; we shall see her bestride his Baggage-horse, and follow him to the Campaign.

HELL: So, so, now you are provided for, there's no care taken of poor me – but since you have set my heart a wishing, I am resolved to know for what. I will not die of the Pip,[73] so I will not.

FLOR: Art thou mad to talk so? who will like thee well enough to have thee, that hears what a mad Wench thou art?

HELL: Like me! I don't intend every he that likes me shall have me, but he that I like; I should have stayed in the Nunnery still, if I had liked my Lady Abbess as well as she liked me – no, I came thence, not (as my wise Brother imagines) to take an Eternal Farewell of the World, but to Love and to be beloved; and I will be beloved or I'll get one of your Men, so I will.

VAL: Am I put into the number of Lovers?

HELL: You? why Cuz, I know thou art too good natured to leave us in any design: thou would venture a Cast,[74] though thou comest off a loser, especially with such a Gamester. – I observed your Man, and your willing Ears incline that way; and if you are not a Lover, 'tis an Art soon learnt – that I find. [*Sighs*.

FLOR: I wonder how you learnt to Love so easily, I had a 1000 Charms to meet my Eyes and Ears, ere I could yield; and 'twas the knowledge of *Belvile*'s merit, not the surprising Person, took my Soul – thou art too rash to give a heart at first sight.

HELL: Hang your considering Lover; I ne'er thought beyond the fancy that 'twas a very pretty, idle, silly kind of pleasure to pass one's time with, to write little, soft, Nonsensical Billets, and with great difficulty and danger receive Answers; in which I shall have my Beauty praised, my Wit admired (though little or none) and have the vanity and power to know I am desirable; then I have the more inclination that way, because I am to be a Nun, and so shall not be suspected to have any such Earthly thoughts about me – but when I walk thus – and sigh thus – they'll think my mind's upon my Monastery, and cry, 'how happy 'tis she's so resolved!' – But not a word of Man.

FLOR: What a mad Creature's this!

Notes

[72] *Deuce* devil.

[73] *Pip* malaise.

[74] *Cast* a turn; a throw of the dice.

HELL: I'll warrant, if my Brother hears either of you sigh, he cries (gravely) – 'I fear you have the indiscretion to be in Love, but take heed of the Honour of our House, and your own unspotted Fame'; and so he Conjures on till he has laid the soft-winged God in your Hearts, or broke the Bird's Nest – but see here comes your Lover: but where's my Inconstant? let's step aside, and we may learn something. [*Go aside.*

Enter Belvile, Fred. *and* Blunt.

BELV: What means this? the Picture's taken in.

BLUNT: It may be the Wench is good Natured, and will be kind *Gratis*. Your Friend's a proper handsome Fellow.

BELV: I rather think she has cut his Throat and is fled: I am mad he should throw himself into dangers – pox on't, I shall want him too at Night – let's knock and ask for him.

HELL: My Heart goes a-pit, a-pat, for fear 'tis my Man they talk of.

Knock, Moretta *above.*

MORE: What would you have?

BELV: Tell the stranger that entered here about two hours ago, that his Friends stay here for him.

MORET: A Curse upon him for *Moretta*, would he were at the Devil – but he's coming to you. [*Enter* Willmore.

HELL: Aye, aye, 'tis he! Oh how this vexes me.

BELV: And how, and how, dear Lad, has Fortune smiled! are we to break her Windows! or raise up Altars to her! hah!

WILL: Does not my Fortune sit Triumphant on my Brow? dost not see the little wanton God there all gay and smiling? Have I not an Air about my Face and Eyes, that distinguish me from the Crowd of common Lovers? By Heaven, *Cupid*'s Quiver has not half so many Darts as her Eyes! – Oh such a *Bona Rota*:[75] to sleep in her Arms is lying in Fresco,[76] all perfumed Air about me.

HELL: Here's fine encouragement for me to fool on. [*Aside.*

WILL: Hark ye, where didst thou purchase that rich Canary we drank today?[77] tell me, that I may Adore the Spigot, and sacrifice to the Butt! the Juice was Divine, into which I must dip my Rosary, and then bless all things that I would have bold or Fortunate.

BELV: Well Sir, let's go take a Bottle, and hear the story of your Success.

FRED: Would not *French* Wine do better?

WILL: Damn the hungry Balderdash;[78] cheerful Sack[79] has a generous Virtue in't, inspiring a successful Confidence, gives Eloquence to the Tongue! and vigour to the Soul! and has in a few hours completed all my hopes and wishes! There's nothing left to raise a new desire in me – come let's be gay and wanton – and, Gentlemen, study, study what you want, for here are Friends, – that will supply, Gentlemen, – hark! what a charming sound they make – 'tis he and she Gold whilst here, and shall beget new pleasures every Moment.

BLUNT: But hark ye, Sir, you are not Married, are you?

Notes

[75] *Bona Rota* good fortune and Buonarroti (i.e. the artist Michelangelo).

[76] *in Fresco* al fresco; outside; in the air; or in the heavenly frescos of Michelangelo.

[77] *Canary* a sweet wine from the Canary Islands.

[78] *hungry* unsatisfying; *Balderdash* a mixture of liquors.

[79] *Sack* a class of white wines including Canary.

WILL: All the honey of Matrimony, but none of the sting, Friend.

BLUNT: 'Sheartlikins, thou'rt a Fortunate Rogue!

WILL: I am so, Sir, let these inform you! – ha, how sweetly they Chime! – pox of Poverty, it makes a Man a slave, makes Wit and Honour sneak; my Soul grew lean and rusty for want of credit.

BLUNT: 'Sheartlikins, this I like well; it looks like my lucky Bargain! Oh how I long for the approach of my Squire, that is to conduct me to her House again. Whe! here's two provided for.

FRED: By this light y're happy Men.

BLUNT: Fortune is pleased to smile on us, Gentlemen – to smile on us.

Enter Sancho, *and pulls* Blunt *by the sleeve. They go aside.*

SANCHO: Sir, my Lady expects you – she has removed all that might oppose your will and pleasure – and is impatient till you come.

BLUNT: Sir, I'll attend you – oh the happiest Rogue! I'll take no leave, lest they either dog me, or stay me. [*Exit with* Sancho.

BELV: But then the little Gipsy is forgot?

WILL: A mischief on thee for putting her into my thoughts; I had quite forgot her else, and this Night's debauch had drunk her quite down.

HELL: Had it so, good Captain? [*Claps him on the Back.*

WILL: Hah! I hope she did not hear me. [*Aside.*

HELL: What, afraid of such a Champion?

WILL: Oh! you're a fine Lady of your word, are you not? to make a Man languish a whole day –

HELL: In tedious search of me.

WILL: Egad Child, thou'rt in the right, hadst thou seen what a Melancholy Dog I have been ever since I was a Lover, how I have walked the streets like a *Capuchin*,[80] with my Hands in my Sleeves – Faith, Sweetheart, thou wouldst pity me.

HELL: Now, if I should be hanged, I can't be angry with him, he dissembles so Heartily [*aside*] – alas good Captain, what pains you have taken – now were I ungrateful not to reward so true a Servant.

WILL: Poor Soul! that's kindly said, I see thou bearest a Conscience – come then for a beginning, show me thy dear Face.

HELL: I'm afraid, my small acquaintance, you have been staying that swingeing Stomach[81] you boasted of this Morning; I remember then my little Collation would have gone down with you, without the Sauce of a handsome Face – is your Stomach so queasy now?

WILL: Faith long fasting, Child, spoils a Man's Appetite – yet if you durst treat, I could so lay about me still –

HELL: And would you fall to, before a Priest says Grace?

WILL: Oh fie, fie, what an old out-of-fashioned thing hast thou named? thou couldst not dash me more out of Countenance, shouldst thou show me an ugly Face.

Whilst he is seemingly courting Hellena, *enter* Angellica, Moretta, Biskey, *and* Sebastian, *all in Masquerade:* Ang. *sees* Will. *and stares.*

ANG: Heavens, 'tis he? and passionately fond to see another Woman.

MORET: What could you expect less from such a swaggerer?

Notes

[80] *Capuchin* a monk of the order of St. Francis.

[81] *swingeing stomach* huge appetite.

ANG: Expect! as much as I paid him, a Heart entire,
Which I had Pride enough to think when e'er I gave
It would have raised the Man above the Vulgar,
Made him all Soul! and that all soft and constant.

HELL: You see, Captain, how willing I am to be Friends with you, till time and ill-luck make us Lovers; and ask you the Question first, rather than put your Modesty to the blush, by asking me: (for alas!) I know you Captains are such strict Men and such severe observers of your Vows to Chastity, that 'twill be hard to prevail with your tender Conscience to Marry a young willing Maid.

WILL: Do not abuse me, for fear I should take thee at thy word, and Marry thee indeed, which I'm sure will be revenge sufficient.

HELL: O my Conscience, that will be our Destiny, because we are both of one humour; I am as inconstant as you, for I have considered, Captain, that a handsome Woman has a great deal to do whilst her Face is good, for then is our Harvest time to gather Friends; and should I in these days of my Youth, catch a fit of foolish Constancy, I were undone; 'tis loitering by daylight in our great Journey: therefore I declare, I'll allow but one year for Love, one year for indifference, and one year for hate – and then – go hang yourself – for I profess myself the gay, the kind, and the Inconstant – the Devil's in't if this won't please you.

WILL: Oh most damnably – I have a Heart with a hole quite through it too: no Prison mine to keep a Mistress in.

ANG: Perjured Man! how I believe thee now. [*Aside.*

HELL: Well, I see our business as well as humours are alike, yours to cozen as many Maids as will trust you, and I as many Men as have Faith – see if I have not as desperate a lying look, as you can have for the heart of you.

Pulls off her Vizard; he starts.

– How do you like it, Captain?

WILL: Like it! by Heaven, I never saw so much beauty! Oh the Charms of those sprightly black Eyes! that strangely fair Face! full of smiles and dimples! those soft round melting Cherry Lips! and small even white Teeth! not to be expressed, but silently adored! – oh one look more! and strike me dumb, or I shall repeat nothing else till I'm mad. [*He seems to Court her to pull off her Vizard: she refuses.*

ANG: I can endure no more – nor is it fit to interrupt him; for if I do, my Jealousy has so destroyed my Reason, – I shall undo him – therefore I'll retire – and you, *Sebastian,* [*To one of her Bravoes*] follow that Woman, and learn who 'tis; while you tell the Fugitive I would speak to him instantly. [*To the other Bravo. Exit.*

This while Flor. *is talking to* Belvile, *who stands sullenly.* Fred. *courting Valeria.*

VAL: Prithee, dear stranger, be not so sullen; for though you have lost your Love, you see my Friend frankly offers you hers to play with in the meantime.

BELV: Faith, Madam, I am sorry I can't play at her Game.

FRED: Pray leave your Intercession, and mind your own Affair, they'll better agree apart; he's a modest sigher in Company, but alone no Woman escapes him.

FLOR: Sure he does but rally[82] – yet if it should be true – I'll tempt him farther – believe me, Noble Stranger, I'm no common Mistress – and for a little proof on't – wear this Jewel – nay, take it, Sir, 'tis right, and Bills of Exchange[83] may sometimes miscarry.

Notes

82 *rally* tease, jest.

83 *Bill of Exchange* a kind of monetary draft, promising money in exchange for goods or services.

BELV: Madam, why am I chose out of all Mankind to be the Object of your Bounty?

VAL: There's another civil Question asked.

FRED: Pox of 'is Modesty, it spoils his own Markets, & hinders mine.

FLOR: Sir, from my Window I have often seen you; and Women of Quality have so few opportunities for Love, that we ought to lose none.

FRED: Ay, this is something! here's a Woman! – when shall I be blessed with so much kindness from your fair Mouth? – take the Jewel, Fool. [*Aside to* Belv.

BELV: You tempt me strangely, Madam, every way –

FLOR: So, if I find him false, my whole Repose is gone. [*Aside.*

BELV: And but for a Vow I've made to a very fine Lady, this goodness had subdued me.

FRED: Pox on't be kind, in pity to me be kind, for I am to thrive here but as you treat her Friend.

HELL: Tell me what did you in yonder House, and I'll unmask.

WILL: Yonder House – oh – I went to – a – to – why, there's a Friend of mine lives there.

HELL: What, a She, or a He Friend?

WILL: A Man upon Honour! a Man – A She Friend – no, no, Madam, you have done my business,[84] I thank you.

HELL: And was't your Man Friend, that had more Darts in's Eyes than *Cupid* carries in a whole Budget[85] of Arrows?

WILL: So –

HELL: Ah such a *Bona Rota*! to be in her Arms is lying in *Fresco*, all perfumed Air about me – was this your Man Friend too?

WILL: So –

HELL: That gave you the He, and the She Gold, that begets young Pleasures.

WILL: Well, well, Madam, then you see there are Ladies in the World, that will not be cruel – there are, Madam, there are –

HELL: And there be Men too, as fine, wild, Inconstant Fellows as yourself, there be, Captain, there be, if you go to that now – therefore I'm resolved –

WILL: Oh! –

HELL: To see your Face no more –

WILL: Oh!

HELL: Till tomorrow.

WILL: Egad you frighted me.

HELL: Nor then neither, unless you'll swear never to see that Lady more.

WILL: See her! – whe never to think of Womankind again?

HELL: Kneel, – and swear – [*Kneels, she gives him her hand.*

HELL: I do, never to think – to see – to Love – nor Lie with any but thyself.

HELL: Kiss the Book.

WILL: Oh, most Religiously. [*Kisses her hand.*

HELL: Now what a wicked Creature am I, to damn a proper Fellow.

CALL: Madam, I'll stay no longer, 'tis e'en dark. [*To* Flor.

FLOR: However, Sir, I'll leave this with you – that when I'm gone, you may repent the opportunity you have lost, by your Modesty.

Notes

84 *done my Business* killed me, figuratively.

85 *Budget* leather bag.

Gives him the Jewel, which is her Picture, and Ex. He gazes after her.

WILL: 'Twill be an Age till tomorrow, – and till then I will most impatiently expect you – Adieu, my Dear pretty Angel. [*Ex. all the Women.*

BELV: Ha! *Florinda's* Picture – 'twas she herself – what a dull Dog was I? I would have given the World for one minute's discourse with her –

FRED: This comes of your modesty! – ah pox o' your vow, 'twas ten to one, but we had lost the Jewel by't.

BELV: *Willmore!* the blessedest Opportunity lost! – *Florinda*, Friends, *Florinda!*

WILL: Ah Rogue! such black Eyes! such a Face! such a Mouth! such Teeth – and so much Wit! –

BELV: All, all, and a Thousand Charms besides.

WILL: Why, dost thou know her?

BELV: Know her! Ay, Ay, and a pox take me with all my Heart for being Modest.

WILL: But hark ye, Friend of mine, are you my Rival? and have I been only beating the Bush[86] all this while?

BELV: I understand thee not – I'm mad – see here – [*Shows the Picture.*

WILL: Ha! whose Picture's this? – 'tis a fine Wench!

FRED: The Colonel's Mistress, Sir.

WILL: Oh, oh, here – I thought 't had been another prize – come, come, a Bottle will set thee right again. [*Gives the Picture back.*

52

BELV: I am content to try, and by that time 'twill be late enough for our design.

WILL: Agreed.

Love does all day the Soul's great Empire keep,
But Wine at night Lulls the soft God asleep.

Exeunt.

Scene II. Lucetta's *House.*

Enter Blunt *and* Lucetta *with a Light.*

LUC: Now we are safe and free, no fears of the coming home of my Old Jealous Husband, which made me a little thoughtful when you came in first – but now Love is all the business of my Soul.

BLUNT: I am transported – pox on't, that I had but some fine things to say to her, such as Lovers use – I was a Fool not to learn of *Fred*, a little by heart before I came – something I must say. – [*Aside.*] 'Sheartlikins, sweet Soul, I am not used to Compliment, but I'm an honest Gentleman, and thy humble Servant.

LUC: I have nothing to pay for so great a Favour, but such a Love as cannot but be great, since at first sight of that sweet Face and Shape it made me your absolute Captive.

BLUNT: Kind heart! how prettily she talks! Egad I'll show her Husband a *Spanish*[87] trick; send him out of the World and Marry her: she's damnably in Love with me, and will ne'er mind Settlements,[88] and so there's that saved. [*Aside.*

LUC: Well, Sir, I'll go and undress me, and be with you instantly.

Notes

[86] *beating the bush* driving the game to another hunter.

[87] *Spanish* deceitful (*OED*, 3a).

[88] *Settlements* marriage settlements or legal arrangements.

BLUNT: Make haste then, for 'adsheartlikins, dear Soul, thou canst not guess at the pain of a longing Lover, when his Joys are drawn within the compass of a few Minutes.

LUC: You speak my sense, and I'll make haste to provide it. [*Exit.*

BLUNT: 'Tis a rare Girl, and this one Night's enjoyment with her will be worth all the days I ever passed in *Essex.* – would she would go with me into *England*, though to say truth, there's plenty of Whores already. – But a pox on 'em; they are such Mercenary – Prodigal Whores, that they want such a one as this, that's Free and Generous, to give 'em good Examples: – Whe what a house she has, how rich and fine!

Enter Sancho.

SANCHO: Sir, my Lady has sent me to conduct you to her Chamber.

BLUNT: Sir, I shall be proud to follow – here's one of her Servants too! 'Sheartlikins, by his garb and gravity he might be a Justice of Peace in *Essex*, and is but a Pimp here. [*Exeunt:*

The Scene Changes to a Chamber with an Alcove-Bed[89] *in't, a Table, &c.*
Lucetta *in Bed. Enter* Sancho *and* Blunt, *who takes the Candle of* Sancho *at the Door.*

SANCH: Sir, my Commission reaches no farther.

BLUNT: Sir, I'll excuse your Compliment – what, in Bed, my sweet Mistress?

LUC: You see, I still outdo you in kindness.

BLUNT: And thou shall see what haste I'll make to quit scores[90] – oh the luckiest Rogue! [*He Undresses himself.*

LUC: Should you be false or cruel now!

BLUNT: False! 'Sheartlikins, what dost thou take me for? A *Jew?*[91] an insensible heathen – a Pox of thy Old Jealous Husband: and[92] he were dead, Egad, sweet Soul, it should be none of my fault, if I did not Marry thee.

LUC: It never should be mine.

BLUNT: Good Soul, I'm the fortunatest Dog!

LUC: Are you not undressed yet?

BLUNT: As much as my impatience will permit.

Goes *towards the Bed in his shirt, Drawers.*

LUC: Hold, Sir, put out the Light, it may betray us else.

BLUNT: Anything, I need no other Light but that of thine Eyes! – 'Sheartlikins, there I think I had it. [*Aside.*

Puts out the Candle, the Bed descends, he gropes about to find it.

– Whe – whe – where am I got? what, not yet? – where are you sweetest? – ah, the Rogue's silent now – a pretty Love-trick this – how she'll laugh at me anon! – you need not, my dear Rogue! you need not! – I'm all on a fire already – come, come, now call me in pity – Sure I'm Enchanted! I have been round the Chamber, and can find neither Woman, nor Bed – I locked the Door, I'm sure she cannot go that way – or if she could, the Bed could not – Enough, enough, my pretty wanton, do not carry the jest too far – ha, Betrayed! Dogs! Rogues! Pimps! – help! help! [*Lights on a Trap,*[93] *and is let down.*

Notes

[89] *Alcove-Bed* a bed of state, sometimes with seats around it (Johnson).

[90] *quit scores* even the game.

[91] *Jew* a miser.

[92] *and* if.

[93] *Lights on a Trap* finds a trap door beneath the floor, under which the bed has already descended.

Enter Lucetta, Philippo, *and* Sancho *with a Light*.

PHIL: Ha, ha, ha, he's dispatched finely.

LUC: Now, Sir, had I been Coy, we had missed of this Booty.

PHIL: Nay when I saw 'twas a substantial Fool, I was mollified; but when you dote upon a Serenading Coxcomb, upon a Face, fine Clothes, and a Lute, it makes me rage.

LUC: You know I never was guilty of that Folly, my dear *Philippo*, but with yourself – but come let's see what we have got by this.

PHIL: A rich Coat! – Sword and Hat – these Breeches too – are well lined – see here, a Gold Watch! – a Purse – ha! – Gold! – at least Two Hundred Pistoles! a bunch of Diamond Rings! and one with the Family Arms! – a Gold Box! – with a Medal of his King! and his Lady Mother's Picture![94] – these were Sacred Relics, believe me! – see, the Waistband of his Breeches have a Mine of Gold! – Old Queen *Bess*'s.[95] We have a quarrel to her ever since *Eighty Eight*, and may therefore justify the Theft; the Inquisition might have committed it.

LUC: – See, a Bracelet of bowed Gold! these his Sister tied about his Arm at parting – but well – for all this, I fear his being a Stranger may make a noise, and hinder our Trade with them hereafter.

PHIL: That's our security; he is not only a Stranger to us, but to the Country too – the Common-Shore[96] into which he is descended, thou know'st, conducts him into another Street, which this Light will hinder him from ever finding again – he knows neither your Name, nor the Street where your House is, nay, nor the way to his own Lodgings.

LUC: And art not thou an unmerciful Rogue! not to afford him one Night for all this? – I should not have been such a *Jew*.

PHIL: Blame me not, *Lucetta*, to keep as much of thee as I can to myself – come, that thought makes me wanton! – let's to Bed! – *Sancho*, lock up these.

This is the Fleece which Fools do bear,
Designed for witty Men to sheer.

[*Exeunt*.

The Scene changes, and discovers Blunt, *creeping out of a Common Shore, his Face, &c., all dirty.*

BLUNT: Oh Lord! [*Climbing up*. I am got out at last, and (which is a Miracle) without a Clue[97] – and now to Damning and Cursing! – but if that would ease me, where shall I begin? with my Fortune, myself, or the Quean[98] that cozened me – what a dog was I to believe in Women! oh Coxcomb! – Ignorant conceited Coxcomb! to fancy she could be enamoured with my Person, at the first sight enamoured! – oh, I'm a cursed Puppy! 'tis plain, Fool was writ upon my Forehead! she perceived it! – saw the *Essex* Calf there – for what Allurements could there be in this Countenance? which I can endure, because I'm acquainted with it – oh, dull silly Dog! to be thus soothed

Notes

[94] *his King! and his Lady Mother's Picture* images of Charles II and his mother Henrietta Maria.

[95] *Old Queen Bess* Elizabeth I, whose forces defeated the Spanish Armada in 1588.

[96] *Common-Shore* sewer.

[97] *Clue* a string, such as Ariadne gave to Theseus, to lead him out of a maze.

[98] *Quean* whore.

into a Cozening! had I been drunk, I might fondly have credited the young Quean! but as I was in my right Wits, to be thus cheated, confirms it: I am a dull believing *English* Country Fop – but my Comrades! death and the Devil! there's the worst of all – then a Ballad will be Sung Tomorrow on the *Prado*,[99] to a Lousy Tune of 'The Enchanted Squire, and the Annihilated Damsel' – But *Fred.*, that Rogue! and the Colonel, will abuse me beyond all Christian patience – had she left me my Clothes, I have a Bill of Exchange at home would have saved my Credit – but now all hope is taken from me – well, I'll home (if I can find the way) with this Consolation, that I am not the first kind believing Coxcomb; but there are, Gallants, many such good Natures amongst ye.

And though you've better Arts to hide your Follies,
'Adsheartlikins y'are all as errant Cullies.[100]

Scene III. *The Garden, in the Night.*

Enter Florinda *in an undress, with a Key and a little Box.*

Flor: Well, thus far I'm in my way to happiness; I have got myself free from *Callis*; my Brother too, I find by yonder light, is gone into his Cabinet, and thinks not of me; I have by good Fortune got the Key of the Garden back door. – I'll open it, to prevent *Belvile's* knocking – a little noise will now Alarm my Brother. Now am I as fearful as a young Thief. *[Unlocks the Door.]* – hark – what noise is that – oh,'twas the Wind that played amongst the Boughs – *Belvile* stays long, methinks – it's time – stay – for fear of a surprise – I'll hide these Jewels in yonder Jessamin. *[She goes to lay down the Box.*

Enter Willmore *drunk.*

Will: What the Devil is become of these fellows, *Belvile* and *Frederick*? They promised to stay at the next Corner for me, but who the Devil knows the Corner of a Full Moon? – now – whereabouts am I? – hah – what have we here? a Garden! – a very convenient place to sleep in – hah – what has God sent us here? – a Female! – by this light, a Woman! – I'm a Dog if it be not a very Wench! –

Flor: He's come! – hah – who's there?

Will: Sweet Soul! let me salute thy Shoestring.

Flor: 'Tis not my *Belvile*. – good Heavens! I know him not – who are you, and from whence come you?

Will: Prithee – prithee, Child – not so many hard questions – let it suffice I am here, Child – come, come kiss me.

Flor: Good Gods! what luck is mine?

Will: Only good luck, Child, parlous[101] good luck – come hither, – 'tis a delicate shining Wench – by this hand she's perfumed, and smells like any Nosegay – prithee, dear Soul, let's not play the Fool, and lose time – precious time – for as God shall save me, I'm as honest a Fellow as breathes, though I am a little disguised at present – come, I say, – whe, thou may'st be free with me, I'll be very secret. I'll not boast who 'twas obliged me, not I – for hang me if I know thy name.

Flor: Heavens! what a filthy beast is this!

Notes

[99] *Prado* any public park, but the Prado is in Madrid.

[100] *Cullies* dupes.

[101] *parlous* extraordinary.

WILL: I am so, and thou oughtst the sooner to lie with me for that reason – for look you, Child, there will be no sin in't, because 'twas neither designed nor premeditated. 'Tis pure Accident on both sides – that's a certain thing now – indeed should I make love to you, and you vow Fidelity – and swear and lie till you believed and yielded – that were to make it wilful Fornication – the crying Sin of the Nation – Thou art therefore (as thou art a good Christian) obliged in Conscience to deny me nothing. Now – come, be kind, without any more idle prating.

FLOR: Oh, I am ruined – Wicked Man, unhand me.

WILL: Wicked! Egad, Child, a Judge, were he young and vigorous, and saw those Eyes of thine, would know 'twas they gave the first blow – the first provocation – come, prithee let's lose no time, I say – this is a fine convenient place.

FLOR: Sir, let me go, I conjure you, or I'll call out.

WILL: Ay, ay, you were best to call Witness to see how finely you treat me – do –

FLOR: I'll cry Murder! Rape! or anything! if you do not instantly let me go.

WILL: A Rape! Come, come, you lie, you Baggage, you lie: what, I'll warrant you would fain have the World believe now that you are not so forward as I. No, not you – why at this time of Night was your Cobweb Door set open, dear Spider – but to catch Flies? – Hah – come – or I shall be damnably angry. – Whe what a Coil[102] is here –

FLOR: Sir, can you think –

WILL: That you'd do it for nothing? – oh, oh, I find what you would be at – look here, here's a Pistole for you – here's a work indeed – here – take it, I say –

FLOR: For Heaven's sake, Sir, as you're a Gentleman –

WILL: So – now – now – she would be wheedling me for more – what, you will not take it then – you're resolved you will not – come, take it, or I'll put it up again – for, look ye, I never give more – whe, how now, Mistress, are you so high i' th' Mouth a Pistole won't down with you? – hah – whe what a work's here – in good time – come, no struggling to be gone – but an' y'are good at a dumb Wrestle, I'm for ye – look ye – I'm for ye – [*She struggles with him.*

Enter Belvile *and* Frederick.

BEL: The Door is open; a pox of this mad Fellow, I'm angry that we've lost him, I durst have sworn he had followed us.

FRED: But you were so hasty, Colonel, to be gone.

FLOR: Help! help! – Murder! – help – oh, I am ruined.

BELV: Ha! sure that's *Florinda's* Voice. [*Comes up to them.*
– A Man! Villain, let go that Lady. [*A noise.* [Will: *turns and draws*, Fred. *interposes.*

FLOR: *Belvile!* Heavens! my Brother too is coming, and 'twill be impossible to escape – *Belvile*, I conjure you to walk under my Chamber-window, from whence I'll give you some Instructions what to do – this rude Man has undone us. *Exit.*

WILL: *Belvile!*

Enter Pedro, Stephano, *and other Servants with Lights.*

PED: I'm betrayed! run, *Stephano*, and see if *Florinda* be safe. [*Exit* Steph.
So whoe'er they be, all is not well, I'll to *Florinda's* Chamber.

Notes

102 *Coil* "tumult, turmoil, bustle, stir, hurry, confusion" (Johnson).

They fight, and Ped.'s *Party beats 'em out; going out, meets* Steph.

STEPH: You need not, Sir, the poor Lady's fast asleep, and thinks no harm. I would not wake her, Sir, for fear of frightening her with your danger.

PED: I'm glad she's there – Rascals, how came the Garden Door open?

STEPH: That Question comes too late, Sir: some of my Fellow Servants Masquerading I'll warrant.

PED: Masquerading! a lewd Custom to debauch our youth, – there's something more in this than I imagine. [*Exeunt.*

Scene IV. *Changes to the Street.*

Enter Belvile *in Rage,* Fred. *holding him, and* Willmore *Melancholy.*

WILL: Whe, how the Devil should I know *Florinda?*

BELV: A plague of your Ignorance! If it had not been *Florinda*, must you be a Beast? – a Brute? a Senseless Swine?

WILL: Well, Sir, you see I am endued with Patience – I can bear – though Egad y'are very free with me, methinks. – I was in good hopes the Quarrel would have been on my side, for so uncivilly interrupting me.

BELV: Peace, Brute! whilst thou'rt safe – oh, I'm distracted.

WILL: Nay, nay, I'm an unlucky Dog, that's certain.

BELV: A curse upon the Star that Ruled my Birth! or whatsoever other Influence that makes me still so wretched.

WILL: Thou break'st my Heart with these Complaints; there is no Star in fault, no Influence but Sack, the cursed Sack I drank.

FRED: Whe, how the Devil came you so drunk?

WILL: Whe, how the Devil came you so sober?

BELV: A Curse upon his thin Skull, he was always beforehand that way.

FRED: Prithee, Dear Colonel, forgive him, he's sorry for his Fault.

BELV: He's always so after he has done a mischief – a plague on all such Brutes.

WILL: By this Light I took her for an Errant Harlot.

BELV: Damn your debauched opinion! tell me, Sot, hadst thou so much sense and light about thee to distinguish her Woman, and couldst not see something about her Face and Person, to strike an awful Reverence into thy Soul?

WILL: Faith no, I considered her as mere a Woman as I could wish.

BELV: 'Sdeath, I have no patience – draw, or I'll kill you.

WILL: Let that alone till Tomorrow, and if I set not all right again, use your pleasure.

BELV: Tomorrow! damn it.
The Spiteful Light will lead me to no happiness.
Tomorrow is *Antonio*'s, and perhaps
Guides him to my undoing; – oh that I could meet
This Rival! this powerful Fortunate!

WILL: What then?

BELV: Let thy own Reason, or my Rage instruct thee.

WILL: I shall be finely informed then, no doubt; hear me, Colonel – hear me – show me the Man and I'll do his Business.[103]

Notes

[103] *do his Business* kill him, literally.

BELV: I know him no more than thou, or if I did, I should not need thy Aid.

WILL: This you say is *Angellica's* House, I promised the kind Baggage to lie with her Tonight. [*Offers to go in.*

Enter Antonio *and his Page.* Ant. *knocks on the Hilt of his Sword.*

ANT: You paid the Thousand Crowns I directed?

PAGE: To the Lady's old Woman, Sir, I did.

WILL: Who the Devil have we here?

BELV: I'll now plant myself under *Florinda*'s Window, and if I find no comfort there, I'll die. [*Ex.* Belv. *and* Fred.

Enter Moretta

MORET: Page!

PAGE: Here's my Lord.

WILL: How is this, a Piccaroon going to board my Frigate? here's one Chase-Gun[104] for you.

Drawing his Sword, justles Ant. *who turns and draws. They fight,* Ant. *falls.*

MORET: Oh, bless us! we're all undone! [*Runs in and shuts the Door.*

PAGE: Help! Murder! [Belvile *returns at the noise of fighting.*

BELV: Ha! the mad Rogue's engaged in some unlucky Adventure again.

Enter two or three Masqueraders.

MASQ: Ha, a Man killed!

WILL: How! a Man killed! then I'll go home to sleep.

Puts up, and reels out. Exeunt *Masquers another way.*

BELV: Who should it be! pray Heaven the Rogue is safe, for all my Quarrel to him.

As Belvile *is groping about, Enter an Officer and six Soldiers.*

SOLD: Who's there?

OFFIC: So, here's one dispatched – secure the Murderer.

BELV: Do not mistake my Charity for Murder! I came to his Assistance.

Soldiers seize on Belvile.

OFFIC: That shall be tried, Sir. – St. *Jago*,[105] Swords drawn in the Carnival time!

Goes to Antonio.

ANT: Thy Hand, prithee.

OFFIC: Ha, *Don Antonio!* look well to the Villain there. – How is it, Sir?

ANT: I'm hurt.

BELV: Has my humanity made me a Criminal?

OFFIC: Away with him.

BELV: What a cursed chance is this! [*Exeunt Soldiers with* Belv.

ANT: This is the Man that has set upon me twice – carry him to my Apartment till you have further Orders from me. *To the Officer. Ex.* Ant. *led.*

Notes

104 *Chase-Gun* naval artillery.

105 *St. Jago* Santiago, St. James the apostle, patron saint of Spain.

ACT IV.

Scene I. *A fine Room.*

Discovers Belvile, *as by Dark alone.*

BELV: When shall I be weary of railing on Fortune, who is resolved never to turn with smiles upon me? – Two such Defeats in one Night – none but the Devil and that mad Rogue could have contrived to have plagued me with – I am here a Prisoner – but where – Heaven knows – and if there be Murder done, I can soon decide the Fate of a Stranger in a Nation without Mercy – Yet this is nothing to the Torture my Soul bows with, when I think of losing my fair, my dear *Florinda* – hark – my door opens – a Light – a Man – and seems of Quality – armed too! – now shall I die like a Dog without defence.

Enter Antonio *in a Nightgown, with a Light; his Arm in a Scarf, and a Sword under his Arm: He sets the Candle on the Table.*

ANT: Sir, I come to know what Injuries I have done you, that could provoke you to so mean an Action, as to Attack me basely, without allowing time for my defence.

BELV: Sir, for a Man in my Circumstances to plead Innocence, would look like fear – but view me well, and you will find no marks of a Coward on me, nor anything that betrays that Brutality you accuse me of.

ANT: In vain, Sir, you impose upon my sense.
You are not only he who drew on me last Night,
But yesterday before the same House, that of *Angellica*.
Yet there is something in your Face and Mien
That makes me wish I were mistaken.

BELV: I own I fought today in the defence of a Friend of mine, with whom you (if you're the same) and your Party were first engaged.
Perhaps you think this Crime enough to kill me,
But if you do, I cannot fear you'll do it basely.

ANT: No, Sir, I'll make you fit for a defence with this. [*Gives him the Sword.*

BELV: This Gallantry surprises me – nor know I how to use this Present, Sir, against a Man so brave.

ANT: You shall not need
For know, I come to snatch you from a danger
That is decreed against you:
Perhaps your Life, or long Imprisonment,
And 'twas with so much Courage you offended,
I cannot see you punished.

BELV: How shall I pay this Generosity?

ANT: It had been safer to have killed another,
Than have attempted me:
To show your Danger, Sir, I'll let you know my Quality,
And 'tis the Viceroy's Son whom you have wounded.

BELV: The Viceroy's Son!
Death and Confusion! was this Plague reserved
To complete all the rest? – obliged by him!
The Man of all the World I would destroy. [*Aside.*

ANT: You seem disordered, Sir.

BELV: Yes, trust me, Sir, I am, and 'tis with pain
That Man receives such Bounties,
who wants the Power to pay 'em back again.

ANT: To gallant Spirits 'tis indeed uneasy,
– But you may quickly overpay me, Sir.
BELV: Then I am well – kind Heaven! but set us even,
That I may fight with him and keep my Honour safe. [*Aside.*
– Oh, I'm impatient, Sir, to be discounting
The mighty Debt I owe you; Command me quickly –
ANT: I have a Quarrel with a Rival, Sir,
About the Maid we love.
BELV: Death,'tis *Florinda* he means –
That thought destroys my Reason, and I shall kill him – [*Aside.*
ANT: My Rival, Sir.
Is one has all the Virtues Man can boast of.
BELV: Death! who should this be? [*Aside.*
ANT: He challenged me to meet him on the *Molo,*
As soon as day appeared; but last Night's quarrel
Has made my Arm unfit to guide a Sword.
BELV: I apprehend you, Sir, you'd have me kill the Man
That lays a claim to the Maid you speak of.
– I'll do't – I'll fly to do it.
ANT: Sir, do you know her?
BELV: – No, Sir, but 'tis enough she is admired by you.
ANT: Sir, I shall rob you of the Glory on't,
For you must fight under my Name and Dress.
BELV: That Opinion must be strangely obliging that makes
You think I can personate the brave *Antonio,*
Whom I can but strive to imitate.
ANT: You say too much to my Advantage
– Come, Sir, the Day appears that calls you forth.
– Within, Sir, is the habit. [*Exit* Antonio.
BELV: Fantastic Fortune, thou deceitful Light,
That Cheats the wearied Traveller by Night,
Though on a Precipice each step you tread,
I am resolved to follow where you lead. [*Exit.*

Scene II. *The Molo.*

Enter Florinda *and* Callis *in Masks, with* Stephano.

FLOR: I'm dying with my fears; *Belvile*'s not coming as I expected, under my Window, Makes me believe that all those fears are true. [*Aside.* – Canst thou not tell with whom my Brother fights?

STEPH: No, Madam, they were both in Masquerade, I was by when they challenged one another, and they had decided the Quarrel then, but were prevented by some Cavaliers; which made 'em put it off till now – but I am sure 'tis about you they fight.

FLOR: Nay, then 'tis with *Belvile*, for what other Lover have I that dares fight for me, except *Antonio*? and he is too much in favour with my Brother – if it be he, for whom shall I direct my Prayers to Heaven? [*Aside.*

STEPH: Madam, I must leave you, for if my Master see me, I shall be hanged for being your Conductor – I escaped narrowly for the excuse I made for you last Night i' th' Garden.

FLOR: And I'll reward thee for't – prithee no more. [*Exit. Steph.*

Enter Don Pedro *in his Masquing Habit.*

PEDRO: *Antonio*'s late today, the place will fill, and we may be prevented.

Walk about.

FLOR: *Antonio!* sure I heard amiss. [*Aside.*
PEDRO: But who will not excuse a happy Lover.
When soft fair Arms confine the yielding Neck;
And the kind whisper languishingly breathesm,
– Must you be gone so soon? –
Sure I had dwelt forever on her Bosom.
– But stay, he's here.

Enter Belvile *dressed in* Antonio's *Clothes.*

FLOR: 'Tis not *Belvile*, half my Fears are vanished.
PEDRO: *Antonio!*
BELV: This must be he. [*Aside.*] You're early, Sir, – I do not use to be outdone this way.
PEDRO: The wretched, Sir, are watchful, and 'tis enough
You have the advantage of me in *Angellica*.
BELV: *Angellica!* or I've mistook my Man! or else *Antonio.*[106]
– Can he forget his Interest in *Florinda*,
And fight for common Prize? [*Aside.*
PEDRO: Come, Sir, you know our terms –
BELV: By Heaven, not I. [*Aside.*] – No talking, I am ready, Sir.

Offers to fight. Flor. *runs in.*

FLOR: Oh, hold! whoe'er you be, I do conjure you hold.
If you strike here – I die – [*To* Belv.
PEDRO: *Florinda!*
BELV: *Florinda* imploring for my Rival!
PEDRO: Away, this kindness is unseasonable.

Puts her by, they fight; she runs in just as Belv. *disarms* Pedro.

FLOR: Who are you, Sir, that dares deny my Prayers?
BELV: Thy Prayers destroy him; if thou wouldst preserve him,
Do that thou'rt unacquainted with, and curse him. [*She holds him.*
FLOR: By all you hold most dear, by her you love,
I do conjure you, touch him not.
BELV: By her I love!
See – I obey – and at your feet resign
The useless Trophy of my Victory. [*Lays his sword at her feet.*
PEDRO: *Antonio*, you've done enough to prove you love *Florinda*.
BELV: Love *Florinda!*
Does Heaven love Adoration, Prayer, or Penitence?
Love her! here, Sir, – your Sword again. [*Snatches up the Sword and gives it him.*
Upon this truth I'll fight my life away.
PEDRO: No, you've redeemed my Sister, and my Friendship.
BELV: *Don Pedro!*

Notes

[106] *Or* … *or* either … or.

He gives him Flor. *and pulls off his Vizard to show his Face, and puts it on again.*

PEDRO: Can you resign your Claims to other Women,
And give your heart entirely to *Florinda?*
BELV: Entire! as dying Saints' Confessions are!
I can delay my happiness no longer.
This Minute let me make *Florinda* mine.
PEDRO: This Minute let it be – no time so proper,
This Night my Father will arrive from *Rome,*
And possibly may hinder what we propose!
FLOR: Oh Heavens! this Minute!

Enter Masqueraders, and pass over.

BELV: Oh, do not ruin me!
PEDRO: The place begins to fill; and that we may not be observed, do you walk off to St. *Peter's* Church, where I will meet you, and conclude your happiness.
BELV: I'll meet you there – if there be no more Saints' Churches in *Naples.* [*Aside.*
FLOR: Oh stay, Sir, and recall your hasty doom:
alas I have not yet prepared my Heart
To entertain so strange a Guest.
PEDRO: Away, this silly modesty is Assumed too late.
BELV: Heaven, Madam! what do you do?
FLOR: Do! despise the Man that lays a Tyrant's Claim
To what he ought to Conquer by submission.[107]
BELV: You do not know me – move a little this way. [*Draws her aside.*
FLOR: Yes, you may even force me to the Altar,
But not the holy Man that offers there
Shall force me to be thine. [Pedro *talks to* Callis *this while.*
BELV: Oh do not lose so blessed an opportunity!
– See – 'tis your *Belvile* – not *Antonio,*
Whom your mistaken Scorn & Anger ruins. [*Pulls off his Vizard.*
FLOR: *Belvile!*
Where was my Soul it could not meet thy Voice,
And take this knowledge in?

As they are talking, enter Willmore *finely dressed, and* Frederick.

WILL: No Intelligence! no News of *Belvile* yet – well I am the most unlucky Rascal in Nature – ha! – am I deceived – or is it he – look, *Fred.* – 'tis he – my dear *Belvile.*

Runs and embraces him. Belv. *Vizard falls out on's Hand.*

BELV: Hell and confusion seize thee!
PEDRO: Ha! *Belvile!* I beg your Pardon, Sir. [*Takes* Flor. *from him.*
BELV: Nay, touch her not, she's mine by Conquest, Sir. I won her by my Sword.
WILL: Didst thou so – and Egad, Child, we'll keep her by the Sword.

Draws on Pedro, Belv. *goes between.*

BELV: Stand off.

Notes

[107] *Submission* "Agreement to abide by a decision or to obey an authority" (*OED*).

Thou'rt so profanely Lewd, so cursed by Heaven,
All quarrels thou espousest must be Fatal.
WILL: Nay, an you be so hot, my Valour's Coy,
And shall be Courted when you want it next. [*Puts up his Sword.*
BELV: You know I ought to claim a Victor's right, [*To Pedro.*
But you're the Brother to divine *Florinda*,
To whom I'm such a Slave – to purchase her,
I durst not hurt the Man she holds so dear.
PEDRO: 'Twas by *Antonio*'s, not by *Belvile*'s Sword,
This question should have been decided, Sir:
I must confess much to your Bravery's due,
Both now, and when I met you last in Arms.
But I am nicely punctual in my word,
As Men of Honour ought, and beg your Pardon.
– For this mistake another time shall clear.
– This was some Plot between you and *Belvile*:
But I'll prevent you. [*Aside to* Flor. *as they are going out.*

Belv. *looks after her, and begins to walk up and down in a Rage.*

WILL: Do not be Modest now, and lose the Woman: but if we shall fetch her back, so –
BELV: Do not speak to me –
WILL: Not speak to you! – Egad, I'll speak to you, and will be answered too.
BELV: Will you, Sir? –
WILL: I know I've done some mischief, but I'm so dull a Puppy, that I am the Son of a Whore, if I know how, or where – prithee inform my understanding –
BELV: Leave me I say, and leave me instantly.
WILL: I will not leave you in this humour, nor till I know my Crime.
BELV: Death, I'll tell you, Sir –

Draws and runs at Will. *he runs out;* Belv. *after him,* Fred. *interposes.*
Enter Angellica, Moretta, *and* Sebastian.

ANG: Ha – *Sebastian* – Is not that *Willmore?* – haste – haste, and bring him back.
FRED: The Colonel's mad – I never saw him thus before; I'll after 'em, lest he do some mischief, for I am sure *Willmore* will not draw on him. [*Exit.*
ANG: I am all Rage! my first desires defeated
For one, for ought he knows, that has no
Other Merit than her Quality,
– Her being *Don Pedro's* Sister – He loves her!
I know 'tis so – dull, dull, Insensible –
He will not see me now though oft invited,
And broke his word last Night – false perjured Man!
– He that but Yesterday fought for my Favours,
And would have made his Life a Sacrifice
To've gained one Night with me,
Must now be hired and Courted to my Arms.
MORET: I told you what would come on't, but *Moretta*'s an old doting Fool – why did you give him five Hundred Crowns, but to set himself out for other Lovers? you should have kept him Poor, if you had meant to have had any good from him.
ANG: Oh, name not such mean Trifles; – had I given him all
My Youth has earned from Sin,
I had not lost a thought nor sigh upon't.
But I have given him my Eternal rest,

My whole repose, my future joys, my Heart!
My Virgin heart, *Moretta*! Oh 'tis gone!

MORET: Curse on him, here he comes,
How fine she has made him too!

Enter Willmore *and* Sebast. Ang. *turns and walks away.*

WILL: How now, turned shadow? Fly when I pursue! and follow when I fly!

Stay gentle shadow of my Dove, [*Sings.*
And tell me ere I go,
Whether the substance may not prove
A Fleeting thing like you.

There's a soft kind look remaining yet. [*As she turns she looks on him.*

ANG: Well, Sir, you may be gay; all happiness, all joys pursue you still, Fortune's your Slave, and gives you every hour choice of new Hearts and Beauties, till you are cloyed with the repeated Bliss, which others vainly languish for – But know, false Man, that I shall be revenged. [*Turns away in a Rage.*

WILL: So, 'gad, there are of those faint-hearted Lovers, whom such a sharp Lesson next their hearts would make as Impotent as Fourscore – pox o' this whining. – My Business is to laugh and love – a pox on't; I hate your sullen Lover, a Man shall lose as much time to put you in humour now, as would serve to gain a new Woman.

ANG: I scorn to cool that Fire I cannot raise,
Or do the Drudgery of your virtuous Mistress.

WILL: A virtuous Mistress! death, what a thing thou hast found out for me! why what the Devil should I do with a virtuous Woman? – a sort of ill-natured Creatures, that take a Pride to torment a Lover. Virtue is but an Infirmity in Women, a Disease that renders even the handsome ungrateful; whilst the ill-favoured, for want of Solicitations and Address, only fancy themselves so. – I have lain with a Woman of Quality, who has all the while been railing at Whores.

ANG: I will not answer for your Mistress's Virtue,
Though she be Young enough to know no Guilt:
And I could wish you would persuade my heart,
'Twas the Two hundred Thousand Crowns you Courted.

WILL: Two Hundred Thousand Crowns! what Story's this? – what Trick? – what Woman? – ha!

ANG: How strange you make it! have you forgot the Creature you entertained on the Piazza last night?

WILL: Ha! my Gipsy worth Two Hundred Thousand Crowns! – oh how I long to be with her – pox, I knew she was of Quality. [*Aside.*

ANG: False Man! I see my Ruin in thy Face.
How many vows you breathed upon my Bosom,
Never to be unjust – have you forgot so soon?

WILL: Faith no, I was just coming to repeat 'em – but here's a humour indeed – would make a Man a Saint – would she would be angry enough to leave me, and Command me not to wait on her. [*Aside.*

Enter Hellena, *dressed in Man's Clothes.*

HELL: This must be *Angellica*, I know it by her mumping Matron here – Ay, ay, 'tis she! my Mad Captain's with her too, for all his swearing – how this unconstant humour makes me love him! – Pray, good grave Gentlewoman, is not this *Angellica*?

MORET: My too young Sir, it is – I hope 'tis one from *Don Antonio*.

Goes to Angellica.

HELL: Well, something I'll do to vex him for this. [*Aside.*
ANG: I will not speak with him; am I in humour to receive a Lover?
WILL: Not speak with him! whe I'll be gone – and wait your idler Minutes – can I show less obedience to the thing I love so fondly? [*Offers to go.*
ANG: A fine excuse this! – stay –
WILL: And hinder your advantage! should I repay your Bounties so ungratefully?
ANG: Come hither, Boy, – that I may let you see
How much above the advantages you name
I prize one Minute's joy with you.
WILL: Oh, you destroy me with this endearment. [*Impatient to be gone.*
– Death! how shall I get away? – Madam, 'twill not be fit I should be seen with you – besides, it will not be convenient – and I've a Friend – that's dangerously sick.
ANG: I see you're impatient – yet you shall stay.
WILL: And miss my Assignation with my Gipsy. [*Aside, and walks about impatiently.*
HELL: Madam,

Moretta *brings* Hellena, *who addresses herself to* Angellica.

You'll hardly pardon my Intrusion,
When you shall know my business!
And I'm too young to tell my Tale with Art:
But there must be a wondrous store of goodness,
Where so much Beauty dwells.
ANG: A pretty Advocate, whoever sent thee.
– Prithee proceed – Nay, Sir, you shall not go. [*To* Will. *who is stealing off.*
WILL: Then shall I lose my dear Gipsy forever.
– Pox on't, she stays me out of spite. [*Aside.*
HELL: I am related to a Lady, Madam,
Young, Rich, and nobly born, but has the Fate
To be in Love with a young *English* Gentleman.
Strangely she loves him, at first sight she loved him,
But did Adore him when she heard him speak;
For he, she said, had Charms in every word,
That failed not to surprise, to Wound, and Conquer.
WILL: Ha! Egad I hope this concerns me. [*Aside.*
ANG: 'Tis my false Man, he means – would he were gone.
This Praise will raise his Pride and ruin me – well,
Since you are so impatient to be gone,
I will release you, Sir. [*To* Will.
WILL: Nay, then I'm sure 'twas me he spoke of; this cannot be the effects of kindness in her. [*Aside.*
– No, Madam, I've considered better on't,
And will not give you Cause of Jealousy.
ANG: But, Sir, I've – business, that –
WILL: This shall not do, I know 'tis but to try me.
ANG: Well, to your Story, Boy, – though 'twill undo me. [*Aside.*
HELL: With this addition to his other Beauties,
He won her unresisting tender heart,
He vowed and sighed, and swore he loved her dearly;

And she believed the cunning flatterer,
And thought herself the happiest Maid alive:
Today was the appointed time by both,
To consummate their Bliss;
The Virgin, Altar, and the Priest were dressed,
And whilst she languished for th' expected Bridegroom,
She heard, he paid his broken Vows to you.

WILL: So, this is some dear Rogue that's in Love with me, and this way lets me know it; or if it be not me, she means someone whose place I may supply. [*Aside.*

ANG: Now I perceive
The cause of thy impatience to be gone,
And all the business of this Glorious Dress.

WILL: Damn the young Prater, I know not what he means.

HELL: Madam,
In your fair Eyes I read too much concern
To tell my farther business.

ANG: Prithee, sweet Youth, talk on, thou may'st perhaps
Raise here a storm that may undo my passion,
And then I'll grant thee anything.

HELL: Madam, 'tis to entreat you (oh unreasonable!)
You would not see this stranger,
For if you do, she Vows you are undone,
Though Nature never made a Man so Excellent,
And sure he'd been a God, but for inconstancy.

WILL: Ah, Rogue, how finely he's instructed! [*Aside.*] – 'Tis plain; some Woman that has seen me *en passant*.[108]

ANG: Oh, I shall burst with Jealousy! do you know the Man you speak of? –

HELL: Yes, Madam, he used to be in Buff and Scarlet.

ANG: Thou, false as Hell, what canst thou say to this? [*To* Will.

WILL: By Heaven –

ANG: Hold, do not Damn thyself –

HELL: Nor hope to be believed.

He walks about, they follow.

ANG: Oh, perjured Man!
Is't thus you pay my generous Passion back?

HELL: Why would you, Sir, abuse my Lady's Faith?

ANG: And use me so inhumanely?

HELL: A Maid so young, so innocent –

WILL: Ah, young Devil!

ANG: Dost thou not know thy life is in my power?

HELL: Or think my Lady cannot be revenged?

WILL: So, so, the storm comes finely on. [*Aside.*

ANG: Now thou art silent, guilt has struck thee dumb.
Oh, hadst thou still been so, I'd lived in safety.

She turns away and weeps.

WILL: Sweetheart, the Lady's Name and House, – quickly: I'm impatient to be with her. –

Notes

[108] *En passant* in passing.

Aside to Hellena, *looks towards* Angel. *to watch her turning; and as she comes towards them, he meets her.*

HELL: So now is he for another Woman. [*Aside.*
WILL: The impudentest young thing in Nature,
I cannot persuade him out of his Error, Madam.
ANG: I know he's in the right, – yet thou'st a tongue
That would persuade him to deny his Faith.

In rage walks away.

WILL: Her Name, her Name, dear Boy. – [*Said softly to* Hell.
HELL: Have you forgot it, Sir?
WILL: Oh, I perceive he's not to know I am a stranger to his Lady. [*Aside.*
– Yes, yes, I do know – but – I have forgot the –

Angel. *turns.*

– By Heaven, such early confidence I never saw.
ANG: Did I not charge you with this Mistress, Sir?
Which you denied, though I beheld your Perjury.
This little generosity of thine has rendered back my heart. [*Walks away.*
WILL: So, you have made sweet work here, my little mischief,
Look your Lady be kind and good-natured now, or
I shall have but a Cursed Bargain on't.

Ang. *turns towards them.*

– The Rogue's bred up to mischief,
Art thou so great a Fool to credit him?
ANG: Yes, I do; and you in vain impose upon me.
– Come hither, Boy, – Is not this he you spoke of?
HELL: I think – it is; I cannot swear, but I vow he has just such another lying Lover's look.

Hell. *looks in his face, he gazes on her.*

WILL: Hah! do not I know that face? –
By Heaven, my little Gipsy! what a dull Dog was I?
Had I but looked that way, I'd known her.
Are all my hopes of a new Woman banished? [*Aside.*
– Egad, if I don't fit thee for this, hang me.[109]
– Madam, I have found out the Plot.
HELL: Oh Lord, what does he say? am I discovered now?
WILL: Do you see this young Spark here? –
HELL: He'll tell her who I am.
WILL: – Who do you think this is?
HELL: Ay, ay, he does know me – Nay, dear Captain! I am undone if you discover me.
WILL: Nay, nay, no cogging; she shall know what a precious Mistress I have.
HELL: Will you be such a Devil?
WILL: Nay, nay, I'll teach you to spoil sport you will not make. – this small Ambassador comes not from a Person of Quality, as you Imagine, and he says; but from a very Errant Gipsy, the talking'st, prating'st, canting'st little Animal thou ever saw'st.

Notes

[109] *fit* punish.

ANG: What news you tell me! that's the thing I mean.

HELL: Would I were well off the place, if ever I go a Captain-hunting again. – [*Aside.*

WILL: Mean that thing? that Gipsy thing? thou may'st as well be jealous of thy Monkey or Parrot as of her: a *German* Motion[110] were worth a dozen of her, and a Dream were a better enjoyment, a Creature of a Constitution fitter for Heaven than Man.

HELL: Though I'm sure he lies, yet this vexes me. [*Aside.*

ANG: You are mistaken; she's a Spanish Woman
Made up of no such dull Materials.

WILL: Materials! Egad, and she be made of any that will either dispense or admit of Love, I'll be bound to continence.

HELL: Unreasonable Man, do you think so? [*Aside to him.*

WILL: You may Return, my little Brazen Head, and tell your Lady, that till she be handsome enough to be beloved, or I dull enough to be Religious, there will be small hopes of me.

ANG: Did you not promise then to marry her?

WILL: Not I, by Heaven.

ANG: You cannot undeceive my fears and torments, till you have vowed you will not marry her.

HELL: If he Swears that, he'll be revenged on me indeed for all my Rogueries.

ANG: I know what Arguments you'll bring against me, Fortune and Honour. –

WILL: Honour, I tell you, I hate it in your Sex, and those that fancy themselves possessed of that Foppery, are the most impertinently troublesome of all Womankind, and will transgress Nine Commandments to keep one, and to satisfy your Jealousy I swear –

HELL: Oh, no swearing, dear Captain – [*Aside to him.*

WILL: If it were possible I should ever be inclined to marry, it should be some kind young Sinner, one that has generosity enough to give a favour handsomely to one that can ask it discreetly, one that has Wit enough to Manage an intrigue of Love – oh, how civil such a Wench is, to a Man that does her the Honour to marry her.

ANG: By Heaven, there's no Faith in anything he says.

Enter Sebastian.

SEBAST: Madam, *Don Antonio* –

ANG: Come hither.

HELL: Ha, *Antonio!* he may be coming hither, and he'll certainly discover me. I'll therefore retire without a Ceremony. [*Exit* Hellena.

ANG: I'll see him, get my Coach ready.

SEBAST: It waits you, Madam.

WILL: This is lucky: what, Madam, now I may be gone and leave you to the enjoyment of my Rival?

ANG: Dull man, that canst not see how Ill, how poor
That false dissimulation looks – be gone,
And never let me see thy Cozening Face again,
Lest I relapse and kill thee.

WILL: Yes, you can spare me now, – farewell till you're in better Humour – I'm glad of this release – Now for my Gipsy:
For though to worse we change, yet still we find
New Joys, new Charms, in a new Miss that's kind. [*Ex.* Will.

Notes

110 *Motion* puppet.

ANG: He's gone, and in this Ague of My Soul
The Shivering fit returns,
Oh with what willing haste he took his leave,
As if the longed for Minute were arrived,
Of some blessed assignation.
In vain I have Consulted all my Charms
In vain this Beauty prized, in vain believed
My Eyes could kindle any lasting Fires.
I had forgot my Name, my Infamy,
And the reproach that Honour lays on those
That dare pretend a sober passion here.
Nice reputation, though it leave behind
More Virtues than inhabit where that dwells,
Yet that once gone, those Virtues shine no more.
– Then since I am not fit to be beloved,
I am resolved to think on a revenge
On him that soothed me thus to my undoing. [*Exeunt.*

Scene III. *A Street.*

Enter Florinda *and* Valeria *in Habits different from what they have been seen in.*

FLOR: We're happily escaped, and yet I tremble still.

VAL: A Lover and fear! whe, I am but half a one, and yet I have Courage for any attempt. Would *Hellena* were here, I would fain have had her as deep in this Mischief as we; she'll fare but ill else I doubt.[111]

FLOR: She pretended a Visit to the *Augustine* Nuns,[112] but I believe some other design carried her out; pray Heaven we light on her. – Prithee what didst do with *Callis*?

VAL: When I saw no reason would do good on her, I followed her into the Wardrobe, and as she was looking for something in a great Chest, I toppled her in by the heels, snatched the Key of the Apartment where you were confined, locked her in, and left her bawling for help.

FLOR: 'Tis well you resolve to follow my Fortunes, for thou darest never appear at home again after such an action.

VAL: That's according as the young Stranger and I shall agree – but to our business – I delivered your Letter, your Note to *Belvile*, when I got out under pretence of going to Mass, I found him at his Lodging, and believe me it came seasonably; for never was Man in so desperate a Condition. I told him of your resolution of making your Escape today, if your Brother would be absent long enough to permit you; if not, to die rather than be *Antonio*'s.

FLOR: Thou shouldst have told him I was confined to my chamber upon my Brother's suspicion, that the business on the *Molo* was a Plot laid between him and I.

VAL: I said all this, and told him your Brother was now gone to his Devotion, and he resolves to visit every Church till he find him; and not only undeceive him in that, but caress[113] him so as shall delay his return home.

FLOR: Oh Heavens! he's here, and *Belvile* with him too.

Notes

111 *doubt* believe.

112 *Augustine Nuns* members of a female monastery.

113 *caress* treat with kindness.

They put on their Vizards.

Enter Don Pedro, Belvile, Willmore; Belvile *and* Don Pedro *seeming in serious discourse.*

VAL: Walk boldly by them, I'll come at distance, lest he suspect us.

She walks by them, and looks back on them.

WILL: Ha! a Woman, and of an Excellent Mien.

PED: She throws a kind look back on you.

WILL: Death, 'tis a likely Wench, and that kind look shall not be cast away – I'll follow her.

BELV: Prithee do not.

WILL: Do not! By Heavens to the Antipodes, with such an invitation.

She goes out, and Will. *follows her.*

BELV: 'Tis a mad Fellow for a Wench.

Enter Fred.

FRED: Oh Col., such News.

BELV: Prithee what?

FRED: News that will make you laugh in spite of Fortune.

BELV: What, *Blunt* has had some Damned Trick put upon him, Cheated, Banged, or Clapped?

FRED: Cheated, Sir, rarely Cheated of all but his Shirt & Drawers; the unconscionable Whore too turned him out before Consummation, so that traversing the Streets at Midnight, the Watch found him in this *Fresco*, and conducted him home: By Heaven 'tis such a sight, and yet I durst as well been hanged as laughed at him, or pity him; he beats all that do but ask him a question, and is in such an Humour.

PED: Who is't has met with this Ill usage, Sir?

BELV: A Friend of ours, whom you must see for mirth's sake. I'll employ him to give *Florinda* time for an escape. [*Aside.*

PED: What is he?

BELV: A Young Countryman of ours, one that has been Educated at so plentiful a rate, he yet ne'er knew the want of Money, and 'twill be a great Jest to see how simply he'll look without it. For my part I'll lend him none, and the Rogue knows not how to put on a Borrowing face, and ask first. I'll let him see how good 'tis to play our parts whilst I play his – prithee, *Fred.* do go home and keep him in that posture till we come. [*Exeunt.*

Enter Florinda *from the farther end of the Scene, looking behind her.*

FLOR: I am followed still – hah – my Brother too advancing this way, good Heavens defend me from being seen by him.

She goes off.

Enter Willmore, *and after him* Valeria, *at a little distance.*

WILL: Ah! There she sails; she looks back as she were willing to be boarded; I'll warrant her Prize.[114] [*He goes out,* Valeria *following.*

Notes

[114] *warrant her Prize* be sure of the value of her treasure.

Enter Hellena, *just as he goes out, with a Page.*

HELL: Hah, is not that my Captain that has a Woman in chase? – 'tis not *Angellica*. Boy, follow those people at a distance, and bring me an account where they go in, – I'll find his haunts, and plague him everywhere, – ha – my Brother! –

Exit Page.

Bel. Wil. Ped. *cross the Stage:* Hell. *runs off.*

Scene changes to another Street. Enter Florinda.

FLOR: What shall I do, my Brother now pursues me.
Will no kind Power protect me from his tyranny?
– Hah, here's a door open, I'll venture in, since nothing can be worse than to fall into his hands; my life and honour are at stake, and my Necessity has no choice.

She goes in.

Enter Valeria, *and* Hellena's *Page peeping after* Florinda.

PAG: Here she went in, I shall remember this house. [*Exit Boy.*

VAL: This is *Belvile*'s Lodgings; she's gone in as readily as if she knew it, – hah – here's that Mad Fellow again, I dare not venture in, – I'll watch my opportunity.

Goes aside.

Enter Willmore, *gazing about him.*

WILL: I have lost her hereabouts – Pox on't, she must not scape me so.

Goes out.

Scene changes to Blunt's *Chamber, discovers him sitting on a Couch in his Shirt and Drawers, reading.*

BLUNT: So, now my mind's a little at peace, since I have resolved revenge – A Pox on this Tailor though, for not bringing home the Clothes I bespoke; and a Pox of all poor Cavaliers, a Man can never keep a spare Suit for 'em; and I shall have these Rogues come in and find me naked; and then I'm undone; but I'm resolved to arm myself – the Rascals shall not insult over me too much.

Puts on an old rusty Sword and Buff-belt.

– Now, how like a Morris Dancer[115] I am Equipped – a fine Lady-like Whore to Cheat me thus, without affording me a kindness for my Money, a Pox light on her, I shall never be reconciled to the Sex more, she has made me as faithless as a Physician, as uncharitable as a Churchman, and as ill-natured as a Poet. O how I'll use all womankind hereafter! what would I give to have one of 'em within my reach now! any Mortal thing in Petticoats, kind Fortune, send me! and I'll forgive thy last night's Malice – Here's a Cursed Book too (a warning to all young Travellers) that can instruct me how to prevent such Mischiefs now 'tis too late. Well 'tis a rare convenient thing to read a little now and then, as well as Hawk and Hunt.

Notes

[115] *Morris Dancer* traditional English dancer wearing a costume with bells and ribbons.

Sits down again and Reads.

Enter to him Florinda.

FLOR: This House is haunted sure; 'tis well furnished and no living thing inhabits it – hah – a Man! Heavens how he's attired! sure 'tis some Rope-dancer, or Fencing-master; I tremble now for fear, and yet I must venture now to speak to him – Sir, if I may not interrupt your Meditations –

He starts up and gazes.

BLUNT: Hah – what's here? are my wishes granted? and is not that a she Creature? 'Adsheartlikins 'tis! what wretched thing art thou? – hah!

FLOR: Charitable Sir, you've told yourself already what I am; a very wretched Maid, forced by a strange unlucky accident, to seek a safety here, and must be ruined, if you do not grant it.

BLUNT: Ruined! Is there any ruin so inevitable as that which now threatens thee? dost thou know, miserable Woman, into what Den of Mischiefs thou art fallen? what abyss of Confusion? – hah! – dost not see something in my looks that frights thy guilty Soul, and makes thee wish to change that shape of Woman for any humble Animal, or Devil? for those were safer for thee, and less mischievous.

FLOR: Alas, what mean you, Sir? I must confess, your looks have something in 'em makes me fear; but I beseech you, as you seem a Gentleman, pity a harmless Virgin, that takes your house for Sanctuary.

BLUNT: Talk on, talk on, and weep too, till my Faith return. Do, flatter me out of my Senses again – a harmless Virgin with a Pox, as much one as t'other, 'adsheartlikins. Whe, what the Devil can I not be safe in my House for you? not in my Chamber? nay, even being naked too cannot secure me. This is an Impudence greater than has invaded me yet – Come, no resistance.

Pulls her rudely.

FLOR: Dare you be so cruel?

BLUNT: Cruel, 'adsheartlikins as a Galley slave, or a *Spanish* Whore: Cruel, yes, I will kiss and beat thee all over; kiss, and see thee all over; thou shalt lie with me too, not that I care for the enjoyment, but to let you see I have ta'en deliberated Malice to thee, and will be revenged on one Whore for the Sins of another; I will smile and deceive thee, flatter thee, and beat thee, kiss and swear, and lie to thee, embrace thee and rob thee, as she did me, fawn on thee, and strip thee stark naked, then hang thee out at my window by the heels, with a Paper of scurvy Verses fastened to thy breast, in praise of damnable women – Come, come along.

FLOR: Alas, Sir, must I be sacrificed for the Crimes of the most infamous of my Sex? I never understood[116] the sins you name.

BLUNT: Do, persuade the Fool you Love him, or that one of you can be just or honest; tell me I was not an easy Coxcomb, or any strange impossible tale: it will be believed sooner than thy false Showers or Protestations. A generation of damned Hypocrites, to flatter my very Clothes from my Back! dissembling Witches! are these the returns you make an honest Gentleman that trusts, believes, and loves you? – but if I be not even with you – Come along – or I shall –

Notes

[116] *understood* was familiar with.

Pulls her again.

Enter Frederick.

FRED: Hah, what's here to do?

BLUNT: 'Adsheartlikins, *Fred*. I am glad thou art come, to be a witness of my dire Revenge.

FRED: What's this, a Person of Quality too, who is upon the ramble to supply the defects of some grave impotent Husband?

BLUNT: No, this has another Pretence, some very unfortunate accident brought her hither, to save a life pursued by I know not who, or why, and forced to take sanctuary here at Fool's Haven. 'Adsheartlikins to me of all Mankind for protection? Is the Ass to be Cajoled again, think ye? No, young one, no Prayers or Tears shall mitigate my rage; therefore prepare for both my pleasures of enjoyment and revenge, for I am resolved to make up my loss here on thy body; I'll take it out in kindness and in beating.

FRED: Now, Mistress of mine, what do you think of this?

FLOR: I think he will not – dares not be so barbarous.

FRED: Have a care, *Blunt*; she fetched a deep sigh; she is enamoured with thy Shirt and Drawers; she'll strip thee even of that. There are of her calling such unconscionable Baggages, and such dexterous Thieves, they'll flay a man, and he shall ne'er miss his skin, till he feels the cold. There was a Countryman of ours Robbed of a Row of Teeth whilst he was sleeping, which the Jilt made him buy again when he waked – you see, Lady, how little reason we have to trust you.

BLUNT: 'Adsheartlikins, whe, this is most abominable.

FLOR: Some such Devils there may be, but by all that's holy I am none such, I entered here to save a Life in danger.

BLUNT: For no goodness I'll warrant her.

FRED: Faith, Damsel, you had e'en confess the plain truth, for we are fellows not to be caught twice in the same Trap: look on that Wreck, a tight Vessel when he set out of Haven, well Trimmed and Laden, and see how a Female Piccaroon of this Island of Rogues has shattered him, and canst thou hope for any Mercy?

BLUNT: No, no, Gentlewoman, come along; 'adsheartlikins we must be better acquainted – we'll both lie with her, and then let me alone to bang her.

FRED: I am ready to serve you in matters of Revenge: that has a double pleasure in't.

BLUNT: Well said. You hear, little one, how you are condemned by public Vote to the Bed within, there's no resisting your Destiny, sweetheart.

Pulls her.

FLOR: Stay, Sir, I have seen you with *Belvile*, an *English* Cavalier; for his sake use me kindly; you know him, Sir.

BLUNT: *Belvile!* whe, yes, sweeting, we do know *Belvile*, and wish he were with us now; he's a Cormorant at Whore and Bacon; he'd have a Limb or two of thee, my Virgin Pullet: but 'tis no matter; we'll leave him the bones to pick.

FLOR: Sir, if you have any Esteem for that *Belvile*, I conjure you to treat me with more gentleness; he'll thank you for the Justice.

FRED: Hark ye, *Blunt*, I doubt we are mistaken in this Matter.

FLOR: Sir, If you find me not worth *Belvile*'s care, use me as you please; and that you may think I merit better treatment than you threaten – pray take this present – [*Gives him a Ring: He looks on it.*

BLUNT: Hum – a Diamond! whe, 'tis a wonderful Virtue now that lies in this Ring, a mollifying Virtue; 'adsheartlikins there's more persuasive Rhetoric in't, than all her Sex can utter.

FRED: I begin to suspect something; and 'twould anger us vilely to be trussed up[117] for a rape upon a Maid of quality, when we only believe we ruffle a Harlot.

BLUNT: Thou art a credulous Fellow, but 'adsheartlikins I have no Faith yet; whe, my Saint prattled as parlously[118] as this does; she gave me a Bracelet too; a Devil on her: but I sent my Man to sell it today for Necessaries, and it proved as counterfeit as her Vows of Love.

FRED: However let it reprieve her till we see *Belvile.*

BLUNT: That's hard, yet I will grant it.

Enter a Servant.

SERV: Oh, Sir, the Colonel is just come with his new Friend and a *Spaniard* of Quality, and talks of having you to Dinner with 'em.

BLUNT: 'Adsheartlikins, I'm undone – I would not see 'em for the World: Hark ye, *Fred.*, lock up the Wench in your Chamber.

FRED: Fear nothing, Madam, whate'er he threatens, you are safe whilst in my Hands. [*Ex.* Fred. *and* Flor.

BLUNT: And, Sirrah – upon your life, say – I am not at home, – or that I am asleep – or – or anything – away – I'll prevent them coming this way.

Locks the Door and Exeunt.

ACT V.

Scene I. *Blunt's Chamber.*

After a great knocking as at his Chamber-door, enter Blunt *softly, crossing the Stage in his Shirt and Drawers, as before.*

[VOICES] *Ned, Ned Blunt, Ned Blunt.* [*Call within.*

BLUNT: The Rogues are up in Arms, 'adsheartlikins, this Villainous *Frederick* has betrayed me, they have heard of my blessed Fortune.

Ned Blunt, Ned, Ned – [*and knocking within.*

BELV: Whe, he's dead, Sir, without dispute dead; he has not been seen today; let's break open the door – here – Boy –

BLUNT: Ha, break open the door! 'adsheartlikins that mad Fellow will be as good as his word.

BELV: Boy, bring something to force the door.

A great noise within at the door again.

BLUNT: So, now must I speak in my own defence, I'll try what Rhetoric will do – hold – hold, what do you mean, Gentlemen, what do you mean?

BELV: Oh Rogue, art alive? prithee open the door and convince us.

BLUNT: Yes, I am alive, Gentlemen – but at present a little busy.

BELV: How! *Blunt* grown a Man of business! come, come, open, and let's see this Miracle. [*within.*

BLUNT: No, no, no, no, Gentlemen, 'tis no great business – but – I am – at – my Devotion – 'adsheartlikins, will you not allow a Man time to Pray?

Notes

[117] *trussed up* strung up; hanged.

[118] *parlously* shrewdly; cunningly.

Belv: Turned religious! a greater wonder than the first; therefore open quickly, or we shall unhinge, we shall. [*within.*

Blunt: This won't do – whe, hark ye, Col.; to tell you the plain truth, I am about a necessary affair of life – I have a wench with me – you apprehend me? the Devil's in't if they be so uncivil as to disturb me now.

Will: How, a Wench! Nay, then we must enter and partake; no resistance, – unless it be your Lady of Quality, and then we'll keep our distance.

Blunt: So, the business is out.

Will: Come, come, lend more hands to the Door, – now heave altogether – so, well done, my Boys – [*Breaks open the Door.*

Enter Belvile, Willmore, Fred. Pedro *and* Belvile's *Page:*
Blunt *looks simply;*[119] *they all laugh at him; he lays his hand on his Sword, and comes up*[120] *to* Willmore.

Blunt: Hark ye, Sir, laugh out your laugh quickly, d'ye hear, and be gone, I shall spoil your sport else; 'adsheartlikins, Sir, I shall – the Jest has been carried on too long – a plague upon my Tailor – [*Aside.*

Will: 'Sdeath, how the Whore has dressed him! Faith, Sir, I'm sorry.

Blunt: Are you so, Sir? keep't to yourself then, Sir, I advise you, d'ye hear? for I can as little endure your pity as his Mirth. [*Lays his Hand on's Sword.*

Belv: Indeed, *Willmore*, thou wert a little too rough with *Ned Blunt*'s Mistress; call a Person of Quality whore, and one so young, so handsome, and so Eloquent! – ha, ha, he. –

Blunt: Hark ye, Sir, you know me, and know I can be angry; have a care – for 'adsheartlikins I can fight too – I can, Sir, – do you mark me – no more –

Belv: Why so peevish, good *Ned?* some disappointments, I'll warrant – what! did the Jealous Count her Husband return just in the nick?

Blunt: Or the Devil, Sir, – d'ye laugh? [*They laugh.*] Look ye, settle me a good sober countenance, and that quickly too, or you shall know *Ned Blunt* is not –

Belv: Not Everybody, we know that.

Blunt: Not an Ass to be laughed at, Sir.

Will: Unconscionable Sinner, to bring a Lover so near his happiness, a vigorous passionate Lover, and then not only cheat him of his moveables, but his very desires too.

Belv: Ah! Sir, a Mistress is a trifle with *Blunt*, he'll have a dozen the next time he looks abroad; his Eyes have Charms not to be resisted: There needs no more than to expose that taking Person to the view of the Fair, and he leads 'em all in Triumph.

Ped: Sir, though I'm a stranger to you, I'm ashamed at the rudeness of my Nation; and could you learn who did it, would assist you to make an Example of 'em.

Blunt: Whe, ay, there's one speaks Sense now, and handsomely; and let me tell you Gentlemen, I should not have showed myself like a Jack-Pudding,[121] thus to have made you Mirth, but that I have revenge within my power; for know, I have got into my possession a Female, who had better have fallen under any Curse, than the ruin I design her: 'adsheartlikins, she assaulted me here in my own Lodgings, and had doubtless committed a Rape upon me, had not this Sword defended me.

Fred: I knew not that, but O' my conscience thou hadst ravished her, had she not redeemed herself with a Ring – let's see't, *Blunt*.

Notes

[119] *simply* stupidly; abashedly.

[120] *conies up* sidles up timidly.

[121] *Jack-Pudding* clown; buffoon.

Blunt *shows the Ring.*

Belv: Hah! – the Ring I gave *Florinda* when we exchanged our Vows! – hark ye, *Blunt* – [*Goes to whisper to him.*

Will: No whispering, good Colonel, there's a Woman in the case, no whispering.

Belv: Hark ye, Fool, be advised, and conceal both the Ring and the Story, for your Reputation's sake; don't let people know what despised Cullies we *English* are: to be cheated and abused by one Whore, and another rather bribe thee than be kind to thee, is an Infamy to our Nation.

Will: Come, come, where's the Wench? we'll see her; let her be what she will, we'll see her.

Ped: Ay, ay, let us see her; I can soon discover whether she be of quality, or for your diversion.

Blunt: She's in *Fred's* Custody.

Will: Come, come, the Key.

To Fred. *who gives him the Key, they are going.*

Belv: Death! what shall I do? – Stay, Gentlemen – yet if I hinder 'em, I shall discover all – hold, let's go one at once – give me the Key.

Will: Nay, hold there, Colonel, I'll go first.

Fred: Nay, no Dispute, *Ned* and I have the propriety of her.

Will: Damn Propriety – then we'll draw cuts. [Belv. *goes to whisper* Will.] nay, no corruption, good Colonel: come, the longest Sword carries her. –

They all draw, forgetting Don Pedro, *being a Spaniard, had the longest.*

Blunt: I yield up my interest to you Gentlemen, and that will be revenge sufficient.

Will: The Wench is yours – [*To* Ped.] Pox of his *Toledo*,[122] I had forgot that.

Fred: Come, Sir, I'll conduct you to the Lady.

Ex: Fred. *and* Ped.

Belv: To hinder him will certainly discover her – [*Aside.*] Dost know, Dull beast, what mischief thou hast done?

Will. *walking up and down out of Humour.*

Will: Ay, ay, to trust our Fortune to Lots, a Devil on't; 'twas madness, that's the truth on't.

Belv: Oh intolerable Sot! –

Enter Florinda, *running masked,* Pedro *after her,* Will. *gazing round her.*

Flor: Good Heaven, defend me from discovery. [*Aside.*

Pedro: 'Tis but in vain to fly me; you are fallen to my Lot.

Belv: Sure she is undiscovered yet, but now I fear there is no way to bring her off.

Will: Whe, what a Pox is not this my woman, the same I followed but now?

[Ped. *talking to* Florinda, *who walks up and down.*

Ped: As if I did not know ye, and your business here.

Flor: Good Heaven! I fear he does indeed – [*Aside.*

Ped: Come, pray be kind, I know you meant to be so when you entered here, for these are proper Gentlemen.

Notes

[122] *Toledo* a sword made at Toledo, Spain.

WILL: But, Sir – perhaps the Lady will not be imposed upon, She'll choose her Man.

PED: I am better bred, than not to leave her choice free.

Enter Valeria, *and is surprised at the sight of* Don Pedro.

VAL: *Don Pedro* here! there's no avoiding him. [*Aside.*

FLOR: *Valeria!* then I'm undone – [*Aside.*

VAL: Oh! have I found you, Sir – [*To* Pedro, *running to him.*] – the strangest accident – if I had breath – to tell it.

PED: Speak – is *Florinda* safe? *Hellena* well?

VAL: Ay, Ay, Sir – *Florinda* – is safe – from any fears of you.

PED: Why, where's *Florinda?* – speak –

VAL: Ay, where indeed, Sir? I wish I could inform you, – but to hold you no longer in doubt –

FLOR: Oh, what will she say! [*Aside.*

VAL: She's fled away in the habit – of one of her Pages, Sir – but *Callis* thinks you may retrieve her yet, if you make haste away; she'll tell you, Sir, the rest – if you can find her out. [*Aside.*

PED: Dishonourable Girl, she has undone my Aim – Sir – you see my necessity of leaving you, and I hope you'll Pardon it: my Sister, I know, will make her flight to you; and if she do, I shall Expect she should be rendered back.

BELV: I shall consult my Love and Honour, Sir. [*Exit* Ped.

FLOR: My dear Preserver, let me embrace thee. [*To* Val.

WILL: What the Devil's all this?

BLUNT: Mystery by this light.

VAL: Come, come, make haste and get yourselves married quickly, for your Brother will return again.

BELV: I am so surprised with fears and joys, so amazed to find you here in safety, I can scarce persuade my heart into a faith of what I see –

WILL: Hark ye, Colonel, is this that Mistress who has cost you so many sighs, and me so many quarrels with you?

BELV: It is – pray give him the honour of your hand. [*To* Flor.

WILL: Thus it must be received then. [*Kneels and kisses her hand.*] And with it give your Pardon too.

FLOR: The Friend to *Belvile* may command me anything.

WILL: Death, would I might, 'tis a surprising Beauty. [*Aside.*

BELV: Boy, run and fetch a Father instantly.

Exit Boy.

FRED: So, now do I stand like a Dog, and have not a syllable to plead my own Cause with: by this Hand, Madam, I was never thoroughly confounded before, nor shall I ever more dare look up with confidence, till you are pleased to Pardon me.

FLOR: Sir, I'll be reconciled to you on one condition, that you'll follow the Example of your Friend, in Marrying a Maid that does not hate you, and whose fortune (I believe) will not be unwelcome to you.

FRED: Madam, had I no Inclinations that way, I should obey your kind Commands.

BELV: Who, *Fred.* marry; he has so few inclinations for Womankind, that had he been possessed of Paradise, he might have continued there to this day, if no Crime but Love could have disinherited him.

FRED: Oh, I do not use to boast of my intrigues.

BELV: Boast! why thou dost nothing but boast; and I dare swear, wert thou as Innocent from the sin of the Grape, as thou art from the Apple, thou might'st yet claim that right in *Eden* which our first Parents lost by too much Loving.

FRED: I wish this Lady would think me so modest a man.

VAL: She would be sorry then, and not like you half so well, and I should be loath to break my word with you; which was, That if your Friend and mine are agreed, it should be a Match between you and I.

She gives him her hand.

FRED: Bear witness, Colonel, 'tis a Bargain.

Kisses her hand.

BLUNT: I have a Pardon to beg too; but 'adsheartlikins I am so out of Countenance, that I am a Dog if I can say anything to Purpose. [*To* Florinda.

FLOR: Sir, I heartily forgive you all.

BLUNT: That's nobly said, sweet Lady – *Belvile*, prithee present her her Ring again, for I find I have not Courage to approach her myself.

Gives him the Ring; he gives it to Florinda.

Enter Boy.

BOY: Sir, I have brought the Father that you sent for.

BELV: 'Tis well, and now my dear *Florinda*, let's fly to complete that mighty joy we have so long wished and sighed for: – Come, *Fred.* – you'll follow?

FRED: Your Example, Sir, 'twas ever my ambition in War, and must be so in Love.

WILL: And must not I see this juggling knot tied?[123]

BELV: No, thou shalt do us better service, and be our Guard, lest *Don Pedro*'s sudden return interrupt the Ceremony.

WILL: Content – I'll secure this pass.

Ex: Bel. Flor. Fred. *and* Val.

Enter Boy.

BOY: Sir, there's a Lady without would speak to you. [*To* Will.

WILL: Conduct her in; I dare not quit my Post.

BOY: And, Sir, your Tailor waits you in your Chamber.

BLUNT: Some comfort yet; I shall not dance naked at the Wedding.

Ex: Blunt *and* Boy.

Enter again the Boy, conducting in Angellica *in a Masquing Habit and a Vizard,* Will. *runs to her.*

WILL: This can be none but my pretty Gipsy – Oh, I see you can follow as well as fly – Come, confess thyself the most malicious Devil in Nature, you think you have done my business with *Angellica*. –

ANG: Stand off, base Villain –

She draws a Pistol and holds it to his Breast.

WILL: Hah, 'tis not she: who art thou? and what's thy business?

ANG: One thou hast injured, and who comes to kill thee for't.

Notes

[123] *This juggling Knot tied* this cheating, deceiving marriage made.

WILL: What the Devil canst thou mean?
ANG: By all my hopes to kill thee –

Holds still the Pistol to his Breast, he going back, she following still.

WILL: Prithee on what acquaintance? for I know thee not.
ANG: Behold this face! – so lost to thy remembrance,
And then call all thy sins about thy Soul,
And let 'em die with thee. [*Pulls off her Vizard.*
WILL: *Angellica!*
ANG: Yes, Traitor.
Does not thy guilty blood run shivering through thy Veins?
Hast thou no horror at this sight, that tells thee,
Thou hast not long to boast thy shameful Conquest?
WILL: Faith, no Child, my blood keeps its old Ebbs and Flows still, and that usual heat too, that could oblige thee with a kindness, had I but opportunity.
ANG: Devil! dost wanton with my pain – have at thy heart.
WILL: Hold, dear Virago! hold thy hand a little, I am not now at leisure to be killed – hold and hear me – Death, I think she's in earnest. [*Aside.*
ANG: Oh if I take not heed,
My coward heart will leave me to his mercy. [*Aside, turning from him.*
– What have you, Sir, to say? – but should I hear thee,
Thoud'st talk away all that is brave about me:

Follows him with the Pistol to his Breast.

And I have vowed thy death, by all that's Sacred.
WILL: Whe, then there's an end of a proper handsome Fellow, that might have lived to have done good service yet: – That's all I can say to't.
ANG: Yet – I would give thee – time for – penitence. [*Pausingly.*
WILL: Faith, Child, I thank God, I have ever took care to lead a good, sober, hopeful Life, and am of a Religion that teaches me to believe, I shall depart in peace.
ANG: So will the Devil! tell me
How many poor believing Fools thou hast undone,
How many Hearts thou hast betrayed to ruin!
– Yet these are little mischiefs to the Ills
Thou'st taught mine to commit: thou'st taught it Love.
WILL: Egad, 'twas shrewdly hurt the while.
ANG: – Love, that has robbed it of its unconcern,
Of all that Pride that taught me how to value it,
And in its room a mean submissive Passion was conveyed,
That made me humbly bow, which I ne'er did
To anything but Heaven.
– Thou, perjured Man, didst this, and with thy Oaths,
Which on thy Knees, thou didst devoutly make,
Softened my yielding heart – And then, I was a slave –
Yet still had been content to've worn my Chains:
Worn 'em with vanity and joy forever,
Hadst thou not broke those Vows that put them on.
– 'Twas then I was undone.

All this while follows him with a Pistol to his Breast.

WILL: Broke my Vows! whe, where hast thou lived?
Amongst the Gods? for I never heard of mortal Man,
That has not broke a thousand Vows.

ANG: Oh, Impudence!

WILL: *Angellica*! that Beauty has been too long tempting,
Not to have made a thousand Lovers languish,
Who in the Amorous Favour, no doubt have sworn
Like me; did they all die in that Faith? still Adoring?
I do not think they did.

ANG: No, faithless Man: had I repaid their Vows, as I did thine, I would have killed the ungrateful that had abandoned me.

WILL: This old General has quite spoiled thee; nothing makes a Woman so vain, as being flattered; your old Lover ever supplies the defects of Age, with intolerable Dotage, vast Charge, and that which you call Constancy; and attributing all this to your own Merits, you domineer, and throw your Favours in's Teeth, upbraiding him still with the defects of Age, and Cuckold him as often as he deceives your Expectations. But the Gay, Young, Brisk Lover, that brings his equal Fires, and can give you dart for dart, he'll be as nice[124] as you sometimes.

ANG: All this thou'st made me know, for which I hate thee.
Had I remained in innocent security,
I should have thought all men were born my slaves;
And worn my power like lightning in my Eyes,
To have destroyed at pleasure when offended:
– But when Love held the Mirror, the undeceiving Glass
Reflected all the weakness of my Soul, and made me know,
My richest treasure being lost, my Honour,
All the remaining spoil could not be worth
The Conqueror's Care or Value.
– Oh how I fell like a long worshipped Idol,
Discovering all the Cheat.
Would not the Incense and rich Sacrifice,
Which blind Devotion offered at my Altars,
Have fall'n to thee?
Why wouldst thou then destroy my fancied power?

WILL: By Heaven thou'rt brave, and I admire thee strangely.
I wish I were that dull, that constant thing,
Which thou wouldst have, and Nature never meant me:
I must, like cheerful Birds, sing in all Groves,
And perch on every Bough,
Billing the next kind she that flies to meet me,
Yet after all could build my Nest with thee,
Thither repairing when I'd loved my round,
And still reserve a tributary Flame.
– To gain your credit, I'll pay you back your Charity,
And be obliged for nothing but for Love.

Notes

[124] *nice* precise; accurate; deadly.

Offers her a Purse of Gold.

ANG: Oh that thou wert in earnest!
So mean a thought of me,
Would turn my rage to scorn, and I should pity thee,
And give thee leave to live,
Which for the public safety of our Sex,
And my own private Injuries, I dare not do.
Prepare –

Follows still, as before.

– I will no more be tempted with replies.
WILL: Sure –
ANG: Another word will damn thee! I've heard thee talk too long.

She follows him with a Pistol ready to shoot: he retires still amazed.
Enter Don Antonio, *his Arm in a Scarf, and lays hold on the Pistol.*

ANT: Hah! *Angellica*!
ANG: *Antonio*! what Devil brought thee hither?
ANT: Love and Curiosity, seeing your Coach at door. Let me disarm you of this unbecoming instrument of death – [*Takes away the Pistol.*] Amongst the Number of your slaves, was there not one worthy the Honour to have fought your quarrel?
– Who are you, Sir, that are so very wretched
To merit death from her?
WILL: One, Sir, that could have made a better End of an Amorous quarrel without you, than with you.
ANT: Sure 'tis some Rival, – hah – the very Man took down her Picture yesterday – the very same that set on me last night – blessed opportunity –

Offers to shoot him.

ANG: Hold, you're mistaken, Sir.
ANT: By Heaven the very same!
– Sir, what pretensions have you to this Lady?
WILL: Sir, I do not use to be Examined, and am ill at all disputes but this –

Draws; Anton. *offers to shoot.*

ANG: Oh, hold! you see he's Armed with certain death:
To Will.
– And you, *Antonio*, I command you hold,
By all the Passion you've so lately vowed me.

Enter Don Pedro, *sees Antonio, and stays.*

PED: Hah, *Antonio*! and *Angellica*! [*Aside.*
ANT: When I refuse obedience to your Will,
May you destroy me with your Mortal hate.
By all that's Holy I Adore you so,
That even my Rival, who has Charms enough
To make him fall a Victim to my jealousy,
Shall live, nay, and have leave to love on still.
PED: What's this I hear? [*Aside.*
ANG: Ah thus! 'twas thus he talked, and I believed. [*Pointing to* Will.

– *Antonio*, yesterday,
I'd not have sold my Interest in his heart,
For all the Sword has won and lost in Battle.
– But now to show my utmost of contempt,
I give thee Life – which if thou wouldst preserve,
Live where my Eyes may never see thee more,
Live to undo someone, whose Soul may prove

Goes out; Ant. *follows, but* Ped. *pulls him back.*

PED: *Antonio* – stay.
ANT: *Don Pedro* –
PED: What Coward fear was that prevented thee
From meeting me this morning on the *Molo*?
ANT: Meet thee?
PED: Yes me; I was the Man that dared thee to't.
ANT: Hast thou so often seen me fight in War,
To find no better Cause to excuse my absence?
– I sent my Sword and one to do thee right,
Finding myself uncapable to use a Sword.
PED: But 'twas *Florinda*'s Quarrel that we fought,
And you to show how little you esteemed her,
Sent me your Rival, giving him your Interest.
– But I have found the cause of this affront,
But when I meet you fit for the dispute,
– I'll tell you my resentment.
ANT: I shall be ready, Sir, ere long to do you reason. [*Exit* Ant.
PED: If I could find *Florinda*, now whilst my anger's high, I think I should be kind, and give her to *Belvile* in revenge.
WILL: Faith, Sir, I know not what you would do, but I believe the Priest within has been so kind.
PED: How! my Sister Married?
WILL: I hope by this time she is, and bedded too, or he has not my longings about him.
PED: Dares he do thus? does he not fear my Power?
WILL: Faith, not at all. If you will go in, and thank him for the favour he has done your Sister, so; if not, Sir, my Power's greater in this house than yours; I have a damned surly Crew here, that will keep you till the next Tide, and then clap you on board for Prize; my Ship lies but a League off the *Molo*, and we shall show your Donship a damned *Tramontana* Rover's[125] Trick.

Enter Belvile.

BELV: This Rogue's in some new Mischief – hah, *Pedro* returned!
PED: Colonel *Belvile*, I hear you have Married my Sister.
BELV: You have heard truth then, Sir.
PED: Have I so? then, Sir, I wish you Joy.
BELV: How!
PED: By this embrace I do, and I am glad on't.

Notes

[125] *Tramontana Rover* a pirate from beyond the Alps; a non-Italian pirate.

Belv: Are you in earnest?

Ped: By our long Friendship and my obligations to thee, I am. The sudden Change I'll give you reasons for anon. Come lead me to my Sister, that she may know I now approve her choice. [*Exit* Bel. *with* Ped.

Will: *goes to follow them. Enter* Hellena *as before in Boy's Clothes, and pulls him back.*

Will: Ha! my Gipsy: – now a thousand blessings on thee for this kindness. Egad, Child, I was e'en in despair of ever seeing thee again; my Friends are all provided for within, each Man his kind woman.

Hell: Hah! I thought they had served me some such trick!

Will: And I was e'en resolved to go aboard, condemn myself to my lone Cabin, and the Thoughts of thee.

Hell: And could you have left me behind? would you have been so ill-natured?

Will: Whe, 'twould have broke my Heart, Child – but since we are met again, I defy foul weather to part us.

Hell: And would you be a Faithful Friend now, if a Maid should trust you?

Will: For a Friend I cannot promise, thou art of a form so Excellent, a Face and Humour too good for cold dull Friendship; I am parlously afraid of being in Love, Child, and you have not forgot how severely you have used me?

Hell: That's all one;[126] such Usage you must still look for, to find out all your Haunts, to rail at you to all that Love you, till I have made you love only me in your own defence, because nobody else will love.

Will: But hast thou no better quality to recommend thyself by?

Hell: Faith none, Captain: – Whe, 'twill be the greater Charity to take me for thy Mistress, I am a lone Child, a kind of Orphan Lover; and why I should die a Maid, and in a Captain's hands too, I do not understand.

Will: Egad, I was never clawed away with Broadsides from any Female before, thou hast one Virtue I Adore, good Nature; I hate a Coy demure Mistress; she's as troublesome as a Colt; I'll break none; no, give me a mad Mistress when Mewed, and in flying, one I dare trust upon the wing, that whilst she's kind will come to the Lure.[127]

Hell: Nay, as kind as you will, good Captain, whilst it lasts, but let's lose no time.

Will: My time's as precious to me, as thine can be; therefore, dear creature, since we are so well agreed, let's retire to my Chamber, and if ever thou were treated with such Savoury[128] Love! – come – my bed's prepared for such a guest, all clean and Sweet as thy fair self; I love to steal a Dish and a Bottle with a Friend, and hate long Graces – come, let's retire and fall to.

Hell: 'Tis but getting my consent, and the business is soon done; let but old Gaffer *Hymen* and his Priest say amen to't, and I dare lay my Mother's daughter by as proper a Fellow as your Father's Son, without fear or blushing.

Will: Hold, hold, no Bug[129] Words, Child, Priest and *Hymen*:[130] prithee add Hangman to 'em to make up the consort – no, no, we'll have no Vows but Love, Child, nor witness but the Lover; the kind Deity enjoins naught but Love! and enjoy! *Hymen* and Priest wait still upon Portion, and Jointure;[131] Love and Beauty have their own Ceremonies. Marriage is as certain a bane to Love, as lending Money is to Friendship: I'll neither

Notes

126 *That's all one* it doesn't matter now.

127 *mewed, flying,* and *lure* are terms of falconry meaning fastened to a perch; hunting; and the apparatus used to bring the bird back to the perch.

128 *savoury* pleasing.

129 *bug* pompous.

130 *Hymen* the god of marriage or marriage itself.

131 *Portion, and Jointure* legal terms in a marriage contract.

ask nor give a Vow, – though I could be content to turn Gipsy, and become a left-hand bridegroom,[132] to have the pleasure of working that great Miracle of making a Maid a Mother, if you durst venture; 'tis upse[133] Gipsy that, and if I miss, I'll lose my Labour.

HELL: And if you do not lose, what shall I get? a cradle full of noise and mischief, with a pack of repentance at my back? can you teach me to weave Inkle[134] to pass my time with? 'tis upse Gipsy that too.

WILL: I can teach thee to Weave a true love's knot better.

HELL: So can my dog.

WILL: Well, I see we are both upon our Guards, and I see there's no way to conquer good Nature, but by yielding, – here – give me thy hand – one kiss and I am thine –

HELL: One kiss! how like my Page he speaks; I am resolved you shall have none, for asking such a sneaking sum – he that will be satisfied with one kiss, will never die of that longing; good Friend single-kiss, is all your talking come to this? – a kiss, a caudle![135] farewell, Captain single-kiss.

Going out; he stays her.

WILL: Nay, if we part so, let me die like a bird upon a bough, at the Sheriff's charge. By Heaven, both the *Indies* shall not buy thee from me. I adore thy Humour and will marry thee, and we are so of one Humour, it must be a bargain – give me thy hand. – [*Kisses her hand.*

AND now let the blind ones (Love and Fortune) do their worst.

HELL: Why, God-a-mercy, Captain!

WILL: But hark ye – the bargain is now made; but is it not fit we should know each other's Names? that when we have reason to curse one another hereafter, and People ask me who 'tis I give to the Devil, I may at least be able to tell what Family you came of.

HELL: Good reason, Captain; and where I have cause (as I doubt not but I shall have plentiful) that I may know at whom to throw my – blessings – I beseech ye your Name.

WILL: I am called *Robert the Constant*.

HELL: A very fine name! pray was it your Falconer or Butler that Christened you? do they not use to Whistle when they call you?

WILL: I hope you have a better, that a man may name without crossing himself, you are so merry with mine.

HELL: I am called *Hellena the Inconstant*.

Enter Pedro, Belvile, Florinda, Fred. Valeria.

PED: Hah! *Hellena*!

FLOR: *Hellena*!

HELL: The very same – hah my Brother! now, Captain, show your Love and Courage; stand to your Arms, and defend me bravely, or I am lost Forever.

PED: What's this I hear? false Girl, how came you hither, and what's your business? Speak. [*Goes roughly to her.*

Notes

132 *Left-hand Bridegroom* one who does not gain property rights through marriage.

133 *upse* in the manner of.

134 *Inkle* linen tape; inkle weavers are proverbially intimate because the inkle looms are so narrow and close together (*OED*, s.v. *inkle-weaver*).

135 *caudle* a warm drink, chiefly for sick people.

WILL: Hold off, Sir, you have leave to parley only. [*Puts himself between.*

HELL: I had e'en as good tell it, as you guess it. Faith, Brother, my business is the same with all living Creatures of my Age, to love, and be beloved, and here's the Man.

PED: Perfidious Maid, hast thou deceived me too, deceived thyself and Heaven?

HELL: 'Tis time enough to make my Peace with that: Be you but kind, let me alone with Heaven.

PED: *Belvile,* I did not expect this false play from you; was't not enough you'd gain *Florinda* (which I pardoned) but your lewd Friends too must be enriched with the spoils of a noble Family?

BELV: Faith, Sir, I am as much surprised at this as you can be: Yet, Sir, my Friends are Gentlemen, and ought to be Esteemed for their Misfortunes, since they have the Glory to suffer with the best of Men and Kings; 'tis true, he's a Rover of Fortune, Yet a Prince aboard his little wooden World.

PED: What's this to the maintenance of a Woman of her Birth and Quality?

WILL: Faith, Sir, I can boast of nothing but a Sword which does me right where'er I come, and has defended a worse Cause than a Woman's: and since I loved her before I either knew her Birth or Name, I must pursue my resolution, and marry her.

PED: And is all your holy intent of becoming a Nun debauched into a desire of Man?

HELL: Why – I have considered the matter, Brother, and find the Three hundred thousand Crowns my Uncle left me (and you cannot keep from me) will be better laid out in Love than in Religion, and turn to as good an account, – let most voices carry it, for Heaven or the Captain?

All cry, a Captain! a Captain!

HELL: Look ye, Sir, 'tis a clear case.

PED: Oh I am mad – if I refuse, my life's in danger – [*Aside.*] – Come – there's one motive induces me – take her – I shall now be free from the fear of her Honour; guard it you now, if you can; I have been a slave to't long enough.

Gives her to him.

WILL: Faith, Sir, I am of a Nation, that are of opinion a woman's Honour is not worth guarding when she has a mind to part with it.

HELL: Well said, Captain.

PED: This was your Plot, Mistress, but I hope you have married one that will revenge my quarrel to you – [*To* Valeria.

VAL: There's no altering Destiny, Sir.

PED: Sooner than a Woman's Will, therefore I forgive you all – and wish you may get my Father's Pardon as Easily; which I fear.

Enter Blunt *dressed in a* Spanish *Habit, looking very ridiculously; his Man adjusting his Band.*[136]

MAN: 'Tis very well, Sir –

BLUNT: Well, Sir, 'adsheartlikins I tell you 'tis damnable Ill, Sir, – a *Spanish* habit, good Lord! could the Devil and my Tailor devise no other punishment for me, but the Mode of a Nation I abominate?

BELV: What's the matter, *Ned*?

BLUNT: Pray view me round, and judge – [*Turns round.*

Notes

[136] *Band* neck-band or collar.

BELV: I must confess thou art a kind of an odd Figure.

BLUNT: In a Spanish habit with a Vengeance! I had rather be in the Inquisition for Judaism, than in this Doublet and Breeches; a Pillory were an easy Collar to this, three handfuls high; and these Shoes too are worse than the stocks, with the sole an Inch shorter than my Foot: In fine, Gentlemen, methinks I look altogether like a Bag of Bays[137] stuffed full of Fools' Flesh.

BELV: Methinks 'tis well, and makes thee look *en Cavalier*: Come, Sir, settle your face, and salute our Friends, Lady –

BLUNT: Hah! – say'st thou so, my little Rover? – [*To* Hell.] Lady – (if you be one) give me leave to kiss your hand, and tell you, 'adsheartlikins, for all I look so, I am your humble Servant, – a Pox of my *Spanish* habit.

WILL: Hark – what's this? [*Music is heard to play.*

Enter Boy.

BOY: Sir, as the Custom is, the gay people in Masquerade, who make every man's House their own, are coming up.

Enter several Men and Women in Masquing Habits, with Music, they put themselves in order and Dance.

BLUNT: 'Adsheartlikins, would 'twere lawful to pull off their false faces, That I might see if my Doxy[138] were not amongst 'em.

BELV: Ladies and Gentlemen, since you are come so *a propos*, you must take a small Collation with us. [*To the Masquers.*

WILL: Whilst we'll to the Good Man within, who stays to give us a Cast[139] of his Office. [*To* Hell.
– Have you no trembling at the near approach?

HELL: No more than you have in an Engagement or a Tempest.

WILL: Egad, thou'rt a brave Girl, and I admire thy Love and Courage.
LEAD on, no other Dangers they can dread
WHO venture in the Storms o'th' Marriage-bed.

Exeunt.

Epilogue

The Banished Cavaliers! a Roving Blade!
A Popish Carnival! a Masquerade!
The Devil's in't if this will please the Nation,
In these our blessed times of Reformation,
When Conventicling is so much in Fashion. [140]
And yet –
That Mutinous Tribe less Factions do beget,
Than your continual differing in Wit;
Your Judgment's (as your Passion's) a disease:
Nor Muse nor Miss your Appetite can please;
You're grown as Nice as queasy Consciences,
Whose each Convulsion, when the Spirit moves,

Notes

[137] *Bag of Bays* a bag of bay leaves for cooking.

[138] *doxy* wench; sweetheart.

[139] *cast* specimen; taste.

[140] *conventicling* meetings of Puritans.

Damns everything that Maggot disapproves.
With Canting Rule you would the Stage refine,[141]
And to Dull Method all our Sense confine.
With th' Insolence of Commonwealths you rule,
Where each gay Fop, and politic brave Fool,
On Monarch Wit impose without control.
As for the last who seldom sees a Play,
Unless it be the old Black Friars way,[142]
Shaking his empty Noddle o'er Bamboo,[143]
He cries, – 'Good Faith, these Plays will never do.
– Ah, Sir, in my young days, what lofty Wit,
What high-strained Scenes of Fighting there were Writ:
These are slight airy Toys. But tell me, pray,
What has the House of Commons *done today?'*
Then shows his Politics, to let you see
Of State Affairs he'll judge as notably,
As he can do of Wit and Poetry.
The younger Sparks, who hither do resort,
Cry, –
'Pox o' your gentle things, give us more Sport;
– Damn me, I'm sure 'twill never please the Court'.
Such Fops are never pleased, unless the Play
Be stuffed with Fools, as brisk and dull as they:
Such might the Half-Crown spare, and in a Glass
At home behold a more Accomplished Ass,
Where they may set their Cravats, Wigs and Faces,
And Practise all their Buffoon'ry Grimaces;
See how this – Huff becomes, – this Dammy, – stare, –
Which they at home may act, because they dare,
But – must with prudent caution do elsewhere.
Oh that our Nokes, *or* Tony Lee *could show*[144]
A Fop but half so much to th' life as you.

Oroonoko: or, the Royal Slave. A True History (1688)

I do not pretend, in giving you the History of this *Royal Slave*, to entertain my Reader with the Adventures of a feigned *Hero*, whose Life and Fortunes Fancy may manage at the Poet's Pleasure; nor in relating the truth, design to adorn it with any Accidents, but such as arrived in earnest to him: And it shall come simply into the World, recommended by its own proper Merits, and natural Intrigues; there being enough of Reality to support it, and to render it diverting, without the Addition of Invention.[1]

I was myself an Eye-Witness, to a great part, of what you will find here set down; and what I could not be Witness of, I received from the Mouth of the chief Actor in

Notes

141 *canting* jargony or hypocritical.

142 *Black Friars way* like those produced at Black Friars, a pre-Civil War theater.

143 *Bamboo* a walking stick.

144 *Nokes, or Tony Lee* prominent comedians.

Oroonoko: or, the Royal Slave. A True History

1 *Invention* "Fiction" (Johnson).

this History, the *Hero* himself, who gave us the whole Transactions of his Youth; and though I shall omit, for Brevity's sake, a thousand little Accidents of his Life, which, however pleasant to us, where History was scarce, and Adventures very rare; yet might prove tedious and heavy to my Reader, in a World where he finds Diversions for every Minute, new and strange: But we who were perfectly charmed with the character of this great Man, were curious to gather every Circumstance of his Life.

The Scene of the last part of his Adventures lies in a Colony in *America*, called *Surinam*,[2] in the *West-Indies*.

But before I give you the Story of this *Gallant Slave*, 'tis fit I tell you the manner of bringing them to these new *Colonies*; for those they make use of there, are not *Natives* of the place; for those we live with in perfect Amity, without daring to command them; but on the contrary, caress them with all the brotherly and friendly Affection in the World; trading with them for their Fish, Venison, Buffalo Skins, and little Rarities; as Marmosets, a sort of *Monkey* as big as a Rat or Weasel, but of a marvellous and delicate shape, and has Face and Hands like an Human Creature; and Cousheries, a little Beast in the form and fashion of a Lion, as big as a Kitten, but so exactly made in all parts like that noble Beast, that it is it in *Miniature*: then for little *Parakeetoes*, great Parrots, *Macaws* and a thousand other Birds and Beasts of wonderful and surprising Forms, Shapes, and Colours: for Skins of prodigious Snakes, of which there are some three-score Yards in length; as is the Skin of one that may be seen at His Majesty's *Antiquaries*:[3] Where are also some rare Flies, of amazing Forms and Colours, presented to them by myself; some as big as my Fist, some less; and all of various Excellencies, such as Art cannot imitate. Then we trade for Feathers, which they order into all Shapes, make themselves little short Habits of them, and glorious Wreaths for their Heads, Necks, Arms and Legs, whose Tinctures are inconceivable. I had a Set of these presented to me, and I gave them to the King's Theatre,[4] and it was the dress of the *Indian Queen*,[5] infinitely admired by Persons of Quality; and were unimitable. Besides these, a thousand little Knacks,[6] and Rarities in Nature; and some of Art; as their Baskets, Weapons, Aprons, &c. We dealt with them with Beads of all Colours, Knives, Axes, Pins and Needles; which they used only as Tools to drill Holes with in their Ears, Noses and Lips, where they hang a great many little things; as long Beads, bits of Tin, Brass, or Silver, beat thin, and any shining Trinket. The Beads they weave into Aprons about a quarter of an Ell[7] long, and of the same breadth; working them very prettily in Flowers of several Colours of Beads; which Apron they wear just before them, as *Adam* and *Eve* did the Fig-leaves; the Men wearing a long Stripe of Linen, which they deal with us for. They thread these Beads also on long Cotton-threads, and make Girdles to tie their Aprons to, which come twenty times, or more, about the Waist; and then cross, like a Shoulder-belt, both ways, and round their Necks, Arms and Legs. This Adornment, with their long black Hair, and the Face painted in little Specks or Flowers here and there, makes them a wonderful Figure to behold. Some of the Beauties, which indeed are finely shaped, as almost all are, and who have pretty Features, are charming and novel; for they have all that is called Beauty, except the

Notes

[2] *Surinam* Dutch Guiana, on the northeast coast of South America.

[3] *His Majesty's Antiquaries* the natural history museum in Gresham College, catalogued by Nehemiah Grew in 1681.

[4] *King's Theatre* the Bridges Street Theater, home of the King's Company of Actors from 1663.

[5] *Indian Queen* title role in a play by Dryden and Robert Howard, first produced in 1664.

[6] *Knack* "A little machine; a petty contrivance; a toy" (Johnson).

[7] *Ell* a measure of forty-five inches.

Colour, which is a reddish Yellow; or after a new Oiling, which they often use to themselves, they are of the colour of a new Brick, but smooth, soft and sleek. They are extreme modest and bashful, very shy, and nice[8] of being touched. And though they are all thus naked, if one lives for ever among them, there is not to be seen an indecent Action, or Glance; and being continually used to see one another so unadorned, so like our first Parents before the Fall, it seems as if they had no Wishes; there being nothing to heighten Curiosity, but all you can see, you see at once, and every Moment see; and where there is no Novelty, there can be no Curiosity. Not but I have seen a handsome young *Indian*, dying for Love of a very beautiful young *Indian* Maid; but all his Courtship was, to fold his Arms, pursue her with his Eyes, and Sighs were all his Language: whilst she, as if no such Lover were present; or rather, as if she desired none such, carefully guarded her eyes from beholding him; and never approached him, but she looked down with all the blushing Modesty I have seen in the most severe and cautious of our World. And these People represented to me an absolute *Idea* of the first State of Innocence, before Man knew how to sin: And 'tis most evident and plain, that simple Nature is the most harmless, inoffensive and virtuous mistress. 'Tis she alone, if she were permitted, that better instructs the World, than all the Inventions of Man: Religion would here but destroy that Tranquillity, they possess by Ignorance; and Laws would but teach them to know Offence, of which now they have no Notion. They once made Mourning and Fasting for the Death of the *English* Governor, who had given his Hand to come on such a day to them, and neither came, nor sent; believing, when once a Man's Word was passed, nothing but Death could or should prevent his keeping it: And when they saw he was not dead, they asked him, what Name they had for a Man who promised a thing he did not do? The Governor told them, Such a man was a 'Liar', which was a Word of Infamy to a Gentleman. Then one of them replied, 'Governor, you are a Liar, and guilty of that Infamy'. They have a Native Justice, which knows no Fraud; and they understand no Vice, or Cunning, but when they are taught by the *White Men*. They have Plurality of Wives, which, when they grow old, they serve those that succeed them, who are young; but with a Servitude easy and respected; and unless they take Slaves in War, they have no other Attendants.

Those on that *Continent* where I was, had no King; but the oldest War-Captain was obeyed with great Resignation.

A War-Captain is a Man who has led them on to Battle with Conduct,[9] and Success; of whom I shall have Occasion to speak more hereafter, and of some other of their Customs and Manners, as they fall in my way.

With these People, as I said, we live in perfect Tranquillity, and good Understanding, as it behooves us to do; they knowing all the places where to seek the best Food of the Country, and the Means of getting it; and for very small and unvaluable Trifles, supply us with what it is almost impossible for us to get; for they do not only in the Wood, and over the *Savannas*, in hunting, supply the parts of Hounds, by swiftly scouring through those almost impassable places, and by the mere activity of their Feet, run down the nimblest Deer, and other eatable Beasts: But in the water, one would think they were Gods of the Rivers, or Fellow-Citizens of the Deep; so rare an Art they have in Swimming, Diving, and almost Living in Water; by which they command the less swift Inhabitants of the Floods. And then for Shooting; what they cannot take, or reach with their Hands, they do with Arrows; and have so admirable an Aim, that they will split

Notes

[8] *nice* "Fastidious; squeamish" (Johnson).

[9] *Conduct* "The act of leading troops; the duty of a general" (Johnson).

almost an Hair; and at any distance that an Arrow can reach, they will shoot down Oranges, and other Fruit, and only touch the Stalk with the Dart's Points, that they may not hurt the Fruit. So that they being, on all Occasions, very useful to us, we find it absolutely necessary to caress them as Friends, and not to treat them as Slaves; nor dare we do other, their numbers so far surpassing ours in that *Continent*.

Those then whom we make use of to work in our Plantations of Sugar, are *Negroes*, *Black-Slaves* altogether; who are transported thither in this manner.

Those who want Slaves, make a Bargain with a Master, or Captain of a Ship, and contract to pay him so much apiece, a matter of twenty Pound a Head for as many as he agrees for, and to pay for them when they shall be delivered on such a Plantation: So that when there arrives a Ship laden with Slaves, they who have so contracted, go aboard, and receive their Number by Lot; and perhaps in one Lot that may be ten, there may happen to be three or four Men; the rest, Women and Children: Or be there more or less of either Sex, you are obliged to be contented with your Lot.

Coramantien,[10] a Country of *Blacks* so called, was one of those places in which they found the most advantageous Trading for these Slaves; and thither most of our great Traders in that Merchandise trafficked; for that Nation is very war-like and brave; and having a continual Campaign, being always in Hostility with one neighbouring Prince or other, they had the fortune to take a great many Captives; for all they took in Battle, were sold as Slaves; at least, those common Men who could not ransom themselves. Of these Slaves so taken, the General only has all the profit; and of these Generals our Captains and Masters of Ships buy all their Freights.

The King of *Coramantien* was of himself a Man of an Hundred and odd Years old, and had no Son, though he had many beautiful *Black* Wives; for most certainly, there are Beauties that can charm of that Colour. In his younger Years he had had many gallant Men to his Sons, thirteen of which died in Battle, conquering when they fell; and he had only left him for his Successor, one Grandchild, Son to one of these dead Victors; who, as soon as he could bear a Bow in his Hand, and a Quiver at his Back, was sent into the Field, to be trained up by one of the oldest Generals, to War; where, from his natural Inclination to Arms, and the Occasions given him, with the good Conduct of the old General, he became, at the Age of Seventeen, one of the most expert Captains, and bravest Soldiers that ever saw the Field of *Mars*:[11] So that he was adored as the Wonder of all that World, and the Darling of the Soldiers. Besides, he was adorned with a native Beauty so transcending all those of his gloomy Race, that he struck an Awe and Reverence, even in those that knew not his Quality; as he did in me, who beheld him with Surprise and Wonder, when afterwards he arrived in our World.

He had scarce arrived at his Seventeenth Year, when, fighting by his Side, the General was killed with an Arrow in his Eye, which the Prince *Oroonoko* (for so was this gallant *Moor* called) very narrowly avoided; nor had he, if the General, who saw the Arrow shot, and perceiving it aimed at the Prince, had not bowed his Head between, on purpose to receive it in his own Body rather than it should touch that of the Prince, and so saved him.

'Twas then, afflicted as *Oroonoko* was, that he was proclaimed General in the old Man's place; and then it was, at the finishing of that War, which had continued for two Years, that the Prince came to Court; where he had hardly been a Month together, from the time of his fifth Year to that of Seventeen; and 'twas amazing to imagine where it was he learned so much Humanity; or, to give his Accomplishments a juster

Notes

[10] *Coramantien* on the Gold Coast of Africa.

[11] *the Field of Mars* i.e., war, after the Roman god of war.

Name, where 'twas he got that real Greatness of Soul, those refined Notions of true Honour, that absolute Generosity, and that Softness that was capable of the highest Passions of Love and Gallantry, whose Objects were almost continually fighting Men, or those mangled, or dead; who heard no Sounds, but those of War and Groans: Some part of it we may attribute to the Care of a *French* Man of Wit and Learning; who finding it turn to a very good Account to be a sort of Royal Tutor to this young *Black*, & perceiving him very ready, apt, and quick of Apprehension, took a great pleasure to teach him Morals, Language and Science; and was for it extremely beloved and valued by him. Another Reason was, He loved when he came from War, to see all the *English* Gentlemen that traded thither; and did not only learn their Language, but that of the *Spaniards* also, with whom he traded afterwards for Slaves.

I have often seen and conversed with this great Man, and been a Witness to many of his mighty Actions; and do assure my Reader, the most Illustrious Courts could not have produced a braver Man, both for Greatness of Courage and Mind, a Judgement more solid, a Wit more quick, and a Conversation more sweet and diverting. He knew almost as much as if he had read much: He had heard of, and admired the *Romans*: he had heard of the late Civil Wars in *England*, and the deplorable Death of our great Monarch; and would discourse of it with all the Sense and Abhorrence of the Injustice imaginable. He had an extreme good and graceful Mien, and all the Civility of a well-bred great Man. He had nothing of Barbarity in his Nature, but in all Points addressed himself, as if his Education had been in some *European* Court.

This great and just Character of *Oroonoko* gave me an extreme Curiosity to see him, especially when I knew he spoke *French* and *English*, and that I could talk with him. But though I had heard so much of him, I was as greatly surprised when I saw him, as if I had heard nothing of him; so beyond all Report I found him. He came into the Room, and addressed himself to me, and some other Women, with the best Grace in the World. He was pretty tall, but of a Shape the most exact[12] that can be fancied: The most famous Statuary could not form the Figure of a Man more admirably turned from Head to Foot. His Face was not of that brown, rusty Black which most of that Nation are, but a perfect Ebony, or polished Jet.[13] His Eyes were the most awful that could be seen, and very piercing; the White of them being like Snow, as were his Teeth. His Nose was rising and *Roman*, instead of *African* and flat. His Mouth, the finest shaped that could be seen; far from those great turned lips, which are so natural to the rest of the *Negroes*. The whole Proportion and Air of his Face was so noble, and exactly formed, that, bating[14] his Colour, there could be nothing in nature more beautiful, agreeable and handsome. There was no one Grace wanting, that bears the Standard of true Beauty. His Hair came down to his Shoulders, by the Aids of Art; which was, by pulling it out with a Quill, and keeping it combed; of which he took particular Care. Nor did the Perfections of his Mind come short of those of his Person; for his Discourse was admirable upon almost any Subject; and whoever had heard him speak, would have been convinced of their Errors, that all fine Wit[15] is confined to the *White* Men, especially to those of *Christendom*; and would have confessed that *Oroonoko* was as capable even of reigning well, and of governing as wisely, had as great a Soul, as politic Maxims, and was as sensible[16] of Power as any Prince civilized in the most refined Schools of Humanity and Learning, or the most Illustrious Courts.

Notes

12 *exact* "Nice; without failure; without deviation from rule" (Johnson).

13 *Jet* "a very beautiful fossil ... of a fine deep black colour, having a grain resembling that of wood" (Johnson, quoting John Hill).

14 *bating* except.

15 *Wit* "The powers of the mind; the mental faculties" (Johnson).

16 *sensible* "having moral perception; having the quality of being affected by moral good or ill" (Johnson, sense 5).

This Prince, such as I have described him, whose Soul and Body were so admirably adorned, was (while yet he was in the Court of his Grandfather) as I said, as capable of Love, as 'twas possible for a brave and gallant Man to be; and in saying that, I have named the highest Degree of Love; for sure, great Souls are most capable of that Passion.

I have already said, the old General was killed by the shot of an Arrow, by the Side of this Prince, in Battle; and that *Oroonoko* was made General. This old dead *Hero* had one only Daughter left of his race, a Beauty that, to describe her truly, one need say only, she was Female to the noble Male; the beautiful *Black Venus* to our young *Mars*; as charming in her Person as he, and of delicate Virtues. I have seen an hundred *White* Men sighing after her, and making a thousand Vows at her Feet, all vain, and unsuccessful: And she was, indeed, too great for any, but a Prince of her own Nation to adore.

Oroonoko coming from the Wars (which were now ended), after he had made his Court to his Grandfather, he thought in Honour he should make a Visit to *Imoinda*, the Daughter of his Foster-father, the dead General; and to make some Excuses to her, because his Preservation was the Occasion of her Father's Death; and to present her with those Slaves that had been taken in this last Battle, as the Trophies of her Father's Victories. When he came, attended by all the young Soldiers of any Merit, he was infinitely surprised at the Beauty of this fair Queen of Night, whose Face and Person was so exceeding all he had ever beheld, that lovely Modesty with which she received him, that Softness in her Look, and Sighs, upon the melancholy Occasion of this Honour that was done by so great a Man as *Oroonoko*, and a Prince of whom she had heard such admirable things; the Awfulness[17] wherewith she received him, and the Sweetness of her Words and Behaviour while he stayed, gained a perfect Conquest over his fierce Heart, and made him feel the Victor could be subdued. So that having made his first Compliments, and presented her an hundred and fifty Slaves in Fetters, he told her with his Eyes that he was not insensible of her Charms; while *Imoinda*, who wished for nothing more than so glorious a Conquest, was pleased to believe, she understood that silent Language of new-born Love; and from that Moment, put on all her Additions to Beauty.

The Prince returned to Court with quite another Humour[18] than before; and though he did not speak much of the fair *Imoinda*, he had the pleasure to hear all his followers speak of nothing but the Charms of that Maid; insomuch that, even in the Presence of the old King, they were extolling her, and heightening, if possible, the Beauties they had found in her: So that nothing else was talked of, no other Sound was heard in every Corner where there were Whisperers, but 'Imoinda! Imoinda!'

'Twill be imagined *Oroonoko* stayed not long before he made his second Visit; nor, considering his Quality, not much longer before he told her, he adored her. I have often heard him say, that he admired by what strange Inspiration he came to talk things so soft, and so passionate, who never knew Love, nor was used to the Conversation of Women; but (to use his own Words) he said, 'Most happily, some new, and till then unknown Power instructed his Heart and Tongue in the Language of Love, and at the same time, in favour of him, inspired *Imoinda* with a Sense of his Passion'. She was touched with what he said, and returned it all in such Answers as went to his very Heart, with a Pleasure unknown before: Nor did he use those Obligations ill, that Love had done him; but turned all his happy Moments to the best advantage; and as he

Notes

[17] *Awfulness* "The quality of striking with awe; solemnity" (Johnson).

[18] *Humour* "Present disposition" (Johnson).

knew no Vice, his Flame aimed at nothing but Honour, if such a distinction may be made in Love; and especially in that Country, where Men take to themselves as many as they can maintain; and where the only Crime and Sin with Woman is, to turn her off, to abandon her to Want, Shame and Misery: Such ill Morals are only practised in *Christian* Countries, where they prefer the bare Name of Religion; and, without Virtue or Morality, think that's sufficient. But *Oroonoko* was none of those Professors; but as he had right Notions of Honour, so he made her Propositions as were not only and barely such; but contrary to the Custom of his Country, he made her Vows she should be the only woman he would possess while he lived; that no Age or Wrinkles should incline him to change, for her Soul would always be fine, and always young; and he should have an eternal *Idea* in his Mind of the Charms she now bore, and should look into his Heart for that *Idea*, when he could find it no longer in her Face.

After a thousand Assurances of his lasting flame, and her eternal Empire over him, she condescended to receive him for her Husband; or rather, received him, as the greatest Honour the Gods could do her.

There is a certain Ceremony in these Cases to be observed, which I forgot to ask how performed; but 'twas concluded on both sides, that, in Obedience to him, the Grandfather was to be first made acquainted with the Design: for they pay a most absolute Resignation to the Monarch, especially when he is a Parent also.

On the other side, the old King, who had many Wives, and many Concubines, wanted not Court-flatterers to insinuate in his Heart a thousand tender Thoughts for this young Beauty; and who represented her to his Fancy, as the most charming he had ever possessed in all the long Race of his numerous Years. At this Character, his old Heart, like an extinguished Brand, most apt to take Fire, felt new Sparks of Love, and began to kindle; and now grown to his second Childhood, longed with Impatience to behold this gay thing, with whom, alas! he could but innocently play. But how he should be confirmed she was this *Wonder*, before he used his Power to call her to Court (where Maidens never came, unless for the King's private Use) he was next to consider; and while he was so doing, he had Intelligence brought him, that *Imoinda* was most certainly Mistress to the Prince *Oroonoko*. This gave him some *Shagrien*:[19] however, it gave him also an Opportunity, one Day, when the Prince was a-hunting, to wait on a Man of Quality, as his Slave and Attendant, who should go and make a Present to *Imoinda*, as from the Prince; he should then, unknown, see this fair Maid, and have an Opportunity to hear what Message she would return the Prince for his Present, and from thence gather the state of her heart, and degree of her Inclination. This was put in Execution, and the old Monarch saw, and burnt: He found all he had heard, and would not delay his Happiness, but found he should have some Obstacle to overcome her Heart; for she expressed her Sense of the Present the Prince had sent her, in terms so sweet, so soft and pretty, with an Air of Love and Joy that could not be dissembled; insomuch that 'twas past doubt whether she loved *Oroonoko* entirely. This gave the old King some Affliction; but he salved it with this, that the Obedience the People pay their King, was not at all inferior to what they paid their Gods: And what Love would not oblige *Imoinda* to do, Duty would compel her to.

He was therefore no sooner got to his Apartment, but he sent the Royal Veil to *Imoinda*; that is, the Ceremony of Invitation; he sends the Lady he has a Mind to honour with his Bed, a Veil, with which she is covered, and secured for the King's Use; and 'tis Death to disobey; besides, held a most impious Disobedience.

Notes

19 *Shagrien* chagrin, "Ill humour; vexation. ... It is pronounced *shagreen*" (Johnson).

'Tis not to be imagined the Surprise and Grief that seized this lovely Maid at this News and Sight. However, as Delays in these Cases are dangerous, and Pleading worse than Treason; trembling, and almost fainting, she was obliged to suffer herself to be covered, and led away.

They brought her thus to Court; and the King, who had caused a very rich Bath to be prepared, was led into it, where he sat under a Canopy, in State, to receive this longed-for Virgin; whom he having commanded should be brought to him, they (after disrobing her) led her to the Bath, and making fast the Doors, left her to descend. The King, without more Courtship, bade her throw off her Mantle, and come to his Arms. But *Imoinda*, all in Tears, threw herself on the Marble, on the brink of the Bath, and besought him to hear her. She told him, as she was a Maid, how proud of the Divine Glory she should have been of having it in her power to oblige her King: but as by the Laws, he could not; and from his Royal Goodness would not take from any Man his wedded Wife: So she believed she should be the Occasion of making him commit a great Sin, if she did not reveal her State and Condition; and tell him, she was another's, and could not be so happy to be his.

The King, enraged at this Delay, hastily demanded the Name of the bold Man that had married a Woman of her Degree, without his Consent. *Imoinda*, seeing his Eyes fierce, and his Hands tremble (whether with Age, or Anger, I know not, but she fancied the last), almost repented she had said so much, for now she feared the Storm would fall on the Prince; she therefore said a thousand things to appease the raging of his Flame, and to prepare him to hear who it was with Calmness; but before she spoke, he imagined who she meant, but would not seem to do so, but commanded her to lay aside her Mantle, and suffer herself to receive his Caresses; or, by his Gods, he swore, that happy Man whom she was going to name should die, though it were even *Oroonoko* himself. 'Therefore', said he, 'deny this Marriage, and swear thyself a Maid'. 'That', replied Imoinda, 'by all our powers I do; for I am not yet known to my husband'. ' 'Tis enough', said the King, ' 'tis enough to satisfy my Conscience, and my Heart'. And rising from his Seat, he went, and led her into the Bath; it being in vain for her to resist.

In this time, the Prince, who was returned from Hunting, went to visit his *Imoinda*, but found her gone; and not only so, but heard she had received the Royal Veil. This raised him to a Storm; and in his Madness, they had much ado to save him from laying violent Hands on himself. Force first prevailed, and then Reason: They urged all to him, that might oppose his Rage; but nothing weighed so greatly with him as the King's Old Age uncapable of injuring him with *Imoinda*. He would give way to that Hope, because it pleased him most, and flattered best his Heart. Yet this served not altogether to make him cease his different Passions, which sometimes raged within him, and sometimes softened into Showers. 'Twas not enough to appease him to tell him his Grandfather was old, and could not that way injure him, while he retained that awful Duty which the young Men are used there to pay their grave Relations. He could not be convinced that he had no Cause to sigh and mourn for the Loss of a Mistress he could not with all his Strength and Courage retrieve. And he would often cry, 'Oh, my Friends! were she in walled Cities, or confined from me in Fortifications of the greatest Strength; did Enchantments or Monsters detain her from me, I would venture through any Hazard to free her: But here, in the Arms of a feeble old Man, my Youth, my violent Love, my Trade in Arms, and all my vast Desire of Glory, avail me nothing: Imoinda is as irrecoverably lost to me, as if she were snatched by the cold Arms of Death. Oh! She is never to be retrieved. If I would wait tedious Years, till Fate should bow the old King to his Grave; even that would not leave me *Imoinda* free; but still that Custom that makes it so vile a Crime for a Son to marry his Father's Wives or Mistresses, would hinder my Happiness; unless I would either ignobly set an ill Precedent to my

Successors, or abandon my Country, and fly with her to some unknown World, who never heard our Story.'

But it was objected to him, that his Case was not the same: for *Imoinda* being his lawful Wife, by solemn Contract, 'twas he that was the injured Man, and might, if he so pleased, take *Imoinda* back, the Breach of law being on his Grandfather's side; and that if he could circumvent him, and redeem her from the *Otan*, which is the Palace of the King's Women, a sort of *Seraglio*, it was both just and lawful for him so to do.

This Reasoning had some force upon him, and he should have been entirely comforted, but for the Thought that she was possessed by his Grandfather. However, he loved so well, that he was resolved to believe what most favoured his hope, and to endeavour to learn from *Imoinda*'s own Mouth, what only she could satisfy him in; whether she was robbed of that Blessing, which was only due to his Faith and Love. But as it was very hard to get a Sight of the Women, for no Men ever entered into the *Otan*, but when the King went to entertain himself with some one of his Wives, or Mistresses; and 'twas death, at any other time, for any other to go in; so he knew not how to contrive to get a Sight of her.

While *Oroonoko* felt all the Agonies of Love, and suffered under a Torment the most painful in the World, the old King was not exempted from his share of Affliction. He was troubled, for having been forced by an irresistible passion, to rob his Son of a Treasure, he knew, could not but be extremely dear to him, since she was the most beautiful that ever had been seen, and had besides, all the Sweetness and Innocence of Youth and Modesty, with a Charm of Wit surpassing all. He found that, however she was forced to expose her lovely Person to his withered Arms, she could only sigh and weep there, and think of *Oroonoko*; and oftentimes could not forbear speaking of him, though her Life were, by Custom, forfeited by owning her Passion. But she spoke not of a lover only, but of a Prince dear to him, to whom she spoke; and of the Praises of a Man, who, till now, filled the old Man's Soul with Joy at every Recital of his Bravery, or even his Name. And 'twas this Dotage on our young *Hero* that gave *Imoinda* a thousand Privileges to speak of him, without offending; and this Condescension in the old King, that made her take the Satisfaction of speaking of him so very often.

Besides, he many times enquired how the Prince bore himself; and those of whom he asked, being entirely Slaves to the Merits and Virtues of the Prince, still answered what they thought conduced best to his Service, which was to make the old King fancy that the Prince had no more Interest in *Imoinda*, and had resigned her willingly to the Pleasure of the King; that he diverted himself with his Mathematicians, his Fortifications, his Officers, and his Hunting.

This pleased the old Lover, who failed not to report these things again to *Imoinda*, that she might, by the Example of her young Lover, withdraw her Heart, and rest better contented in his Arms. But, however she was forced to receive this unwelcome News, in all Appearance, with Unconcern, and Content, her Heart was bursting within, and she was only happy when she could get alone, to vent her Griefs and Moans with Sighs and Tears.

What Reports of the Prince's Conduct were made to the King, he thought good to justify, as far as possibly he could by his Actions; and when he appeared in the Presence of the King, he showed a Face not at all betraying his Heart: So that in a little time the old Man, being entirely convinced that he was no longer a Lover of *Imoinda*, he carried him with him, in his Train, to the *Otan*, often to banquet with his Mistress. But as soon as he entered, one Day, into the Apartment of *Imoinda*, with the King, at the first Glance from her Eyes, notwithstanding all his determined Resolution, he was ready to sink in the place where he stood; and had certainly done so, but for the Support of *Aboan*, a young Man who was next to him, which, with his Change of Countenance, had betrayed him, had the King chanced to look that way. And I have observed, 'tis a very great Error in those who laugh when one says, 'A *Negro* can change colour'; for I have seen them as frequently blush, and look pale, and that as visibly as ever I saw in the most beautiful *White*. And it is certain that both these Changes were evident, this Day, in both these Lovers. And *Imoinda*, who saw with some Joy the Change in the Prince's Face, and found it in her own, strove to divert the King from beholding either by a forced Caress, with which she met him, which was a new Wound in the heart of the poor dying Prince. But soon as the King was busied in looking on some fine thing of *Imoinda*'s making, she had time to tell the Prince with her angry, but Love-darting Eyes, that she resented his Coldness, and bemoaned her own miserable Captivity. Nor were his Eyes silent, but answered hers again, as much as eyes could do, instructed by the most tender, and most passionate Heart that ever loved: And they spoke so well, and so effectually, as *Imoinda* no longer doubted but she was the only Delight, and the Darling of that Soul she found pleading in them its Right of Love, which none was more willing to resign than she. And it was this powerful Language alone that in an Instant conveyed all the Thoughts of their Souls to each other; that they both found, there wanted but Opportunity to make them both entirely happy. But when he saw another Door opened by *Onahal*, a former old wife of the King's, who now had charge of *Imoinda*; and saw the prospect of a Bed of State made ready, with Sweets and Flowers for the Dalliance of the King; who immediately led the trembling Victim from his Sight, into the prepared Repose. What Rage! what wild Frenzies seized his Heart! which forcing to keep within Bounds, and to suffer without Noise, it became the more insupportable, and rent his Soul with ten thousand Pains. He was forced to retire, to vent his Groans, where he fell down on a Carpet, and lay struggling a long time, and only breathing now and then – 'O Imoinda!' When *Onahal* had finished her necessary Affair within, shutting the Door, she came forth to wait, till the King called; and hearing some one sighing in the other Room, she passed on, and found the Prince in that deplorable Condition, which she thought needed her Aid. She gave him Cordials, but all in vain, till finding the nature of his Disease, by his Sighs, and naming *Imoinda*. She told him he had not so much Cause as he imagined to afflict himself; for if he knew the King so well as she did, he would not lose a Moment in Jealousy; and that she was confident that *Imoinda* bore, at this Minute, part in his Affliction. *Aboan* was of the same Opinion; and both together, persuaded him to reassume his Courage; and all sitting down on the Carpet, the Prince said so many obliging things to *Onahal*, that he half persuaded her to be of his Party. And she promised him, she would thus far comply with his just Desires, that she would let *Imoinda* know how faithful he was, what he suffered, and what he said.

This Discourse lasted till the King called, which gave *Oroonoko* a certain Satisfaction; and with the hope *Onahal* had made him conceive, he assumed a Look as gay as 'twas possible a man in his Circumstances could do; and presently after, he was called in with the rest who waited without. The King commanded Music to be brought, and several of his young Wives and Mistresses came all together by his Command to dance before him, where *Imoinda* performed her Part with an Air and Grace so passing all the rest, as her Beauty was above them, and received the Present, ordained as a Prize. The Prince was every Moment more charmed with the new Beauties and Graces he beheld in this fair One; and while he gazed, and she danced, *Onahal* was retired to a Window with *Aboan*.

This *Onahal*, as I said, was one of the Cast-Mistresses[20] of the old King; and 'twas these (now past their Beauty) that were made Guardians or Governants to the new,

Notes

[20] *Cast-Mistress* former, cast-off mistress.

and the young Ones; and whose Business it was, to teach them all those wanton Arts of Love, with which they prevailed and charmed heretofore in their Turn; and who now treated the triumphing happy Ones with all the Severity, as to Liberty and Freedom, that was possible, in revenge of those Honours they rob them of; envying them those Satisfactions, those Gallantries and Presents, that were once made to themselves, while Youth and Beauty lasted, and which they now saw pass regardless by, and paid only to the Bloomings.[21] And certainly, nothing is more afflicting to a decayed Beauty, than to behold in itself declining Charms, that were once adored; and to find those Caresses paid to new Beauties, to which once she laid a Claim; to hear them whisper as she passes by, 'That once was a delicate Woman'. These abandoned Ladies therefore endeavour to revenge all the Despites[22] and Decays of Time on these flourishing happy Ones. And 'twas this Severity that gave *Oroonoko* a thousand Fears he should never prevail with *Onahal* to see *Imoinda*. But, as I said, she was now retired to a window with *Aboan*.

This young Man was not only one of the best Quality,[23] but a Man extremely well made, and beautiful; and coming often to attend the King to the *Otan*, he had subdued the Heart of the antiquated *Onahal*, which had not forgot how pleasant it was to be in Love: And though she had some Decays in her Face, she had none in her Sense and Wit; she was there agreeable still, even to *Aboan*'s Youth, so that he took pleasure in entertaining her with Discourses of Love. He knew also that to make his Court to these She-Favourites was the way to be great, these being the Persons that do all Affairs and Business at Court. He had also observed that she had given him Glances more tender and inviting than she had done to others of his Quality: And now, when he saw that her Favour could so absolutely oblige the Prince, he failed not to sigh in her Ear, and look with Eyes all soft upon her, and give her Hope that she had made some Impressions on his Heart. He found her pleased at this, and making a thousand Advances to him; but the Ceremony ending, and the King departing, broke up the Company for that Day, and his Conversation.

Aboan failed not that night to tell the Prince of his Success, and how advantageous the Service of *Onahal* might be to his Amour with *Imoinda*. The Prince was overjoyed with this good News, and besought him, if it were possible to caress her so, as to engage her entirely, which he could not fail to do, if he complied with her Desires: 'For then', said the Prince, 'her Life lying at your Mercy, she must grant you the Request you make in my Behalf'. *Aboan* understood him and assured him he would make Love so effectually that he would defy the most expert Mistress of the Art to find out whether he dissembled it, or had it really. And 'twas with Impatience they waited the next Opportunity of going to the *Otan*.

The Wars came on, the Time of taking the Field approached, and 'twas impossible for the Prince to delay his going at the Head of his Army, to encounter the Enemy: So that every Day seemed a tedious Year, till he saw his *Imoinda*; for he believed he could not live, if he were forced away without being so happy. 'Twas with Impatience therefore that he expected the next Visit the King would make; and, according to his Wish, it was not long.

The Parley of the Eyes of these two Lovers had not passed so secretly, but an old jealous Lover could spy it; or rather, he wanted not Flatterers, who told him they observed it: So that the Prince was hastened to the Camp, and this was the last Visit he

Notes

21 *Bloomings* women in the bloom of youth.

22 *Despite* "Act of malice; act of opposition" (Johnson).

23 *Quality* "Comparative or relative rank" (Johnson).

found he should make to the *Otan*; he therefore urged *Aboan* to make the best of this last Effort, and to explain himself so to *Onahal*, that she, deferring her Enjoyment of her young Lover no longer, might make way for the Prince to speak to *Imoinda*.

The whole Affair being agreed on between the Prince and *Aboan*, they attended the King, as the Custom was, to the *Otan*; where, while the whole Company was taken up in beholding the Dancing and antic[24] Postures the Women Royal made to divert the King, *Onahal* singled out *Aboan*, whom she found most pliable to her Wish. When she had him where she believed she could not be heard, she sighed to him, and softly cried, 'Ah, *Aboan*! When will you be sensible[25] to my Passion? I confess it with my Mouth, because I would not give my Eyes the Lie; and you have but too much already perceived they have confessed my Flame: Nor would I have you believe, that because I am the abandoned Mistress of a King, I esteem myself altogether divested of Charms: No, *Aboan*; I have still a Rest[26] of Beauty enough engaging, and I have learned to please too well, not to be desirable. I can have Lovers still, but will have none but *Aboan*'.

'Madam', replied the half-feigning youth, 'you have already, by my Eyes, found, you can still conquer; and I believe 'tis in pity of me, you condescend to this kind Confession. But, Madam, Words are used to be so small a part of our Country-Courtship, that it is rare one can get so happy an Opportunity as to tell one's Heart; and those few Minutes we have are forced to be snatched for more certain Proofs of Love, than speaking and sighing; and such I languish for'.

He spoke this wish with such a Tone, that she hoped it true, and could not forbear believing it; and being wholly transported with Joy, for having subdued the finest of all the King's Subjects to her Desires, she took from her Ears two large pearls, and commanded him to wear them in his. He would have refused them, crying, 'Madam, these are not the Proofs of your Love that I expect; 'tis Opportunity, 'tis a Lone-hour only, that can make me happy'. But forcing the Pearls into his Hand, she whispered softly to him, 'Oh! Do not fear a Woman's Invention, when Love sets her a-thinking'. And pressing his hand, she cried, 'This Night you shall be happy. Come to the Gate of the Orange Groves, behind the *Otan*, and I will be ready, about Midnight, to receive you'. 'Twas thus agreed, and she left him, that no notice might be taken of their speaking together.

The Ladies were still dancing, and the King, laid on a Carpet, with a great deal of pleasure, was beholding them, especially *Imoinda*; who that Day appeared more lovely than ever, being enlivened with the good Tidings *Onahal* had brought her of the constant Passion the Prince had for her. The Prince was laid on another Carpet, at the other end of the Room, with his Eyes fixed on the Object of his Soul; and as she turned, or moved, so did they; and she alone gave his Eyes and Soul their Motions: Nor did *Imoinda* employ her Eyes to any other Use, than in beholding with infinite Pleasure the Joy she produced in those of the Prince. But while she was more regarding him, than the Steps she took, she chanced to fall; and so near him, as that leaping with extreme force from the carpet, he caught her in his Arms as she fell; and 'twas visible to the whole Presence, the Joy wherewith he received her: He clasped her close to his Bosom, and quite forgot that Reverence that was due to the Mistress of a King, and that Punishment that is the Reward of a Boldness of this nature; and had not the Presence of Mind of *Imoinda* (fonder of his Safety, than her own) befriended him, in making her spring from his Arms, and fall into her Dance again, he had, at that Instant, met his Death; for the old King, jealous to the last degree, rose up in Rage, broke all

Notes

[24] *antic* "Odd; ridiculously wild" (Johnson).

[25] *sensible* "Perceiving by either mind or senses" (Johnson).

[26] *Rest* remainder; remnant.

the Diversion, and led *Imoinda* to her Apartment, and sent out Word to the Prince to go immediately to the Camp; and that if he were found another Night in Court, he should suffer the Death ordained for disobedient Offenders.

You may imagine how welcome this News was to *Oroonoko*, whose unseasonable Transport and Caress of *Imoinda* was blamed by all Men that loved him; and now he perceived his Fault, yet cried, 'That for such another Moment, he would be content to die'.

All the *Otan* was in disorder about this Accident; and *Onahal* was particularly concerned, because on the Prince's Stay depended her Happiness; for she could no longer expect that of *Aboan*. So that, ere they departed, they contrived it so, that the Prince and he should come both that Night to the Grove of the *Otan*, which was all of Oranges and Citrons; and that there they should wait her Orders.

They parted thus, with Grief enough, till Night; leaving the King in possession of the lovely Maid. But nothing could appease the Jealousy of the old Lover: He would not be imposed on, but he would have it, that *Imoinda* made a false Step on purpose to fall into *Oroonoko*'s Bosom, and that all things looked like a Design on both sides, and 'twas in vain she protested her Innocence: He was old and obstinate, and left her more than half-assured that his Fear was true.

The King going to his Apartment, sent to know where the Prince was, and if he intended to obey his Command. The Messenger returned, and told him, he found the Prince pensive, and altogether unpreparing for the Campaign; that he lay negligently on the Ground, and answered very little. This confirmed the Jealousy of the King, and he commanded that they should very narrowly and privately watch his Motions; and that he should not stir from his Apartment, but one spy or another should be employed to watch him: so that the Hour approaching, wherein he was to go to the Citron-Grove; and taking only *Aboan* along with him, he leaves his Apartments, and was watched to the very Gate of the *Otan*; where he was seen to enter, and where they left him, to carry back the Tidings to the King.

Oroonoko and *Aboan* were no sooner entered, but *Onahal* led the Prince to the apartment of *Imoinda*; who, not knowing any thing of her Happiness, was laid in Bed. But *Onahal* only left him in her chamber, to make the best of his Opportunity, and took her dear *Aboan* to her own; where he showed the highth of Complaisance[27] for his Prince, when, to give him an Opportunity, he suffered himself to be caressed in bed by *Onahal*.

The Prince softly wakened *Imoinda*, who was not yet a little surprised with Joy to find him there; and yet she trembled with a thousand Fears. I believe he omitted saying nothing to this young Maid that might persuade her to suffer him to seize his own, and take the Rights of Love; and I believe she was not long resisting those Arms where she so longed to be; and having Opportunity, Night and Silence, Youth, Love and Desire, he soon prevailed, and ravished in a Moment, what his old Grandfather had been endeavouring for so many Months.

'Tis not to be imagined the Satisfaction of these two young Lovers; nor the Vows she made him, that she remained a spotless Maid, till that Night, and that what she did with his Grandfather had robbed him of no part of her Virgin-Honour; the Gods, in Mercy and Justice, having reserved that for her plighted[28] Lord, to whom of Right it belonged. And 'tis impossible to express the Transports he suffered, while he listened to a Discourse so charming, from her loved Lips; and clasped that Body in his Arms,

Notes

[27] *Complaisance* "Civility; desire of pleasing; act of adulation" (Johnson).

[28] *plighted* promised, avowed.

for whom he had so long languished; and now nothing afflicted him, but his sudden Departure from her; for he told her the Necessity, and his Commands; but should depart satisfied in this, that since the old King had not been able to deprive him of those Enjoyments which only belonged to him, he believed for the future he would be less able to injure him; so that, abating the Scandal of the Veil, which was no otherwise so, than that she was Wife to another: He believed her safe, even in the Arms of the King, and innocent; yet would he have ventured at the Conquest of the World, and given it all, to have had her avoided that Honour of receiving the *Royal Veil*. 'Twas thus, between a thousand Caresses, that both bemoaned the hard Fate of Youth and Beauty, so liable to that cruel Promotion: 'Twas a Glory that could well have been spared here, though desired and aimed at by all the young Females of that Kingdom.

But while they were thus fondly employed, forgetting how Time ran on, and that the Dawn must conduct him far away from his only Happiness, they heard a great Noise in the *Otan*, and unusual Voices of Men; at which the Prince, starting from the Arms of the frighted *Imoinda*, ran to a little Battle-Axe he used to wear by his Side; and having not so much leisure, as to put on his Habit, he opposed himself against some who were already opening the Door; which they did with so much Violence, that *Oroonoko* was not able to defend it; but was forced to cry out with a commanding Voice, 'Whoever ye are that have the Boldness to attempt to approach this Apartment thus rudely; know, that I, the Prince *Oroonoko*, will revenge it with the certain death of him that first enters: therefore stand back, and know, this place is sacred to Love, and me this Night; Tomorrow 'tis the King's'.

This he spoke with a Voice so resolved and assured, that they soon retired from the Door; but cried, ' 'Tis by the King's command we are come; and being satisfied by thy Voice, O Prince, as much as if we had entered, we can report to the King the Truth of all his Fears, and leave thee to provide for thy own Safety, as thou art advised by thy Friends'.

At these Words they departed, and left the Prince to take a short and sad Leave of *Imoinda*; who, trusting in the strength of her Charms, believed she should appease the Fury of a jealous King, by saying, She was surprised, and that it was by force of Arms he got into her Apartment. All her Concern now was for his Life, and therefore she hastened him to the Camp, and with much ado prevailed on him to go. Nor was it she alone that prevailed; *Aboan* and *Onahal* both pleaded, and both assured him of a Lie that should be well enough contrived to secure *Imoinda*. So that, at last, with a Heart sad as Death, dying Eyes, and sighing Soul, *Oroonoko* departed, and took his way to the Camp.

It was not long after the King in Person came to the *Otan*; where beholding *Imoinda*, with Rage in his Eyes, he upbraided her Wickedness and Perfidy and threatening[29] her Royal Lover; she fell on her Face at his Feet, bedewing the floor with her Tears, and imploring his Pardon for a Fault which she had not with her Will committed; as *Onahal*, who was also prostrate with her, could testify: That, unknown to her, he had broke into her Apartment, and ravished her. She spoke this much against her Conscience; but to save her own Life, 'twas absolutely necessary she should feign this Falsity. She knew it could not injure the Prince, he being fled to an Army that would stand by him, against any Injuries that should assault him. However, this last Thought of *Imoinda*'s being ravished, changed the Measures of his Revenge; and whereas before he designed

Notes

[29] *threatening* the participle is confusing; the subject is probably the king, despite the lack of parallelism.

to be himself her Executioner, he was now resolved she should not die. But as it is the greatest Crime in nature amongst them to touch a Woman after having been possessed by a Son, a Father, or a Brother; so now he looked on *Imoinda* as a polluted thing, wholly unfit for his Embrace; nor would he resign her to his Grandson, because she had received the *Royal Veil*: he therefore removed her from the *Otan*, with *Onahal*; whom he put into safe Hands, with the Order they should be both sold off as Slaves to another Country, either *Christian*, or *Heathen*; 'twas no matter where.

This cruel Sentence, worse than Death, they implored might be reversed; but their Prayers were vain, and it was put in Execution accordingly, and that with so much secrecy, that none, either without, or within the *Otan*, knew anything of their Absence, or their Destiny.

The old King, nevertheless, executed this with a great deal of Reluctancy; but he believed he had made a very great Conquest over himself, when he had once resolved, and had performed what he resolved. He believed now, that his Love had been unjust; and that he could not expect the Gods, or the Captain of the Clouds (as they call the unknown Power) would suffer a better Consequence from so ill a Cause. He now begins to hold *Oroonoko* excused; and to say, he had Reason for what he did: And now Everybody could assure the King, how passionately *Imoinda* was beloved by the Prince; even those confessed it now, who said the contrary before his Flame was abated. So that the King being old, and not able to defend himself in War, and having no Sons of all his Race remaining alive, but only this, to maintain him on his Throne; and looking on this as a Man disobliged, first by the Rape of his Mistress, or rather wife, and now by depriving him wholly of her, he feared, might make him desperate, and do some cruel thing, either to himself, or his old Grandfather, the Offender; he began to repent him extremely of the Contempt he had, in his Rage, put on *Imoinda*. Besides, he considered he ought in Honour to have killed her for this Offence, if it had been one; He ought to have had so much Value and Consideration for a Maid of her Quality, as to have nobly put her to death; and not to have sold her like a common Slave, the greatest Revenge, and the most disgraceful of any; and to which they a thousand times prefer Death, and implore it, as *Imoinda* did, but could not obtain that Honour. Seeing therefore it was certain that *Oroonoko* would highly resent this Affront, he thought good to make some Excuse for his Rashness to him; and to that End he sent a Messenger to the Camp with orders to treat with him about the Matter, to gain his Pardon, and to endeavour to mitigate his Grief; but that by no means he should tell him she was sold, but secretly put to death; for he knew he should never obtain his Pardon for the other.

When the Messenger came, he found the Prince upon the point of engaging with the Enemy; but as soon as he heard of the Arrival of the Messenger, he commanded him to his Tent, where he embraced him, and received him with Joy; which was soon abated by the downcast Looks of the Messenger, who was instantly demanded the Cause by *Oroonoko*; who impatient of Delay, asked a thousand Questions in a Breath, and all concerning *Imoinda*. But there needed little Return, for he could almost answer himself of all he demanded, from his Sighs and Eyes. At last, the Messenger casting himself at the Prince's Feet, and kissing them with all the Submission of a Man that had something to implore which he dreaded to utter, he besought him to hear with Calmness what he had to deliver to him, and to call up all his noble and Heroic Courage, to encounter with his Words, and defend himself against the ungrateful things he must relate. *Oroonoko* replied, with a deep Sigh, and a languishing Voice, – 'I am armed against their worst Efforts –; for I know they will tell me, *Imoinda* is no more –; and after that, you may spare the rest'. Then, commanding him to rise, he laid himself on a Carpet, under a rich Pavilion, and remained a good while silent, and was hardly heard to sigh. When he was come a little to himself, the Messenger asked him leave to deliver that part of his Embassy, which the Prince had not yet divined: and the Prince cried, 'I permit thee' – Then he told him the Affliction the old King was in, for the Rashness he had committed in his Cruelty to *Imoinda*; and how he deigned to ask Pardon for his Offence, and to implore the Prince would not suffer that Loss to touch his Heart too sensibly, which now all the Gods could not restore him, but might recompense him in Glory, which he begged he would pursue; and that Death, that common Revenger of all Injuries, would soon even the Account between him and a feeble old Man.

Oroonoko bade him return his Duty to his Lord and Master; and to assure him, there was no Account of Revenge to be adjusted between them; if there was, he was the Aggressor, and that Death would be just, and maugre[30] his Age, would see him righted; and he was contented to leave his Share of Glory to Youths more fortunate and worthy of that Favour from the Gods. That henceforth he would never lift a Weapon, or draw a Bow; but abandon the small Remains of his Life to Sighs and Tears, and the continual Thoughts of what his Lord and Grandfather had thought good to send out of the World, with all that Youth, that Innocence, and Beauty.

After having spoken this, whatever his greatest Officers and Men of the best Rank could do, they could not raise him from the Carpet, or persuade him to Action and Resolutions of Life; but commanding all to retire, he shut himself into his Pavilion all that Day, while the Enemy was ready to engage; and wondering at the Delay, the whole Body of the chief of the Army then addressed themselves to him, and to whom they had much ado to get Admittance. They fell on their Faces at the Foot of his Carpet; where they lay, and besought him with earnest Prayers and Tears to lead them forth to Battle, and not let the Enemy take Advantages of them; and implored him to have regard to his Glory, and to the World, that depended on his Courage and Conduct. But he made no other Reply to all their Supplications but this, That he had now no more Business for Glory; and for the World, it was a Trifle not worth his Care. 'Go', continued he, sighing, 'and divide it amongst you; and reap with Joy what you so vainly prize, and leave me to my more welcome Destiny'.

They then demanded what they should do, and whom he would constitute in his Room, that the Confusion of ambitious Youth and Power might not ruin their Order, and make them a Prey to the Enemy. He replied, He would not give himself the Trouble –; but wished them to chose the bravest Man amongst them, let his Quality or Birth be what it would: 'For, oh my Friends', said he! 'it is not Titles that make Men brave, or good; or Birth that bestows Courage and Generosity, or makes the Owner happy. Believe this, when you behold *Oroonoko*, the most wretched, and abandoned by Fortune, of all the Creation of the Gods'. So turning himself about, he would make no more Reply to all they could urge or implore.

The Army beholding their Officers return unsuccessful, with sad Faces, and ominous Looks, that presaged no good Luck, suffered a thousand Fears to take possession of their Hearts, and the Enemy to come even upon them, before they would provide for their Safety, by any Defence: and though they were assured by some, who had a mind to animate them, that they should be immediately headed by the Prince, and that in the meantime *Aboan* had Orders to command as General; yet they were so dismayed for want of that great Example of Bravery, that they could make but a very feeble Resistance; and, at last, downright fled before the Enemy, who pursued them to the very Tents, killing them: Nor could all *Aboan*'s Courage, which that Day gained him immortal Glory,

Notes

30 *maugre* in spite of.

shame them into a Manly Defence of themselves. The Guards that were left behind, about the Prince's Tent, seeing the Soldiers flee before the Enemy, and scatter themselves all over the Plain, in great Disorder, made such Outcries, as roused the Prince from his amorous Slumber, in which he had remained buried for two Days, without permitting any Sustenance to approach him. But, in spite of all his Resolutions, he had not the Constancy of Grief to that Degree, as to make him insensible of the Danger of his Army; and in that Instant he leaped from his Couch, and cried, – 'Come, if we must die, let us meet Death the noblest Way; and 'twill be more like *Oroonoko* to encounter him at an Army's Head, opposing the Torrent of a conquering Foe, than lazily, on a Couch, to wait his lingering Pleasure, and die every Moment by a thousand wrecking Thoughts; or be tamely taken by an Enemy, and led a whining, Love-sick Slave to adorn the Triumphs of *Jamoan*, that young Victor, who already is entered beyond the Limits I had prescribed him'.

While he was speaking, he suffered his People to dress him for the Field; and sallying out of his Pavilion, with more Life and Vigour in his Countenance than ever he showed, he appeared like some Divine Power descended to save his Country from Destruction; and his People had purposely put on him all things that might make him shine with most Splendour, to strike a reverend Awe into the Beholders. He flew into the thickest of those that were pursuing his Men; and being animated with Despair, he fought as if he came on purpose to die, and did such things as will not be believed that Human Strength could perform; and such as soon inspired all the rest with new Courage, and new Order: And now it was, that they began to fight indeed; and so, as if they would not be outdone, even by their adored *Hero*; who turning the Tide of Victory, changing absolutely the Fate of the Day, gained an entire Conquest; and *Oroonoko* having the good Fortune to single out *Jamoan*, he took him Prisoner with his own Hand, having wounded him almost to death.

This *Jamoan* afterwards became very dear to him, being a Man very gallant, and of excellent Graces, and fine Parts; so that he never put him amongst the Rank of Captives, as they used to do, without distinction, for the common Sale, or Market, but kept him in his own Court, where he retained nothing of the Prisoner, but the Name, and returned no more into his own Country, so great an Affection he took for *Oroonoko*, and by a thousand Tales and Adventures of Love and Gallantry, flattered[31] his Disease of Melancholy and Languishment; which I have often heard him say, had certainly killed him, but for the Conversation of this Prince and *Aboan*, the *French* Governor he had from his Childhood, of whom I have spoken before, and who was a Man of admirable Wit, great Ingenuity and Learning; all which he had infused into his young Pupil. This *French*-Man was banished out of his own Country, for some Heretical Notions he held; and though he was a man of very little Religion, he had admirable Morals, and a brave Soul.

After the total Defeat of *Jamoan*'s Army, which all fled, or were left dead upon the Place, they spent some time in the Camp; *Oroonoko* choosing rather to remain awhile there in his Tents, than to enter into a Place, or live in a Court where he had so lately suffered so great a Loss. The Officers therefore, who saw and knew his Cause of Discontent, invented all sorts of Diversions and Sports, to entertain their Prince: So that what with those Amusements abroad, and others at home, that is, within their Tents, with the Persuasions, Arguments, and Care of his Friends and Servants that he more peculiarly prized, he wore off in time a great part of that *Shagrien*, and Torture of Despair, which the first Efforts[32] of *Imoinda*'s Death had given him: Insomuch as

Notes

[31] *flatter* "To please; to soothe. This sense is purely Gallic" (Johnson).

[32] *Efforts* a typographical error for "Effects," I think.

having received a thousand kind Embassies from the King, and Invitations to return to Court, he obeyed, though with no little Reluctancy; and when he did so, there was a visible Change in him, and for a long time he was much more melancholy than before. But Time lessens all Extremes, and reduces them to *Mediums*, and Unconcern; but no Motives or Beauties, though all endeavoured it, could engage him in any sort of Amour, though he had all the Invitations to it, both from his own Youth, and other Ambitions and Designs.

Oroonoko was no sooner returned from this last Conquest, and received at Court with all the Joy and Magnificence that could be expressed to a young Victor, who was not only returned triumphant, but beloved like a Deity, when there arrived in the Port an *English* Ship.

This Person had often before been in these Countries, and was very well known to *Oroonoko*, with whom he had trafficked for Slaves, and had used to do the same with his Predecessors.

This Commander was a Man of a finer sort of Address, and Conversation, better bred, and more engaging, than most of that sort of Men are; so that he seemed rather never to have been bred out of a Court, than almost all his Life at Sea. This Captain therefore was always better received at Court, than most of the Traders to those Countries were; and especially by *Oroonoko*, who was more civilized, according to the *European* Mode, than any other had been, and took more Delight in the *White* Nations; and, above all, Men of Parts and Wit. To this Captain he sold abundance of his Slaves; and for the Favour and Esteem he had for him, made him many Presents, and obliged him to stay at Court as long as possibly he could. Which the Captain seemed to take as a very great Honour done him, entertaining the Prince every Day with Globes and Maps, and Mathematical Discourses and Instruments; eating, drinking, hunting, and living with him with so much Familiarity, that it was not to be doubted, but he had gained very greatly upon the Heart of this gallant young Man. And the Captain, in Return of all these mighty Favours, besought the Prince to honour his Vessel with his Presence some Day or other, to Dinner, before he should set Sail; which he condescended[33] to accept, and appointed his Day. The Captain, on his part, failed not to have all things in a Readiness, in the most magnificent Order he could possibly: And the Day being come, the Captain, in his Boat, richly adorned with Carpets and Velvet-Cushions, rowed to the Shore to receive the Prince; with another Long-Boat, where was placed all his Music and Trumpets, with which *Oroonoko* was extremely delighted; who met him on the Shore, attended by his *French* Governor, *Jamoan, Aboan*, and about an hundred of the noblest of the Youths of the Court: And after they had first carried the Prince on Board, the boats fetched the rest off; where they found a very splendid Treat, with all sorts of fine Wines; and were as well entertained, as 'twas possible in such a place to be.

The Prince having drunk hard of Punch, and several Sorts of Wine, as did all the rest (for great Care was taken, they should want nothing of that part of the Entertainment) was very merry, and in great Admiration of the Ship, for he had never been in one before; so that he was curious of beholding every place where he decently might descend. The rest, no less curious, who were not quite overcome with Drinking, rambled at their pleasure *Fore* and *Aft*, as their fancies guided them: So that the Captain, who had well laid his Design before, gave the Word, and seized on all his Guests; they

Notes

[33] *condescend* "To consent to do more than mere justice can require" (Johnson).

clapping great Irons suddenly on the Prince, when he was leaped down in the Hold, to view that part of the Vessel; and locking him fast down, secured him. The same Treachery was used to all the rest; and all in one Instant, in several places of the Ship, were lashed fast in Irons, and betrayed to Slavery. That great Design over, they set all Hands to work to hoist Sail; and with as treacherous and fair a Wind, they made from the Shore with this innocent and glorious Prize, who thought of nothing less than such an Entertainment.

Some have commended this Act, as brave, in the Captain; but I will spare my Sense of it, and leave it to my Reader, to judge as he pleases.

It may be easily guessed in what manner the Prince resented this Indignity, who may be best resembled to a Lion taken in a Toil;[34] so he raged, so he struggled for Liberty, but all in vain; and they had so wisely managed his Fetters, that he could not use a Hand in his Defence, to quit himself of a Life that would by no Means endure Slavery; nor could he move from the Place, where he was tied, to any solid part of the Ship, against which he might have beat his Head, and have finished his Disgrace that way: So that being deprived of all other means, he resolved to perish for want of Food: And pleased at last with that Thought, and toiled[35] and tired by Rage and Indignation, he laid himself down, and sullenly resolved upon dying, and refused all things that were brought him.

This did not a little vex the Captain, and the more so, because, he found almost all of them of the same Humour; so that the loss of so many brave Slaves, so tall and goodly to behold, would have been very considerable: He therefore ordered one to go from him (for he would not be seen himself) to *Oroonoko*, and to assure him he was afflicted for having rashly done so inhospitable a Deed, and which could not be now remedied, since they were far from shore; but since he resented it in so high a nature, he assured him he would revoke his Resolution, and set both him and his Friends ashore on the next Land they should touch at; and of this the Messenger gave him his Oath, provided he would resolve to live: And *Oroonoko*, whose Honour was such as he never had violated a Word in his Life himself, much less a solemn Asseveration, believed in an instant what this Man said, but replied, He expected for a Confirmation of this, to have his shameful Fetters dismissed. This Demand was carried to the *Captain*, who returned him answer, That the Offence had been so great which he had put upon the Prince, that he durst not trust him with Liberty while he remained in the Ship, for fear lest by a Valour natural to him, and a Revenge that would animate that Valour, he might commit some Outrage fatal to himself and the *King* his Master, to whom the Vessel did belong. To this *Oroonoko* replied, he would engage his Honour to behave himself in all friendly Order and Manner, and obey the Command of the *Captain*, as he was Lord of the *King*'s Vessel, and General of those Men under his Command.

This was delivered to the still doubting *Captain*, who could not resolve to trust a *Heathen* he said, upon his *Parole*,[36] a Man that had no sense or notion of the God that he Worshipped. *Oroonoko* then replied, He was very sorry to hear that the *Captain* pretended to the Knowledge and Worship of any *Gods*, who had taught him no better Principles, than not to Credit as he would be Credited: but they told him, the Difference of their Faith occasioned that Distrust: for the *Captain* had protested to him upon the Word of a *Christian*, and sworn in the Name of a Great *GOD*; which if he should violate, he must expect eternal Torment in the World to come. 'Is that all the Obligation

Notes

[34] *Toil* net.

[35] *toiled* wearied.

[36] *Parole* "Word given as an assurance" (Johnson).

he has to be Just to his Oath', replied Oroonoko? 'Let him know I Swear by my Honour, which to violate, would not only render me contemptible and despised by all brave and honest Men, and so give myself perpetual pain, but it would be eternally offending and diseasing[37] all Mankind, harming, betraying, circumventing and outraging all Men; but Punishments hereafter are suffered by oneself; and the World takes no cognizances whether this God has revenged them, or not, 'tis done so secretly, and deferred so long; While the Man of no Honour suffers every moment the scorn and contempt of the honester World, and dies every day ignominiously in his Fame,[38] which is more valuable than Life: I speak not this to move Belief, but to show you how you mistake when you imagine. That he who will violate his Honour will keep his Word with his *Gods*'. So turning from him with a disdainful smile, he refused to answer him, when he urged him to know what Answer he should carry back to his *Captain*; so that he departed without saying any more.

The Captain pondering and consulting what to do, it was concluded that nothing but *Oroonoko*'s Liberty would encourage any of the rest to eat, except the *French*-man, whom the *Captain* could not pretend to keep Prisoner, but only told him he was secured because he might act something in favour of the Prince, but that he should be freed as soon as they came to Land. So that they concluded it wholly necessary to free the Prince from his Irons, that he might show himself to the rest; that they might have an Eye upon him, and that they could not fear a single Man.

This being resolved, to make the Obligation the greater, the Captain himself went to *Oroonoko*; where, after many Compliments, and Assurances of what he had already promised, he receiving from the Prince his *Parole*, and his Hand, for his good Behaviour, dismissed his Irons, and brought him to his own Cabin; where, after having treated and reposed him a while, for he had neither eaten nor slept in four Days before, he besought him to visit those obstinate People in Chains, who refused all manner of Sustenance; and entreated him to oblige them to eat, and assure them of their Liberty the first Opportunity.

Oroonoko, who was too generous not to give Credit to his Words, showed himself to his People, who were transported with Excess of Joy at the sight of their Darling Prince, falling at his Feet, and kissing and embracing them, believing, as some Divine Oracle, all he assured them. But he besought them to bear their Chains with that Bravery that became those whom he had seen act so nobly in Arms; and that they could not give him greater Proofs of their Love and Friendship, since it was all the Security the Captain (his Friend) could have against the Revenge, he said, they might possibly justly take, for the Injuries sustained by him. And they all, with one Accord, assured him, that they could not suffer enough, when it was for his Repose and Safety.

After this they no longer refused to eat, but took what was brought them, and were pleased with their Captivity, since by it they hoped to redeem the Prince, who, all the rest of the Voyage, was treated with all the Respect due to his Birth, though nothing could divert his Melancholy; and he would often sigh for *Imoinda*, and think this a Punishment due to his Misfortune, in having left that noble Maid behind him, that fatal Night, in the *Otan*, when he fled to the Camp.

Possessed with a thousand Thoughts of past Joys with this fair young Person, and a thousand Griefs for her eternal Loss, he endured a tedious Voyage, and at last arrived at the Mouth of the River of *Surinam*, a Colony belonging to the King of *England*, and

Notes

[37] *disease* "To put to pain; to pain; to make uneasy" (Johnson).

[38] *Fame* reputation.

where they were to deliver some part of their Slaves. There the Merchants and Gentlemen of the Country going on Board, to demand those Lots of Slaves they had already agreed on; and amongst those, the Overseers of those Plantations where I then chanced to be, the Captain, who had given the Word, ordered his men to bring up those noble Slaves in Fetters, whom I have spoken of; and having put them, some in one, and some in other Lots, with Women and Children (which they call *Pickaninies*,[39]) they sold them off, as Slaves, to several Merchants and Gentlemen; not putting any two in one Lot, because they would separate them far from each other; not daring to trust them together, lest Rage and Courage should put them upon contriving some great Action, to the Ruin of the Colony.

Oroonoko was first seized on, and sold to our Overseer, who had the first Lot, with seventeen more of all sorts and sizes, but not one of Quality with him. When he saw this, he found what they meant; for, as I said, he understood *English* pretty well; and being wholly unarmed and defenceless, so as it was in vain to make any Resistance, he only beheld the Captain with a Look all fierce and disdainful, upbraiding him with Eyes, that forced Blushes on his guilty Cheeks, he only cried, in passing over the Side of the Ship: 'Farewell, Sir: 'Tis worth my Suffering, to gain so true a Knowledge both of you, and of your Gods by whom you swear'. And desiring those that held him to forbear their pains, and telling them he would make no Resistance, he cried, 'Come, my Fellow-Slaves, let us descend, and see if we can meet with more Honour and Honesty in the next World we shall touch upon'. So he nimbly leaped into the Boat, and showing no more Concern, suffered himself to be rowed up the River, with his seventeen Companions.

The Gentleman that bought him was a young *Cornish* Gentleman, whose Name was *Trefry*;[40] a man of great Wit, and fine Learning, and was carried into those Parts by the Lord —— Governor, to manage all his Affairs. He reflecting on the last Words of *Oroonoko* to the Captain, and beholding the Richness of his Vest, no sooner came into the Boat, but he fixed his Eyes on him; and finding something so extraordinary in his Face, his Shape and Mien, a Greatness of Look, and Haughtiness in his Air, and finding he spoke *English*, had a great mind to be inquiring into his Quality and Fortune; which, though *Oroonoko* endeavoured to hide, by only confessing he was above the Rank of common Slaves, *Trefry* soon found he was yet something greater than he confessed; and from that Moment began to conceive so vast an Esteem for him, that he ever after loved him as his dearest Brother, and showed him all the Civilities due to so great a Man.

Trefry was a very good Mathematician, and a Linguist; could speak *French* and *Spanish*; and in the three Days they remained in the Boat (for so long were they going from the Ship to the Plantation) he entertained *Oroonoko* so agreeably with his *Art* and *Discourse*, that he was no less pleased with *Trefry*, than he was with the Prince; and he thought himself, at least, fortunate in this, that since he was a Slave, as long as he would suffer himself to remain so, he had a Man of so excellent Wit and Parts for a Master: So that before they had finished their Voyage up the River, he made no scruple of declaring to *Trefry* all his Fortunes, and most part of what I have here related, and put himself wholly into the Hands of his new Friend, whom he found resenting all the Injuries were done him, and was charmed with all the Greatness of his Actions; which were recited with that Modesty, and delicate Sense, as wholly vanquished him, and

Notes

39 *Pickaninies* from Portuguese *pequenino*; first use recorded in the *OED* is 1657.

40 *Trefry* John Trefry, the actual overseer for the governor, Francis Willoughby, to whom Charles II had issued letters patent for control of the region in 1663; Willoughby died in a storm at sea in 1666, as Behn correctly suggests later.

subdued him to his Interest. And he promised him on his Word and Honour, he would find the Means to re-conduct him to his own Country again: assuring him, he had a perfect Abhorrence of so dishonourable an Action; and that he would sooner have died, than have been the author of such a Perfidy. He found the Prince was very much concerned to know what became of his Friends, and how they took their Slavery; and *Trefry* promised to take care about the inquiring after their Condition, and that he should have an Account of them.

Though, as *Oroonoko* afterwards said, he had little reason to credit the words of a *Backearary*;[41] yet he knew not why; but he saw a kind of Sincerity, and awful Truth in the Face of *Trefry*; he saw an Honesty in his Eyes, and he found him wise and witty enough to understand Honour: for it was one of his Maxims, A Man of Wit could not be a Knave or Villain.

In their passage up the River, they put in at several Houses for Refreshment; and ever when they landed, numbers of People would flock to behold this Man; not but their Eyes were daily entertained with the sight of Slaves; but the Fame of *Oroonoko* was gone before him, and all People were in Admiration of his Beauty. Besides, he had a rich Habit on, in which he was taken, so different from the rest, and which the Captain could not strip him of, because he was forced to surprise[42] his Person in the Minute he sold him. When he found his Habit made him liable, as he thought, to be gazed at the more, he begged *Trefry* to give him something more befitting a Slave; which he did, and took off his Robes. Nevertheless, he shone through all; and his *Osenbrigs* (a sort of brown *Holland Suit* he had on) could not conceal the Graces of his Looks and Mien; and he had no less Admirers, than when he had his dazzling Habit on: The Royal Youth appeared in spite of the Slave, and People could not help treating him after a different manner, without designing it: As soon as they approached him, they venerated and esteemed him; his Eyes insensibly commanded Respect, and his Behaviour insinuated it into every Soul. So that there was nothing talked of but this young and gallant Slave, even by those who yet knew not that he was a Prince.

I ought to tell you, that the *Christians* never buy any Slaves but they give them some Name of their own, their native ones being likely very barbarous,[43] and hard to pronounce; so that Mr. *Trefry* gave *Oroonoko* that of *Cæsar*; which Name will live on in that Country as long as that (scarce more) glorious one of the great *Roman*: for 'tis most evident, he wanted no part of the Personal Courage of that *Cæsar*, and acted things as memorable, had they been done in some part of the World replenished with People, and Historians, that might have given him his due. But his Misfortune was, to fall in an obscure World, that afforded only a Female Pen to celebrate his Fame; though I doubt not but it had lived from others' Endeavours, if the *Dutch*, who immediately after his Time took that Country, had not killed, banished and dispersed all those that were capable of giving the World this great Man's Life, much better than I have done. And Mr. *Trefry*, who designed it, died before he began it; and bemoaned himself for not having undertook it in time.

For the future therefore I must call *Oroonoko, Cæsar*, since by that Name only he was known in our Western World, and by that name he was received on Shore at *Parham House*,[44] where he was destined a Slave. But if the King himself (God bless him) had

Notes

[41] *Backearary* white man.

[42] *surprise* reveal, display.

[43] *barbarous* foreign or "A form of speech contrary to the purity and exactness of any language" (Johnson, s.v. "barbarism").

[44] *Parham House* part of Lord Willoughby's estate.

come ashore there could not have been greater Expectations by all the whole Plantation, and those neighbouring ones, than was on ours at that time; and he was received more like a Governor than a Slave. Notwithstanding, as the Custom was, they assigned him his Portion of Land, his House, and his Business, up in the Plantation. But as it was more for Form, than any Design, to put him to his Task, he endured no more of the Slave but the Name, and remained some Days in the House, receiving all Visits that were made him, without stirring towards that part of the Plantation where the *Negroes* were.

At last, he would needs go view his Land, his House, and the Business assigned him. But he no sooner came to the Houses of the Slaves, which are like a little Town by itself, the *Negroes* all having left Work, but they all came forth to behold him, and found he was that Prince who had, at several times, sold most of them to these Parts; and from a Veneration they pay to great Men, especially if they know them, and from the Surprise and Awe they had at the sight of him, they all cast themselves at his Feet, crying out, in their Language, 'Live, O King! Long live, O King!' And kissing his Feet, paid him even Divine Homage.

Several *English* Gentlemen were with him; and what Mr. *Trefry* told them, was here confirmed; of which he himself before had no other Witness than *Cæsar* himself: But he was infinitely glad to find his Grandeur confirmed by all the Adoration of the Slaves.

Cæsar, troubled with their Over-Joy, and Over-Ceremony, besought them to rise, and to receive him as their Fellow-Slave, assuring them, he was no better. At which they set up with one Accord a most terrible and hideous Mourning and condoling, which he and the *English* had much ado to appease; but at last they prevailed with them, and they prepared all their barbarous Music, and everyone killed and dressed something of his own Stock (for every Family has their Land apart, on which, at their leisure times, they breed all eatable things); and clubbing it together, made a most magnificent Supper, inviting their *Grandee Captain*, their *Prince*, to honour it with his Presence; which he did, and several *English* with him; where they all waited on him, some playing, others dancing before him all the time, according to the Manners of their several Nations, and with unwearied Industry endeavouring to please and delight him.

While they sat at Meat, Mr. *Trefry* told *Cæsar*, that most of these young *Slaves* were undone in Love with a fine she *Slave*, whom they had had about Six Months on their Land; the *Prince*, who never heard the Name of *Love* without a Sigh, nor any mention of it without the Curiosity of examining further into that tale, which of all Discourses was most agreeable to him, asked, how they came to be so Unhappy, as to be all Undone for one fair *Slave*? *Trefry*, who was naturally Amorous, and loved to talk of Love as well as anybody, proceeded to tell him, they had the most charming Black that ever was beheld on their *Plantation*, about Fifteen or Sixteen Years old, as he guessed; that for his part, he had done nothing but Sigh for her ever since she came; and that all the white Beauties he had seen, never charmed him so absolutely as this fine Creature had done; and that no Man, of any Nation, ever beheld her, that did not fall in Love with her; and that she had all the *Slaves* perpetually at her Feet; and the whole Country resounded with the Fame of *Clemene*, for so, said he, we have Christened her: But she denies us all with such noble Disdain, that 'tis a Miracle to see, that she, who can give such eternal Desires, should herself be all Ice, and all Unconcern. She is adorned with the most Graceful Modesty that ever beautified Youth; the softest Sigher – that, if she were capable of Love, one would swear she languished for some absent happy Man; and so retired, as if she feared a Rape even from the God of Day; or that the Breezes would steal Kisses from her delicate Mouth. Her Task of Work some sighing Lover every day makes it his Petition to perform for her, which she accepts blushing, and with reluctancy, for fear he will ask her a Look for a Recompense, which he dares not presume to hope, so great an Awe she strikes into the Hearts of her Admirers. 'I do not wonder', replied the Prince, 'that *Clemene* should refuse Slaves, being as you say so Beautiful, but wonder how she escapes those who entertain her as you can do; or why, being your Slave, you do not oblige her to yield'.

'I confess', said Trefry, 'when I have, against her will, entertained her with Love so long, as to be transported with my Passion, even above Decency, I have been ready to make use of those advantages of Strength and Force Nature has given me. But oh! she disarms me with that Modesty and Weeping so tender and so moving, that I retire, and thank my Stars she overcame me'. The Company laughed at his Civility to a *Slave*, and *Cæsar* only applauded the nobleness of his Passion and Nature; since that Slave might be Noble, or, what was better, have true Notions of Honour and Virtue in her. Thus passed they this night, after having received, from the *Slaves* all imaginable Respect and Obedience.

The next day, *Trefry* asked *Cæsar* to walk when the heat was allayed, and designedly carried him by the cottage of the *fair Slave*; and told him, she whom he spoke of last Night lived there retired: 'But', says he, 'I would not wish for you to approach, for, I am sure you will be in Love as soon as you behold her'. *Cæsar* assured him, he was proof against all the Charms of that Sex; and that if he imagined his Heart could be so perfidious to Love again, after *Imoinda*, he believed he should tear it from his Bosom: They had no sooner spoke, but a little shock Dog,[45] that *Clemene* had presented her, which she took great Delight in, ran out; and she, not knowing anybody was there, ran to get it in again, and bolted out on those who were just Speaking of her: When seeing them, she would have run in again; but *Trefry* caught her by the Hand, and cried, '*Clemene*, however you fly a Lover, you ought to pay some respect to this Stranger', pointing to *Cæsar*. But she, as if she had resolved never to raise her Eyes to the Face of a Man again, bent them the more to the Earth, when he spoke, and gave the *Prince* the Leisure to look the more at her. There needed no long-Gazing, or Consideration, to examine who this fair Creature was; he soon saw *Imoinda* all over her; in a Minute he saw her Face, her Shape, her Air, her Modesty, and all that called forth his Soul with Joy at his Eyes, and left his Body destitute of almost life; it stood without Motion, and for a Minute, knew not that it had a Being; and, I believe, he had never come to himself, so oppressed he was with over-Joy, if he had not met with this Allay, that he perceived *Imoinda* fall dead in the Hands of *Trefry*: This awakened him, and he ran to her aid, and caught her in his Arms, where, by degrees, she came to herself; and 'tis needless to tell what transports, what ecstasies of Joy, they both a while beheld each other, without Speaking; then Snatched each other to their Arms; then Gaze again, as if they still doubted whether they possessed the Blessing They Grasped, but when they recovered their Speech, 'tis not to be imagined, what tender things they expressed to each other, wondering what strange Fate had brought them again together. They soon informed each other of their Fortunes, and equally bewailed their Fate; but, at the same time they mutually protested, that even Fetters and Slavery were Soft and Easy, and would be supported with Joy and Pleasure, while they could be so happy to possess each other, and to be able to make good their Vows. *Cæsar* swore he disdained the Empire of the World, while he could behold his *Imoinda*; and she despised Grandeur and Pomp, those Vanities of her sex, when she could Gaze on *Oroonoko*. He adored the very Cottage where she resided, and said, That little Inch of the World would give him

Notes

[45] *shock Dog* "[from *shagg*] A rough dog" (Johnson).

more Happiness than all the Universe could do; and she vowed, It was a Palace, while adorned with the Presence of *Oroonoko*.

Trefry was infinitely pleased with this Novel,[46] and found this *Clemene* was the Fair Mistress of whom *Cæsar* had before spoke; and was not a little satisfied, that Heaven was so kind to the *Prince*, as to sweeten his Misfortunes by so lucky an Accident; and leaving the Lovers to themselves, was impatient to come down to *Parham House* (which was on the same *Plantation*) to give me an Account of what had happened. I was as impatient to make these Lovers a Visit, having already made a Friendship with *Cæsar*; and from his own Mouth learned what I have related, which was confirmed by his French-man, who was set on Shore to seek his Fortunes, and of whom they could not make a Slave, because a Christian; and he came daily to *Parham Hill* to see and pay his Respects to his Pupil *Prince*: So that concerning and interesting myself, in all that related to *Cæsar*, whom I had assured of Liberty, as soon as the Governor arrived, I hasted presently to the Place where the Lovers were, and was infinitely glad to find this Beautiful young *Slave* (who had already gained all our Esteems, for her Modesty and extraordinary Prettiness) to be the same I had heard *Cæsar* speak so much of. One may imagine then, we paid her a treble Respect; and though from her being carved in fine Flowers and Birds all over her body, we took her to be of Quality before, yet when we knew *Clemene* was *Imoinda*, we could not enough admire her.

I had forgot to tell you, that those who are Nobly born of that Country, are so delicately Cut and Raced[47] all over the fore-part of the Trunk of their Bodies, that it looks as if it were Japanned,[48] the Works being raised like high Point[49] round the Edges of the Flowers: Some are only Carved with a little Flower, or Bird, at the Sides of the Temples, as was *Cæsar*; and those who are so Carved over the Body, resemble our Ancient *Picts*[50] that are figured in the Chronicles,[51] but these Carvings are far more delicate.

From that happy Day *Cæsar* took *Clemene* for his Wife, to the general Joy of all People; and there was as much Magnificence as the Country would afford at the Celebration of this Wedding: and in a very short time after she conceived with Child, which made *Cæsar* even adore her, knowing he was the last of his Great Race. This new Accident made him more Impatient of Liberty, and he was every Day treating with *Trefry* for his and *Clemene*'s Liberty, and offered either Gold, or a vast quantity of Slaves, which should be paid before they let him go, provided he could have any Security that he should go when his Ransom was paid: They fed him from Day to Day with Promises, and delayed him, till the Lord-Governor should come; so that he began to suspect them of falsehood, and that they would delay him till the time of his Wife's delivery, and make a slave of that too, for all the Breed is theirs to whom the Parents belong: This Thought made him very uneasy, and his Sullenness gave them some Jealousies[52] of him; so that I was obliged, by some Persons, who feared a Mutiny (which is very Fatal sometimes in those Colonies that abound so with Slaves, that they exceed the Whites in vast Numbers) to discourse with *Cæsar*, and to give him all the Satisfaction I possibly could; they knew he and *Clemene* were scarce an Hour in a Day from my Lodgings; that they eat with me, and that I obliged them in all things I was capable of: I entertained them with the Lives of the Romans, and great Men, which charmed him

Notes

46 *Novel* "A small tale, generally of love" (Johnson).

47 *race* "Cut or slash (shoes or clothes) in an ornamental fashion" (*OED*).

48 *Japan* "To varnish, and embellish with gold and raised figures" (Johnson).

49 *high Point* fancy embroidery or lace.

50 *Picts* early inhabitants of Scotland.

51 *Chronicles* any of a number of early British historical writings and later imitations thereof.

52 *Jealousy* "Suspicious fear" (Johnson).

to my Company; and her, with teaching her all the pretty Works I was Mistress of, and telling her Stories of Nuns, and endeavouring to bring her to the knowledge of the true God. But of all Discourses, *Cæsar* liked that the worst, and would never be reconciled to our Notions of the Trinity, of which he ever made a Jest; it was a Riddle, he said, would turn his Brain[53] to conceive, and one could not make him understand what Faith was. However, these Conversations failed not altogether so well to divert him, that he liked the Company of us Women much above the Men; for he could not Drink, and he is but an ill Companion in that Country that cannot: So that obliging him to love us very well, we had all the Liberty of Speech with him, especially myself, whom he called his *Great Mistress*; and indeed my Word would go a great way with him. For these reasons I had Opportunity to take notice to him, that he was not well pleased of late, as he used to be (was more retired and thoughtful) and told him, I took it ill he should Suspect we would break our Words with him, and not permit both him and *Clemene* to return to his own Kingdom, which was not so long a way, but when he was once on his Voyage he would quickly arrive there. He made me some Answers that showed a doubt in him, which made me ask him, what advantage it would be to doubt? it would but give us a Fear of him, and possibly compel us to treat him so as I should be very loath to behold: that is, it might occasion his Confinement. Perhaps this was not so Luckily spoke of me,[54] for I perceived he resented that Word, which I strove to Soften again in vain: However, he assured me, that whatsoever Resolutions he should take, he would Act nothing upon the White-People; and as for myself, and those upon that *Plantation* where he was, he would sooner forfeit his eternal Liberty, and Life it self, than lift his Hand against his greatest Enemy on that Place: He besought me to suffer no Fears upon his Account, for he could do nothing that Honour should not dictate; but he accused himself for having suffered Slavery so long; yet he charged that weakness on Love alone, who was capable of making him neglect even Glory itself, and, for which, now he reproaches himself every moment of the Day. Much more to this effect he spoke, with an Air impatient enough to make me know he would not be long in Bondage; and though he suffered only the Name of a Slave, and had nothing of the Toil and Labour of one, yet that was sufficient to render him Uneasy; and he had been too long Idle, who used to be always in Action, and in Arms: He had a Spirit all Rough and Fierce, and that could not be tamed to lazy Rest; and though all endeavours were used to exercise himself in such Actions and Sports as this World afforded, as Running, Wrestling, Pitching the Bar,[55] Hunting and Fishing, Chasing and Killing *Tigers* of a monstrous Size, which this Continent affords in abundance; and wonderful *Snakes*, such as *Alexander* is reported to have encountered at the River of *Amazons*,[56] and which *Cæsar* took great Delight to overcome; yet these were not Actions great enough for his large Soul, which was still panting after more renowned Action.

Before I parted that Day with him, I got, with much ado, a Promise from him to rest yet a little longer with Patience, and wait the coming of the Lord Governor, who was every Day expected on our Shore; he assured me he would, and this Promise he desired me to know was given perfectly in Complaisance to me, in whom he had an entire Confidence.

Notes

[53] *turn his Brain* "To infatuate; to make mad" (Johnson, sense 22).

[54] *spoke of me* spoken by me.

[55] *Pitching the Bar* a kind of weight-throwing contest (see *Spectator* 434).

[56] *Alexander is reported … Amazons* in one of the many romances of Alexander based on the fictional history of Pseudo-Callisthenes.

After this, I neither thought it convenient to trust him much out of our View, nor did the Country who feared him; but with one accord it was advised to treat him Fairly, and oblige him to remain within such a compass, and that he should be permitted, as seldom as could be, to go up to the Plantations of the Negroes; or, if he did, to be accompanied by some that should be rather in appearance Attendants than Spies. This Care was for some time taken, and *Cæsar* looked upon it as a Mark of extraordinary Respect, and was glad his discontent had obliged them to be more observant to him; he received new assurance from the Overseer, which was confirmed to him by the Opinion of all the Gentlemen of the Country, who made their court of him: During this time that we had his Company more frequently than hitherto we had had, it may not be unpleasant to relate to you the Diversions we entertained him with, or rather he us.

My stay was to be short in that Country, because my Father died at Sea, and never arrived to possess the Honour was designed him (which was Lieutenant-General of Six and thirty Islands, besides the Continent[57] of *Surinam*) nor the advantages he hoped to reap by them; so that though we were obliged to continue on our Voyage, we did not intend to stay upon the Place: Though, in a Word, I must say this much of it, That certainly had his late Majesty,[58] of sacred Memory, but seen and known what a vast and charming World he had been Master of in that Continent, he would never have parted so easily with it to the Dutch.[59] 'Tis a Continent whose vast Extent was never yet known, and may contain more Noble Earth than all the Universe besides; for, they say, it reaches from East to West one way as far as *China*, and another to *Peru*:[60] It affords all things both for Beauty and Use; 'tis there Eternal Spring, always the very Months of *April*, *May*, and *June*; the Shades are perpetual, the Trees, bearing at once all degrees of Leaves, and Fruit, from blooming Buds to ripe Autumn; Groves of Oranges, Lemons, Citrons, Figs, Nutmegs, and noble Aromatics, continually bearing their Fragrancies. The trees appearing all like Nosegays adorned with Flowers of different kind; some are all White, some Purple, some Scarlet, some Blue, some Yellow; bearing, at the same time, Ripe Fruit and Blooming Young, or producing every Day new. The very Wood of all these Trees has an intrinsic Value, above common Timber; for they are, when cut, of different Colours, glorious to behold, and bear a Price considerable, to inlay withal. Besides this, they yield rich Balm, and Gums; so that we make our Candles of such an Aromatic Substance, as does not only give a sufficient Light, but, as they Burn, they cast their Perfumes all about. Cedar is the common Firing, and all the Houses are built with it. The very Meat we eat, when set on the Table, if it be Native, I mean of the Country, perfumes the whole Room; especially a little Beast called an *Armadilly*, a thing which I can liken to nothing so well as a *Rhinoceros*; 'tis all in white Armour so jointed, that it moves as well in it, as if it had nothing on; this Beast is about the bigness of a pig Six Weeks old. But it were endless to give an Account of all the divers Wonderful and Strange things that Country affords, and which we took a great Delight to go in search of; though those adventures are oftentimes Fatal, and at least Dangerous. But while we had *Cæsar* in our Company on these Designs we feared no harm, nor suffered any.

Notes

57 *Continent* "Land not disjoined by the sea from other lands" (Johnson).

58 *his late Majesty* Charles II.

59 *Dutch* The English gave up Surinam to the Dutch in the Treaty of Breda (1667) and took control of New York.

60 *'Tis a Continent ... to Peru* the description reflects the fact that the region was thought to contain the fabulous city of El Dorado; Raleigh sailed up the Orinoco River in search of that golden world in 1595.

As soon as I came into the Country, the best House in it was presented me, called St. *John's Hill*.[61] It stood on a vast Rock of white Marble, at the Foot of which the River ran a vast depth down, and not to be descended on that side; the little Waves still dashing and washing the foot of this Rock, made the softest Murmurs and Purlings in the World; and the Opposite Bank was adorned with such vast quantities of different Flowers eternally Blowing,[62] and every Day and Hour new, fenced behind them with lofty Trees of a Thousand rare Forms and Colours, that the Prospect was the most ravishing that Sands[63] can create. On the Edge of this white Rock, towards the River, was a Walk or Grove of Orange and Lemon Trees, about half the length of the Mall[64] here, whose Flowery and Fruit-bearing Branches met at the top, and hindered the sun, whose Rays are very fierce there, from entering a Beam into the Grove; and the cool Air that came from the River made it not only fit to entertain People in, at all the hottest Hours of the Day, but refresh the sweet Blossoms, and made it always Sweet and Charming; and sure the whole Globe of the World cannot show so delightful a Place as this Grove was: Not all the Gardens of boasted *Italy* can produce a Shade to outvie this, which Nature had joined with Art to render so exceeding Fine; and 'tis a marvel to see how such vast Trees, as big as English Oaks, could take footing on so solid a Rock, and in so little Earth, as covered that Rock. But all things by Nature there are Rare, Delightful and Wonderful. But to our Sports.

Sometimes we would go surprising and in search of young *Tigers* in their Dens, watching when the old Ones went forth to forage for Prey; and oftentimes we have been in great Danger, and have fled apace for our Lives, when surprised by the Dams. But once, above all other times, we went on this Design, and *Cæsar* went with us, who had no sooner stolen a young *Tiger* from her Nest, but going off, we encountered the Dam, bearing a Buttock of a Cow, which she had torn off with her mighty Paw, and going with it towards his *Den*; we had only four Women, *Cæsar*, and an English Gentleman, Brother to *Harry Martin*, the great *Oliverian*;[65] we found there was no escaping this enraged and ravenous Beast. However, we Women fled as fast as we could from it; but our Heels had not saved our Lives, if *Cæsar* had not laid down his *Cub*, when he found the *Tiger* quit her Prey to make the more speed towards him; and taking Mr. *Martin*'s Sword desired him to stand aside, or follow the Ladies. He obeyed him, and *Cæsar* met this monstrous Beast of might, size, and vast Limbs, who came with open Jaws upon him; and fixing his Awful stern Eyes full upon those of the Beast, and putting himself into a very steady and good aiming posture of Defence, ran his Sword quite through his Breast, down to his very Heart, home to the Hilt of the Sword; the dying Beast stretched forth her Paw, and going to grasp his Thigh, surprised with Death in that very moment, did him no other harm than fixing her long Nails in his Flesh very deep, feebly wounded him, but could not grasp the Flesh to tear off any. When he had done this, he hallooed us to return, which, after some assurance of his Victory, we did, and found him lugging out the Sword from the Bosom of the *Tiger*, who was laid in her Blood on the Ground; he took up the *Cub*, and with an unconcern, that had nothing of the Joy or Gladness of a Victory, he came and laid the Whelp at my Feet: We all extremely wondered at his Daring, and at the Bigness of the Beast, which was about the highth of an Heifer, but of mighty, great, and strong Limbs.

Notes

[61] *St. John's Hill* an estate probably sold to Willoughby in 1664 by Robert Harley (1626–73), uncle of the more famous Robert, first earl of Oxford (1661–1724).

[62] *Blowing* blooming.

[63] *Sands* emended to "Fancy" in some later editions.

[64] *Mall* a fashionable walk in St James's Park, London.

[65] *Harry Martin, the great Oliverian* Henry Marten, a Republican Politician, though not a supporter of Oliver Cromwell; there was a plantation owner in Surinam named Martin (or Marten) who may have been the brother of Henry.

Another time, being in the Woods, he killed a *Tiger*, which had long infested that part, and borne away abundance of Sheep and Oxen, and other things, that were for the support of those to whom they belonged; abundance of People assailed this Beast, some affirming they had shot her with several Bullets quite through the Body, at several times; and some swearing they shot her through the very Heart, and they believed she was a Devil rather than a Mortal thing. *Cæsar*, had often said, he had a mind to encounter this Monster, and spoke with several Gentlemen who had attempted her, one crying, 'I shot her with so many poisoned Arrows', another with his Gun in this part of her, and another in that; so that he remarking all these Places where she was shot, fancied still he should overcome her, by giving her another sort of Wound than any had yet done; and one day said (at the Table) 'What Trophies and Garlands Ladies will you make me if I bring you home the Heart of this Ravenous Beast, that eats up all your Lambs and Pigs?' We all promised he should be rewarded at all our Hands. So taking a Bow, which he chose out of a great many, he went up into the Wood with two Gentlemen, where he imagined this Devourer to be. They had not passed very far into it when they heard her Voice growling and grumbling, as if she were pleased with something she was doing. When they came in view, they found her muzzling in the Belly of a new ravished Sheep, which she had torn open; and seeing herself approached, she took fast hold of her Prey with her fore Paws, and set a very fierce raging look on *Cæsar*, without offering to approach him; for fear, at the same time of losing what she had in Possession. So that *Cæsar* remained a good while, only taking aim, and getting an opportunity to shoot her where he designed; 'twas some time before he could accomplish it, and to wound her, and not kill her, would but have enraged her more, and endangered him: He had a Quiver of Arrows at his side, so that if one failed he could be supplied; at last, retiring a little, he gave her opportunity to eat, for he found she was Ravenous, and fell to as soon as she saw him retire, being more eager of her Prey than of doing new Mischiefs. When he going softly to one side of her, and hiding his Person behind certain Herbage that grew high and thick, he took so good aim, that, as he intended, he shot her just into the Eye, and the Arrow was sent with so good a will, and so sure a hand, that it stuck in her Brain, and made her caper, and become mad for a moment or two; but being seconded by another Arrow, he[66] fell dead upon the Prey. *Cæsar* cut him open with a Knife, to see where those Wounds were that had been reported to him, and why she did not Die of them. But I shall now relate a thing that possibly will find no Credit among Men, because 'tis a Notion commonly received with us, That nothing can receive a Wound in the Heart and Live; but when the Heart of this courageous Animal was taken out, there were Seven Bullets of Lead in it, and the Wounds seamed up with great Scars, and she lived with the Bullets a great while, for it was long since they were shot: This Heart the Conqueror brought up to us, and 'twas a very great Curiosity, which all the Country came to see; and which gave *Cæsar* occasion of many fine Discourses of Accidents in War, and Strange Escapes.

At other times he would go a Fishing; and discoursing on that Diversion, he found we had in that Country a very Strange Fish, called, a *Numb Eel*[67] (an *Eel* of which I have eaten) that while it is alive, it has a quality so Cold, that those who are Angling, though with a Line of ever so great a length, with a Rod at the end of it, it shall, in the same minute the Bait is touched by this *Eel*, seize him or her that holds the Rod with benumbedness, that shall deprive them of Sense, for a while; and some have fallen into the Water, and others dropped as dead on the Banks of the Rivers where they stood, as soon

Notes

[66] *he* the gender of the beast seems to change.

[67] *Numb Eel* electric eel.

as this Fish touches the Bait. *Cæsar* used to laugh at this, and believed it impossible a Man could lose his Force at the touch of a Fish; and could not understand that Philosophy,[68] that a cold Quality should be of that Nature: However, he had a great Curiosity to try whether it would have the same effect on him it had on others, and often tried, but in vain; at last, the sought for Fish came to the Bait, as he stood Angling on the Bank; and instead of throwing away the Rod, or giving it a sudden twitch out of the Water, whereby he might have caught both the *Eel*, and have dismissed the Rod, before it could have too much Power over him; for Experiment sake, he grasped it but the harder, and fainting fell into the River; and still being possessed of the Rod, the Tide carried him senseless as he was a great way, till an *Indian* Boat took him up and perceived, when they touched him, a Numbness seize them, and by that knew the Rod was in his Hand, which, with a Paddle (that is a short Oar) they struck away, and snatched it into the Boat, *Eel* and all. If *Cæsar* was almost Dead, with the effect of this Fish, he was more so with that of the Water, where he had remained the space of going a League;[69] and they found they had much ado to bring him back to Life: But, at last, they did, and brought him home, where he was in a few Hours well Recovered and Refreshed, and not a little Ashamed to find he should be overcome by an *Eel*; and all the People, who heard his Defiance, would Laugh at him. But we cheered him up; and he, being convinced, we had the *Eel* at Supper, which was a quarter of an Ell about, and most delicate Meat; and was of the more Value, since it cost so Dear, as almost the Life of so gallant a Man.

About this time we were in many mortal Fears, about some Disputes the *English* had with the *Indians*; so that we could scarce trust ourselves, without great Numbers, to go to any *Indian* Towns, or Place, where they abode for fear they should fall upon us, as they did immediately after my coming away; and that it was in the possession of the *Dutch*, who used them not so civilly as the *English*; so that they cut in pieces all they could take, getting into Houses, and hanging up the Mother, and all her Children about her; and cut a Footman I left behind me, all in Joints,[70] and nailed him to Trees.

This feud began while I was there; so that I lost half the satisfaction I proposed, in not seeing and visiting the *Indian* Towns. But one Day, bemoaning of our Misfortunes upon this account, *Cæsar* told us, we need not Fear; for if we had a mind to go, he would undertake to be our Guard: Some would, but most would not venture; about Eighteen of us resolved, and took Barge; and, after Eight Days, arrived near an *Indian* Town: But approaching it, the Hearts of some of our Company failed, and they would not venture on Shore; so we Polled who would, and who would not: For my part, I said, if *Cæsar* would, I would go; he resolved, so did my Brother, and my Woman, a Maid of good Courage. Now none of us speaking the Language of the People, and imagining we should have a half Diversion in Gazing only; and not knowing what they said, we took a Fisherman that lived at the Mouth of the River, who had been a long Inhabitant there, and obliged him to go with us: But because he was known to the *Indians*, as trading among them; and being, by long Living there, become a perfect Indian in colour, we, who resolved to surprise them, by making them see something they never had seen (that is, White People), resolved only myself, my Brother and Woman should go; so *Cæsar*, the Fisherman, and the rest, hiding behind some thick Reeds and Flowers, that grew on the Banks, let us pass on towards the Town, which was on the Bank of the River all along. A little distant from the Houses, or Huts; we saw

Notes

[68] *Philosophy* scientific principle.

[69] *League* a nautical measurement; three miles.

[70] *Joint* "One of the limbs of an animal cut up by the butcher" (Johnson).

some Dancing, others busied in fetching and carrying of Water from the River: They had no sooner spied us, but they set up a loud Cry, that frighted us at first; we thought it had been for those that should Kill us, but it seems it was of Wonder and Amazement. They were all Naked, and we were Dressed, so as is most comode[71] for the hot Countries, very Glittering and Rich; so that we appeared extremely fine; my own Hair was cut short, and I had a Taffaty[72] Cap, with Black Feathers, on my Head; my Brother was in a Stuff [73] Suit, with Silver Loops and Buttons, and abundance of Green Ribbon; this was all infinitely surprising to them, and because we saw them stand still till we approached them, we took Heart and advanced, came up to them and offered them our Hands, which they took, and looked on us round about, calling still for more Company, who came swarming out, all wondering, and crying out *Tepeeme*; taking their Hair up in their Hands, and spreading it wide to those they called out too; as if they would say (as indeed it signified) *Numberless Wonders*, or not to be recounted, no more than to number the Hair of their Heads. By degrees they grew more bold, and from gazing upon us round, they touched us; laying their Hands upon all the Features of our Faces, feeling our Breasts and Arms, taking up one Petticoat, then wondering to see another; admiring our Shoes and Stockings, but more our Garters, which we gave them; and they tied about their Legs, being Laced with Silver Lace at the ends, for they much Esteem any shining things: In fine,[74] we suffered them to survey us as they pleased, and we thought they would never have done admiring us. When *Cæsar*, and the rest, saw we were received with such wonder, they came up to us; and finding the *Indian* Trader whom they knew (for 'tis by these Fishermen, called *Indian* Traders, we hold a Commerce with them; for they love not to go far from home, and we never go to them) when they saw him therefore they set up a new Joy; and cried, in their language, 'Oh! here's our *Tiguamy*, and we shall now know whether those things can speak': So advancing to him, some of them gave him their Hands, and cried, '*Amora Tiguamy*'; which is as much as, 'How do you, or Welcome Friend'; and all, with one din, began to gabble to him, and asked, If we had Sense, and Wit? if we could talk of affairs of Life, and War, as they could do? if we could Hunt, Swim, and do a thousand things they use? He answered them, We could. Then they invited us into their Houses, and dressed Venison and Buffalo for us; and, going out, gathered a Leaf of a Tree, called a *Sarumbo* leaf, of Six Yards long, and spread it on the Ground for a Table-Cloth; and cutting another in pieces instead of Plates, setting us on little low *Indian* Stools, which they cut out of one entire piece of Wood, and Paint, in a sort of Japan Work:[75] They serve every one their Mess on these pieces of Leaves, and it was very good, but too high seasoned with Pepper. When we had eat, my Brother and I took out our Flutes, and played to them, which gave them new Wonder; and I soon perceived, by an admiration, that is natural to these People; and by the Extreme Ignorance and Simplicity of them, it were not difficult to establish any unknown or extravagant Religion among them, and to impose any Notions or Fictions upon them. For seeing a Kinsman of mine set some Paper afire with a Burning-glass, a Trick they had never before seen, they were like to have Adored him for a God; and begged he would give them the Characters or Figures of his Name, that they might oppose it against Winds and Storms; which he did, and they held it up in those Seasons, and fancied it had a

Notes

71 *comode* suitable.

72 *Taffaty* taffeta, "A thin silk" (Johnson).

73 *Stuff* "Textures of wool thinner and slighter than cloth" (Johnson).

74 *In fine* in brief.

75 *Japan Work* an elaborate lacquer finish.

Charm to conquer them, and kept it like a Holy Relic. They are very Superstitious, and called him the Great *Peeie*, that is, *Prophet*. They showed us their *Indian Peeie*, a youth of about Sixteen Years old, as handsome as Nature could make a Man. They consecrate a beautiful Youth from his Infancy, and all Arts are used to complete him in the finest manner, both in Beauty and Shape: He is bred to all the little Arts and cunning they are capable of, to all the Legerdemain Tricks, and Sleight of Hand, whereby he imposes upon the Rabble, and is both a Doctor in Physic[76] and Divinity. And by these Tricks [that he] makes the Sick believe he sometimes eases their Pains – by drawing from the afflicted part little Serpents, or odd Flies, or Worms, or any Strange thing – and though they have besides undoubted good Remedies, for almost all their Diseases, they cure the Patient more by Fancy than by Medicines, and make themselves Feared, Loved, and Reverenced. This young *Peeie* had a very young Wife, who seeing my Brother kiss her, came running and kissed me; after this, they kissed one another, and made it a very great Jest, it being so Novel; and new Admiration and Laughing went round the Multitude, that they never will forget that Ceremony, never before used or known. *Cæsar* had a mind to see and talk with their War *Captains*, and we were conducted to one of their Houses; where we beheld several of the great *Captains*, who had been at Council: But so frightful a Vision it was to see them no Fancy can create; no such Dreams can represent so dreadful a Spectacle. For my part, I took them for Hobgoblins, or Fiends, rather than Men; but however their Shapes appeared, their Souls were very Human and Noble; but some wanted their Noses, some their Lips, some both Noses and Lips, some their Ears, and others Cut through each Cheek, with long Slashes, through which their Teeth appeared; they had other several formidable Wounds and Scars, or rather Dismemberings; they had *Comitias*, or little Aprons before them; and Girdles of Cotton, with their Knives naked, stuck in it; a Bow at their Backs, and a Quiver of Arrows on their Thighs; and most had Feathers on their Heads of divers Colours. They cried '*Amora Tiguame*' to us, at our entrance, and were pleased we said as much to them; they seated us, and gave us Drink of the best Sort; and wondered, as much as the others had done before, to see us. *Cæsar* was marvelling as much at their Faces, wondering how they should all be so Wounded in War; he was Impatient to know how they all came by those frightful Marks of Rage or Malice, rather than Wounds got in Noble Battle: They told us by our Interpreter, That when any War was waging, two Men chosen out by some old *Captain*, whose Fighting was past, and who could only teach the Theory of War, these two Men were to stand in Competition for the Generalship, or Great War Captain; and being brought before the old Judges, now past Labour, they are asked, What they dare do to show they are worthy to lead an Army? When he, who is first asked, making no Reply, Cuts off his Nose, and throws it contemptibly on the Ground; and the other does something to himself that he thinks surpasses him, and perhaps deprives himself of Lips and an Eye; so they slash on till one gives out, and many have died in this Debate. And 'tis by a passive Valour they show and prove their Activity; a sort of Courage too Brutal to be applauded by our Black Hero; nevertheless he expressed his Esteem of them.

In this Voyage *Cæsar* begot so good an understanding between the *Indians* and the *English*, that there were no more Fears or Heart-burnings during our stay; but we had a perfect, open, and free Trade with them. Many things Remarkable, and worthy Reciting, we met with in this short Voyage; because *Cæsar* made it his Business to search out and provide for our Entertainment, especially to please his dearly Adored

Notes

[76] *Physic* medicine.

Imoinda, who was a sharer in all our Adventures; we being resolved to make her Chains as easy as we could, and to Compliment the Prince in that manner that most obliged him.

As we were coming up again, we met with some *Indians* of strange Aspects, that is, of a larger Size, and other sort of Features, than those of our Country. Our *Indian Slaves*, that Rowed us, asked them some Questions, but they could not understand us; but showed us a long Cotton String, with several Knots on it; and told us, they had been coming from the Mountains so many Moons as there were Knots; they were habited in Skins of a strange Beast, and brought along with them Bags of Gold Dust; which, as well as they could give us to understand, came streaming in little small Channels down the high Mountains, when the Rains fell;[77] and offered to be the Convoy to anybody, or Persons, that would go to the Mountains. We carried these Men up to *Parham*, where they were kept till the Lord Governor came: And because all the Country was mad to be going on this Golden Adventure, the Governor, by his Letters, commanded (for they sent some of the Gold to him) that a Guard should be set at the Mouth of the River of *Amazons* (a River so called, almost as broad as the River of *Thames*[78]) and prohibited all People from going up that River, it conducting to those Mountains of Gold. But we going off for *England* before the Project was further prosecuted, and the Governor being drowned in a Hurricane, either the Design died, or the *Dutch* have the Advantage of it: And it is to be bemoaned what his Majesty lost by losing that part of *America*.

Though this digression is a little from my Story, however since it contains some Proofs of the Curiosity and Daring of this great Man, I was content to omit nothing of his Character.

It was thus, for some time we diverted him; but now *Imoinda* began to show she was with Child, and did nothing but Sigh and Weep for the Captivity of her Lord, herself, and the Infant yet Unborn; and believed, if it were so hard to gain the Liberty of Two, 'twould be more difficult to get that for Three. Her Griefs were so many Darts in the great Heart of *Cæsar*; and taking his Opportunity one *Sunday*, when all the Whites were overtaken in Drink, as there were abundance of several Trades, and *Slaves* for Four Years, that Inhabited among the *Negro* Houses; and Sunday being their Day of Debauch (otherwise they were a sort of Spies upon *Cæsar*), went pretending, out of Goodness to them, to Feast among them, and sent all his Music, and ordered a great Treat for the whole Gang, about Three Hundred *Negroes*, and about a Hundred and Fifty were able to bear Arms, such as they had, which were sufficient to do Execution with Spirits accordingly: For the *English* had none but rusty Swords that no Strength could draw from a Scabbard, except the People of particular Quality, who took care to Oil them and keep them in good Order: The Guns also, unless here and there one, or those newly carried from *England*, would do no good or harm; for 'tis the Nature of that Country to Rust and Eat upon Iron, or any Metals, but Gold and Silver. And they are very Unexpert at the Bow, which the *Negroes* and *Indians* are perfect Masters of.

Cæsar, having singled out these Men from the Women and Children, made a Harangue to them of the Miseries, and Ignominies of Slavery; counting up all their Toils and Sufferings, under such Loads, Burdens, and Drudgeries as were fitter for Beasts than Men; [for] Senseless Brutes, [rather] than Human Souls. He told them, it was not for Days, Months or Years, but for Eternity; there was no end to be of their

Notes

77 *Gold ... when the Rains fell* this may not be part of the mythic description; the same phenomenon is reported in the review of *The Description and Natural History of Peru*, in *Literary Magazine* 10 (January 1757), pp. 10–11, 13.

78 *Thames* the comparison suggests Behn did not see the Amazon.

Misfortunes: They suffered not like Men, who might find a Glory, and Fortitude in Oppression, but like Dogs that loved the Whip and Bell,[79] and fawned the more they were beaten: That they had lost the Divine Quality of Men, and were become insensible Asses, fit only to bear; nay worse: an Ass, or Dog, or Horse having done his duty, could lie down in Retreat, and rise to work again, and while he did his Duty endured no Stripes; but Men, Villainous, Senseless Men, such as they, Toiled on all the tedious Week till Black *Friday*; and then, whether they Worked or not, whether they were Faulty or Meriting, they promiscuously, the Innocent with the Guilty, suffered the infamous Whip, the sordid Stripes, from their Fellow *Slaves* till their Blood trickled from all Parts of their Body – Blood, whose every drop ought to be Revenged with a Life of some of those Tyrants, that impose it; 'And why', said he, 'my dear Friends and Fellow-sufferers, should we be Slaves to an unknown People? Have they Vanquished us Nobly in Fight? Have they Won us in Honourable Battle? And are we, by the chance of War, become their Slaves? This would not anger a Noble Heart, this would not animate a Soldier's Soul; no, but we are Bought and Sold like Apes, or Monkeys, to be the Sport of Women, Fools and Cowards; and the Support of Rogues, Renegades, that have abandoned their own Countries, for Rapine, Murders, Thefts and Villainies. Do you not hear every Day how they upbraid each other with infamy of Life, below the Wildest Savages; And shall we render Obedience to such a degenerate Race, who have no one Human Virtue left, to distinguish them from the vilest Creatures? Will you, I say, suffer the Lash from such Hands?' They all Replied, with one accord, 'No, no, no; *Cæsar* has spoke like a Great Captain, like a Great King'.

After this he would have proceeded, but was interrupted by a tall *Negro* of some more Quality than the rest, his Name was *Tuscan*; who Bowing at the Feet of *Cæsar*, cried, 'My Lord, we have listened with Joy and Attention to what you have said; and, were we only Men, would follow so great a Leader through the World: But oh! consider, we are Husbands and Parents too, and have things more dear to us than Life – our Wives and Children unfit for Travel, in these unpassable Woods, Mountains and Bogs; we have not only difficult Lands to overcome, but Rivers to Wade, and Monsters to Encounter, Ravenous Beasts of Prey –'

To this, *Cæsar* replied, That 'Honour was the First Principle in Nature, that was to be Obeyed; but as no Man would pretend to that, without all the Acts of Virtue, Compassion, Charity, Love, Justice and Reason; he found it not inconsistent with that, to take an equal Care of their Wives and Children, as they would of themselves; and that he did not Design, when he led them to Freedom, and Glorious Liberty, that they should leave that better part of themselves to Perish by the Hand of the Tyrant's Whip: But if there were a Woman among them so degenerate from Love and Virtue, to choose Slavery before the pursuit of her Husband, and with the hazard of her Life, to share with him in his Fortunes; that such an one ought to be Abandoned, and left as a Prey to the common Enemy'.

To which they all Agreed, – and Bowed. After this, he spoke of the Impassable Woods and Rivers; and convinced them, the more Danger, the more Glory. He told them that he had heard of one *Hannibal*, a Great Captain, had Cut his Way through Mountains of Solid Rocks;[80] and should a few Shrubs oppose them, which they could Fire before them? No, 'twas a trifling Excuse to Men resolved to die, or overcome. As for Bogs, they are with a little Labour filled and hardened; and the Rivers could be no

Notes

[79] *Whip and [a] Bell* anything that causes discomfort, according to the *OED*, from the Roman custom of putting these items on a general's chariot to ward off evil spirits.

[80] *Hannibal … Cut his Way through Mountains of Solid Rocks* with fire and vinegar, according to Plutarch in his *Life of Hannibal*.

Obstacle, since they Swam by Nature – at least by Custom – from the First Hour of their Birth: That when the Children were weary they must carry them by turns, and the Woods and their own Industry would afford them Food. To this they all assented with Joy.

Tuscan then demanded, What he would[81] do? He said, they would travel towards the Sea, Plant a New Colony, and Defend it by their Valour; and when they could find a Ship, either driven by stress of Weather, or guided by Providence that way, they would Seize it, and make it a Prize, till it had transported them to their own Countries; at least, they should be made Free in his Kingdom, and be Esteemed as his Fellow-Sufferers, and Men that had the Courage, and the Bravery to attempt, at least, for Liberty; and if they Died in the attempt, it would be more brave than to Live in perpetual Slavery.

They bowed and kissed his Feet at this Resolution, and with one accord Vowed to follow him to Death. And that Night was appointed to begin their March. They made it known to their Wives, and directed them to tie their Hamaca[82] about their Shoulders, and under their Arms like a scarf; and to lead their Children that could go, and carry those that could not. The Wives, who pay an entire Obedience to their Husbands obeyed, and stayed for them where they were appointed: The Men stayed but to furnish themselves with what defensive Arms they could get; and All met at the Rendezvous, where *Cæsar* made a new encouraging Speech to them and led them out.

But as they could not march far that Night, on Monday early, when the Overseers went to call them all together, to go to Work, they were extremely surprised, to find not one upon the Place, but all fled with what Baggage they had. You may imagine this News was not only suddenly spread all over the *Plantation*, but soon reached the Neighbouring ones; and we had by Noon about Six hundred Men, they call the *Militia* of the Country, that came to assist us in the pursuit of the Fugitives: But never did one see so comical an Army march forth to War. The Men, of any fashion, would not concern themselves, though it were almost the common Cause; for such Revoltings are very ill Examples, and have very fatal Consequences oftentimes in many Colonies: But they had a Respect for *Cæsar*, and all hands were against the *Parhamites*, as they called those of *Parham Plantation*; because they did not in the first place love the Lord Governor; and secondly, they would have it, that *Cæsar* was ill-used, and Baffled with;[83] and 'tis not impossible but some of the best in the Country was of his Council in this Flight, and depriving us of all the *Slaves*; so that they of the better sort would not meddle in the matter. The Deputy Governor, of whom I have had no great occasion to speak, and who was the most Fawning fair-tongued Fellow in the World, and one that pretended the most friendship to *Cæsar*, was now the only violent Man against him; and though he had nothing, and so need fear nothing, yet talked and looked bigger than any Man: He was a Fellow, whose Character is not fit to be mentioned with the worst of the *Slaves*. This Fellow would lead his Army forth to meet *Cæsar*, or rather to pursue him; most of their arms were of those sort of cruel Whips they call *Cat with Nine tails*; some had rusty useless Guns for show; others old Basket-hilts, whose Blades had never seen the Light in this Age; and others had long Staffs and Clubs. Mr. *Trefry* went along, rather to be a Mediator than a Conqueror, in such a Battle; for he foresaw, and knew, if by fighting they put the *Negroes* into despair, they were a sort of sullen Fellows, that would drown, or kill themselves, before they would yield; and he advised

Notes

81 *would* wished or planned to.

82 *Hamaca* hammock; this is the Spanish source of the English word.

83 *Baffled with* from "baffle," "to defeat with some confusion … to baffle is sometimes less than to conquer" (Johnson).

that fair means was best. But *Byam*[84] was one that abounded in his own Wit, and would take his own Measures.

It was not hard to find these Fugitives; for as they fled they were forced to fire and cut the Woods before them, so that Night or Day they pursued them by the light they made, and by the path they had cleared. But as soon as *Cæsar* found he was pursued, he put himself in a Posture of Defence, placing all the Women and Children in the rear; and himself, with *Tuscan* by his side, or next to him, all promising to Die or Conquer. Encouraged thus, they never stood to Parley, but fell Pell-mell upon the *English*, and killed some and wounded a great many – they having recourse to their Whips, as the best of their Weapons – And as they observed no Order, they perplexed the Enemy so sorely, with Lashing them in the Eyes; and the Women and Children, seeing their Husbands so treated, being of fearful Cowardly Dispositions, and hearing the *English* cry out, 'Yield and live, Yield and be pardoned'; they all ran in amongst their Husbands and Fathers, and hung about them, crying out, 'Yield, Yield, and leave *Cæsar* to their Revenge'; that by degrees the *Slaves* abandoned *Cæsar*, and left him only *Tuscan* and his heroic *Imoinda*; who, grown as big as she was, did nevertheless press near her Lord, having a Bow and a Quiver full of poisoned Arrows, which she managed with such dexterity, that she wounded several, and shot the *Governor* into the Shoulder; of which Wound he had liked to have Died, but that an *Indian* Woman, his Mistress, sucked the Wound, and cleansed it from the Venom: But however, he stirred not from the Place till he had Parleyed with *Cæsar*, who he found was resolved to die Fighting, and would not be Taken; no more would *Tuscan* or *Imoinda*. But he, more thirsting after Revenge of another sort, than that of depriving him of Life, now made use of all his Art of talking, and dissembling; and besought *Cæsar* to yield himself upon Terms, which he himself should propose, and should be Sacredly assented to, and kept by him: He told him, it was not that he any longer feared him, or could believe the force of Two Men, and a young Heroine, could overcome all them, and with all the Slaves on their side also; but it was the vast Esteem he had for his Person; the desire he had to serve so Gallant a Man; and to hinder himself from the Reproach hereafter, of having been the occasion of the Death of a *Prince*, whose Valour and Magnanimity deserved the Empire of the World. He protested to him, he looked upon this Action, as Gallant and Brave; however tending to the prejudice of his Lord and Master, who would by it have lost so considerable a number of *Slaves*; that this Flight of his should be looked on as a heat of Youth, and rashness of a too forward Courage, and an unconsidered impatience of Liberty, and no more; and that he laboured in vain to accomplish that which they would effectually perform, as soon as any Ship arrived that would touch on his Coast. 'So that if you will be pleased', continued he, 'to surrender yourself, all imaginable Respect shall be paid to you; and yourself, your Wife and Child, if it be born here, shall depart free out of our Land'. But *Cæsar* would hear of no Composition;[85] though *Byam* urged, If he pursued and went on in his Design, he would inevitably Perish, either by great *Snakes*, wild Beasts or Hunger; and he ought to have regard to his Wife, whose Condition required ease, and not the fatigues of tedious Travel, where she could not be secured from being devoured. But *Cæsar* told him, there was no Faith in the White Men, or the Gods they Adored, who instructed them in Principles so false, that honest Men could not live amongst them; though no People professed so much, none performed so little; that he knew what he had to do, when he dealt with

Notes

[84] *Byam* William Byam, the deputy governor.

[85] *Composition* "Compact; agreement; terms on which differences are settled" (Johnson).

Men of Honour; but with them a Man ought to be eternally on his Guard, and never to Eat and Drink with *Christians* without his Weapon of Defence in his Hand; and, for his own Security, never to credit one Word they spoke. As for the rashness and inconsiderateness of his Action, he would confess the Governor is in the right; and that he was ashamed of what he had done, in endeavouring to make those Free, who were by Nature *Slaves*, poor wretched Rogues, fit to be used as *Christians'* Tools – Dogs, treacherous and cowardly, fit for such Masters – and they wanted only but to be whipped into the knowledge of the *Christian Gods* to be the vilest of all creeping things – to learn to Worship such Deities as had not Power to make them Just, Brave, or Honest. In fine, after a thousand things of this Nature, not fit here to be recited, he told *Byam*, he had rather Die than Live upon the same Earth with such Dogs. But *Trefry* and *Byam* pleaded and protested together so much that *Trefry* believing the *Governor* to mean what he said, and speaking very cordially himself, generously put himself into *Cæsar*'s Hands, and took him aside, and persuaded him, even with Tears, to Live, by Surrendering himself, and to name his Conditions. *Cæsar* was overcome by his Wit and Reasons, and in consideration of *Imoinda*; and demanding what he desired, and that it should be ratified by their Hands in Writing, because he had perceived that was the common way of contract between Man and Man, amongst the Whites: All this was performed, and *Tuscan*'s Pardon was put in, and they Surrender to the Governor, who walked peacefully down into the *Plantation* with them, after giving order to bury their dead. *Cæsar* was very much toiled with the bustle of the Day; for he had fought like a Fury; and what Mischief was done he and *Tuscan* performed alone; and gave their Enemies a fatal Proof that they durst do anything, and feared no mortal Force.

But they were no sooner arrived at the Place, where all the Slaves receive their Punishments of Whipping, but they laid hands on *Cæsar* and *Tuscan*, faint with heat and toil; and, surprising them, Bound them to two several Stakes, and Whipped them in a most deplorable and inhumane Manner, rending the very Flesh from their Bones, especially *Cæsar*, who was not perceived to make any Moan or to alter his Face, only to roll his Eyes on the Faithless *Governor*, and those he believed Guilty, with Fierceness and Indignation; and, to complete his Rage, he saw every one of those *Slaves*, who, but a few Days before, Adored him as something more than Mortal, now had a Whip to give him some Lashes, while he strove not to break his Fetters; though, if he had, it were impossible: But he pronounced a Woe and Revenge from his Eyes, that darted Fire, that 'twas at once both Awful[86] and Terrible to behold.

When they thought they were sufficiently Revenged on him, they untied him, almost Fainting, with loss of Blood, from a thousand Wounds all over his Body; from which they had rent his Clothes, and led him Bleeding and Naked as he was; and loaded him all over with Irons; and then rubbed his Wounds, to complete their Cruelty, with *Indian Pepper*, which had like to have made him raving Mad; and, in this Condition, made him so fast to the Ground that he could not stir, if his Pains and Wounds would have given him leave. They spared *Imoinda*, and did not let her see this Barbarity committed towards her Lord, but carried her down to *Parham*, and shut her up; which was not in kindness to her, but for fear she should Die with the Sight, or Miscarry; and then they should lose a young *Slave*, and perhaps the Mother.

You must know, that when the News was brought on Monday Morning that *Cæsar* had betaken himself to the Woods, and carried with him all the *Negroes*, we were

Notes

[86] *Awful* "That which strikes with awe, or fills with reverence" (Johnson).

possessed with extreme Fear, which no persuasions could Dissipate, that he would secure himself till Night; and then, that he would come down and Cut all our Throats. This apprehension made all the Females of us fly down the River, to be secured; and while we were away, they acted this Cruelty: for I suppose I had Authority and Interest enough there, had I suspected any such thing, to have prevented it; but we had not gone many Leagues, but the news overtook us that *Cæsar* was taken, and Whipped like a common *Slave*. We met on the River with Colonel *Martin*, a Man of great Gallantry, Wit, and Goodness, and whom I have celebrated in a Character of my New *Comedy*,[87] by his own Name, in memory of so brave a Man: He was Wise and Eloquent; and, from the fineness of his Parts, bore a great Sway over the Hearts of all the *Colony*: He was a Friend to *Cæsar*, and resented this false Dealing with him very much. We carried him back to *Parham*, thinking to have made an Accommodation; when he came, the First News we heard was, that the *Governor* was Dead of a Wound that *Imoinda* had given him; but it was not so well: But it seems he would have the Pleasure of beholding the Revenge he took on *Cæsar*; and before the cruel Ceremony was finished, he dropped down; and then they perceived the Wound he had on his Shoulder, was by a venomed Arrow, which, as I said, his *Indian* Mistress healed, by Sucking the Wound.

We were no sooner Arrived, but we went up to the *Plantation* to see *Cæsar*, whom we found in a very Miserable and Unexpressible Condition; and I have a Thousand times admired how he lived in so much tormenting Pain. We said all things to him, that Trouble, Pity and Good Nature could suggest; Protesting our Innocency of the Fact, and our abhorrence of such Cruelties. Making a Thousand Professions and Services to him, and Begging as many Pardons for the Offenders, till we said so much, that he believed that we had no Hand in his ill Treatment; but told us, he could never Pardon *Byam*; as for *Trefry*, he confessed he saw his Grief and Sorrow, for his Suffering, which he could not hinder, but was like to have been beaten down by the very *Slaves*, for Speaking in his Defence. But for *Byam*, who was their Leader, their Head – and should, by his Justice, and Honour, have been an Example to them – For him, he wished to Live, to take a dire Revenge of him, and said, 'It had been well for him, if he had Sacrificed me, instead of giving me the contemptible Whip'. He refused to Talk much; but Begging us to give him our Hands; he took them, and Protested never to lift up his, to do us any Harm. He had a great Respect for Colonel *Martin*, and always took his Counsel, like that of a Parent; and assured him, he would obey him in anything, but his Revenge on *Byam*: 'Therefore', said he, 'for his own Safety, let him speedily dispatch me; for if I could dispatch myself, I would not, till that Justice were done to my injured Person, and the contempt of a Soldier: No, I would not kill myself, even after a Whipping, but will be content to live with that Infamy, and be pointed at by every grinning Slave, till I have completed my Revenge; and then you shall see that *Oroonoko* scorns to live with the Indignity that was put on *Cæsar*'. All we could do could get no more Words from him; and we took care to have him put immediately into a healing Bath, to rid him of his Pepper, and ordered a Chirurgeon[88] to anoint him with healing Balm, which he suffered, and in some time he began to be able to Walk and Eat; we failed not to visit him every Day, and, to that end, had him brought to an apartment at *Parham*.

The *Governor* was no sooner recovered, and had heard of the menaces of *Cæsar*, but he called his Council; who (not to disgrace them, or Burlesque the Government there) consisted of such notorious Villains as *Newgate*[89] never transported;[90] and, possibly,

Notes

[87] *my New Comedy The Younger Brother: or the Amorous Jilt* (published 1696).

[88] *Chirurgeon* surgeon.

[89] *Newgate* an old prison in London.

[90] *transport* "To carry into banishment: as a felon" (Johnson); at this time the place of banishment was often America.

originally were such, who understood neither the laws of *God* or *Man*; and had no sort of Principles to make them worthy the Name of Men: But at the very Council Table would Contradict and Fight with one another; and Swear so bloodily, that 'twas terrible to hear, and see them. (Some of them were afterwards Hanged, when the *Dutch* took possession of the place; others sent off in Chains:) But calling these special Rulers of the Nation together, and requiring their counsel in this weighty Affair, they all concluded, that (Damn them) it might be their own Cases; and that *Cæsar* ought to be made an Example to all the *Negroes*, to fright them from daring to threaten their Betters, their Lords and Masters; and, at this rate, no Man was safe from his own *Slaves*; and concluded, *nemine contradicente*[91] that *Cæsar* should be Hanged.

Trefry then thought it time to use his Authority; and told *Byam* his Command did not extend to his Lord's *Plantation*; and that *Parham* was as much exempt from the Law as *Whitehall*;[92] and that they ought no more to touch the Servants of the Lord (who there represented the King's Person) than they could those about the King himself; and that *Parham* was a Sanctuary; and though his Lord were absent in Person, his Power was still in Being there; which he had entrusted with him, as far as the Dominions of his particular *Plantations* reached, and all that belonged to it; the rest of the *Country*, as *Byam* was Lieutenant to his Lord, he might exercise his Tyranny upon. *Trefry* had others as powerful, or more, that interested themselves in *Cæsar*'s Life, and absolutely said, He should be Defended. So turning the *Governor*, and his wise Council, out of Doors (for they sat at *Parham-house*) they set a Guard upon our Landing Place, and would admit none but those we called Friends to us and *Cæsar*.

The *Governor* having remained wounded at *Parham*, till his recovery was completed, *Cæsar* did not know but he was still there; and indeed for the most part, his time was spent there; for he was one that loved to Live at other People's Expense, and if he were a Day absent, he was Ten present there; and used to Play, and Walk, and Hunt, and Fish, with *Cæsar*. So that *Cæsar* did not at all doubt, if he once recovered Strength, but he should find an opportunity of being Revenged on him: Though, after such a Revenge, he could not hope to Live; for if he escaped the Fury of the *English* Mobile,[93] who perhaps would have been glad of the occasion to have killed him, he was resolved not to survive his Whipping; yet he had, some tender Hours, a repenting Softness, which he called his fits of Coward; wherein he struggled with Love for the Victory of his Heart, which took part with his charming *Imoinda* there; but, for the most part, his time was passed in melancholy Thought, and black Designs; he considered, if he should do this Deed, and Die, either in the Attempt, or after it, he left his lovely *Imoinda* a Prey, or at best a *Slave*, to the enraged Multitude; his great Heart could not endure that Thought: 'Perhaps', said he, 'she may be first Ravished by every Brute; exposed first to their nasty Lusts, and then a shameful Death'. No, he could not Live a Moment under that Apprehension, too insupportable to be borne. These were his Thoughts, and his silent Arguments with his Heart, as he told us afterwards; so that now resolving not only to kill *Byam*, but all those he thought had enraged him; pleasing his great Heart with the fancied Slaughter he should make over the whole Face of the *Plantation*. He first resolved on a Deed, that (however Horrid it at first appeared to us all) when we had heard his Reasons, we thought it Brave and Just: Being able to Walk, and, as he believed, fit for the Execution of his great Design, he begged *Trefry* to trust him into the Air, believing a Walk would do him good; which was granted him, and taking

Notes

91 *nemine contradicente* with no dissenting votes.

92 *Whitehall* the king's palace in London.

93 *Mobile* "The populace; the rout; the mob" (Johnson).

Imoinda with him, as he used to do in his more happy and calmer Days, he led her up into a Wood, where, after (with a thousand Sighs, and long Gazing silently on her Face, while Tears gushed, in spite of him, from his Eyes) he told her his Design first of Killing her, and then his Enemies, and next himself, and the impossibility of Escaping, and therefore he told her the necessity of Dying; he found the Heroic Wife faster pleading for Death than he was to propose it, when she found his fixed Resolution; and, on her Knees, besought him, not to leave her a Prey to his Enemies. He (grieved to Death) yet pleased at her noble Resolution, took her up, and embracing of her, with all the Passion and Languishment of a dying Lover, drew his Knife to kill this Treasure of his Soul, this Pleasure of his Eyes; while Tears trickled down his Cheeks, hers were Smiling with Joy she should die by so noble a Hand, and be sent into her own Country (for that's their Notion of the next World) by him she so tenderly Loved, and so truly Adored in this; for Wives have a respect for their Husbands equal to what any other People pay a Deity; and when a Man finds any occasion to quit his Wife, if he love her, she dies by his Hand; if not, he sells her, or suffers some other to kill her. It being thus, you may believe the Deed was soon resolved on; and 'tis not to be doubted, but the Parting, the eternal Leave taking of Two such Lovers, so greatly Born, so Sensible,[94] so Beautiful, so Young, and so Fond, must be very Moving, as the Relation of it was to me afterwards.

All that Love could say in such cases, being ended, and all the intermitting Irresolutions being adjusted, the Lovely, Young and Adored Victim lays herself down, before the Sacrificer, while he, with a Hand resolved, and a Heart breaking within, gave her the Fatal Stroke, first, cutting her Throat, and then severing her yet Smiling Face from that Delicate Body, pregnant as it was with the Fruits of tenderest Love. As soon as he had done, he laid the Body decently on Leaves and Flowers, of which he made a Bed, and concealed it under the same cover-lid of Nature; only her Face he left yet bare to look on: But when he found she was Dead, and past all Retrieve, never more to bless him with her Eyes, and soft Language, his Grief swelled up to Rage; he Tore, he Raved, he Roared, like some Monster of the Wood, calling on the loved Name of *Imoinda*; a thousand times he turned the Fatal Knife that did the Deed, toward his own Heart, with a Resolution to go immediately after her; but dire Revenge, which now was a thousand times more fierce in his Soul than before, prevents him; and he would cry out, 'No, since I have sacrificed *Imoinda* to my revenge, shall I lose that glory which I have purchased so dear, as at the price of the fairest, dearest, softest creature that ever nature made? No, no!' Then, at her Name, grief would get the ascendant of Rage, and he would lie down by her side, and water her Face with showers of Tears, which were never wont to fall from those Eyes: And however bent he was on his intended Slaughter, he had not the power to stir from the Sight of this dear Object, now more Beloved, and more Adored than ever.

He remained in this deploring Condition for two Days, and never rose from the Ground where he had made his sad Sacrifice; at last, rousing from her side, and accusing himself for living too long, now *Imoinda* was dead; and that the Deaths of those barbarous Enemies were deferred too long, he resolved now to finish the great Work; but offering to rise, he found his Strength so decayed, that he reeled to and fro, like Boughs assailed by contrary Winds; so that he was forced to lie down again, and try to summon all his Courage to his Aid; he found his Brains turn round, and his Eyes were

Notes

94 *Sensible* "Having quick intellectual feeling; being easily or strongly affected" (Johnson).

dizzy; and Objects appeared not the same to him they were wont to do; his Breath was short; and all his Limbs surprised with a Faintness he had never felt before: He not Eaten in two Days, which was one occasion of this Feebleness, but excess of Grief was the greatest; yet still he hoped he should recover Vigour to act his Design; and lay expecting it yet six Days longer; still mourning over the dead Idol of his Heart, and striving every Day to rise, but could not.

In all this time you may believe we were in no little affliction for *Cæsar*, and his Wife; some were of Opinion he was escaped never to return; others thought some Accident had happened to him: But however, we failed not to send out a hundred People several ways to search for him; a Party, of about forty, went that way he took; among whom was *Tuscan*, who was perfectly reconciled to *Byam*; they had not gone very far into the Wood, but they smelt an unusual Smell, as of a dead Body; for Stinks must be very noisome that can be distinguished among such a quantity of Natural Sweets, as every Inch of that Land produces. So that they concluded they should find him dead, or somebody that was so; they passed on towards it, as Loathsome as it was, and made such a rustling among the Leaves that lie thick on the Ground, by continual Falling, that *Cæsar* heard he was approached; and though he had, during the space of these eight Days, endeavoured to rise, but found he wanted Strength, yet looking up, and seeing his Pursuers, he rose, and reeled to a Neighbouring Tree, against which he fixed his Back; and being within a dozen Yards of those that advanced, and saw him; he called out to them, and bid them approach no nearer, if they would be safe: So that they stood still, and hardly believing their Eyes, that would persuade them that it was *Cæsar* that spoke to them, so much was he altered; they asked him, What he had done with his Wife? for they smelt a Stink that almost struck them dead? He, pointing to the dead Body, sighing, cried, 'Behold her there'; they put off the flowers that covered her with their Sticks, and found she was killed; and cried out, 'Oh, Monster! that hast murdered thy Wife'. Then asking him, Why he did so cruel a deed? He replied, he had no leisure to answer impertinent Questions: 'You may go back', continued he, 'and tell the Faithless Governor, he may thank Fortune that I am breathing my last; and that my Arm is too feeble to obey my Heart, in what it had designed him': But his Tongue faltering, and trembling, he could scarce end what he was saying. The *English* taking Advantage by his weakness, cried, 'Let us take him alive by all means': He heard them; and, as if he had revived from a Fainting, or a Dream, he cried out, 'No, Gentlemen, you are deceived; you will find no more *Cæsars* to be Whipped; no more find a Faith in me: Feeble as you think me, I have Strength yet left to secure me from a second Indignity'. They swore all anew; and he only shook his Head, and beheld them with Scorn; then they cried out, 'Who will venture on this single Man? Will nobody?' They stood all silent, while *Cæsar* replied, 'Fatal will be the Attempt of the first Adventurer; let him assure himself', and, at that Word, held up his Knife in a menacing Posture. 'Look ye, ye faithless Crew', said he, ''tis not Life I seek, nor am I afraid of Dying', and, at that Word, cut a piece of Flesh from his own Throat, and threw it at them; 'yet still I would Live if I could, till I had perfected my Revenge. But oh! it cannot be; I feel Life gliding from my Eyes and Heart; and, if I make not haste, I shall yet fall a Victim to the shameful Whip'. At that, he ripped up his own Belly, and took his Bowels and pulled them out, with what Strength he could; while some, on their Knees imploring, besought him to hold his Hand. But when they saw him tottering, they cried out, 'Will none venture on him?' A bold *English* cried, 'Yes, if he were the Devil' (taking Courage when he saw him almost Dead), and swearing a horrid Oath for his farewell to the World; he rushed on *Cæsar*, [who] with his Armed Hand met him so fairly, as stuck him to the Heart, and he fell Dead at his Feet. *Tuscan* seeing that, cried out, 'I love thee, O Cæsar; and therefore will not let thee Die, if possible': And running to him, took him in his Arms; but, at the same time, warding a Blow that *Cæsar* made at his Bosom, he received it quite through his Arm; and *Cæsar* having not Strength to pluck the Knife forth, though he attempted it, *Tuscan* neither pulled it out himself, nor suffered it to be pulled out; but came down with it sticking in his Arm; and the reason he gave for it was, because the Air should not get into the Wound: They put their Hands across, and carried *Cæsar* between Six of them, fainting as he was; and they thought Dead, or just Dying; and they brought him to *Parham*, and laid him on a Couch, and had the Chirurgeon immediately to him, who dressed his Wounds, and sowed up his Belly, and used means to bring him to Life, which they effected. We ran all to see him; and, if before we thought him so beautiful a Sight, he was now so altered, that his Face was like a Death's Head[95] blacked over; nothing but Teeth, and Eye-holes: For some Days we suffered nobody to speak to him, but caused Cordials to be poured down his Throat, which sustained his Life; and in six or seven Days he recovered his Senses: For, you must know, that Wounds are almost to a Miracle cured in the *Indies*; unless Wounds in the Legs, which rarely ever cure.

When he was well enough to speak, we talked to him; and asked him some Questions about his Wife, and the Reasons why he killed her; and he then told us what I have related of that Resolution, and of his Parting; and he besought us we would let him Die, and was extremely Afflicted to think it was possible he might Live; he assured us, if we did not Dispatch him, he would prove very Fatal to a great many. We said all we could to make him Live, and gave him new Assurances; but he begged we would not think so poorly of him, or his love to *Imoinda*, to imagine we could Flatter him to Life again; but the Chirurgeon assured him, he could not Live, and therefore he need not Fear. We were all (but *Cæsar*) afflicted at this News, and the Sight was gashly;[96] his Discourse was sad; and the earthly Smell about him so strong, that I was persuaded to leave the Place for some time (being myself but Sickly, and very apt to fall into Fits of dangerous Illness upon any extraordinary Melancholy); the Servants, and *Trefry*, and the Chirurgeons, promised all to take what possible care they could of the Life of *Cæsar*; and I, taking Boat, went with other Company to Colonel *Martin*'s, about three Days' Journey down the River; but I was no sooner gone, but the *Governor* taking *Trefry*, about some pretended earnest Business, a Day's Journey up the River; having communicated his Design to one *Banister*,[97] a wild *Irish* Man, and one of the Council – a Fellow of absolute Barbarity, and fit to execute any Villainy, but was Rich. He came up to *Parham*, and forcibly took *Cæsar*, and had him carried to the same Post where he was Whipped; and causing him to be tied to it, and a great Fire made before him, he told him he should Die like a Dog, as he was. *Cæsar* replied, this was the first piece of Bravery that ever *Banister* did; and he never spoke Sense till he pronounced that Word; and, if he would keep it, he would declare, in the other World, that he was the only Man, of all the Whites, that ever he heard speak Truth. And turning to the Men that bound him, he said, 'My friends, am I to Die, or to be Whipped?' And they cried, 'Whipped! no; you shall not escape so well'. And then he replied, smiling, 'A blessing on thee'; and assured them, they need not tie him, for he would stand fixed, like a Rock, and endure Death so as should encourage[98] them to Die. 'But if you Whip me', said he, 'be sure you tie me fast'.

He had learned to take Tobacco; and when he was assured he should Die, he desired they would give him a Pipe in his Mouth, ready Lighted, which they did; and the

Notes

[95] *a Death's Head* a skull, sometimes kept by scholars as a reminder of death.

[96] *gashly* ghastly.

[97] *Banister* Major James Bannister.

[98] *encourage* "To raise confidence; to make confident" (Johnson, sense 3).

Executioner came, and first cut off his Members, and threw them in the Fire; after that, with an ill-favoured Knife, they cut his Ears, and his Nose, and burned them; he still Smoked on, as if nothing had touched him; then they hacked off one of his Arms, and still he bore up, and held his Pipe; but at the cutting off the other Arm, his Head sunk, and his Pipe dropped; and he gave up the Ghost, without a Groan, or a Reproach. My Mother and Sister were by him all the while, but not suffered to save him; so rude and wild were the Rabble, and so inhuman were the Justices, who stood by to see the Execution, who after paid dearly enough for their Insolence. They cut *Cæsar* in Quarters, and sent them to several of the chief *Plantations*: One Quarter was sent to Colonel *Martin*, who refused it; and swore, he had rather see the Quarters of *Banister*, and the *Governor* himself, than those of *Cæsar*, on his *Plantations*; and that he could govern his *Negroes* without Terrifying and Grieving them with frightful Spectacles of a mangled King.

Thus Died this Great Man, worthy of a better Fate, and a more sublime Wit than mine to write his Praise; yet, I hope, the Reputation of my Pen is considerable enough to make his Glorious Name to survive to all Ages; with that of the Brave, the Beautiful and the Constant *Imoinda*.

John Wilmot, Second Earl of Rochester (1647–1680)

Rochester entered Wadham College, Oxford at age twelve and was given his MA at fourteen. Graduating at such an early age was more common in the seventeenth century than it is now, but in Rochester's case it was a sign of his considerable literary talent and his high degree of personal appeal. From College he went to the court of King Charles where he became a favorite and one of the rowdiest rakes in a society infamous for profligacy. He drank, whored, vandalized, and publicly appeared both naked and in full disguise. He abducted an heiress named Elizabeth Malet, for which he spent some time imprisoned in the Tower of London, but later he married her. Very late in his short life, Rochester repented and became serious about religion. He called in Gilbert Burnet, and according to the bishop's spiritual biography, Rochester presented his Maker with a penitent soul.

Rochester's bawdy poetry is still considered scandalous by some, but many readers admire his most outrageous works because of their insistence on the glories of what the world calls immoral behavior. The more philosophical poems also turn conventional beliefs upside down, but they do so in the service of conventional satirical aims. The paradoxical or apparently false positions that Rochester delights in arguing inevitably reveal arbitrary and irrational aspects of our own unexamined suppositions about the world. By so doing, Rochester's poetry achieves a certain philosophical astuteness even in its impudence.

Modern editorial work on Rochester begins with David Vieth (Yale University Press, 1968). It was importantly advanced by Keith Walker (Blackwell, 1984) and rigorously pursued by Harold Love (Oxford University Press, 1999). In these successive editions, greater and greater account was taken of the manuscript tradition in which the poems circulated and for which they were written in the first place. The extensive work that went into establishing the texts of Rochester is beyond the brief of any mere anthologist. I have therefore relied on the texts in Nicholas Fisher's revision of Keith Walker's edition – *John Wilmot, Earl of Rochester: The Poems and Lucina's Rape* (Wiley-Blackwell, 2013) – which takes into account Harold Love's extensive research. I have, however, also applied the protocols of this anthology: modernized spelling when the sound is not affected and occasional liberties with the punctuation for the sake of sense. Works like these derived from manuscript traditions are naturally more various than works with a print history. An extreme case is "Signior Dildo," which I present in hybrid form, including some but not all of the stanzas in all manuscripts. I am nonetheless indebted to Fisher, Walker, and Love throughout these selections.

from *Poems on Several Occasions* (1680?)

The Imperfect Enjoyment

Naked she lay, clasped in my longing Arms
I filled with Love, and she all over Charms
Both equally inspired with eager fire

Melting through kindness, flaming in desire.
With Arms, Legs, Lips close clinging to embrace
She clips me to her Breast, and sucks me to her face.[1]
Her nimble tongue (love's lesser lightning) played
Within my Mouth, and to my thoughts conveyed
Swift Orders that I should prepare to throw
The all-dissolving Thunderbolt below.
My fluttering soul, sprung with the pointed Kiss
Hangs hovering o'er her balmy brinks of bliss.
But whilst her busy hand would guide that part
Which should convey my soul up to her Heart,
In liquid raptures I dissolve all o'er,
Melt into sperm, and spend at every pore.
A touch from any part of her had done 't:
Her hand, her foot, her very look's a C—t.
Smiling, she chides in a kind, murmuring noise,
And from her body wipes the clammy joys
When with a Thousand kisses wand'ring o'er
My panting bosom, 'Is there then no more?'
She cries; 'all this to Love, and Rapture's due;
Must we not pay a debt to pleasure too?'
But I the most forlorn lost man alive
To show my wished obedience vainly strive:
I sigh, 'alas!' and Kiss, but cannot sw—ve.[2]
Eager desires Confound first intent
Succeeding shame does more success prevent,
And Rage at last Confirms me Impotent.
Even her fair hand which might bid heat return
To frozen Age, and make cold Hermits burn,
Applied to my Dead Cinder, warms no more
Than fire to ashes could past flames Restore.
Trembling, Confused, Despairing, limber, dry,
A wishing weak, unmoving lump I lie.
This Dart of Love whose piercing point, oft Tried
With Virgin blood Ten Thousand Maids have dyed,
Which Nature still Directed with such Art
That it through every C—t reached every heart,
Stiffly Resolved 'twould Carelessly invade
Woman, nor Man, nor ought its fury stayed;
Where'er it pierced a C—t it found or made,
Now languid lies in this unhappy hour,
Shrunk up and sapless like a withered flower.
Thou Treacherous base Deserter of my Flame,
False to my passion, fatal to my Fame,
Through what mistaken Magic dost thou prove
So true to Lewdness, so untrue to Love?

Notes

THE IMPERFECT ENJOYMENT

[1] *clips* hugs.

[2] *sw—ve* swive, copulate.

What Oyster, Cinder, Beggar, Common whore[3]
Didst thou e'er fail in all thy Life before?
When Vice, Disease, and scandal lead the way,
With what officious haste dost thou obey!
Like a rude Roaring Hector in the streets[4]
Who scuffles Cuffs and Jostles all he meets
But if his *King* or Country claim his Aid
The Rakehell villain shrinks and hides his head.
Even so thy brutal valour is displayed,
Break'st every stew, dost each small whore invade,[5]
But when great Love the onset does Command
Base Recreant to thy Prince thou durst not stand.
Worst part of me and henceforth hated most,
Through all the Town a common F—cking Post,
On whom each Wh—re Relieves her tingling C—t
As Hogs on Gates do rub themselves and grunt,
Mayst thou to Ravenous Shankers be a prey
Or in Consuming weepings waste away;
May strangury and stone thy days attend;[6]
Mayest thou ne'er piss who didst Refuse to spend
When all my Joys did on false Thee depend.
And may Ten Thousand abler Pr—cks agree
To do the wrong'd *Corinna* Right for Thee.

A Ramble in Saint James's Park

Much wine had passed with grave discourse
Of who F—cks who and who does worse,
Such as you usually do hear
From those that diet at the *Bear*,[1,2]
When I who still take care to see
Drunkenness Relieved by Lechery
Went out to Saint James's Park
To cool my head, and fire my heart.
But though St. James has the Honor on't
'Tis consecrate to P—ck and C—t.
There by a most incestuous Birth
Strange woods spring from the Teeming Earth
For they relate how heretofore,

Notes

[3] *Oyster ... Whore* oysterwench, "A woman whose business is to sell oysters. Proverbially. A low woman" (Johnson; see Shakespeare, *Richard II*, I.iv.31).

[4] *Hector* "A bully; a blustering, turbulent, pervicacious, noisy fellow" (Johnson).

[5] *stew* brothel.

[6] *strangury* "A difficulty of urine attended with pain" (Johnson); *Stone* a concretion in the kidneys or bladder that blocks urination.

A Ramble in Saint James's Park

[1] *diet* take regular meals or board.

[2] *the Bear* a common name for a pub.

When ancient Pict, began to whore,[3]
Deluded of his Assignation,
Jilting it seems was then in fashion,
Poor pensive Lover in this place
Would frigg upon his Mother's face;[4]
Whence Rows of Mandrakes tall did rise[5]
Whose lewd Tops F—ckt the very Skies.
Each imitative branch does twine
In some loved fold of *Aretine*,[6]
And nightly now beneath their shade
Are Buggeries, Rapes, and Incests made:
Unto this all-sin-sheltering Grove
Whores of the Bulk, and the Alcove,[7]
Great Ladies, Chamber-Maids, and Drudges,
The Rag-picker, and Heiress Trudges,
Car-men, Divines, Great Lords, and Tailors,[8]
Prentices, Poets, Pimps, and Gaolers,
Footmen, Fine Fops, do here arrive,
And here promiscuously they sw—ve.
Along these hallowed walks it was
That I beheld *Corinna* pass;
Whoever had been by to see
The proud disdain she cast on Me
Through charming eyes he would have swore
She dropped from Heaven that very Hour
Forsaking the Divine abode
In scorn of some despairing God.
But mark what Creatures women are
So infinitely vile when fair:
Three Knights of the Elbow, and the slur[9]
With wriggling tails made up to her.
The first was of your *Whitehall* Blades[10]
Near kin to the Mother of the Maids,[11]
Graced by whose favour he was able
To bring a Friend to the Waiter's Table[12]
Where he had heard *Sir Edward Sutton*[13]
Say how the King liked *Bansted* Mutton.[14]
Since when he'd ne'er be brought to eat
By's good will any other meat.

Notes

[3] *Pict* a Celt of Scotland; a native of the British Isles.

[4] *frigg* masturbate; *Mother's face* the earth.

[5] *Mandrakes* a poisonous plant thought to have magical powers, sometimes used to promote conception because of the phallic shape of its roots.

[6] *Aretine* Pietro Aretino (1492–1556) author of sonnets designed to accompany his contemporary Giulio Romano's pornographic drawings.

[7] *Bulk, and the Alcove* of the shop front (i.e., common or cheap) and the bedroom (i.e., expensive).

[8] *Car-men* carters.

[9] *Knights of the Elbow* dice-throwers; *slur* a way of cheating by keeping the thrown die from turning.

[10] *Whitehall Blades* court gallants.

[11] *Mother of the Maids* an official in charge of the queen's maids of honor.

[12] *Waiter* Daily Waiter, another court post.

[13] *Edward Sutton* the daily waiter at this time.

[14] *Bansted* Banstead, a place in Surrey where sheep are raised; *Mutton* slang for a woman or a woman's genitals.

In this, as well as all the rest
He ventures to do like the best
But wanting Common Sense, th' ingredient
In choosing well not least expedient,
Converts abortive imitation
To universal affectation.
Thus he not only eats and Talks
But feels and smells, sits down and walks,
Nay looks, and lives, and loves by Rote
In an old Tawdry Birthday Coat.[15]
  The second was a *Gray's Inn* Wit,[16]
A great Inhabiter of the Pit,[17]
Where *Critic*-like he sits and squints,
Steals Pocket-Handkerchiefs and hints
From 's Neighbour and the Comedy
To Court and pay his Landlady.
  The third a Lady's Eldest Son,
Within few years of Twenty-one;
Who hopes from his propitious Fate,
Against he comes to his Estate
By these Two Worthies to be made
A most accomplished tearing blade.
  One in a strain 'twixt Tune and Nonsense,
Cries, 'Madam, I have loved you long since;
Permit me your fair hand to kiss,'
When at her *Mouth* her *C—t* cries yes.
In short without much more ado
Joyful and pleased away she flew
And with these Three Confounded Asses,
From *Park* to Hackney Coach she passes.
  So a proud Bitch does lead about
Of Humble *Curs* the Amorous Rout
Who most obsequiously do hunt
The savoury scent of Salt-swol'n *C—t*.
Some power more patient now Relate
The sense of this surprising Fate;
Gods! that a thing admired by me
Should fall to so much Infamy.
Had she picked out to rub her Arse on
Some stiff-pr—cked Clown or well-hung Parson,
Each job of whose spermatic sluice[18]
Had filled her C—t with wholesome Juice,
I the proceeding should have praised
In hope she had quenched a fire I raised;
Such natural freedoms are but Just,

Notes

[15] *Birthday Coat* attire worn on the occasion of the king's birthday.

[16] *Gray's Inn* one of the Inns of Court for training lawyers.

[17] *Pit* the flat part of theater seating, below the stage.

[18] *job* "A sudden stab with a sharp instrument" (Johnson).

There's something Gen'rous in mere lust.
But to turn damned abandoned Jade,
When neither Head nor Tail persuade
To be a Whore in understanding,
A passive pot for Fools to spend in,
The Devil played booty sure with Thee[19]
To bring a blot on Infamy.
But why am I of all *Mankind*,
To so severe a Fate designed?
Ungrateful! Why this Treachery
To humble fond, believing me
Who gave you Privilege above
The nice allowances of Love?
Did ever I refuse to bear
The meanest part your Lust could spare?
When your lewd C—t came spewing home
Drenched with the Seed of half the Town,
My dram of sperm was supped up after
For the digestive surfeit water.[20]
Full gorgèd at another time
With a vast meal of nasty slime,
Which your devouring C—t had drawn
From *Porters' Backs* and *Footmen's* brawn,
I was content to serve you up
My Ballock full for your Grace cup,[21]
Nor ever thought it an abuse
While you had pleasure for excuse.
You that could make my heart away
For Noise and Colour and betray
The secrets of my tender hours
To such knight errant Paramours,
When leaning on your faithless breast
Wrapped in security and rest
Soft kindness all my powers did move
And Reason lay dissolved in Love.
May stinking vapours Choke your womb
Such as the Men you dote upon;
May your depravèd Appetite
That could in Whiffling Fools delight[22]
Beget such Frenzies in your Mind
You may go mad for the North wind,
And fixing all your hopes upon't
To have him Bluster in your C—t,
Turn up your longing Arse to the Air
And perish in a wild despair.
    But Cowards shall forget to rant,

Notes

19 *played booty* cheated.
20 *surfeit water* "Water that cures surfeits" (Johnson).
21 *Grace cup* "The cup or health drank after grace" (Johnson).
22 *Whiffling* insignificant.

Schoolboys to Frigg, old whores to paint,[23]
The *Jesuits* Fraternity
Shall leave the use of Buggery,
Crab-louse inspired with Grace divine
From Earthy Cod to Heaven shall climb,[24]
Physicians shall believe in *Jesus*,
And Disobedience cease to please us
Ere I desist with all my Power
To plague this Woman and undo her.
But my Revenge will best be timed
When she is *Married*, that is limed;[25]
In that most lamentable state
I'll make her feel my scorn, and hate,
Pelt her with scandals, Truth or lies,
And her poor *Cur* with Jealousies
Till I Have torn him from her Breech
While she whines like a Dog-drawn Bitch,
Loathed, and despised, Kicked out o' the Town
Into some dirty Hole alone
To chew the Cud of Misery,
And know she owes it all to Me.
  And may no *Woman* better thrive
  That dares profane the C—t I sw—ve.

A Satyr against Reason and Mankind

Were I (who to my cost already am
One of those strange, prodigious Creatures Man)
A Spirit free to choose for my own share,
What case of flesh and blood I'd please to wear;
I'd be a Dog, a Monkey, or a Bear,
Or anything but that vain Animal
Who boasts so much of being Rational.
The senses are too gross, and he'll contrive
A sixth to contradict the other five:
And before certain Instinct will prefer
Reason, which fifty times for one doth err.
Reason, an Ignis fatuus in the Mind,[1]
Which, leaving Light of Nature, sense, behind;
Pathless and dangerous wand'ring ways it takes,
Through Error's fenny bogs and thorny brakes:
Whilst the misguided follower climbs with pain
Mountains of whimsies heaped in his own brain;

Notes

[23] *frigg* masturbate; *paint* use make-up.
[24] *Cod* scrotum.
[25] *limed* impregnated or coupled.

A Satyr against Reason and Mankind
[1] *Ignis fatuus* false fire, will-o'-the-wisp, luminous marsh gases, which travelers mistake for beacons.

Stumbling from thought to thought, falls headlong down
Into doubt's boundless Sea, where like to drown,
Books bear him up awhile, and make him try
To swim with Bladders of Philosophy:[2]
In hopes still to o'ertake th' escaping Light,
The Vapour dances in his dazzled sight,
Till spent, it leaves him to Eternal night.
Then old Age and Experience hand in hand,
Lead him to Death, and make him understand,
After a Search so painful and so long
That all his Life he has been in the wrong.
Huddled in dirt the reasoning Engine lies,
Who was so proud, so witty and so wise,
Pride drew him in (as Cheats their Bubbles catch)[3]
And made him venture to become a Wretch.
His Wisdom did his Happiness destroy,
Aiming to know that World he should enjoy;
And Wit was his vain frivolous pretence,
Of pleasing others at his own expense:
For Wits are treated just like common Whores,
First they're enjoyed and then kicked out of doors.
The Pleasure past, a threatening doubt remains,
That frights th' enjoyer with succeeding pains.
Women and men of Wit are dangerous tools,
And always fatal to admiring Fools.
Pleasure allures, and when the fops escape,
'Tis not that they're belov'd, but fortunate;
And therefore what they fear, at heart they hate.
    But now, methinks, some formal band and beard[4]
Takes me to task. Come on, Sir, I'm prepared:
    'Then, by your favour, anything that's writ
Against this gibing, jingling knack called Wit,
Likes me abundantly, but you take care[5]
Upon this point not to be too severe.
Perhaps my Muse were fitter for this part,
For, I profess, I can be very smart
On Wit, which I abhor with all my heart.
I long to lash it in some sharp essay,
But your grand indiscretion bids me stay,
And turns my tide of Ink another way.
What rage foments[6] in your degenerate mind,
To make you rail at Reason and Mankind?
Blessed, glorious Man! to whom alone kind Heaven

Notes

[2] *Bladders* "It is usual for those that learn to swim, to support themselves with blown bladders" (Johnson).

[3] *Bubbles* dupes.

[4] *band and beard* the neckcloth and tonsorial style of a clergyman or professor.

[5] *Likes me* pleases me.

[6] *foments* becomes heated.

An Everlasting Soul hath freely given:
Whom his great Maker took such care to make,
That from himself he did the Image take:
And this fair frame in shining reason dressed,
To dignify his Nature above Beast.
Reason, by whose aspiring Influence
We take a flight beyond Material sense;
Dive into Mysteries, then soaring pierce
The flaming limits of the Universe:
Search Heaven and Hell, find out what's acted there,
And give the World true grounds of hope and fear.'
'Hold mighty Man', I cry: 'all this I know,
From the pathetic pen of Ingelo,[7]
From Patrick's Pilgrim, Sibbes' Soliloquies;[8]
And 'tis this very Reason I despise.
This supernatural Gift, that makes a mite
Think he's the Image of the Infinite;
Comparing his short life, void of all rest,
To the Eternal, and the ever blessed.
This busy puzzling stirrer up of doubt,
That frames deep Mysteries, then finds them out;
Filling with frantic crowds of thinking Fools
Those Reverend Bedlams, Colleges and Schools;[9]
Borne on whose wings each heavy Sot can pierce
The limits of the boundless Universe.
So charming Ointments make an old Witch fly,[10]
And bear a crippled carcass through the sky,
'Tis this exalted power whose business lies
In Nonsense and Impossibilities,
This made a whimsical Philosopher[11]
Before the spacious World his Tub prefer.
And we have modern Cloistered Coxcombs, who[12]
Retire to think, 'cause they have naught to do:
But Thoughts are given for Action's government,
Where Action ceases, Thought's impertinent.
Our sphere of Action is Life's happiness,
And he who thinks beyond, thinks like an Ass.
Thus whilst against false Reasoning I inveigh,
I own right reason, which I would obey;
That Reason which distinguishes by Sense,
And gives us Rules of Good and Ill from thence:
That bounds Desires with a reforming Will,

Notes

[7] *pathetic* productive of painful feelings; *Ingelo* Nathaniel Ingelo (1621?–83), a religious writer.

[8] *Patrick's Pilgrim The Parable of the Pilgrim* (1664) by Simon Patrick; *Sibbe's Soliloquies* any of the works of Richard Sibbes (1577?–1635), a Church of England priest and preacher with a reputation for puritan beliefs.

[9] *Bedlam* an asylum for the insane in London.

[10] *charming Ointments* magic oils, which were believed to be used by witches.

[11] *whimsical Philosopher* Diogenes the Cynic.

[12] *Cloistered Coxcombs* academic fools.

To keep them more in vigour, not to kill.
Your Reason hinders, mine helps to enjoy,
Renewing appetites yours would destroy.
My Reason is my friend, Yours is a cheat,
Hunger calls out, my Reason bids me eat;
Perversely yours your appetites doth mock,
They ask for food, that answers, 'What's o'clock?'
This plain distinction, Sir, your doubt secures,
'Tis not true Reason I despise, but yours.
'Thus I think Reason righted; but for Man,
I'll ne'er recant, defend him if you can.
For all his Pride and his Philosophy,
'Tis evident Beasts are in their Degree,
As wise at least, and better far than he.
Those Creatures are the wisest who attain
By surest means, the ends at which they aim:
If therefore Jowler finds and kills his Hares[13]
Better than Meres supplies Committee chairs;[14]
Though one's a Statesman, th' other but a Hound,
Jowler in Justice will be wiser found.
You see how far Man's wisdom here extends;
Look next if human nature makes amends:
Whose Principles most generous are and just,
And to whose Morals you would sooner trust.
Be Judge yourself, I'll bring it to the test,
Which is the Basest Creature, Man or Beast.
Birds feed on Birds, Beasts on each other prey,
But savage Man alone does man betray:
Pressed by necessity they kill for food,
Man undoes Man to do himself no good.
With teeth and claws by nature armed, they hunt
Nature's allowance to supply their want.
But Man with Smiles, embraces, friendship, praise,
Most humanely his fellow's life betrays:[15]
With voluntary pains works his distress,
Not through Necessity, but Wantonness.
For hunger or for Love they fight and tear,
Whilst wretched man is still in arms for Fear:
For fear he Arms, and is of arms afraid,
By fear to fear successively betrayed.
Base Fear! The source whence his best passion came,
His boasted Honour, and his dear-bought Fame:
That lust of Power, to which he's such a slave,
And for the which alone he dares be brave,
To which his various projects are designed;

Notes

[13] *Jowler* the name of a dog.

[14] *Meres* Sir Thomas Meres (1634–1715), Whig MP and commissioner of the admiralty.

[15] *Humanely* in seventeenth-century spelling indistinguishable from humanly.

Which makes him generous, affable and kind;
For which he takes such pains to be thought wise
And screws his Actions in a forced disguise;[16]
Leading a tedious Life in Misery
Under laborious mean Hypocrisy:
Look to the bottom of his vast design,
Wherein Man's Wisdom, Power and Glory join;
The Good he acts, the Ill he doth endure,
'Tis all from Fear to make himself secure.
Merely for safety after fame we thirst;
For all men would be Cowards if they durst.
And Honesty's against all common sense;
Men must be Knaves, 'tis in their own defence.
Mankind's dishonest: If you think it fair
Among known Cheats to play upon the Square,[17]
You'll be undone—
Nor can weak Truth your Reputation save;
The Knaves will all agree to call you Knave.
Wronged shall he live, insulted o'er, oppressed,[18]
Who dares be less a Villain than the rest.
'Thus, Sir, you see what Human Nature craves,
Most men are Cowards, all men should be Knaves.
The difference lies, as far as I can see,
Not in the thing itself, but the degree:
And all the subject matter of debate,
Is only who's a Knave of the first rate.
All this with indignation have I hurled
At the pretending part of the proud World,
Who swollen with selfish vanity, devise
False Freedoms, Holy Cheats and formal Lies,
Over their fellow Slaves to tyrannize.
'But if in Court so just a Man there be,
(In Court a just man yet unknown to me)
Who doth his needful Flattery direct,
Not to Oppress and Ruin, but protect.
(Since Flattery, which way so ever laid,[19]
Is still a Tax on that unhappy trade)
If so upright a Statesman you can find,
Whose Passions bend to his unbiased mind;
Who doth his Arts and Policies apply,
To raise his Country, not his Family.
Nor whilst his Pride owned Avarice withstands,[20]
Receives close Bribes through Friends' corrupted hands.
'Is there a Churchman who on God relies,
Whose life his Faith, and Doctrine justifies?

Notes

[16] *screw* "To force; to bring by violence" (Johnson).
[17] *to play upon the Square* to deal fairly.
[18] *insult* "To trample upon; to triumph over" (Johnson).
[19] *which way so ever laid* however you look at it.
[20] *owned* admitted.

Not one blown up with vain Prelatic pride,
Who for Reproof of sins doth Man deride;
Whose Envious heart makes preaching a pretence,
With his obstreperous saucy Eloquence,
To chide at Kings, and rail at Men of Sense
Who from his pulpit vents more peevish lies;
More bitter railings, Scandals, Calumnies;[21]
Than at a Gossiping are thrown about,[22]
When the good Wives get drunk and then fall out,
None of that Sensual Tribe, whose Talents lie
In Avarice, Pride, Sloth and Gluttony,
Who hunt good Livings, but abhor good Lives,
Whose Lust exalted to that height arrives,
They act Adultery with their own Wives;
And ere a score of Years completed be,
Can from the lofty Pulpit proudly see
Half a large Parish their own Progeny.
Nor doting Bishop, who would be adored
For domineering at the Council Board,[23]
A greater Fop in business at Fourscore,
Fonder of serious Toys, affected more
Than the gay glittering Fool at twenty proves,
With all his Noise, his tawdry Clothes and Loves.
  'But a meek humble Man of honest sense,
Who Preaching peace doth practise Continence;
Whose pious life's a proof he doth believe
Mysterious Truths, which no man can conceive.
If upon Earth there dwell such God-like men,
I'll here Recant my Paradox to them;[24]
Adore those Shrines of Virtue, homage pay,
And with the rabble World, their Laws obey.
  'If such there are, yet grant me this at least,
Man differs more from Man, than Man from Beast.'

The Disabled Debauchee

As some brave Admiral, in former War
  Deprived of force, yet pressed with courage still,
Two Rival Fleets appearing from afar,
  Crawls to the top of an Adjacent Hill,
From whence, with thoughts full of concern, he views
  The wise and daring conduct of the Fight,

Notes

[21] *Calumnies* slanders.

[22] *Gossiping* "a merry meeting of Gossips at a woman's lying-in" (Bailey).

[23] *Council Board* episcopal council table.

[24] *Paradox* a statement that is apparently false but arguably true; Rochester's paradox is that, despite the apparent and accepted superiority of human beings, it is actually better to be a beast.

While each bold action to his mind renews
  His present glory and his past delight;
From his fierce eyes flashes of Rage he throws,
  As from black Clouds when Lightning breaks away;
Transported, thinks himself amidst his Foes,
  And absent, yet enjoys the bloody Day:
So, when my days of Impotence approach,
  And I'm by Pox and Wine's unhappy chance[1]
Forced from the pleasing Billows of Debauch
  On the Dull Shores of lazy Temperance;
My pains at least some respite shall afford
  While I behold the Battles you maintain,
When Fleets of Glasses Sail about the Board,
  From whose broadsides Volleys of Wit shall Rain.
Nor shall the sight of honourable Scars,
  Which my too forward valour did procure,
Frighten new-listed Soldiers from the Wars;[2]
  Past joys have more than paid what I endure.
Should hopeful youths, worth being drunk, prove nice,[3]
  And from their fair Inviters meanly shrink,
'Twill please the Ghost of my departed Vice
  If, at my counsel, they repent, and Drink.
Or should some cold-complexioned Sot forbid,
  With his Dull Morals, your bold Night-Alarms,
I'll fire his blood, by telling what I did
  When I was strong, and able to bear Arms.
I'll tell of Whores attacked, their Lords at home;
  Bawds' Quarters beaten up, and Fortress won:[4]
Windows demolished, Watches overcome;[5]
  And handsome ills, by my contrivance, done.
Nor shall our Love-fits *Cloris* be forgot,
  When each the well-looked Linkboy strove t' enjoy;[6]
And the best Kiss was the deciding Lot,
  Whether the Boy Fucked you, or I the Boy.
With Tales like these, I will such thoughts inspire
  As to important mischief shall incline;
I'll make him long some Ancient Church to fire,
  And fear no lewdness he's called to by Wine.
Thus, Statesmanlike, I'll saucily Impose,
  And, safe from Action, valiantly advise;
Sheltered in impotence, urge you to blows:
  And now, being good for nothing else, be Wise.

Notes

THE DISABLED DEBAUCHEE

1 *Pox* venereal disease.

2 *new-listed* newly enlisted.

3 *nice* peevish, delicate, shy.

4 *Beaten up* visited by surprise.

5 *Watches* night watchmen, guards.

6 *well-looked* handsome; *Linkboy* candle bearer for hire in the dark streets of seventeenth-century cities.

Lampoon

Too Long the Wise Commons have been in debate
About Money, and Conscience (those Trifles of State)[1]
Whilst dangerous Grievances daily increase,
And the Subject can't riot in Safety, and Peace;
Unless (as against Irish Cattle before)[2]
You now make an Act, to forbid Irish whore.
The Coots (black, and white) Clenbrazell, and Fox,[3]
Invade us with Impudence, beauty and Pox.[4]
They carry a Fate, which no man can oppose;
The loss of his heart, and the fall of his Nose.[5]
Should he dully resist, yet will each take upon her,
To beseech him to do it, and engage him in honour.
O! Ye merciful powers, which of Mortals take Care,
Make the Women more modest, more sound, or less fair.
Is it just, that with death cruel Love should conspire,
And our Tails be burnt by our hearts taking fire?
There's an end of Communion, if humble Believers
Must be damned in the Cup, like unworthy Receivers.[6]

[Signior Dildo]

To the Tune of 'Peg's Gone to Sea with a Soldier' ['The Lame Soldier']

O! all ye young Ladies of merry England,
That have been to kiss the Duchess's hand,[1]
I pray you, inquire, the next time you do go,
For a noble Italian called *Signior Dildo*.
This *Signior Dildo* was the chief of the Train
That came, to conduct her safe over the *Main;*
I could not in Conscience, but let you all know
The happy arrival of *Signior Dildo*.
At the Sign of the Cross in St James's Street,[2]
When next you endeavour, to make yourself sweet,

Notes

Lampoon

1 *Money and Conscience* Parliament was then (1673) discussing the Money Bill to support the war against the Dutch and the Test Act, which required government appointees to take communion in the Church of England.

2 *Irish Cattle* the importation of Irish livestock was forbidden by an act of Parliament.

3 *Coots (black, and white)* simpletons, but also blonde and brunette women related to Charles Coote, second earl of Mountrath and a Lord Justice of Ireland; *Clenbrazell, and Fox* women in the running for the honor of being mistress to Charles II; at least one of them was Irish.

4 *Pox* venereal disease.

5 *fall of his Nose* in the advanced stages of syphilis, the mucous membrane decays, and in the centuries before antibiotics brass noses were sometimes fitted over the mutilated flesh.

6 *unworthy Receivers* those who take holy communion in a state of sin damn themselves, according to St. Paul.

Signior Dildo

1 *Duchess* Mary of Modena, second wife of James II (then duke of York), arrived in London in 1673; she brought many of her countrymen (Italians) with her in her entourage.

2 *Sign of the Cross* unidentified "toyshop," a place for buying cosmetics and other trinkets.

By buying of Powder, Gloves, Essence, or so,
You may chance get a sight of this *Signior Dildo.*
You will take him at first for no Person of Note
Because he'll appear in a plain *Leather Coat,*
But when you his virtuous Abilities know,
You'll fall down, and worship this *Signior Dildo.*
This *Signior* once dwelt with the Countess of *Rafe,*[3]
And from all the fierce Harrys preserved her safe:[4]
She had smothered him almost under her Pillow:
'Tis a barbarous Nation, quoth Signior Dildo.
My Lady *Southesk* (Heaven prosper her for't)[5]
First clothed him in *Satin*, and brought him to Court,
When scarce in the Circle his face he durst show;[6]
So modest a youth was this *Signior Dildo.*
My good Lady *Suffolk* thinking no harm,
Had hid this poor Stranger under her Arm;
Lady Betty by chance came the *Secret* to know,
And from her own Mother stole *Signior Dildo.*
Her undutiful Daughter, whom dearly she loved,
With tears in her Eyes severely reproved:
Lamentably, 'Betty, why would you do so?
I charge you of my blessing, restore the Dildo'.
'Pray, pardon me, Madam', said Lady Betty,
I am not such a Fool, as you take me to be:
For all you are my Mother, I'll have you to know,
Either give me a P—, or I'll keep the Dildo'.
Saint Albans with wrinkles, and smiles in his face,
Whose kindness to strangers becomes his high place,
In a *Coach, and Six Horses* is gone to *Pyrgo,*[7]
To take the fresh Air with this *Signior Dildo.*
Red *Howard*, Red *Sheldon*, and *Temple* so tall[8]
Complain of his absence thus long from Whitehall
But *Signior Bernard* hath promised, a journey to go,[9]
And bring back his Countryman *Signior Dildo.*
Doll Howard no more with his Highness can range,[10]
We'll proffer her therefore this civil exchange,
Her Teeth being rotten, the Smell's best below,
And needs must be fitter for *Signior Dildo.*
This Signior is sound, safe, and ready, and dumb,
As ever was Candle, Finger, or Thumb;

Notes

[3] *Countess of Rafe* wife of Ralph (pronounced Rafe) Montagu, later duke of Montagu.

[4] Suitors named Henry, including Henry Savile, Rochester's friend (Fisher).

[5] *Lady Southesk* one of the duke of York's mistresses.

[6] *Circle* "An assembly surrounding the principal person" (Johnson).

[7] *Pyrgo* a park now in the northeast London borough of Havering.

[8] *Howard, Sheldon, Temple* maids of honor to the queen.

[9] *Signior Bernard* perhaps Francesco Bernardi (d. 1657), a Genovese ex-patriot banker and friend to Cromwell, but identified by Love as a dealer in rare books.

[10] *Doll Howard* maid of honor to the duchess of York, sister of *Red* (Anne), l. 49.

Then away with these nasty devices, to show,
How you rate the merits of *Signior Dildo*.
If he were but well used by the Citizen Fops,
He'd keep their fine Wives from the Foremen o' th' Shops;
But the Rascals deserve, that their Horns should still grow,
For burning the Pope, and his Nephew *Dildo*.[11]
Tom Killigrew's wife, North Holland's fine Flower,[12]
At the Sight of this *Signior*, did fart, and Belch Sour,
And her Dutch Breeding further to Show,
Says, 'Welcome to England, Mijn Heer Van *Dildo*'.
He civilly came to the Cockpit one night,
And proffered his Service to fair Madam Knight,[13]
Quoth she, 'I intrigue with Captain Cazzo.[14]
Your Nose in mine Arse good *Signior Dildo*'.
Count Cazzo who carries his Nose very high,
In Passion he Swore, his Rival should Die,
Then Shut up himself, to let the world know,
Flesh and Blood could not bear it from *Signior Dildo*.
A Rabble of Pricks, who were welcome before,
Now finding the Porter denied 'em the Door,
Maliciously waited his coming below,
And inhumanely fell on *Signior Dildo*.
Nigh wearied out, the poor Stranger did fly
And along the Pall Mall, they followed full Cry[15]
The Women concerned from every Window,
Cried, 'Oh! for Heaven's sake save *Signior Dildo*'.
The good Lady Sandys, burst into a Laughter
To see how the Ballocks came wobbling after,
And had not their weight retarded the Foe
Indeed 't had gone hard with *Signior Dildo*.

A Satire on Charles II[1]

In the Isle of Britain long since famous grown
For breeding the best C—ts in Christendom,
Not long since Reigned (oh may he long survive)
The easiest King and best bred Man alive.
Him no Ambition moved to get Renown
Like a French Fool still wandering up and down,[2]

Notes

[11] *burning the Pope* in effigy on Guy Fawkes' Day, November 5, which celebrates the discovery of the Gunpowder Plot, a Roman Catholic scheme to burn down Parliament and destabilize Protestant England; *his Nephew Dildo* in 1671 Rochester was informed by a correspondent that a box of dildos had been seized and burned by the Customs Office.

[12] *Tom Killigrew* courtier and playwright, father of Anne (see p. 218 above).

[13] *Madam Knight* Mary, a singer.

[14] *Cazzo* Italian for penis.

[15] *Pall Mall* a fashionable street in London.

A Satire on Charles II

[1] This poem caused Rochester to flee the court early in 1674 when he delivered it by mistake to the king.

[2] *French Fool* Louis XIV, who pursued the current war with the Dutch, even after the English withdrew from their alliance in 1674.

Starving his People, hazarding his Crown,
Peace was his Aim, his gentleness was such
And Love, he loved, For he loved Fucking much,
Nor was his high desire above his Strength;
His Sceptre and his Prick were of a Length,
And she may Sway the one who plays with t'other
Which makes him little wiser than his Brother.[3]
For Princes' Pricks like to Buffoons at Court
Do govern Us, because they make Us Sport.
His was the sauciest that did ever swive,
The proudest peremptory Prick alive,
Though Safety, Law, Religion, Life lay on't
'Twould break through all to make its way to C—t.
Restless he Rolls about from Whore to Whore
With Dog and Bastard, always going before,
A merry Monarch, scandalous and poor.
Ah my dear Carwell, dearest of all Dears![4]
Thou best Relief of my declining years![5]
O How I mourn thy Fortune and My Fate
To love so well and to be Loved too late.
Yet his Graceless Ballocks hang an Arse,[6]
But ill agreeing with his limber Tarse.[7]
This to evince would be too long to tell ye
The painful Tricks of the laborious Nelly[8]
Employing Hands, Arms, Fingers, Mouth and Thighs
To raise the Limb which she each Night enjoys.
  I hate all Monarchs and the Thrones they sit on
From the Hector of France to th' Cully of Britain.[9]

A Letter from Artemiza in the Town to Chloe in the Country

Chloe, in Verse by your command I write;
Shortly you'll bid me ride astride, and fight.[1]
These Talents better with our Sex agree,
Than lofty flights of dangerous Poetry.
Amongst the Men (I mean) the Men of Wit
(At least they passed for such, before they writ)
How many bold Adventurers for the Bays,[2]
(Proudly designing large returns of Praise)
Who durst that stormy pathless World explore,

Notes

[3] *his Brother* the future James II.

[4] *Carwell* Louise de Kéroualle, duchess of Portsmouth.

[5] *my declining years* Charles was forty-three when the much younger Rochester wrote this poem.

[6] *hang an Arse* hold back; be reluctant.

[7] *limber* easily bent; *Tarse* "A man's yard" (Nathan Bailey, *Dictionarium Britannicum*; not in Johnson); penis.

[8] *Nelly* Eleanor Gwyn (1650–87), actress and mistress of Charles.

[9] *Hector* bully; *Cully* dupe.

A Letter from Artemiza in the Town to Chloe in the Country

[1] *Ride astride* ride in the male fashion, rather than the lady-like side-saddle.

[2] *Bays* a crown of bay leaves, symbolic of literary achievement

Were soon dashed back, and wrecked on the dull Shore,
Broke of that little Stock, they had before?
How would a Woman's tottering Bark be tossed,[3]
Where stoutest Ships (the Men of Wit) are lost?
When I reflect on this, I straight grow wise,
And my own self thus gravely I advise.
'Dear Artemiza, Poetry's a snare:
Bedlam has many Mansions: have a Care.[4]
Your Muse diverts you, makes the Reader sad;
You fancy, you're inspired, he thinks, you're mad.
Consider too, 'twill be discreetly done,
To make Yourself the Fiddle of the Town,[5]
To find th' ill-humoured pleasure at their need,
Cursed, if you fail, and scorned, though you succeed'.
Thus, like an Arrant Woman, as I am,[6]
No sooner well convinced, writing's a shame,
That Whore is scarce a more reproachful name,
Than Poetess:
As Men, that marry, or as Maids, that Woo,
Because 'tis the worst thing, that they can do,
Pleased with the Contradiction, and the Sin,
Methinks, I stand on Thorns, till I begin.
Y' expect at least, to hear, what Loves have passed
In this Lewd Town, since you, and I met last.
What change has happened of Intrigue, and whether
The Old ones last, and who, and who's together.
But how, my dearest Chloe, shall I set
My pen to write, what I would fain forget,
Or name that lost thing (Love) without a tear,
Since so debauched by ill-bred Customs here?
Love, the most generous Passion of the mind,
The softest refuge Innocence can find,
The safe director of unguided youth,
Fraught with kind wishes, and secured by Truth,
That Cordial drop Heaven in our Cup has thrown,
To make the nauseous draught of life go down,
On which one only blessing God might raise[7]
In lands of Atheists Subsidies of Praise
(For none did e'er so dull, and stupid prove,
But felt a God, and blessed his power in *Love*)
This only Joy, for which poor We were made,
Is grown like Play, to be an Arrant Trade;[8]
The Rooks creep in, and it has got of late[9]
As many little Cheats, and Tricks, as that.

Notes

3 *Bark* ship; ship of state; the individual soul or self.

4 *Bedlam* an asylum for the insane in London.

5 *Fiddle* fool, jester

6 *Arrant* "Bad in a high degree" (Johnson).

7 *only* sole.

8 *play* gambling.

9 *Rooks* "A cheat; a trickish rapacious fellow" (Johnson).

But what yet more a Woman's heart would vex,
'Tis chiefly carried on by Our own Sex,
Our silly Sex, who born, like Monarchs, free,
Turn Gypsies for a meaner liberty,
And hate restraint, though but from Infamy.
They call whatever is not Common, nice,[10]
And deaf to Nature's rule, or *Love*'s advice,
Forsake the Pleasure, to pursue the Vice.
To an exact perfection they have wrought
The Action *Love*, the Passion is forgot.
'Tis below Wit, they tell you, to admire,
And ev'n without approving they desire.
Their private wish obeys the public Voice,
'Twixt good, and bad Whimsy decides, not Choice.
Fashions grow up for taste, at Forms they strike;
They know, what they would have, not what they like.
Bovey is a beauty, if some few agree,[11]
To call him so, the rest to that degree
Affected are, that with their Ears they see.
Where I was visiting the other night,
Comes a fine Lady with her humble Knight,
Who had prevailed on her, through her own skill,
At his request, though much against his will,
To come to London.
As the Coach stopped, we heard her Voice more loud,
Than a great-bellied Woman's in a Crowd,
Telling the Knight, that her affairs require,
He for some hours obsequiously retire.[12]
I think, she was ashamed, to have him seen
(Hard fate of Husbands) the Gallant had been,
Though a diseased ill-favoured Fool, brought in.
'Dispatch', says she, 'that business you pretend,
Your beastly Visit to your drunken friend;
A Bottle ever makes you look so fine!
Methinks I long, to smell you stink of Wine.
Your Country drinking breath's enough to kill—
Sour Ale corrected with a Lemon Peel.
Prithee farewell—We'll meet again anon'.
The necessary thing bows, and is gone.
She flies up stairs, and all the haste does show,
That fifty Antic postures will allow,[13]
And then bursts out – 'Dear Madam, am not I
The alter'dst Creature breathing? Let me die,[14]
I find myself ridiculously grown
Embarrassée with being out of Town,

Notes

[10] *Nice* fussy.
[11] *Bovey* Sir Ralph Bovey (d. 1679).
[12] *obsequiously* obediently.
[13] *Antic* "Odd; ridiculously wild" (Johnson).
[14] *Let me die* an affected, high-society expression, like many others in the speech of this "fine lady."

Rude, and untaught, like any Indian Queen;
My Country nakedness is strangely seen.
How is *Love* governed? *Love*, that rules the State,
And, pray, who are the Men most worn of late?
When I was married, Fools were *à la mode*,
The Men of Wit were then held *incommode*,[15]
Slow of belief, and fickle in desire,
Who ere they'll be persuaded, must inquire,
As if they came to spy, not to admire.
With searching Wisdom fatal to their ease
They still find out, why, what may, should not please;
Nay take themselves for injured, when We dare,
Make 'em think better of us, than We are:
But if we hide Our frailties from their sights,
Call Us deceitful Jilts, and Hypocrites.[16]
They little guess, who at Our Arts are grieved,
The perfect Joy of being well deceived.
Inquisitive, as jealous Cuckolds, grow,
Rather, than not be knowing, they will know,
What being known creates their certain woe.
Women should these of all Mankind avoid;
For Wonder by clear knowledge is destroyed.
Woman, who is an Arrant Bird of night,
Bold in the Dusk, before a Fool's dull sight,
Should fly, when Reason brings the glaring light.
But the Kind easy Fool apt, to admire
Himself, trusts us, his Follies all conspire,
To flatter his, and favour Our desire.[17]
Vain of his proper Merit he with ease
Believes, We love him best, who best can please.
On him Our gross dull common Flatteries pass,
Ever most joyful, when most made an Ass.
Heavy, to apprehend, though all Mankind
Perceive Us false, the Fop concerned is blind,
Who doting on himself,
Thinks everyone, that sees him, of his mind.
These are true Women's Men. – Here forced, to cease
Through Want of Breath, not Will, to hold her peace,
She to the Window runs, where she had spied
Her much esteemed dear Friend the Monkey tied.[18]
With forty smiles, as many Antic bows,
As if 't had been the Lady of the House,
The dirty chattering Monster she embraced,
And made it this fine tender speech at last:
'Kiss me, thou curious Miniature of Man;

Notes

[15] *Incommode* inconvenient, tiresome.

[16] *Jilts* "A woman who gives her lover hopes, and deceives him" (Johnson).

[17] *flatter* "To raise false hopes" (Johnson).

[18] *Monkey* a fashionable pet at this time.

How odd thou art? How pretty? How Japan?[19]
Oh I could live, and die with thee'—then on
For half an hour in Compliment she run.
I took this time, to know, what Nature meant,
When this mixed thing into the World she sent,
So very wise, yet so impertinent.
One who knew everything, who, God thought fit,
Should be an Ass through choice, not want of Wit:
Whose Foppery, without the help of Sense,
Could ne'er have rose to such an Excellence.
Nature's as lame, in making a true Fop,
As a Philosopher, the very top,
And Dignity of Folly we attain
By studious Search, and labour of the Brain,
By observation, Counsel, and deep thought:
God never made a Coxcomb worth a groat.[20]
We owe that name to Industry, and Arts:
An Eminent Fool must be a Fool of Parts;[21]
And such a One was she, who had turned o'er
As many Books, as men, loved much, read more,
Had a discerning Wit, to her was known
Everyone's fault, and merit, but her own.
All the good qualities, that ever blessed
A Woman, so distinguished from the rest,
Except discretion only, she possessed.
But now, '*Mon cher* dear Pug', she cries, '*adieu*',
And the Discourse broke off does thus renew.
You smile, to see me, whom the World perchance
Mistakes, to have some Wit, so far advance
The Interest of Fools, that I approve
Their Merit more, than Men's of Wit, in Love.
But in Our Sex too many proofs there are
Of such, whom Wits undo, and Fools repair.
This in my time was so observed a Rule,
Hardly a Wench in Town, but had her Fool.
The meanest Common Slut, who long was grown
The Jest, and Scorn of every Pit-Buffoon,[22]
Had yet left Charms enough, to have subdued
Some Fop or Other, fond to be thought lewd,[23]
Foster could make an Irish Lord a Nokes,[24]
And Betty Morris had her City Cokes.[25]
A Woman's ne'er so ruined, but she can
Be still revenged on her undoer Man.

Notes

[19] *Japan* a high varnish with gold embellishments once used on fashionable furniture.

[20] *groat* a coin worth only a few pence.

[21] *Parts* "Qualities; powers; faculties; or accomplishments" (Johnson).

[22] *Pit-Buffoon* theatre troublemaker.

[23] *fond* eager.

[24] *Foster* a lower-class girl on whom Rochester had designs; *Nokes* an actor known for his ability to play solemn fools.

[25] *Betty Morris* a well-known prostitute; *City* the financial center of London; *Cokes* fools.

How lost so e'er, she'll find some Lover more
A lewd abandoned Fool, than she a whore.
That wretched thing Corinna, who had run
Through all the several Ways of being undone,
Cozened at first by Love, and living then
By turning the too-dear-bought trick on Men:
Gay were the hours, and winged with Joys they flew,
When first the Town her early Beauties knew,
Courted, admired, and loved, with Presents fed,
Youth in her looks, and pleasure in her bed,
Till Fate, or her ill Angel thought it fit,
To make her dote upon a Man of Wit,
Who found, 'twas dull, to love above a day,
Made his ill-natured Jest, and went away.
Now scorned by all, forsaken, and oppressed,
She's a Memento Mori to the rest.[26]
Diseased, decayed, to take up half a Crown,
Must mortgage her long Scarf, and Mantua Gown.[27]
Poor Creature! Who unheard of, as a Fly,
In some dark hole must all the Winter lie,
And Want, and dirt endure a whole half year,
That for one Month she tawdry may appear.[28]
In Easter Term she gets her a new Gown,
When my young Master's Worship comes to Town,[29]
From Pedagogue, and Mother just set free,
The Heir, and Hopes of a great Family,
Which with strong Ale, and Beef the Country Rules,
And ever since the Conquest have been Fools:[30]
And now with careful prospect to maintain
This Character, lest crossing of the strain
Should mend the Booby-breed, his Friends provide[31]
A Cousin of his own, to be his Bride;
And thus set out—
With an Estate, no Wit, and a young Wife
(The solid comforts of a Coxcomb's Life)
Dunghill, and Pease forsook, he comes to Town,[32]
Turns Spark, learns to be lewd, and is undone.[33]
Nothing suits worse with Vice, than want of Sense;
Fools are still wicked at their own Expense.
This o'ergrown Schoolboy lost—Corinna wins,
And at first dash, to make an Ass, begins:
Pretends, to like a Man, who has not known

Notes

26 *Memento Mori* salutary reminder of death.

27 *Mantua Gown* a loose upper garment worn in preference to a straight-bodied dress (*OED*, citing the Phillips-Kersey dictionary [1706]).

28 *tawdry* "Meanly showy; splendid without cost; fine without grace; shewy without elegance" (Johnson).

29 *Worship* "A character of honour" (Johnson).

30 *The Conquest* the Norman Conquest (1066) when many noble titles were created.

31 *Booby* "A dull, heavy, stupid fellow; a lubber" (Johnson).

32 *Pease* food made from peas, but with a pun on the word *peace*.

33 *Spark* "a lively, showy, gay man. It is usually used in contempt" (Johnson).

The Vanities, nor Vices of the Town,
Fresh in his youth, and faithful in his Love,
Eager of Joys, which he does seldom prove,[34]
Healthful, and strong, he does no pains endure,
But what the Fair One, he adores, can cure.
Grateful for favours does the Sex esteem,[35]
And libels none, for being kind to him.
Then of the Lewdness of the times complains,
Rails at the Wits, and Atheists, and maintains,
'Tis better, than good Sense, than power, or Wealth,
To have alone untainted youth, and health.
The unbred puppy, who had never seen
A Creature look so gay, or talk so fine,
Believes, then falls in Love, and then in Debt,
Mortgages all, ev'n to th' Ancient Seat,[36]
To buy this Mistress a new house for life;
To give her Plate, and Jewels, robs his wife;
And when to the height of fondness he is grown,
'Tis time, to poison him, and all's her own.
Thus meeting in her Common Arms his Fate,
He leaves her Bastard Heir to his Estate,
And as the Race of such an Owl deserves,[37]
His own dull lawful Progeny he starves.
Nature, who never made a thing in vain,
But does each Insect to some end ordain,
Wisely provides kind-keeping Fools, no doubt,[38]
To patch up Vices, Men of Wit wear out.
Thus she ran on two hours, some grains of Sense
Still mixed with Volleys of Impertinence.
But now 'tis time, I should some pity show
To Chloe, since I cannot choose, but know,
Readers must reap the dullness Writers sow.
By the next Post such stories I will tell,
As joined with these shall to a Volume swell,
As true, as Heaven, more infamous, than Hell;
But you are tired, and so am I. Farewell.

Notes

[34] *Prove* experience.
[35] *the Sex* women.
[36] *Seat* principal residence of the family.
[37] *Owl* a solemn fool.
[38] *keeping* Supporting a mistress.

Daniel Defoe (1660–1731)

Robinson Crusoe is one of three books that Samuel Johnson said he wished longer than it was. This undeniably great, groundbreaking, and remarkably durable novel may be Defoe's best creation, but it represents a tiny fraction of the immense amount of invention with which he filled his life. He wrote literally hundreds of works of all sorts; so industrious was he and so mercurial in his interests, and in the surprising slants he could take on various issues, that a full and accurate accounting of his works will probably never be achieved. Most of his work can be broadly described as journalism, and to a large degree Defoe created that highly various kind of writing. His works are based largely on contemporary events and experiences, though they often have historical frameworks and also, very often, depart from ascertainable facts. Defoe shows that it is possible to be an author on this model, and not only on the "higher" model followed by fellow journalists like Addison and Johnson, in which the present is viewed mainly through the spectacles of classical literature.

Although he was desperate and venal enough at times to serve Tory as well as Whig politicians, as a spy and counter-spy, most of Defoe's works are imbued with his democratic, Whiggish political outlook. A religious dissenter, he believed in the Lockean, and later American, values of individual life, liberty, and the pursuit of happiness in preference to the protection of the established society, church, or government. His literary works were entrepreneurial projects designed to further his interest, and they were very much of a piece with his operation of a brick and tile factory, his investment and development of land, and his sales of timber. He launched businesses, established markets, and undertook mortgages with the same speed and industry that he created new forms of literature. Insofar as the laws and customs of society could be flexed to permit it, Defoe's life was itself a creation of his own. There is an emblem of his self-fashioning in the fact that he changed his name from that of his butcher father, Foe, to the classier Norman-sounding name by which he is known.

Defoe could, of course, change the names of other people even more easily in his artistic life as a kind of fictionalizing journalist. *A Journal of the Plague Year* and *Moll Flanders* are only two of the best known of Defoe's transformations. It was long thought that *The Apparition of Mrs. Veal* was one of Defoe's most obvious hoaxes, but it appears now that in this case he did nothing but transmit the same report heard by another in the very consistent and largely unimpeachable accounts of Mrs. Bargrave. A much trickier work is Defoe's *Shortest-Way with the Dissenters*; here he presents a speaker who rabidly supports the position on toleration that Defoe despises, but he is so realistic a creation that many who shared his views did not at first understand that they were being lampooned. Defoe paid dearly for this trick; he lost his business through fines and imprisonment and was exposed in the public stocks. The irony in *The True-Born Englishman* is more obvious; in fact, the whole poem is dedicated to ridiculing its title phrase and showing that virtually all Englishmen are immigrants of mixed national heritage. The conclusion, proclaiming virtue rather than birth the measure of a man, was meant to support King William's image in Britain, but it might be used as a credo for members of the underclasses in many parts of the world today. Along with the rights of immigrants and the poor, Defoe also championed the rights of women. He was not the only person in

British Literature 1640–1789: An Anthology, Fourth Edition. Edited by Robert DeMaria, Jr.

England in the seventeenth century to decry the miserable state of women's education, but he was in the minority, and his call for women's colleges was not fully heeded until the second half of the nineteenth century.

The following texts are all based on first editions, with somewhat more modernization in the prose than in the poetry. There is not, and may never be, a standard edition of Defoe's works, although a great many of his works are in print. In recent years three important scholars have published biographies of Defoe: Paula Backscheider (Johns Hopkins University Press, 1989); Maximillian Novak (Oxford University Press, 2001); and John Richetti (Blackwell, 2005). For a thorough treatment of the bibliography see P. N. Furbank and W. R. Owens, *A Critical Bibliography of Daniel Defoe* (Pickering and Chatto, 1998). The accompanying edition of Defoe's collected works runs to 63 volumes.

from *An Essay upon Projects* (1698)

An Academy for Women

I have often thought of it as one of the most barbarous Customs in the world, considering us as a Civilized and a Christian Country, that we deny the advantages of Learning to Women. We reproach the Sex[1] every day with Folly and Impertinence, while I am confident, had they the advantages of Education equal to us, they would be guilty of less than ourselves.

One would wonder indeed how it should happen that Women are conversable at all, since they are only beholding to Natural Parts[2] for all their Knowledge. Their Youth is spent to teach them to Stitch and Sow, or make Baubles: They are taught to Read, indeed, and perhaps to write their Names, or so; and that is the height of a Woman's Education. And I would but ask any who slight the Sex for their Understanding, what is a Man (a Gentleman, I mean) good for, that is taught no more?

I need not give Instances, or examine the Character of a Gentleman with a good Estate, and of a good Family, and with tolerable Parts, and examine what Figure he makes for want of Education.

The Soul is placed in the Body like a rough Diamond, and must be polished, or the Lustre of it will never appear: And 'tis manifest, that as the Rational Soul distinguishes us from Brutes, so Education carries on the distinction, and makes some less brutish than others: This is too evident to need any demonstration. But why then should Women be denied the benefit of Instruction? If Knowledge and Understanding had been useless additions to the Sex, God Almighty would never have given them Capacities; for he made nothing needless: Besides, I would ask such, What they can see in Ignorance, that they should think it a necessary Ornament to a Woman? Or how much worse is a Wise Woman than a Fool? Or what has the Woman done to forfeit the Privilege of being taught? Does she plague us with her Pride and Impertinence? Why did we not let her learn, that she might have had more Wit? Shall we upbraid Women with Folly, when 'tis only the Error of this inhuman Custom that hindered them being made wiser?

The Capacities of Women are supposed to be greater, and their Senses quicker than those of the Men; and what they might be capable of being bred to, is plain from some

Notes

AN ACADEMY FOR WOMEN

1 *the Sex* women.

2 *Parts* abilities.

Instances of Female-Wit, which this Age is not without; which upbraids us with Injustice, and looks as if we denied Women the advantages of Education, for fear they should *vie* with the Men in their Improvements.

To remove this Objection, and that Women might have at least a needful Opportunity of Education in all sorts of Useful Learning, I propose the Draught[3] of an Academy for that purpose.

I know 'tis dangerous to make Public Appearances of the Sex; they are not either to be *confined* or *exposed*; the first will disagree with their Inclinations, and the last with their Reputations; and therefore it is somewhat difficult; and I doubt[4] a Method proposed by an Ingenious Lady, in a little Book, called, *Advice to the Ladies*[5] would be found impracticable. For, saving my Respect to the Sex, the Levity, which perhaps is a little peculiar to them, at least in their Youth, will not bear the Restraint; and I am satisfied, nothing but the height of Bigotry can keep up a Nunnery: Women are extravagantly desirous of going to Heaven, and will punish their *Pretty Bodies* to get thither; but nothing else will do it; and even in that case sometimes it falls out that *Nature will prevail*.

When I talk therefore of an Academy for Women, I mean both the Model, the Teaching, and the Government, different from what is proposed by that Ingenious Lady, for whose Proposal I have a very great Esteem, and also a great Opinion of her Wit; different too from all sorts of Religious Confinement, and above all, from *Vows of Celibacy*.

Wherefore the Academy I propose should differ but little from Public Schools, wherein such Ladies as were willing to study, should have all the advantages of Learning suitable to their Genius.

But since some Severities of Discipline more than ordinary would be absolutely necessary to preserve the Reputation of the House, that Persons of Quality and Fortune might not be afraid to venture their Children thither, I shall venture to make a small Scheme by way of Essay.

The House I would have built in a Form by itself, as well as in a Place by itself

The Building should be of Three plain Fronts, without any Jettings, or Bearing-Work, that the Eye might at a Glance see from one Coign[6] to the other; the Gardens walled in the same Triangular Figure, with a large Moat, and but one Entrance.

When thus every part of the Situation was contrived well as might be for discovery, and to render *Intriguing* dangerous, I would have no Guards, no Eyes, no Spies set over the Ladies, but shall expect them to be tried by the Principles of Honour and strict Virtue.

And if I am asked, 'Why?' I must ask Pardon of my own Sex for giving this reason for it:

I am so much in Charity with Women, and so well acquainted with Men, that 'tis my opinion, There needs no other Care to prevent Intriguing than to keep the men effectually away: For though *Inclination*, which we prettily call *Love*, does sometimes move a little too visibly in the Sex, and Frailty often follows; yet I think verily, *Custom*,

Notes

[3] *Draught* sketch.

[4] *doubt* expect, believe.

[5] *Advice to the Ladies* Defoe is misremembering the title of Mary Astell's *A Serious Proposal to the Ladies*, as Patricia Springborg notes in her edition of Astell's essay (Broadview Press, 2002), p. 268, n. 1.

[6] *Coign* projecting corner.

which we miscall *Modesty*, has so far the Ascendant over the Sex, that *Solicitation* always goes before it.

Custom with Women 'stead of Virtue rules;
It leads the Wisest, and commands the Fools;
For this alone, when Inclinations reign,
Though Virtue's fled, will Acts of Vice restrain.
Only by Custom 'tis that Virtue lives,
And Love requires to be asked, before it gives.
For that which we call Modesty is Pride:
They scorn to ask, and hate to be denied.
'Tis Custom thus prevails upon their Want;
They'll never beg, what asked they eas'ly grant.
And when the needless Ceremony's over,
Themselves the Weakness of the Sex discover.
If then Desires are strong, and Nature free,
Keep from her Men, and Opportunity.
Else 'twill be vain to curb her by Restraint;
But keep the Question off, you keep the Saint.

In short, let a Woman have never such a Coming-Principle,[7] she will let you ask before she complies, at least if she be a Woman of any Honour.

Upon this ground I am persuaded such Measures might be taken, that the Ladies might have all the Freedom in the world within their own Walls, and yet no Intriguing, no Indecencies, nor Scandalous Affairs happen; and in order to this, the following Customs and Laws should be observed in the Colleges; of which I would propose One at least in every County in *England*, and about Ten for the City of *London*.

After the Regulation of the Form of the Building as before;

(1.) All the Ladies who enter into the House, should set their Hands[8] to the Orders of the House, to signify their Consent to submit to them.

(2.) As no Woman should be received, but who declared herself willing, and that it was the Act of her Choice to enter herself, so no Person should be confined to continue there a moment longer than the same voluntary Choice inclined her.

(3.) The Charges of the House being to be paid by the Ladies, everyone that entered should have only this Incumbrance, That she should pay for the whole Year, though her mind should change as to her continuance.

(4.) An Act of Parliament should make it Felony without Clergy,[9] for any man to enter by Force or Fraud into the House, or to solicit any Woman, *though it were to Marry*, while she was in the House. And this Law would by no means be severe; because any Woman who was willing to receive the Addresses of a Man, might discharge herself of the House when she pleased; and on the contrary, any Woman who had occasion, might discharge herself of the Impertinent Addresses of any Person she had an Aversion to, by entering into the House.

Notes

[7] *Coming-Principle* natural forwardness.

[8] *set their Hands* sign their names.

[9] *Felony without Clergy* a capital offense with no possibility of appeal.

In this House

The Persons who Enter, should be taught all sorts of Breeding suitable to both their Genius and their Quality; and in particular, *Music* and *Dancing*, which it would be cruelty to bar the Sex of, because they are their Darlings: But besides this, they should be taught Languages, as particularly *French* and *Italian*; and I would venture the Injury of giving a Woman more Tongues than one.

They should, as a particular Study, be taught all the Graces of Speech, and all the necessary Air of Conversation; which our common Education is so defective in, that I need not expose it: They should be brought to read Books, and especially History, and so to read as to make them understand the World, and be able to know and judge of things when they hear of them.

To such whose Genius would lead them to it, I would deny no sort of Learning; but the chief thing in general is to cultivate the Understandings of the Sex, that they may be capable of all sorts of Conversation; that their Parts and Judgements being improved, they may be as Profitable in their Conversation as they are Pleasant.

Women, in my observation, have little or no difference in them, but as they are, or are not distinguished by Education. Tempers indeed may in some degree influence them, but the main distinguishing part is their Breeding.

The whole Sex are generally Quick and Sharp: I believe I may be allowed to say generally so, for you rarely see them lumpish and heavy when they are Children, as Boys will often be. If a Woman be well-bred, and taught the proper Management of her Natural Wit, she proves generally very sensible and retentive: And without partiality, a Woman of Sense and Manners is the Finest and most Delicate Part of God's Creation; the Glory of her Maker, and the greatest Instance of his singular regard to Man, his Darling Creature, to whom he gave the best Gift either God could bestow, or man receive: And 'tis the sordidest Piece of Folly and Ingratitude in the world, to withhold from the Sex the due Lustre which the advantages of Education gives to the Natural Beauty of their Minds.

A Woman well Bred and well Taught, furnished with the additional Accomplishments of Knowledge and Behaviour, *is a Creature without comparison*; her Society is the Emblem of sublimer Enjoyments; her Person is Angelic, and her Conversation heavenly; she is all Softness and Sweetness, Peace, Love, Wit, and Delight: She is every way suitable to the sublimest Wish; and the man that has such a one to his Portion, has nothing to do but to rejoice in her, and to be thankful.

On the other hand, Suppose her to be the *very same* Woman, and rob her of the Benefit of Education, and it follows thus;

If her Temper be Good, want of Education makes her Soft and Easy.

Her Wit, for want of Teaching, makes her Impertinent and Talkative.

Her Knowledge, for want of Judgement and Experience, makes her Fanciful and Whimsical.

If her Temper be Bad, want of Breeding makes her worse, and she grows Haughty, Insolent, and Loud.

If she be Passionate, want of Manners makes her Termagant,[10] and a Scold, *which is much at one with Lunatic*.

If she be Proud, want of Discretion (which still is Breeding) makes her Conceited, Fantastic, and Ridiculous.

Notes

[10] *Termagant* "Quarrelsome; scolding; furious" (Johnson).

And from these she degenerates to be Turbulent, Clamorous, Noisy, Nasty, *and the Devil.*

Methinks Mankind for their own sakes, since say what we will of the Women, we all think fit one time or other to be concerned with 'em,[11] should take some care to breed them up to be *suitable* and *serviceable*, if they expected no such thing as *Delight* from 'em. Bless us! What Care do we take to Breed up a good Horse, and to Break him well! and what a Value do we put upon him when it is done, and all because he should be fit for our use! and why not a Woman? Since all her Ornaments and Beauty, without suitable Behaviour, is a Cheat in Nature, like the false Tradesman, who puts the best of his Goods uppermost, that the Buyer may think the rest are of the same Goodness.

Beauty of the Body, which is the Woman's Glory, seems to be now unequally bestowed, and Nature, or rather Providence, to lie under some Scandal about it, as if 'twas given a Woman for a Snare to Men, and so made a kind of *She-Devil* of her: Because they say Exquisite Beauty is *rarely* given with Wit; *more rarely* with Goodness of Temper, and *never at all* with Modesty. And some, pretending to justify the Equity of such a Distribution, will tell us 'tis the Effect of the Justice of Providence in dividing particular Excellencies among all his Creatures: *share and share alike, as it were*, that all might for something or other be acceptable to one another, else some would be despised.

I think both these Notions false; and yet the last, which has the show of Respect to Providence, is the worst; for it supposes Providence to be Indigent and Empty; as if it had not wherewith to furnish all the Creatures it had made, but was fain to be parsimonious in its Gifts, and distribute them by *piecemeal*, for fear of being exhausted.

If I might venture my Opinion against an almost universal Notion, I would say, Most men mistake the Proceedings of Providence in this case, and all the world at this day are mistaken in their Practice about it. And because the Assertion is very bold, I desire to explain myself.

That Almighty First Cause which made us all, is certainly the Fountain of Excellence, as it is of Being, and by an Invisible Influence could have diffused Equal Qualities and Perfections to all the Creatures it has made, as the Sun does its Light, without the least Ebb or Diminution to himself; and has given indeed to every individual sufficient to the Figure his Providence had designed him in the world.

I believe it might be defended, if I should say, That I do suppose God has given to all Mankind equal Gifts and Capacities, in that he has given them all *Souls* equally capable; and that the whole difference in Mankind proceeds either from Accidental Difference in the Make of their Bodies, or from the *foolish Difference* of Education.

From Accidental Difference in Bodies. I would avoid discoursing here of the Philosophical Position of the Soul in the Body: But if it be true, as Philosophers do affirm, That the Understanding and Memory is dilated or contracted according to the accidental Dimensions of the Organ through which 'tis conveyed; then though God has given a Soul as capable to me as another, yet if I have any Natural Defect in those Parts of the Body by which the Soul should act, I may have the same Soul infused as another man, and yet he be a Wise Man, and I a very Fool. *For example*, If

Notes

[11] *'em* an old form of "them," not slang.

a Child naturally have a Defect in the Organ of Hearing, so that he could never distinguish any Sound, that Child shall never be able to speak or read, though it have a Soul capable of all the Accomplishments in the world. The Brain is the Centre of the Soul's actings, where all the distinguishing Faculties of it reside; and 'tis observable, A man who has a narrow contracted Head, in which there is not room for the due and necessary Operations of Nature by the Brain, is never a man of very great Judgement; and that Proverb, *A Great Head and Little Wit*, is not meant by Nature, but is a Reproof upon Sloth; as if one should, by way of wonder, say, *Fie, fie, you that have a Great Head, have but Little Wit, that's strange! that must certainly be your own fault*. From this Notion I do believe there is a great matter in the Breed of Men and Women; not that Wise Men shall always get Wise Children; but I believe Strong and Healthy Bodies have the Wisest Children; and Sickly Weakly Bodies affect the Wits as well as the Bodies of their Children. We are easily persuaded to believe this in the Breeds of Horses, Cocks, Dogs, and other Creatures; and I believe 'tis as visible in Men.

But to come closer to the business; the great distinguishing difference which is seen in the world between Men and Women, is in their Education; and this is manifested by comparing it with the difference between one Man or Woman, and another.

And herein it is that I take upon me to make such a bold Assertion, That all the World are mistaken in their Practice about Women: For I cannot think that God Almighty ever made them so delicate, so glorious Creatures, and furnished them with such Charms, so Agreeable and so Delightful to Mankind, with Souls capable of the same Accomplishments with Men, and all to be only Stewards of our Houses, *Cooks, and Slaves*.

Not that I am for exalting the Female Government in the least: But, in short, *I would have Men take Women for Companions, and Educate them to be fit for it*. A Woman of Sense and Breeding will scorn as much to encroach upon the Prerogative of the Man, as a Man of Sense will scorn to oppress the 'Weakness' of the Woman. But if the Women's Souls were refined and improved by Teaching, that word would be lost; to say, 'The Weakness of the Sex', as to Judgement, would be Nonsense; for Ignorance and Folly would be no more found among Women than Men. I remember a Passage which I heard from a very Fine Woman; she had Wit and Capacity enough, an Extraordinary Shape and Face, and a Great Fortune, but had been cloistered up all her time, and for fear of being stolen, had not had the liberty of being taught the common necessary knowledge of Women's Affairs; and when she came to converse in the world, her Natural Wit made her so sensible of the want of Education that she gave this short Reflection on herself:

'I am ashamed to talk with my very Maids', says she, 'for I don't know when they do right or wrong: I had more need to go to School, than be Married'.

I need not enlarge on the Loss the Defect of Education is to the Sex, nor argue the Benefit of the contrary Practice; 'tis a thing will be more easily granted than remedied: This Chapter is but an Essay[12] at the thing, and I refer the Practice to those Happy Days, if ever they shall be, when men shall be wise enough to mend it.

Notes

[12] *Essay* attempt.

from *The True-Born Englishman: A Satire* (1700)

Part I

Wherever God erects a House of Prayer,[1]
The Devil always builds a Chapel there:
And 'twill be found upon Examination,
The latter has the largest Congregation:
For ever since he first debauched the Mind,
He made a perfect Conquest of Mankind.
With Uniformity of Service, he
Reigns with a general Aristocracy.
No Nonconforming Sects disturb his Reign,
For of his Yoke there's very few complain.[2]
He knows the Genius and the Inclination,
And matches proper Sins for every Nation.
He needs no Standing-Army Government;[3]
He always rules us by our own Consent:
His Laws are easy, and his gentle Sway
Makes it exceeding pleasant to obey.
The List of his Vicegerents and Commanders,
Outdoes your *Cæsars*, or your *Alexanders*.
They never fail of his Infernal Aid,
And he's as certain ne'er to be betrayed.
Through all the World they spread his vast Command,
And Death's Eternal Empire's maintained.
They rule so politically and so well,
As if they were *L———J———* of Hell.[4]
Duly divided to debauch Mankind,
And plant Infernal Dictates in his Mind.
Pride, the first Peer, and President of Hell,
To his share *Spain*, the largest Province, fell.
The subtle Prince thought fittest to bestow
On these the Golden Mines of *Mexico*;
With all the Silver Mountains of *Peru*;
Wealth which would in wise hands the World undo:
Because he knew their Genius was such;
Too Lazy and too Haughty to be Rich.

Notes

FROM THE TRUE-BORN ENGLISHMAN

[1] An English Proverb, "Where God has a Church, the Devil has a Chapel" [Defoe's note].

[2] *Yoke* a reference to Christ's description of the discipline he enjoins: "my yoke is easy, and my burden is light" (Matthew 11.30).

[3] *Standing-Army* whether or not there was a need for a permanent military force was one of the most hotly contested issues in politics in the seventeenth and eighteenth centuries; Defoe wrote against King William's retention of his standing army.

[4] *L[ords] J[ustices]* the officers left in charge of England when King William made his annual return to the Netherlands.

So proud a People, so above their Fate,
That if reduced to beg, they'll beg in State.
Lavish of Money, to be counted Brave,
And Proudly starve, because they scorn to save.
Never was a Nation in the World before,
So very Rich, and yet so very Poor.
Lust chose the Torrid Zone of *Italy*,
Where Blood ferments in Rapes and Sodomy:
Where swelling Veins o'erflow with livid Streams,
With Heat impregnate from *Vesuvian* Flames:[5]
Whose flowing Sulphur forms Infernal Lakes,
And human Body of the Soil partakes.
There Nature ever burns with hot Desires,
Fanned with Luxuriant Air from Subterranean Fires:
Here undisturbed in Floods of scalding Lust,
Th' Infernal King reigns with Infernal Gust.[6]
Drunkenness, the Darling Favourite of Hell,
Chose *Germany* to Rule; and rules so well,
No Subjects more obsequiously obey,
None please so well, or are so pleased as they.
The cunning Artist manages so well,
He lets them Bow to Heav'n, and Drink to Hell.
If but to Wine and him they Homage pay,
He cares not to what Deity they Pray,
What God they worship most, or in what way.
Whether by *Luther, Calvin*, or by *Rome*,[7]
They sail for Heav'n, by Wine he steers them home.
Ungoverned Passion settled first in *France*,
Where Mankind Lives in haste, and Thrives by Chance,
A *Dancing Nation*, Fickle and Untrue:
Have oft undone themselves, and others too:
Prompt the Infernal Dictates to Obey,
And in Hell's Favour none more great than they.
The *Pagan* World he blindly leads away,
And Personally rules with Arbitrary Sway:
The Mask thrown off, *Plain Devil* his Title stands;
And what elsewhere he Tempts, he there Commands.
There with full Gust th' Ambition of his Mind
Governs, as he of old in Heav'n designed.
Worshipped as God, his *Painim Altars*[8] smoke,
Embrued with Blood of those that him Invoke.
The rest by Deputies he rules as well,
And plants the distant Colonies of Hell.

Notes

[5] *Vesuvian* from the volcanic Mount Vesuvius near Pompeii and Naples.

[6] *Gust* "height of sensual enjoyment" (Johnson).

[7] *Luther, Calvin* founders of important Protestant sects in opposition to the Roman Catholic Church.

[8] *Painim Altars* pagan places of worship where Defoe imagines human sacrifices.

By them his secret Power he well maintains,
And binds the World in his Infernal Chains.
By Zeal the *Irish*; and the *Rush* by Folly:[9]
Fury the *Dane*: The *Swede* by Melancholy:[10]
By stupid Ignorance, the *Muscovite*:
The *Chinese* by a *Child of Hell*, called Wit:
Wealth makes the *Persian* too Effeminate:
And Poverty the *Tartars* Desperate:
The *Turks* and *Moors* by *Mah'met* he subdues:
And God has given him leave to rule the Jews:
Rage rules the *Portuguese*; and Fraud the *Scotch*:
Revenge the *Pole*; and Avarice the *Dutch*.
Satire be kind, and draw a silent Veil,
Thy *Native England's* Vices to conceal:
Or if that Task's impossible to do,
At least be just, and show her Virtues too;
Too Great the first, Alas! the last too Few.
England unknown as yet, unpeopled lay;
Happy, had she remained so to this day,
And not to every Nation been a Prey.
Her Open Harbours, and her Fertile Plains,
The Merchant's Glory these, and those the Swains,
To every Barbarous Nation have betrayed her,
Who conquer her as oft as they Invade her.
So Beauty guarded but by Innocence,
That ruins her which should be her Defence.
Ingratitude, a Devil of Black *Renown*,
Possessed her very early for his own.
An Ugly, Surly, Sullen, Selfish Spirit,
Who Satan's *worst Perfections does inherit*:
Second to him in Malice and in Force,
All *Devil without*, and all *within* him *Worse*.
He made her First-born Race to be so rude,
And suffered her to be so oft subdued:
By several Crowds of Wand'ring Thieves o'errun,
Often unpeopled, and as oft undone.
While every Nation that her Powers reduced,
Their Languages and Manners introduced.
From whose mixed Relics our compounded Breed,
By Spurious Generation does succeed;
Making a Race uncertain and unev'n,
Derived from all the Nations under Heav'n.
The *Romans* first with *Julius Cæsar* came,
Including all the Nations of that Name,
Gauls, Greeks, and *Lombards*; and by Computation,[11]

Notes

[9] *Rush* Russ, Russians.

[10] *Melancholy* madness.

[11] *Gauls, Greeks, and Lombards* peoples conquered by the Romans and pressed into military service for them.

Auxiliaries, or Slaves of every Nation.
With *Hengist, Saxons*; Danes with *Sueno* Came,[12]
In search of Plunder, not in search of Fame.
Scots, Picts and *Irish* from th' *Hibernian* Shore;[13]
And Conqu'ring *William* brought the *Normans* o'er.
   All these their Barb'rous offspring left behind
The Dregs of Armies, they of all Mankind;
Blended with *Britons* who before were here,
Of whom the *Welsh* have blessed the Character.
   From this Amphibious Ill-born Mob began
That vain ill-natured thing, an Englishman.
The Customs, Surnames, Languages, and Manners,
Of all these Nations are their own Explainers:
Whose Relics are so lasting and so strong,
They have left a *Shibboleth* upon our Tongue;[14]
By which with easy search you may distinguish
Your *Roman-Saxon-Danish-Norman* English.
   The great Invading *Norman* let us know[15]
What Conquerors in After-Times might do.
To every *Musketeer* he brought to *Town*,[16]
He gave the Lands which never were his own.
When first the *English* Crown he did obtain,
He did not send his *Dutchmen* home again.[17]
No Reassumptions in his Reign were known,[18]
Davenant might there have let his Book alone.[19]
No Parliament his Army could disband;
He raised no Money, for he paid in Land.
He gave his Legions their Eternal Station,
And made them all Freeholders of the Nation.
He cantoned out the Country to his Men,
And every Soldier was a Denizen.
The Rascals thus enriched, he called them *Lords*,
To please their Upstart Pride with new-made Words;
And *Doomsday-Book* his Tyranny records.[20]
   And here begins the Ancient Pedigree
That so exalts our Poor Nobility:
'Tis that from some *French* Trooper they derive,
Who with the *Norman* Bastard did arrive:[21]

Notes

12 *Hengist* with his brother Horsa, he came from the region of southern Denmark to found Kent in England around 449; *Sueno* King Sweyn II (d. 1075) assisted Anglo-Saxon rebels in England for a year but settled with William the Conqueror and withdrew in 1070.

13 *Picts* an ancient Celtic people inhabiting parts of what is now Scotland; *Hibernian* Irish.

14 *Shibboleth* a test word that identifies a speaker as belonging to an ethnic, political, religious, or other such group (see Judges 12.6).

15 *Invading Norman* William the Conqueror [Defoe's note].

16 *Musketeer* Or Archer [Defoe's note].

17 *Dutchmen* the nationality of King William's guard, not William the Conqueror's.

18 *Reassumption* the act of the crown in reassuming ownership of lands once granted to others.

19 *Davenant* Charles Davenant, *A Discourse upon Grants and Resumptions* (1700).

20 *Doomsday-Book* the record of the survey of lands made by William the Conqueror in 1086.

21 *Norman Bastard* William I of England was the bastard son and heir of Robert the Devil, duke of Normandy.

The Trophies of the Families appear;
Some show the Sword, the Bow, and some the Spear,
Which their Great Ancestor, *forsooth*, did wear.
These in Herald's Register remain,
Their Noble Mean Extraction to explain.
Yet who the Hero was, no man can tell,
Whether a Drummer, or a Colonel:
The silent Record blushes to reveal
Their Undescended Dark Original.
But grant the best, How came the Change to pass;
A *True-Born Englishman* of *Norman* Race?
A *Turkish* Horse can show more History,
To prove his Well-descended Family.
Conquest, as by the Moderns 'tis expressed,
May give a Title to the Lands possessed:
But that the Longest Sword should be so Civil,
To make a *Frenchman English*, that's the Devil.
These are the Heroes that despise the *Dutch*,
And rail at new-come Foreigners so much;
Forgetting that themselves are all derived
From the most Scoundrel Race that ever lived,
A horrid Medley of Thieves and Drones,
Who ransacked Kingdoms, and dispeopled Towns.
The *Pict* and Painted *Briton*, Treach'rous *Scot*,[22]
By Hunger, Theft, and Rapine, hither brought.
Norwegian Pirates, Buccaneering *Danes*,
Whose Red-haired Offspring everywhere remains.
Who joined with *Norman-French* compound the Breed
From whence your *True-Born Englishmen* proceed.
And lest by Length of Time it be pretended,
The Climate may this Modern Breed have mended,
Wise Providence, to keep us where we are,
Mixes us daily with exceeding Care:
We have been *Europe*'s Sink, *the Jakes* where she[23]
Voids all her Offal Outcast Progeny.
From our Fifth *Henry*'s time, the Strolling Bands
Of banished Fugitives from Neighb'ring Lands,
Have here a certain Sanctuary found:
The Eternal Refuge of the Vagabond.
Where in but half a common Age of Time,
Borr'wing new Blood and Manners from the Clime,
Proudly they learn all Mankind to contemn,
And all their Race are *True-Born Englishmen*.

Notes

[22] *Painted Britain* Roman conquerors described the inhabitants of Britain as painted for ceremony or war.

[23] *Jakes* "A house of office" (Johnson); privy; toilet.

Dutch, *Walloons*, *Flemings*, *Irishmen*, and *Scots*,[24]
Vaudois and *Valtolins*, and *Huguenots*,[25]
In good Queen *Bess*'s Charitable Reign,[26]
Supplied us with Three hundred thousand Men.
Religion, *God we thank thee*, sent them hither,
Priests, Protestants, the Devil and all together:
Of all Professions, and of every Trade,
All that were persecuted or afraid;
Whether for Debt or other Crimes they fled,
David at *Hackelah* was still their Head.[27]
The Offspring of this Miscellaneous Crowd,
Had not their new Plantations long enjoyed,
But they grew *Englishmen*, and raised their Votes
At Foreign Shoals of *Interloping Scots*.
The Royal Branch from *Pict-land* did succeed,[28]
With Troops of *Scots* and Scabs from *North-by-Tweed*.[29]
The Seven first Years of his Pacific Reign,
Made him and half his Nation *Englishmen*.
Scots from the *Northern* Frozen Banks of *Tay*,
With Packs and Plods came *Whigging* all away:[30]
Thick as the Locusts which in *Egypt* swarmed,[31]
With Pride and hungry Hopes completely armed:
With Native Truth, Diseases, and no Money,
Plundered our *Canaan* of the Milk and Honey.[32]
Here they grew quickly Lords and Gentlemen,
And all their Race are *True-Born Englishmen*.
The Civil Wars, the common Purgative,
Which always use to make the Nation thrive,
Made way for all the strolling Congregation,[33]
Which thronged in Pious *Ch——s* 's Restoration.[34]
The *Royal Refugee* our Breed restores,
With *Foreign Courtiers*, and with *Foreign Whores*:
And carefully repeopled us again,
Throughout his Lazy, Long, Lascivious Reign;
With such a blessed and True-Born *English* Fry,

Notes

24 *Walloons* a people of Gallic origin inhabiting southern Belgium in the sixteenth century; *Flemings* Flemish people; inhabitants of Flanders.

25 *Vaudois* a Protestant sect of southern France; *Valtolins* natives of Valtellina in present-day Switzerland; *Huguenots* a sect of French Protestants.

26 *Queen Bess* Queen Elizabeth I reigned from 1558 to 1603; some members of sects persecuted in Roman Catholic countries took refuge in Protestant England.

27 *David at Hackelah* David and his followers fled from King Saul and sheltered in a stronghold on the hill of Hachilah (1 Samuel 23.19).

28 James VI of Scotland *(Pict-land)* became James I of England in 1603, thus beginning the reign of the House of Stuart.

29 *Scab* "A paltry fellow, so named from the itch often incident to negligent poverty" (Johnson); *North-by-Tweed* Scotland, which is divided from England by the River Tweed.

30 *Whigging* jogging.

31 *Locusts* "they covered the face of the whole earth" (Exodus 10.15).

32 *Canaan* the Promised Land of the Israelites in the Bible, "a land that floweth with milk and honey" (Joshua 5.6).

33 *strolling* from "stroll," "To wander; to ramble; to rove; to be a vagrant" (Johnson).

34 *Ch[arle]s* II, restored to the throne in 1660, after a long, enforced sojourn in France.

As much Illustrates our Nobility.[35]
A Gratitude which will so black appear,
As future Ages must abhor to hear:
When they look back on all that Crimson Flood,
Which streamed in *Lindsey*'s, and *Caernarvon*'s Blood:[36]
Bold *Strafford, Cambridge, Capel, Lucas, Lisle,*
Who crowned in Death his Father's Fun'ral Pile,
The loss of whom, in order to supply,
With True-Born *English* Nobility,
Six Bastard Dukes survive his Luscious Reign,[37]
The Labours of *Italian C———n,*[38]
French P———h, Taby S——t, and Cambrian.
Besides the Num'rous Bright and Virgin Throng,
Whose Female Glories shade them from my Song.
This Offspring, if one Age they multiply,
May half the House with *English* Peers supply:[39]
There with true *English* Pride they may contemn
S——g and *P——d*, new-made Noblemen.[40]
French Cooks, *Scotch* Pedlars, and *Italian* Whores,
Were all made Lords, or Lords' Progenitors.
Beggars and Bastards by his new Creation,
Much multiplied the Peerage of the Nation;
Who will be all, ere one short Age runs o'er,
As *True-Born* Lords as those we had before.
Then to recruit the Commons he prepares,
And heal the latent Breaches of the Wars:
The Pious Purpose better to advance,
H' invites the banished Protestants of *France*:
Hither for God's sake and their own they fled,
Some for Religion came, and some for Bread:
Two hundred thousand Pair of Wooden Shoes,[41]
Who, God be thanked, had nothing left to lose;
To Heav'n great Praise did for Religion fly,
To make us starve our Poor in Charity.
In every Port they plant their fruitful Train,
To get a Race of *True-Born Englishmen*:
Whose Children will, when Riper Years they see,
Be as Ill-natured and as Proud as we:
Call them *English*, Foreigners despise,
Be Surly like us all, and just as Wise.

Notes

[35] *Illustrate* "To brighten with honour" (Johnson); Charles created a great many new nobles upon his return.

[36] *Lindsey … Caernarvon … Strafford, Cambridge, Capel, Lucas, Lisle* all noblemen killed in the Civil War.

[37] *Six Bastard Dukes* Charles created six of his illegitimate sons dukes.

[38] *Italian C[astlemai]n, French P[ortsmout]h, Taby S[lu]t, and Cambrian* mothers of Charles's illegitimate children, Barbara Villiers, Louise de Kéroualle, Nell Gwyn, and Lucy Walter.

[39] *House* the House of Lords, the non-elective branch of Parliament.

[40] *S[chomber]g* Frederick Herman von Schomberg (1640–90), German-born English noble and gallant soldier killed at Boyne; *P[ortlan]d* William Bentinck, first earl of Portland (1649–1709), Dutch-born English noble, close confidant of William III.

[41] *Wooden Shoes* a sign of indigence or rusticity.

Thus from a Mixture of all Kinds began,
That Het'rogeneous *Thing, An Englishman*:
In eager Rapes, and furious Lust begot,
Betwixt a Painted *Briton* and a *Scot*:
Whose gend'ring Offspring quickly learnt to bow,[42]
And Yoke their Heifers to the *Roman* Plough:
From whence a Mongrel half-bred Race there came,
With neither Name nor Nation, Speech nor Fame.
In whose hot Veins new Mixtures quickly ran,
Infused betwixt a *Saxon* and a *Dane*.
While their Rank Daughters, to their Parents just,
Received all Nations with Promiscuous Lust.
This Nauseous Blood directly did contain
The well-extracted Blood of *Englishmen*.
Which Medley cantoned in a Heptarchy,[43]
A Rhapsody of Nations to supply,
Among themselves maintained eternal Wars,
And still the Ladies loved the Conquerors.
The *Western* Angles all the rest subdued;
A bloody Nation, barbarous and rude:
Who by the Tenure of the Sword possessed
One part of *Britain*, and subdued the rest.
And as great things denominate the small,
The Conqu'ring part gave Title to the Whole.
The *Scot, Pict, Briton, Roman, Dane* submit,
And with the *English-Saxon* all unite:
And these the Mixture have so close pursued,
The very Name and Memory's subdued:
No *Roman* now, no *Britain* does remain;
Wales strove to separate, but strove in vain:
The silent Nations undistinguished fall,
And *Englishman*'s the common Name for all.
Fate jumbled them together, *God knows how*;
Whate'er they were, they're *True-Born English* now.
The Wonder which remains is at our Pride,
To value that which all wise men deride.
For *Englishmen* to boast of Generation,[44]
Cancels their Knowledge, and lampoons the Nation.
A *True-Born Englishman*'s a Contradiction,
In Speech an Irony, in Fact a Fiction.
A Banter made to be a Test of Fools,
Which those that use it justly ridicules.
A Metaphor invented to express
A Man *a-kin* to all the Universe.

Notes

[42] *gender* "To copulate; to breed" (Johnson).
[43] *Heptarchy* the seven kingdoms of the Angles and Saxons (sixth to ninth centuries CE).
[44] *Generation* "A family; a race" (Johnson).

For as the *Scots*, as Learned Men have said,
Throughout the World their Wand'ring Seed have spread;
So open-handed *England*, 'tis believed,
Has all the Gleanings of the World received.
Some think of *England* 'twas our Saviour meant,
The Gospel should to all the World be sent:
Since when the blessèd Sound did hither reach,
They to all Nations might be said to Preach.
'Tis well that Virtue gives Nobility,
Else God knows where we had our Gentry;
Since scarce one Family is left alive,
Which does not from some Foreigner derive.
Of Sixty thousand *English* Gentlemen,
Whose Names and Arms in Registers remain,
We challenge all our Heralds to declare
Ten Families which *English-Saxons* are.
France justly boasts the Ancient Noble Line
Of *Bourbon, Mommorency*, and *Lorrain*.
The *Germans* too their House of *Austria* show,
And *Holland* their Invincible *Nassau*,
Lines which in Heraldry were Ancient grown,
Before the Name of *Englishman* was known.
Even *Scotland* too, her Elder Glory shows,
Her *Gordons, Hamiltons*, and her *Monroes*;
Douglas, Mackays, and *Grahams*, Names well known,
Long before Ancient *England* knew her own.
But *England*, Modern to the last degree,
Borrows or makes her own Nobility,
And yet she boldly boasts of Pedigree:
Repines that Foreigners are put upon her,
And talks of her Antiquity and Honour:
Her *S*[ackvi]*lls*, *S*[avi]*ls*, *C*[eci]*ls*, *De-la-M*[ere]*s*,
M[ohu]*ns* and *M*[ontag]*ues*, *D*[urase]*s* and *V*[ere]*s*,
Not one have *English* Names, yet all are *English* Peers.
Your *H*[*oublons*], *P*[*apillons*], and *L*[*ethuliers*],
Pass now for True-Born *English* Knights and Squires,
And make good Senate-Members, or Lord-Mayors.
Wealth, howsoever got, in *England* makes
Lords of Mechanics, Gentlemen of Rakes.
Antiquity and Birth are needless here;
'Tis Impudence and Money makes a P[ee]r.
Innumerable City-Knights we know,
From *Bluecoat Hospitals* and *Bridewell* flow.[45]
Draymen and Porters fill the City Chair,
And Footboys Magisterial Purple wear.

Notes

[45] *Bluecoat Hospitals and Bridewell* Christ's Hospital, and other charity schools where the pupils wore blue uniforms, and Bridewell Hospital, a training school for apprentices.

Fate has but very small Distinction set
Betwixt the *Counter* and the Coronet.[46]
Tarpaulin Lords, Pages of high Renown,[47]
Rise up by Poor Men's Valour, not their own.
Great Families of yesterday we show,
And Lords, whose Parents were *the Lord knows who.*

The Shortest-Way with the Dissenters:[1] Or Proposals for the Establishment of the Church (1702)

Sir *Roger L'Estrange* tells us a Story in his Collection of Fables,[2] of the Cock and the Horses. The Cock was gotten to Roost in the Stable, among the Horses, and there being no Racks or other Conveniences for him, it seems, he was forced to roost upon the Ground; the Horses jostling about for room, and putting the Cock in danger of his Life, he gives them this grave Advice: 'Pray Gentlefolks let us stand still, for fear we should tread upon one another'.

There are some People in the World, who now they are *unperched*, and reduced to an Equality with other People, and under strong and very just Apprehensions of being further treated as they deserve, begin with *Æsop*'s Cock, to Preach up to Peace and Union, and the Christian Duties of Moderation, forgetting, that when they had the Power in their Hands, those Graces were Strangers in their Gates.

It is now near Fourteen Years,[3] that the Glory and Peace of the purest and most flourishing Church in the World has been Eclipsed, Buffeted, and Disturbed by a sort of Men, who God in his Providence has suffered to insult over her, and bring her down; these have been the Days of her Humiliation and Tribulation: She has borne with an invincible Patience the Reproach of the Wicked, and God has at last heard her Prayers, and delivered her from the Oppression of the Stranger.[4]

And now they find their Day is over, their Power gone, and the Throne of this Nation possessed by a Royal, *English*, True, and ever Constant Member of, and Friend to the Church of *England*. Now they find that they are in danger of the Church of *England*'s just Resentments; now they cry out, *Peace, Union, Forbearance*, and *Charity*, as if the Church had not too long harboured her Enemies under her Wing, and nourished the viperous Brood, till they hiss and fly in the Face of the Mother that cherished them.[5]

Notes

[46] *Counter* debtors' prison.

[47] *Tarpaulin* nickname for a common sailor.

The Shortest-Way with the Dissenters

[1] *Dissenters* nonconformists, members of religious sects separate from the Church of England; these people and their educational academies were tolerated during the reign of William III, but when Queen Anne ascended the throne in March 1702 she made it clear that she would favor members of the national church. High Tory clergymen, especially a charismatic speaker named Henry Sacheverell, pressed the point and called for the suppression of dissenters and the extirpation of their academies. Defoe's brilliant essay is an answer to Sacheverell so deeply ironical that it was at first taken by many people as a defense of the High Tory position. When its meaning became clear, a warrant was issued for Defoe's arrest (see below, p. 431); he was very heavily fined, made to stand in the public stocks, and imprisoned.

[2] *Roger L'Estrange* Tory journalist and voluminous writer; author of *The Fables of Aesop* (1692).

[3] *Fourteen Years* the length of William III's reign.

[4] *Stranger* "deliver thee from the strange woman, even from the stranger ... Which forsaketh the guide of her youth, and forgetteth the covenant of her God" (Proverbs 2.16–17).

[5] *viperous Brood ... them* it was popularly believed that snakes tore through the mother's womb in birth, in revenge of the mother's biting off the head of the father in conception (Browne, *Pseudodoxia Epidemica*, chapter 16).

No Gentlemen, the Time of Mercy is past, your *Day of Grace is over*; you should have practised Peace, and Moderation, and Charity, if you expected any yourselves.

We have heard none of this Lesson for Fourteen Years past: We have been huffed and bullied with your Act of Toleration;[6] you have told us that you are the *Church established by Law*, as well as others; have set up your Canting-Synagogues at our Church Doors, and the Church and her Members have been loaded with Reproaches, with Oaths, Associations, Abjurations, and what not; where has been the Mercy, the Forbearance, the Charity you have shown to *tender Consciences of the Church of England*, that could not take Oaths *as fast as you made 'em*; that having sworn Allegiance to their lawful and rightful King,[7] could not dispense with that Oath, *their King being still alive*, and swear to your new *Hodge-podge of a Dutch-Government*.[8] These ha' been turned out of their Livings, and they and their Families left to starve; their Estates double Taxed to carry on a War[9] they had *no Hand in*, and you *got nothing by*: What Account can you give of the Multitudes you have forced to comply, against their Consciences, with your new *sophistical Politics*, who like the new Converts[10] in *France*, Sin because they can't Starve. And now the Tables are turned upon you, *you must not be Persecuted, 'tis not a Christian Spirit*.

You have *Butchered* one King, *Deposed* another King, and made a *mock King* of a Third; and yet you could have the Face to expect to be employed and trusted by the Fourth;[11] anybody that did not know the Temper of your Party, would stand amazed at the Impudence, as well as Folly, to think of it.

Your Management of your *Dutch Monarch*, whom you reduced to a mere *King of Cl[ub]s*, is enough to give any future Princes such an Idea of your Principles, as to warn them sufficiently from coming into your Clutches; and God be thanked, the Queen is out of your Hands, knows you, and will have a care of you.

There is no doubt but the supreme Authority of a Nation has in itself a Power, *and a Right to that Power*, to execute the Laws upon any Part of that nation it governs. The execution of the known Laws of the Land, and that with but a weak and gentle Hand neither, was all that the fanatical Party of this Land have ever called Persecution; this they have magnified to a height, that the sufferings of the *Huguenots* in *France*[12] were not to be compared with – Now to execute the known Laws of a Nation upon those who transgress them, after having first been voluntarily consenting to the making those Laws, can never be called Persecution, but Justice. But Justice is always Violence to the Party offending, for every Man is Innocent in his own Eyes. The first execution of the Laws against Dissenters in *England*, was in the Days of King *James* the First; and what did it amount to, truly? the worst they suffered, was at their own request, to let them go to *New-England*, and erect a new Colony,[13] and give them great Privileges, Grants, and suitable Powers, keep them under Protection, and defend them against all Invaders, and receive no Taxes or Revenue from them. This was the cruelty of the

Notes

6 *Act of Toleration* a bill passed on May 24, 1689, granting freedom of worship to Protestant dissenters, provided they took an oath of allegiance.

7 *rightful King* James II.

8 *Dutch-Government* the government of William III.

9 *War* one phase of the war against France, initiated in the Treaty of Vienna (1689).

10 *new Converts* French Protestants forced to convert to Roman Catholicism.

11 *Fourth* Queen Anne, following Charles I, James II, and William III in this list.

12 *Huguenots in France* thousands were slain in the infamous Massacre of St. Bartholomew's Day on the night of August 24/25, 1572.

13 *New Colony* Plymouth, in present-day Massachusetts, was founded by the Pilgrims who sailed on the *Mayflower* in 1620.

Church of *England*, fatal Lenity! 'Twas the ruin of that excellent Prince, King *Charles* the First. Had King *James* sent all the Puritans in *England* away to the *West Indies*, we had been a national unmixed Church; the Church of *England* had been kept undivided and entire.

To requite the Lenity of the Father, they take up Arms against the Son; Conquer, Pursue, Take, Imprison, and at last put to Death the anointed of God, and destroy the very Being and Nature of Government, setting up a sordid Impostor,[14] who had neither Title to Govern, nor Understanding to Manage, but supplied that want with Power, bloody and desperate Counsels and Craft, without Conscience.

Had not King *James* the First withheld the full execution of the Laws; had he given them strict Justice, he had cleared the Nation of them, and the Consequences had been plain; his *Son had never been murdered by them*, nor the Monarchy overwhelmed; 'twas *too much Mercy* shown them, was the ruin of his Posterity, and the ruin of the Nation's Peace. One would think the Dissenters should not have the Face to believe that we are to be wheedled and canted into Peace and Toleration, when they know that they have once requited us with a civil War, and once with an intolerable and unrighteous Persecution for our former Civility.

Nay, to encourage us to be Easy with them, 'tis apparent, that they never had the Upper hand of the Church, but[15] they treated her with all the Severity, with all the Reproach and Contempt as was possible: What Peace, and what Mercy did they show the Loyal Gentry of the Church of *England* in the time of their Triumphant Common-Wealth? How did they put all the Gentry of *England* to ransom, whether they were actually in Arms for the King or Not, making People compound[16] for their Estates, and starve their Families? How did they treat the Clergy of the Church of *England*, sequestered the Ministers, devoured the Patrimony of the Church, and divided the Spoil, by sharing the Church-Lands among their Soldiers, and turning her Clergy out to starve; just such Measure as they have mete, should be measured to them again.

Charity and Love is the known Doctrine of the Church of *England*, and 'tis plain she has put it in practice towards the Dissenters, even beyond what they ought, till she has been wanting to herself, and in effect, unkind to her own Sons; particularly, in the too much Lenity of King *James* the First, mentioned before, had he so rooted the Puritans from the Face of the Land, which he had an opportunity early to have done, they had not the Power to vex the Church, as since they have done.

In the Days of King *Charles* the Second, how did the Church reward their bloody Doings with Lenity and Mercy,[17] *except the barbarous Regicides of the pretended Court of Justice*; not a Soul suffered for the Blood in an unnatural War: King *Charles* came in all Mercy and Love, cherished them, preferred them, employed them, withheld the rigour of the Law, and oftentimes, even against the Advice of his Parliament, gave them liberty of Conscience; and how did they requite him with the villainous Contrivance to Depose and Murder him and his Successor at the *Rye-Plot*.[18]

King *James*, as if Mercy was the inherent Quality of the Family, began his Reign with unusual Favour to them: Nor could their joining with the Duke of *Monmouth* against him, move him to do himself Justice upon them; but that mistaken Prince thought to

Notes

14 *sordid Impostor* Oliver Cromwell, Lord Protector of the Commonwealth of England, Scotland, and Ireland, 1653–8.

15 *they never had … but they treated* whenever they had … they treated.

16 *compound* "To come to terms" (Johnson).

17 *Lenity and Mercy* shown in An Act of Indemnity (August 1660), pardoning almost everyone who had fought against the king.

18 *Rye-Plot* Rye-House Plot, an attempt in 1683 to murder King Charles II and his Catholic brother, who became James II.

win them by Gentleness and Love, proclaimed an universal Liberty[19] to them and rather discountenanced the Church of *England* than them; how they requited him all the World knows.

The late Reign is too fresh in the Memory of all the World to need a Comment; how under Pretence of joining with the Church in redressing some Grievances, they pushed things to that extremity, in conjunction with some mistaken Gentlemen, as to Depose the late King, as if the Grievance of the Nation could not have been redressed but by the absolute ruin of the Prince: Here's an Instance of their Temper, their Peace, and Charity. To what height they carried themselves during the Reign of a King of their own; how they crope[20] into all Places of Trust and Profit; how they insinuated into the Favour of the King, and were at first preferred to the highest Places in the Nation; how they engrossed the Ministry, and, *above* all, *how pitifully they Managed*, is too plain to need any Remarks.

But particularly, their Mercy and Charity, the Spirit of Union, they tell us so much of, has been remarkable in *Scotland*, there they made entire Conquest of the Church, trampled down the sacred Orders, and suppressed the Episcopal Government, with an absolute, and as they suppose, irretrievable Victory, though 'tis possible, *they may find themselves mistaken*: Now 'twould be a very proper Question to ask their *Impudent Advocate, the Observator*,[21] Pray how much Mercy and Favour did the Members of the Episcopal Church find in *Scotland*, from the *Scotch* Presbyterian-Government; and I shall undertake for the Church of *England*, that the Dissenters shall still receive as much here, though they deserve but little.

In a small Treatise[22] of the Sufferings of the Episcopal Clergy in *Scotland*, 'twill appear, what Usage they met with, how they not only lost their Livings, but in several Places, were plundered and abused in their Persons; the Ministers that could not conform, turned out, with numerous Families, and no Maintenance, and hardly Charity enough left to relieve them with a bit of Bread; and the Cruelties of the Party[23] are innumerable, and are not to be attempted in this short Piece.

And now to prevent the distant Cloud which they perceived to hang over their Heads from *England*; with a true Presbyterian Policy, they put in for *a union of Nations*,[24] that *England* might unite their Church with the Kirk of *Scotland*, and their Presbyterian Members sit in our House of Commons, and their Assembly of *Scotch* canting Long-Cloaks[25] in our Convocation;[26] what might have been, if our Fanatic, Whiggish-Statesmen had continued, God only knows; but we hope we are out of fear of that now.

'Tis alleged by some of the Faction,[27] and they began to Bully us with it; that if we won't unite with them, they will not settle the Crown with us again, but when her majesty dies, will choose a King for themselves.

If they won't, we must make them, and 'tis not the first time we have let them know that we are able: The Crowns of these Kingdoms have not so far disowned the right of

Notes

[19] *universal Liberty* in *A Declaration of Indulgence* (1687 and 1688), which was issued mostly for the benefit of his fellow-Catholics.

[20] *crope* old past tense of "creep."

[21] *the Observator* John Tutchin, who wrote a Whig journal under that name from 1702 to 1712; he defended Defoe after his imprisonment in 1703.

[22] *Treatise The Sufferings of the Episcopal Clergy* (1691).

[23] *the Party* the Whigs.

[24] *a union of Nations* the Act of Union joining Scotland to the United Kingdom became law in 1707; as an agent of the Whigs, Defoe spent time in Edinburgh campaigning for ratification.

[25] *Long-Cloaks* Presbyterians.

[26] *Convocation* "An assembly of the clergy for consultation on matters ecclesiastical, in time of Parliament" (Johnson, quoting John Cowell).

[27] *the Faction* the Whigs.

Succession; but they may retrieve it again, and if *Scotland* thinks to come off from a Successive to an Elective State of Government, *England* has not promised not to assist the right Heir, and put him into possession, without any regard to their ridiculous Settlements.[28]

These are the Gentlemen, these their ways of treating the Church, both at home and abroad. Now let us examine the Reasons they pretend to give why we should be favourable to them, why we should continue and tolerate them among us.

First, They are very Numerous, they say, they are a great Part of the Nation, and we cannot suppress them.

To this may be answered, 1. They are not so Numerous as the Protestants in *France*, and yet the *French* King effectually cleared the Nation[29] of them at once, and we don't find he misses them at home.

But I am not of the Opinion that they are so Numerous as is pretended; their Party is more Numerous than their Persons, and those mistaken People of the Church, who are misled and deluded by their wheedling Artifices, to join with them, make their Party the greater; but those will open their Eyes, when the Government shall set heartily about the work, and come off from them, as some Animals, which they say, always desert a House when 'tis likely to fall.

2dly. The more Numerous, the more Dangerous, and therefore the more need to suppress them; and God has suffered us to bear them as Goads in our sides, for not utterly extinguishing them long ago.

3dly. If we are to allow them, only because we cannot suppress them, then it ought to be tried whether we can or no; and I am of the Opinion 'tis easy to be done, and could prescribe Ways and Means, if it were proper, but I doubt not but the Government will find effectual Methods for the rooting the Contagion from the Face of this Land.

Another Argument they use, which is this, That 'tis a time of War, and we have need to unite against the common Enemy.

We answer, this common Enemy had been no Enemy, if they had not made him so; he was quiet, in peace, and no way disturbed, or encroached upon us, and we know no reason we had to quarrel with him.

But further, We make no question but we are able to deal with this common Enemy without their help; but why must we unite with them because of the Enemy? will they go over to the Enemy, if we do not prevent it by a union with them – We are very well contented they should; and make no question, we shall be ready to deal with them and the common Enemy too, and better without them than with them.

Besides, if we have a common Enemy, there is the more need to be secure against our private Enemies; if there is one common Enemy, we have the less need to have an Enemy in our Bowels.

'Twas a great Argument some People used against suppressing the Old-Money,[30] that 'twas a time of War, and was too great a Risk for the Nation to run; if we should not master it, we should be undone; and yet the Sequel proved the Hazard was not so great, but it might be mastered; and the Success was answerable. The suppressing the

Notes

28 *Settlements* the Act of Settlement (1701) maintained the Protestant succession and shifted the regal line to the House of Hanover (1714).

29 *cleared the Nation* in 1685 Louis XIV revoked the Edict of Nantes (1598), which had given religious freedom to the Huguenots, and in a few succeeding years 400,000 of them and other unprotected Protestants fled to the Americas and elsewhere.

30 *suppressing the Old-Money* the debased silver coinage of the realm was called in and replaced in 1695 in what is known as the great recoinage.

Dissenters is not a harder Work, nor a Work of less necessity to the Public; we can never enjoy a settled uninterrupted Union and Tranquillity in this Nation, till the Spirit of Whiggism, Faction, and Schism is melted down like the Old-Money.

To talk of the Difficulty, is to Frighten ourselves with Chimeras and Notions of a Powerful Party, which are indeed a Party without Power; Difficulties often appear greater at a distance, than when they are searched into with Judgement, and distinguished from the Vapours and Shadows that attend them.

We shall not be frighten'd with it; this Age is wiser than that, by all our own Experience, *and theirs too*; King *Charles* the First, had early suppressed this Party, if he had took more deliberate Measures. In short, 'tis not worth arguing, to talk of their Arms, their *Monmouths*,[31] and *Shaftesburys*, and *Argylls* are gone, their *Dutch-Sanctuary* is at an end; Heaven has made way for their Destruction, and if we do not close with the Divine occasion, we are to blame ourselves, and may remember that we once had an opportunity to serve the Church of *England*, by extirpating her implacable Enemies, and having let slip the Minute that Heaven presented, may experimentally[32] Complain, *Post est Occasio Calva*.[33]

Here are some popular Objections in the way.

As first, The Queen has promised them, to continue them in their tolerated Liberty; and has told us she will be a religious Observer of her Word.

What her Majesty will do we cannot help, but what, as the Head of the Church, she ought to do, is another Case: Her Majesty has promised to Protect and Defend the Church of *England*, and if she cannot effectually do that without the Destruction of the Dissenters, she must of course dispense with one Promise to comply with another. But to answer *this Cavil more effectually*: Her Majesty did never promise to maintain the Toleration, to the Destruction of the Church; but this is upon supposition that it may be compatible with the well being and safety of the Church, which she had declared she would take especial Care of: Now if these two Interests clash, 'tis plain her Majesty's Intentions are to Uphold, Protect, Defend, and Establish the Church, and this we conceive is impossible.

Perhaps it may be said, That the Church is in no immediate danger from the Dissenters, and therefore 'tis time enough: But this is a weak Answer.

For first. If a Danger be real, the Distance of it is no Argument against, but rather a Spur to quicken us to prevention, lest it be too late hereafter.

And 2ndly, Here is the Opportunity, and the only one perhaps that ever the Church had to secure herself, and destroy her Enemies.

The Representatives of the Nation have now an Opportunity; the Time is come when all good Men have wished for, that the Gentlemen of *England* may serve the Church of *England*; now they are protected and encouraged by a Church of *England* Queen.

What will ye do for your Sister in the Day that she shall be spoken for?[34]

Notes

[31] *Monmouths* James Scott, Charles's illegitimate son by Lucy Walter, the favorite of Protestants to succeed to the throne instead of Catholic James II; Anthony Ashley Cooper, first earl of Shaftesbury and Archibald Campbell, ninth earl of Argyll were important supporters.

[32] *experimentally* on the basis of experience.

[33] *Post est Occasio Calva* "opportunity is bald behind," a proverb illustrated by emblematical pictures of Opportunity with a forelock that must be seized.

[34] *What will ye do … spoken for?* see Song of Solomon 8.8, where the text reads "we" instead of "ye"; the female speaker of these lines was allegorically interpreted as Christ's Church, and here she could be construed to be enjoining establishment of the church.

If ever you establish the best Christian Church in the World.

If ever you will suppress the Spirit of Enthusiasm.

If ever you will free the Nation from the viperous Brood that have so long sucked the Blood of their Mother.

If [ever] you will leave your Posterity free from Faction and Rebellion, this is the time.

This is the time to pull up this hysterical Weed of Sedition, that has so long disturbed the Peace of the Church, and poisoned the good Corn.

But, says another Hot and Cold Objector, this is renewing Fire and Faggot, reviving the Act *De Heret[ico] Comburendo*:[35] This will be Cruelty in its Nature, and Barbarous to all the World.

I answer, 'tis Cruelty to kill a Snake or a Toad in cold Blood, but the Poison of their Nature makes it a Charity to our Neighbours, to destroy those Creatures, not for any personal Injury received, but for prevention; not for the Evil they have done, but the Evil they may do.

Serpents, Toads, Vipers, *&c.* are noxious to the Body, and poison the sensitive Life;[36] these poison the Soul, corrupt our Posterity, ensnare our Children, destroy the Vitals of our Happiness, our future Felicity, and contaminate the whole Mass.

Shall any Law be given to such wild Creatures? Some Beasts are for Sport, and the Huntsmen give them advantages of Ground;[37] but some are knocked on their head by all possible ways of Violence and Surprise.

I do not prescribe Fire and Faggot; but as *Scipio* said of *Carthage, Delenda est Carthago*,[38] they are to be rooted out of this Nation, if we will ever live in Peace, serve God, or enjoy our own: As for the Manner, I leave it to those Hands, who have a right to execute God's Justice on the Nation's and the Church's Enemies.

But if we must be frighted from this Justice, under the specious Pretences, and odious Sense of Cruelty, nothing will be effected: 'Twill be more Barbarous and Cruel to our own children, and dear Posterity, when they shall reproach their Fathers, as we do ours, and tell us, 'You had an Opportunity to root out this cursed Race from the World, under the Favour and Protection of a true *English* Queen; and out of your foolish Pity you spared them, because, forsooth, you would not be Cruel, and now our Church is suppressed and persecuted, our Religion trampled under Foot, our Estates plundered, our Persons imprisoned and dragged to Jails, Gibbets, and Scaffolds; your sparing this *Amalekite* Race[39] is our Destruction, your Mercy to them proves Cruelty to your poor Posterity'.

How just will such Reflections be, when our Posterity shall fall under the merciless Clutches of this uncharitable Generation, when our Church shall be swallowed up in Schism, Faction, Enthusiasm, and Confusion; when our Government shall be devolved upon Foreigners, and our Monarchy dwindled into a Republic.

'Twould be more rational for us, if we must spare this Generation, to summon our own to a general Massacre, and as we have brought them into the World Free, send

Notes

35 *Act De Heret[ico] Comburendo* concerning the burning of heretics (1382), which empowered bishops to pass such a sentence without royal approval.

36 *sensitive Life* the life of sense and perception, rather than reason or soul.

37 *Ground* "The intervening space between the flyer and pursuer" (Johnson; sense 16).

38 *Delenda est Carthago* "Carthage must be destroyed," frequently repeated by Cato the Censor, or the Elder, Marcus Porcius Cato (234–149 BCE), in framing his nationalistic foreign policy.

39 *Amalekite Race* an enemy of the Israelites condemned to annihilation by the Lord in a revelation to Moses (Exodus 17.14).

them out so, and not betray them to Destruction by our supine negligence, and then cry, 'it is Mercy'.

Moses was a merciful meek Man, and yet with what Fury did he run through the Camp, and cut the Throats of Three and thirty thousand of his dear *Israelites*,[40] that were fallen into Idolatry; what was the reason? 'twas Mercy to the rest, to make these be Examples, to prevent the Destruction of the whole Army.

How many Millions of future Souls we [should] save from Infection and Delusion, if the present Race of poisoned Spirits were purged from the Face of the Land.

'Tis vain to trifle in this matter, the light foolish handling of them by Mulcts,[41] Fines, *&c.* 'tis their Glory and their Advantage; if the Gallows instead of the Counter,[42] and the Galleys instead of the Fines, were the Reward of going to a Conventicle,[43] to preach or hear, there would not be so many Sufferers. The Spirit of Martyrdom is over; they that will go to Church to be chosen Sheriffs and Mayors,[44] would go to forty Churches rather than be Hanged.

If one severe Law were made, and punctually executed, that who was ever found at a Conventicle, should be Banished the Nation, and the Preacher be Hanged, we should soon see an end of the Tale; they would all come to Church, and one Age would make us all One again.

To talk of five shillings a Month for not coming to the Sacrament, and one shilling *per* Week for not coming to Church, this is such a way of converting People as never was known; this is selling them a Liberty to transgress for so much Money: If it be not a Crime, why don't we give them full Licence? And if it be, no Price ought to compound for the committing it, for that is selling a Liberty to People to sin against God and the Government.

If it be a Crime of the highest Consequence, both against the Peace and Welfare of the Nation, the Glory of God, the Good of the Church, and the Happiness of the Soul, let us rank it among capital Offences, and let it receive a Punishment in proportion to it.

We Hang Men for Trifles, and Banish them for things not worth naming, but that an Offence against God and the Church, against the Welfare of the World, and the Dignity of Religion, shall be bought off for five shillings, this is such a shame to Christian Government, that 'tis with regret I transmit it to Posterity.

If Men sin against God, affront his Ordinances, rebel against his Church, and disobey the Precepts of their Superiors, let them suffer as such capital Crimes deserve, so will Religion flourish, and this divided Nation be once again united.

And yet the Title of Barbarous and Cruel will soon be taken off from this Law too. I am not supposing that all the Dissenters in *England* should be Hanged or Banished, but as in cases of Rebellions and Insurrections, if a few of the Ring-leaders suffer, the Multitude are dismissed, so a few obstinate People being made Examples, there's no doubt but the Severity of the Law would find a stop in the Compliance of the Multitude.

Notes

40 *Three and thirty thousand of his dear Israelites* see Exodus 33.25–9; the correct number is merely 3,000.

41 *Mulcts* fines.

42 *Counter* prison.

43 *Conventicle* "An assembly for worship. Generally used in an ill sense, including heresy or schism" (Johnson).

44 *go to Church to be chosen Sheriffs and Mayors* dissenters could avoid the Test Act and hold public office if they occasionally took communion in the Church of England; the Tory Act of Occasional Conformity (1711) sought to put an end to the practice.

To make the reasonableness of this matter out of question, and more unanswerably plain, let us examine for what it is that this Nation is divided into Parties and Factions, and let us see how they can justify a Separation, or we of the Church of *England* can justify our bearing the Insults and Inconveniences of the Party.

One of their leading Pastors, and a Man of as much Learning as most among them, in his Answer to a Pamphlet entitled *An Enquiry into the Occasional Conformity*,[45] hath these Words, P. 27: 'Do the Religion of the Church and the Meeting-houses make two Religions? Wherein do they differ? The Substance of the same Religion is common to them both; and the Modes and Accidents are the things in which only they differ'. P. 28: 'Thirty nine Articles[46] are given us for the summary of our Religion. Thirty six contain the Substance of it, wherein we agree. Three [are] the additional Appendices, about which we have some differences'.

Now, if as by their own acknowledgement, the Church of *England* is a true Church, and the Difference between them is only in a few *Modes and Accidents*, Why should we expect that they will suffer Gallows and Gallies, corporeal Punishment and Banishment for these Trifles; there is no question but they will be wiser; even their own Principles won't bear them out in it; they will certainly comply with the Laws, and with Reason, and though at the first, Severity may seem hard, the next Age will feel nothing of it; the Contagion will be rooted out; the Disease being cured, there will be no need of the Operation, but if they should venture to transgress, and fall into the Pit, all the World must condemn their Obstinacy, as being without Ground from their own Principles.

Thus the Pretence of Cruelty will be taken off, and the Party actually suppressed, and the Disquiets they have so often brought upon the Nation, prevented.

Their Numbers, and their Wealth, makes them Haughty, and that is so far from being an Argument to persuade us to forbear them, that 'tis a Warning to us, without any more delay, to reconcile them to the Unity of the Church, or remove them from us.

At present, Heaven be praised, they are not so Formidable as they have been, and 'tis our own fault if ever we suffer them to be so; Providence, and the Church of *England*, seems to join in this particular, that now the Destroyers of the Nation's Peace may be overturned, and to this end the present Opportunity seems to be put into our Hands.

To this end her present Majesty seems reserved[47] to enjoy the Crown, that the Ecclesiastic as well as Civil Rights of the Nation may be restored by her Hand.

To this end the Face of Affairs have received such a Turn in the process of a few Months, as has never been before; the leading Men of the Nation, the universal Cry of the People, the unanimous Request of the Clergy, agree in this, that the Deliverance of our Church is at hand.

For this end has Providence given us such a Parliament, such a Convocation, such a Gentry, and such a Queen as we never had before.

And what may be the Consequences of a Neglect of such Opportunities? The Succession of the Crown has but a dark Prospect, another *Dutch* Turn may make the Hopes of it ridiculous, and the Practice impossible: Be the House of our future Princes ever so well inclined, they will be Foreigners; and many Years will be spent in suiting

Notes

[45] *An Enquiry into the Occasional Conformity* a pamphlet by Defoe himself, published in 1698.

[46] *Thirty nine Articles* the articles of faith to which individuals had to subscribe in order to enjoy privileges such as government positions and matriculation at Oxford or Cambridge; the Act of Toleration had released dissenters from subscribing to three of the thirty-nine.

[47] *reserved* kept in store, by Providence.

the Genius of Strangers to the Crown, and to the Interests of the Nation; and how many Ages it may be before the *English* Throne be filled with so much Zeal and Candour, so much Tenderness, and hearty Affection to the Church, as we see it now covered with, who can imagine.

'Tis high time then for the Friends of the Church of *England*, to think of Building up, and Establishing her, in such a manner, that she may be no more Invaded by Foreigners, nor Divided by Factions, Schisms, and Error.

If this could be done by gentle and easy Methods, I should be glad, but the Wound is corroded, the Vitals begin to mortify,[48] and nothing but Amputation of Members can complete the Cure; all the ways of Tenderness and Compassion, all persuasive Arguments have been made use of in vain.

The Humour[49] of the Dissenters has so increased among the People, that they hold the Church in Defiance, and the House of God is an Abomination among them: Nay, they have brought up their Posterity in such prepossessed Aversions to our Holy Religion, that the ignorant Mob think we are all Idolaters, and Worshippers of *Baal*;[50] and account it a Sin to come within the Walls of our Churches.

The primitive Christians were not more shy of a Heathen-Temple, or of Meat offered to Idols, nor the *Jews* of Swine's-Flesh, than some of our Dissenters are of the Church, and the Divine Service solemnized therein.

This Obstinacy must be rooted out with the Profession of it; while the Generation are left at liberty daily to affront God Almighty, and Dishonour his Holy Worship, we are wanting in our Duty to God, and our Mother the Church of *England*.

How can we answer it to God, to the Church, and to our Posterity, to leave them entangled with Fanaticism, Error, and Obstinacy, in the Bowels of the Nation; to leave them an Enemy in their Streets, that in time may involve them in the same Crimes, and endanger the utter Extirpation of Religion in the Nation.

What's the Difference betwixt this, and being subjected to the Power of the Church of *Rome*, from whence we have reformed? If one be an extreme on one Hand, and one on another, 'tis equally destructive to the Truth, to have Errors settled among us, let them be of what Nature they will.

Both are Enemies of our Church, and of our Peace, and why should it not be as criminal to admit an Enthusiast as a Jesuit? Why should the *Papist* with his Seven Sacraments be worse than the *Quaker* with no Sacraments at all? Why should Religious-houses be more intolerable than Meeting-Houses – *Alas the Church of England*! What with Popery on one Hand, and Schismatics on the other, how has she been Crucified between two Thieves.

Now, *let us Crucify the Thieves*. Let her Foundations be established upon the Destruction of her Enemies: The Doors of Mercy being always open to the returning Part of the deluded People: Let the Obstinate be ruled with the Rod of Iron.

Let all true Sons of so Holy an Oppressed Mother, exasperated by her Afflictions, harden their Hearts against those who have oppressed her.

And may God Almighty put it into the Hearts of all the Friends of Truth, to lift up a Standard against Pride and Antichrist, that the Posterity of the Sons of Error may be rooted out from the Face of this Land for ever—.

FINIS

Notes

[48] *mortify* "To gangrene; to corrupt" (Johnson).

[49] *Humour* inclination, temper.

[50] *Baal* Jehovah's chief competition in the Old Testament.

A True Relation of the Apparition of one Mrs. Veal, The next Day after Her Death: To One Mrs. Bargrave at Canterbury. The 8th of September, 1705 (1706)[1]

The Preface

This relation is Matter of Fact, and attended with such Circumstances as may induce any Reasonable Man to believe it. It was sent by a Gentleman, a Justice of Peace of *Maidstone* in *Kent*, and a very Intelligent Person, to his Friend in *London*, as it is here worded; which Discourse is attended by a very sober and understanding Gentlewoman, a Kinswoman of the said Gentleman's, who lives in *Canterbury*, within a few Doors of the House in which the within named Mrs. *Bargrave* lives; who believes his Kinswoman to be of so discerning a Spirit, as not to be put upon by any Fallacy, and who positively assured him, that the whole Matter, as it is here released and laid down, is what is really True; and what She herself had in the same Words (as near as may be) from Mrs. *Bargrave's* own Mouth, who she knows had no Reason to invent and publish such a Story, nor any design to forge and tell a Lie, being a Woman of much Honesty and Virtue, and her whole Life a Course as it were of Piety. The use which we ought to make of it is, to consider, That there is a Life to come after this, and a Just God, who will retribute to everyone according to the Deeds done in the Body; and therefore, to reflect upon our past Course of Life we have led in the World, That our Time is Short and Uncertain, and that if we would escape the Punishment of the Ungodly, and receive the Reward of the Righteous, which is the laying hold of Eternal Life, we ought for the time to come, to turn to God by a speedy Repentance, ceasing to do Evil and learning to do Well: To seek after God Early, if happily he may be found of us, and lead such Lives for the future, as may be well pleasing in his Sight.

A Relation of the Apparition of Mrs. Veal

This thing is so rare in all its Circumstances, and on so good Authority, that my Reading and Conversation has not given me anything like it; it is fit to gratify the most Ingenious and Serious Enquirer. Mrs. *Bargrave* is the Person to whom Mrs. *Veal* Appeared after her Death; she is my Intimate Friend, and I can avouch for her Reputation, for these last fifteen or sixteen Years, on my own Knowledge; and I can confirm the Good Character she had from her Youth, to the time of my Acquaintance. Though since this Relation, she is Calumniated by some People, that are Friends to the Brother of Mrs. *Veal* who Appeared;[2] who think the Relation of this Appearance to be a Reflection,[3] and endeavour what they can to Blast Mrs. *Bargrave*'s Reputation; and to Laugh the Story out of Countenance. But the Circumstances thereof, and the Cheerful Disposition of Mrs. *Bargrave*, notwithstanding the unheard of ill Usage of a very wicked Husband, there is not yet the least sign of Dejection in her Face; nor did I ever hear her let fall a Desponding or Murmuring Expression; nay, not when actually under her Husband's Barbarity; which I have been Witness to, and several other Persons of undoubted Reputation.

Notes

A True Relation

1 *Mrs. Veal* Mrs. Veal was a real person, and Defoe's account has proven to be an accurate relation of the facts as they were consistently reported by Bargrave.

2 *Appear* "To become visible as a spirit" (Johnson).

3 *Reflection* "A thought or idea occurring to, or occupying, the mind" (*OED*, 9a)

Now you must know, that Mrs. *Veal* was a Maiden Gentlewoman of about 30 Years of Age, and for some Years last past,[4] had been troubled with Fits; which were perceived coming on her, by her going off from her Discourse very abruptly, to some impatience: She was maintained by an only Brother, and kept his House in *Dover*. She was a very Pious Woman, and her Brother a very Sober Man to all Appearance: But now he does all he can to Null and Quash the Story. Mrs. *Veal* was intimately acquainted with Mrs. *Bargrave* from her Childhood. Mrs. *Veal*'s Circumstances were then Mean; her Father did not take care of his Children as he ought, so that they were exposed to Hardships: And Mrs. *Bargrave* in those days, had as unkind a father, though She wanted neither for Food nor Clothing, whilst Mrs. *Veal* wanted for both: So that it was in the Power of Mrs. *Bargrave* to be very much her Friend in several Instances, which mightily endeared Mrs. *Veal*; insomuch that she would often say, 'Mrs. Bargrave, you are not only the best, but the only Friend I have in the World; and no Circumstances of Life, shall ever dissolve my Friendship'. They would often condole each other's adverse Fortunes, and read together, *Drelincourt upon Death*:[5] and other good Books: and so like two Christian Friends, they comforted each other under their Sorrow.

Sometime after, Mr. *Veal*'s Friends got him a Place in the Custom-House at *Dover*, which occasioned Mrs. *Veal* by little and little, to fall off from her Intimacy with Mrs. *Bargrave*, though there was never any such thing as a Quarrel; but an Indifferency came on by degrees, till at last Mrs. *Bargrave* had not seen her in two Years and a half; though above a Twelve Month of the time, Mrs. *Bargrave* had been absent from *Dover*, and this last half Year, has been in *Canterbury* about two Months of the time, dwelling in a House of her own.

In this House, on the Eighth of *September* last, *viz*. 1705. She was sitting alone in the Forenoon, thinking over her Unfortunate Life, and arguing herself into a due Resignation to Providence, though her Condition seemed hard. And said she, 'I have been provided for hitherto, and doubt not but I shall be still; and am well satisfied, that my Afflictions shall end, when it is most fit for me': And then took up her Sewing Work, which she had no sooner done, but she hears a Knocking at the Door; she went to see who was there, and this proved to be Mrs. *Veal*, her Old Friend, who was in a Riding Habit: At that Moment of Time, the Clock struck Twelve at Noon.

'Madam', says Mrs. *Bargrave*, 'I am surprised to see you; you have been so long a stranger', but told her, she was glad to see her and offered to Salute[6] her, which Mrs. *Veal* complied with, till their Lips almost touched, and then Mrs. *Veal* drew her hand cross her own Eyes, and said, 'I am not very well', and so waived it. She told Mrs. *Bargrave*, she was going a Journey, and had a great mind to see her first: 'But', says Mrs. *Bargrave*, 'how came you to take a Journey alone? I am amazed at it, because I know you have so fond a Brother'.

'O!' says Mrs. Veal, 'I gave my Brother the Slip, and came away, because I had so great a Mind to see you before I took my Journey'. So Mrs. *Bargrave* went in with her, into another Room within the first, and Mrs. *Veal* sat her down in an Elbow-chair,[7] in which Mrs. *Bargrave* was sitting when she heard Mrs. *Veal* Knock. Then says Mrs. *Veal*, 'My Dear Friend, I am come to renew our Old Friendship again, and to beg your Pardon for my breach of it, and if you can forgive me, you are the best of Women'.

Notes

4 *last past* the last years she passed in life.

5 *Drelincourt upon Death The Christian's Defence against the Fears of Death* (English translation, 1675).

6 *Salute* kiss.

7 *Elbow-chair* "A chair with arms to support the elbows" (Johnson).

'O!' says Mrs. Bargrave, 'don't mention such a thing. I have not had an uneasy thought about it; I can easily forgive it'.

'What did you think of me?' says Mrs. *Veal*. Says Mrs. *Bargrave*, 'I thought you were like the rest of the World, and that Prosperity had made you forget yourself and me'. Then Mrs. *Veal* reminded Mrs. *Bargrave* of the many Friendly Offices she did her in former Days, and much of the Conversation they had with each other in time of their Adversity; what Books they Read, and what Comfort in particular they received from *Drelincourt's Book of Death*, which was the best she said on that Subject was ever Wrote. She also mentioned Dr. *Sherlock*,[8] and two *Dutch* Books which were Translated, Wrote upon Death, and several others: But *Drelincourt* she said, had the clearest Notions of Death, and of the Future State, of any who have handled that Subject. Then she asked Mrs. *Bargrave*, whether she had *Drelincourt*. She said yes. Says Mrs. *Veal*, 'Fetch it', and so Mrs. *Bargrave* goes up Stairs, and brings it down. Says Mrs. *Veal*, 'Dear Mrs. *Bargrave*, If the Eyes of our Faith were as open as the Eyes of our Body, we should see numbers of Angels about us for our Guard: The Notions we have of Heaven now, are nothing like what it is, as *Drelincourt* says. Therefore be comforted under your Afflictions, and believe that the Almighty has a particular regard to you; and that your Afflictions are Marks of God's Favour: And when they have done the business they were sent for, they shall be removed from you. And believe me my Dear Friend, believe what I say to you, One Minute of future Happiness will infinitely reward you for all your Sufferings. For I can never believe' (and claps her Hand upon her Knee, with a great Earnestness, which indeed ran through all her Discourse) 'that ever God will suffer you to spend all your Days in this afflicted State: But be assured, that your Afflictions shall leave you, or you them in a short time'. She spake in that Pathetical and Heavenly manner, that Mrs. *Bargrave* wept several times; she was so deeply affected with it. Then Mrs. *Veal* mentioned Dr. *Horneck's Ascetic*,[9] at the end of which, he gives an Account of the Lives of the Primitive Christians. Their Pattern she recommended to our Imitation, and said, 'their Conversation was not like this of our Age. For now', says she, 'there is nothing but frothy vain Discourse, which is far different from theirs. Theirs was to Edification, and to Build one another up in Faith: So that they were not as we are, nor are we as they are; but', said she, 'We might do as they did. There was a Hearty Friendship among them; but where is it now to be found?'

Says Mrs. *Bargrave*, ''tis hard indeed to find a true Friend in these days'.

Says Mrs. *Veal*, 'Mr. *Norris*[10] has a Fine Copy of Verses, called *Friendship in Perfection*, which I wonderfully admire. Have you seen the Book?' says Mrs. *Veal*.

'No', says Mrs. *Bargrave*, 'but I have the Verses, of my own writing out'.

'*Have you?*' says Mrs. *Veal*, 'then fetch them'; which she did from above Stairs, and offered them to Mrs. *Veal* to read, who refused, and waived the thing, saying, holding down her Head would make it ache, and then desired Mrs. *Bargrave* to read them to her, which she did. As they were admiring Friendship, Mrs. *Veal* said, 'Dear Mrs. *Bargrave*, I shall love you for ever'. In the Verses there is twice used the Word 'Elysium'. 'Ah!', says Mrs. *Veal*, 'These Poets have such Names for Heaven'. She would often draw her hand cross her own Eyes and say, 'Mrs. *Bargrave*, Don't you think I am mightily impaired by my Fits?'

Notes

[8] *Dr. Sherlock* William Sherlock, *A Practical Discourse concerning Death* (1689).

[9] *Dr. Horneck's Ascetic* Anthony Horneck, *The Happy Ascetic* (1681).

[10] *Mr. Norris* John Norris of Bemerton, *A Collection of Miscellanies* (1687).

'No', says Mrs. *Bargrave*, 'I think you look as well as ever I knew you'.

After all this discourse, which the Apparition put in Words much finer than Mrs. *Bargrave* said she can remember (for it cannot be thought, that an hour and three-quarters' Conversation could all be retained, though the main of it, she thinks she does), she said to Mrs. *Bargrave*, she would have her write a Letter to her Brother, and tell him, she would have him give Rings to such and such; and that there was a Purse of Gold in her Cabinet, and that she would have Two Broad Pieces given to her Cousin Watson. Talking at this Rate, Mrs. *Bargrave* thought that a Fit was coming upon her, and so placed herself in a Chair just before her Knees, to keep her from falling to the Ground, if her Fits should occasion it; for the Elbow-Chair she thought would keep her from falling on either side. And to divert Mrs. *Veal* as she thought, took hold of her Gown Sleeve several times, and commended it. Mrs. *Veal* told her, it was a Scoured[11] Silk, and newly made up. But for all this Mrs. *Veal* persisted in her Request, and told Mrs. *Bargrave* that she must not deny her: and she would have her tell her Brother all their Conversation, when she had an opportunity.

'Dear Mrs. *Veal*', said Mrs. *Bargrave*, 'this seems so impertinent, that I cannot tell how to comply with it; and what a mortifying Story will our Conversation be to a Young Gentleman?'

'Well', says Mrs. *Veal*, 'I must not be denied'.

'Why', says Mrs. *Bargrave*, ''tis much better methinks to do it yourself'.

'No', says Mrs. *Veal*; 'though it seems impertinent to you now, you will see more reason for it hereafter'. Mrs. *Bargrave* then to satisfy her importunity, was going to fetch a Pen and Ink: but Mrs. *Veal* said, 'let it alone now, but do it when I am gone; but you must be sure to do it': which was one of the last things she enjoined her at parting; and so she promised her.

Then Mrs. *Veal* asked for Mrs. *Bargrave's* Daughter; she said she was not at home. 'But if you have a mind to see her', says Mrs. *Bargrave*, 'I'll send for her'.

'Do', says Mrs. *Veal*. On which she left her, and went to a Neighbour's to send for her; and by the Time Mrs. *Bargrave* was returning, Mrs. *Veal* was got without the Door into the Street, in the face of the *Beast-Market* on a Saturday (which is Market day) and stood ready to part, as soon as Mrs. *Bargrave* came to her. She asked her why she was in such haste? She said she must be going; though perhaps she might not go to her journey till Monday, and told Mrs. *Bargrave* she hoped she should see her again, at her Cousin *Watson*'s before she went whither she was a going. Then she said she would take Leave of her, and walked from Mrs. *Bargrave* in her view, till a turning interrupted the sight of her, which was three quarters after One in the Afternoon.

Mrs. *Veal* Died the 7th of *September* at 12 o'Clock at Noon, of her Fits, and had not above four hours' Senses before her Death, in which time she received the Sacrament. The next day after Mrs. *Veal's* appearing being Sunday, Mrs. *Bargrave* was so mightily indisposed with a Cold, and a Sore Throat, that she could not go out that day: but on Monday morning she sends a person to Captain *Watson*'s to know if Mrs. *Veal* was there. They wondered at Mrs. *Bargrave*'s enquiry, and sent her Word, that she was not there, nor was expected. At this Answer Mrs. *Bargrave* told the Maid she had certainly mistook the Name, or made some blunder. And though she was ill, she put on her Hood, and went herself to Captain *Watson*'s, though she knew none of the Family, to see if Mrs. *Veal* was there or not. They said, they wondered at her asking, for that she

Notes

11 *Scoured* bleached.

had not been in Town; they were sure, if she had, she would have been there. Says Mrs. *Bargrave*, 'I am sure she was with me on Saturday almost two hours'. They said it was impossible, for they must have seen her if she had. In comes Captain *Watson*, while they were in Dispute, and said that Mrs. *Veal* was certainly Dead, and her Escutcheons[12] were making. This strangely surprised Mrs. *Bargrave*, who went to the Person immediately who had the care of them, and found it true. Then she related the whole Story to Captain *Watson*'s Family, and what Gown she had on, and how striped. And that Mrs. *Veal* told her it was Scoured. Then Mr. *Watson* cried out, 'you have seen her indeed, for none knew but Mrs. *Veal* and my self, that the Gown was Scoured'; and Mrs. *Watson* owned that she described the Gown exactly; for, said she, 'I helped her to make it up'. This, Mrs. *Watson* blazed all about the Town, and avouched the Demonstration of the Truth of Mrs. *Bargrave*'s seeing Mrs. *Veal*'s Apparition. And Captain *Watson* carried two Gentlemen immediately to Mrs. *Bargrave*'s House, to hear the Relation from her own Mouth. And then it spread so fast, that Gentlemen and Persons of Quality, the Judicious and Sceptical part of the World, flocked in upon her, which at last became such a Task, that she was forced to go out of the way. For they were in general, extremely satisfied of the truth of the thing; and plainly saw, that Mrs. *Bargrave* was no Hypochondriac,[13] for she always appears with such a cheerful Air, and pleasing Mien, that she has gained the favour and esteem of all the Gentry. And it's thought a great favour if they can but get the Relation from her own Mouth.

I should have told you before, that Mrs. *Veal* told Mrs. *Bargrave*, that her Sister and Brother in Law, were just come down from *London* to see her.

Says Mrs. *Bargrave*, 'how came you to order Matters so strangely?'

'It could not be helped', said Mrs. *Veal*; and her Sister and Brother did come to see her, and entered the Town of *Dover*, just as Mrs. *Veal* was expiring. Mrs. *Bargrave* asked her, whether she would drink some Tea. Says Mrs. *Veal*, 'I do not care if I do: but I'll Warrant this Mad Fellow' (meaning Mrs. *Bargrave's* Husband) 'has broke all your Trinkets'.

'But', says Mrs. *Bargrave*, 'I'll get something to Drink in for all that'; but Mrs. *Veal* waived it, and said, 'it is no matter, let it alone', and so it passed.

All the time I sat with Mrs. *Bargrave*, which was some Hours, she recollected fresh Sayings of Mrs. *Veal*. And one material thing more she told Mrs. *Bargrave*, that Old Mr. *Breton* allowed Mrs. *Veal* Ten Pounds a Year, which was a Secret, and unknown to Mrs. *Bargrave*, till Mrs. *Veal* told it to her. Mrs. *Bargrave* never varies in her Story, which puzzles those who doubt of the Truth, or are unwilling to believe it. A Servant in the Neighbour's Yard adjoining to Mrs. *Bargrave*'s House, heard her talking to somebody, an Hour of the Time Mrs. *Veal* was with her. Mrs. *Bargrave* went out to her next Neighbour's the very Moment she parted with Mrs. *Veal*, and told her what Ravishing Conversation she had with an Old Friend, and told the whole of it. *Drelincourt*'s *Book of Death* is, since this happened, Bought up strangely. And it is to be observed, that notwithstanding all this Trouble and Fatigue Mrs. *Bargrave* has undergone upon this Account, she never took the value of a Farthing, nor suffered her Daughter to take anything of anybody, and therefore can have no Interest in telling the Story.

Notes

12 *Escutcheons* armorial badges for the hearse.

13 *Hypochondriac* one who is "melancholy; disordered in the imagination" (Johnson).

But Mr. *Veal* does what he can to stifle the matter, and said he would see Mrs. *Bargrave*; but yet it is certain matter of fact, that he has been at Captain *Watson*'s since the Death of his Sister, and yet never went near Mrs. *Bargrave*; and some of his Friends report her to be a great Liar, and that she knew of Mr. *Breton*'s Ten Pounds a Year. But the Person who pretends to say so, has the Reputation of a Notorious Liar, among persons which I know to be of undoubted Repute. Now Mr. *Veal* is more a Gentleman, than to say, she Lies; but says, a bad Husband has Crazed her. But she needs only to present herself, and it will effectually confute that Pretence. Mr. *Veal* says he asked his Sister on her Death Bed, whether she had a mind to dispose of anything, and she said, No. Now the things which Mrs. *Veal*'s Apparition would have disposed of, were so Trifling, and nothing of Justice aimed at in their disposal, that the design of it appears to me to be only in order to make Mrs. *Bargrave*, so to demonstrate the Truth of her Appearance, as to satisfy the World of the Reality thereof, as to what she had seen and heard: and to secure her Reputation among the Reasonable and understanding part of Mankind. And then again, Mr. *Veal* owns that there was a Purse of Gold; but it was not found in her Cabinet, but in a Comb-Box. This looks improbable, for that Mrs. *Watson* owned that Mrs. *Veal* was so very careful of the Key of her Cabinet, that she would trust nobody with it. And if so, no doubt she would not trust her Gold out of it. And Mrs. *Veal* often drawing her hand over her Eyes, and asking Mrs. *Bargrave*, whether her Fits had not impaired her, looks to me as if she did it on purpose to remind Mrs. *Bargrave* of her Fits, to prepare her not to think it strange that she should put her upon Writing to her Brother to dispose of Rings and Gold, which looked so much like a dying Person's Bequest; and it took accordingly with Mrs. *Bargrave*, as the effect of her Fits coming upon her; and was one of the many Instances of her Wonderful Love to her, and Care of her, that she should not be affrighted: which indeed appears in her whole management; particularly, in her coming to her in the day time, waiving the Salutation,[14] and when she was alone; and then the manner of her parting, to prevent a second attempt to Salute her.

Now, why Mr. *Veal* should think this Relation a Reflection (as 'tis plain he does by his endeavouring to stifle it) I can't imagine, because the Generality believe her to be a good Spirit; her Discourse was so Heavenly. Her two great Errands were to comfort Mrs. *Bargrave* in her Affliction, and to ask her forgiveness for her Breach of Friendship, and with a Pious Discourse to encourage her. So that after all, to suppose that Mrs. *Bargrave* could Hatch such an Invention as this from *Friday-Noon* till *Saturday-Noon* (supposing that she knew of Mrs. *Veal*'s Death the very first Moment) without jumbling Circumstances, and without any Interest too; she must be more Witty, Fortunate, and Wicked too, than any indifferent Person I dare say, will allow. I asked Mrs. *Bargrave* several times, If she was sure she felt the Gown. She answered Modestly, 'if my Senses be to be relied on, I am sure of it'. I asked her, If she heard a Sound, when she clapped her Hand upon her Knee: She said, she did not remember she did: And she said, she Appeared to be as much a Substance as I did, who talked with her. 'And I may', said she, 'be as soon persuaded that your Apparition is talking to me now, as that I did not really see her; for I was under no manner of Fear; I received her as a Friend, and parted with her as such. I would not', says she, 'give one Farthing to make anyone believe it, I have no Interest in it; nothing but trouble is entailed upon me for a long time for ought I know; and had it not come to Light by Accident, it would never have been made

Notes

[14] *Salutation* kiss.

Public'. But now, she says, she will make her own Private Use of it, and keep herself out of the way as much as she can. And so she has done since. She says, she had a Gentleman who came thirty Miles to her to hear the Relation; and that she had told it to a Room full of People at a time. Several particular Gentlemen have had the Story from Mrs. *Bargrave*'s own Mouth.

This thing has very much affected me, and I am well satisfied, as I am of the best grounded Matter of Fact. And why we should dispute Matter of Fact, because we cannot solve things, of which we can have no certain or demonstrative Notions, seems strange to me: Mrs. *Bargrave*'s Authority and Sincerity alone, would have been undoubted in any other Case.

FINIS

Advertisement

Drelincourt's Book of Consolations against the Fear of Death, has been four times Printed already in *English* of which many Thousands have been Sold, and not without great Applause: And its bearing so great a Character in this Relation the Impression is near Sold off.

from the *London Gazette*[1]

Monday, 11 January to Thursday, 14 January 1702

Deal, January 12. Admiral *Allemonde* arrived here Yesterday from *Holland*, on Board a *Dutch* Man of War, which immediately after his landing sailed for *Spithead*.

St. James's, Jan. 10. Whereas *Daniel de Foe* alias *de Fooe*, is charged with writing a Scandalous and Seditious Pamphlet. Entitled [*The Shortest way with the Dissenters*]. Whoever shall discover the said *Daniel de Foe* alias *de Fooe* to one of Her Majesty's Principal Secretaries of State, or any of Her Majesty's Justices of the Peace, so as he may be apprehended, shall have a Reward of £50 which Her Majesty has ordered immediately to be paid upon such Discovery.

He is a middle Sized Spare Man, about 40 years old, of a brown Complexion, and dark brown coloured Hair, but wears a Wig, a hooked Nose, a sharp Grin, grey Eyes, and a large Mould[2] near his Mouth, was born in *London*, and for many years was a Hose Factor in Freeman's-yard, in Cornhill, and now is Owner of the Brick and Pantile Works near *Tilbury-Fort* in *Essex*.

Notes

FROM THE *LONDON GAZETTE*

1 Begun in 1665 as the *Oxford Gazette*, the *London Gazette* was perhaps the first regularly published newspaper in England. It was always a government organ, and Samuel Johnson expressed a common, though largely anti-government view in his second definition of "gazetteer": "It was lately a term of the utmost infamy, being applied to wretches who were hired to vindicate the court." The court in 1702 belonged to the newly crowned Queen Anne, and Defoe had earned its displeasure with his highly ironical *Shortest-Way with the Dissenters*. This notice of a reward for information leading to Defoe's arrest appears amidst other news and contains the only known physical description of the author.

2 *Mould* mole.

Anne Kingsmill Finch, Countess of Winchilsea (1661–1720)

The year 1688 marked a watershed in Finch's life as well as that of the nation's. She and her husband held positions in the court of James II, and after his deposition, they refused to swear allegiance to William and Mary. Outcast from the political world of London, they went to live with relations in Kent. Heneage Finch eventually became the earl of Winchilsea, and Anne devoted herself to reading, writing, and an appreciation of her beautiful natural surroundings. However, contact with literary London was not altogether lost. In 1713, for example, she dined with Alexander Pope in London and heard a play read with him, as the great poet's correspondence for December of that year attests. On January 12, 1709 Jonathan Swift wrote to a friend in Paris, "I amuse myself sometimes with writing verses to Mrs. Finch, and sometimes with Projects for uniting of Parties, which I perfect over night, and burn in the morning; sometimes Mr. Addison and I steal a pint of bad wine. ..." Finch was enough of a figure to be on Swift's mind and to require no more explanation in a friendly letter than Addison.

Finch published "The Spleen" anonymously in 1701, but one of the three editions of her *Miscellany Poems* in 1713 actually printed her name on the title page, a fairly good indication of celebrity. "The Spleen" was revised and reprinted for *Miscellany Poems*, and most of the texts printed here are based on that edition. Three poems, however, "The Introduction," "The Unequal Fetters," and "The Answer," are among the many that were not published in Finch's lifetime, and I draw them from a much later edition of her poems by Myra Reynolds (University of Chicago Press, 1903). Like many seventeenth- and eighteenth-century poets, but particularly women, Finch wrote numerous poems that she would have been uncomfortable publishing in her lifetime. The reasons for this have partly to do with changed standards of decorum but also with the nearly complete disappearance of manuscript "publication" – the informal circulation of poetry among the coterie of friends or fellow-writers for whom the works were mainly intended. *The Works of Anne Finch: A Critical Edition*, edited by Jennifer Keith and Claudia Thomas Kairoff, 2 vols. (Cambridge University Press, 2016) finally brings together the manuscript and print publications of this important poet.

The Introduction

Did I, my lines intend for public view,
How many censures, would their faults pursue,
Some would, because such words they do affect,
Cry they're insipid, empty, uncorrect.
And many, have attained, dull and untaught
The name of Wit, only by finding fault.
True judges, might condemn their want of wit,
And all might say, they're by a Woman writ.
Alas! a woman that attempts the pen,
Such an intruder on the rights of men,

British Literature 1640–1789: An Anthology, Fourth Edition. Edited by Robert DeMaria, Jr.

Such a presumptuous Creature, is esteemed,
The fault, can by no virtue be redeemed.
They tell us, we mistake our sex and way;
Good breeding, fashion, dancing, dressing, play
Are the accomplishments we should desire;
To write, or read, or think, or to enquire
Would cloud our beauty, and exhaust our time,
And interrupt the Conquests of our prime;
Whilst the dull manage, of a servile house
Is held by some, our utmost art, and use.
   Sure 'twas not ever thus, nor are we told
Fables, of Women that excelled of old;[1]
To whom, by the diffusive hand of Heaven
Some share of wit, and poetry was given.
On that glad day, on which the Ark returned,[2]
The holy pledge, for which the Land had mourned,
The joyful Tribes, attend it on the way,
The Levites do the sacred Charge convey,
Whilst various Instruments, before it play;
Here, holy Virgins in the Concert join,
The louder notes, to soften, and refine,
And with alternate verse, complete the Hymn Divine.[3]
Lo! the young Poet, after God's own heart,
By Him inspired, and taught the Muses' Art,
Returned from Conquest, a bright Chorus meets,[4]
That sing his slain ten thousand in the streets.
In such loud numbers they his acts declare,[5]
Proclaim the wonders, of his early war,
That Saul upon the vast applause does frown,
And feels, its mighty thunder shake the Crown.
What, can the threatened Judgement now prolong?[6]
Half of the Kingdom is already gone;
The fairest half, whose influence guides the rest,
Have David's Empire, o'er their hearts confessed.
   A Woman here, leads fainting Israel on,[7]
She fights, she wins, she triumphs with a song,
Devout, Majestic, for the subject fit,
And far above her arms, exalts her wit,
Then, to the peaceful, shady Palm withdraws,

Notes

THE INTRODUCTION

1 *Fables* false stories.

2 *Ark* the ark of the covenant, the chest containing agreements between God and the Israelites, such as the tablets on which the Ten Commandments were written, the central object of the tabernacle; the most elaborate description of the return of the ark from an enemy is in 1 Chronicles 15–16.

3 *Hymn Divine* David the young Poet's psalm of thanks for the return of the ark (1 Chronicles 16.7–36).

4 *a bright Chorus* women greet David on his return from his miraculous conquest of Goliath; King Saul envies him (1 Samuel 18.6–7).

5 *numbers* verses, poetry.

6 *Judgement* the prophecy of Samuel that a "neighbour" would rule instead of Saul (1 Samuel 15.28).

7 *A Woman* Queen Anne.

And rules the rescued Nation, with her Laws.
How are we fal'n, fal'n by mistaken rules?
And Education's, more than Nature's fools,
Debarred from all improvements of the mind,
And to be dull, expected and designed;
And if some one, would Soar above the rest,
With warmer fancy, and ambition pressed,
So strong, th' opposing faction still appears,
The hopes to thrive, can ne'er outweigh the fears,
Be cautioned then my Muse, and still retired;
Nor be despised, aiming to be admired;
Conscious of wants, still with contracted wing,
To some few friends, and to thy sorrow sing;
For groves of Laurel, thou wert never meant;[8]
Be dark enough thy shades, and be thou there content.

Life's Progress

How gayly is at first begun
  Our *Life*'s uncertain Race!
Whilst yet that sprightly Morning Sun,
With which we just set out to run
  Enlightens all the Place.

How smiling the World's Prospect lies
  How tempting to go through!
Not *Canaan* to the Prophet's Eyes,[1]
From *Pisgah* with a sweet Surprise,[2]
Did more inviting show.

How promising's the Book of Fate,
  Till throughly understood!
Whilst partial Hopes such Lots create,
As may the youthful Fancy treat
  With all that's Great and Good.

How soft the first Ideas prove,
  Which wander through our Minds!
How full the Joys, how free the Love,
Which does that early Season move;
  As Flowers the Western Winds!

Our Sighs are then but Vernal Air;
  But *April*-drops our Tears,

Notes

[8] *Laurel* bay laurel, symbolic of poetic or some other public achievement.

LIFE'S PROGRESS

[1] *Canaan* the promised land of the Israelites.

[2] *Pisgah* the mountain from which Moses viewed the Promised Land which he was never able to enter (Deuteronomy 34.1–4).

Which swiftly passing, all grows Fair,
Whilst Beauty compensates our Care,
And Youth each Vapour clears.

But oh! too soon, alas, we climb;
Scarce feeling we ascend
The gently rising Hill of *Time*,
From whence with Grief we see that Prime,
And all its Sweetness end.

The Die now cast, our Station known,
Fond Expectation past;
The Thorns, which former Days had sown,[3]
To Crops of late Repentance grown,
Through which we toil at last.[4]

Whilst every Care's a driving Harm,
That helps to bear us down;
Which faded Smiles no more can charm,
But every Tear's a Winter-Storm,
And every Look's a Frown.

Till with succeeding Ills oppressed,
For Joys we hoped to find;
By Age too, rumpled and undressed,
We gladly sinking down to rest,
Leave following Crowds behind.

Adam Posed[1]

Could our First Father, at his toilsome Plough,
Thorns in his Path, and Labour on his Brow,
Clothed only in a rude, unpolished Skin,
Could he a vain Fantastic Nymph have seen,[2]
In all her Airs, in all her antic Graces,[3]
Her various Fashions, and more various Faces;
How had it posed that Skill, which late assigned
Just Appellations to Each several Kind![4]
A right Idea of the Sight to frame;
T' have guessed from what New Element she came;
T' have hit the wav'ring Form, or giv'n this Thing a Name.

Notes

[3] *Thorns* an echo of Jeremiah 12.13: "They have sown wheat, but shall reap thorns."

[4] *Through which we toil* "The way of the slothful man is as an hedge of thorns" (Proverbs 15.19).

Adam Posed

[1] *Posed* puzzled.

[2] *Nymph* "A lady. In poetry" (Johnson).

[3] *antic* "Odd; ridiculously wild" (Johnson).

[4] *Just Appellations* Adam named all the animals of Eden (Genesis 2.20).

The Petition for an Absolute Retreat

Inscribed to the Right Honourable CATHARINE Countess of THANET, mentioned in the Poem under the Name of ARMINDA[1]

Give me, O indulgent Fate!
Give me yet, before I Die,
A sweet, but absolute Retreat,
'Mongst Paths so lost, and Trees so high,
That the World may ne'er invade,
Through such Windings and such Shade,
My unshaken Liberty.
No Intruders thither come!
Who visit, but to be from home;
None who their vain Moments pass,
Only studious of their Glass,[2]
News, that charm to list'ning Ears;
That false Alarm to Hopes and Fears;
That common Theme for every Fop,[3]
From the Statesman to the Shop,
In those Coverts ne'er be spread,
Of who's Deceased, or who's to Wed,
Be no Tidings thither brought,
But Silent, as a Midnight Thought,
Where the World may ne'er invade,
Be those Windings, and that Shade:
Courteous Fate! afford me there
A *Table* spread without my Care,
With what the neighb'ring Fields impart,
Whose Cleanliness be all its Art,
When, of old, the Calf was dressed,
(Though to make an Angel's Feast)
In the plain, unstudied Sauce
Nor *Treufle*, nor *Morillia* was;[4]
Nor could the mighty Patriarch's Board[5]
One far-fetched *Ortolane* afford.[6]
Courteous Fate, then give me there
Only plain, and wholesome Fare.
Fruits indeed (would Heaven bestow)
All, that did in *Eden* grow,
All, but the *Forbidden Tree*,
Would be coveted by me;
Grapes, with Juice so crowded up,

Notes

THE PETITION FOR AN ABSOLUTE RETREAT

[1] *Catharine, Countess of Thanet* member of a prominent Kent family.

[2] *Glass* mirror.

[3] *Fop* a dandy, a fashionable, superficial fellow.

[4] *Treufle* truffle, an edible fungus; *Morillia* morel, another edible fungus.

[5] *Patriarch* Abraham, who entertains three messengers of the Lord in plain but hospitable fashion (Genesis 18).

[6] *Ortolane* a small bird with a delicate flavor.

As breaking through the native Cup;
Figs (yet growing) candied o'er,
By the Sun's attracting Pow'r;
Cherries, with the downy Peach,
All within my easy Reach;
Whilst creeping near the humble Ground,
Should the Strawberry be found
Springing wheresoe'er I strayed,
Through those Windings and that Shade.
For my *Garments*; let them be
What may with the Time agree;
Warm, when *Phœbus* does retire,[7]
And is ill-supplied by Fire:
But when he renews the Year,
And verdant all the Fields appear;
Beauty every thing resumes,
Birds have dropped their Winter-Plumes;
When the Lily full displayed,
Stands in purer White arrayed,
Than that Vest, which heretofore
The Luxurious Monarch wore,[8]
When from *Salem*'s Gates he drove,[9]
To the soft Retreat of Love,
Lebanon's all burnished House,
And the dear *Egyptian* Spouse.[10]
Clothe me, Fate, though not so Gay;
Clothe me light, and fresh as *May*:
In the Fountains let me view
All my Habit cheap and new;
Such as, when sweet *Zephyrs* fly,[11]
With their Motions may comply;
Gently waving, to express
Unaffected Carelessness:
No Perfumes have there a Part,
Borrowed from the *Chemist*'s Art;
But such as rise from flow'ry Beds,
Or the falling *Jasmine* Sheds!
'Twas the Odour of the Field,
Esau's rural Coat did yield,[12]
That inspired his Father's Prayer,
For Blessings of the Earth and Air:

Notes

[7] *Phœbus* Apollo, the Greek god of the sun.

[8] *Luxurious Monarch* Solomon; Finch inserts a long note here, citing the historian Josephus' account of Solomon's very white robe, or "vest."

[9] *Salem* Jerusalem.

[10] *Egyptian Spouse* the daughter of Pharaoh, for whom Solomon built a house of Lebanon cedar, covered with jewels (1 Kings 7.8–12).

[11] *Zephyrs* light westerly winds.

[12] *Esau's rural Coat* the "goodly raiment" of animal skins in which Rebekah clothed Jacob so he could deceive his aged father Isaac into giving him the blessing meant for his older brother (Genesis 27.6–29).

Of Gums, or Powders had it smelt;
The Supplanter, then unfelt,
Easily had been descried,
For One that did in Tents abide;
For some beauteous Handmaid's Joy,
And his Mother's darling Boy.
Let me then no Fragrance wear,
But what the Winds from Gardens bear,
In such kind, surprising Gales,[13]
As gathered from *Fidentia*'s Vales,
All the Flowers that in them grew;
Which intermixing, as they flew,
In wreathen Garlands dropped again,
On *Lucullus*, and his Men;
Who, cheered by the victorious Sight,
Trebled Numbers put to Flight.[14]
Let me, when I must be fine,
In such natural Colours shine;
Wove, and painted by the Sun,
Whose resplendent Rays to shun,
When they do too fiercely beat,
Let me find some close Retreat,
Where they have no Passage made,
Through those Windings, and that Shade.
Give me there (since Heaven has shown
It was not Good to be alone)
A *Partner* suited to my Mind,
Solitary, pleased and kind;
Who, partially, may something see
Preferred to all the World in me;
Slighting, by my humble Side,
Fame and Splendour, Wealth and Pride.
When but Two the Earth possessed,
'Twas their happiest Days, and best;
They by Business, nor by Wars,
They by no Domestic Cares,
From each other e'er were drawn,
But in some Grove, or flow'ry Lawn,
Spent their own, and Nature's Prime,
In Love; that only Passion given
To perfect Man, whilst Friends with Heaven.
Rage, and Jealousy, and Hate,
Transports of his fallen State
(When by *Satan*'s Wiles betrayed),
Fly those Windings, and that Shade!

Notes

[13] *Gales* gentle breezes.

[14] *Lucullus and his Men … put to Flight* as Finch notes, the story is in Plutarch's life of Sulla (27.7–8); the flowers from *Fidentia* (in northern Italy) seemed to the Roman soldiers as garlands crowning them and their weapons with victory; this inspired them to kill 18,000 of the enemy (c.83 BCE).

Thus from Crowds, and Noise removed,
Let each Moment be improved;
Every Object still produce,
Thoughts of Pleasure, and of Use:
When some River slides away,
To increase the boundless Sea;
Think we then, how Time does haste,
To grow Eternity at last,
By the Willows, on the Banks,
Gathered into social Ranks,
Playing with the gentle Winds,
Straight the Boughs, and smooth the Rinds,
Moist each Fibre, and each Top,
Wearing a luxurious Crop,
Let the time of Youth be shown,
The time alas! too soon outgrown;
Whilst a lonely stubborn Oak,
Which no Breezes can provoke,
No less Gusts persuade to move,
Than those, which in a Whirlwind drove,
Spoiled the old Fraternal Feast,
And left alive but one poor Guest;[15]
Rivelled the distorted Trunk,[16]
Sapless Limbs all bent, and shrunk,
Sadly does the Time presage,
Of our too near approaching Age.
When a helpless Vine is found,
Unsupported on the Ground,
Careless all the Branches spread,
Subject to each haughty Tread,
Bearing neither Leaves, nor Fruit,
Living only in the Root;
Back reflecting let me say,
So the sad *Ardelia* lay;[17]
Blasted by a Storm of Fate,[18]
Felt, through all the *British* State;
Fall'n, neglected, lost, forgot,
Dark Oblivion all her Lot;
Faded till *Arminda*'s Love,
(Guided by the Pow'rs above)
Warmed anew her drooping Heart,
And Life diffused through every Part;
Mixing Words, in wise Discourse,
Of such Weight and wond'rous Force,

Notes

15 *one poor Guest* the messenger who reports the destruction of his son's house to Job (Job 1.18–19).

16 *Rivelled* shrivelled, wrinkled.

17 *Ardelia* Finch's poetic name for herself.

18 *Storm of Fate* the Glorious Revolution (1688–9), which sent Finch and her husband into retirement in Kent because they remained loyal to the Stuarts and would not swear allegiance to William III.

As could all her Sorrows charm,
And transitory Ills disarm;
Cheering the delightful Day,
When disposed to be more Gay,
With Wit, from an unmeasured Store,
To Woman ne'er allowed before.
What Nature, or refining Art,
All that Fortune could impart,
Heaven did to *Arminda* send;
Then gave her for *Ardelia*'s Friend:
To her cares the Cordial drop,
Which else had overflowed the Cup.
So, when once the Son of *Jesse*,[19]
Every Anguish did oppress,
Hunted by all kinds of Ills,
Like a *Partridge* on the Hills;
Trains were laid to catch his Life,
Baited with a Royal Wife,
From his House, and Country torn,
Made a Heathen Prince's Scorn;
Fate, to answer all these Harms,
Threw a *Friend* into his Arms.[20]
Friendship still has been designed,
The Support of Human-kind;
The safe delight, the useful Bliss,
The next World's Happiness, and this.
Give then, O indulgent Fate!
Give a Friend in that Retreat
(Though withdrawn from all the rest)
Still a Clue, to reach my Breast.[21]
Let a Friend be still conveyed
Through those Windings, and that Shade!
Where, may I remain secure,
Waste, in humble Joys and pure, A Life, that can no Envy yield;
Want of Affluence my Shield.
Thus, had *Crassus* been content,[22]
When from *Marius*' Rage he went,
With the Seat that Fortune gave,
The commodious ample Cave,
Formed, in a divided Rock,
By some mighty Earthquake's Shock,
Into Rooms of every Size,
Fair, as Art could e'er devise,

Notes

[19] *Son of Jesse* King David.

[20] *a Friend* Jonathan, the son of King Saul who envied and persecuted David (1 Samuel 18.24).

[21] *Clue* the thread given by Ariadne to Theseus to help him from the labyrinth once he had killed the Minotaur.

[22] *Crassus* Marcus Licinius Crassus (115–53 BCE), later a Roman triumvir, fled from the slaughter of real and imagined enemies launched by Cinna and Gaius Marius in 86 BCE and lived in a spacious cave (Plutarch, *Crassus* 4–5); Finch notes that her description of the cave is "exactly taken" from Plutarch.

Leaving, in the marble Roof
('Gainst all Storms and Tempests proof),
Only Passage for the Light,
To refresh the cheerful Sight,
Whilst Three Sharers in his Fate,
On th' Escape with joy dilate,
Beds of Moss their Bodies bore,
Canopied with Ivy o'er;
Rising Springs, that round them played,
O'er the native Pavement strayed;
When the Hour arrived to Dine,
Various Meats, and sprightly Wine,
On some neighb'ring Cliff they spied;
Every Day anew supplied
By a Friend's entrusted Care;
Had He still continued there,
Made that lonely wond'rous Cave
Both his Palace, and his Grave;
Peace and Rest he might have found
(Peace and Rest are under Ground),
Nor have been in that Retreat,
Famed for a Proverbial Fate;[23]
In pursuit of Wealth been caught,
And punished with a golden Draught.
Nor had He, who Crowds could blind,[24]
Whisp'ring with a snowy Hind,
Made 'em think that from above,
(Like the great Impostor's Dove)[25]
Tidings to his Ears she brought,
Rules by which he marched and fought,
After *Spain* he had o'er-run,
Cities sacked, and Battles won,
Drove *Rome*'s Consuls from the Field,
Made her darling *Pompey* yield,[26]
At a fatal, treacherous Feast,
Felt a Dagger in his Breast;
Had he his once-pleasing Thought
Of Solitude to Practice brought;
Had no wild Ambition swayed;
In those Islands had he stayed,[27]
Justly called the Seats of Rest,

Notes

[23] *a Proverbial Fate* his life was said to have ended like a tragedy; he sought wealth in Syria, but was killed by the Parthians; his head was brought to the Parthian courtduring a performance of Euripides' *Bacchae* and used as the head of slaughtered Pentheus in the final act (Plutarch, *Crassus* 33).

[24] *He* Sertorius [Finch's note; he deceived locals into believing his tame doe was a gift from heaven and could speak its prophecies; see Plutarch, *Sertorius* 11].

[25] *great Impostor* the French playwright Molière's title character Tartuffe.

[26] *Pompey* great Roman general forced to bring in reserves to deal with Sertorius.

[27] *those Islands* the Canary Islands, called by the Ancients the Fortunate Islands and taken by some of the Poets for Elysium [Finch's note; see Plutarch, *Sertorius* 8–9].

Truly Fortunate, and Blest,
By the ancient Poets giv'n
As their best discovered Heav'n.
Let me then, indulgent Fate!
Let me be still, in my Retreat,
From all roving Thoughts be freed,
Or Aims, that may Contention breed:
Nor be my Endeavours led
By Goods, that perish with the Dead!
Fitly might the Life of Man
Be indeed esteemed a Span,[28]
If the present Moment were
Of Delight his only Share;
If no other Joys he knew
Than what round about him grew:
But as those, who Stars would trace
From a subterranean Place,
Through some Engine lift their Eyes[29]
To the outward, glorious Skies;
So th' immortal Spirit may,
When descended to our Clay,
From a rightly governed Frame
View the Height, from whence she came;
To her Paradise be caught,
And things unutterable taught.
Give me then, in that Retreat,
Give me, O indulgent Fate!
For all Pleasures left behind,
Contemplations of the Mind.
Let the Fair, the Gay, the Vain
Courtship and Applause obtain;
Let th' Ambitious rule the Earth;
Let the giddy Fool have Mirth;
Give the Epicure his Dish,
Everyone their several Wish;
Whilst my Transport I employ
On that more extensive Joy,
When all Heaven shall be surveyed
From those Windings and that Shade.

To the Nightingale

Exert thy Voice, sweet Harbinger of Spring!
  This Moment is thy Time to Sing,
  This Moment I attend to Praise,

Notes

[28] *Span* "Any short duration" (Johnson).

[29] *Engine* instrument, device.

And set my Numbers to thy Lays.
  Free as thine shall be my Song;
  As thy Music, short, or long.
Poets, wild as thee, were born,
  Pleasing best when unconfined,
  When to Please is least designed,
Soothing but their Cares to rest;
  Cares do still their Thoughts molest,
  And still th' unhappy Poet's Breast,
Like thine, when best he sings, is placed against a Thorn.
She begins, Let all be still!
  Muse, thy Promise now fulfil!
Sweet, oh! sweet, still sweeter yet
Can thy Words such Accents fit,
Canst thou Syllables refine,
Melt a Sense that shall retain
Still some Spirit of the Brain,
Till with Sounds like these it join.
  'Twill not be! then change thy Note;
  Let Division shake thy Throat.[1]
Hark! Division now she tries;
Yet as far the Muse outflies.
  Cease then, prithee, cease thy Tune;
  Trifler, wilt thou sing till *June*?
Till thy Business all lies waste,
And the Time of Building's past!
  Thus we Poets that have Speech,
Unlike what thy Forests teach,
  If a fluent Vein be shown
  That's transcendent to our own,
Criticize, reform, or preach,
Or censure what we cannot reach.

A Poem for the Birth-day of the Right Honourable the Lady Catharine Tufton[1]

Occasioned by sight of some Verses upon that Subject for the preceding Year, composed by no Eminent Hand

'Tis fit *SERENA* should be sung.
High-born *SERENA*, Fair and Young,
Should be of every Muse and Voice
The pleasing, and applauded Choice.
But as the Meanest of the Show

Notes

To the Nightingale

[1] *Division* in music, a run or variation, in which several notes are interpolated between those of the main melody.

A Poem for the Birth-Day

[1] *Catharine Tufton* (b. 1692), daughter of the countess of Thanet (see "Petition for an Absolute Retreat," p. 436); called Serena in Finch's poetry.

Do First in all Processions go:
So, let my Steps pursue that Swain
The humblest of th' inspired Train;
Whose well-meant Verse did just appear,
To lead on the preceding Year:
So let my Pen, the next in Fame,
Now wait on fair *SERENA*'s Name;
The second Tribute gladly pay,
And hail this blessed returning Day.
But let it not attempt to raise
Or rightly speak *SERENA*'s Praise:
Since with more ease we might declare
How Great that more distinguished Peer,[2]
To whom she owes her Being here;
In whom our *Britain* lets us see
What once they were, and still should be;
As, when the earliest Race was drowned,
Some Patterns, from amongst them found,
Were kept to show succeeding Times
Their Excellence without their Crimes:
More easily we might express
What Virtues do her Mother dress;
What does her Form and Mind adorn,
Of whom th' engaging Nymph was born:
What Piety, what generous Love,
Does the enlargèd Bosom move
Of her, whose Favourite she appears,[3]
Who more than as a Niece endears.
Such full Perfections obvious lie,
And strike, at first, a Poet's Eye.
Deep lines of Honour all can hit,
Or mark out a superior Wit;
Consummate Goodness all can show,
And where such Graces shine below:
But the more tender Strokes to trace,
T' express the Promise of a Face,
When but the Drawings of the Mind
We from an Air unripened find;
Which alt'ring, as new Moments rise,
The Pen or Pencil's Art defies;
When Flesh and Blood in Youth appears,
Polished like what our Marble wears;
Fresh as that Shade of op'ning Green,
Which first upon our Groves is seen;
Enlivened by a harmless Fire,
And brightened by each gay Desire;

Notes

[2] *more distinguished Peer* Thomas Tufton, sixth earl of Thanet.

[3] *her* the Lady Coventry [Finch's note, meaning Margaret Tufton].

These nicer Touches would demand
A *Cowley*'s or a *Waller*'s Hand,[4]
T' explain, with undisputed Art,
What 'tis affects th' enlightened Heart,
When every darker Thought gives way,
Whilst blooming Beauty we survey;
To show how All, that's soft and sweet,
Does in the fair *SERENA* meet;
To tell us, with a sure Presage,
The Charms of her maturer Age.
When *Hothfield*[5] shall (as heretofore
From its far-sought and virtuous Store
It Families of great Renown
Did with illustrious Hymens crown)[6]
When *Hothfield* shall such Treasure know,
As fair *SERENA* to bestow:
Then should some Muse of loftier Wing
The Triumphs of that Season sing;
Describe the Pains, the Hopes, the Fears
Of noble Youths, th' ambitious Cares
Of Fathers, the long-framed Design,
To add such Splendour to their Line,
Whilst all shall strive for such a Bride
So Educated, and Allied.

The Atheist and the Acorn

'Methinks this World is oddly made,
And every thing's amiss',
A dull presuming Atheist said,
As stretched he lay beneath a Shade;
And instancèd in this:

'Behold', quoth he, 'that mighty thing,
A *Pumpkin*, large and round,
Is held but by a little String,
Which upwards cannot make it spring,
Or bear it from the Ground.

'Whilst on this *Oak*, a Fruit so small,
So disproportioned, grows;
That, who with Sense surveys this *All*,
This universal Casual Ball,[1]
Its ill Contrivance knows.

Notes

[4] *Cowley … Waller* Abraham Cowley (1618–67) and Edmund Waller (1606–86), poets.

[5] *Hothfield* the family seat of the Tuftons in Kent.

[6] *Hymen* god of marriage or marriage itself.

The Atheist and the Acorn

[1] *Casual* "arising from chance; depending upon chance" (Johnson), rather than divine government.

'My better Judgement would have hung
That Weight upon a Tree,
And left this Mast, thus slightly strung,[2]
'Mongst things which on the Surface sprung,
And small and feeble be'.

No more the Caviller could say,
Nor farther Faults descry;
For, as he upwards gazing lay,
An *Acorn*, loosened from the Stay,
Fell down upon his Eye.

Th' offended Part with Tears ran o'er,
As punished for the Sin:
Fool! had that Bough a *Pumpkin* bore,
Thy Whimsies must have worked no more,
Nor Skull had kept them in.

The Unequal Fetters

Could we stop the time that's flying
Or recall it when 'tis past
Put far off the day of Dying
Or make Youth forever last
To Love would then be worth our cost.

But since we must lose those Graces
Which at first your hearts have won
And you seek for in new Faces
When our Spring of Life is done,
It would but urge our ruin on.

Free as Nature's first intention
Was to make us, I'll be found,
Nor by subtle Man's invention
Yield to be in Fetters bound
By one that walks a freer round.

Marriage does but slightly tie Men
Whilst close Pris'ners we remain;
They the larger Slaves of Hymen[1]
Still are begging Love again
At the full length of all their chain.

Notes

[2] *Mast* "The fruit of the oak and beech" (Johnson).

The Unequal Fetters

[1] *larger* freer; *Hymen* god of marriage.

The Answer (to Pope's Impromptu)[1]

Disarmed with so genteel an air,
The contest I give o'er;
Yet, Alexander, have a care,
And shock the sex no more.
We rule the world our life's whole race,
Men but assume that right;
First slaves to every tempting face,
Then martyrs to our spite.
You of one Orpheus sure have read,[2]
Who would like you have writ
Had he in London town been bred,
And polished too his wit;
But he poor soul thought all was well,
And great should be his fame,
When he had left his wife in hell,
And birds and beast could tame.
Yet venturing then with scoffing rhymes
The women to incense,
Resenting Heroines of those times
Soon punished his offence.
And as the Hebrus rolled his skull,
And harp besmeared with blood,
They clashing as the waves grew full,
Still harmonized the flood.
But you our follies gently treat,
And spin so fine the thread
You need not fear his awkward fate,
The lock won't cost the head.
Our admiration you command
For all that's gone before;
What next we look for at your hand
Can only raise it more.
Yet sooth the Ladies I advise
(As me too pride has wrought),
We're born to wit, but to be wise
By admonitions taught.

Notes

THE ANSWER

1 Pope's Impromptu, Alexander Pope's verse reply to Finch's lost attack on *The Rape of the Lock*, Canto IV, ll. 59–62.

2 *Orpheus* a legendary pre-Homeric poet whose music charmed wild beasts and made rocks and trees move; he failed to recover his wife Eurydice from Hades; maenads, followers of Dionysus, tore him to pieces and sent his head floating down the River Hebrus in Thrace.

The *Spleen*: A Pindaric Poem[1] (1701; revised 1713)

What art thou,*SPLEEN*, which everything dost ape?
Thou *Proteus* to abused Mankind,[2]
Who never yet thy real Cause could find,
Or fix thee to remain in one continued Shape.
Still varying thy perplexing Form,
Now a Dead sea thou'lt represent,
A Calm of stupid Discontent,
Then, dashing on the Rocks wilt rage into a Storm.
Trembling sometimes thou dost appear,
Dissolved into a Panic fear;
On Sleep intruding dost thy Shadows spread,
Thy gloomy Terrors round the silent Bed,
And crowd with boding Dreams the Melancholy Head;
Or, when the Midnight Hour is told,
And drooping Lids thou still dost waking hold,
Thy fond Delusions cheat the Eyes,
Before them antic Spectres dance,[3]
Unusual Fires their pointed Heads advance,
And airy Phantoms rise.
Such was the monstrous *Vision* seen,
When *Brutus* (now beneath his Cares oppressed,[4]
And all *Rome's* Fortunes rolling in his Breast,
Before *Philippi*'s latest Field,
Before his Fate did to *Octavius* lead)
Was vanquished by the *Spleen*.

Falsely, the Mortal part we blame
Of our depressed, and pond'rous Frame,
Which, till the First degrading Sin
Let Thee, its dull Attendant, in,
Still with the Other did comply,
Nor clogged the Active Soul, disposed to fly,
And range the Mansions of its native Sky.
Nor, whilst in his own Heaven he dwelt,
Whilst Man his Paradise possessed,
His fertile Garden in the fragrant East,
And all united Odours smelt,
No armèd Sweets, until thy Reign,
Could shock the Sense, or in the Face

Notes

THE *SPLEEN*: A PINDARIC POEM

[1] *Pindaric* after the great praise poet of fifth-century BCE Greece, but meaning largely that the poem uses a variety of prosodical forms and is somewhat irregular, as Pindar was thought to be because of his difficulty and the rapid rhetorical shifts in his verse; *Spleen* "Melancholy; hypochondriacal vapours" (Johnson); the name of a variety of mental ailments.

[2] *Proteus* a shape-shifting, prophetic old man of the sea in Greek myth.

[3] *antic*"Odd; ridiculously wild" (Johnson).

[4] *Brutus* Marcus Junius Brutus (85–42 BCE), Roman general and statesman; participated in the assassination of Julius Caesar; committed suicide after his defeat by Antony and Octavius Caesar in the second battle of *Philippi*.

A flushed, unhandsome Colour place.
Now the *Jonquille* o'ercomes the feeble Brain;[5]
We faint beneath the Aromatic Pain,
Till some offensive Scent thy Pow'rs appease,
And Pleasure we resign for short, and nauseous Ease.

In every One thou dost possess,
New are thy Motions, and thy Dress:
Now in some Grove a list'ning Friend
Thy false Suggestions must attend,
Thy whispered Griefs, thy fancied Sorrows hear,
Breathed in a Sigh, and witnessed by a Tear;
Whilst in the light, and vulgar Crowd,
Thy Slaves, more clamorous and loud,
By Laughters unprovoked, thy Influence too confess.
In the Imperious *Wife* thou Vapours art,[6]
Which from o'erheated Passions rise
In clouds to the attractive Brain,
Until descending thence again,
Through the o'ercast, and show'ring Eyes,
Upon her Husband's softened Heart,
He the disputed Point must yield,
Something resign of the contested Field;
Till Lordly *Man*, born to Imperial Sway,
Compounds for Peace, to make that Right away,[7]
And *Woman*, armed with *Spleen*, does servilely Obey.

The *Fool*, to imitate the Wits,
Complains of thy pretended Fits,
And Dullness, born with him, would lay
Upon thy accidental Sway,
Because, sometimes, thou dost presume
Into the ablest heads to come:
That, often, Men of Thoughts refined,
Impatient of unequal Sense,[8]
Such slow Returns, where they so much dispense,
Retiring from the Crowd, are to thy Shades inclined.
O'er me alas! thou dost too much prevail:
I feel thy Force, whilst I against thee rail;
I feel my Verse decay, and my cramped Numbers fail.
Through thy black Jaundice I all Objects see,

Notes

5 *Jonquille* "A species of daffodil. The flowers of this plant … are greatly esteemed for their strong sweet scent, though few ladies can bear the smell of them, it being so powerful as to overcome their spirits" (Johnson, quoting Miller's *Gardener's Dictionary*).

6 *Vapours* "Mental fume; vain imagination" or, in the plural only, "hypochondriacal maladies; melancholy; spleen" (Johnson).

7 *Compounds* comes to compromising terms.

8 *unequal Sense* experiential life, which is unequal to the flights of thoughts.

As Dark, and Terrible as Thee,
My Lines decried, and my Employment thought
An useless Folly, or presumptuous Fault:
Whilst in the *Muses'* Path I stray,
Whilst in their Groves, and by their secret Springs
My Hand delights to trace unusual Things,
And deviates from the known, and common way;
Nor will in fading Silks compose
Faintly th' inimitable *Rose*,
Fill up an ill-drawn *Bird*, or paint on Glass
The *Sovereign*'s blurred and undistinguished Face,[9]
The threat'ning *Angel*, and the speaking *Ass*.[10]
Patron thou art to every gross Abuse,
The sullen *Husband*'s feigned Excuse,
When the ill Humour with his Wife he spends,
And bears recruited Wit, and Spirits to his Friends.
The Son of *Bacchus* pleads thy Pow'r,
As to the Glass he still repairs,
Pretends but to remove thy Cares,
Snatch from thy Shades one gay, and smiling Hour,
And drown thy Kingdom in a purple Show'r.
When the *Coquette*, whom every Fool admires,
Would in Variety be Fair,
And, changing hastily the Scene
From Light, Impertinent, and Vain,
Assumes a soft, a melancholy Air,
And of her Eyes rebates the wand'ring Fires,[11]
The careless Posture, and the Head reclined,
The thoughtful, and composèd Face,
Proclaiming the withdrawn, the absent Mind,
Allows the Fop more liberty to gaze,
Who gently for the tender Cause inquires;
The Cause, indeed, is a Defect in Sense,
Yet is the *Spleen* alleged, and still the dull Pretence.
But these are thy fantastic Harms,
The Tricks of thy pernicious Stage,
Which do the weaker Sort engage;
Worse are the dire Effects of thy more pow'rful Charms.
By Thee *Religion*, all we know,
That should enlighten here below,
Is veiled in Darkness, and perplexed
With anxious Doubts, with endless Scruples vexed,
And some Restraint implied from each perverted Text.
Whilst *Touch* not, *Taste* not, what is freely giv'n,

Notes

[9] *undistinguished* indistinguishable.

[10] *speaking Ass* it speaks when God places an angel in its path to prevent its master Balaam from disobeying him (Numbers 22.22–33); a hackneyed subject of amateur art.

[11] *rebates* blunts, damps.

Is but thy niggard Voice, disgracing bounteous Heav'n.
From Speech restrained, by thy Deceits abused,
To Deserts banished, or in Cells reclused,
Mistaken Vot'ries to the Pow'rs Divine,
Whilst they a purer Sacrifice design,
Do but the *Spleen* obey, and worship at thy Shrine.
In vain to chase thee every Art we try,
In vain all Remedies apply,
In vain the *Indian* Leaf infuse,[12]
Or the parched *Eastern* Berry bruise;[13]
Some pass, in vain, those Bounds, and nobler Liquors use.
Now *Harmony*, in vain, we bring,
Inspire the Flute, and touch the String.
From Harmony no help is had;
Music but soothes thee, is too sweetly sad,
And if too light, but turns thee gaily Mad.
Though the Physician's greatest Gains,[14]
Although his growing Wealth he sees
Daily increased by Ladies' Fees,
Yet dost thou baffle all his studious Pains.
Not skilful *Lower* thy Source could find,[15]
Or through the well-dissected Body trace
The secret, the mysterious ways,
By which thou dost surprise, and prey upon the Mind.
Though in the Search, too deep for Human Thought,
With unsuccessful Toil he wrought,
'Till thinking Thee to've catched, Himself by thee was caught,
Retained thy Pris'ner, thy acknowledged Slave,
And sunk beneath thy Chain to a lamented Grave.

Notes

[12] *Indian Leaf* tea.

[13] *Eastern Berry* coffee, from Turkey.

[14] *Though* in spite of.

[15] *Lower* Richard Lower (1631–91), the most famous physician and physiologist of his time.

Mary Astell (1666–1731)

Bishop Tillotson, John Locke, John Norris, and Daniel Defoe were among the foremost writers and religious thinkers that Astell was bold enough, committed enough, and intelligent enough to oppose in her life as a controversialist. She was passionately committed to the Church of England, to the monarchy, and to the unification of church and state. She believed in a religion of love and feeling, which drew her, like several other women writers, into correspondence with Norris. Even more than Norris she favored faith, hope, and charity above the rational and abstract elements of religion. The most prominent feature of Astell's constellation of beliefs, however, was her conviction that women were tragically failing in modern society to cultivate their immortal souls and their minds. As a response to this situation, Astell proposed the formation of an academy for women. It was to be primarily religious in its aims, although it was also meant to provide intellectual training. Defoe was very favorably impressed, even though the monastic elements of the scheme suggested Roman Catholic oppression to him and to many others. His own scheme (see pp. 400–405 above) emphasized the secular parts of Astell's. Although a charity school for girls was formed shortly after her death along lines proposed by Astell, it was the fate of her ideas only to be realized much later and in a much more progressive, liberal, and secular form than she had conceived them. She may not have approved of them in many respects, but the women's colleges finally established in the nineteenth century owe a great deal to the groundbreaking ideas and forceful thinking of Mary Astell.

The small portion of *A Serious Proposal* (1694) presented here is based on the third edition, corrected, of 1696. The entire work has been edited by Patricia Springborg (Chatto and Pickering, 1997). There is a recent and important biography by Ruth Perry, *The Celebrated Astell* (University of Chicago Press, 1986).

from *A Serious Proposal to the Ladies, for the Advancement of their True and Greatest Interest. By a Lover of her Sex* (1694)

Ladies,

Since the Profitable Adventures[1] that have gone abroad in the World have met with so great Encouragement, though the highest advantage they can propose, is an uncertain Lot for such matters as Opinion, not real worth, give a value to; things which if obtained are as flitting and fickle as that Chance which is to dispose of them; I therefore persuade myself, you will not be less kind to a Proposition that comes attended with more certain and substantial Gain, whose only design is to improve your Charms and heighten your Value by suffering you no longer to be cheap and contemptible. Its aim is to fix that Beauty, to make it lasting and permanent, which Nature with all the helps of Art cannot secure, and to place it out of the reach of Sickness and Old Age, by

Notes

FROM *A SERIOUS PROPOSAL TO THE LADIES*

[1] *Profitable Adventures* successful economic ventures; Astell is thinking of some fad in fashion or makeup.

transferring it from a corruptible Body to an immortal Mind. An obliging Design, which would procure them *inward* Beauty, to whom Nature has unkindly denied the *outward*, and not permit those Ladies who have comely Bodies to tarnish their Glory with deformed Souls. Would have you all be wits, or what is better, Wise. Raise you above the Vulgar by something more truly illustrious, than a founding Title[2] or a great Estate. Would excite in you a generous Emulation to excel in the best things, and not in such Trifles as every mean person who has but Money enough may purchase as well as you. Not suffer you to take up with the low thought of distinguishing yourselves by anything that is not truly valuable, and procure you such Ornaments as all the Treasures of the *Indies* are not able to purchase. Would help you to surpass the Men as much in Virtue and Ingenuity, as you do in Beauty; that you may not only be as lovely, but as wise as Angels. Exalt and Establish your Fame, more than the best wrought *Poems* and loudest *Panegyrics*,[3] by ennobling your Minds with such Graces as really deserve it. And instead of the Fustian[4] Compliments and Fulsome Flatteries of your Admirers, obtain for you the Plaudit of Good Men and Angels, and the approbation of Him who cannot err. In a word, render you the Glory and Blessing of the present Age, and the Admiration and Pattern of the next.

And sure, I shall not need many words to persuade you to close with[5] this *Proposal*. The very offer is a sufficient inducement, nor does it need the set-offs of *Rhetoric* to recommend it, were I capable, which yet I am not, of applying them with the greatest force. Since you can't be so unkind to yourselves, as to refuse your *real* Interest, I only entreat you to be so wise as to examine wherein it consists; for nothing is of worse consequence than to be deceived in a matter of so great concern. 'Tis as little beneath your Grandeur as your Prudence, to examine curiously what is in this case offered you; and to take care that cheating Hucksters don't impose upon you with deceitful Ware. This is a Matter infinitely more worthy your Debates, than what Colours are the most agreeable, or what's the Dress becomes you best. Your *Glass*[6] will not do you half so much service as a serious reflection on your own Minds, which will discover Irregularities more worthy your Correction, and keep you from being either too much elated or depressed by the representations of the other. 'Twill not be near so advantageous to consult with your Dancing-Master as with your own Thoughts, how you may with greatest exactness tread in the Paths of Virtue, which has certainly the most attractive *Air*, and Wisdom the most graceful and becoming *Mien*: Let these attend you and your Carriage will be always well composed, and everything you do will carry its Charm with it. No solicitude in the adornation of yourselves is discommended, provided you employ your care about that which is really your *self*; and do not neglect that particle of Divinity within you, which must survive, and may (if you please) be happy and perfect when its unsuitable and much inferior Companion is mouldering into Dust. Neither will any pleasure be denied you, who are only desired not to catch at the Shadow and let the Substance go. You may be as ambitious as you please, so you aspire to the best things; and contend with your Neighbours as much as you can, that they may not outdo you in any commendable Quality. Let it never be said, That they to whom pre-eminence is so very agreeable, can be tamely content that others should surpass them in *this*, and precede them in a *better* World! Remember, I pray you, the famous Women of former Ages,

Notes

2 *founding Title* one that comes with a perpetual fund.
3 *Panegyrics* speeches or poems of praise.
4 *Fustian* "Swelling; unnaturally pompous" (Johnson).
5 *close with* agree to.
6 *Glass* mirror.

the *Orinda's*[7] of late and the more Modern Heroines, and blush to think how much is now, and will hereafter be said of them, when you yourselves (as great a Figure as you make) must be buried in silence and forgetfulness! Shall your Emulation fail *there only* where it is commendable? Why are you so preposterously humble, as not to contend for one of the highest Mansions in the Court of Heaven? Believe me, Ladies, this is the only *Place* worth contending for; you are neither better nor worse in yourselves for going before, or coming after *now*; but you are really so much the better, by how much the higher your station is in an Orb of Glory. How can you be content to be in the World like Tulips in a Garden, to make a fine *show* and be good for nothing; have all your Glories set in the Grave, or perhaps much sooner! What your own sentiments are I know not, but I can't without pity and resentment reflect, that those Glorious Temples on which your kind Creator has bestowed such exquisite workmanship, should enshrine no better than *Ægyptian* Deities; be like a garnished Sepulchre, which for all its glittering, has nothing within but emptiness or putrefaction! What a pity it is, that whilst your Beauty casts a lustre round about, your Souls which are infinitely more bright and radiant (of which if you had but a clear Idea, as lovely as it is, and as much as you now value it, you would then despise and neglect the mean *Case* that encloses it) should be suffered to overrun with Weeds, lie fallow and neglected, unadorned with any Grace! Although the Beauty of the mind is necessary to secure those Conquests which your Eyes have gained, and Time that mortal Enemy to handsome Faces, has no influence on a lovely Soul, but to better and improve it. For shame let us abandon that *Old*, and therefore one would think, unfashionable employment of pursuing Butterflies and Trifles! No longer drudge on in the dull beaten road of Vanity and Folly, which so many of us have gone before us, but dare to break the enchanted Circle that custom has placed us in, and scorn the vulgar way of imitating all the Impertinencies of our Neighbours. Let us learn to pride ourselves in something more excellent than the invention of a Fashion; And not entertain such a degrading thought of our own *worth*, as to imagine that our Souls were given us only for the service of our Bodies, and that the best improvement we can make of these, is to attract the Eyes of Men. We value *them* too much, and our *selves* too little, if we place any part of our worth in their Opinion; and don't think ourselves capable of Nobler Things than the pitiful Conquest of some worthless heart. She who has opportunities of making an interest in Heaven, in obtaining the love and admiration of GOD and Angels, is too prodigal of her Time, and injurious to her Charms, to throw them away on vain insignificant men. She need not make herself so cheap, as to descend to court their Applauses; for at the greater distance she keeps, and the more she is above them, the more effectually she secures their esteem and wonder. Be so generous then, Ladies, as to do nothing unworthy of you; so true to your Interest, as not to lessen your Empire and depreciate your Charms. Let not your Thoughts be wholly busied in observing what respect is paid you, but a part of them at least, in studying to deserve it. And after all, remember that Goodness is the truest Greatness; to be wise of yourselves the greatest Wit; and *that* Beauty the most desirable which will endure to Eternity.

Notes

[7] *Orinda* a general name for a heroine, particularly recalling Katherine Philips (see p. 237 above).

Jonathan Swift (1667–1745)

Editing Swift and commenting on his writing makes one part of the universe of minds that his work ridicules. The complexities and ironies of his best-known books and essays invite (even demand) commentary and explanation because they are subtle in tone, allusive, and stocked with arcana from his classical and theological studies. Yet, Swift's message is often about the folly of sophisticated study and the simplicity of the basic, Christian truths that a good person needs to know and follow. "Sophisticated study," in fact, defines the object of Swift's satire too narrowly: it often seems that reading and writing and everything that goes along with modern print culture is ridiculous in his eyes. That means that you, "Gentle Reader," or "Candid Reader," as Swift will sarcastically address you, are also part of the joke by virtue merely of the fact that you are reading and trying to interpret the printed page in front of you.

Swift perpetually reveals the potential of print to lie, to conceal, to obfuscate, to prevaricate and sophisticate the truth; as you read, you enter this world of falsehood. Perhaps we are meant to realize that all other printed works, all the constructions of the print world (the rhetoric of politics, law, and business, for example) are just as baseless as the hypothetical speakers and bizarre visions that Swift creates. But what then? Silence (or illiteracy) is no solution. The ugly, savage life led by the Yahoos in Part 4 of *Gulliver's Travels* makes it clear that Swift has no illusions about the beauty of a life devoid of cultural sophistication. Yet much of his writing shows that no degree of sophistication can eradicate the weakness and insufficiency of humanity. The human body reveals human weakness, as Swift shows, for example, in the hideous images in the poem "A Beautiful Young Nymph Going to Bed." Swift's attitude to the body, especially his apparent fixation on the organs of digestion and defecation, is striking and likely to arouse a wish for psychological inquiry about his childhood. It is true that an accident of weather and the hasty decision of a nurse caused him to be separated from his recently widowed mother for the first three years of his life, and you may make of this what you will, but it is possible to explain Swift's attack on the body in terms of conventional religious exhortations about the infirmity of human life and the consequent necessity of placing our faith in God.

For all its obvious attention to the body, however, what makes Swift's work perpetually interesting is its distressing, complex satire of the human mind. *A Tale of a Tub* is one of the most original, alarming, and amusing critiques of mentality ever written. Its involvement with religious beliefs and with the contemporary critical debate about the superiority of modern or ancient writers makes it more obscure to twenty-first-century readers than it was to Swift's contemporaries. On the other hand, the work contains elements which resemble representations of elliptical, fragmented, or deconstructive perceptions that are more familiar to us than to the astonished purchasers of the first edition in 1704. *Gulliver's Travels*, which Swift wrote later in life, is more entertaining, but *A Tale of a Tub* is Swift's most concise and uncompromising expression of his creative vision.

British Literature 1640–1789: An Anthology, Fourth Edition. Edited by Robert DeMaria, Jr.

The edition of Swift's collected works, begun by the Dublin publisher George Faulkner, was four volumes in 1735, and eventually ran to twenty volumes (1772), as more and more of Swift's essays and poems were attributed or came to light. Swift probably participated in the assembly of Faulkner's edition, although he denied it; earlier, beginning in 1711, he also participated in bringing together many of his own scattered (or sometimes previously unpublished) works in a series of volumes called *Miscellanies*. His diverse body of work contains various political writings, spoofs, send-ups, and satires, as well as carefully reasoned arguments. His poetry as well as his prose often defies categorization, because both tend to mock the standard forms, even when they depend upon them. Perhaps the most famous short work in this large body of miscellaneous work is "A Modest Proposal." The unreliable speaker in this essay has long been the textbook case for English students, but, like many of Swift's works, it is just such a textbook approach that he ridicules in hopes of making readers more alive to the simple fact that people are starving, and there are practical ways to alleviate their suffering, though they are unpopular and require some sacrifice for the wealthy and middle classes.

A few years after barely escaping expulsion and obtaining his BA from Trinity College, Dublin, Swift made the first of his many trips to England and served as a secretary to the diplomat and writer William Temple at his home, Moor Park. There he met the young Esther Johnson ("Stella"), a woman whom he loved and depended upon until her death in 1728. Later, he established her in Ireland, where he was ordained as a priest in the Church of Ireland and received successively better appointments until he became Dean of St. Patrick's in 1713. *Swift's Journal to Stella*, his letters home to her from England, provide much of what we know about his private life and sensibility. On one of his trips he met Esther Vanhomrigh, with whom he also had a long and intimate association. Swift was also close to some important literary figures of his time, especially Alexander Pope and John Gay, with whom he collaborated on several elaborate lampoons. Although he came to England first as a Whig, his most active participation in English political life was in the service of the Tory ministry from 1710 to 1714. After the death of Queen Anne, Swift spent most of his time in Dublin. His few surviving sermons are remarkably simple, straightforward, if somewhat condescending, exhortations to simple virtue. It is tempting to think that in those works one hears the "real" Swift, but no such construction will really stand up to modern scrutiny of the very kind that Swift helped create.

I have based my text of the *Tale* on the first edition (1704), of "A Modest Proposal" on the second edition (1730), and the texts of the poems on those in Faulkner's edition (1735). The edition of the *Tale* by A. C. Guthkeltch and D. N. Smith (second edition, Clarendon Press, 1958) supplied me with a great deal of the information I print in my notes to that work. I also profited from the notes and collations in Harold Williams's edition of the poems (second edition, Clarendon Press, 1958). The comprehensive biography is by Irvin Ehrenpreis, *Swift: The Man, His Works, and the Age*, 3 vols. (Methuen, 1962–83). *Jonathan Swift: His Life and His World*, by Leopold Damrosch (Yale University Press, 2013) is an excellent shorter biography. Earlier editions of Swift's works are all being superseded by the Cambridge Edition, ed. Claude Rawson et al., 14 vols. (2006–).

A Tale of a Tub Written for the Universal Improvement of Mankind (1704)

Diu multumque desideratum[1]
Basima eacabasa irraurista, diarba da caeotaba fobor camelanthi.
Iren. Lib. I. C. 18[2]
———*Juvatque novos decerpere flores,*
Insignemque meo capiti petere inde coronam,
Unde prius nulli velarunt tempore Musæ. Lucret.[3]

Treatises written by the same Author, most of them mentioned in the following Discourses, which will be speedily published.[4]

A Character of the present set of Wits *in this Island.*
A panegyrical Essay upon the Number THREE.
A dissertation upon the principal Productions of Grub Street.[5]
Lectures upon a Dissection of Human Nature.
A Panegyric upon the World.
An analytical Discourse upon Zeal, histori-theo-physi-logically *considered.*
A general History of Ears.
A modest Defence of the Proceedings of the Rabble *in all ages.*
A Description of the Kingdom of Absurdities.
A Voyage into England, *by a Person of Quality in* Terra Australis incognita, *translated from the Original.*
A critical Essay upon the Art of Canting, *philosophically, physically, and musically considered.*

To the Right Honourable John *Lord* Somers[6]

My Lord,
Though the author has written a large Dedication, yet That being addressed to a Prince,[7] whom I am never likely to have the Honour of being known to; a Person, besides, as far as I can observe, not at all regarded, or thought on by any of our present Writers; And, I being wholly free from that Slavery, which Booksellers usually lie under, to the Caprices

Notes

A Tale of a Tub

1 *Diu multumque desideratum* "having been long and much needed."

2 *Basima eacabasa, etc.* The Citation out of Irenaeus [second-century Christian theologian who wrote a treatise "Against Heresies"] in the Title-Page, which seems to be all Gibberish, is a Form of Initiation used anciently by the Marcosian Heretics. W[illiam] Wotton. [Note added in the fifth edition, taken from Wotton's *Defence of the Reflections upon Ancient Learning* (1705); the Marcosians believed in a complete separation between the creating and judgmental God of the Old Testament and the redeeming God of the New; they preached rejection of the old creator's world and concentration on the totally unworldly God whom they could only know in Heaven; Wotton translates Irenaeus' transliteration of the Syriac, "I call upon this, which is above all the Power of the Father, which is called Light, and Spirit, and Life, because thou hast reigned in the Body."]

3 *Juvatque ... Musae* "I love to pluck new flowers, and to seek an illustrious chaplet for my head from fields whence before this the Muses have crowned the brows of none" (Lucretius, *De Rerum Natura* 4.2–5; Loeb Library translation).

4 *Treatises ... published* This mock advertising page faced the title page in the first edition.

5 *Grub Street* "Originally the name of a street in Moorfields in London, much inhabited by writers of small histories, dictionaries, and temporary poems; whence any mean production is called *grubstreet*" (Johnson).

6 *Lord Somers* Lord High Chancellor of England (1697), patron of many writers of the time, and very influential politician; in the fifth edition, Swift inserted "An Apology" and a postscript between the title page and this dedication.

7 *Prince* Posterity, see below, p. 460.

of Authors, I think it a wise Piece of Presumption, to inscribe these Papers to your Lordship, and to implore your Lordship's Protection of them. God and your Lordship know their Faults and their Merits; for as to my own Particular, I am altogether a Stranger to the Matter, and though everybody else should be equally ignorant, I do not fear the Sale of the Book at all the worse, upon that Score. Your Lordship's Name on the Front, in Capital Letters, will at any time get off one Edition: Neither would I desire any other Help to grow an Alderman, than a Patent for the sole Privilege of dedicating to your Lordship.

I should now, in right of a dedicator, give your Lordship a List of your own Virtues, and at the same time, be very unwilling to offend your Modesty; But, chiefly, I should celebrate your Liberality towards Men of great Parts and small Fortunes, and give you broad Hints, that I mean myself. And, I was just going on in the usual Method, to peruse a hundred or two of Dedications, and transcribe an Abstract to be applied to your Lordship; But, I was diverted by a certain Accident. For, upon the Covers of these Papers, I casually observed written in large Letters, the two following Words, *DETUR DIGNISSIMO*; which, for ought I knew, might contain some important Meaning. But it unluckily fell out that none of the Authors I employ, understood *Latin* (though I have them often in pay, to translate out of that Language) I was therefore compelled to have recourse to the Curate of our Parish, who Englished it thus, *Let it be given to the Worthiest:* And his Comment was, that the Author meant, his Work should be dedicated to the sublimest Genius of the Age, for Wit, Learning, Judgement, Eloquence and Wisdom. I called at a Poet's Chamber (who works for my Shop) in an Alley hard by, showed him the Translation, and desired his Opinion, who it was that the Author could mean; He told me, after some Consideration, that Vanity was a Thing he abhorred; but by the Description, he thought Himself to be the Person aimed at; And, at the same time, he very kindly offered his own Assistance *gratis* towards penning a Dedication to Himself. I desired him, however, to give a second Guess. Why, then, said he, It must be I, or my Lord Somers. From thence I went to several other Wits of my Acquaintance, with no small Hazard and Weariness to my Person, from a prodigious Number of dark, winding Stairs;[8] But found them all in the same Story, both of your Lordship and themselves. Now, your Lordship is to understand that this Proceeding was not of my own Invention; For, I have somewhere heard, it is a Maxim, that those, to whom every Body allows the second Place, have an undoubted Title to the First.

This, infallibly, convinced me, that your Lordship was the Person intended by the Author. But, being very unacquainted in the style and form of dedications, I employed those wits aforesaid to furnish me with hints and materials towards a panegyric upon your Lordship's virtues.

In two Days, they brought me ten Sheets of Paper, filled up on every Side. They swore to me, that they had ransacked whatever could be found in the Characters of *Socrates, Aristides,*[9] *Epaminondas,*[10] *Cato,*[11] *Tully,*[12] *Atticus,*[13] and other hard names which I cannot now recollect. However, I have Reason to believe, they imposed upon my Ignorance, because when I came to read over their Collections, there was not a Syllable there, but what I and everybody else, knew as well as themselves: Therefore I grievously suspect a Cheat, and that these Authors of mine, stole and transcribed every Word, from the universal Report of Mankind. So that I look upon myself, as fifty Shillings[14] out of Pocket, to no manner of Purpose.

Notes

8 *dark, winding Stairs* Grubstreet wits, or writers, were infamous for dwelling in garrets or attics, the cheapest places to live.

9 *Aristides* Athenian statesman of the fifth century BCE.

10 *Epaminondas* Theban general of the fourth century BCE.

11 *Cato* Roman writer and general of the second century BCE.

12 *Tully* Marcus Tullius Cicero.

13 *Atticus* friend of Cicero, scholar, and patron.

14 *fifty shillings* £2.50, several hundred pounds and many hundred dollars in today's money.

If, by altering the Title, I could make the same Materials serve for another Dedication (as my Betters have done) it would help to make up my Loss; but I have made several persons dip here and there in those Papers, and before they read three Lines, they have all assured me, plainly, that they cannot possibly be applied to any Person, besides your Lordship.

I expected, indeed, to have heard of your Lordship's Bravery, at the Head of an Army; of your undaunted Courage in mounting a Breach, or scaling a Wall; Or, to have had your Pedigree traced in a Lineal Descent from the House of *Austria*; Or, of your wonderful talent at Dress and Dancing; Or, your Profound Knowledge in *Algebra, Metaphysics*, and the Oriental Tongues: But to ply the World with an old beaten Story of your Wit, and Eloquence, and Learning, and Wisdom, and Justice, and Politeness, and Candour, and Evenness of Temper in all Scenes of Life; Of that great Discernment in Discovering, and Readiness in Favouring deserving Men; with forty other common Topics: I confess, I have neither Conscience, nor Countenance to do it. Because there is no Virtue, either of a Public or Private Life, which some Circumstances of your own, have not often produced upon the Stage of the World; and those few, which for want of Occasions to exert them, might otherwise have passed unseen or unobserved by your *Friends*, your *Enemies* have at length brought them to Light.[15]

'Tis true, I should be very loath, the Bright Example of your Lordship's Virtues should be lost to after Ages, both for their sake and your own; but chiefly, because they will be so very necessary to adorn the History of a *late Reign*;[16] And That is another Reason, why I would forbear to make a Recital of them here; Because, I have been told by Wise Men, that as Dedications have run for some Years past, a good Historian will not be apt to have Recourse thither, in search of Characters.[17]

There is one Point, wherein I think we Dedicators would do well to change our Measures; I mean, instead of running on so far upon the Praise of our Patron's *liberality*, to spend a Word or two, in admiring their *Patience*. I can put no greater Compliment on your Lordship's, than by giving you so ample an Occasion to exercise it at present. Though, perhaps I shall not be apt to reckon much Merit to your Lordship upon that Score, who having been formerly used to tedious Harangues, and sometimes, to as little Purpose, will be the readier to pardon this, especially, when it is offered by one, who is with all Respect and Veneration,

My Lord,
Your Lordship's most obedient,
and most faithful servant,
The Bookseller

The Bookseller to the Reader

It is now Six Years, since these Papers came first to my Hands, which seems to have been about a Twelvemonth after they were writ: for the Author tells us in his Preface to the first Treatise, that he has calculated it for the Year 1697, and in several Passages of that Discourse, as well as the second, it appears, they were written about that Time.

As to the Author, I can give no manner of Satisfaction; However, I am credibly informed, that this Publication is without his Knowledge, for he concludes the Copy is lost, having lent it to a Person, since dead, and being never in Possession of it after: So that whether the

Notes

15 *Enemies have ... brought them to Light* in a failed impeachment proceeding in Parliament in 1701.

16 *a late Reign* that of King William III.

17 *Character* "A representation of any man as to his personal qualities" (Johnson).

Work received his last Hand, or, whether he intended to fill up the defective Places, is like to remain a Secret.

If I should go about to tell the Reader, by what Accident, I became Master of these Papers, it would, in this unbelieving Age, pass for little more than the Cant, or Jargon of the Trade. I, therefore, gladly spare both him and myself so unnecessary a Trouble. There yet remains a difficult Question, why I published them no sooner. I forbore upon two Accounts: First, because I thought I had better Work upon my Hands; and Secondly, because, I was not without some Hope of hearing from the Author, and receiving his Directions. But, I have been lately alarmed with Intelligence of a surreptitious Copy which a certain great Wit had new polished and refined, or, as our present Writers express themselves, fitted to the Humour of the Age, *as they have already done with great Felicity, to* Don Quixote, Boccalini, la Bruyere, *and other Authors.*[18] *However, I thought it fairer Dealing to offer the whole Work in its Naturals.*

If any Gentleman will please to furnish me with a Key,[19] *in order to explain the more difficult Parts, I shall very gratefully acknowledge the Favour, and print it by itself.*

The Epistle Dedicatory to His Royal Highness Prince Posterity

SIR,

I here present Your Highness with the Fruits of a very few leisure Hours, stolen from the short Intervals of a World of Business and of an Employment quite alien from such Amusements as this: The poor Production of that Refuse of Time, which has lain heavy upon my Hands, during a long Prorogation[20] of Parliament, a great Dearth of Foreign News, and a tedious Fit of rainy Weather: For which, and other Reasons, it cannot choose extremely to deserve such a Patronage as that of *Your Highness*, whose numberless Virtues in so few Years, make the World look upon You as the future Example to all Princes: For although *Your Highness* is hardly got clear of Infancy, yet has the universal learned World already resolved upon appealing to Your future Dictates with the lowest and most resigned Submission; Fate having decreed You sole Arbiter of the Productions of human Wit, in this polite and most accomplished Age. Methinks, the Number of Appellants were enough to shock and startle any Judge of a Genius less unlimited than Yours: but in order to prevent such glorious Trials, the *Person*[21] (it seems) to whose Care the Education of Your Highness is committed, has resolved (as I am told) to keep You in almost an universal Ignorance of our Studies, which it is your inherent Birthright to inspect.

It is amazing to me, that this *Person* should have Assurance in the face of the Sun, to go about persuading *Your Highness* that our Age is almost wholly illiterate, and has hardly produced one Writer upon any Subject. I know very well that when *Your Highness* shall come to riper Years, and have gone through the Learning of Antiquity, You will be too curious to neglect inquiring into the Authors of the very Age before You; and to think that this *Insolent*, in the Account he is preparing for Your View, designs to reduce them to a Number so insignificant as I am ashamed to mention; it moves my Zeal and my Spleen[22] for the Honour and Interest of our vast flourishing Body, as well as of myself, for whom I know by long Experience, he has professed, and Still continues a peculiar Malice.

Notes

18 *they have already done ... and other Authors* such adaptive translations or imitations were, in fact, common.

19 *Key* such a work was printed in 1710; it was compiled by Benjamin Tooke, and some parts of it, perhaps worked over by Swift, came into the fifth edition as footnotes.

20 *Prorogation* "Interruption of the session of Parliament by regal authority" (Johnson).

21 *Person* Time.

22 *Spleen* "It is supposed the seat of anger and melancholy" (Johnson).

'Tis not unlikely that when *Your Highness* will one Day peruse what I am now writing, You may be ready to expostulate with Your *Governor* upon the Credit of what I here affirm, and command Him to show You some of our Productions. To which he will answer (for I am well informed of his Designs) by asking *Your Highness*, where they are? and what is become of them? and pretend it a Demonstration that there never were any, because they are not then to be found: Not to be found! Who has mislaid them? Are they sunk in the Abyss of Things? 'Tis certain, that in their own Nature they were *light* enough to swim upon the Surface for all Eternity: Therefore the Fault is in Him, who tied Weights so heavy to their Heels, as to depress them to the Centre. Is their very Essence destroyed? Who has annihilated them? Were they drowned by *Purges*, or martyred by *Pipes*?[23] Who administered them to the posteriors of———[?] But that it may no longer be a Doubt with *Your Highness*, who is to be the Author of this universal Ruin; I beseech you to observe that large and terrible *Scythe* which Your *Governor* affects to bear continually about him. Be pleased to remark the Length and Strength, the Sharpness and Hardness, of his *Nails* and *Teeth*; Consider his baneful, abominable *Breath*, Enemy to Life and Matter, infectious and corrupting: And then reflect whether it be possible for any mortal Ink and Paper of this Generation to make a suitable Resistance. Oh, that *Your Highness* would one day resolve to disarm this Usurping *Maitre de Palais*,[24] of his furious Engines, and bring Your Empire *hors de Page*.[25]

It were endless to recount the several Methods of Tyranny and Destruction, which Your *Governor* is pleased to practise upon this Occasion. His inveterate Malice is such to the Writings of our Age, that of several Thousands produced yearly from this renowned City, before the next Revolution of the Sun, there is not one to be heard of: Unhappy Infants, many of them barbarously destroyed, before they have so much as learnt their *Mother-Tongue* to beg for Pity. Some he stifles in their Cradles; others he frights into Convulsions, whereof they suddenly die; Some he flays alive; others he tears Limb from Limb. Great Numbers are offered to *Moloch*,[26] and the rest tainted by his Breath, die of a languishing Consumption.

But the Concern I have most at Heart, is for our Corporation[27] of *Poets*, from whom I am preparing a Petition to *Your Highness*, to be subscribed with the Names of one hundred thirty six of the first Rate, but whose immortal Productions are never likely to reach your Eyes, though each of them is now an humble and an earnest Appellant for the Laurel,[28] and has large comely Volumes ready to show for a Support to his Pretensions. The *never-dying* Works of these illustrious Persons, *Your Governor*, sir, has devoted to unavoidable Death, and *Your Highness* is to be made believe, that our Age has never arrived at the Honour to produce one single Poet.

We confess *Immortality* to be a great and powerful Goddess, but in vain we offer up to her our Devotions and our Sacrifices, if *Your Highness's Governor*, who has usurped the *Priesthood*, must by an unparalleled Ambition and Avarice, wholly intercept and devour them.

To affirm that our Age is altogether Unlearned, and devoid of Writers in any kind, seems to be an Assertion so bold and so false, that I have been some time thinking, the contrary may almost be proved by uncontrollable Demonstration.[29] 'Tis true indeed,

Notes

23 *Purges ... Pipes* unsold copies of books, especially if, as was common, they were unbound, could be used for toilet paper or wadding in pipes or pistols.

24 *Maitre de Palais* chamberlain, or master of the king's palace.

25 *hors de Page* out of its childhood.

26 *Moloch* a false god in the Old Testament, to whom sacrifices of burning children were made.

27 *Corporation* society or fellowship.

28 *Laurel* crown of bay leaves symbolic of literary achievement.

29 *uncontrollable Demonstration* irrefutable proof.

that although their Numbers be vast, and their Productions numerous in proportion, yet are they hurried so hastily off the Scene, that they escape our Memory, and delude our Sight. When I first thought of this Address, I had prepared a copious List of *Titles* to present *Your Highness* as an undisputed Argument for what I affirm. The Originals were posted fresh upon all Gates and Corners of Streets; but returning in a very few Hours to take a Review, they were all torn down, and fresh ones in their Places: I inquired after them among Readers and Booksellers, but I inquired in vain, 'the Memorial of them was lost among Men, their Place was no more to be found';[30] and I was laughed to scorn, for a *Clown* and a *Pedant*, devoid of all Taste and Refinement, little versed in the Course of *present* Affairs, and that knew nothing of what had passed in the best Companies of Court and Town. So that I can only avow in general to *Your Highness*, that we *do* abound in Learning and Wit; but to fix upon Particulars, is a Task too slippery for my slender Abilities. If I should venture in a windy Day, to affirm to *Your Highness* that there is a huge Cloud near the *Horizon* in the Form of a *Bear*, another in the *Zenith* with the Head of an *Ass*, a third to the Westward with Claws like a *Dragon*, and *Your Highness* should in a few Minutes think fit to examine the Truth; 'tis certain, they would be all changed in Figure and Position, new ones would arise, and all we could agree upon would be, that Clouds there were, but that I was grossly mistaken in the *Zoography*[31] and *Topography* of them.

But Your *Governor*, perhaps, may still insist, and put the Question: 'What is then become of those immense Bales of Paper, which must needs have been employed in such Numbers of Books? Can these also be wholly annihilate, and so of a sudden as I pretend?' What shall I say in return of so invidious an Objection? It ill befits the Distance between *Your Highness* and Me, to send You for ocular Conviction to a *Jakes*[32] or an *Oven*; to the Windows of a *Bawdy-House*, or to a sordid *Lantern*.[33] Books like Men their Authors have no more than one Way of coming into the World, but there are ten Thousand to go out of it and return no more.

I profess to *Your Highness*, in the Integrity of my Heart, that what I am going to say is literally true this Minute I am writing; What Revolutions may happen before it shall be ready for Your Perusal, I can by no means warrant; However, I beg You to accept it as a Specimen of our Learning, our Politeness and our Wit. I do therefore affirm upon the Word of a sincere Man, that there is now actually in being, a certain Poet called *John Dryden*, whose Translation of *Virgil* was lately[34] printed in a large Folio, well bound, and if diligent search were made, for ought I know, is yet to be seen. There is another called *Nahum Tate*,[35] who is ready to make Oath that he has caused many Reams of Verse to be published, whereof both himself and his Bookseller (if lawfully required) can still produce authentic Copies, and therefore wonders why the World is pleased to make such a Secret of it. There is a Third, known by the Name of *Tom Durfey*,[36] a Poet of a vast Comprehension, an universal Genius, and most profound Learning. There are also one Mr. *Rymer*,[37] and one Mr. *Dennis*,[38] most profound Critics.

Notes

30 *Memorial … found* an echo of Revelation 12.8 and other biblical passages.

31 *Zoography* animal outlines.

32 *Jakes* "A house of office" (Johnson); lavatory.

33 *Lantern* lighthouse.

34 *lately* 1697.

35 *Nahum Tate* (1652–1715), much maligned poet and dramatist, famous for revising Shakespeare's *King Lear* in a more optimistic version that held the stage for an age.

36 *Tom Durfey* Thomas D'Urfey (1653–1723), frequently lampooned poet and dramatist.

37 *Rymer* Thomas Rymer (1641–1713), dramatic critic.

38 *Dennis* John Dennis (1657–1734), dramatist and critic of contemporary poetry, satirized by Pope.

There is a person styled Dr. *B—tl—y*,[39] who has written near a thousand Pages of immense Erudition, *giving a full and true Account* of a certain *Squabble*, of wonderful importance between himself and a Bookseller: He is a Writer of infinite Wit and Humour; no Man rallies with a better Grace, and in more sprightly Turns. Further, I avow to *Your Highness*, that with these Eyes I have beheld the Person of *William W—tt—n*, BD,[40] who has written a good sizeable Volume against a *Friend of Your Governor* (from whom, alas! he must therefore look for little Favour) in a most gentlemanly Style, adorned with utmost Politeness and Civility: replete with Discoveries equally valuable for their Novelty and Use; and embellished with *Traits* of Wit so poignant and so apposite, that he is a worthy Yokemate to his fore-mentioned *Friend*.

Why should I go upon further Particulars, which might fill a Volume with the just Elogies[41] of my contemporary Brethren? I shall bequeath this Piece of Justice to a larger Work; wherein I intend to write a Character of the present Set of *Wits* in our Nation: Their persons I shall describe particularly and at Length, their Genius and Understandings in *Miniature*.

In the meantime, I do here make bold to present *Your Highness* with a faithful Abstract drawn from the Universal Body of all Arts and Sciences, intended wholly for Your Service and Instruction: Nor do I doubt in the least, but *Your Highness* will peruse it as carefully, and make as considerable Improvements, as *other* young *Princes* have already done by the many Volumes of late Years written for a Help to their Studies.

That *Your Highness* may advance in Wisdom and Virtue, as well as Years, and at last outshine all Your Royal Ancestors, shall be the daily Prayer of,

SIR,
Your Highness's
Most devoted, &c.

Decemb. 1697.

The Preface

The Wits of the present Age being so very numerous and penetrating, it seems, the Grandees of *Church* and *State* begin to fall under horrible Apprehensions, lest these Gentlemen during the Intervals of a long Peace, should find leisure to pick Holes in the weak sides of Religion and Government. To prevent which, there has been much Thought employed of late upon certain Projects for taking off the Force and Edge of those formidable Enquirers, from canvassing and reasoning upon such delicate Points. They have at length fixed upon one which will require some Time as well as cost to perfect. Meanwhile, the Danger hourly increasing, by new Levies[42] of Wits all appointed (as there is Reason to fear) with Pen, Ink, and Paper, which may at an hour's Warning be drawn out into Pamphlets, and other Offensive Weapons, ready for immediate Execution: It was judged of absolute necessity, that some present Expedient be thought

Notes

39 *B—tl—y* Richard Bentley (1662–1742), important classical scholar; supported William Wotton and the moderns in a famous debate about the relative merit of the ancient and modern writers, in which Swift fought for the ancients alongside his patron William Temple.

40 *William W—tt—n, BD* Wotton (1666–1727), like Bentley, an accomplished classicist who supported the claims of the moderns against the excesses of Temple's preference for the ancients in *Reflections upon Ancient and Modern Learning* (1694). BD stands for Bachelor of Divinity.

41 *Elogies* praises.

42 *Levies* conscription.

on, till the main Design can be brought to Maturity. To this End, at a Grand Committee, some Days ago, this important Discovery was made by a certain curious and refined Observer; That Seamen have a Custom when they meet a *Whale*, to fling him out an empty *Tub* by way of Amusement, to divert him from laying violent Hands upon the Ship. This Parable was immediately mythologized; The *Whale* was interpreted to be *Hobbes*'s *Leviathan*,[43] which tosses and plays with all Schemes of Religion and Government, whereof a great many are hollow, and dry, and empty, and noisy, and wooden, and given to Rotation.[44] This is the *Leviathan* from whence the terrible Wits of our Age are said to borrow their Weapons. The *Ship* in danger, is easily understood to be its old Antitype the *Commonwealth*. But, how to analyse the *Tub*, was a Matter of Difficulty; when, after long Enquiry and Debate, the literal Meaning was preserved: And it was decreed, that in order to prevent these *Leviathans* from tossing and sporting with the *Commonwealth* (which itself is too apt to *fluctuate*) they should be diverted from that Game by *a Tale of a Tub*. And my Genius being conceived to lie not unhappily that way, I had the Honour done me to be engaged in the Performance.

This is the sole Design in publishing the following Treatise, which I hope will serve for an *Interim* of some Months to employ those unquiet Spirits, till the perfecting of that great Work; into the Secret of which, it is reasonable the courteous Reader should have some little Light.

It is intended that a large Academy be erected, capable of containing nine thousand seven hundred forty and three Persons, which by modest Computation is reckoned to be pretty near the current Number of *Wits* in this Island. These are to be disposed into the several Schools of this Academy, and there pursue those Studies to which their Genius most inclines them. The Undertaker himself will publish his Proposals with all convenient speed, to which I shall refer the curious Reader for a more particular Account, mentioning at present only a few of the principal Schools. There is, first, a large *Pederastic* School, with French and Italian masters. There is also, the *Spelling* School, *a very spacious Building*: The School of *Looking-Glasses*: The School of *Swearing*: The School of *Critics*: The School of *Salivation*: The School of *Hobby-horses*: The School of *Poetry*: The School of *Tops*: The School of *Spleen*: The School of *Gaming*: with many others too tedious to recount. No Person to be admitted Member into any of these Schools, without an Attestation under two sufficient Persons' Hands, certifying him to be a *Wit*.

But, to return. I am sufficiently instructed in the principal Duty of a Preface, if my Genius were capable of arriving at it. Thrice have I forced my Imagination to make the *Tour* of my Invention, and thrice it has returned empty; the latter having been wholly drained by the following Treatise. Not so, my more successful Brethren the *Moderns*, who will by no means let slip a Preface or Dedication, without some notable distinguishing Stroke, to surprise the Reader at the Entry, and kindle a wonderful Expectation of what is to ensue. Such was that of a most ingenious Poet, who soliciting his Brain for something new, compared himself to the *Hangman*, and his Patron to the *Patient*: This was *Insigne, recens, indictum ore alio*.[45] When I went through that necessary and noble course of Study, I had the happiness to observe many such egregious Touches, which I shall not injure the Authors by transplanting: Because I have remarked, that nothing is so very tender as a *Modern* Piece of Wit, and which is apt to suffer so much

Notes

[43] *Hobbes's Leviathan* see above, pp. 10–13.

[44] *Rotation* a reference to the Rota Club, and in particular, to James Harrington, author of *The Commonwealth of Oceana* (1656), a republican utopia.

[45] *Insigne ... alio* "extraordinary, recent, untold by another author" (Horace, *Odes* 3.25.7–8).

in the Carriage. Some things are extremely witty *today*, or *fasting*, or *in this Place*, or *at eight o'Clock*, or *over a Bottle*, or *spoken by Mr.* Whatdicall'um, or *in a Summer's Morning*: Any of which, by the smallest Transposal or Misapplication, is utterly annihilate. Thus, *Wit* has its Walks and Purlieus, out of which it may not stray the breadth of a Hair, upon peril of being lost. The *Moderns* have artfully fixed this *Mercury*,[46] and reduced it to the Circumstances of Time, Place, and Person. Such a Jest there is, that will not pass out of *Covent-Garden*, and such a one, that is nowhere intelligible but at *Hyde-Park* Corner.[47] Now, though it sometimes tenderly affects me to consider, that all the towardly Passages I shall deliver in the following Treatise, will grow quite out of date and relish with the first shifting of the present Scene; yet I must need subscribe to the Justice of this Proceeding: because, I cannot imagine why we should be at Expense to furnish Wit for succeeding Ages, when the former have made no sort of Provision for ours; wherein I speak the Sentiment of the very newest, and consequently the most Orthodox Refiners, as well as my own. However, being extremely solicitous that every accomplished Person who has got into the Taste of Wit calculated for this present Month of *August* 1697, should descend to the very *bottom* of all the *Sublime*[48] throughout this Treatise; I hold fit to lay down this general Maxim. Whatever Reader desires to have a thorough Comprehension of an Author's Thoughts, cannot take a better Method, than by putting himself into the Circumstances and Posture of Life, that the Writer was in, upon every important Passage as it flowed from his Pen; For this will introduce a Parity and strict Correspondence of Ideas between the Reader and the Author. Now, to assist the diligent Reader in so delicate an Affair, as far as brevity will permit, I have recollected, that the shrewdest Pieces of this Treatise, were conceived in Bed, in a Garret: at other times (for a Reason best known to myself) I thought fit to sharpen my Invention with Hunger; and in general, the whole Work was begun, continued, and ended, under a long course of Physic,[49] and a great want of Money. Now, I do affirm, it will be absolutely impossible for the candid Peruser to go along with me in a great many bright Passages, unless upon the several Difficulties emergent, he will please to capacitate and prepare himself by these Directions. And this I lay down as my principal *Postulatum*.

Because I have professed to be a most devoted Servant of all *Modern* Forms; I apprehend some curious *Wit* may object a-me for proceeding thus far in a Preface, without declaiming according to the Custom, against the Multitude of Writers, whereof the whole Multitude of Writers most reasonably complains. I am just come from perusing some hundreds of Prefaces, wherein the Authors do at the very beginning address the gentle Reader concerning this enormous Grievance. Of these I have preserved a few Examples, and shall set them down as near as my Memory has been able to retain them.

One begins thus;

'For a Man to set up for a Writer, when the Press swarms with, &c.'

Another;

'The Tax upon Paper does not lessen the Number of Scribblers, who daily pester, &c.'

Another;

'When every little Would-be wit takes Pen in hand, 'tis in vain to enter the Lists, &c.'

Another;

Notes

46 *Mercury* "Sprightly qualities" (Johnson), from the properties of the element, as chemists described them.

47 *Covent-Garden … Hyde-Park Corner* neighborhoods in London.

48 *the Sublime* "The grand or lofty style. The sublime is a Gallicism but now naturalised" (Johnson).

49 *Physic* medication, especially purgatives.

'To observe what Trash the Press swarms with, &c.'

Another;

'SIR. It is merely in Obedience to your Commands that I venture into the Public; for who upon a less Consideration would be of a Party with such a Rabble of Scribblers, &c.'

Now, I have two Words in my own Defence against this Objection. First: I am far from granting the Number of Writers, a Nuisance to our Nation, having strenuously maintained the contrary in several Parts of the following Discourse. Secondly: I do not well understand the Justice of this Proceeding, because I observe many of these polite Prefaces to be not only from the same Hand, but from those who are most voluminous in their several Productions: Upon which I shall tell the Reader a short Tale.

'A Mountebank in *Leicester-Fields*[50] had drawn a huge Assembly about him. Among the rest, a fat unwieldy Fellow, half stifled in the Press, would be every fit[51] crying out, "Lord! what a filthy Crowd is here; Pray, good People, give way a little; Bless me! what a Devil has raked this Rabble together: Z——ds,[52] what squeezing is this! Honest Friend, remove your Elbow". At last a Weaver that stood next him could hold no longer. "A plague confound you", said he, "for an overgrown Sloven; and who (in the Devil's Name) I wonder, helps to make up the Crowd half so much as yourself? Don't you consider (with a Pox[53]) that you take up more room with that Carcass than any five here? Is not the Place as free for us as for you? Bring your own Guts to a reasonable Compass (and be d——n'd) and then I'll engage we shall have room enough for us all."'

There are certain common Privileges of a Writer, the Benefit whereof, I hope there will be no Reason to doubt; particularly, that where I am not understood, it shall be concluded, that something very useful and profound is couched underneath: And again, that whatever Word or Sentence is printed in a different Character, shall be judged to contain something extraordinary either of *Wit* or *Sublime*.

As for the Liberty I have thought fit to take of praising myself, upon some Occasions or none; I am sure it will need no Excuse, if a Multitude of great Examples be allowed sufficient Authority: For, it is here to be noted, that *Praise* was originally a Pension paid by the World; but the *Moderns* finding the trouble and charge too great in collecting it, have lately brought out the *Fee-Simple*;[54] since which time, the Right of Presentation is wholly in ourselves. For this Reason it is, that when an Author makes his own Elogy, he uses a certain Form to declare and insist upon his Title, which is commonly in these or the like Words, 'I speak without vanity'; which I think plainly shows it to be a Matter of Right and Justice. Now, I do here once for all declare, that in every Encounter of this Nature, through the following Treatise, the Form aforesaid is implied; which I mention, to save the Trouble of repeating it on so many Occasions.

'Tis a great Ease to my Conscience that I have writ so elaborate and useful a Discourse without one grain of Satire intermixed; which is the sole Point wherein I have taken Leave to dissent from the famous Originals of our Age and Country. I have observed some Satirists to use the Public much at the rate that Pedants do a naughty Boy ready horsed[55] for Discipline; First expostulate the Case, then plead the Necessity of the Rod, from great Provocations, and conclude every Period[56] with a Lash. Now, if

Notes

[50] *Leicester-Fields* now Leicester Square, London.

[51] *fit* short interval of time.

[52] *Z[oun]ds* "God's wounds," a mild curse.

[53] *Pox* venereal disease, a curse.

[54] *Fee-Simple* an unconditional gift or grant.

[55] *horsed* raised up, on a man's back, for flogging.

[56] *Period* sentence.

I know anything of Mankind, these Gentlemen might very well spare their Reproof and Correction: For, there is not through all Nature another so callous and insensible a Member as *the World's Posteriors*, whether you apply to it with the *Toe* or the *Birch*.[57] Besides, most of our late Satirists seem to lie under a sort of Mistake, that because *Nettles* have the Prerogative to Sting, therefore all *other Weeds* must do so too. I make not this Comparison out of the least Design to detract from these worthy Writers: For it is well known among *Mythologists*, that *Weeds* have the Pre-eminence over all other Vegetables; and therefore the first *Monarch* of this Island,[58] whose Taste and Judgement were so acute and refined, did very wisely root out the *Roses* from the Collar of *the Order*, and plant the *Thistles*[59] in their stead, as the nobler Flower of the two. For which Reason it is conjectured by profounder Antiquaries, that the Satirical Itch, so prevalent in this Part of our Island, was first brought among us from beyond the *Tweed*.[60] Here may it long flourish and abound: May it survive and neglect the Scorn of the World, with as much Ease and Contempt, as the World is insensible to the Lashes of it. May their own Dullness, or that of their Party, be no Discouragement for the Authors to proceed; but let them remember, it is with *Wits* as with *Razors*, which are never so apt to *cut* those they are employed on, as when they have *lost their Edge*: Besides, those whose Teeth are too rotten to bite, are best of all others qualified to revenge that Defect with their Breath.

I am not like other Men, to envy or undervalue the Talents I cannot reach; for which Reason I must needs bear a true Honour to this large eminent Sect of our *British* Writers. And I hope this little panegyric will not be offensive to their Ears, since it has the Advantage of being only designed for themselves. Indeed, Nature herself has taken Order, that Fame and Honour should be purchased at a better Pennyworth by Satire, than by any other Productions of the Brain; the World being soonest provoked to *Praise* by *Lashes*, as Men are to *Love*. There is a Problem in an ancient Author, why Dedications, and other Bundles of Flattery run all upon stale, musty Topics, without the smallest Tincture of anything New; not only to the torment and nauseating of the *Christian* Reader, but (if not suddenly prevented) to the universal spreading of that pestilent Disease, the Lethargy, in this Island: Whereas there is very little Satire which has not something in it untouched before. The Defects of the former are usually imputed to the want of Invention among those who are Dealers in that kind: But, I think, with a great deal of Injustice; the Solution being easy and natural. For, the Materials of Panegyric being very few in Number, have been long since exhausted: For, as Health is but one Thing and has been always the same, whereas Diseases are by thousands, besides new and daily Additions: So, all the Virtues that have been ever in Mankind, are to be counted upon a few Fingers; but his Follies and Vices are innumerable, and Time adds hourly to the Heap. Now, the utmost a poor poet can do, is to get by heart a List of the Cardinal Virtues, and deal them with his utmost Liberality to his Hero or his Patron: He may ring the Changes as far as it will go, and vary his Phrase till he has talked round; but the Reader quickly finds, it is all *Pork*, with a little variety of Sauce. For there is no inventing Terms of Art beyond our Ideas; and when Ideas are exhausted, Terms of Art must be so too.

Notes

57 *Birch* a bundle of sticks used for flogging.

58 *Monarch of this Island* James I, because he was King of England, Scotland, and Wales.

59 *Thistles* a Scottish order of knights, revived or begun by James II; it coexisted with the Order of the Garter, which has roses in its ceremonial collar, but the House of Stuart was seen to favor it.

60 *Tweed* river dividing England from Scotland.

But, though the matter for Panegyric were as fruitful as the Topics of Satire, yet would it not be hard to find out a sufficient Reason, why the latter will be always better received than the first. For, this being bestowed only upon one or a few Persons at a time, is sure to raise Envy, and consequently ill Words from the rest, who have no share in the Blessing: But Satire being levelled at all, is never resented for an Offence by any, since every individual Person makes bold to understand it of others, and very wisely removes his particular Part of the Burden upon the Shoulders of the World, which are broad enough, and able to bear it. To this purpose, I have sometimes reflected upon the Difference between *Athens* and *England*, with respect to the Point before us. In the *Attic* Commonwealth,[61] it was the Privilege and Birthright of every Citizen and Poet, to rail aloud and in public, or to expose upon the Stage by Name, any Person they pleased, though of the greatest Figure, whether a *Creon*, an *Hyperbolus*, an *Alcibiades*, or a *Demosthenes*:[62] But, on the other side, the least reflecting Word let fall against the *People* in general, was immediately caught up, and revenged upon the Authors, however considerable for their Quality or their Merits. Whereas, in *England* it is just the Reverse of all this. Here, you may securely display your utmost *Rhetoric* against Mankind, in the Face of the World; tell them, 'That all are gone astray; That there is none that doth good, no not one;[63] That we live in the very Dregs of Time; That Knavery and Atheism are Epidemic as the Pox; That Honesty is fled with Astræa';[64] with any other Common Places *equally* new and eloquent, which are furnished by the *Splendida bilis*.[65] And when you have done, the whole Audience, far from being offended, shall return you Thanks, as a Deliverer of precious and useful Truths. Nay further; it is but to venture your Lungs, and you may Preach in *Covent-Garden*[66] against Foppery and Fornication, and *something else*: Against Pride, and Dissimulation, and Bribery, at *White-Hall*:[67] You may expose Rapine and Injustice in the *Inns of Court*[68] Chapel: And in a *City*[69] Pulpit be as fierce as you please against Avarice, Hypocrisy, and Extortion. 'Tis but a *Ball* bandied to and fro, and every man carries a *Racket* about Him to strike it from himself among the rest of the Company. But on the other side, whoever should mistake the Nature of things so far, as to drop but a single Hint in public, How *such a one* starved half the Fleet, and half poisoned the rest: How *such a one*, from a true principle of *Love* and *Honour*, pays no Debts but for *Wenches* and *Play*: How *such a one* has got a Clap,[70] and runs out of his Estate: How *Paris* bribed by *Juno* and *Venus*, loath to offend either Party, slept out the whole Cause on the Bench: Or, how *such an Orator* makes long Speeches in the Senate, with much Thought, little Sense, and to no Purpose. Whoever, I say, should venture to be thus particular, must expect to be imprisoned for *Scandalum Magnatum*;[71] to have *Challenges* sent him; to be sued for *Defamation*, and to be *brought before the Bar of the House*.[72]

But, I forget that I am expatiating on a Subject, wherein I have no Concern, having neither a Talent nor an Inclination for Satire; On the other side, I am so entirely satisfied

Notes

61 *Attic Commonwealth* vid. Xenoph. [Swift's marginal note; "see Xenophon," meaning *On the Polity of the Athenians*, a work then but not now attributed to Xenophon].

62 *Creon* [a mistake for Cleon], *Hyperbolus, Alcibiades, Demosthenes* all Athenian generals and politicians in the late fifth century BCE, all critically discussed by Thucydides.

63 *all are gone astray… not one* Psalm 14.3 [note in edition of 1720].

64 *Astræa* goddess of justice, who left the world in disgust.

65 *Splendida bilis* "gleaming (black) bile, or anger" (Horace, *Satires* 2.3.141).

66 *Covent-Garden* a district then known for prostitution.

67 *White-Hall* the seat of government.

68 *Inns of Court* center of London's legal system.

69 *City* the commercial center.

70 *Clap* venereal disease.

71 *Scandalum Magnatum* libel against a high personage of the land.

72 *Bar of the House* the House of Commons, constituted as a court of judgment.

with the whole present Procedure of human Things, that I have been for some Years preparing Materials towards *A Panegyric upon the World*; to which I intended to add a Second Part entitled, *A Modest Defence of the Proceedings of the Rabble in all Ages*. Both these I had Thoughts to publish by way of Appendix to the following Treatise; but finding my Common-Place Book fill much slower than I had reason to expect, I have chosen to defer them to another Occasion. Besides, I have been unhappily prevented in that Design, by a certain Domestic Misfortune, in the Particulars whereof, though it would be very seasonable and much in the *Modern* way, to inform the *gentle Reader*, and would also be of great Assistance towards extending this Preface into the Size now in Vogue, which by Rule ought to be *large* in Proportion as the subsequent Volume is *small*; Yet I shall now dismiss our impatient Reader from any further Attendance at the *Porch*, and having duly prepared his Mind by a preliminary Discourse, shall gladly introduce Him to the sublime Mysteries that ensue.

A Tale of a Tub, &C.

SECT. I
The Introduction

Whoever hath an Ambition to be heard in a Crowd, must press, and squeeze, and thrust, and climb, with indefatigable Pains, till he has exalted himself to a certain Degree of Altitude above them. Now, in all Assemblies, though you wedge them ever so close, we may observe this peculiar Property: that, over their Heads there is Room enough; but how to reach it, is the difficult Point; It being as hard to get quit of *Number* as of *Hell*;

——Evadere ad auras,
Hoc opus, hic labor est.——[73]

To this End, the Philosopher's Way in all Ages, has been by erecting certain *Edifices in the Air*; But, whatever Practice and Reputation these kind of Structures have formerly possessed, or may still continue in; not excepting even that of *Socrates*, when he [was] suspended in a Basket to help Contemplation;[74] I think, with due Submission, they seem to labour under two Inconveniences. First, that the Foundations being laid too high, they have been often out of *Sight*, and ever out of *Hearing*. Secondly, that the Materials being very transitory, have suffered much from Inclemencies of Air, especially in these North-West Regions.

Therefore, towards the just Performance of this great Work, there remain but three Methods that I can think on; Whereof the Wisdom of our Ancestors being highly sensible, has, to encourage all aspiring Adventurers, thought fit to erect three wooden Machines, for the Use of those Orators who desire to talk much without Interruption. These are, the *Pulpit*, the *Ladder*, and the *Stage-Itinerant*. For, as to the *Bar*, though it be compounded of the same Matter, and designed for the same Use, it cannot however

Notes

[73] *Evadere ... est* "But to return, and view the cheerful Skies;/ In this the Task and mighty Labour lies" [note in fifth edition, citing Dryden's translation of *Aeneid* 6.128–9].

[74] *Socrates ... Contemplation* he arrives on stage in this manner in Aristophanes' comedy *The Clouds*, l. 218.

be well allowed the Honour of a fourth, by reason of its level or inferior Situation, exposing it to perpetual Interruption from Collaterals. Neither can the *Bench* itself, though raised to a proper Eminency, put in a better Claim, whatever its Advocates insist on. For if they please to look into the original Design of its Erection, and the Circumstances or Adjuncts subservient to that Design, they will soon acknowledge the present Practice exactly correspondent to the Primitive Institution, and both to answer the Etymology of the Name, which in the *Phœnician* Tongue is a Word of great Signification, importing, if literally interpreted, 'The Place of Sleep'; but in common Acceptation, 'a Seat well bolstered and cushioned, for the Repose of old and gouty Limbs': *Senes ut in otia tuta recedant.*[75] Fortune being indebted to them this Part of Retaliation, that, as formerly they have long *Talked*, whilst others *Slept*, so now they may *Sleep* as long whilst others *Talk*.

But if no other Argument could occur to exclude the *Bench* and the *Bar* from the List of Oratorial Machines, it were sufficient that the Admission of them would overthrow a Number which I was resolved to establish whatever Argument it might cost me: In imitation of that prudent Method observed by many other Philosophers and great Clerks, whose chief Art in Division has been, to grow fond of some proper mystical Number, which their Imaginations have rendered Sacred, to a Degree, that they force common Reason to find room for it in every part of Nature; reducing, including, and adjusting, every *Genus* and *Species* within that Compass, by coupling some against their Wills, and banishing others at any Rate. Now, among all the rest, the profound Number *THREE* is that which hath most employed my sublimest Speculations, nor ever without wonderful Delight. There is now in the Press (and will be published next Term) a Panegyrical Essay of mine upon this Number, wherein I have by most convincing Proofs, not only reduced the *Senses* and the *Elements* under its Banner, but brought over several Deserters from its two great Rivals *SEVEN* and *NINE*.

Now, the first of these Oratorial Machines in Place as well as Dignity, is the *Pulpit*. Of *Pulpits* there are in this Island several sorts; but I esteem only That made of Timber from the *Sylva Caledonia*,[76] which agrees very well with our Climate. If it be upon its Decay, 'tis the better, both for Conveyance of Sound and for other Reasons to be mentioned by and by. The Degree of Perfection in Shape and Size, I take to consist, in being extremely narrow, with little Ornament, and, best of all, without a Cover (for by ancient Rule it ought to be the only uncovered *Vessel* in every Assembly where it is rightfully used) by which means, from its near Resemblance to a Pillory, it will ever have a mighty Influence on human Ears.

Of *Ladders* I need say nothing: 'Tis observed by Foreigners themselves, to the Honour of our Country, that we excel all Nations in our Practice and Understanding of this Machine. The ascending Orators do not only oblige their Audience in the agreeable Delivery, but the whole World in their *early* Publication of their Speeches; which I look upon as the choicest Treasury of our British Eloquence, and whereof I am informed, that worthy Citizen and Bookseller, Mr. *John Dunton*,[77] hath made a faithful and a painful Collection which he shortly designs to publish in Twelve Volumes in Folio, illustrated with Copper-Plates. A Work highly useful and curious, and altogether worthy of such a Hand.

Notes

[75] *Senes ... recedant* "so that when they are old they may retire to a life of ease" (Horace, *Satires* 1.1.31).

[76] *Sylva Caledonia* "Scottish forest"; Scotland was already notoriously deforested.

[77] *John Dunton* (1659–1733); published over 600 books, but was plagued by poverty and growing insanity by 1704.

The last Engine of Orators, is the *stage-itinerant*,[78] erected with much Sagacity, *sub Jove pluvio, in triviis & quadriviis*.[79] It is the great Seminary of the two former, and its Orators are sometimes preferred to the One, and sometimes to the Other, in proportion to their Deservings, there being a strict and perpetual Intercourse between all three.

From this accurate Deduction it is manifest that for obtaining Attention in Public, there is of necessity required *a superior Position of Place*. But, although this Point be generally granted, yet the Cause is little agreed in; and it seems to me, that very few Philosophers have fallen into a true, natural Solution of this *Phenomenon*. The deepest Account, and the most fairly digested of any I have yet met with, is this, That Air being a heavy Body, and therefore (according to the System of *Epicurus*[80]) continually descending, must needs be more so, when loaden and pressed down by Words, which are also Bodies of much Weight and Gravity, as it is manifest from those deep *Impressions* they make and leave upon us; and therefore must be delivered from a due Altitude, or else they will neither carry a good Aim, nor fall down with a sufficient Force.

> *Corpoream quoque enim vocem constare fatendum est,*
> *Et sonitum, quoniam possunt impellere Sensus.*
> LUCR. Lib. 4.[81]

And I am the readier to favour this Conjecture, from a common Observation; that in the several Assemblies of these Orators, Nature itself has instructed the Hearers to stand with their Mouths open, and erected parallel to the Horizon, so as they may be intersected by a perpendicular Line from the Zenith to the Centre of the Earth. In which Position, if the Audience be well compact, every one carries home a Share, and little or nothing is lost.

I confess there is something yet more refined in the Contrivance and Structure of our Modern Theatres. For, First; the Pit is sunk below the Stage with due Regard to the Institution above deduced; that whatever *weighty* Matter shall be delivered thence (whether it be *Lead* or *Gold*) may fall plumb into the Jaws of certain *Critics* (as I think they are called) which stand ready open to devour them. Then, the Boxes are built round, and raised to a Level with the Scene, in deference to the Ladies, because, That large Portion of Wit laid out in raising Pruriences[82] and Protuberances, is observed to run much upon a Line, and ever in a Circle. The whining Passions, and little starved Conceits, are gently wafted up by their own extreme Levity, to the middle Region, and there fix and are frozen by the frigid Understandings of the Inhabitants. Bombast and Buffoonery, by nature lofty and light, soar highest of all, and would be lost in the Roof, if the prudent Architect had not with much Foresight contrived for them a fourth Place, called the *Twelve-Penny Gallery*, and there planted a suitable Colony, who greedily intercept them in their Passage.

Now this Physico-logical Scheme of Oratorial Receptacles or Machines, contains a great Mystery, being a Type, a Sign, an Emblem, a Shadow, a Symbol, bearing Analogy to the spacious Commonwealth of Writers, and to those Methods by which they must exalt

Notes

[78] *stage-itinerant* Is the Mountebank's Stage [note in fifth edition].

[79] *sub Jove ... quadriviis* In the open Air, and in Streets where the greatest Resort is [note in fifth edition].

[80] *Epicurus* Lucret. [De *Rerum Natura*] Lib. 2 [Swift's marginal note].

[81] *Corpoream ... Lib.* 4 "'Tis certain then, that Voice that thus can wound/Is all Material; Body every Sound" [note in fifth edition from Creech's Lucretius (1683), 4.526–7].

[82] *Prurience* "An itching or a great desire or appetite to any thing" (Johnson, quoting Swift).

themselves to a certain Eminency above the inferior World. By the *Pulpit* are adumbrated the Writings of our *Modern Saints* in *Great Britain*, as they have spiritualized and refined them from the Dross and Grossness of *Sense* and *Human Reason*. The Matter, as we have said, is of rotten Wood, and that upon two Considerations; Because it is the Quality of rotten Wood to give *Light* in the Dark: And secondly, Because its Cavities are full of Worms: Which is a Type with a Pair of Handles, having a Respect to the two principal Qualifications of the Orator, and the two different Fates attending upon his Works.[83]

The *Ladder* is an adequate Symbol of *Faction*[84] and of *Poetry*, to both of which so noble a Number of Authors are indebted for their Fame. Of *Faction* because * *
* * * * * * * * * * * *
* * * * * * * * [*Hiatus in MS*]* *
* * * * * * * * * * * *
* * Of *poetry*, because its Orators do *perorare*[85] with a Song; and because climbing up by slow Degrees, Fate is sure to turn them off before they can reach within many Steps of the Top: And because it is a Preferment attained by transferring of Propriety, and a confounding of *Meum* and *Tuum*.[86]

Under the *Stage-itinerant* are couched those Productions designed for the Pleasure and Delight of Mortal Man, such as, *Six-penny-worth of Wit*, Westminster *Drolleries, Delightful Tales, Complete Jesters*,[87] and the like, by which the Writers of and for *GRUBSTREET*, have in these later Ages so nobly triumphed over *Time*; have clipped his Wings, pared his Nails, filed his Teeth, turned back his Hour-Glass, blunted his Scythe, and drawn the Hob-Nails out of his Shoes. It is under this *Classis*, I have presumed to list my present Treatise, being just come from having the Honour conferred upon me to be adopted a Member of that illustrious Fraternity.

Now, I am not unaware, how the Productions of the *Grub-Street* Brotherhood, have of late years fallen under many Prejudices; nor how it has been the perpetual Employment of two *Junior* start-up Societies to ridicule them and their Authors, as unworthy their established Post in the Commonwealth of Wit and Learning. Their own Consciences will easily inform them, whom I mean; Nor has the World been so negligent a Looker on, as not to observe the continual Efforts made by the Societies of *Gresham*[88] and of *Will's*[89] to edify a Name and Reputation upon the Ruin of OURS. And this is yet a more feeling Grief to Us upon the Regards of Tenderness as well as of Justice, when we reflect on their Proceedings, not only as unjust, but as ungrateful, undutiful, and unnatural. For, how can it be forgot by the World or themselves (to say nothing of our own Records, which are full and clear in the Point) that they both are Seminaries not only of our *Planting*, but our *Watering* too? I am informed, Our two *Rivals* have lately made an Offer to enter into the Lists with united Forces, and challenge Us to a Comparison of Books, both as to *Weight* and *Number*. In Return to which (with Licence from our *President*) I humbly offer two Answers: First, We say, the Proposal is like that which *Archimedes*[90] made upon a *smaller* Affair, including an Impossibility in the Practice; For, where can

Notes

[83] *Type ... Works* The Two Principal Qualifications of a fanatic Preacher are his Inward Light, and his Head full of Maggots, and the Two different Fates of his Writings are to be burnt or Worm eaten [note in fifth edition].

[84] *Faction* political partisanship; dissension; tumult.

[85] *perorare* deliver the final part of a speech.

[86] *Meum and Tuum* mine and yours.

[87] *Six-penny-worth of Wit ... Complete Jesters* real and typical titles of cheap publications or chapbooks.

[88] *Gresham* the Royal Society, which met at Gresham College until 1710.

[89] *Will's* a coffeehouse made a famous center for writers and wits by Dryden's patronage.

[90] *Archimedes* Syracusan mathematician and philosopher of the third century BCE; Swift probably refers to one of his works, *The Sand-reckoner*, which demonstrates how the number of grains of sand in the universe could be calculated.

they find Scales of *Capacity* enough for the first, or an Arithmetician of *Capacity* enough for the second. Secondly, We are ready to accept the Challenge, but with this Condition, that a third indifferent Person be assigned, to whose impartial Judgement it shall be left to decide, which Society each Book, Treatise or Pamphlet do most properly belong to. This Point, God knows, is very far from being fixed at present; For, We are ready to produce a Catalogue of some Thousands, which in all common Justice ought to be entitled to Our Fraternity, but by the revolted and newfangled Writers most perfidiously ascribed to the others. Upon all which, we think it very unbecoming our Prudence, that the Determination should be remitted to the Authors themselves; when our Adversaries by Briguing and Caballing,[91] have caused so universal a Defection from us, that the greatest Part of our Society hath already deserted to them, and our nearest Friends begin to stand aloof, as if they were half ashamed to own Us.

This is the utmost I am authorized to say upon so ungrateful and melancholy a Subject; because We are extreme unwilling to inflame a Controversy, whose Continuance may be so fatal to the Interests of Us All, desiring much rather that Things be amicably composed. And We shall so far advance on our Side, as to be ready to receive the two *Prodigals*[92] with open Arms, whenever they shall think fit to return from their *Husks*[93] and their *Harlots*; which I think from the present Course of their Studies they most properly may be said to be engaged in; and like an indulgent Parent, continue to them our Affection and our Blessing.

But the greatest Maim given to that general Reception, which the Writings of our Society have formerly received, next to the transitory State of all sublunary Things, hath been a superficial Vein among many Readers of the present Age, who will by no means be persuaded to inspect beyond the Surface and the Rind of Things; whereas, *Wisdom* is a *Fox*, who after long hunting, will at last cost you the Pains to dig out: 'Tis a *Cheese*, which by how much the richer, has the thicker, the homelier, and the coarser Coat; and whereof, to a judicious Palate, the *Maggots* are the best. 'Tis a *Sack-Posset*,[94] wherein the deeper you go, you will find it the sweeter. *Wisdom* is a *Hen*, whose *Cackling* we must value and consider, because it is attended with an *Egg*; But then, lastly, 'tis a *Nut*, which unless you choose with Judgement, may cost you a Tooth, and pay you with nothing but a *Worm*. In consequence of these momentous Truths, the *Grubæan* Sages have always chosen to convey their Precepts and their Arts, shut up within the Vehicles of Types and Fables, which having been perhaps more careful and curious in adorning, than was altogether necessary, it has fared with these Vehicles after the usual Fate of Coaches over-finely painted and gilt; that the transitory Gazers have so dazzled their Eyes, and filled their Imaginations with the outward Lustre, as neither to regard nor consider the Person or the Parts of the Owner within. A Misfortune we undergo with somewhat less Reluctancy, because it has been common to us with *Pythagoras*,[95] *Æsop*, *Socrates*, and other of our Predecessors.

However, that neither the World nor ourselves may any longer suffer by such Misunderstandings, I have been prevailed on, after much importunity from my Friends, to travail in a complete and laborious Dissertation upon the prime Productions of our Society, which besides their beautiful Externals for the Gratification of superficial

Notes

91 *Briguing and Caballing* intriguing.

92 *Prodigals*recalling the parable of the prodigal son (Luke 15.11–32).

93 *Husks* corn husks in the biblical story, the only food left for the prodigal son before he returns home, but here, the Royal Society's meaningless objects of inquiry, as Swift saw it.

94 *Sack-Posset* a kind of alcoholic eggnog.

95 *Pythagoras* his precepts were collected in the form of pithy sayings requiring interpretation.

Readers, have darkly and deeply couched under them, the most finished and refined Systems of all Sciences and Arts; as I do not doubt to lay open by Untwisting or Unwinding, and either to draw up by Exantlation,[96] or display by Incision.

This great Work was entered upon some Years ago, by one of our most eminent Members: He began with the History of *Reynard* the *Fox* but neither lived to publish his Essay, nor to proceed further in so useful an Attempt, which is very much to be lamented, because the Discovery he made, and communicated with his Friends, is now universally received; Nor, do I think, any of the Learned will dispute, that famous Treatise to be a complete Body of Civil Knowledge, and the *Revelation*, or rather the *Apocalypse*, of all State *Arcana*. But the Progress I have made is much greater, having already finished my Annotations upon several Dozens: From some of which, I shall impart a few Hints to the candid Reader, as far as will be necessary to the Conclusion at which I aim.

The first Piece I have handled is that of *Tom Thumb*, whose Author was a *Pythagorean* Philosopher. This dark Treatise contains the whole Scheme of the *Metempsychosis*,[97] deducing the Progress of the Soul through all her Stages.

The next is *Doctor Faustus*, penned by *Artephius*,[98] an Author *bonæ notæ* and an *Adeptus*. He published it in the nine hundred eighty fourth Year of his Age; this Writer proceeds wholly by *Reincrudation*, or in the *via humida*: And the marriage between *Faustus* and *Helen*, does most conspicuously dilucidate the fermenting of the *Male* and *Female Dragon*.

Whittington and his Cat, is the Work of that Mysterious *Rabbi, Jehuda Hannasi*; containing a Defence of the *Gemara* of the *Jerusalem Misna*, and its just preference to that of *Babylon*, contrary to the vulgar Opinion.

The Hind and Panther. This is the Masterpiece of a famous Writer now living,[99] intended for a complete Abstract of sixteen thousand Schoolmen from *Scotus* to *Bellarmine*.[100]

Tommy Pots.[101] Another Piece supposed by the same Hand, by way of Supplement to the former.

The Wise Men of Gotham,[102] *cum Appendice*. This is a Treatise of immense Erudition, being the great Original and Fountain of those Arguments, bandied about both in *France* and *England*, for a just Defence of the *Modern* Learning and Wit, against the Presumption, the Pride, and the Ignorance of the *Ancients*. This unknown Author hath so exhausted the Subject that a penetrating Reader will easily discover, whatever hath been written since upon that Dispute, to be little more than Repetition. An Abstract of this Treatise[103] hath been lately published by a *worthy Member* of our Society.

These Notices may serve to give the Learned Reader an Idea, as well as a Taste, of what the whole Work is likely to produce: wherein I have now altogether circumscribed my Thoughts and my Studies; and if I can bring it to a Perfection before I die, shall reckon I have well employed the poor Remains of an unfortunate Life.[104]

Notes

96 *Exantlation* "The act of drawing out; exhaustion" (Johnson).

97 *Metempsychosis* transmigration of the soul in rebirth, a Pythagorean belief.

98 *Artephius* an alchemist; the paragraph is full of alchemical terms.

99 *Writer now living* Viz. in the Year 1697 [Swift's marginal note; the writer is John Dryden (d. 1700)].

100 *Scotus* Duns Scotus, thirteenth-century Scottish theologian; *Bellarmine* Cardinal Robert Bellarmine, sixteenth-century Roman Catholic theologian.

101 *Tommy Pots* a romantic ballad, formally entitled *The Lovers' Quarrel*.

102 *The Wise Men of Gotham* another chapbook romance.

103 *An Abstract of this Treatise* This I suppose to be understood of Mr. W[o]tt[o]n's *Discourse of Ancient and Modern Learning* [note in fifth edition].

104 *an unfortunate Life* Here the Author seems to [im]personate [Roger] L'Estrange [1616–1704], Dryden, and some others, who after having passed their Lives in Vice, Faction and Falsehood, have the Impudence to talk of Merit and Innocence and Sufferings [note in fifth edition].

This indeed is more than I can justly expect from a Quill worn to the Pith in the Service of the State, in *Pro's* and *Con's* upon *Popish Plots*, and *Meal Tubs*, and *Exclusion Bills*, and *Passive Obedience*, and *Addresses of Lives and Fortunes*; and *Prerogative*, and *Property*, and *Liberty of Conscience*, and *Letters to a Friend*:[105] From an Understanding and a Conscience, threadbare and ragged with perpetual turning; From a Head broken in a hundred places, by the Malignants of the opposite Factions; and from a Body spent with Poxes ill-cured, by trusting to Bawds and Surgeons, who (as it afterwards appeared) were professed Enemies to Me and the Government, and revenged their Party's Quarrel upon my Nose and Shins. Fourscore and eleven Pamphlets have I writ under three Reigns, and for the service of six and thirty Factions. But finding the State has no further Occasion for Me and my Ink, I retire willingly to draw it out into Speculations more becoming a Philosopher, having to my unspeakable Comfort, passed a long Life, with a *Conscience void of Offence towards God and towards Men*.

But to return. I am assured from the Reader's Candour that the brief Specimen I have given, will easily clear all the rest of our Society's Productions, from an Aspersion grown, as it is manifest, out of Envy and Ignorance: That they are of little further Use or Value to Mankind, beyond the common Entertainments of their Wit and their Style: For, these I am sure have never yet been disputed by our keenest Adversaries: In both which, as well as the more profound and mystical Part, I have throughout this Treatise closely followed the most applauded Originals. And to render all complete, I have with much Thought and Application of Mind, so ordered that the chief Title prefixed to it (I mean, That under which I design it shall pass in the common Conversations of Court and Town) is modelled exactly after the Manner peculiar to *Our* Society.

I confess to have been somewhat liberal in the Business of Titles,[106] having observed the Humour of multiplying them, to bear great Vogue among certain Writers, whom I exceedingly Reverence. And indeed, it seems not unreasonable, that Books, the Children of the Brain, should have the Honour to be Christened with a variety of Names, as well as other Infants of Quality. Our famous *Dryden* has ventured to proceed a Point further, endeavouring to introduce also a Multiplicity of *Godfathers*;[107] which is an Improvement of much more Advantage, upon a very obvious Account. 'Tis a Pity this admirable invention has not been better cultivated, so as to grow by this time into general Imitation, when such an Authority serves it for a Precedent. Nor have my Endeavours been wanting to second so useful an Example: But it seems, there is an unhappy Expense usually annexed to the Calling of a Godfather, which was clearly out of my Head, as it is very reasonable to believe. Where the Pinch lay, I cannot certainly affirm; but having employed a World of Thoughts and Pains, to split my Treatise into forty Sections, and having entreated forty Lords of my Acquaintance, that they would do me the Honour to stand, they all made it a Matter of Conscience and sent me their Excuses.

Notes

[105] *Pro's and Con's … Letters to a Friend* polemical publications and issues addressed by Dryden and L'Estrange.

[106] *Titles* The Title Page in the Original was so torn, that it was not possible to recover several Titles which the Author here speaks of [Swift's marginal note].

[107] *Multiplicity of Godfathers* Dryden dedicated his *Aeneas* to three patrons.

Sect. II

Once upon a Time, there was a Man who had three Sons[108] by one Wife, and all at a Birth, neither could the Midwife tell certainly which was the Eldest. Their Father died while they were young, and upon his Death-Bed, calling the Lads to him, spoke thus.

'Sons; Because I have purchased no Estate, nor was born to any, I have long considered of some good Legacies to bequeath You; And at last, with much Care as well as Expense, have provided each of you (here they are) a new Coat.[109] Now, you are to understand, that these Coats have two Virtues contained in them: One is, that with good wearing, they will last you fresh and sound as long as you live: The other is, that they will grow in the same Proportion with your Bodies, lengthening and widening of themselves, so as to be always fit. Here, let me see them on you before I die. So, very well, Pray Children, wear them clean, and brush them often. You will find in my Will[110] (here it is) full Instructions in every Particular concerning the Wearing and Management of your Coats; wherein you must be very exact, to avoid the Penalties I have appointed for every Transgression or Neglect, upon which your future Fortunes will entirely depend. I have also commanded in my Will, that you should live together in one House like Brethren and Friends, for then you will be sure to thrive, and not otherwise'.

Here the story says, this good Father died, and the three Sons went all together to seek their Fortunes.

I shall not trouble you with recounting, what Adventures they met for the first seven Years, any further than by taking notice, that they carefully observed their Father's Will, and kept their Coats in very good Order; That they travelled through several Countries, encountered a reasonable Quantity of Giants, and slew certain Dragons.

Being now arrived at the proper Age for producing themselves, they came up to Town, and fell in love with the Ladies, but especially three, who about that time were in chief Reputation: The Duchess *d'Argent, Madame de Grands Titres*, and the Countess *d'Orgueil*.[111] On their first Appearance, our three Adventurers met with a very bad Reception; and soon with great Sagacity guessing out the Reason, they quickly began to improve in the good Qualities of the Town: They Writ, and Rallied, and Rhymed, and Sung, and Said, and said Nothing; They Drank, and Fought, and Whored, and Slept, and Swore, and took Snuff; They went to new Plays on the first Night, haunted the *Chocolate*-Houses, beat the Watch, lay on Bulks,[112] and got Claps: They bilked[113] Hackney-Coachmen, ran in Debt with Shopkeepers, and lay with their Wives: They killed Bailiffs, kicked Fiddlers down Stairs, eat at *Locket's*,[114] loitered at *Will's*: They talked of the Drawing-Room and never came there; Dined with Lords they never saw; Whispered a Duchess, and spoke never a Word; exposed the Scrawls of their Laundress for Billets-doux[115] of Quality; came ever just from Court, and were never seen in it; attended the Levee *sub dio*;[116] Got a List of the Peers by heart in one Company, and with great Familiarity retailed them in another. Above all, they constantly attended those

Notes

108 *three Sons* By these three Sons, Peter, Martin and Jack, Popery, the Church of England, and our Protestant Dissenters are designed. W. Wotton [note in fifth edition].

109 *Coat* the Doctrine and Faith of Christianity [note in fifth edition].

110 *Will* The New Testament [note in fifth edition].

111 *d'Argent, Grands Titres, d'Orgueil* Covetousness, Ambition and Pride [note in fifth edition].

112 *Bulks* stalls outside of shops.

113 *bilked* cheated (of fares or other profits).

114 *Locket's* a fashionable restaurant in Charing Cross, London.

115 *Billets-doux* love letters.

116 *Levee sub dio* sunrise (or morning) entertainment of a nobleman in the open air.

Committees of Senators who are silent in the *House*, and loud in the *CoffeeHouse*, where they nightly adjourn to chew the Cud of Politics, and are encompassed with a Ring of Disciples, who lie in wait to catch up their Droppings. The three Brothers had acquired forty other Qualifications of the like Stamp, too tedious to recount, and by consequence, were justly reckoned the most accomplished Persons in Town: But all would not suffice, and the Ladies aforesaid continued still inflexible: To clear up which Difficulty, I must with the Reader's good Leave and Patience, have recourse to some Points of Weight which the Authors of that Age have not sufficiently illustrated.

For, about this Time it happened, a Sect arose, whose Tenets obtained and spread very far, especially in the *Grand monde*, and among every Body of good Fashion. They worshipped a sort of *Idol*,[117] who as their Doctrine delivered, did daily create Men, by a kind of Manufactory Operation. This *Idol* they placed in the highest Parts of the House, on an Altar erected about three Foot: He was shown in the Posture of a *Persian* Emperor, sitting on a *Superficies*,[118] with his Legs interwoven under him. This God had a *Goose*[119] for his Ensign; whence it is, that some Learned Men pretend to deduce his Original from *Jupiter Capitolinus*.[120] At his left Hand, beneath the Altar, *Hell* seemed to open, and catch at the Animals the *Idol* was creating; to prevent which, certain of his Priests hourly flung in Pieces of the uninformed Mass, or Substance, and sometimes whole Limbs already enlivened, which that horrid Gulf insatiably swallowed, terrible to behold. The *Goose* was also held a Subaltern Divinity, or *Deus minorum gentium*,[121] before whose Shrine was sacrificed that Creature, whose hourly Food is Human Gore, and who is in so great Renown abroad, for being the Delight and Favourite of the *Ægyptian Cercopithecus*.[122] Millions of these Animals were cruelly slaughtered every Day, to appease the Hunger of that consuming Deity. The chief *Idol* was also worshipped as the Inventor of the *Yard*[123] and *Needle*,[124] whether as the God of Seamen, or on Account of certain other mystical Attributes, hath not been sufficiently cleared.

The Worshippers of this Deity had also a System of their Belief, which seemed to turn upon the following Fundamentals. They held the Universe to be a large *Suit of Clothes*, which *invests* every Thing: That the Earth is *invested* by the Air; The Air is *invested* by the Stars; and the Stars are *invested* by the *Primum Mobile*.[125] Look on this Globe of Earth, you will find it to be a very complete and fashionable *Dress*. What is that which some call *Land*, but a fine Coat faced with Green? or the Sea, but a Waistcoat of Water-Tabby?[126] Proceed to the particular Works of the Creation, you will find how curious [a] *Journey-man* Nature hath been, to trim up the *vegetable* Beaux: Observe how sparkish a Periwig adorns the Head of a *Beech*, and what a fine Doublet of white Satin is worn by the *Birch*. To conclude from all, What is Man himself but a *Micro-Coat*,[127] or rather a complete Suit of Clothes with all its Trimmings. As to his Body, there can be no Dispute; but examine even the Acquirements of his Mind, you will find them all contribute in their Order, towards furnishing out an

Notes

[117] *Idol* By this idol is meant a Tailor [note in fifth edition].

[118] *Superficies* "A flat or level surface" (*OED*, 2.b.).

[119] *Goose* after the gooseneck of the tailor's iron.

[120] *Jupiter Capitolinus* Jupiter's temple, the Roman capitol, was said to have been saved by geese.

[121] *Deus minorum gentium* "God of lesser people."

[122] *Ægyptian Cercopithecus* The Ægyptians worshipped a Monkey, which Animal is very fond of eating Lice, styled here Creatures that feed on Human Gore [note in fifth edition].

[123] *Yard* the support of a sail on a ship.

[124] *Needle* compass.

[125] *Primum Mobile* the first mover or outermost sphere in the Ptolemaic system of the universe.

[126] *Tabby* "A kind of waved silk" (Johnson).

[127] *Micro-Coat* Alluding to the Word *Microcosm*, or a little World, as Man hath been called by Philosophers [note in fifth edition].

exact Dress: To instance no more; Is not Religion a *Cloak*, Honesty a *Pair of Shoes*, worn out in the Dirt, Self-love a *surtout*,[128] Vanity a *Shirt*, and Conscience a *Pair of Breeches*, which though a Cover for Lewdness as well as Nastiness, is easily slipped down for the Service of both?

These *Postulata* being admitted, it will follow in due course of Reasoning, that those Beings which the World calls improperly *Suits of Clothes*, are in Reality the most refined Species of Animals, or to proceed higher, that they are Rational Creatures, or Men. For, is it not manifest, that They live, and move, and talk, and perform all other Offices of Human Life? Are not Beauty, and Wit, and Mien, and Breeding, their inseparable Proprieties? In short, we see nothing but them, hear nothing but them. Is it not They who walk the Streets, fill up *Parliament-*, *Coffee-*, *Play-*, *Bawdy-houses*. 'Tis true indeed, that these Animals, which are vulgarly called *Suits of Clothes*, or *Dresses*, do according to certain Compositions receive different Appellations. If one of them be trimmed up with a Gold Chain, and a red Gown, and a white Rod, and a great Horse, it is called a *Lord Mayor*; If certain Ermines and Furs be placed in a certain Position, we style them a *Judge*; and so, an apt conjunction of Lawn and black Satin, we entitle a *Bishop*.

Others of these Professors, though agreeing in the main System, were yet more refined upon certain Branches of it; and held that Man was an Animal compounded of two *Dresses*, the *Natural* and the *Celestial Suit*, which were the Body and the Soul: That the Soul was the outward, and the Body the inward Clothing; that the latter was *ex traduce*;[129] but the former, of daily Creation and Circumfusion. This last they proved by *Scripture*, because, 'in Them we Live, and Move, and have our Being';[130] As likewise by Philosophy, because they are 'All in All, and All in every Part'.[131] 'Besides', said they, 'Separate these two, and you will find the Body to be only a senseless unsavoury Carcass. By all which it is manifest, that the outward Dress must needs be the Soul'.

To this System of Religion were tagged several subaltern Doctrines, which were entertained with great Vogue; as particularly, the Faculties of the Mind were deduced by the Learned among them in this manner: *Embroidery*, was *Sheer Wit*; *Gold Fringe* was *agreeable Conversation; Gold Lace* was *Repartee*; a huge long *Periwig* was *Humour*; and a *Coat full of Powder* was very good *Raillery*: All which required abundance of *Finesse* and *Delicatesse* to manage with Advantage, as well as a strict Observance after Times and Fashions.

I have with much Pains and Reading, collected out of ancient Authors, this short Summary of a Body of Philosophy and Divinity, which seems to have been composed by a Vein and Race of Thinking, very different from any other Systems, either *Ancient* or *Modern*. And it was not merely to entertain or satisfy the Reader's Curiosity, but rather to give him Light into several Circumstances of the following Story: that knowing the State of Dispositions and Opinions in an Age so remote, he may better comprehend those great Events which were the Issue of them. I advise therefore the courteous Reader, to peruse with a world of Application, again and again, whatever I have written upon this Matter. And so leaving these broken Ends, I carefully gather up the chief Thread of my Story, and proceed.

These Opinions therefore were so universal, as well as the Practices of them, among the refined Part of Court and Town, that our three Brother Adventurers, as their

Notes

128 *surtout* "A large coat worn over all the rest" (Johnson).

129 *ex traduce* "by traduction" (see Dryden's "Ode to Anne Killigrew," l. 23, p. 218 above).

130 *"in Them ... Being"* see Acts 17.28, where it says "in him," meaning God.

131 *All in All ... Part* I Corinthians 15.28,where God is meant.

Circumstances then stood, were strangely at a loss. For, on the one side, the three Ladies they addressed themselves to (whom we have named already) were ever at the very Top of the Fashion, and abhorred all that were below it, but the breadth of a Hair. On the other side, their Father's Will was very precise, and it was the main Precept in it, with the greatest Penalties annexed, not to add to, or diminish from their Coats, one Thread, without a positive Command in the Will. Now, the Coats their Father had left them, were, 'tis true, of very good Cloth, and besides, so neatly sewn, you would swear they were all of a Piece, but at the same time, very plain, and with little or no Ornament; And it happened, that before they were a Month in Town, great *Shoulder-knots*[132] came up: Straight, all the World was *Shoulder-knots*; no approaching the Ladies' *Ruelles*[133] without the *Quota* of *Shoulder-knots*: *That Fellow*, cries one, *has no Soul; where is his Shoulder-knot?* Our three Brethren soon discovered their Want by sad Experience, meeting in their Walks, with forty Mortifications and Indignities. If they went to the *Playhouse*, the Door-keeper showed them into the Twelve-penny Gallery. If they called a Boat, says a Waterman, 'I am first Sculler':[134] If they stepped to the *Rose* to take a Bottle, the Drawer would cry, 'Friend we sell no ale'. If they went to visit a Lady, a Footman met him at the Door with, 'Pray send up your message'. In this unhappy Case, they went immediately to consult their Father's Will, read it over and over, but not a Word of the *Shoulder-knots*. What should they do? What Temper should they find? Obedience was absolutely necessary, and yet *Shoulder-knots* appeared extremely requisite. After much Thought, one of the Brothers who happened to be more *Book-learned* than the other two, said, he had found an Expedient. ''Tis true', said he, 'there is nothing here in this Will, *totidem verbis*,[135] making mention of *Shoulderknots*, but I dare conjecture, we may find them *inclusivè*,[136] or *totidem syllabis*.'[137] This Distinction was immediately approved by all; and so they fell again to examine the Will. But their evil Star had so directed the Matter, that the first Syllable was not to be found in the whole Writing. Upon which Disappointment, he who found the former Evasion, took heart, and said, 'Brothers, there is yet Hopes; for though we cannot find them *totidem verbis*, nor *totidem syllabis*, I dare engage we shall make them out *tertio modo*, or *totidem literis*'.[138] This Discovery was also highly commended, upon which they fell once more to the Scrutiny, and soon picked out *S,H,O,U,L,D,E,R*; when the same Planet,[139] Enemy to their Repose, had wonderfully contrived, that a *K* was not to be found. Here was a weighty Difficulty! But the distinguishing Brother (for whom we shall hereafter find a Name) now his Hand was in, proved by a very good Argument that *K* was a modern illegitimate Letter, unknown to the Learned Ages nor anywhere to be found in ancient Manuscripts. ''Tis true', said he, 'the Word *Calendæ* hath in *Q.V.C.*[140] been sometimes writ with a *K*, but erroneously, for in the best Copies it is ever spelt with a *C*. And by consequence it was a gross Mistake in our Language to spell *Knot* with a *K*, but that from henceforward, he would take care it should be writ with a *C*. Upon this, all further Difficulty vanished; *Shoulder-knots* were made clearly out, to be *Jure Paterno*,[141] and our three Gentlemen swaggered with as large and as flaunting ones as the best.

Notes

[132] *Shoulder-knots* By this is understood the first introducing of Pageantry, and unnecessary Ornaments in the Church ... [note in fifth edition; another note indicates that the Roman Catholic Church is represented in this section on Peter].

[133] *Ruelle* "circle" or "assembly at a private house" (Johnson).

[134] *Sculler* a one-man scull or small boat.

[135] *totidem verbis* "in so many words."

[136] *inclusivè* medieval Latin, "included" or "by inclusion."

[137] *totidem syllabis* "in so many syllables."

[138] *totidem literis* "in so many letters."

[139] *Planet* astrological influence, fortune.

[140] *Q.V.C. Quibusdam Veteribus Codicibus* [Swift's marginal note; "certain old books"].

[141] *Jure Paterno* "by the father's law," in imitation of *iure divino*.

But, as Human Happiness is of a very short Duration, so in those Days were Human Fashions, upon which it entirely depends. *Shoulder-knots* had their Time, and we must now imagine them in their Decline; for a certain Lord came just from *Paris* with fifty Yards of *Gold Lace* upon his Coat, exactly trimmed after the Court Fashion of *that Month*. In two Days all Mankind appeared closed up in Bars of *Gold Lace*: Whoever durst peep abroad without his Complement of *Gold Lace*, was as scandalous as a——, and as ill received among the Women. What should our three Knights do in this momentous Affair; They had sufficiently strained a Point already, in the Affair of *Shoulder-knots*: Upon recourse to the Will, nothing appeared there but *altum silentium*.[142] That of the *Shoulder-knots* was a loose, flying, circumstantial Point; but this of *Gold Lace*, seemed too considerable an Alteration without better Warrant; it did *aliquo modo essentiæ adhærere*,[143] and therefore required a positive Precept. But about this Time it fell out, that the learned Brother aforesaid, had read *Aristotelis Dialectica*, and especially that wonderful Piece *de Interpretatione*, which has the Faculty of teaching its Readers to find out a Meaning in every Thing but itself, like Commentators on the *Revelations*, who proceed Prophets without understanding a Syllable of the Text. 'Brothers', said he, 'you are to be informed, that, of Wills, *duo sunt genera*,[144] Nuncupatory [145] and Scriptory; that in the Scriptory Will here before us, there is no Precept or Mention about Gold Lace, *conceditur*; But, *si idem affirmetur de nuncupatorio, negatur*.[146] 'For, Brothers, if you remember, we heard a Fellow say when we were Boys, that he heard my Father's Man say, that he heard my Father say, that he would advise his Sons to get *Gold Lace* on their Coats, as soon as ever they could Procure Money to buy it'. 'By G—that is very true', cries the other. 'I remember it perfectly well', said the third. And so without more ado they got the largest *Gold Lace* in the Parish, and walked about as fine as Lords.

A while after, there came up *all in Fashion*, a pretty sort of *flame-coloured Satin* for Linings, and the *Mercer* brought a Pattern of it immediately to our three Gentlemen. 'An please your worships', said he, 'my Lord C[utts] and Sir J[ohn] W[alters] had Linings out of this very Piece last Night, it takes wonderfully, and I shall not have a Remnant left, enough to make my Wife a Pincushion by tomorrow Morning at ten o'Clock'. Upon this they fell again to rummage the Will, because the present Case also required a positive Precept, the Lining being held by Orthodox Writers to be of the Essence of the Coat. After long search, they could fix upon nothing to the Matter in hand, except a short Advice of their Father's in the Will, to take Care of *Fire*, and put out their *Candles* before they went to Sleep. This, though a good deal for the Purpose, and helping very far towards Self-Conviction, yet not seeming wholly of Force to establish a Command; and being resolved to avoid further Scruple,[147] as well as future Occasion for Scandal, says He that was the Scholar, 'I remember to have read in Wills, of a Codicil annexed, which is indeed a Part of the Will, and what it contains hath equal Authority with the rest. Now, I have been considering of this same Will here before us, and I cannot reckon it to be complete, for want of such a Codicil. I will therefore fasten one in its proper Place very dexterously; I have had it by me some Time, it was written by a Dog-keeper of my Grandfather's, and talks a great deal (as good Luck would have it) of this very flame-coloured Satin'. The Project was

Notes

142 *altum silentium* "deep silence."

143 *aliquo modo ... adhærere* "belonged to another category."

144 *duo sunt genera* "there are two kinds."

145 *Nuncupatory* "verbally pronounced" (Johnson).

146 *conceditur... negatur* "it is conceded, but if it is affirmed concerning the nuncupatory kind, it is denied."

147 *Scruple* doubt.

immediately approved by the other two; an old Parchment Scroll was tagged on according to Art, in the Form of a *Codicil annexed*, and the *Satin* bought and worn.

Next Winter, a *Player*, hired for the Purpose by the Corporation of *Fringe-makers*, acted his Part in a new Comedy, all covered with *Silver Fringe*, and according to the laudable Custom gave Rise to that Fashion. Upon which, the Brothers consulting their Father's Will, to their great Astonishment found these Words, '*Item*, I charge and command my said three sons to wear no sort of *Silver Fringe* upon, or about their said coats', &c., with a Penalty in case of Disobedience, too long here to insert. However, after some Pause, the Brother so often mentioned for his Erudition, who was well skilled in Criticisms, had found in a certain Author which he said should be nameless, that the same Word which in the Will is called *Fringe*, does also signify a *Broomstick*, and doubtless ought to have the same Interpretation in this Paragraph. This, another of the Brothers disliked, because of that Epithet, *Silver*, which could not, he humbly conceived, in Propriety of Speech be reasonably applied to a *Broomstick*: But it was replied upon him, that this Epithet was understood in a *Mythological*, and *Allegorical* Sense. However, he objected again, why their Father should forbid them to wear a *Broomstick* on their Coats, a Caution that seemed unnatural and impertinent: Upon which he was taken up short, as one that spoke irreverently of a *Mystery*, which doubtless was very useful and significant, but ought not to be over-curiously pried into, or nicely reasoned upon. And in short, their Father's Authority being now considerably sunk, this Expedient was allowed to serve as a lawful Dispensation, for wearing their full Proportion of *Silver Fringe*.

A while after, was revived an old Fashion, long antiquated, of *Embroidery* with *Indian Figures* of Men, Women, and Children. Here they had no Occasion to examine the Will. They remembered but too well, how their Father had always abhorred this Fashion; that he made several Paragraphs on purpose, importing his utter Detestation of it, and bestowing his everlasting Curse to his Sons, whenever they should wear it. For all this, in a few Days, they appeared higher in the Fashion than anybody else in Town. But they solved the Matter by saying, that these Figures were not at all the *same* with those that were formerly worn, and were meant in the Will: Besides, they did not wear them in that Sense, as forbidden by their Father, but as they were a commendable Custom, and of great use to the Public. That these rigorous Clauses in the Will did therefore require some *Allowance*, and a favourable Interpretation, and ought to be understood *cum grano Salis*.[148]

But, Fashions perpetually altering in that Age, the Scholastic Brother grew weary of searching further Evasions, and solving everlasting Contradictions. Resolved therefore at all Hazards to comply with the Modes of the World, they concerted Matters together, and agreed unanimously, to lock up their Father's Will in a *Strong-Box*, brought out of *Greece* or *Italy*[149] (I have forgot which) and trouble themselves no further to examine it, but only refer to its Authority whenever they thought fit. In consequence whereof, a while after, it grew a general Mode to wear an infinite Number of *Points*,[150] most of them *tagged with Silver*: Upon which the Scholar pronounced *ex Cathedra*, that *Points* were absolutely *Jure Paterno*, as they might very well remember. 'Tis true indeed, the Fashion prescribed somewhat more than were directly named in

Notes

148 *cum grano Salis* "with a grain of salt," i.e., loosely.

149 *Greece or Italy* Greek or Latin, the languages of scripture in the Roman Catholic Church, as a note in the fifth edition explains.

150 *Point* "A string with a tag" (Johnson), for lacing.

the Will; However, that they, as Heirs general of their Father, had Power to make and add certain Clauses for public Emolument, though not deducible *totidem verbis* from the Letter of the Will, or else, *Multa absurda sequerentur*.[151] This was understood for *Canonical*, and therefore on the following *Sunday* they came to Church all covered with *Points*.

The Learned Brother so often mentioned, was reckoned the best Scholar in all that, or the next Street to it; insomuch, as having run something behindhand with the World, he obtained the Favour from a *certain Lord*, to receive him into his House and to teach his Children. A while after, the *Lord* died, and He by long practice upon his Father's Will, found the Way of contriving a *Deed of Conveyance*[152] of that House to Himself and his Heirs: Upon which he took Possession, turned the young Squires out, and received his Brothers in their stead.

Sect. III
A Digression concerning Critics

Though I have been hitherto as cautious as I could, upon all Occasions, most nicely to follow the Rules and Methods of Writing, laid down by the Example of our illustrious *Moderns*; yet has the unhappy shortness of my Memory led me into an Error, from which I must immediately extricate myself, before I can decently pursue my principal Subject. I confess with Shame, it was an unpardonable Omission to proceed so far as I have already done, before I had performed the due Discourses, Expostulatory, Supplicatory, or Deprecatory, with my *good Lords* the *Critics*. Towards some Atonement for this grievous Neglect, I do here make humbly bold to present them with a short Account of Themselves and their *Art*, by looking into the Original and Pedigree of the Word, as it is generally understood among us, and very briefly considering the ancient and present State thereof.

By the Word, *Critic*, at this Day so frequent in all Conversations, there have sometime been distinguished three very different Species of Mortal Men, according as I have read in *Ancient Books and Pamphlets*. For first, by this Term was understood such Persons as invented or drew up Rules for Themselves and the World, by observing which, a careful Reader might be able to pronounce upon the Productions of the *Learned*, form his Taste to a true Relish of the *Sublime* and the *Admirable*, and divide every Beauty of Matter or of Style from the Corruption that Apes it: In their common Perusal of Books, singling out the Errors and Defects, the Nauseous, the Fulsome, the Dull, and the Impertinent, with the Caution of a Man that walks through *Edinburgh* Streets in a Morning, who is indeed as careful as he can, to watch diligently, and spy out the Filth in his Way; not that he is curious to observe the Colour and Complexion of the Ordure, or take its Dimensions, much less to be paddling in, or tasting it: but only with a Design to come out as cleanly as he may. These Men seem, though very erroneously, to have understood the Appellation of *Critic* in a literal Sense; That, one principal Part of his Office was, to Praise and Acquit; and, that a *Critic* who sets up to Read only for an Occasion of Censure and Reproof, is a

Notes

[151] *Multa absurda sequerentur* "much absurdity would follow."

[152] *Deed of Conveyance* allegorical reference to the Donation of Constantine, a document that discusses the supposed grant of spiritual and temporal authority by the Emperor Constantine to Pope Sylvester I (314–35) and his successors; the validity of this forgery was still being debated in Swift's time.

Creature as barbarous, as a *Judge*, who should take up a Resolution to *hang* all Men that came before Him upon a Trial.

Again; by the Word, *Critic*, have been meant, the Restorers of Ancient Learning from the Worms, and Graves, and Dust of Manuscripts.

Now, the Races of those two have been for some Ages utterly extinct; and besides, to Discourse any further of them would not be at all to my Purpose.

The Third, and noblest Sort, is that of the *TRUE CRITIC*, whose Original is the most Ancient of all. Every *True Critic* is a Hero born, descending in a direct Line from a Celestial Stem, by *Momus* and *Hybris*, who begat *Zoilus*, who begat *Tigellius*,[153] who begat *Etcætera* the Elder, who begat *B—t—ly*, and *Rym—r*, and *W—tt—n*, and *Perrault*,[154] and *Dennis*, who begat *Etcætera* the Younger.

And these are the *Critics*, from whom the Commonwealth of Learning has in all Ages received such immense Benefits, that the Gratitude of their Admirers placed their Origin in Heaven, among those of *Hercules, Theseus, Perseus*, and other great Deservers of Mankind. But Heroic Virtue itself hath not been exempt from the Obloquy of evil Tongues. For it hath been objected, that those Ancient Heroes, famous for their Combating so many Giants, and Dragons, and Robbers, were in their own Persons a greater Nuisance to Mankind, than any of those Monsters they subdued; And therefore, to render their Obligations more Complete, when all *other* Vermin were destroyed, should in Conscience have concluded with the same Justice upon themselves: as *Hercules* most generously did,[155] and hath upon that Score, procured to himself more Temples and Votaries than the best of his Fellows. For these Reasons, I suppose it is, why some have conceived, it would be very expedient for the Public Good of Learning, that every *True Critic*, as soon as he had finished his Task assigned, should immediately deliver himself up to Ratsbane or Hemp, or from some convenient *Altitude*; and that no Man's Pretensions to so Illustrious a Character, should by any means be received, before That Operation were performed.

Now, from this Heavenly Descent of *Criticism*, and the close Analogy it bears to *Heroic Virtue*, 'tis easy to assign the proper Employment of a *True, Ancient, Genuine Critic*; which is, to travel through this vast World of Writings: to pursue and hunt those Monstrous Faults bred within them: to drag out the lurking Errors, like *Cacus* from his Den; to multiply them like *Hydra*'s Heads; and rake them together like *Augeas*'s Dung.[156] Or else to drive away a sort of *dangerous Fowl*, who have a perverse inclination to plunder the best Branches of the *Tree of Knowledge*, like those *Stymphalian* Birds that eat up the Fruit.[157]

These Reasonings will furnish us with an adequate Definition of a *True Critic*: that, he is a *Discoverer and Collector of Writers' Faults*. Which may be further put beyond Dispute by the following Demonstration: That whoever will examine the Writings in all kinds, wherewith this ancient Sect has honoured the World, shall immediately find from the whole Thread and Tenor of them, that the Ideas of the Authors have been altogether conversant, and taken up with the Faults, and Blemishes, and Oversights, and Mistakes of other Writers; and let the Subject treated on be whatever it will, their imaginations

Notes

153 *Momus, Hybris, Zoilus, Tigellius* the first is mythological, the second allegorical (overweening pride), and the last two are real critics, of Homer and Horace, respectively.

154 *Perrault* Charles (1628–1703), French champion of the moderns in the debate in which Swift is always for the ancients.

155 *Hercules ... did* he immolated himself on Mount Oeta to end his suffering from the poisonous shirt of Nessus.

156 *Cacus* (a fire-breathing giant) and *Hydra* (a nine-headed monster) were slain by Hercules; *Augeas* was a king whose huge, filthy stables Hercules had to cleanse.

157 *Stymphalian Birds* Hercules killed them, or at least expelled them from Arcadia.

are so entirely possessed and replete with the defects of other pens that the very quintessence of what is bad, does of necessity distil into their own; by which means the whole appears to be nothing else but an *abstract* of the *criticisms* themselves have made.

Having thus briefly considered the Original and Office of a *Critic*, as the Word is understood in its most noble and universal Acceptation, I proceed to refute the Objections of those who argue from the Silence and Pretermission[158] of Authors; by which they pretend to prove, that the very Art of *Criticism*, as now exercised, and by me explained, is wholly *Modern*; and consequently, that the *Critics* of *Great Britain* and *France* have no Title to an Original so Ancient and Illustrious as I have deduced. Now, if I can clearly make out on the contrary, that the most ancient Writers have particularly described, both the Person and the Office of a *True Critic*, agreeable to the Definition laid down by me; their grand Objection from the Silence of Authors will fall to the Ground.

I confess to have for a long time borne a Part in this general Error; From which I should never have acquitted myself, but through the Assistance of our Noble *Moderns* whose most edifying Volumes I turn indefatigably over Night and Day, for the Improvement of my Mind, and the Good of my Country: These have with unwearied Pains made many useful Searches into the weak Sides of the *Ancients*, and given us a comprehensive List of them. Besides, they have proved[159] beyond Contradiction, that the very finest Things delivered of old, have been long since invented, and brought to Light by much later Pens, and that the noblest Discoveries those *Ancients* ever made of Art or of Nature, have all been produced by the transcending Genius of the present Age. Which clearly shows, how little Merit those *Ancients* can justly pretend to; and takes off that blind Admiration paid them by Men in a Corner, who have the Unhappiness of conversing too little with *present Things*. Reflecting maturely upon all this, and taking in the whole Compass of Human Nature, I easily concluded, that these *Ancients*, highly sensible of their many Imperfections, must needs have endeavoured from some Passages in their Works, to obviate, soften, or divert the Censorious Reader, by *Satire*, or *Panegyric* upon the *True Critics*, in Imitation of their *Masters* the *Moderns*. Now, in the *Common-Places* of both these, I was plentifully instructed, by a long Course of useful Study in *Prefaces* and *Prologues*; and therefore immediately resolved to try what I could discover of either, by a diligent Perusal of the most Ancient Writers, and especially those who treated of the earliest Times. Here I found to my great Surprise, that although they all entered, upon Occasion, into particular Descriptions of the *True Critic*, according as they were governed by their Fears or their Hopes: yet whatever they touched of that kind, was with abundance of Caution, adventuring no further than *Mythology* and *Hieroglyphic*. This, I suppose, gave ground to superficial Readers, for urging the Silence of Authors, against the Antiquity of the *True Critic*, though the *Types* are so apposite, and the Applications so necessary and natural, that it is not easy to conceive, how any Reader of a *Modern Eye* and *Taste* could overlook them. I shall venture from a great Number to produce a few, which I am very confident, will put this Question beyond Dispute.

It well deserves considering, that these *Ancient Writers* in treating Enigmatically upon this Subject, have generally fixed upon the very *same Hieroglyph*, varying only the Story according to their Affections or their Wit. For first; *Pausanias*[160] is of Opinion,

Notes

158 *Pretermission* "The act of omitting" (Johnson).

159 *they have proved* See Wotton, *Of Ancient and Modern Learning* [Swift's marginal note].

160 *Pausanias* Greek traveller and geographer of the second century CE.

that the Perfection of Writing correct, was entirely owing to the Institution of *Critics*; and, that he can possibly mean no other than the *True Critic*, is, I think, manifest enough from the following Description. He says, 'They were a Race of Men, who delighted to nibble at the Superfluities, and Excrescencies of Books; which the Learned at length observing, took Warning of their own Accord, to lop the Luxuriant, the Rotten, the Dead, the Sapless, and the Overgrown Branches from their Works'. But now, all this he cunningly shades under the following Allegory; that the *Nauplians* in *Argia*, learned the Art of pruning their Vines, by observing, that when an *ASS* had browsed upon one of them, it thrived the better, and bore fairer Fruit.[161] But *Herodotus*, holding the very same Hieroglyph, speaks much plainer, and almost *in terminis*. He hath been so bold to tax the *True Critics* of Ignorance and Malice; telling us openly, for I think nothing can be plainer, that in the Western Part of *Libya*, there were *ASSES* with *HORNS*:[162] Upon which Relation *Ctesias* yet refines, mentioning the very same animal about *India*, adding, That 'whereas all other *ASSES* wanted a *Gall*, these horned ones were so redundant in that Part that their Flesh was not to be eaten, because of its extreme *Bitterness*'.

Now, the Reason why those Ancient Writers treated this Subject only by Types and Figures, was, because they durst not make open Attacks against a Party so Potent and Terrible, as the *Critics* of those Ages were: whose very Voice was so Dreadful, that a Legion of Authors would tremble, and drop their Pens at the Sound; For so *Herodotus* tells us expressly in another Place, how a vast Army of *Scythians* was put to flight in a Panic Terror, by the Braying of an *ASS*.[163] From hence it is conjectured by certain profound *Philologers*, that the great Awe and Reverence paid to a *True Critic* by the Writers of *Britain*, have been derived to Us, from those our *Scythian* Ancestors. In short, this Dread was so universal, that in process of Time, those Authors who had a mind to publish their Sentiments more freely, in describing the *True Critics* of their several Ages, were forced to leave off the use of the former Hieroglyph, as too nearly approaching the *Prototype*, and invented other Terms instead thereof, that were more cautious and mystical; so *Diodorus* speaking to the same purpose, ventures no further than to say, that 'in the Mountains of *Helicon* there grows a certain *Weed*, which bears a Flower of so damned a Scent, as to poison those who offer to smell it'. *Lucretius* gives exactly the same Relation:

> *Est etiam in magnis Heliconis montibus arbos,*
> *Floris odore hominem retro consueta necare.*
> Lib. 6.[164]

But *Ctesias*, whom we lately quoted, hath been a great deal bolder; He had been used with much severity by the *True Critics* of his own Age, and therefore could not forbear to leave behind him, at least one deep Mark of his Vengeance, against the whole Tribe. His Meaning is so near the Surface, that I wonder how it possibly came to be overlooked by those who deny the Antiquity of the *True Critics*. For pretending to make a Description of many strange Animals about *India*, he hath set down these remarkable Words. 'Among the rest', says he, 'there is a *Serpent* that wants *Teeth*, and consequently cannot bite, but if its *Vomit* (to which it is much addicted) happens to fall upon any

Notes

161 *ASS … Fruit* Pausanias 2.38.

162 *HORNS* Herodotus 4.191.

163 *Braying of an ASS* Herodotus 4.129.

164 *Lib. 6* "Near Helicon, and round the Learned Hill, Grow Trees, whose Blossoms with their Odour kill" [note in fifth edition, citing Creech's Lucretius, 6.786–7].

Thing, a certain Rottenness or Corruption ensues: These Serpents are generally found among the Mountains where *Jewels* grow, and they frequently emit a *poisonous juice*, whereof, whoever drinks, that Person's *Brains* flies out of his Nostrils'.[165]

There was also among the *Ancients* a sort of *Critic*, not distinguished in *Specie* from the Former, but in Growth or Degree, who seem to have been only the *Tyros* or *junior Scholars*; yet because of their differing Employments, they are frequently mentioned as a Sect by themselves. The usual exercise of these younger Students, was to attend constantly at Theatres, and learn to spy out the *worst Parts* of the Play, whereof they were obliged carefully to take Note and render a rational Account, to their tutors. Fleshed at these smaller Sports, like young Wolves, they grew up in Time, to be nimble and strong enough for hunting down large Game. For it hath been observed both among Ancients and Moderns, that a *True Critic* hath one Quality in common with a *Whore* and an *Alderman*, never to change his Title or his Nature; that a *Grey Critic* has been certainly a *green* one, the Perfections and Acquirements of his Age being only the improved Talents of his Youth; like *Hemp*, which some Naturalists inform us, is bad for *Suffocations*, though taken but in the *Seed*. I esteem the invention, or at least the Refinement of *Prologues*, to have been owing to these younger Proficients, of whom *Terence*[166] makes frequent and honourable mention, under the Name of *Malevoli*.

Now, 'tis certain, the Institution of the *True Critics*, was of absolute Necessity to the Commonwealth of Learning. For all Human Actions seem to be divided like *Themistocles* and his Company; One Man can *Fiddle*, and another can make *a Small Town a great City*;[167] and he that cannot do either one or the other, deserves to be kicked out of the Creation. The avoiding of which Penalty, has doubtless given the first Birth to the Nation of *Critics*, and withal, an Occasion for their secret Detractors to report that a *True Critic* is a sort of Mechanic,[168] set up with a Stock and Tools for his Trade, at as little Expense as a *Tailor*; and that there is much Analogy between the Utensils and Abilities of both: That the *Tailor's Hell*[169] is the Type of a Critic's *Commonplace-Book*, and his Wit and Learning held forth by the *Goose*:[170] That it requires at least as many of these, to the making up of one Scholar, as of the other to the Composition of a Man:[171] That the Valour of both is equal, and their *Weapons* near of a Size. Much may be said in answer to those invidious Reflections; and I can positively affirm the first to be a Falsehood. For, on the contrary, nothing is more certain, than that it requires greater Layings out, to be free of the *Critic*'s Company, than of any other you can name. For, as to be a *true Beggar*, it will cost the richest Candidate every Groat he is worth; so, before one can commence a *True Critic* it will cost a Man all the good Qualities of his Mind; which, perhaps, for a less Purchase, would be thought but an indifferent Bargain.

Having thus amply proved the Antiquity of *Criticism* and described the Primitive State of it; I shall now examine the present Condition of this Empire, and show how well it agrees with its ancient self. A certain Author whose Works have many Ages since been entirely lost, does in his fifth Book and eighth Chapter, say of *Critics*, that 'their Writings are the Mirrors of Learning'.[172] This I understand in a literal Sense, and

Notes

165 This and the other citations from Ctesias (fourth-century BCE Greek physician and historian of Persia and India) are genuine.

166 *Terence* Roman comic dramatist of the second century BCE.

167 *Themistocles ... City* the Greek general's boyhood claim for himself, in contrast to his schoolmates, according to Plutarch, *Life of Themistocles* 2.

168 *Mechanic* "A manufacturer; a low workman" (Johnson).

169 *Tailor's Hell* "The place into which the tailor throws his shreds" (Johnson).

170 *Goose* "A tailor's smoothing iron" (Johnson).

171 *as many... of a Man* "Nine tailors make a man" (*Oxford Dictionary of English Proverbs*).

172 *A certain Author... Learning* A Quotation after the manner of a great Author. Vide Bentley's Dissertation &c. [Swift's marginal note].

suppose our Author must mean, that whoever designs to be a perfect Writer, must inspect into the Books of *Critics*, and correct his Invention there as in a Mirror. Now, whoever considers, that the *Mirrors* of the Ancients were made of Brass, and *sine Mercurio*,[173] may presently apply the two principal Qualifications of a *True Modern Critic*, and consequently, must needs conclude, that these have always been and must be for ever the same. For, *Brass* is an Emblem of Duration, and when it is skilfully burnished, will cast *Reflections* from its own *Superficies*, without any Assistance of *Mercury* from behind. All the other Talents of a *Critic* will not require a particular Mention, being included, or easily deducible to these. However, I shall conclude with three Maxims, which may serve both as Characteristics to distinguish a *True Modern Critic* from a Pretender, and will be also of admirable Use to those worthy Spirits, who engage in so useful and honourable an Art.

The first is, That *Criticism*, contrary to all other Faculties of the Intellect, is ever held the truest and best, when it is the very *first* Result of the *Critic*'s Mind: As Fowlers reckon the first Aim for the surest, and seldom fail of missing the Mark if they stay for a Second.

Secondly, the *True Critics* are known by their Talent of swarming about the noblest Writers, to which they are carried merely by Instinct, as a Rat to the best Cheese, or a wasp to the fairest Fruit. So, when the *King* is a Horseback, he is sure to be the *dirtiest* Person of the Company, and they that make their Court best, are such as *bespatter* him most.

Lastly, a *True Critic*, in the Perusal of a Book, is like a *Dog* at a Feast, whose Thoughts and Stomach are wholly set upon what the Guests *fling away*, and consequently, is apt to *Snarl* most, when there are the fewest *Bones*.

Thus much, I think, is sufficient to serve by way of Address to my Patrons, the *True Modern Critics*, and may very well atone for my past Silence, as well as That which I am like to observe for the future. I hope, I have deserved so well of their whole *Body*, as to meet with generous and tender Usage at their *Hands*. Supported by which Expectation, I go on boldly to pursue those Adventures already so happily begun.

Sect. IV
A Tale of a Tub

I have now, with much Pains and Study, conducted the Reader to a Period, where he must expect to hear of great Revolutions. For no sooner had Our *Learned Brother*, so often mentioned, got a warm House of his own over his Head, than he began to look big, and to take mightily upon him; insomuch, that unless the Gentle Reader, out of his great Candour, will please a little to exalt his Idea, I am afraid he will henceforth hardly know the *Hero* of the Play, when he happens to meet Him; his Part, his Dress, and his Mien being so much altered.

He told his Brothers, he would have them to know, that he was their Elder, and consequently his Father's sole Heir; Nay, a while after, he would not allow them to call Him *Brother*, but *Mr. PETER*; and then he must be styled, *Father PETER*; and sometimes, *My Lord PETER*. To support this Grandeur, which he soon began to consider, could not be maintained without a Better *Fonde*[174] than what he was born to; after much Thought, he cast about at last, to turn *Projector* and *Virtuoso*; wherein he so well

Notes

[173] *sine Mercurio* "without Mercury," or without talent, since Mercury is associated with wit.

[174] *Fonde* foundation.

succeeded, that many famous Discoveries, Projects, and Machines, which bear great Vogue and Practice at present in the World, are owing entirely to *Lord Peter*'s Invention. I will deduce the best Account I have been able to collect of the Chief amongst them, without considering much the Order they came out in; because I think Authors are not well agreed as to that Point.

I hope, when this Treatise of mine shall be translated into Foreign Languages (as I may without Vanity affirm, That the Labour of collecting, the Faithfulness in recounting, and the great Usefulness of the Matter to the Public, will amply deserve that Justice) that the worthy Members of the several *Academies* abroad, especially those of *France* and *Italy*, will favourably accept these humble Offers, for the advancement of Universal Knowledge. I do also advertise the most Reverend Fathers, the *Eastern* Missionaries, that I have purely for their sakes, made use of such Words and Phrases, as will best admit an easy Turn into any of the *Oriental* Languages, especially the *Chinese*. And so I proceed with great Content of Mind, upon reflecting, how much Emolument this whole Globe of the Earth is like to reap by my Labours.

The first Undertaking of *Lord Peter* was to purchase a large Continent,[175] lately said to have been discovered in *Terra Australis incognita*.[176] This Tract of Land he bought at a very great Pennyworth from the Discoverers themselves (though some pretended to doubt whether they had ever been there) and then retailed it into several Cantons to certain Dealers, who carried over Colonies but were all Shipwrecked in the Voyage. Upon which, *Lord Peter* sold the said Continent to other Customers *again*, and *again*, and *again*, with the same Success.

The second Project I shall mention, was his Sovereign Remedy for the *Worms*, especially those in the *Spleen*.[177] The Patient was to eat nothing after Supper for three Nights: As soon as he went to Bed, he was carefully to lie on one Side, and when he grew weary, to turn upon the other: He must also duly confine his two Eyes to the same Object; and by no means break Wind at both Ends together, without manifest Occasion. These Prescriptions diligently observed, the *Worms* would void insensibly by Perspiration, ascending through the Brain.

A third Invention, was the erecting of a *Whispering-Office*,[178] for the Public Good and Ease of all such as were Hypochondriacal, or troubled with the Colic; likewise of all Eavesdroppers, Physicians, Midwives, small Politicians, Friends fallen out, Repeating Poets, Lovers Happy or in Despair, Bawds, Privy-Counsellors, Pages, Parasites, and Buffoons; In short, of all such as are in Danger of bursting with too much *Wind*. An *Ass*'s Head was placed so conveniently, that the Party affected might easily with his Mouth accost either of the Animal's Ears; which he was to apply close for a certain Space, and by a fugitive Faculty, peculiar to the Ears of that Animal, receive immediate Benefit either by Eructation, or Expiration, or Evomition.

Another very beneficial Project of *Lord Peter*'s, was an *Office of Insurance*[179] for Tobacco-Pipes, Martyrs of the Modern Zeal, Volumes of Poetry, Shadows, ———and Rivers: That these, nor any of these shall receive Damage by *Fire*. From whence our *Friendly Societies* may plainly find themselves, to be only Transcribers from this

Notes

[175] *a large Continent* Purgatory [note in fifth edition].

[176] *Terra Australis incognita* "unexplored southern land," the West Indies.

[177] *Sovereign Remedy… Spleen* Here the Author ridicules the Penances of the Church of Rome, which may be made as easy to the Sinner as he pleases, provided he will pay for them accordingly [note in fifth edition].

[178] *Whispering-Office* confession.

[179] *Office of Insurance* insurance policies; indulgences, according to later notes, which could subtract time from one's future stay in Purgatory.

Original; though the one and the other have been of *great* Benefit to the Undertakers, as well as of *equal* to the Public.

Lord Peter was also held the Original Author of *Puppets* and *Raree-Shows*;[180] the great Usefulness whereof being so generally known, I shall not enlarge further upon this Particular.

But, another Discovery for which he was much renowned, was his famous universal *Pickle*.[181] For, having remarked how your common *Pickle* in use among Housewives, was of no further Benefit than to preserve dead Flesh, and certain kinds of Vegetables; *Peter*, with great Cost as well as Art, had contrived a *Pickle* proper for Houses, Gardens, Towns, Men, Women, Children, and Cattle; wherein he could preserve them as Sound as Insects in Amber. Now, this *Pickle* to the Taste, the Smell, and the Sight, appeared exactly the same, with what is in common Service for Beef, and Butter, and Herrings (and has been often that way applied with great Success) but for its many Sovereign Virtues, was quite a different Thing. For *Peter* would put in a certain Quantity of his *Powder Pimperlin-pimp*, after which it never failed of Success. The Operation was performed by *Spargefaction*[182] in a proper Time of the Moon. The Patient who was to be *pickled*, if it were a House, would infallibly be preserved from all Spiders, Rats, and Weasels; If the Party affected were a Dog, he should be exempt from Mange, and Madness, and Hunger. It also infallibly took away all Scabs and Lice, and scalled Heads[183] from Children never hindering the Patient from any Duty, either at Bed or Board.

But of all *Peter's* Rarities, he most valued a certain Set of *Bulls*,[184] whose Race was by great Fortune preserved in a lineal Descent from those that guarded the *Golden-Fleece*. Though some who pretended to observe them curiously, doubted the Breed had not been kept entirely chaste; because they had degenerated from their Ancestors in some Qualities, and had acquired others very extraordinary, but a Foreign Mixture. The *Bulls of Colchos* are recorded to have *brazen Feet*; But whether it happened by ill Pasture and Running, by an Allay[185] from Intervention of other Parents, from stolen Intrigues; Whether a Weakness in their Progenitors had impaired the seminal Virtue; Or by a Decline necessary through a long Course of Time, the Originals of Nature being depraved in these latter sinful Ages of the World; Whatever was the Cause, 'tis certain that *Lord Peter's Bulls* were extremely vitiated by the Rust of Time in the Metal of their Feet, which was now sunk into common *Lead*. However, the terrible *roaring* peculiar to their Lineage, was preserved; as likewise that Faculty of breathing out *Fire* from their Nostrils; which notwithstanding, many of their Detractors took to be a Feat of Art, and to be nothing so terrible as it appeared; proceeding only from their usual Course of Diet, which was of *Squibs* and *Crackers*.[186] However, they had two peculiar Marks which extremely distinguished them from the *Bulls* of *Jason*, and which I have not met together in the Description of any other Monster, beside that in Horace;

Varias inducere plumas;
and
Atrum desinit in piscem.[187]

Notes

180 *Puppets and Raree-Shows* ceremonies.

181 *Pickle* holy water.

182 *Spargefaction* "The act of sprinkling" (Johnson).

183 *scalled Heads* or "scall," "Leprosy; morbid baldness" (Johnson).

184 *Bulls* The Papal *Bulls* [pronouncements] are ridiculed by Name, So that here we are at no loss for the Author's Meaning. W. Wotton [note in fifth edition].

185 *Allay* repression, check (*OED*, 9).

186 *Squibs and Crackers* firecrackers and, metaphysically, sarcasms and empty boasts.

187 *Varias ... piscem* "to put in parti-coloured feathers" and "[a woman above] who ends as an ugly fish"; parts of the description of a ridiculous monster in the opening of Horace's *Ars Poetica*.

For, these had *Fishes' Tails*, yet upon Occasion could *out-fly* any Bird in the Air. *Peter* put these *Bulls* upon several Employs. Sometimes he would set them a *roaring* to fright *Naughty Boys*, and make them quiet. Sometimes he would send them out upon Errands of great Importance; where it is wonderful to recount, and perhaps the cautious Reader may think much to believe it; an *Appetitus Sensibilis*,[188] deriving itself through the whole Family, from their Noble Ancestors, Guardians of the *Golden Fleece*; they continued so extremely fond of *Gold*, that if *Peter* sent them abroad, though it were only upon a Compliment;[189] they would *Roar*, and *Spit*, and *Belch*, and *Piss*, and *Fart*, and *Snivel* out *Fire*, and keep a perpetual Coil, till you flung them a Bit of *Gold*; but then *Pulveris exigui jactu*,[190] they would grow calm and quiet as Lambs. In short, whether by secret Connivance or Encouragement from their Master, or out of their own liquorish[191] Affection to Gold, or both; it is certain they were no better than a sort of sturdy, swaggering Beggars; and where they could not prevail to get an Alms, would make Women miscarry, and Children fall into Fits, who to this day usually call Sprites and Hobgoblins by the Name of *Bull-Beggars*.[192] They grew at last so very troublesome to the Neighbourhood, that some Gentlemen of the *North-West* got a Parcel of right *English Bull-Dogs*, and baited them so terribly, that they felt it ever after.[193]

I must needs mention one more of *Lord Peter*'s Projects, which was very extraordinary and discovered him to be a Master of a high Reach, and profound Invention. Whenever it happened that any Rogue of *Newgate* was condemned to be hanged, *Peter* would offer him a Pardon for a certain Sum of Money, which when the poor Caitiff had made all Shifts to scrape up and send, *His Lordship* would return a Piece of Paper in this Form:

> To all Mayors, Sheriffs, Jailors, Constables, Bailiffs, Hangmen, &c. Whereas we are informed that *A. B.* remains in the Hands of you, or any of you, under the Sentence of Death, We will and command you upon Sight hereof, to let the said Prisoner depart to his own Habitation, whether he stands condemned for Murder, Sodomy, Rape, Sacrilege, Incest, Treason, Blasphemy, &c. for which this shall be your Sufficient Warrant. And if you fail hereof, G—d—mn You and Yours to all Eternity. And so we bid you heartily Farewell.
>
> Your most Humble
> Man's Man,
> EMPEROR PETER.

The Wretches trusting to this, lost their Lives and Money too.

I desire of those whom the *Learned* among Posterity will appoint for Commentators upon this elaborate Treatise; that they will proceed with great Caution upon certain dark Points, wherein all who are not *Verè adepti*,[194] may be in Danger to form rash and

Notes

188 *Appetitus Sensibilis* fleshly or carnal desire, as opposed to an intellectual interest.

189 *upon a Compliment* as a formal greeting.

190 *Pulveris exigui jactu* "after a little dusting" (Virgil, *Georgics* 4.87), a method of controlling bees.

191 *liquorish* lickerish, lustful.

192 *Bull-Beggars* "This word probably came from the insolence of those who begged, or raised money by the pope's bull. Something terrible; something to fright children with" (Johnson).

193 *baited them ... ever after* in the formation of the Church of England under Henry VIII.

194 *Verè adepti* Latin, "truly in possession (of the requisite knowledge)"; in its anglicized form, "adept" was a name for accomplished alchemists and practitioners of other arts.

hasty Conclusions, especially in some mysterious Paragraphs where certain *Arcana* are joined for Brevity sake, which in the Operation must be divided. And, I am certain, that future Sons of Art, will return large Thanks to my Memory, for so grateful, so useful an *Innuendo*.

It will be no difficult Part to persuade the Reader, that so many worthy Discoveries met with Great success in the World, though I may justly assure him, that I have related much the smallest Number; My Design having been only to single out such, as will be of most Benefit for Public Imitation, or which best served to give some Idea of the Reach and Wit of the Inventor. And therefore it need not be wondered, if by this Time, *Lord Peter* was become exceeding Rich. But alas, he had kept his Brain so long, and so violently upon the Rack, that at last it *shook* itself and began to *turn round* for a little Ease. In short, what with Pride, Projects, and Knavery, poor *Peter* was grown distracted, and conceived the strangest Imaginations in the World. In the Height of his Fits (as it is usual with those who run Mad out of Pride) he would call Himself *God Almighty*, and sometimes, *Monarch of the Universe*. 'I have seen him', says my Author,[195] 'take three old *high-crowned Hats*, and clap them all on his Head, three Storey high, with a huge Bunch of *Keys* at his Girdle, and an *Angling-Rod* in his Hand. In which Guise, whoever went to take him by the Hand in the Way of Salutation, *Peter* with much Grace, like a well-educated Spaniel, would present them with his *Foot*; and if they refused his Civility, then he would raise it as high as their Chops, and give them a damned Kick on the Mouth, which hath ever since been called a *Salute*. Whoever walked by without paying him their Compliments, having a wonderful strong Breath, he would blow their Hats off into the Dirt'. Meantime, his Affairs at home went upside down; and his two Brothers had a wretched Time; where his first *Boutade*[196] was to kick both their *Wives* one Morning out of Doors, and his own too, and in their stead, gave Orders to pick up the first three Strollers could be met with in the Streets. A while after, he nailed up the Cellar Door, and would not allow his Brothers a Drop of *Drink* to their Victuals. Dining one Day at an Alderman's in the City, *Peter* observed him expatiating after the manner of his Brethren, in the Praises of his Sirloin of Beef. 'Beef', said the Sage Magistrate, 'is the King of Meat; Beef comprehends in it the Quintessence of Partridge, and Quail, and Venison, and Pheasant, and Plum-pudding, and Custard'. When *Peter* came home, he would needs take the Fancy of cooking up this Doctrine into use, and apply the Precept in default of a Sirloin, to his brown Loaf. 'Bread', says he, 'Dear Brothers, is the Staff of Life; in which Bread is contained, *inclusivè*, 'the Quintessence of Beef, Mutton, Veal, Venison, Partridge, Plum-pudding, and Custard: And to render all complete, there is intermingled a due Quantity of Water, whose Crudities are also corrected by Yeast or Barm, through which means it becomes a wholesome fermented Liquor, diffused through the Mass of the Bread'. Upon the Strength of these Conclusions, next Day at Dinner[197] was the brown Loaf served up in all the Formality of a City Feast. 'Come, Brothers', said Peter, 'fall to, and spare not; here is excellent good Mutton; or hold, now my Hand is in, I'll help you'. At which word, in much Ceremony, with Fork and Knife, he carves out two good Slices of the Loaf, and presents each on a Plate to his Brothers. The Elder of the two, not suddenly entering into *Lord Peter's* Conceit, began with very civil Language to examine the Mystery. 'My Lord', said he, 'I doubt, with great Submission, there may be some Mistake'. 'What', says Peter, 'you are pleasant; Come then, let us hear this Jest, your Head is so big with'.

Notes

195 *Author* authority, whom the speaker quotes.

196 *Boutade* sudden motion.

197 *Dinner* Holy Communion.

'None in the World, my Lord; but unless I am very much deceived, your Lordship was pleased a while ago, to let fall a word about Mutton, and I would be glad to see it with all my Heart'. 'How', said *Peter*, appearing in great Surprise, 'I do not comprehend this at all'. Upon which, the younger interposing to set the Business right, 'My Lord', said he, 'My Brother, I suppose, is hungry, and longs for the Mutton, your Lordship hath promised us to Dinner'. 'Pray', said Peter, 'take me along with you; either you are both Mad, or disposed to be merrier than I approve of: If *You* there, do not like your Piece I will carve you another, though I should take that to be the choice Bit of the whole Shoulder'.

'What then, my Lord', replied the first, 'it seems this is a Shoulder of Mutton all this while'.

'Pray, Sir', says Peter, 'eat your Vittles and leave off your Impertinence, if you please, for I am not disposed to relish it at present'. But the other could not forbear, being over provoked at the affected Seriousness of *Peter*'s Countenance. 'By G—, My Lord', said he, 'I can only say, that to my Eyes, and Fingers, and Teeth, and Nose, it seems to be nothing but a Crust of Bread'. Upon which the second put in his Word: 'I never saw a piece of Mutton in my Life, so nearly resembling a Slice from a Twelve-penny Loaf'.

'Look ye, Gentlemen', cries Peter in a Rage, 'to convince you what a couple of blind, positive, ignorant, wilful Puppies you are, I will use but this plain Argument: By G—, it is true, good, natural Mutton as any in Leaden-Hall Market; and G—confound you both eternally, if you offer to believe otherwise'. Such a thundering Proof as this, left no further Room for Objection: The two Unbelievers began to gather and pocket up their Mistake as hastily as they could. 'Why, truly', said the first, 'upon more mature Consideration' – 'Ay', says the other, interrupting him, 'now I have thought better on the Thing, your Lordship seems to have a great deal of Reason'.

'Very well', said Peter, 'Here Boy, fill me a Beer-Glass of Claret. Here's to you both with all my Heart'. The two Brethren much delighted to see him so readily appeased, returned their most humble Thanks and said they would be glad to pledge His Lordship. 'That you shall', said Peter, 'I am not a Person to refuse you any Thing that is reasonable; Wine moderately taken, is a Cordial; Here is a Glass a piece for you; 'Tis true natural Juice from the Grape; none of your damned *Vintners*' Brewings'. Having spoke thus, he presented to each of them another large dry Crust, bidding them drink it off, and not be bashful, for it would do them no Hurt. The two Brothers, after having performed the usual Office in such delicate Conjectures, of staring a sufficient Period at *Lord Peter*, and each other; and finding how Matters were like to go, resolved not to enter on a new Dispute, but let him carry the Point as he pleased; for he was now got into one of his mad Fits, and to Argue or Expostulate further, would only serve to render him a hundred times more untractable.

I have chosen to relate this worthy Matter in all its Circumstances, because it gave a principal Occasion to that great and famous *Rupture*,[198] which happened about the same time among these Brethren, and was never afterwards made up. But of that, I shall treat at large in another Section.

However, it is certain that *Lord Peter*, even in his lucid Intervals, was very lewdly given in his common Conversation, extreme wilful and positive, and would at any time rather argue to the Death, than allow himself once to be in an Error. Besides, he

Notes

198 *Rupture* By this Rupture is meant the Reformation [note in fifth edition].

had an abominable Faculty of telling huge palpable *Lies* upon all Occasions; and swearing, not only to the Truth, but cursing the whole Company to Hell, if they pretended to make the least Scruple of believing Him. One time, he swore, he had a *Cow*[199] at home, which gave as much Milk at a Meal as would fill three thousand Churches; and what was yet more extraordinary, would never turn Sour. Another time, he was telling of an old *Sign-Post*[200] that belonged to his *Father*, with Nails and Timber enough on it, to build sixteen large Men of War. Talking one Day of *Chinese* Wagons, which were made so light as to sail over Mountains: 'Z—ds', said Peter, 'where's the Wonder of that? By G—, I saw a Large House[201] of Lime and Stone travel over Sea and Land (granting that it stopped sometimes to bait[202]) above two thousand German Leagues'. And that which was the good of it, he would swear desperately all the while that he never told a Lie in his Life; And at every Word, 'By G—, Gentlemen, I tell you nothing but the Truth, and the D—l broil them eternally that will not believe me'.

In short, *Peter* grew so scandalous, that all the Neighbourhood began in plain Words to say, he was no better than a Knave. And his two Brothers long weary of his ill Usage, resolved at last to leave him; but first, they humbly desired a Copy of their Father's *Will*, which had now lain by neglected, time out of Mind. Instead of granting this Request he called them 'damned Sons of Whores, Rogues, Traitors', and the rest of the vile Names he could muster up. However, while he was abroad one Day upon his Projects, the two Youngsters watched their Opportunity, made a Shift to come at the *Will*, and took a *Copia vera*,[203] by which they presently saw how grossly they had been abused: Their Father having left them equal Heirs, and strictly commanded, that whatever they got, should lie in common among them all. Pursuant to which, their next Enterprise was to break open the Cellar-Door, and get a little good *Drink* to spirit and comfort their Hearts. In copying the *Will*, they had met another Precept against Whoring, Divorce, and separate Maintenance; Upon which their next Work was to discard their Concubines, and send for their Wives. Whilst all this was in agitation, there enters a Solicitor from *Newgate*, desiring *Lord Peter* would please procure a *Pardon* for a *Thief* that was to be *hanged* tomorrow. But the two Brothers told him, he was a Coxcomb to seek Pardons from a Fellow, who deserved to be hanged much better than his Client; and discovered all the Method of that Imposture, in the same Form I delivered it a while ago, advising the Solicitor to put his Friend upon obtaining *a Pardon from the King*.[204] In the midst of all this Clutter and Revolution, in comes *Peter* with a File of Dragoons at his Heels, and gathering from all Hands what was in the Wind, he and his Gang, after several Millions of Scurrilities and Curses, not very important here to repeat, by main Force, very fairly kicks them both out of Doors, and would never let them come under his Roof from that Day to this.

Notes

199 *Cow* The ridiculous Multiplying of the Virgin *Mary's Milk* among the Papists, under the Allegory of a *Cow*, which gave as much Milk at a Meal, as would fill three thousand Churches. W. Wotton [note in fifth edition].

200 *Sign-Post* the Cross of our Blessed Saviour [note in fifth edition].

201 *Large House* The Chapel of Loreto [note in fifth edition; the shrine is supposed to be the house of the Virgin Mary, converted to a church, and later carried by angels in increments to Italy].

202 *Bait* "to stop for food and rest when traveling" (Merriam-Webster).

203 *took a Copia vera* Translated the Scriptures into the vulgar Tongues [note in fifth edition].

204 *Pardon from the King* to implore the Mercy of God [note in fifth edition].

Sect. V
A Digression in the Modern Kind

We whom the World is pleased to honour with the Title of *Modern Authors*, should never have been able to compass our great Design of an everlasting Remembrance, and never-dying Fame, if our Endeavours had not been so highly serviceable to the general Good of Mankind. This, *O Universe*, is the adventurous Attempt of me thy Secretary;

> —*Quemvis perferre laborem*
> *Suadet, et inducit noctes vigilare serenas.*[205]

To this End, I have some time since, with a World of Pains and Art, dissected the Carcass of *Human Nature*, and read many useful Lectures upon the several Parts, both *Containing* and *Contained*, till at last it *smelt* so strong, I could preserve it no longer. Upon which, I have been at a great Expense to fit up all the Bones with exact Contexture and in due Symmetry; so that I am ready to show a complete Anatomy thereof to all curious *Gentlemen and others*. But not to Digress further in the midst of a Digression, as I have known some Authors enclose Digressions in one another, like a Nest of Boxes, I do affirm, that having carefully cut up *Human Nature*, I have found a very strange, new, and important Discovery; that the Public Good of Mankind is performed by two Ways, *Instruction*, and *Diversion*. And I have further proved in my said several Readings (which, perhaps, the World may one day see, if I can prevail on any Friend to steal a Copy, or on certain Gentlemen of my Admirers, to be very Importunate) that, as Mankind is now disposed, he receives much greater Advantage by being *Diverted* than *Instructed*; His Epidemical Diseases being *Fastidiosity, Amorphy*, and *Oscitation*;[206] whereas in the present universal Empire of Wit and Learning, there seems but little Matter left for *Instruction*. However, in Compliance with a Lesson of great Age and Authority, I have attempted carrying the Point in all its Heights; and accordingly, throughout this Divine Treatise, have skilfully kneaded up both together with a *Layer* of *Utile*, and a *Layer* of *Dulce*.[207]

When I consider how exceedingly our Illustrious *Moderns* have eclipsed the weak glimmering lights of the *Ancients*, and turned them out of the Road of all fashionable Commerce, to a degree, that our choice Town Wits of most refined Accomplishments, are in grave Dispute whether there have been ever any *Ancients* or no: In which Point we are like to receive wonderful Satisfaction from the most useful Labours and Lucubrations of that Worthy *Modern*, Dr. *B—tly*. I say, when I consider all this, I cannot but bewail, that no famous *Modern* hath ever yet attempted an universal System in a small portable Volume, of all Things that are to be Known, or Believed, or Imagined, or Practised in Life. I am, however, forced to acknowledge that such an Enterprise was thought on some Time ago by a great Philosopher of *O. Brazile*.[208] The Method he proposed, was by a certain curious *Receipt*, a *Nostrum*,[209] which after his untimely Death, I found among his Papers; and do here out of my great Affection to the *Modern Learned*, present them with it, not doubting, it may one Day encourage some worthy Undertaker:

Notes

205 *Quemvis … serenas* "it urges me to shoulder the burden and induces me to study through the calm nights" (Lucretius, *De Rerum Natura* 1.141–2).

206 *Oscitation* "The act of yawning" (Johnson).

207 *Utile … Dulce* usefulness and pleasure, age-old categories.

208 *O. Brazile* an imaginary island … [note in fifth edition].

209 *Receipt, a Nostrum* prescription; it follows, full of alchemical jargon.

You take fair correct Copies, well bound in Calf's Skin, and Lettered at the Back, of all Modern Bodies of Arts and Sciences whatsoever, and in what Language you please. These you distil *in balneo Mariæ*, infusing *Quintessence of Poppy Q.S.*, together with three Pints of *Lethe*, to be had from the Apothecaries. You cleanse away carefully the *Sordes* and *Caput mortuum*, letting all that is volatile evaporate. You preserve only the first Running, which is again to be distilled seventeen times, till what remains will amount to about two Drams. This you keep in a Glass Vial, *Hermetically* sealed, for one and twenty Days. Then you begin your Catholic Treatise, taking every Morning fasting (first shaking the Vial) three Drops of this *Elixir*, snuffing it strongly up your Nose. It will dilate itself about the Brain (where there is any) in fourteen Minutes, and you immediately perceive in your Head an infinite Number of *Abstracts, Summaries, Compendiums, Extracts, Collections, Medullas, Excerpta quædams, Florilegas*, and the like, all disposed into great Order, and reducible upon Paper.

I must needs own, it was by the Assistance of this *Arcanum*, that I, though otherwise *impar*, have adventured upon so daring an Attempt; never achieved or undertaken before, but by a certain Author called *Homer*, in whom, though otherwise a Person, not without some Abilities, and *for an Ancient*, of a tolerable Genius; I have discovered many gross Errors, which are not to be forgiven his very Ashes, if by chance any of them are left. For whereas, we are assured, he designed his Work for a complete Body of all Knowledge, Human, Divine, Political, and Mechanic; it is manifest he hath wholly neglected some, and been very imperfect in the rest. For, first of all, as eminent a *Cabalist*[210] as his Disciples would represent Him, his account of the *Opus magnum* is extremely poor and deficient; he seems to have read but very superficially, either *Sendivogius, Behmen*, or *Anthroposophia Theomagica*. He is also quite mistaken about the *Sphæra Pyroplastica*, a neglect not to be atoned for; and (if the Reader will admit so severe a Censure) *Vix crederem Autorem hunc, unquam audivisse ignis vocem.*[211] His Failings are not less prominent in several Parts of the *Mechanics*. For, having read his Writings with the utmost Application usual among *Modern Wits*, I could never yet discover the least Direction about the Structure of that useful Instrument, a *Save-all.*[212] For want of which, if the *Moderns* had not lent their Assistance, we might yet have wandered *in the Dark*. But I have still behind, a Fault far more notorious to tax this Author with; I mean, his gross Ignorance in the *Common Laws of this Realm*, and in the Doctrine as well as Discipline of the Church of England. A Defect indeed, for which both he and all the Ancients stand most justly censured by my worthy and ingenious Friend Mr. W—tt—n, Bachelor of Divinity, in his incomparable Treatise of *Ancient and Modern Learning*; A Book never to be sufficiently valued, whether we consider the happy Turns and Flowings of the Author's Wit, the great Usefulness of his sublime Discoveries upon the Subject of *Flies* and *Spittle*, or the laborious Eloquence of his Style. And I cannot forbear doing that Author the Justice of my public Acknowledgements, for the great *Helps* and *Liftings* I had out of his incomparable Piece, while I was penning this Treatise.

But, besides these Omissions in *Homer* already mentioned, the curious Reader will also observe several Defects in that Author's Writings, for which he is not altogether so

Notes

210 *Cabalist* mystic philosopher, therefore familiar with the occult works and writers whose names follow.

211 *Vix ... vocem* "I can hardly believe that this author ever heard the voice of fire."

212 *Save-all* "A small pan inserted into a candlestick to save the ends of candles" (Johnson).

accountable. For whereas every Branch of Knowledge has received such wonderful Acquirements since his Age, especially within these last three Years, or thereabouts; it is almost impossible, he could be so very perfect in Modern Discoveries, as his Advocates pretend. We freely acknowledge him to be the Inventor of the *Compass*, of *Gunpowder*, and the *Circulation of the Blood*: But, I challenge any of his Admirers to show me in all his Writings, a complete Account of the *Spleen*; Does he not also leave us wholly to seek in the Art of *Political Wagering*? What can be more defective and unsatisfactory than his long Dissertation upon *Tea*? and as to his Method of *Salivation without Mercury*, so much celebrated of late, it is to my own Knowledge and Experience, a Thing very little to be relied on.

It was to supply such momentous Defects, that I have been prevailed on after long Solicitation, to take Pen in Hand; and I dare venture to Promise, the Judicious Reader shall find nothing neglected here, that can be of Use upon any Emergency of Life. I am confident to have included and exhausted all that Human Imagination can *Rise* or *Fall* to. Particularly, I recommend to the Perusal of the Learned, certain Discoveries that are wholly untouched by others; whereof I shall only mention among a great many more; *My New Help of Smatterers*, or the *Art of being Deep learned, and Shallow read*; *A curious Invention about Mouse-Traps*; *An Universal Rule of Reason, or every Man his own Carver*; Together with a most useful Engine for *catching of Owls*. All which the judicious Reader will find largely treated on, in the several Parts of this Discourse.

I hold myself obliged to give as much Light as is possible, into the Beauties and Excellencies of what I am writing, because it is become the Fashion and Humour most applauded among the first Authors of this Polite and Learned Age, when they would correct the ill Nature of Critical, or inform the Ignorance of Courteous Readers. Besides, there have been several famous Pieces lately published both in Verse and Prose; wherein, if the Writers had not been pleased, out of their great Humanity and Affection to the Public, to give us a nice Detail of the *Sublime*, and the *Admirable* they contain; it is a thousand to one, whether we should ever have discovered one Grain of either. For my own particular, I cannot deny, that whatever I have said upon this Occasion had been more proper in a Preface, and more agreeable to the Mode, which usually directs it there. But I here think fit to lay hold on that great and honourable Privilege of being the *Last Writer*; I claim an absolute Authority in Right, as the *freshest Modern*, which gives me a Despotic Power over all Authors before me. In the Strength of which Title, I do utterly disapprove and declare against that pernicious Custom, of making the Preface a Bill of Fare to the Book. For I have always looked upon it as a high Point of Indiscretion in *Monster-mongers* and other *Retailers of strange Sights*; to hang out a fair large Picture over the door, drawn after the Life, with a most eloquent description underneath: This hath saved me many a Threepence, for my Curiosity was fully satisfied, and I never offered to go in, though often invited by the urging and attending Orator, with his last *moving* and *standing* Piece of Rhetoric, 'Sir, Upon my Word, we are just going to begin'. Such is exactly the Fate, at this time of *Prefaces, Epistles, Advertisements, Introductions, Prolegomenas, Apparatuses, To-the-Reader's*. This Expedient was admirable at first; Our Great *Dryden* has long carried it as far as it would go, and with incredible Success. He has often said to me in Confidence, that the world would have never suspected him to be so great a Poet, if he had not assured them so frequently in his Prefaces, that it was impossible they could either doubt or forget it. Perhaps it may be so; However, I much fear his Instructions have edified out of their Place, and taught Men to grow wiser in certain Points, where he never intended they should: For it is lamentable to behold, with what a lazy Scorn, many of the yawning Readers in our Age, do nowadays twirl over forty or fifty Pages of *Preface* and *Dedication* (which is the usual *Modern* Stint) as if it were so much *Latin*. Though it must be also allowed on the other Hand, that a very considerable Number is known to proceed[213] *Critics* and *Wits*, by reading nothing else. Into which two Factions, I think, all present Readers may justly be divided. Now, for myself, I profess to be of the former Sort; and therefore having the *Modern* Inclination to expatiate upon the Beauty of my own Productions, and display the bright Parts of my Discourse; I thought best to do it in the Body of the Work, where, as it now lies, it makes a very considerable Addition to the Bulk of the Volume, *a Circumstance by no means to be neglected by a skilful Writer*.

Having thus paid my due Deference and Acknowledgment to an established Custom of our newest Authors, by *a long Digression unsought for*, and *an universal Censure unprovoked*; By forcing into the Light, with much Pains and Dexterity, my own Excellencies and other Men's Defaults, with great Justice to myself and Candour to them; I now happily resume my Subject, to the infinite Satisfaction both of the Reader and the Author.

Sect. VI
A Tale of a Tub

We left *Lord Peter* in open Rupture with his two Brethren; both for ever discarded from his House, and resigned to the wide World, with little or nothing to trust to. Which are Circumstances that render them proper Subjects for the Charity of a Writer's Pen to work on; Scenes of Misery ever affording the fairest Harvest for great Adventures. And in this, the World may perceive the Difference between the Integrity of a generous Author and that of a common Friend. The latter is observed to adhere close in Prosperity, but on the Decline of Fortune, to drop suddenly off. Whereas, the generous Author, just on the contrary, finds his Hero on the Dunghill, from thence by gradual Steps, raises Him to a Throne, and then immediately withdraws, expecting not so much as Thanks for his Pains: In imitation of which Example, I have placed *Lord Peter* in a Noble House, given him a Title to wear, and Money to spend. There I shall leave Him for some Time, returning where common Charity directs me, to the Assistance of his two Brothers, at their lowest Ebb. However, I shall by no means forget my Character of an Historian, to follow the Truth step by step, whatever happens or wherever it may lead me.

The two Exiles so nearly united in Fortune and Interest, took a Lodging together; Where, at their first Leisure, they began to reflect on the numberless Misfortunes and Vexations of their Life past, and could not tell, of the sudden, to what Failure in their Conduct they ought to impute them; When, after some Recollection, they called to Mind the Copy of their Father's *Will*, which they had so happily recovered. This was immediately produced, and a firm Resolution taken between them, to alter whatever was already amiss, and reduce all their future Measures to the strictest Obedience prescribed therein. The main Body of the *Will* (as the Reader cannot easily have forgot) consisted in certain admirable Rules about the wearing of their Coats; in the Perusal whereof, the two Brothers at every Period duly comparing the Doctrine with the Practice, there was never seen a wider Difference between two Things; horrible downright Transgressions of every Point. Upon which, they both resolved without further Delay, to fall immediately upon reducing the Whole, exactly after their Father's Model.

Notes

[213] *proceed* to advance beyond the Bachelor of Arts degree to a higher academic degree or position.

But, here it is good to stop the hasty Reader, ever impatient to see the End of an Adventure, before We Writers can duly prepare him for it. I am to record, that these two Brothers began to be distinguished at this Time, by certain Names. One of them desired to be called *MARTIN*,[214] and the other took the Appellation of *JACK*.[215] These two had lived in much Friendship and Agreement under the Tyranny of their Brother *Peter*, as it is the Talent of Fellow-Sufferers to do; Men in Misfortune, being like Men in the Dark, to whom all Colours are the same: But when they came forward into the World, and began to display themselves to each other, and to the Light, their Complexions appeared extremely different, which the present Posture of their Affairs gave them sudden Opportunity to discover.

But, here the severe Reader may justly tax me as a Writer of short Memory, a Deficiency to which a true *Modern* cannot but of Necessity be a little subject. Because, *Memory* being an Employment of the Mind upon things past, is a Faculty for which the Learned, in our Illustrious Age, have no manner of Occasion, who deal entirely with *Invention*, and strike all Things out of themselves, or at least, by Collision, from each other: Upon which Account, we think it highly reasonable to produce our great Forgetfulness, as an Argument unanswerable for our great Wit. I ought in Method, to have informed the Reader about fifty Pages ago, of a Fancy *Lord Peter* took, and infused into his Brothers, to wear on their Coats whatever Trimmings came up in Fashion; never pulling off any, as they went out of the Mode, but keeping on all together; which amounted in time to a Medley the most Antic[216] you can possibly conceive; and this to a Degree, that upon the Time of their Falling out, there was hardly a Thread of the Original Coat to be seen, but an infinite Quantity of *Lace*, and *Ribbands*, and *Fringe*, and *Embroidery*, and *Points*; (I mean only those *tagged with Silver*, for the rest fell off). Now, this material Circumstance, having been forgot in due Place, as good Fortune hath ordered, comes in very properly here, when the two Brothers are just going to reform their Vestures into the Primitive State, prescribed by their Father's *Will*.

They both unanimously entered upon this great Work, looking sometimes on their Coats, and sometimes on the *Will*. Martin laid the first Hand; at one Twitch brought off a large Handful of *Points*; and with a second Pull, stripped away ten dozen Yards of *Fringe*. But when He had gone thus far, he demurred a while. He knew very well, there yet remained a great deal to be done; however, the first Heat being over, his Violence began to cool, and he resolved to proceed more moderately in the rest of the Work; having already narrowly scaped a swinging Rent in pulling off the *Points*, which being *tagged with Silver* (as we have observed before) the judicious Workman had with much Sagacity, double-sewn to preserve them from *falling*. Resolving therefore to rid his Coat of a huge Quantity of *Gold Lace*; he picked up the Stitches with much Caution, and diligently gleaned out all the loose Threads as he went, which proved to be a Work of Time. Then he fell about the embroidered *Indian* Figures of Men, Women, and Children; against which, as you have heard in its due Place, their Father's Testament was extremely exact and severe: These, with much Dexterity and Application, were after a while, quite eradicated, or utterly defaced. For the rest, where he observed the Embroidery to be worked so close, as not to be got away without damaging the Cloth, or where it served to hide or strengthened any Flaw in the Body of the Coat, contracted by the perpetual tampering of Workmen upon it, he concluded the wisest

Notes

[214] *MARTIN* Martin Luther [note in fifth edition].

[215] *JACK* John Calvin [note in fifth edition; with Luther, Calvin was a principal theologian of the Protestant Reformation; Swift sees him as much more radical than Luther].

[216] *Antic* absurd.

Course was to let it remain, resolving in no Case whatsoever that the Substance of the Stuff should suffer Injury; which he thought the best Method for serving the true Intent and Meaning of his Father's *Will*. And this is the nearest Account I have been able to collect, of *Martin*'s Proceedings upon this great Revolution.

But, his Brother *Jack*, whose Adventures will be so extraordinary, as to furnish a great Part in the Remainder of this Discourse; entered upon the Matter with other Thoughts, and a quite different Spirit. For, the Memory of *Lord Peter*'s Injuries, produced a Degree of Hatred and Spite, which had a much greater Share of inciting Him, than any Regards after his Father's Commands, since these appeared at best, only Secondary and Subservient to the other. However, for this Medley of Humour, he made a Shift to find a very plausible Name, honouring it with the Title of *Zeal*; which is, perhaps, the most significant Word that hath been ever yet produced in any Language: As, I think, I have fully proved in my excellent *Analytical* Discourse upon that Subject; wherein I have deduced a *Histori-theo-physi-logical* Account of *Zeal*, showing how it first proceeded from a *Notion* into a *Word*, and from thence in a hot Summer, ripened into a *tangible Substance*. This Work containing three large Volumes in Folio, I design very shortly to publish by the *Modern* way of *Subscription*,[217] not doubting but the Nobility and Gentry of the Land will give me all possible Encouragement, having already had such a Taste of what I am able to perform.

I record therefore, that Brother *Jack*, brim-full of this miraculous Compound, reflecting with Indignation upon *PETER*'s Tyranny, and further provoked by the Despondency of *Martin*; prefaced his Resolutions to this purpose: 'What?' said he, 'A Rogue that locked up his Drink, turned away our Wives, cheated us of our Fortunes; palmed his damned Crusts upon us for Mutton; and at last kicked us out of Doors; must we be in his Fashions with a Pox? a Rascal, besides, that all the Street cries out against'. Having thus kindled and inflamed himself as high as possible, and by Consequence, in a delicate Temper for beginning a Reformation, he set about the Work immediately, and in three Minutes, made more Dispatch than *Martin* had done in as many Hours. For, Courteous Reader, you are given to understand, that *Zeal* is never so highly obliged, as when you set it a *Tearing*; and *Jack*, who doted on that Quality in himself, allowed it at this Time its full Swinge.[218] Thus it happened, that stripping down a Parcel of *Gold Lace*, a little too hastily, he rent the *main Body* of his *Coat* from Top to Bottom;[219] and whereas his Talent was not of the happiest in *taking up a Stitch*, he knew no better way, than to darn it again with *Packthread* and a *Skewer*. But the Matter was yet infinitely worse (I record it with Tears) when he proceeded to the *Embroidery*: For being clumsy by Nature, and of Temper, Impatient; withal, beholding Millions of Stitches that required the nicest Hand, and sedatest Constitution, to extricate; in a great Rage, he tore off the whole Piece, Cloth and all, and flung them into the Kennel,[220] and furiously thus continuing his Career: 'Ah, good brother *Martin*', said he, 'do as I do, for the Love of God; Strip, Tear, Pull, Rent, Flay off all, that we may appear as unlike that Rogue *Peter*, as it is possible: I would not for a hundred Pounds carry the least Mark about me, that might give Occasion to the Neighbours, of suspecting I was related to such a Rascal'. But *Martin*, who at this Time happened to be

Notes

217 *Subscription* a way of financing publication by soliciting advance purchases from subscribers, whose names are then listed in the preliminary matter of the book.

218 *Swinge* "Sway; a sweep of any thing in motion. Not in use" (Johnson).

219 *he rent the main Body of his Coat from Top to Bottom* removed Episcopacy and set up Presbyterian church government.

220 *Kennel* gutter.

extremely phlegmatic and sedate, begged his Brother, of all Love, not to damage his Coat by any Means; for he never would get such another: Desired him to consider, that it was not their Business to form their Actions by any Reflection upon *Peter*'s, but by observing the Rules prescribed in their Father's *Will*. That he should remember, *Peter* was still their Brother, whatever Faults or Injuries he had committed; and therefore they should by all means avoid such a Thought, as that of taking Measures for Good and Evil, from no other Rule, than of Opposition to Him. That it was true, the Testament of their good Father was very exact in what related to the wearing of their *Coats*; yet it was no less penal and strict in prescribing Agreement, and Friendship, and Affection between them. And therefore, if straining a Point were at all dispensable, it would certainly be so, rather to the Advance of Unity, than Increase of Contradiction.

Martin had still proceeded as gravely as he began; and doubtless would have delivered an admirable Lecture of Morality, which might have exceedingly contributed to my Reader's *Repose, both of Body and Mind*: (the true ultimate End of *Ethics*); But *Jack* was already gone a Flight-shot[221] beyond his Patience. And as in Scholastic Disputes, nothing serves to rouse the Spleen of him that *Opposes*, so much as a kind of Pedantic affected Calmness in the *Respondent*; Disputants being for the most part like unequal Scales, where the *Gravity* of one Side advances the *Lightness* of the Other, and causes it to fly up and kick the Beam; So it happened here that the *Weight* of *Martin*'s Argument exalted *Jack*'s *Levity*, and made him fly out and spurn against his Brother's Moderation. In short, *Martin*'s *Patience* put *Jack* in a *Rage*; but that which most afflicted him was to observe his Brother's Coat so well reduced into the State of Innocence; while his own was either wholly rent to his Shirt; or those Places which had scaped his cruel Clutches, were still in *Peter*'s Livery. So that he looked like a drunken *Beau*, half rifled by *Bullies*; Or like a Fresh Tenant of *Newgate*,[222] when he has refused the Payment of *Garnish*;[223] Or like a discovered *Shoplifter*, left to the mercy of *Exchange-Women*;[224]Or like a *Bawd* in her old Velvet Petticoat, resigned into the secular Hands of the *Mobile*.[225] Like any, or like all of these, a Medley of *Rags*, and *Lace*, and *Rents*, and *Fringes*, unfortunate *Jack* did now appear: He would have been extremely glad to see his Coat in the Condition of *Martin*'s, but infinitely gladder to find that of *Martin*'s in the same Predicament with his. However, since neither of these was likely to come to pass, he thought fit to lend the whole Business another Turn, and to dress up Necessity as a Virtue. Therefore, after as many of the *Fox*'s Arguments[226] as he could muster up, for bringing Martin to *Reason*, as he called it; or, as he meant it, into his own ragged, bobtailed Condition; and observing he said all to little purpose; what, alas, was left for the forlorn *Jack* to do, but after a Million of Scurrilities against his Brother, to run mad with Spleen, and Spite, and Contradiction. To be short, here began a mortal Breach between these two. *Jack* went immediately to *New Lodgings*, and in a few Days it was for certain reported, that he had run out of his Wits. In a short time after, he appeared abroad, and confirmed the Report, by falling into the oddest Whimsies that ever a sick Brain conceived.

And now the little Boys in the Streets began to salute him with several Names. Sometimes they would call Him, *Jack the Bald*;[227] sometimes, *Jack with a Lantern*;[228]

Notes

221 *Flight-shot* bowshot, distance an arrow can travel in the air.

222 *Newgate* a prison in London.

223 *Garnish* the fee paid by prisoners to the jailer for food and other necessaries.

224 *Exchange-Women* shop-women running stores in the galleries of a center for merchants.

225 *Mobile* the mob.

226 *the Fox's Arguments* having lost his tail in a trap, the fox tries to persuade the other foxes to cut off their tails (Aesop).

227 *Jack the Bald* from Calvus [Latin], Bald [note in fifth edition].

228 *Jack with a Lantern* All those who pretend to Inward Light [note in fifth edition].

sometimes, *Dutch Jack*;[229] sometimes, *French Hugh*;[230] sometimes, *Tom the Beggar*;[231] and sometimes, *Knocking Jack of the North*.[232] And it was under one, or some, or all of these Appellations (which I leave the Learned Reader to determine) that he hath given Rise to the most Illustrious and Epidemic Sect of *Æolists*,[233] who, with honourable Commemoration, do still acknowledge the Renowned *JACK* for their Author and Founder. Of whose Originals, as well as Principles, I am now advancing to gratify the World with a very particular Account.

—*Mellœo contingens cuncta Lepore*.[234]

Sect. VII
A Digression in Praise of Digressions

I have sometimes *heard* of an *Iliad* in a *Nutshell*; but it hath been my Fortune to have much oftener *seen* a *Nutshell* in an *Iliad*. There is no doubt, that Human Life has received most wonderful Advantages from both; but to which of the two the World is chiefly indebted, I shall leave among the Curious, as a Problem worthy of their utmost Enquiry. For the Invention of the latter, I think the Commonwealth of Learning is chiefly obliged to the great *Modern* Improvement of *Digressions*: The late Refinements in Knowledge, running parallel to those of Diet in our Nation, which among Men of a judicious Taste are dressed up in various Compounds, consisting in *Soups* and *Olios*,[235] *Fricassees* and *Ragouts*.

'Tis true, there is a sort of morose, detracting, ill-bred People, who pretend utterly to disrelish these polite Innovations; And as to the Similitude from Diet, they allow the Parallel, but are so bold to pronounce the Example itself a Corruption and Degeneracy of Taste. They tell us, that the Fashion of jumbling fifty Things together in a Dish, was at first introduced in Compliance to a depraved and *debauched Appetite*, as well as to a *crazy Constitution*; And to see a Man hunting through an *Olio* after the *Head* and *Brains* of a *Goose*, a *Wigeon*, or a *Woodcock*, is a Sign he wants a Stomach and Digestion for more substantial Victuals. Further, they affirm, that *Digressions* in a Book, are like *Foreign Troops* in a *State*, which argue the Nation to want a *Heart* and *Hands* of its own, and often, either *subdue* the *Natives*, or drive them into the most *unfruitful Corners*.

But, after all that can be objected by these supercilious Censors, 'tis manifest, the Society of Writers would quickly be reduced to a very inconsiderable Number, if Men were put upon making Books, with the fatal Confinement of delivering nothing beyond what is to the Purpose. 'Tis acknowledged, that were the Case the same among Us as with the *Greeks* and *Romans*, when Learning was in its *Cradle*, to be reared and fed, and clothed by *Invention*, it would be an easy Task to fill up Volumes upon particular Occasions, without further expatiating from the Subject than by moderate Excursions, helping to advance or clear the main Design. But with *Knowledge*, it has

Notes

229 *Dutch Jack* Jack of Leyden who gave rise to the Anabaptists [note in fifth edition].

230 *French Hugh* The Huguenots [note in fifth edition].

231 *Tom the Beggar* The Gueuses [French, "beggars"] by which Name some Protestants in Flanders were called [note in fifth edition].

232 *Knocking Jack of the North* John Knox, the Reformer of *Scotland* [note in fifth edition].

233 *Æolists* after Æolus, the Greek god of the winds; spiritualists, but also those who are in any sense windy.

234 *Mellœo contingens cuncta Lepore* "Touching all with sweet grace" (Lucretius, *De Rerum Natura* 1.934, inaccurately).

235 *Olios* stews.

fared as with a numerous Army, encamped in a fruitful Country; which for a few Days maintains itself by the Product of the Soil it is on; till Provisions being spent, they send to forage many a Mile, among Friends or Enemies it matters not. Meanwhile the neighbouring Fields trampled and beaten down, become barren and dry, affording no Sustenance but Clouds of Dust.

The whole Course of Things being thus entirely changed between *Us* and the *Ancients*; and the *Moderns* wisely sensible of it, we of this Age have discovered a shorter, and more prudent Method, to become *Scholars* and *Wits*, without the fatigue of *Reading* or of *Thinking*. The most accomplished Way of using Books at present, is two-fold: Either first, to serve them as some Men do *Lords*, learn their *Titles* exactly, and then brag of their Acquaintance. Or Secondly, which is indeed the choicer, the profounder, and politer Method, to get a thorough Insight into the *Index*, by which the whole Book is governed and turned, like *Fishes* by the *Tail*. For, to enter the Palace of Learning at the *great Gate*, requires an Expense of Time and Forms; therefore Men of much Haste and little Ceremony, are content to get in by the *Back-Door*. For, the Arts are all in a *flying* March, and therefore more easily subdued by attacking them in the *Rear*. Thus Physicians discover the State of the whole Body, by consulting only what comes from *Behind*. Thus Men catch Knowledge by throwing their *Wit* on the Posteriors of a Book, as Boys do Sparrows with flinging *Salt* upon their *Tails*. Thus Human Life is best understood by the wise man's Rule of *Regarding the End*. Thus are the Sciences found like *Hercules*'s Oxen, by *tracing them backwards*. Thus are *old Sciences* unravelled like *old Stockings*, by beginning at the *Foot*.

Besides all this, the Army of Sciences hath been of late with a World of Martial Discipline, drawn into its *close Order*, so that a View, or a Muster may be taken of it with abundance of Expedition. For this great Blessing we are wholly indebted to *Systems* and *Abstracts*, in which the *Modern* Fathers of Learning, like prudent Usurers, spent their Sweat for the Ease of Us their Children. For *Labour* is the Seed of *Idleness*, and it is the peculiar Happiness of our Noble Age to gather the *Fruit*.

Now the Method of growing Wise, Learned, and *Sublime*, having become so regular an Affair, and so established in all its Forms, the Number of Writers must needs have increased accordingly, and to a Pitch that has made it of absolute Necessity for them to interfere continually with each other. Besides, it is reckoned that there is not at this present, a sufficient Quantity of new Matter left in Nature, to furnish and adorn any one particular Subject to the Extent of a Volume. This I am told by a very skilful *Computer*, who hath given a full Demonstration of it from Rules of *Arithmetic*.

This, perhaps, may be objected against by those, who maintain the Infinity of Matter, and therefore will not allow that any *Species* of it can be exhausted. For Answer to which, let us examine the noblest Branch of *Modern* Wit or Invention, planted and cultivated by the present Age, and, which of all others, hath borne the most and the fairest Fruit. For though some Remains of it were left us by the *Ancients*, yet have not any of those, as I remember, been translated or compiled into Systems for *Modern* Use. Therefore we may affirm, to our own Honour, that it has in some sort, been both invented, and brought to a Perfection by the same Hands. What I mean, is that highly celebrated Talent among the *Modern* Wits, of deducing Similitudes, Allusions, and Applications, very Surprising, Agreeable, and Apposite, from the *Genitals* of either Sex, together with *their proper Uses*. And truly, having observed how little Invention bears any Vogue, besides what is derived into these *Channels*, I have sometimes had a Thought, That the happy Genius of our Age and Country, was prophetically held forth by that ancient typical Description of the *Indian* Pygmies; 'whose Stature did not exceed above two Foot; sed quorum pudenda crassa, & ad talos usque pertingentia'.[236] Now, I have been very curious to inspect the late Productions, wherein the Beauties of this kind have most prominently appeared. And although this *Vein* hath bled so freely, and all Endeavours have been used in the Power of Human Breath to dilate, extend, and keep it open: Like the Scythians, 'who had a Custom, and an Instrument, to blow up the Privities of their Mares, that they might yield the more Milk';[237] Yet I am under an Apprehension, it is near growing dry, and past all Recovery; And that either some new *Fonde* of Wit should, if possible, be provided, or else that we must e'en be content with Repetition here, as well as upon all other Occasions.

This will stand as an uncontestable Argument, that our *Modern* Wits are not to reckon upon the Infinity of Matter, for a constant Supply. What remains therefore but that our last Recourse must be had to large *Indexes*, and little *Compendiums*; *Quotations* must be plentifully gathered, and booked in Alphabet; To this End, though Authors need be little consulted, yet *Critics*, and *Commentators*, and *Lexicons* carefully must. But above all, those judicious Collectors of *Bright Parts*, and *Flowers*, and *Observandas*, are to be nicely dwelt on; by some called the *Sieves* and *Bolters*[238] of Learning; though it is left undetermined, whether they dealt in *Pearls* or *Meal*, and consequently, whether we are more to value that which *passed through*, or what *stayed behind*.

By these Methods, in a few Weeks, there starts up many a Writer capable of managing the profoundest and most universal Subjects. For, what though his *Head* be empty, provided his *Commonplace Book* be full; And if you will bate him but the Circumstances of *Method*, and *Style*, and *Grammar*, and *Invention*; allow him but the common Privileges, of transcribing from others, and digressing from himself, as often as he shall see Occasion; He will desire no more Ingredients towards fitting up a Treatise, that shall make a very comely Figure on a Bookseller's Shelf; there to be preserved neat and clean, for a long Eternity, adorned with the Heraldry of its Title, fairly inscribed on a Label; never to be thumbed or greased by Students, nor bound to everlasting Chains of Darkness in a Library:[239] But when the Fullness of Time is come, shall haply undergo the Trial of Purgatory in order *to ascend the Sky*.

Without these Allowances, how is it possible we *Modern* Wits should ever have an Opportunity to introduce our Collections, listed under so many thousand Heads of a different Nature? for want of which, the Learned World would be deprived of infinite Delight, as well as Instruction, and we ourselves buried beyond Redress in an inglorious and undistinguished Oblivion.

From such Elements as these, I am alive to behold the Day, wherein the Corporation of Authors can outvie all its Brethren in the *Yield*. A Happiness derived to us with a great many others, from our *Scythian* Ancestors, among whom, the Number of *Pens* was so infinite, that the *Grecian* Eloquence had no other way of expressing it, than by saying, That 'in the Regions, far to the North, it was hardly possible for a Man to travel, the very Air was so replete with *Feathers*'.[240]

The Necessity of this Digression, will easily excuse the Length, and I have chosen for it as proper a Place as I could readily find. If the judicious Reader can assign a fitter, I do here empower him to remove it into any other Corner he please. And so I return with great Alacrity to pursue a more important Concern.

Notes

236 *sed quorum pudenda crassa, & ad talos usque pertingentia* ["but whose genitals are thick, hanging down even to their ankles"] Ctesiae fragm. apud Photium [Swift's marginal note; a correct citation].

237 *"who had a Custom ... Milk"* Herodotus 4.2.1.

238 *Bolter* "A sieve to separate meal from bran or husks" (Johnson).

239 *Chains ... in a Library* libraries still had many chained books in Swift's time.

240 *"in the Regions ... Feathers"* Herodotus 4 [7 and 13; Swift's marginal gloss].

Sect. VIII
A Tale of a Tub

The Learned *Æolists*,[241] maintain the Original Cause of all Things to be *Wind*, from which Principle this whole Universe was at first produced, and into which it must at last be resolved; that the same Breath which had kindled and blew *up* the Flame of Nature, should one Day blow it *out*.

Quod procul à nobis flectat Fortuna gubernans.[242]

This is what the *Adepti* understand by their *Anima Mundi*; that is to say, the *Spirit*, or *Breath*, or *Wind* of the World: Or Examine the whole System by the Particulars of Nature, and you will find it not to be disputed. For, whether you please to call the *Forma informans*[243] of a Man by the name of *Spiritus, Animus, Afflatus*, or *Anima*; what are all these, but several Appellations for *Wind*? which is the ruling *Element* in every Compound, and into which they all resolve upon their Corruption. Farther, what is Life itself, but as it is commonly called, the *Breath* of our Nostrils? Whence it is very justly observed by Naturalists, that *Wind* still continues of great Emolument in *certain Mysteries* not to be named, giving Occasion for those happy Epithets of *Turgidus*, and *Inflatus*, applied either to the *Emittent*, or *Recipient* Organs.

By what I have gathered out of ancient Records, I find, the *Compass* of their Doctrine took in two and thirty Points; wherein it would be tedious to be very particular. However, a few of their most important Precepts, deducible from it, are by no means to be omitted; among which, the following Maxim was of much Weight; That since *Wind* had the Master Share, as well as Operation in every Compound, by Consequence, those Beings must be of chief Excellence wherein that *Primordium* appears most prominently to abound; and therefore, *Man* is in the highest Perfection of all created Things, as having by the great Bounty of Philosophers,[244] been endued with three distinct *Animas* or *Winds*, to which the sage *Æolists*, with much Liberality, have added a fourth, of equal Necessity, as well as Ornament with the other three; by this *quartum Principium*, taking in the four Corners of the World. Which gave Occasion to that Renowned *Cabalist*, *Bumbastus*,[245] of placing the Body of Man, in due position to the four *Cardinal* Points.

In Consequence of this, their next Principle was, that *Man* brings with Him into the World a peculiar Portion, or Grain of *Wind*, which may be called a *Quinta essentia*, extracted from the other four. This *Quintessence* is of a Catholic Use upon all Emergencies of Life, is improveable into all Arts and Sciences, and may be wonderfully refined, as well as enlarged by certain Methods in Education. This, when *blown* up to its Perfection, ought not to be covetously hoarded up, stifled, or hid under a Bushel, but freely communicated to Mankind. Upon these Reasons, and others of equal Weight, the Wise *Æolists*, affirm the Gift of *BELCHING* to be the noblest Act of a Rational Creature. To cultivate which Art and render it more serviceable to Mankind, they made Use of several Methods. At certain Seasons of the Year, you might behold the Priests amongst

Notes

241 *Æolists* All Pretenders to Inspiration whatever [note in fifth edition].

242 *Quod procul à nobis flectat Fortuna gubernans* "Which [earthquakes and other evidence of his prediction that the earth will someday dissolve] may governing Fortune steer far from us" (Lucretius 5.107).

243 *Forma informans* a scholastic category, the material form or idea, which sounds like a contradiction in terms.

244 *Philosophers* scholastic philosophers attribute three functional kinds of anima, or spirit, to man: vegetative, animal, and rational; the "Æolists" add spirit, or wind, as a fourth dimension of the soul's activity.

245 *Bumbastus* part of the name of Paracelsus, a sixteenth-century alchemist.

them in vast Numbers, with their *Mouths gaping wide against a Storm*. At other Times were to be seen, several Hundreds linked together in a circular Chain, with every Man a Pair of Bellows applied to his Neighbour's Breech, by which they blew up each other to the Shape and Size of a *Tun*;[246] and for that Reason, with great Propriety of Speech, did usually call their Bodies, their *Vessels*. When, by these and the like Performances, they were grown sufficiently replete, they would immediately depart, and disembogue for the Public Good a plentiful Share of their Acquirements into their Disciples' Chaps.[247] For we must here observe, that all Learning was esteemed among them, to be compounded from the same Principle. Because, First, it is generally affirmed, or confessed, that Learning *puffeth Men up*:[248] And Secondly, they proved it by the following Syllogism: 'Words are but Wind; and Learning is nothing but Words'; *Ergo*, 'Learning is nothing but Wind'. For this Reason, the Philosophers among them, did in their Schools, deliver to their Pupils, all their Doctrines and Opinions by *Eructation*, wherein they had acquired a wonderful Eloquence, and of incredible Variety. But the great Characteristic by which their chief Sages were best distinguished, was a certain Position of Countenance, which gave undoubted Intelligence to what Degree or Proportion, the Spirit agitated the inward Mass. For, after certain Gripings,[249] the *Wind* and Vapours issuing forth, having first by their Turbulence and Convulsions within caused an Earthquake in Man's little World; distorted the Mouth, bloated the Cheeks, and gave the Eyes a terrible kind of *Relievo*. At which Junctures all their *Belches* were received for Sacred, the Sourer the better, and swallowed with infinite Consolation by their meagre Devotees. And to render these yet more complete, because the Breath of Man's Life is in his Nostrils, therefore, the choicest, most edifying, and most enlivening *Belches*, were very wisely conveyed through that Vehicle, to give them a Tincture as they passed.

Their Gods were the four *Winds*, whom they worshipped, as the Spirits that pervade and enliven the Universe, and as those from whom alone all *Inspiration* can properly be said to proceed. However, the Chief of these, to whom they performed the Adoration of *Latria*,[250] was the *Almighty North*. An Ancient Deity whom the Inhabitants of *Megalopolis* in *Greece*, had likewise in highest Reverence. *Omnium deorum Boream maxime celebrant*.[251] This God, though endued with Ubiquity, was yet supposed by the profounder *Æolists*, to possess one peculiar Habitation, or, to speak in Form, a *Cælum Empyræum*,[252] wherein he was more intimately present. This was situated in a certain Region, well known to the Ancient *Greeks*, by them called, *Σκοτία*,[253] or the *Land of Darkness*. And although many Controversies have arisen upon that Matter, yet so much is undisputed that from a Region of the *like Denomination*, the most refined *Æolists* have borrowed their Original, from whence in every Age, the zealous among their Priesthood, have brought over their choicest *Inspiration*, fetching it with their own Hands, from the Fountain Head, in certain *Bladders*, and disploding it among the Sectaries in all Nations, who did, and do, and ever will, daily Gasp and Pant after it.

Now, their Mysteries and Rites were performed in this Manner. 'Tis well known among the Learned, that the Virtuosos[254] of former Ages, had a Contrivance for

Notes

246 *Tun* barrel.

247 *Chaps* jaws, mouths.

248 *Learning puffeth Men up* "Knowledge puffeth up but Charity edifieth" (1 Corinthians 8.1).

249 *Gripings* colic.

250 *Latria* "The highest kind of worship; distinguished by the papists from dulia, or inferior worship" (Johnson).

251 *Omnium deorum Boream maxime celebrant* "They worshipped Boreas (the north wind) the most of all the gods" (Pausanias 8.36.6).

252 *Cælum Empyræum* the highest part of the heavens.

253 *Σκοτία* Scotia, which means "darkness" as well as Scotland.

254 *Virtuoso* "A man skilled in antique or natural curiosities" (Johnson), but Swift uses it of inventors.

carrying and preserving *Winds* in Casks or Barrels, which was of great Assistance upon long Sea Voyages; And the loss of so useful an Art at present, is very much to be lamented, though, I know not how, with great Negligence omitted by *Pancirolius*.[255] It was an Invention ascribed to *Æolus* himself, from whom this Sect is denominated, and who in Honour of their Founder's Memory, have to this Day preserved great Numbers of those *Barrels*, whereof they fix one in each of their Temples, first beating out the Top. Into this *Barrel*, upon solemn Days, the Priest enters; where, having before duly prepared himself by the Methods already described, a secret Funnel is also conveyed from his Posteriors, to the Bottom of the Barrel, which admits new Supplies of Inspiration, from a *Northern* Chink or Cranny. Whereupon, You behold him swell immediately to the Shape and Size of his *Vessel*. In this Posture he disembogues whole Tempests upon his Auditory, as the Spirit from beneath gives him Utterance; which issuing *ex adytis* and *penetralibus*,[256] is not performed without much Pain and Gripings. And the Wind in breaking forth deals with his Face,[257] as it does with that of the Sea; first *blackening*, then *wrinkling*, and at last *bursting it into a Foam*. It is in this Guise, the Sacred *Æolist* delivers his oracular *Belches* to his panting Disciples; Of whom, some are greedily gaping after the sanctified Breath, others are all the while hymning out the Praises of the *Winds*, and gently wafted to and fro by their own Humming, do thus represent the soft Breezes of their Deities appeased.

It is from this Custom of the Priests that some Authors maintain these *Æolists* to have been very ancient in the World. Because the Delivery of their Mysteries, which I have just now mentioned, appears exactly the same with that of other Ancient Oracles, whose Inspirations were owing to certain subterraneous *Effluviums* of *Wind*, delivered with the *same* Pain to the Priest, and much about the *same* Influence on the People. It is true indeed, that these were frequently managed and directed by *Female* Officers, whose Organs were understood to be better disposed for the Admission of those Oracular *Gusts*, as entering, and passing up through a Receptacle of greater Capacity, and causing also a Pruriency by the Way, such as with due Management, hath been refined from Carnal, into a Spiritual Ecstasy. And to strengthen this profound Conjecture, it is further insisted, that this Custom of *Female* Priests[258] is kept up still in certain refined Colleges of our *modern Æolists*, who are agreed to receive their Inspiration, derived through the Receptacle aforesaid, like their Ancestors, the *Sibyls*.[259]

And whereas the Mind of Man, when he gives the Spur and Bridle to his Thoughts, doth never stop, but naturally sallies out into both extremes of High and Low, of Good and Evil; his first Flight of Fancy commonly transports him to Ideas of what is most Perfect, finished, and exalted; till having soared out of his own Reach and Sight, not well perceiving how near the Frontiers of Height and Depth border upon each other; With the same Course and Wing, he falls down plumb into the lowest Bottom of Things; like one who travels the *East* into the *West*; or like a straight Line drawn by its own Length into a Circle. Whether a Tincture of Malice in our Natures,

Notes

[255] *Pancirolius* Guido Panciroli (1523–99), author of a treatise on the inventions of the ancients and the moderns.

[256] *ex adytis and penetralibus* "out of the inmost part of the temple or sanctuary [where the household gods are kept]" (Virgil, *Aeneid* 2.297).

[257] *Face* This is an exact Description of the Changes made in the Face by Enthusiastic Preachers [note in fifth edition].

[258] *Female Priests* Quakers who suffer their Women to preach and pray [note in fifth edition].

[259] *Sibyls* prophetesses of the classical world, the most famous of whom was the Cumaean Sibyl, consulted by Aeneas before he visited Hades.

makes us fond of furnishing every bright Idea with its Reverse; Or, whether Reason reflecting upon the Sum of Things, can like the Sun serve only to enlighten one half of the Globe, leaving the other half, by Necessity, under Shade and Darkness; Or, whether Fancy, flying up to the Imagination of what is Highest and Best, becomes over-shot, and spent, and weary, and suddenly falls like a dead Bird of Paradise, to the Ground. Or, whether after all these *Metaphysical* Conjectures, I have not entirely missed the true Reason; The Proposition, however, which hath stood me in so much Circumstance, is altogether true; That, as the most uncivilized Parts of Mankind have in some way or other, climbed up into the Conception of a *God*, or Supreme Power, so they have seldom forgot to provide their Fears with certain ghastly Notions, which instead of better, have served them pretty tolerably for a *Devil*. And this Proceeding seems to be natural enough; for it is with Men, whose Imaginations are lifted up very high, after the same Rate, as with those whose Bodies are so; that, as they are delighted with the Advantage of a nearer Contemplation upwards, so they are equally terrified with the dismal Prospect of the Precipice below. Thus, in the Choice of a *Devil*, it hath been the usual Method of Mankind to single out some Being, either in Act or in Vision, which was in most Antipathy to the God they had framed. Thus, also, the Sect of *Æolists*, possessed themselves with a Dread, and Horror, and Hatred of two malignant Natures, betwixt whom, and the Deities they adored, perpetual Enmity was established. The first of these, was the *Chameleon*,[260] sworn Foe to *Inspiration*, who in Scorn, devoured large Influences of their God, without refunding the smallest Blast by *Eructation*. The other was a huge terrible Monster, called *Moulinavent*,[261] who with four strong Arms, waged eternal Battle with all their Divinities, dexterously turning to avoid their Blows, and repay them with Interest.

Thus furnished, and set out with *Gods*, as well as *Devils*, was the renowned Sect of *Æolists*; which makes at this Day so illustrious a Figure in the World, and whereof, that polite Nation of *Laplanders*, are beyond all Doubt, a most Authentic Branch; Of whom I therefore cannot, without Injustice, here omit to make honourable Mention, since they appear to be so closely allied in Point of Interest as well as Inclinations with their Brother *Æolists* among Us, as not only to buy their *Winds* by wholesale from the *same* Merchants, but also to retail them after the *same* Rate and Method, and to Customers much alike.

Now, whether the System here delivered, was wholly compiled by *Jack*, or, as some Writers believe, rather copied from the Original at *Delphos*, with certain Additions and Emendations suited to Times and Circumstances, I shall not absolutely determine. This I may affirm, that *Jack* gave it at least a new Turn, and formed it into the same Dress and Model as it lies deduced by me.

I have long sought after this Opportunity of doing Justice to a Society of Men, for whom I have a peculiar Honour, and whose Opinions, as well as Practices, have been extremely misrepresented, and traduced by the Malice or Ignorance of their Adversaries. For, I think it one of the greatest, and best of human Actions to remove Prejudices, and place Things in their truest and fairest Light; which I therefore boldly undertake without any Regards of my own, besides the Conscience, the Honour, and the Thanks.

Notes

260 *Chameleon* because this animal was popularly believed to feed on air (Browne, *Pseudodoxia Epidemica* 3.21).

261 *Moulinavent* French, "windmill."

Sect. IX
A Digression concerning the Original, the Use, and Improvement of Madness in a Commonwealth

Nor shall it anyways detract from the just Reputation of this famous Sect, that its Rise and Institution are owing to such an Author as I have described *Jack* to be; A Person whose Intellectuals were overturned, and his Brain shaken out of its natural Position; which we commonly suppose to be a Distemper, and call by the name of *Madness* or *Frenzy*. For, if we take a Survey of the greatest Actions that have been performed in the World, under the Influence of Single Men, which are, *the Establishment of New Empires by Conquest; The Advance and Progress of New Schemes in Philosophy; and the contriving, as well as the propagating of New Religions*; we shall find the Authors of them all, to have been Persons, whose natural Reason hath admitted great Revolutions from their Diet, their Education, the Prevalency of some certain Temper, together with the particular Influence of Air and Climate. Besides, there is something Individual in human Minds, that easily kindles at the accidental Approach and Collision of certain Circumstances, which though of paltry and mean Appearance, do often flame out into the greatest Emergencies of Life. For, great Turns are not always given by strong Hands, but by lucky Adaptation, and at proper Seasons; and it is of no Import, where the Fire was kindled, if the Vapour has once got up into the Brain. For, the *upper Region* of Man, is furnished like the *middle Region* of the Air; The Materials are formed from Causes of the widest Difference, yet produce at last the same Substance and Effect. Mists arise from the Earth, Steams from Dunghills, Exhalations from the Sea, and Smoke from Fire; yet all Clouds are the same in Composition as well as Consequences: And the Fumes issuing from a Jakes,[262] will furnish as comely and useful a Vapour as Incense from an Altar. Thus far, I suppose, will be easily granted me: And then it will follow; that as the Face of Nature never produces Rain, but when it is overcast and disturbed; so Human Understanding, seated in the Brain, must be troubled and overspread by Vapours, ascending from the lower Faculties to water the Invention, and render it fruitful. Now, although these Vapours (as it hath been already said) are of as various Original as those of the Skies, yet the Crop they produce, differs both in Kind and Degree, merely according to the Soil. I will produce two Instances to prove and Explain what I am now advancing.

A certain Great Prince[263] raised a mighty Army, filled his Coffers with infinite Treasures, provided an invincible Fleet; and all this without giving the least Part of his Design to his greatest Ministers, or his nearest Favourites. Immediately the whole World was alarmed; the neighbouring Crowns, in trembling Expectation, towards what Point the Storm would burst; the small Politicians everywhere forming profound Conjectures. Some believed he had laid a Scheme for Universal Monarchy: Others, after much Insight, determined the Matter to be a Project for pulling down the *Pope*, and setting up the *Reformed* Religion, which had once been his own. Some, again, of a deeper Sagacity, sent him into *Asia* to subdue the *Turk*, and recover *Palestine*. In the midst of all these Projects and Preparations; a certain *State-Surgeon*, gathering the Nature of the Disease by these Symptoms, attempted the Cure, at one Blow performed

Notes

262 *Jakes* privy, toilet.

263 *Great Prince* This was *Harry* the Great of France [Henry IV, assassinated in 1610 by a fanatical Roman Catholic; note in fifth edition].

the Operation, broke the Bag, and out flew the *Vapour*; nor did anything want to render it a complete Remedy, only, that the Prince unfortunately happened to Die in the Performance. Now, is the Reader exceeding curious to learn from whence this *Vapour* took its Rise, which had so long set the Nations at a Gaze? What secret Wheel, what hidden Spring could put into Motion so wonderful an Engine? It was afterwards discovered, that the Movement of this whole Machine had been directed by an absent *Female*, whose Eyes had raised a Protuberancy, and before Emission, she was removed into an Enemy's Country. What should an unhappy Prince do in such ticklish Circumstances as these? He tried in vain the Poet's never-failing Receipt of *Corpora quæque*;[264] For,

> *Idque petit corpus mens unde est saucia amore;*
> *Unde feritur, eo tendit, gestitque coire.* Lucr.[265]

Having to no purpose used all peaceable Endeavours, the collected Part of the *Semen*, raised and inflamed, became adust,[266] converted to Choler, turned head upon the spinal Duct, and ascended to the Brain. The very same Principle that influences a *Bully* to break the Windows of a Whore, who has jilted him, naturally stirs up a Great Prince to raise Mighty Armies, and dream of nothing, but Sieges, Battles, and Victories.

> *—Cunnus teterrima belli*
> *Causa—*[267]

The other Instance[268] is, what I have read somewhere, in a very ancient Author, of a Mighty King, who for the space of above thirty Years, amused himself to take and lose Towns; beat Armies, and be beaten; drive Princes out of their Dominions; fright Children from their Bread and Butter; burn, lay waste, plunder, dragoon, massacre, Subject and Stranger, Friend and Foe, Male and Female. 'Tis recorded, that the Philosophers of each Country were in grave Dispute, upon Causes Natural, Moral, and Political, to find out where they should assign an original Solution of this *Phenomenon*. At last the *Vapour* or *Spirit*, which animated the Hero's Brain, being in perpetual Circulation, seized upon that Region of the Human Body so renowned for furnishing the *Zibeta Occidentalis*,[269] and gathering there into a Tumour, left the rest of the World for that Time in Peace. Of such mighty Consequence it is, where those Exhalations fix, and of so little, from whence they proceed. The same Spirits which in their superior Progress, would conquer a Kingdom, descending upon the *Anus*, conclude in a *Fistula*.[270]

Let us next examine the great Introducers of new Schemes in Philosophy, and search till we can find from what Faculty of the Soul, the Disposition arises in mortal Man, of taking it into his Head, to advance new Systems with such an eager Zeal in Things

Notes

264 *Corpora quæque* "any body," part of a prescription of promiscuity to avoid love (Lucretius 4.1065).

265 *Idque ... Lucr* "The body seeks the source of the mind's love-wound; it goes for the source and is eager for coition with it" (Lucretius 4.1048, 1055).

266 *adust* hot, burnt up; a description of bodily "humours" or psychological qualities, such as anger or melancholy, at one extreme.

267 *Cunnus teterrima belli/Causa* "Cunt [was, long before Helen of Troy] the most hideous cause of war" (Horace, *Satires* 1.3.107); "cunnus" was deleted in the fifth edition.

268 *other Instance* This is meant of the Present *French* King [Louis XIV; note in fifth edition].

269 *Zibeta Occidentalis* Paracelsus ... tried an Experiment upon human Excrement, to make a Perfume of it, which when he had brought to Perfection, he called *Zibeta Occidentalis*, or Western-Civet, the back Parts of Man (according to his Division mentioned by the Author, page [407]) being West [note in fifth edition].

270 *Fistula* "A sinuous ulcer, callous within" (Johnson).

agreed on all Hands impossible to be known: From what Seeds this Disposition springs, and to what Quality of human Nature these Grand Innovators have been indebted for their Number of Disciples. Because, it is plain, that several of the Chief among them, both *Ancient* and *Modern*, were usually mistaken by their Adversaries, and indeed by all except their own Followers, to have been Persons crazed, or out of their Wits, having generally proceeded in the common Course of their Words and Actions, by a Method very different from the vulgar Dictates of *unrefined* Reason, agreeing for the most Part in their several Models, with their present undoubted Successors in the *Academy* of *Modern Bedlam* [271] (whose Merits and Principles I shall further examine in due Place.) Of this Kind were *Epicurus*,[272] *Diogenes*,[273] *Apollonius*,[274] *Lucretius*, *Paracelsus*,[275] *Descartes*, and others; who, if they were now in the World, tied fast, and separate from their Followers, would in this our undistinguishing Age, incur manifest Danger of *Phlebotomy*,[276] and *Whips*, and *Chains*, and *dark Chambers*, and *Straw*. For, what Man in the natural State, or Course of Thinking, did ever conceive it in his Power, to reduce the Notions of all Mankind, exactly to the same Length, and Breadth, and Height of his own? Yet this is the first humble and civil Design of all Innovators in the Empire of Reason. *Epicurus*, modestly hoped, that one Time or other, a certain Fortuitous Concourse of all Men's Opinions, after perpetual Justlings, the Sharp with the Smooth, the Light and the Heavy, the Round and the Square, would by certain *Clinamina*,[277] unite in the Notions of *Atoms* and *Void*, as these did in the Originals of all things. *Cartesius* reckoned to see before he died, the Sentiments of all Philosophers, like so many lesser Stars in his *Romantic* [278] System, rapt and drawn within his own *Vortex*.[279] Now, I would gladly be informed, how it is possible to account for such Imaginations as these in particular Men, without recourse to my *Phenomenon* of *Vapours*, ascending from the lower Faculties to overshadow the Brain, and thence distilling into Conceptions for which the Narrowness of our Mother-Tongue has not yet assigned any other Name, beside that of *Madness* or *Frenzy*. Let us therefore now conjecture how it comes to pass, that none of these great Prescribers, do ever fail providing themselves and their Notions, with a number of implicit Disciples. And, I think, the Reason is easy to be assigned: For, there is a peculiar *String* in the Harmony of Human Understanding which in several Individuals, is exactly of the same Tuning. This, if you can dexterously screw up to its right Key, and then strike gently upon it; Whenever you have the good Fortune to light among those of the same Pitch, they will, by a secret necessary Sympathy, strike exactly at the same Time. And in this one Circumstance, lies all the Skill or Luck of the Matter; for if you chance to jar the String among those who are either above or below your own Height, instead of subscribing to your Doctrine, they will tie you fast, call you Mad, and feed you with Bread and Water. It is therefore a Point of the nicest Conduct to distinguish and adapt this noble Talent, with respect to the Differences of Persons and Times. *Cicero* understood this very well, when writing to a Friend in

Notes

[271] *Bedlam* London asylum for the insane.

[272] *Epicurus* founded a radical third school in Athens, opposed to Plato's Academy and Aristotle's Lyceum, but his materialism or atomism, like *Lucretius'* and *Descartes'*, is what singles him out for ridicule here.

[273] *Diogenes* the Cynic, famous for taking up residence in a barrel and carrying a lighted candle symbolic of his search for an honest man.

[274] *Apollonius* of Tyana, a neo-Pythagorean of the first century CE, said to have performed miracles.

[275] *Paracelsus* Bombast von Hohenheim, Philippus Aureolus Theophrastus (1493–1541), alchemist and physician, known as Paracelsus after the ancient medical writer Celsus.

[276] *Phlebotomy* bloodletting; a treatment for insanity.

[277] *Clinamina* the principle of swerving that explains the concourse of atoms in Lucretius' cosmology.

[278] *Romantic* "Improbable; false" (Johnson).

[279] *Vortex* a feature of Descartes' materialist cosmology.

England, with a Caution, among other Matters, to beware of being cheated by our *Hackney-Coachmen* (who, it seems, in those Days were as arrant Rascals, as they are now) has these remarkable Words, *Est quod gaudeas te in ista loca venisse, ubi aliquid sapere viderere.*[280] For, to speak a bold Truth, it is a fatal Miscarriage, so ill to order Affairs, as to pass for a *Fool* in one Company, when in another, you might be treated as a *Philosopher*. Which I desire *some certain Gentlemen of my Acquaintance*, to lay up in their Hearts, as a very seasonable *Innuendo*.

This, indeed, was the Fatal Mistake of that worthy Gentleman, my most ingenious Friend, Mr. *W—tt—n*: A Person, in Appearance, ordained for great Designs, as well as Performances; whether you will consider his *Notions* or his *Looks*. Surely, no Man ever advanced into the Public with fitter Qualifications of Body and Mind for the Propagation of a new Religion. Oh, had those happy Talents, misapplied to vain Philosophy, been turned into their proper Channels of *Dreams* and *Visions*, where *Distortion* of Mind and Countenance are of such Sovereign Use; the base detracting World would not then have dared to report, that something is amiss, that his Brain hath undergone an unlucky Shake, which even his Brother *Modernists* themselves, like Ungrates, do whisper so loud, that it reaches up to the very *Garret* I am now writing in.

Lastly, whoever pleases to look into the Fountains of *Enthusiasm*, from whence in all Ages, have eternally proceeded such fattening Streams, will find the Spring Head to have been as *Troubled* and *Muddy* as the Current; Of such great Emolument, is a Tincture of this *Vapour*, which the World calls *Madness*, that without its Help, the World would not only be deprived of those two great Blessings, *Conquests* and *Systems*, but even all Mankind would unhappily be reduced to the same Belief in Things Invisible. Now, the former *Postulatum* being held, that it is of no Import, from what Originals this *Vapour* proceeds, but either in what *Angles* it strikes and spreads over the Understanding, or upon what *Species* of Brain it ascends; It will be a very delicate Point, to cut the Feather, and divide the several Reasons to a nice and curious Reader, how this numerical Difference in the Brain can produce Effects of so vast a Difference from the same *Vapour*, as to be the sole Point of Individuation between *Alexander the Great, Jack* of *Leyden*, and *Monsieur Des Cartes*. The present Argument, is the most abstracted that I ever engaged in; it strains my Faculties to their highest Stretch; and I desire the Reader to attend with the utmost Perpensity; For, I now proceed to unravel this knotty Point.

There is in mankind a certain[281] * * * * * *

* * * * * * * * * * * * *

Hic multa * * * * * * * * * *

desiderantur.[282] * * * * * * * * *

* * * * * * * * * * * * *

* * * * * And this I take to be a clear Solution of the Matter. Having therefore so narrowly passed through this intricate Difficulty, the Reader will, I am sure, agree with me in the Conclusion; that if the *Moderns* mean by *Madness*, only a Disturbance or Transportation of the Brain, by Force of certain *Vapours* issuing up from the lower Faculties; then has this *Madness* been the Parent of all those mighty

Notes

[280] *Est quod … viderere* "You may well congratulate yourself on having reached those regions where you pass for a man who knows something [of the law]" (Cicero, *Letters to his Friends* 7.10; Loeb 216.33).

[281] a certain … Here is another Defect in the Manuscript, but I think the Author did wisely, and that the Matter which thus strained his Faculties, was not worth a Solution; and it were well if all Metaphysical Cobweb Problems were no otherwise answered [note in fifth edition].

[282] *Hic multa desiderantur* "Here much is lacking."

Revolutions, that have happened in *Empire*, in *Philosophy*, and in *Religion*. For, the Brain, in its natural Position and State of Serenity, disposeth its Owner to pass his Life in the common Forms, without any Thought of subduing Multitudes to his own *Power*, his *Reasons*, or his *Visions*; And the more he shapes his Understanding by the Pattern of Human Learning, the less he is inclined to form Parties after his particular Notions; Because that instructs him in his private Infirmities, as well as in the stubborn Ignorance of the People. But when a Man's Fancy gets *astride* on his Reason, when Imagination is at Cuffs with the Senses, and common Understanding as well as common Sense, is kicked out of Doors; the first Proselyte he makes is Himself, and when that is once compassed, the Difficulty is not so great in bringing over others; A strong Delusion always operating from *without*, as vigorously as from *within*. For Cant and Vision are to the Ear and the Eye, the same that Tickling is to the Touch. Those Entertainments and Pleasures we most value in Life are such as *Dupe* and play the Wag with the Senses. For, if we take an Examination of what is generally understood by *Happiness*, as it has Respect either to the Understanding or the Senses; We shall find all its Properties and Adjuncts will herd under this short Definition; That, *it is a perpetual Possession of being well Deceived*. And first, with Relation to the Mind or Understanding; 'tis manifest, what mighty Advantages Fiction has over Truth; and the Reason is just at our Elbow; because Imagination can build nobler Scenes and produce more wonderful Revolution than Fortune or Nature will be at Expense to furnish. Nor is Mankind so much to blame in his Choice, thus determining him, if we consider that the Debate merely lies between *Things past*, and *Things conceived*; And so the Question is only this; Whether Things that have Place in the *Imagination*, may not as properly be said to *Exist*, as those that are seated in the *Memory*; which may be justly held in the Affirmative, and very much to the Advantage of the former, since this is acknowledged to be the *Womb* of Things, and the Other allowed to be no more than the *Grave*. Again, if we take this Definition of Happiness, and examine it with Reference to the Senses, it will be acknowledged wonderfully adapt. How fade and insipid do all Objects accost us, that are not conveyed in the Vehicle of *Delusion*? How shrunk is every Thing, as it appears in the Glass of Nature! So, that if it were not for the Assistance of artificial *Mediums*, false Lights, refracted Angles, Varnish, and Tinsel; there would be a mighty Level in the Felicity and Enjoyments of Mortal Men. If this were seriously considered by the World, as I have a certain Reason to Suspect it hardly will; Men would no longer reckon among their high Points of Wisdom the Art of exposing weak Sides, and publishing Infirmities; an Employment, in my Opinion, neither better nor worse than that of *Unmasking*, which, I think has never been allowed fair Usage, either in the *World* or the *Playhouse*.

In the Proportion that Credulity is a more peaceful Possession of the Mind than Curiosity, so far preferable is that Wisdom, which converses about the Surface, to that pretended Philosophy which enters into the Depth of Things, and then comes gravely back with Informations and Discoveries, that in the Inside they are good for nothing. The two Senses, to which all Objects first Address themselves, are the Sight and the Touch; These never examine further than the Colour, the Shape, the Size, and whatever other Qualities dwell, or are drawn by Art upon the Outward of Bodies; and then comes Reason, officiously, with Tools for cutting, and opening, and mangling, and piercing, offering to demonstrate that they are not of the same consistence quite through. Now, I take all this to be the last Degree of perverting Nature; one of whose eternal Laws it is, to put her best Furniture[283] forward. And therefore, in order to save

Note

[283] *Furniture* "Equipage; embellishments; decorations" (Johnson).

the Charges of all such expensive Anatomy for the Time to come; I do here think fit to inform the Reader, that in such Conclusions as these, Reason is certainly in the Right; And that in most Corporeal Beings which have fallen under my Cognisance, the Outside hath been infinitely preferable to the *In*: Whereof I have been further convinced from some late Experiments. Last Week I saw a Woman *flayed*, and you will hardly believe, how much it altered her Person for the worse. Yesterday I ordered the Carcass of a *Beau* to be stripped in my Presence; when we were all amazed to find so many unsuspected Faults under one Suit of Clothes: Then I laid open his *Brain*, his *Heart*, and his *Spleen*; But, I plainly perceived at every Operation, that the further we proceeded, we found the Defects increase upon us in Number and Bulk: From all which, I justly formed this Conclusion to myself. That whatever Philosopher or Projector can find out an Art to solder and patch up the Flaws and Imperfections of Nature, will deserve much better of Mankind, and teach us a more useful Science, than that so much in present Esteem, of widening and exposing them (like him who held *Anatomy* to be the ultimate End of *Physic*). And he, whose Fortunes and Dispositions have placed him in a convenient Station to enjoy the Fruits of this noble Art; He that can with *Epicurus* content his Ideas with the *Films* and *Images* that fly off upon his Senses from the *Superficies* of Things; Such a Man truly Wise, creams off Nature, leaving the Sour and the Dregs for Philosophy and Reason to lap up. This is the sublime and refined Point of Felicity, called, *the Possession of being well deceived*; The Serene peaceful State of being a Fool among Knaves.

But to return to *Madness*. It is certain, that according to the System I have above deduced; every *Species* thereof proceeds from a Redundancy of *Vapour*, therefore, as some Kinds of *Frenzy* give a double Strength to the Sinews, so there are of other *Species* which add Vigour, and Life, and Spirit to the Brain: Now, it usually happens, that these active Spirits, getting Possession of the Brain, resemble those that haunt other Waste and Empty Dwellings, which for want of Business, either vanish, and carry away a piece of the House, or else stay at home, and fling it all out of the Windows. By which are mystically displayed the two principal Branches of *Madness*; and which some Philosophers not considering so well as I, have mistook to be different in their Causes, over-hastily assigning the first to Deficiency, and the other to Redundance.

I think it therefore manifest, from what I have here advanced, that the main Point of Skill and Address is to furnish Employment for this Redundancy of *Vapour*, and prudently to adjust the Seasons of it; by which Means it may certainly become of cardinal and catholic Emolument in a Commonwealth. Thus, one Man choosing a proper Juncture, leaps into a Gulf, from thence proceeds a Hero, and is called the Saver of his Country; Another achieves the same Enterprise, but unluckily timing it, has left the Brand of *Madness* fixed as a Reproach upon his Memory; Upon so nice a Distinction are we taught to repeat the Name of *Curtius*[284] with Reverence and Love; that of *Empedocles*,[285] with Hatred and Contempt. Thus, also it is usually conceived, that the elder *Brutus*[286] only personated the *Fool* and *Madman*, for the good of the Public: but this was nothing else, than a Redundancy of the same *Vapour*, long misapplied, called by the *Latins, Ingenium par negotiis*:[287] Or, (to translate it as nearly as I can) a sort of *Frenzy*, never in its right Element, till you take it up in Business of the State.

Notes

284 *Curtius* Marcus Curtius sacrificed himself for Rome in 352 BCE.

285 *Empedocles* jumped into flaming Mount Etna in an attempt to gain immortal fame.

286 *Brutus* Lucius Junius Brutus, consul of Rome (509 BCE); feigned madness to escape murder by Tarquin, the last Roman king.

287 *Ingenium par negotiis* ability equal to the tasks at hand.

Upon all which, and many other Reasons of equal Weight, though not equally curious; I do here gladly Embrace an Opportunity I have long sought for, of Recommending it as a very noble Undertaking, to Sir E——d S——r, Sir C——r M——ve, Sir J—n B——ls, J—n H——, Esq;[288] and other Patriots [289] concerned, that they would move for Leave to bring in a Bill, for appointing Commissioners to Inspect into *Bedlam*, and the Parts adjacent; who shall be empowered to *send for Persons, Papers, and Records*, to examine into the Merits and Qualifications of every Student and Professor; to observe with utmost Exactness their several Dispositions and Behaviour; by which means, duly distinguishing and adapting their Talents, they might produce admirable Instruments for the several Offices in a State, *****, [290] *Civil*, and *Military*, proceeding in such Methods, as I shall here humbly propose. And, I hope, the Gentle Reader will give some Allowance to my great Solicitudes in this important Affair, upon Account of the high Esteem I have ever borne that honourable Society, whereof I had some time the Happiness to be an unworthy Member.

Is any Student [291] tearing his Straw in piece-meal, Swearing and Blaspheming, biting his Grate, foaming at the Mouth, and emptying his Pisspot in the Spectators' Faces? Let the Right Worshipful, the *Commissioners of Inspection*, give him a Regiment of Dragoons, and send him into Flanders among the *rest*. Is another eternally talking, sputtering, gaping, bawling, in a Sound without Period or Article? What wonderful Talents are here mislaid! Let him be furnished immediately with a green Bag and Papers and *three Pence*[292] in his Pocket, and away with Him to *Westminster-Hall*. You will find a Third, gravely taking the Dimensions of his Kennel, a Person of Foresight and Insight, though kept quite in the Dark; for why, like *Moses, Ecce cornuta erat ejus facies*.[293] He walks duly in one Pace, entreats your Penny with due Gravity and Ceremony, talks much of hard Times, and Taxes, and the *Whore of Babylon*;[294] Bars up the wooden Window of his Cell constantly at eight o'Clock, Dreams of *Fire*, and *Shoplifters*, and *Court-Customers*, and *Privileged Places*. Now, what a Figure would all these Acquirements amount to, if the Owner were sent into the *City* among his Brethren! Behold a Fourth, in much and deep Conversation with himself, biting his Thumbs at proper Junctures; his Countenance chequered with Business and Design; sometimes walking very fast, with his Eyes nailed to a Paper that he holds in his Hands, a great Saver of Time, somewhat thick of Hearing, very short of Sight, but more of Memory. A Man ever in Haste, a great Hatcher and Breeder of Business, and excellent at the Famous Art of *whispering Nothing*. A huge Idolater of Monosyllables and Procrastination: so ready to *Give* his Word to every Body that he never *keeps* it. One that has forgot the common *Meaning* of Words, but an admirable Retainer of the *Sound*. Extremely subject to the *Looseness*, for his *Occasions* are perpetually *calling him away*. If you approach his Grate in his familiar Intervals; 'Sir', says he, 'Give me a Penny, and I'll sing you a Song: But give me the Penny first'. (Hence comes the common Saying, and commoner Practice of parting with Money for a *Song*.) What a complete System of *Court-Skill* is here described in every Branch of it, and all utterly lost with wrong Application? Accost the Hole of

Notes

288 *Sir E[dwar]d S[eymou]r, Sir C[hristophe]r M[usgra]ve, Sir J[oh]n B[ow]l[e]s, J[oh]n H[o]we, Esq* leading Tory politicians of the time.

289 *Patriots* a name adopted by anti-government Tories.

290 * * ... * Ecclesiastical.

291 *Student* inmate of Bedlam, the London asylum for the insane.

292 *three Pence* A Lawyer's Coach-hire [Swift's marginal note].

293 *Ecce cornuta erat ejus facies* "Lo, his face was horned," a well-known mistranslation in the Latin or Vulgate Bible for a Hebrew word meaning "shining," like the surface of polished horn; a note in the fifth edition suggests this.

294 *Whore of Babylon* a figure in the Book of Revelation taken by some Protestants to represent the Roman Catholic Church.

another Kennel, first stopping your Nose, you will behold a surly, gloomy, nasty, slovenly Mortal, raking in his own Dung, and dabbling in his Urine. The best Part of his Diet, is the Reversion of his own Ordure, which expiring into Steams, whirls perpetually about, and at last reinfunds. His Complexion is of a dirty Yellow, with a thin scattered Beard, exactly agreeable to that of his Diet upon its first Declination; like other Insects, who having their Birth and Education in an Excrement, from thence borrow their Colour and their Smell. The Student of this Apartment is very sparing of his Words, but somewhat over-liberal of his Breath; He holds his Hand out ready to receive your Penny, and immediately upon Receipt, withdraws to his former Occupations. Now, is it not amazing to think, the society of *Warwick-Lane*,[295] should have no more Concern for the Recovery of so useful a Member, who, if one may judge from these Appearances, would become the greatest Ornament to that Illustrious Body? Another Student struts up fiercely to your Teeth, puffing with his Lips, half squeezing out his Eyes, and very graciously holds you out his Hand to kiss. The *Keeper* desires you not to be afraid of this Professor, for he will do you no Hurt: To him alone is allowed the Liberty of the Ante-chamber, and the *Orator* of that Place gives you to understand, that this solemn Person is a *Tailor* run mad with Pride. This considerable Student is adorned with many other Qualities, upon which, at present, I shall not further enlarge ——*Hark in your Ear* ————[296] I am strangely mistaken, if all his Address, his Motions, and his Airs, would not then be very natural, and in their proper Element.

I shall not descend so minutely, as to insist upon the vast Number of *Beaux, Fiddlers, Poets*, and *Politicians*, that the World might recover by such a Reformation: But what is more material, beside the clear Gain redounding to the Commonwealth, by so large an Acquisition of Persons to employ, whose Talents and Acquirements, if I may be so bold to affirm it, are now buried, or at least misapplied: It would be a mighty Advantage accruing to the Public from this Enquiry, that all these would very much excel, and arrive at great Perfection in their several Kinds; which, I think, is manifest from what I have already shown; and shall enforce by this one plain Instance; That even I myself, the Author of these momentuous Truths, am a Person, whose Imaginations are hard-mouthed,[297] and exceedingly disposed to run away with his *Reason*, which I have observed from long Experience, to be a very light Rider, and easily shook off; upon which Account, my Friends will never trust me alone, without a solemn Promise, to vent my Speculations in this, or the like manner, for the universal Benefit of Human kind; which, perhaps, the gentle, courteous, and candid Reader, brim-full of that *Modern* Charity and Tenderness, usually annexed to his *Office*, will be very hardly persuaded to believe.

Sect. X
A Tale of a Tub

It is an unanswerable Argument of a very refined Age, the wonderful Civilities that have passed of late Years, between the Nation of *Authors*, and that of *Readers*. There can hardly pop out a *Play*, a *Pamphlet*, or a *Poem*, without a Preface full of

Notes

[295] *society of Warwick-Lane* the Royal College of Physicians.

[296] ——*Hark in your Ear* ———— I cannot conjecture what the Author means here, or how this Chasm could be filled, though it is capable of more than one Interpretation [note in fifth edition].

[297] *hard-mouthed* like a disobedient horse that does not feel the bit.

Acknowledgements to the World, for the general Reception and Applause they have given it, which the Lord knows where, or when, or how, or from whom it received. In due Deference to so laudable a Custom, I do here return my humble Thanks to *His Majesty*, and both Houses of *Parliament*; To the *Lords* of the King's most honourable Privy-Council; To the Reverend the *Judges*; To the *Clergy*, and *Gentry*, and *Yeomanry* of this Land: But in a more especial manner to my worthy Brethren and Friends at *Will's Coffee-house*, and *Gresham-College*, and *Warwick-Lane*, and *Moor-Fields*,[298] and *Scotland-Yard*, and *Westminster-Hall*, and *Guild-hall*; [299]In short, to all Inhabitants and Retainers whatsoever, either in Court, or Church, or Camp, or City, or Country, for their generous and universal Acceptance of this Divine Treatise. I accept their Approbation, and good Opinion with extreme Gratitude, and to the utmost of my poor Capacity, shall take hold of all Opportunities to return the Obligation.

I am also happy that Fate has flung me into so blessed an Age for the mutual Felicity of *Booksellers* and *Authors*, whom I may safely affirm to be at this Day the two only satisfied Parties in *England*. Ask an *Author* how his last Piece hath succeeded; 'Why, truly he thanks his Stars, the World has been very favourable, and he has not the least Reason to complain: And yet, By G—, He writ it in a Week, at Bits and Starts, when he could steal an Hour from his urgent Affairs'; as, it is a hundred to one, you may see further in the Preface; to which he refers you, and for the rest, to the Bookseller. There you go as a Customer, and make the same Question: He blesses his God the *Thing* takes wonderfully, he is just printing a Second Edition, and has but three left in his Shop. You beat down the Price: 'Sir, we shall not differ'; and in hopes of your Custom another Time, lets you have it as reasonable as you please; 'And, pray send as many of your Acquaintance as you will, I shall, upon your Account furnish them all at the same Rate'.

Now, it is not well enough considered, to what Accidents and Occasions the World is indebted for the greatest Part of these noble Writings, which hourly start up to entertain it. If it were not for a *rainy Day, a drunken Vigil, a Fit of the Spleen, a Course of Physic, a sleepy Sunday, an ill Run at Dice, a long Tailor's Bill, a Beggar's Purse, a factious Head, a hot Sun, costive Diet, Want of Books, and a just Contempt of Learning*. But for these Events, I say, and some Others too long to recite (especially *a prudent Neglect of taking Brimstone inwardly*) I doubt the Number of *Authors* and of *Writings* would dwindle away to a Degree most woeful to behold. To confirm this Opinion, hear the Words of the famous *Troglodyte* Philosopher: ''Tis certain', said he, 'some Grains of Folly are of course annexed, as Part in the Composition of Human Nature, only the Choice is left us, whether we please to wear them *Inlaid* or *Embossed*: And we need not go very far to seek how That is usually determined, when we remember, it is with Human Faculties as with Liquors, the lightest will be ever at the Top'.

There is in this famous Island of *Britain* a certain paltry *Scribbler*, very voluminous, whose Character the Reader cannot wholly be Stranger to. He deals in a pernicious Kind of Writings called *Second Parts*, and usually passes under the Name of *The Author of the First*. I easily foresee, that as soon as I lay down my Pen, this nimble *Operator* will have stole it, and treat me as inhumanly as he hath already done Dr. B——re,[300]L——ge,[301] and many others who shall here be nameless. I therefore fly for Justice and Relief,

Notes

[298] *Moor-Fields* the location of Bedlam.

[299] *Guild-hall* a London courthouse.

[300] *B——re* Richard Blackmore (1655–1729), physician and author of two epic poems.

[301] *L——ge* Roger L'Estrange (1616–1704), Tory journalist, prolific writer, and translator.

into the Hands of that great *Rectifier of Saddles*, and *Lover of Mankind*, Dr. B——tly, begging he will take this enormous Grievance into his most *Modern* Consideration: And if it should so happen that the *Furniture*[302] *of an Ass*, in the Shape of a *Second Part*, must for my Sins, be clapped by a Mistake, upon my Back, that he will immediately please, in the Presence of the World, to lighten me of the Burthen, and take it Home to *his own House*, till the *true Beast* thinks fit to call for it.

In the meantime I do here give this public Notice, that my Resolutions are to circumscribe within this Discourse the whole Stock of Matter I have been so many Years providing. Since my *Vein* is once opened, I am content to exhaust it all at a Running, for the peculiar Advantage of my dear Country, and for the universal Benefit of Mankind. Therefore, hospitably considering the Number of my Guests, they shall have my whole Entertainment at a Meal; And I scorn to set up the *Leavings* in the Cupboard. What the *Guests* cannot eat may be given to the *Poor*, and the *Dogs* under the Table may gnaw the *Bones*; This I understand for a more generous Proceeding, than to turn the Company's Stomachs, by inviting them again tomorrow to a scurvy Meal of *Scraps*.

If the Reader fairly considers the Strength of what I have advanced in the foregoing Section, I am convinced it will produce a wonderful Revolution in his Notions and Opinions; And he will be abundantly better prepared to receive and to relish the concluding Part of this miraculous Treatise. Readers may be divided into three Classes – the *Superficial*, the *Ignorant*, and the *Learned*: and I have with much Felicity fitted my Pen to the Genius and Advantage of each. The *Superficial* Reader will be strangely provoked to *Laughter*; which clears the Breast and the Lungs, is Sovereign against the *Spleen*, and the most innocent of all *Diuretics*. The *Ignorant* Reader (between whom and the former, the Distinction is extremely nice) will find himself disposed to *Stare*; which is an admirable Remedy for ill Eyes, serves to raise and enliven the Spirits, and wonderfully helps *Perspiration*. But the Reader truly *Learned*, chiefly for whose Benefit, I wake when others sleep, and sleep when others wake, will here find sufficient Matter to employ his Speculations for the rest of his Life. It were much to be wished, and I do here humbly propose for an Experiment, that every Prince in *Christendom* will take seven of the *deepest Scholars* in his Dominions, and shut them up close for *seven* Years in *seven* Chambers, with a Command to write *seven* ample Commentaries on this comprehensive Discourse. I shall venture to affirm, that whatever Difference may be found in their several Conjectures, they will be all without the least Distortion, manifestly deducible from the Text. Meantime, it is my earnest Request, that so useful an Undertaking may be entered upon (if their Majesties please) with all convenient Speed; because, I have a strong Inclination, before I leave the World, to taste a Blessing which we *Mysterious* Writers can seldom reach, till we have got into our Graves. Whether it is that *Fame*, being a Fruit grafted on the Body, can hardly grow, and much less ripen, till the *Stock*[303] is in the Earth: Or, whether she be a Bird of Prey, and is lured among the rest, to pursue after the Scent of a *Carcass*: Or, whether she conceives her Trumpet sounds best and farthest, when she stands on a *Tomb*, by the Advantage of a rising Ground, and the Echo of a hollow Vault.

'Tis true, indeed, the Republic of *dark* Authors, after they once found out this excellent Expedient of *Dying*, have been peculiarly happy in the Variety as well as extent of their Reputation. For, *Night* being the universal Mother of things, wise Philosophers hold all Writings to be *fruitful*, in the Proportion they are *dark*; And therefore, the *true*

Notes

302 *Furniture* saddle, stirrups, etc.

303 *Stock* "The trunk into which a graft is inserted" (Johnson).

Illuminated (that is to say, the *Darkest* of all) have met with such numberless Commentators, whose *Scholiastic*[304] Midwifery hath delivered them of Meanings that the Authors themselves perhaps never conceived, and yet may very justly be allowed the Lawful Parents of them: the Words of such Writers being like Seed, which, however scattered at random, when they light upon a fruitful Ground, will multiply far beyond either the Hopes or Imagination of the Sower.

And therefore in order to promote so useful a Work, I will here take Leave to glance a few *Innuendoes*, that may be of great Assistance to those sublime Spirits, who shall be appointed to labour in a universal Comment upon this wonderful Discourse. And First, I have couched a very profound Mystery in the Number of O's multiplied by *Seven*, and divided by *Nine*. Also, if a devout Brother of the *Rosy-cross*[305] will pray fervently for sixty-three Mornings, with a lively Faith, and then transpose certain Letters and Syllables according to Prescription in the second and fifth Section; they will certainly reveal into a full Receipt of the *Opus Magnum*. Lastly, Whoever will be at the Pains to calculate the whole Number of each Letter in this Treatise, and sum up the Difference exactly between the several Numbers, assigning the true natural Cause for every such Difference, the Discoveries in the Product, will plentifully Reward his Labour. But then he must beware of *Bythus* and *Sigè*,[306] and be sure not to forget the Qualities of *Acamoth; A cujus lacrymis humecta prodit Substantia, à risu lucida, à tristitia solida, et à timore mobilis;*[307] wherein *Eugenius Philalethes*[308] hath committed an unpardonable Mistake.

Sect. XI
A Tale of a Tub

After so wide a Compass as I have wandered, I do now gladly overtake and close in with my Subject, and shall henceforth hold on with it an even Pace to the End of my Journey, except some beautiful Prospect appears within sight of my Way; whereof, though at present I have neither Warning nor Expectation, yet upon such an Accident, come when it will, I shall beg my Reader's Favour and Company, allowing me to conduct him through it along with myself. For in *Writing*, it is as in *Travelling*: If a Man is in haste to be at home (which I acknowledge to be none of my Case, having never so little Business, as when I am there), if his *Horse* be tired with long Riding and ill Ways or be naturally

Notes

304 *Scholiastic* having to do with commentary, or the practice of adding scholia (notes).

305 *Rosy-cross* Rosicrucian Society, a Christian brotherhood with mystical beliefs.

306 *Bythus and Sigè* I was told by an Eminent Divine, whom I consulted on this Point, that these two Barbarous Words, with that of *Acamoth* [Hebrew, "wisdom"] and its Qualities, as here set down, are quoted from *Irenaeus*. This he discovered by searching that Ancient Writer for another Quotation of our Author, which he has placed in the Title Page, and refers to the Book and Chapter; the Curious were very Inquisitive, whether those Barbarous Words, *Basima Eacabasa*, &c. are really in *Irenaeus* [*Against Heresies* 1.4.2], and upon enquiry 'twas found they were a sort of Cant or Jargon of certain Heretics, and therefore very properly prefixed to such a Book as this is of our Author [note in fifth edition].

307 *A cujus lacrymis ... mobilis* "from the tears of which come damp essences, from the laughter light ones, from the sadness solid ones, and from the fear moving essences."

308 *Eugenius Philalethes* To the abovementioned [in Swift's marginal note] Treatise, called *Anthroposophia Theomagica*, there is another annexed, called *Anima Magica Abscondita*, written by the same Author [Thomas] Vaughan, under the Name of Eugenius Philalethes, but in neither of those Treatises is there any mention of Acamoth or its Qualities, so that this is nothing but Amusement, and a Ridicule of dark, unintelligible Writers; only the Words, A cujus lacrymis, &c. are as we have said, transcribed from *Irenaeus*, though I know not from what part. I believe one of the Author's Designs was to set curious Men a hunting through Indexes, and enquiring for Books out of the common Road [note in fifth edition].

a Jade, I advise him clearly to make the straightest and the commonest Road, be it ever so dirty; But then surely we must own such a Man to be a scurvy Companion at best; He *spatters* himself and his Fellow-Travellers at every Step: All their Thoughts, and Wishes, and Conversation turn entirely upon the Subject of their Journey's End; and at every Splash, and Plunge, and Stumble, they heartily wish one another at the Devil.

On the other side, when a Traveller and his *Horse* are in Heart and Plight, when his Purse is full and the Day before him; he takes the Road only where it is clean or convenient; entertains his Company there as agreeably as he can; but upon the first Occasion, carries them along with him to every delightful Scene in View, whether of Art, of Nature, or of both; and if they chance to refuse out of Stupidity or Weariness; let them jog on by themselves, and be d—n'd; He'll overtake them at the next Town; at which arriving, he Rides furiously through, the Men, Women, and Children run out to gaze, a hundred *noisy Curs*[309] run *barking* after him, of which, if he honours the boldest with a *Lash of his Whip*, it is rather out of Sport than Revenge: But should some *sourer Mongrel* dare too near an Approach, he receives a *Salute* on the Chaps by an accidental Stroke from the Courser's Heels (nor is any Ground lost by the Blow) which sends him yelping and limping home.

I now proceed to sum up the singular Adventures of my renowned *Jack*; the State of whose Dispositions and Fortunes, the careful Reader does, no doubt, most exactly remember, as I last parted with them in the Conclusion of a former Section. Therefore, his next Care must be from two of the foregoing, to extract a Scheme of Notions, that may best fit his Understanding for a true Relish of what is to ensue.

Jack had not only calculated the first Revolution of his Brain so prudently, as to give Rise to that Epidemic Sect of *Æolists*, but succeeding also into a new and strange Variety of Conceptions, the Fruitfulness of his Imagination led him into certain Notions, which, although in Appearance very unaccountable, were not without their Mysteries and their Meanings, nor wanted Followers to countenance and improve them. I shall therefore be extremely careful and exact in recounting such material Passages of this Nature, as I have been able to collect, either from undoubted Tradition, or indefatigable Reading; and shall describe them as graphically as it is possible, and as far as Notions of that Height and Latitude can be brought within the Compass of a Pen. Nor do I at all question, but they will furnish Plenty of noble Matter for such, whose converting Imaginations dispose them to reduce all Things into *Types*; who can make *Shadows*, no thanks to the Sun; and then mould them into Substances, no thanks to Philosophy; whose peculiar Talent lies in fixing Tropes and Allegories to the *Letter*, and refining what is Literal into Figure and Mystery.

Jack had provided a fair Copy of his Father's *Will* engrossed in Form upon a large Skin of Parchment; and resolving to act the Part of a most dutiful Son, he became the fondest Creature of it imaginable. For, although, as I have often told the Reader, it consisted wholly in certain plain, easy Directions about the management and wearing of their Coats, with Legacies and Penalties in case of Obedience or Neglect; yet He began to entertain a Fancy, that the matter was *deeper* and *darker*, and therefore must needs have a great deal more of Mystery at the Bottom. 'Gentlemen', said he, 'I will prove this very Skin of Parchment to be Meat, Drink, and Cloth, to be the Philosopher's Stone,[310] and the Universal Medicine'. In consequence of which Raptures, he resolved to make use of it in the most necessary, as well as the most paltry Occasions of Life.

Notes

[309] *noisy Curs* By these are meant what the Author calls, The *True Critics* [note in fifth edition].

[310] *Philosopher's Stone* "A stone dreamed of by alchemists, which, by its touch, converts base metals into gold" (Johnson).

He had a Way of working it into any Shape he pleased; so that it served him for a Nightcap when he went to Bed, and for an Umbrella in rainy Weather. He would lap a Piece of it about a sore Toe, or when he had Fits, burn two Inches under his Nose; or if any Thing lay heavy on his Stomach, scrape off and swallow as much of the Powder as would lie on a silver Penny, they were all infallible Remedies. With Analogy to these Refinements, his common Talk and Conversation, ran wholly in the Phrase of his Will, and he circumscribed the utmost of his Eloquence within that Compass, not daring to let slip a Syllable without Authority from thence. Once at a strange House he was suddenly taken short, upon an urgent Juncture, whereon it may not be allowed too particularly to dilate; and being not able to call to mind, with that Suddenness, the Occasion required, an Authentic Phrase for demanding the Way to the Backside;[311] he chose rather as the more prudent Course, to incur the Penalty in such Cases usually annexed. Neither was it possible for the united Rhetoric of Mankind to prevail with him to make himself clean again: Because having consulted the Will upon this Emergency, he met with a Passage near the Bottom[312] (whether foisted in by the Transcriber, is not known) which seemed to forbid it.

He made it a Part of his Religion, never to say Grace to his Meat, nor could all the World persuade him, as the common Phrase is, to eat his Victuals *like a Christian*.

He bore a strange kind of Appetite to *Snap-Dragon*,[313] and to the livid Snuffs of a burning Candle, which he would catch and swallow with an Agility, wonderful to conceive; and by this Procedure, maintained a perpetual Flame in his Belly, which issuing in a glowing Stream from both his Eyes as well as his Nostrils, and his Mouth; made his Head appear in a dark Night, like the Skull of an Ass, wherein a roguish Boy hath conveyed a Farthing Candle, *to the Terror of his Majesty's Liege Subjects*. Therefore, he made use of no other Expedient to light himself home, but was wont to say, That 'a Wise Man was his own Lantern'.

He would shut his Eyes as he walked along the Streets, and if he happened to bounce his Head against a Post, or fall into the Kennel (as he seldom missed either to do one or both) he would tell the gibing Prentices, who looked on, that he submitted with entire Resignation, as to a Trip, or a Blow of Fate, with whom he found by long Experience, how vain it was either to wrestle or to cuff; and whoever durst undertake to do either, would be sure to come off with a swinging Fall, or a bloody Nose. 'It was ordained', said he, 'some few Days before the Creation, that my Nose and this very Post should have a Rencounter, and therefore Nature thought fit to send us both into the World in the same Age, and to make us Countrymen and Fellow-Citizens. Now, had my Eyes been open it is very likely, the Business might have been a great deal worse: For how many a confounded Slip is daily got by Man, with all his Foresight about him? Besides, the Eyes of the Understanding see best, when those of the Senses are out of the way; and therefore, blind Men are observed to tread their Steps with much more Caution, and Conduct, and Judgement, than those who rely with too much Confidence, upon the Virtue of the visual Nerve which every little Accident shakes out of Order, and a Drop, or a Film, can wholly disconcert; like a Lantern among a Pack of roaring Bullies,

Notes

311 *Backside* backyard.

312 I cannot guess the Author's meaning here, which I would be very glad to know, because it seems to be of Importance [note in fifth edition; an industrious editor has identified the passage as Revelation 22.11, "he which is filthy, let him be filthy still"].

313 *Snap-Dragon* "A kind of play, in which brandy is set on fire, and raisins thrown into it, which those who are unused to the sport are afraid to take out; but which may be safely snatched by a quick motion, and put blazing into the mouth, which being closed, the fire is at once extinguished" (Johnson).

when they scour the Streets; exposing its Owner and itself to outward Kicks and Buffets, which both might have escaped if the Vanity of Appearing would have suffered them to walk in the Dark. But further, if we examine the *Conduct* of these boasted Lights, it will prove yet a great deal worse than their *Fortune*: 'Tis true, I have broke my Nose against this Post because Providence either forgot, or did not think it convenient, to twitch me by the Elbow, and give me notice to avoid it. But let not this encourage either the present Age or Posterity, to trust their *Noses* into the keeping of their Eyes, which may prove the fairest Way of losing them for good and all. For, O ye Eyes, Ye blind Guides; miserable Guardians are Ye of our frail Noses; Ye, I say, who fasten upon the first Precipice in view, and then tow our wretched willing Bodies after You, to the very Brink of Destruction: But, alas, that Brink is rotten, our Feet slip, and we tumble down prone into a Gulf, without one hospitable Shrub in the Way to break the Fall; a Fall, to which not any Nose of mortal Make is equal, except that of the Giant *Lauralco*,[314] who was Lord of the *Silver Bridge*. Most properly therefore, O Eyes, and with great Justice, may You be compared to those foolish Lights, which conduct Men through Dirt and Darkness, till they fall into a deep Pit, or a noisome Bog'.

This I have produced as a Scantling of *Jack*'s great Eloquence and the Force of his Reasoning upon such abstruse Matters.

He was, besides, a Person of great Design and Improvement in Affairs of *Devotion*, having introduced a new Deity, who hath since met with a vast Number of Worshippers; by some called *Babel*, by others, *Chaos*; who had an ancient temple of *Gothic* Structure upon *Salisbury* Plain;[315] famous for its Shrine and Celebration by Pilgrims.

When he had some Roguish Trick to play, he would down with his Knees, up with his Eyes, and fall to Prayers, though in the midst of the Kennel. Then it was that those who understood his Pranks, would be sure to get far enough out of his Way; And whenever Curiosity attracted Strangers to Laugh, or to Listen; he would of a sudden, with one Hand, out with his *Gear*, and piss full in their Eyes, and with the other, all to-bespatter them with Mud.

In Winter he went always loose and unbuttoned, and clad as thin as possible, to let *in* the ambient Heat; and in Summer, lapped himself close and thick to keep it *out*. In all Revolutions of Government, he would make his Court for the Office of *Hangman* General; and in the Exercise of that Dignity, wherein he was very dexterous, would make use of no other *Vizard*[316] than a *long Prayer*.

He had a Tongue so Musculous and Subtle, that he could twist it up into his Nose, and deliver a strange Kind of Speech from thence. He was also the first in these Kingdoms, who began to improve the *Spanish* Accomplishment of *Braying*;[317] and having large Ears, perpetually exposed and erect, he carried his Art to such a Perfection, that it was a Point of great Difficulty to distinguish either, by the View or the Sound, between the *Original* and the *Copy*.

He was troubled with a Disease, reverse to that called the Stinging of the *Tarantula*; and would run Dog-mad at the Noise of *Music*,[318] especially a *Pair of Bag-Pipes*. But he would cure himself again, by taking two or three Turns in *Westminster-Hall*, or *Billingsgate*,[319] or in a *Boarding-School*, or the *Royal-Exchange*, or a *State Coffee-House*.

Notes

[314] *Lauralco* Vide *Don Quixote* [Swift's marginal note].

[315] *Gothic Structure upon Salisbury Plain* Stonehenge.

[316] *Vizard* mask.

[317] *Braying* an allusion to *Don Quixote*, chapters 25 and 27.

[318] *Music* the poison of the tarantula was supposed to be counteracted by the effects of music.

[319] *Billingsgate* the fish market.

He was a Person that *feared* no *Colours* but mortally *hated* all, and upon that Account, bore a cruel Aversion to *Painters*; insomuch, that in his Paroxysms, as he walked the Streets, he would have his Pockets loaden with Stone, to pelt at the *Signs*.

Having from this manner of Living, frequent Occasions to *wash* himself, he would often leap over Head and Ears into the Water, though it were in the midst of the Winter, but was always observed to come out again much *dirtier*, if possible, than he went in.

He was the first that ever found out the Secret of contriving a *Soporiferous* Medicine to be conveyed in at the *Ears*; It was a Compound of *Sulphur* and *Balm of Gilead*,[320] with a little *Pilgrim's Salve*.

He wore a large Plaster of artificial *Caustics* on his Stomach, with the Fervour of which, he could set himself a *groaning*, like the famous *Board*[321] upon Application of a red-hot Iron.

He would stand in the Turning of a Street, and calling to those who passed by, would cry to One; 'Worthy Sir, do me the Honour of a good Slap in the Chaps'. To another, 'Honest Friend, pray, favour me with a handsome Kick on the Arse'. 'Madam, shall I entreat a small Box in the Ear from your Ladyship's fair Hands?' 'Noble Captain, Lend a reasonable Thwack, for the Love of God, with that Cane of yours, over these poor Shoulders'. And when he had by such earnest Solicitations, made a shift to procure a Basting sufficient to swell up his Fancy and his Sides; He would return home extremely comforted, and full of terrible Accounts of what he had undergone for the *Public Good*. 'Observe this Stroke', said he, showing his bare Shoulders, 'a plaguey *Janissary* gave it me this very Morning at seven o'Clock, as, with much ado, I was driving off the *Great Turk*. Neighbours mine, this broken Head deserves a Plaster; had poor *Jack* been tender of his Noddle you would have seen the *Pope*, and the *French* King, long before this time of Day, among your Wives and your Warehouses. Dear *Christians*, the *Great Mogul was come as far as White-Chapel*, and you may thank these poor Sides that he hath not (God bless us) already swallowed up Man, Woman, and Child'.

It was highly worth observing the singular Effects of that Aversion, or Antipathy, which *Jack* and his Brother *Peter* seemed, even to an Affectation, to bear towards each other. *Peter* had lately done *some Rogueries*, that forced him to abscond; and he seldom ventured to stir out before Night, for fear of Bailiffs. Their Lodgings were at the two most distant Parts of the Town, from each other; and whenever their Occasions, or Humours called them abroad, they would make Choice of the oddest unlikely Times, and most uncouth Rounds they could invent, that they might be sure to avoid one another: Yet after all this, it was their perpetual Fortune to meet. The Reason of which, is easy enough to apprehend: For, the Frenzy and the Spleen of both, having the same Foundation, we may look upon them as two Pair of Compasses, equally extended, and the fixed Foot of each, remaining in the same Centre; which, though moving contrary Ways at first, will be sure to encounter somewhere or other in the Circumference. Besides, it was among the great Misfortunes of *Jack*, to bear a huge Personal Resemblance with his Brother *Peter*. Their Humour and Dispositions were not only the same, but there was a close Analogy in their Shape, their Size, and their Mien. Insomuch, as nothing was more frequent than for a Bailiff to seize *Jack* by the Shoulders,

Notes

320 *Balm of Gilead* "juice drawn from the balsam tree" (Johnson, translating Calmet's *Dictionary of the Bible*).

321 *famous Board* a board of wood which, when surreptitiously heated, would give off whining sounds because it contained hidden air pockets; the so-called *groaning board* was for a time a popular marvel in London.

and cry: 'Mr. *Peter*, You are the king's Prisoner'. Or, at other Times, for one of *Peter*'s nearest Friends, to accost *Jack* with open Arms, 'Dear *Peter*, I am glad to see thee, pray send me one of your best Medicines for the Worms'. This we may suppose, was a mortifying Return of those Pains and Proceedings, *Jack* had laboured in so long; And finding, how directly opposite all his Endeavours had answered to the sole End and Intention, which he had proposed to himself; How could it avoid having terrible Effects upon a Head and Heart so furnished as his? However, the poor Remainders of his *Coat* bore all the Punishment; The orient Sun never entered upon his diurnal Progress, without missing a Piece of it. He hired a Tailor to stitch up the Collar so close, that it was ready to choke him, and squeezed out his Eyes at such a Rate, as one could see nothing but the White. What little was left of the main Substance of the Coat, he rubbed every Day for two hours, against a rough-cast Wall, in order to grind away the Remnants of *Lace* and *Embroidery*; but at the same time went on with so much Violence, that he proceeded a *Heathen Philosopher*. Yet after all he could do of this kind, the Success continued still to disappoint his Expectation. For, as it is the Nature of Rags, to bear a kind of mock Resemblance to Finery; there being a sort of fluttering Appearance in both, which is not to be distinguished at a Distance, in the Dark, or by short-sighted Eyes; So, in those Junctures, it fared with *Jack* and his Tatters, that they offered to the first View, a ridiculous Flaunting, which, assisting the Resemblance in Person and Air, thwarted all his Projects of Separation, and left so near a Similitude between them, as frequently deceived the very Disciples and followers of both.

* * * * * * * * * * * * *

* * * * * * * * * * * * *

Desunt non- * * * * * * * * * * *

nulla[322] * * * * * * * * * *

* * * * * * * * * * * * *

* * * * * * * * * * * * *

The old *Sclavonian* Proverb said well, That 'it is with *Men* as with Asses; whoever would keep them fast, may find a very good Hold at their *Ears*'. Yet, I think, we may affirm, and it hath been verified by repeated Experience, that,

Effugiet tamen hæc sceleratus vincula Proteus.[323]

It is good, therefore, to read the Maxims of our Ancestors, with great Allowances to Times and Persons: For, if we look into Primitive Records, we shall find, that no Revolutions have been so great, or so frequent, as those of human *Ears*. In former Days, there was a curious Invention to catch and keep them; which, I think, we may justly reckon among the *Artes perditæ*:[324] And how can it be otherwise, when in these latter Centuries, the very Species is not only diminished to a very lamentable Degree, but the poor Remainder is also degenerated so far, as to mock our skilfullest *Tenure*? For, if the only slitting of one *Ear* in a Stag, hath been found sufficient to propagate the Defect through a whole Forest; Why should we wonder at the greatest Consequences, from so many Loppings and Mutilations, to which the *Ears* of our Fathers and our own, have been of late so much exposed? 'Tis true, indeed, that while this *Island* of ours, was under the *Dominion of Grace*, many Endeavours were made to improve the

Notes

322 *Desunt non-nulla* "Much is missing."

323 Effugiet tamen hæc sceleratus vincula Proteus "Nevertheless, that rascal Proteus escapes all these chains" (Horace, *Satires* 2.3.71, where Proteus is a debtor from whom it is impossible to collect).

324 *Artes perditæ* lost arts.

Growth of *Ears* once more among us. The Proportion of Largeness was not only looked upon as an Ornament of the *Outward* Man, but as a Type of Grace in the *Inward*.[325] Besides, it is held by Naturalists, that if there be a Protuberancy of Parts in the *Superior* Region of the Body, as in the *Ears* and *Nose*, there must be a Parity also in the *Inferior*: And therefore in that truly pious Age, the *Males* in every Assembly, according as they were gifted, appeared very forward in exposing their *Ears* to view, and the Regions about them; because *Hippocrates*[326] tells us, 'that when the Vein behind the *Ear* happens to be cut, a Man becomes a Eunuch'. And the *Females* were nothing backwarder in beholding and edifying by them: Whereof those who had already *used the Means*, looked about them with great Concern, in hopes of conceiving a suitable Offspring by such a Prospect: Others, who stood Candidates for *Benevolence*, found there a plentiful Choice, and were sure to fix upon such as discovered the largest *Ears*, that the Breed might not dwindle between them. Lastly, the devouter Sisters, who looked upon all extraordinary Dilatations of that Member, as Protrusions of Zeal, or spiritual Excrescencies, were sure to honour every Head they sat upon, as if they had been *cloven Tongues*;[327] but, especially, that of the Preacher, whose *Ears* were usually of the prime Magnitude: which upon that Account, he was very frequent and exact in exposing with all Advantages to the people: in his Rhetorical *Paroxysms*, turning sometimes to *hold forth* the one, and sometimes to *hold forth* the other: From which Custom, the whole Operation of Preaching is to this very Day among their Professors, styled by the Phrase of *Holding forth*.

Such was the Progress of the *Saints*, for advancing the Size of that Member. And it is thought, the Success would have been every way answerable, if in process of time, a cruel King[328] had not arose, who raised a bloody Persecution against all *Ears*, above a certain Standard: Upon which, some were glad to hide their flourishing Sprouts in a black Border, others crept wholly under a Periwig: some were slit, others cropped, and a great Number sliced off to the Stumps. But of this, more hereafter, in my *general History of Ears*; which I design very speedily to bestow upon the Public.

From this brief Survey of the falling State of *Ears*, in the last Age, and the small Care had to advance their ancient Growth in the present, it is manifest, how little Reason we can have to rely upon a Hold so short, so weak, and so slippery; and that, whoever desires to catch Mankind fast, must have Recourse to some other Methods. Now, he that will examine Human Nature with Circumspection enough, may discover several *Handles*, whereof the *Six* Senses afford one apiece, beside a great Number that are screwed to the Passions, and some few riveted to the Intellect. Among these last, *Curiosity* is one, and of all others, affords the firmest Grasp; *Curiosity*, that Spur in the side, that Bridle in the Mouth, that Ring in the Nose, of a lazy, an impatient, and a grunting Reader. By this *Handle* it is, that an Author should seize upon his Readers; which as soon as he hath once compassed, all Resistance and struggling are in vain; and they become his Prisoners as close as he pleases, till Weariness or Dullness force him to let go his Grip.

Notes

[325] *Grace in the Inward* Protestants who look for signs of inner grace, or Roundheads in the Civil War, who wore short hair and thus exposed their ears.

[326] *Hippocrates* Lib. de aëre locis & aquis [Swift's marginal note, which gives true citations of the early Greek physician and aphorist].

[327] *cloven Tongues* part of the Pentecostal vision described in Acts 2.3.

[328] *cruel King* This was King *Charles* the Second, who at his Restoration turned out all the Dissenting Teachers that would not conform [note in fifth edition].

And therefore, I the Author of this miraculous Treatise, having hitherto, beyond Expectation, maintained by the aforesaid *Handle*, a firm Hold upon my gentle Readers; it is with great Reluctance, that I am at length compelled to remit my Grasp; leaving them in the Perusal of what remains, to that natural *Oscitancy* inherent in the Tribe. I can only assure thee, Courteous Reader, for both our Comforts, that my Concern is altogether equal to thine, for my Unhappiness in losing, or mislaying among my Papers the remaining Part of these Memoirs; which consisted of Accidents, Turns, and Adventures, both New, Agreeable, and Surprising; and therefore, calculated in all due Points, to the delicate Taste of this our noble Age. But, alas, with my utmost Endeavours, I have been able only to retain a few of the Heads. Under which, there was a full Account, how *Peter* got a *Protection* out of the *King's-Bench*; And of a Reconcilement between *Jack* and Him, upon a Design they had in a certain *rainy Night* to trepan [329] Brother *Martin* into a *Spunging-house*,[330] and there strip him to the Skin. How *Martin*, with much ado, showed them both a fair pair of Heels. How a *new Warrant* came out against *Peter;* upon which, how *Jack* left him in the lurch, *stole his Protection, and made use of it himself.* How *Jack*'s Tatters came into Fashion in *Court* and *City*; How *he got upon a great Horse, and eat Custard.*[331] But the Particulars of all these, with several others, which have now slid out of my Memory, are lost beyond all Hopes of Recovery. For, which Misfortune, leaving my Readers to condole with each other, as far as they shall find it to agree with their several Constitutions; but conjuring them by all the Friendship that hath passed between Us, from the Title-Page to this, not to proceed so far as to injure their Healths, for an Accident past Remedy; I now go on to the Ceremonial Part of an accomplished Writer and therefore, by a Courtly *Modern*, least of all others to be omitted.

The Conclusion

Going too long is a Cause of Abortion as effectual, though not so frequent, as *Going too short*; and holds true especially in the *Labours* of the Brain. Well fare the Heart of that Noble *Jesuit*,[332] who first adventured to confess in Print, that Books must be suited to their several Seasons, like Dress, and Diet, and Diversions: And better fare our noble Nation, for refining upon this, among other *French* Modes. I am living fast, to see the Time, when a *Book* that misses its Tide shall be neglected, as the *Moon* by Day, or like *Mackerel* a Week after the Season. No Man hath more nicely observed our Climate, than the Bookseller who bought the Copy of this Work; He knows to a Tittle,[333] what Subjects will best go off in a *dry Year*, and which it is proper to expose foremost, when the Weather-glass is fallen to *much Rain*. When he had seen this Treatise, and consulted his *Almanac* upon it; he gave me to understand, that he had maturely considered the two Principal Things, which were the *Bulk* and the *Subject*; and found, it would never *take*, but after a long Vacation, and then only, in case it should happen to be a hard Year for Turnips. Upon which I desired to know, *considering my urgent Necessities*, what he thought might be acceptable this Month. He looked *Westward*, and said, I doubt we

Notes

329 *trepan* trick, ensnare.

330 *Spunging-house* "A house to which debtors are taken before commitment to prison, where the bailiffs spunge upon them, or riot at their cost" (Johnson).

331 *Custard* Custard is a famous Dish at a Lord-Mayor's Feast [a note in the fifth edition suggests the passage is about a particular Protestant mayor, Sir Humphrey Edwin].

332 *Jesuit* Père d' Orleans [Swift's accurate marginal note].

333 *Tittle* small part of a piece of writing, a dot or whit.

shall have a fit of bad Weather; However, if you could prepare some pretty little *Banter* (*but not in Verse*) or a small Treatise upon the——, it would run like Wild Fire. But, *if it hold up*, I have already hired an Author to write something against Dr. B—tl—y, which, I am sure will turn to Account.

At length we agreed upon this Expedient; That when a Customer comes for one of these, and desires in Confidence to know the Author; he will tell him very privately, as a Friend, naming whichever of the Wits shall happen to be that Week in the Vogue; and if *D'Urfey*'s last Play should be in Course, I had as lieve he may be[334] the Person as *Congreve*. This I mention, because I am wonderfully well acquainted with the present Relish of Courteous Readers; and have often observed, with singular Pleasure, that a *Fly* driven from a *Honey-pot*, will immediately, with very good Appetite alight, and finish his Meal on an *Excrement*.

I have one Word to say upon the Subject of *Profound Writers*, who are grown very numerous of late; And, I know very well, the judicious World is resolved to list me in that Number. I conceive therefore, as to the Business of being *Profound*, that it is with *Writers* as with *Wells*; A Person with good Eyes may see to the Bottom of the deepest, provided any *Water* be there; and, that often, when there is nothing in the world at the Bottom, besides *Dryness* and *Dirt*, though it be but a Yard and half under Ground, it shall pass, however, for wondrous *Deep*, upon no wiser a Reason than because it is wondrous *Dark*.

I am now trying an Experiment very frequent among Modern Authors; which is *to write upon Nothing*: When the Subject is utterly exhausted, to let the Pen still move on; by some called the Ghost of Wit, delighting to walk after the Death of its Body. And to say the Truth, there seems to be no Part of Knowledge in fewer Hands, than That of Discerning *when to have Done*. By the Time that an Author has writ out a Book, he and his Readers are become old Acquaintance, and grow very loath to part: So that I have sometimes known it to be in Writing, as in Visiting, where the Ceremony of taking Leave, has employed more Time than the whole Conversation before. The Conclusion of a Treatise, resembles the Conclusion of Human Life, which hath sometimes been compared to the End of a Feast, where few are satisfied to depart, *ut plenus vitæ conviva*:[335] For men will sit down after the fullest Meal, though it be only to *doze*, or to *sleep* out the rest of the Day. But, in this latter, I differ extremely from other Writers; and shall be too proud, if by all my Labours, I can have anyways contributed to the *Repose* of Mankind, in Times so turbulent and unquiet as these. Neither, do I think such an Employment so very alien from the Office of a *Wit*, as some would suppose. For among a very polite Nation in *Greece*, there were the *same* Temples built and consecrated to *Sleep* and the *Muses*, between which two Deities they believed the strictest Friendship was established.

I have one concluding Favour, to request of my Reader; that he will not expect to be equally diverted and informed by every Line, or every Page of this Discourse; but give some Allowance to the Author's Spleen, and short Fits or Intervals of Dullness, as well as his own; And lay it seriously to his Conscience, whether, if he were walking the Streets in dirty Weather, or a rainy Day, he would allow it fair dealing in Folks at their Ease from a Window, to critic his Gait, and ridicule his Dress at such a Juncture.

In my Disposure of Employments of the Brain, I have thought fit to make *Invention* the *Master*, and to give *Method* and *Reason*, the Office of its *Lackeys*. The Cause of this

Notes

[334] *I had as lieve he may be* it is all the same to me if he is.

[335] *ut plenus vitæ conviva* "[why not withdraw calmly into death] like a banqueter fed full of life" (Lucretius 3.938).

Distribution was, from observing it my peculiar Case, to be often under a Temptation of being *Witty* upon Occasions, where I could be neither *Wise* nor *Sound*, nor anything to the Matter in hand. And, I am too much a Servant of the *Modern* Way, to neglect any such Opportunities, whatever Pains or Improprieties I may be at, to introduce them. For, I have observed, that from a laborious Collection of Seven Hundred Thirty Eight *Flowers*, and *shining Hints* of the best *Modern* Authors, digested with great Reading, into my Book of *Common-Places*; I have not been able after five Years to draw, hook, or force, into common Conversation, any more than a Dozen. Of which Dozen, the one Moiety failed of Success, by being dropped among unsuitable Company; and the other cost me so many Strains, and Traps, and *Ambages* to introduce, that I at length resolved to give it over. Now, this Disappointment (to discover a Secret) I must own gave me the first Hint of setting up for an *Author*, and I have since found, among some particular Friends, that it is become a very general Complaint and has produced the same Effects upon many others. For, I have remarked many a *towardly Word*, to be wholly neglected or despised in *Discourse*, which has passed very smoothly, with some Consideration and Esteem, after its Preferment and Sanction in *Print*. But, now, since by the Liberty and Encouragement of the Press, I am grown absolute Master of the Occasions and Opportunities, to expose the Talents I have acquired; I already discover that the *Issues* of my *Observanda* begin to grow too large for the *Receipts*. Therefore, I shall here pause awhile, till I find, by feeling the World's Pulse, and my own, that it will be of absolute Necessity for us both, to resume my Pen.

FINIS

A Modest Proposal for Preventing the Children of Poor People from Being a Burden to Their Parents or the Country, and for Making Them Beneficial to the Public (1729)

It is a melancholy Object to those who walk through this great town,[1] or travel in the Country, when they see the *Streets*, the *Roads*, and *Cabin-Doors* crowded with Beggars of the Female Sex, followed by three, four, or six Children, *all in Rags*, and importuning every Passenger for an Alms. These *Mothers* instead of being able to work for their honest Livelihood, are forced to employ all their Time in strolling[2] to beg Sustenance for their *helpless Infants* who, as they grow up, either turn *Thieves* for want of Work or leave their *dear native Country to fight for the Pretender*[3] *in Spain*, or sell themselves to the *Barbadoes*.[4]

I think it is agreed by all Parties that this prodigious Number of Children, in the Arms, or on the Backs, or at the *Heels* of their *Mothers*, and frequently of their *Fathers*, is *in the present deplorable State of the Kingdom*,[5] a very great additional Grievance; and therefore whoever could find out a Fair, Cheap and Easy Method of making these Children Sound and Useful Members of the Common-wealth would deserve so well of the Public, as to have his Statue set up for a Preserver of the Nation.

Notes

A Modest Proposal

1 *this great town* Dublin.

2 *strolling* from "stroll," "To wander; to ramble; to rove; to be a vagrant" (Johnson).

3 *Pretender* James Francis Edward (1688–1766), son of James II, recognized as James III in some Catholic countries.

4 *Barbadoes* where the sugar mills attracted slave and indentured labor.

5 *Kingdom* Ireland.

But my Intention is very far from being confined to provide only for the Children of *professed Beggars*; it is of a much greater Extent, and shall take in the whole Number of Infants at a certain Age, who are born of Parents in effect as little able to support them as those who demand our Charity in the Streets.

As to my own Part, having turned my Thoughts for many Years upon this important Subject, and maturely weighed the several *Schemes of other Projectors*,[6] I have always found them grossly mistaken in their *Computation*. 'Tis true, a Child *just dropped from its Dam* may be supported by her Milk for a Solar Year with little other Nourishment, at most not above the Value of two Shillings,[7] which the mother may certainly get, or the Value in *Scraps*, by *her lawful Occupation of Begging*; and it is exactly at one Year old that I propose to provide for them, in such a manner, as, instead of being a *Charge* upon their *Parents*, or the *Parish*, or *wanting Food and Raiment* for the rest of their Lives, they shall, on the contrary, contribute to the *Feeding* and partly to the *Clothing* of many Thousands.

There is likewise another great Advantage in my Scheme, that it will prevent those *voluntary Abortions*, and that horrid practice of *Women murdering their Bastard Children*, alas! too frequent among us; Sacrificing the poor innocent Babes, I doubt,[8] more to avoid the Expense than the Shame, which would move Tears and Pity in the most savage and inhuman Breast.

The Number of Souls in this Kingdom being usually reckoned One million and a half; of these I calculate there may be about Two hundred Thousand Couple whose Wives are Breeders, from which Number I subtract Thirty thousand Couples who are able to maintain their own Children; although I apprehend there cannot be as many under *the present Distresses of the Kingdom*: but this being granted, there will remain One hundred and seventy thousand Breeders.

I again subtract Fifty thousand for those Women who miscarry, or whose Children die by Accident, or Disease within the Year; there only remain One hundred and twenty thousand Children of poor Parents annually born: the Question therefore is, How this Number shall be reared and provided for; which, as I have already said, under the present Situation of Affairs is utterly impossible, by all the Methods hitherto proposed: for we can neither employ them in Handicraft, or Agriculture; we neither build Houses (I mean in the country) nor cultivate land.[9] They can very seldom pick up a Livelihood by Stealing till they arrive at six Years old, except where they are of Towardly Parts, although I confess they learn the Rudiments much earlier, during which time they can however be properly looked upon only as Probationers, as I have been informed by a principal gentleman in the County of Cavan, who protested to me that he never knew above one or two Instances under the Age of Six, even in a part of the Kingdom *so renowned for the quickest Proficiency in that Art*.

I am assured by our Merchants, that a Boy or a Girl, *before twelve Years old*, is no saleable Commodity; and even when they come to this Age, they will not yield above three Pounds, or three Pounds and half a Crown[10] at most on the Exchange: which cannot turn to Account either to the *Parents* or the *Kingdom*, the Charge of Nutriment and Rags having been at least four times that Value.

Notes

6 *Projector* "1. One who forms schemes or designs; 2. One who forms wild impracticable schemes" (Johnson).

7 *two shillings* ten pence, perhaps £25 or $40 in present value.

8 *doubt* believe, think.

9 *we neither build Houses … land* absentee landlords and British restrictions on Irish agricultural trade contributed to the impoverishment of Ireland.

10 *Crown* five shillings, or twenty-five pence.

I shall now therefore humbly propose my own Thoughts, which I hope will not be liable to the least Objection.

I have been assured by a very knowing *American*[11] of my acquaintance in *London*, that a young healthy child, well nursed, is at a Year old a most *delicious, nourishing*, and *wholesome* Food, whether *stewed, roasted, baked*, or *boiled*; and I make no doubt that it will equally serve in a *Fricassee*, or a *Ragout*.

I do therefore humbly offer it to *public Consideration*, that of the Hundred and twenty thousand Children already computed, Twenty thousand may be reserved for *Breed*, whereof only one Fourth part to be Males, which is more than we allow to *Sheep, black Cattle*,[12] or *Swine*, and my Reason is that these Children are seldom the Fruits of Marriage, *a Circumstance not much regarded by our Savages*; therefore *one Male* will be sufficient to serve *four Females*. That the remaining Hundred thousand may, at a Year old, be offered *in Sale* to the *Persons of Quality* and *Fortune* through the Kingdom, always advising the Mother to let them suck plentifully of the last Month, so as to *render them plump and fat for a good Table*. A Child will make two Dishes at an Entertainment for Friends, and when the Family dines alone, the fore or hind *Quarter* will make a reasonable Dish, and seasoned with a little *Pepper* or *Salt* will be very good boiled on the fourth Day, especially in *Winter*.

I have reckoned upon a Medium, that a Child just born will weigh twelve Pounds, and, in a solar Year, if tolerably nursed, increaseth to Twenty-eight Pounds.

I grant this Food will be somewhat dear, and therefore *very proper for Landlords*, who, as they have already devoured most of the *Parents*, seem to have the best Title to the *Children*.

Infants' Flesh will be in Season throughout the Year, but more plentiful in *March*, and a little *before* and *after*, for we are told by a grave Author,[13] an eminent *French* physician, that *Fish being a prolific Diet*,[14] there are more children born in *Roman Catholic Countries* about nine Months after *Lent*, than at any other Season: therefore, reckoning a Year after *Lent*, the Markets will be more glutted than usual, because the Number of *Popish Infants* is at least three to one in this Kingdom, and therefore it will have one other collateral Advantage by lessening the Number of Papists among us.

I have already computed the Charge of Nursing a Beggar's Child (in which list I reckon all *Cottagers*,[15] *Labourers*, and Four Fifths of the *Farmers*) to be about two Shillings *per Annum*, Rags included; and I believe no Gentleman would repine to give Ten Shillings for the *Carcass of a good fat Child*, which, as I have said, will make four Dishes of excellent Nutritive Meat, when he hath only some particular Friend, or his own Family to dine with him. Thus the Esquire[16] will learn to be a good Landlord, and grow popular among his Tenants, the Mother will have Eight Shillings net Profit, and be fit for Work till she produces another Child.

Those who are more thrifty (*as I must confess the Times require*) may flay the Carcass; the Skin of which, artificially[17] dressed, will make admirable *Gloves for Ladies*, and *Summer Boots for fine Gentlemen*.

Notes

[11] *American* American Indian.

[12] *black Cattle* "Oxen; bull; and cows. 'The other part of the grazier's business is what we call *black-cattle*, producing hides, tallow, and beef, for exportation' Swift" (Johnson).

[13] *a grave Author* the sixteenth-century physician and satirist François Rabelais.

[14] *prolific Diet* one that promotes productive sexual activity.

[15] *Cottagers* tenant farmers.

[16] *Esquire* "A title of dignity and next in degree below a knight" (Johnson).

[17] *artificially* skillfully.

As to our City of *Dublin*, shambles[18] may be appointed for this Purpose in the most convenient Parts of it, and Butchers we may be assured will not be wanting; although I rather recommend buying the Children alive, and dressing them hot from the Knife, as we do *Roasting Pigs*.

A very worthy Person, *a true Lover of his Country*, and whose virtues I highly esteem, was lately pleased in discoursing on this Matter, to offer a Refinement upon my Scheme. He said that many Gentlemen of this Kingdom, having of late destroyed their Deer, he conceived that the want of Venison might be well supplied by the Bodies of young Lads and Maidens, not exceeding fourteen Years of Age, nor under twelve; so great a Number of both Sexes in every County being now ready to starve for want of Work and Service:[19] And these to be disposed of by their Parents, if alive, or otherwise by their nearest Relations. But with due deference to so excellent a Friend, and so deserving a Patriot,[20] I cannot be altogether in his Sentiments: for as to the Males, my *American* Acquaintance assured me from frequent Experience that their Flesh was generally Tough and Lean, like that of our School-Boys, by continual Exercise, and their Taste disagreeable; and to Fatten them would not answer the Charge. Then as to the Females, it would, I think, with humble Submission, *be a Loss to the Public*, because they soon would become Breeders themselves: And besides, it is not improbable that some scrupulous People might be apt to censure such a Practice (although indeed very unjustly) as a little bordering upon Cruelty; which, I confess, hath always been with me the strongest Objection against any Project, however well intended.

But in order to justify my Friend, he confessed that this Expedient was put into his head by the famous *Psalmanaazar*,[21] a native of the island of Formosa, who came from thence to *London* above twenty Years ago; and in Conversation told my Friend that in his Country when any young Person happened to be put to death, the Executioner sold the Carcass to *Persons of Quality*, as a prime Dainty, and that, in his Time, the Body of a plump Girl of fifteen, who was crucified for an Attempt to poison the Emperor, was sold to his *Imperial Majesty's Prime Minister of State*, and other great *Mandarins* of the Court, *in Joints from the Gibbet*, at four hundred Crowns. Neither indeed can I deny, that if the same Use were made of several plump young Girls in this Town, who, without one single Groat[22] to their Fortunes, cannot stir abroad without a Chair,[23] and appear at the *Play-House* and *Assemblies* in foreign Fineries, which they never will pay for, the Kingdom would not be the worse.

Some Persons of a desponding Spirit are in great concern about that vast Number of poor People who are aged, diseased, or maimed; and I have been desired to employ my Thoughts what Course may be taken to ease the Nation of so grievous an Encumbrance. But I am not in the least Pain upon that Matter, because it is very well known that they are every Day *dying*, and *rotting*, by *Cold* and *Famine*, and *Filth*, and *Vermin*, as fast as can be reasonably expected. And as to the younger Labourers, they are now in almost as hopeful a Condition. They cannot get Work, and consequently pine away for want of Nourishment, to a Degree that if at any time they are accidentally

Notes

18 *shambles* "The place where butchers kill or sell their meat" (Johnson).

19 *Service* position as a servant.

20 *Patriot* a name taken by some Tories at this time.

21 *Psalmanaazar* George Psalmanazar (c.1679–1763); although he had never been out of Europe, he pretended to be from Formosa (modern Taiwan), and wrote a fictional account of the island's customs. Psalmanazar does in fact describe cannibalism of this kind (see *An Historical and Geographical Description of Formosa*, second edition, 1705, pp. 112–13).

22 *Groat* a very small amount of money.

23 *Chair* "A vehicle borne by men; a sedan" (Johnson).

hired to common Labour, they have not Strength to perform it: and thus the Country and themselves are happily delivered from the Evils to come.

I have too long digressed, and therefore shall return to my Subject. I think the Advantages by the Proposal which I have made are obvious and many, as well as of the highest Importance.

For first, as I have already observed, it would greatly lessen *the Number of Papists*, with whom we are yearly over-run, being the principal Breeders of the Nation, as well as our most dangerous Enemies; and who stay at Home on purpose with a design *to deliver the Kingdom to the Pretender*; hoping to take their Advantage by the Absence *of so many good Protestants*, who have chosen rather to leave their Country, than stay at home and pay Tithes[24] against their Conscience to an Episcopal Curate.

2dly, the poorer Tenants will have something valuable of their own, which by Law may be made liable to Distress,[25] and help to pay their Landlord's Rent; their Corn and Cattle being already seized, and *Money a thing unknown*.

3dly, Whereas the Maintenance of an hundred thousand Children, from two Years old and upwards, cannot be computed at less than ten Shillings apiece *per Annum*, the Nation's Stock will be thereby increased fifty thousand Pounds *per Annum*, besides the Profit of a new Dish introduced to the Tables of all *Gentlemen of Fortune* in the Kingdom who have any refinement in Taste; and the Money will circulate among ourselves, the Goods being entirely of our own Growth and Manufacture.

4ly, the constant Breeders, besides the Gain of eight Shillings sterling *per Annum* by the Sale of their Children, will be rid of the Charge of maintaining them after the first Year.

5ly, this Food would likewise bring great *Customs to Taverns*, where the Vintners will certainly be so prudent as to procure the best Receipts[26] for dressing it to Perfection, and consequently have their Houses frequented by all the *fine Gentlemen*, who justly value themselves upon their Knowledge in good Eating; and a skilful Cook, who understands how to oblige his Guests, will contrive to make it as expensive as they please.

6ly, This would be a great Inducement to Marriage, which all wise Nations have either encouraged by Rewards, or enforced by Laws and Penalties. It would increase the Care and Tenderness of Mothers toward their Children, when they were sure of a Settlement for Life to the poor Babes, provided in some Sort by the Public to their annual Profit instead of Expense; we should soon see an honest Emulation among the married Women, *which of them could bring the fattest Child to Market*; Men would become as fond of their *Wives*, during the Time of their Pregnancy, as they are now of their *Mares* in Foal, their *Cows* in Calf, or *Sows* when they are ready to farrow; nor offer[27] to beat or kick them (as it is too frequent a Practice) for fear of a Miscarriage.

Many other Advantages might be enumerated: For Instance, the Addition of some thousand Carcasses in our Exportation of barrelled Beef: The Propagation of *Swine's Flesh* and Improvement in the Art of making good *Bacon*, so much wanted among us by the great Destruction of *Pigs*, too frequent at our Tables, which are no way comparable in Taste, or Magnificence to a well-grown, fat Yearling Child, which roasted

Notes

[24] *Tithes* taxes to support the ministry of the Church of Ireland; nonconformists or lower-church Christians (*Protestants*) become absentee landlords in order to avoid the tax, Swift suggests.

[25] *Distress* "The act of making a legal seizure" (Johnson).

[26] *Receipts* recipes.

[27] *offer* attempt, begin.

whole will make a considerable Figure at a *Lord Mayor's Feast*, or any other public Entertainment. But this and many others I omit, being studious of Brevity.

Supposing that One thousand Families in this City, would be constant Customers for Infants' Flesh, besides others who might have it at Merry-meetings, particularly *Weddings* and *Christenings*, I compute that *Dublin* would take off annually about Twenty thousand Carcasses, and the rest of the Kingdom (where probably they will be sold somewhat cheaper) the remaining Eighty thousand.

I can think of no one Objection that will possibly be raised against this Proposal, unless it should be urged that the number of People will be thereby much lessened in the Kingdom. This I freely own, and it was indeed one principal Design in offering it to the World. I desire the Reader will observe, that I calculate my Remedy *for this one individual Kingdom of* Ireland, *and for no other that ever was, is, or, I think, ever can be upon Earth*. Therefore let no Man talk to me of other Expedients: *Of taxing our Absentees at five Shillings a Pound: Of using neither Clothes, nor Household Furniture, except what is of our own Growth and Manufacture: Of utterly rejecting the* materials *and* instruments *that promote Foreign Luxury: Of curing the Expensiveness of Pride, Vanity, Idleness, and Gaming in our Women: Of introducing a Vein of Parsimony, Prudence and Temperance: Of learning to love our Country, wherein we differ even from* Laplanders, *and the inhabitants of* Topinanmou:[28] *Of quitting our Animosities and Factions, nor act any longer like the Jews, who were murdering one another at the very moment their City was taken:*[29] *Of being a little cautious not to sell our Country and Consciences for nothing: Of teaching Landlords to have at least one Degree of Mercy toward their Tenants: Lastly, Of putting a Spirit of Honesty, Industry and Skill into our Shop-Keepers, who, if a Resolution could now be taken to buy only our Native Goods, would immediately unite to cheat and exact upon us in the Price, the Measure, and the Goodness, nor could ever yet be brought to make one fair Proposal of just Dealing, though often in earnest invited to it.*

Therefore I repeat, let no Man talk to me of these and the like Expedients, till he hath at least some Glimpse of Hope that there will ever be some hearty and sincere Attempt to put them in practice.

But as to myself, having been wearied out for many Years with offering vain, idle, visionary Thoughts, and at length utterly despairing of Success, I fortunately fell upon this Proposal; which, as it is wholly new, so it hath something solid and real, of no Expense and little Trouble, full in our own Power, and whereby we can incur no Danger in disobliging *England*. For this kind of Commodity will not bear exportation, the Flesh being of too tender a Consistence to admit a long Continuance in Salt, although perhaps I could name a Country which would be glad to eat up our whole Nation without it.

After all, I am not so violently bent upon my own Opinion as to reject any Offer proposed by wise Men, which shall be found equally innocent, cheap, easy and effectual. But before something of that kind shall be advanced in contradiction to my Scheme, and offering a better, I desire the Author, or Authors, will be pleased maturely to consider two Points.

1st, As things now stand, how they will be able to find Food and Raiment for One hundred thousand useless Mouths and Backs.

Notes

[28] *Topinanmou* part of modern Brazil.

[29] *Jews ... their City was taken* Titus destroyed Jerusalem and the Temple in 70 CE; Flavius Josephus, who was with Titus during the siege, wrote the history that Swift knew.

And *2dly*, There being a round Million of Creatures in human Figure throughout this Kingdom, whose whole Subsistence put into a common Stock would leave them in Debt Two million of Pounds *Sterling*, adding those who are Beggars by Profession, to the Bulk of Farmers, Cottagers and Labourers, with their Wives and Children, who are Beggars in effect.

I desire those *Politicians* who dislike my Overture and may perhaps be so bold to attempt an Answer, that they will first ask the Parents of these Mortals, whether they would not at this Day think it a great Happiness to have been sold for Food at a Year old, in the manner I prescribe, and thereby have avoided such a perpetual Scene of Misfortunes as they have since gone through, by *the Oppression of Landlords*, the Impossibility of paying Rent without Money or Trade, the want of common Sustenance, with neither House nor Clothes to cover them from the Inclemencies of the Weather, and the most inevitable Prospect of entailing the like, or greater Miseries upon their *Breed* for ever.

I profess in the Sincerity of my Heart, that I have not the least Personal Interest in endeavouring to promote this necessary Work, having no other Motive than the *Public Good of my Country*, by *advancing our Trade, providing for Infants, relieving the Poor, and giving some Pleasure to the Rich*. I have no Children by which I can propose to get a single Penny, the youngest being nine Years old, and my Wife past Child-bearing.

A Description of the Morning (1709)

Now hardly here and there a Hackney-coach[1]
Appearing, showed the ruddy Morn's approach.
Now *Betty* from her Master's Bed had flown,[2]
And softly stole to discompose her own.
The Slip-shod 'Prentice from his master's door
Had pared the street, and sprinkled round the floor[3]
Now *Moll* had whirled her Mop with dext'rous Airs,
Prepared to scrub the Entry and the Stairs.
The youth with broomy stumps began to trace
The kennel edge, where wheels had worn the place.[4]
The Small-coal Man was heard with Cadence deep,[5]
Till drowned in shriller Notes of *Chimney Sweep*.
Duns at his lordship's gate began to meet;[6]
And brickdust-*Moll* had screamed through half a Street.[7]
The Turnkey now his flock Returning sees,
Duly let out a-Nights to steal for Fees.[8]
The watchful Bailiffs take their silent Stands;
And School-boys lag with Satchels in their Hands.

Notes

1 *hardly* "Unwelcomely; harshly" (Johnson); *Hackney-coach* coach and horses for hire, a version of Apollo's chariot.

2 *Betty* typical name for a maid.

3 *pared* trimmed, or cleaned; *sprinkled … floor* with fresh sawdust to absorb dirt.

4 *The Youth … place* To find old Nails [note in Faulkner's edition, probably by Swift]; *kennel* gutter.

5 *Small-coal* bits of wood coal used to light fires.

6 *Dun* "A clamorous, importunate, troublesome creditor" (Johnson).

7 *brickdust* used for sharpening knives.

8 *Fees* the "garnish" paid by prisoners to the Bailiff or Turnkey for food and other things in jail.

The Lady's Dressing Room (1732)

Five Hours (and who can do it less in?)
By haughty *Celia* spent in Dressing;
The Goddess from her Chamber issues,
Arrayed in Lace, Brocades and Tissues.
Strephon, who found the Room was void,
And *Betty* otherwise employed;
Stole in, and took a strict Survey,
Of all the Litter as it lay;
Whereof, to make the Matter clear,
An Inventory follows here.

And first a dirty Smock appeared,
Beneath the Armpits well besmeared.
Strephon, the Rogue, displayed it wide,
And turned it round on every Side.
On such a Point few Words are best,
And *Strephon* bids us guess the rest;
But swears how damnably the Men lie,
In calling *Celia* sweet and cleanly.
Now listen while he next produces,
The various Combs for various Uses,
Filled up with Dirt so closely fixed,
No Brush could force a way betwixt.
A Paste of Composition rare,
Sweat, Dandruff, Powder, Lead, and Hair;
A Forehead Cloth with Oil upon't
To smooth the wrinkles on her Front;
Here Alum Flour to stop the Steams,[1]
Exhaled from sour unsavoury Streams,
There Night-gloves made of Tripsy's Hide,
Bequeathed by Tripsy when she died,
With Puppy Water, Beauty's Help[2]
Distilled from Tripsy's darling Whelp;
Here Gallipots and Vials placed,[3]
Some filled with Washes, some with Paste,
Some with Pomatum, Paints and Slops,[4]
And Ointments good for scabby Chops,[5]
Hard by a filthy Basin stands,
Fouled with the Scouring of her Hands;

Notes

THE LADY'S DRESSING ROOM

1 *Alum Flour* powdered alum, used as an astringent in dentifrices and cosmetics (Johnson).

2 *Puppy Water* "the urine of a puppy, formerly used as a cosmetic" (OED, *puppy*, 6).

3 *Gallipots* "A pot painted and glazed, commonly used for medicines" (Johnson).

4 *Pomatum* a scented ointment for the skin; *Slops* "Mean and vile liquor of any kind. Generally some nauseous or useless medicinal liquor" (Johnson).

5 *Chops* "The mouth of a beast" (Johnson).

The Basin takes whatever comes
The Scrapings of her Teeth and Gums,
A nasty Compound of all Hues,
For here she spits, and here she spues.
But oh! it turned poor *Strephon*'s Bowels,
When he beheld and smelt the Towels,
Begummed, bemattered, and beslimed
With Dirt, and Sweat, and Ear-Wax grimed.
No Object *Strephon*'s Eye escapes,
here Petticoats in frowzy Heaps;
Nor be the Handkerchiefs forgot
All varnished o'er with Snuff and Snot.
The Stockings, why should I expose,
Stained with the Marks of stinking Toes;
Or greasy Coifs and Pinners reeking[6]
Which *Celia* slept at least a Week in?
A Pair of Tweezers next he found
To pluck her Brows in Arches round,
Or Hairs that sink the Forehead low,
Or on her Chin like Bristles grow.

The Virtues we must not let pass,
Of *Celia's* magnifying Glass.
When frighted *Strephon* cast his Eye on't
It showed the Visage of a Giant.
A Glass that can to Sight disclose,
The smallest Worm in *Celia*'s Nose,
And faithfully direct her Nail
To squeeze it out from Head to Tail;
For catch it nicely by the Head,
It must come out alive or dead.

Why *Strephon* will you tell the rest?
And must you needs describe the Chest?
That careless Wench! no Creature warn her
To move it out from yonder Corner;
But leave it standing full in Sight
For you to exercise your Spite.
In vain, the Workman showed his Wit
With Rings and Hinges counterfeit
To make it seem in this Disguise,
A Cabinet to vulgar Eyes;
For *Strephon* ventured to look in,
Resolved to go through thick and thin;
He lifts the Lid, there needs no more,
He smelt it all the Time before.

Notes

[6] *Coifs and Pinners* close-fitting caps and their long side-flaps.

As from within *Pandora*'s Box,[7]
When *Epimetheus* op'd the Locks,
A sudden universal Crew
Of human Evils upwards flew;
He still was comforted to find
That *Hope* at last remained behind;
So *Strephon* lifting up the Lid,
To view what in the Chest was hid.
The Vapours flew from out the Vent,
But *Strephon* cautious never meant
The Bottom of the Pan to grope,
And foul his Hands in Search of *Hope*.
O never may such vile Machine[8]
Be once in *Celia*'s Chamber seen!
O may she better learn to keep
'Those Secrets of the hoary deep![9]

As Mutton Cutlets, Prime of Meat,
Which though with Art you salt and beat,
As laws of Cookery require,
And toast them at the clearest Fire;
If from adown the hopeful Chops
The Fat upon a Cinder drops,
To stinking Smoke it turns the Flame
Pois'ning the Flesh from whence it came;
And up exhales a greater Stench,
For which you curse the careless Wench;
So Things, which must not be expressed,
When plumped into the reeking chest;
Send up an excremental Smell
To taint the Parts from whence they fell.
The Petticoats and Gown perfume,
Which waft a Stink round every Room.

Thus finishing his grand Survey,
Disgusted *Strephon* stole away
Repeating in his amorous Fits,
Oh! *Celia, Celia, Celia* shits!

But Vengeance, Goddess never sleeping,
Soon punished *Strephon* for his Peeping;
His foul Imagination links
Each Dame he sees with all her Stinks:

Notes

[7] *Pandora* The first woman in Greek mythology, she received gifts from all the gods, but Hermes taught her flattery and brought her, at the request of Jove, to *Epimetheus*, the brother of Prometheus. She then opened a jar containing all the ills of mankind; hope only remained inside, under the lid, as a consolation to man; cf. *Paradise Lost* 4.714.

[8] *Machine* "Any complicated piece of workmanship" (Johnson).

[9] *Those … deep!* Milton [Swift's note; *Paradise Lost* 2.891].

And, if unsav'ry Odours fly,
Conceives a Lady standing by;
All Women his Description fits,
And both Ideas jump like Wits:
By vicious Fancy coupled fast,
And still appearing in Contrast.
I pity wretched *Strephon* blind
To all the Charms of Female Kind;
Should I the Queen of Love refuse,[10]
Because she rose from stinking Ooze?
To him that looks behind the Scene,
Statira's but some pocky Quean.[11]
When *Celia* in her Glory shows,
If *Strephon* would but stop his Nose
(Who now so impiously blasphemes
Her Ointments, Daubs, and Paints and Creams,
Her Washes, Slops, and every Clout,[12]
With which he makes so foul a Rout),
He soon would learn to think like me,
And bless his ravished Sight to see
Such Order from Confusion sprung,
Such gaudy Tulips raised from Dung.

A Beautiful Young Nymph Going to Bed Written for the Honour of the Fair Sex (1734)

Corinna, Pride of *Drury Lane*,[1]
For whom no Shepherd sighs in vain;
Never did *Covent Garden* boast
So bright a battered, strolling Toast;
No drunken Rake to pick her up,
No Cellar where on Tick to sup;[2]
Returning at the Midnight Hour;
Four Stories climbing to her Bow'r;
Then, seated on a three-legg'd Chair,
Takes off her artificial Hair:
Now, picking out a Crystal Eye,
She wipes it clean, and lays it by.
Her Eye-brows from a Mouse's Hide,
Stuck on with Art on either Side,
Pulls off with Care, and first displays 'em,

Notes

[10] *Queen of Love* Aphrodite, whom Hesiod describes as born fully formed from the foam of the sea.

[11] *Statira* Persian princess and wife of Alexander the Great; *Quean* harlot.

[12] *Clout* rag.

A Beautiful Young Nymph Going to Bed

[1] *Drury Lane* street in *Covent Garden*, a theater and red-light district.

[2] *Tick* credit.

Then in a Play-book smoothly lays 'em.
Now dext'rously her Plumpers draws,[3]
That serve to fill her hollow Jaws.
Untwists a Wire; and from her Gums
A Set of Teeth completely comes.
Pulls out the Rags contrived to prop
Her flabby Dugs, and down they drop.
Proceeding on, the lovely Goddess
Unlaces next her Steel-ribbed Bodice;
Which, by the Operator's Skill,
Press down the Lumps, the Hollows fill.
Up goes her Hand, and off she slips
The Bolsters that supply her Hips.
With gentlest Touch, she next explores
Her Shankers, Issues, running Sores;[4]
Effects of many a sad Disaster,
And then to each applies a Plaster.
But must, before she goes to Bed,
Rub off the Daubs of White and Red.[5]
And smooth the Furrows in her Front,[6]
With greasy Paper stuck upon't.
She takes a *Bolus* ere she sleeps;[7]
And then between two Blankets creeps.
With Pains of Love tormented lies;
Or, if she chance to close her Eyes,
Of *Bridewell* and the *Compter* dreams,[8]
And feels the Lash, and faintly screams.
Or, by a faithless Bully drawn,
At some Hedge-Tavern lies in Pawn.[9]
Or to Jamaica seems transported,[10]
Alone, and by no Planter courted;[11]
Or, near *Fleet-Ditch*'s oozy Brinks,[12]
Surrounded with a Hundred Stinks,
Belated, seems on Watch to lie,
And snap some Cully passing by;[13]
Or, struck with Fear, her Fancy runs[14]
On Watchmen, Constables and Duns,[15]

Notes

[3] *Plumper* "Something worn in the mouth to swell out the cheeks" (Johnson).

[4] *Shankers* canker sores; *Issues* medical incisions made to drain boils or other infections.

[5] *Daubs of White and Red* facial makeup.

[6] *Front* forehead.

[7] *Bolus* "A form of medicine in which the ingredients are made up into a soft mass, larger than pills, to be swallowed at once" (Johnson).

[8] *Bridewell and the Compter* correctional facilities in London.

[9] *Hedge-Tavern* a low, rough tavern.

[10] *transported* a common punishment of convicted prostitutes and thieves.

[11] *Alone Et longam incomitata videtur/Ire viam* [Swift's note: "She seemed to be going on a long journey alone"; this is the feverish dream of Dido that precedes her determination to commit suicide (*Aeneid* 4.467–8)].

[12] *Fleet-Ditch* a creek carrying filth southeast through the City and emptying into the Thames.

[13] *Cully* dupe or victim.

[14] *Fancy* imagination.

[15] *Dun* "A clamorous, importunate, troublesome creditor" (Johnson).

From whom she meets with frequent Rubs;[16]
But, never from religious Clubs;[17]
Whose Favour she is sure to find,
Because she pays them all in Kind.
  Corinna wakes. A dreadful Sight!
Behold the Ruins of the Night!
A wicked Rat her Plaster stole,
Half eat, and dragged it to his Hole.[18]
The Crystal Eye, alas, was missed;
And Puss had on her plumpers p——sed;
A Pigeon picked her Issue-peas;[19]
And *Shock* her *Tresses* filled with fleas.[20]
  The Nymph, though in this mangled Plight,
Must every Morn her Limbs unite;
But, how shall I describe her Arts
To recollect her scattered Parts?
Or show the Anguish, Toil, and Pain,
Of gathering up herself again?
The bashful Muse will never bear
In such a Scene to interfere.
Corinna in the Morning dizened,[21]
Who sees will spew; who smells be poisoned.

A Description of a City Shower (1710)

Careful Observers may foretell the Hour
By sure Prognostics when to dread a Show'r:
While Rain depends, the pensive Cat gives o'er
Her Frolics, and pursues her Tail no more.
Returning Home at Night, you find the Sink[1]
Strike your offended Sense with double Stink.
If you be wise, then go not far to dine:
You spend in Coach-hire more than save in Wine.
A coming Show'r your shooting Corns presage;
Old Aches throb, your hollow Tooth will rage:[2]
Saunt'ring in Coffee-house is *Dulman* seen;
He damns the Climate, and complains of Spleen.[3]
Meanwhile the South, rising with dabbled Wings,[4]
A sable Cloud athwart the Welkin flings,[5]

Notes

[16] *Rub* "Collision; hindrance; obstruction" (Johnson).

[17] *religious Clubs* dissenting Protestant societies, which Swift derides for their pretensions to visionary understanding.

[18] *eat* an old form of the past tense.

[19] *Issue-peas* rolled-up bits of ivy-root inserted in an issue to keep it running.

[20] *Shock* stock name for a lap dog.

[21] *dizen* "To dress; to deck; to rig out. A low word" (Johnson).

A Description of a City Shower

[1] *Sink* "A drain; a jakes [outhouse]" (Johnson); a lavatory.

[2] *Aches* a disyllable (as if "aitch-es").

[3] *Spleen* "Melancholy; hypochondriacal vapours" (Johnson); the name of a variety of ills.

[4] *dabbled* muddy.

[5] *Welkin* sky (consciously archaic).

That swilled more Liquor than it could contain,
And, like a Drunkard, gives it up again.
Brisk *Susan* whips her Linen from the Rope,[6]
While the first drizzling Show'r is borne aslope:[7]
Such is that Sprinkling, which some careless Quean[8]
Flirts on you from her Mop; but not so clean:[9]
You fly, invoke the Gods; then turning, stop
To rail; she singing, still whirls on her Mop.
Nor yet the Dust had shunned th' unequal Strife,
But, aided by the Wind, fought still for Life;
And wafted with its Foe by violent Gust,
'Twas doubtful which was Rain, and which was Dust.
Ah! where must needy Poet seek for Aid,
When Dust and Rain at once his Coat invade?
Sole Coat, where Dust, cemented by the Rain,
Erects the Nap, and leaves a cloudy Stain.
Now, in contiguous Drops the Flood comes down,
Threat'ning with Deluge this *devoted* Town.
To Shops in Crowds the daggled Females fly,[10]
Pretend to cheapen Goods, but nothing buy.[11]
The Templer spruce, while every Spout's abroach,[12]
Stays till 'tis fair, yet *seems* to call a Coach.
The tucked-up Sempstress walks with hasty Strides,
While Streams run down her oiled Umbrella's Sides.[13]
Here various Kinds, by various Fortunes led,
Commence Acquaintance underneath a Shed.
Triumphant Tories, and desponding Whigs,[14]
Forget their Feuds, and join to save their Wigs.
Boxed in a Chair the Beau impatient sits,[15]
While Spouts run clatt'ring o'er the Roof by Fits,
And ever and anon with frightful Din
The Leather sounds; he trembles from within.
So when *Troy* Chairmen bore the wooden Steed,
Pregnant with *Greeks*, impatient to be freed;
(Those Bully *Greeks*, who, as the Moderns do,
Instead of paying Chair-men, run them through)
Laocoon struck the Out-side with his Spear,
And each imprisoned Hero quaked for Fear.[16]

Notes

6 *Susan* a typical maid's name.

7 *aslope* on a slant; obliquely (a word used to describe the way a lance or sword might strike a knight's shield).

8 *Quean* "A worthless woman; generally a strumpet" (Johnson).

9 *Flirt* "To throw anything with a quick, elastic motion" (Johnson).

10 *daggled* muddied.

11 *cheapen* "Attempt to purchase" (Johnson); shop for.

12 *Templer* law student; *abroach* overflowing.

13 *oil'd* so as to be waterproof.

14 *Triumphant Tories, and desponding Whigs* the poem was written in 1710, the first year of the Tory ministry under Queen Anne.

15 *Chair* "An enclosed chair or covered vehicle for one person, carried on poles by two men; a sedan" (*OED*, 10).

16 *Troy Chairmen ... quaked for fear* tricked into believing the Greeks had given up the siege, the Trojans carried a wooden horse (supposedly an offering to the gods) concealing lethal soldiers into their city; the priest *Laocoon* advised against this, struck the horse, and frightened the Greeks (Virgil, *Aeneid* 2.50–2).

Now from all Parts the swelling Kennels flow,
And bear their Trophies with them, as they go:
Filths of all Hues and Odours seem to tell
What Street they sailed from, by the Sight and Smell.
They, as each Torrent drives with rapid Force,
From *Smithfield*, or *St. Pulchre*'s shape their course,[17]
And in huge Confluent join at *Snow-hill* Ridge,
Fall from the *Conduit* prone to *Holborn-Bridge*.
Sweepings from Butchers' Stalls, Dung, Guts, and Blood,
Drowned Puppies, stinking Sprats, all drenched in Mud,
Dead Cats, and Turnip-Tops come tumbling down the Flood[18]

Stella's Birth-Day[1] (13 March 1719)

Stella this Day is Thirty-four
(We shan't dispute a Year or more).
However, *Stella*, be not troubled,
Although thy Size and Years be doubled,
Since first I saw thee at Sixteen,[2]
The brightest Virgin on the Green.
So little is thy Form declined,
Made up so largely in thy Mind.
 Oh! would it please the Gods to *split*
Thy Beauty, Size, and Years, and Wit,
No Age could furnish out a Pair
Of Nymphs so graceful, wise, and fair;
With half the Lustre of your Eyes,
With half your Wit, your Years, and Size.
And then, before it grew too late,
How should I beg of gentle Fate,
(That either Nymph might have her Swain),
To split my Worship too in twain.

Notes

17 *Smithfield* an open area just northwest of the City, used as a cattle market and sometimes for hangings; *St. Pulchre's* suburban parish just west of Newgate Prison; the water would flow southeast, past the other places mentioned, on its way into the Fleet and through the City to the Thames.

18 These three last lines were intended against that licentious Manner of modern Poets, in making three Rhymes together, which they call *Triplets*; and the last of the three, was two or sometimes more Syllables longer, called an *Alexandrine*. These *Triplets* and *Alexandrines* were brought in by Dryden, and other Poets in the Reign of Charles II. They were the mere Effect of Haste, Idleness, and want of Money; and have been wholly avoided by the best Poets, since these Verses were written [Note in Faulkner's edition, probably by Swift].

STELLA'S BIRTH-DAY

1 *Stella* Esther Johnson (1681–1728), whom Swift loved and supported almost from the time he met her in 1689 until her death; written in 1719, when Stella turned thirty-eight, this is the first in a series of annual birthday poems that concluded with her last birthday in 1727.

2 *sixteen* she was eight, but perhaps Swift first looked on her as a woman at sixteen, or perhaps this is part of his gentlemanly looseness about her age.

Delarivier Manley (c.1670–1724)

Soon after she was orphaned, with £200 and a share in her late father's estate, Delarivier Manley was seduced into a bigamous marriage by her cousin John Manley. When he abandoned her, she lived briefly with the duchess of Cleveland and undoubtedly began collecting the kind of "intelligence" or gossip about the nobility that she would later exploit in her sensational novels. The duchess expelled Manley from her house by accusing her of intriguing with her son; this seems to be the beginning of Manley's career as a writer, for, after two years away from London, she reappeared with a pair of plays ready for production. She had some success, but she got into trouble with the law through her dealings with Mary Thompson, a known criminal, and their plot to extort money from a man named Pheasant. With no bird in hand, Manley nevertheless made a name for herself as a wit among the London writers who taunted the court, and each other, in the coffeehouses and taverns. In 1705 she published a satire on the duchess of Marlborough called *The Secret History of Queen Zarah*. She followed this first attempt at mixing the conventions of romance and scandal with a more wide-ranging send-up of the Whig nobility, full of gossip and scandal about all its most prominent members. The whole work is a *roman à clef*, but the veil of allegory is thin, and gossip, followed by published "keys," made everything clear to her readers. Shortly after the appearance of *Secret Memoirs and Manners of Several Persons of Quality of Both Sexes. From the New Atalantis*, Manley was arrested along with the two publishers and the printer. (She was eventually tried and discharged.)

With its numerous erotic scenes of seduction and its inside accounts of the private lives of many members of the nobility, the *New Atalantis* was a sensation. It became an emblem of dissolute, upper-class reading in Pope's more gently satirical picture of that life, *The Rape of the Lock*. Manley published a number of sequels to the *New Atalantis* and some similar works, including *The Adventures of Rivella* (1714), which is mainly about herself and is the principal source of information about her early life. (Her birth on a boat sailing near the Channel Islands suggests the reason for her unusual first name.) Manley's novels are racy romances that excite our curiosity as readers, even without intimate knowledge of the "key," but the allegory was fraught with political meaning for her contemporaries. She was a sharp-tongued enemy of the Whigs and fought in print with Richard Steele and, early on, with Jonathan Swift. They were reconciled, however, and Manley referred in her will to her "much honoured friend, the dean of St Patrick, Dr. Swift."

Manley is one of the women writers of the eighteenth century who have recently emerged from the obscurity imposed first by morally censorious Victorian judgments of her work and then by formalist aesthetics of the earlier twentieth century. In fact, she performs excellently in her somewhat purplish genre; she is not only sensational, and she does not simply look back to earlier French *romans à clef*: there is also an archness and self-assuredness in her tone that help prepare the way for the greater, more measured accomplishments of later novelists, such as Jane Austen.

The text here presented is based on the first edition of 1709. I have profited from the notes in the Penguin edition (1991), edited by Ros Ballaster.

British Literature 1640–1789: An Anthology, Fourth Edition. Edited by Robert DeMaria, Jr.

from *Secret Memoirs and Manners of Several Persons of Quality of Both Sexes. From the New Atalantis, an Island in the Mediterranean* (1709)

Astrea:][1] We are entertained with another Object; who is that Person[2] not very *young* nor *handsome*, yet something august and solemn in his *Mien*, he that walks up the *Vista*?[3] He sees us not; 'tis certainly one that loved the departed Monarch,[4] his Handkerchief is in his Hand, his Eyes red and full of Tears; he comes hither doubtless to weep in Solitude, a Master upon whom his Fortune probably depended.

Intell:][5] He weeps indeed, and he loved his Master, but his Fortune is the greatest of all the Favourites; therefore are his Tears the more Meritorious, yet he is not free from the Vices of Men in Power; the greediness of Gain and unbounded Ostentation in expending with Noise and Splendour in Foreign Courts what he by Cunning had acquired in this. Love has had his turn, in a fatal manner! Fatal I mean to the unhappy Object of his Flame; raised from a mean degree, 'tis no wonder his Head is giddy with the highth. If Pride and Contempt of those beneath them be fashionable Manners, worn even by those that are born Great, we need not wonder to find 'em assumed by Persons that oftner by Chance than true Merit, touch a Fortune unexpected; yet is the Duke's Fidelity to his Master to be applauded, and as well as he loves *Riches*, he could never be brought to depart from the King's Interest. He has been bred to the Business of the State and Cabinet; he perfectly knows the management of Affairs, the posture of his own and that of his Neighbour-Nations; their true and their false Interests. He is not Eloquent but Wise; to be short, few Princes but would be glad of such a Servant, for since in the Composition of the Human Frame, Vices are generally blended with the Virtues, we are to Reverence that Man, who suffers not, to the Prejudice of his Master, the former to get the ascendant.

If I be not tiresome, I design a short sketch of the Amour he had with a Lady, truly named Unfortunate. I will take the Duke as high as from his first coming to Court, a Boy, to attend Prince *Henriquez*,[6] as his Page of *Honour*. When Persons have their Fortune to make, and are born with little or no Estate, 'tis necessary that they have a lucky hit, a happy Introduction, a leading Card to make a prosperous Game. Such the Duke met with, and had the Courage and Address to lay hold of the Opportunity. Prince *Henriquez* fell ill of a malignant Distemper; *Medicine* was at a loss; it seemed as if Art were no more; the *Physicians* could find no Drugs of sufficient Heat to throw out the Distemper, without which, inevitable Death was all that could be expected. One of those Sons of *Esculapius*[7] proposed that a Youth of Warmth and Vigour should be put to Bed to him, by that natural glow of Body, to draw out the Malignancy of the Distemper. The Duke was the only Person, that with Pleasure and Boldness, offered his own, to save the Life of his Master; he would not even stay to take his leave of any of his Friends, but with the greatest Bravery throwing off his Clothes got into Bed to the *Prince*, embracing closely his Feverish Body, from whence he never stirred, 'till the

Notes

FROM SECRET MEMOIRS AND MANNERS

1 *Astrea* a Greek goddess associated with justice, who was supposed to have left the world after the Golden Age; in Manley's fiction, she returns "to see if humankind were still as defective, as when she in disgust forsook it."

2 *Person* William Bentinck, first earl of Portland (1649–1709), a Dutchman created an English earl by William III, who relied on him in military matters and foreign affairs (see Defoe, *The True-Born Englishman*, p. 412, n. 40 above).

3 *Vista* "an avenue or glade" (*OED*).

4 *departed Monarch* William III.

5 *Intell[igence]* Astrea's guide in New Atalantis, which stands for England; her name means "Commerce of information" (Johnson) or news.

6 *Prince Henriquez* the Dutch title of William III was Willem Hendrik, Prins Van Oranje.

7 *Esculapius* or Aesculapius, the Greek god of healing.

happy Effects of his kind Endeavours, were visible. The Disease passed from the *Heart* into the *Blood*, from thence by the Application of a kindly Warmth, 'twas thrown into the Flesh and Skin; after which, the Symptoms being favourable, they no longer doubted the Life of the Prince. But the generous Youth could not escape the Infection; it seized him in such a terrible manner that Destiny was expected to be fatal to him. They removed him to another Bed. The Prince tenderly regretted his Sufferings, assured him, That he hoped he would live to find in his *Friendship* and *Gratitude* the Rewards of *Fidelity* and *Generosity*. The Gods were too-well pleased at so glorious an Action to let him sink under it; after an unusual and bitter Conflict, they restored him to his former Health and Vigour. And if he still wears the cruel Marks of so malignant a Distemper, they are in him but glorious Proofs of *Love* and *Duty* to his Prince, no less to be revered, than the most flourishing Laurels of others.

Not one of the most fortunate Courtiers but dreaded the towering Genius[8] of the Youth; they saw he was resolved to push, though at the expense of Life; rather than not to make his Fortune, to sink under the Endeavour. *Henriquez* was young, *Human*, disposed by Nature (all Hero as he was) to the soft Trusts and Joys of Friendship: He called the Youth near to his Confidence, found in him a strength of Mind, a Capacity far above his Years, a projecting[9] Brain, with a height of Courage, able to put in practice the boldest Resolutions. The Prince had in his Nonage been oppressed by a potent faction, that left him only a titular Sovereignty[10]; he had no longer the Command of his own Fleet and Armies, all were at the disposal of those who pretended to Administer to Public Good. He would often lament with his young Favourite the Oppression. His inborn courage, and boiling Youth, made him long to rush into the Field of Glory, to snatch from thence those Laurels that were not to be attained but with the greatest Difficulty! At the head of his own Armies, to meet the Enemy of his Country,[11] who with hostile Fire, and cruel slaughter, had successfully Invaded it. The young Statesman (by his intrigue and management with some of the Head Officers) procured that a Battle should be lost. The Event was fatal to the two Brothers that opposed the Prince, and were at the Head of the State. The People (dreading the approach of the Conqueror) called aloud for their own Sovereign to defend 'em. They rushed unanimously upon the two Usurpers,[12] with as much Ease and Fierceness, as a hungry Lion the devouring Wolf, or Tiger falls upon the harmless Flock; and, with the same Expedition (animated by the Intrigues, Cabals,[13] and Spirit of our young Favourite) rends 'em piecemeal! Scatters their Body, small as the Dust thrown in to the air! Swift as Destruction, as mortal Plagues fall from Hands of the avenging Deities, when by the accumulated Sins of Mortals, they are justly provoked.

This was no sooner performed, but they rush into the Palace, seize upon *Henriquez*, bear him (with Exultings of Rapturous Joy) upon their Shoulders, force open the Door of the *Divan*, and with Acclamations that pierced the Skies, seat the Prince upon the Royal Throne! Invest him with the Purple Robe, the Sword of Defence, the awful Diadem, and all other Ensigns of Sovereignty! take a voluntary Oath of Fidelity! perform their Homage! and then with the same Exclamations (of rude and hasty Joy) present him to the Army! who echoed back with loud Shootings their

Notes

[8] *Genius* "Disposition; nature" (Johnson).

[9] *projecting* contriving, resourceful.

[10] *titular Sovereignty* after the death of William's father, eight days before his heir's birth, a republican oligarchy designed laws that limited the power of the princes of Orange.

[11] *the Enemy of his Country* the French invaded the United Provinces in June 1672, with the support of the British.

[12] *the two Usurpers* Johann de Witt and his brother were killed by an angry mob at the Hague on August 20, 1672.

[13] *Cabal* "Intrigue" (Johnson).

Approbation of what was done. The *Prince* and his *young Favourite*, harangue and caress the Soldiers and People; he tells 'em (like his glorious Ancestors) he longs to lose his Blood in defence of his Country! That he will either die or relieve 'em from the Oppression of the Invader! They one and all demand him to lead 'em on to Conquest and Revenge.

No Age has ever shown us a Hero made up of greater Compositions! *Henriquez* was ardent for Battle, yet cautiously prudent to watch all the Advantages of it. His young Favourite, with his Valour, maintained that Opinion he had acquired; by Conduct and politic Management, they put a stop to the rapid Course of the Enemy's Victories, and regained the Towns that were lost. …

After this the young Favourite (though formerly but of his Pleasures) became his first Minister. He was always trusted and extreme *habile*[14] in the Affairs of State; he followed the wise Maxims of *Machiavel*,[15] who aimed to make his Prince Great, let what would be the Price. He it was that encouraged *Count Fortunatus*, and the Disaffected Lords of *Atalantis*, to expel their Bigoted Monarch.[16] By his politic Management the young *Caesario* was sacrificed, and the Prince called to take possession of the Government. Without such a Head as his (cunning to conceal, crafty to foresee, wise to Project, and valiant to undertake) the whole Fabric[17] had tottered. He was the solid Foundation upon which the greatest *Hero* of the Age has raised himself to be such; though in all his Advices the finishing Stroke still came from *Henriquez*.

Now raised to be *Duke* and *Peer*, *General* of the *Army*, in Possession of the Ear and Cabinet of the Prince, whom we must henceforward (if we have occasion to speak of him) call King, he gave up himself to amass up Riches! his Ambition was not satisfied! he aimed at something more! 'Twas Glorious to be a Sovereign Prince, though but of a Petty State! He offered sixteen hundred thousand Crowns for the Succession, where only a Princess Dowager was in Possession, and to become her Husband. Affairs of that Consequence, that depend not upon Action but Treaty, are generally tedious: Whilst it was depending, our Duke felt the Sting of a Passion, which (at the Expense of the Ladies) he had hitherto only played with. There was a young Girl, named *Mademoiselle Charlot*,[18] left to his Care by her Father, for whom he had as great a Friendship, as a Statesman can be supposed to have. The young *Charlot* had lost her Mother long before: Her Dowry amounted to forty thousand Crowns; the Family was Noble, and there was almost nothing but what she might pretend to. The Duke had been some considerable time a Widower[19]; his Wife was of the Family of the Favourites, naturally Born to the soothing Arts of the Courts. *Fame* is not afraid to speak aloud, that *Henriquez* saw what was agreeable in her; and when wearied with the Fatigues of Hunting, would go to Bed between her and her Husband, but you may be sure all very Innocent, especially where such a Witness was in Place. When she died, he transferred his Esteem, with an additional Tenderness, to her Sister. She affected first to be in Love

Notes

[14] *habile* able.

[15] *Machiavel* Niccolò Macchiavelli (1469–1527), Florentine diplomat, author of *Il Principe* (1513), *The Prince*, a book of practical statecraft; his name is somewhat unjustly synonymous with unscrupulous diplomacy.

[16] *Bigoted Monarch* James II, who was Catholic.

[17] *Fabric* construction.

[18] *Mademoiselle Charlot* Stuarta Werburge Howard, daughter of James Howard, third earl of Suffolk (d. 1688) and Charlotte Jemima Henrietta Maria, an illegitimate daughter of Charles II (d. 1684).

[19] *Widower* Anne Villiers, his first wife, died in 1688; her sister Elizabeth (d. 1733) was William III's mistress.

with the *Hero*, not the *Prince*. Personal Lovers are so rarely found among People of their Station; so few are acquainted with the Delicacy of dividing the *Monarch* from the *Man*, that out of Gratitude he gave into those Endearments that were necessary to bespeak a reciprocal Passion. And as his Temper to his Favourites was magnificently Lavish, she tasted all the Sweets of unlimited Majesty, and the charming Effects of unbounded Generosity!

But to return to the Duke. He spared for no Expense in the Education of young *Charlot*. She was brought up at his own House with his Children; but having something the Advantage in Age of his Daughters, the Precepts were proportionably advanced. He designed her (in those early Days of his Power) as a Wife for his Son, before the increase of his own Ambition and Riches taught him other Desires; that is to say, to look out a Lady for the young Lord with more than six times *Charlot*'s Fortune. ...

Charlot was no great Beauty, her Shape was [not] the best; but Youth and Dress make all Things agreeable. To have prepossessed you in her Favour, I should, as I was inclined, have advanced a System of her Charms; but *Truth*, who too well foresaw my Intentions, has repelled 'em with a Frown; not but *Charlot* had many Admirers. There's something so touching in the *agreeable*, that I know not whether it does not enchant us deeper than Beauty; we are oftentimes upon our guard against the Attack of that, whilst the unwary Heart, Careless and Defenceless, as dreading no Surprise, permits the *agreeable* to manage as they please.

The Duke had a seeming Admiration for *Virtue* wherever he found it, but he was a Statesman, and held it incompatible (in an age like this) with a Man's making his Fortune. *Ambition, Desire of Gain, Dissimulation, Cunning*, all these were meritoriously Serviceable to him. 'Twas enough he always applauded Virtue, and in his Discourse decried Vice. As long as he stuck close in his Practice, no matter what became of his Words; these are times where the Heart and the Tongue do not agree! However, young *Charlot* was to be Educated in the high road to Applause and Virtue. He banished far from her Conversation whatever would not Edify, airy *Romances, Plays*, dangerous Novels, *loose* and *insinuating Poetry*, artificial Introductions of *Love*, well-painted Landscapes of that dangerous Poison; her Diversions were always among the sort that were most Innocent and Simple, such as Walking, but not in public Assemblies. Music, in Airs all Divine; reading and improving Books of Education and Piety; as well knowing, that if a Lady be too early used to violent Pleasures, it debauches their Tastes forever to any others. He taught her to beware of *Hopes* and *Fears*, never to desire anything with too much eagerness; to guard herself from those dangerous Convulsions of the Mind, that upon the least Disappointment precipitates into a million of Inconveniences. He endeavoured to cure her of those number of Affections and Aversions, so natural to young People, by showing her that nothing truly deserved to be passionately beloved, but the *Gods*, because they alone were perfect; though nothing on the other Hand ought to be hated but Vice, because we are all the Image of our Divinities. He wisely and early forewarned her, for what seemed natural to her, a desire of being applauded for her Wit. She had a brightness of Genius, that would often break out in dangerous Sparkles; he showed her that true Wit consisted not in much speaking, but in speaking much in a few Words; that whatever carried her beyond the knowledge of her Duty, carried her too far; all other Embellishments of the Mind were more dangerous than useful, and to be avoided as her Ruin. That the possession of 'em were attended with *Self-Love, Vanity* and *Coquetry*, things incompatible, and never mingled in the Character of a Woman of true Honour. He recommended *Modesty* and *Silence*, that she should shun all occasions of speaking upon Subjects not necessary to a Lady's Knowledge, though it were true she spoke never so well. He remembered[20] her, that so Great, so wise a man as *Zeno*,[21] of all the Virtues made choice of Silence, for by it he heard other Men's Imperfections and concealed his own; that the more Wit she was Mistress of, the less occasion she had to show it; that if want of it gave a disgust, too much does not generally please better. That assuming Air that generally accompanies it, is distasteful to the Company, where all pretend an equal right to be heard. The weakness of Human Nature is such, the chiefest Pleasure of Conversation lies in the speaking, not the hearing part; and if a presumptuous Person (though with never so great a Capacity) pretends to usurp once upon that Privilege, they look upon her as a Tyrant, that would ravish from 'em the Freedom of their Votes. But his strongest Battery was united against *Love*, that invader of the *Heart*; he showed her how shameful it was for a young Lady ever so much as to think of any tenderness for a Lover, 'till he was become her Husband; that true Piety and Duty would instruct her in all that was necessary for a good Wife to feel of that dangerous Passion; that she should not so much as ever seek to know what was meant by that shameful Weakness called Jealousy. 'Twas abominable in us to give others occasion to be Jealous, and painful to be so ourselves: that 'tis generally attended with *Slander* and *Hatred*, two base and contemptible Qualities. That that violent *inborn* desire of pleasing, so natural to Ladies, is the pest of Virtue; they would by the Charms of their Beauty, and their sweet and insinuating way of Conversation, assume that native Empire over Mankind, which seems to be politically denied them, because the way to Authority and Glory is stopped up. Hence it is, that with their acquired Arts and languishing Charms, they risk their *Virtue* to gain a little contemptible Dominion over a Heart, that at the same time it surrenders itself a Slave, refuses to bestow esteem upon the Victor; that Friendship was far nobler in its Nature, and much to be preferred to Love, because a 'Friend loves always, a Lover but for a time'. That under the most flattering appearances it concealed inevitable Ruin; the very first Impressions were dreadful, and to be carefully suppressed. *Pythagoras* taught, 'The assaults of Love were to be beaten back at the first Sight, lest they undermine at the second'. *And* Plato, That 'the first step to Wisdom was not to love; the second so to love, as not to be perceived'.

Fraught with these, and a number more of such Precepts as these, the young *Charlot* seemed to intend herself a Pattern for the Ladies of this degenerate Age, who divide their Hours between the *Toilet* and the *Basset*-Table,[22] which is grown so totally the Business of the Fair, that even the Diversions of the *Opera, Gallantry* and *Love* are but second Pleasures. A Person who has once given herself up to Gaming, neglects all her Duties, disorders her Family, breaks her Rest, forgets her Husband, and by her Expense often inconveniences him irreparably, together with their waste of time. The Passions of Anger and Avarice, concur to make her odious to all, but those who engage with her at the dangerous Diversion; not to instance [those] who have compounded[23] for the loss of Money, with the loss of their Chastity and Honour: Nor is it a new, though frequent way of paying of Play-Debts, in this entirely corrupted Age.

The Duke had a magnificent *Villa* within five Leagues of the Capitol, adorned with all that's imaginable Beautiful, either in Art or Nature; the pride of Conquest, the Plunder of Victory, the homage of the Vanquished, the Presents of Neighbouring

Notes

20 *remembered* reminded.

21 *Zeno* Zeno of Citium (c.335–263 BCE), founder of Stoicism, had many maxims about the value of listening and the dangers of speaking.

22 *Basset* a card game.

23 *compounded* settled, made an agreement on compromising terms.

Monarchs, and whatever Curiosity could inform, or Money recover, were the Ornaments of this Palace.[24] *Henriquez* had received a new Favourite into his Bosom, but it was a Favourite not at all interfering with the Duke, who was ever trusted and esteemed; by this means he oftener found a recess from Court; his great Master would sometimes in Goodness dismiss him to his *Villa*, to take a rest from Power, a calm of Greatness, a suspense of Business, a respiration of Glory. Here it was that he used to confirm the young *Charlot* in that early love of Virtue that had been taught her, to unbend her Mind from the more serious Studies. He sometimes permitted her those of *Poetry*, not loose Descriptions, lascivious Joys, or wanton heightenings of the Passions. They sung and acted the History of the *Gods*, the Rape of *Proserpine*,[25] the Descent of *Ceres*, the Chastity of *Diana*,[26] and such Pieces that tended to the instruction of the Mind. One Evening at a Representation, where *Charlot* personated the Goddess, and the Duke's Son *Acteon*, she Acted with so animated a Spirit, cast such Rays of Divinity about her, gave every Word so twanging,[27] yet so sweet an Accent, that awakened the Duke's Attention; and so admirably she varied the Passions, that gave Birth in his Breast, to what he had never felt before. He applauded, embraced, and even kissed the charming *Diana*. 'Twas Poison to his Peace, the cleaving sweetness thrilled[28] swiftly to his Heart, thence tingled his Blood, and cast Fire throughout his whole Person; he Sighed with Pleasure! he wondered what those Sighs meant! he repeats his Kisses, to find if *Charlot* were the occasion of his Disorder. Confirmed by this new taste of Joy, he throws the young Charmer hastily from him, folds his Arms, and walks off with continued Sighs! The innocent Beauty makes after him, modest and afraid, insinuatingly,[29] and with trembling she inquires, if she have not offended? Begs to know her Fault, and that she will endeavour to repair it. He answers her not but with his Eyes, which have but too tender an Aspect. The Maid (by them) improving her Courage, comes nearer, spreads her fond Arms about him, and in her usual fawning Language calls him dear *Papa*; joins her Face, her Eyes, her Cheeks, her Mouth, close to his. By this time the Duke was fallen upon a Chair that stood next him, he was fully in her reach, and without any opposition she had leisure to diffuse the irremediable Poison through his Veins. He sat immovable to all Kindness, but with the greatest taste of Joy, he had ever been sensible of. Whilst he was thus dangerously entertained, the young *Acteon*, and the rest of the Company, join 'em; the Duke was forced to rouse himself from his Love-sick Lethargy; *Charlot* would not leave him, till he would tell her in what she had done amiss. He only answered her, That he had nothing to object; she had acted her part but too well. The young Lady had been taught (in her cold Precepts of Education) that it was a degree of fault to excel, even in an Accomplishment. Occasion was not to be sought of eminently distinguishing oneself in anything but solid Virtue; she feared she had shown too great a Transport in representing *Diana*; that the Duke would possibly think she was prepossessed more than she ought with that Diversion; and in this Despondence she took resolutions to regulate herself hereafter more to his satisfaction.

Notes

[24] *Palace* Windsor Castle.

[25] *the Rape of Proserpine* Hades takes Proserpine to the underworld, and her mother Ceres, after searching in anguish for her daughter, leaves the world in winter half the year (Ovid, *Metamorphoses*, 5.391–571).

[26] *the Chastity of Diana* Artemis, or Diana, the chaste huntress of the gods, was seen bathing with her followers by Actaeon; in revenge she turned him into a stag; in that form he was hunted down and torn to pieces by his own hounds (Ovid, *Metamorphoses* 3.138–252).

[27] *twanging* from "twang," "An affected modulation of the voice" (Johnson).

[28] *thrilled* pierced.

[29] *insinuatingly* from "insinuate," "To push gently into favour or regard" (Johnson).

That fatal Night the Duke felt hostile Fires in his Breast. *Love* was entered with all his dreadful Artillery; he took possession in a moment of the Avenues that led to the Heart; neither did the resistance he found there serve for anything but to make his Conquest more illustrious. The Duke tried every corner of his uneasy Bed! whether shut or open, *Charlot* was still before his Eyes! his Lips and Face retained the deep Impression of her Kisses! the Idea of her innocent and charming Touches, wandered o'er his Mind! he wished again to be so blessed! but then, with a deep and dreadful Sigh, he remembered who she was, the Daughter of his Friend! of a Friend who had at his Death left the charge of her Education to him! His Treaty with the Princess Dowager, would not admit him to think of marrying of her; Ambition came in to rescue him (in that particular) from the Arms of Love. To possess her without [love], was a villainous detestable thought! but not to possess her at all, was loss of Life! was Death inevitable! Not able to gain one wink of Sleep, he arose with the first dawn, and posted back to *Angela*.[30] He hoped the hurry of Business and the Pleasures of the Court, would stifle so guilty a Passion; he was too well persuaded of his Distemper, the Symptoms were right, the Malignity was upon him! he was regularly possessed! Love in all its forms, had took in that formidable Heart of his! He began to be jealous of his Son, whom he had always designed for *Charlot*'s Husband; he could not bear the thoughts that he should be beloved by her, though all beautiful as the lovely Youth was. She had never any tender Inclinations for him, nothing that exceeded the warmth of a Sister's love! whether it were that he were designed for [her], or that the Precepts of Education had warned her from too precipitate a liking. She was bred up with him, accustomed to his Charms; they made no impression upon her Heart; neither was the Youth more sensible. The Duke could distress neither of 'em by his love of that side, but this he was not so happy to know. He wrote up for the young Lord to come to Court, and gave immediate Orders for forming his Equipage, that he might be sent to Travel. Meantime *Charlot* was never from his Thoughts. Who knows not the violence of beginning Love! especially a Love that we hold opposite to our Interest and Duty. "'Tis an unreasonable excess of Desire, which enters swiftly, but departs slowly. The love of Beauty is the loss of Reason. Neither is it to be suppressed by Wisdom, because it is not to be comprehended with Reason'. And the Emperor *Aurelius*[31]; 'Love is a cruel Impression of that wonderful Passion, which to define is impossible, because no Words reach to the strong Nature of it, and only they know which inwardly feel it'.

The Duke vainly struggled in the Snare; he would live without seeing *Charlot*, but then he must live in Pain, in inexplicable Torture! He applies the relief of Business, the Pleasures of Woman! *Charlot*'s Kisses were still upon his Lips, and made all others insipid to him. In short, he tried so much to divert his Thoughts from her, that it but more perfectly confirmed him of the vanity and unsuccessfulness of the Attempt. He could neither eat nor sleep! Love and Restlessness raised Vapours[32] in him to that degree, he was no longer Master of his Business! Wearied with all things, hurried by a secret Principle of *Self-Love* and *Self-Preservation*, the Law of Nature! he orders his Coach to carry him down once more to his *Villa*, there to see his Dear! This dangerous *Charlot*! that little innocent Sweetness! that embittered his Happiness. She loved him tenderly as a Benefactor, a Father, or something more; that she had been used to love

Notes

30 *Angela* London.

31 *Aurelius* Marcus Aurelius (Emperor of Rome 161–80 CE), author of *Meditations*, in Greek, which had been recently translated by Jeremy Collier (1701).

32 *Vapours* "Mental fume; vain imagination; fancy unreal" (Johnson).

without that severe mixture of Fear that mingles in the love we bear to Parents. She ran to meet him as he alighted; her young Face, over-spread with blushing Joys! his transport exceeded hers! he took her in his Arms with eagerness! he exchanged all his Pains for Pleasures! there was the Cure of his past Anguish! her Kisses were the Balm of his wounded Mind! he wondered at the immediate Alteration! she caressed and courted him, showed him all Things that could divert or entertain. He knew not what to resolve upon; he could not prudently marry her, and how to attempt to corrupt her! those excellent Principles that had been early infused into her were all against him; but yet he must love her! He found he could not live without her! He opened a *Machiavel*, and read there a Maxim, 'That none but great Souls could be completely Wicked'.[33] He took it for an Oracle to him. He would be loath to tell himself, his 'Soul was not great enough for any Attempt'. He closed the Book, took some turns about the Gallery to digest what he had read, and from thence concluded, that neither *Religion, Honour, Gratitude*, nor *Friendship*, were ties sufficient to deprive us of an essential Good! *Charlot* was necessary to his very Being! all his Pleasures faded without her! and, which was worse, he was in Torture! in actual Pain as well as want of Pleasure! therefore *Charlot* he would have. He had struggled more than sufficient; Virtue ought to be satisfied with the terrible Conflict he had suffered! but Love was become Master, and 'twas time for her to abscond. After he had settled his Thoughts, he grew more calm and quiet; nothing should now disturb him, but the manner how to corrupt her. He was resolved to change her whole Form of Living, to bring her to Court, to show her the World; *Balls, Assemblies, Operas, Comedies, Cards*, and *Visits*, everything that might enervate the Mind, and fit it for the soft Play and Impression of Love. One Thing he a little scrupled, lest in making her susceptible of that Passion, it should be for another, and not for him. He did not doubt but upon her first Appearance at Court she would have many Admirers. Lovers have this Opinion peculiar to themselves, they believe that others see with their Eyes. He knew that were she less agreeable, the Gloss of Novelty was enough to recommend her; but the Remedy he found for this, was, to caress and please her above all others, to show such a particular regard for her, that should frighten any new Pretender. Few are willing to cross a first Minister, especially in such a tender Point, where all Mankind are tenacious of their Pretensions.

He had observed, that *Charlot* had been, but with Disgust[34] denied the gay part of Reading. 'Tis natural for young People to choose the Diverting, before the Instructive; he sent for her into the Gallery, where was a noble Library in all Languages, a Collection of the most valuable Authors, with a mixture of the most Amorous. He told her, that now her Understanding was increased, with her Stature, he resolved to make her Mistress of her own Conduct; and as the first thing that he intended to oblige her in, that *Governante*, who had hitherto had the care of her Actions, should be dismissed, because he had observed the Severity of her Temper had sometimes been displeasing to her. That she should henceforth have none above her that she should need to stand in awe of; and to confirm to her that good Opinion he seemed to have, he presented her with the Key of that Gallery, to improve her Mind, and seek her Diversion among those Authors he had formerly forbid her the Use of. *Charlot* made him a very low Curtsy, and, with a blushing Grace, returned him Thanks for the two Favours he bestowed upon her. She assured him, That no Action of hers should make him repent the Distinction: That her whole endeavour should be to walk in that Path he had made

Notes

[33] *none but great Souls … Wicked Il Principe* ,chapter 8.

[34] *Disgust* "ill-humour; malevolence; offence conceived" (Johnson).

familiar to her; and that Virtue should ever be her only Guide. Though this was not what the Duke wanted, 'twas nothing but what he expected. He observed formerly, that she was a great lover of Poetry, especially when 'twas forbid her; he took down an *Ovid*, and opening it just at the love of *Myrra* for her Father,[35] conscious red overspread his Face; he gave it her to read, she obeyed him with a visible delight: Nothing is more pleasing to young Girls, than in being first considered as Women. *Charlot* saw the Duke entertained her with an Air of Consideration more than usual, passionate and respectful; this taught her to refuge in the native Pride and cunning of the Sex[36]; she assumed an air more haughty. Then, leaving a Girl just beginning to believe herself capable of attaining that Empire over Mankind, which they are all born and are taught by Instinct to expect, she took the Book, and placed herself by the Duke; his Eyes feasted themselves upon her Face, thence wandered over her snowy Bosom, and saw the young swelling Breasts just beginning to distinguish themselves, and which were gently heaved at the Impression of *Myrra*'s Sufferings made upon her Heart.

By this dangerous reading he pretended to show her, that there were Pleasures her Sex were born for, and which she might consequently long to taste! Curiosity is an early and dangerous Enemy to Virtue. The young *Charlot*, who had by a noble Inclination of Gratitude, a strong Propension of Affection for the Duke, whom she called and esteemed her *Papa*, being a Girl of wonderful reflection and consequently Application, wrought her Imagination up to such a lively height at the Father's Anger after the Possession of his Daughter, which she judged highly unkind and unnatural, that she dropped her Book, Tears filled her Eyes, Sobs rose to oppress her, and she pulled out her Handkerchief to cover the Disorder. The Duke, who was Master of all Mankind, could trace 'em in all the *Meanders* of Dissimulation and Cunning, was not at a loss how to interpret the Agitation of a Girl who knew no Hypocrisy. All was Artless, the beautiful Product of Innocence and Nature. He drew her gently to him, drank her Tears with his Kisses, sucked her Sighs, and gave her by that dangerous Commerce (her Soul before prepared to Softness) new and unfelt Desires. Her Virtue was becalmed, or rather unapprehensive of him for an Invader. He pressed her Lips with his; the nimble Beatings of his Heart, apparently seen and felt through his open Breast! the Glowings! the Tremblings of his Limbs! the Glorious Sparkles from his guilty Eyes! his Shortness of Breath, and eminent Disorder, were things all new to her that had never seen, heard, or read before of those powerful Operations, struck from the Fire of the two meeting Sex. Nor had she Leisure to examine his Disorders, possessed by greater of her own! Greater! because that Modesty opposing Nature, forced a struggle of Dissimulation. But the Duke's pursuing Kisses overcame the very Thoughts of anything; but the new and lazy Poison stealing to her Heart, and spreading swiftly and imperceptibly through all her Veins, she closed her Eyes with languishing Delight! Delivered up the Possession of her Lips and Breath to the amorous Invader; returned his eager Grasps; and, in a word, gave her whole Person into his Arms, in meltings full of Delight! The Duke by that lovely Ecstasy carried beyond himself, sunk over the expiring Fair in Raptures too powerful for Description! calling her his admirable *Charlot*! his charming Angel! his adorable Goddess! But all was so far modest that he attempted not beyond her Lips and Breast, but cried that she should

Notes

[35] *the love of Myrra for her Father Metamorphoses* 10.312–518; aided by her nurse, she succeeds in sleeping with her father, but when he discovers the deceit, she is forced to flee and in pity the gods transform her into the myrrh tree, which sheds balm as she shed tears; the child of her incestuous conception lives and is named Adonis.

[36] *the Sex* women.

never be another's. The Empire of his Soul was hers; enchanted by inexplicable, irresistible Magic! she had the Power beyond the Gods themselves!

Charlot, returned from that amiable Disorder, was anew charmed at the Duke's Words – words that set her so far above what was Mortal, the Woman assumed in her, and she would have no Notice taken of the Transports she had shown. He saw and favoured her Modesty, secure of that fatal Sting he had fixed within her Breast, that Taste of Delight, which powerful Love and Nature would call upon her to repeat. He owned he loved her; that he never could love any other; that 'twas impossible for him to live a Day, an Hour, without seeing her; that in her Absence he had felt more than ever had been felt by Mortal. He begged her to have pity on him, to return his Love, or else he should be the most lost, undone Thing alive. *Charlot*, amazed and charmed, felt all those dangerous Perturbations of Nature that arise from an amorous Constitution; with Pride and Pleasure, she saw herself necessary to the Happiness of one, that she had hitherto esteemed so much above her, ignorant of the Power of Love, that Leveller of Mankind, that blender of Distinction and Hearts. Her soft Answer was, That she was indeed reciprocally Charmed, she knew not how; all he had said and done was wonderful and pleasing to her; and if he would still more please her (if there were a more) it should be never to be parted from her. The Duke had one of those violent Passions, where, to heighten it, Resistance was not at all necessary; it had already reached the Ultimate; it could not be more ardent; yet was he loath to rush upon the Possession of the Fair, lest the too early Pretension might disgust her. He would steal himself into her Soul; he would make himself necessary to her Quiet, as she was to his.

From the Library he led her to his Cabinet[37]; from forth his strong Box he took a set of Jewels that had been her Mother's; he told her she was now of an Age to expect the Ornaments, as well as Pleasures, of a Woman. He was pleased to see her look down with a seeming contempt upon what most other Girls would have been transported with. He had taught her other Joys, those of the Mind and Body. She sighed, she raved to herself, she was all charmed and uneasy! The Duke casting over the rest of his Jewels, made a Collection of such as were much more valuable than her Mother's; he presented her with, and would force her to accept 'em. But *Charlot*, as tender and gallant as the Duke, seeing his picture in little, set round with Diamonds, begged that he would only honour her with that Mark of his Esteem. The ravished Duke consented, conditionally, that she would give him hers in return.

After this tender, dangerous Commerce, *Charlot* found everything insipid, nothing but the Duke's Kisses could relish with her; all those Conversations she had formerly delighted in, were insupportable. He was obliged to return to Court, and had recommended to her Reading the most dangerous Books of Love, *Ovid, Petrarch, Tibullus*,[38] those moving Tragedies that so powerfully expose the Force of Love, and corrupt the Mind. He went even farther, and left her such as explained the Nature, Manner, and Raptures of Enjoyment. Thus he infused Poison into the Ears of the lovely Virgin. She easily (from those Emotions she had found in herself) believed as highly of those Delights as was imaginable; her waking Thoughts, her golden Slumber, ran all of a Bliss only imagined, but never proved. She even forgot, as one that wakes from Sleep and the Visions of the Night, all those Precepts of airy Virtue, which she had found had nothing to do with Nature. She longed again to renew those dangerous Delights.

Notes

[37] *Cabinet* "A set of boxes or drawers for curiosities; a private box" (Johnson).

[38] *Ovid, Petrarch, Tibullus* Ovid's *Amores*; Petrarch's sonnets; and the Latin love poetry of Albius Tibullus (d. 19 BCE).

The Duke was an Age absent from her; she could only in Imagination possess what she believed so pleasing. Her Memory was prodigious, she was indefatigable in Reading. The Duke had left Orders she should not be controlled in anything: Whole Nights were wasted by her in that Gallery; she had too well informed herself of the speculative Joys of Love. There are Books dangerous to the Community of Mankind,[39] abominable for Virgins, and destructive to Youth; such as explain the Mysteries of Nature, the congregated Pleasures of *Venus*, the full Delights of mutual Lovers, and which rather ought to pass the Fire than the Press. The Duke had laid in her way such as made no mention of *Virtue* or *Hymen*,[40] but only advanced native, generous and undissembled Love. She was become so great a Proficient, that nothing of the Theory was a stranger to her.

Whilst *Charlot* was thus employed, the Duke was not idle; he had prepared her a Post at Court with *Henriquez*'s Queen. The young Lady was sent for; neither Art, Money, nor Industry was wanting, to make her Appearance glorious. The Duke awed and trembling with his Passion, approached her as a Goddess; conscious of his and her own Desires. The mantling Blood would smile upon her Cheeks, sometimes glowing with Delight, then afterwards, by a feeble Recollection of Virtue, sink apace, to make room for a guilty succeeding Paleness. The Duke knew all the Motions of her Heart; he debated with himself whether it were best to attempt the Possession of her whilst so young, or permit her time to know and set a Value upon what she granted. His Love was highly Impatient, but Respectful; he longed to be Happy, but he dreaded to displease her. The Ascendant she had over him was wonderful; he had let slip those first Impressions which strike deepest in the Hearts of Women; to be successful, 'One ought never to allow 'em time to think, their Vivacity being prodigious, and their foresight exceeding short, and limited: The first hurry of their Passions, if they are but vigorously followed, is what is generally most favourable to Lovers'. *Charlot* by this time had informed herself, that there were such terrible Things such as Perfidy and Inconstancy in Mankind; that even the very Favours they received, often disgusted, and that to be entirely Happy, one ought never to think of the faithless Sex. This brought her back to those Precepts of Virtue that had embellished her dawn of Life; but alas! these Admonitions were too feeble, the Duke was all submissive, passionate, eager to obey, and to oblige. He watched her Uprisings,[41] scarce could eat without her; she was Mistress of his Heart and Fortune; his own Family, and the whole Court imagined that he resolved her for his Duchess; they almost looked upon her as such; she went often to his Palace, where all were devoted to her Service; the very glance of her Eyes commanded their Attention; at her least Request, as soon as her Mouth was opened to speak, before her Words were half formed, they started to obey her.

She had learnt to manage the Duke, and to distrust herself; she would no more permit of Kisses, that sweet and dangerous Commerce. The Duke had made her wise at his own Cost, and vainly languished for a Repetition of Delight. He guessed at the Interest he had in her Heart, had proved the Warmth of her Constitution, and was resolved he would no more be wanting to his own Happiness; he omitted no occasion by which he might express his Love, pressing her to crown his Longings. Her courage did not reach to ask him that honourable Proof of his Passion, which 'tis believed he would not have refused, if she had but insisted on it. The Treaty was still depending:

Notes

39 *Books dangerous to… Mankind* for a discussion of some of these, see David Foxon, *Libertine Literature in England, 1660–1745*.

40 *Hymen* Greek god of marriage.

41 *watched her Uprisings* was anxious for her rising in the morning.

he might marry the Princess Dowager. *Charlot* tenderly dropped a Word that spoke her Apprehensions of it; he assured her there was nothing in it; all he aimed at was to purchase the Succession, that he might make her a Princess, as she deserved. Indeed the Hopes his Agent had given the Lady of becoming her Husband was not the smallest Inducement to the Treaty; therefore he delayed his Marriage to *Charlot*; for if that were but once confirmed, the Princess (by resenting, as she ought, the Abuse that had been laid upon her) would put an end to it, infinitely to his Prejudice.

Charlot, very well satisfied with these Reasons, and unwilling to do anything against the Interest of a Man whom she tenderly loved, accustomed herself to hear his eager Solicitations. He could no longer contend with a Fire that consumed him, he must be gratified, or die. She languished under the same Disquiets. The Season of the Year[42] was come that he must make the Campaign with the King; he could not resolve to depart unblessed; *Charlot* still refused him that last Proof of her Love. He took a tender and passionate Farewell. *Charlot*, drowned in Tears, told him, 'twas impossible she should support his Absence; all the Court would ridicule her Melancholy. This was what he wanted; he bid her take care of that; a Maid was but an ill Figure that brought herself to be the sport of Laughters; but since her Sorrow (so pleasing and glorious to him) was like to be visible, he advised her to pass some days at his *Villa*, till the height of Melancholy should be over, under the Pretence of Indisposition. He would take care that the Queen should be satisfied of the necessity of her Absence. He advised her even to depart that Hour; since the King was already on his Journey, he must be gone that moment, and endeavour to overtake him. He assured her he would write by every Courier, and begged her not to admit of another lover, though he was sensible there were many (taking the advantage of his Absence) would endeavour to please her. To this all she answered so as to quiet his Distrust and Fears; her Tears drowned her Sighs; her Words were lost in Sobs and Groans! The Duke did not show less concern, but led her all trembling to put her in a Coach that was to carry her to his *Villa*; where he had often wished to have her, but she distrusted herself, and would not go with him; nor had she have ventured now, but that she thought he was to follow the King, who could not be without him.

Charlot no sooner arrived, but the Weather being very hot, she ordered a Bath to be prepared for her. Soon as she was refreshed with that, she threw herself down upon a Bed, with only one thin Petticoat and a loose Nightgown, the Bosom of her Gown and Shift open; her Night-clothes tied carelessly together with a Cherry-coloured Ribbon, which answered well to the yellow and Silver Stuff of her Gown. She lay uncovered in a melancholy careless Posture, her Head resting upon one of her Hands; the other held a Handkerchief that she employed to dry those Tears that sometimes fell from her Eyes; when raising herself a little at a gentle noise she heard from the opening of a Door that answered to the Bedside, she was quite astonished to see enter the amorous Duke. Her first Emotions were all Joy; but in a minute she recollected herself, thinking he was not come there for nothing. She was going to rise; but he prevented her by flying to her Arms, where, as we may call it, he nailed her down to the Bed with Kisses; his Love and Resolution gave him double Vigour; he would not stay a moment to capitulate[43] with her; whilst yet her Surprise made her doubtful of his Designs, he took advantage of her confusion to accomplish 'em; neither her Prayers, Tears, nor Strugglings could prevent him, but in her Arms he made himself a full amends for all those Pains he had suffered for her.

Notes

[42] *Season of the Year* summer, when armies were traditionally "on campaign" or in the field.

[43] *capitulate* "to draw up articles of agreement; to parley" (*OED*).

Thus *Charlot* was undone! thus ruined by him that ought to have been her Protector! 'Twas very long before he could appease her; but so artful, so amorous, so submissive was his Address, so violent his Assurances, he told her, that he must have died without the Happiness. *Charlot* espoused[44] his Crime, by sealing[45] his Forgiveness. He passed the whole Night in her Arms, pleased, transported, and out of himself; whilst the ravished Maid was not at all behind-hand in Ecstasies and guilty Transports. He stayed a whole Week with *Charlot* in a surfeit of Love and Joy! that Week more inestimable than all the Pleasures of his Life before! whilst the Court believed him with the King, posting to the Army. He neglected *Mars* to devote himself wholly to *Venus*; abstracted from all Business, that happy Week sublimed him almost to an Immortal. *Charlot* was formed to give and take all those Raptures necessary to accomplish the Lover's Happiness; none were ever more Amorous; none were ever more Happy!

The two Lovers separated, the Duke for the Army, *Charlot* returned to the Court; one of the Royal-Secretaries[46] fell in Love with her, but his being of the precise[47] Party, and a married Man, it behooved to carry himself discreetly. He omitted no private Devoirs to please her, but her Heart entirely fixed upon the Duke, neglected the Attempt. She had made an intimate Friendship with a young Countess,[48] who was a *lovely Widow*, full of *Air, Life* and *Fire*; her Lord purchased her from his Rival, by the Point of his Sword, but he did not long survive to enjoy the Fruits of his *Victory*. He made her Circumstances as easy as he could, but that was not extraordinary; however, she appeared well at Court, knew the management of Mankind, and how to procure herself universal Love and Admiration. *Charlot* made her the unwary Confidant of her Passion for the Duke; the Countess had the Goodness, or Complaisance,[49] which you please, to hearken to the Over-flowings of a Love-sick-Heart. …

Notes

44 *espouse* "To adopt; to take to h[er]self" (Johnson).

45 *sealing* confirming, ratifying.

46 *one of the Royal-Secretaries* Sir John Trenchard (1640–95), an influential Whig.

47 *precise* "Formal; finical; solemnly and superstitiously exact" (Johnson).

48 *a young Countess* Martha Jane Temple; her first husband fought a duel for her; she married Bentinck (Charlot's Duke) in 1700.

49 *Complaisance* civility.

William Congreve (1670–1729)

William Congreve was born in Yorkshire in 1670 but moved with his parents to Ireland at age four. Like Jonathan Swift, his elder by only three years, Congreve attended Kilkenny College and Trinity College, Dublin. Also like Swift, Congreve fled Ireland in 1688 because he feared the uprising of Catholics loyal to James II and the prospect of its violent demise at the hands of William III. After a stay at the family house, Stretton Manor, Staffordshire, Congreve went to London to study law at the Middle Temple. Although he left those hallowed halls quickly, there is much evidence of his legal learning in *The Way of the World* and his other plays. In 1692 Congreve published a short moral novel called *Incognita: or Love and Duty Reconciled*, which is unjustly known mainly as the occasion for Samuel Johnson's deathless remark that he would rather praise it than read it. Congreve followed his novel with translations of parts of Horace, Juvenal, and Homer, which earned him literary patronage and praise from John Dryden. The excellence of these early works notwithstanding, the success of his first play, *The Old Batchelor* (1693), was so great that London felt he had burst upon the scene with that work. He wrote only three more comedies: *The Double-Dealer* (1694), *Love for Love* (1695), and *The Way of the World* (1700). Between the last two he wrote his only tragedy, *The Mourning Bride*, which was a very great success with the public and with the critics both of his age and the next: Johnson selected a passage of *The Mourning Bride* as "the most poetical paragraph" in "the whole mass of English Poetry."

After 1700 Congreve's production as a writer fell off dramatically. He wrote a couple of operas in the first few years of the new century and continued to produce occasional pieces of poetry and prose throughout his life, but for most of his last twenty years he lived as a private gentleman rather than a writer. Part of the reason for this may have been his relationship with Henrietta, the second duchess of Marlborough, which naturally incited gossip, although the duke apparently chose to be oblivious to the affair, even when it led to the birth of a child in 1723. Another reason for his reserve after 1700 may have been Congreve's steadily declining health. He was overweight; suffered from gout and other chronic ailments; and was increasingly myopic. Whatever the reason, his retreat into gentlemanly life earned him the condemnation of two unlikely bedfellows, Johnson and Voltaire, both of whom considered him a traitor to their Grubstreet brethren.

Like *The Double-Dealer*, *The Way of the World* enjoyed only moderate success in comparison with Congreve's other plays. It has been said that his disappointment over the reception of *The Way of the World* led Congreve to abandon writing for the general public. The play is partly an answer to Jeremy Collier's vexing attack on him in *A Short View of the Immorality and Profaneness of the English Stage* (1698), and the public's tepid response may have indicated to Congreve that they were irredeemably like Collier in their literalness and rigidity. Later readers have seen that the work is not only Congreve's but Restoration comedy's masterpiece. The complexity of the plot may still confuse some and it makes productions difficult, but such a plot suits the urbanity of the protagonist and his pleasing combination of wit and passion.

John C. Hodges is the author of the standard biography, *William Congreve, the Man* (Modern Language Association, 1941), as well as other informative works on the facts as they are ascertainable. Equally learned and more engaging is

British Literature 1640–1789: An Anthology, Fourth Edition. Edited by Robert DeMaria, Jr.

Maximillian Novak's *William Congreve* (Twayne, 1971). *The Works of William Congreve*, 3 vols. (Oxford University Press, 2011), ed. D. F. McKenzie and prepared for publication by C. Y. Ferdinand, is definitive and unlikely ever to be surpassed. The text of *The Way of the World* presented here is based on *The Works of Mr. William Congreve* (London, 1710), a collected edition which Congreve saw through the press, and in which he adjusted the scene divisions. McKenzie defends the use of the collected edition with his usual brilliance in "When Congreve Made a Scene," *Transactions of the Cambridge Bibliographical Society* 7 (1979), 338–42.

The Way of the World (1700)

Prologue
Spoken by Mr *Betterton*

Of those few Fools, who with ill Stars are cursed,
Sure scribbling Fools, called Poets, fare the worst:
For they're a sort of Fools which Fortune *makes,*
And after she has made 'em Fools, forsakes.
With Nature's Oafs 'tis quite a different Case,
For Fortune *favours all her* Idiot-Race:
In her own Nest the Cuckoo-Eggs we find,[1]
O'er which she broods to hatch the Changeling-Kind.[2]
No Portion for her own she has to spare,
So much she dotes on her adopted Care.
Poets are Bubbles, by the Town drawn in,[3]
Suffered at first some trifling Stakes to win:
But what unequal Hazards do they run!
Each time they write they venture all they've won:
The Squire that's buttered still, is sure to be undone.[4]
This Author, heretofore, has found your Favour,
But pleads no Merit from his past Behaviour.
To build on that might prove a vain Presumption,
Should Grants to Poets made, admit Resumption:[5]
And in Parnassus he must lose his Seat,[6]
If that be found a forfeited Estate.
He owns, with Toil, he wrought the following Scenes,
But if they're naught ne'er spare him for his Pains:
Damn him the more; have no Commiseration
For Dullness on mature Deliberation.

Notes

THE WAY OF THE WORLD

[1] *Cuckoo-Eggs* The cuckoo was "said to suck the eggs of other birds and lay her own to be hatched in their place" (Johnson).

[2] *Changeling-Kind* "the word [*changeling*] arises from an odd superstitious opinion, that the fairies steal away children, and put others that are ugly and stupid in their places" (Johnson).

[3] *Bubble* the victim of a cheat or con artist.

[4] *buttered* "To encrease the stakes every throw, or every game: a cant term among gamesters. 'It is a fine simile in one of Mr. Congreve's prologues, which compares a writer to a *buttering* gamester, that stakes all his winning upon one cast; so that if he loses the last throw, he is sure to be undone.' Addison. *Freeholder*, No. 40." (Johnson, s.v. *to butter*, sense 2).

[5] *Resumption* in law, "the action, on the part of the Crown or other authority, of reassuming possession of lands, rights, etc., which have been bestowed on others" (*OED*).

[6] *Parnassus* a mountain in Greece sacred to Apollo, the god of poetry; *Seat* "Mansion; residence; dwelling; abode" (Johnson, sense 3).

He swears he'll not resent one hissed-off Scene,
Nor, like those peevish Wits, his Play maintain,
Who, to assert their Sense, your Taste arraign.
Some Plot we think he has, and some new Thought;
Some Humour too, no Farce; but that's a Fault.
Satire, he thinks, you ought not to expect;
For so reformed a Town, who dares Correct?
To Please, this Time, has been his sole Pretence,
He'll not Instruct, lest it should give Offence.
Should he by Chance a Knave or Fool expose,
That hurts none here, sure here are none of those.
In short, our Play shall (with your Leave to show it)
Give you one Instance of a Passive Poet.
Who to your Judgements yields all Resignation;
So Save or Damn, after your own Discretion.

Dramatis Personae

Men

Fainall, in Love with *Mrs Marwood*	Mr *Betterton*
Mirabell, in Love with Mrs *Millamant*	Mr *Verbruggen*
Witwoud, } Followers of Mrs *Millamant*	Mr *Bowen*
Petulant, } Followers of Mrs *Millamant*	Mr *Bowman*
Sir *Wilfull Wilwoud*, half Brother to *Witwoud*, and Nephew to Lady *Wishfort*	Mr *Underhill*
Waitwell, Servant to *Mirabell*	Mr *Bright*

Women

Lady *Wishfort*, Enemy to *Mirabell*, for having falsely pretended Love to her	Mrs *Leigh*
Mrs *Millamant*, A fine Lady, Niece to Lady *Wishfort*, and loves *Mirabell*	Mrs *Bracegirdle*
Mrs *Marwood*, Friend to Mr *Fainall*, and likes *Mirabell*	Mrs *Barry*
Mrs *Fainall*, Daughter to Lady *Wishfort*, and Wife to *Fainall*, formerly Friend to *Mirabell*	Mrs *Bowman*
Foible, Woman [7] to Lady *Wishfort*	Mrs *Willis*
Mincing, Woman to Mrs *Millamant*	Mrs *Prince*
Dancers, Footmen *and* Attendants	

Notes

[7] *Woman* female servant

Scene London

The Time equal to that of the Presentation

The Way of the World

ACT I. SCENE I

A Chocolate-House[8]

Mirabell and *Fainall* [*Rising from Cards*]*Betty waiting*

MIRABELL: You are a fortunate Man, Mr *Fainall.*

FAINALL: Have we done?

MIRABELL: What you please. I'll play on to entertain you.

FAINALL: No, I'll give you your Revenge another time, when you are not so indifferent; you are thinking of something else now, and play too negligently; the Coldness of a losing Gamester lessens the Pleasure of the Winner. I'd no more play with a Man that slighted his ill Fortune than I'd make Love to a Woman who undervalued the Loss of her Reputation.

MIRABELL: You have a Taste extremely delicate, and are for refining on your Pleasures.

FAINALL: Prithee, why so reserved? Something has put you out of Humour.

MIRABELL: Not at all: I happen to be grave today; and you are gay:[9] that's all.

FAINALL: Confess, *Millamant* and you quarrelled last Night, after I left you; my fair Cousin has some Humours that would tempt the Patience of a Stoic. What, some Coxcomb came in, and was well received by her, while you were by.

MIRABELL: *Witwoud* and *Petulant*; and what was worse, her Aunt, your Wife's Mother, my evil Genius; or to sum up all in her own Name, my old Lady *Wishfort* came in.——

FAINALL: O there it is then——She has a lasting Passion for you, and with Reason.—— What, then my Wife was there?

MIRABELL: Yes, and Mrs *Marwood* and three or four more, whom I never saw before; seeing me, they all put on their grave Faces, whispered one another; then complained aloud of the Vapours, and after fell into a profound Silence.

FAINALL: They had a Mind to be rid of you.

MIRABELL: For which Reason I resolved not to stir. At last the good old Lady broke through her painful Taciturnity, with an Invective against long Visits. I would not have understood her, but *Millamant* joining in the Argument, I rose and with a constrained Smile told her, I thought nothing was so easy as to know when a Visit began to be troublesome; she reddened, and I withdrew without expecting her Reply.

FAINALL: You were to blame to resent what she spoke only in Compliance with her Aunt.

MIRABELL: She is more Mistress of herself, than to be under the Necessity of such a Resignation.

Notes

[8] *Chocolate-House* a fashionable but somewhat disreputable hangout.

[9] *gay* happy, blithe; the opposite of *grave.*

FAINALL: What? though half her Fortune depends upon her marrying with my Lady's Approbation?

MIRABELL: I was then in such a Humour, that I should have been better pleased if she had been less discreet.

FAINALL: Now I remember, I wonder not they were weary of you; last Night was one of their Cabal-Nights;[10] they have 'em three times a Week, and meet by turns, at one another's Apartments, where they come together like the Coroner's Inquest, to sit upon the murdered Reputations of the Week. You and I are excluded; and it was once proposed that all the Male Sex should be excepted; but some Body moved that to avoid Scandal there might be one Man of the Community; upon which Motion *Witwoud* and *Petulant* were enrolled Members.

MIRABELL: And who may have been the Foundress of this Sect? My Lady *Wishfort*, I warrant, who publishes her Detestation of Mankind; and full of the Vigour of fifty-five, declares for a Friend and *Ratafia*;[11] and let Posterity shift for itself, she'll breed no more.

FAINALL: The Discovery of your sham Addresses to her, to conceal your Love to her Niece, has provoked this Separation: Had you dissembled better, Things might have continued in the State of Nature.

MIRABELL: I did as much as Man could, with any reasonable Conscience; I proceeded to the very last Act of Flattery with her, and was guilty of a Song in her Commendation. Nay, I got a Friend to put her into a Lampoon[12] and compliment her with the Imputation of an Affair with a young Fellow, which I carried so far, that I told her the malicious Town took notice that she was grown fat of a sudden; and when she lay in of a Dropsy,[13] persuaded her she was reported to be in Labour. The Devil's in 't, if an old Woman is to be flattered further, unless a Man should endeavour downright personally to debauch her; and that my Virtue forbade me. But for the Discovery of this Amour, I am indebted to your Friend, or your Wife's Friend, Mrs *Marwood*.

FAINALL: What should provoke her to be your Enemy, unless she has made you Advances, which you have slighted? Women do not easily forgive Omissions of that Nature.

MIRABELL: She was always civil to me, till of late; I confess I am not one of those Coxcombs who are apt to interpret a Woman's good Manners to her Prejudice; and think that she who does not refuse 'em everything, can refuse 'em nothing.

FAINALL: You are a gallant Man, *Mirabell*; and though you may have Cruelty enough, not to satisfy a Lady's Longing, you have too much Generosity, not to be tender of her Honour. Yet you speak with an Indifference which seems to be affected; and confesses you are conscious of a Negligence.

MIRABELL: You pursue the Argument with a Distrust that seems to Be unaffected, and confesses that you are conscious of a Concern for which the Lady is more indebted to you, than is your Wife.

FAINALL: Fie, fie, Friend; if you grow censorious I must leave you;——I'll look upon the Gamesters in the next Room.

MIRABELL: Who are they?

FAINALL: *Petulant* and *Witwoud*——Bring me some Chocolate.

Notes

[10] *Cabal* a secret society or meeting for the purposes of intrigue.

[11] *Ratafia* "A fine liquor, prepared from the kernels of apricots and spirits" (Bailey).

[12] *Lampoon* a published, personal satire.

[13] *Dropsy* "A collection of water in the body" (Johnson, quoting John Quincy).

MIRABELL: *Betty*, what says your Clock?
BETTY: Turned of the last Canonical Hour,[14] Sir.
MIRABELL: How pertinently the Jade answers me! Ha? almost one o'clock! [*Looking on his Watch.*] O, y'are come——

Scene II

Mirabell and *Footman*

MIRABELL: Well; is the grand Affair over? You have been something tedious.
SERVANT: Sir, there's such coupling at *Pancras*,[15] that they stand behind one another, as 'twere in a Country Dance. Ours was the last Couple to lead up; and no Hopes appearing of Dispatch, besides, the Parson growing hoarse, we were afraid his Lungs would have failed before it came to her Turn; so we drove round to *Duke's-Place*; and there they were riveted in a trice.
MIRABELL: So, so, you are sure they are married.
SERVANT: Married and Bedded, Sir: I am Witness.
MIRABELL: Have you the Certificate?
SERVANT: Here it is, Sir.
MIRABELL: Has the Tailor brought *Waitwell*'s Clothes home, and the new Liveries?
SERVANT: Yes, Sir.
MIRABELL: That's well. Do you go home again, d'ye hear, and adjourn the Consummation till farther Order; bid *Waitwell* shake his Ears, and Dame *Partlet*[16] rustle up her Feathers, and meet me at One o'clock by *Rosamond*'s Pond[17] that I may see her before she returns to her Lady: And as you tender your Ears be secret.

Scene III

Mirabell, Fainall, Betty

FAINALL: Joy of your Success, *Mirabell*; you look pleased.
MIRABELL: Ay; I have been engaged in a Matter of some sort of Mirth, which is not yet ripe for Discovery. I am glad this is not a Cabal-Night. I wonder, *Fainall*, that you who are married, and of consequence should be discreet, will suffer your Wife to be of such a Party.
FAINALL: Faith, I am not jealous. Besides, most who are engaged are Women and Relations; and for the Men, they are of a Kind too contemptible to give Scandal.
MIRABELL: I am of another Opinion. The greater the Coxcomb always the more the Scandal: For a Woman who is not a Fool, can have but one Reason for associating with a Man who is one.
FAINALL: Are you jealous as often as you see *Witwoud* entertained by *Millamant*?
MIRABELL: Of her Understanding I am, if not of her Person.

Notes

14 *Canonical Hour* a time "within which marriage can be legally performed in a parish church in England" (*OED*); the hours were 8 A.M. to noon at this time.

15 *Pancras* St. Pancras, a church exempt from the jurisdiction of the bishop and therefore free to offer a venue for unlicensed, clandestine marriages; the *Duke's Place* in St. James enjoyed the same freedom.

16 *Dame Partlet* the wife of the rooster Chaunticleer in Chaucer's mock-heroic *Nun's Priest's Tale*, part of *The Canterbury Tales*.

17 *Rosamond's Pond* a meeting place in St. James's Park.

FAINALL: You do her wrong; for to give her her Due, she has Wit.

MIRABELL: She has Beauty enough to make any Man think so; and Complaisance enough not to contradict him who shall tell her so.

FAINALL: For a passionate Lover, methinks you are a Man somewhat too discerning in the Failings of your Mistress.

MIRABELL: And for a discerning Man, somewhat too passionate a Lover; for I like her with all her Faults; nay, like her for her Faults. Her Follies are so natural, or so artful, that they become her; and those Affectations which in another Woman would be odious, serve but to make her more agreeable. I'll tell thee, *Fainall*, she once used me with that Insolence, that in Revenge I took her to pieces; sifted her, and separated her Failings; I studied 'em, and got 'em by Rote. The Catalogue was so large, that I was not without Hopes, one Day or other, to hate her heartily: To which end I so used myself to think of 'em, that at length, contrary to my Design and Expectation, they gave me every Hour Less Disturbance; till in a few Days it became habitual to me, to remember 'em without being displeased. They are now grown as familiar to me as my own Frailties; and in all probability in a little time longer I shall like 'em as well.

FAINALL: Marry her, marry her; be half as well acquainted with her Charms, as you are with her Defects, and my Life on 't, you are your own Man again.

MIRABELL: Say you so?

FAINALL: I, I, I have Experience: I have a Wife, and so forth.

Scene IV

[To them] Messenger

MESSENGER: Is one Squire *Witwoud* here?

BETTY: Yes; What's your Business?

MESSENGER: I have a Letter for him, from his Brother Sir *Wilfull* which I am charged to deliver into his own Hands.

BETTY: He's in the next Room, Friend——That way.

Scene V

Mirabell, Fainall, Betty

MIRABELL: What, is the chief of that noble Family in Town, Sir *Wilfull Witwoud*!

FAINALL: He is expected today. Do you know him?

MIRABELL: I have seen him, he promises to be an extraordinary Person; I think you have the Honour to be related to him.

FAINALL: Yes; he is half Brother to this *Witwoud* by a former Wife, who was Sister to my Lady *Wishfort*, my Wife's Mother. If you marry *Millamant*, you must call Cousins too.

MIRABELL: I had rather be his Relation than his Acquaintance.

FAINALL: He comes to Town in order to Equip himself for Travel.

MIRABELL: For Travel! Why the Man that I mean is above Forty.

FAINALL: No matter for that; 'tis for the Honour of England, that all Europe should know we have Blockheads of all Ages.

MIRABELL: I wonder there is not an Act of Parliament to save the Credit of the Nation, and prohibit the Exportation of Fools.

FAINALL: By no means, 'tis better as 'tis; 'tis better to Trade with a little Loss, than to be quite eaten up, with being overstocked.

MIRABELL: Pray, are the Follies of this Knight-Errant, and those of the Squire his Brother, anything related?

FAINALL: Not at all; *Witwoud* grows by the Knight, like a Medlar[18] grafted on a Crab. One will melt in your Mouth, and t'other set your Teeth on Edge; one is all Pulp, and the other all Core.

MIRABELL: So one will be Rotten before he be Ripe, and the other will be Rotten without ever being Ripe at all.

FAINALL: Sir *Wilfull* is an odd Mixture of Bashfulness and Obstinacy——But when he's drunk, he's as loving as the monster in The Tempest;[19] and much after the same manner. To give t'other his due; he has something of good nature, and does not always want Wit.

MIRABELL: Not always; but as often as his Memory fails him, and his common-Place[20] of Comparisons. He is a Fool with a good Memory, and some few Scraps of other Folks' Wit. He is one whose Conversation can never be approved, yet it is now and then to be endured. He has indeed one good Quality, he is not Exceptious;[21] for he passionately affects the Reputation of understanding Raillery, that he will construe an Affront into a Jest; and call downright Rudeness and ill Language Satire and Fire.

FAINALL: If you have a mind to finish his Picture, you have an Opportunity to do it at full length. Behold the Original.

Scene VI

[*To them*] *Witwoud*

WITWOUD: Afford me your Compassion, my Dears; pity me, *Fainall; Mirabell*, pity me.

MIRABELL: I do from my Soul.

FAINALL: Why, what's the Matter?

WITWOUD: No Letters for me, *Betty*?

BETTY: Did not a Messenger bring you one but now, Sir?

WITWOUD: Ay, but no other?

BETTY: No, Sir.

WITWOUD: That's hard, that's very hard;——A Messenger, a Mule, a Beast of Burden, he has brought me a Letter from the Fool my Brother, as heavy as a Panegyric in a Funeral Sermon or a Copy of Commendatory Verses from one Poet to another. And what's worse, 'tis as sure a Forerunner of the Author, as an Epistle Dedicatory.

MIRABELL: A Fool, and your Brother, *Witwoud*!

WITWOUD: Ay, ay, my half Brother. My half Brother he is, no nearer, upon Honour.

MIRABELL: Then 'tis possible he may be but half a Fool.

WITWOUD: Good, good, *Mirabell*, le Drole![22] Good, good: hang him, don't let's talk of him;—— *Fainall*, how does your Lady? Gad, I say anything in the World to

Notes

[18] *Medlar* a fruit tree "native of the middle and south of Europe, and found in hedges and woods in England" (*OED*).

[19] *the monster in The Tempest* Caliban, a wild man in Shakespeare's play and Davenant and Dryden's version of it (1670) (McKenzie).

[20] *common-Place* commonplace book, a notebook full of quotations or familiar phrases for the assistance of writers and speakers.

[21] *Exceptious* "Peevish; froward; full of objections; quarrelsome" (Johnson).

[22] *le Drole* French, *droll*, "One whose business is to raise mirth by petty tricks; a jester; a buffoon; a jackpudding" (Johnson).

get this Fellow out of my Head. I beg Pardon that I should ask a Man of Pleasure, and the Town, a Question at once so Foreign and Domestic. But I talk like an old Maid at a Marriage, I don't know what I say: she's the best Woman in the World.

FAINALL: 'Tis well you don't know what you say, or else your Commendation would go near to make me either Vain or Jealous.

WITWOUD: No Man in Town lives well with a Wife but *Fainall*. Your Judgement, *Mirabell*?

MIRABELL: You had better step and ask his Wife; if you would be credibly informed.

WITWOUD: *Mirabell*.

MIRABELL: Ay.

WITWOUD: My Dear, I ask ten Thousand Pardons;——Gad I have forgot what I was going to say to you.

MIRABELL: I thank you heartily, heartily.

WITWOUD: No, but prithee excuse me,——my Memory is such a Memory.

MIRABELL: Have a care of such Apologies, *Witwoud*;——for I never knew a Fool but he affected to complain, either of the Spleen or his Memory.

FAINALL: What have you done with *Petulant*?

WITWOUD: He's reckoning his Money——my Money it was——I have no Luck today.

FAINALL: You may allow him to win of you at Play;——for you are sure to be too hard for him at Repartee: Since you monopolize the Wit that is between you, the Fortune must be his of Course.

MIRABELL: I don't find that *Petulant* confesses the Superiority of Wit to be your Talent, *Witwoud*.

WITWOUD: Come, come, you are malicious now, and would breed Debates——Petulant's my Friend, and a very pretty[23] Fellow, and a very honest Fellow, and has a smattering——Faith and Troth[24] a pretty deal of an odd sort of a small Wit: Nay, I'll do him Justice. I'm his Friend, I won't wrong him——And if he had any Judgement in the World,——he would not be altogether contemptible. Come, come, don't detract from the Merits of my Friend.

FAINALL: You don't take your Friend to be over-nicely bred.

WITWOUD: No, no, hang him, the Rogue has no Manners at all, that I must own——No more Breeding than a Bumbaily,[25] that I grant you,——'Tis pity; the Fellow has Fire and Life.

MIRABELL: What, Courage?

WITWOUD: Hum, faith I don't know as to that, I can't say as to that. Yes, faith, in a Controversy he'll contradict anybody.

MIRABELL: Though 'twere a Man whom he feared, or a Woman whom he loved.

WITWOUD: Well, well, he does not always think before he speaks;——We have all our Failings; you are too hard upon him, you are, faith. Let me excuse him,——I can defend most of his Faults, except one or two; one he has, that's the Truth on 't, if he were my Brother, I could not acquit him——That indeed I could wish were otherwise.

MIRABELL: Ay marry,[26] what's that, *Witwoud*?

Notes

[23] *pretty* "Beautiful without grandeur or dignity. … It is used in a kind of diminutive contempt in poetry, and in conversation: as, *a pretty fellow indeed!*" (Johnson, senses 2–3).

[24] *Troth* "Belief; faith; fidelity" (Johnson, 1773).

[25] *Bumbaily* a sergeant or undersheriff (see Johnson, s.v. *catch-poll*).

[26] *marry* an interjection expressing surprise or indignation (*OED*).

WITWOUD: O pardon me——Expose the Infirmities of my Friend!——No, my dear, excuse me there.

FAINALL: What I warrant he's unsincere, or 'tis some such Trifle.

WITWOUD: No, no, what if he be? 'Tis no matter for that, his wit will excuse that: A Wit should no more be sincere, than a Woman constant; one argues a Decay of Parts, as t'other of Beauty.

MIRABELL: May be you think him too positive?[27]

WITWOUD. No, no, his being positive is an Incentive to Argument, and keeps up Conversation.

FAINALL: Too illiterate.

WITWOUD. That! that's his Happiness——His want of Learning gives him the more Opportunities to show his natural Parts.

MIRABELL: He wants Words.

WITWOUD: Ay; but I like him for that now; for his want of Words gives me the Pleasure very often to explain his Meaning.

FAINALL: He's Impudent.

WITWOUD: No, that's not it.

MIRABELL: Vain.

WITWOUD: No.

MIRABELL: What, he speaks unseasonable Truths sometimes, because he has not Wit enough to invent an Evasion.

WITWOUD: Truths! Ha, ha, ha! No, no; since you will have it——I mean, he never speaks Truth at all,——That's all. He will lie like a Chambermaid, or a Woman of Quality's Porter. Now that is a Fault.

Scene VII

[To them] Coachman

COACHMAN: Is Master *Petulant* here, Mistress?

BETTY: Yes.

COACHMAN: Three Gentlewomen in a Coach would speak with him.

FAINALL: O brave *Petulant*, Three!

BETTY: I'll tell him.

COACHMAN: You must bring Two Dishes of Chocolate and a Glass of cinnamon-water.[28]

Scene VIII

Mirabell, Fainall, Witwoud

WITWOUD: That should be for Two fasting Strumpets, and a Bawd[29] troubled with the Wind. Now you may know what the Three are.

MIRABELL: You are very free with your Friend's Acquaintance.

Notes

[27] *positive* opinionated.

[28] *Cinnamon-water* a drink used as a tonic or astringent.

[29] *Bawd* "A procurer, or procuress; one that introduces men and women to each other, for the promotion of debauchery" (Johnson).

WITWOUD: Ay, ay. Friendship without Freedom is as dull as Love without Enjoyment, or Wine without Toasting; but to tell you a Secret, these are Trulls[30] whom he allows Coach-hire, and something more by the Week, to call on him once a Day at public Places.

MIRABELL: How!

WITWOUD: You shall see he won't go to 'em because there's no more Company here to take notice of him——Why this is nothing to what he used to do;——Before he found out this way, I have known him call for himself——

FAINALL: Call for himself? What dost thou mean?

WITWOUD: Mean! Why, he would slip you out of this Chocolate-house, just when you had been talking to him——As soon as your Back was turned——Whip he was gone;——Then trip to his Lodging, clap on a Hood and Scarf, and a Mask, slap into a Hackney-Coach and drive hither to the Door again in a trice! where he would send in for himself, that is, I mean, call for himself, wait for himself, nay and what's more, not finding himself, sometimes leave a Letter for himself.

MIRABELL: I confess this is something extraordinary——I believe he waits for himself now, he is so long a coming; O I ask his Pardon.

Scene IX

Petulant, Mirabell, Fainall, Witwoud, Betty

BETTY: Sir, the Coach stays.

PETULANT: Well, well; I come——'Sbud[31] a Man had as good be a professed Whore-master, at this rate; to be knocked up and raised at all Hours, and in all Places. Pox on 'em, I won't come——D' ye hear, tell 'em I won't come.——Let 'em snivel and cry their hearts out.

FAINALL: You are very cruel, *Petulant*.

PETULANT: All's one, let it pass——I have a Humour[32] to be cruel.

MIRABELL: I hope they are not Persons of Condition[33] that you use at this rate.

PETULANT: Condition! Condition's a dried Fig, if I am not in Humour——By this Hand, if they were your——a——a——your What-d'ye-call-'ems themselves, they must wait or rub off, if I want Appetite.

MIRABELL: What-d'ye-call-'ems! What are they, *Witwoud*?

WITWOUD: Empresses, my Dear——By your What-d'ye-call-'ems he means Sultana Queens.

PETULANT: Ay, *Roxolanas*.[34]

MIRABELL: Cry you Mercy.

FAINALL: *Witwoud* says they are——

PETULANT: What does he say th'are?——

WITWOUD: I? fine Ladies, I say.

PETULANT: Pass on, *Witwoud*——Harkee; by this Light, his Relations——Two Coheiresses his Cousins, and an old Aunt, who loves Catterwauling[35] better than a Conventicle.[36]

Notes

30 *Trull* "A low whore; a vagrant strumpet" (Johnson).

31 *'Sbud* "God's blood," a mild curse; part of the canned language of would-be wits.

32 *Humour* present disposition.

33 *Persons of Condition* men or women of distinction or importance.

34 *Roxolana* "The Turkish sultana in [Sir William] Davenant's *The Siege of Rhodes*" (Womersley).

35 *Catterwauling* "Going after the opposite sex; lecherous motions or pursuits" (*OED*, sense 2).

36 *Conventicle* a then illegal meeting of dissenters from the Church of England.

WITWOUD: Ha, ha, ha; I had a Mind to see how the Rogue would come off—— Ha, ha, ha; Gad I can't be angry with him; if he had said they were my Mother and my Sisters.

MIRABELL: No!

WITWOUD: No; the Rogue's Wit and Readiness of Invention charm me. Dear *Petulant.*

BETTY: They are gone, Sir, in great Anger.

PETULANT: Enough, let 'em trundle.[37] Anger helps Complexion, saves Paint.

FAINALL: This Continence is all dissembled; this is in order to have something to brag of the next time he makes Court to *Millamant*, and swear he has abandoned the whole Sex for her Sake.

MIRABELL: Have you not left off your impudent Pretensions there yet? I shall cut your Throat, sometime or other, *Petulant*, about that Business.

PETULANT: Aye, aye, let that pass——There are other Throats to be cut——

MIRABELL: Meaning mine, sir?

PETULANT: Not I——I mean nobody——I know nothing. But there are uncles and nephews in the world——and they may be rivals——What then? All's one for that——

MIRABELL: How! Harkee, *Petulant*, come hither——explain, or I shall call your interpreter.

PETULANT: Explain? I know nothing——Why, you have an Uncle, have you not, lately come to Town, and lodges by my Lady Wishfort's?

MIRABELL: True.

PETULANT: Why, that's enough——You and he are not Friends; and if he should marry and have a child, you may be disinherited, ha?

MIRABELL: Where hast thou stumbled upon all this Truth?

PETULANT: All's one for that; why, then, say I know something.

MIRABELL: Come, thou art an honest fellow, *Petulant*, and shalt make Love to my mistress, thou sha't,[38] Faith. What hast thou heard of my Uncle?

PETULANT: I? nothing, I. If Throats are to be cut, let Swords clash; Snug's the Word, I shrug and am silent.

MIRABELL: O Raillery, Raillery. Come, I know thou art in the Women's Secrets——What you're a Cabalist, I know you stayed at *Millamant*'s last Night, after I went. Was there any Mention made of my Uncle, or me? Tell me. If thou hadst but good Nature equal to thy Wit, *Petulant, Tony Witwoud*, who is now thy Competitor in Fame, would show as dim by thee as a dead Whiting's Eye by a Pearl of Orient; he would no more be seen by thee, than *Mercury* is by the Sun: Come, I'm sure thou wo't[39] tell me.

PETULANT: If I do, will you grant me common Sense then, for the future?

MIRABELL: Faith I'll do what I can for thee, and I'll pray that Heaven may grant it thee in the mean time.

PETULANT: Well, harkee.

FAINALL: *Petulant* and you both will find *Mirabell* as warm a Rival as a Lover.

WITWOUD: Pshaw, pshaw, that she laughs at *Petulant* is plain. And for my part——But that it is almost a Fashion to admire her, I should——Harkee——To tell you a Secret, but let it go no further——Between Friends, I shall never break my Heart for her.

FAINALL: How!

Notes

[37] *trundle* to go away, but with some sense of rolling off, perhaps unsteadily.

[38] *sha't* shalt.

[39] *wo't* would wish to.

WITWOUD: She's handsome; but she's a sort of an uncertain Woman.

FAINALL: I thought you had died for her.

WITWOUD: Umh——No——

FAINALL: She has Wit.

WITWOUD: 'Tis what she will hardly allow anybody else——Now, Demme, I should hate that, if she were as handsome as *Cleopatra*. *Mirabell* is not so sure of her as he thinks for.

FAINALL: Why do you think so?

WITWOUD: We stayed pretty late there last Night; and heard something of an Uncle to *Mirabell*, who is lately come to Town,——and is between him and the best part of his Estate; *Mirabell* and he are at some Distance, as my Lady *Wishfort* has been told; and you know she hates *Mirabell*, worse than a Quaker[40] hates a Parrot, or than a Fishmonger hates a hard Frost. Whether this Uncle has seen Mrs *Millamant* or not, I cannot say; but there were Items of such a Treaty being in Embryo; and if it should come to Life, poor *Mirabell* would be in some sort unfortunately fobbed,[41] i' faith.

FAINALL: 'Tis impossible *Millamant* should hearken to it.

WITWOUD: Faith, my Dear, I can't tell; she's a Woman and a kind of a Humorist.[42]

MIRABELL: And this is the Sum of what you could collect last Night?

PETULANT: The Quintessence. Maybe *Witwoud* knows more, he stayed longer——Besides, they never mind him; they say anything before him.

MIRABELL: I thought you had been the greatest Favourite.

PETULANT: *Ay tete a tete;*[43] But not in public, because I make Remarks.

MIRABELL: You do?

PETULANT: Ay, ay, pox I'm malicious, Man. Now he's soft, you know, they are not in awe of him——The Fellow's well bred, he's what you call a——What d'ye-call-'em. A fine Gentleman, but he's silly withal.

MIRABELL: I thank you. I know as much as my Curiosity requires. *Fainall*, are you for the *Mall* ?[44]

FAINALL: Ay, I'll take a turn before Dinner.

WITWOUD: Ay, we'll all walk in the Park; the Ladies talked of being there.

MIRABELL: I thought you were obliged to watch for your Brother Sir *Wilfull*'s Arrival.

WITWOUD: No, no, he comes to his Aunt's, my Lady *Wishfort*. Pox on him, I shall be troubled with him too; what shall I do with the Fool?

PETULANT: Beg him for his Estate; that I may beg you afterwards; and so have but one Trouble with you both.

WITWOUD: O rare *Petulant*; thou art as quick as Fire in a frosty Morning; thou shalt to the *Mall* with us; and we'll be very severe.

PETULANT: Enough, I'm in a Humour to be severe.

MIRABELL: Are you? Pray then walk by yourselves,——Let not us be accessary to your putting the Ladies out of Countenance, with your senseless Ribaldry; which you roar out aloud as often as they pass by you; and when you have made a handsome Woman blush, then you think you have been severe.

Notes

[40] *Quaker* member of a religious sect then known for silence.

[41] *fobbed* cheated.

[42] *Humorist* a person subject to his or her own odd fancies or whimsies.

[43] *tete a tete* face to face, in private.

[44] *Mall* a fashionable walk in St. James's Park.

PETULANT: What, what? Then let 'em either show their Innocence by not understanding what they hear, or else show their Discretion by not hearing what they would not be thought to understand.

MIRABELL: But hast not thou then Sense enough to know that thou ought'st to be most ashamed thyself, when thou hast put another out of Countenance?

PETULANT: Not I, by this Hand——I always take Blushing either for a Sign of Guilt, or ill Breeding.

MIRABELL: I confess you ought to think so. You are in the right, that you may plead the Error of your Judgement in defence of your Practice.

Where Modesty's ill Manners, 'tis but fit
That Impudence and Malice pass for Wit.

ACT II. SCENE I

St. James's Park

Mrs *Fainall* and Mrs *Marwood*

MRS FAINALL: Ay, ay, dear *Marwood*, if we will be happy, we must find the Means in ourselves, and among ourselves. Men are ever in Extremes; either doting, or averse. While they are Lovers, if they have Fire and Sense, their Jealousies are insupportable: And when they cease to Love (we ought to think at least), they loathe; they look upon us with Horror and Distaste; they meet us like the Ghosts of what we were, and as from such, fly from us.

MRS MARWOOD: True, 'tis an unhappy Circumstance of Life, that Love should ever die before us; and that the Man so often should outlive the Lover. But say what you will, 'tis better to be left, than never to have been loved. To pass our Youth in dull Indifference, to refuse the Sweets of Life because they once must leave us, is as preposterous as to wish to have been born Old, because we one Day must be Old. For my part, my Youth may wear and waste, but it shall never rust in my Possession.

MRS FAINALL: Then it seems you dissemble an Aversion to Mankind, only in compliance to my Mother's Humour.

MRS MARWOOD: Certainly. To be free; I have no Taste of those insipid dry Discourses, with which our Sex of force must entertain themselves, apart from Men. We may affect Endearments to each other, profess eternal Friendships, and seem to dote like Lovers; but 'tis not in our Natures long to persevere. Love will resume his Empire in our Breasts, and every Heart, or soon or late,[45] receive and readmit him as its lawful Tyrant.

MRS FAINALL: Bless me, how have I been deceived! Why you profess a Libertine.

MRS MARWOOD: You see my Friendship by my Freedom. Come, be as sincere, acknowledge that your Sentiments agree with mine.

MRS FAINALL: Never.

MRS MARWOOD: You hate Mankind?

MRS FAINALL: Heartily, Inveterately.

MRS MARWOOD: Your Husband?

MRS FAINALL: Most transcendently; ay, though I say it, meritoriously.

MRS MARWOOD: Give me your Hand upon it.

MRS FAINALL: There.

Notes

[45] *or…or* either…or.

MRS MARWOOD: I join with you; what I have said has been to try you.

MRS FAINALL: Is it possible? Dost thou hate those Vipers, Men?

MRS MARWOOD: I have done hating 'em, and am now come to despise 'em; the next thing I have to do, is eternally to forget 'em.

MRS FAINALL: There spoke the Spirit of an *Amazon*, a *Penthesilea*.[46]

MRS MARWOOD: And yet I am thinking sometimes to carry my Aversion farther.

MRS FAINALL: How?

MRS MARWOOD: Faith, by marrying; if I could but find one that loved me very well, and would be throughly sensible of ill Usage, I think I should do myself the Violence of undergoing the Ceremony.

MRS FAINALL: You would not make him a Cuckold?

MRS MARWOOD: No; but I'd make him believe I did, and that's as bad.

MRS FAINALL: Why, had not you as good do it?

MRS MARWOOD: O if he should ever discover it, he would then know the worst, and be out of his Pain; but I would have him ever to continue upon the Rack of Fear and Jealousy.

MRS FAINALL: Ingenious Mischief! Would thou wert married to *Mirabell*.

MRS MARWOOD: Would I were.

MRS FAINALL: You change Colour.

MRS MARWOOD: Because I hate him.

MRS FAINALL: So do I; but I can hear him named. But what Reason have you to hate him in particular?

MRS MARWOOD: I never loved him; he is, and always was insufferably proud.

MRS FAINALL: By the Reason you give for your Aversion, one would think it dissembled; for you have laid a Fault to his Charge, of which his Enemies must acquit him.

MRS MARWOOD: O then it seems you are one of his favourable Enemies. Methinks you look a little pale, and now you flush again.

MRS FAINALL: Do I? I think I am a little sick o' the sudden.

MRS MARWOOD: What ails you?

MRS FAINALL: My Husband. Don't you see him? He turned short upon me unawares, and has almost overcome me.

Scene II

[To them] Fainall and *Mirabell*

MRS MARWOOD: Ha, ha, ha; he comes opportunely for you.

MRS FAINALL: For you, for he has brought *Mirabell* with him.

FAINALL: My Dear.

MRS FAINALL: My Soul.

FAINALL: You don't look well today, Child.

MRS FAINALL: D'ye think so?

MIRABELL: He is the only Man that does, Madam.

MRS FAINALL: The only Man that would tell me so at least; and the only Man from whom I could hear it without Mortification.

FAINALL: O my Dear, I am satisfied of your Tenderness; I know you cannot resent anything from me; especially what is an effect of my Concern.

Notes

[46] *Penthesilea* queen of the Amazons, a mythical tribe of warrior women who excluded men from their society.

MRS FAINALL: Mr *Mirabell*, my Mother interrupted you in a pleasant Relation last Night: I would fain hear it out.

MIRABELL: The Persons concerned in that Affair, have yet a tolerable Reputation.——I am afraid Mr *Fainall* will be censorious.

MRS FAINALL: He has a Humour more prevailing than his Curiosity, and will willingly dispense with the hearing of one scandalous Story, to avoid giving an Occasion to make another by being seen to walk with his Wife. This way, Mr *Mirabell*, and I dare promise you will oblige us both.

Scene III

Fainall, Mrs *Marwood*

FAINALL Excellent Creature! Well, sure if I should live to be rid of my Wife, I should be a miserable Man.

MRS MARWOOD. Ay.

FAINALL: For having only that one Hope, the Accomplishment of it, of Consequence, must put an end to all my Hopes; and what a Wretch is he who must survive his Hopes! Nothing remains when that Day comes, but to sit down and weep like *Alexander*,[47] when he wanted other Worlds to conquer.

MRS MARWOOD: Will you not follow 'em?

FAINALL: Faith, I think not.

MRS MARWOOD. Pray let us; I have a Reason.

FAINALL: You are not jealous?

MRS MARWOOD: Of whom?

FAINALL: Of *Mirabell*.

MRS MARWOOD: If I am, is it inconsistent with my Love to you that I am tender of your Honour?

FAINALL: You would intimate then, as if there were a fellow feeling between my Wife and him.

MRS MIRABELL: I think she does not hate him to that degree she would be thought.

FAINALL: But he, I fear, is too insensible.

MRS MARWOOD: It may be you are deceived.

FAINALL: It may be so. I do not now begin to apprehend it.

MRS MARWOOD: What?

FAINALL: That I have been deceived, Madam, and you are false.

MRS MARWOOD: That I am false! What mean you?

FAINALL: To let you know I see through all your little Arts——Come, you both love him; and both have equally dissembled your Aversion. Your mutual Jealousies of one another have made you clash till you have both struck Fire. I have seen the warm Confession reddening on your Cheeks, and sparkling from your Eyes.

MRS MARWOOD: You do me wrong.

FAINALL: I do not——'Twas for my Ease to oversee and wilfully neglect the gross Advances made him by my Wife; that by permitting her to be engaged, I might continue unsuspected in my Pleasures; and take you oftener to my Arms in full Security. But could you think, because the nodding Husband would not wake, that e'er the watchful Lover slept?

Notes

47 *Alexander* Alexander the Great of Macedonia; for the story of Alexander weeping because there were no territories left for him to conquer, see Valerius Maximus 8.14 (McKenzie).

MRS MARWOOD: And wherewithal can you reproach me?

FAINALL: With Infidelity, with loving another, with Love of *Mirabell*.

MRS MARWOOD: 'Tis false. I challenge you to show an Instance that can confirm your groundless Accusation. I hate him.

FAINALL: And wherefore do you hate him? He is insensible, and your Resentment follows his Neglect. An Instance? The Injuries you have done him are a Proof: Your interposing in his Love. What Cause had you to make discoveries of his pretended Passion? To undeceive the credulous Aunt, and be the Officious Obstacle of his match with *Millamant*?

MRS MARWOOD: My Obligations to my Lady urged me: I had professed Friendship to her; and could not see her easy Nature abused by that Dissembler.

FAINALL: What, was it Conscience then? Professed a Friendship! O the pious Friendships of the Female Sex!

MRS MARWOOD: More tender, more sincere, and more enduring, than all the vain and empty Vows of Men, whether professing Love to us, or mutual Faith to one another.

FAINALL: Ha, ha, ha; you are my Wife's Friend too.

MRS MARWOOD: Shame and Ingratitude! Do you reproach me? You, you upbraid me! Have I been false to her, through strict Fidelity to you, and sacrificed my Friendship to keep my Love inviolate? And have you the Baseness to charge me with the guilt, unmindful of the Merit! To you it should be meritorious that I have been vicious: And do you reflect that Guilt upon me, which should lie buried in your Bosom?

FAINALL: You misinterpret my Reproof. I meant but to remind you of the slight Account you once could make of strictest Ties, when set in Competition with your Love to me.

MRS MARWOOD: 'Tis false, you urged it with deliberate Malice——'Twas spoke in Scorn, and I never will forgive it.

FAINALL: Your Guilt, not your Resentment, begets your Rage. If yet you loved, you could forgive a Jealousy: But you are stung to find you are discovered.

MRS MARWOOD: It shall be all discovered. You too shall be discovered; be sure you shall. I can but be exposed——if I do it myself, I shall prevent your Baseness.

FAINALL: Why, what will you do?

MRS MARWOOD: Disclose it to your Wife; own what has passed between us.

FAINALL: Frenzy!

MRS MARWOOD: By all my Wrongs I'll do't——I'll publish to the World the Injuries you have done me, both in my Fame and Fortune: With both I trusted you, you Bankrupt in Honour, as indigent of Wealth.

FAINALL: Your Fame I have preserved. Your Fortune has been bestowed as the Prodigality of your Love would have it, in Pleasures which we both have shared. Yet, had not you been false, I had ere this repaid it——'Tis true——had you permitted *Mirabell* with *Millamant* to have stolen their Marriage, my Lady had been incensed beyond all Means of Reconcilement: *Millamant* had forfeited the Moiety[48] of her Fortune; which then would have descended to my Wife;——And wherefore did I marry, but to make lawful Prize of a rich Widow's Wealth, and squander it on Love and you?

MRS MARWOOD: Deceit, and frivolous Pretence.

FAINALL: Death, am I not married? What's Pretence? Am I not imprisoned fettered? Have I not a Wife? Nay a Wife that was a Widow, a young Widow. A handsome

Notes

[48] *Moiety* half.

Widow; and would be again a Widow, but that I have a Heart of Proof,[49] and something of a Constitution to bustle through the ways of Wedlock and this World. Will you yet be reconciled to Truth and me?

MRS MARWOOD: Impossible. Truth and you are inconsistent——I hate you, and shall for ever.

FAINALL: For loving you?

MRS MARWOOD: I loathe the Name of Love after such Usage; and next to the Guilt with which you would asperse me, I scorn you most. Farewell.

FAINALL: Nay, we must not part thus.

MRS MARWOOD: Let me go.

FAINALL: Come, I'm sorry.

MRS MARWOOD: I care not——Let me go——Break my Hands, do——I'd leave 'em to get loose.

FAINALL: I would not hurt you for the World. Have I no other Hold to keep you here?

MRS MARWOOD: Well, I have deserved it all.

FAINALL: You know I love you.

MRS MARWOOD: Poor dissembling!——O that——Well, it is not yet——

FAINALL: What? What is it not? What is not yet? It is not yet too late——

MRS MARWOOD: No, it is not yet too late——I have that Comfort.

FAINALL: It is, to love another.

MRS MARWOOD: But not to loathe, detest, abhor Mankind, myself, and the whole treacherous World.

FAINALL: Nay, this is Extravagance——Come, I ask your Pardon——No Tears——I was to blame. I could not love you and be easy in my Doubts——Pray forbear——I believe you; I'm convinced I've done you wrong; and any way, every way will make amends;——I'll hate my Wife yet more, Damn her, I'll part with her, rob her of all she's worth, and we'll retire somewhere, anywhere, to another World. I'll marry thee——Be pacified——'Sdeath! They come, hide your Face, your Tears—— You have a Mask, wear it a Moment. This way, this way, be persuaded.

Scene IV

Mirabell and Mrs *Fainall*

MRS FAINALL They are here yet.

MIRABELL: They are turning into the other Walk.

MRS FAINALL: While I only hated my Husband, I could bear to see him but since I have despised him, he's too offensive.

MIRABELL: O you should hate with Prudence.

MRS FAINALL: Yes, for I have loved with indiscretion.

MIRABELL: You should have just so much Disgust for your Husband as may be sufficient to make you relish your Lover.

MRS FAINALL: You have been the Cause that I have loved without bounds, and would you set Limits to that Aversion, of which you have been the Occasion? Why did you make me marry this Man?

Notes

[49] *Proof* "Firm temper; impenetrability; the state of being wrought and hardened, till the expected strength is found by trial to be attained" (Johnson).

Mirabell: Why do we daily commit disagreeable and dangerous actions? To save that Idol Reputation. If the Familiarities of our Loves had produced that Consequence, of which you were apprehensive, where could you have fixed a father's Name with Credit, but on a Husband? I knew *Fainall* to be a Man lavish of his Morals, an interested and professing Friend, a false and a designing Lover; yet one whose Wit and outward fair Behaviour have gained a Reputation with the Town, enough to make that Woman stand excused, who has suffered herself to be won by his Addresses. A better Man ought not to have been sacrificed to the Occasion; a worse had not answered to the Purpose. When you are weary of him, you know your remedy.

Mrs Fainall: I ought to stand in some Degree of Credit with you, *Mirabell*.

Mirabell: In Justice to you, I have made you privy to my whole Design, and put it in your Power to ruin or advance my Fortune.

Mrs Fainall: Whom have you instructed to represent your pretended Uncle?

Mirabell: *Waitwell*, my Servant.

Mrs Fainall: He is an humble Servant[50] to *Foible*, my Mother's Woman, and may win her to your Interest.

Mirabell: Care is taken for that——She is won and worn by this time. They were married this Morning.

Mrs Fainall: Who?

Mirabell: *Waitwell* and *Foible*. I would not tempt my Servant to betray me by trusting him too far. If your Mother, in hopes to ruin me, should consent to marry my pretended Uncle, he might, like *Mosca* in the *Fox*, stand upon Terms;[51] so I made him sure before-hand.

Mrs Fainall: So, if my poor Mother is caught in a Contract, you will discover the Imposture betimes; and release her by producing a Certificate of her Gallant's former Marriage.

Mirabell: Yes, upon Condition that she consent to my Marriage with her Niece, and surrender the Moiety of her Fortune in her Possession.

Mrs Fainall: She talked last Night of endeavouring at a Match between *Millamant* and your Uncle.

Mirabell: That was by *Foible*'s Direction; and my Instruction, that she might seem to carry it more privately.

Mrs Fainall: Well, I have an Opinion of your Success; for I believe my Lady will do anything to get an Husband; and when she has this, which you have provided for her, I suppose she will submit to anything to get rid of him.

Mirabell: Yes, I think the good Lady would marry anything that resembled a Man, though 'twere no more than what a Butler could pinch out of a Napkin.

Mrs Fainall: Female Frailty! We must all come to it, if we live to be Old, and feel the craving of a false Appetite when the true is decayed.

Mirabell: An old Woman's Appetite is depraved like that of a Girl——'Tis the Green Sickness[52] of a second Childhood; and like the faint Offer of a latter Spring, serves but to usher in the Fall; and withers in an affected Bloom.

Mrs Fainall: Here's your Mistress.

Notes

[50] *an humble Servant* a devoted lover.

[51] *Mosca…stands upon terms* Mosca, the fly, is the intriguing servant in Ben Jonson's play *Volpone, or the Fox* who finally gets the upper hand on his master and makes his own terms for a settlement, or "stands upon terms."

[52] *Green Sickness* "The disease of maids [i.e., virgins], so called from the paleness which it produces" (Johnson); associated with love longing as early as Sappho.

Scene V

[*To them*] Mrs *Millamant, Witwoud, Mincing*

MIRABELL: Here she comes i' faith full Sail, with her Fan spread and Streamers out, and a Shoal of Fools for Tenders[53]——Ha, no, I cry her Mercy. Here she comes i' faith full Sail, with her Fan spread and Streamers out, and a Shoal of Fools for Tenders——Ha, no, I cry her Mercy.

MRS FAINALL: I see but one poor empty Sculler;[54] and he tows her Woman after him.

MIRABELL: You seem to be unattended, Madam,——You used to have the *Beau-monde* throng after you; and a Flock of fine Perukes[55] hovering round you.

WITWOUD: Like Moths about a Candle——I had like to have lost my Companion for want of Breath.

MILLAMANT: O I have denied myself Airs to Day. I have walked as fast through the Crowd——

WITWOUD: As a Favourite[56] just disgraced; and with as few Followers.

MILLAMANT: Dear Mr *Witwoud*, Truce with your Similitudes——No, you met her Husband, and did not ask him for her.

MIRABELL: By your leave, *Witwoud*, that were like enquiring after an old Fashion, to ask a Husband for his Wife.

WITWOUD: Hum, a hit, a hit, a palpable hit, I confess it.[57]

MRS FAINALL: You were dressed before I came abroad.

MILLAMANT: Ay, that's true——O but then I had——*Mincing*, what had I? Why was I so long?

MINCING: Mem, your La'ship stayed to peruse a Pacquet of Letters.

MILLAMANT: O ay, Letters——I had Letters——I am persecuted by Letters——I hate Letters——Nobody knows how to write Letters; and yet one has 'em, one does not know why——They serve one to pin up one's Hair.

WITWOUD: Is that the way? Pray, Madam, do you pin up your Hair with all your Letters? I find I must keep Copies.

MILLAMANT: Only with those in Verse, Mr *Witwoud*. I never pin my Hair with Prose. I think I tried once, *Mincing*.

MINCING: O Mem, I shall never forget it.

MILLAMANT: Ay, poor *Mincing* tiffed[58] and tiffed all the Morning.

MINCING: 'Till I had the Cramp in my Fingers, I'll vow Mem. And all to no Purpose. But when your La'ship pins it up with Poetry, it sits so pleasant the next Day, as anything, and is so pure and so crips.[59]

WITWOUD: Indeed, so crips?

MINCING: You're such a Critic, Mr *Witwoud*.

MILLAMANT: *Mirabell*, Did you take Exceptions last Night? O ay, and went away——Now I think on't I'm angry——no, I think on't I'm pleased——For I believe I gave you some Pain.

Notes

[53] *Tenders* ships or boats attending a larger vessel.

[54] *Sculler* "A cockboat; a boat in which there is but one rower" (Johnson), or the solitary rower.

[55] *Perukes* "A cap of false hair; a periwig" (Johnson); a metaphor for suitors in fancy dress.

[56] *Favourite* "One chosen as a companion by his superior; a mean wretch whose whole business is by any means to please" (Johnson, sense 2).

[57] *Hum … confess it* an allusion to *Hamlet* V.ii.232, 238.

[58] *tiffed tiff*, "To attire, dress, deck out, trick out, 'tittivate' [sic] (one's person, hair, etc.)" (*OED*).

[59] *crips* obsolete, dialect form of *crisp* (*OED*).

MIRABELL: Does that please you?

MILLAMANT: Infinitely; I love to give Pain.

MIRABELL: You would affect a Cruelty which is not in your Nature; your true Vanity is in the Power of pleasing.

MILLAMANT: O I ask your Pardon for that——One's Cruelty is one's Power, and when one parts with one's Cruelty, one parts with one's Power; and when one has parted with that I fancy one's old and ugly.

MIRABELL: Ay, ay, suffer your Cruelty to ruin the Object of your Power, to destroy your Lover——And then how vain, how lost a Thing you'll be? Nay, 'tis true: You are no longer handsome when you've lost your Lover; your Beauty dies upon the Instant: For Beauty is the Lover's Gift; 'tis he bestows your Charms——Your Glass is all a Cheat. The Ugly and the Old, whom the Looking-glass mortifies, yet after Commendation can be flattered by it and discover Beauties in it: For that reflects our Praises, rather than your Face.

MILLAMANT: O the Vanity of these Men! *Fainall*, d'ye hear him? If they did not commend us, we were not handsome! Now you must know they could not commend one, if one was not handsome. Beauty the Lover's Gift——Lord, what is a Lover, that it can give? Why one makes Lovers as fast as one pleases, and they live as long as one pleases, and they die as soon as one pleases: And then if one pleases one makes more.

WITWOUD: Very pretty. Why you make no more of making Lovers, Madam, than of making so many Card-matches.[60]

MILLAMANT: One no more owes one's Beauty to a Lover, than one's Wit to an Echo——They can but reflect what we look and say; vain empty Things if we are silent or unseen, and want a Being.

MIRABELL: Yet, to those two vain empty Things, you owe two the greatest Pleasures of your Life.

MILLAMANT: How so?

MIRABELL: To your Lover you owe the Pleasure of hearing yourselves praised; and to an Echo the Pleasure of hearing yourselves talk.

WITWOUD: But I know a Lady that loves Talking so incessantly, she won't give an Echo fair play; she has that everlasting Rotation of Tongue, that an Echo must wait till she dies, before it can catch her last Words.

MILLAMANT: O Fiction! *Fainall*, let us leave these Men.

MIRABELL: Draw off *Witwoud*. [*Aside to Mrs* Fainall]

MRS FAINALL: Immediately. I have a Word or two for Mr *Witwoud*.

Scene VI

Millamant, Mirabell, Mincing

MIRABELL: I Would beg a little private Audience too——You had the Tyranny to deny me last Night; though you knew I came to impart a Secret to you that concerned my love.

Notes

[60] *Card-matches* homemade cardboard matches; pieces of card dipped in sulphur.

MILLAMANT: You saw I was engaged.

MIRABELL: Unkind. You had the Leisure to entertain a Herd of Fools; Things who visit you from their excessive Idleness; bestowing on your Easiness that Time, which is the Encumbrance of their Lives. How can you find Delight in such Society? It is impossible they should admire you, they are not capable: Or if they were, it should be to you as a Mortification; for sure to please a Fool is some degree of Folly.

MILLAMANT: I please myself——Besides, sometimes to converse with Fools is for my Health.

MIRABELL: Your Health! Is there a worse Disease than the Conversation of Fools?

MILLAMANT: Yes, the Vapours;[61] Fools are Physic[62] for it, next to Assa-foetida.[63]

MIRABELL: You are not in a Course of Fools?

MILLAMANT: *Mirabell*, if you persist in this offensive Freedom——you'll displease me——I think I must resolve, after all not to have you——We shan't agree.

MIRABELL: Not in our Physic, it may be.

MILLAMANT: And yet our Distemper in all likelihood will be the same; for we shall be sick of one another. I shan't endure to be reprimanded, nor instructed; 'tis so dull to act always by Advice, and so tedious to be told of one's Faults——I can't bear it. Well, I won't have you, *Mirabell*——I'm resolved——I think——you may go——Ha, ha, ha. What would you give, that you could help loving me?

MIRABELL: I would give something that you did not know I could not help it.

MILLAMANT: Come, don't look grave then. Well, what do you say to me?

MIRABELL: I say that a Man may as soon make a Friend by his Wit, or a Fortune by his Honesty, as win a Woman with Plain-dealing and Sincerity.

MILLAMANT: Sententious *Mirabell*! Prithee don't look with that violent and inflexible wise Face, like Solomon at the dividing of the Child[64] in an old Tapestry Hanging.

MIRABELL: You are merry, Madam, but I would persuade you for a Moment to be serious.

MILLAMANT: What, with that Face? No, if you keep your Countenance, 'tis impossible I should hold mine. Well, after all, there is something very moving in a Lovesick Face. Ha, ha, ha——Well I won't laugh, don't be peevish——Heigho! Now I'll be melancholy, as melancholy as a Watch-light.[65] Well *Mirabell*, if ever you will win me, woo me now——Nay, if you are so tedious, fare you well;——I see they are walking away.

MIRABELL: Can you not find in the variety of your Disposition one Moment——

MILLAMANT: To hear you tell me *Foible*'s Married and your Plot like to speed——No.

MIRABELL: But how came you to know it——

MILLAMANT: Without the help of the Devil, you can't imagine; unless she should tell me herself. Which of the two it may have been, I will leave you to consider; and when you have done thinking of that, think of me.

Notes

61 *Vapours* "Diseases caused by flatulence, or by diseased nerves; hypochondriacal maladies; melancholy; spleen" (Johnson, sense 5).

62 *Physic* medicine.

63 *Assa-foetida asafoetida*, "A gum or resin brought from the East Indies … of known efficacy in some uterine disorders … " (Johnson, citing Ephraim Chambers).

64 *Solomon … Child* for the story of Solomon recommending this division to determine which of two women truthfully claimed to be the mother, see 1 Kings 3.16–28.

Scene VII

Mirabell alone

I Have something more——Gone——Think of you! To think of a Whirlwind though 'twere in a Whirlwind, were a Case of more steady Contemplation; a very Tranquillity of Mind and Mansion.[66] A Fellow that lives in a Windmill, has not a more whimsical Dwelling than the Heart of a Man that is lodged in a Woman. There is no Point of the Compass to which they cannot turn, and by which they are not turned; and by one as well as another; for Motion, not Method is their Occupation. To know this, and yet continue to be in Love, is to be made wise from the Dictates of Reason, and yet persevere to play the Fool by the force of Instinct——O here come my Pair of Turtles——What, billing so sweetly! Is not *Valentine's Day* over with you yet?

Scene VIII

[*To him*] *Waitwell, Foible*

MIRABELL: Sirrah, *Waitwell*, why sure you think you were married for your own Recreation, and not for my Conveniency.

WAITWELL: Your Pardon, Sir. With Submission, we have indeed been solacing in lawful Delights; but still with an Eye to Business, Sir. I have instructed her as well as I could. If she can take your Directions as readily as my Instructions, Sir, your Affairs are in a prosperous way.

MIRABELL: Give you Joy, Mrs *Foible*.

FOIBLE: O-las, sir, I'm so ashamed——I'm afraid my Lady has been in a thousand Inquietudes for me. But I protest, Sir, I made as much haste as I could.

WAITWELL: That she did indeed, Sir. It was my Fault that she did not make more.

MIRABELL: That I believe.

FOIBLE: But I told my Lady as you instructed me, Sir. That I had a Prospect of seeing Sir *Rowland* your Uncle, and that I would put her Ladyship's Picture in my Pocket to show him; which I'll be sure to say has made him so enamoured of her Beauty, that he burns with Impatience to lie at her Ladyship's Feet, and worship the original.

MIRABELL: Excellent *Foible*! Matrimony has made you eloquent in Love.

WAITWELL: I think she has profited, Sir. I think so.

FOIBLE: You have seen Madam *Millamant*, Sir?

MIRABELL: Yes.

FOIBLE: I told her, Sir, because I did not know that you might find an Opportunity; she had so much Company last Night.

MIRABELL: Your Diligence will merit more——In the meantime. [*Gives money*]

FOIBLE: O dear Sir, your humble Servant.

WAITWELL: Spouse.

MIRABELL: Stand off, Sir, not a Penny——Go on and prosper, *Foible*——The Lease shall be made good and the Farm stocked, if we succeed.

Notes

[65] *Watch-light* a night light, especially "a slow-burning candle with a rush wick," which gives off a "dismal" light (*OED*, definition and citation of Gilbert White, 1775).

[66] *Mansion* dwelling place.

FOIBLE: I don't question your Generosity, Sir: And you need not doubt of Success. If you have no more Commands, Sir, I'll be gone; I'm sure my Lady is at her Toilet,[67] and can't dress till I come.——O dear, I'm sure that [*Looking out*] was Mrs *Marwood* that went by in a Mask; if she has seen me with you I'm sure she'll tell my Lady. I'll make haste home and prevent her. Your Servant, Sir. B'w'y,[68] *Waitwell.*

Scene IX

Mirabell, Waitwell

WAITWELL: Sir *Rowland*, if you please. The Jade's so pert upon her Preferment she forgets herself.

MIRABELL: Come Sir, will you endeavour to forget yourself——and transform into Sir *Rowland*.

WAITWELL: Why Sir; it will be impossible I should remember myself——Married, knighted and attended all in one Day! 'Tis enough to make my Man forget himself. The Difficulty will be how to recover my Acquaintance and Familiarity with my former self; and fall from my Transformation to a Reformation into *Waitwell*. Nay, I shan't be quite the same *Waitwell* neither——for now I remember me, I'm married and can't be my own Man again.

Ay, there's my Grief; that's the sad change of Life:
To lose my Title, and yet keep my Wife.

ACT III. SCENE I

A Room in Lady Wishfort's House

Lady *Wishfort* at her Toilet, *Peg* waiting

LADY WISHFORT: Merciful! no News of *Foible* yet?

PEG: No, Madam.

LADY WISHFORT: I have no more Patience——If I have not fretted myself till I am pale again, there's no veracity in me. Fetch me the Red——the Red, do you hear, Sweetheart? An errant Ash Colour, as I'm a Person. Look you how this Wench stirs! Why dost thou not fetch me a little Red? Didst thou not hear me, Mopus?

PEG: The Red *Ratafia* does your Ladyship mean, or the Cherry-Brandy?

LADY WISHFORT: *Ratafia*, Fool? No, Fool. Not the *Ratafia*, Fool——Grant me Patience! I mean the *Spanish* Paper,[69] Idiot——Complexion Darling. Paint, Paint, Paint, dost thou understand that, changeling,[70] dangling thy Hands like Bobbins before thee? Why dost thou not stir, Puppet? Thou wooden Thing upon Wires.

PEG: Lord, Madam, your Ladyship is so impatient.——I cannot come at the Paint, Madam, Mrs *Foible* has locked it up, and carried the Key with her.

LADY WISHFORT: Pox take you both——Fetch me the Cherry-Brandy then.

Notes

[67] *Toilet* "The process of washing oneself, dressing, and attending to one's appearance" (*Concise OED*).

[68] *B'w'y* God be with you.

[69] *Spanish Paper* or Spanish wool, a cosmetic, like rouge (see *Spectator* 41).

[70] *changeling* "An idiot; a fool; a natural" (Johnson).

Scene II

Lady *Wishfort*

I'm as pale and as faint, I look like Mrs *Qualmsick* the Curate's Wife, that's always breeding——Wench, come, come, Wench, what art thou doing, Sipping? Tasting? Save thee, dost thou not know the Bottle?

Scene III

Lady *Wishfort, Peg* with a Bottle and *China* Cup

PEG: Madam, I was looking for a Cup.

LADY WISHFORT: A Cup, save thee, and what a Cup hast thou brought! Dost thou take me for a *Fairy*, to drink out of an *Acorn*? Why didst thou not bring thy Thimble? Hast thou ne'er a Brass-Thimble clinking in thy Pocket with a bit of Nutmeg? I warrant thee. Come, fill, fill.——So——again. See who that is——[*One knocks*] Set down the Bottle first. Here, here, under the Table——What, wouldst thou go with the Bottle in thy Hand like a Tapster.[71] As I'm a Person, this Wench has lived in an Inn upon the Road, before she came to me, like *Maritornes* the *Asturian* in *Don Quixote*.[72] No *Foible* yet?

PEG: No Madam, Mrs *Marwood*.

LADY WISHFORT: O *Marwood*, let her come in. Come in, good *Marwood*.

Scene IV

[*To them*] Mrs *Marwood*

MRS MARWOOD: I'm surprised to find your Ladyship in *dishabille*[73] at this time of Day.

LADY WISHFORT: *Foible*'s a lost Thing; has been abroad since Morning, and never heard of since.

MRS MARWOOD: I saw her but now, as I came masked through the Park in Conference with *Mirabell*:

LADY WISHFORT: With *Mirabell*! You call my Blood into my Face, with mentioning that Traitor. She durst not have the Confidence. I sent her to negotiate an Affair, in which if I'm detected I'm undone. If that wheedling Villain has wrought upon *Foible* to detect me, I'm ruined. Oh my dear Friend, I'm a Wretch of Wretches if I'm detected.

MRS MARWOOD: O Madam, you cannot suspect Mrs *Foible*'s Integrity.

LADY WISHFORT: O, he carries Poison in his Tongue that would corrupt Integrity itself. If she has given him an Opportunity she has as good as put her Integrity into his Hands. And dear *Marwood*, what's Integrity to an Opportunity?——Hark! I hear her——Dear Friend retire into my Closet that I may examine her with more Freedom——You'll pardon me, dear Friend, I can make bold with you——There are

Notes

71 *Tapster* "One whose business is to draw beer in an alehouse" (Johnson).

72 *Maritornes the Asturian in Don Quixote* the innkeeper's daughter in Cervantes' novel.

73 *dishabille* fashionable undress; a loose nightgown worn over a smock (Waller, 158).

Books over the Chimney——*Quarles* and *Prynne*, and the *Short View of the Stage*, with Bunyan's Works[74] to entertain you.——Go, you Thing, and send her in. [*to* Peg]

Scene V

Lady *Wishfort, Foible*

LADY WISHFORT: O *Foible*, where hast thou been? what hast thou been doing?

FOIBLE: Madam, I have seen the party.

LADY WISHFORT: But what hast thou done?

FOIBLE: Nay, 'tis your Ladyship has done, and are to do, I have only promised. But a Man so enamoured——so transported! Well, if worshipping of Pictures be a Sin——poor Sir *Rowland*, I say.

LADY WISHFORT: The Miniature has been counted like——But hast thou not betrayed me, *Foible*? Hast thou not detected me to that faithless *Mirabell*?——What hadst thou to do with him in the Park? Answer me, has he got nothing out of thee?

FOIBLE: So, the Devil has been beforehand with me. What shall I say?——Alas, Madam, could I help it, if I met that confident Thing? Was I in Fault? If you had heard how he used me, and all upon your Ladyship's Account, I'm sure you would not suspect my Fidelity. Nay, if that had been the worst I could have borne: But he had a Fling at your Ladyship too; and then I could not hold; but i' faith I gave him his own.

LADY WISHFORT: Me? What did the Filthy Fellow say?

FOIBLE: O Madam; 'tis a Shame to say what he said——his Taunts and his Fleers, tossing up his Nose. 'Humh', says he, 'what you are a hatching some Plot', says he, 'you are so early abroad, or catering', says he, 'ferreting for some disbanded Officer,[75] I warrant——Half Pay is but thin Subsistence', says he——'Well, what Pension does your Lady propose? Let me see', says he, 'what she must come down pretty deep now, she's superannuated', says he, 'and——'[76]

LADY WISHFORT: Ods my Life, I'll have him, I'll have him murdered. I'll have him poisoned. Where does he eat? I'll marry a Drawer[77] to have him poisoned in his Wine. I'll send for *Robin* from *Locket's*——immediately.[78]

FOIBLE: Poison him? Poisoning's too good for him. Strangle him, Madam, starve him; marry Sir *Rowland*, and get him disinherited. O you would bless yourself, to hear what he said.

LADY WISHFORT: A Villain! superannuated!

FOIBLE: 'Humh', says he, 'I hear you are laying Designs against me too', says he, 'and Mrs *Millamant* is to marry my Uncle'; he does not suspect a Word of your Ladyship, 'but', says he, 'I'll fit you for that, I warrant you', says he, 'I'll hamper you for that', says he, 'you and your old Frippery too', says he, 'I'll handle you——'

LADY WISHFORT: Audacious Villain! handle me, would he durst——Frippery? old Frippery! Was there ever such a foul-mouthed Fellow? I'll be married tomorrow, I'll be contracted tonight.

Notes

[74] *Quarles ... Bunyan's Works* Francis Quarles (1592–1644), author of many works of piety and morals; William Prynne (1600–69), Puritan moralist and opponent of stage-plays; *A Short View of the Immorality and Profaneness of the Stage* (1698) by Jeremy Collier (1650–1726); John Bunyan (1628–88), moralist, author of *Pilgrim's Progress*.

[75] *disbanded Officer* a soldier not on active duty.

[76] *Ods my Life* "God save my life," an oath.

[77] *Drawer* "One whose business is to draw liquors from the cask" (Johnson, sense 2).

[78] *Robin from Locket's* stock name for a servant at London's most fashionable restaurant of the time.

Foible: The sooner the better, Madam.

Lady Wishfort: Will Sir *Rowland* be here, say'st thou? when, *Foible*?

Foible: Incontinently, Madam. No new Sheriff's Wife expects the Return of her Husband after Knighthood, with that Impatience in which Sir *Rowland* burns for the dear Hour of kissing your Ladyship's Hand after Dinner.

Lady Wishfort: Frippery! superannuated Frippery! I'll Frippery the Villain; I'll reduce him to Frippery and Rags: A Tatterdemalion[79]——I hope to see him hung with Tatters, like a *Long-Lane* Pent-house,[80] or a Gibbet Thief.[81] A slander-mouthed Railer: I warrant the Spendthrift Prodigal's in Debt as much as the Million Lottery,[82] or the whole Court upon a Birthday.[83] I'll spoil his Credit with his Tailor. Yes, he shall have my Niece with her Fortune, he shall.

Foible: He! I hope to see him lodge in *Ludgate*[84] first, and angle into *Blackfriars*[85] for Brass Farthings,[86] with an old Mitten.[87]

Lady Wishfort: Ay dear *Foible*; thank thee for that, dear *Foible*. He has put me out of all Patience. I shall never recompose my Features, to receive Sir *Rowland* with any Economy of Face. This Wretch has fretted me that I am absolutely decayed. Look, *Foible*.

Foible: Your Ladyship has frowned a little too rashly, indeed Madam. There are some Cracks discernible in the white Varnish.

Lady Wishfort: Let me see the Glass——Cracks say'st thou? Why I am arrantly flayed——I look like an old peeled Wall. Thou must repair me, *Foible*, before Sir *Rowland* comes; or I shall never keep up to my Picture.

Foible: I warrant you, Madam; a little Art once made your Picture like you; and now a little of the same Art must make you like your Picture. Your Picture must sit for you, Madam.

Lady Wishfort: But art thou sure Sir *Rowland* will not fail to come? Or will he not fail when he does come? Will he be Importunate, *Foible*, and push? For if he should not be importunate——I shall never break Decorums——I shall die with Confusion, if I am forced to advance——Oh, no, I can never advance——I shall swoon if he should expect Advances. No, I hope Sir *Rowland* is better bred than to put a Lady to the Necessity of breaking her Forms. I won't be too coy neither.——I won't give him Despair——But a little Disdain is not amiss; a little Scorn is alluring.

Foible: A little Scorn becomes your Ladyship.

Lady Wishfort: Yes, but Tenderness becomes me best——A sort of Dyingness——You see that Picture has a sort of a——Ha *Foible*? A Swimmingness in the Eyes—— Yes, I'll look so——My Niece affects it; but she wants Features. Is Sir *Rowland* handsome? Let my Toilet be removed——I'll dress above. I'll receive Sir *Rowland* here. Is he handsome? Don't answer me. I won't know: I'll be surprised; I'll be taken by Surprise.

Notes

79 *Tatterdemalion* "a ragged fellow" (Johnson).

80 *a Long-Lane Penthouse* a shed hanging out from the main wall of stores in the second-hand clothes district of London; these *penthouses* formed arcades and were hung with goods for sale.

81 *Gibbet Thief* one who steals the clothes of executed criminals, who were hung on the gibbet, a wooden post, as an admonition to others; it was customary for the condemned to wear their Sunday best to their executions (Waller, 153).

82 *the Million Lottery* a state lottery, made illegal in 1699.

83 *Birthday* birthday of a member of the royal family, especially the prince, when there was much celebration and elaborate dress.

84 *Ludgate* a high-class debtors' prison in London.

85 *Blackfriars* a district of London on the Thames near Ludgate.

86 *Brass Farthings* emphatic expression for coins of very low denomination.

87 *Mittens* "Gloves that cover the arm without covering the fingers" (Johnson, sense 2).

FOIBLE: By Storm, Madam. Sir *Rowland*'s a brisk Man.

LADY WISHFORT: Is he! O then he'll importune, if he's a brisk Man; I shall save Decorums if Sir *Rowland* importunes. I have a moral Terror at the Apprehension of offending against Decorums. O I'm glad he's a brisk Man. Let my Things be removed, good *Foible*.

Scene VI

Mrs *Fainall, Foible*

MRS FAINALL: O *Foible*, I have been in a Fright, lest I should come too late. That Devil, *Marwood*, saw you in the Park with *Mirabell*, and I'm afraid will discover it to my Lady.

FOIBLE: Discover what, Madam?

MRS FAINALL: Nay, nay, put not on that strange Face. I am privy to the whole Design, and know that *Waitwell*, to whom thou wert this Morning married, is to personate *Mirabell*'s Uncle, and as such, winning my Lady, to involve her in those Difficulties from which *Mirabell* only must release her, by his making his Conditions to have my Cousin and her Fortune left to her own Disposal.

FOIBLE: O dear Madam, I beg your Pardon. It was not my Confidence in your Ladyship that was deficient; but I thought the former good Correspondence between your Ladyship and Mr *Mirabell*, might have hindered his communicating this Secret.

MRS FAINALL: Dear *Foible*, forget that.

FOIBLE: O dear Madam. Mr *Mirabell* is such a sweet winning Gentleman——But your Ladyship is the Pattern of Generosity.——Sweet Lady, to be so good! Mr *Mirabell* cannot choose but be grateful. I find your Ladyship has his Heart still. Now, Madam, I can safely tell your Ladyship our Success; Mrs *Marwood* had told my Lady; but I warrant I managed myself. I turned it all for the better. I told my Lady that Mr *Mirabell* railed at her. I laid horrid Things to his Charge, I'll vow; and my Lady is so incensed that she'll be contracted to Sir *Rowland* tonight, she says;——I warrant I worked her up that he may have her for asking for, as they say of a *Welsh* Maiden-Head.

MRS FAINALL: O rare *Foible*!

FOIBLE: Madam, I beg your Ladyship to acquaint Mr *Mirabell* of his Success. I would be seen as little as possible to speak to him——besides, I believe Madam *Marwood* watches me——She has a Month's Mind;[88] but I know Mr *Mirabell* can't abide her.——[*Calls*] John——remove my Lady's Toilet. Madam, your Servant. My Lady is so impatient, I fear she'll come for me, if I stay.

MRS FAINALL: I'll go with you up the back Stairs, lest I should meet her.

Scene VII

Mrs *Marwood* alone

Indeed, Mrs Engine,[89] is it thus with you? Are you become a go-between of this Importance? Yes, I shall watch you. Why this Wench is the Passe-partout, a very Master-Key to everybody's strong Box. My Friend *Fainall*, have you carried it so

Notes

[88] *Month's Mind* inclination, liking, fancy (*OED*, sense 2).

[89] *Engine* "An agent for another. In contempt" (Johnson, sense 6).

swimmingly? I thought there was something in it; but it seems it's over with you. Your Loathing is not from a want of Appetite then, but from a Surfeit. Else you could never be so cool to fall from a Principal to be an Assistant; to procure for him! A Pattern of Generosity, that I confess. Well, Mr *Fainall*, you have met with your Match.——O Man, Man! Woman, Woman! The Devil's an Ass: If I were a Painter, I would draw him like an Idiot, a Driveller with a Bib and Bells. Man should have his Head and Horns, and Woman the rest of him. Poor simple Fiend! Madam *Marwood* has a Month's Mind, but he can't abide her——'Twere better for him you had not been his Confessor in that Affair, without you could have kept his Counsel closer. I shall not prove another Pattern of Generosity——he has not obliged me to that with those Excesses of himself; and now I'll have none of him. Here comes the good Lady, panting ripe; with a Heart full of Hope, and a Head full of Care, like any Chemist upon the Day of Projection.[90]

Scene VIII

[*To her*] Lady *Wishfort*

Lady Wishfort: O Dear *Marwood*, what shall I say for this rude Forgetfulness——But my dear Friend is all Goodness.

Mrs Marwood: No Apologies, dear Madam. I have been very well entertained.

Lady Wishfort: As I'm a Person I am in a very Chaos to think I should forget myself——But I have such an Olio[91] of Affairs really I know not what to do—— [*Calls*]——*Foible*——expect my Nephew Sir *Wilfull* every Moment too:——why *Foible*——He means to travel for Improvement.

Mrs Marwood: Methinks Sir *Wilfull* should rather think of marrying than travelling at his Years. I hear he is turned of forty.

Lady Wishfort: O he's in less Danger of being spoiled by his Travels——I am against my Nephew's marrying too young. It will be time enough when he comes back, and has acquired Discretion to choose for himself.

Mrs Marwood: Methinks Mrs *Millamant* and he would make a very fit Match. He may travel afterwards. 'Tis a Thing very usual with young Gentlemen.

Lady Wishfort: I promise you I have thought on't——And since your Judgement, I'll think on't again. I assure you I will; I value your Judgement extremely. On my Word I'll propose it.

Scene IX

[*To them*] *Foible*

Lady Wishfort: Come, come *Foible*——I had forgot my Nephew will be here before Dinner——I must make haste.

Foible: Mr *Witwoud* and Mr *Petulant* are come to dine with your Ladyship.

Lady Wishfort: O Dear, I can't appear till I am dressed. Dear *Marwood* shall I be free with you again, and beg you to entertain 'em? I'll make all imaginable Haste. Dear Friends, excuse me.

Notes

90 *Chemist upon the Day of Projection* alchemist at the climax of his procedure of turning baser metals into gold.

91 *Olio* mixture, hodgepodge.

Scene X

Mrs Marwood, Mrs Millamant, Mincing

MILLAMANT: Sure never anything was so unbred as that odious Man.——*Marwood*, your Servant.

MRS MARWOOD: You have a Colour, what's the Matter?

MILLAMANT: That horrid Fellow *Petulant* has provoked me into a flame——I have broke my Fan——*Mincing*, lend me yours;——Is not all the Powder out of my Hair?

MRS MARWOOD: No. What has he done?

MILLAMANT: Nay, he has done nothing; he has only talked——Nay, he has said nothing neither; but he has contradicted everything that has been said. For my part, I thought *Witwoud* and he would have quarrelled.

MINCING: I vow Mem, I thought once they would have fit.[92]

MILLAMANT: Well, 'tis a lamentable thing I swear that one has not the Liberty of choosing one's Acquaintance as one does one's Clothes.

MRS MARWOOD: If we had that Liberty, we should be as weary of one Set of Acquaintance, though never so good, as we are of one Suit though never so fine. A Fool and a *Doily Stuff* [93] would now and then find Days of Grace, and be worn for Variety.

MILLAMANT: I could consent to wear 'em, if they would wear alike; but Fools never wear out——They are such *Drap-de-Berry*[94] Things! Without one could give 'em to one's Chambermaid after a Day or two.

MRS MARWOOD: 'TWERE BETTER SO INDEED. Or what think you of the Play-House? A fine gay glossy Fool should be given there like a new masking Habit after the Masquerade is over and we have done with the Disguise. For a Fool's visit is always a Disguise; and never admitted by a Woman of Wit, but to blind her Affair with a Lover of Sense. If you would but appear bare-faced now, and own *Mirabell*, you might as easily put off *Petulant* and *Witwoud*, as your Hood and Scarf. And indeed 'tis time, for the Town has found it: The Secret is grown too big for the Pretence: 'Tis like Mrs *Primly*'s great Belly; she may lace it down before, but it burnishes on her Hips. Indeed, *Millamant*, you can no more conceal it, than my Lady *Strammel* can her Face, that goodly Face, which in Defiance of her Rhenish-Wine Tea,[95] will not be comprehended in a Mask.

MILLAMANT: I'LL TAKE MY DEATH, *MARWOOD*, YOU ARE MORE CENSORIOUS THAN A DECAYED BEAUTY OR A DISCARDED TOAST.[96] *Mincing*, tell the Men they may come up. My Aunt is not dressing here; their Folly is less provoking than your Malice.

Scene XI

Millamant, Marwood

MILLAMANT: The Town has found it! What has it found? That *Mirabell* loves me is no more a Secret, than it is a Secret that you discovered it to my Aunt, or than the Reason why you discovered it is a Secret.

Notes

92 *fit* dialectal or vulgar form of *fought*.

93 *Doily Stuff* "A species of woollen stuff, so called, I suppose, from the name of the first maker" (Johnson).

94 *Drap-de-Berry* a kind of wool manufactured in Berry, France (*OED*).

95 *Rhenish-Wine Tea* an infusion perhaps used to induce urination.

96 *Toast* a woman frequently toasted, the belle of the ball.

Mrs Marwood: You are nettled.

Millamant: You're mistaken. Ridiculous!

Mrs Marwood: Indeed, my Dear, you'll tear another Fan, if you don't mitigate those violent Airs.

Millamant: O silly! Ha, ha, ha. I could laugh immoderately. Poor *Mirabell*! His Constancy to me has quite destroyed his Complaisance for all the World beside. I swear, I never enjoined it him, to be so coy——If I had the Vanity to think he would obey me; I would command him to show more Gallantry——'Tis hardly well bred to be so particular on one Hand, and so insensible on the other. But I despair to prevail, and so let him follow his own Way. Ha, ha, ha. Pardon me, dear Creature, I must laugh, ha, ha, ha; though I grant you 'tis a little barbarous, ha, ha, ha.

Mrs Marwood: What Pity 'tis, so much fine Raillery, and delivered with so significant Gesture, should be so unhappily directed to miscarry.

Millamant: Ha? Dear Creature I ask your Pardon——I swear I did not mind you.

Mrs Marwood: Mr *Mirabell* and you both may think a Thing impossible, when I shall tell him by telling you——

Millamant: O dear, what? for it is the same thing, if I hear it——Ha, ha, ha.

Mrs Marwood. That I detest him, Madam.

Millamant: O Madam, why so do I——And yet the Creature loves me, ha, ha. How can one forbear laughing to think of it——I am a Sybil[97] if I am not amazed to think what he can see in me. I'll take my Death, I think you are handsomer——and within a Year or two as young——If you could but stay for me, I should overtake you——But that cannot be——Well, that Thought makes me melancholic——Now I'll be sad.

Mrs Marwood: Your merry Note may be changed sooner than you think.

Millamant: D' ye say so? Then I'm resolved I'll have a Song to keep up my Spirits.

Scene XII

[To them] Mincing

Mincing: The Gentlemen stay but to Comb,[98] Madam; and will wait on you.

Millamant: Desire Mrs —— that is in the next Room to sing the Song I would have learnt Yesterday. You shall hear it, Madam——Not that there's any great Matter in it——But 'tis agreeable to my Humour.

Song

Set by *Mr John Eccles*[99]

I

Love's but the Frailty of the Mind,
When 'tis not with Ambition joined;
A sickly Flame, which if not fed expires;
And feeding, wastes in Self-consuming Fires.

Notes

[97] *Sybil* prophet (see, especially, *Aeneid* 6.98–123).

[98] *Comb* dress their wigs.

[99] *John Eccles* composer (d. 1735) who also wrote nine pieces for the play (McKenzie, II.535).

II

'Tis not to wound a wanton Boy
Or am'rous Youth, that gives the Joy;
But 'tis the Glory to have pierced a Swain,
For whom inferior Beauties sighed in vain.

III

Then I alone the conquest prize,
When I insult a Rival's Eyes:
If there's Delight in Love, 'tis when I see
That heart which others bleed for, bleed for me.

Scene XIII

[*To them*] *Petulant, Witwoud*

MILLAMANT: Is your Animosity composed, Gentlemen?

WITWOUD: Raillery, Raillery, Madam, we have no Animosity——We hit off a little Wit now and then, but no Animosity——The falling out of Wits is like the falling out of Lovers——We agree in the main, like Treble and Bass. Ha, *Petulant*!

PETULANT: Ay, in the main——But when I have a Humour to contradict——

WITWOUD: Ay, when he has a Humour to contradict, then I contradict too. What, I know my Cue. Then we contradict one another like two Battledores,[100] for Contradictions beget one another like *Jews*.[101]

PETULANT: If he says Black's Black——If I have a Humour to say Blue——Let that pass——All's one for that. If I have a Humour to prove it, it must be granted.

WITWOUD: Not positively must——But it may——It may.

PETULANT: Yes, it positively must, upon Proof positive.

WITWOUD: Ay, upon Proof positive it must; but upon Proof presumptive it only may. That's a Logical Distinction now, Madam.

MRS MARWOOD: I perceive your Debates are of Importance, and very learnedly handled.

PETULANT: Importance is one Thing, and Learning's another; but a Debate's a Debate, that I assert.

WITWOUD: *Petulant*'s an Enemy to Learning; he relies altogether on his Parts.[102]

PETULANT: No, I'm no Enemy to anybody, but them that have it.

MILLAMANT: Well, an illiterate Man's my Aversion. I wonder at the Impudence of any illiterate Man, to offer to make Love.

WITWOUD: That I confess I wonder at too.

MILLAMANT: Ah! to marry an Ignorant! that can hardly Read or Write.

PETULANT: Why should a Man be any further from being married though he can't read, than he is from being hanged. The Ordinary's[103] paid for setting the Psalm, and the

Notes

[100] *Battledores* "An instrument with a handle and a flat blade, used in play to strike a ball, or shuttlecock" (Johnson).

[101] *Contradictions beget … Jews* because the word beget is used so frequently in the English translations of Old Testament genealogies (see, e.g., 1 Chronicles 6.4–14).

[102] *Parts* "Qualities; powers; faculties; or accomplishments" (Johnson, sense 13).

[103] *Ordinary* the chaplain of Newgate Prison, who would prepare prisoners for execution.

Parish Priest for reading the Ceremony.[104] And for the rest which is to follow in both Cases, a Man may do it without a book——So all's one for that.

MILLAMANT: D'ye hear the Creature? Lord, here's Company, I'll be gone.

Scene XIV

Sir *Wilfull Witwoud* in a riding Dress, Mrs *Marwood, Petulant, Witwoud, Footman*

WITWOUD: In the Name of *Bartlemew* and his Fair,[105] what have we here?

MRS MARWOOD: 'Tis your Brother, I fancy. Don't you know him?

WITWOUD: Not I——Yes, I think it is he——I've almost forgot him; I have not seen him since the Revolution.[106]

FOOTMAN: Sir, my Lady's dressing. Here's Company; if you please to walk in, in the mean time.

SIR WILFULL. Dressing! What, it's but Morning here I warrant with you in *London*; we should count it towards Afternoon in our Parts, down in *Shropshire*——Why then belike my Aunt han't dined yet——Ha, Friend?

FOOTMAN: Your Aunt, Sir?

SIR WILFULL: My Aunt, Sir? yes my Aunt, Sir, and your Lady, Sir; your Lady is my Aunt, Sir——Why, what dost thou not know me, Friend? Why then send somebody hither that does. How long hast thou lived with thy Lady, Fellow, ha?

FOOTMAN: A Week, Sir; longer than any in the House, except my Lady's Woman.

SIR WILFULL: Why then belike thou dost not know thy Lady, if thou see'st her, ha, Friend!

FOOTMAN: Why truly, Sir, I cannot safely swear to her Face in the Morning, before she is dressed. 'Tis like I may give a shrewd guess at her by this time.

SIR WILFULL: Well, prithee try what thou canst do; if thou canst not guess, inquire her out, do'st hear, Fellow? And tell her her Nephew, Sir *Wilfull Witwoud*, is in the House.

FOOTMAN: I shall, Sir.

SIR WILFULL: Hold ye, hear me, Friend; a Word with you in my Ear: Prithee who are these Gallants?

FOOTMAN: Really, Sir, I can't tell; here come so many here, 'tis hard to know 'em all.

Scene XV

Sir *Wilfull Witwoud, Petulant, Witwoud,* Mrs *Marwood*

SIR WILFULL: Oons,[107] this Fellow knows less than a Starling; I don't think a' knows his own Name.

MRS MARWOOD: Mr *Witwoud*, your Brother is not behindhand in Forgetfulness——I fancy he has forgot you too.

WITWOUD: I hope so——The Devil take him that remembers first, I say.

SIR WILFULL: Save you Gentlemen and Lady.

Notes

[104] *Ceremony* marriage ceremony.

[105] *Bartlemew and his Fair* St. Bartholomew, one of the twelve apostles, and the fair held in London on his feast day; also the name of a comedy by Ben Jonson in which a country fellow is cheated out of all his belongings at the fair.

[106] *Revolution* the Glorious Revolution of 1688–9, which brought William and Mary to the throne.

[107] *Oons* God's wounds, a mild curse.

MRS MARWOOD: For shame, Mr *Witwoud*; why won't you speak to him?——And you, Sir.

WITWOUD: *Petulant*, speak.

PETULANT: And you, Sir.

SIR WILFULL: No Offence, I hope. [*Salutes* Marwood.]

MRS MARWOOD: No sure, Sir.

WITWOUD: This is a vile Dog, I see that already. No Offence! Ha, ha, ha! To him; to him, *Petulant*, smoke[108] him.

PETULANT: It seems as if you had come to a Journey, Sir; hem, hem. [*Surveying him round*]

SIR WILFULL: Very likely, Sir, that it may seem so.

PETULANT: No Offence! I hope, Sir.

WITWOUD: Smoke the Boots, the Boots; *Petulant*, the Boots; Ha, ha, ha.

SIR WILFULL: Maybe not, Sir; thereafter as 'tis meant, Sir.

PETULANT: Sir, I presume upon the Information of your Boots.

SIR WILFULL: Why, 'tis like you may, Sir: If you are not satisfied with the Information of my Boots, Sir, if you will step to the Stable, you may inquire further of my Horse.

PETULANT: Your Horse, Sir! Your Horse is an Ass, Sir!

SIR WILFULL: Do you speak by way of Offence, Sir?

MRS MARWOOD: The Gentleman's merry, that's all, Sir——'Slife,[109] we shall have a Quarrel betwixt an Horse and an Ass, before we find one another out. You must not take anything amiss from your Friends, Sir. You are among your Friends, here, though it may be you don't know it——If I am not mistaken, you are Sir *Wilfull Witwoud*.

SIR WILFULL: Right, Lady; I am Sir *Wilfull Witwoud*, so I write myself; no Offence to anybody, I hope; and Nephew to the Lady *Wishfort* of this Mansion.

MRS MARWOOD: Don't you know this Gentleman, Sir?

SIR WILFULL: Hum! What, sure 'tis not——Yea by'r Lady, but 'tis——'Sheart,[110] I know not whether 'tis or no——Yea but 'tis, by the *Wrekin*.[111] Brother *Antony*! What *Tony*, i' faith! What do'st thou not know me? By'r Lady nor I thee, thou art so Becravated, and so Beperiwigged——'Sheart why do'st thou not speak? Art thou o'erjoyed?

WITWOUD: Odso Brother, is it you? Your Servant, Brother.

SIR WILFULL: Your Servant! Why yours, Sir. Your Servant again——'Sheart, and your Friend and Servant to that——And a——(*puff*) and a Flap Dragon[112] for your Service, Sir: And a Hare's Foot, and a Hare's Scut[113] for your Service, Sir; an you be so cold and so courtly!

WITWOUD: No Offence, I hope, Brother.

SIR WILFULL: 'Sheart, Sir, but there is, and much Offence.——A Pox, is this your Inns o' Court[114] Breeding, not to know your Friends and your Relations, your Elders, and your Betters?

WITWOUD: Why Brother *Wilfull* of *Salop*,[115] you may be as short as a *Shrewsbury* Cake,[116] if you please. But I tell you 'tis not modish to know Relations in Town. You think

Notes

108 *smoke* "To sneer; to ridicule to the face" (Johnson, sense 3).

109 *'Slife* God's life, a mild curse.

110 *'Sheart* God's heart, a mild curse.

111 *Wrekin* a hill near Shrewsbury in Shropshire, England (McKenzie).

112 *Flap Dragon* a raisin or a small bit of something easily swallowed, in a drinking game of the same name; perhaps with a pun on a kind of clap or venereal disease.

113 *Hare's Scut* a hare's tail; perhaps, like a rabbit's foot, a lucky charm.

114 *Inns o' Court* the college-like institutions where young men were trained in law.

115 *Salop* an old name for Shropshire or the county town, Shrewsbury.

116 *Shrewsbury Cake* "a flat round crisp biscuit-like cake" (*OED*).

you're in the Country, where great lubberly Brothers slabber and kiss one another when they meet, like a Call of Serjeants.[117]——'Tis not the Fashion here; 'tis not indeed, dear Brother.

SIR WILFULL: The Fashion's a Fool; and you're a Fop, dear Brother. 'Sheart, I've suspected this——By'r Lady I conjectured you were a Fop, since you began to change the Style of your Letters, and write in a scrap of Paper gilt round the Edges, no bigger than a *Subpoena*. I might expect this when you left off 'Honoured Brother; and hoping you are in good Health', and so forth——To begin with a 'Rat me, Knight, I'm so sick of a last Night's Debauch——O'ds Heart', and then tell a familiar Tale of a Cock and a Bull, and a Whore and a Bottle, and so conclude——You could write News before you were out of your Time, when you lived with honest *Pumple-Nose* the Attorney of *Furnival*'s Inn——You could entreat to be remembered then to your Friends round the *Wrekin*. We could have *Gazettes* then, and *Dawks*'s Letter, and the Weekly Bill,[118] till of late Days.

PETULANT: 'Slife, *Witwoud*, were you ever an Attorney's Clerk? Of the Family of the *Furnivals*. Ha, ha, ha!

WITWOUD: Ay, ay, but that was but for a while. Not long, not long; pshaw, I was not in my own Power then. An Orphan, and this Fellow was my Guardian; ay, ay, I was glad to consent to that, Man, to come to *London*. He had the Disposal of me then. If I had not agreed to that, I might have been bound Prentice to a Felt-maker in *Shrewsbury*; this Fellow would have bound me to a Maker of Felts.

SIR WILFULL: 'Sheart, and better than to be bound to a Maker of Fops; where, I suppose, you have served your Time; and now you may set up for yourself.

MRS MARWOOD: You intend to Travel, Sir, as I'm informed.

SIR WILFULL: Belike I may, Madam. I may chance to sail upon the salt Seas, if my Mind hold.[119]

PETULANT: And the Wind serve.

SIR WILFULL: Serve or not serve, I shan't ask Licence of you, Sir; nor the Weather-Cock your Companion. I direct my Discourse to the Lady, Sir; 'Tis like my Aunt may have told you, Madam——Yes, I have settled my Concerns, I may say now, and am minded to see Foreign Parts. If an how that the Peace[120] holds, whereby that is Taxes abate.

MRS MARWOOD: I thought you had designed for *France* at all Adventures.

SIR WILFULL: I can't tell that; 'tis like I may, and 'tis like I may not. I am somewhat dainty in making a Resolution,——because when I make it I keep it. I don't stand shill I, shall I, then; if I say't, I'll do't: But I have Thoughts to tarry a small matter in Town, to learn somewhat of your *Lingo* first, before I cross the Seas. I'd gladly have a spice of your *French* as they say, whereby to hold Discourse in Foreign Countries.

MRS MARWOOD: Here's an Academy in Town for that use.

SIR WILFULL: There is? 'Tis like there may.

MRS MARWOOD: No doubt you will return very much improved.

WITWOUD: Yes, refined like a *Dutch* Skipper from a Whale-fishing.

Notes

[117] *Call of Serjeants* call to the bar; admission to the status of barrister; serjeants of the law were members of a superior order of barristers.

[118] *Gazettes ... the Weekly Bill* the *London Gazette*, a government newspaper; *Dawks's Newsletter*, by the author of the *Protestant Mercury*; and the *Bills of Mortality*, a list of deaths.

[119] *if my Mind hold* if my desire to do so continues.

[120] *the Peace* the Peace of Ryswick (1697); it ended the War of the Grand Alliance between France, and Great Britain in alliance with the Netherlands, Spain, and the Holy Roman Empire.

Scene XVI

[To them] Lady *Wishfort*, and *Fainall*

Lady Wishfort: Nephew, you are welcome.

Sir Wilfull: Aunt, your Servant.

Fainall: Sir *Wilfull*, your most faithful Servant.

Sir Wilfull: Cousin *Fainall*, give me your Hand.

Lady Wishfort: Cousin *Witwoud*, your Servant; Mr *Petulant*, your Servant——Nephew, you are welcome again. Will you drink anything after your Journey, Nephew, before you eat? Dinner's almost ready.

Sir Wilfull: I'm very well I thank you, Aunt——However, I thank you for your courteous Offer. 'Sheart I was afraid you would have been in the Fashion too, and have remembered to have forgot your Relations. Here's your Cousin *Tony*, belike, I mayn't call him Brother for fear of Offence.

Lady Wishfort: O he's a Rallier, Nephew——My Cousin's a Wit: And your great Wits always rally their best Friends to choose.[121] When you have been Abroad, Nephew, you'll understand Raillery better.

Sir Wilfull: Why then let him hold his Tongue in the mean Time; and rail when that Day comes.

[Fainall *and Mrs* Marwood *talk apart*]

Scene XVII

[To them] Mincing

Mincing: Mem, I am come to acquaint your La'ship that Dinner is impatient.

Sir Wilfull: Impatient? Why then belike it won't stay till I pull off my Boots. Sweetheart, can you help me to a pair of Slippers?——My Man's with his Horses, I warrant.

Lady Wishfort: Fie, fie, Nephew, you would not pull off your Boots here——Go down into the Hall——Dinner shall stay for you——My Nephew's a little unbred; you'll pardon him, Madam,——Gentlemen, will you walk? *Marwood*?

Mrs Marwood: I'll follow you, Madam,——Before Sir *Wilfull* is ready.

Scene XVIII

Mrs *Marwood, Fainall*

Fainall: Why then *Foible*'s a Bawd,[122] an Errant, Rank, Match-making Bawd. And I it seems am a Husband; a Rank-Husband; and my Wife a very Errant, Rank-Wife,——all in the Way of the *World*. 'Sdeath! to be a Cuckold by Anticipation, a Cuckold in Embryo? Sure I was born with budding Antlers like a young Satyr,[123] or a Citizen's Child.[124] 'Sdeath! to be Out-witted, to be Out-jilted——Out-Matrimonied,——If I

Notes

121 *to choose* by choice or preference.

122 *Bawd* pimp.

123 *Satyr* "A sylvan god" (Johnson) with the hind legs and horns of a goat.

124 *Citizen's Child* child conceived by a gentleman and the wife of a citizen (i.e., "A townsman; a man of trade; not a gentleman"; Johnson, sense 2).

had kept my Speed like a Stag, 'twere somewhat——but to crawl after, with my Horns like a Snail, and be out-stripped by my Wife——'tis Scurvy Wedlock.

Mrs Marwood: Then shake it off; you have often wished for an Opportunity to part; and now you have it. But first prevent their Plot,——the half of *Millamant*'s Fortune is too considerable to be parted with, to a Foe, to *Mirabell*.

Fainall: Damn him, that had been mine——had you not made that fond[125] Discovery——That had been forfeited, had they been Married. My Wife had added Lustre to my Horns, by that Increase of Fortune. I could have worn them tipped with Gold, though my Forehead had been furnished like a Deputy-Lieutenant's Hall.[126]

Mrs Marwood: They may prove a Cap of Maintenance[127] to you still, if you can away with[128] your Wife. And she's no worse than when you had her——I dare swear she had given up her Game, before she was Married.

Fainall: Hum! That may be——[She might throw up her Cards; but I'll be hanged if she did not put Pam[129] in her Pocket.]

Mrs Marwood: You Married her to keep you; and if you can contrive to have her keep you better than you expected; why should you not keep her longer than you intended?

Fainall: The Means, the Means.

Mrs Marwood: Discover to my Lady your Wife's Conduct; threaten to part with her——My Lady loves her, and will come to any Composition[130] to save her Reputation. Take the Opportunity of breaking it, just upon the Discovery of his Imposture. My Lady will be enraged beyond Bounds, and sacrifice Niece, and Fortune, and all at that Conjuncture. And let me alone to keep her warm; if she should flag in her part, I will not fail to prompt her.

Fainall: Faith, this has an Appearance.[131]

Mrs Marwood: I'm sorry I hinted to my Lady to endeavour a Match between *Millamant* and Sir *Wilfull*; that may be an Obstacle.

Fainall: O for that Matter leave me to manage him; I'll disable him for that; he will drink like a *Dane*: After Dinner, I'll set his Hand in.

Mrs Marwood: Well, how do you stand affected towards your Lady?

Fainall: Why faith I'm thinking of it.——Let me see——I am Married already; so that's over——My Wife has played the Jade with me——Well, that's over too——I never loved her, or if I had, why that would have been over too by this time——Jealous of her I cannot be, for I am certain; so there's an end of Jealousy. Weary of her, I am and shall be——No, there's no end of that; No, no, that were too much to hope. Thus far concerning my Repose. Now for my Reputation,——As to my own, I married not for it; so that's out of the Question.——And as to my Part in my Wife's——Why she had parted with hers before; so bringing none to me, she can take none from me; 'tis against all rule of Play, that I should lose to one, who has not wherewithal to stake.

Notes

125 *fond* foolish.

126 *like a Deputy-Lieutenant's Hall* with the horns of animals mounted as trophies.

127 *Cap of Maintenance* "A kind of cap, with two points like horns behind, borne in the arms of certain families either as a charge or in the place of a wreath, is described by heralds as a 'cap of maintenance' " (*OED*).

128 *away with* tolerate, endure (*OED*, sense 16).

129 *Pam* Jack of trumps, the most powerful card in the fashionable game of Loo.

130 *Composition* settlement, agreement.

131 *this has an Appearance* it's a promising scheme.

MRS MARWOOD: Besides you forget, Marriage is honourable.

FAINALL: Hum! Faith and that's well thought on; Marriage is honourable, as you say; and if so, wherefore should Cuckoldom be a Discredit, being derived from so honourable a Root?

MRS MARWOOD: Nay I know not; if the Root be honourable, why not the Branches?

FAINALL: So, so, why this Point's clear——Well, how do we proceed?

MRS MARWOOD: I will contrive a Letter which shall be delivered to my Lady at the time when that Rascal who is to act Sir *Rowland* is with her. It shall come as from an unknown Hand——for the less I appear to know of the Truth, the better I can play the Incendiary. Besides, I would not have *Foible* provoked if I could help it,——because you know she knows some Passages——Nay I expect all will come out——But let the Mine be sprung first, and then I care not if I am discovered.

FAINALL: If the worst come to the worst,——I'll turn my Wife to Grass[132]——I have already a Deed of Settlement of the best Part of her Estate; which I wheedled out of her; and that you shall partake at least.

MRS MARWOOD: I hope you are convinced that I hate *Mirabell* now: You'll be no more Jealous?

FAINALL: Jealous, no,——by this Kiss——let Husbands be Jealous; but let the Lover still believe: Or if he doubt, let it be only to endear his Pleasure, and prepare the Joy that follows, when he proves his Mistress true. But let Husbands' Doubts convert to endless Jealousy; or if they have Belief, let it corrupt to Superstition, and blind Credulity. I am single, and will herd no more with 'em. True, I wear the Badge, but I'll disown the Order. And since I take my Leave of 'em, I care not if I leave 'em a common Motto to their common Crest.[133]

All Husbands must, or Pain, or Shame endure;
The Wise too jealous are, Fools too secure.

ACT IV. SCENE I

SCENE CONTINUES

Lady *Wishfort* and *Foible*

LADY WISHFORT: Is Sir *Rowland* coming, say'st thou, *Foible*? and are things in order?

FOIBLE: Yes, Madam. I have put Wax-Light in the Sconces,[134] and placed the Footmen in a Row in the Hall, in their best Liveries, with the Coachman and Postilion[135] to fill up the Equipage.

LADY WISHFORT: Have you pulvilled[136] the Coachman and Postilion, that they may not stink of the Stable, when Sir *Rowland* comes by?

FOIBLE: Yes, Madam.

Notes

[132] *turn my Wife to Grass* dismiss her from her position; separate from, or divorce, her.

[133] *Crest* in heraldry, a device borne above the helmet and shield in a coat of arms (*OED*).

[134] *Sconces* "A pensile [i.e., hanging] candlestick, generally with a looking-glass to reflect the light" (Johnson, sense 3).

[135] *Postilion* "One who guides the first pair of a set of six horses in a coach" (Johnson).

[136] *pulvilled* perfumed with powder.

LADY WISHFORT: And are the Dancers and the Music ready, that he must be entertained in all Points with Correspondence to his Passion?
FOIBLE: All is ready, Madam.
LADY WISHFORT: And——well——and how do I look, *Foible*?
FOIBLE: Most killing well, Madam.
LADY WISHFORT: Well, and how shall I receive him? In what Figure shall I give his Heart the first Impression? There is a great deal in the first Impression. Shall I sit?——No, I won't sit——I'll walk——ay I'll walk from the Door upon his Entrance; and then turn full upon him——No, that will be too sudden. I'll lie——ay, I'll lie down——I'll receive him in my little Dressing-Room. There's a Couch——Yes, yes, I'll give the first Impression on a Couch——I won't lie neither, but loll and lean upon one Elbow; with one Foot a little dangling off, jogging in a thoughtful Way——Yes——and then as soon as he appears, start, ay, start and be surprised, and rise to meet him in a pretty Disorder——Yes——O, nothing is more alluring than a Levee[137] from a Couch in some Confusion——It shows the Foot to advantage, and furnishes with Blushes, and recomposing Airs beyond Comparison. Hark! There's a Coach.
FOIBLE: 'Tis he, Madam.
LADY WISHFORT: O dear, has my Nephew made his Addresses to *Millamant*? I ordered him.
FOIBLE: Sir *Wilfull* is set in to Drinking, Madam, in the Parlour.
LADY WISHFORT: Ods my Life, I'll send him to her. Call her down, *Foible*; bring her hither. I'll send him as I go——When they are together, then come to me, *Foible*, that I may not be too long alone with Sir *Rowland*.

Scene II

Mrs *Millamant*, Mrs *Fainall*, *Foible*

FOIBLE: Madam, I stayed here, to tell your Ladyship that Mr *Mirabell* has waited this half Hour for an Opportunity to talk with you. Though my Lady's Orders were to leave you and Sir *Wilfull* together. Shall I tell Mr *Mirabell* that you are at Leisure?
MILLAMANT: No——What would the dear Man have? I am thoughtful, and would amuse myself——bid him come another time.

There never yet was Woman made,
Nor shall, but to be cursed.[138]

[*Repeating and walking about.*]

That's hard!
MRS FAINALL: You are very fond of Sir John Suckling today, *Millamant*, and the Poets.
MILLAMANT: He? Ay, and filthy Verses——So I am.
FOIBLE: Sir *Wilfull* is coming, Madam. Shall I send Mr *Mirabell* away?
MILLAMANT: Ay, if you please, *Foible*, send him away——Or send him hither.——just as you will, dear *Foible*——I think I'll see him——Shall I? Ay, let the Wretch come.

Notes

[137] *Levee* French, "rising"; also the name of a morning audience with a great lord or lady.

Thyrsis, a Youth of the Inspired Train.[139]

Dear *Fainall*, entertain Sir *Wilfull*——Thou hast Philosophy to undergo a Fool, thou art married and hast Patience——I would confer with my own Thoughts.

MRS FAINALL: I am obliged to you, that you would make me your Proxy in this Affair; but I have Business of my own.

Scene III

[*To them*] Sir *Wilfull*

MRS FAINALL: O Sir *Wilfull*; you are come at the critical Instant. There's your Mistress up to the Ears in Love and Contemplation; pursue your Point, now or never.

SIR WILFULL: Yes; my Aunt will have it so,——I would gladly have been encouraged with a Bottle or two, because I'm somewhat wary at first, before I am acquainted;——But I hope, after a time, I shall break my Mind[140]——that is upon further Acquaintance——So for the present, Cousin, I'll take my Leave If so be you'll be so kind to make my Excuse, I'll return to my Company——

MRS FAINALL: O fie, Sir *Wilfull*! What, you must not be daunted.

SIR WILFULL: Daunted, no, that's not it, it is not so much for that——for if so be that I set on't, I'll do't. But only for the present, 'tis sufficient till further Acquaintance, that's——your Servant.

MRS FAINALL: Nay, I'll swear you shall never lose so favourable an Opportunity, if I can help it. I'll leave you together, and lock the Door.

Scene IV

Sir *Wilfull*, *Millamant*

SIR WILFULL: Nay, nay Cousin,——I have forgot my Gloves,——What d'ye do? 'Sheart a' has locked the Door indeed, I think——Nay, Cousin *Fainall*, open the Door——Pshaw, what a Vixen Trick is this?——Nay, now a' has seen me too.—— Cousin, I made bold to pass through as it were——I think this Door's enchanted——

MILLAMANT: *[repeating]*

I prithee spare me, gentle Boy,
Press me no more for that slight Toy.[141]

SIR WILL: Anan? Cousin, your Servant.

MILLAMANT: ——*That foolish Trifle of a Heart* ——Sir *Wilfull*!

SIR WILFULL: Yes——your Servant. No Offence I hope, Cousin.

MILLAMANT: [*Repeating*]

I swear it will not do its Part,
THOUGH thou dost thine, employ'st thy Power and Art.

NATURAL, easy *Suckling*!

SIR WILFULL: Anan? *Suckling*? No such Suckling neither, Cousin nor Stripling: I thank Heaven, I'm no Minor.

Notes

138 *There never... cursed* opening lines of a poem by Sir John Suckling.

139 *Thyrsis, a Youth of the Inspired Train* from "The Story of *Phoebus and Daphne* applied" by Edmund Waller, 1.32 (McKenzie).

140 *break my Mind* "reveal my intentions."

141 *I prithee ... slight Toy* opening lines of another poem by Suckling; continued in Millamant's next lines.

Millamant: Ah Rustic, ruder than *Gothic*.

Sir Wilfull: Well, well, I shall understand your *Lingo* one of these Days, Cousin, in the meanwhile I must answer in plain *English*.

Millamant: Have you any Business with me, Sir *Wilfull*?

Sir Wilfull: Not at present, Cousin,——Yes, I made bold to see, to come and know if that how you were disposed to fetch a Walk this Evening, if so be that I might not be troublesome, I would have sought a Walk with you.

Millamant: A Walk? What then?

Sir Wilfull: Nay nothing——Only for the Walk's sake, that's all——

Millamant: I nauseate Walking; 'tis a Country Diversion; I loathe the Country and everything that relates to it.

Sir Wilfull: Indeed! Hah! Look ye, look ye, you do? Nay, 'tis like you may——Here are choice of Pastimes here in Town, as Plays and the like, that must be confessed indeed——

Millamant: Ah *l'etourdie*![142] I hate the Town too.

Sir Wilfull: Dear Heart, that's much——Hah! that you should hate 'em both! Hah! 'tis like you may; there are some can't relish the Town, and others can't away with the Country,——'tis like you may be one of those, Cousin.

Millamant: Ha, ha, ha. Yes, 'tis like I may.——You have nothing further to say to me?

Sir Wilfull: Not at present, Cousin——'Tis like when I have an Opportunity to be more private——I may break my Mind in some Measure——I conjecture you partly guess——However that's as time shall try,——But spare to speak and spare to speed,[143] as they say.

Millamant: If it is of no great Importance, Sir *Wilfull*, you will oblige me to leave me: I have just now a little Business——

Sir Wilfull: Enough, enough, Cousin: Yes, yes, all a case——When you're disposed. Now's as well as another time and another time as well as now. All's one for that,——Yes, yes, if your Concerns call you, there's no haste; it will keep cold, as they say——Cousin, your Servant——I think this Door's locked.

Millamant: You may go this way, Sir.

Sir Wilfull: Your Servant, then with your leave I'll return to my Company.

Millamant: Ay, ay; ha, ha, ha.

Like Phoebus sung the no less am'rous Boy.[144]

Scene V

Millamant, Mirabell

Like Daphne she, as Lovely and as Coy.

Mirabell: Do you lock yourself up from me, to make my Search more curious? Or is this pretty Artifice contrived to signify that here the Chase must end, and my Pursuit be crowned, for you can fly no further?——

Millamant: Vanity! No——I'll fly and be followed to the last Moment, though I am upon the very Verge of Matrimony, I expect you should solicit me as much as if I were wavering at the Grate of a Monastery,[145] with one Foot over the Threshold. I'll be solicited to the very last, nay and afterwards.

Notes

142 *l'etourdie* a giddy, thoughtless creature.

143 *spare to speak and spare to speed* a proverb recorded as early as the fifteenth century (*OED*); to speed means to attain one's purpose (*OED*).

144 *Like Phoebus sung the no less am'rous Boy* from "The Story of *Phoebus and Daphne* applied," ll. 3–4; Mirabell completes the couplet in the next line (McKenzie).

145 *Monastery* a convent, where she would take vows of chastity and become a nun.

MIRABELL: What, after the last?

MILLAMANT: O, I should think I was poor and had nothing to bestow, if I were reduced to an inglorious Ease; and freed from the agreeable Fatigues of Solicitation.

MIRABELL: But do not you know, that when Favours are conferred upon instant[146] and tedious Solicitation, that they diminish in their Value, and that both the Giver loses the grace, and the Receiver lessens his Pleasure?

MILLAMANT: It may be in Things of common Application;[147] but never sure in Love. O, I hate a Lover, that can dare to think he draws a Moment's Air, independent on the Bounty of his Mistress. There is not so impudent a Thing in Nature, as the saucy Look of an assured Man, confident of Success. The Pedantic Arrogance of a very Husband, has not so Pragmatical[148] an Air. Ah! I'll never marry, unless I am first made sure of my Will and Pleasure.

MIRABELL: Would you have 'em both before Marriage? Or will you be contented with the first now, and stay for the other till after Grace?

MILLAMANT: Ah don't be impertinent——My dear Liberty, shall I leave thee? My faithful Solitude, my darling Contemplation, must I bid you then Adieu? Ay-h adieu——My morning Thoughts, agreeable Wakings, indolent Slumbers, all *ye douceurs, ye Sommeils du Matin,*[149] adieu——I can't do't, 'tis more than impossible——Positively *Mirabell*, I'll lie abed in a Morning as long as I please.

MIRABELL: Then I'll get up in a Morning as early as I please.

MILLAMANT: Ah! Idle Creature, get up when you will——And d'ye hear, I won't be called Names after I'm married; positively I won't be called Names.

MIRABELL: Names!

MILLAMANT: Ay, as Wife, Spouse, my Dear, Joy, Jewel, Love, Sweetheart, and the rest of that nauseous Cant, in which Men and their Wives are so fulsomely familiar——I shall never bear that——Good *Mirabell*, don't let me be familiar or fond, nor kiss before Folks, like my Lady *Fadler* and Sir *Francis*: Nor go to *Hyde Park* together the first *Sunday* in a new Chariot, to provoke Eyes and Whispers; And then never be seen there together again; as if we were proud of one another the first Week and ashamed of one another ever after. Let us never Visit together, not go to a Play together, but let us be very strange and well bred: Let us be as strange as if we had been married a great while; and as well bred as if we were not married at all.

MIRABELL: Have you any more Conditions to offer? Hitherto your Demands are pretty reasonable.

MILLAMANT: Trifles——As Liberty to pay and receive Visits to and from whom I please; to write and receive Letters, without Interrogatories or wry Faces on your Part; to wear what I please; and choose Conversation with regard only to my own Taste; to have no Obligation upon me to converse with Wits that I don't like, because they are your Acquaintance; or to be intimate with Fools because they may be your Relations. Come to Dinner when I please, dine in my Dressing-Room when I'm out of Humour, without giving a Reason. To have my Closet inviolate; to be sole Empress of my Tea Table, which you must never presume to approach without first asking Leave. And lastly, wherever I am, you shall always knock at the Door before you

Notes

146 *instant* "Pressing; urgent; importunate; earnest" (Johnson).

147 *Application* "The act of applying to any person" (Johnson, sense 3).

148 *Pragmatical* "Meddling; impertinently busy; assuming business without leave or invitation" (Johnson).

149 *ye douceurs, ye Sommeils du Matin* "you sweetnesses, you morning sleeps."

come in. These Articles subscribed, if I continue to endure you a little longer, I may by degrees dwindle into a Wife.

MIRABELL: Your Bill of Fare is something advanced in this latter Account. Well, have I Liberty to offer Conditions——That when you are dwindled into a Wife, I may not be beyond Measure enlarged into a Husband.

MILLAMANT: You have free leave, propose your utmost, speak and spare not.

MIRABELL: I thank you. *Imprimis*[150] then, I covenant that your Acquaintance be general; that you admit no sworn Confidante, or Intimate of your own Sex: No she Friend to screen her Affairs under your Countenance, and tempt you to make Trial of a mutual Secrecy. No Decoy-Duck to wheedle you a *fop-scrambling* to the Play in a Mask——Then bring you home in a pretended Fright, when you think you shall be found out——And rail at me for missing the Play, and disappointing the Frolic which you had to pick me up[151] and prove my Constancy.

MILLAMANT: Detestable *Imprimis*! I go to the Play in a Mask!

MIRABELL: *Item*, I Article, that you continue to like your own Face, as long I shall: And while it passes current with me, that you endeavour not to new coin it. To which end, together with all Vizards for the Day, I prohibit all Masks for the Night, made of Oiled-skins and I know not what——Hog's Bones, Hare's Gall, Pig Water, and the Marrow of a roasted Cat. In short, I forbid all Commerce with the Gentlewomen in *what-d'ye-call-it* court. *Item*, I shut my Doors against all Bawds with Baskets, and Pennyworths of *Muslin*, *China*, *Fans*, *Atlases*,[152] &c.——*Item*, when you shall be Breeding——

MILLAMANT: Ah! Name it not.

MIRABELL: Which may be presumed, with a Blessing on our Endeavours——

MILLAMANT: Odious Endeavours!

MIRABELL: I denounce against all strait Lacing, squeezing for a Shape, till you mould my Boy's Head like a Sugar-loaf[153] and instead of a Man-Child, make me Father to a crooked Billet.[154] Lastly, to the Dominion of the *Tea-Table* I submit——But with *proviso*, that you exceed not in your Province; but restrain yourself to native and simple *Tea-Table* Drinks, as *Tea*, *Chocolate*, and *Coffee*. As likewise to Genuine and authorized *Tea-Table* Talk——such as mending of Fashions, spoiling Reputations, railing at absent Friends, and so forth——But that on no Account you encroach upon the Men's Prerogative, and presume to drink Healths, or toast Fellows; for Prevention of which I banish all *Foreign Forces*, all Auxiliaries at the *Tea-Table*, as *Orange-Brandy*, all *Aniseed*, *Cinnamon*, *Citron* and *Barbados-Waters*,[155] together with *Ratafia* and the most noble Spirit of *Clary*.[156]——But for Cowslip-Wine, Poppy Water, and all Dormitives,[157] those I allow——The Provisos admitted, in other Things I may prove a tractable and complying Husband.

MILLAMANT: O horrid *Provisos*! filthy strong Waters! I toast Fellows, odious Men! I hate your odious *Provisos*.

MIRABELL: Then we're agreed. Shall I kiss your Hand upon the Contract? and here comes one to be a Witness to the Sealing of the Deed.

Notes

150 *Imprimis* in the first place.

151 *pick me up* select me for a sexual encounter; for this kind of game, see Eliza Haywood's *Fantomina*, below.

152 *Atlases* "A rich kind of silk or stuff made for women's clothes" (Johnson, sense 4).

153 *Sugar-loaf* "A moulded conical mass of hard refined sugar" (*OED*).

154 *Billet* "A small log of wood for the chimney" (Johnson, sense 4).

155 *Barbados-Waters* an orange and lemon liquor.

156 *Clary* like the others in this list, a sweet liquor.

157 *Dormitives* drinks that induce drowsiness or sleep.

Scene VI

[*To them*] Mrs *Fainall*

MILLAMANT: *Fainall*, what shall I do? Shall I have him? I think I must have him.

MRS FAINALL: Ay, ay, take him; what should you do?

MILLAMANT: Well then——I'll take my Death I'm in a horrid Fright——*Fainall*, I shall never say it——Well——I think——I'll endure you.

MRS FAINALL: Fy, fy, have him, have him, and tell him so in plain Terms: For I am sure you have a Mind to him.

MILLAMANT: Are you? I think I have——and the horrid Man looks as if he thought so too——Well, you ridiculous thing, you, I'll have you——I won't be kissed, nor I won't be thanked——Here kiss my Hand though——So, hold your Tongue now, don't say a Word.

MRS FAINALL: Mirabell, there's a Necessity for your Obedience;——You have neither time to talk nor stay. My Mother is coming; and in my Conscience if she should see you, would fall into Fits, and maybe not recover, time enough to return to Sir *Rowland*; who, as *Foible* tells me, is in a fair Way to succeed. Therefore spare your Ecstasies for another Occasion, and slip down the back Stairs, here *Foible* waits to consult you.

MILLAMANT: Ay, go, go. In the mean time I suppose you have said something to please me.

MIRABELL: I am all Obedience.

Scene VII

Millamant, Mrs *Fainall*

MRS FAINALL: Yonder Sir *Wilfull*'s drunk; and so noisy that my Mother has been forced to leave Sir *Rowland* to appease him; but he answers her only with Singing and Drinking——What they may have done by this time I know not; but *Petulant* and he were upon quarrelling as I came by.

MILLAMANT: Well, if *Mirabell* should not make a good Husband, I am a lost thing; for I find I love him violently.

MRS FAINALL: So it seems; for you mind not what's said to you——If you doubt him, you had best take up with Sir *Wilfull*.

MILLAMANT: How can you name that superannuated Lubber?[158] foh!

Scene VIII

[*To them*] *Witwoud* from drinking

MRS FAINALL: So, is the Fray made up that you have left 'em?

WITWOUD: Left 'em? I could stay no longer——I have laughed like ten Christenings——I am tipsy with laughing——If I had stayed any longer I should have burst,—— I must have been let out and pieced[159] in the Sides like an unsized Camlet[160]——Yes,

Notes

[158] *Lubber* "A sturdy drone; an idle, fat, bulky losel; a booby" (Johnson).

[159] *pieced* pieced out, augmented with extra material.

[160] *unsized Camlet* a rich dress fabric untreated with size, a moistening, glutinous substance.

yes, the Fray is composed; my Lady came in like a *Noli prosequi*,[161] and stopped the Proceedings.

MILLAMANT: What was the Dispute?

WITWOUD: That's the Jest; there was no Dispute. They could neither of 'em speak for Rage; and so fell a sputt'ring at one another like two roasting Apples.

Scene IX

[*To them*] *Petulant* Drunk

WITWOUD: Now *Petulant*? all's over, all's well? Gad my Head begins to whim it about——Why dost thou not speak? thou art both as drunk and as mute as a Fish.

PETULANT: Look you, Mrs *Millamant*——if you can love me, dear Nymph——say it——and that's the Conclusion——pass on, or pass off,——that's all.

WITWOUD: Thou hast uttered *Volumes, Folios,* in less than *Decimo Sexto,*[162] my dear *Lacedemonian.*[163] Sirrah, *Petulant,* thou art an Epitomizer[164] of Words.

PETULANT: *Witwoud*——You are an Annihilator of Sense.

WITWOUD: Thou art a Retailer of Phrases; and dost deal in Remnants of Remnants, like a Maker of Pincushions——thou art in truth (metaphorically speaking) a Speaker of Shorthand.

PETULANT: Thou art (without a Figure) just one half of an Ass, and Baldwin[165] yonder, thy half Brother, is the rest——A *Gemini* of Asses split, would make just four of you.

WITWOUD: Thou dost bite, my dear Mustard-seed;[166] kiss me for that.

PETULANT: Stand off——I'll kiss no more Males,——I have kissed your *Twin* yonder in a humour of Reconciliation, till he (*hiccup*) rises upon my Stomach like a Radish.

MILLAMANT: Eh! filthy Creature——what was the Quarrel?

PETULANT: There was no Quarrel——there might have been a Quarrel.

WITWOUD. If there had been Words enow[167] between 'em to have expressed Provocation, they had gone together by the Ears like a pair of Castanets.

PETULANT: You were the Quarrel.

MILLAMANT: Me!

PETULANT: I if I have a Humour to quarrel, I can make less Matters conclude Premises,——If you are not handsome, what then; If I have a Humour to prove it?——If I shall have my Reward, say so; if not, fight for your Face the next time yourself——I'll go sleep.

WITWOUD: Do, wrap thyself up like a *Woodlouse*, and dream Revenge——And hear me, if thou canst learn to write by tomorrow Morning, pen me a Challenge——I'll carry it for thee.

PETULANT: Carry your Mistress's *Monkey*[168] a *Spider,*——go flea Dogs, and read Romances——I'll go to Bed to my Maid.

MRS FAINALL: He's horridly Drunk——how came you all in this Pickle?

WITWOUD: A Plot, a Plot, to get rid of the Knight,——Your Husband's Advice; but he sneaked off.

Notes

[161] *Noli prosequi* a legal phrase (literally, "I do not wish to pursue") indicating the end of contention in a trial.

[162] *Decimo Sexto* a small printing format in which sixteen pages are printed on each side of the sheets of paper laid on the press.

[163] *Lacedemonian* Spartan, and therefore terse.

[164] *Epitomizer* one who condenses or abstracts.

[165] *Baldwin* the name of the ass in the fable of Reynard the Fox.

[166] *Mustard-seed* one of the fairies attending Bottom when he has an ass's head in Shakespeare's *A Midsummer Night's Dream*.

[167] *enow* enough.

[168] *Monkey* a fashionable, exotic pet.

Scene X

Sir *Wilfull* Drunk, Lady *Wishfort, Witwoud, Millamant,* Mrs *Fainall*

LADY WISHFORT: Out upon't, out upon't! at Years of Discretion, and comport yourself at this Rantipole[169] rate!

SIR WILFULL: No Offence, Aunt.

LADY WISHFORT: Offence? As I'm a Person, I'm ashamed of you——Fogh! how you stink of Wine! D'ye think my Niece will ever endure such a *Borachio*![170] you're an absolute *Borachio*.

SIR WILFULL: *Borachio*!

LADY WISHFORT: At a time when you should commence an Amour, and put our best Foot foremost——

SIR WILFULL: 'Sheart, an you grutch me your Liquor, make a Bill——Give me more Drink, and take my Purse.

Sings.

Prithee fill me the Glass
'Till it laugh in my Face,
With Ale that is potent and Mellow;
He that whines for a Lass
Is an ignorant Ass,
For a Bumper[171] *has not its Fellow.*

But if you would have me marry my Cousin,——say the Word, and I'll do 't——*Wilfull* will do 't, that's the Word.——*Wilfull* will do't; that's my Crest——my Motto I have forgot.

LADY WISHFORT: My Nephew's a little overtaken, Cousin——but 'tis with drinking your Health——O' my Word, you are obliged to him——

SIR WILFULL: *In Vino Veritas*,[172] Aunt:——If I drunk your Health today, Cousin,——I am a *Borachio*. But if you have a Mind to be married, say the Word, and send for the Piper, *Wilfull* will do 't. If not, dust it away, and let's have t'other Round——*Tony*, Ods-heart where's *Tony*?——*Tony*'s an honest Fellow, but he spits after a Bumper, and that's a Fault. Sings.

We'll drink, and we'll never ha' done, Boys.
Put the Glass then around with the Sun, Boys,
Let Apollo's Example invite us;
For he's drunk every Night,
And that makes him so bright,
That he's able next Morning to light us.

The Sun's a good Pimple,[173] an honest Soaker,[174] he has a Cellar at your *Antipodes*. If I travel, Aunt, I touch at your *Antipodes*——your *Antipodes* are a good rascally sort of

Notes

169 *Rantipole* "Wild; roving; rakish" (Johnson).

170 *Borachio* drunk.

171 *Bumper* "A cup filled till the liquour swells over the brims" (Johnson).

172 *In Vino Veritas* "there's truth in wine."

173 *Pimple* drinking companion.

174 *Soaker* "A great drinker. In low language" (Johnson, 1773, sense 2).

175 *Tallow-Chandler* maker of candles from animal fat.

176 *quotha* "said he," sarcastically; hence, "indeed!"

topsy-turvy Fellows——If I had a Bumper I'd stand upon my Head and drink a Health to 'em——A Match or no Match, Cousin, with the hard name——Aunt, *Wilfull* will do 't. If she has her Maidenhead let her look to 't; if she has not, let her keep her own Counsel in the mean time, and cry out at the nine Months' End.

MILLAMANT: Your Pardon, Madam, I can stay no longer——Sir *Wilfull* grows very powerful. Egh! how he smells! I shall be overcome if I stay. Come, Cousin.

Scene XI

Lady *Wishfort*, Sir *Wilfull*, Mr *Witwoud*, *Foible*

LADY WISHFORT: Smells! He would poison a Tallow-Chandler[175] and his Family. Beastly Creature, I know not what to do with him——Travel quotha;[176] ay travel, travel, get thee gone, get thee gone, get thee but far enough, to the Saracens, or the Tartars, or the Turks——for thou art not fit to live in a Christian Commonwealth, thou beastly Pagan.

SIR WILFULL: *Turks*! no; no *Turks*, Aunt; Your *Turks* are Infidels, and believe not in the Grape. Your *Mahometan*, your *Mussulman* is a dry Stinkard——No Offence, Aunt. My Map says that your Turk is not so honest a Man as your Christian——I cannot find by the Map that your *Mufti*[177] is Orthodox——Whereby it is a plain Case, that Orthodox is a hard Word, Aunt, and (*hiccup*) Greek for Claret.

Sings.

To drink is a Christian Diversion,
Unknown to the Turk or the Persian:
Let Mahometan *Fools*
Live by Heathenish Rules,
And be damned over Tea-Cups and Coffee.
But let British Lads sing,
Crown a Health to the King,
And a Fig for your Sultan and Sophy.

Ah, *Tony*! [Foible *Whispers Lady* Wishfort]

LADY WISHFORT: Sir *Rowland* impatient? Good lack! What shall I do with this beastly Tumbrel?[178] ——Go lie down and sleep, you Sot——Or as I'm a Person, I'll have you bastinadoed with Broomsticks. Call up the Wenches with Broomsticks.

SIR WILFULL: Ahey? Wenches, where are the Wenches?

LADY WISHFORT: Dear Cousin *Witwoud* get him away, and you will bind me to you inviolably. I have an Affair of Moment that invades me with some Precipitation——You will oblige me to all Futurity.

WITWOUD: Come, Knight——Pox on him, I don't know what to say to him——Will you go to a Cock-Match?

SIR WILFULL: With a Wench, *Tony*? Is she a shake-bag,[179] Sirrah? Let me bite your Cheek for that.

Notes

[177] *Mufti* "The high priest of the Mahometans" (Johnson).
[178] *Tumbrel* "A dungcart" (Johnson).
[179] *shake-bag* a large fighting cock; also a "poor sneaking fellow" (*Dictionary of the Vulgar Tongue*).

Witwoud: Horrible! He has a Breath like a Bagpipe——Ay, ay, come will you march, my *Salopian*?[180]

Sir Wilfull: Lead on, little *Tony*——I'll follow thee my *Anthony*, my *Tantony*; Sirrah thou shalt be my *Tantony*, and I'll be thy Pig.[181]——*And a Fig for your Sultan and* Sophy.

Lady Wishfort: This will never do. It will never make a Match——At least before he has been abroad.

Scene XII

Lady *Wishfort*, *Waitwell* disguised as for Sir *Rowland*

Lady Wishfort: Dear Sir *Rowland*, I am confounded with Confusion at the Retrospection of my own Rudeness,——I have more Pardons to ask than the *Pope* distributes in the Year of *Jubilee*.[182] But I hope where there is likely to be so near an Alliance,——we may unbend the Severity of *Decorum*——and dispense with a little Ceremony.

Waitwell: My Impatience, Madam, is the Effect of my Transport;——and till I have the Possession of your adorable Person, I am tantalized[183] on the Rack; and do but hang, Madam, on the Tenter of Expectation.

Lady Wishfort: You have Excess of Gallantry, Sir *Rowland*; and press Things to a Conclusion, with a most prevailing Vehemence——But a Day or two for Decency of Marriage——

Waitwell: For Decency of Funeral, Madam. The Delay will break my Heart——or if that should fail, I shall be poisoned. My Nephew will get an inkling of my Designs, and poison me,——and I would willingly starve him before I die——I would gladly go out of the World with that Satisfaction.——That would be some Comfort to me, if I could live so long as to be revenged on that unnatural Viper.

Lady Wishfort: Is he so unnatural, say you? Truly I would contribute much both to the saving of your Life, and the Accomplishment of your Revenge——Not that I respect myself; though he has been a perfidious Wretch to me.

Waitwell: Perfidious to you!

Lady Wishfort: O Sir *Rowland* the Hours that he has died away at my Feet, the Tears that he has shed, the Oaths that he has sworn, the Palpitations that he has felt, the Trances and the Tremblings, the Ardours and the Ecstasies, the Kneelings and the Risings, the Heart heavings and the Hand-gripings, the Pangs and the Pathetic Regards of his protesting Eyes! Oh no Memory can Register.

Waitwell: What, my Rival! Is the Rebel my Rival? a' dies.

Lady Wishfort: No, don't kill him at once, Sir *Rowland*, starve him gradually Inch by Inch.

Waitwell: I'll do't. In three Weeks he shall be barefoot; in a Month out at Knees with begging an Alms,——he shall starve upward and upward, 'till he has nothing living but his Head, and then go out in a Stink like a Candle's End upon a Save-all.[184]

Notes

180 *Salopian* a resident of Shropshire.

181 *Tantony, and I'll be thy Pig* St. Anthony, the father of Catholic monasticism (d. 356) and patron saint of swineherds; hence a "tantony" is a small pig, which obsequiously follows another (McKenzie).

182 *Year of Jubilee* a year of special pardon celebrated once every twenty-five years in the Catholic Church.

183 *tantalized* "torment[ed] by the show of pleasures which cannot be reached" (Johnson).

184 *Save-all* "A small pan inserted into a candlestick to save the ends of candles" (Johnson).

LADY WISHFORT: Well, Sir *Rowland*, you have the way,——You are no novice in the Labyrinth of Love——You have the Clue[185]——But as I am a Person, Sir *Rowland*, you must not attribute my yielding to any sinister Appetite, or Indigestion of Widowhood; nor impute my Complacency to any Lethargy of Continence—— I hope you do not think me prone to any Iteration of Nuptials.——

WAITWELL: Far be it from me——

LADY WISHFORT: If you do, I protest I must recede——or think that I have made a Prostitution of Decorums, but in the Vehemence of Compassion, and to save the Life of a Person of so much Importance——

WAITWELL: I esteem so——

LADY WISHFORT: Or else you wrong my Condescension——

WAITWELL: I do not, I do not——

LADY WISHFORT: Indeed you do.

WAITWELL: I do not, fair Shrine of Virtue.

LADY WISHFORT: If you think the least Scruple of Carnality was an Ingredient——

WAITWELL: Dear Madam, no. You are all *Camphor* and *Frankincense*[186] all *Chastity* and *Odour*.

LADY WISHFORT: Or that——

Scene XIII

[To them] Foible

FOIBLE: Madam, the Dancers are ready, and there's one with a Letter, who must deliver it into your own Hands.

LADY WISHFORT: Sir *Rowland* will you give me Leave? Think favourably, judge candidly, and conclude you have found a Person who would suffer Racks in Honour's Cause, dear Sir *Rowland*, and will wait on you incessantly.

Scene XIV

Waitwell, Foible

WAITWELL: Fie, fie!——What a Slavery have I undergone! Spouse, hast thou any *Cordial*, I want *Spirits*.

FOIBLE: What a washy Rogue art thou, to pant thus for a Quarter of an Hour's Lying and Swearing to a fine Lady?

WAITWELL: O, she is the Antidote to Desire. Spouse, thou wilt fare the worse for't——I shall have no Appetite to Iteration of Nuptials——this eight and forty Hours——By this Hand, I'd rather be a Chairman in the Dog-days[187]——than act Sir *Rowland* till this time to Morrow.

Notes

185 *the Clue* the thread supplied by Ariadne to lead Theseus out of the labyrinth of King Minos.

186 *Camphor and Frankincense* a crystalline substance thought to be an antaphrodisiac and an aromatic resin gum often burned as incense in church ceremonies (*OED*).

187 *Chairman in the Dog-days* bearer of a sedan chair in late summer.

Scene XV

[*To them*] Lady *Wishfort* with a Letter

LADY WISHFORT: Call in the Dancers;——Sir *Rowland*, we'll sit, if you please, and see the Entertainment. [*Dance*]

Now with your Permission, Sir *Rowland*, I will peruse my Letter——I would open it in your Presence, because I would not make you uneasy. If it should make you uneasy I would burn it——speak if it does——but you may see, the Superscription is like a Woman's Hand.

FOIBLE: By Heaven! Mrs *Marwood*'s. I know it——My Heart aches——get it from her——

[*To him*]

WAITWELL: A Woman's Hand? No Madam, that's no Woman's Hand, I see that already. That's somebody whose Throat must be cut.

LADY WISHFORT: Nay, Sir *Rowland*, since you give me a Proof of your Passion by your Jealousy, I promise you I'll make a Return, by a frank Communication——You shall see it——we'll open it together——look you here. *Reads.——Madam, though unknown to you* [Look you there, 'tis from nobody that I know.]——*I have that Honour for your Character, that I think myself obliged to let you know you are abused. He who pretends to be Sir* Rowland *is a Cheat and a Rascal*——

Oh Heavens? what's this?

FOIBLE: Unfortunate, all 's ruined!

WAITWELL: How, how; let me see, let me see——*reading, A Rascal and disguised, and suborned for that Imposture*——O Villainy! O Villainy!——*By the Contrivance of*——

LADY WISHFORT: I shall faint, I shall die, oh!

FOIBLE: Say 'tis your Nephew's Hand——Quickly, his Plot, swear, swear it.——

[*To him*]

WAITWELL: Here's a Villain! Madam, don't you perceive it, don't you see it?

LADY WISHFORT: Too well, too well. I have seen too much.

WAITWELL: I told you at first I knew the Hand——A Woman's Hand? The Rascal writes a sort of large Hand; your *Roman* Hand[188]——I saw there was a Throat to be cut presently. If he were my Son, as he is my Nephew, I'd pistol him——

FOIBLE: O Treachery! But are you sure, Sir *Rowland*, it is his Writing?

WAITWELL: Sure? Am I here? Do I live? do I love this Pearl of *India*? I have twenty Letters in my Pocket from him, in the same Character.

LADY WISHFORT: How!

FOIBLE: O what Luck it is, Sir *Rowland*, that you were present at this Juncture! This was the Business that brought Mr *Mirabell* disguised to Madam *Millamant* this Afternoon. I thought something was contriving, when he stole by me and would have hid his Face.

LADY WISHFORT: How, how!——I heard the Villain was in the House indeed; and now I remember, my Niece went away abruptly, when Sir *Wilfull* was to have made his Addresses.

FOIBLE: Then, then, Madam, Mr *Mirabell* waited for her in her Chamber; but I would not tell your Ladyship, to discompose you when you were to receive Sir *Rowland*.

WAITWELL: Enough; his Date is short.

FOIBLE: No, good Sir *Rowland*, don't incur the Law.

Notes

[188] *Roman Hand* a "round and bold" style of handwriting (*OED*).

WAITWELL: Law! I care not for Law. I can but die, and 'tis in a good Cause——My Lady shall be satisfied of my Truth and Innocence, though it cost me my Life.

LADY WISHFORT: No, dear Sir *Rowland*, don't fight; if you should be killed I must never show my Face; or hanged——consider my Reputation, Sir *Rowland*——No, you shan't fight,——I'll go in and examine my Niece; I'll make her confess. I conjure you, Sir *Rowland*, by all your Love not to fight.

WAITWELL: I am charmed Madam, I obey. But some Proof you must let me give you;——I'll go for a black Box, which contains the Writings of my whole Estate, and deliver that into your Hands.

LADY WISHFORT: Ay, dear Sir *Rowland*, that will be some Comfort, bring the black Box.

WAITWELL: And may I presume to bring a Contract to be signed this Night? May I hope so far?

LADY WISHFORT: Bring what you will; but come alive, pray come alive. O this is a happy Discovery.

WAITWELL: Dead or alive I'll come——and married we will be in fright of Treachery; ay and get an Heir that shall defeat the last remaining Glimpse of Hope in my abandoned Nephew. Come, my Buxom Widow:

Ere long you shall substantial Proof receive
That I'm an arrant Knight——

FOIBLE: ——Or arrant Knave.

ACT V. SCENE I

[SCENE *CONTINUES*]

Lady *Wishfort* and *Foible*

LADY WISHFORT: Out of my House, out of my House, thou *Viper*, thou *Serpent*, that I have fostered; thou bosom Traitress, that I raised from nothing——Begone, begone, begone, go, go,——That I took from washing of old Gauze and weaving of dead Hair, with a bleak blue[189] Nose, over a Chafing dish of starved Embers, and Dining behind a Traverse Rag in a Shop no bigger than a Birdcage,——go, go, starve again, do, do.

FOIBLE: Dear Madam, I'll beg Pardon on my Knees.

LADY WISHFORT: Away, out, out, go set up for yourself again——do, drive a Trade, do, with your Three-penny worth of small Ware, flaunting upon a Packthread, under a Brandy-seller's Bulk, or against a dead Wall by a Ballad-monger. Go, hang out an old frisoneer-gorget,[190] with a Yard of Yellow Colbertine[191] again; do; an old gnawed Mask, two Rows of Pins and a Child's Fiddle; A Glass Necklace, with the Beads broken, and a Quilted Nightcap with one Ear. Go, go, drive a Trade,——These were your Commodities, you treacherous Trull, this was the Merchandise you dealt in, when I took you into my House, placed you next myself, and made you Governante[192] of my whole Family. You have forgot this, have you, now you have feathered your Nest?

Notes

[189] *bleak blue* pale blue.

[190] *frisoneer-gorget* a coarse woolen covering for the neck and breast.

[191] *Colbertine* an inferior kind of lace.

[192] *Governante* "A lady who has the care of young girls of quality. The more usual and proper word is governess" (Johnson).

Foible: No, no, dear Madam. Do but hear me, have but a Moment's Patience——I'll confess all. Mr *Mirabell* seduced me; I am not the first that he has wheedled with his dissembling Tongue; Your Ladyship's own Wisdom has been deluded by him, then how should I, a poor Ignorant, defend myself ? O Madam, if you knew but what he promised me, and how he assured me your Ladyship should come to no Damage——Or else the Wealth of the *Indies* should not have bribed me to conspire against so Good, so Sweet, so Kind a Lady as you have been to me.

Lady Wishfort: No Damage? What, to betray me, to marry me to a Cast-Serving-Man; to make me a Receptacle, an Hospital for a decayed Pimp? No Damage! O thou frontless[193] Impudence, more than a big-bellied Actress.

Foible: Pray do but hear me, Madam; he could not marry your Ladyship, Madam——No indeed his Marriage was to have been void in Law; for he was married to me first, to secure your Ladyship. He could not have bedded your Ladyship; for if he had consummated with your Ladyship, he must have run the risk of the Law, and been put upon his Clergy[194]——Yes indeed, I inquired of the Law in that case before I would meddle or make.

Lady Wishfort: What, then I have been your Property, have I? I have been convenient to you, it seems,——while you were catering for *Mirabell*; I have been Broker for you? What have you made a passive Bawd of me?——this exceeds a Precedent; I am brought to fine Uses, to become a Botcher[195] of second-hand Marriages between *Abigails* and *Andrews*![196] I'll couple you. Yes, I'll baste you together, you and your *Philander*. I'll *Duke's-Place* you, as I'm a Person. Your Turtle is in Custody already: You shall Coo in the same Cage, if there be a Constable or Warrant in the Parish.

Foible: O that ever I was born, O that I was ever married——a Bride, ay I shall be a *Bridewell*[197] Bride. Oh!

Scene II

Mrs *Fainall, Foible*

Mrs Fainall: Poor *Foible*, what's the matter?

Foible: O Madam, my Lady's gone for a Constable; I shall be had to a Justice, and put to *Bridewell* to beat Hemp; poor *Waitwell*'s gone to Prison already.

Mrs Fainall: Have a good Heart, *Foible; Mirabell*'s gone to give Security for him. This is all *Marwood*'s and my Husband's doing.

Foible: Yes, yes; I know it, Madam; she was in my Lady's Closet, and overheard all that you said to me before Dinner. She sent the Letter to my Lady; and that missing Effect, Mr *Fainall* laid this Plot to arrest *Waitwell*, when he pretended to go for the Papers; and in the mean time Mrs *Marwood* declared all to my Lady.

Mrs Fainall: Was there no Mention made of me in the Letter?——My Mother does not suspect my being in the Confederacy: I fancy *Marwood* has not told her, though she has told my Husband.

Foible: Yes, Madam; but my Lady did not see that Part: We stifled the Letter before she read so far. Has that mischievous Devil told Mr *Fainall* of your Ladyship then?

Notes

193 *frontless* shameless.

194 *put upon his Clergy* the benefit of clergy, a plea in court that allowed defendants who read a little Latin (like a clergyman) to escape severe penalties for serious crimes; once widely used in cases of felony, the plea was retained at this time only in cases of bigamy and manslaughter.

195 *Botcher* "A mender of old clothes" (Johnson).

196 *Abigails and Andrews* stock names of servants.

197 *Bridewell* a correctional facility in London.

MRS FAINALL: Ay, all's out, my Affair with *Mirabell*, everything discovered. This is the last Day of our living together, that's my Comfort.

FOIBLE: Indeed Madam, and so 'tis a Comfort if you knew all,——he has been even with your Ladyship; which I could have told you long enough since, but I love to keep Peace and Quietness by my good Will: I had rather bring Friends together, than set them at Distance. But Mrs *Marwood* and he are nearer related than ever their Parents thought for.

MRS FAINALL: Say'st thou so, *Foible*? Canst thou prove this?

Foible. I can take my Oath of it, Madam, so can Mrs *Mincing*; we have had many a fair Word from Madam *Marwood*, to conceal something that passed in our Chamber one Evening when you were at Hyde Park;——and we were thought to have gone a Walking: But we went up unawares,——though we were sworn to Secrecy too; Madam *Marwood* took a Book and swore us upon it: But it was but a Book of Poems,——So long as it was not Bible-Oath, we may break it with a safe Conscience.

MRS FAINALL: This Discovery is the most opportune Thing I could wish——Now, *Mincing*?

Scene III

[*To them*] *Mincing*

MINCING: My Lady would speak with Mrs *Foible, Mem*, Mr *Mirabell* is with her; he has set your Spouse at Liberty, Mrs *Foible*, and would have you hide yourself in my Lady's Closet, till my old Lady's Anger is abated. O, my old Lady is in a perilous Passion, at something Mr *Fainall* has said; he swears, and my old Lady cries. There's a fearful Hurricane, I vow. He says, *Mem*, how that he'll have my Lady's Fortune made over to him, or he'll be divorced.

MRS FAINALL: Does your Lady or *Mirabell* know that?

MINCING: Yes *Mem*, they have sent me to see if Sir *Wilfull* be sober, and to bring him to them. My Lady is resolved to have him, I think, rather than lose such a vast Sum as Six Thousand Pound. O, come Mrs *Foible*, I hear my old Lady.

MRS FAINALL: *Foible*, You must tell *Mincing*, that she must prepare to vouch when I call her.

FOIBLE: Yes, yes, Madam.

MINCING: O, yes, *Mem*, I'll vouch anything for your Ladyship's Service, be what it will.

Scene IV

Mrs *Fainall*, Lady *Wishfort*, *Marwood*

LADY WISHFORT: O My dear Friend, how can I enumerate the Benefits that I have received from your Goodness? To you I owe the timely Discovery of the false Vows of *Mirabell*; to you I owe the Detection of the Impostor Sir *Rowland*. And now you are become an Intercessor with my Son-in-Law, to save the Honour of my House, and compound for the Frailties of my Daughter. Well Friend, you are enough to reconcile me to the bad World, or else I would retire to Deserts and Solitudes; and feed harmless Sheep by Groves and purling Streams. Dear *Marwood*, let us leave the World, and retire by ourselves and be Shepherdesses.

MRS MARWOOD: Let us first dispatch the Affair in Hand, Madam. We shall have Leisure to think of Retirement afterwards. Here is one who is concerned in the Treaty.

LADY WISHFORT: Daughter, Daughter, is it possible thou should'st be a Child, Bone of my Bone, and Flesh of my Flesh, and as I may say, another Me, and yet transgress the most minute Particle of severe Virtue? Is it possible you should lean aside into Iniquity, who have been cast in the direct Mould of Virtue? I have not only been a Mould but a Pattern for you, and a Model for you, after you were brought into the World.

MRS FAINALL: I don't understand your Ladyship.

LADY WISHFORT: Not understand? Why, have you not been Naught? Have you not been Sophisticated?[198] Not understand? Here am I ruined to compound for your Caprices and your Cuckoldoms. I must pawn my Mate and my Jewels, and ruin my Niece, and all little enough——

MRS FAINALL: I am wronged and abused, and so are you. 'Tis a false Accusation, as false as Hell, as false as your Friend there, ay, or your Friend's Friend, my false Husband.

MRS MARWOOD: My Friend, Mrs *Fainall*? Your Husband my Friend, what do you mean?

MRS FAINALL: I know what I mean, Madam, and so do you; and so shall the World at a Time convenient.

MRS MARWOOD: I am sorry to see you so passionate, Madam. My Temper would look more like Innocence. But I have done. I am sorry my Zeal to serve your Ladyship and Family should admit of Misconstruction, or make me liable to Affronts. You will pardon me, Madam, if I meddle no more with an Affair, in which I am not personally concerned.

LADY WISHFORT: O dear Friend, I am so ashamed that you should meet with such Returns;——You ought to ask Pardon on your Knees, ungrateful Creature; she deserves more from you than all your Life can accomplish——O, don't leave me destitute in this Perplexity;——No, stick to me, my good Genius.

MRS FAINALL: I tell you, Madam, you're abused——Stick to you? Ay, like a Leech, to suck your best Blood——She'll drop off when she's full. Madam, you shan't pawn a Bodkin nor part with a Brass Counter,[199] in Composition[200] for me. I defy 'em all. Let 'em prove their Aspersions: I know my own Innocence, and dare stand a Trial.

Scene V

Lady *Wishfort, Marwood*

LADY WISHFORT: Why, if she should be innocent, if she should be wronged after all, ha? I don't know what to think,——and I promise you, her Education has been very unexceptionable——I may say it; for I chiefly made it my own Care to initiate her very Infancy in the Rudiments of Virtue, and to impress upon her tender years a young Odium and Aversion to the very Sight of Men——ay Friend, she would ha' shrieked if she had but seen a Man, till she was in her Teens. As I'm a Person, 'tis true——She was never suffered to play with a Male-Child though but in Coats; Nay, her very Babies[201] were of the *Feminine Gender,*——O, she never looked a Man in the Face, but her own Father, or the Chaplain, and him we made a shift to put upon her for a Woman, by the help of his long Garments, and his sleek Face; till she was going in her Fifteen.

MRS MARWOOD: 'Twas much she should be deceived so long.

LADY WISHFORT: I warrant you, or she would never have borne to have been catechized by him; and have heard his long Lectures against Singing and Dancing, and such

Notes

[198] *Sophisticated* corrupted.

[199] *Counter* "A false piece of money" (Johnson).

[200] *Composition* "The act of discharging a debt by paying part; the sum paid" (Johnson, sense 9).

[201] *Babies* dolls.

Debaucheries; and going to filthy Plays; and profane Music-meetings, where the lewd Trebles squeak nothing but Bawdy, and the Basses roar Blasphemy. O, she would have swooned at the Sight or Name of an obscene Play-Book——and can I think after all this, that my Daughter can be Naught? What, a Whore? And thought it Excommunication to set her Foot within the Door of a Playhouse. O dear Friend, I can't believe it, no, no; as she says, let him prove it, let him prove it.

MRS MARWOOD: Prove it, Madam? What, and have your Name prostituted in a public Court; yours and your Daughter's Reputation worried at the Bar by a Pack of bawling Lawyers? To be ushered in with an *O Yes* of Scandal; and have your Case opened by an old fumbling Lecher in a Quoif like a Man-Midwife, to bring your Daughter's Infamy to Light; to be a Theme for legal Punsters, and Quibblers by the Statute; and become a Jest, against a Rule of Court, where there is no Precedent for a Jest in a Record; not even in *Domesday Book*:[202] To discompose the Gravity of the Bench, and provoke naughty Interrogatories in more naughty Law *Latin*; while the good Judge, tickled with the Proceeding, simpers under a Grey Beard and fidges off and on his Cushion, as if he had swallowed *Cantharides*,[203] or sat upon *Cow-Itch*.[204]

LADY WISHFORT: O, 'tis very hard!

MRS MARWOOD: And then to have my young Revellers of the Temple[205] take Notes, like Prentices at a Conventicle; and after talk it over again in Commons, or before Drawers in an Eating-House.

LADY WISHFORT: Worse and worse.

MRS MARWOOD: Nay, this is nothing; if it would end here 'twere well. But it must after this be consigned by the Shorthand writers to the public Press; and from thence be transferred to the Hands, nay into the Throats and Lungs of Hawkers, with Voices more licentious than the loud Flounderman's: And this you must hear till you are stunned; nay, you must hear nothing else for some Days.

LADY WISHFORT: O, 'tis insupportable. No, no, dear Friend, make it up, make it up; ay, ay, I'll compound. I'll give up all, myself and my all, my Niece and her all——anything, everything for Composition.

MRS MARWOOD: Nay, Madam, I advise nothing; I only lay before you, as a Friend, the Inconveniencies which perhaps you have overseen.[206] Here comes Mr *Fainall*, if he will be satisfied to huddle up all in Silence, I shall be glad. You must think I would rather congratulate than condole with you.

Scene VI

Fainall, Lady *Wishfort*, Mrs *Marwood*

LADY WISHFORT: Ay, ay, I do not doubt it, dear *Marwood*: No, no, I do not doubt it.

FAINALL: Well, Madam; I have suffered myself to be overcome by the Importunity of this Lady your Friend; and am content you shall enjoy your own proper Estate

Notes

202 *Domesday Book* a record of landownership ordered by William I of England in 1086.

203 *Cantharides* Spanish flies, used to raise blisters and reputed to be an aphrodisiac.

204 *Cow-Itch* cowage, the stinging, scratchy hairs of a tropical plant, used to treat cases of worms.

205 *Temple* the collegiate institution where lawyers were trained in London.

206 *overseen* overlooked.

during Life; on Condition you oblige yourself never to marry, under such Penalty as I think convenient.

LADY WISHFORT: Never to marry?

FAINALL: No more Sir *Rowlands*,——the next Imposture may not be so timely detected.

MRS MARWOOD: That Condition, I dare answer, my Lady will consent to, without Difficulty; she has already but too much experienced the Perfidiousness of Men. Besides, Madam, when we retire to our Pastoral Solitude we shall bid adieu to all other Thoughts.

LADY WISHFORT: Ay, that's true; but in case of Necessity; as of Health, or some such Emergency——

FAINALL: O, if you are prescribed Marriage, you shall be considered; I will only reserve to myself the Power to choose for you. If your Physic be wholesome, it matters not who is your Apothecary. Next, my Wife shall settle on me the remainder of her Fortune, not made over already; and for her Maintenance depend entirely on my discretion.

LADY WISHFORT: This is most inhumanly savage; exceeding the Barbarity of a *Muscovite* Husband.[207]

FAINALL: I learned it from his *Czarish* Majesty's[208] Retinue, in a Winter Evening's conference over Brandy and Pepper, amongst other Secrets of Matrimony and Policy, as they are at present practised in the Northern Hemisphere. But this must be agreed unto, and that positively. Lastly, I will be endowed, in right of my Wife, with that Six thousand Pound, which is the Moiety of Mrs *Millamant's* Fortune in your Possession; and which she has forfeited (as will appear by the last Will and Testament of your deceased Husband, Sir *Jonathan Wishfort*) by her Disobedience in contracting herself against your Consent or Knowledge; and by refusing the offered Match with Sir *Wilfull Witwoud*, which you, like a careful Aunt, had provided for her.

LADY WISHFORT: My Nephew was *non Compos*,[209] and could not make his Addresses.

FAINALL: I come to make Demands——I'll hear no Objections.

LADY WISHFORT: You will grant me Time to consider?

FAINALL: Yes, while the Instrument is drawing, to which you must set your Hand till more sufficient Deeds can be perfected: Which I will take Care shall be done with all possible Speed. In the meanwhile I will go for the said Instrument, and till my Return you may balance this matter in your own Discretion.

Scene VII

Lady Wishfort, *Mrs* Marwood

LADY WISHFORT: This Insolence is beyond all Precedent, all Parallel; must I be subject to this merciless Villain?

MRS MARWOOD: 'Tis severe indeed, Madam; that you should smart for your Daughter's Wantonness.

LADY WISHFORT: 'Twas against my Consent that she married this Barbarian; but she would have him, though her Year[210] was not out——Ah! her first Husband, my

Notes

207 *the Barbarity of a Muscovite Husband* according to Adam Olearius, *Voyages and Travels* (trans., 1669), they beat their wives (McKenzie).

208 *Czarish Majesty* When Peter the Great visited England in 1698, he rented John Evelyn's house in Deptford and ruined it (McKenzie).

209 *non Compos non compos mentis*, "not of sound mind," a legal term.

210 *her Year* a loosely defined period of life, in this case for mourning or for matrimonial eligibility (*OED*, sense 3b).

Son[211] *Languish*, would not have carried it thus. Well, that was my Choice, this is hers; she is matched now with a Witness[212]——I shall be mad, dear Friend; is there no Comfort for me? Must I live to be confiscated at this Rebel-rate?[213]——Here come two more of my *Egyptian* Plagues, too.

Scene VIII

[*To them*] *Millamant*, Sir *Wilfull*

Sir Wilfull: Aunt, your Servant.

Lady Wishfort: Out *Caterpillar*, call not me Aunt; I know thee not.

Sir Wilfull: I confess I have been a little in Disguise, as they say——'Sheart! and I'm sorry for't. What would you have? I hope I committed no Offence, Aunt——and if I did I am willing to make Satisfaction; and what can a Man say fairer? If I have broke anything I'll pay for't an it cost a Pound. And so let that content for what's past, and make no more Words. For what's to come, to please you, I'm willing to marry my Cousin. So pray let's all be Friends, she and I are agreed upon the Matter before a Witness.

Lady Wishfort: How's this, dear Niece? Have I any Comfort? Can this be true?

Millamant: I am content to be a Sacrifice to your Repose, Madam; and to convince you that I had no hand in the Plot as you were misinformed, I have laid my Commands on *Mirabell* to come in Person, and be a Witness that I give my Hand to this Flower of *Knighthood*; and for the Contract that passed between *Mirabell* and me, I have obliged him to make a Resignation of it in your Ladyship's Presence;——He is without, and waits your Leave for Admittance.

Lady Wishfort: Well, I'll swear I am something revived at this Testimony of your Obedience; but I cannot admit that Traitor,——I fear I cannot fortify myself to support his Appearance. He is as terrible to me as a Gorgon; if I see him I fear I shall turn to Stone, and petrify incessantly.

Millamant: If you disoblige him he may resent your Refusal, and insist upon the Contract still. Then 'tis the last time he will be offensive to you.

Lady Wishfort: Are you sure it will be the last time?——If I were sure of that——shall I never see him again?

Millamant: Sir *Wilfull*, you and he are to travel together, are you not?

Sir Wilfull: 'Sheart, the Gentleman's a civil Gentleman, Aunt, let him come in; why we are sworn Brothers and Fellow-Travellers.——We are to be *Pylades* and *Orestes*,[214] he and I——He is to be my Interpreter in Foreign Parts. He has been Overseas once already; and with *proviso* that I marry my Cousin, will cross 'em once again, only to bear me Company.——'Sheart, I'll call him in,——an I set on't once, he shall come in; and see who'll hinder him.

[*Goes to the Door and hems*]

Mrs Marwood: This is precious Fooling, if it would pass; but I'll know the Bottom of it.

Lady Wishfort: O dear *Marwood*, you are not going?

Mrs Marwood: Not far, Madam; I'll return immediately.

Notes

211 *Son* son-in-law.

212 *with a Witness* "Effectually; to a great degree, so as to leave some lasting mark or testimony behind. A low phrase" (Johnson).

213 *Rebel-rate* a wilfully unlawful financial arrangement.

214 *Pylades and Orestes* in classical mythology, Orestes, the son of Agamemnon, and Pylades, his cousin's husband, are constant friends and fellow-travelers.

Scene IX

Lady *Wishfort, Millamant,* Sir *Wilfull, Mirabell*

Sir Wilfull: Look up, Man, I'll stand by you; 'sbud, an she do frown, she can't kill you;——Besides——harkee, she dare not frown desperately, because her Face is none of her own; 'Sheart, an she should, her Forehead would wrinkle like the Coat of a Cream-Cheese; but mum for that, Fellow-Traveller.

Mirabell: If a deep Sense of the many Injuries I have offered to so good a Lady, with a sincere Remorse, and a hearty Contrition, can but obtain the least Glance of Compassion, I am too happy,——Ah Madam, there was a time——But let it be forgotten——I confess I have deservedly forfeited the high Place I once held, of sighing at your Feet; nay kill me not, by turning from me in Disdain——I come not to plead for Favour;——Nay, not for Pardon; I am a Suppliant only for Pity——I am going where I never shall behold you more.——

Sir Wilfull: How, Fellow-Traveller!——You shall go by yourself then.

Mirabell: Let me be pitied first; and afterwards forgotten——I ask no more.

Sir Wilfull: By'r Lady a very reasonable Request, and will cost you nothing, Aunt,——Come, come, forgive and forget, Aunt; why you must, an you are a Christian.

Mirabell: Consider, Madam, in Reality, you could not receive much Prejudice; it was an innocent Device; though I confess it had a Face of Guiltiness,——it was at most an Artifice which Love contrived——And Errors which Love produces have ever been accounted *Venial*. At least think it is Punishment enough, that I have lost what in my Heart I hold most dear; that to your cruel Indignation, I have offered up this Beauty and with her my Peace and Quiet; nay all my Hopes of future Comfort.

Sir Wilfull: An he does not move me, would I may never be O' *the Quorum*,[215]——An it were not as good a Deed as to drink, to give her to him again,——I would I might never take Shipping——Aunt, if you don't forgive quickly, I shall melt, I can tell you that. My Contract went no farther than a little Mouth-Glue,[216] and that's hardly dry;——One doleful Sigh more from my Fellow-Traveller, and 'tis dissolved.

Lady Wishfort: Well, Nephew, upon your Account——Ah, he has a false insinuating Tongue——Well, Sir, I will stifle my just Resentment, at my Nephew's Request——I will endeavour what I can to forget,——but on *proviso* that you resign the Contract with my Niece immediately.

Mirabell: It is in Writing, and with Papers of Concern; but I have sent my Servant for it, and will deliver it to you, with all Acknowledgements for your transcendent Goodness.

Lady Wishfort: Oh, he has Witchcraft in his Eyes and Tongue;——When I did not see him, I could have bribed a Villain to his Assassination; but his Appearance rakes the Embers which have so long lain smothered in my Breast.——

[*Aside*]

Notes

[215] *Quorum* bench of county justices.

[216] *Mouth-Glue* literally, a glue that works when moistened with the tongue; hence, a merely verbal contract.

Scene X

[*To them*] *Fainall*, Mrs *Marwood*

FAINALL: Your Date of Deliberation, Madam is expired. Here is the Instrument, are you prepared to sign?

LADY WISHFORT: If I were prepared, I am not empowered. My Niece exerts a lawful Claim, having matched herself by my Direction to Sir *Wilfull*.

FAINALL: That Sham is too gross to pass on me——though 'tis imposed on you, Madam.

MILLAMANT: Sir, I have given my Consent.

MIRABELL: And, Sir, I have resigned my Pretensions.

SIR WILFULL: And, Sir, I assert my Right; and will maintain it in Defiance of you. Sir, and of your Instrument. S'heart, an you talk of an Instrument, Sir, I have an old Fox by my Thigh shall hack your Instrument or *Ram Vellum*[217] to Shreds, Sir. It shall not be sufficient for a *Mittimus*[218] or Tailor's Measure; therefore withdraw your Instrument, Sir, or by'r Lady I shall draw mine.

LADY WISHFORT: Hold, Nephew, hold.

MILLAMANT: Good Sir *Wilfull* respite your Valour.

FAINALL: Indeed? Are you provided of your Guard, with your single Beefeater[219] there? But I am prepared for you; and insist upon my first Proposal. You shall submit your own Estate to my Management, and absolutely make over my Wife's to my sole Use; as pursuant to the Purport and Tenor of this other Covenant.——I suppose, Madam, your Consent is not requisite in this Case; nor, Mr *Mirabell*, your Resignation; nor, Sir *Wilfull*, your Right——You may draw your Fox if you please, Sir, and make a *Bear-Garden*[220] Flourish somewhere else: For here it will not avail. This, my Lady *Wishfort*, must be subscribed, or your Darling Daughter's turned adrift, like a leaky Hulk to sink or swim, as she and the Current of this lewd Town can agree.

LADY WISHFORT: Is there no Means, no Remedy, to stop my Ruin? Ungrateful Wretch! Dost thou not owe thy Being, thy Subsistence to my Daughter's Fortune?

FAINALL: I'll answer you when I have the rest of it in my Possession.

MIRABELL: But that you would not accept of a Remedy from my Hands——I own I have not deserved you should owe my Obligation to me; or else perhaps I could advise——

LADY WISHFORT: O what? what? to save me and my Child from Ruin, from Want I'll forgive all that's past; nay I'll consent to anything to come, to be delivered from this Tyranny.

MIRABELL: Ay Madam; but that is too late, my Reward is intercepted. You have disposed of her, who only could have made me a Compensation for all my Services;——but be it as it may, I am resolved I'll serve you, you shall not be wronged in this Savage Manner.

LADY WISHFORT: How! Dear Mr *Mirabell*, can you be so generous at last! But it is not possible.——Harkee, I'll break my Nephew's Match, you shall have my Niece yet, and all her Fortune, if you can but save me from this imminent Danger.

MIRABELL: Will you? I take you at your Word. I ask no more. I must have leave for two Criminals to appear.

LADY WISHFORT: Ay, ay, anybody, anybody.

MIRABELL: *Foible* is one, and a Penitent.

Notes

217 *Ram Vellum* sheepskin parchment, on which legal documents were written.

218 *Mittimus* "A warrant by which a justice commits an offender to prison" (Johnson).

219 *Beefeater* "A yeoman of the [king's] guard" (Johnson).

220 *Bear-garden* "Any place of tumult or misrule" (Johnson, sense 2).

Scene XI

[*To them*] Mrs *Fainall, Foible, Mincing*

Mrs Marwood: O my Shame! [Mirabell *and Lady* Wishfort *go to Mrs* Fainall *and* Foible] these corrupt Things are brought hither to expose me.

[*To* Fainall]

Fainall: If it must all come out, why let 'em know it, 'tis but the *Way of the World*. That shall not urge me to relinquish or abate one Tittle of my Terms, no, I will insist the more.

Foible: Yes indeed Madam, I'll take my Bible-Oath of it.

Mincing: And so will I, *Mem*.

Lady Wishfort: O *Marwood, Marwood*, art thou false? My Friend deceive me? Hast thou been a wicked Accomplice with that profligate Man?

Mrs Marwood: Have you so much Ingratitude and Injustice, to give Credit against your Friend, to the Aspersions of two such mercenary Trulls?

Mincing: Mercenary, *Mem*? I scorn your Words. 'Tis true, we found you and Mr *Fainall* in the blue Garret; by the same Token, you swore us to Secrecy upon *Messalina*'s Poems.[221] Mercenary? No, if we would have been Mercenary, we should have held our Tongues; you would have bribed us sufficiently.

Fainall: Go, you are an insignificant Thing——Well, what are you the better for this! Is this Mr *Mirabell*'s Expedient? I'll be put off no longer——You, Thing, that was a Wife, shall smart for this. I will not leave thee wherewithal to hide thy Shame: Your Body shall be Naked as your Reputation.

Mrs Fainall: I despise you, and defy your Malice——You have aspersed me wrongfully——I have proved your Falsehood——Go, you and your treacherous——I will not name it, but starve together——Perish.

Fainall: Not while you are worth a Groat, indeed my Dear. Madam, I'll be fooled no longer.

Lady Wishfort: Ah Mr *Mirabell*, this is small Comfort, the Detection of this Affair.

Mirabell: O in good time——Your leave for the other Offender and Penitent to appear, Madam.

Scene XII

[*To them*] *Waitwell* with a Box of Writings

Lady Wishfort: O Sir *Rowland*——Well, Rascal.

Waitwell: What your Ladyship pleases——I have brought the Black Box at last, Madam.

Mirabell: Give it me. Madam, you remember your Promise.

Lady Wishfort: Ay, dear Sir.

Mirabell: Where are the Gentlemen?

Notes

221 *Messalina's Poems* a malapropism for the common title *Miscellany of Poems* (McKenzie); Messalina was the notoriously promiscuous wife of the Emperor Claudius.

WAITWELL: At hand, Sir, rubbing their Eyes——just risen from Sleep.
FAINALL: S'death! what's this to me? I'll not wait your private Concerns.

Scene XIII

[To them] Petulant, Witwoud

PETULANT: How now? what's the matter? whose Hand's out?
WITWOUD: Hey day! what, are you all got together, like Players at the End of the last Act?
MIRABELL: You may remember, Gentlemen, I once requested your Hands as Witnesses to a certain Parchment.
WITWOUD: Ay I do, my Hand I remember——*Petulant* set his Mark.
MIRABELL: You wrong him, his Name is fairly written, as shall appear——You do not remember, Gentlemen, anything of what that Parchment contained——

[Undoing the Box]

WITWOUD: No.
PETULANT: Not I. I writ, I read nothing.
MIRABELL: Very well; now you shall know——Madam, your Promise.
LADY WISHFORT: Ay, ay, Sir, upon my Honour.
MIRABELL: Mr *Fainall*, it is now Time that you should know, that your Lady, while she was at her own Disposal, and before you had by your Insinuations wheedled her out of a pretended Settlement of the greatest Part of her Fortune——
FAINALL: Sir! pretended!
MIRABELL: Yes, Sir. I say, that this Lady while a Widow, having, it seems received some Cautions respecting your Inconstancy and Tyranny of Temper, which from her own partial Opinion and Fondness of you she could never have suspected——she did, I say, by the wholesome Advice of Friends, and of Sages learned in the Laws of this Land, deliver this same as her Act and Deed to me in Trust, and to the Uses within mentioned. You may read if you please——*[holding out the Parchment]* though perhaps what is written on the Back may serve your Occasions.
FAINALL: Very likely, Sir. What's here? Damnation?

[Reads]

A Deed of Conveyance of the whole Estate real of Arabella Languish, *Widow, in Trust to* Edward Mirabell.

Confusion!
MIRABELL: Even so, Sir; 'tis *the Way of the World*, Sir; of the Widows of the World. I suppose this Deed may bear an elder Date than what you have obtained from your Lady.
FAINALL: Perfidious Fiend! then thus I'll be revenged.——

[Offers to run at Mrs Fainall*]*

SIR WILFULL: Hold, Sir; now you may make your *Bear-Garden* Flourish somewhere else, Sir.
FAINALL: *Mirabell*, you shall hear of this, Sir, be sure you shall——Let me pass, Oaf.
MRS FAINALL: Madam, you seem to stifle your Resentment: You had better give it Vent.
MRS MARWOOD: Yes, it shall have Vent——and to your Confusion, or I'll perish in the Attempt.

Scene the Last

Lady *Wishfort, Millamant, Mirabell, Mrs Fainall,* Sir *Wilfull, Petulant, Witwoud, Foible, Mincing, Waitwell*

LADY WISHFORT: O Daughter, Daughter, 'tis plain thou hast inherited thy Mother's Prudence.

MRS FAINALL: Thank Mr *Mirabell*, a cautious Friend, to whose Advice all is owing.

LADY WISHFORT: Well, Mr *Mirabell*, you have kept your Promise——and I must perform mine.——First I pardon for your sake Sir *Rowland* there and *Foible*——The next thing is to break the Matter to my Nephew——and how to do that——

MIRABELL: For that, Madam, give yourself no Trouble——let me have your Consent——Sir *Wilfull* is my Friend, he has had Compassion upon Lovers, and generously engaged a Volunteer in this Action, for our Service; and now designs to prosecute his Travels.

SIR WILFULL: 'Sheart, Aunt, I have no mind to marry. My Cousin's a fine Lady, and the Gentleman loves her, and she loves him, and they deserve one another; my Resolution is to see Foreign Parts——I have set on't——and when I'm set on't, I must do't. And if these two Gentlemen would travel too, I think they may be spared.

PETULANT: For my part, I say little——I think things are best; off or on.

WAITWELL: I'gad I understand nothing of the matter,——I'm in a Maze yet, like a Dog in a Dancing-School.

LADY WISHFORT: Well Sir, take her, and with her all the Joy I can give you.

MILLAMANT: Why does not the Man take me? Would you have me give myself to you over again?

MIRABELL: Ay, and over and over again; [*Kisses her Hand*] I would have you as often as possibly I can. Well, Heaven grant I love you not too well, that's all my Fear.

SIR WILFULL: 'Sheart, you'll have time enough to toy after you're married; or if you will toy now, let us have a Dance in the mean time; that we who are not Lovers may have some other Employment, besides looking on.

MIRABELL: With all my Heart, dear Sir *Wilfull*. What shall we do for Music?

FOIBLE: O Sir, some that were provided for Sir *Rowland*'s Entertainment are yet within Call.

[*A Dance*]

LADY WISHFORT: NAs I am a Person I can hold out no longer;——I have wasted my Spirits so today already, that I am ready to sink under the Fatigue; and I cannot but have some Fears upon me yet, that my Son *Fainall* will pursue some desperate Course.

MIRABELL: NMadam, disquiet not yourself on that account; to my Knowledge his Circumstances are such, he must of Force comply. For my part, I will contribute all that in me lies to a Reunion: In the mean time, Madam, [*To Mrs* Fainall] let me before these Witnesses restore to you this Deed of Trust; it may be a Means, well managed, to make you live easily together.

From hence let those be warned, who mean to wed;
Lest mutual Falsehood stain the Bridal Bed:
For each Deceiver to his Cost may find,
That Marriage Frauds too oft are paid in kind.

[*Exeunt Omnes*]

Epilogue

Spoken by Mrs *Bracegirdle*[222]

After our Epilogue *this Crowd dismisses,*
I'm thinking how this Play'll be pulled to Pieces.
But pray consider, ere you doom its Fall,
How hard a thing 'twould be, to please you all.
There are some Critics so with Spleen[223] *diseased,*
They scarcely come inclining to be Pleased:
And sure he must have more than mortal Skill,
Who pleases anyone against his Will.
Then, all bad Poets we are sure are Foes,
And how their Number's swelled the Town well knows:
In shoals, I've marked 'em judging in the Pit;
Though they're on no Pretence for Judgement fit,
But that they have been Damned for Want of Wit.
Since when, they, by their own Offences taught,
Set up for Spies on Plays, and finding Fault.
Others there are whose Malice we'd prevent;
Such, who watch Plays, with scurrilous Intent,
To mark out who by Characters *are meant.*
And though no perfect Likeness they can trace;
Yet each pretends to know the Copied Face.
These with false Glosses feed their own Ill-nature,
And turn to Libel, *what was meant a* Satire.
May such malicious Fops *this Fortune find,*
To think themselves alone the Fools *designed:*
If any are so arrogantly Vain,
To think they singly can support a Scene,
And furnish Fool *enough to entertain.*
For well the Learned and the Judicious know,
That Satire *scorns to stoop so meanly low,*
As any one abstracted Fop *to show.*
For, as when Painters form a matchless Face,
They from each Fair one *catch some different Grace;*
And shining Features in one Portrait blend,
To which no single Beauty must pretend:
So Poets oftn do in one Piece expose
Whole Belles Assemblées *of* Coquettes *and* Beaux[224]

Notes

[222] *Mrs. Bracegirdle* Anne Bracegirdle (1671–1748), Millamant in the play, was a fixture in Congreve's productions. He was probably in love with her.

[223] *Spleen* "Anger; spite; ill-humour" (Johnson, sense 2).

[224] *Belles Assemblées of Coquettes and Beaux* French, lovely gatherings of well-dressed, superficial flirts.

Joseph Addison (1672–1719) and Richard Steele (1672–1729)

The names of Addison and Steele are permanently linked in literary history because of their collaboration on the most important, broadly influential, and popular journal published in the eighteenth century. The *Spectator* began appearing on March 1, 1711, just about two months after the last issue of Steele's immensely popular *Tatler*, a series of thrice-weekly papers he wrote under the name of Isaac Bickerstaff. Steele was a well-known man about town with several successful plays to his credit and a conspicuous record of service as a writer under the Whig government of Queen Anne. The public immediately recognized the *Spectator* as his, although, as was usual, the essays were signed in code only. Since the papers appeared every day, it was clear there must be a collaborator. The wit and learning of the papers made Swift a candidate, but readers knew that he had defected from Steele's political party to join the newly formed Tory administration. Because of the change in government, Addison was unemployed and available to bring his considerable accomplishments as a classicist to the task of writing a daily paper. He was soon identified by the public as a principal in the new paper.

There were several other contributors to the *Spectator*, but Addison and Steele divided the vast majority of the 555 numbers that appeared continuously into December of 1712. There was a brief revival in 1714, but the real longevity of the paper came from the numerous collected editions, which were considered essential across a broad spectrum of the reading public, and, in fact, were influential in shaping that public. The papers employ a set of dramatis personae, led by Mr. Spectator, who visit places, mostly in London, and supply information and opinion from an urbane yet learned and witty point of view. As a kind of extension and apotheosis of coffeehouse chat, the *Spectator* helped create the public sphere of private individuals, which recent sociologists have seen as so important in the formation of modern society.

When the Whigs returned to power after 1714, Addison rose high, probably too high for his abilities, in the state department. Steele became the commissioner for forfeited Scottish estates and went on to become embroiled in further controversies in politics and literature. But it was their collaboration, during only two of the scant four years that their party was out of office, that has given them their lasting fame. Here are one number by Steele and one by Addison. Each is a moral fable that enjoyed immediate and long-lasting popularity. The text is based on the collected edition of 1712, in which both authors, but especially the more deliberate Addison, made numerous small changes. The standard edition of the *Spectator* is by Donald Bond (Clarendon Press, 1965). I am indebted to Bond's notes, his introduction, and his textual apparatus.

British Literature 1640–1789: An Anthology, Fourth Edition. Edited by Robert DeMaria, Jr.

Number 11, *Tuesday*, March 13, 1711 [Inkle and Yarico]

Dat veniam corvis, vexat censura columbas. Juv.[1]

Arietta is visited by all Persons of both Sexes, who have any Pretence to Wit and Gallantry. She is in that time of Life which is neither affected with the Follies of Youth, or Infirmities of Age; and her Conversation is so mixed with Gaiety and Prudence, that she is agreeable both to the Young and the Old. Her Behaviour is very frank, without being in the least blameable; and she is out of the Tract[2] of any amorous or ambitious Pursuits of her own, her Visitants entertain her with Accounts of themselves very freely, whether they concern their Passions or their Interests. I made her a Visit this Afternoon, having been formerly introduced to the Honour of her Acquaintance, by my Friend WILL HONEYCOMB,[3] who has prevailed upon her to admit me sometimes into her Assembly, as a civil inoffensive Man. I found her accompanied with one Person only, a Common-Place Talker,[4] who, upon my Entrance, rose, and after a very slight Civility sat down again; then turning to *Arietta*, pursued his Discourse, which I found was upon the old Topic, of Constancy in Love. He went on with great Facility in repeating what he talks every Day of his Life; and, with the Ornaments of insignificant Laughs and Gestures, enforced his Arguments by Quotations out of Plays and Songs, which allude to the Perjuries of the Fair, and the general Levity of Women. Methought he strove to shine more than ordinarily in his Talkative Way, that he might insult my Silence, and distinguish himself before a Woman of *Arietta*'s Taste and Understanding. She had often an Inclination to interrupt him, but could find no Opportunity, till the Larum[5] ceased on itself; which it did not till he had repeated and murdered the celebrated Story of the *Ephesian* Matron.[6]

Arietta seemed to regard this Piece of Raillery as an Outrage done to her Sex; as indeed I have always observed that Women, whether out of a nicer Regard to their Honour, or what other Reason, I cannot tell, are more sensibly touched with those general Aspersions, which are cast upon their Sex, than Men are by what is said of theirs.

When she had a little recovered herself from the serious Anger she was in, she replied in the following manner.

'Sir, When I consider, how perfectly new all you have said on this Subject is, and that the Story you have given us is not quite Two thousand Years Old, I cannot but think it a Piece of Presumption to dispute with you: But your Quotations put me in Mind of the Fable of the Lion and the Man. The Man walking with that noble Animal, showed him, in the Ostentation of Human Superiority, a Sign of a Man killing a Lion. Upon which the Lion said very justly, "We Lions are none of us Painters, else we could show a hundred

Notes

NUMBER 11 *TUESDAY*

1 *Dat veniam ... Juv.* "He pardons the ravens and crucifies the doves" (Juvenal 2.63), a proverbial sentence, given by the female speaker of the poem, when she has shown the folly of criticizing women when men are so much worse.

2 *Tract* period or duration.

3 *WILL HONEYCOMB* one of the characters who appears repeatedly in the essays; he is a friend of Mr. Spectator, whose opinions about women are valued.

4 *Common-Place Talker* one who rehashes well-known subjects, or commonplaces.

5 *Larum* alarm.

6 *the Ephesian Matron* Petronius (d. 65 CE) tells this story in the *Satyricon* about a woman from Ephesus who is courted by a soldier, as she weeps by the tomb of her recently killed husband; in the end, she gives in to the soldier and saves his life by offering to let him put her husband's body on the cross he, in his ardor, has left unguarded (Loeb edition, pp. 268–76).

Men killed by Lions, for one Lion killed by a Man". You Men are Writers, and can represent us Women as Unbecoming as you please in your Works, while we are unable to return the Injury. You have twice or thrice observed in your Discourse, that Hypocrisy is the very Foundation of our Education; and that an Ability to dissemble our Affections, is a professed Part of our Breeding. These, and such other Reflections, are sprinkled up and down the Writings of all Ages, by Authors, who leave behind them Memorials of their Resentment against the Scorn of particular Women, in Invectives against the whole Sex. Such a Writer, I doubt not, was the celebrated *Petronius*, who invented the pleasant Aggravations of the Frailty of the *Ephesian* Lady; but when we consider this Question between the Sexes, which has been either a Point of Dispute or Raillery ever since there were Men and Women, let us take Facts from plain People, and from such as have not either Ambition or Capacity to embellish their Narrations with any Beauties of Imagination. I was the other Day amusing myself with *Ligon*'s Account of *Barbadoes*;[7] and, in Answer to your well-wrought Tale, I will give you (as it dwells upon my Memory) out of that honest Traveller, in his Fifty-fifth Page, the History of *Inkle* and *Yarico*.

Mr. *Thomas Inkle*, of *London*, aged twenty Years, embarked in the *Downs* on the good Ship called the *Achilles*, bound for the *West Indies*, on the 16th of *June* 1647, in order to improve his Fortune by Trade and Merchandise. Our Adventurer was the third Son of an eminent Citizen, who had taken particular Care to instil into his Mind an early Love of Gain, by making him a perfect Master of Numbers, and consequently giving him a quick View of Loss and Advantage, and preventing the natural Impulses of his Passions, by Prepossession towards his Interests. With a Mind thus turned, young *Inkle* had a Person every way agreeable, a ruddy Vigour in his Countenance, Strength in his Limbs, with Ringlets of fair Hair loosely flowing on his Shoulders. It happened, in the Course of the Voyage, that the *Achilles*, in some Distress, put into a Creek on the Main of *America*, in Search of Provisions: The Youth, who is the Hero of my Story, among others, went ashore on this Occasion. From their first Landing they were observed by a Party of *Indians*, who hid themselves in the Woods for that Purpose. The *English* unadvisedly marched a great distance from the Shore into the Country, and were intercepted by the Natives, who slew the greatest Number of them. Our Adventurer escaped among others, by flying into a Forest. Upon his coming into a remote and pathless Part of the Wood, he threw himself, tired and breathless, on a little Hillock, when an *Indian* Maid rushed from a Thicket behind him: After the first Surprise, they appeared mutually agreeable to each other. If the *European* was highly Charmed with the Limbs, Features, and wild Graces of the Naked *American*; the *American* was no less taken with the Dress, Complexion and Shape of an *European*, covered from Head to Foot. The *Indian* grew immediately enamoured of him, and consequently solicitous for his Preservation: She therefore conveyed him to a Cave, where she gave him a Delicious Repast of Fruits, and led him to a Stream to slake his Thirst. In the midst of these good Offices, she would sometimes play with his Hair, and delight in the Opposition of its Colour, to that of her Fingers: Then open his Bosom, then laugh at him for covering it. She was, it seems, a Person of Distinction, for she every day came to him in a different Dress, of the most beautiful Shells, Bugles and Bredes.[8] She likewise brought him a great many Spoils, which her other Lovers had presented to her; so that his Cave was richly adorned with all the spotted Skins of Beasts, and most Party-coloured Feathers of Fowls, which that World afforded. To make his Confinement

Notes

[7] *Ligon's ... Barbadoes* Richard Ligon, *A True and Exact History of the Island of Barbadoes* (1657).

[8] *Bugles* "Shining beads of black glass" (Johnson); *Bredes* braids.

more tolerable, she would carry him in the Dusk of the Evening, or by the favour of Moonlight, to unfrequented Groves and Solitudes, and show him where to lie down in Safety, and sleep amidst the Falls of Waters, and Melody of Nightingales. Her Part was to watch and hold him in her Arms, for fear of her Countrymen, and wake him on Occasions to consult his Safety. In this manner did the Lovers pass away their Time, till they had learned a Language of their own, in which the Voyager communicated to his Mistress, how happy he should be to have her in his Country, where she should be Clothed in such Silks as his Waistcoat was made of, and be carried in Houses drawn by Horses, without being exposed to Wind or Weather. All this he promised her the Enjoyment of, without such Fears and Alarms as they were there Tormented with. In this tender Correspondence these Lovers lived for several Months, when *Yarico*, instructed by her Lover, discovered a Vessel on the Coast, to which she made the Signals; and in the Night, with the utmost Joy and Satisfaction accompanied him to a Ship's-Crew of his Countrymen, bound for *Barbadoes*. When a Vessel from the Main arrives in that Island, it seems the Planters come down to the Shore, where there is an immediate Market of the *Indians* and other Slaves, as with us of Horses and Oxen.

To be short, Mr. *Thomas Inkle*, now coming into *English* Territories, began seriously to reflect upon his loss of Time, and to weigh with himself how many Days' Interest of his Money he had lost during his stay with *Yarico*. This Thought made the Young Man very pensive, and careful what Account he should be able to give his Friends of his Voyage. Upon which Considerations, the prudent and frugal young Man sold *Yarico* to a *Barbadian* Merchant; notwithstanding that the poor Girl, to incline him to commiserate her Condition, told him that she was with Child by him: But he only made use of that Information to rise in his Demands upon the Purchaser.

I was so touched with this Story (which I think should be always a Counterpart to the *Ephesian* Matron) that I left the Room with Tears in my Eyes; which a Woman of *Arietta*'s good Sense, did, I am sure, take for greater Applause, than any Compliments I could make her.

Number 159, Saturday, September 1, 1711
[The Visions of Mirzah]

Omnem quæ nunc obducta tuenti
Mortales hebetat visus tibi, & humida circum
Caligat, nubem eripiam....

Virgil[1]

When I was at *Grand Cairo*, I picked up several Oriental Manuscripts, which I have still by me. Among others I met with one entitled, *The Visions of Mirzah*, which I have read over with great Pleasure. I intend to give it to the Public when I have no other Entertainment for them; and shall begin with the first Vision,[2] which I have translated Word for Word as follows.

On the fifth Day of the Moon, which according to the Custom of my Forefathers I always keep holy, after having washed myself, and offered up my Morning Devotions,

Notes

NUMBER 159 SATURDAY

1 Aeneid, 2.604-6: "[Now cast your Eyes around;] while I dissolve/The Mists and Films that mortal Eyes involve:/ Purge from your sight the Dross" (Dryden's *Aeneas*, 2.819–21). These are the words of Athena to Aeneas when she shows him that Troy is lost and he must flee.

2 Addison never added others.

I ascended the high Hills of *Baghdad*, in order to pass the rest of the Day in Meditation and Prayer. As I was here airing myself on the Tops of the Mountains, I fell into a profound Contemplation on the Vanity of human Life; and passing from one Thought to another, 'Surely,' said I, 'Man is but a Shadow and Life a Dream'. Whilst I was thus musing, I cast my Eyes towards the Summit of a Rock that was not far from me, where I discovered one in the Habit of a Shepherd, with a little Musical Instrument in his Hand. As I looked upon him he applied it to his Lips, and began to play upon it. The Sound of it was exceeding sweet, and wrought into a Variety of Tunes that were inexpressibly melodious, and altogether different from anything I had ever heard. They put me in mind of those heavenly Airs that are played to the departed Souls of good Men upon their first Arrival in Paradise, to wear out the Impressions of the last Agonies, and qualify them for the Pleasures of that happy Place. My Heart melted away in secret Raptures.

I had been often told that the Rock before me was the Haunt of a Genius;[3] and that several had been entertained with Music who had passed by it, but never heard that the Musician had before made himself visible. When he had raised my Thoughts by those transporting Airs which he played, to taste the Pleasures of his Conversation, as I looked upon him like one astonished, he beckoned to me, and by the waving of his Hand directed me to approach the Place where he sat. I drew near with that Reverence which is due to a superior Nature; and as my Heart was entirely subdued by the captivating Strains I had heard, I fell down at his Feet and wept. The Genius smiled upon me with a Look of Compassion and Affability that familiarized him to my Imagination,[4] and at once dispelled all the Fears and Apprehensions with which I approached him. He lifted me from the Ground, and taking me by the hand, '*Mirzah*', said he, 'I have heard thee in thy Soliloquies; follow me'.

He then led me to the highest Pinnacle of the Rock, and placing me on the Top of it, 'Cast thy Eyes Eastward', said he, 'and tell me what thou seest'. 'I see', said I, 'a huge Valley, and a prodigious Tide of Water rolling through it'. 'The Valley that thou seest', said he, 'is the Vale of Misery, and the Tide of Water that thou seest is part of the great Tide of Eternity'. 'What is the Reason', said I, 'that the Tide I see rises out of a thick Mist at one End, and again loses itself in a thick Mist at the other?' 'What thou seest', said he, 'is that Portion of Eternity which is called Time, measured out by the Sun, and reaching from the Beginning of the World to its Consummation. Examine now', said he, 'this Sea that is bounded with Darkness at both Ends, and tell me what thou discoverest in it'. 'I see a Bridge', said I, 'standing in the Midst of the Tide'. 'The Bridge thou seest', said he, 'is human Life; consider it attentively'. Upon a more leisurely Survey of it, I found that it consisted of threescore and ten entire Arches, with several broken Arches, which added to those that were entire, made up the Number about an hundred. As I was counting the Arches, the Genius told me that this Bridge consisted at first of a thousand Arches; but that a great Flood swept away the rest, and left the Bridge in the ruinous Condition I now beheld it. 'But tell me further', said he, 'what thou discoverest on it'. 'I see Multitudes of People passing over it', said I, 'and a black Cloud hanging on each End of it'. As I looked more attentively, I saw several of the Passengers dropping through the Bridge, into the great Tide that flowed underneath it; and upon further Examination, perceived there were innumerable Trap-doors that lay concealed in the Bridge, which the Passengers no sooner trod upon, but they fell through them into the Tide and immediately disappeared. These hidden Pitfalls were

Notes

[3] *Genius* a presiding spirit.

[4] *Imagination* mind; the image-making faculty.

set very thick at the Entrance of the Bridge, so that the Throngs of People no sooner broke through the Cloud, but many of them fell into them. They grew thinner towards the Middle, but multiplied and lay closer together towards the End of the Arches that were entire.

There were indeed some Persons, but their Number was very small, that continued a kind of hobbling March on the broken Arches, but fell through one after another, being quite tired and spent with so long a Walk.

I passed some Time in the Contemplation of this wonderful Structure, and the great Variety of Objects which it presented. My Heart was filled with a deep Melancholy to see several dropping unexpectedly in the midst of Mirth and Jollity, and catching at everything that stood by them to save themselves. Some were looking up towards the Heavens in a thoughtful Posture, and in the midst of a Speculation stumbled and fell out of Sight. Multitudes were very busy in the Pursuit of Bubbles[5] that glittered in their Eyes and danced before them, but often when they thought themselves within the Reach of them their Footing failed, and down they sunk. In this Confusion of Objects, I observed some with Scimitars in their Hands, and others with Urinals,[6] who ran to and fro upon the Bridge, thrusting several Persons on Trap-doors which did not seem to lie in their Way, and which they might have escaped had they not been thus forced upon them.

The Genius seeing me indulge myself in this melancholy Prospect, told me I had dwelt long enough upon it: 'Take thine Eyes off the Bridge', said he, 'and tell me if thou yet seest anything thou dost not comprehend'. Upon looking up, 'What mean', said I, 'those great Flights of Birds that are perpetually hovering about the Bridge, and settling upon it from time to time? I see Vultures, Harpies,[7] Ravens, Cormorants, and among many other feathered Creatures several little winged Boys, that perch in great Numbers upon the middle Arches'. 'These', said the Genius, 'are Envy, Avarice, Superstition, Despair, Love, with the like Cares and Passions that infest human Life'.

I here fetched a deep Sigh, 'Alas', said I, 'Man was made in vain! How is he given away to Misery and Mortality! tortured in Life, and swallowed up in Death!' The Genius being moved with Compassion towards me, bid me quit so uncomfortable a Prospect: 'Look no more', said he, 'on Man in the first Stage of his Existence, in his setting out for Eternity; but cast thine Eye on that thick Mist into which the Tide bears the several Generations of Mortals that fall into it'. I directed my Sight as I was ordered, and (whether or no the good Genius strengthened it with any supernatural Force, or dissipated Part of the Mist that was before too thick for the Eye to penetrate) I saw the Valley opening at the further End, and spreading forth into an immense Ocean, that had a huge Rock of Adamant running through the Midst of it, and dividing it into two equal Parts. The Clouds still rested on one Half of it, insomuch that I could discover nothing in it; but the other appeared to me a vast Ocean planted with innumerable Islands, that were covered with Fruits and Flowers, and interwoven with a thousand little shining Seas that ran among them. I could see Persons dressed in glorious Habits with Garlands upon their Heads, passing among the Trees, lying down by the Sides of Fountains, or resting on Beds of Flowers; and could hear a confused Harmony of singing Birds, falling Waters, human Voices, and musical Instruments. Gladness grew in

Notes

5 *Bubble* "Anything fragile, unsubstantial, empty, or worthless" (*OED*, 3a).

6 *Urinals* glass vessels used in alchemy.

7 *Harpy* a kind of buzzard or a mythological creature with wings and claws but a woman's face and body.

me upon the Discovery of so delightful a Scene. I wished for the Wings of an Eagle, that I might fly away to those happy Seats; but the Genius told me there was no Passage to them, except through the Gates of Death that I saw opening every Moment upon the Bridge. 'The Islands', said he, 'that lie so fresh and green before thee, and with which the whole Face of the Ocean appears spotted as far as thou canst see, are more in Number than the Sands on the Sea-shore; there are Myriads of Islands behind those which thou here discoverest, reaching further than thine Eye, or even thine Imagination can extend itself. These are the Mansions of good Men after Death, who according to the Degree and Kinds of Virtue in which they excelled, are distributed among these several Islands, which abound with Pleasures of different Kinds and Degrees, suitable to the Relishes and Perfections of those who are settled in them; every Island is a Paradise accommodated to its respective Inhabitants. Are not these, O *Mirzah*, Habitations worth contending for? Does Life appear miserable, that gives thee Opportunities of earning such a Reward? Is Death to be feared, that will convey thee to so happy an Existence? Think not Man was made in vain, who has such an Eternity reserved for him'. I gazed with inexpressible Pleasure on these happy Islands. At length said I, 'show me now, I beseech thee, the Secrets that lie hid under those dark Clouds which cover the Ocean on the other side of the Rock of Adamant. The Genius making me no Answer, I turned about to address myself to him a second time, but I found that he had left me; I then turned again to the Vision which I had been so long contemplating; but Instead of the rolling Tide, the arched Bridge, and the happy Islands, I saw nothing but the long hollow Valley of *Baghdad*, with Oxen, Sheep, and Camels, grazing upon the Sides of it.

The End of the first Vision of Mirzah.

C.[8]

Notes

[8] The code signature of Addison.

Isaac Watts (1674–1748)

Watts was one of the five poets whom Samuel Johnson personally recommended for inclusion in *The Works of the English Poets*, for which he wrote his famous biographical prefaces known as *The Lives of the Poets*. Watts was a dissenting minister who wrote against the established church, but his piety, his evident sincerity, and his determination to write for the purpose of improving his readers were irresistible to Johnson. Watts was also a skillful versifier, and a great number of his songs have found their way into all sorts of Christian hymnals. He wrote a great deal of verse and prose for children and students, and he gave generously of his own meager property to assist educational projects, such as a fledgling American college called Yale that so badly needed books.

The texts presented here come from *Divine Songs Attempted in Easy Language for the Use of Children* (1715).

from *Divine Songs Attempted in Easy Language for the Use of Children* (1715)

Against Quarrelling and Fighting

Let Dogs delight to bark and bite,
For GOD hath made them so;
Let Bears and Lions growl and fight,
For 'tis their Nature too.

But, Children, you should never let
Such angry Passions rise;
Your little Hands were never made
To tear each other's Eyes.

Let Love through all your Actions run,
And all your Words be mild;
Live like the blessèd Virgin's Son,
That sweet and lovely Child.

His Soul was gentle as a Lamb;
And as his Stature grew,
He grew in Favour both with Man
And God his Father too.

Now, Lord of all, he reigns above,
And from his heav'nly Throne,
He sees what Children dwell in Love,
And marks them for his own.

British Literature 1640–1789: An Anthology, Fourth Edition. Edited by Robert DeMaria, Jr.

The Sluggard[1]

'Tis the Voice of the Sluggard. I hear him complain
'You have waked me too soon, I must slumber again'.
As the Door on it Hinges, so he on his Bed,
Turns his Sides, and his Shoulders, and his heavy Head.

'A little more Sleep, and a little more Slumber';
Thus he wastes half his Days, and his Hours without number:
And when he gets up, he sits folding his Hands
Or walks about saunt'ring, or trifling he stands.

I passed by his Garden, and saw the wild Briar
The Thorn and the Thistle grow broader and higher:
The Clothes that hang on him are turning to Rags;
And his Money still wastes, till he starves, or he begs.

I made him a Visit, still hoping to find
He had took better care for improving his Mind:
He told me his Dreams, talked of eating and drinking,
But he scarce reads his Bible, and never loves thinking.

Said I then to my Heart, 'Here's a Lesson for me',
That Man's but the Picture of what I might be:
But thanks to my Friends for their care in my Breeding:
Who taught me betimes to love Working and Reading.[2]

Notes

THE SLUGGARD

[1] *The Sluggard* he is one kind of "fool" mentioned frequently in the Book of Proverbs, which supplies the background of Watts's poem.

[2] *betimes* early.

Allan Ramsay (1684–1758)

It was under the auspices of the Easy Club, which Ramsay helped found in Edinburgh, that the poet began to make a name for himself. He read his poems to the other young men, and under the poetical name of Gawin (or Gavin) Douglas (a sixteenth-century Scots translator of Virgil) became poet laureate to the group. His first hit was an elegy (1713) on a country woman who brewed and sold beer to the local lads. Filled with Scottish words, it begins:

Auld Reeky, mourn in sable hue,[1]
Let fouth of tears dreep like May dew;[2]
To braw tippony bid adieu,[3]
  Which we with greed
Bended as fast as she could brew:
  But ah! she's dead.

Ramsay went on to publish volumes of his own poetry, collections of songs and ballads, a play, a mock epic, and loosely edited versions of old Scots poetry. His songs remain his most famous works, but he also produced a good deal of interesting satire, mingling, like Gay, classic forms and modern, often rural, imagery. He was an admirer of Pope, whom he celebrated as "Sandy" in several tributes to his favorite British writers.

For convenience's sake, I have used *The Poems of Allan Ramsay* (London, 1800) as my copy-text. Like the collections that began coming out in 1721, this edition includes a glossary of Scottish words, and I have used it in my notes.

from *The Poems of Allan Ramsay* (1800)

Polwart on the Green (1721)

At Polwart on the green,
If you'll meet me the morn,
Where lasses do convene
To dance about the thorn;
A kindly welcome ye shall meet
  Frae her wha likes to view
A lover and a lad complete,
  The lad and lover you.
  Let dorty dames say na,[1]
As lang as e'er they please,
Seem caulder than the sna',
While inwardly they bleeze;

Notes

Allan Ramsay

1 *Auld Reeky* "old smoky," Edinburgh.

2 *fouth* "plenty."

3 *braw tippony* ["brave twopenny"] She sold the Scots pint, which is near two quarts English for two pence [Ramsay's note].

Polwart on the Green

1 *dorty* proud, not to be spoken to.

But I will frankly shaw my mind,
And yield my heart to thee;
Be ever to the captive kind,
That langs na to be free.
At Polwart on the Green,
Among the new-mawn hay,
With sangs and dancing keen
We'll pass the heartsome day,
At night if beds be o'er thrang laid,[2]
And thou be twined of thine,[3]
Thou shalt be welcome, my dear lad,
To take a part of mine.

Give Me a Lass with a Lump of Land (1721)

Gi'e me a lass with a lump of land,
And we for life shall gang the gither;[1]
Though daft or wise I'll never demand,
Or black or fair it maks na whether.
I'm aff with wit, and beauty will fade,[2]
And blood alane is no worth a shilling;
But she that's rich, her market's made,
For ilka charm about her is killing.[3]
Gi'e me a lass with a lump of land,
And in my bosom I'll hug my treasure;
Gin I had anes her gear in my hand,[4]
Should love turn dowf, it will find pleasure.[5]
Laugh on wha likes, but there's my hand,
I hate with poortith, though bonny, to meddle;[6]
Unless they bring cash, or a lump of land,
They'se never get me to dance to their fiddle.
There's meikle good love in bands and bags,[7]
And siller and gowd's a sweet complexion;[8]
But beauty, and wit, and virtue in rags,
Have tint the art of gaining affection.[9]
Love tips his arrows with woods and parks,
And castles, and riggs, and moors, and meadows;[10]
And nathing can catch our modern sparks,[11]
But well tochered lasses, or jointured widows.[12]

Notes

2 *thrang* crowded.
3 *twined of* separated from.

Give Me a Lass with a Lump of Land
1 *gang the gither* go together.
2 *aff with* off, finished with.
3 *ilka* every.
4 *Gin* if; *anes* once; *gear* stuff.
5 *dowf* mournful, wanting variety.
6 *poortith* poverty.
7 *meikle* mighty.
8 *siller and gowd* silver and gold.
9 *tint* lost.
10 *rigg* measure of land.
11 *sparks* beaux, men about town.
12 *tocher* dowry; *jointure* "Estate settled on a wife to be enjoyed after her husband's decease" (Johnson).

John Gay (1685–1732)

At age seventy Samuel Johnson recognized in Gay a quality that he knew himself to lack, at least as a younger man: "Gay is represented as a man easily incited to hope and deeply depressed when his hopes were disappointed. This is not the character of a hero; but it may naturally imply something more generally welcome, a soft and civil companion. Whoever is apt to hope good from others is diligent to please them; but he that believes his powers strong enough to force their own way, commonly tries only to please himself" (*Life of Gay*, Yale ed., II.795). Gay's attempts to please brought him from Devon to London, where he was an apprentice to a silk mercer and learned things about the world of fashion that show up consistently in his poetry. To increase his available time for writing, however, he became a steward in the house of the duchess of Monmouth, the first of his many noble patrons. About the same time he established what would be a lifelong friendship with Alexander Pope and became acquainted with Swift, Arbuthnot, and other important writers. Gay's success at pleasing the public was more variable than his happiness in his friendships with writers and patrons. His drinking songs, burlesque plays, and farces about modern life had some popularity, and *Trivia* (1716), a poem about life in London, was both a great success and a work of enduring merit.

However, Gay could not manage his money. Like many other Englishmen he lost a small fortune in the South Sea Company investment scheme, when the so-called "Bubble" burst in 1720, and he was forever falling back on the help of patrons, despite bouts of tremendous success. *The Beggar's Opera* (1728) is Gay's most famous work; it established the genre of musical comedy, and its popularity has continued into the present; it made Gay somewhat wealthy, but it ruined his hopes for political preferment because of its satire of Walpole. Equally popular and even more frequently reprinted are Gay's *Fables*. More than 350 editions have appeared since they first came out in 1727. When he died at forty-seven, Gay was living in the household of the duke and duchess of Queensberry. He had savings of £6,000 and could finance his own publications, but he never married, never had his own house, and never achieved the sort of independence that Pope enjoyed or that Johnson so highly valued.

The text of *The Beggar's Opera* is based on the so-called "second edition" of 1728 with some corrections from the "third edition" of 1729 and without the large section reserved in both for the music of the many songs. I have benefited from the commentary and textual notes in the standard edition of Gay's dramatic works, edited by John Fuller (Oxford University Press, 1983), and in the excellent edition by Edgar V. Roberts (University of Nebraska Press, 1969). There is a sound and entertaining critical biography by David Nokes, *John Gay: A Profession of Friendship* (Oxford University Press, 1995).

British Literature 1640–1789: An Anthology, Fourth Edition. Edited by Robert DeMaria, Jr.

The Beggar's Opera *(1728)*
As it is Acted at the THEATRE-ROYAL IN *LINCOLNS-INN-FIELDS*.

Written by Mr. Gay.

—Nos haec novimus esse nihil. Mart.[1]

Dramatis Personae.

MEN.
Mr. *Hippesley*, Peachum.[2]
Mr. *Hall*, Lockit.
Mr. *Walker*, Macheath.[3]
Mr. *Clark*, Filch.

Macheath's Gang:
Mr. *H Bullock*, Jemmy Twitcher.
Mr. *Houghton*, *Crook-fingered* Jack.
Mr. *Smith*, Wat Dreary.
Mr. *Lacy*, Robin *of* Bagshot.
Mr. *Pit*, *Nimming* Ned.[4]
Mr. *Eaton*, Harry Padington.[5]
Mr. *Spiller*, Mat *of the* Mint.
Mr. *Morgan*, Ben Budge.

Mr. *Chapman*, *Beggar*.
Mr. *Milward*, *Player*.
Constables, Drawer, Turnkey, etc.

WOMEN.
Mrs. *Martin*, *Mrs.* Peachum.
Miss *Fenton*, Polly Peachum.
Mrs. *Egleton*, Lucy Lockit.

Women of the town:
Mrs. *Martin*, Diana Trapes.
Mrs. *Holiday*, *Mrs.* Coaxer.
Mrs. *Lacy*, Dolly Trull.
Mrs. *Rice*, *Mrs.* Vixen.
Mrs. *Rogers*, Betty Doy.
Mrs. *Clarke*, Jenny Diver.[6]
Mrs. *Morgan*, *Mrs.* Slammekin.[7]
Mrs. *Palin*, Suky Tawdry.
Mrs. *Sallee*, Molly Brazen.

Notes

THE BEGGAR'S OPERA

1 From Martial's *Epigrams*, 13.2.8: "I myself know my work is worth nothing." The poem goes on, however, to say, "but it's not entirely worthless, if you listen genially, and don't eye it very soberly and sternly."

2 *To peach* to inform and so to betray one's companions.

3 *Macheath* of the Heath, any wild park in or near London known for robberies, such as Bagshot Heath (see Robin of Bagshot below).

4 *To nim* to nab or steal.

5 The Tyburn gallows were in the parish of Paddington; a Paddington Fair Day was an execution day (*Dictionary of the Vulgar Tongue*).

6 *Diver* pickpocket (*Dictionary of the Vulgar Tongue*).

7 *Slammekin* "A female sloven … a careless trapes" (*Dictionary of the Vulgar Tongue*).

INTRODUCTION.

BEGGAR. PLAYER.

BEGGAR: If Poverty be a Title to Poetry, I am sure Nobody can dispute mine. I own myself of the Company of Beggars; and I make one at their Weekly Festivals at St. *Giles*'s.[8] I have a small Yearly Salary for my Catches,[9] and am welcome to a Dinner there whenever I please, which is more than most Poets can say.

PLAYER: As we live by the Muses, 'tis but Gratitude in us to encourage Poetical Merit wherever we find it. The Muses, contrary to all other Ladies, pay no Distinction to Dress, and never partially mistake the Pertness of Embroidery for Wit, nor the Modesty of Want for Dullness. Be the Author who he will, we push his Play as far as it will go. So (though you are in Want) I wish you Success heartily.

BEGGAR: This Piece I own was originally writ for the celebrating the Marriage of *James Changer* and *Moll Lay*, two most excellent Ballad-Singers. I have introduced the Similes that are in all your celebrated *Operas*: The *Swallow*, the *Moth*, the *Bee*, the *Ship*, the *Flower*, etc.[10] Besides, I have a Prison Scene which the Ladies always reckon charmingly pathetic. As to the Parts, I have observed such a nice Impartiality to our two ladies, that it is impossible for either of them to take Offence. I hope I may be forgiven, that I have not made my Opera throughout unnatural, like those in vogue; for I have no Recitative:[11] Excepting this, as I have consented to have neither Prologue nor Epilogue, it must be allowed an Opera in all its forms. The Piece indeed hath been heretofore frequently represented by ourselves in our great Room at St. *Giles*'s, so that I cannot too often acknowledge your Charity in bringing it now on the Stage.

PLAYER: But I see 'tis time for us to withdraw; the Actors are preparing to begin. Play away the Overture.[12] [*Exeunt*].

ACT I. SCENE I.

SCENE Peachum's *House.*

Peachum *sitting at a Table with a large Book of Accounts before him.*

AIR I. An old Woman clothed in Gray, etc.[13]

Through all the Employments of Life
Each Neighbour abuses his Brother;
Whore and Rogue they call Husband and Wife:
All Professions berogue one another.
The Priest calls the Lawyer a Cheat,
The Lawyer beknaves the Divine;
And the Statesman, because he's so great,
Thinks his Trade as honest as mine.

Notes

8 *St. Giles* a parish in central London known for poverty at this time.

9 *Catches* musical rounds, in which the singers perform a succession of overlapping lines.

10 Songs with these names follow.

11 *Recitative* "A style of musical declamation" (*OED*).

12 The second edition included the musical scores of the overture and the other music in the play.

13 The airs, or tunes, are associated throughout with well-known ballads.

A Lawyer is an honest Employment, so is mine. Like me too he acts in a double Capacity, both against Rogues and for 'em; for 'tis but fitting that we should protect and encourage Cheats, since we live by them.[14]

SCENE II.

Peachum, Filch.

FILCH: Sir, Black *Moll* hath sent word her Trial comes on in the Afternoon, and she hopes you will order Matters so as to bring her off.

PEACH: Why, she may plead her Belly at worst;[15] to my Knowledge she hath taken care of that Security. But as the Wench is very active and industrious, you may satisfy her that I'll soften the Evidence.

FILCH: *Tom Gagg*, Sir, is found guilty.

PEACH: A lazy Dog! When I took him the time before, I told him what he would come to if he did not mend his Hand. This is Death without Reprieve. I may venture to Book him. [*writes*] For *Tom Gagg*, forty Pounds. Let *Betty Sly* know that I'll save her from Transportation, for I can get more by her staying in *England*.

FILCH: *Betty* hath brought more Goods into our Lock[16] to-year than any five of the Gang; and in truth, 'tis a pity to lose so good a Customer.

PEACH: If none of the Gang take her off, she may, in the common course of Business, live a Twelve-month longer. I love to let Women 'scape. A good Sportsman always lets the Hen Partridges fly, because the breed of the Game depends upon them. Besides, here the Law allows us no Reward; there is nothing to be got by the Death of Women—except our wives.[17]

FILCH: Without dispute, she is a fine Woman! 'Twas to her I was obliged for my Education, and (to say a bold Word) she hath trained up more young Fellows to the Business than the Gaming table.

PEACH: Truly, *Filch*, thy Observation is right. We and the Surgeons are more beholden to Women than all the Professions besides.[18]

AIR II. The bonny gray-eyed Morn, etc.

Filch. *'Tis Woman that seduces all Mankind,*
By her we first were taught the wheedling Arts:
Her very eyes can cheat; when most she's kind,
She tricks us of our Money with our Hearts.
For her, like Wolves by night we roam for Prey,
And practice every Fraud to bribe her Charms;
For Suits of Love, like Law, are won by Pay,
And beauty must be feed into our Arms.[19]

Notes

[14] Jonathan Wild, the notorious criminal on whom Peachum is loosely based, profited both by informing on thieves (reaping a reward of £40) and by returning for a reward goods stolen in schemes often plotted by Wild himself. He ran an "Office for the Recovery of Lost and Stolen Property" located in the Central Criminal Court, or "Old Bailey" (Fuller). He was eventually convicted and hanged at Tyburn on May 24, 1725.

[15] *Plead her belly* evidence of pregnancy could commute a sentence of capital punishment to "transportation," exile to the colonies.

[16] *Lock* warehouse.

[17] Jonathan Wild was reputed to have had six "wives," some simultaneously (*ODNB*).

[18] The surgeons benefited from treating sexually transmitted diseases.

[19] *feed* bribed (*OED*, s.v. *fee*, v. 1, 3b).

PEACH: But make haste to *Newgate*, Boy, and let my Friends know what I intend; for I love to make them easy one way or other.

FILCH: When a Gentleman is long kept in suspense, Penitence may break his Spirit ever after. Besides, Certainty gives a Man a good Air upon his Trial, and makes him risk another without Fear or Scruple. But I'll away, for 'tis a Pleasure to be the Messenger of Comfort to Friends in Affliction.

SCENE III.

Peachum.

But 'tis now high time to look about me for a decent Execution against next Sessions.[20] I hate a lazy Rogue, by whom one can get nothing till he is hanged. A Register of the Gang, [reading] Crook-fingered *Jack*. A Year and a half in the Service; Let me see how much the Stock owes to his Industry; one, two, three, four, five Gold Watches, and seven Silver ones. A mighty clean-handed Fellow! Sixteen Snuff-boxes, five of them of true Gold. Six dozen of Handkerchiefs, four silver-hilted Swords, half a dozen of Shirts, three Tie Periwigs,[21] and a piece of Broad Cloth. Considering these are only the Fruits of his leisure Hours, I don't know a prettier Fellow, for no Man alive hath a more engaging Presence of Mind upon the Road. *Wat Dreary*, alias *Brown Will*, an irregular Dog, who hath an underhand way of disposing of his Goods. I'll try him only for a Session or two longer upon his good Behaviour. *Harry Padington*, a poor petty-larceny Rascal, without the least Genius; that Fellow, though he were to live these six Months, will never come to the Gallows with any Credit. Slippery *Sam*; he goes off the next Sessions, for the Villain hath the Impudence to have views of following his Trade as a Tailor, which he calls an honest Employment. *Mat of the Mint*; listed[22] not above a Month ago, a promising sturdy Fellow, and diligent in his way; somewhat too bold and hasty, and may raise good Contributions on the Public, if he does not cut himself short by Murder. *Tom Tipple*, a guzzling soaking Sot, who is always too drunk to stand himself, or to make others stand. A Cart is absolutely necessary for him. *Robin* of *Bagshot*, alias *Gorgon*, alias *Bluff Bob*, alias *Carbuncle*, alias *Bob Booty*.[23]

SCENE IV.

Peachum, *Mrs*. Peachum.

MRS. PEACH: What of *Bob Booty*, Husband? I hope nothing bad hath betided him. You know, my Dear, he's a favourite Customer of mine. 'Twas he made me a Present of this Ring.

PEACH: I have set his Name down in the Black-List, that's all, my Dear; he spends his Life among Women, and as soon as his Money is gone, one or other of the Ladies will hang him for the Reward, and there's forty Pound lost to us for ever.

Notes

[20] *Sessions* criminal trials at the Old Bailey.

[21] *Tie Periwig* a stylized wig, like those worn by judges and barristers in Britain.

[22] *Listed* enlisted.

[23] This character is meant to recall Robert Walpole (1676–1745), the immensely powerful Whig minister and Lord of the Treasury, often accused of using his power to increase his personal wealth.

MRS. PEACH: You know, my Dear, I never meddle in matters of Death; I always leave those Affairs to you. Women indeed are bitter bad Judges in these cases, for they are so partial to the Brave that they think every Man handsome who is going to the Camp or the Gallows.

AIR III. Cold and Raw, etc.

If any Wench Venus's *Girdle wear,*[24]
Though she be never so ugly;
Lilies and Roses will quickly appear,
And her Face look wondrous smugly.[25]
Beneath the left Ear so fit but a Cord,
(A Rope so charming a Zone is!)[26]
The Youth in his Cart hath the Air of a Lord,
And we cry, There dies an Adonis!

But really, Husband, you should not be too hard-hearted, for you never had a finer, braver set of Men than at present. We have not had a Murder among them all, these seven Months. And truly, my Dear, that is a great Blessing.

PEACH: What a dickens is the Woman always a-whimpering about Murder for? No Gentleman is ever looked upon the worse for killing a Man in his own Defence; and if Business cannot be carried on without it, what would you have a Gentleman do?

MRS. PEACH: If I am in the wrong, my Dear, you must excuse me, for Nobody can help the Frailty of an over-scrupulous Conscience.

PEACH: Murder is as fashionable a Crime as a Man can be guilty of. How many fine Gentlemen have we in *Newgate*[27] every Year, purely upon that Article! If they have wherewithal to persuade the Jury to bring it in Manslaughter, what are they the worse for it? So, my Dear, have done upon this Subject. Was Captain *Macheath* here this Morning, for the Banknotes he left with you last Week?

MRS. PEACH: Yes, my Dear; and though the Bank hath stopped Payment, he was so cheerful and so agreeable! Sure there is not a finer Gentleman upon the Road than the Captain! If he comes from *Bagshot* at any reasonable Hour he hath promised to make one this Evening with *Polly* and me, and *Bob Booty*, at a Party of Quadrille.[28] Pray, my Dear, is the Captain rich?

PEACH: The Captain keeps too good Company ever to grow rich. *Marylebone*[29] and the Chocolate Houses are his undoing. The Man that proposes to get Money by Play should have the Education of a fine Gentleman, and be trained up to it from his Youth.

MRS. PEACH: Really, I am sorry upon *Polly*'s Account the Captain hath not more Discretion. What business hath he to keep Company with Lords and Gentlemen? he should leave them to prey upon one another.

PEACH: Upon *Polly*'s Account! What, a Plague, does the Woman mean?—Upon *Polly*'s Account!

Notes

[24] The girdle or belt, containing all of Venus's charms, is described in *Iliad* 14.214–21.

[25] *Smugly* "neat and spruce" (*Dictionary of the Vulgar Tongue*).

[26] *Zone* belt, band.

[27] *Newgate* a famous prison in London.

[28] *Quadrille* a popular card game resembling bridge.

[29] *Marylebone* a parish in London then known for gambling.

MRS. PEACH: Captain *Macheath* is very fond of the Girl.

PEACH: And what then?

MRS. PEACH: If I have any Skill in the Ways of Women, I am sure *Polly* thinks him a very pretty Man.

PEACH: And what then? You would not be so mad to have the Wench marry him! Gamesters and Highwaymen are generally very good to their Whores, but they are very Devils to their Wives.

MRS. PEACH: But if *Polly* should be in love, how should we help her, or how can she help herself? Poor Girl, I am in the utmost Concern about her.

AIR IV. Why is your faithful Slave disdained? etc.

If Love the Virgin's Heart invade,
How, like a Moth, the simple Maid
Still plays about the Flame!
If soon she be not made a Wife,
Her Honour's singed, and then for Life,
She's—what I dare not name.

PEACH: Look ye, Wife. A handsome Wench in our way of Business is as profitable as the Bar of a *Temple*[30] Coffeehouse, who looks upon it as her Livelihood to grant every Liberty but one. You see I would indulge the Girl as far as prudently we can. In anything, but Marriage! After that, my Dear, how shall we be safe? Are we not then in her Husband's Power? For a Husband hath the absolute Power over all a Wife's Secrets but her own. If the Girl had the Discretion of a Court Lady, who can have a dozen young Fellows at her Ear without complying with one, I should not matter it; but *Polly* is Tinder, and a Spark will at once set her on a Flame. Married! If the Wench does not know her own Profit, sure she knows her own Pleasure better than to make herself a Property![31] My Daughter to me should be, like a Court Lady to a Minister of State, a Key to the whole Gang. Married! If the affair is not already done, I'll terrify her from it, by the Example of our Neighbours.

MRS. PEACH: Mayhap, my Dear, you may injure the Girl. She loves to imitate the fine Ladies, and she may only allow the Captain Liberties in the View of Interest.

PEACH: But 'tis your Duty, my Dear, to warn the Girl against her Ruin, and to instruct her how to make the most of her Beauty. I'll go to her this moment, and sift[32] her. In the meantime, Wife, rip out the Coronets and Marks[33] of these dozen of Cambric Handkerchiefs, for I can dispose of them this Afternoon to a Chap in the City.

SCENE V.

Mrs. Peachum.

Never was a Man more out of the way in an Argument than my Husband! Why must our *Polly*, forsooth, differ from her Sex, and love only her Husband? And why must *Polly*'s Marriage, contrary to all Observation, make her the less followed by

Notes

[30] *Temple* the part of London dominated by legal offices and law schools.

[31] In marriage the woman's property was legally transferred to the husband.

[32] *Sift* question.

[33] *Coronets and Marks* emblems signifying noble ownership and monograms.

other Men? All Men are Thieves in Love, and like a Woman the better for being another's Property.

AIR V. Of all the simple Things we do, etc.

A Maid is like the golden Ore,
Which hath Guineas intrinsical in't
Whose Worth is never known, before
It is tried and impressed in the Mint.[34]
A wife's like a Guinea in Gold,
Stamped with the Name of her Spouse;
Now here, now there; is bought, or is sold;
And is current in every House.

SCENE VI.

Mrs. Peachum, Filch.

MRS. PEACH: Come hither *Filch*. I am as fond of this Child, as though my Mind misgave me he were my own. He hath as fine a Hand at picking a Pocket as a Woman, and is as nimble-fingered as a Juggler. If any unlucky Session does not cut the Rope of thy Life, I pronounce, Boy, thou wilt be a great Man in History. Where was your Post last Night, my Boy?

FILCH: I plied at the Opera, Madam; and considering 'twas neither dark nor rainy, so that there was no great Hurry in getting Chairs and Coaches, made a tolerable hand on't. These seven Handkerchiefs, Madam.

MRS. PEACH: Coloured ones, I see. They are of sure Sale from our Warehouse at *Redriff*[35] among the Seamen.

FILCH: And this Snuffbox.

MRS. PEACH: Set in Gold! A pretty Encouragement this to a young Beginner.

FILCH: I had a fair tug at a charming Gold Watch. Pox take the Tailors for making the Fobs[36] so deep and narrow! It stuck by the way, and I was forced to make my Escape under a Coach. Really, Madam, I fear I shall be cut off in the Flower of my Youth, so that every now and then (since I was pumped[37]) I have thoughts of taking up and going to Sea.

MRS. PEACH: You should go to *Hockley-in-the-Hole,*[38] and to Marylebone, Child, to learn Valour. These are the Schools that have bred so many brave Men. I thought, Boy, by this time, thou hadst lost Fear as well as Shame. Poor Lad! how little does he know as of yet of the *Old Bailey*! For the first Fact I'll insure thee from being hanged; and going to Sea, *Filch* will come time enough upon a Sentence of Transportation. But now, since you have nothing better to do, even go to your Book, and learn your Catechism; for really a Man makes but an ill Figure in the Ordinary's Paper,[39] who

Notes

34 Refined and made into coins.

35 *Redriff* or Rotherhithe, a dock district in east London; Lemuel Gulliver's putative place of residence.

36 *Fobs* small, tight pockets for watches.

37 *pumped* held under a water pump as punishment for theft.

38 *Hockley-in-the-Hole* a part of Clerkenwell, Islington, then known for bear-baiting and other blood sports.

39 *Ordinary's Paper* reports of the Chaplain of Newgate, sometimes including accounts of confession and conversion.

cannot give a satisfactory Answer to his Questions. But, hark you, my Lad. Don't tell me a Lie; for you know I Hate a Liar. Do you know of anything that hath past between Captain *Macheath* and our Polly?

FILCH: I beg you, Madam, don't ask me; for I must either tell a Lie to you or to Miss *Polly*; for I promised her I would not tell.

MRS. PEACH: But when the Honour of our Family is concerned—

FILCH: I shall lead a sad Life with Miss *Polly*, if ever she come to know that I told you. Besides, I would not willingly forfeit my own Honour by betraying anybody.

MRS. PEACH: Yonder comes my Husband and *Polly*. Come, *Filch*, you shall go with me into my own Room, and tell me the whole Story. I'll give thee a Glass of a most delicious Cordial that I keep for my own drinking.

SCENE VII.

Peachum, Polly.

POLLY: I know as well as any of the fine Ladies how to make the most of myself and of my Man too. A Woman knows how to be mercenary, though she hath never been in a Court or at an Assembly. We have it in our Natures, Papa. If I allow Captain *Macheath* some trifling Liberties, I have this Watch and other visible Marks of his Favour to show for it. A Girl who cannot grant some Things, and refuse what is most material, will make but a poor hand of her Beauty, and soon be thrown upon the Common.

AIR VI. What shall I do to show how much I love her, etc.

Virgins are like the fair Flower in its Lustre,
Which in the Garden enamels the Ground;
Near it the Bees in Play flutter and cluster,
And gaudy Butterflies frolic around.
But, when once plucked, 'tis no longer alluring,
To Covent Garden *'tis sent (as yet sweet),*
There fades, and shrinks, and grows past all enduring,
Rots, stinks, and dies, and is trod under feet.

PEACH: You know, *Polly*, I am not against your toying and trifling with a Customer in the way of Business, or to get out a Secret, or so. But if I find out that you have played the fool and are married, you Jade you, I'll cut your Throat, Hussy. Now you know my Mind.

SCENE VIII.

Peachum, Polly, Mrs. *Peachum.*

AIR VII. Oh *London* is a fine Town.

Mrs. Peachum, *in a very great Passion.*

Our Polly *is a sad Slut! nor heeds what we have taught her.*
I wonder any Man alive will ever rear a Daughter!

For she must have both Hoods and Gowns and Hoops[40] *to swell her Pride,*
With Scarfs and Stays,[41] *and Gloves and Lace; and she will have Men beside;*
And when she's dressed with Care and Cost, all-tempting, fine and gay,
As Men should serve a Cucumber, she flings herself away.[42] *Our* Polly *is a sad Slut, etc.*

You Baggage! you Hussy! you inconsiderate Jade! had you been hanged, it would not have vexed me, for that might have been your Misfortune; but to do such a mad thing by Choice! The Wench is married, Husband.

PEACH: Married! The Captain is a bold Man, and will risk anything for Money; to be sure he believes her a Fortune. Do you think your Mother and I should have lived comfortably so long together, if ever we had been married? Baggage!

MRS. PEACH: I knew she was always a proud Slut; and now the Wench hath played the Fool and married, because forsooth she would do like the Gentry. Can you support the Expense of a Husband, Hussy, in gaming, drinking and whoring? have you Money enough to carry on the daily Quarrels of Man and Wife about who shall squander most? There are not many Husbands and Wives, who can bear the Charges of plaguing one another in a handsome way. If you must be married, could you introduce nobody into our Family but a Highwayman? Why, thou foolish Jade, thou wilt be as ill-used, and as much neglected, as if thou hadst married a Lord!

PEACH: Let not your Anger, my Dear, break through the Rules of Decency, for the Captain looks upon himself in the Military Capacity, as a Gentleman by his Profession. Besides what he hath already, I know he is in a fair way of getting, or of dying, and both these ways, let me tell you, are most excellent Chances for a Wife. Tell me, Hussy, are you ruined or no?

MRS. PEACH: With *Polly*'s Fortune, she might very well have gone off to a Person of Distinction. Yes, that you might, you pouting Slut!

PEACH: What, is the Wench dumb? Speak, or I'll make you plead by squeezing out an Answer from you. Are you really bound Wife to him, or are you only upon liking? [Pinches *her.*

POLLY: Oh! [*Screaming.*

MRS. PEACH: How the Mother is to be pitied who hath handsome Daughters! Locks, Bolts, Bars, and Lectures of Morality are nothing to them: They break through them all. They have as much Pleasure in cheating a Father and Mother, as in cheating at Cards.

PEACH: Why, *Polly*, I shall soon know if you are married, by *Macheath*'s keeping from our House.

AIR VIII. Grim King of the Ghosts, etc.

Polly. *Can Love be controlled by Advice?*
Will Cupid *our Mothers obey?*
Though my Heart were as frozen as Ice,
At his Flame 'twould have melted away.

Notes

40 *Hoops* circular structures used to expand skirts and petticoats.

41 *Stays* corsets; girdles.

42 Alludes to the jocular medical prescription that a cucumber should be well dressed, served, and discarded as worthless (Fuller, citing Boswell's *Tour to the Hebrides*, October 5, 1773).

When he kissed me so closely he pressed,
'Twas so sweet that I must have complied:
So I thought it both safest and best
To marry, for fear you should chide.

MRS. PEACH: Then all the Hopes of our Family are gone for ever and ever!

PEACH: And *Macheath* may hang his Father and Mother-in-Law, in hope to get into their Daughter's Fortune.

POLLY: I did not marry him (as 'tis the Fashion) coolly and deliberately for Honour or Money. But, I love him.

MRS. PEACH: Love him! worse and worse! I thought the Girl had been better bred. Oh, Husband, Husband her Folly makes me mad! my Head swims! I'm distracted! I can't support myself—Oh! [*Faints.*

PEACH: See, Wench, to what a Condition you have reduced your poor Mother! a Glass of Cordial, this instant. How the poor Woman takes it to Heart!

[Polly *goes out, and returns with it.*

AH, Hussy, now this is the only Comfort your Mother has left!

POLLY: Give her another Glass, Sir; my Mama drinks double the Quantity whenever she is out of Order. This, you see, fetches her.

MRS. PEACH: The Girl shows such a Readiness, and so much Concern, that I could almost find in my Heart to forgive her.

AIR IX. O *Jenny*, O *Jenny*, where hast thou been.

O Polly, *you might have toyed and kissed.*
By keeping Men off, you keep them on.
Polly. *But he so teased me,*
And he so pleased me,
What I did, you must have done.

MRS. PEACH: Not with a Highwayman.—You sorry Slut!

PEACH: A Word with you, Wife. 'Tis no new thing for a Wench to take Man without consent of Parents. You know 'tis the Frailty of Woman, my Dear.

MRS. PEACH: Yes, indeed, the Sex is frail. But the first time a Woman is frail, she should be somewhat nice[43] methinks, for then or never is the time to make her Fortune. After that, she hath nothing to do but to guard herself from being found out, and she may do what she pleases.

PEACH: Make yourself a little easy; I have a Thought shall soon set all Matters again to rights. Why so melancholy, *Polly*? since what is done cannot be undone, we must all endeavour to make the best of it.

MRS. PEACH: Well, *Polly*; as far as one Woman can forgive another, I forgive thee.—Your Father is too fond of you, Hussy.

POLLY: Then all my Sorrows are at an end.

MRS. PEACH: A mighty likely Speech in troth, for a Wench who is just married!

Notes

[43] *Nice* discriminating.

AIR X. *Thomas*, I cannot, etc.

Polly. *I, like a Ship in Storms, was tossed;*
Yet afraid to put into Land;
For seized in the Port of the Vessel's lost,
Whole Treasure is contraband.
The Waves are laid,
My Duty's paid.
O Joy beyond Expression!
Thus, safe ashore,
I ask no more,
My All is in my possession.

PEACH: I hear Customers in the other Room; Go, talk with 'em, Polly; but come to us again, as soon as they are gone.—But, hark ye, Child, if 'tis the Gentleman who was here Yesterday about the Repeating Watch;[44] say, you believe we can't get Intelligence[45] of it, till tomorrow. For I lent it to *Suky Straddle*, to make a Figure with it tonight at a Tavern in *Drury Lane.*[46] If the other Gentleman calls for the Silver-hilted Sword; you know Beetle-browed[47] *Jemmy* hath it on, and he doth not come from *Tunbridge*[48] till *Tuesday* Night; so that it cannot be had till then.

SCENE IX.

Peachum, *Mrs*. Peachum.

PEACH: Dear Wife, be a little pacified. Don't let your Passion run away with your Senses. *Polly*, I grant you, hath done a rash thing.

MRS. PEACH: If she had had only an Intrigue with the Fellow, why the very best Families have excused and huddled up a Frailty of that sort. 'Tis Marriage, Husband, that makes it a Blemish.

PEACH: But Money, Wife, is the true Fuller's Earth[49] for Reputations, there is not a Spot or a Stain but what it can take out. A rich Rogue nowadays is fit Company for any Gentleman; and the World, my Dear, hath not such a Contempt for Roguery as you imagine. I tell you, Wife, I can make this Match turn to our Advantage.

MRS. PEACH: I am very sensible, Husband, that Captain *Macheath* is worth Money, but I am in doubt whether he hath not two or three Wives already, and then if he should die in a Session or two, *Polly*'s Dower would come into Dispute.

PEACH: That, indeed, is a Point which ought to be considered.

AIR XI. A Soldier and a Sailor.

A Fox may steal your Hens, Sir,
A Whore your Health and Pence, Sir,
Your Daughter rob your Chest, Sir,

Notes

44 *Repeating Watch* a watch with chimes to tell the time in the dark.

45 *Intelligence* news.

46 *Drury Lane* famous for the theater of that name and infamous for prostitution.

47 *Beetle-browed* "Having prominent brows" (Johnson).

48 *Tunbridge* a popular resort town in Kent.

49 *Fuller's Earth* a cleansing agent; to full is cleanse or thicken cloth (*OED*, s.v. *full*, v.3).

Your Wife may steal your Rest, Sir,
A Thief your Goods and Plate.
But this is all but picking,
With Rest, Pence, Chest and Chicken;
It ever was decreed, Sir,
If Lawyer's Hand is feed, Sir,
He steals your whole Estate.

The Lawyers are bitter Enemies to those in our Way. They don't care that Anybody should get a Clandestine Livelihood but themselves.

SCENE X.

Mrs. Peachum, Peachum, Polly.

Polly: 'Twas only Nimming *Ned*. He brought in a Damask Window Curtain, a Hoop Petticoat, a Pair of Silver Candlesticks, a Periwig, and one Silk Stocking, from the Fire that happened last Night.

Peach: There is not a Fellow that is cleverer in his way, and saves more Goods out of the Fire than *Ned*. But now, *Polly*, to your Affair; for Matters must not be left as they are. You are married then, it seems?

Polly: Yes, Sir.

Peach: And how do you propose to live, Child?

Polly: Like other Women, Sir, upon the Industry of my Husband.

Mrs. Peach: What is the Wench turned Fool? A Highwayman's Wife, like a Soldier's, hath as little of his Pay, as of his Company.

Peach: And had not you the common Views of a Gentlewoman in your Marriage, *Polly*?

Polly: I don't know what you mean, Sir.

Peach: Of a Jointure,[50] and of being a Widow.

Polly: But I love him, Sir: how then could I have Thoughts of parting with him?

Peach: Parting with him! Why, that is the whole Scheme and Intention of all Marriage Articles. The comfortable Estate of Widowhood, is the only Hope that keeps up a Wife's Spirits. Where is the Woman who would scruple[51] to be a Wife, if she had it in her Power to be a Widow whenever she pleased? If you have any Views of this sort, *Polly*, I shall think the Match not so very unreasonable.

Polly: How I dread to hear your Advice! Yet I must beg you to explain yourself.

Peach: Secure what he hath got, have him peached the next Sessions, and then at once you are made a rich Widow.

Polly: What, murder the Man I love! The Blood runs cold at my Heart with the very Thought of it.

Peach: Fie, *Polly*! What hath Murder to do in the Affair? Since the thing sooner or later must happen, I dare say, the Captain himself would like that we should get the Reward for his Death sooner than a Stranger. Why, *Polly*, the Captain knows, that as 'tis his Employment to rob so 'tis ours to take Robbers; every Man in his Business. So that there is no Malice in the Case.

Notes

[50] *Jointure* "Estate settled on a wife to be enjoyed after husband's decease" (Johnson)

[51] *scruple* hesitate.

MRS. *PEACH*: Ay, Husband, now you have nicked the Matter.[52] To have him peached is the only thing could ever make me forgive her.

AIR XII. Now ponder well, ye Parents dear.

Polly. *Oh, ponder well! be not severe;*
So save a wretched Wife!
For on the Rope that hangs my Dear
Depends poor Polly's *Life.*

MRS. *PEACH*: But your Duty to your Parents, Hussy, obliges you to hang him. What would many a Wife give for such an Opportunity!

POLLY: What is a Jointure, what is Widowhood to me? I know my Heart. I cannot survive him.

AIR XIII. Le printemps rappelle aux armes.[53]

The Turtle thus with plaintive crying,[54]
Her Lover dying,
The Turtle thus with plaintive crying,
Laments her Dove.
Down she drops quite spent with sighing,
Paired in Death, as paired in Love.

Thus, Sir, it will happen to your poor *Polly*.

MRS. *PEACH*: What, is the Fool in Love in earnest then? I hate thee for being particular:[55] Why, Wench, thou art a Shame to thy very Sex.

POLLY: But hear me, Mother.—If you ever loved—

MRS. *PEACH*: Those cursed Playbooks she reads have been her Ruin. One Word more, Hussy, and I shall knock your Brains out, if you have any.

PEACH: Keep out of the way, Polly, for fear of Mischief, and consider of what is proposed to you.

MRS. *PEACH*: Away, Hussy. Hang your Husband, and be dutiful.

SCENE XI.

Mrs. Peachum, Peachum.

[Polly *listening.*

MRS. *PEACH*: The Thing, Husband, must and shall be done. For the sake of Intelligence[56] we must take other Measures, and have him peached the next Session without her Consent. If she will not know her Duty, we know ours.

PEACH: But really, my Dear, it grieves one's Heart to take off a great Man. When I consider his Personal Bravery, his fine Stratagem,[57] how much we have already got by

Notes

[52] *nicked the Matter* cut to the chase; got to the point.

[53] Spring issues a call to arms.

[54] *Turtle* turtle-dove.

[55] *Particular* peculiar; odd.

[56] *Intelligence* damaging information in Macheath's hands.

[57] *Stratagem* "artifice, cunning" (OED, sense 3).

him, and how much more we may get, methinks I can't find in my Heart to have a Hand in his Death. I wish you could have made *Polly* undertake it.

MRS. *PEACH*: But in a Case of Necessity—our own Lives are in danger.

PEACH: Then, indeed, we must comply with the Customs of the World, and make Gratitude give way to Interest.—He shall be taken off.

MRS. *PEACH*: I'll undertake to manage *Polly*.

PEACH: And I'll prepare Matters for the *Old Bailey*.

SCENE XII.

Polly.

Now I'm a Wretch, indeed.—Methinks I see him already in the Cart,[58] sweeter and more lovely than the Nosegay in his Hand!—I hear the Crowd extolling his Resolution and Intrepidity!—What Volleys of Sighs are sent from the Windows of *Holborn*,[59] that so comely a Youth should be brought to disgrace! I see him at the Tree![60] The whole Circle are in Tears!—even Butchers weep!—*Jack Ketch*[61] himself hesitates to perform his Duty, and would be glad to lose his Fee, by a Reprieve. What then will become of *Polly*!—As yet I may inform him of their Design, and aid him in his Escape.—It shall be so.—But then he flies, absents himself, and I bar myself from his dear dear Conversation! That too will distract me.—If he keep out of the way, my Papa and Mama may in time relent, and we may be happy.—If he stays, he is hanged, and then he is lost for ever!—He intended to lie concealed in my Room, 'till the Dusk of the Evening: If they are abroad, I'll this Instant let him out, lest some Accident should prevent him. [*Exit, and returns.*

SCENE XIII.

Polly, Macheath.

AIR XIV. Pretty Parrot, say—

Mach. *Pretty Polly, say,*
When I was away,
Did your Fancy never stray
To some newer Lover?
Polly. *Without Disguise.*
Heaving Sighs,
Doting Eyes,
My constant Heart discover.
Fondly let me loll!
Mach. *O pretty, pretty* Poll.

Notes

[58] Being carried to the gallows at Tyburn.

[59] *Holborn* a parish in central London on the way from Newgate to Tyburn.

[60] *Tree* gallows.

[61] *Jack Ketch* "An appellation for the common executioner or hangman" (*OED*).

POLLY: And are *you* as fond as ever, my Dear?

MACH: Suspect my Honour, my Courage, suspect anything but my Love.—May my Pistols Misfire, and my Mare flip her Shoulder[62] while I am pursued, if I ever forsake thee!

POLLY: Nay, my Dear, I have no Reason to doubt you, for I find in the Romance you lent me, none of the great Heroes were ever false in Love.

AIR XV. Pray, Fair One, be kind—

Mach. *My Heart was so free,*
It roved like the Bee,
Till Polly *my Passion requited;*
I sipped each Flower,
I changed every Hour,
But here every Flower is united.

POLLY: Were you sentenced to Transportation, sure, my Dear, you could not leave me behind you—could you?

MACH: Is there any Power, any Force that could tear me from thee? You might sooner tear a Pension[63] out of the Hands of a Courtier, a Fee from a Lawyer, a pretty Woman from a Looking-glass, or any Woman from *Quadrille*.—But to tear me from thee is impossible!

AIR XVI. Over the Hills and far away.

Were I laid on Greenland's *Coast,*
And in my Arms embraced my Lass;
Warm amidst eternal Frost,
Too soon the Half Year's Night would pass.
Polly. *Were I sold on* Indian *Soil,*
Soon as the burning Day was closed,
I could mock the sultry Toil,
When on my Charmer's Breast reposed.
Mach. *And I would love you all the Day,*
Polly. *Every Night would kiss and play,*
Mach. *If with me you'd fondly stray*
Polly. *Over the Hills and far away.*

POLLY: Yes, I would go with thee. But oh!—how shall I speak it? I must be torn from thee. We must part.

MACH: How! Part!

POLLY: We must, we must.—My papa and Mama are set against thy Life. They now, even now are in Search after thee. They are preparing Evidence against thee. Thy Life depends upon a Moment.

Notes

62 *Slip her shoulder* go lame in the shoulder due to nerve damage.

63 *Pension* "An allowance given to anyone without an equivalent. In England it is generally understood to mean pay given to a state hireling for treason to his country" (Johnson).

AIR XVII. Gin thou wert mine awn thing—[64]

O what Pain it is to part!
Can I leave thee, can I leave thee?
O what Pain it is to part!
Can thy Polly *ever leave thee?*
But lest Death my Love should thwart,
And bring thee to the fatal Cart,
Thus I tear thee from my bleeding Heart!
Fly hence, and let me leave thee.

One kiss and then—one Kiss—begone—farewell.

MACH: My Hand, my Heart, my Dear, is so riveted to thine, that I cannot unloose my Hold.

POLLY: But my Papa may intercept thee, and then I should lose the very glimmering of Hope. A few Weeks, perhaps, may reconcile us all. Shall thy *Polly* hear from thee?

MACH: Must I then go?

POLLY: And will not Absence change your Love?

MACH: If you doubt it, let me stay—and be hanged.

POLLY: Oh how I fear! how I tremble!—Go—but when Safety will give you leave, you will be sure to see me again; for till then *Polly* is wretched.

AIR XVIII. O the Broom, etc.

[Parting, and looking back at each other with fondness; he at *one Door, she at the other.*

Mach. *The Miser thus a Shilling sees,*
Which he's obliged to pay,
With Sighs resigns it by degrees,
And fears 'tis gone for aye.[65]
Polly. *The Boy, thus, when his Sparrow's flown,*
The Bird in Silence eyes;
But soon as out of Sight 'tis gone,
Whines, whimpers, sobs and cries.

ACT II. SCENE I.

A Tavern near Newgate.

Jemmy Twitcher, *Crook-fingered* Jack, Wat Dreary, Robin *of* Bagshot, Nimming Ned, Henry Padington, Matt *of the* Mint, Ben Budge, *and the rest of the Gang, at the Table, with Wine, Brandy and Tobacco.*

BEN: But prithee, *Matt*, what is become of thy Brother *Tom*? I have not seen him since my Return from Transportation.

Notes

[64] *Gin* Scottish for *if*.

[65] *Aye* Scottish for *ever*.

MATT: Poor Brother *Tom* had an Accident this time Twelve-month, and so clever a made Fellow he was, that I could not save him from those flaying Rascals the Surgeons; and now, poor Man, he is among the Atomies at *Surgeon's Hall.*[66]

BEN: So it seems, his Time was come.

JEM: But the present Time is ours, and Nobody alive hath more. Why are the Laws levelled at us? are we more dishonest than the rest of Mankind? What we win, Gentlemen, is our own by the Law of Arms, and the Right of Conquest.

CROOK: Where shall we find such another Set of practical Philosophers, who to a Man are above the Fear of Death?

WAT: Sound Men, and true!

ROBIN: Of tried Courage, and indefatigable Industry!

NED: Who is there here that would not die for his Friend?

HARRY: Who is there here that would betray him for his Interest?

MAT: Show me a Gang of Courtiers that can say as much.

BEN: We are for a just Partition of the World, for every Man hath a Right to enjoy Life.

MAT: We retrench the Superfluities of Mankind. The World is avaricious, and I hate Avarice. A covetous fellow, like a Jackdaw,[67] steals what he was never made to enjoy, for the sake of hiding it. These are the Robbers of Mankind, for Money was made for the Free-hearted and Generous, and where is the Injury of taking from another, what he hath not the Heart to make use of?

JEM: Our several Stations for the Day are fixed. Good luck attend us all. Fill the Glasses.

AIR XIX. Fill every Glass, etc.

Matt. *Fill every Glass, for Wine inspires us,*
And fires us
With Courage, Love and Joy.
Women and Wine should Life employ.
Is there ought else on Earth desirous?
Chorus. *Fill every Glass, etc.*

SCENE II.

To them enter Macheath.

MACH: Gentlemen, well met. My Heart hath been with you this Hour; but an unexpected Affair hath detained me. No Ceremony, I beg you.

MATT: We were just breaking up to go upon Duty. Am I to have the Honour of taking the Air with you. Sir, this Evening upon the Heath? I drink a Dram now and then with the Stage-Coachmen in the way of Friendship and Intelligence; and I know that about this Time there will be Passengers upon the Western Road, who are worth speaking with.

MACH: I was to have been of that Party—but—

Notes

[66] *atomies* skeletons; Surgeon's Hall or Barber-Surgeons Hall, redesigned by Christopher Wren after the Great Fire of 1666, destroyed in 1740 when the surgeons moved to Royal College. The bodies of executed criminals were sometimes brought there for dissection.

[67] *Jackdaw* a bird in the crow family noted for thievery.

MATT: But what, Sir?

MACH: Is there any man who suspects my Courage?

MATT: We have all been witness of it.

MACH: My Honour and Truth to the Gang?

MATT: I'll be answerable for it.

MACH: In the Division of our Booty, have I ever shown the least Marks of Avarice or Injustice?

MATT: By these Questions something seems to have ruffled you. Are any of us suspected?

MACH: I have a fixed Confidence, Gentlemen, in you all, as Men of Honour, and as such I value and respect you. *Peachum* is a Man that is useful to us.

MATT: Is he about to play us any foul Play? I'll shoot him through the Head.

MACH: I beg you, Gentlemen, act with Conduct and Discretion. A Pistol is your last resort.

MATT: He knows nothing of this Meeting.

MACH: Business cannot go on without him. He is a Man who knows the World, and is a necessary Agent to us. We have had a slight Difference, and till it is accommodated I shall be obliged to keep out of this way. Any private Dispute of mine shall be of no ill consequence to my Friends. You must continue to act under his Direction, for the moment we break loose from him, our Gang is ruined.

MATT: As a Bawd[68] to a Whore, I grant you, he is to us of great Convenience.

MACH: Make him believe I have quitted the Gang, which I can never do but with Life. At our private Quarters I will continue to meet you. A Week or so will probably reconcile us.

MATT: Your Instructions shall be observed. 'Tis now high time for us to repair our several Duties; so till the Evening at our Quarters in *Moorfields* we bid you farewell.

MACH: I shall wish myself with you. Success attend you.

[*Sits down melancholy at the Table.*

AIR XX. March in *Rinaldo*,[69] with Drums and Trumpets.

Matt. *Let us take the Road.*
Hark! I hear the sound of Coaches!
The hour of Attack approaches,
To your Arms, brave Boys, and load.
See the Ball I hold!
Let the Chemists toil like Asses,
Our Fire their Fire surpasses,
And turns all our Lead to Gold.

[The Gang, ranged in the Front of the Stage, load their Pistols, and stick them under their Girdles; then go off singing the first Part in Chorus.

Notes

68 *Bawd* a madam or "female procuress" (*Dictionary of the Vulgar Tongue*).

SCENE III.

Macheath, Drawer.

MACH: What a Fool is a fond Wench! *Polly* is most confoundedly bit.[70]—I love the Sex. And a Man who loves Money, might as well be contented with one Guinea, as I with one Woman. The Town perhaps hath been as much obliged to me, for recruiting it with free-hearted Ladies, as to any Recruiting Officer in the Army. If it were not for us and the other Gentlemen of the Sword, *Drury Lane* would be uninhabited.

AIR XXI. Would you have a Young Virgin, etc.

If the Heart of a Man is depressed with Cares;
The Mist is dispelled when a Woman appears;
Like the Notes of a Fiddle, she sweetly, sweetly
Raises the Spirits, and charms our Ears,
Roses and Lilies her Cheeks disclose,
But her ripe Lips are more sweet than those.
Press her,
Caress her
With Blisses,
Her Kisses
Dissolve us in Pleasure, and soft Repose.

I must have Women. There is nothing unbends the Mind like them. Money is not so strong a Cordial for the Time. Drawer.[71]—[*Enter Drawer.*] Is the Porter gone for all the Ladies, according to my directions?

DRAW: I expect him back every Minute. But you know, Sir, you sent him as far as *Hockley-in-the-Hole*, for three of the Ladies, for one in *Vinegar Yard*, and for the rest of them somewhere about *Lewkner's Lane*.[72] Sure some of them are below, for I hear the Bar Bell. As they come I will show them up. Coming, Coming.

SCENE IV.

Macheath, *Mrs.* Coaxer, Dolly Trull, *Mrs.* Vixen, Betty Doxy,
Jenny Diver, *Mrs.* Slammekin, *Suky* Tawdry, and Molly Brazen.

MACH: Dear Mrs. *Coaxer*, you are welcome. You look charmingly today. I hope you don't want the Repairs of Quality, and lay on Paint.—*Dolly Trull*! kiss me, you Slut; are you amorous as ever, Hussy? You are always so taken up with stealing Hearts, that you don't allow yourself Time to steal anything else.—Ah *Dolly*, thou wilt ever be a Coquette!—Mrs. *Vixen*, I'm yours, I always loved a Woman of Wit and Spirit; they make charming Mistresses, but plaguy Wives.—*Betty Doxy*! Come hither, Hussy. Do you drink as hard as ever? You had better stick to good wholesome Beer; for in troth, *Betty*, Strong-Waters[73] will in time ruin your Constitution. You should leave those to your Betters.—What! and my pretty *Jenny Diver* too! As prim and demure as ever!

Notes

69 *Rinaldo* an opera (1711) by Frederic Handel.
70 *Bit* conned; tricked.
71 *Drawer* bartender.
72 *Vinegar Yard* and *Lewkner's Lane* places near Drury Lane in the red light district.
73 *Strong-Waters* hard liquor.

There is not any Prude, though ever so high bred, hath a more sanctified Look, with a more mischievous Heart. Ah! thou art a dear artful Hypocrite.—Mrs. *Slammekin*! as careless and genteel as ever! all you fine Ladies, who know your own Beauty, affect an Undress.—But see, there's *Suky Tawdry* come to contradict what I was saying. Everything she gets one way she lays out upon her Back. Why, *Suky*, you must keep at least a dozen Tallymen.[74] *Molly Brazen*! [*She kisses him.*] That's well done. I love a free-hearted Wench. Thou hast a most agreeable Assurance, Girl, and art as willing as a Turtle.—But hark! I hear music. The Harper is at the Door. *If Music be the Food of Love, play on.* Ere you seat yourselves, Ladies, what think you of a Dance? Come in. [*Enter Harper.*] Play the *French* Tune, that Mrs. *Slammekin* was so fond of.

[*A Dance à la ronde in the* French *Manner;*[75] *near the End of it this Song and Chorus.*

AIR XXII. Cotillion.

Youth's the Season made for Joys,
Love is then our Duty,
She alone who that employs,
Well deserves her Beauty.
Let's be gay,
While we may,
Beauty's a Flower, despised in decay.
Youth's the Season etc.
Let us drink and sport today,
Ours is not tomorrow.
Love with Youth flies swift away,
Age is naught but Sorrow.
Dance and sing,
Time's on the Wing,
Life never knows the return of Spring.
Chorus. *Let us drink etc.*

MACH: Now pray Ladies, take your Places. Here Fellow. [*Pays the Harper.*] Bid the Drawer bring us more Wine. [*Ex. Harper.*] If any of the Ladies choose Gin, I Hope they will be so free to call for it.

JENNY: You look as if you meant me. Wine is strong enough for me. Indeed, Sir, I never drink Strong-Waters, but when I have the Colic.

MACH: Just the Excuse of the fine Ladies! Why, a Lady of Quality is never without the Colic. I hope, Mrs. *Coaxer*, you have had a good Success of late in your Visits among the Mercers.[76]

COAX: We have so many Interlopers—Yet with Industry, one may still have a little Picking. I carried a silver-flowered Lutestring,[77] and a Piece of black Padesoy[78] to Mr. *Peachum*'s Lock but last Week.

Notes

[74] *Tallymen* "Brokers that let out clothes to the women of the town" (*Dictionary of the Vulgar Tongue*).

[75] *A Dance à la ronde in the* French *Manner* a formal dance involving several participants forming a circle.

[76] *Mercer* a dealer in fine fabrics.

[77] *Lutestring* glossy kind of silk or a dress or ribbon made with this material.

[78] *Padesoy* rich, silky fabric, usually embossed, or a garment of this material.

VIX: There's *Molly Brazen* hath the Ogle[79] of a Rattlesnake. She riveted a Linen-draper's Eye so fast upon her, that he was nicked of three Pieces of Cambric[80] before he could look off.

BRAZ: Oh dear Madam!—But sure nothing can come up to your handling of Laces! And then you have such a sweet deluding Tongue! To cheat a Man is nothing; but the Woman must have fine Parts indeed who cheats a Woman!

VIX: Lace, Madam, lies in a small Compass, and is of easy Conveyance. But you are apt, Madam, to think too well of your Friends.

COAX: If any Woman hath more Art than another, to be sure, 'tis *Jenny Diver*. Though her Fellow be never so agreeable, she can pick his Pocket as coolly, as if Money were her only Pleasure. Now that is a Command of the Passions uncommon in a Woman!

JENNY: I never go to the Tavern with a Man, but in the View of Business. I have other Hours, and other sort of Men for my Pleasure. But had I your Address, Madam—

MACH: Have done with your Compliments, Ladies; and drink about: You are not so fond of me, *Jenny*, as you use to be.

JENNY: 'Tis not convenient, Sir, to show my Fondness among so many Rivals. 'Tis your own Choice, and not the warmth of my Inclination that will determine you.

AIR XXIII. All in a misty Morning, etc.

Before the Barn-door crowing,
The Cock by Hens attended,
His Eyes around him throwing,
Stands for a while suspended.
Then One he singles from the Crew,
And cheers the happy Hen;
With how do you do, and how do you do,
And how do you do again.

MACH: Ah *Jenny*! thou art a dear Slut.

TRULL: Pray, Madam, were you ever in keeping?

TAWD: I hope, Madam, I haven't been so long upon the Town, but I have met with some good Fortune as well as my Neighbours.

TRULL: Pardon me, Madam, I meant no harm by the Question; 'twas only in the way of Conversation.

TAWD: Indeed, Madam, if I had not been a Fool, I might have lived very handsomely with my last Friend. But upon his missing five Guineas, he turned me off. Now I never suspected he had counted them.

SLAM: Who do you look upon, Madam, as your best sort of Keepers?

TRULL: That, Madam, is thereafter as they be.

SLAM: I, Madam, was once kept by a *Jew*; and bating their religion, to Women they are a good sort of People.

TAWD: Now for my part, I own I like an old Fellow: for we always make them pay for what they can't do.

VIX: A spruce Prentice, let me tell you, Ladies, is no ill thing, they bleed freely.[81] I have sent at least two or three dozen of them in my time to the Plantations.

Notes

79 *Ogle* lecherous stare.

80 *Cambric* lightweight fabric of linen or cotton.

81 *bleed freely* spend money liberally.

JEN: But to be sure, Sir, with so much good Fortune as you have had upon the Road, you must be grown immensely rich.
MACH: The Road, indeed, hath done me justice, but the Gaming-Table hath been my ruin.

AIR XXIV. When once I lay with another Man's Wife, etc.

Jen. *The Gamesters and Lawyers are Jugglers alike,*
If they meddle your All is in danger.
Like Gypsies, if once they can finger a Souse,
Your Pockets they pick, and they pilfer your House,
And give your Estate to a Stranger.

A Man of Courage should never put Anything to the Risk, but his Life. These are the Tools of a Man of Honour. Cards and Dice are only fit for cowardly Cheats, who prey upon their Friends.

[*She takes up his Pistol.* Tawdry *takes up the other.*

TAWD: This, Sir, is fitter for your Hand. Besides your Loss of Money, 'tis a Loss to the Ladies. Gaming takes you off from Women. How fond could I be of you! but before Company, 'tis ill bred.
MACH: Wanton Hussies!
JEN: I must and will have a Kiss to give my Wine a zest.

[*They take him about the Neck, and make Signs to* Peachum *and Constables, who rush in upon him.*

SCENE V.

To them, Peachum *and Constables.*

PEACH: I seize you, Sir, as my Prisoner.
MACH: Was this well done, *Jenny*?—Women are Decoy Ducks; who can trust them! Beasts, Jades, Jilts, Harpies, Furies, Whores!
PEACH: Your Case, Mr. *Macheath*, is not particular. The greatest Heroes have been ruined by Women. But, to do them justice, I must own they are a pretty sort of Creatures, if we could trust them. You must now, Sir, take your leave of the Ladies, and if they have a Mind to make you a Visit, they will be sure to find you at home. The Gentleman, Ladies, lodges in *Newgate*. Constables, wait upon the Captain to his Lodgings.

AIR XXV. When first I laid Siege to my *Cloris*, etc.

Mac. *At the Tree I shall suffer with pleasure,*
At the Tree I shall suffer with pleasure,
Let me go where I will,
In all kinds of Ill,
I shall find no such Furies as these are.

PEACH: Ladies, I'll take care the Reckoning shall be discharged.

[*Ex.* Macheath, *guarded with* Peachum *and Constables.*

SCENE VI.

The Women remain.

VIX: Look ye, Mrs. *Jenny*, though Mr. *Peachum* may have made a private Bargain with you and *Suky Tawdry* for betraying the Captain, as we were all assisting, we ought all to share alike.

COAX: I think Mr. *Peachum*, after so long an acquaintance, might have trusted me as well as *Jenny Diver*.

SLAM: I am sure at least three Men of his hanging, and in a Year's time too (if he did me justice) should be set down to my account.

TRULL: Mrs. *Slammekin*, that is not fair. For you know one of them was taken in Bed with me.

JENNY: As far as a Bowl of Punch or a Treat, I believe Mrs. *Suky* will join with me.—As for anything else, Ladies, you cannot in conscience expect it.

SLAM: Dear Madam—

TRULL: I would not for the World—

SLAM: 'Tis impossible for me—

TRULL: As I hope to be saved, Madam—

SLAM: Nay, then I must stay here all Night—

TRULL: Since you command me. [*Exeunt with great Ceremony.*

SCENE VII. *Newgate.*

Lockit, Turnkeys, Macheath, Constables.

LOCK: Noble Captain, you are welcome. You have not been a Lodger of mine this Year and half. You know the custom, Sir. Garnish, Captain, Garnish.[82] Hand me down those Fetters there.

MACH: Those, Mr. *Lockit*, seem to be the heaviest of the whole set. With your leave, I should like the further pair better.

LOCK: Look ye, Captain, we know what is fittest for our Prisoners. When a Gentleman uses me with Civility, I always do the best I can to please him.—Hand them down I say.—We have them of all Prices, from one Guinea to ten, and 'tis fitting every Gentleman should please himself.

MACH: I understand you, Sir. [*Gives Money.*] The Fees here are so many, and so exorbitant, that few Fortunes can bear the Expense of getting off handsomely, or of dying like a Gentleman.

LOCK: Those, I see, will fit the Captain better.—Take down the further Pair. Do but examine them, Sir.—Never was better work.—How gently they are made!—They will fit as easy as a Glove, and the nicest Man in *England* might not be ashamed to wear them. [*He puts on the Chains.*] If I had the best Gentleman in the Land in my Custody I could not equip him more handsomely. And so, Sir—I now leave you to your private Mediations.

Notes

[82] *Garnish* the money that prisoners had to pay their jailers.

SCENE VIII.

Macheath.

AIR XXVI. Courtiers, Courtiers think it no harm, etc.

Man may escape from Rope and Gun;
Nay, some have outlived the Doctor's Pill;
Who takes a Woman must be undone,
That Basilisk is sure to kill.[83]
The Fly that sips Treacle is lost in the Sweets,
So he that tastes Woman, Woman, Woman,
He that tastes Woman, Ruin meets.

To what a woeful plight have I brought myself! Here must I (all day long, till I am hanged) be confined to hear the Reproaches of a Wench who lays her Ruin at my Door.—I am in the Custody of her Father, and to be sure if he knows of the matter, I shall have a fine time on't betwixt this and my Execution.—But I promised the Wench Marriage.—What signifies a Promise to a Woman? Does not Man in Marriage itself promise a hundred things that he never means to perform? Do all we can, Women will believe us; for they look upon a Promise as an Excuse for following their own Inclinations.—But here comes *Lucy*, and I cannot get from her—Would I were deaf!

SCENE IX.

Macheath, Lucy.

LUCY: You Base Man you,—how can you look me in the Face after what hath passed between us?—See here, perfidious Wretch, how I am forced to bear about the load of Infamy you have laid upon me—O *Macheath*! thou hast robbed me of my Quiet—to see thee tortured would give me pleasure.

AIR XXVII. A lovely Lass to a Friar came, etc.

Thus when a good Housewife sees a Rat
In her Trap in the Morning taken,
With pleasure her Heart goes pit a pat,
In Revenge for her loss of Bacon.
Then she throws him
To the Dog or Cat,
To be worried, crushed and shaken.

MAC: Have you no Bowels, no Tenderness, my dear *Lucy*, to see a Husband in these Circumstances?
LUCY: A Husband!

Notes

[83] *Basilisk* a mythical reptile whose gaze was fatal.

MAC: In every respect but the Form, and that, my Dear, may be said over us at any time.—Friends should not insist upon Ceremonies. From a Man of Honour, his Word is as good as his Bond.

LUCY: 'Tis the Pleasure of all you fine Men to insult the Women you have ruined.

AIR XXVIII. 'Twas when the Sea was roaring, etc.

How cruel are the Traitors,
Who lie and swear in jest,
To cheat unguarded Creatures
Of Virtue, Fame, and Rest!
Whoever steals a Shilling,
Through Shame the Guilt conceals:
In Love the perjured Villain
With Boasts the Theft reveals.

MAC: The very first Opportunity, my Dear, (have but Patience) you shall be my Wife in whatever manner you please.

LUCY: Insinuating Monster! And so you think I know nothing of the Affair of Miss *Polly Peachum.*—I could tear thy Eyes out!

MAC: Sure *Lucy*, you can't be such a Fool as to be jealous of *Polly*!

LUCY: Are you not married to her, you Brute, you?

MAC: Married! Very good. The Wench gives it out only to vex thee, and to ruin me in thy good Opinion. 'Tis true, I go to the House; I chat with the Girl, I kiss her, I say a thousand things to her (as all Gentlemen do) that mean nothing, to divert myself; and now the silly Jade hath set it about that I am married to her, to let me know what she would be at. Indeed, my dear *Lucy*, these violent Passions may be of ill consequence to a Woman in your condition.

LUCY: Come, come, Captain, for all your Assurance, you know that Miss *Polly* hath put it out of your power to do me the Justice you promised me.

MAC: A jealous Woman believes everything her Passion suggests. To convince you of my Sincerity, if we can find the Ordinary, I shall have no Scruples of making you my Wife; and I know the consequence of having two at a time.

LUCY: That you are only to be hanged, and so get rid of them both.

MAC: I am ready, my dear *Lucy*, to give you satisfaction—if you think there is any in Marriage.—What can a Man of Honour say more?

LUCY: So then it seems, you are not married to Miss *Polly*.

MAC: You know, *Lucy*, the Girl is prodigiously conceited. No man can say a civil thing to her, but (like other fine Ladies) her Vanity makes her think he's her own for ever and ever.

AIR XXIX. The Sun had loosed his weary Teams, etc.[84]

The first time at the Looking-glass
The Mother sets her Daughter,
The Image Strikes the Smiling Lass
With Self-love ever after

Notes

[84] *Weary teams* Apollo, the god of the Sun, was described as driving a team of horses across the sky to light the day.

Each time she looks, she fonder grown,
Thinks every Charm grows stronger.
But alas, vain Maid, all Eyes but your own
Can see you are not younger.

When Women consider their own Beauties, they are all alike unreasonable in their demands; for they expect their Lovers should like them as long as they like themselves.

LUCY: Yonder is my Father—perhaps this way we may light upon the Ordinary, who shall try if you will be as good as your Word.—For I long to be made an honest Woman.

SCENE X.

Peachum, Lockit *with an Account Book.*

LOCK: In this last Affair, Brother *Peachum*, we are agreed. You have consented to go halves in *Macheath*.

PEACH: We shall never fall out about an Execution.—But as to that Article, pray how stands our last Year's account?

LOCK: If you will run your Eye over it, you'll find 'tis fair and clearly stated.

PEACH: This long Arrear[85] of the Government is very hard upon us! Can it be expected that we should hang our Acquaintance for nothing, when our Betters will hardly save theirs without being paid for it. Unless the People in employment pay better, I promise them for the future, I shall let other Rogues live besides their own.

LOCK: Perhaps, Brother, they are afraid these matters may be carried too far. We are treated too by them with Contempt, as if our Profession were not reputable.

PEACH: In one respect indeed, our Employment may be reckoned dishonest, because, like Great Statesmen, we encourage those who betray their Friends.

LOCK: Such Language, Brother, anywhere else, might turn to your prejudice. Learn to be more guarded, I beg you.

AIR XXX. How happy are we, etc.

When you censure the Age,
Be cautious and sage,
Lest the Courtiers offended should be:
If you mention Vice or Bribe,
'Tis so pat to all the Tribe;
Each cries—That was levelled at me.

PEACH: Here's poor *Ned Clincher*'s[86] Name, I see. Sure, Brother *Lockit*, there was a little unfair proceeding in *Ned*'s case: for he told me in the Condemned Hold, that for Value received, you had promised him a Session or two longer without Molestation.

LOCK: Mr. *Peachum*, This is the first time my Honour was ever called in Question.

PEACH: Business is at an end—if once we act dishonourably.

LOCK: Who accuses me?

Notes

[85] *Arrear* delay in payment of the £40 bounty.

[86] *Clincher* one who makes clinches—puns or other kinds of word-play.

Peach: You are warm, Brother.

Lock: He that attacks my Honour, attacks my Livelihood.—And this Usage—Sir—is not to be borne.

Peach: Since you provoke me to speak—I must tell you too, that Mrs. *Coaxer* charges you with defrauding her of her Information-Money, for the apprehending of curl-pated *Hugh*. Indeed, indeed, Brother, we must punctually pay our Spies, or we shall have no Information.

Lock: Is this Language to me, Sirrah—who have saved you from the Gallows, Sirrah!

[*Collaring each other.*

Peach: If I am hanged, it shall be for ridding the World of an arrant Rascal.

Lock: This Hand shall do the office of the Halter you deserve, and throttle you—you Dog!—

Peach: Brother, Brother,—We are both in the Wrong—We shall be both Losers in the Dispute—for you know we have it in our Power to hang each other. You should not be so passionate.

Lock: Nor you so provoking.

Peach: 'Tis our mutual Interest; 'tis for the Interest of the World we should agree. If I said anything, Brother, to the Prejudice of your Character, I ask pardon.

Lock: Brother *Peachum*—I can forgive as well as resent.—Give me your Hand. Suspicion does not become a Friend.

Peach: I only meant to give you occasion to justify yourself: But I must now step home, for I expect the Gentleman about this Snuffbox, that *Filch* nimmed two Nights ago in the Park. I appointed him at this hour.

SCENE XI.

Lockit, Lucy.

Lock: Whence come you, Hussy?

Lucy: My Tears might answer that Question.

Lock: You have then been whimpering and fondling, like a Spaniel, over the Fellow that hath abused you.

Lucy: One can't help Love; one can't cure it. 'Tis not in my Power to obey you, and hate him.

Lock: Learn to bear your Husband's Death like a reasonable Woman. 'Tis not the fashion, nowadays, so much as to affect Sorrow upon these Occasions. No Woman would ever marry, if she had not the Chance of Mortality for a Release. Act like a Woman of Spirit, Hussy, and thank your Father for what he is doing.

AIR XXXI. Of a noble Race was *Shenkin.*[87]

Lucy. *Is then his Fate decreed, Sir?*
Such a Man can I think of quitting?
When first we met, so moves me yet,
O see how my Heart is splitting!

Lock: Look ye, *Lucy*—There is no saving him.—So, I think, you must even do like other Widows—Buy yourself Weeds,[88] and be cheerful.

Notes

[87] *Shenkin* a Welsh hero.

[88] *Weeds* mourning clothes.

AIR XXXII.

You'll think ere many Days ensue
This Sentence not severe;
I hang your Husband, Child, 'tis true,
But with him hang your Care.
Twang dang dillo dee.

Like a good Wife, go moan over your dying Husband. That, Child, is your Duty—Consider, Girl, you can't have the Man and the Money too—so make yourself as easy as you can by getting all you can from him.

SCENE XII.

Lucy, Macheath.

Lucy: Though the Ordinary was out of the way today, I hope, my Dear, you will, upon the first opportunity, quiet my Scruples—Oh Sir!—my Father's hard Heart is not to be softened, and I am in the utmost Despair.

Mac: But if I could raise a small Sum—Would not twenty Guineas, think you, move him?—Of all the Arguments in the way of Business, the Perquisite[89] is the most prevailing.—Your Father's Perquisites for the Escape of Prisoners must amount to a considerable Sum in the Year. Money well timed, and properly applied, will do anything.

AIR XXXIII. *London* Ladies.

If you at an Office solicit your Due,
And would not have Matters neglected;
You must quicken the Clerk with the Perquisite too,
To do what his Duty directed.
Or would you the Frowns of a Lady prevent,
She too has this palpable Failing,
The Perquisite softens her into Consent;
That Reason with all is prevailing.

Lucy: What Love or Money can do shall be done: for all my Comfort depends upon your Safety.

SCENE XIII.

Lucy, Macheath, Polly.

Polly: Where is my dear Husband?—Was a Rope ever intended for this Neck!—O let me throw my Arms about it, and throttle thee with Love!—Why dost thou turn away from me?—'Tis thy *Polly*—'Tis thy Wife.

Mac: Was ever such an unfortunate Rascal as I am!

Lucy: Was there ever such another Villain!

Notes

[89] *Perquisite* gratuity.

Polly: O *Macheath*! was it for this we parted? Taken! Imprisoned! Tried! Hanged!—cruel Reflection! I'll stay with thee till Death—no Force shall tear thy dear Wife from thee now.—What means my Love?—Not one kind Word! not one kind Look! think what thy *Polly* suffers to see thee in this Condition.

AIR XXXIV. All in the Downs, etc.

Thus when the Swallow, seeking Prey,
Within the Sash is closely pent,
His Comfort, with bemoaning Lay,
Without sits pining for th' Event.
Her chattering Lovers all around her skim;
She heeds them not (poor Bird!*) her Soul's with him.*

Mac: I must disown her. [*Aside.*] The Wench is distracted.

Lucy: Am I then bilked of my Virtue? Can I have no Reparation? Sure Men were born to lie, and Women to believe them! O Villain! Villain!

Polly: Am I not thy Wife?—Thy Neglect of me, thy Aversion to me too severely proves it.—Look on me.—Tell me, am I not thy Wife?

Lucy: Perfidious Wretch!

Polly: Barbarous Husband!

Lucy: Hadst thou been hanged five Months ago, I had been happy.

Polly: And I too—If you had been kind to me till Death, it would not have vexed me—And that's no very unreasonable Request, (though from a Wife) to a Man who hath not above seven or eight Days to live.

Lucy: Art thou then married to another? Hast thou two Wives, Monster?

Mac: If Women's Tongues can cease for an Answer—hear me.

Lucy: I won't.—Flesh and Blood can't bear my Usage.

Polly: Shall I not claim my own? Justice bids me speak.

AIR XXXV. Have you heard of a frolicsome Ditty, etc.

Mac. How happy could I be with either,
Were t'other dear Charmer away!
But while you thus tease me together,
To neither a Word will I say;
But tol de rol, etc.

Polly: Sure, my Dear, there ought to be some Preference shown to a Wife! At least she may claim the Appearance of it. He must be distracted with his Misfortunes, or he could not use me thus!

Lucy: O Villain, Villain! thou hast deceived me—I could even inform against thee with Pleasure. Not a Prude wishes more heartily to have Facts against her intimate Acquaintance, than I now wish to have Facts against thee. I would have her Satisfaction, and they should all out.

AIR XXXVI. Irish Trot.

Polly. *I'm bubbled.*[90]
Lucy. *I'm bubbled.*
Polly. *Oh how I am troubled!*

Notes

[90] *Bubbled* cheated.

Lucy. *Bamboozled, and bit!*
Polly. *My differences are doubled.*
Lucy. *When you come to the Tree, should the Hangman refuse*
These Fingers, with Pleasure, could fasten the Noose.
Polly. *I'm bubbled, etc.*

MAC: Be pacified, my dear Lucy—This is all a Fetch[91] of *Polly*'s, to make me desperate with you in case I get off. If I am hanged, she would fain have the Credit of being thought my Widow—Really, Polly, this is no time for a Dispute of this sort; for whenever you are talking of Marriage, I am thinking of Hanging.

POLLY: And hast thou the Heart to persist in disowning me?

MAC: And hast thou the Heart to persist in persuading me that I am married? Why, *Polly*, dost thou seek to aggravate my Misfortunes?

LUCY: Really, Miss *Peachum*, you but expose yourself. Besides, 'tis barbarous in you to worry a Gentleman in his Circumstances.

AIR XXXVII.

Polly. *Cease your Funning;*
Force or Cunning
Never shall my heart trapan[92].
All these Sallies
Are but Malice
To seduce my constant Man.
'Tis most certain,
By their flirting
Women oft have Envy shown:
Pleased, to ruin
Others' wooing;
Never happy in their own!

POLLY: Decency, Madam, methinks might teach you to behave yourself with some Reserve with the Husband, while his Wife is present.

MAC: But seriously, *Polly*, this is carrying the Joke a little too far.

LUCY: If you are determined, Madam, to raise a Disturbance in the Prison, I shall be obliged to send for the Turnkey to show you the Door. I am sorry, Madam, you force me to be so ill-bred.

POLLY: Give me leave to tell you, Madam; These forward Airs don't become you in the least, Madam. And my Duty, Madam, obliges me to stay with my Husband, Madam.

AIR XXXVIII. Good-morrow, Gossip *Joan.*

Lucy. *Why how now, Madam* Flirt?
If you thus must chatter;
And are for flinging Dirt,
Let's try who best can spatter;
Madam Flirt!

Notes

[91] *Fetch* contrivance.

[92] *Trapan* beguile.

Polly. *Why how now, saucy Jade;*
Sure the Wench is Tipsy!
How can you see me made [To him.
The Scoff of such a Gipsy?
Saucy Jade! [To her.

SCENE XIV.

Lucy, Macheath, Polly, Peachum.

PEACH: Where's my Wench? Ah Hussy! Hussy!—Come you home, you Slut; and when your Fellow is hanged, hang yourself, to make your Family some amends.

POLLY: Dear, dear Father, do not tear me from him—I must speak; I have more to say to him—Oh! twist thy Fetters about me, that he may not haul me from thee!

PEACH: Sure all Women are alike! If ever they commit the Folly, they are sure to commit another by exposing themselves—Away—Not a Word more—You are my Prisoner now Hussy.

AIR XXXIX. *Irish* Howl.

Polly. *No Power on Earth can e'er divide,*
The Knot that Sacred Love hath tied.
When Parents draw against our Mind,
The True-love's Knot they faster bind.
Oh, oh ray, oh Amborah—oh, oh, etc.

[Holding *Macheath*, *Peachum* pulling her.

SCENE XV.

Lucy, Macheath.

MAC: I am naturally compassionate, Wife; so that I could not use the Wench as she deserved; which made you at first suspect there was something in what she said.

LUCY: Indeed, my Dear, I was strangely puzzled.

MAC: If that had been the Case, her Father would never have brought me into this Circumstance—No, *Lucy*,—I had rather die than be false to thee.

LUCY: How happy am I, if you say this from your Heart! For I love thee so, that I could sooner bear to see thee hanged than in the Arms of another.

MAC: But couldst thou bear to see me hanged?

LUCY: O *Macheath*, I can never live to see that Day.

MAC: You see, *Lucy*; in the Account of Love you are in my debt, and you must now be convinced, that I rather choose to die than be another's.—Make me, if possible, love thee more, and let me owe my Life to thee—If you refuse to assist me, *Peachum* and your Father will immediately put me beyond all means of Escape.

LUCY: My Father, I know, hath been drinking hard with the Prisoners: and I fancy he is now taking his Nap in his own Room—If I can procure the Keys, shall I go off with thee, my Dear?

MAC: If we are together, 'twill be impossible to lie concealed. As soon as the Search begins to be a little cool, I will send to thee—Till then my Heart is thy Prisoner.

LUCY: Come then, my dear Husband—owe thy Life to me—and though you love me not—be grateful—But that *Polly* runs in my Head strangely.

MAC: A Moment of time may make us unhappy for ever.

AIR XL. The lass of *Patie*'s Mill, etc.

Lucy. *I like the Fox shall grieve,*
Whose Mate hath left her side,
Whom Hounds, from Morn to Eve,
Chase o'er the Country wide.
Where can my Lover hide?
Where cheat the wary Pack?
If Love be not his Guide,
He never will come back!

ACT III. SCENE. I.

SCENE *Newgate.*

LOCK: To be sure, Wench, you must have been aiding and abetting to help him to this Escape.

LUCY: Sir, here hath been *Peachum* and his Daughter *Polly*, and to be sure they know the Ways of *Newgate* as well as if they had been born and bred in the Place all their Lives. Why must all your Suspicion light upon me?

LOCK: *Lucy*, *Lucy*, I will have none of these shuffling Answers.

LUCY: Well then—If I know Anything of him I wish I may be burnt!

LOCK: Keep your Temper, *Lucy*, or I shall pronounce you guilty.

LUCY: Keep yours, Sir,—I do wish I may be burnt. I do—And what can I say more to convince you?

LOCK: Did he tip handsomely?—How much did he come down with? Come, Hussy, don't cheat your Father; and I shall not be angry with you—Perhaps you have made a better Bargain with him than I could have done—How much, my good Girl?

LUCY: You know, Sir, I am fond of him, and would have given Money to have kept him with me.

LOCK: Ah *Lucy*! thy Education might have put thee more upon thy Guard; for a Girl in the Bar of an Alehouse is always besieged.

LUCY: Dear Sir, mention not my Education—for 'twas to that I owe my Ruin.

AIR XLI. If Love's a sweet Passion, etc.

When young at the Bar you first taught me to score,
And bid me be free of my Lips, and no more;
I was kissed by the Parson, the Squire, and the Sot.
When the Guest was departed, the Kiss was forgot.
But his Kiss was so sweet, and so closely he pressed,
That I languished and pined till I granted the rest.

If you can forgive me, Sir, I will make a fair Confession, for to be sure he hath been a most barbarous Villain to me.

Lock. And so you have let him escape, Hussy—Have you?

Lucy: When a Woman loves; a kind Look, a tender Word can persuade her to anything—And I could ask no other Bribe.

Lock: Thou wilt always be a vulgar Slut, *Lucy*—If you would not be looked upon as a Fool, you should never do anything but upon the Foot of Interest. Those that act otherwise are their own Bubbles.

Lucy: But Love, Sir, is a Misfortune that may happen to the most discreet Woman, and in Love we are all Fools alike—Notwithstanding all he swore, I am now fully convinced that *Polly Peachum* is actually his Wife.—Did I let him escape (Fool that I was!) to go to her?—*Polly* will wheedle herself into his Money, and then *Peachum* will hang him, and cheat us both.

Lock: So I am to be ruined, because, forsooth, you must be in Love!—a very pretty Excuse!

Lucy: I could murder that impudent happy Strumpet:—I gave him his Life, and that Creature enjoys the Sweets of it.—Ungrateful *Macheath*!

AIR XLII. *South-Sea* Ballad.

My Love is all Madness and Folly,
Alone I lie,
Toss, tumble, and cry,
What a happy Creature is Polly!
Was e'er such a Wretch as I!
With Rage I redden like Scarlet,
That my dear inconstant Varlet,
Stark blind to my Charms,
Is lost in the Arms
Of that Jilt, that inveigling Harlot!
Stark blind to my Charms,
Is lost in the Arms
Of that Jilt, that inveigling Harlot!
This, this my Resentment alarms.

Lock: And so, after all this Mischief, I must stay here to be entertained with your caterwauling, Mistress Puss!—Out of my Sight, wanton Strumpet! you shall fast and mortify yourself into Reason, with now and then a little handsome Discipline to bring you to your Senses.—Go.

SCENE II.

Lockit.

Peachum then intends to outwit me in this Affair; but I'll be even with him.—The Dog is leaky in his Liquor, so I'll ply him that way, get the Secret from him, and turn this Affair to my own Advantage.—Lions, Wolves, and Vultures don't live together in Herds, Droves, or Flocks.—Of all Animals of Prey, Man is the only sociable one. Every one of us preys upon his Neighbour, and yet we herd together.—*Peachum* is my Companion, my Friend—According to the Custom of the World, indeed, he may quote thousands of Precedents for cheating me—And shall I not make use of the Privilege of Friendship to make him a Return?

AIR XLIII. *Packington's* Pound.

Thus Gamesters united in Friendship are found,
Though they know that their Industry all is a Cheat;
They flock to their Prey at the Dice-Box's Sound,
And join to promote one another's Deceit.
But if by mishap,
They fail of a Chap,[93]
To keep in their Hands, they each other entrap.
Like Pikes, lank with Hunger, who miss of their Ends,[94]
They bite their Companions, and prey on their Friends.

Now, *Peachum,* you and I, like honest Tradesmen, are to have a fair Trial which of us two can overreach the other.—*Lucy.*—[*Enter* Lucy.] Are there any of *Peachum*'s People now in the House?

LUCY: *Filch,* Sir, is drinking a Quartern[95] of Strong-Waters in the next Room with Black *Moll.*

LOCK: Bid him come to me.

SCENE III.

Lockit, Filch.

LOCK: Why, Boy, thou lookest as if thou wert half starved; like a shotten Herring.[96]

FILCH: One had need have the Constitution of a Horse to go through the Business.—Since the favourite Child-getter was disabled by a Mishap, I have picked up a little Money by helping the Ladies to a Pregnancy against their being called down to Sentence.—But if a Man cannot get an honest Livelihood any easier way, I am sure, 'tis what I can't undertake for another Session.

LOCK: Truly, if that great Man should tip off, 'twould be an irreparable Loss. The Vigour and Prowess of a Knight-Errant never saved half the Ladies in Distress that he hath done.—But, Boy, canst thou tell me where thy Master is to be found?

FILCH: At his Lock, Sir, at the *Crooked Billet.*

LOCK: Very well.—I have nothing more with you. [*Ex.* Filch.] I'll go to him there, for I have many important Affairs to settle with him; and in the way of those Transactions, I'll artfully get into his Secret.—So that *Macheath* shall not remain a Day longer out of my Clutches.

SCENE IV. *A Gaming-House.*

Macheath *in a fine tarnished coat,* Ben Budge, Matt *of the Mint.*

MAC: I am sorry, Gentlemen, the Road was so barren of Money. When my Friends are in Difficulties, I am always glad that my Fortune can be serviceable to them. [*Gives them Money.*] You see, Gentlemen, I am not a mere Court Friend, who professes everything and will do nothing.

Notes

[93] *Chap* buyer; a mark in their hustle.
[94] *Pike* a predatory fish notorious for cannibalism.
[95] *Quartern* a quarter of a pint.
[96] *Shotten herring* a fish that has spawned; worn out; emaciated.

AIR XLIV. Lillibullero.

The Modes of the Court so common are grown,
That a true Friend can hardly be met;
Friendship for Interest is but a Loan,
Which they let out for what they can get.
'Tis true, you find
Some Friends so kind,
Who will give you good Counsel themselves to defend.
In Sorrowful Ditty,
They promise, they pity,
But shift you for Money, from Friend to Friend.

But we, Gentlemen, have still Honour enough to break through the Corruptions of the World.—And while I can serve you, you may command me.

BEN: It grieves my Heart that so generous a Man should be involved in such Difficulties, as oblige him to live with such ill Company, and herd with Gamesters.

MAT: See the Partiality of Mankind!—One Man may steal a Horse, better than another look over a Hedge[97]—Of all Mechanics,[98] of all servile Handicraftsmen, a Gamester is the vilest. But yet, as many of the Quality are of the Profession, he is admitted amongst the politest Company. I wonder we are not more respected.

MACH: There will be deep Play tonight at *Marylebone*, and consequently Money may be picked up upon the Road. Meet me there, and I'll give you the Hint who is worth Setting.

MAT: The Fellow with a brown Coat with a narrow Gold Binding, I am told, is never without Money.

MACH: What do you mean, *Mat*?—Sure you will not think of meddling with him!—He's a good honest kind of a Fellow, and one of us.

BEN: To be sure, Sir, we will put ourselves under your Direction.

MACH: Have an Eye upon the Money-Lenders.—A *Rouleau*,[99] or two, would prove a pretty sort of an Expedition. I hate Extortion.

MAT: Those *Rouleaus* are very pretty Things.—I hate your Bank Bills.—There is such a Hazard in putting them off.[100]

MACH: There is a certain Man of Distinction, who in his Time hath nicked me out of a great deal of the Ready. He is in my Cash,[101] Ben;—I'll point him out to you this Evening, and you shall draw upon him for the Debt.—The Company are met; I hear the Dice-box in the other Room. So, Gentlemen, your Servant. You'll meet me at *Marylebone*.

SCENE V. Peachum's *Lock*.

A Table with Wine, Brandy, Pipes, and Tobacco. Peachum, Lockit.

LOCK: The Coronation Account,[102] Brother *Peachum*, is of so intricate a Nature, that I believe it will never be settled.

Notes

97 "One Man may steal a Horse, better than another look over a Hedge" an old saying, meaning some people get in trouble for nothing while others get away with murder.

98 *Mechanics* manual laborers.

99 *Rouleau* a stack of gold coins (*OED*).

100 *putting them off* passing or cashing them.

101 *In my cash* stealing from me.

102 *Coronation Account* the list of items stolen during the coronation of George II in October 1727 (Fuller).

PEACH: It consists indeed of a great Variety of Articles.—It was worth to our People, in Fees of different Kinds, above ten Instalments.[103]—This is part of the Account, Brother, that lies open before us.

LOCK: A Lady's Tail[104] of rich Brocade—that, I see, is disposed of.

PEACH: To Mrs. *Diana Trapes*, the Tally-woman, and she will make a good Hand on't in Shoes and Slippers, to trick out young Ladies, upon their going into Keeping.—

LOCK: But I don't see any Article of the Jewels.

PEACH: Those are so well known, that they must be sent abroad—You'll find them entered under the Article of Exportation.—As for the Snuffboxes, Watches, Swords, etc.—I thought it best to enter them under their several Heads.

LOCK: Seven and twenty Women's Pockets complete; with the several things therein contained; all Sealed, Numbered, and entered.

PEACH: But, Brother, it is impossible for us now to enter upon this Affair.—We should have the whole Day before us.—Besides, the Account of the last Half Year's Plate is in a book by itself, which lies at the other Office.

LOCK: Bring us then more Liquor.—Today shall be for Pleasure—Tomorrow for Business.—Ah Brother, those Daughters of ours are two slippery Hussies—Keep a watchful Eye upon *Polly*, and *Macheath* in a Day or two shall be our own again.

AIR XLV. Down in the North Country, etc.

Lock. *What Gudgeons are we Men!*[105]
Every Woman's easy Prey.
Though we have felt the Hook, again
We bite and they betray.
The Bird that hath been trapped,
When he hears his calling Mate,
To her he flies, again he's clapped,
Within the wiry Grate.

PEACH: But what signifies catching the Bird, if your Daughter *Lucy* will set open the Door of the Cage?

LOCK: If Men were answerable for the Follies and Frailties of their Wives and Daughters, no Friends could keep a good Correspondence together for two Days.—This is unkind of you, Brother; for among good Friends, what they say or do goes for nothing.

Enter a Servant.

SERV: Sir, here's Mrs. *Diana Trapes* wants to speak with you.

PEACH: Shall we admit her, Brother *Lockit*?

LOCK: By all means—She's a good Customer, and a fine-spoken Woman—And a Woman who drinks and talks so freely, will enliven the Conversation.

PEACH: Desire her to walk in. [*Exit Servant.*

Notes

103 *Instalments* ceremonies installing a lord mayor.

104 *Tail* the train of a formal gown.

105 *Gudgeons* a kind of easily caught fish.

SCENE VI.

Peachum, Lockit, *Mrs.* Trapes.

Peach: Dear Mrs. *Dye*, your Servant—One may know by your Kiss, that your Gin is excellent.

Trapes: I was always very curious in my Liquors.

Lock: There is no perfumed Breath like it—I have been long acquainted with the Flavour of those Lips—Haven't I, Mrs. *Dye*?

Trapes: Fill it up.—I take as large Draughts of Liquor, as I did of Love.—I hate a Flincher in either.

AIR XLVI. A Shepherd kept Sheep, etc.

In the Days of my Youth I could bill like a Dove, fa, la, la, etc.
Like a Sparrow at all times was ready for Love, fa, la, la, la, etc.
The Life of all Mortals in Kissing should pass,
Lip to Lip while we're young—then the Lip to the Glass, fa, etc.

But now, Mr. *Peachum*, to our Business—If you have Blacks of any kind, brought in of late; Mantoes[106]—Velvet Scarves—Petticoats—Let it be what it will—I am your Chap—for all my Ladies are very fond of Mourning.

Peach: Why, look ye, Mrs. *Dye*—you deal so hard with us, that we can afford to give the Gentlemen, who venture their Lives for the Goods, little or nothing.

Trapes: The hard Times oblige me to go very near in my Dealing.—To be sure, of late Years I have been a great Sufferer by the Parliament.—Three thousand Pounds would hardly make me amends.—The Act for destroying the Mint,[107] was a severe Cut upon our Business—Till then, if a Customer stepped out of the way—we knew where to have her—No doubt you know Mrs. *Coaxer*—there's a Wench now (till today) with a good Suit of Clothes of mine upon her Back, and I could never set Eyes upon her for three Months together.—Since the Act too against Imprisonment for small Sums,[108] my Loss there too hath been very considerable, and it must be so, when a Lady can borrow a handsome Petticoat, or a clean Gown, and I not have the least Hank[109] upon her! And, o' my Conscience, nowadays most Ladies take a Delight in cheating, when they can do it with Safety.

Peach: Madam, you had a handsome Gold Watch of us t'other Day for seven Guineas.—Considering we must have our Profit—To a Gentleman upon the Road, a Gold Watch will be scarce worth the taking.

Trap: Consider, Mr. *Peachum*, that Watch was remarkable, and not of very safe Sale.—If you have any black Velvet Scarves—they are a handsome Winter-wear; and take with most Gentlemen who deal with my Customers.—'Tis I that put the Ladies upon a good Foot. 'Tis not Youth or Beauty that fixes their Price. The Gentlemen always pay according to their Dress, from half a Crown to two Guineas; and yet those Hussies make nothing of bilking of me.—Then too, allowing for Accidents.—I have eleven fine Customers now down under the Surgeon's Hands,—what with Fees and other

Notes

106 *Mantoes* mantles; cloaks.

107 *Act for destroying the Mint* a law passed in 1722 eliminating "the Mint," the parish of St. George in Surrey, as a safe haven for thieves fleeing arrest (Fuller).

108 *Act against Imprisonment for small Sums* a law passed in 1725 restricting arrest for small debts (Fuller).

109 *Hank* hold; advantage.

Expenses, there are great Goings-out, and no Comings-in, and not a Farthing to pay for at least a Month's clothing.—We run great Risks—great Risks indeed.

PEACH: As I remember, you said something just now of Mrs. *Coaxer.*

TRAP: Yes, Sir.—To be sure I stripped her of a Suit of my own Clothes about two hours ago and have left her as she should be, in her Shift, with a Lover of hers at my House. She called him Upstairs, as he was going to *Marylebone* in a Hackney Coach.—And I hope, for her own sake and mine, she will persuade the Captain to redeem her, for the Captain is very generous to the Ladies.

LOCK: What Captain?

TRAP: He thought I did not know him—An intimate Acquaintance of yours, Mr. *Peachum*—Only Captain *Macheath*—as fine as a Lord.

PEACH: Tomorrow, dear Mrs. *Dye*, you shall set your own Price upon any of the Goods you like—We have at least half a dozen Velvet Scarves, and all at your service. Will you give me leave to make you a Present of this Suit of Nightclothes for your own wearing?—But you are sure it is Captain *Macheath*?

TRAP: Though he thinks I have forgot him; Nobody knows him better. I have taken a great deal of the Captain's Money in my Time at second-hand, for he always loved to have his Ladies well dressed.

PEACH: Mr. *Lockit* and I have a little business with the Captain;—You understand me—and we will satisfy you for Mrs. *Coaxer*'s Debt.

LOCK: Depend upon it—we will deal like Men of Honour.

TRAP: I don't enquire after your Affairs—so whatever happens, I wash my Hands on't.—It hath always been my Maxim, that one Friend should assist another—But if you please—I'll take one of the Scarves home with me, 'Tis always good to have something in Hand.

SCENE VII. *Newgate.*

Lucy.

Jealousy, Rage, Love and Fear are at once tearing me to pieces. How I am weather-beaten and shattered with distresses!

AIR XLVII. One Evening, having lost my Way, etc.

I'm like a Skiff on the Ocean tossed,
Now high, now low, with each Billow born,
With her Rudder broke, and her Anchor lost,
Defeated and all forlorn.
While thus I lie rolling and tossing all Night,
That Polly *lies sporting on Seas of Delight!*
Revenge, Revenge, Revenge,
Shall appease my restless Sprite.

I have the Rat's-bane ready.—I run no Risk; for I can lay her Death upon the Gin, and so many die of that naturally that I shall never be called in Question.—But say, I were to be hanged—I never could be hanged for anything that would give me greater Comfort, than the poisoning that Slut.

Enter Filch.

FILCH: Madam, here's our Miss *Polly* come to wait upon you.

LUCY: Show her in.

SCENE VIII.

Lucy, Polly.

Lucy: Dear Madam, your Servant.—I hope you will pardon my Passion, when I was so happy to see you last.—I was so overrun with the Spleen,[110] that I was perfectly out of myself. And really when one hath the Spleen, everything to is to be excused by a Friend.

AIR XLVIII. Now *Roger*, I'll tell thee, because thou'rt my Son.

When a Wife's in her Pout,
(As she's sometimes, no doubt;)
The good Husband as meek as a Lamb,
Her Vapours to still,[111]
First grants her her Will,
And the quieting Draught is a Dram.
Poor Man! And the quieting Draught is a Dram.

—I wish all our Quarrels might have so comfortable a Reconciliation.

Polly: I have no Excuse for my own Behaviour, Madam, but my Misfortunes.—And really, Madam, I suffer too upon your Account.

Lucy: But, Miss *Polly*—in the way of Friendship, will you give me leave to propose a Glass of Cordial to you?

Polly: Strong-Waters are apt to give me the Headache—I hope, Madam, you will excuse me.

Lucy: Not the greatest Lady in the Land could have better in her Closet, for her own private drinking.—You seem mighty low in Spirits, my Dear.

Polly: I am sorry, Madam, my Health will not allow me to accept of your Offer.—I should not have left you in the rude Manner I did when we met last, Madam, had not my Papa hauled me away so unexpectedly—I was indeed somewhat provoked, and perhaps might use some Expressions that were disrespectful.—But really, Madam, the Captain treated me with so much Contempt and Cruelty, that I deserved your Pity, rather than your Resentment.

Lucy: But since his Escape, no doubt all Matters are made up again.—Ah *Polly*! *Polly*! 'tis I am the unhappy Wife; and he loves you as if you were only his Mistress.

Polly: Sure, Madam, you cannot think me so happy as to be the Object of your Jealousy.—A Man is always afraid of a Woman who loves him too well—so that I must expect to be neglected and avoided.

Lucy: Then our Cases, my dear *Polly*, are exactly alike. Both of us indeed have been too fond.

AIR XLIX. O Bessy Bell.

Polly. *A Curse attends that Woman's Love,*
Who always would be pleasing.
Lucy. *The Pertness of the billing Dove,*
Like tickling, is but teasing.
Polly. *What then in Love can Woman do?*

Notes

110 *Spleen* bad temper; melancholy.

111 *Vapours* bad mood.

Lucy. *If we grow fond they shun us.*
Polly. *And when we fly them, they pursue:*
Lucy. *But leave us when they've won us.*

LUCY: Love is so very whimsical in both Sexes, that it is impossible to be lasting.—But my Heart is particular, and contradicts my own Observation.

POLLY: But really, Mistress *Lucy*, by his last Behaviour, I think I ought to envy you.—When I was forced from him, he did not show the least Tenderness.—But perhaps, he hath a Heart not capable of it.

AIR L. Would Fate to me *Belinda* give—

Among the Men, Coquettes we find,
Who Court by turns all Womankind;
And we grant all their Hearts desired,
When they are flattered, and admired.

The Coquettes of both Sexes are Self-lovers, and that is a Love no other whatever can dispossess. I fear, my dear *Lucy*, our Husband is one of those.

LUCY: Away with these melancholy Reflections,—indeed, my dear *Polly*, we are both of us a Cup too low.—Let me prevail upon you, to accept of my Offer.

AIR LI. Come, sweet Lass, etc.

Come, sweet Lass,
Let's banish Sorrow
Till Tomorrow;
Come, sweet Lass,
Let's take a chirping Glass.[112]
Wine can clear
The Vapours of Despair;
And make us light as Air;
Then drink and banish Care.

I can't bear, Child, to see you in such low Spirits.—And I must persuade you to what I know will do you good.—shall now soon be even with the hypocritical Strumpet. [Aside.

SCENE IX.

Polly.

POLLY: All this wheedling of *Lucy* cannot be for nothing.—At this time too! when I know she hates me!—The Dissembling of a Woman is always the Forerunner of Mischief.—By pouring Strong-Waters down my Throat, she thinks to pump some Secrets out of me.—I'll be upon my Guard, and won't taste a Drop of her Liquor, I'm resolved.

Notes

[112] *Chirping* making cheer.

SCENE X.

Lucy, *with Strong-Waters*. Polly.

LUCY: Come, Miss *Polly*.

POLLY: Indeed, Child, you have given yourself trouble to no purpose.—You must, my Dear, excuse me.

LUCY: Really, Miss *Polly*, you are so squeamishly affected about taking a Cup of Strong-Waters as a Lady before Company. I vow, *Polly*, I shall take it monstrously ill if you refuse me.—Brandy and Men (though Women love them never so well) are always taken by us with some Reluctance—unless 'tis in private.

POLLY: I protest, Madam, it goes against me.—What do I see! *Macheath* again in Custody!—Now every glimmering of Happiness is lost.

[Drops the Glass of Liquor on the Ground.

LUCY: Since things are thus, I'm glad the Wench hath escaped: for by this Event, 'tis plain, she was not happy enough to deserve to be poisoned.

SCENE XI.

Lockit, Macheath, Peachum, Lucy, Polly.

LOCK: Set your Heart to rest, Captain.—You have neither the Chance of Love or Money for another Escape,—for you are ordered to be called down upon your Trial immediately.

PEACH: Away, Hussies!—This is not a time for a Man to be hampered with his Wives.—You see, the Gentleman is in Chains already.

LUCY: O Husband, Husband, my Heart longed to see thee; but to see thee thus distracts me!

POLLY: Will not my dear Husband look upon his *Polly*? Why hast thou not flown to me for Protection? with me thou hadst been safe.

AIR LII. The last time I went o'er the Moor.

Polly. *Hither, dear Husband, turn your Eyes.*
Lucy. *Bestow one Glance to cheer me.*
Polly. *Think with that Look, thy* Polly *dies.*
Lucy. *O shun me not—but hear me.*
Polly. *'Tis* Polly *sues.*
Lucy. *'Tis* Lucy *speaks.*
Polly. *Is thus true Love requited?*
Lucy. *My heart is bursting.*
Polly. *Mine too breaks.*
Lucy. *Must I*
Polly. *Must I be slighted?*

MACH: What would you have me say, Ladies?—You see, this Affair will soon be at an end, without my disobliging either of you.

PEACH: But the settling this Point, Captain, might prevent a Lawsuit between your two Widows.

AIR LIII. *Tom Tinker's* my true Love.

Mach. *Which way shall I turn me—How can I decide?*
Wives, the Day of our Death, are as fond as a Bride.
One Wife is too much for most Husbands to hear,
But two at a time there's no Mortal can bear.
This way, and that way, and which way I will,
What would comfort the one, t'other Wife would take ill.

POLLY: But if his own Misfortunes have made him insensible to mine—A father sure will be more compassionate—Dear, dear Sir, sink the material Evidence, and bring him off at his Trial—*Polly* upon her Knees begs it of you.

AIR LIV. I am a poor Shepherd undone.

When my Hero in Court appears,
And stands arraigned for his Life;
Then think of poor Polly*'s Tears;*
For Ah! Poor Polly*'s his Wife.*
Like the Sailor he holds up his Hand,
Distressed on the dashing Wave.
To die a dry Death at Land,
Is as bad as a watery Grave.
And alas, poor Polly*!*
Alack, and well-a-day!
Before I was in Love,
Oh! every Month was May.

LUCY: If *Peachum*'s Heart is hardened; sure you, Sir, will have more Compassion on a Daughter.—I know the Evidence is in your Power.—How then can you be a Tyrant to me? [Kneeling.

AIR LV. *Ianthe* the lovely, etc.

When he holds up his Hand arraigned for his Life,
O think of your Daughter, and think I'm his Wife!
What are Cannons, or Bombs, or clashing of Swords?
For Death is more certain by Witnesses' Words.
Then nail up their Lips; that dread Thunder allay;
And each Month of my Life will hereafter be May.

LOCK: *Macheath*'s time is come, *Lucy*.—We know our own Affairs, therefore let us have no more Whimpering or Whining

AIR LVI. A Cobbler there was, etc.

Ourselves, like the Great, to secure a Retreat,
When Matters require it, must give up our Gang:
And good reason why,
Or, instead of the Fry,
Even Peachum *and I,*
Like poor petty Rascals, might hang, hang;
Like poor petty Rascals, might hang.

PEACH: Set your Heart at rest, *Polly*.—Your Husband is to die today.—Therefore, if you are not already provided, 'tis high time to look about for another. There's Comfort for you, you Slut.

LOCK: We are ready, Sir, to conduct you to the *Old Bailey*.

AIR LVII. Bonny *Dundee*.

Mach. *The Charge is prepared the Lawyers are met,*
The Judges all ranged (a terrible Show!)
I go, undismayed.—For Death is a Debt,
A Debt on demand.—So, take what I owe.
Contented I die—'Tis the better for you.
Here ends all Dispute the rest of our Lives,
For this way at once I please all my Wives.

Now, Gentlemen, I am ready to attend you.

SCENE XII.

Lucy, Polly, Filch.

POLLY: Follow them, *Filch*, to the Court. And when the Trial is over, bring me a particular Account of his Behaviour, and of everything that happened.—You'll find me here with Miss *Lucy*. [*Ex.* Filch.] But why is all this Music?

LUCY: The Prisoners, whose Trials are put off till next Session, are diverting themselves.

POLLY: Sure there is nothing so charming as Music! I'm fond of it to distraction!—But alas!—now, all Mirth seems an Insult upon my Affliction.—Let us retire, my dear *Lucy*, and indulge our Sorrows.—The noisy Crew, you see, are coming upon us. [*Exeunt.*

A Dance of Prisoners in Chains, etc.

SCENE XIII.

The Condemned Hold.
Macheath, *in a melancholy Posture.*

AIR LVIII. Happy Groves.

O cruel, cruel, cruel Case!
Must I suffer this Disgrace?

AIR LIX. Of all the Girls that are so smart.

Of all the Friends in time of Grief,
When threatening Death looks grimmer,
Not one so sure can bring Relief,
As this best Friend, a Brimmer.[113] [Drinks.

Notes

[113] *Brimmer* a glass full to the brim.

AIR LX. *Britons* strike home.

Since I must swing,—I scorn, I scorn to wince or whine. [Rises.

AIR LXI. Chevy Chase.

But now again my Spirits sink;
I'll raise them high with Wine. [Drinks a Glass of Wine.

AIR LXII. To old Sir *Simon* the King.

But Valour, the stronger grows,
The stronger Liquor we're drinking.
And how can we feel our Woes,
When we've lost the Trouble of Thinking? [Drinks.

AIR LXIII. Joy to great *Caesar.*

If thus—A Man can die
Much bolder with Brandy. [Pours out a Bumper of Brandy.

There was an old Woman.

So I drink off this Bumper.—And now I can stand the Test.
And my Comrades shall see, that I die as brave as the Best. [Drinks.

AIR LXV. Did you ever hear of a gallant Sailor.

But can I leave my pretty Hussies,
Without one Tear, or tender Sigh?

AIR LXVI. Why are mine Eyes still flowing.

Their Eyes, their Lips, their Busses[114]
Recall my Love.—Ah must I die!

AIR LXVII. Green Sleeves.

Since Laws were made for every Degree,
To curb Vice in others, as well as me,
I wonder we han't better Company,
Upon Tyburn *Tree!*
But Gold from Law can take out the Sting;
And if rich Men like us were to swing,
'Twould thin the Land, such Numbers to string
Upon Tyburn *Tree!*

Jailor: Some Friends of yours, Captain, desire to be admitted.—I leave you together.

Notes

[114] *Busses* kisses, especially loud and vigorous ones (*OED*).

SCENE XIV.

Macheath, Ben Budge, Matt *of the Mint.*

MACH: For my having broke Prison, you see, Gentlemen, I am ordered immediate Execution.—The Sheriff's Officers, I believe, are now at the Door.—That *Jemmy Twitcher* should peach me, I own surprised me!—'Tis a plain Proof that the World is all alike, and that even our Gang can no more trust one another than other People. Therefore, I beg you, Gentlemen, look well to yourselves, for in all probability you may live some Months longer.

MAT: We are heartily sorry, Captain, for your Misfortune.—But 'tis what we must all come to.

MACH: *Peachum* and *Lockit*, you know, are infamous Scoundrels. Their Lives are as much in your Power, as yours are in theirs.—Remember your dying Friend!—'Tis my last Request.—Bring those Villains to the Gallows before you, and I am satisfied.

MATT: We'll do't.

JAILOR: Miss *Polly* and Miss *Lucy* entreat a Word with you.

MACH: Gentlemen, adieu.

SCENE XV.

Lucy, Macheath, Polly.

MACH: My dear *Lucy*—My dear *Polly*—Whatsoever hath passed between us is now at an end.—If you are fond of marrying again, the best Advice I can give you, is to Ship yourselves off for the *West Indies*, where you'll have a fair chance of getting a Husband apiece; or by good Luck, two or three, as you like best.

POLLY: How can I support this Sight!

LUCY: There is nothing moves one so much as a great Man in Distress.

AIR LXVIII. All you that must take a Leap, etc.

Lucy. *Would I might be hanged!*
Polly. *And I would so too!*
Lucy. *To be hanged with you.*
Polly. *My Dear, with you.*
Mach. *O Leave me to Thought! I fear! I doubt!*
I tremble! I droop!—See, my Courage is out.
[Turns up the empty Bottle.
Polly. *No token of Love?*
Mach. *See, my Courage is out.* [Turns up the empty Pot.
Lucy. *No token of Love?*
Polly. *Adieu.*
Lucy. *Farewell.*
Mach. *But hark! I hear the Toll of the Bell.*
Chorus. *Tol de rol lol, etc.*

JAILOR: Four Women more, Captain, with a Child apiece! See, here they come.

[*Enter Women and Children.*

MACH: What—four Wives more!—This is too much.—Here—tell the Sheriff's Officers I am ready. [*Exit* Macheath *guarded.*

SCENE XVI.

To them, Enter Player *and* Beggar.

PLAY: But, honest Friend, I hope you don't intend that *Macheath* shall be really executed.

BEG: Most certainly, Sir.—To make the Piece perfect, I was for doing strict poetical Justice.—*Macheath* is to be hanged; and for the other Personages of the Drama, the Audience must have supposed they were all either hanged or transported.

PLAY: Why then, Friend, this is a downright deep Tragedy. The Catastrophe is manifestly wrong, for an Opera must end happily.

BEG: Your Objection, Sir, is very just; and is easily removed. For you must allow, that in this kind of Drama, 'tis no matter how absurdly things are brought about—So—you Rabble there—run and cry a Reprieve—let the Prisoner be brought back to his Wives in Triumph.

PLAY: All this we must do, to comply with the Taste of the Town.

BEG: Through the whole Piece you may observe such a similitude of Manners in high and low Life, that it is difficult to determine whether (in the fashionable Vices) the fine Gentlemen imitate the Gentlemen of the Road, or the Gentlemen of the Road the fine Gentlemen.—Had the Play remained, as I at first intended, it would have carried a most excellent Moral. 'Twould have shown that the lower Sort of People have their Vices in a degree as well as the Rich: And that they are punished for them.

SCENE XVII.

To them, Macheath *with Rabble, etc.*

MACH: So, it seems, I am not left to my Choice, but must have a Wife at last.—Look ye, my Dears, we will have no Controversy now. Let us give this Day to Mirth, and I am sure she who thinks herself my Wife will testify her Joy by a Dance.

ALL: Come, a Dance—a Dance.

MACH: Ladies, I hope you will give me leave to present a Partner to each of you. And (if I may without Offence) for this time, I take *Polly* for mine.—And for Life, you Slut,—for we were really married.—As for the rest.—[*To* Polly.] But at present keep your own Secret.

A DANCE.

AIR LXIX. Lumps of Pudding, etc.

Thus I stand like the Turk, *with his Doxies around;*[115]
From all Sides their Glances his Passion confound;
For black, brown, and fair, his Inconstancy burns,

Notes

[115] *Doxies* mistresses or wenches.

And the different Beauties subdue him by turns:
Each calls forth her Charms, to provoke his Desires:
Though willing to all; with but one he retires.
But think of this Maxim, and put off your Sorrow,
The Wretch of Today, may be happy Tomorrow.
Chorus. *But think of this Maxim, etc.*

FINIS.

Alexander Pope (1688–1744)

Pope was the most important, popular, and influential poet of his time. He excelled at versification, and set a standard in manipulation of the heroic couplet that every young poet emulated but none could match. He also went a long way toward defining poetic diction, the sort of language that is proper for and to poetry, for his age. No poet has ever been more adept at putting lines of verse together, and few poets have worked over their lines with more care and attention. Pope was the consummate literary craftsman, but there is disagreement about the importance and penetration of the thoughts he put into such memorable and excellently wrought poetry.

His first major work, published when he was twenty-three, was *An Essay on Criticism*. Modelled on Horace's *Ars Poetica, An Essay* is filled with commonplaces of literary theory. But Pope exemplifies them so well and embodies them in his own composition so nicely that he redefines the standards he adopts. Pope is the master of "true wit" (insight as well as mere repartee), as he himself defines it: "What oft was thought but ne'er so well expressed." The work that made him famous and financially independent was, appropriately, a translation. Pope's Homer began appearing in 1715. It is not the work of a Hellenistic scholar, but it represents a transmission of poetry from one great poetic talent to another. The work now seems anachronistically marked by the trappings of its own historical period; it makes Homer's heroes live to an extent in Queen Anne's age. But it is a triumph of versification and diction. Later in his career Pope wrote numerous looser translations, called imitations, in which he consciously substitutes contemporary names and manners for those described in Horace and some other important classical writers. These learned, elegant, yet sometimes gossipy works are also emblematic of the literary era that Pope did so much to create.

Despite the fact that all his poetry is written in heroic couplets, Pope was a terrifically versatile writer, and he is particularly difficult to anthologize for that reason. However, *The Rape of the Lock* (1714) is too attractive to leave out, and *The Dunciad* seems essential both to Pope and his age. Both works are mock-epics that readers of *Paradise Lost* must appreciate for their ironic application of the heroic mode to modern life. *The Dunciad*, first published in 1728, is a much sharper satire than the *Rape*, and in its final version and expansion (1743) becomes the most philosophical and universal of Pope's satires, despite its deep involvement with now obscure, real people. For inclusion here I have selected Book I of *The Dunciad Variorum* (1729), including much of the preliminary matter and many of the notes that Pope (with a little help from his friends) added to the first edition. Also included here are Pope's *Essay on Criticism* and his sensitive and romantic *Eloisa to Abelard*, which, set beside the heroic mockery of *The Dunciad*, shows Pope's great literary range.

Because of his Roman Catholic background Pope was excluded from the sort of university education his talents deserved. Early in life, Pope's aspirations to elite society were also blocked by his creed. Later, when fame might have brought him into any company and conferred any honor on him, Pope was understandably somewhat bitter. The final book of *The Dunciad* is in many ways a rejection of the Oxford honors that were offered too late to be acceptable. Pope's private life was restricted by poor health and congenital scoliosis, which made him small and stooped. He had some kind of infatuation with Lady Mary

British Literature 1640–1789: An Anthology, Fourth Edition. Edited by Robert DeMaria, Jr.

Wortley Montagu (as the letter below to her suggests), although her marriage made anything like consummation unthinkable. He had a deeper attachment to Martha Blount, who was his life-long friend and endured public obloquy to live as his mistress. Both of these important women in Pope's life suffered permanent disfigurement from smallpox. In his comprehensive biography (Norton, 1985) Maynard Mack suggests that Pope's consciousness of his own infirmities may have led him to a kind of fellow-feeling with these women, who were like Pope highly intelligent and physically marred.

Pope is blessed with a sumptuous standard edition of his poetry, *The Twickenham Edition of the Poems of Alexander Pope*, edited by John Butt and others, 11 vols. (Methuen, 1938–68). Although I take my texts of the poems from the first editions specified here, I rely on the *Twickenham Pope* for those of Pope's corrections to later editions which I incorporate; he was a relentless corrector and reviser. I am also indebted to the *Twickenham* editors for much help with my footnotes. For the letter from Pope I draw on *The Correspondence of Alexander Pope*, edited by George Sherburn, 5 vols. (Clarendon Press, 1956).

An Essay on Criticism (1711)

———Si quid novisti rectius istis,
Candidus imperti; si non, his utere mecum.
HORAT.[1]

'Tis hard to say, if greater Want of Skill
Appear in *Writing* or in *Judging* ill;
But, of the two, less dangerous is th' Offence,
To tire our *Patience*, than mislead our *Sense*:
Some few in *that*, but Numbers err in *this*,
Ten Censure wrong for one who Writes amiss;
A *Fool* might once *himself* alone expose,
Now *One* in *Verse* makes many more in *Prose*.
'Tis with our *Judgments* as our *Watches*, none
Go just *alike*, yet each believes his own.
In *Poets* as true *Genius* is but rare,
True *Taste* as seldom is the *Critic*'s Share;
Both must alike from Heaven derive their Light,
These *born* to Judge, as well as those to Write.
Let such teach others who themselves excel,
And *censure freely* who have *written well*.
Authors are partial to their *Wit*, 'tis true,
But are not *Critics* to their *Judgment* too?
Yet if we look more closely, we shall find
Most have the *Seeds* of Judgment in their Mind;
Nature affords at least a *glimmering Light*;

Notes

An Essay on Criticism

[1] Horace, *Epistles*, I.vi.67–8: "If you know something better than this advice, impart it, dear reader; if not, make use of it along with me."

The *Lines*, though touched but faintly, are drawn right.
But as the slightest Sketch, if justly traced,
Is by ill *Colouring* but the more disgraced,
So by *false Learning* is *good Sense* defaced;
Some are bewildered in the Maze of Schools,
And some made *Coxcombs* Nature meant but *Fools*.
In search of *Wit* these lose their *common Sense*,
And then turn Critics in their own Defence.
Each burns alike, who can, or cannot write
Or with a *Rival*'s, or an Eunuch's spite.
All *Fools* have still an Itching to deride,
And fain *would* be upon the *Laughing Side*:
If *Mævius* Scribble in *Apollo*'s spite,[2]
There are, who *judge* still *worse* than he can *write*.
Some have at first for *Wits*, then *Poets* passed,
Turned *Critics* next, and proved plain *Fools* at last;
Some neither can for *Wits* nor *Critics* pass,
As heavy Mules are neither *Horse* nor *Ass*.
Those half-learn'd Witlings, num'rous in our Isle,
As half-formed Insects on the Banks of *Nile*;
Unfinished Things, one knows not what to call,
Their Generation's so *equivocal*:[3]
To tell 'em, would a *hundred Tongues* require,
Or *one vain Wit*'s, that might a hundred tire.
But *you* who seek to *give* and *merit* Fame,
And justly bear a Critic's noble Name,
Be sure *yourself* and your own *Reach* to know,
How far your *Genius*, *Taste*, and *Learning* go;
Launch not beyond your Depth, but be discreet,
And mark *that Point* where Sense and Dullness *Meet*.
Nature to all things fixed the Limits fit,
And wisely curbed proud Man's pretending Wit:
As on the *Land* while *here* the *Ocean* gains,
In *other Parts* it leaves wide sandy Plains;
Thus in the *Soul* while *Memory* prevails,
The solid Power of *Understanding* fails;
Where Beams of warm *Imagination* play,
The *Memory*'s soft Figures melt away.
One *Science* only will one *Genius* fit;[4]
So *vast* is Art, so *narrow* Human Wit:[5]
Not only bounded to *peculiar Arts*,[6]
But oft in *those*, confined to *single Parts*.
Like Kings we lose the Conquests gained before,

Notes

[2] *Mævius* a hack writer ridiculed by Virgil and Horace; Apollo is the god of poetry.

[3] "Equivocal generation is the production of plants without seed, or insects or animals without parents" (Johnson, sense 2, quoting John Harris).

[4] *Science* any branch of learning.

[5] *Art* "A science; as, the liberal arts" (Johnson, sense 2).

[6] *peculiar* particular.

By vain Ambition still to make them more:
Each might his *several Province* well command,
Would all but *stoop* to what they *understand.*
First follow NATURE, and your Judgment frame
By her just Standard, which is still the same:
Unerring Nature, still divinely bright,
One *clear*, *unchanged*, and *Universal* Light,
Life, Force, and Beauty, must to all impart,
At once the *Source*, and *End*, and *Test* of *Art*.
Art from that Fund each just Supply provides;
Works without *Show*, and without *Pomp presides*:
In some fair Body thus th' informing Soul
With Spirits feeds, with Vigour fills the whole,
Each Motion guides, and every Nerve sustains;
Itself unseen, but in th' *Effects*, remains.
There are whom Heaven has blessed with store of Wit,
Yet want as much again to manage it;
For *Wit* and *Judgment* ever are at strife,
Though meant each other's Aid, like *Man* and *Wife*.
'Tis more to *guide* than *spur* the Muse's Steed;
Restrain his Fury, than provoke his Speed;
The wingèd Courser, like a gen'rous Horse,
Shows most true Mettle when you *check* his Course.
Those RULES of old *discovered*, not *devised*,
Are *Nature* still, but *Nature Methodized*;
Nature, like *Monarchy*, is but restrained[7]
By the same Laws which first *herself* ordained.
Hear how learn'd *Greece* her useful Rules indites,[8]
When to repress, and when indulge our Flights:
High on *Parnassus*' Top her Sons she showed,
And pointed out those arduous Paths they trod,
Held from afar, aloft, th' Immortal Prize,
And urged the rest by equal Steps to rise;
Just *Precepts* thus from great *Examples* given,
She drew from *them* what they derived from *Heaven*,
The gen'rous Critic *fanned* the *Poet's Fire*,
And taught the World, *with Reason* to *Admire*.
Then Criticism the Muses' Handmaid proved,
To dress her Charms, and make her more belov'd;
But following Wits from that Intention strayed;
Who could not win the Mistress, wooed the Maid,
Against the Poets *their own Arms* they turned,
Sure to hate most the Men from whom they *learned*.
So modern *'Pothecaries*, taught the Art
By *Doctor's Bills* to play the *Doctor's Part*,
Bold in the Practice of *mistaken Rules*,
Prescribe, apply, and call their *Masters Fools*.

Notes

[7] In 1744, *"Monarchy"* was changed to *"Liberty."*

[8] *indites* proclaims; dictates; or inscribes.

Some on the Leaves of ancient Authors prey,
Nor Time nor Moths e'er spoiled so much as they:
Some dryly plain, without Invention's Aid,
Write dull *Receipts* how Poems may be made:
These lose the Sense, the Learning to display,
And those explain the Meaning quite away.
You then whose Judgment the right Course would steer,
Know well each ANCIENT's proper *Character*,
His *Fable*, *Subject*, *Scope* in every Page,
Religion, *Country*, *Genius* of his *Age*:
Without all these at once before your Eyes,
Cavil you may, but never *Criticize*.
Be *Homer's* Works your *Study*, and *Delight*,
Read them by Day, and meditate by Night,
Thence form your Judgment, thence your Maxims bring,
And trace the Muses *upward* to their *Spring*;
Still with *Itself compared*, his *Text* peruse;
And let your *Comment* be the *Mantuan Muse*.[9]
When first young *Maro*[10] in his boundless Mind
A Work, t' outlast Immortal *Rome* designed,
Perhaps he seemed *above* the Critic's Law,
And but from *Nature's Fountains* scorned to draw:
But when t' examine every Part he came,
Nature and *Homer* were, he found, the *same*:
Convinced, amazed, he checks the bold Design,
And Rules as strict his laboured Work confine,
As if the *Stagyrite* o'erlooked each Line.[11]
Learn hence for Ancient *Rules* a just Esteem;
To copy *Nature* is to copy *Them*.
Some Beauties yet, no Precepts can declare,
Fore there's a *Happiness* as well as *Care*.[12]
Music resembles *Poetry*, in each
Are *nameless Graces* which no Methods teach,
And which a *Master-Hand* alone can reach.
If, where the *Rules* not far enough extend,
(Since Rules were made but to promote their End)
Some Lucky LICENCE answers to the full
Th' Intent proposed, *that Licence* is a *Rule*.
Thus *Pegasus*, a nearer way to take,[13]
May boldly deviate from the common Track.
Great Wits sometimes may *gloriously offend*,
And *rise* to *Faults* true Critics *dare not mend*;

Notes

9 *Mantuan* is a name for Virgil because he was born in that Italian city.

10 *Maro* the family name of Virgil, author of the *Aeneid*.

11 *Stagyrite* Aristotle, who was from Stagira in Macedonia. The combat might break several of the rules established by neo-classical critics claiming the authority of Aristotle: unity of place; and unity of time; unity of action; and an injunction against violence portrayed on stage.

12 *Happiness* good fortune; good luck.

13 *Pegasus* the winged horse of the muses; hence, poetic inspiration.

From *vulgar Bounds* with *brave Disorder* part,
And *snatch* a *Grace* beyond the Reach of Art,
Which, without passing through the *Judgment*, gains
The *Heart*, and all its End *at once* attains.
In *Prospects*, thus, some *Objects* please our Eyes,
Which *out of* Nature's *common Order* rise,
The shapeless *Rock*, or hanging *Precipice*.
But Care in Poetry must still be had,
It asks *Discretion* even in *running Mad*;
And though the *Ancients* thus their *Rules* invade,
(As *Kings* dispense with *Laws* Themselves have made):
Moderns, beware! Or if you must offend
Against the *Precept*, ne'er transgress its *End*,
Let it be *seldom*, and *compelled by Need*,
And have, at least, *Their Precedent* to plead.
The Critic else proceeds without Remorse,
Seizes your Fame, and puts his Laws in force.
I know there are, to whose presumptuous Thoughts
Those *Freer Beauties*, even in *Them*, seem Faults:
Some Figures *monstrous* and *misshaped* appear,
Considered *singly*, or beheld too *near*,
Which, but *proportioned* to their *Light*, or *Place*,
Due Distance *reconciles* to Form and Grace.
A prudent Chief not always must display
His Powers in *equal Ranks*, and *fair Array*,
But with th' *Occasion* and the *Place* comply,
Conceal his Force, nay seem sometimes to *Fly*.
Those oft are *Stratagems* which *Errors* seem,
Nor is it *Homer Nods*, but *We* that *Dream*.
Still green with Bays each *ancient* Altar stands,
Above the reach of *Sacrilegious Hands*,
Secure from *Flames*, from *Envy*'s fiercer Rage,
Destructive *War*, and all-devouring *Age*.
See, from *each Clime* the Learn'd their Incense bring;
Hear, in *all Tongues* consenting *Paeans* ring!
In Praise so just, let every Voice be joined,
And fill the *Gen'ral Chorus* of *Mankind*!
Hail *Bards Triumphant*! born in *happier Days*,
Immortal Heirs of *Universal* Praise!
Whose Honours with Increase of Ages grow,
As Streams roll down, *enlarging* as they flow!
Nations *unborn* your mighty Names shall sound,
And Worlds applaud that must not yet be *found*!
Oh may some Spark of *your* Celestial Fire
The last, the meanest of your Sons inspire,
(That on weak Wings, from far, pursues your Flights;
Glows while he *reads*, but *trembles* as he *writes*)
To teach vain Wits a Science *little known*,
T' admire Superior Sense, and *doubt* their own!
Of all the causes which conspire to blind
Man's erring Judgment, and misguide the Mind,

What the weak Head with Strongest Bias rules,
Is *Pride*, the *never-failing Vice of Fools*.
Whatever Nature has in *Worth* denied,
She gives in large Recruits of *needful Pride*;
For as in *Bodies*, thus in *Souls*, we find
What wants in *Blood* and *Spirits*, swelled with *Wind*;
Pride, where Wit fails, steps in to our Defence,
And fills up all the *mighty Void* of *Sense*!
If once right Reason drives *that Cloud* away,
Truth breaks upon us with *resistless Day*;
Trust not yourself; but your Defects to know,
Make use of every *Friend*—and every *Foe*.
   A *little Learning* is a dangerous Thing;
Drink deep, or taste not the *Pierian* Spring:
There *shallow Draughts* intoxicate the Brain,
And drinking *largely* sobers us again.
Fired at first Sight with what the *Muse* imparts,
In *fearless Youth* we tempt the Heights of Arts;
While from the bounded *Level* of our Mind,
Short Views we take, nor see the *Lengths behind*,
But *more advanced*, behold with strange Surprise
New, distant Scenes of *endless* Science rise!
So pleased at first, the towering *Alps* we try,
Mount o'er the Vales, and seem to tread the Sky;
Th' Eternal Snows appear already past,
And the first *Clouds* and *Mountains* seem the last:
But those attained, we tremble to survey
The growing Labours of the lengthened Way,
Th' *increasing* Prospect *tires* our wand'ring Eyes,
Hills peep o'er Hills, and *Alps* on *Alps* arise!
   A perfect Judge will *read* each Work of Wit
With the same Spirit that its Author *writ*,
Survey the *Whole*, nor seek slight Faults to find
Where Nature *moves*, and *Rapture warms* the Mind;
Nor lose, for that malignant dull Delight,
The *generous Pleasure* to be charmed with Wit.
But in such Lays as neither *ebb*, nor *flow*,
Correctly cold, and *regularly low*,
That shunning Faults, one quiet *Tenor* keep;
We cannot *blame* indeed—but we may *sleep*.
In Wit, as Nature, what affects our Hearts
Is not th' Exactness of peculiar Parts;
'Tis not a *Lip*, or *Eye*, we Beauty call,
But the joint Force and full *Result* of *all*.
Thus when we view some well-proportioned Dome,
(The *World*'s just Wonder, and even *thine* O *Rome*!)[14]

Notes

[14] *Dome* any grand kind of building; Pope refers to St. Peter's Basilica, which is crowned with its famous dome.

No single Parts unequally surprise;
All comes united to th' admiring Eyes;
No monstrous Height, or Breadth, or Length appear;
The *Whole* at once is *Bold*, and *Regular*.
Whoever thinks a faultless Piece to see,
Thinks what ne'er was, nor is, nor e'er shall be.
In every Work regard the *Writer's End*,
Since none can compass more than they *Intend*;
And if the *Means* be just, the *Conduct* true,
Applause, in spite of trivial Faults, is due.
As Men of Breeding, sometimes Men of Wit,
T' avoid *great Errors*, must the *less* commit,
Neglect the Rules each *Verbal Critic* lays,[15]
For *not* to know some Trifles, is a Praise.
Most Critics, fond of some subservient Art,
Still make the *Whole* depend upon a *Part*,
They talk of *Principles*, but Notions prize,
And All to one loved Folly Sacrifice.
Once on a time, *La Mancha*'s Knight, they say,[16]
A certain *Bard* encountering on the Way,
Discoursed in Terms as just, with Looks as Sage,
As e'er could *Dennis*, of the *Grecian* Stage;[17]
Concluding all were desp'rate Sots and Fools,
Who durst depart from *Aristotle*'s Rules.
Our Author, happy in a Judge so nice,
Produced his Play, and begged the Knight's Advice,
Made him observe the *Subject* and the *Plot*,
The *Manners*, *Passions*, *Unities*, what not?
All which, exact to *Rule* were brought about,
Were but a *Combat in the Lists* left out.
What! Leave the Combat out? Exclaims the Knight;
Yes, or we must renounce the *Stagyrite*.
Not so by Heaven (he answers in a Rage)
Knights, Squires, and Steeds must enter on the Stage.
The Stage can ne'er so vast a Throng contain.
Then build a New, or act it in a Plain.
Thus Critics, of less *Judgment* than *Caprice*,
Curious, not *Knowing*, not *exact*, but *nice*,
Form *short* Ideas; and offend in *Arts*
(As most in *Manners*) by a *Love to Parts*.
Some to *Conceit* alone their Taste confine,
and glitt'ring Thoughts struck out at every Line;
Pleased with a Work where nothing's just or fit;
One *glaring Chaos* and *wild Heap* of *Wit*:

Notes

[15] *Verbal Critic* one "interested in, attending to, the mere words of a literary composition" (*OED*, s.v. *verbal*, 1c).

[16] *La Mancha's Knight* Don Quixote, the hero of Cervantes' famous romance.

[17] John Dennis (1658–1734), author of *The Grounds of Criticism in Poetry* (1704), a formal critic much concerned with rules derived from Aristotle's *Poetics*, to some of which Pope alludes in the following lines.

Poets like Painters, thus, unskilled to trace
The *naked Nature* and the *living Grace*,
With *Gold* and *Jewels* cover every Part,
And hide with *Ornaments* their *Want of Art*.
True Wit is *Nature* to Advantage dressed,
What oft was *Thought*, but ne'er so well *Expressed*,
Something, whose Truth convinced at Sight we find,
That gives us back the Image of our Mind:
As Shades more sweetly recommend the Light,
So modest Plainness sets off spritely Wit:
For *Works* may have more *Wit* than does 'em good,
As *Bodies* perish through Excess of *Blood*.[18]
    Others for *Language* all their Care express,
And value *Books* as Women *Men*, for *Dress*:
Their Praise is still—*The Style is excellent*:
The *Sense*, they humbly take upon Content.
Words are like *Leaves*; and where they most abound,
Much *Fruit* of *Sense* beneath is rarely found.
False Eloquence, like the *Prismatic Glass*,
Its gaudy Colours spreads on *every place*;
The Face of Nature we no more Survey,
All glares *alike*, without *Distinction* gay:
But true *Expression*, like th' unchanging *Sun*,
Clears, and *improves* whate'er it shines upon,
It *gilds* all Objects, but it *alters* none.
Expression is the *Dress* of *Thought*, and still
Appears more *decent* as more *suitable*;
A vile Conceit in pompous Words expressed,
Is like a Clown in regal Purple dressed;
For different *Styles* with different *Subjects* sort,
As several Garbs with Country, Town, and Court.
Some by *Old Words* to Fame have made Pretence,
Ancients in *Phrase*, mere Moderns in their *Sense*!
Such *laboured Nothings*, in so *strange* a Style,
Amaze th' unlearn'd, and make the Learnèd *Smile*.
Unlucky, as *Fungoso* in the Play,[19]
These Sparks with awkward Vanity display
What the Fine Gentleman wore *Yesterday*!
And but so mimic ancient Wits at best,
As Apes our Grandsires in their *Doublets dressed*.
In *Words*, as *Fashions*, the same Rule will hold;
Alike Fantastic, if *too New*, or *Old*;
Be not the *first* by whom the *New* are tried,
Nor yet the *last* to lay the *Old* aside.
    But most by *Numbers* judge a Poet's Song,[20]
And *smooth* or *rough*, with them, is *right* or *wrong*;

Notes

[18] "Excess of Blood" could also indicate a build-up of fluid causing pleurisy or congestive heart failure.

[19] See Ben Jonson's *Every Man in His Humour* [Pope's note].

[20] *Numbers* prosody or meter; the rhythm of verse.

In the bright *Muse* though thousand *Charms* conspire,
Her *Voice* is all these tuneful Fools admire,
Who haunt *Parnassus* but to please their Ear,
Not mend their Minds as some to *Church* repair,
Not for the *Doctrine*, but the *Music* there.
These *Equal Syllables* alone require,
Though oft the Ear the *open Vowèls* tire,[21]
While *Expletives* their feeble Aid do join,[22]
And ten low Words oft creep in one dull Line,
While they ring round the same *unvaried Chimes*,
With sure *Returns* of still *expected Rhymes*.
Where'er you find *the cooling Western Breeze*,
In the next Line, it *whispers through the Trees*;
If *Crystal Streams with pleasing Murmurs creep*,
The reader's threatened (not in vain) with *Sleep*.
Then, at the *last*, and *only* Couplet fraught
With some *unmeaning* Thing they call a *Thought*,
A needless Alexandrine ends the Song,[23]
That like a wounded Snake, drags its slow Length along.
Leave such to tune their own dull Rhymes, and know
What's *roundly smooth*, or *languishingly slow*;
And praise the *Easy Vigour* of a Line,
Where *Denham*'s Strength, and *Waller*'s Sweetness join.[24]
'Tis not enough no Harshness gives Offence,
The *Sound* must seem an *Echo* to the *Sense*.
Soft is the Strain when *Zephyr* gently blows,[25]
And the *smooth Stream* in *smoother Numbers* flows;
But when loud Surges lash the sounding Shore,
The *hoarse, rough Verse* should like the *Torrent* roar.
When *Ajax* strives, some Rock's vast Weight to throw,[26]
The Line too *labours*, and the Words move *slow*;
Not so, when swift *Camilla* scours the Plain,[27]
Flies o'er th' unbending Corn, and skims along the Main.
Hear how *Timotheus'* varied Lays surprise, [28]
And bid Alternate Passions fall and rise!
While, at each Change, the Son of *Libyan Jove*[29]
Now *burns* with Glory, and then *melts* with Love,
Now his *fierce Eyes* with *sparkling Fury* glow;
Now *Sighs* steal out, and *Tears begin to flow*:

Notes

21 An open vowel is pronounced with "a wide opening of the mouth," but Pope may mean an open syllable (i.e. one ending in a vowel) (*OED*, s.v. open, 13.a and b).

22 *Expletive* "Something used only to take up room" (Johnson).

23 *Alexandrine* a line with twelve syllables.

24 John Denham (1614/15–69) and Edmund Waller (1606–87), poets whose strengths Dryden summarized in *Of Dramatic Poesy: An Essay* (1668), writing that the Elizabethans had "nothing so even, sweet, and flowing as Mr. *Waller*; nothing so Majestic, so correct as Sir *John Denham*."

25 *Zephyr* the west wind.

26 *Ajax* the brawniest hero among the Greeks in the Trojan War.

27 *Camilla* a mythical warrior whose speed is celebrated by Virgil (*Aeneid*, 7.803–17).

28 See *Alexander's Feast, or the Power of Music; an Ode* by Mr. Dryden [Pope's note; see p. 225 above].

29 Alexander the Great was called the son of Zeus Ammon, the Greek version of the Egyptian god Amun.

Persians and *Greeks* like *Turns of Nature* found,
And the *World's Victor* stood subdued by *Sound*!
The Power of Music all our Hearts allow;
And what *Timotheus* was, is *Dryden* now.
Avoid *Extremes*; and shun the Fault of such,
Who still are pleased *too little*, or *too much*.
At every Trifle scorn to take Offence,
That always shows *Great Pride*, or *Little Sense*;
Those *Heads* as *Stomachs* are not sure the best
Which nauseate all, and nothing can digest.
Yet let not each gay *Turn* thy Rapture move,
For Fools *Admire*, but Men of Sense *Approve*;
As things seem *large* which we through Mists descry,
Dullness is ever apt to *Magnify*.
Some the *French* Writers, some our *own* despise;
The *Ancients* only, or the *Moderns* prize:
(Thus *Wit*, like *Faith*, by each Man is applied
To *one small Sect*, and All are *damned beside*.)
Meanly they seek the Blessing to confine,
And force *that Sun* but on a *Part* to Shine;
Which not alone the *Southern Wit* sublimes,
But ripens Spirits in cold *Northern Climes*;
Which from the first has shone on *Ages past*,
Enlights the *present*, and shall warm the *last*:
(Though *each* may feel *Increases* and *Decays*,
And see now *clearer* and now *darker Days*)
Regard not then if Wit be *Old or New*,
But blame the *False*, and value still the *True*.
Some ne'er advance a Judgment of their own,
But *catch* the *spreading Notion* of the Town;
They reason and conclude by *Precedent*,
And own *stale Nonsense* which they ne'er invent.[30]
Some judge of Authors' *Names*, not *Works*, and then
Nor praise nor blame the *Writings*, but the *Men*.
Of all this *Servile Herd* the worst is He
That in *proud Dullness* joins with *Quality*,[31]
A constant Critic at the Great man's Board,
To *fetch and carry* Nonsense for my Lord.
What *woeful stuff* this Madrigal would be,
In some starved Hackney Sonneteer, or me?
But let a *Lord* once own the *happy Lines*,
How the *Wit brightens*! How the *Style refines*!
Before *his* sacred Name flies every Fault,
And each *exalted* Stanza *teems* with *Thought*!
The *Vulgar* thus through *Imitation* err;
As oft the *Learn'd* by being *Singular*;
So much they scorn the Crowd, that if the Throng

Notes

[30] *Own* "To claim as being one's own" (*OED*, 3).

[31] *Quality* nobility.

By *Chance* go right, they *purposely* go wrong;
So Schismatics the *plain Believers* quit,[32]
And are but damned for having *too much Wit.*
Some praise at Morning what they blame at Night;
But always think the *last* Opinion *right.*
A Muse by these is like a Mistress used,
This hour she's *idolized*, the next *abused*,
While their weak Heads, like Towns unfortified,
'Twixt Sense and Nonsense daily change their Side.
Ask them the Cause; *They're wiser still*, they say;
And still Tomorrow's wiser than Today.
We think our *Fathers* Fools, so *wise* we grow;
Our *wiser Sons*, no doubt, will think *us* so.
Once *School-Divines* this zealous Isle o'erspread;[33]
Who knew most *Sentences* was *deepest read*;
Faith, Gospel, All, seemed made to be *disputed*,
And none had *Sense enough to be Confuted.*
Scotists and *Thomists*, now, in Peace remain,
Amidst their *kindred Cobwebs* in *Duck Lane.*[34]
If *Faith* itself has different Dresses worn,
What wonder *Modes* in *Wit* should take their Turn?
Oft, leaving what is Natural and fit,
The *current Folly* proves the *ready Wit*,
And Authors think their Reputation safe,
Which lives as long as *Fools* are pleased to *Laugh.*
Some valuing those of their own *Side*, or *Mind*,
Still make themselves the measure of Mankind;
Fondly we think we honour Merit then,
When we but praise *Ourselves* in *Other Men.*
Parties in *Wit* attend on those of *State*,
And public Faction doubles private Hate.
Pride, Malice, Folly, against *Dryden* rose,
In various Shapes of *Parsons, Critics, Beaus*;
But *Sense* survived, when *merry Jests* were past;
For rising Merit will *buoy up* at last.
Might he return, and bless once more our Eyes,
New *Blackmores* and new *Milbourns* must arise;[35]
Nay should great *Homer* lift his awful Head,
Zoilus again would start up from the Dead.[36]
Envy will *Merit* as its *Shade* pursue,
But like a Shadow, proves the *Substance* true;

Notes

[32] *Schismatics* Those who separate themselves from the established church.

[33] *School-divines* scholastic philosophers, such as Duns Scotus (c.1265–1308) and Thomas Aquinas (1225–74) given to creating vast systems of knowledge and concerned with modes (l. 447) and categories of all things, as well as compilations of sentences (l. 441), pithy remarks.

[34] *Duck Lane* a place in the City of London where used or second-hand books were sold.

[35] Richard Blackmore (1654–1729), a "critic" who attacked Dryden in his epic poem, *Prince Arthur* (1695); Luke Milbourn (1622–88), a "parson", author of *Notes on Dryden's Virgil* (1698).

[36] *Zoilus* fourth-century BCE Greek grammarian and critic of Homer.

For envied Wit, like *Sol* Eclipsed, makes known
Th' *opposing Body's* Grossness, not its *own*.
When first that Sun too powerful Beams displays,
It draws up Vapours which obscure its Rays;
But even those Clouds at last adorn its Way,
Reflect new Glories, and augment the Day.
  Be thou the *first* true Merit to befriend;
His Praise is lost, who stays till *All* commend;
Short is the Date, alas, of *Modern Rhymes*;
And 'tis but just to let 'em live *betimes*.[37]
No longer now that Golden Age appears,
When *Patriarch-Wits* survived a *thousand Years*;[38]
Now Length of *Fame* (our *second* Life) is lost,
And bare Threescore is all even That can boast:
Our Sons their Fathers' *failing Language* see,
And such as *Chaucer* is, shall *Dryden* be.
So when the faithful *Pencil* has designed
Some *bright Idea* of the Master's Mind,
Where a *new World* leaps out at his command,
And ready Nature waits upon his Hand;
When the ripe Colours *soften* and *unite*,
And sweetly *melt* into just Shade and Light,
When mellowing Years their full Perfection give,
And each Bold Figure just begins to *Live*;
The *treacherous Colours* the fair Art betray,
And all the bright Creation fades away!
Unhappy *Wit*, like most mistaken Things,
Atones not for that *Envy* which it brings:
In *Youth* alone its empty Praise we boast,
But soon the Short-lived Vanity is lost!
Like some fair *Flower* the early *Spring* supplies,
That gaily Blooms, but even in blooming *Dies*.
What is this *Wit* which must our Cares employ?
The *Owner's Wife*, that *other Men* enjoy,
The most our trouble still when most *admired*;
The more we *give*, the more is still *required*:
The Fame with Pains we gain, but lose with ease;
Sure *some* to *vex*, but never *all* to *please*;
'Tis what the *Vicious fear*, the *Virtuous shun*;
By *Fools* 'tis *hated*, and by *Knaves undone*!
  If Wit so much from *Ignorance* undergo,
Ah let not *Learning* too commence its Foe!
Of old, those met *Rewards* who could *excel*,
And such were *Praised* who but *endeavoured well*:
Though *Triumphs* were to *Generals* only due,

Notes

[37] *Betimes* early in the day; early in life.
[38] Abraham and the other patriarchs in Genesis are said to have lived a long time.

Crowns were reserved to grace the *Soldiers* too.
Now they who reach *Parnassus'* lofty Crown,
Employ their Pains to spurn some others down;
And while Self-Love each jealous Writer rules,
Contending Wits become the *Sport of Fools*:
But still the *Worst* with most Regret commend,
And each *Ill Author* is as bad a *Friend*.
To what base Ends, and by what abject Ways,
Are Mortals urged through *Sacred Lust of Praise*!
Ah ne'er so *dire* a *Thirst of Glory* boast,
Nor in the *Critic* let the *Man* be lost!
Good-Nature and *Good-Sense* must ever join;
To Err is *Human*; to Forgive, *Divine*.
  But if in Noble Minds some Dregs remain,
Not yet purged off, of Spleen and sour Disdain,
Discharge that Rage on more Provoking Crimes,
Nor fear a Dearth in these Flagitious Times.[39]
No Pardon vile *Obscenity* should find,
Though *Wit* and *Art* conspire to move your Mind;
But *Dullness* with *Obscenity* must prove
As Shameful sure as *Impotence* in *Love*.
In the fat Age of Pleasure, Wealth, and Ease,
Sprung the rank Weed, and thrived with large Increase;
When *Love* was all an easy Monarch's Care;[40]
Seldom at *Council*, never in a *War*:
Jilts ruled the State, and Statesmen *Farces* writ;
Nay *Wits* had *Pensions*, and *young Lords* had *Wit*:
The Fair sat panting at a *Courtier's Play*,
And not a Mask went *unimproved* away
The modest Fan was lifted up no more,
And Virgins *smiled* at what they *blushed* before—
The following Licence of a Foreign Reign[41]
Did all the Dregs of bold *Socinus* drain;[42]
Then Unbelieving Priests reformed the Nation,
And taught more *Pleasant* Methods of Salvation;
Where Heaven's Free Subjects might their *Rights* dispute,
Lest God himself should seem too *Absolute*.
Pulpits their *Sacred Satire* learned to spare,
And Vice *admired* to find a *Flatterer there*!
Encouraged thus, Wit's *Titans* braved the Skies,
And the Press groaned with Licensed *Blasphemies*—[43]
These Monsters, Critics! with your Darts engage,

Notes

39 *Flagitious* wicked.

40 *easy Monarch* Charles II, whose court (1660–85) was known for powerful *jilts* (mistresses), such as Barbara Villiers and Louise de Kéroualle, and bawdy wits, such as John Wilmot, 2nd earl of Rochester (see p. 376 above).

41 *Foreign Reign* that of William of Orange, William III (1685–1702).

42 *Socinus* Lelio Sozzini (1525–62) gave his name to the heresy of doubting the divinity of Christ.

43 Pope conflates Whiggish politics, weak Christian belief, and corruption among ambitious churchmen.

Here point your Thunder, and exhaust your Rage!
Yet shun their Fault, who, *Scandalously nice*,
Will needs *mistake* an Author *into Vice*;
All seems Infected that th' Infected spy,
As all looks yellow to the Jaundiced Eye.[44]
Learn then what MORALS Critics ought to show,
For 'tis but *half* a *Judge's Task*, to *Know*.
'Tis not enough, Wit, Art, and Learning join;
In all you speak, let Truth and Candour shine:
That not alone what to your *Judgment*'s due,
All may allow; but seek your *Friendship* too.
Be *silent* always when you *doubt* your Sense;
And *Speak*, tho' sure, with *seeming Diffidence*;
Some positive persisting Fops we know,[45]
That if *once wrong*, will needs be *always so*;
But you, with Pleasure own your Errors past,
And make each Day a *Critic* on the last.[46]
'Tis not enough your Counsel still be *true*,
Blunt Truths more Mischief than *nice Falsehoods* do;
Men must be *taught* as if you taught them *not*;
And Things *unknown* proposed as Things *forgot*:
Without *Good Breeding*, *Truth* is disapproved,
That only makes *Superior* Sense belov'd.
Be Niggards of Advice on no Pretence;
For the *worst Avarice* is that of *Sense*:
With mean Complacence ne'er betray your Trust,[47]
Nor be so *Civil* as to prove *Unjust*;
Fear not the Anger of the Wise to raise;
Those best can *bear Reproof*, who *merit Praise*.
'Twere well, might Critics still this Freedom take;
But *Appius* reddens at each Word you speak,[48]
And *stares*, *Tremendous*! with a *threatening Eye*,
Like some *fierce Tyrant* in *Old Tapestry*!
Fear most to tax an *Honourable* Fool,
Whose Right it is, *uncensured* to be dull;
Such without *Wit* are Poets when they please,
As without *Learning* they can take *Degrees*.
Leave dangerous *Truths* to unsuccessful *Satires*,
And *Flattery* to fulsome *Dedicators*,
Whom, when they *Praise*, the World believes no more,
Than when they promise to give *Scribbling* o'er.
'Tis best sometimes your Censure to restrain,
And *charitably* let the Dull be *vain*:
Your Silence there is better than your *Spite*,
For who can *rail* so long as they can *write*?

Notes

[44] *Jaundiced* physically colored yellow from hepatitis, or colored, or biased, through jealousy or envy.

[45] *Positive* opinionated.

[46] *Critic* criticism or critique.

[47] *Complacence* "Disposition to please … complaisance" (*OED*, 3).

[48] *Appius* John Dennis, a critic of Pope and author of the unsuccessful play *Appius and Virginia* (1709).

Still humming on, their drowsy Course they keep,
And *lashed* so long, like *Tops*, are lashed *asleep*.[49]
False Steps but help them to renew the Race,
As after *Stumbling*, Jades will *mend* their Pace.[50]
What Crowds of these, impenitently bold,
In *Sounds* and jingling *Syllables* grown old,
Still *run on* Poets in a raging Vein,
Even to the Dregs and *Squeezings* of the *Brain*,
Strain out the last, dull droppings of their Sense,
And Rhyme with all the *Rage* of *Impotence*!
    Such shameless *Bards* we have; and yet 'tis true,
There are as mad, abandoned *Critics* too.
The Bookful Blockhead, ignorantly read,
With *Loads of Learned Lumber* in his Head,
With his own Tongue still edifies his Ears,
And always *Listening to Himself* appears.
All Books he reads, and all he reads assails,
From *Dryden's Fables* down to *Durfey's Tales*.[51]
With *him*, most Authors steal their Works, or buy;
Garth did not write his own *Dispensary*.[52]
Name a new *Play*, and *he*'s the Poet's *Friend*,
Nay showed his Faults—but when would Poets mend?
No Place so Sacred from such Fops is barred,
Nor is *Paul's Church* more safe than *Paul's Churchyard*:[53]
Nay, fly to *Altars*; *there* they'll talk you dead;
For *Fools* rush in where *Angels* fear to tread.
Distrustful *Sense* with modest Caution speaks;
It still *looks home*, and *short Excursions* makes;
But *rattling Nonsense* in full *Volleys* breaks;
And never shocked, and never turned aside,
Bursts out, resistless, with a thundering Tide!
    But where's the Man, who Counsel *can* bestow,
Still *pleased* to *teach*, and yet not *proud* to *know*?
Unbiased, nor by *Favour* or by *Spite*;
Not *dully prepossessed*, or *blindly right*;
Though Learn'd, well-bred; and though well-bred, sincere;
Modestly bold, and Humanly severe?
Who to a *Friend* his Faults can freely show,
And gladly praise the Merit of a *Foe*?
Blessed with a *Taste* exact, yet unconfined;
A *Knowledge* both of *Books* and *Humankind*;
Generous Converse; a *Soul* exempt from *Pride*;
And *Love to Praise*, with *Reason* on his Side?

Notes

49 A top, spun around, or lashed, with a string, is said to sleep when its movement becomes quiet and regular (*OED*, 3c). To sleep like a top is to sleep well (*OED*, 1e).

50 *Jade* a worn-out or ill-tempered horse, a hack.

51 John Dryden, *Fables Ancient and Modern* (1700; see p. 230 above); Thomas D'Urfey, *Tales Tragical and Comical* (1704).

52 Samuel Garth's *Dispensary* (1699), like Pope's *Rape of the Lock*, took Boileau's *Le lutrin* (1674) as a model.

53 St. Paul's churchyard was then full of bookstalls; loitering in the church was common.

Such once were *Critics*, such the Happy *Few*,
Athens and *Rome* in better Ages knew.
The mighty *Stagyrite* first left the Shore,
Spread all his Sails, and durst the Deeps explore;
He steered securely, and discovered far,
Led by the Light of the *Mæonian Star.*[54]
Poets, a *Race* long unconfined and free,
Still fond and proud of *Savage Liberty*,
Received his Laws, and stood convinced 'twas fit
Who conquered *Nature*, should preside o'er *Wit.*
Horace still charms with graceful Negligence,
And without Method *talks* us into Sense,
Will like a *Friend* familiarly convey
The *truest Notions* in the *easiest way*.
He, who Supreme in Judgment, as in Wit,
Might boldly censure, as he boldly writ,
Yet *judged* with *Coolness* though he sung with *Fire*;
His *Precepts* teach but what his *Works* inspire.
Our Critics take a contrary Extreme,
They *judge* with *Fury*, but they *write* with *Phlegm*:[55]
Nor suffers *Horace* more in wrong translations
By *Wits*, than *Critics* in as wrong *Quotations*.
See Dionysius Homer's Thoughts refine,[56]
And Call new Beauties forth from every Line!
Fancy and Art in gay *Petronius* please,[57]
The *Scholar's* Learning, with the *Courtier's Ease*.
In grave *Quintilian's* copious Work we find[58]
The justest *Rules*, and clearest *Method* joined;
Thus *useful Arms* in Magazines we place,[59]
All ranged in *Order*, and disposed with *Grace*,
Nor thus alone the Curious Eye to please,
But to be *found*, when Need requires, with Ease.
Thee, bold *Longinus*! All the Nine inspire,[60]
And bless *their Critic* with a *Poet's Fire*.
An ardent *Judge*, who Zealous in his Trust,
With *Warmth* gives Sentence, yet is always *Just*;
Whose *own Example* strengthens all his Laws,
And *Is himself* that great *Sublime* he draws.
Thus long succeeding Critics justly reigned,
Licence repressed, and *useful Laws* ordained;

Notes

[54] *Mæonian Star* Homer, supposedly from Maeonia, in Asia Minor.

[55] *Phlegm* one of the four "humours" in the human constitution, it is associated with laziness and turgor.

[56] Dionysius of Halicarnassus [Pope's note; a first-century BCE critic and rhetorician].

[57] Gaius Petronius Arbiter, first-century CE Roman courtier, author of the *Satyricon*.

[58] *Quintilian* a first-century CE author of a famous textbook of oratory.

[59] *Magazine* a storehouse for military weapons.

[60] *Longinus* supposed author of *On the Sublime*, an influential Greek treatise of the second century CE.

Learning and *Rome* alike in Empire grew,
And *Arts* still *followed* where her *Eagles flew*;
From the same Foes, at last, both felt their Doom,
And the same Age saw *Learning* fall, and *Rome*.
With *Tyranny*, then *Superstition* joined,
As that the *Body*, this enslaved the *Mind*;
Much was *Believed*, but little *understood*,
And to be *dull* was construed to be *good*;
A *second* Deluge Learning thus o'errun,
And the *Monks* finished what the *Goths* begun.
At length, *Erasmus*, that *great, injured* Name,[61]
(The Glory of the Priesthood, and the *Shame*!)
Stemmed the *wild Torrent* of a *barbarous Age*,
And drove those *Holy Vandals* off the Stage.
But see! each *Muse*, in *Leo*'s Golden Days,[62]
Starts from her Trance, and trims her withered Bays!
Rome's ancient *Genius*, o'er its *Ruins* spread,
Shakes off the *Dust*, and rears his reverend Head!
Then *Sculpture* and her *Sister-Arts* revive;
Stones leaped to *Form*, and *Rocks* began to *live*;
With *Sweeter Notes* each *rising Temple* rung;
A *Raphael* painted, and a *Vida* sung![63]
Immortal *Vida*! on whose honoured Brow
The Poet's *Bays* and Critic's *Ivy* grow:
Cremona now shall ever boast thy Name,
As next in Place to *Mantua*, next in Fame!
But soon by Impious Arms from *Latium* chased,[64]
Their *ancient Bounds* the banished Muses past;
Thence Arts o'er all the *Northern World* advance;
But *Critic Learning* flourished most in *France*.
The *Rules*, a Nation born to serve, obeys,[65]
And *Boileau* still in Right of *Horace* sways.[66]
But *we*, brave *Britons*, *Foreign Laws* despised,
And kept *unconquered*, and *uncivilized*,
Fierce for the *Liberties of Wit*, and bold,
We still defied the *Romans*, as *of old*.
Yet *some* there were, among the *sounder Few*
Of those who *less presumed*, and *better knew*,
Who durst assert the *juster Ancient Cause*,
And here *restored* Wit's *Fundamental Laws*.
Such was the Muse, whose Rules and Practice tell,

Notes

[61] Desiderius Erasmus (1466–1536), greatest of the Christian humanists, Catholic priest but critic of the church.

[62] Leo X, Pope from 1513–21.

[63] Raffaello Sanzio da Urbino (1483–1520); Marco Girolamo Vida (1485?–1566), born in Cremona, Italy, author of a didactic poem "The Art of Poetry."

[64] "Impious Arms" refers to the attack on Rome by Emperor Charles V in 1527.

[65] Rules such as the three "unities," which were taken as laws for judging dramatic works. The French were regarded by the British as politically servile under the rule of Louis XIV.

[66] Nicolas Boileau-Despréaux (1636–1711), author of *L'art poétique*, an imitation of Horace's *Ars Poetica*.

Nature's chief Masterpiece is writing well.[67]
Such was *Roscommon*—not more *learn'd* than *good*,[68]
With Manners generous as his Noble Blood;
To him the Wit of *Greece* and *Rome* was known,
And every Author's *Merit*, but his own.
Such late was *Walsh*,—the Muses' Judge and Friend,[69]
Who justly knew to blame or to commend;
To Failings *mild*, but *zealous* for Desert;
The *clearest Head*, and the *sincerest Heart*.
This humble Praise, lamented Shade! receive,
This Praise at least a grateful Muse may give!
The Muse, whose early Voice you taught to Sing,
Prescribed her Heights, and pruned her tender Wing,
(Her Guide now lost) no more attempts to *rise*,
But in low Numbers short Excursions tries:
Content, if hence th' Unlearn'd their Wants may view,
The Learn'd reflect on what before they knew:
Careless of *Censure*, nor too fond of *Fame*,
Still pleased to *praise*, yet not afraid to *blame*,
Averse alike to *Flatter*, or *Offend*,
Not *free* from Faults, nor yet too vain to *mend*.

The RAPE of the LOCK. An Heroi-Comical Poem (1714) In Five Canto's

—*A tonso est hoc nomen adepta capillo.*
Ovid.[1]

TO
MRS. ARABELLA FERMOR[2]

Madam,

It will be in vain to deny that I have some Value for this Piece, since I Dedicate it to You. Yet You may bear me Witness, it was intended only to divert a few young Ladies, who have good Sense and good Humour enough, to laugh not only at their Sex's little unguarded Follies, but at their own. But as it was communicated with the Air of a

Notes

[67] *Essay on Poetry, by the Duke of* Buckingham [Pope's note; referring to John Sheffield's *Essay* (1709) and quoting its second line].

[68] Wentworth Dillon, fourth earl of Roscommon (1637–85), a translator of Horace's *Art of Poetry* (1679) and the verse *Essay on Translated Verse* (1684).

[69] William Walsh (1662–1708), poet and Pope's mentor, who perhaps saw *An Essay on Criticism* in draft (*ODNB*).

The RAPE of the LOCK

[1] *A tonso ... Ovid* "the name taken from a shorn lock of hair" (*Metamorphoses* 8.151), from the story of Scylla, who is turned into a bird and renamed Ciris (Latin, "lock," "curl") after she betrays her father by cutting off a special lock of his hair and presenting it to his handsome enemy. In later editions, Pope replaced the motto with a quotation from Martial: "Nolueram, [Belinda], tuos violare capillos/Sed juvat hoc precibus me tribuisse tuis" (*Epigrams* 12.84.1–2; "I did not wish, [Belinda], to violate your locks, but I rejoice to have yielded this to your wishes").

[2] *Arabella Fermor* (c.1689–1738), Belinda in the poem, who really was the victim of the prank that Pope describes with such grandeur; "Mrs.," as usual in the eighteenth century, is a title of respect rather than one that indicates marriage; Fermor married in 1714, shortly after this expanded version of the poem was first published.

Secret, it soon found its Way into the World. An imperfect Copy having been offered to a Bookseller, You had the Good Nature for my Sake to consent to the Publication of one more correct:[3] This I was forced to before I had executed half my Design, for the *Machinery* was entirely wanting to complete it.

The *Machinery*, Madam, is a Term invented by the Critics, to signify that Part which the Deities, Angels, or Dæmons, are made to act in a Poem: For the ancient Poets are in one respect like many modern Ladies; Let an Action be never so trivial in itself, they always make it appear of the utmost Importance. These Machines I determined to raise on a very new and odd Foundation, the *Rosicrucian* Doctrine of Spirits.

I know how disagreeable it is to make use of hard Words before a Lady; but 'tis so much the Concern of a Poet to have his Works understood, and particularly by your Sex, that You must give me leave to explain two or three difficult Terms.

The *Rosicrucians* are a People I must bring You acquainted with. The best Account I know of them is in a French Book called *Le Comte de Gabalis*,[4] which both in its Title and Size is so like a *Novel*, that many of the Fair Sex have read it for one by Mistake. According to these Gentlemen, the four Elements are inhabited by Spirits, which they call *Sylphs*, *Gnomes*, *Nymphs*, and *Salamanders*.[5] The *Gnomes*, or Dæmons of Earth, delight in Mischief; but the *Sylphs*, whose Habitation is in the Air, are the best-conditioned Creatures imaginable. For they say, any Mortals may enjoy the most intimate Familiarities with these gentle Spirits, upon a Condition very easy to all true *Adepts*, an inviolate Preservation of Chastity.

As to the following Cantos, all the Passages of them are as Fabulous, as the Vision at the Beginning, or the Transformation at the End (except the Loss of your Hair, which I always mention with Reverence). The Human Persons are as Fictitious as the Airy ones; and the Character of *Belinda*, as it is now managed, resembles You in nothing but in Beauty.

If this Poem had as many Graces as there are in Your Person, or in Your Mind, yet I could never hope it should pass through the World half so Uncensured as You have done. But let its Fortune be what it will, mine is happy enough, to have given me this Occasion of assuring You that I am, with the truest Esteem,

Madam,
Your Most Obedient
Humble Servant.
A. Pope

The *Rape* of the Lock

Canto I

What dire Offence from am'rous Causes springs,
What mighty Quarrels rise from trivial Things,
I sing – This Verse to *C—l*, Muse! is due;[6]
This, ev'n *Belinda* may vouchsafe to view:
Slight is the Subject, but not so the Praise,
If she inspire, and He approve my Lays.

Notes

3 *Publication of one more correct* this was the version in two cantos, published in 1712.

4 *Le Comte de Gabalis* by Abbé de Montfaucon de Villars (1670).

5 *Salamanders* elemental, fire-inhabiting beings.

6 *C—l* John Caryll (1667–1736), a wealthy landowner, friend and correspondent of Pope; he was related both to Robert, Lord Petre (the Baron of the poem) and to Arabella Fermor (Belinda), and wished for continued good relations among the three well-to-do Catholic families.

Say what strange Motive, Goddess! could compel
A well-bred *Lord* t'assault a gentle *Belle*?
Oh say what stranger Cause, yet unexplored
Could make a gentle *Belle* reject a *Lord*?
And dwells such Rage in softest Bosoms then?
And lodge such daring Souls in Little Men?
Sol through white Curtains shot a tim'rous Ray,[7]
And op'd those Eyes that must eclipse the Day;
Now Lapdogs give themselves the rousing Shake,
And sleepless Lovers, just at Twelve, awake:
Thrice rung the Bell, the Slipper knocked the Ground,[8]
And the pressed Watch returned a silver Sound.[9]
Belinda still her downy Pillow pressed,
Her Guardian *Sylph* prolonged the balmy Rest.
'Twas he had summoned to her silent Bed
The Morning Dream that hovered o'er her Head.
A Youth more glitt'ring than a *Birthnight Beau*,[10]
(That ev'n in Slumber caused her Cheek to glow)
Seemed to her Ear his winning Lips to lay,
And thus in Whispers said, or seemed to say,
'Fairest of Mortals, thou distinguished Care
Of thousand bright Inhabitants of Air!
If e'er one Vision touched thy infant Thought,
Of all the Nurse and all the Priest have taught,
Of airy Elves by Moonlight Shadows seen,
The silver Token, and the circled Green,[11]
Or Virgins visited by Angel-Powers,[12]
With Golden Crowns and Wreaths of heav'nly Flowers,
Hear and believe! thy own Importance know,
Nor bound thy narrow Views to Things below.
Some secret Truths from Learned Pride concealed,
To Maids alone and Children are revealed:
What though no Credit doubting Wits may give?
The Fair and Innocent shall still believe.
Know then, unnumbered Spirits round thee fly,
The light *Militia* of the lower Sky;
These, though unseen, are ever on the Wing,
Hang o'er the *Box*, and hover round the *Ring*.[13]
Think what an Equipáge thou hast in Air,[14]
And view with scorn *Two Pages* and a *Chair*.[15]

Notes

7 *Sol* Latin for "sun."

8 *Slipper knocked* to call the maid from her station downstairs.

9 *pressed Watches* or "repeaters," sounded when pressed open.

10 *Birthnight Beau* a fashionable suitor, dressed up for the celebration of a royal birthday.

11 *circled Green* a fairy ring, a circle of grass with a different color than the rest, supposed to be left, like silver coins, by fairies (but actually caused by fungus).

12 *Virgins* particularly, the Virgin Mary at the Annunciation, which is depicted with similar images.

13 *the Ring* a track cruised by fashionable coaches on the north side of Hyde Park, London.

14 *Equipáge* "Attendance; retinue" (Johnson).

15 *Chair* a sedan chair borne by two pages.

As now your own, our Beings were of old,
And once enclosed in a Woman's beauteous Mould;
Thence, by a soft Transition, we repair
From earthly Vehicles to these of Air.
Think not, when Woman's transient Breath is fled,
That all her Vanities at once are dead:
Succeeding Vanities she still regards,
And though she plays no more, o'erlooks the Cards.
Her Joy in gilded Chariots, when alive,
And Love of *Ombre*, after Death survive.[16]
For when the Fair in all their Pride expire,
To their first Elements their Souls retire:[17]
The Sprites of fiery Termagants in Flame[18]
Mount up, and take a *Salamander*'s Name.[19]
Soft yielding Minds to Water glide away,
And sip with *Nymphs*, their Elemental Tea.
The graver Prude sinks downward to a *Gnome*,
In search of Mischief still on Earth to roam.
The light Coquettes in *Sylphs* aloft repair,
And sport and flutter in the Fields of Air.
'Know farther yet; Whoever fair and chaste
Rejects Mankind, is by some *Sylphs* embraced:
For Spirits, freed from mortal Laws, with ease
Assume what Sexes and what Shapes they please.
What guards the Purity of melting Maids,
In Courtly Balls, and Midnight Masquerades,
Safe from the treach'rous Friend, the daring Spark,[20]
The Glance by Day, the Whisper in the Dark;
When kind Occasion prompts their warm Desires,
When Music softens, and when Dancing fires?
'Tis but their *Sylph*, the wise Celestials know,
Though *Honour* is the Word with Men below.
'Some Nymphs there are, too conscious of their Face,
For Life predestined to the *Gnomes'* Embrace.
These swell their Prospects and exalt their Pride,
When Offers are disdained, and Love denied.
Then gay Ideas crowd the vacant Brain;
While Peers and Dukes, and all their sweeping Train,
And Garters, Stars and Coronets appear,[21]
And in soft Sounds, "Your Grace" salutes their Ear.
'Tis these that early taint the Female Soul,
Instruct the Eyes of young *Coquettes* to roll,

Notes

[16] *Ombre* a card game in which one player (the ombre), depending on the deal, declares which cards are trumps and competes for tricks with the other two players.

[17] *first elements* predominant of the four "elements" of fire, water, earth, and air, supposed to comprise all things and, by their proportions in the soul, to determine personality.

[18] *Termagant* "A scold; a brawling, turbulent woman" (Johnson).

[19] *Salamander's Name* because *salamanders* were popularly believed to live in fire (Browne, *Pseudodoxia Epidemica*, chapter 14).

[20] *Spark* dashing, bold man about town.

[21] *Garters, Stars and Coronets* badges of nobility.

Teach Infant Cheeks a bidden Blush to know,
And little Hearts to flutter at a *Beau*.
'Oft when the World imagine Women stray,
The *Sylphs* through mystic Mazes guide their Way,
Through all the giddy Circle they pursue,
And old Impertinence expel by new.
What tender Maid but must a Victim fall
To one Man's Treat, but for another's Ball?[22]
When *Florio* speaks, what Virgin could withstand,
If gentle *Damon* did not squeeze her Hand?
With varying Vanities, from every Part,
They shift the moving Toyshop of their Heart;
Where Wigs with Wigs, with Sword-knots Sword-knots strive,[23]
Beaus banish Beaus, and Coaches Coaches drive.
This erring Mortals Levity may call,
Oh blind to Truth! the *Sylphs* contrive it all.
'Of these am I, who thy Protection claim,
A watchful Sprite, and *Ariel* is my Name.
Late, as I ranged the Crystal Wilds of Air,
In the clear Mirror of thy ruling *Star*
I saw, alas! some dread Event impend,
Ere to the Main this Morning's Sun descend.[24]
But Heav'n reveals not what, or how, or where:
Warned by thy *Sylph*, oh Pious Maid beware!
This to disclose is all thy Guardian can.
Beware of all, but most beware of Man!'
He said; when *Shock*, who thought she slept too long,[25]
Leapt up, and waked his Mistress with his Tongue.
'Twas then *Belinda*! if Report say true,
Thy Eyes first opened on a *Billet-doux*;[26]
Wounds, *Charms*, and *Ardours*, were no sooner read,
But all the Vision vanished from thy Head.
And now, unveiled, the *Toilet* stands displayed,[27]
Each Silver Vase in mystic Order laid.
First, robed in White, the Nymph intent adores
With Head uncovered, the *Cosmetic* Powers.
A heav'nly Image in the Glass appears,
To that she bends, to that her Eyes she rears;
Th' inferior Priestess, at her Altar's side,
Trembling, begins the sacred Rites of Pride.
Unnumbered Treasures ope at once, and here
The various Off'rings of the World appear;
From each she nicely culls with curious Toil,

Notes

[22] *Treat* "An entertainment given" (Johnson).
[23] *Sword-knot* "Ribband tied to the hilt of the sword" (Johnson), worn in fancy dress.
[24] *Main* ocean.
[25] *Shock* stock name for a lap dog, as well as a breed from Iceland.
[26] *Billet-doux* love letter.
[27] *Toilet* dressing table.

And decks the Goddess with the glitt'ring Spoil.
This Casket *India's* glowing Gems unlocks,
And all *Arabia* breathes from yonder Box.
The Tortoise here and Elephant unite,
Transformed to *Combs*, the speckled and the white.
Here Files of Pins extend their shining Rows,
Puffs, Powders, Patches, Bibles, Billet-doux.[28]
Now awful Beauty puts on all its Arms;
The Fair each moment rises in her Charms,
Repairs her Smiles, awakens every Grace,
And calls forth all the Wonders of her Face;
Sees by Degrees a purer Blush arise,
And keener Lightnings quicken in her Eyes.
The busy *Sylphs* surround their darling Care;
These set the Head, and those divide the Hair,
Some fold the Sleeve, whilst others plait the Gown;
And *Betty's* praised for Labours not her own.

Canto II

Not with more Glories, in th' Ethereal Plain,
The Sun first rises o'er the purpled Main,
Than issuing forth, the Rival of his Beams
Launched on the Bosom of the Silver *Thames*.
Fair Nymphs, and well-dressed Youths around her shone,
But every Eye was fixed on her alone.
On her white Breast a sparkling *Cross* she wore,
Which *Jews* might kiss, and Infidels adore.
Her lively Looks a sprightly Mind disclose,
Quick as her Eyes, and as unfixed as those:
Favours to none, to all she Smiles extends,
Oft she rejects, but never once offends.
Bright as the Sun, her Eyes the Gazers strike,
And, like the Sun, they shine on all alike.
Yet graceful Ease, and Sweetness void of Pride,
Might hide her Faults, if *Belles* had Faults to hide:
If to her share some Female Errors fall,
Look on her Face, and you'll forget 'em all.
    This Nymph, to the Destruction of Mankind,
Nourished two Locks, which graceful hung behind
In equal Curls, and well conspired to deck
With shining Ringlets the smooth Iv'ry Neck.
Love in these Labyrinths his Slaves detains,
And mighty Hearts are held in slender Chains.
With hairy Springes we the Birds betray,[29]

Notes

[28] *Patch* "A small spot of black silk put on the face."

[29] *Springès* "A gin; noose which fastened to any elastic body catches by a spring or jerk" (Johnson).

Slight Lines of Hair surprise the Finny Prey,
Fair Tresses Man's Imperial Race ensnare,
And Beauty draws us with a single Hair.
Th' Advent'rous *Baron* the bright Locks admired,[30]
He saw, he wished, and to the Prize aspired:
Resolved to win, he meditates the way,
By Force to ravish, or by Fraud betray;
For when Success a Lover's Toil attends,
Few ask, if Fraud or Force attained his Ends.
For this, ere *Phœbus* rose, he had implored,
Propitious Heav'n, and every Power adored,
But chiefly *Love* – to *Love* an Altar built,
Of twelve vast *French* Romances, neatly gilt.
There lay three Garters, half a Pair of Gloves;
And all the Trophies of his former Loves.
With tender *Billet-doux* he lights the Pyre,
And breathes three am'rous Sighs to raise the Fire.
Then prostrate falls, and begs with ardent Eyes
Soon to obtain, and long possess the Prize:
The Pow'rs gave Ear, and granted half his Prayer,
The rest, the Winds dispersed in empty Air.
But now secure the painted Vessel glides,
The Sunbeams trembling on the floating Tides,
While melting Music steals upon the Sky,
And softened Sounds along the Waters die.
Smooth flow the Waves, the Zephyrs gently play,
Belinda smiled, and all the World was gay.
All but the *Sylph* – With careful Thought oppressed,
Th' impending Woe sate heavy on his Breast.
He summons straight his Denizens of Air;
The lucid Squadrons round the Sails repair:
Soft o'er the Shrouds Aerial Whispers breathe,
That seemed but *Zephyrs* to the Train beneath.
Some to the Sun their Insect-Wings unfold,
Waft on the Breeze, or sink in Clouds of Gold.
Transparent Forms, too fine for mortal Sight,
Their fluid Bodies half dissolved in Light.
Loose to the Wind their airy Garments flew,
Thin glitt'ring Textures of the filmy Dew;
Dipped in the richest Tincture of the Skies,
Where Light disports in ever-mingling Dyes,
While every Beam new transient Colours flings,
Colours that change whene'er they wave their Wings.
Amid the Circle, on the gilded Mast,
Superior by the Head, was *Ariel* placed;
His Purple Pinions opening to the Sun,
He raised his Azure Wand, and thus begun.

Notes

[30] *Baron* Robert, Lord Petre (1690–1713); on March 1, 1712, just before the publication of the short version of the *Rape*, Lord Petre married Catherine Walmesley, a younger, richer belle than Arabella Fermor.

'Ye *Sylphs* and *Sylphids*, to your Chief give Ear,
Fays, Fairies, Genii, Elves and *Dæmons* hear![31]
Ye know the Spheres and various Tasks assigned,
By Laws Eternal, to th' Aerial Kind.
Some in the Fields of purest *Æther* play,[32]
And bask and whiten in the Blaze of Day.
Some guide the Course of wand'ring Orbs on high,
Or roll the Planets through the boundless Sky.
Some less refined, beneath the Moon's pale Light
Pursue the Stars that shoot athwart the Night,
Or suck the Mists in grosser Air below,
Or dip their Pinions in the painted Bow,
Or brew fierce Tempests on the wintry Main,
Or o'er the Glebe distil the kindly Rain.
Others on Earth o'er human Race preside,
Watch all their Ways, and all their Actions guide:
Of these the Chief the Care of Nations own,
And guard with Arms Divine the *British Throne*.
'Our humbler Province is to tend the Fair,
Not a less pleasing, though less glorious Care.
To save the Powder from too rude a Gale,[33]
Nor let th' imprisoned Essences exhale,
To draw fresh Colours from the vernal Flow'rs,
To steal from Rainbows ere they drop in Show'rs
A brighter Wash; to curl their waving Hairs,[34]
Assist their Blushes, and inspire their Airs;
Nay oft, in Dreams, Invention we bestow,
To change a *Flounce*, or add a *Furbelow*.[35]
'This Day, black Omens threat the brightest Fair
That e'er deserved a watchful Spirit's Care;
Some dire Disaster, or by Force, or Slight,[36]
But what, or where, the Fates have wrapped in Night.
Whether the Nymph shall break *Diana*'s Law,[37]
Or some frail *China* Jar receive a Flaw,
Or stain her Honour, or her new Brocade,
Forget her Prayers, or miss a Masquerade,
Or lose her Heart, or Necklace at a Ball;
Or whether Heav'n has doomed that *Shock* must fall.
Haste then ye Spirits! to your Charge repair;
The flutt'ring Fan be *Zephyretta*'s Care;
The Drops to thee, *Brillantè*, we consign;[38]
And, *Momentilla*, let the Watch be thine;

Notes

[31] *Fays, Fairies, Genii, Elves and Dæmons hear*! in imitation of *Paradise Lost* 5.601.

[32] *Æther* "An element more fine and subtle than air" (Johnson).

[33] *Gale* "A wind not tempestuous, yet stronger than a breeze" (Johnson).

[34] *Wash* "A medical or cosmetic lotion" (Johnson).

[35] *Furbelo* "Fur sewed on the lower part of the garment; an ornament of dress" (Johnson).

[36] *or … or* either…or.

[37] *Diana* goddess of chastity.

[38] *Drop* "Diamond hanging in the ear" (Johnson).

Do thou, *Crispissa*, tend her favourite Lock;
Ariel himself shall be the Guard of *Shock*.
'To Fifty chosen *Sylphs*, of special Note,
We trust th' important Charge, the *Petticoat*:
Oft have we known that sev'nfold Fence to fail,[39]
Though stiff with Hoops, and armed with Ribs of Whale.
Form a strong Line about the Silver Bound,
And guard the wide Circumference around.
'Whatever Spirit, careless of his Charge,
His Post neglects, or leaves the Fair at large,
Shall feel sharp Vengeance soon o'ertake his Sins,
Be stop't in *Vials*, or transfixed with *Pins*;
Or plunged in Lakes of bitter *Washes* lie,
Or wedged whole Ages in a *Bodkin*'s Eye:[40]
Gums and *Pomatums* shall his Flight restrain,[41]
While clogged he beats his silken Wings in vain;
Or Alum-*Styptics* with contracting Power[42]
Shrink his thin Essence like a rivelled Flower.[43]
Or as *Ixion* fixed, the Wretch shall feel[44]
The giddy Motion of the whirling Mill,
In Fumes of burning Chocolate shall glow,
And tremble at the Sea that froths below!'
He spoke; the Spirits from the Sails descend;
Some, Orb in Orb, around the Nymph extend,
Some thrid the mazy Ringlets of her Hair,[45]
Some hang upon the Pendants of her Ear;
With beating Hearts the dire Event they wait,
Anxious, and trembling for the Birth of Fate.

Canto III

Close by those Meads for ever crowned with Flow'rs,
Where *Thames* with Pride surveys his rising Tow'rs,
There stands a Structure of Majestic Frame,[46]
Which from the neighb'ring *Hampton* takes its Name.
Here *Britain*'s Statesmen oft the Fall foredoom
Of Foreign Tyrants, and of Nymphs at home;
Here Thou, Great *Anna*! whom three Realms obey,[47]
Dost sometimes Counsel take – and sometimes *Tea*.

Notes

39 *sev'nfold Fence* with its seven layers and silver band, the petticoat is a version of an epic hero's shield (see *Iliad* 18 or *Aeneid* 8).

40 *Bodkin* "An instrument to draw a thread or ribband through a loop" (Johnson).

41 *Gums and Pomatums* cosmetic ointments.

42 *Alum-Styptics* an astringent used to close small cuts and blemishes.

43 *rivel* "To contract into wrinkles and corrugations" (Johnson).

44 *Ixion* the first Greek to murder a kinsman; for this crime Zeus had him bound to a perpetually revolving wheel of fire.

45 *thrid* "To slide through a narrow passage" (Johnson).

46 *Structure of Majestic Frame* Hampton Court, a palace built by Cardinal Wolsey in the sixteenth century, renovated and enlarged by William III.

47 *three Realms* England, Ireland, and Scotland.

Hither the Heroes and the Nymphs resort,
To taste awhile the Pleasures of a Court;
In various Talk th' instructive hours they passed,
Who gave the *Ball*, or paid the *Visit* last:
One speaks the Glory of the *British Queen*,
And one describes a charming *Indian Screen*;
A third interprets Motions, Looks, and Eyes;
At every Word a Reputation dies.
Snuff, or the *Fan*, supply each Pause of Chat,
With singing, laughing, ogling, and all that.[48]
Meanwhile declining from the Noon of Day,
The Sun obliquely shoots his burning Ray;
The hungry Judges soon the Sentence sign,
And Wretches hang that Jurymen may Dine;
The Merchant from th' *Exchange* returns in Peace,[49]
And the long Labours of the *Toilette* cease –
Belinda now, whom Thirst of Fame invites,
Burns to encounter two advent'rous Knights,
At *Ombre* singly to decide their Doom;
And swells her Breast with Conquests yet to come.
Straight the three Bands prepare in Arms to join,
Each Band the number of the Sacred Nine.[50]
Soon as she spreads her Hand, th' Aerial Guard
Descend, and sit on each important Card:
First *Ariel* perched upon a *Matadore*,[51]
Then each, according to the Rank they bore;
For *Sylphs*, yet mindful of their ancient Race,
Are, as when Women, wondrous fond of Place.
Behold, four *Kings* in Majesty revered,
With hoary Whiskers and a forky Beard;
And four fair *Queens* whose hands sustain a Flower,
Th' expressive Emblem of their softer Power;
Four *Knaves* in Garbs succinct, a trusty Band,
Caps on their heads, and Halberds in their hand;
And Particoloured Troops, a shining Train,
Draw forth to Combat on the Velvet Plain.
The skilful Nymph reviews her Force with Care;
'Let Spades be Trumps!', she said, and Trumps they were.[52]
Now move to War her Sable *Matadores*,
In Show like Leaders of the swarthy *Moors*.
Spadillio first, unconquerable Lord![53]
Led off two captive Trumps, and swept the Board.

Notes

[48] *ogle* "To view with side glances, as in fondness" (Johnson).

[49] *Exchange* one of several merchants' centers, such as New Exchange.

[50] *Sacred Nine* the muses.

[51] *Matadore* one of the three best cards in the game: the black aces, plus the 2 or 7 of the trumps suit.

[52] *'Let Spades be Trumps'* in imitation of "Let there be light ..." (Genesis 1.3).

[53] *Spadillio* ace of spades.

As many more *Manillio* forced to yield,[54]
And marched a Victor from the verdant Field.
Him *Basto* followed, but his Fate more hard[55]
Gained but one Trump and one *Plebeian* Card.
With his broad Sabre next, a Chief in Years,
The hoary Majesty of *Spades* appears;
Puts forth one manly Leg, to sight revealed;
The rest his many-coloured Robe concealed.
The Rebel-*Knave*, who dares his Prince engage,
Proves the just Victim of his Royal Rage.
Ev'n mighty *Pam* that Kings and Queens o'erthrew,[56]
And mowed down Armies in the Fights of *Loo*,
Sad Chance of War! now, destitute of Aid,
Falls undistinguished by the Victor *Spade*!
Thus far both Armies to *Belinda* yield;
Now to the *Baron* Fate inclines the Field.
His warlike *Amazon* her Host invades,
Th' Imperial Consort of the Crown of *Spades*.
The *Club*'s black Tyrant first her Victim died,
Spite of his haughty Mien, and barb'rous Pride:
What boots the Regal Circle on his Head,
His Giant Limbs in State unwieldy spread?
That long behind he trails his pompous Robe,
And of all the Monarchs only grasps the Globe?
The *Baron* now his *Diamonds* pours apace;
Th' embroidered *King* who shows but half his Face,
And his refulgent *Queen*, with Pow'rs combined,
Of broken Troops an easy Conquest find.
Clubs, *Diamonds*, *Hearts*, in wild Disorder seen,
With Throngs promiscuous strow the level Green.
Thus when dispersed a routed Army runs,
Of *Asia*'s Troops, and *Afric*'s Sable Sons,
With like Confusion different Nations fly,
Of various Habit and of various Dye,
The pierced Battalions disunited fall,
In Heaps on Heaps; one Fate o'erwhelms them all.
The *Knave of Diamonds* tries his wily Arts,
And wins (oh shameful Chance!) the *Queen of Hearts*.[57]
At this, the Blood the Virgin's Cheek forsook,
A livid Paleness spreads o'er all her Look;
She sees, and trembles at th' approaching Ill,
Just in the Jaws of Ruin, and *Codille*.[58]
And now (as oft in some distempered State),

Notes

[54] *Manillio* 2 of spades, second-highest card when spades are trumps.

[55] *Basto* ace of clubs, the third-best card.

[56] *Pam* jack, or knave, of clubs, the best card in the equally popular game of Lu.

[57] *Knave of Diamonds … Hearts* because diamonds was led, even the higher heart loses.

[58] *Codille* to give codille to the ombre means to defeat her; see n. 16 above.

On one nice *Trick* depends the gen'ral Fate,
An *Ace* of Hearts steps forth: The *King* unseen
Lurked in her Hand, and mourned his captive *Queen*.
He springs to Vengeance with an eager pace,
And falls like Thunder on the prostrate *Ace*.[59]
The Nymph exulting fills with *Shouts* the Sky,[60]
The Walls, the Woods, and long Canals reply.
Oh thoughtless Mortals! ever blind to Fate,
Too soon dejected, and too soon elate!
Sudden these Honours shall be snatched away,
And cursed for ever this Victorious Day.
For lo! the Board with Cups and Spoons is crowned,
The Berries crackle, and the Mill turns round.[61]
On shining Altars of *Japan* they raise[62]
The silver Lamp, the fiery Spirits blaze.
From silver Spouts the grateful Liquors glide,
While *China*'s Earth receives the smoking Tide.
At once they gratify their Scent and Taste,
And frequent Cups prolong the rich Repast.
Straight hover round the Fair her Airy Band;
Some, as she sipped, the fuming Liquor fanned,
Some o'er her Lap their careful Plumes displayed,
Trembling, and conscious of the rich Brocade.
Coffee (which makes the Politician wise,
And see through all things with his half-shut Eyes)
Sent up in Vapours to the *Baron*'s Brain[63]
New Stratagems, the radiant Lock to gain.
Ah cease rash Youth! desist ere 'tis too late,
Fear the just Gods, and think of *Scylla*'s Fate![64]
Changed to a Bird, and sent to flit in Air,
She dearly pays for *Nisus'* injured Hair!
But when to Mischief Mortals bend their Mind,
How soon fit Instruments of Ill they find!
Just then, *Clarissa* drew with tempting Grace
A two-edged Weapon from her shining Case;
So Ladies in Romance assist their Knight,
Present the Spear, and arm him for the Fight.
He takes the Gift with rev'rence, and extends
The little Engine on his Finger's Ends,[65]
This just behind *Belinda*'s Neck he spread,
As o'er the fragrant Steams she bends her Head:
Swift to the Lock a thousand Sprites repair,
A thousand Wings, by turns, blow back the Hair,

Notes

59 *Ace* with spades as trumps, the ace of hearts has no value, unless Belinda fails to follow suit.

60 *Shouts* like those issued by a conquering Homeric warrior.

61 *Berries* coffee beans.

62 *Altars of Japan* japanned (heavily lacquered) tables.

63 *Vapours* "Mental fume; vain imagination" as well as "steam" (Johnson).

64 *Scylla* see epigraph and n. 1 above.

65 *Engine* "Any instrument" (Johnson).

And thrice they twitched the Diamond in her Ear,
Thrice she looked back, and thrice the Foe drew near.
Just in that instant, anxious *Ariel* sought
The close Recesses of the Virgin's Thought;
As on the Nosegay in her Breast reclined,
He watched th' Ideas rising in her Mind,[66]
Sudden he viewed, in spite of all her Art,
An Earthly Lover lurking at her Heart.
Amazed, confused, he found his Pow'r expired,
Resigned to Fate, and with a Sigh retired.
The Peer now spreads the glitt'ring *Forfex* wide,[67]
T' enclose the Lock; now joins it, to divide.
Ev'n then, before the fatal Engine closed,
A wretched *Sylph* too fondly interposed;
Fate urged the Sheers, and cut the *Sylph* in twain,
(But Airy Substance soon unites again)[68]
The meeting Points the sacred Hair dissever
From the fair Head, for ever and for ever!
Then flashed the living Lightning from her Eyes,
And Screams of Horror rend th' affrighted Skies.
Not louder Shrieks by Dames to Heav'n are cast,
When Husbands or when Monkeys breathe their last,
Or when rich *China* Vessels, fall'n from high,
In glitt'ring Dust and painted Fragments lie!
'Let Wreaths of Triumph now my Temples twine',
The Victor cried, 'the glorious Prize is mine!
While Fish in Streams, or Birds delight in Air,
Or in a Coach and Six the *British* Fair,
As long as *Atalantis* shall be read,[69]
Or the small Pillow grace a Lady's Bed,
While *Visits* shall be paid on solemn Days,
When numerous Wax-lights in bright Order blaze,[70]
While Nymphs take Treats, or Assignations give,
So long my Honour, Name, and Praise shall live!'
What Time would spare, from Steel receives its date,
And Monuments, like Men, submit to Fate!
Steel did the Labour of the Gods destroy,[71]
And strike to Dust th' Imperial Tow'rs of *Troy*;
Steel could the Works of mortal Pride confound,
And hew Triumphal Arches to the Ground.
What Wonder then, fair Nymph! thy Hairs should feel
The conqu'ring Force of unresisted Steel?

Notes

[66] *Idea* "Mental imagination. 'Whatsoever the mind perceives in itself, or is the immediate object of perception, thought, or understanding, that I call idea.' Locke" (Johnson).

[67] *Forfex* Latin, "scissors."

[68] *Airy Substance … again* See *Milton* lib. 6 [Pope's note; *Paradise Lost* 6.344].

[69] *Atalantis* Delarivier Manley, *Secret Memoirs and Manners of Several Persons of Quality* (1709) (see selection above, pp. 543–555).

[70] *Wax-lights* candles made of wax, rather than the cheaper, greasy tallow.

[71] *Labour of the Gods* Apollo and Poseidon were the legendary builders of the city of Troy.

Canto IV

But anxious Cares the pensive Nymph oppressed,
And secret Passions laboured in her Breast.
Not youthful Kings in Battle seized alive,
Not scornful Virgins who their Charms survive,
Not ardent Lovers robbed of all their Bliss,
Not ancient Ladies when refused a Kiss,
Not Tyrants fierce that unrepenting die,
Not *Cynthia* when her *Manteau*'s pinned awry,[72]
E'er felt such Rage, Resentment and Despair,
As Thou, sad Virgin! for thy ravished Hair.
For, that sad moment, when the *Sylphs* withdrew,
And *Ariel* weeping from *Belinda* flew,
Umbriel, a dusky melancholy Sprite,
As ever sullied the fair face of Light,
Down to the Central Earth, his proper Scene,
Repaired to search the gloomy Cave of *Spleen*.[73]
Swift on his sooty Pinions flits the *Gnome*,
And in a Vapour reached the dismal Dome.
No cheerful Breeze this sullen Region knows,
The dreaded *East* is all the Wind that blows.[74]
Here, in a Grotto, sheltered close from Air,[75]
And screened in Shades from Day's detested Glare,
She sighs for ever on her pensive Bed,
Pain at her Side, and *Megrim* at her Head.[76]
Two Handmaids wait the Throne: Alike in Place,
But diff'ring far in Figure and in Face.
Here stood *Ill-nature* like an *ancient Maid*,
Her wrinkled Form in *Black* and *White* arrayed;
With store of Prayers, for Mornings, Nights, and Noons,
Her Hand is filled; her Bosom with Lampoons.
There *Affectation* with a sickly Mien
Shows in her Cheek the Roses of Eighteen,
Practised to Lisp, and hang the Head aside,
Faints into Airs, and languishes with Pride;
On the rich Quilt sinks with becoming Woe,
Wrapped in a Gown, for Sickness, and for Show.
The Fair ones feel such Maladies as these,
When each new Night-Dress gives a new Disease.
A constant *Vapour* o'er the Palace flies;
Strange Phantoms rising as the Mists arise;
Dreadful, as Hermit's Dreams in haunted Shades,

Notes

[72] *Manteau* or "mantua," a loose-fitting gown.

[73] *Spleen* "The milt; one of the viscera, of which the use is scarcely known. It is supposed to be the seat of anger and melancholy [meaning all sorts of psychological ills]" (Johnson); also the name of an ill-defined constellation of ailments.

[74] *East* the east wind was supposed to bring on spleen.

[75] *Grotto* "A cavern or cave made for coolness. It is not used properly of a dark, horrid cavern" (Johnson); Pope had a grotto on his estate in Twickenham.

[76] *Megrim* or "migraine," severe headache.

Or bright as Visions of expiring Maids.[77]
Now glaring Fiends, and Snakes on rolling Spires,
Pale Spectres, gaping Tombs, and Purple Fires:
Now Lakes of liquid Gold, *Elysian* Scenes,[78]
And Crystal Domes, and Angels in Machines.
  Unnumbered Throngs on every side are seen
Of Bodies changed to various Forms by *Spleen*.
Here living *Teapots* stand, one Arm held out,[79]
One bent; the Handle this, and that the Spout:
A Pipkin there like *Homer's Tripod* walks;[80]
Here sighs a Jar, and there a Goose-pie talks;[81]
Men prove with Child, as powerful Fancy works,
And Maids turned Bottles, call aloud for Corks.
  Safe passed the *Gnome* through this fantastic Band,
A Branch of healing *Spleenwort* in his hand.[82]
Then thus addressed the Power – 'Hail wayward Queen!
Who rule the Sex to Fifty from Fifteen,
Parent of Vapours and of Female Wit,
Who give th' *Hysteric* or *Poetic* Fit,
On various Tempers act by various ways,
Make some take Physic, others scribble Plays;[83]
Who cause the Proud their Visits to delay,
And send the Godly in a Pet, to pray.
A Nymph there is, that all thy Pow'r disdains,
And thousands more in equal Mirth maintains.
But oh! if e'er thy *Gnome* could spoil a Grace,
Or raise a Pimple on a beauteous Face,
Like Citron-Waters Matrons' Cheeks inflame,[84]
Or change Complexions at a losing Game;
If e'er with airy Horns I planted Heads,[85]
Or rumpled Petticoats, or tumbled Beds,
Or caused Suspicion when no Soul was rude,
Or discomposed the Head-dress of a Prude,
Or e'er to costive Lap-Dog gave Disease,
Which not the Tears of brightest Eyes could ease:
Hear me, and touch *Belinda* with Chagrin;
That single Act gives half the World the Spleen'.
  The Goddess with a discontented Air
Seems to reject him, though she grants his Prayer.

Notes

77 *Hermit's Dreams ... Visions of ... Maids* these are religious hallucinations of Hell and Heaven.

78 *Elysian* the best part of the classical underworld.

79 *living Teapots* Robert Burton records two instances of insane persons who think they are pitchers (*Anatomy of Melancholy* 1.3.1.3).

80 *Pipkin* "A small earthen boiler" (Johnson, 1773); *Tripod* See Hom. *Iliad* 18 [373–7], of *Vulcan's Walking tripods* [Pope's note; they have wheels and move at his command].

81 *Goose-pie* Alludes to a real fact, a Lady of distinction imagined herself in this condition [Pope's note].

82 *Spleenwort* an herb said to be good for the spleen; this is a version of the golden bough that Aeneas used to pass safely through the Cave of Avernus into Hades (*Aeneid* 6)

83 *Physic* any medicine, but also, specifically, a purgative.

84 *Citron-Waters* a flavored liquor.

85 *airy Horns* imagined signs that the wearer has been cuckolded.

A wondrous Bag with both her Hands she binds,
Like that where once *Ulysses* held the Winds;[86]
There she collects the Force of Female Lungs,
Sighs, Sobs, and Passions, and the War of Tongues.
A Vial next she fills with fainting Fears,
Soft Sorrows, melting Griefs, and flowing Tears.
The *Gnome* rejoicing bears her Gifts away,
Spreads his black Wings, and slowly mounts to Day.
Sunk in *Thalestris*' Arms the Nymph he found,[87]
Her Eyes dejected and her Hair unbound.
Full o'er their Heads the swelling Bag he rent,
And all the Furies issued at the Vent.
Belinda burns with more than mortal Ire,
And fierce *Thalestris* fans the rising Fire.
'O wretched Maid!' she spread her Hands, and cried,
(While *Hampton*'s Echoes, 'wretched Maid!' replied),
'Was it for this you took such constant Care
The *Bodkin*, *Comb*, and *Essence* to prepare;
For this your Locks in Paper-Durance bound,
For this with tort'ring Irons wreathed around?
For this with Fillets strained your tender Head,[88]
And bravely bore the double Loads of Lead?[89]
Gods! shall the Ravisher display your Hair,
While the Fops envy, and the Ladies stare!
Honour forbid! at whose unrivalled Shrine
Ease, Pleasure, Virtue, All, our Sex resign.
Methinks already I your Tears survey,
Already hear the horrid things they say,
Already see you a degraded Toast,
And all your Honour in a Whisper lost!
How shall I, then, your helpless Fame defend?
'Twill then be Infamy to seem your Friend!
And shall this Prize, th' inestimable Prize,
Exposed through Crystal to the gazing Eyes,
And heightened by the Diamond's circling Rays,
On that Rapacious Hand for ever blaze?
Sooner shall Grass in *Hyde*-Park *Circus* grow,[90]
And Wits take Lodgings in the Sound of *Bow*;[91]
Sooner let Earth, Air, Sea to *Chaos* fall,
Men, Monkeys, Lap-dogs, Parrots, perish all!'
She said; then raging to *Sir Plume* repairs,[92]
And bids her *Beau* demand the precious Hairs:

Notes

[86] *Ulysses held the Winds* in the bag given him by Aeolus at the beginning of *Odyssey* Book 10.

[87] *Thalestris* name of a queen of the Amazons; here, Mrs. Morley, Arabella's second cousin by her marriage to Sir George Browne (Sir Plume).

[88] *Fillet* "A band tied around the head" (Johnson).

[89] *Leads* soft wire ties.

[90] *Hyde-Park Circus* the Ring (cf. canto 1, l. 44 above).

[91] *Sound of Bow* the bells of the church of St. Mary-le-Bow in Cheapside, which had become expensive and commercial.

[92] *Sir Plume* Arabella's second cousin, Sir George Browne.

(*Sir Plume*, of *Amber Snuff-box* justly vain,
And the nice Conduct of a *clouded Cane*)[93]
With earnest Eyes, and round unthinking Face,
He first the Snuff-box opened, then the Case,
And thus broke out – 'My Lord, why, what the Devil?
Z—ds! damn the Lock! 'fore Gad, you must be civil![94]
Plague on't! 'tis past a Jest – nay prithee, Pox!
Give her the Hair' – he spoke, and rapped his Box.
'It grieves me much', replied the Peer again,
'Who speaks so well should ever speak in vain.
But by this Lock, this sacred Lock I swear.
(Which never more shall join its parted Hair,
Which never more its Honours shall renew,
Clipped from the lovely Head where late it grew)
That while my Nostrils draw the vital Air,
This Hand, which won it, shall for ever wear'.
He spoke, and speaking, in proud Triumph spread
The long-contended Honours of her Head.
But *Umbriel*, hateful *Gnome*! forbears not so;
He breaks the Vial whence the Sorrows flow.
Then see! the *Nymph* in beauteous Grief appears,
Her Eyes half-languishing, half-drowned in Tears;
On her heaved Bosom hung her drooping Head,
Which, with a Sigh, she raised; and thus she said.
'Forever cursed be this detested Day,
Which snatched my best, my fav'rite Curl away!
Happy! ah ten times happy, had I been,
If *Hampton-Court* these Eyes had never seen!
Yet am not I the first mistaken Maid,
By Love of *Courts* to num'rous Ills betrayed.
Oh had I rather un-admired remained
In some lone Isle, or distant *Northern* Land;
Where the gilt *Chariot* never marked the way,
Where none learn *Ombre*, none e'er taste *Bohea*![95]
There kept my Charms concealed from mortal Eye,
Like Roses that in Deserts bloom and die.
What moved my Mind with youthful Lords to roam?
O had I stayed, and said my Prayers at home!
'Twas this, the Morning *Omens* did foretell;
Thrice from my trembling hand the *Patch-box* fell;
The tott'ring *China* shook without a Wind,
Nay, *Poll* sate mute, and *Shock* was most Unkind!
A *Sylph* too warned me of the Threats of Fate,
In mystic Visions, now believed too late!
See the poor Remnants of these slighted Hairs!
My hands shall rend what ev'n thy Rapine spares:

Notes

[93] *clouded Cane* one with a head of polished stone, variegated with dark veins.

[94] *Z—ds!* "God's wounds," a mild curse.

[95] *Bohea* a fancy tea.

These, in two sable Ringlets taught to break,
Once gave new Beauties to the snowy Neck.
The Sister-Lock now sits uncouth, alone,
And in its Fellow's Fate foresees its own;
Uncurled it hangs, the fatal Sheers demands;
And tempts once more thy sacrilegious Hands.
Oh hadst thou, Cruel! been content to seize
Hairs less in sight, or any Hairs but these!'

Canto V

She said: the pitying Audience melt in Tears,
But *Fate* and *Jove* had stopped the *Baron*'s Ears.
In vain *Thalestris* with Reproach assails,
For who can move when fair *Belinda* fails?
Not half so fixed the *Trojan* could remain,[96]
While *Anna* begged and *Dido* raged in vain.
Then grave Clarissa graceful waved her Fan;[97]
Silence ensued, and thus the Nymph began.
'Say, why are Beauties praised and honoured most,
The wise Man's Passion, and the vain Man's Toast?
Why decked with all that Land and Sea afford,
Why Angels called, and Angel-like adored?
Why round our Coaches crowd the white-gloved Beaus,
Why bows the Side-box from its inmost Rows?[98]
How vain are all these Glories, all our Pains,
Unless good Sense preserve what Beauty gains:
That Men may say, when we the Front-box grace,
Behold the first in Virtue, as in Face!
Oh! if to dance all Night, and dress all Day,
Charmed the Small-pox, or chased old Age away;
Who would not scorn what Housewife's Cares produce?
Who would learn one earthly Thing of Use?
To patch, nay ogle, might become a Saint,
Nor could it sure be such a Sin to paint.
But since, alas! frail Beauty must decay,
Curled or uncurled, since Locks will turn to grey,
Since painted, or not painted, all shall fade,
And she who scorns a Man, must die a Maid;
What then remains, but well our Pow'r to use,
And keep good Humour still whate'er we lose?

Notes

[96] *Trojan* Aeneas, beseeched to stay in Carthage by Dido and her sister Anna (*Aeneid* 4).

[97] *Clarissa* A new Character introduced in the subsequent Editions, to open more clearly the Moral of the Poem, in a parody of the speech of Sarpedon to Glaucus in Homer [*Iliad* 12; Pope's note; lines 7–36 were added in 1717; Clarissa is new in that she now has a speaking part; she appeared in the earlier edition of the poem, as here in canto 3, line 127, as the silent supplier of the forfex for the Baron's wicked deed].

[98] *side-box* "A seated compartment in a theatre, at first specially for ladies" (*OED*, s.v. *box*, II.8).

And trust me, Dear! good Humour can prevail,
When Airs, and Flights, and Screams, and Scolding fail.
Beauties in vain their pretty Eyes may roll;
Charms strike the Sight, but Merit wins the Soul'.
So spoke the Dame, but no Applause ensued;
Belinda frowned, *Thalestris* called her Prude.
'To Arms, to Arms!' the fierce Virago cries,[99]
And swift as Lightning to the Combat flies.
All side in Parties, and begin th' Attack;
Fans clap, Silks rustle, and tough Whalebones crack;
Heroes' and Heroines' Shouts confus'dly rise,
And bass, and treble Voices strike the Skies.
No common Weapons in their Hands are found,
Like Gods they fight, nor dread a mortal Wound.
So when bold *Homer* makes the Gods engage,
And heav'nly Breasts with human Passions rage;
'Gainst *Pallas, Mars; Latona, Hermes* Arms;[100]
And all *Olympus* rings with loud Alarms.
Jove's Thunder roars, Heav'n trembles all around;
Blue *Neptune* storms, the bellowing Deeps resound;
Earth shakes her nodding Towers, the Ground gives way;
And the pale Ghosts start at the Flash of Day!
Triumphant *Umbriel* on a Sconce's Height[101]
Clapped his glad Wings, and sate to view the Fight,
Propped on their Bodkin Spears, the Sprites survey
The growing Combat, or assist the Fray.
While through the Press enraged *Thalestris* flies,
And scatters Deaths around from both her Eyes,
A *Beau* and *Witling* perished in the Throng,
One died in *Metaphor*, and one in *Song*.
'O cruel Nymph! a living Death I bear',
Cried *Dapperwit*, and sunk beside his Chair.
A mournful Glance Sir *Fopling* upwards cast,
'Those Eyes are made so killing' – was his last:[102]
Thus on *Meander*'s flow'ry Margin lies
Th' expiring Swan, and as he sings he dies.[103]
When bold Sir *Plume* had drawn *Clarissa* down,
Chloe stepped in, and killed him with a Frown;
She smiled to see the doughty Hero slain,
But at her Smile, the Beau revived again.
Now *Jove* suspends his golden Scales in Air,[104]
Weighs the Men's Wits against the Lady's Hair;

Notes

99 *Virago* "A female warrior; a woman with the qualities of a man" (Johnson).

100 *Latona* mother of Artemis and Apollo.

101 *Sconce* a flat candlestick with a handle for hanging.

102 *"Those Eyes are made so killing"* A song in the opera of *Camilla* [Pope's note].

103 *Th' expiring Swan* as Pope noted in later editions, this is a reference to the opening of Ovid's *Heroides* 7, a lament from Dido to Aeneas.

104 *golden Scales* Vid. *Homer* Il. 22 & *Virg.* Æn. 12 [Pope's note; see *Paradise Lost* 4.996–8].

The doubtful Beam long nods from side to side;
At length the Wits mount up, the Hairs subside.
See fierce *Belinda* on the *Baron* flies
With more than usual Lightning in her Eyes;
Nor feared the Chief th' unequal Fight to try,
Who sought no more than on his Foe to die.
But this bold Lord, with manly Strength endued,
She with one Finger and a Thumb subdued:
Just where the Breath of Life his Nostrils drew,
A Charge of *Snuff* the wily Virgin threw;
The *Gnomes* direct, to ev'ry Atom just,
The pungent Grains of titillating Dust.
Sudden, with starting Tears each Eye o'erflows,
And the high Dome re-echoes to his Nose.
'Now meet thy Fate', th' incensed *Virago* cried,
And drew a deadly *Bodkin* from her Side.
(The same, his ancient Personage to deck,
Her great great Grandsire wore about his Neck
In three *Seal-Rings*; which after, melted down,
Formed a vast *Buckle* for his Widow's Gown:
Her infant Grandame's *Whistle* next it grew,
The *Bells* she jingled, and the *Whistle* blew;
Then in a *Bodkin* graced her Mother's Hairs,
Which long she wore, and now *Belinda* wears.)
'Boast not my Fall', he cried, 'insulting Foe!
Thou by some other shalt be laid as low.
Nor think, to die dejects my lofty Mind;
All that I dread, is leaving you behind!
Rather than so, ah let me still survive,
And burn in *Cupid*'s Flames, – but burn alive'.
'Restore the Lock!' she cries; and all around
'Restore the Lock!' the vaulted Roofs rebound.
Not fierce *Othello* in so loud a Strain
Roared for the Handkerchief that caused his Pain.
But see how oft Ambitious Aims are crossed,
And Chiefs contend till all the Prize is lost!
The Lock, obtained with Guilt, and kept with Pain.
In every place is sought, but sought in vain:
With such a Prize no Mortal must be blest,
So Heav'n decrees! with Heav'n who can contest?
Some thought it mounted to the Lunar Sphere,[105]
Since all things lost on Earth, are treasured there.
There Heroes' Wits are kept in pond'rous Vases,

Notes

[105] *the Lunar Sphere* Pope refers this vision to Ariosto's *Orlando Furioso*, but see also *Paradise Lost* 3.444ff.

And Beaus' in *Snuff-boxes* and *Tweezer-Cases*.
There broken Vows, and Death-bed Alms are found,
And Lovers' Hearts with Ends of Ribband bound;
The Courtier's Promises, and Sick Man's Prayers,
The Smiles of Harlots, and the Tears of Heirs,
Cages for Gnats, and Chains to Yoke a Flea;
Dried Butterflies, and Tomes of Casuistry.[106]
  But trust the Muse – she saw it upward rise,
Though marked by none but quick Poetic Eyes:
(So *Rome*'s great Founder to the Heav'ns withdrew,
To *Proculus* alone confessed in view.)[107]
A sudden Star, it shot through liquid Air,
And drew behind a radiant *Trail of Hair*.
Not *Berenice*'s Locks first rose so bright,[108]
The Skies bespangling with dishevelled Light.
The *Sylphs* behold it kindling as it flies,
And pleased pursue its Progress through the Skies.
  This the *Beau-monde* shall from the *Mall* survey,[109]
And hail with Music its propitious Ray.
This, the blessed Lover shall for *Venus* take,
And send up Vows from *Rosamonda*'s Lake.[110]
This *Partridge* soon shall view in cloudless Skies,[111]
When next he looks through *Galileo*'s Eyes;
And hence th' Egregious Wizard shall foredoom
The Fate of *Louis*, and the Fall of *Rome*.
  Then cease, bright Nymph! to mourn thy ravished Hair
Which adds new Glory to the shining Sphere!
Not all the Tresses that fair Head can boast
Shall draw such Envy as the Lock you lost.
For, after all the Murders of your Eye,
When after Millions slain, yourself shall die;
When those fair Suns shall set, as set they must,
And all those Tresses shall be laid in Dust;
This Lock, the Muse shall consecrate to Fame,
And mid'st the Stars inscribe *Belinda*'s Name!

FINIS

Notes

[106] *Casuistry* "the doctrine of cases of conscience" (Johnson).

[107] *Rome's great Founder … in view* Romulus was killed in a storm (or by angry senators), and Proculus, to calm the bereaved populace, supported the explanation that he had been swept up into heaven with a story about seeing him descend to give a prophecy of Rome's greatness (Livy 1.16).

[108] *Berenice's Locks* the votive offering of hair from a queen of Egypt for the safe return of her husband; when it was lost, the court astronomer claimed to find it in a hitherto unnamed constellation; Callimachus and Catullus used the myth in poetry before Pope.

[109] *Beau-monde* fashionable society; *Mall* a walk in St. James's Park, as fashionable for cruising as the Ring.

[110] *Rosamonda's Lake* a pond in St. James's Park, famous as a meeting place for lovers.

[111] *Partridge* John Partridge [1644–1715] was a ridiculous Star-gazer, who in his Almanacs every year, never failed to predict the downfall of the Pope, and the King of *France*, then at war with the *English* [Pope's note].

Eloisa to Abelard (1717)
The Argument

Abelard and *Eloisa* flourished in the twelfth Century; they were two of the most distinguished persons of their age in learning and beauty, but for nothing more famous than for their unfortunate passion. After a long course of calamities, they retired each to a several Convent, and consecrated the remainder of their days to religion. It was many years after this separation that a letter of *Abelard*'s to a friend, which contained the history of his misfortunes, fell into the hands of *Eloisa*. This awakening all her tenderness, occasioned those celebrated letters (out of which the following is partly extracted) which give so lively a picture of the struggles of grace and nature, virtue and passion.

Eloisa to Abelard

'In these deep solitudes and awful cells,
Where heav'nly-pensive, contemplation dwells,
And ever-musing melancholy reigns;
What means this tumult in a Vestal's veins?[1]
Why rove my thoughts beyond this last retreat?
Why feels my heart its long-forgotten heat?
Yet, yet I love! – From *Abelard* it came,
And *Eloisa* yet must kiss the name.
'Dear fatal name! rest ever unrevealed,
Nor pass these lips in holy silence sealed.
Hide it, my heart, within that close disguise,
Where, mixed with God's, his loved Idea lies.
Oh write it not, my hand – The name appears
Already written – wash it out, my tears!'
In vain lost *Eloisa* weeps and prays,
Her heart still dictates, and her hand obeys.
'Relentless walls! whose darksome round contains
Repentant sighs, and voluntary pains:
Ye rugged rocks! Which holy knees have worn;
Ye grots and caverns shagged with horrid thorn:
Shrines! Where their vigils pale-eyed virgins keep,
And pitying saints, whose statues learn to weep!
Though cold like you, unmoved, and silent grown,
I have not yet forgot myself to stone.
Heav'n claims me all in vain, while he has part,
Still rebel nature holds out half my heart;
Nor prayers nor fasts its stubborn pulse restrain,
Nor tears, for ages, taught to flow in vain.

Notes

ELOISA TO ABELARD

[1] *Vestal* a virgin, like the priestesses of the Roman temple to Vesta.

'Soon as thy letters trembling I unclose,
That well-known name awakens all my woes.
O name for ever sad! for ever dear!
Still breathed in sighs, still ushered with a tear.
I tremble too where-e'er my own I find,
Some dire misfortune follows close behind,
Line after line my gushing eyes o'erflow,
Led through a sad variety of woe:
Now warm in love, now with'ring in thy bloom,
Lost in a convent's solitary gloom!
There stern religion quenched th' unwilling flame,
There died the best of passions, Love and Fame.
'Yet write, oh write me all, that I may join
Griefs to thy griefs, and echo sighs to thine.
Nor foes nor fortune take this power away:
And is my *Abelard* less kind than they?
Tears still are mine, and those I need not spare,
Love but demands what else were shed in prayer;
No happier task these faded eyes pursue,
To read and weep is all they now can do.
'Then share thy pain, allow that sad relief;
Ah more than share it! Give me all thy grief.
Heav'n first taught letters for some wretch's aid,
Some banished lover, or some captive maid;
They live, they speak, they breathe what love inspires,
Warm from the soul, and faithful to its fires,
The virgin's wish without her fears impart,
Excuse the blush, and pour out all the heart,
Speed the soft intercourse from soul to soul,
And waft a sigh from *Indus* to the *Pole*.
'Thou know'st how guiltless first I met thy flame,
When Love approached me under Friendship's name;
My fancy formed thee of Angelic kind,
Some emanation of th' all-beauteous Mind.
Those smiling eyes, attemp'ring ev'ry ray,
Shone sweetly lambent with celestial day:
Guiltless I gazed; heav'n listened while you sung;
And truths divine came mended from that tongue.
From lips like those what precept failed to move?
Too soon they taught me 'twas no sin to love.
Back through the paths of pleasing sense I ran,
Nor wished an Angel whom I loved a Man.
Dim and remote the joys of saints I see,
Nor envy them, that heav'n I lose for thee.
'How oft, when pressed to marriage, have I said,
Curse on all laws but those which love has made!
Love, free as air, at sight of human ties,
Spreads his light wings, and in a moment flies.
Let wealth, let honour, wait the wedded dame,
August her deed, and sacred be her fame;
Before true passion all those views remove,
Fame, wealth, and honour! what are you to Love?

The jealous God, when we profane his fires,
Those restless passions in revenge inspires;
And bids them make mistaken mortals groan,
Who seek in love for ought but love alone.
Should at my feet the world's great master fall,
Himself, his throne, his world, I'd scorn them all:
Not *Caesar's* empress would I deign to prove;
No, make me mistress of the man I love:
If there be yet another name more free,
More fond than mistress, make me that to thee!
O happy fate! when souls each other draw,
When love is liberty, and nature law:
All then is full, possessing, and possessed,
No craving Void left aching in the breast:
Ev'n thought meets thought ere from the lips it part,
And each warm wish springs mutual from the heart.
This sure is bliss (if bliss on earth there be)
And once the lot of *Abelard* and me.
   Alas how changed! what sudden horrors rise!
A naked Lover bound and bleeding lies!
Where, where was *Eloise*? her voice, her hand,
Her poniard had opposed the dire command.
Barbarian stay! that bloody hand restrain;
The crime was common, common be the pain.
I can no more; by shame, by rage suppressed,
Let tears, and burning blushes speak the rest.
   'Canst thou forget that sad, that solemn day,
When victims at yon altar's foot we lay?
Canst thou forget what tears that moment fell,
When, warm in youth, I bade the world farewell?
As with cold lips I kissed the sacred veil,
The shrines all trembled, and the lamps grew pale:
Heav'n scarce believed the conquest it surveyed.
And Saints with wonder heard the vows I made.
Yet then, to those dread altars as I drew,
Not on the Cross my eyes were fixed, but you;
Not grace, or zeal, love only was my call,
And if I lose thy love, I lose my all.
Come! with thy looks, thy words, relieve my woe;
Those still at least are left thee to bestow.
Still on that breast enamoured let me lie,
Still drink delicious poison from thy eye,
Pant on thy lip, and to thy heart be pressed;
Give all thou canst – and let me dream the rest.
Ah no! instruct me other joys to prize,
With other beauties charm my partial eyes,
Full in my view set all the bright abode,
And make my soul quit *Abelard* for God.
   'Ah think at least thy flock deserve thy care,
Plants of thy hand, and children of thy prayer.
From the false world in early youth they fled,
By thee to mountains, wilds, and deserts led.

You raised these hallowed walls; the desert smiled,
And Paradise was opened in the Wild.
No weeping orphan saw his father's stores
Our shrines irradiate, or emblaze the floors;
No silver saints, by dying misers giv'n,
Here bribed the rage of ill-requited heav'n:
But such plain roofs as piety could raise,
And only vocal with the Maker's praise.
In these lone walls (their days eternal bound)
These moss-grown domes with spiry turrets crowned,[2]
Where awful arches make a noon-day night,
And the dim windows shed a solemn light;
Thy eyes diffused a reconciling ray,
And gleams of glory brightened all the day.
But now no face divine contentment wears,
'Tis all blank sadness, or continual tears.
See how the force of others' prayers I try,
(Oh pious fraud of am'rous charity!)
But why should I on others' prayers depend?
Come thou, my father, brother, husband, friend!
Ah let thy handmaid, sister, daughter move,
And, all those tender names in one, thy love!
The darksome pines that o'er yon rocks reclined
Wave high, and murmur to the hollow wind,
The wand'ring streams that shine between the hills,
The grots that echo to the tinkling rills,[3]
The dying gales that pant upon the trees,[4]
The lakes that quiver to the curling breeze;
No more these scenes my meditation aid,
Or lull to rest the visionary maid:
But o'er the twilight groves, and dusky caves,
Long-founded isles, and intermingled graves,
Black Melancholy sits, and round her throws
A death-like silence, and a dread repose:
Her gloomy presence saddens all the scene,
Shades ev'ry flower, and darkens ev'ry green,
Deepens the murmur of the falling floods,
And breathes a browner horror on the woods.
'Yet here for ever, ever must I stay;
Sad proof how well a lover can obey!
Death, only death, can break the lasting chain;
And here ev'n then, shall my cold dust remain,
Here all its frailties, all its flames resign,
And wait, till 'tis no sin to mix with thine.
'Ah wretch! believed the spouse of God in vain,
Confessed within the slave of love and man.

Notes

[2] *domes* buildings.
[3] *grots* grottos; caves.
[4] *gales* gentle breezes.

Assist me heav'n! but whence arose that prayer?
Sprung it from piety, or from despair?
Ev'n here, where frozen chastity retires,
Love finds an altar for forbidden fires.
I ought to grieve, but cannot what I ought;
I mourn the lover, not lament the fault;
I view my crime, but kindle at the view,
Repent old pleasures, and solicit new:
Now turned to heav'n, I weep my past offence,
Now think of thee, and curse my innocence.
Of all, affliction taught a lover yet,
'Tis sure the hardest science to forget!
How shall I lose the sin, yet keep the sense,
And love th' offender, yet detest th' offence?
How the dear object from the crime remove,
Or how distinguish penitence from love?
Unequal task! a passion to resign,
For hearts so touched, so pierced, so lost as mine.
Ere such a soul regains its peaceful state,
How often must it love, how often hate!
How often hope, despair, resent, regret,
Conceal, disdain – do all things but forget.
But let heav'n seize it, all at once 'tis fired,
Not touched, but rapt; not weakened, but inspired!
Oh come! oh teach me nature to subdue,
Renounce my love, my life, myself – and you.
Fill my fond heart with God alone, for he
Alone can rival, can succeed to thee.
　'How happy is the blameless Vestal's lot?
The world forgetting, by the world forgot.
Eternal sunshine of the spotless mind!
Each prayer accepted, and each wish resigned;
Labour and rest, that equal periods keep;
　Obedient slumbers that can wake and weep;
Desires composed, affections ever even,
Tears that delight, and sighs that waft to heav'n.
Grace shines around her with serenest beams,
And whisp'ring Angels prompt her golden dreams.
For her the Spouse prepares the bridal ring,
For her white virgins *Hymeneals* sing;[5]
For her th' unfading Rose of *Eden* blooms,
And wings of Seraphs shed divine perfumes;
To sounds of heav'nly harps, she dies away,
And melts in visions of eternal day.
　'Far other dreams my erring soul employ,
Far other raptures, or unholy joy:
When at the close of each sad, sorrowing day,

Notes

[5] *Hymeneals* wedding-hymns.

Fancy restores what vengeance snatched away,
Then conscience sleeps, and leaving nature free,
All my loose soul unbounded springs to thee.
O cursed, dear horrors of all-conscious nights!
How glowing guilt exalts the keen delight!
Provoking Demons all restraint remove,
And stir within me every source of love.
I hear thee, view thee, gaze o'er all thy charms,
And round thy phantom glue my clasping arms.
I wake – no more I hear, no more I view,
The phantom flies me, as unkind as you.
I call aloud; it hears not what I say;
I stretch my empty arms; it glides away:
To dream once more I close my willing eyes;
Ye soft illusions, dear deceits, arise!
'Alas no more! – methinks we wand'ring go
Through dreary wastes, and weep each other's woe;
Where round some mould'ring tower pale ivy creeps,
And low-browed rocks hang nodding o'er the deeps.
Sudden you mount, you beckon from the skies;
Clouds interpose, waves roar, and winds arise.
I shriek, start up, the same sad prospect find,
And wake to all the griefs I left behind.
'For thee the fates, severely kind, ordain
A cool suspense from pleasure and from pain;
Thy life a long, dead calm of fixed repose;
No pulse that riots, and no blood that glows.
Still as the sea, ere winds were taught to blow,
Or moving Spirit bade the waters flow;
Soft as the slumbers of a saint forgiv'n,
And mild as opening gleams of promised heav'n.
'Come *Abelard*! for what hast thou to dread?
The torch of *Venus* burns not for the dead;
Cut from the root my perished joys I see,
And love's warm tide for ever stopped in thee.
Nature stands checked; Religion disapproves;
Ev'n thou art cold – yet *Eloisa* loves.
Ah hopeless, lasting flames! like those that burn
To light the dead, and warm th' unfruitful urn.
'What scenes appear where'er I turn my view,
The dear Ideas, where I fly pursue,[6]
Rise in the grove, before the altar rise,
Stain all my soul, and wanton in my eyes!
I waste the Matin lamp in sighs for thee,
Thy image steals between my God and me,
Thy voice I seem in every hymn to hear,
With every bead I drop too soft a tear.

Notes

[6] *Ideas* mental images.

When from the Censer clouds of fragrance roll,
And swelling organs lift the rising soul;
One thought of thee puts all the pomp to flight:
Priests, Tapers, Temples, swim before my sight:
In seas of flame my plunging soul is drowned,
While Altars blaze, and Angels tremble round.
'While prostrate here in humble grief I lie,
Kind, virtuous drops just gath'ring in my eye,
While praying, trembling, in the dust I roll,
And dawning grace is opening on my soul.
Come, if thou dar'st, all charming as thou art!
Oppose thyself to heav'n; dispute my heart;
Come, with one glance of those deluding eyes,
Blot out each bright Idea of the skies.
Take back that grace, those furrows, and those tears,
Take back my fruitless penitence and prayers,
Snatch me, just mounting, from the blessed abode,
Assist the Fiends, and tear me from my God!
'No, fly me, fly me! far as Pole from Pole;
Rise *Alps* between us! and whole oceans roll!
Ah come not, write not, think not once of me,
Nor share one pang of all I felt for thee.
Thy oaths I quit, thy memory resign,
Forget, renounce me, hate whate'er was mine.
Fair eyes, and tempting looks (which yet I view!)
Long loved, adored ideas! all adieu!
O grace serene! Oh virtue heav'nly fair!
Divine oblivion of low-thoughted care!
Fresh blooming hope, gay daughter of the sky!
And faith, our early immortality!
Enter each mild, each amicable guest;
Receive, and wrap me in eternal rest!
'See in her Cell sad *Eloisa* spread,
Propped in some tomb, a neighbour of the dead!
In each low wind methinks a spirit calls,
And more than echoes talk along the walls.
Here, as I watched the dying lamps around,
From yonder shrine I heard a hollow sound.
"Come, sister come!" it said, or seemed to say,
"Thy place is here, sad sister come away!
Once like thyself, I trembled, wept, and prayed,
Love's victim then, though now a sainted maid:
But all is calm in this eternal sleep;
Here grief forgets to groan, and love to weep.
Ev'n superstition loses every fear:
For God, not man, absolves our frailties here."
'I come, ye ghosts! Prepare your roseate bowers,
Celestial palms, and ever-blooming flowers.
Thither, where sinners may have rest, I go,
Where flames refined in breasts seraphic glow.
Thou, *Abelard*! the last sad office pay,
And smooth my passage to the realms of day:

See my lips tremble, and my eyeballs roll,
Suck my last breath, and catch the flying soul!
Ah no – in sacred vestments may'st thou stand,
The hallowed taper trembling in thy hand,
Present the Cross before my lifted eye,
Teach me at once, and learn of me to die.
Ah then, thy once-loved *Eloisa* see!
It will be then no crime to gaze on me.
See from my cheek the transient roses fly!
See the last sparkle languish in my eye!
Till every motion, pulse, and breath, be o'er;
And ev'n my *Abelard* beloved no more.
O death all-eloquent! you only prove
What dust we dote on, when 'tis man we love.
'Then too, when fate shall thy fair frame destroy,
(That cause of all my guilt, and all my joy)
In trance ecstatic may thy pangs be drowned,
Bright clouds descend, and Angels watch thee round,
From opening skies may streaming glories shine,
And Saints embrace thee with a love like mine.
'May one kind grave unite each hapless name,
And graft my love immortal on thy fame.
Then ages hence, when all my woes are o'er,
When this rebellious heart shall beat no more;
If ever chance two wand'ring lovers brings
To *Paraclete*'s white walls, and silver springs,[7]
O'er the pale marble shall they join their heads,
And drink the falling tears each other sheds,
Then sadly say, with mutual pity moved,
Oh may we never love as these have loved!
From the full quire when loud *Hosanna*'s rise,
And swell the pomp of dreadful sacrifice,
Amid the scene, if some relenting eye
Glance on the stone where our cold relics lie,
Devotion's self shall steal a thought from heav'n,
One human tear shall drop, and be forgiv'n.
And sure if fate some future Bard shall join
In sad similitude of griefs to mine,
Condemned whole years in absence to deplore,
And image charms he must behold no more;
Such if there be, who loves so long, so well,
Let him our sad, our tender story tell;
The well-sung woes shall soothe my pensive ghost;
He best can paint 'em, who shall feel 'em most'.

Notes

[7] *Paraclete* the title given in the Christian church to the Holy Spirit, or sometimes to Jesus, and the name of the monastery where Eloisa and Abelard were interred.

from *The Dunciad Variorum* (1729)

Martinus Scriblerus, of the Poem

This Poem, as it celebrateth the most grave and ancient of things, Chaos, Night and Dullness, so is it of the most grave and ancient kind. *Homer*, saith *Aristotle*, was the first who gave the *Form*, and, saith *Horace*, who adapted the *Measure*, to heroic poetry. But even before this, [as] may be rationally presumed from what the ancients have left written, was a piece by *Homer* composed, of like nature and matter with this of our Poet. For of Epic sort it appeareth to have been, yet of matter surely not unpleasant, witness what is reported of it by the learned Archbishop *Eustathius*,[1] in Odyss. K. And accordingly *Aristotle* in his poetic, chap. 4. doth further set forth, that as the Iliad and Odyssey gave example to Tragedy, so did this poem to Comedy its first Idæa.

From these authors also it should seem, that the Hero or chief personage of it was no less *obscure*, and his *understanding* and *sentiments* no less quaint and strange (if indeed not more so) than any of the actors in our poem. MARGITES was the name of this personage, whom Antiquity recordeth to have been *Dunce the First*; and surely from what we hear of him, not unworthy to be the root of so spreading a tree, and so numerous a posterity. The poem therefore celebrating him, was properly and absolutely a *Dunciad*; which though now unhappily lost, yet is its nature sufficiently known by the infallible tokens aforesaid. And thus it doth appear, that the first Dunciad was the first Epic poem, written by *Homer* himself, and anterior even to the Iliad or Odyssey.

Now forasmuch as our Poet had translated those two famous works of *Homer* which are yet left; he did conceive it in some sort his duty to imitate that also which was lost: And was therefore induced to bestow on it the same Form which *Homer*'s is reported to have had, namely that of Epic poem, with a title also framed after the ancient *Greek* manner, to wit, that of *Dunciad*.

Wonderful it is, that so few of the moderns have been stimulated to attempt some Dunciad! Since in the opinion of the multitude, it might cost less pain and oil, than an imitation of the greater Epic. But possible it is also that on due reflection, the maker might find it easier to paint a *Charlemagne*, a *Brute*[2] or a *Godfry*,[3] with just pomp and dignity heroic, than a *Margites*,[4] a *Codrus*,[5] a *Flecknoe*,[6] or *Tibbald*.[7]

We shall next declare the occasion and the cause which moved our Poet to this particular work. He lived in those days, when (after providence had permitted the Invention of Printing as a scourge for the Sins of the learned) Paper also became so cheap, and printers so numerous, that a deluge of authors covered the land: Whereby not only the peace of the honest unwriting subject was daily molested, but unmerciful demands were made of his applause, yea of his money, by such as would neither earn the one, or deserve the other: At the same time, the Liberty of the Press was so unlimited, that it grew dangerous to refuse them either: For they would forthwith publish slanders unpunished, the

Notes

FROM *THE DUNCIAD VARIORUM*

1 *Archbishop Eustathius* of Thessalonica, twelfth-century commentator on Homer.

2 *Brute* the grandson of Aeneas, founder of Britain in fables.

3 *Godfry* Godfrey of Bouillon, eleventh-century crusader, the perfect knight.

4 *Margites* hero and title of a lost mock-heroic poem attributed to Homer.

5 *Codrus* a poor garret-dweller (hence, prototypical Grubstreet hack) in Juvenal, *Satire* 3.203–11.

6 *Flecknoe* Richard (d. 1678), a poet ridiculed by Marvell and Dryden (see "Mac Flecknoe," p. 186 above).

7 *Tibbald* Lewis Theobald (1688–1744), author of *Shakespeare Restored* (1726), a critique of Pope's edition of Shakespeare.

authors being anonymous; nay the immediate publishers thereof lay skulking under the wings of an Act of Parliament,[8] assuredly intended for better purposes.

Now our author living in those times, did conceive it an endeavour well worthy an honest satirist, to dissuade the dull and punish the malicious, *the only way that was left*. In that public-spirited view he laid the plan of this Poem, as the greatest service he was capable (without much hurt or being slain) to render his dear country. First, taking things from their original, he considereth the Causes creative of such authors, namely *Dullness* and *Poverty*; the one born with them, the other contracted, by neglect of their proper talent through self-conceit of great abilities. This truth he wrapped in an *Allegory* (as the constitution of Epic poesy requires) and feigns, that one of these Goddesses had taken up her abode with the other, and that they jointly inspired all such writers and such works. He proceedeth to show the *qualities* they bestow on these authors, and the *effects* they produce: Then the *materials* or *stock* with which they furnish them, and (above all) that *self-opinion* which causeth it to seem to themselves vastly greater than it is, and is the prime motive of their setting up in this sad and sorry merchandise. The great power of these Goddesses acting in alliance (whereof as the one is the mother of industry, so is the other of plodding) was to be exemplified in some *one, great* and *remarkable action*. And none could be more so than that which our poet hath chosen, the introduction of the lowest diversions of the rabble in *Smithfield* to be the entertainment of the court and town; or in other words, the Action of the Dunciad is the Removal of the Imperial seat of Dullness from the City to the polite world; as that of the Æneid is the Removal of the Empire of *Troy* to *Latium*. But as *Homer*, singing only the *Wrath* of *Achilles*, yet includes in his poem the whole history of the *Trojan* war, in like manner our author hath drawn into this single action the whole history of Dullness and her children. To this end she is represented at the very opening of the poem, taking a view of her forces, which are distinguished into these three kinds, Party writers, dull poets, and wild critics.

A *Person* must be fixed upon to support this action, who (to agree with the said design) must be such an one as is capable of being all three. This *phantom* in the poet's mind, must have a *name*: He seeks for one who hath been concerned in the *Journals*, written bad *Plays* or *Poems*, and published low *Criticisms*: He finds his name to be *Tibbald*, and he becomes of course the Hero of the poem.

The *Fable* being thus according to best example one and entire, as contained in the proposition; the *Machinery* is a continued chain of Allegories, setting forth the whole power, ministry, and empire of Dullness, extended through her subordinate instruments, in all her various operations.

This is branched into *Episodes*, each of which hath its Moral apart, though all conducive to the main end. The crowd assembled in the second book demonstrates the design to be more extensive than to bad poets only, and that we may expect other Episodes, of the Patrons, Encouragers, or Paymasters of such authors, as occasion shall bring them forth. And the third book, if well considered, seemeth to embrace the whole world. Each of the Games relateth to some or other vile class of writers. The first concerneth the Plagiary, to whom he giveth the name of *More*; the second the libellous Novelist, whom he styleth *Eliza*; the third the flattering Dedicator; the fourth the bawling Critic or noisy Poet; the fifth the dark and dirty Party-writer; and so of the rest, assigning to each some *proper name* or other, such as he could find.

Notes

8 *an Act of Parliament* 10 Anne, C. 19.113 required that the publisher's real name appear on all publications; it was frequently ignored, and false publishers' names were often given.

As for the *Characters*, the public hath already acknowledged how justly they are drawn: The manners are so depicted, and the sentiments so peculiar to those to whom applied, that surely to transfer them to any other, or wiser, personages, would be exceeding difficult. And certain it is, that every person concerned, being consulted apart, will readily own the resemblance of every portrait, his own excepted.

The Descriptions are singular; the Comparisons very quaint; the Narrations various, yet of one colour. The purity and chastity of Diction is so preserved, that in the places most suspicious not the *words* but only the *images* have been censured, and yet are those images no other than have been sanctified by ancient and classical authority (though as was the manner of those good times, not so curiously wrapped up) yea and commented upon by most grave doctors, and approved critics.

As it beareth the name of Epic, it is thereby subjected to such severe indispensable rules as are laid on all Neotericks,[9] a strict imitation of the ancient; insomuch that any deviation accompanied with whatever poetic beauties, hath always been censured by the sound critic. How exact that Imitation hath been in this piece, appeareth not only by its general structure, but by particular allusions infinite, many whereof have escaped both the commentator and poet himself; yea divers by his exceeding diligence are so altered and interwoven with the rest, that several have already been, and more will be, by the ignorant abused, as altogether and originally his own.

In a word, the whole poem proveth itself to be the work of our Author when his faculties were in full vigour and perfection: at that exact time of life when years have ripened the judgement, without diminishing the imagination; which by good critics is held to be punctually at *forty*. For, at that season it was that *Virgil* finished his *Georgics*; and Sir *Richard Blackmore*[10] at the like age composing his Epic poesy: though since he hath altered it to *sixty*, the year in which he published his *Alfred*. True it is, that the talents for Criticism, namely smartness, quick censure, vivacity of remark, certainty of asseveration, indeed all but acerbity, seem rather the gifts of Youth than of riper age: But it is far otherwise in *Poetry*; witness the works of Mr. *Rymer* and Mr. *Dennis*,[11] who beginning with criticism, became afterwards such Poets as no age hath paralleled. With good reason therefore did our author choose to write his *Essay* on that subject at twenty, and reserve for his maturer years, this great and wonderful work of the *Dunciad*.

Dunciados Periocha:
or,
Arguments to the Books

Book the First

The Proposition of the subject. The Invocation, and the Inscription. Then the Original of the great empire of *Dullness*, and cause of the continuance thereof. The beloved seat of the Goddess is described, with her chief attendants and officers, her functions, operations, and effects. Then the poem hastes into the midst of things, presenting her on the evening of a Lord Mayor's day, revolving the long succession of her sons, and the glories past, and to come. She fixes her eye on *Tibbald* to be the instrument of that

Notes

9 *Neotericks* moderns.

10 *Richard Blackmore* (1655–1729), physician and epic poet.

11 *Rymer and Dennis* Thomas Rymer (1641–1713) and John Dennis (1657–1734), two of the best-known critics of their time, not much valued for their poetry.

great event which is the subject of the poem. He is described pensive in his study, giving up the cause, and apprehending the period of her empire from the old age of the present monarch *Settle*. Wherefore debating whether to betake himself to law or politics, he raises an altar of proper books, and (making first his solemn prayer and declaration) purposes thereon to sacrifice all his unsuccessful writings. As the pile is kindled, the Goddess beholding the flame from her seat, flies in person and puts it out, by casting upon it the poem of *Thule*. She forthwith reveals herself to him, transports him to her Temple, unfolds all her arts, and initiates him into her mysteries; then announcing the death of *Settle* that night, anoints, and proclaims him Successor.

Book the Second

The King being proclaimed, the solemnity is graced with public Games and sports of various kinds; not instituted by the Hero, as by *Æneas* in *Virgil*, but for greater honour by the Goddess in person; in like manner as the games *Pythia*, *Isthmia*, *&c.* were anciently said to be by the Gods, and as *Thetis* herself appearing according to *Homer* Odyss. 24. proposed the prizes in honour of her son *Achilles*. Hither flock the Poets and Critics, attended (as is but just) with their Patrons and Booksellers. The Goddess is first pleased for her disport to propose games to the latter, and setteth up the phantom of a poet which the booksellers contend to overtake. The races described, with their divers accidents: Next, the game for a Poetess: Afterwards the exercises for the *Poets*, of Tickling, Vociferating, Diving: the first holds forth the arts and practices of Dedicators, the second of Disputants and fustian[12] poets, the third of profound, dark, and dirty authors. Lastly, for the *Critics*, the Goddess proposes (with great Propriety) an exercise not of their parts but their patience; in hearing the works of two voluminous authors, one in verse and the other in prose, deliberately read, without sleeping: The various effects of which, with the several degrees and manners of their operation, are here most lively set forth: Till the whole number, not of critics only, but of spectators, actors, and all present fall fast asleep, which naturally and necessarily ends the games.

Book the Third

After the other persons are disposed in their proper places of rest, the Goddess transports the King to her Temple, and there lays him to slumber with his head on her lap; a position of marvellous virtue, which causes all the visions of wild enthusiasts, projectors,[13] politicians, inamorato's, castle-builders, chemists[14] and poets. He is immediately carried on the wings of fancy to the *Elysian* shade, where on the banks of *Lethe* the souls of the dull are dipped by *Bavius*, before their entrance into this world. There he is met by the ghost of *Settle*, and by him made acquainted with the wonders of the place, and with those which he is himself destined to perform. He takes him to a *Mount of Vision*, from whence he shews him the past triumphs of the empire of Dullness, then the present, and lastly the future. How small a part of the world was ever conquered by *Science*, how soon those conquests were stopped, and those very nations again reduced to her dominion. Then distinguishing the Island of *Great Britain*, shows by what aids, and by what persons, it shall be forthwith brought to her empire. These he causes to pass in review before his eyes, describing each by his proper figure, character, and qualifications. On a sudden the Scene shifts, and a vast number of miracles and prodigies appear, utterly surprising and unknown

Notes

[12] *fustian* "Swelling; unnaturally pompous" (Johnson).

[13] *projectors* "One who forms wild, impracticable schemes" (Johnson).

[14] *chemists* alchemists.

to the King himself, till they are explained to be the wonders of his own reign now commencing. On this subject *Settle* breaks into a congratulation, yet not unmixed with concern, that his own times were but the types of these; He prophesies how first the nation shall be overrun with farces, operas, shows: Then how her sons shall preside in the seats of arts and sciences, till in conclusion all shall return to their original Chaos: A scene, of which the present Action of the Dunciad is but a Type or Foretaste, giving a Glimpse or *Pisgah-sight*[15] of the promised Fullness of her Glory; the Accomplishment whereof will, in all probability, hereafter be the Theme of many other and greater Dunciads.

*THE DUNCIAD**

Book the First

Books and the Man I sing, the first who brings[16]
The Smithfield Muses to the Ear of Kings.[17]
Say great Patricians! (since yourselves inspire
These wond'rous works; so Jove and Fate require,)
Say from what cause, in vain decried and cursed,
Still Dunce the second reigns like Dunce the first?

Notes

[15] *Pisgah-sight* an anticipation or view from afar, after the mountain from which Moses glimpsed the Promised Land that he was never to enter.

THE DUNCIAD

* The *Dunciad*, *Sic* M.S. It may be well disputed whether this be a right Reading. Ought it not rather to be spelled *Dunceiad*, as the Etymology evidently demands? *Dunce* with an *e*, therefore *Dunceiad* with an *e*. That accurate and punctual Man of Letters, the Restorer of *Shakespeare*, constantly observes the preservation of this very Letter *e*, in spelling the Name of his beloved Author, and not like his common careless Editors, with the omission of one, nay sometimes of two *ee's* (as *Shak'spear*) which is utterly unpardonable. Nor is the neglect of a *Single Letter* so trivial as to some it may appear; the alteration whereof in a learned language is an *Achievement that brings honour* to the Critic who advances it; and Dr. {*Richard*}*B*{*entley*}. will be remembered to posterity for his performances of *this sort*, as long as the world shall have any Esteem for the Remains of [the Greek comic playwrights] *Menander* and *Philemon*. THEOBALD [Pope's note].

I have a just value for the Letter E, and the same affection for the Name of this Poem, as the forecited Critic for that of his Author; yet cannot it induce me to agree with those who would add yet another *e* to it, and call it the *Dunceiade*, which being a French and foreign Termination, is no way proper to a word entirely English, and Vernacular. One *E* therefore in this case is right, and two *E's* wrong; yet upon the whole I shall follow the Manuscript, and print it without any *E* at all; moved thereto by Authority, at all times with Critics equal if not superior to Reason. In which method of proceeding, I can never enough praise my very good Friend, the exact Mr. *Tho. Hearne* [Wormius in the poem; scholar; antiquary; Bodleian librarian], who, if any word occur which to him and all mankind is evidently wrong, yet keeps he it in the Text with due reverence, and only remarks in the Margin, *sic* M.S. In like manner we shall not amend this error in the Title itself, but only note it *obiter* [incidently], to evince to the learned that it was not our fault, nor any effect of our own Ignorance or Inattention. SCRIBLERUS [Pope's note].

[16] *Books and the Man I sing* ... Wonderful is the stupidity of all the former Critics and Commentators on this Poem! It breaks forth at the very first line. The Author of the Critique prefixed to *Sawney*, a Poem [by James Ralph, 1728], p. 5. hath been so dull as to explain *The Man who brings*, &c. not of the Hero of the Piece, but of our Poet himself, as if he vaunted that *Kings* were to be his Readers (an Honour which though this Poem hath had, yet knoweth he how to receive it with more Modesty.)

We remit this Ignorant to the first lines of the *Æneid*; assuring him, that *Virgil* there speaketh not of himself, but of *Æneas*, *Arma virumq; cano* ... SCRIBLERUS [Pope's note].

[17] *The Smithfield Muses* Smithfield is the place where Bartholomew Fair was kept, whose Shows, Machines, and Dramatical Entertainments, formerly agreeable only to the Taste of the Rabble, were, by the Hero of this Poem and others of equal Genius, brought to the Theatres of Covent-Garden, Lincolns-Inn-Fields, and the Hay-Market, to be the reigning Pleasures of the Court and Town. This happened in the Year 1725, and continued to the Year 1728. See Book 3. Vers. 191, &c. [Pope's note].

In eldest time, ere mortals writ or read,
Ere Pallas issued from the Thund'rer's head,[18]
Dullness o'er all possessed her ancient right,
Daughter of Chaos and eternal Night:[19]
Fate in their dotage this fair idiot gave,
Gross as her sire, and as her mother grave,
Laborious, heavy, busy, bold, and blind,
She ruled, in native Anarchy, the mind.
Still her old empire to confirm, she tries,
For born a Goddess, Dullness never dies.
O thou! whatever Title please thine ear,
Dean, Drapier, Bickerstaff, or Gulliver![20]
Whether thou choose Cervantes' serious air,
Or laugh and shake in Rab'lais' easy Chair,
Or praise the Court, or magnify Mankind,
Or thy grieved Country's copper chains unbind;[21]
From thy Bæotia though Her Pow'r retires[22]
Grieve not at aught our sister realms acquire:
Here pleased behold her mighty wings outspread,
To hatch a new Saturnian age of Lead.[23]
Where wave the tattered ensigns of Rag-Fair,[24]
A yawning ruin hangs and nods in air;
Keen, hollow winds howl through the bleak recess,
Emblem of Music caused by Emptiness:
Here in one bed two shiv'ring sisters lie,
The cave of Poverty and Poetry.
This, the Great Mother dearer held than all[25]
The clubs of Quidnunc's, or her own Guild-hall.
Here stood her Opium, here she nursed her Owls,
And destined here th' imperial seat of Fools.
Hence springs each weekly Muse, the living boast
Of Curl's chaste press, and Lintot's rubric post,[26]
Hence hymning Tyburn's elegiac lay,[27]

Notes

[18] *Pallas* Athena, goddess of wisdom, born from the head of Zeus.

[19] *Daughter of Chaos, &c.*] The beauty of this whole Allegory being purely of the Poetical kind, we think it not our proper business as a Scholiast, to meddle with it; but leave it (as we shall in general all such) to the Reader: remarking only, that Chaos (according to Hesiod, Θεογονία) was the Progenitor of all the Gods. SCRIBL. [Pope's note; see *Paradise Lost* 2.894–6].

[20] *Dean…Gulliver* all names used by Jonathan Swift in his satires.

[21] *copper chains* an allusion to Swift's successful combat against a form of currency imposed on Ireland by England.

[22] *Bæotia* a large Greek island.

[23] *A new Saturnian age of Lead* The ancient Golden Age is by Poets styled *Saturnian*; but in the Chemical language, *Saturn* is Lead [Pope's note].

[24] *Rag-fair* a place near the *Tower of London*, where old clothes and frippery are sold [Pope's note].

[25] *Great Mother Magna mater*, here applied to *Dullness*. The *Quidnunc's* was a name given to the ancient Members of certain political Clubs, who were constantly enquiring, *Quid nunc*? what news? [Pope's note].

[26] [*Edmund*] *Curl*…[*Bernard*] *Lintot* Two Booksellers, of whom see Book 2 [49 ff.]. The former was fined by the Court of King's-Bench for publishing obscene books; the latter usually adorned his shop with Titles in red letters [Pope's note]; *rubric post* a show board or marquee outside the shop on which title pages with their rubrics (titles or headings in red letters) were displayed.

[27] *Tyburn's elegiac lay* It is an ancient English custom for the Malefactors to sing a Psalm at their Execution at *Tyburn*; and no less customary to print Elegies on their deaths, at the same time, or before [Pope's note].

Hence the soft sing-song on Cecilia's day,
Sepulchral lies our holy walls to grace,
And New-year Odes, and all the Grubstreet race.[28]
  'Twas here in clouded majesty she shone;
Four guardian Virtues, round, support her Throne;
Fierce champion Fortitude, that knows no fears
Of hisses, blows, or want, or loss of ears:
Calm Temperance, whose blessings those partake
Who hunger, and who thirst, for scribbling sake:
Prudence, whose glass presents th' approaching jail:[29]
Poetic Justice, with her lifted scale;
Where in nice balance, truth with gold she weighs,
And solid pudding against empty praise.
  Here she beholds the Chaos dark and deep,
Where nameless somethings in their causes sleep,
'Till genial Jacob, or a warm Third-day[30]
Call forth each mass, a poem or a play.
How Hints, like spawn, scarce quick in embryo lie,
How new-born Nonsense first is taught to cry,
Maggots half-formed, in rhyme exactly meet,
And learn to crawl upon poetic feet.
Here one poor Word a hundred clenches makes,[31]
And ductile dullness new meanders takes;
There motley Images her fancy strike,
Figures ill-paired, and Similes unlike.
She sees a Mob of Metaphors advance,
Pleased with the Madness of the mazy dance:
How Tragedy and Comedy embrace;

Notes

[28] *Cecilia's day ... New-year Odes* Allude to the annual Songs composed to Music on St. Cecilia's Feast, and those made by the Poet-Laureate for the time being to be sung at Court, on every New-Years-Day, the words of which are happily drowned in the voices and Instruments. [*Sepulchral lies*] is a just Satire on the Flatteries and Falsehoods admitted to be inscribed on the Walls of Churches in Epitaphs [Pope's notes].

I must not here omit a Reflection, which will occur perpetually through this Poem, and cannot but greatly endear the Author to every attentive Observer of it: I mean that *Candour* and *Humanity* which everywhere appears in him, to those unhappy Objects of the Ridicule of all mankind, the bad Poets. He here imputes all scandalous rhymes, scurrilous weekly papers, lying news, base flatteries, wretched elegies, songs, and verses (even from those sung at Court, to ballads in the streets) not so much to Malice or Servility as to Dullness; and not so much to Dullness, as to Necessity; And thus at the very commencement of his Satire, makes an Apology for all that are to be satirized [Pope's note].

[29] *glass* spyglass or small telescope, with which Prudence was usually represented in allegorical pictures.

[30] *genial Jacob* Jacob Tonson, a very important publisher until 1720 (when his nephew Jacob II took over the business); also secretary and sometime host of the Kit-cat Club, which included Addison, Steele and other prominent Whigs; a *warm Third-day* a prosperous author's night (the profits of every third night of a dramatic production went to the author).

[31] *one poor Word ... clenches* [puns] It may not be amiss to give an instance or two of these operations of *Dullness* out of the Authors celebrated in the Poem. A great Critic [Dennis] formerly held these Clenches in such abhorrence, that he declared, "He that would Pun, would pick a Pocket." Yet Mr. *Dennis*'s Works afford us notable Examples in this kind. "*Alexander* Pope hath sent abroad into the world as many *Bulls* as his Namesake Pope *Alexander*." – "Let us take the initial and final letters of his Surname, viz., *A. P—E*, and they give you the idea of an *Ape*. – *Pope* comes from the Latin word *Popa*, which signifies a little Wart; or from *Poppysma*, because he was continually *popping* out squibs of wit, or rather *Popysmata*, or *Po-pisms*." DENNIS. *Daily-Journal* June 11.1728 [Pope's note; the source, a letter in the *Daily Journal*, is signed Philoscriblerus, a lover of Martinus Scriblerus].

How Farce and Epic get a jumbled race;
How Time himself stands still at her command,
Realms shift their place, and Ocean turns to land.
Here gay Description Ægypt glads with showers;[32]
Or gives to Zembla fruits, to Barca flowers;[33]
Glitt'ring with ice here hoary hills are seen,
There painted valleys of eternal green,
On cold December fragrant chaplets blow,[34]
And heavy harvests nod beneath the snow.
All these and more, the cloud-compelling Queen[35]
Beholds through fogs that magnify the scene:
She, tinselled o'er in robes of varying hues,
With self-applause her wild creation views,
Sees momentary monsters rise and fall,
And with her own fool's colours gilds them all.
'Twas on the day, when Thorold, rich and grave,[36]
Like Cimon triumphed, both on land and wave:
(Pomps without guilt, of bloodless swords and maces,
Glad chains, warm furs, broad banners, and broad faces)[37]
Now Night descending, the proud scene was o'er,
But lived, in Settle's numbers, one day more.[38]
Now May'rs and Shrieves all hushed and satiate lay,[39]
Yet eat in dreams the custard of the day;
While pensive Poets painful vigils keep,
Sleepless themselves to give their readers sleep.
Much to the mindful Queen the feast recalls,
What City-Swans, once sung within the walls;
Much she revolves their arts, their ancient praise,
And sure succession down from Heywood's days.[40]
She saw with joy the line immortal run,
Each sire impressed and glaring in his son;[41]
So watchful Bruin forms with plastic care
Each growing lump, and brings it to a Bear.[42]

Notes

32 *Ægypt glads with showers* In the lower *Ægypt* rain is of no use, the overflowing of the *Nile* being sufficient to impregnate the soil [Pope's note].

33 *Zembla* an arctic island; *Barca* a place in the Libyan desert.

34 *chaplets* garlands.

35 *cloud-compelling* Homer's epithet for Zeus.

36 *Thorold* Sir *George Thorold* Lord Mayor of *London*, in the Year 1720. The Procession of a Lord Mayor is made partly by land, and partly by water. – *Cimon* the famous *Athenian* General obtained a Victory by sea, and another by land, on the same day, over the *Persians* and *Barbarians* [Pope's note].

37 *Glad chains* The Ignorance of these Moderns! This was altered in one Edition to *Gold Chains* … [Pope's note].

38 [*Elkanah*] *Settle* [1648–1724] was alive at this time, and Poet to the City of *London*. His office was to compose yearly panegyrics upon the Lord Mayors, and Verses to be spoken in the Pageants: But that part of the shows being by the frugality of some Lord Mayors at length abolished, the employment of City Poet ceased; so that upon *Settle*'s demise, there was no successor to that place. This important point of time our Poet has chosen, as the Crisis of the Kingdom of *Dullness*, who thereupon decrees to remove her imperial seat from the City, and overspread the other parts of the Town: To which great Enterprise all things being now ripe, she calls the Hero of this Poem [Pope's note].

39 *Shrieves* sheriffs.

40 *Heywood* probably Thomas, a dramatist, like Settle, ridiculed by Dryden (see *Mac Flecknoe*, l. 29), though Pope's note points to John, a Tudor poet.

41 *impressed* as on the face of a medal or coin.

42 *Bruin… Bear* "Bruin" was a name for a bear; it was popularly believed that bears licked their cubs into shape.

She saw old Pryn in restless Daniel shine,[43]
And Eusden eke out Blackmore's endless line;[44]
She saw slow Philips creep like Tate's poor page,[45]
And all the Mighty Mad in Dennis rage.[46]
  In each she marks her image full expressed,
But chief, in Tibbald's monster-breeding breast;
Sees Gods with Demons in strange league engage,
And earth, and heav'n, and hell her battles wage.
  She eyed the Bard, where supperless he sate,[47]
And pined, unconscious of his rising fate;
Studious he sate, with all his books around,
Sinking from thought to thought, a vast profound!
Plunged for his sense, but found no bottom there;
Then writ, and floundered on, in mere despair.
He rolled his eyes that witnessed huge dismay,[48]
Where yet unpawned, much learned lumber lay,
Volumes, whose size the space exactly filled;
Or which fond authors were so good to gild;
Or where, by sculpture made forever known,
The page admires new beauties, not its own.

Notes

43 *Pryn … Daniel William Prynn* [1600–69] and *Daniel Defoe* were writers of Verses, as well as of Politics … Both these Authors had a resemblance in their fates as well as writings, having been alike sentenced to the Pillory [Pope's note; the Protestant Prynne had his ears cut off for writing *HistrioMastix* (1633) and Defoe was pilloried and jailed for *The Shortest Way with the Dissenters*].

44 *Eusden* Lawrence (1688–1730), poet laureate (1718); *Blackmore* Richard (1654–1729), physician and epic poet.

45 *Philips* Ambrose (1674–1749), author of pastorals and Whig journalist; *Tate* Nahum (1652–1715), another poet laureate (1692), famous for revising Shakespeare's *King Lear* so that it ends happily.

46 *And all the mighty Mad* This is by no means to be understood literally, as if Mr. *D.* were really mad … No – it is spoken of that *Excellent* and *Divine Madness*, so often mentioned by *Plato*, that poetical rage and enthusiasm, with which no doubt Mr. *D.* hath, in his time, been highly possessed. SCRIBL …

> It would be unjust not to add his Reasons for this Fury, they are so strong and so coercive. "I regard him," saith he, "as an *Enemy*, not so much to me, as to my King, to my Country, to my Religion, and to that Liberty which has been the sole felicity of my life. A vagary of fortune, who is sometimes pleased to be frolicsome, and the epidemic *Madness of the times*, have given him *Reputation*, and Reputation (as *Hobbes* says) is *Power*, and *that has made him dangerous*. Therefore I look on it as my duty to *King George*, whose faithful subject I am, to my *Country*, of which I have appeared a constant lover; to the *Laws*, under whose protection I have so long lived; and to the *Liberty* of my *Country*, more dear than life to me, of which I have now for forty years been a constant asserter, *&c.* I look upon it as my duty, I say, to do – *you shall see what* – to pull the Lion's skin from this little Ass, which popular error has thrown round him; and to show, that this Author who has been lately so much in vogue, has neither sense in his thoughts, nor English in his expressions". DENNIS, *Rem. on* Hom. *Pref. p. 2 and p. 91, &c* … [Pope's note, which goes on for several pages].

47 *supperless he sate* It is amazing how the sense of this line hath been mistaken by all the former Commentators, who most idly suppose it to imply, that the Hero of the Poem wanted a supper. In truth a great absurdity! Not that we are ignorant that the Hero of *Homer's Odyssey* is frequently in that circumstance, and therefore it can no way derogate from the grandeur of the Epic Poem to represent such [a] Hero under a Calamity, to which the greatest not only of Critics and Poets, but of Kings and Warriors, have been subject. But much more refined, I will venture to say, is the meaning of our author: It was to give us obliquely a curious precept, or what *Bossu* calls a *dignified sentence*, that "Temperance is the life of Study". The language of Poesy brings all into Action; and to represent a Critic encompassed with books, but without a supper, is a picture which lively expresseth how much the true Critic prefers the diet of the mind to that of the body, one of which he always castigates and often totally neglects, for the greater improvement of the other. SCRIBLERUS [Pope's note].

48 *He rolled his eyes* [*Paradise Lost* 1.56–7, incorrect] The progress of a bad Poet in his thoughts being (like the progress of the Devil in *Milton*) through a Chaos, might probably suggest this imitation [Pope's note].

Here swells the shelf with Ogilby the great:[49]
There, stamped with arms, Newcastle shines complete,[50]
Here all his suff'ring brotherhood retire,
And 'scape the martyrdom of jakes and fire;[51]
A Gothic Vatican! of Greece and Rome
Well-purged, and worthy Withers, Quarles, and Blome.[52]
  But high above, more solid Learning shone,
The Classics of an Age that heard of none;
There Caxton slept, with Wynkyn at his side,[53]
One clasped in wood, and one in strong cow-hide.
There saved by spice, like mummies, many a year,
Old Bodies of Philosophy appear.
De Lyra here a dreadful front extends,[54]
And there, the groaning shelves Philemon bends.[55]
  Of these twelve volumes, twelve of amplest size,
Redeemed from tapers and defrauded pies,
Inspired he seizes: These an altar raise:
An hecatomb of pure, unsullied lays
That altar crowns: A folio Common-place[56]
Founds the whole pile, of all his works the base;
Quartos, Octavos, shape the less'ning pyre,
And last, a little Ajax tips the spire.[57]
  Then he. 'Great Tamer of all human art!
First in my care, and nearest at my heart:
Dullness! whose good old cause I yet defend,[58]
With whom my Muse began, with whom shall end!
O thou, of business the directing soul,
To human heads like bias to the bowl,[59]
Which as more pond'rous makes their aim more true,
Obliquely waddling to the mark in view.
O ever gracious to perplexed mankind!
Who spread a healing mist before the mind,
And, lest we err by Wit's wild, dancing light,

Notes

[49] *Ogilby the great John Ogilby* [1600–76] was one, who from a late initiation into literature, made such a progress as might well style him the *Prodigy* of his time! sending into the world so many *large Volumes!*...[Pope's note].

[50] *Newcastle* The *Duchess* of *Newcastle* [Margaret Cavendish] was one who busied herself in the ravishing delights of Poetry; leaving to posterity in print three *ample Volumes* of her studious endeavours ... [Pope's note].

[51] *jakes* "A house of office" (Johnson), a toilet.

[52] *Withers, Quarles, and Blome* [George *Withers* (1588–1667); Francis *Quarles*, author of *Emblemes* (1635); Richard Blome (d. 1705); all three used illustrations and were considered authors of children's or coffee-table books.] *George Withers* was a great pretender to poetical zeal against the vices of the times, and abused the greatest Personages in power, which brought upon him *frequent correction*. The *Marshalsea* and *Newgate* were no strangers to him. WINSTANLY. *Quarles* was as dull a writer, but an honester man. *Blome's* books are remarkable for their cuts [Pope's note].

[53] *Caxton* William Caxton (1422–91), first English printer; *Wynkyn* de Worde (d. 1534), another important early printer; Theobald used Caxton's prose *Aeneid* to correct one of Pope's errors in his edition of Shakespeare; Pope actually included the work in one of the appendices of *The Dunciad* in 1729.

[54] *De Lyra* Nicholas of Lyra (c.1270–1349), French scholar, author of a biblical commentary in fifty volumes.

[55] *Philemon* Holland, [1552–1637] Dr. in Physic. He translated *so many books*, that a man would think he had done *nothing else*, insomuch that he might be called *Translator General of his age* ... [Pope's note].

[56] *folio Common-place* a large notebook full of quotations.

[57] *a little Ajax* In *duodecimo*, translated from *Sophocles* by *Tibbald* [Pope's note].

[58] *good old cause* the cause of the Protestants and republicans in the Civil War.

[59] *bowl* a ball in lawn bowling, which is weighted or biased.

Secure us kindly in our native night.
Ah! still o'er Britain stretch that peaceful wand,
Which lulls th' Helvetian and Batavian land.[60]
Where rebel to thy throne if Science rise,
She does but show her coward face and dies:
There, thy good Scholiasts with unwearied pains
Make Horace flat, and humble Maro's strains;[61]
Here studious I unlucky moderns save,
Nor sleeps one error in its father's grave,
Old puns restore, lost blunders nicely seek,
And crucify poor Shakespeare once a week.[62]
For thee I dim these eyes, and stuff this head,
With all such reading as was never read;[63]
For thee supplying, in the worst of days,
Notes to dull books, and prologues to dull plays;
For thee explain a thing till all men doubt it,
And write about it, Goddess, and about it;
So spins the silkworm small its slender store,
And labours, till it clouds itself all o'er.
Not that my quill to Critiques was confined,
My Verse gave ampler lessons to mankind;
So gravest precepts may successless prove,
But sad examples never fail to move.
As forced from wind-guns, lead itself can fly,
And pond'rous slugs cut swiftly through the sky;
As clocks to weight their nimble motion owe,
The wheels above urged by the load below;
Me, Emptiness and Dullness could inspire,
And were my Elasticity and Fire.
Had heav'n decreed such works a longer date,
Heav'n had decreed to spare the Grubstreet-state.
But see great Settle to the dust descend,
And all thy cause and empire at an end!
Could Troy be saved by any single hand,
His grey-goose-weapon must have made her stand.
But what can I? my Flaccus cast aside,[64]
Take up th' *Attorney's* (once my better) *Guide*?[65]
Or rob the Roman geese of all their glories,[66]
And save the state by cackling to the Tories?
Yes, to my Country I my pen consign,

Notes

[60] *Helvetian and Batavian* Swiss and Netherlandish.

[61] *Maro* Virgil's surname.

[62] *once a week* For some time, once a week or fortnight, he printed in *Mist's Journal* a single remark or poor conjecture on some word or *pointing* of *Shakespeare* [Pope's note].

[63] *such reading as was never read* Such as *Caxton* abovementioned; the three destructions of *Troy* by *Wynkyn*, and other like classics [Pope's note].

[64] *my Flaccus* [surname of Horace] A familiar manner of speaking used by modern Critics of a favourite Author. Mr. *T.* might as justly speak thus of *Horace*, as a French wit did of *Tully* seeing his works in a library, *Ah! mon cher Ciceron! Je le connois bien: c'est le même que Marc Tulle* [Pope's note].

[65] *Attorney* In allusion to his first profession [Pope's note].

[66] *Roman geese* Relates to the well-known story of the geese that saved the Capitol of which Virgil, Æn. 8 [655–6; Pope's note; the geese awakened the Romans to a night attack of Gauls (Livy 5.47)].

Yes, from this moment, mighty Mist! am thine,[67]
And rival, Curtius! of thy fame and zeal,[68]
O'er head and ears plunge for the public weal.
Adieu my children! better thus expire[69]
Un-stalled, unsold; thus glorious mount in fire
Fair without spot; than greased by grocer's hands,
Or shipped with Ward to ape and monkey lands,[70]
Or wafting ginger, round the streets to go,
And visit alehouse where ye first did grow'.
With that, he lifted thrice the sparkling brand,
And thrice he dropped it from his quiv'ring hand:
Then lights the structure, with averted eyes;
The rolling smokes involve the sacrifice.
The opening clouds disclose each work by turns,
Now flames old Memnon, now Rodrigo burns,[71]
In one quick flash see Proserpine expire,[72]
And last, his own cold Æschylus took fire.[73]
Then gushed the tears, as from the Trojan's eyes
When the last blaze sent Ilion to the skies.
Roused by the light, old Dullness heaved the head,
Then snatched a sheet of Thulè from her bed;[74]
Sudden she flies, and whelms it o'er the pyre:
Down sink the flames, and with a hiss expire.
  Her ample presence fills up all the place;
A veil of fogs dilates her awful face;

Notes

67 *mighty Mist!* Nathaniel Mist [d. 1737] was a publisher of a famous Tory Paper ... [Pope's note].

68 *Curtius* the Roman who sacrificed himself for the Republic by riding in full armor into a huge chasm in the Forum (Livy 7.6).

69 *Adieu my children!* This is a tender and passionate Apostrophe to his own Works which he is going to sacrifice, agreeable to the nature of a man in great affliction, and reflecting like a parent, on the many miserable fates to which they would otherwise be subject.

> ——*Felix Priameïa virgo!Jussa mori: quæ sortitus non pertulit ullos,Nec victoris heri tetigit captiva cubile!Nos patriâ incensâ, diversa per æquora vectæ, &c.*Virg. Æn. 3. [321–4] [Pope's note].

70 *Ward Edward Ward* [1667–1731] a very voluminous Poet ... best known by the *London Spy* ... Great numbers of his works are yearly sold into the Plantations [Pope's note].

71 *old Memnon* a Hero in *The Persian Princess* [by Theobald] very apt to take fire, as appears by these lines with which he begins the Play:

> By heav'n it fires my frozen blood with rage, And makes it *scald* my aged Trunk——
>
> *Rodrigo* the chief personage of *The Perfidious Brother*, a play written between T. and a Watchmaker [Pope's notes].

72 *Proserpine* The *Rape of Proserpine*, one of the Farces of this Author, in which *Ceres* sets fire to a Corn-field, which endangered the burning of the Play-house [Pope's note].

73 *his own cold Æschylus* He had been (to use an expression of our Poet) "about Æschylus" for ten years, and had received Subscriptions for the same, but then went "about" other Books. The character of this tragic Poet is Fire and Boldness in a high degree; but our Author supposes it to be very much cooled by the translation; Upon sight of a specimen of it, was made this Epigram,

> Alas! poor Æschylus! unlucky Dog!Whom once a *Lobster* kill'd, and now a *Log*.

But this is a grievous error, for Æschylus was not slain by the fall of a Lobster on his head, but of a Tortoise ... SCRIBL. [Pope's note; Theobald never finished his proposed translation of Aeschylus].

74 *Thulè* [1718] An unfinished Poem of that name, of which one sheet was printed fifteen Years ago; by *A*[*mbrose*] *Ph*[*ilips*] a Northern Author. It is an usual method of putting out a fire, to cast wet sheets upon it. Some Critics have been of opinion, that this sheet was of the nature of the *Asbestos*, which cannot be consumed by fire; but I rather think it only an allegorical allusion to the coldness and heaviness of the writing [Pope's note].

Great in her charms! as when on Shrieves and May'rs
She looks, and breathes herself into their airs.
She bids him wait her to the sacred Dome;[75]
Well-pleased he entered, and confessed his Home:
So spirits ending their terrestrial race,
Ascend, and recognize their native place:
Raptured, he gazes round the dear retreat,
And in sweet numbers celebrates the seat.[76]
  Here to her Chosen all her works she shows;
Prose swelled to verse, Verse loit'ring into prose;
How random Thoughts now meaning chance to find,
Now leave all memory of sense behind:
How Prologues into Prefaces decay,
And these to Notes are frittered quite away.
How Index-learning turns no student pale,
Yet holds the Eel of science by the Tail.
How, with less reading than makes felons 'scape,[77]
Less human genius than God gives an ape,
Small thanks to France and none to Rome or Greece,
A past, vamped, future, old, revived, new piece,[78]
'Twixt Plautus, Fletcher, Congreve, and Corneille,
Can make a Cibber, Johnson, or Ozell.[79]
  The Goddess then o'er his anointed head,
With mystic words, the sacred Opium shed;
And lo! her Bird (a monster of a fowl!
Something betwixt a H***r and Owl)[80]
Perched on his crown. 'All hail! and hail again,
My son! the promised land expects thy reign.
Know, Settle, cloyed with custard and with praise,
Is gathered to the Dull of ancient days,
Safe, where no critics damn, no duns molest,
Where Gildon, Banks, and high-born Howard rest.[81]
I see a King! who leads my chosen sons
To lands, that flow with clenches and with puns:
Till each famed Theatre my empire own,

Notes

[75] *sacred Dome* The *Cave of Poverty* above-mentioned; where he no sooner enters, but he Reconnoitres the place of his original … [Pope's note].

[76] *sweet numbers* He writ a Poem called the *Cave of Poverty*, which concludes with a very extraordinary Wish, "That some great Genius, or man of distinguished merit may be *starved*, in order to celebrate her power, and describe her Cave". It was printed in octavo, 1715 [Pope's note; Pope is misquoting].

[77] *reading* proving that one could read even a few words of Latin at this time still gave some accused criminals "benefit of clergy" and pardon.

[78] *vamp* "To piece an old thing with some new part" (Johnson).

[79] *Cibber* Colly (1671–1757), actor and playwright; his elevation to poet laureate in 1730 helped earn him an equivalent depression as hero of Pope's *New Dunciad* (1742); *Johnson* Charles (1679–1748), dramatist and Whig; *Ozell* John (d. 1743), a voluminous translator.

[80] *a H***r* A strange Bird from *Switzerland* [Pope's note; John James Heidegger (d. 1749), famous for promoting masquerades and other entertainments].

[81] *Gildon* Charles (1665–1724), critic and dramatist; he called Pope "a little diminutive Creature, who had got a sort of Knack in smooth Versification"; *Banks* John (1652/3–1706); *Howard* Edward (1624–1712), author of an epic poem; known as "foolish Ned."

Till Albion, as Hibernia, bless my throne!
I see! I see!' – Then rapt, she spoke no more.
'God save King Tibbald!' Grubstreet alleys roar.
    So when Jove's block descended from on high,
(As sings thy great fore-father, Ogilby)[82]
Loud thunder to its bottom shook the bog,
And the hoarse nation croaked, God save King Log![83]

from *Letters*

To Lady Mary Wortley Montagu (1 September 1718)

Madam, – I have been (what I never was till now) in debt to you for a letter some weeks. I was informed you were at Sea, & that 'twas to no purpose to write, till some news had been heard of your arriving somewhere or other. Besides, I have had a second dangerous Illness, from which I was more diligent to be recovered than from the first, having now some hopes of seeing you again. If you make any Tour in Italy, I shall not easily forgive you for not acquainting me soon enough to have met you there: I am very certain I can never be Polite, unless I travel with you. And it is never to be repaired, the loss that Homer has sustained, for my want of translating him in Asia.[1] You will come hither full of criticisms against a man, who wanted nothing to be in the right but to have kept your company. You have no way of making me amends, but by continuing an Asiatic when you return, to me, whatever English Airs you may put on to other people. I prodigiously long for your Sonnets, your remarks, your oriental learning; but I long for nothing so much as your Oriental Self. You must of necessity be *advanced* so far *Back* into true nature & simplicity of manners, by these 3 years residence in the East, that I shall look upon you as so many years Younger than you was, so much nearer Innocence (that is, Truth) & Infancy (that is Openness). I expect to see your Soul as much thinner dressed as your Body; and that you have left

Notes

[82] *As sings thy great fore-father, Ogilby* See his *Æsop Fab.* where this excellent hemistich [half-line] is to be found [see next note]. Our author shows here and elsewhere, a prodigious Tenderness for a *bad writer*. We see he selects the only good passage perhaps in all that ever *Ogilby writ*; which shows how candid and patient a reader he must have been. What can be more kind and affectionate than these words in the preface to his Poems, quarto, 1717, where he labours to call up all our humanity and forgiveness toward them, by the most moderate representation of their case that has ever been given by any Author? "Much may be said to extenuate the fault of bad Poets: What we call a *Genius* is hard to be distinguished, by a man himself, from a prevalent inclination: And if it be never so great, he can at first discover it no other way, than by that strong propensity, which renders him the more liable to be mistaken. He has no other method but to make the experiment by writing, and so appealing to the judgement of others: And if he happens to write ill (which is certainly no sin in itself) he is immediately made the Object of Ridicule! I wish we had the humanity to reflect, that even the worst Authors might endeavour to please us, and in that endeavour, deserve something at our hands. We have no cause to quarrel with them, but for their obstinacy in persisting, and even that may admit of alleviating circumstances: For their particular friends may be either ignorant, or unsincere; and the rest of the world too well-bred, to shock them with a truth, which generally their Booksellers are the first that inform them of" [Pope's note].

[83] *King Log* in Ogilby's translation of Aesop (1651) the frogs cry *"Jove* save King Log" when Zeus answers their prayers by sending a wooden god; when they are dissatisfied with the stump, he sends them a stork who eats them up.

To Lady Mary Wortley Montagu

[1] *Homer ... Asia* Lady Mary praised Pope's translation of the *Iliad* (vol. 2 came out in 1716) in a letter to him dated April 1, 1717 and told him that it helped explain many customs that she was witnessing on her Turkish travels.

off, as unwieldy & cumbersome, a great many damned European Habits. Without offence to your modesty be it spoken, I have a burning desire to see your Soul stark naked, for I am confident 'tis the prettiest kind of white Soul, in the universe – But I forget whom I am talking to: you may possibly by this time Believe according to the Prophet,[2] that you have none. If so, show me That which comes next to a Soul; you may easily put it upon a poor ignorant Christian for a Soul, & please him as well with it: I mean your Heart: Mahomet I think allows you Hearts: which (together with fine eyes & other agreeable equivalents) are worth all the Souls on this side of the world. But if I must be content with seeing your body only, God send it to come quickly: I honour it more than the Diamond-Casket that held Homer's *Iliads*. For in the very twinkle of one eye of it, there is more Wit; and in the very dimple of one cheek of it, there is more Meaning, than in all the Souls that ever were casually put into Women since Men had the making them.

I have a mind to fill the rest of this paper with an accident that happened just under my eyes, and has made a great Impression upon me. I have passed part of this Summer at an old romantic Seat of my Lord Harcourt's which he lent me; It overlooks a Common-field, where under the Shade of a Hay cock sate two Lovers, as constant as ever were found in Romance, beneath a spreading Beech. The name of one (let it sound as it will) was John Hewet, of the other Sarah Drew. John was a well-set man about five and twenty, Sarah a brown woman of about eighteen. John had for several months borne the labour of the day in the same field with Sarah; When she milked, it was his morning & evening charge to bring the Cows to her pail: Their Love was the Talk, but not the Scandal, of the whole neighbourhood, for all they aimed at was the blameless possession of each other in marriage. It was but this very morning that he had obtained her Parents' consent, and it was but till next week that they were to wait to be happy. Perhaps, this very day in the intervals of their work, they were talking of their wedding clothes, and John was matching several kinds of poppies and field-flowers to her Complexion, to make her a Present of Knots for the day. While they were thus employed (it was on the last of July) a terrible Storm of Thunder and Lightning arose, that drove the Labourers to what Shelter the Trees or hedges afforded. Sarah frighted, and out of breath, sunk down on a Haycock, & John (who never separated from her) sat by her side, having raked two or three heaps together to secure her. Immediately there was heard so loud a Crack as if Heaven had burst asunder: the Labourers, all solicitous for each other's safety, called to one another: those that were nearest our Lovers, hearing no answer, stepped to the place where they lay; they first saw a little Smoke, & after, this faithful Pair. John with one arm about his Sarah's neck, and the other held over her face as if to screen her from the Lightning. They were struck dead, & already grown stiff and cold in this tender posture. There was no mark or discolouring on their bodies, only that Sarah's eyebrow was a little singed, and a small Spot appeared between her breasts. They were buried the next day in one grave, in the Parish of Stanton-Harcourt in Oxfordshire, where my Lord Harcourt, at my request, has erected a monument over them. Of the following Epitaphs which I made, the Critics have chosen the godly one: I like neither, but wish you had been in England to have done this office better; I think 'twas what you could not have refused me on so moving an occasion.

When Eastern Lovers feed the fun'ral fire,
On the same Pile their faithful Fair expire;

Notes

[2] *Prophet* Muhammad.

Here pitying Heav'n that virtue mutual found,
And blasted both, that it might neither wound.
Hearts so sincere, th' Almighty saw well-pleased,
Sent his own Lightning, & the Victims seized.

1

Think not, by rig'rous Judgement seized,
  A Pair so faithful could expire;
Victims so pure Heav'n saw well-pleased,
  And snatched them in celestial fire.

2

Live well, & fear no sudden fate:
  When God calls Virtue to the grave,
Alike 'tis Justice, soon, or late,
  Mercy alike, to kill, or save.
Virtue unmoved, can hear the Call,
And face the Flash that melts the Ball.

Upon the whole, I can't think these people unhappy: The greatest happiness, next to living as they would have done, was to die as they did. The greatest honour people of this low degree could have was to be remembered on a little monument; unless you will give them another, that of being honoured with a Tear from the finest eyes in the world. I know you have Tenderness; you must have it: It is the very Emanation of Good Sense & virtue: The finest minds like the finest metals, dissolve the easiest.

But when you are reflecting upon Objects of pity, pray do not forget one, who had no sooner found out an Object of the highest Esteem, than he was separated from it: And who is so very unhappy as not to be susceptible of Consolation from others, by being so miserably in the right as to think other women what they really are. Such an one can't but be desperately fond of any creature that is quite different from these. If the Circassian[3] be utterly void of such Honour as these have, and such virtue as these boast of, I am content. I have detested the Sound of *honest Woman, & loving Spouse* ever since I heard the pretty name of Odaliche. Dear Madam I am for ever Yours, and your Slave's Slave, & Servant.

My most humble Services to Mr Wortley. Pray let me hear from you soon: Though I shall very soon write again. I am confident half our letters have been lost.

Notes

[3] *Circassian* in an earlier letter Pope jested about Lady Mary procuring him a female slave from that place near southern Russia; Lady Mary had suggested in another letter that such slaves were notoriously dishonorable.

Mary Collier (1688?–1762)

Much that is known of Mary Collier is contained in the following "advertisement" to *The Woman's Labour*, written by the unknown M. B. Collier filled out the picture a little in her preface to her *Poems on Several Occasions* (1762). She continued a washer-woman until age sixty-three and retired from working altogether at seventy.

The Woman's Labour: An Epistle to Mr. Stephen Duck;[1] In Answer to his late Poem, called The Thresher's Labour … (1739)

By Mary Collier, Now a Washer-Woman, at Petersfield in Hampshire

ADVERTISEMENT

It is thought proper to assure the Reader, that the following Verses are the real Productions of the Person to whom the Title-Page ascribes them.

Though She pretends not to the Genius of Mr. Duck, nor hopes to be taken Notice of by the Great, yet her Friends are of Opinion that the Novelty of a *Washer-Woman*'s turning Poetess, will procure her some Readers.

If all that follow the same Employment would amuse themselves, and one another, during the tedious Hours of their Labour, in this, or some other Ways as innocent, instead of tossing Scandal to and fro, many Reputations would remain unwounded, and the Peace of Families be less disturbed.

I think it no Reproach to the Author, whose Life is toilsome, and her Wages inconsiderable, to confess honestly, that the View of her putting a small Sum of Money in her Pocket, as well as the Reader's Entertainment, had its Share of Influences upon this Publication. And she humbly hopes she shall not be absolutely disappointed; since, though she is ready to own that her Performance could by no Means stand a critical Examination, yet she flatters herself that, with all its Faults and Imperfections, the candid Reader will judge it to be something considerably beyond the common Capacity of those of her own Rank and Occupation.

M. B.

Immortal Bard! thou Favourite of the Nine!
Enriched by Peers, advanced by Caroline!
Deign to look down on One that's poor and low,
Remembering you yourself was lately so;
Accept these Lines: Alas! what can you have
From her, who ever was, and's still a Slave?

Notes

THE WOMAN'S LABOUR

[1] *Mr. Stephen Duck* Stephen Duck (1705–56) (see below, p. 802), who was given an income by Queen Caroline.

British Literature 1640–1789: An Anthology, Fourth Edition. Edited by Robert DeMaria, Jr.

No Learning ever was bestowed on me;
My Life was always spent in Drudgery:
And not alone; alas! with Grief I find,
It is the Portion of poor Woman-kind.
Oft have I thought as on my Bed I lay,
Eased from the tiresome Labours of the Day,
Our first Extraction from a Mass refined,
Could never be for Slavery designed;
Till Time and Custom by degrees destroyed
That happy State our sex at first enjoyed.
When Men had used their utmost Care and Toil,
Their Recompense was but a Female Smile;
When they by Arts or Arms were rendered Great,
They laid their Trophies at a Woman's Feet;
They, in those Days, unto our Sex did bring
Their Hearts, their All, a Free-will Offering;
And as from us their Being they derive,
They back again should all due Homage give.
Jove once descending from the Clouds, did drop
In Show'rs of Gold on lovely *Danae*'s Lap;[2]
The sweet-tongued Poets, in those generous Days,
Unto our Shrine still offered up their Lays:
But now, alas! that Golden Age is past,
We are the Objects of your Scorn at last.
And you, great Duck, upon whose happy Brow
The Muses seem to fix the Garland now,
In your late *Poem* boldly did declare[3]
Alcides' Labours can't with yours compare;[4]
And of your annual Task have much to say,
Of threshing, Reaping, Mowing Corn and Hay;
Boasting your daily Toil, and nightly Dream,
But can't conclude your never-dying Theme,
And let our hapless Sex in Silence lie
Forgotten, and in dark Oblivion die;
But on our abject State you throw your Scorn,
And Women wrong, your Verses to adorn.
You of Hay-making speak a Word or two,
As if our Sex but little Work could do:
This makes the honest Farmer smiling say,
He'll seek for Women still to make his Hay;
For if his Back be turned, their Work they mind
As well as men, as far as he can find.
For my own Part, I many a *Summer*'s Day
Have spent in throwing, turning, making Hay;
But ne'er could see, what you have lately found,
Our Wages paid for sitting on the Ground.

Notes

2 *Show'rs of Gold* Jove took this form to penetrate the defenses erected by Danae's father, and with her conceived Perseus.

3 *Poem* "The Thresher's Labour" (1730); see below, p. 802.

4 *Alcides* Heracles or Hercules, as Duck calls him.

'Tis true, that when our Morning's Work is done,
And all our Grass exposed unto the Sun,
While that his scorching Beams do on it shine,
As well as you, we have a Time to dine:
I hope, that since we freely toil and sweat
To earn our Bread, you'll give us Time to eat.
That over, soon we must get up again,
And nimbly turn our Hay upon the Plain;
Nay, rake and prow it in, the Case is clear;[5]
Or how should Cocks in equal Rows appear?[6]
But if you'd have what you have wrote believed.
I find, that you to hear us talk are grieved:
In this, I hope, you do not speak your Mind,
For none but *Turks*, that ever could I find,
Have Mutes to serve them, or did e'er deny
Their Slaves, at Work, to chat it merrily.
Since you have Liberty to speak your Mind,
And are to talk, as well as we, inclined,
Why should you thus repine, because that we,
Like you, enjoy that pleasing Liberty?
What! would you lord it quite, and take away
The only Privilege our Sex enjoy?
  When Evening does approach, we homeward hie,
And our domestic Toils incessant ply:
Against your coming Home prepare to get
Our Work all done, our House in order set;
'Bacon' and 'Dumpling' in the Pot we boil,[7]
Our Beds we make, our Swine we feed the while;
Then wait at Door to see you coming Home,
And set the Table out against you come:
Early next Morning we on you attend;
Our Children dress and feed, their Clothes we mend;
And in the Field our daily Task renew,
Soon as the rising Sun has dried the Dew.
  When Harvest comes, into the Field we go,
And help to reap the Wheat as well as you;
Or else we go the Ears of Corn to glean;
No Labour scorning, be it e'er so mean;
But in the Work we freely bear a Part,
And what we can, perform with all our Heart.
To get a Living we so willing are,
Out tender Babes into the Field we bear,
And wrap them in our Clothes to keep them warm,

Notes

[5] *prow* (not in *OED*) perhaps "plough" or "drow" (a dialectal form of "draw") if the *p* is actually an upside-down *d*.

[6] *Cocks* haycocks, haystacks; the line, like many others in the poem, alludes to one just like it in Duck's poem.

[7] *"Bacon" and "Dumpling"* allusions to Duck's poem.

While round about we gather up the Corn;
And often unto them our Course do bend,
To keep them safe, that nothing them offend:
Our children that are able, bear a Share
In gleaning Corn, such is our frugal care.
When Night comes on, unto our Home we go,
Our Corn we carry, and our Infant too;
Weary, alas! but 'tis not worth our while
Once to complain, or 'rest at every Stile';[8]
We must make haste, for when we Home are come,
Alas! we find our Work but just begun;
So many Things for our Attendance call,
Had we ten Hands, we could employ them all.
Our Children put to Bed, with greatest Care
We all Things for your coming Home prepare:
You sup, and go to Bed without delay,
And rest yourselves till the ensuing Day;
While we, alas! but little Sleep can have,
Because our froward Children cry and rave;[9]
Yet, without fail, soon as Day-light doth spring,
We in the Field again our Work begin,
And there, with all our Strength, our Toil renew,
Till *Titan*'s golden Rays have dried the Dew;
Then home we go unto our Children dear,
Dress, feed, and bring them to the Field with care.
Were this your Case, you justly might complain
That Day nor Night you are secure from Pain;
Those mighty Troubles which perplex your Mind,
(*Thistles* before, and *Females* come behind)
Would vanish soon, and quickly disappear,
Were you, like us, encumbered thus with Care.
What you would have of us we do not know:
We oft take up the Corn that you do mow;
We cut the Pease, and always ready are
In every Work to take our Proper Share;
And from the Time that Harvest doth begin,
Until the Corn be cut and carried in,
Our Toil and Labour's daily so extreme,
That we have hardly ever *Time to dream*.
    The Harvest ended, Respite none we find;
The hardest of our Toil is still behind:
Hard labour we most cheerfully pursue,
And out, abroad, a Charring often go:[10]
Of which I now will briefly tell in part,
What fully to declare is past my Art;

Notes

8 *"rest at every Stile"* the men do this on their way home in Duck's poem.

9 *froward* "Peevish; ungovernable; angry; perverse" (Johnson).

10 *a Charring* from "to char," "To work at others' houses by the day, without being hired as a servant" (Johnson).

So many Hardships daily we go through,
I boldly say, the like *you* never knew.
When bright *Orion* glitters in the Skies
In *Winter* Nights, then early we must rise;
The Weather ne'er so bad, Wind, Rain, or Snow.
Our Work appointed, we must rise and go;
While you on easy Beds may lie and sleep,
Till Light does through your Chamber-windows peep.
When to the House we come where we should go,
How to get in, alas! we do not know:
The Maid quite tir'd with Work the Day before,
O'ercome with Sleep; we standing at the Door
Oppressed with Cold, and often call in vain,
Ere to our Work we can Admittance gain:
But when from Wind and Weather we get in,
Briskly with Courage we our Work begin;
Heaps of fine Linen we before us view,
Whereon to lay our Strength and Patience too;
Cambrics and Muslins, which our ladies wear,[11]
Laces and Edgings, costly, fine, and rare,
Which must be washed with utmost Skill and care;
With Holland Shirts, Ruffles and Fringes too,[12]
Fashions which our Fore-fathers never knew.
For several Hours here we work and slave,
Before we can one Glimpse of Day-light have;
We labour hard before the Morning's past,
Because we fear the Time runs on too fast.
At length bright *Sol* illuminates the Skies,
And summons drowsy Mortals to arise;
Then comes our Mistress to us without fail,
And in her Hand, *perhaps*, a Mug of Ale
To cheer our Hearts, and also to inform
Herself, what Work is done that very Morn;
Lays her Command upon us, that we mind
Her Linen well, nor 'leave the Dirt behind':
Not this alone, but also to take care
We don't her Cambrics nor her Ruffles tear;
And *these* most strictly does of us require,
'To save her Soap, and sparing be of Fire';
Tells us her Charge is great, nay furthermore,
Her Clothes are fewer than the Time before.
Now we drive on, resolved our Strength to try,
And what we can, we do most willingly;
Until with Heat and Work, 'tis often known
Not only Sweat, but Blood runs trickling down
Our Wrists and Fingers; still our Work demands
The constant Action of our lab'ring Hands.

Notes

11 *Cambrics* fine linens from Flanders.

12 *Holland* "Fine linen made in Holland" (Johnson).

Now Night comes on, from whence you have Relief,
But that, alas! does but increase our Grief;
With heavy Hearts we often view the Sun,
Fearing he'll set before our Work is done;
For either in the Morning, or at Night,
We piece the *Summer*'s Day with Candle-light.[13]
Though we all Day with Care our Work attend,
Such is our Fate, we know not when 'twill end:
When Evening's come, you Homeward take your Way,
We, till our Work is done, are forced to stay;
And after all our Toil and Labour past,
Six-pence or Eight-pence pays us off at last;
For all our Pains, no Prospect can we see
Attend us, but *Old Age* and *Poverty*.
The *Washing* is not all we have to do:
We oft change Work for Work as well as you.
Our Mistress of her Pewter doth complain,
And 'tis our Part to make it clean again.
This Work, though very hard and tiresome too,
Is not the worst we hapless Females do:
When Night comes on, and we quite weary are,
We scarce can count what falls unto our Share;
Pots, Kettles, Sauce-pans, Skillets, we may see,
Skimmers and Ladles, and such Trumpery,
Brought in to make complete our Slavery,
Though early in the Morning 'tis begun,
'Tis often very late before we've done;
Alas! our Labours never know an End;
On Brass and Iron we our Strength must spend;
Our tender Hands and Fingers scratch and tear:
All this, and more, with Patience we must bear.
Coloured with Dirt and Filth we now appear;
Your threshing 'sooty Peas' will not come near.
All the Perfections Woman once could boast,
Are quite obscured, and altogether lost.
Once more our Mistress sends to let us know
She wants our Help, because the Beer runs low:
Then in much haste for Brewing we prepare,
The Vessels clean, and scald with greatest care;
Often at Midnight, from our Bed we rise;
At other Times, ev'n *that* will not suffice;
Our Work at Evening oft we do begin,
And ere we've done, the Night comes on again.

Notes

[13] *piece* eke out; stretch.

Water we pump, the Copper we must fill,
Or tend the Fire; for if we e'er stand still,
Like you, when threshing, we a Watch must keep,
Our Wort boils over if we dare to sleep.[14]
But to rehearse all Labour is in vain,
Of which we very justly might complain:
For us, you see, but little Rest is found;
Our Toil increases as the Year runs round.
While you to *Sisyphus* yourselves compare,[15]
With *Danaus' Daughters* we may claim a Share;[16]
For while *he* labours hard against the Hill,
Bottomless Tubs of Water *they* must fill.
So the industrious Bees do hourly strive
To bring their Loads of Honey to the Hive;
Their sordid Owners always reap the Gains,[17]
And poorly recompense their Toil and Pains.

Notes

[14] *Wort* "A plant of the cabbage kind," perhaps with a pun on another meaning, fermenting beer, which the threshers drink.

[15] *Sisyphus* a figure in Greek mythology doomed to push a stone unsuccessfully up an incline in Hades.

[16] *Danaus' Daughters* these Egyptians suffered the specified fate for murdering their husbands at their father's behest.

[17] *sordid* "Covetous; niggardly" (Johnson, sense 3).

Lady Mary Wortley Montagu (1689–1762)

A noblewoman by birth, Lady Mary Pierrepont eloped with Edward Wortley Montagu at age twenty-three. An accomplished, largely self-taught scholar, she accompanied her husband on his embassy to Turkey in 1716 and sent back to friends and family some of the most remarkable letters of the eighteenth century. Not only was she the first European woman to travel in many of the places she visited, she was the first European person to witness the private lives of Islamic women, because they were utterly closed to males. The letters, which are the basis of her literary fame, were not published until after Lady Mary's death. On her return from her two years of travel, however, she enjoyed London literary society, patronized some poets, and wrote a play and some poetry, much of which she did not intend to publish. She also brought back to England knowledge about smallpox inoculation which helped establish the practice there. Her learning and elegance fascinated Alexander Pope and some other great writers of the day, though she was not equally smitten. Her youthful marriage turned cold in the early stages, and some of her poetry reflects a pessimism about the possibility of successful relations between the sexes. However, she enjoyed her daughter, who was born on her journey and married a prime minister, and she suffered through the vicissitudes of a strange and wayward son's life. She became a single émigrée and lived nearly the last twenty years of her life on the Continent, not returning to London once until the death of her estranged husband.

Most of the modern scholarly work on Montagu was done by the late Robert Halsband, who based his editorial work on the manuscripts, many of which are in private hands. I rely on the notes to his edition of the letters (3 vols., Clarendon Press, 1965), and I use his edition of the poems (edited with Isobel Grundy, Clarendon Press, 1977). As a copy-text for the letters I include here, I have used the second edition (1763), but substituted a few readings from Halsband's superior edition. Montagu's romance writings have been edited by Isobel Grundy (Oxford University Press, 1996), and her biography (Oxford University Press, 1999) supersedes Halsband's (Clarendon Press, 1956).

from *LETTERS Of the Right Honourable Lady M—y W——y M———u: Written, during her Travels in EUROPE, ASIA and AFRICA, TO Persons of Distinction, Men of Letters, &c. in different Parts of Europe. WHICH CONTAIN, Among other CURIOUS Relations, Accounts of the POLICY and MANNERS of the TURKS; Drawn from Sources that have been inaccessible to other Travellers*

To the Lady X——

Vienna, Oct. I, O.S. 1716[1]

You desire me, Madam, to send you some accounts of the customs here, and at the same time a description of Vienna. I am always willing to obey your Commands, but you must upon this occasion, take the Will for the deed. If I should undertake to tell you all the particulars, in which the manners here differ from ours, I must write a whole quire[2] of the dullest stuff that was ever read, or printed without being read. Their dress agrees with the French or English in no one article, but wearing petticoats. They have many fashions peculiar to themselves; they think it indecent for a widow ever to wear green or rose colour, but all the other gayest colours at her own discretion. The assemblies here are the only regular diversion, the operas being always at court, and commonly on some particular occasion. Madam *Rabutin* has the assembly constantly every night at her house; and the other ladies whenever they have a mind to display the magnificence of their apartments, or oblige a friend by complimenting them on the day of their Saint, they declare, that on such a day the assembly shall be at their house in honour of the feast of the Count or Countess——*such a one*. These days are called days of *Gala*, and all the friends or relations of the lady, whose Saint it is, are obliged to appear in their best clothes and all their jewels. The mistress of the house takes no particular notice of anybody, nor returns anybody's visit; and, whoever pleases, may go without the formality of being presented. The company are entertained with ice in several forms, winter and summer; afterwards they divide into parties of ombre, piquett[3] or conversation, all games of hazard being forbid.

I saw t'other day the *Gala* for Count *Altheim*, the Emperor's favourite, and never in my life saw so many fine clothes ill fancied. They embroider the richest gold stuffs, and provided they can make their clothes expensive enough, that is all the taste they show in them. On other days the general dress is a scarf, and what you please under it.

But now I am speaking of Vienna, I am sure you expect I should say something of the convents; they are of all sorts and sizes, but I am best pleased with that of *St. Lawrence*, where the ease and neatness they seem to live with, appears to me much more edifying than those stricter orders, where perpetual penance and nastinesses must breed discontent and wretchedness. The nuns are all of quality.[4] I think there are to the number of fifty. They have each of them, a little cell perfectly clean, and all the walls covered with pictures, more or less fine, according to their quality. A long white stone gallery runs by all of them, furnished with the pictures of exemplary sisters; the chapel is extremely neat and richly adorned. But I could not forbear laughing at their showing me a wooden head of our Saviour, which they assured me, spoke during the siege of Vienna;[5] and, as a proof of it, bid me remark his mouth, which had been open ever since. Nothing can be more becoming than the dress of these nuns. It is a fine white camlet,[6] the sleeves turned up with fine white calico, and their head dress the same, excepting a small veil of black crepe that falls behind. They have a lower sort of

Notes

FROM *LETTERS*

1 *O.S.* old style, meaning the Julian calendar (used in England until 1752), which was eleven days behind the reformed Gregorian method and counted March 25 as the first day of the new year.

2 *quire* "A bundle of paper consisting of twenty-four sheets" (Johnson).

3 *ombre, piquett* card games.

4 *of quality* upper-class, ladies.

5 *the siege of Vienna* in 1683 by the Turks.

6 *camlet* "A kind of stuff originally made by a mixture of silk and camel's hair; it is now made with wool and silk" (Johnson).

serving nuns, that wait on them as their chambermaids. They receive all visits of women, and play at ombre in their chambers with permission of the Abbess, which is very easy to be obtained. I never saw an old woman so good-natured; she is near four-score, and yet shows very little sign of decay, being still lively and cheerful. She caressed me as if I had been her daughter, giving me some pretty things of her own work, and sweetness in abundance. The grate[7] is not one of the most rigid; it is not very hard to put a head through; and I don't doubt but a man, a little more slender than ordinary, might squeeze in his whole person. The young Count of *Salmis* came to the grate, while I was there, and the Abbess gave him her hand to kiss. But I was surprised to find here, the only beautiful young woman I have seen at Vienna, and not only beautiful but genteel, witty and agreeable, of a great family, and who had been the admiration of the town. I could not forbear showing my surprise at seeing a nun like her. She made me a thousand obliging compliments, and desired me to come often. 'It will be an infinite pleasure to me', said she, sighing, 'but I avoid, with the greatest care, seeing any of my former acquaintance, and whenever they come to our convent, I lock myself in my cell'. I observed tears come into her eyes, which touched me extremely, and I began to talk to her in that strain of tender pity she inspired me with; but she would not own to me, that she is not perfectly happy. I have since endeavoured to learn the real cause of her retirement, without being able to get any account, but that every-body was surprised at it, and nobody guessed the reason. I have been several times to see her; but it gives me too much melancholy to see so agreeable a young creature buried alive. I am not surprised that Nuns have so often inspired violent passions; the pity one naturally feels for them, when they seem worthy of another destiny, making an easy way for yet more tender sentiments. I never in my life had so little charity for the Roman Catholic religion, as since I see the misery it occasions; so many poor unhappy women! and then the gross superstition of the common people, who are some or other of them, day or night, offering bits of candle to the wooden figures, that are set up almost in every street. The processions I see very often are a pageantry, as offensive and apparently contradictory to common sense, as the pagods[8] of China. God knows whether it be the *womanly* spirit of contradiction that works in me, but there never, before, was so much zeal against popery in the heart of,

Dear Madam, &c. &c.

To the Lady ——

Adrianople, April I, O.S. 1717.

I am now got into a new world, where everything I see, appears to me a change of scene; and I write to your ladyship with some content of mind, hoping, at least that you will find the charm of novelty in my letters, and no longer reproach me, that I tell you nothing extraordinary. I won't trouble you with a relation of our tedious journey; but I must not omit what I saw remarkable at *Sophia*, one of the most beautiful towns in the Turkish Empire, and famous for its hot baths, that are resorted to both for diver-sions and for health. I stopped here one day, on purpose to see them; and designing to go *incognito*, I hired a Turkish coach. These *voitures*[9] are not at all like ours, but much

Notes

[7] *grate* "A partition made with bars placed near to one another, or crossing each other: such as are in cloisters or prisons" (Johnson).

[8] *pagod* Buddhist monastery.

[9] *voitures* French, "carriages."

more convenient for the country, the heat being so great that glasses would be very troublesome. They are made a good deal in the manner of Dutch stage coaches, having wooden lattices painted and gilded; the inside being also painted with baskets and nosegays of flowers, intermixed commonly with little poetical mottoes. They are covered all over with scarlet cloth, lined with silk and very often richly embroidered and fringed. This covering entirely hides the persons in them, but may be thrown back at pleasure, and thus permit the ladies to peep through the lattices. They hold four people very conveniently, seated on cushions, but not raised.

In one of these covered waggons, I went to the *Bagnio*[10] about ten o' clock. It was already full of women. It is built of stone, in the shape of a dome, with no windows but in the roof, which gives light enough. There was five of these domes joined together, the outmost being less than the rest, and serving only as a hall, where the *Portress* stood at the door. Ladies of quality generally give this woman a crown or ten shillings, and I did not forget that ceremony. The next room is a very large one, paved with marble, and all round it are two raised Sofas of marble, one above another. There were four fountains of cold water in this room, falling first into marble basins, and then running on the floor in little channels made for that purpose, which carried the streams into the next room, something less than this, with the same sort of marble Sofas, but so hot with streams of sulphur proceeding from the baths joining to it, 'twas impossible to stay there with one's clothes on. The two other domes were the hot baths, one of which had cocks of cold water turning into it, to temper it to what degree of warmth the bathers have a mind to.

I was in my travelling habit, which is a riding dress, and certainly appeared very extraordinary to them. Yet there was not one of them that showed the least surprise or impertinent curiosity, but received me with all the obliging civility possible. I know no European court, where the ladies would have behaved themselves in so polite a manner to a stranger.

I believe, in the whole, there were 200 women, and yet none of those disdainful smiles, and satiric whispers, that never fail in our assemblies, when anybody appears that is not dressed exactly in fashion. They repeated over and over to me: 'Uzelle, pek, Uzelle', which is nothing but, 'Charming, very Charming'. – The first Sofas were covered with cushions and rich carpets, on which sat the ladies; and on the second, their slaves behind them, but without any distinction of rank by their dress, all being in the state of nature, that is, in plain English, stark naked, without any Beauty or defect concealed. Yet there was not the least wanton smile or immodest gesture amongst them. They walked and moved with the same majestic grace, which Milton describes of our General Mother.[11] There were many amongst them, as exactly proportioned as ever any goddess was drawn by the pencil of Guido or Titian,[12] – and most of their skins shiningly white, only adorned by their beautiful hair, divided into many tresses, hanging on their shoulders, braided either with pearl or ribbon, perfectly representing the figures of the graces.

I was here convinced of the truth of a reflection that I had often made, *that if it were the fashion to go naked, the face would be hardly observed*. I perceived that the Ladies of the most delicate skins and finest shapes, had the greatest share of my admiration, though their faces were sometimes less beautiful than those of their companions. To tell you the truth, I had wickedness enough, to wish secretly, that Mr. *Jervas*[13] could have been

Notes

10 *Bagnio* bath or spa.

11 *General Mother Paradise Lost* 4.304–18.

12 *Guido or Titian* the Italian artists Guido di Pietro, known as Fra Angelico (c.1400–55), and Tiziano Vecelli (1490?–1576).

13 *Mr. Jervas* Charles (1675?–1739), a fashionable portrait artist who had painted Lady Mary as a shepherdess in 1710.

there invisible. I fancy it would have very much improved his art, to see so many fine women naked, in different postures, some in conversation, some working, others drinking coffee or sherbet, and many negligently lying on their cushions, while their slaves (generally pretty girls of 17 or 18) were employed in braiding their hair in several pretty fancies. In short, 'tis the women's coffee-house, where all the news of the town Notes is told, scandal invented, &c. – They generally take this diversion once a week, and stay there at least four or five hours, without getting cold, or immediately coming out of the hot-bath into the cool room, which was very surprising to me. The lady, that seemed the most considerable amongst them, entreated me to sit by her, and would fain have undressed me for the bath. I excused myself with some difficulty. They being all so earnest in persuading me, I was at last forced to open my skirt, and show them my stays, which satisfied them very well; for, I saw, they believed I was locked up in that machine, that it was not in my own power to open it, which contrivance they attributed to my husband. – I was charmed with their civility and beauty, and should have been very glad to pass more time with them; but Mr. Wortley resolving to pursue his journey the next morning early, I was in haste to see the ruins of Justinian's church, which did not afford me so agreeable a prospect as I had left, being little more than a heap of stones.

Adieu, Madam. I am sure I have now entertained you, with an account of such a sight as you have never saw in your life, and what no book of travels could inform you of, as 'tis no less than death for a man to be found in one of these places.

[To Lady Mar]

***Adrianople*, April 18, O.S.**

I wrote to you, dear sister, and to all my other English correspondents, by the last ship, and only Heaven can tell, when I shall have another opportunity of sending to you; but I cannot forbear to write again, though perhaps my letter may lie upon my hands this two months. To confess the truth, my head is so full of my entertainment yesterday, that 'tis absolutely necessary, for my own repose, to give it some vent. Without farther preface I will then begin my story.

I was invited to dine with the Grand *Vizier*'s lady,[14] and it was with a great deal of pleasure I prepared myself for an entertainment, which was never given before to any Christian. I thought, I should very little satisfy her curiosity (which I did not doubt was a considerable motive to the invitation) by going in a dress she was used to see, and therefore dressed myself in the court habit of *Vienna*, which is much more magnificent than ours. However, I chose to go *incognito*, to avoid any disputes about ceremony, and went in a Turkish coach, only attended by my woman that held up my train, and the Greek lady, who was my interpretress. I was met, at the court-door by her black Eunuch, who helped me out of the coach with great respect, and conducted me through several rooms, where her she-slaves, finely dressed, were ranged on each side. In the innermost, I found the lady sitting on her sofa, in a sable vest. She advanced to meet me, and presented me half a dozen of her friends, with great civility. She seemed a very good woman, near fifty years old. I was surprised to observe so little magnificence in her house, the furniture being all very moderate; and except the habits and number of her slaves,

Notes

[14] *Grand Vizier* the principal minister of the Sultan; Arnand Haci Halil Pasha (c.1655–1733) at this time.

nothing about her appeared expensive. She guessed at my thoughts, and told me, that she was no longer of an age to spend either her time or money in superfluities; that her whole expense was in charity, and her employment praying to God. There was no affectation in this speech; both she and her husband are entirely given up to devotion. He never looks upon any other woman; and what is much more extraordinary, touches no bribes, notwithstanding the example of all his predecessors. He is so scrupulous in this point, he would not accept Mr. Wortley's present till he had been assured over and over, that it was a settled perquisite of his place, at the entrance of every Ambassador. She entertained me with all kind of civility, till Dinner came in, which was served, one dish at a time, to a vast number, all finely dressed after their manner, which I do not think so bad as you have perhaps heard it represented. I am a very good judge of their eating, having lived three weeks in the house of an *Effendi*[15] at Belgrade, who gave us very magnificent dinners, dressed by his own cooks. The first week pleased me extremely; but, I own, I then begun to grow weary of their table, and desired our own cook might add a dish or two after our manner. But I attribute this to custom, and am very much inclined to believe that an Indian, who had never tasted of either, would prefer their cookery to ours. Their sauces are very high, all the roast very much done. They use a great deal of very rich spice. The soup is served for the last dish; and they have, at least, as great variety of ragouts, as we have. I was very sorry I could not eat of as many as the good lady would have had me, who was very earnest in serving me of every thing. The treat concluded with coffee and perfumes, which is a high mark of respect; two slaves kneeling *censed* my hair, clothes, and handkerchief. After this ceremony, she commanded her slaves to play and dance, which they did with their guitars in their hands, and she excused to me their want of skill, saying she took no care to accomplish them in that art. I returned her thanks, and soon after took my leave.

I was conducted back in the same manner I entered, and would have gone straight to my own house, but the Greek lady, with me, earnestly solicited me to visit the *Kahya*'s lady,[16] saying he was the second officer in the Empire, and ought indeed to be looked upon as the first, the Grand Vizier having only the name, while he exercised the authority. I had found so little diversion in the Vizier's *Harem*, that I had no mind to go to another. But her importunity prevailed with me, and I am extreme glad, I was so complaisant. All things here were with quite another air than at the Grand Vizier's; and the very house confessed the difference between an old devotee, and a young beauty. It was nicely clean and magnificent. I was met at the door by two black Eunuchs, who led me through a long gallery between two ranks of beautiful young girls with their hair finely plaited almost hanging to their feet, all dressed in fine light damasks, brocaded with silver. I was sorry that decency did not permit me to stop to consider them nearer. But that thought was lost upon my entrance into a large room, or rather pavilion, built round with gilded sashes, which were most of them thrown up, and the trees planted near them gave an agreeable shade, which hindered the Sun from being troublesome. The jessamines and honeysuckles that twisted round their trunks, shed a soft perfume, increased by a white marble fountain playing sweet water in the lower part of the room, which fell into three or four basins, with a pleasing sound. The roof was painted with all sort of flowers, falling out of gilded baskets, that seemed tumbling down. On a Sofa, raised three steps, and covered with fine Persian carpets, sat the Kahya's lady, leaning on cushions of white satin embroidered; and at her feet, sat two young girls about twelve years old, lovely as angels, dressed perfectly rich, and almost

Notes

15 *Effendi* scholar.

16 *Kahya* steward.

covered with jewels. But they were hardly seen near the fair *Fatima* (for that is her name) so much her beauty effaced everything I have seen, nay, all that has been called lovely either in England or Germany. I must own, that I never saw anything so gloriously beautiful, nor can I recollect a face that would have been taken notice of near hers. She stood up to receive me, saluting me, after their fashion, putting her hand upon her heart with a sweetness full of majesty, that no court breeding could ever give. She ordered cushions to be given me, and took care to place me in the corner, which is the place of honour. I confess, though the Greek lady had before me given me a great opinion of her beauty, I was so struck with admiration, that I could not, for some time, speak to her, being wholly taken up in gazing. That surprising harmony of features! That charming result of the whole! That exact proportion of body! That lovely bloom of complexion unsullied by art! The unutterable enchantment of her smile! – But her eyes! – Large and black, with all the soft languishment of the blue! every turn of her face discovering some new charm.

After my first surprise was over, I endeavoured, by nicely examining her face, to find out some imperfection, without any fruit of my search, but being clearly convinced of the error of that vulgar notion, that a face perfectly regular would not be agreeable; nature having done for her, with more success, what *Apelles*[17] is said to have essayed by a collection of the most exact features to form a perfect face. Add to all this, a behaviour so full of grace and sweetness, such easy motions with an air so majestic, yet free from stiffness or affectation, that I am persuaded, could she be transported upon the most polite throne of Europe, nobody would think her other than born and bred to be a Queen, though educated in a country we call barbarous. To say all in a word, our most celebrated English Beauties would vanish near her.

She was dressed in a *Caftan* of gold brocade, flowered with silver, very well fitted to her shape, and showing to advantage the beauty of her bosom, only shaded by the thin gauze of her shift. Her drawers were pale pink, her waistcoat green and silver, her slippers white satin finely embroidered; her lovely arms adorned with bracelets of diamonds, and her broad girdle set round with diamonds; upon her head a rich Turkish handkerchief of pink and silver, her own fine black hair hanging a great length, in various tresses, and on one side of her head some bodkins of jewels.[18] I am afraid you will accuse me of extravagance in this description. I think I have read somewhere, that women always speak in rapture, when they speak of beauty, and I cannot imagine why they should not be allowed to do so. I rather think it a virtue to be able to admire without any mixture of desire or envy. The gravest writers have spoke with great warmth of some celebrated pictures and statues. The workmanship of Heaven, certainly excels all our weak imitations, and I think, has a much better claim to our praise. For me, I am not ashamed to own, I took more pleasure in looking on the beauteous *Fatima*, than the finest piece of sculpture could give me. She told me the two girls at her feet were her daughters, though she appeared too young to be their mother. Her fair maids were ranged below the Sofa to the number of twenty, and put me in mind of the pictures of the ancient nymphs. I did not think all nature could have furnished such a scene of beauty. She made them a sign to play and dance. Four of them immediately begun to play some soft airs on instruments, between a lute and a guitar, which they accompanied with their voices, while the others danced by turns. This dance was very different from what I had seen before. Nothing could be more artful, or more proper

Notes

[17] *Apelles* fourth-century BCE Greek painter.

[18] *bodkins* ornamented hairpins or combs.

to raise *certain ideas*. The tunes so soft! – The motions so languishing! – Accompanied with pauses and dying eyes! half-falling back, and then recovering themselves in so artful a manner, that I am very positive, the coldest and most rigid prude upon earth, could not have looked upon them without thinking of *something not to be spoke of*. – I suppose you may have read that the Turks have no music, but what is shocking to the ears; but this account is from those who never heard any but what is played in the streets, and is just as reasonable as if a foreigner should take his ideas of the English music from the *bladder* and *string*, and *marrow bones* and *cleavers*. I can assure you, that the music is extremely pathetic;[19] 'tis true, I am inclined to prefer the Italian, but perhaps I am partial. I am acquainted with a Greek Lady, who sings better than Mrs. *Robinson*,[20] and is very well skilled in both, who gives the preference to the Turkish. 'Tis certain they have very fine natural voices, these were very agreeable. When the dance was over, four fair slaves came into the room, with silver censers in their hands, and perfumed the air with amber, aloes-wood and other scents. After this, they served me coffee upon their knees, in the finest japan china, with *soucoups*[21] of silver gilt. The lovely *Fatima* entertained me, all this while, in the most polite agreeable manner, calling me often 'Uzelle Sultanam', or the Beautiful Sultana, and desiring my friendship with the best grace in the world, lamenting that she could not entertain me in my own language.

When I took my leave, two maids brought in a fine silver basket of embroidered handkerchiefs; she begged I would wear the richest for her sake, and gave the others to my woman and interpretress. – I retired through the same ceremonies as before, and could not help thinking, I had been some time in Mahomet's paradise, so much I was charmed with what I had seen. I know not how the relation of it appears to you. I wish it may give you part of my pleasure; for I would have my dear sister share in all the diversions of,

Yours, &c. &c.

To Mr. [Alexander] Pope

Belgrade-Village, June 17, O.S.

I hope, before this time, you have received two or three of my letters. I had yours but yesterday, though dated the third of February, in which you suppose me to be dead and buried. I have already let you know that I am still alive; but to say truth, I look upon my present circumstances to be exactly the same with those of departed spirits. The heats of Constantinople have driven me to this place, which perfectly answers the description of the Elysian fields.[22] I am in the middle of a wood, consisting chiefly of fruit trees, watered by a vast number of fountains, famous for the excellency of their water, and divided into many shady walks, upon short grass, that seems to me artificial; but I am assured, is the pure work of nature – within view of the Black Sea, from whence we perpetually enjoy the refreshments of cool breezes, that make us insensible of the heat of the summer. The village is only inhabited by the richest among the Christians, who meet every night at a fountain, forty paces from my house, to sing and dance. The beauty and dress of the women, exactly resemble the ideas of the ancient nymphs, as

Notes

[19] *pathetic* capable of producing feelings in the hearer.

[20] *Mrs. Robinson* Anastasia Robinson (d. 1755).

[21] *soucoups* saucers.

[22] *Elysian fields* the best part of the classical underworld.

they are given us by the representations of the poets and painters. But what persuades me more fully of my decease, is the situation of my own mind, the profound ignorance I am in, of what passes among the living (which only comes to me by chance) and the great calmness with which I receive it. Yet I have still a hankering after my friends and acquaintance left in the world, according to the authority of that admirable author,

That spirits departed are wonderous kind
To friends and Relations left behind,
Which nobody can deny.

Of which Solemn Truth I am a *dead* Instance. I think *Virgil* is of the same opinion, that in human souls there will still be some remains of human passions:

—Curæ non ipsa in morte relinquunt.[23]

And 'tis very necessary to make a perfect Elysium, that there should be a river *Lethe*,[24] which I am not so happy to find. To say truth, I am sometimes very weary of the singing and dancing and sunshine, and wish for the smoke and impertinencies in which you toil; though I endeavour to persuade myself that I live in a more agreeable Variety than you do; and that *Monday*, setting of partridges; *Tuesday*, reading English; *Wednesday*, studying in the Turkish language (in which, by the way, I am already very learned); *Thursday*, classical authors; *Friday*, spent in writing; *Saturday*, at my needle, and *Sunday*, admitting of visits and hearing of music, is a better way of disposing the week, than, *Monday* at the drawing room; *Tuesday*, Lady Mohun's; *Wednesday*, at the opera; *Thursday*, the play; *Friday*, Mrs. Chetwynd's, &c. a perpetual round of hearing the same scandal and seeing the same follies acted over and over, which here affect me more than they do other dead people. I can now hear of displeasing things with pity and without indignation. The reflection on the great gulf between you and me, cools all news that come hither. I can neither be sensibly touched with joy or grief, when I consider that, possibly, the cause of either is removed, before the letter comes to my hands. But (as I said before) this indolence does not extend to my few friendships; I am still warmly sensible of yours and Mr. *Congreve*'s[25] and desire to live in your remembrance, though dead to all the world beside.

I am, &c. &c.

To Mr. [Alexander] P[ope]

***Dover*, Nov.I, O.S. 1718.**

I have this minute received a letter of yours sent me from Paris. I believe and hope I shall very soon see both you and Mr. *Congreve*; but as I am here in an inn where we stay to regulate our march to London, bag and baggage, I shall employ some of my leisure time in answering that part of yours that seems to require an answer.

Notes

[23] *Curæ non ... relinquunt* "not in death itself do the cares leave them" (*Aeneid* 6.444).

[24] *Lethe* the river of forgetfulness, beyond which is Elysium.

[25] *Mr. Congreve* William (1670–1729), greatest English dramatist of his time.

I must applaud your good nature in supposing that your pastoral lovers (vulgarly called Haymakers) would have lived in everlasting joy and harmony if the lightning had not interrupted their scheme of happiness. I see no reason to imagine that *John Hughes* and *Sarah Drew*[26] were either wiser or more virtuous than their neighbours. That a well-set man of twenty-five should have a fancy to marry a brown woman of eighteen is nothing marvellous; and I cannot help thinking that had they married, their lives would have passed in the common track with their fellow-parishioners. His endeavouring to shield her from the storm was a natural action and what he would have certainly done for his horse, if he had been in the same situation. Neither am I of opinion that their sudden death was a reward of their mutual virtue. You know the Jews were reproved for thinking a village destroyed by fire, more wicked than those that had escaped the thunder. Time and chance happen to all men. Since you desire me to try my skill in an *epitaph*, I think the following lines perhaps more just, though not so poetical as yours.

Here lies John Hughes and Sarah Drew;
Perhaps you'll say, what's that to you?
Believe me, friend, much may be said
On this poor couple that are dead.
On Sunday next they should have married;
But see how oddly things are carried!
On Thursday last it rained and lightened,
These tender lovers sadly frightened,
Sheltered beneath the cocking hay
In hopes to pass the time away.
But the BOLD THUNDER found them out
(Commissioned for that end no doubt)
And seizing on their trembling breath,
Consigned them to the shades of death.
Who knows if 'twas not kindly done?
For had they seen the next year's sun,
A beaten wife and cuckold swain
Had jointly cursed the marriage chain;
Now they are happy in their doom,
FOR POPE HAS WROTE UPON THEIR TOMB.

I confess these sentiments are not altogether so heroic as yours; but I hope you will forgive them in favour of the two last lines. You see how much I esteem the honour you have done them; though I am not very impatient to have the same, and had rather continue to be your stupid, *living*, humble servant than be *celebrated* by all the pens in Europe.

I would write to Mr. C[ongreve]; but suppose you will read this to him if he enquires after me.

Notes

[26] *John Hughes and Sarah Drew* see the letter from Pope to Lady Mary (above, p. 738).

The Lover (1721–5)

A Ballad

1

At length by so much Importunity pressed,
Take, Molly, at once the Inside of my Breast:
This stupid Indifference so often you blame
Is not owing to Nature, to fear, or to Shame,
I am not as cold as a Virgin in Lead[1]
Nor is Sunday's Sermon so strong in my Head,
I know but too well how Time flies along,
That we live but few Years and yet fewer are young.

2

But I hate to be cheated, and never will buy
Long years of Repentance for moments of Joy;
Oh was there a Man (but where shall I find
Good sense, and good Nature so equally joined?)
Would value his pleasure, contribute to mine,
Not meanly would boast, nor lewdly design,
Not over severe, yet not stupidly vain,
For I would have the power though not give the pain.

3

No Pedant yet learned, not rakehelly Gay
Or laughing because he has nothing to say,
To all my whole sex, obliging and Free,
Yet never be fond of any but me.
In public preserve the Decorums are just
And show in his Eyes he is true to his Trust,
Then rarely approach, and respectfully Bow,
Yet not fulsomely pert, nor yet foppishly low.

4

But when the long hours of Public are past
And we meet with Champagne and a Chicken at last,
May every fond Pleasure that hour endear,
Be banished afar both Discretion and Fear,
Forgetting or scorning the Airs of the Crowd
He may cease to be formal, and I to be proud,
Till lost in the Joy we confess that we live
And he may be rude, and yet I may forgive.

Notes

The Lover
1 *a Virgin in Lead* the decoration of a funeral casket.

5

And that my Delight may be solidly fixed
Let the Friend, and the Lover be handsomely mixed,
In whose tender Bosom my Soul might confide,
Whose kindness can soothe me, whose Counsel could guide,
From such a dear Lover as here I describe
No danger should fright me, no Millions should bribe,
But till this astonishing creature I know
As I long have lived Chaste I will keep myself so.

6

I never will share with the wanton Coquette
Or be caught by a vain affectation of Wit.
The Toasters, and Songsters may try all their Art
But never shall enter the pass of my Heart;
I loathe the Lewd Rake, the dressed Fopling despise,
Before such pursuers the nice Virgin flies,
And as Ovid has sweetly in Parables told
We harden like Trees, and like Rivers are cold.[2]

The Reasons that Induced Dr. S[wift] to Write a Poem Called the Lady's Dressing Room[1] (1732–4)

The Doctor in a clean starched band,
His Golden Snuff box in his hand,
With care his Diamond Ring displays
And Artful shows its various Rays,
While Grave he stalks down —— Street
His dearest Betty —— to meet.
  Long had he waited for this Hour,
Nor gained Admittance to the Bower,
Had joked and punned, and swore and writ,
Tried all his Gallantry and Wit,[2]
Had told her oft what part he bore
In Oxford's Schemes in days of yore,[3]
But Bawdy, Politics nor Satire
Could move this dull hard hearted Creature.
Jenny her Maid could taste a Rhyme
And grieved to see him lose his Time,

Notes

[2] *harden like Trees, and like Rivers are cold* Daphne turned into a laurel to escape Apollo and Arethusa into a stream to escape Alpheus in Ovid's *Metamorphoses*.

The Reasons that Induced Dr S[wift]

[1] *the Lady's Dressing Room* Swift published this poem in 1734; see p. 534, above.

[2] *Had joked ... and Wit* this couplet is an imitation of one Swift wrote about himself in his long poem *Cadenus and Vanessa* (ll. 542–3).

[3] *Oxford* Robert Harley, first earl of Oxford (1661–1724), formed the Tory administration which ruled from 1710 to 1714 and for which Swift worked; subsequently he was impeached and imprisoned for two years for his "schemes."

Had kindly whispered in his Ear,
For twice two pound you enter here,
My Lady vows without that Sum
It is in vain you write or come.
  The Destined Offering now he brought
And in a paradise of thought
With a low Bow approached the Dame
Who smiling heard him preach his Flame.
His Gold she takes (such proofs as these
Convince most unbelieving shes)
And in her trunk rose up to lock it
(Too wise to trust it in her pocket)
And then returned with Blushing Grace
Expects the Doctor's warm Embrace.
  But now this is the proper place
Where mortals Stare me in the Face
And for the sake of fine Expression
I'm forced to make a small digression.
Alas for wretched Humankind,
With Learning Mad, with wisdom blind!
The Ox thinks he's for Saddle fit
(As long ago Friend Horace writ)[4]
And Men their Talents still mistaking,
The stutterer fancies his is speaking.
With Admiration oft we see
Hard Features heightened by Toupée,[5]
The Beau affects the Politician,
Wit is the citizen's Ambition,
Poor Pope Philosophy displays on
With so much Rhyme and little reason,
And though he argues ne'er so long
That, all is right, his Head is wrong.[6]
  None strive to know their proper merit
But strain for Wisdom, Beauty, Spirit
And lose the Praise that is their due
While they've th' impossible in view.
So have I seen the Injudicious Heir
To add one Window the whole House impair.
  Instinct the Hound does better teach
Who never undertook to preach,
The frighted Hare from Dogs does run
But not attempts to bear a Gun.
Here many Noble thoughts occur
But I prolixity abhor,

Notes

[4] *Horace Epistles* 1.14.43 " … and the horse, when lazy, longs to plough."

[5] *Toupée* the top curl on a fashionable wig.

[6] *all is right* a reference to Pope's philosophical poem *An Essay on Man,* which expounds a kind of theodicy in which all things human and divine are in a harmony, the cosmic benevolence of which is hidden from mere mortals.

And will pursue th'instructive Tale
To show the Wise in some things fail.
  The Reverend Lover with surprise
Peeps in her Bubbies, and her Eyes,
And kisses both, and tries – and tries.
The Evening in this Hellish Play,
Beside his Guineas thrown away,
Provoked the Priest to that degree[7]
He swore, 'the Fault is not in me.
Your damned Close stool so near my Nose,
Your Dirty Smock, and Stinking Toes
Would make a Hercules as tame
As any Beau that you can name'.
  The nymph grown Furious roared by God
'The blame lies all in Sixty odd',
And scornful pointing to the door
Cried, 'Fumbler see my Face no more'.
'With all my Heart I'll go away
But nothing done, I'll nothing pay.
Give back the Money' – 'How', cried she,
'Would you palm such a cheat on me!
For poor 4 pound to roar and bellow,
Why sure you want some new Prunella?'[8]
'I'll be revenged you saucy Quean'
Replies the disappointed Dean,
'I'll so describe your dressing room
The very Irish shall not come'.
She answered short, 'I'm glad you'll write,
You'll furnish paper when I shite'.

To the Memory of Mr Congreve[1] (1729?)

Farewell the best and loveliest of Mankind
Where Nature with a happy hand had joined
The softest temper with the strongest mind,
In pain could counsel and could charm when blind.

In this Lewd age when Honour is a Jest
He found a refuge in his Congreve's breast,
Superior there, unsullied, and entire;
And only could with the last breath expire.

His wit was never by his Malice stained,
No rival writer of his Verse complained,

Notes

[7] *Priest* Swift was an ordained priest and Dean of St. Patrick's Cathedral, Dublin.

[8] *Prunella* a material used in clerical gowns and the name of a heroine in a popular play of the time.

To the Memory of Mr Congreve

[1] *Mr Congreve* William (1670–1729), pre-eminent dramatist of his time.

For neither party drew a venal pen
To praise bad measures or to blast good men.

A Queen indeed he mourned, but such a Queen[2]
Where Virtue mixed with royal Blood was seen,
With equal merit graced each Scene of Life
An Humble Regent and Obedient Wife.

If in a Distant State blessed Spirits know
The Scenes of Sorrow of a World below,
This little Tribute to thy Fame approve,
A Trifling Instance of a boundless Love.

[A Summary of Lord Lyttelton's advice to a Lady][1] (1731–3)

Be plain in Dress, and sober in your Diet,
In short, my Dearee, kiss me, and be quiet.

Notes

[2] *Queen* Mary II, Queen of William III.

[A Summary of Lord Lyttelton's advice to a Lady]
[1] *Summary* Lady Mary wrote this couplet on a scribal copy of Lord Lyttelton's poem "Advice to a Lady" (1733); the title was added by the editor who first printed it in 1803.

Trials at the Old Bailey (1722–1727)

Unlike the proceedings of Parliament, the sessions held in the Central Criminal Court of London (the Old Bailey) were not legally closed to journalists. Court sessions thus provided an early form of eyewitness reporting and news. As in journalism of all times, there was a sensational element in the reports, which tended to focus on trials that excited the most interest – those involving violence and sex. In making the following selection, I have followed the same time-honored principles. I take my texts from the first edition of *Select Trials at the Sessions House in the Old Bailey* (1742). *The Proceedings of the Old Bailey, London 1674 to 1913* is now a website containing 197,745 trials (www.oldbaileyonline.org). In several of my notes I have taken advantage of information in the landmark study by J. M. Beattie, *Crime and the Courts in England, 1660–1800* (Princeton University Press, 1986).

from *Select TRIALS at the Sessions House in the Old Bailey* (1742)

H —— J ——, for a *Rape, 1722*

H—— J——, of *Alhallows, Lombard Street*, was indicted for assaulting, ravishing, and, against her Will, carnally knowing *Mary Hicks*, Spinster,[1] *April* 29.

Mary Hicks. The Prisoner was Journeyman to my Master, Mr. *Allen*, a Confectioner, in *Grace-church-street*. He came hither the 29th of last Month, between 9 and 10 at Night. He went into the Kitchen, where he fell asleep. Between eleven and twelve the Family were going to Bed, and another Journeyman waked him, and said, he should lie with him;[2] but the Prisoner refused, and pretended to fall asleep again, and so he sat till the Journeyman and Boy were a-bed. A young Woman that lodged in the House was going to Bed too; but, upon my desiring her to bear me Company, because I was not willing to be left alone with the Prisoner, she came down, and stayed with me: But it was not long before the Prisoner went up into the Garret, in order, as I supposed, to go to Bed to the Apprentice. Then I and the young Woman both went up, but were greatly surprised to find that the Keys of both our Chamber Doors were taken out; and, as we had no other fastening, and suspected some Design, we were afraid to go to Bed; but, at last, as we thought it was the Prisoner who had taken the Keys out, we went up into the Garret, and asked him for them. He said, he had left them in the young Woman's Room, and would go down and show us the Place where they lay: So down we came, and all three went into the Room, and presently the Prisoner took the Key out of his Pocket, locked the Door, put the Key into his Pocket again, seized upon me, threw me down on upon the Bed, and used me in a violent Manner.

Notes

H—J—, for a Rape

1 *Spinster* "In law, the general term for a girl or maiden woman" (Johnson).

2 *lie with him* beds were still scarce in the eighteenth century, and it was common for people to share them when they were guests in private homes or inns.

Court. What did he do to ye?

Mary Hicks. He threw up my Coats. I strove to save myself as much as I was able for half an Hour, but then I was quite spent, and could resist no longer.

Court. But did not the other Woman help you?

M. H. Yes, as far as she could; but he was so violent, that, notwithstanding all that she and I could do, he overpowered us both.

Court. He did not ravish ye both, I hope?

M. H. No; he did not offer the Thing to her.

Court. You say there was another Man and a Boy in the House.

M. H. Yes.

Court. And could not they have heard you if you had cried out?

M. H. Lord! I was quite spent and out of Breath with struggling, so that I could not call loud enough to be heard.

Court. But sure you might have called loud enough when he had begun to be rude with ye – or at least the other Woman might.

M. H. We did make what Noise we could; but the Door was locked, and the Window-shutters were nailed up, and I suppose the other Man and the Boy were fast asleep.

Court. In what Manner did he use ye?

M. H. He forced my Body with what he had.

Court. You must explain yourself.[3]

M. H. ——

Court. What followed? Did you perceive——

M. H. Yes; —— And the next Day I was so very bad that I could hardly turn myself in my Bed.

Mrs. ——I was present at the same Time. She called out for Help, and I did what I could to prevent his Rudeness with her; but I could do her no good, though I knocked as hard as I could, and would have broke open the Door, if I had been able.

Mr. *Allen*. I was in the Country when this Affair happened. At my coming Home I found my Maid – or House-keeper in some Disorder, and when she saw me, she cried. I inquired what was the Matter, and she gave me an Account how she had been abused.

Prisoner. Whatever I did, I did not force her, nor did she next Morning show any Resentment of the Usage that she met with over Night; for she drank Coffee with me at Breakfast.

Court to the Prosecutrix.[4] What do you say to that?

M. H. I drank Coffee next Morning with the rest of the Family, but we had half breakfasted before he came up, and then it was above half an Hour before I would let him have any.

Another Evidence[5] for the Prisoner deposed, that after he had heard of this Prosecution, he went to *Mary Hicks*, and asked her if she intended to hang the Prisoner, and that she answered, 'No, I had rather marry him than hang him'.[6]

The Jury acquitted him.

Notes

3 *You must explain yourself* conviction for rape depended upon proof that the rape had been accomplished, including full penetration.

4 *Prosecutrix* feminine form of "prosecutor," "one who pursues another by law in a criminal case."

5 *Evidence* witness.

6 *rather marry him than hang him* such settlements could be negotiated in or out of court and were not uncommon; conviction for rape was difficult but did occur and was punished with hanging.

Gabriel Lawrence, for *Sodomy, April, 1726*

GABRIEL LAWRENCE was indicted for committing, with *Thomas Newton*, aged thirty Years, the heinous and detestable Sin of Sodomy,[1] not to be named among Christians, *July* 20, 1725.

Thomas Newton. About the End of *June*, or the Beginning of July, one *Peter Bavidge*, who is not yet taken, and —— *Eccleston*, who died last Week in *Newgate*,[2] carried me to the House of *Margaret Clap*, who is now at the *Compter*,[3] and there I first became acquainted with the Prisoner. Mother *Clap*'s House bore the public Character of a Place of Rendezvous for Sodomites. —— For the more convenient Entertainment of her Customers, she had provided Beds in every Room in the House. She had commonly thirty or forty of such Kind of Chaps every Night, but more especially on *Sunday* Nights. I was conducted to a Bed up one Pair of Stairs, where, by the Persuasion of *Bavidge*, who was present all the while, I suffered the Prisoner to ——. He, and one *Daniel*, having attempted the same since that Time, but I refused, though they bussed[4] me, and stroked me over the Face, and said I was a very pretty fellow. —— When Mother *Clap* was taken up in *February* last, I went to put in Bail for her; at which Time Mr. *Williams* and Mr. *Willis* told me they believed I could give Information; which I promised to do: but at the End of the same Month I was taken up myself.

—— *Willis*. In *March, Newton* was set at Liberty, but he came the next Day, and made a voluntary Information.[5]

—— *Williams*. He informed against several of the Sodomites at that Time, but did not discover the Prisoner till the 2d of this Month, and then I took his Information at Sir *John Fryer*'s.

Samuel Stevens. Mother *Clap*'s House was in *Field lane*, in *Hilburn*, it was next to the *Bunch of Grapes*[6] on one Side, and joined to an Arch on the other Side. It was notorious for being a *Molly-house*.[7] I have been there several Times, in order to detect those who frequented it: I have seen 20 or 30 of them together, kissing and hugging, and making Love (as they called it) in a very indecent Manner. Then they used to go out by Couples into another Room, and, when they came back, they would tell what they had been doing, which, in their Dialect, they called *Marrying*.

Joseph Sellers. I have been twice at that House, and seen the same Practices.

The Prisoner's Defence

Prisoner. I own I have been several Times at Mrs. *Clap*'s House to drink, as any other Person might do; but I never knew that it was a Resort for People that followed such Sort of Practices.

Henry Yoxan. I am a Cow-keeper, and the Prisoner is a Milk-man. I have kept him Company, and served him with Milk these eighteen Years. I have been with him at the *Oxfordshire-Feast*, where we have both got drunk, and then come Home together in a Coach, and yet he never offered any such Indecencies to me.

Notes

GABRIEL LAWRENCE

1 *Sin of Sodomy* "An unnatural form of sexual intercourse, esp. that of one male with another" (*OED*); it is not "named" in Johnson's *Dictionary*.

2 *Newgate* the main prison in the City of London.

3 *Compter* the counter, or sheriff's prison, used for holding those arrested, especially on civil charges, such as debt.

4 *bussed* kissed.

5 *Information* "Charge or accusation exhibited" (Johnson).

6 *Bunch of Grapes* a tavern with that name and, no doubt, a suitable banner, which served as an address before numbers were introduced on buildings later in the century.

7 *Molly* "an effeminate fellow, a sodomite" (Grose's *Dictionary of the Vulgar Tongue*, 1785).

Samuel Pullen. I am a Cow-keeper too, and have served him with Milk several Years, but never heard any such Thing of him before.

Margaret Chapman. I have known him seven Years. He has often been at my House, and, if I had suspected any such Stories of him, he should never have darkened my Doors, I'll assure ye.

William Preston. I know him to be a very *sober* Man, and have often been in his Company when he was *drunk*, but never found any ill by him.

Thomas Fuller. Nor I either. He married my Daughter eighteen Years ago: She has been dead seven Years. He had a Child by her, which is now living, and thirteen Years old.

Charles Bell. He married my Wife's Sister. I never heard the like before of the Prisoner; but, as for the Evidence,[8] *Newton*, I know that he bears a vile Character.

The Jury found him guilty. *Death*.

He was a second Time indicted for committing Sodomy with P——, *November* 10. But, being convicted of the former, he was not tried for this.

The Ordinary's[9] *Account of* Gabriel Lawrence

Gabriel Lawrence, aged 43 Years, was a Papist, and did not make any particular Confessions to me. He kept the Chapel with the rest for the most part; was always very grave, and made frequent Responses with the rest, and said the Lord's Prayer and Creed after me. He owned himself of the *Romish* Communion; but said, that he had *a great liking to the Church of* England, *and could communicate with them*; but this I would not allow, unless he renounced his Error. He said *Newton* had perjured himself, and that in all his Life he had never been guilty of that detestable Sin; but that he had lived many Years with a Wife who had borne several Children, and kept a good sober House.——

At the Place of Execution he said, that a certain Person had injured him when he took him before a Justice of the Peace, who committed him, in swearing or affirming, that fifteen Years ago he had been taken up for that unnatural Sin, and, that it cost him Twenty Pounds, to get himself free, which, he said, was utterly false; for, till this Time, he was never suspected.

He was hanged at *Tyburn*, on *Monday, May* 9, 1726.

Mary Picart, alias Gandon, for Bigamy, June, 1725

MARY PICART, alias *GANDON*, was indicted for marrying *Philip Bouchain* on the 24th of *June* last, her former Husband being then living.

Paul Gandon. Mine Broder,[1] *Jean Gandon*, and dis Voman, de Preesonar, vas marie togader at de *Stapaney-Shursh*, and I vas den prasant – It is vary long time ago, – me no remamber ow long – 'tis more as twanty Year. – Dare vas de Ministar *Anglois*, dare vas de putting de Ring upon de Feengar, dare vas de putting de Hands togader, and de oder tings dat be made use of in de Marriage. Den after dis vas done da bote leeve a togader so as de Man and de Vife: and mine broder *Jean* make von, two, tree Shile upon her:

Notes

[8] *Evidence* witness.

[9] *Ordinary* the chaplain of Newgate Prison, who would prepare prisoners for execution.

MARY PICART

[1] *Mine Broder* the report is trying to represent a foreign accent with a combination of Dutch, French, and, occasionally, Italian imitations.

But now mine Broder be grown von old Man: he no make more Shile, and so she marie vid dis oder Man *Philip Bouchain*.

Philip Bouchain. Me vas marie to dis Voman; dat is de trute, upon the twanty-four of dis Mont, a sis heures after de noon, a l'Engseigne de *Hand* and de *Pen* in de *Fleet Lane*, and my give tree Shilling and tree quartern of *Sheneva*[2] to de Parsoong. But me vas vary mush elevate vid de Liquor, and dis and dat and t'oder, so dat me no cou'd tell vat I do ven de ting vas done. But me no go to de bed vid mine Vife at all, for in tree, four heures atter de Saremonee vas over, dare come in some Relationg of mine Spouse, and dey make de grand Noise and de Uproar, dat me no could tink vat a diable vas de maiter vid 'em. But, in a leetel time da tell me dat I must no do vid mine Vife, for she vas belong to anoder Man: and so da take her avay, and me vas force to go to bed vid mine own salf.

Prisoner. Me ave but von Husband, and dat is *Jean Gandon*; for dis oder Man, *Philip Bouchain*, be none Husband for me. Vat signify de Parsoong and de Ring, all de Saremonee? Vy dat no make a de Husband——Dare be no Husband no Vife, till da go to bed togader. But Monsieur *Bouchain* he do no vid me in bed; he do noting in de Varld.——Noting but de Saremonee.——Vy dat be no Husband.

There being no Proof that the second Marriage was consummated, the Jury acquitted the Prisoner.

Richard Savage, James Gregory, and William Merchant, for Murder, Thursday, Dec. 7, 1727[1]

Richard Savage, James Gregory, and *William Merchant* were indicted for the Murder of *James Sinclair*: *Savage* by giving him with a drawn Sword, one mortal Wound in the lower Part of the Belly, of the Length of half an Inch, and the Depth of nine Inches, on the 20th of *Nov*. last, of which mortal Wound he languished till the next Day, and then died: And *Gregory* and *Merchant* by being present, aiding, abetting, comforting, and maintaining the said *Savage*, in committing the said Murder.

At the Request of the Prisoners, the Witnesses against them were examined a-part.

Mr. *Nuttal*. On *Monday* the 20th of *Nov*. about 11 at Night, the Deceased, and Mr. *Lemery*, and his Brother, and I, went to *Robinson's* Coffee-house, near *Charing Cross*, where we stayed till one or two in the Morning. We had drank two Three-Shilling Bowls of Punch, and were just concluding to go, when the Prisoners came into the Room. *Merchant* entered first, and, turning his Back to the Fire, he kicked down our Table without any Provocation. 'What do ye mean?' says I. And 'what do *you* mean?' says *Gregory*. Presently *Savage* drew his Sword, and we retreated to the farther End of the Room. *Gregory* drawing too, I desired them to put up their Swords, but they refused. I did not see the Deceased draw, but *Gregory*, turning to him, said, 'Villain, deliver your Sword': And, soon after, he took the Sword from the Deceased. *Gregory*'s Sword was broke in the Scuffle; but, with the Deceased's Sword, and Part of his own, he came and demanded mine; and, I refusing to deliver it, he made a Thrust at me. I defended myself.

Notes

2 *Sheneva* gin.

Richard Savage

1 *Richard Savage* a poet and playwright who claimed to be the unacknowledged, illegitimate child of two members of the nobility; he pursued this claim in public and private attacks on his putative mother, Lady Macclesfield; after his death in 1743 Savage's memory was blessed with a powerful apologist in the famous biography by Samuel Johnson (see below, p. 811).

He endeavoured to get my Sword from me; but he either fell of himself, or I threw him, and took the (Deceased's) Sword from him; and three Soldiers coming into the Room, they rescued him.——I did not see *Savage* push at the Deceased, but I heard the Deceased say, 'I am a dead Man!' And soon after the Candles were put out. I afterwards went up to the Deceased, and saw something hang out at his Belly which I took to be his Caul.[2] The Maid of the House came in, and kneeled to suck the Wound, and it was after this, that the Soldiers came in: And I and *Gregory* were carried to the Watch-house.

Gregory. Did not I say, 'Put up your Swords'.

Nuttal. There might be such an Expression, but I can't call to mind when it was spoke.

Mr. *Lemery*. I was with the Deceased, and Mr. *Nuttal*, and my Brother, at *Robinson's* Coffee-house, and we were ready to go Home, when somebody knocked at the (Street) Door. The Landlady opened it, and let in the Prisoners, and lighted them into another Room. They would not stay there, but rudely came into ours. *Merchant* kicked down the Table. Our Company all retreated. *Gregory* came up to the Deceased, and said, 'G-d damn ye, you Rascal, deliver your Sword!' Swords were drawn. *Savage* made a Thrust at the Deceased, who stooped, and cried, 'Oh!' At which *Savage* turned pale, stood for some Time astonished, and then endeavoured to get away: but I held him. The Lights were then put out. We struggled together. The Maid came to my Assistance, pullected[3] off his Hat and Wig, and clung about him. He, in striving to force himself from her, struck at her, cut her in the Head with his Sword, and at last got away. I went to a Night-cellar,[4] and called two or three Soldiers, who took him and *Merchant* in a back Court.——When *Savage* gave the Wound, the Deceased had his Sword drawn, but held it with the Point down towards the Ground, on the Left Side. As to *Merchant*, I did not see that he had any Sword.

Mr. *Nuttal* again. Nor I: Nor did I see him in the Room after the Fray began. But after the Candles were put out, he was taken with *Savage* in a back Court.

Jane Leader. I was in the Room, and saw *Savage* draw first. Then *Gregory* went up to the Deceased, and *Savage* stabbed him; and, turning back, he looked pale. The Deceased cried, 'I am dead! I am dead!'——I opened his Coat, and bid the Maid-Servant suck the Wound. She did, but no Blood came.——I went to see the Deceased upon his Death bed, and desired him to tell me how he was wounded. He said, that the Wound was given him by the least Man in Black.——*That* was *Savage*, for *Merchant* was in coloured Clothes, and had no Sword,——and that the tallest of them,—— which was *Gregory*,—— passed, or struck his Sword, while *Savage* stabbed him.—— I did not see the Deceased's Sword at all, nor did he open his Lips, or speak one Word to the Prisoners.

Mrs. *Endersby*. I keep *Robinson's* Coffee house. When I let the Prisoners in, I perceived they were in Drink. I showed them a Room. They were very rude to me. I told them, if they wanted any Liquor, they should have it; but, if they did not, I desired their Absence. Upon which one of them took up a Chair, and offered to strike me with it——They went into the next Room, which is a public Coffee-Room in the Day-time. *Merchant* kicked down the Table.——Whether the other Company were sitting or standing at that Table I cannot be positive; but it is a folding Table with two Leaves, and there were two other Tables in the same Room.——Swords were drawn,——the Deceased was wounded,——and *Savage* struggled with the Maid-Servant, and cut her over the Head with his Sword.

Notes

[2] *Caul* part of the membrane encasing the stomach and intestines.

[3] *pullected* plucked, tore off.

[4] *Night-cellar* "a tavern or other place serving as a resort at night for persons of the lowest class" (*OED*).

Mary Rock, the Maid. My Mistress and I let the Prisoners into the House. My Mistress showed them a Room. *Merchant* pulled her about very rudely, and she making Resistance, he took up a Chair, and offered to strike her with it. Then asking, who was in the next Room? I answered, 'Some Company that have paid their Reckoning, and are just a going, and you have the Room to yourselves if you'll have but a little Patience': But they would not, and so they ran in. I went in not long after, and saw *Gregory* and *Savage* with their Swords drawn, and the Deceased with his Sword in his Hand, and the Point from him.——Soon after, I heard *Jane Leader* say, 'Poor Dear *Sinclair* is killed! I sucked the Wound, but it would not bleed. *Savage* endeavoured to get away, but I stopped him'.——I did not see the Wound given to the Deceased, but I afterwards saw the Encounter between Mr. *Nuttal* and Mr. *Gregory*.

Mr. *Taylor*, a Clergyman. On the 21st of *November*, I was sent for to pray by the Deceased, and, after I had recommended him to the Mercy of Almighty God, Mr. *Nuttal* desired me to ask him a few Questions; but, as I thought it not belonging to my Province, I declined it. Mr. *Nuttal* however, willing to have a Witness to the Words of a dying Man, persuaded me to stay while he himself asked a Question. And then, turning to the Deceased, he said, 'Do you know from which of the Gentlemen you received the Wound?' The Deceased answered, 'From the shortest in Black', which was Mr. *Savage*, 'the tallest commanded my Sword, and the other stabbed me'.

Rowland Holderness, Watchman. I came to the Room just after the Wound was given, and then I heard the Deceased say, 'I was stabbed barbarously before my Sword was drawn'.

John Wilcox, another Watchman. I saw the Deceased leaning his Head upon his Hand, and heard him then say, 'I am a dead Man, and was stabbed cowardly'.

Mr. *Wilkey*, the Surgeon. I searched the Wound, it was on the left Side of the Belly, as high as the Navel. The Sword had grazed on the Kidney, and I believe that Wound was the Cause of his Death.

Court. Do you think this Deceased could receive that Wound in a Posture of Defence?

Mr. *Wilkey*. I believe he could not, except he was Left-handed.

The Defence of the Prisoners

Mr. *Gregory* said, That the Reason of their going into that Room, was for the Benefit of the Fire: That the Table was thrown down accidentally. That the House bore an infamous Character, and some of the Witnesses lay under the Imputation of being Persons who had no Regard to Justice and Morality.

Mr. *Savage*, having given the Court an Account of his meeting with *Gregory* and *Merchant*, and going with them to *Robinson's* Coffee-house, made some Remarks on what had been sworn by the Witnesses, and declared, that his endeavouring to escape, was only to avoid the Inclemency, of a Jail.

And then the Prisoners called their Witnesses.

Henry Huggins, Thomas Huggins, and *Robert Fish* deposed, That they were present at the latter Part of the Quarrel, and saw Mr. *Nuttal* engaged with Mr. *Gregory*, and struggling with a Sword.——This only confirmed Part of *Nuttal's* Evidence.——They added, that the Coffee-house was a House of ill Fame.

Mary Stanly deposed, That she had seen the Deceased in a Quarrel, before *that* in which he was killed: That Mr. *Nuttal* and he were very well acquainted, and that she had seen Mrs. *Nuttal* and Mr. *Leader* in Bed together.

John Pearse deposed, That *Jane Leader* told him, that when the Swords were drawn, she went out of the Room, and did not see the Wound given: That she was a Woman of ill Reputation, and that the Coffee-house had a bad Character.

Daniel Boyle deposed, That the Deceased bore the Character of an idle Person, who had no settled Place of Residence.

John Eaton deposed, That he had known the Deceased about two Months, and had heard that his Character was but indifferent.

Mr. *Rainby* deposed, That, the Morning after the Accident, he went to the Coffee-House to enquire for Mr. *Merchant*, and then heard Mr. *Nuttal* say, that, if he had any of the Prisoners in a convenient Place, he would cut their Throats, provided he could be sure of escaping the Law.

Mr. *Cheesborough* deposed to the same Effect.

Mr. *Nuttal*. Being moved with the barbarous Treatment my Friend had met with, I believe I might say, That if I had them in an open Field, I would not have Recourse to the Law, but do them Justice myself.

Then Mr. *Nuttal* called some Gentlemen who deposed, that he was a Man of Reputation, Civility, and good Manners.

Several Persons of Distinction appeared in behalf of the Prisoners, and gave them the Characters of good-natured, quiet, peaceable Men, and by no means inclinable to be quarrelling.

And the Prisoners then said, they hoped the good Characters which had been given them, the Suddenness of the unfortunate Accident, and their having no premeditated Malice, would entitle them to some Favour.

The Court, having summed up the Evidence, observed to the Jury, That as the Deceased and his Company were in Possession of the Room, if the Prisoners were the Aggressors by coming into that Room, kicking down the Table, and immediately thereupon drawing their Swords without Provocation, and the Deceased retreated, was pursued, attacked, and killed in the Manner as had been sworn by the Witnesses, it was Murder, not only in him who gave the Wound, but in the others, who aided and abetted him. That as to the Characters of the Prisoners, good Character is of Weight where the Proof is doubtful, but flies up,[5] when put in the Scale against plain and positive Evidence: And, as to the Suddenness of the Action; where there is a sudden Quarrel, and a Provocation is given by him who is killed, or where suddenly and mutually Persons attack each other and fight, and one of them is killed in the Heat of Blood, it is Manslaughter. But, where one is the Aggressor, pursues the Insult, and kills the Person attacked, without any Provocation, though on a sudden, the Law implies Malice, and it is Murder.

The Trial lasted about eight Hours. The Jury found *Richard Savage* and *James Gregory* guilty of Murder, and *William Merchant* guilty of Manslaughter.

On *Monday, December* 11, being the last Day of the Sessions, *Richard Savage*, and *James Gregory*, with four other capitally convicted Prisoners, were brought again to the bar, to receive Sentence of Death. And being severally asked (as is usual on such Occasions) what they had to say, why Judgement should not be passed upon them, Mr. *Savage* addressed himself to the Court in the following Terms:

> It is now, my Lord, too late to offer any Thing by Way of Defence, or Vindication; nor can we expect ought from your Lordships, in this Court, but the Sentence which the Law requires you as Judges to pronounce against Men of our calamitous Condition.—But we are also persuaded, that as mere Men, and out of this

Notes

[5] *flies up* does not count for much; the metaphor is that of a balance with opposing scales holding weights on either end.

Seat of rigorous Justice, you are susceptive of the tender Passions, and too humane, not to commiserate the unhappy Situation of those, whom the Law – sometimes perhaps – exacts from you to pronounce upon. No doubt you distinguish between Offences, which arise out of Premeditation, and a Disposition habitual to Vice or Immorality, and Transgressions, which are the unhappy and unforeseen Effects of a casual Absence of Reason, and sudden Impulse of Passion: We, therefore, hope you will contribute all you can to an Extension of that Mercy, which the Gentlemen of the Jury have been pleased to show Mr. *Merchant*, who (allowing Facts as sworn against us by the Evidence) has led us into this our Calamity. I hope, this will not be construed as if we meant to reflect upon[6] that Gentleman, or remove any Thing from us upon him, or, that we repine the more at our Fate, because he has no Participation of it: No, my Lord! For my Part, I declare nothing could more soften my Grief, than to be without any Companion in so great a Misfortune.

Mr. *Merchant* was burnt in the Hand.

At the End of the next Sessions, which was on *Saturday* the 20th of *January, Richard Savage*, and *James Gregory* were admitted to Bail, in order to their pleading the King's Pardon.[7] And, on the last Day of the following Sessions, being the 5th of *March*, 1727–8, they accordingly pleaded his Majesty's Pardon, and their bail were discharged.[8]

Notes

6 *to reflect upon* criticize.

7 *the King's Pardon* this process would have been initiated by the judge, and he probably did so under pressure of popular sentiment stirred up by a pamphlet biography of Savage, published while the prisoner was under sentence; the report goes on to quote the pamphlet at some length.

8 *their bail were discharged* they were released from any obligation to present themselves to the court; their sentences were dismissed.

Eliza Fowler Haywood (1693–1756)

By 1714 Haywood was married and acting at Smock Alley in Dublin. Within five years, however, her marriage was over, and she was in London. She supported herself in London as a writer, and occasionally as an actress, producing at least sixty separate publications. She wrote plays and translations and both edited, and for the most part wrote, a successful magazine, *The Female Spectator* (1744–6). But the bulk of her work and the most innovative part of it was prose fiction. She produced numerous romances and many other works that combined contemporary gossip and fiction; in both forms she contributed to the development of the novel. In 1724 Haywood had ten new publications, and in that year her first hit, *Love in Excess* (1719–20), reached a fifth edition. Her works are romances in which women are usually the central figures. Haywood's heroines are often intriguers who find ways over, around, and through the web of social conventions that restrict their freedom. The darker side of her work, however, is its recognition that the barriers to women's freedom have their foundations in nature or in the deepest and oldest social assumptions: men are naturally unfaithful; unwanted pregnancy is often the result of pursuing sexual desires; and the most superficial qualities of women are those that count for the most in the world created by males and for males. In some of her works Haywood explores the possibility of more lasting relations between women and of other kinds of sexual freedom. She also wrote some sharp political satire of Walpole's administration, but what really made her a threat to the establishment in London was her successful appeal to female readers. Pope satirizes her nastily in *The Dunciad* not because of her politics but rather because she led a shift in the nature of reading and readership that would displace classically based, relatively highbrow poetry, and then poetry in general, from its central position. In the end, Pope was more successful at defeating the scholarly and antiquarian threats to his kind of literature than he was at staving off the encroachments of popular literature.

Numerous volumes of Haywood's writings have been reprinted in various forms in recent years: Paula Backscheider's *Selected Fiction and Drama* and Patricia Spacks's *Selections from The Female Spectator* (both Oxford University Press, 1999) and *Selected Works*, edited by Alexander Petit, 6 vols. (Pickering and Chatto, 2000–1). Kathryn R. King is the author of an important biographical article, "Eliza Haywood, Savage Love, and Biographical Uncertainty" (*Review of English Studies* 59 (2008), 722–39). The text presented here is based on the edition of *Fantomina* included, with separate title page, in *Secret Histories, Novels and Poems*, 4 vols., second edition (1725).

Fantomina: OR, Love in a Maze (1724)

A Masquerade Novel by Eliza Haywood

A Young Lady of distinguished Birth, Beauty, Wit, and Spirit, happened to be in a Box one Night at the Playhouse; where, though there were a great Number of celebrated Toasts, she perceived several Gentlemen extremely pleased themselves with entertaining a Woman who sat in a Corner of the Pit, and, by her Air and Manner of receiving them,

British Literature 1640–1789: An Anthology, Fourth Edition. Edited by Robert DeMaria, Jr.

might easily be known to be one of those who come there for no other Purpose, than to create Acquaintance with as many as seem desirous of it. She could not help testifying her Contempt of Men, who, regardless either of the Play, or Circle, threw away their Time in such a Manner, to some Ladies that sat by her: But they, either less surprised by being more accustomed to such Sights, than she who had been bred for the most Part in the Country, or not of a Disposition to consider any Thing very deeply, took but little Notice of it. She still thought of it, however; and the longer she reflected on it, the greater was her Wonder, that Men, some of whom she knew were accounted to have Wit, should have Tastes so very depraved. – This excited a Curiosity in her to know in what Manner these Creatures were addressed: – She was young, a Stranger to the World, and consequently to the Dangers of it; and having no Body in Town, at that Time, to whom she was obliged to be accountable for her Actions, did in every Thing as her Inclinations or Humours[1] rendered most agreeable to her: Therefore thought it not in the least a Fault to put in practice a little Whim which came immediately into her Head, to dress herself as near as she could in the Fashion of those Women who make sale of their Favours, and set herself in the Way of being accosted as such a one, having at that Time no other Aim, than the Gratification of an innocent Curiosity. – She no sooner designed this Frolic, than she put it in Execution; and muffling her Hoods over her Face, went the next Night into the Gallery-Box,[2] and practising as much as she had observed, at that Distance, the Behaviour of that Woman, was not long before she found her Disguise had answered the Ends she wore it for: – A Crowd of Purchasers of all Degrees and Capacities were in a Moment gathered about her, each endeavouring to out-bid the other, in offering her a Price for her Embraces. – She listened to 'em all, and was not a little diverted in her Mind at the Disappointment she should give to so many, each of which thought himself secure of gaining her. – She was told by 'em all, that she was the most lovely Woman in the World; and some cried, 'Gad, she is mighty like my fine Lady Such-a-one', – naming her own Name. She was naturally vain, and received no small Pleasure in hearing herself praised, though in the Person of another, and a supposed Prostitute; but she dispatched as soon as she could all that had hitherto attacked her, when she saw the accomplished *Beauplaisir* was making his Way through the Crowd as fast as he was able, to reach the Bench she sat on. She had often seen him in the Drawing-Room, had talked with him; but then her Quality[3] and reputed Virtue kept him from using her with that Freedom she now expected he would do, and had discovered something in him, which had made her often think she should not be displeased, if he would abate some Part of his Reserve. – Now was the Time to have her Wishes answered: – He looked in her Face, and fancied, as many others had done, that she very much resembled that Lady whom she really was; but the vast Disparity there appeared between their Characters, prevented him from entertaining even the most distant Thought that they could be the same. – He addressed her at first with the usual Salutations of her pretended Profession, as, 'Are you engaged, Madam? – Will you permit me to wait on you home after the Play? – By Heaven, you are a fine Girl! – How long have you used this House?' – And such like Questions; but perceiving she had a Turn of Wit, and a genteel Manner in her Raillery, beyond what is frequently to be found among those Wretches, who are for the most part Gentlewomen but by Necessity, few of 'em having had an Education suitable to what they affect to appear, he changed the

Notes

FANTOMINA

[1] *Humour* "Present disposition" (Johnson).

[2] *Gallery-Box* a place for ladies among the highest and cheapest seats in a theatre.

[3] *Quality* nobility.

Form of his Conversation, and showed her it was not because he understood no better, that he had made use of Expressions so little polite. – In fine,[4] they were infinitely charmed with each other: He was transported to find so much Beauty and Wit in a Woman, who he doubted not but on very easy Terms he might enjoy; and she found a vast deal of Pleasure in conversing with him in this free and unrestrained Manner. They passed their Time all the Play with an equal Satisfaction; but when it was over, she found herself involved in a Difficulty, which before never entered into her Head, but which she knew not well how to get over. – The Passion he professed for her, was not of that humble Nature which can be content with distant Adorations: – He resolved not to part from her without the Gratifications of those Desires she had inspired; and presuming on the Liberties which her supposed Function allowed of, told her she must either go with him to some convenient House of his procuring, or permit him to wait on her to her own Lodgings. – Never had she been in such a *Dilemma*: Three or four Times did she open her Mouth to confess her real Quality; but the Influence of her ill Stars prevented it, by putting an Excuse into her Head, which did the Business as well, and at the same Time did not take from her the Power of seeing and entertaining him a second Time with the same Freedom she had done this. – She told him, she was under Obligations to a Man who maintained her, and whom she durst not disappoint, having promised to meet him that Night at a House hard by. – This Story so like what those Ladies sometimes tell, was not at all suspected by *Beauplaisir*; and assuring her he would be far from doing her a Prejudice,[5] desired that in return for the Pain he should suffer in being deprived of her Company that Night, that she would order her Affairs, so as not to render him unhappy the next. She gave a solemn Promise to be in the same Box on the Morrow Evening; and they took Leave of each other; he to the Tavern to drown the Remembrance of his Disappointment; she in a Hackney-Chair[6] hurried home to indulge Contemplation on the Frolic she had taken, designing nothing less on her first Reflections, than to keep the Promise she had made him, and hugging herself with Joy, that she had the good Luck to come off undiscovered.

But these Cogitations were but of a short Continuance, they vanished with the Hurry of her Spirits, and were succeeded by others vastly different and ruinous: – All the Charms of *Beauplaisir* came fresh into her Mind; she languished, she almost died for another Opportunity of conversing with him; and not all the Admonitions of her Discretion were effectual to oblige her to deny laying hold of that which offered itself the next Night. – She depended on the Strength of her Virtue, to bear her fate through Trials more dangerous than she apprehended this to be, and never having been addressed by him as Lady, – was resolved to receive his Devoirs[7] as a Town-Mistress, imagining a world of Satisfaction to herself in engaging him in the Character of such a one, and in observing the Surprise he would be in to find himself refused by a Woman, who he supposed granted her Favours without Exception. – Strange and unaccountable were the Whimsies she was possessed of, – wild and incoherent her Desires, – unfixed and undetermined her Resolutions, but in that of seeing *Beauplaisir* in the Manner she had lately done. As for her Proceedings with him, or how a second Time to escape him, without discovering who she was, she could neither assure herself, nor whether or not in the last Extremity she would do so. – Bent, however, on meeting him, whatever should be the Consequence, she went out some Hours before

Notes

4 *In fine* in conclusion.

5 *Prejudice* "Mischief; detriment; hurt; injury" (Johnson).

6 *Hackney-Chair* a hired sedan chair, an enclosed seat carried by two men.

7 *Devoir* "Act of civility or obsequiousness" (Johnson).

the Time of going to the Playhouse, and took Lodgings in a House not very far from it, intending, that if he should insist on passing some Part of the Night with her, to carry him there, thinking she might with more Security to her Honour entertain him at a Place where she was Mistress, than at any of his own choosing.

The appointed Hour being arrived, she had the Satisfaction to find his Love in his Assiduity: He was there before her; and nothing could be more tender than the Manner in which he accosted her: But from the first Moment she came in, to that of the Play being done, he continued to assure her that no Consideration should prevail with him to part from her again, as she had done the Night before; and she rejoiced to think she had taken that Precaution of providing herself with a Lodging, to which she thought she might invite him, without running any Risk, either of her Virtue or Reputation. Having told him she would admit of his accompanying her home, he seemed perfectly satisfied; and leading her to the Place, which was not above twenty Houses distant, would have ordered a Collation[8] to be brought after them. But she would not permit it, telling him she was not one of those who suffered themselves to be treated at their own Lodgings; and as soon as she was come in, sent a Servant, belonging to the House, to provide a very handsome Supper, and Wine, and every Thing was served to Table in a Manner which showed the Director neither wanted Money, nor was ignorant how it should be laid out.

This Proceeding, though it did not take from him the Opinion that she was what she appeared to be, yet it gave him Thoughts of her, which he had not before. – He believed her a *Mistress*, but believed her to be one of a superior Rank, and began to imagine the Possession of her would be much more Expensive than at first he had expected: But not being of a Humour to grudge any Thing for his Pleasures, he gave himself no further Trouble, than what were occasioned by Fears of not having Money enough to reach her Price, about him.

Supper being over, which was intermixed with a vast deal of amorous Conversation, he began to explain himself more than he had done; and both by his Words and Behaviour let her know, he would not be denied that Happiness the Freedoms she allowed had made him hope. – It was in vain; she would have retracted the Encouragement she had given: – In vain she endeavoured to delay, till the next Meeting, the fulfilling of his Wishes: – She had now gone too far to retreat: – *He* was bold; – he was resolute: *She* fearful, – confused, altogether unprepared to resist in such Encounters, and rendered more so, by the extreme Liking she had to him. – Shocked, however, at the Apprehension of really losing her Honour, she struggled all she could, and was just going to reveal the whole Secret of her Name and Quality, when the Thoughts of the Liberty he had taken with her, and those he still continued to prosecute, prevented her, with representing the Danger of being exposed, and the whole Affair made a Theme for public Ridicule. – Thus much, indeed, she told him, that she was a Virgin, and had assumed this Manner of Behaviour only to engage him. But that he little regarded, or if he had, would have been far from obliging him to desist; – nay, in the present burning Eagerness of Desire, 'tis probable, that had he been acquainted both with who and what she really was, the Knowledge of her Birth would not have influenced him with Respect sufficient to have curbed the wild Exuberance of his luxurious Wishes, or made him in that longing, that impatient Moment, change the Form of his Addresses. In fine, she was undone; and he gained a Victory, so highly rapturous, that had he known over whom, scarce could he have triumphed more. Her Tears, however, and the Distraction she appeared in, after the ruinous Ecstasy was past, as it heightened his

Notes

[8] *Collation* a light meal.

Wonder, so it abated his Satisfaction: – He could not imagine for what Reason a Woman, who, if she intended not to be a *Mistress*, had counterfeited the Part of one, and taken so much Pains to engage him, should lament a Consequence which she could not but expect, and till the last Test, seemed inclinable to grant; and was both surprised and troubled at the Mystery. – He omitted nothing that he thought might make her easy; and still retaining an Opinion that the Hope of Interest had been the chief Motive which had led her to act in the Manner she had done, and believing that she might know so little of him, as to suppose, now that she had nothing left to give, he might not make that Recompense she expected for her Favours: To put her out of that Pain, he pulled out of his Pocket a Purse of Gold, entreating her to accept of that as an Earnest of what he intended to do for her; assuring her, with ten thousand Protestations, that he would spare nothing, which his whole Estate could purchase, to procure her Content and Happiness. This Treatment made her quite forget the Part she had assumed, and throwing it from her with an Air of Disdain, 'Is this a Reward', said she, 'for Condescensions,[9] such as I have yielded to? – Can all the Wealth you are possessed of, make a Reparation for my Loss of Honour? – Oh! no, I am undone beyond the Power of Heaven itself to help me!' – She uttered many more such Exclamations; which the amazed *Beauplaisir* heard without being able to reply to, till by Degrees sinking from that Rage of Temper, her Eyes resumed their softening Glances, and guessing at the Consternation he was in, 'No, my dear *Beauplaisir*', added she, 'your Love alone can compensate for the Shame you have involved me in; be you sincere and constant, and I hereafter shall, perhaps, be satisfied with my Fate, and forgive myself the Folly that betrayed me to you'.

Beauplaisir thought he could not have a better Opportunity than these Words gave him of enquiring who she was, and wherefore she had feigned herself to be of a Profession which he was now convinced she was not; and after he had made her thousand Vows of an Affection, as inviolable and ardent as she could wish to find in him, entreated she would inform him by what Means his Happiness has been brought about, and also to whom he was indebted for the Bliss he had enjoyed. – Some remains of yet unextinguished Modesty, and Sense of Shame, made her Blush exceedingly at this Demand; but recollecting herself in a little Time, she told him so much of the Truth, as to what related to the Frolic she had taken of satisfying her Curiosity in what Manner *Mistresses*, of the sort she appeared to be, were treated by those who addressed them; but forbore discovering her true Name and Quality, for the Reasons she had done before, resolving, if he boasted of this Affair, he should not have it in his Power to touch her Character: She therefore said she was the Daughter of a Country Gentleman, who was come to Town to buy Clothes, and that she was called *Fantomina*. He had no Reason to distrust the Truth of this Story, and was therefore satisfied with it; but did not doubt by the Beginning of her Conduct, but that in the End she would be in Reality, the Thing she so artfully had counterfeited; and had good Nature enough to pity the Misfortunes he imagined would be her Lot: But to tell her so, or offer his Advice in that Point, was not his Business, at least, as yet.

They parted not till towards Morning; and she obliged him to a willing Vow of visiting her the next Day at Three in the Afternoon. It was too late for her to go home that Night; [she] therefore contented herself with lying there. In the Morning she sent for the Woman of the House to come up to her; and easily perceiving, by her Manner,

Notes

[9] *Condescension* "Voluntary humiliation" (Johnson).

that she was a Woman who might be influenced by Gifts, made her a Present of a Couple of Broad Pieces,[10] and desired her, that if the Gentleman, who had been there the Night before, should ask any Questions concerning her, that he should be told, she was lately come out of the Country, had lodged there about a Fortnight, and that her Name was *Fantomina*. I shall (also added she) lie but seldom here; nor, indeed, ever come but in those Times when I expect to meet him: I would, therefore, have you order it so, that he may think I am but just gone out, if he should happen by any Accident to call when I am not here; for I would not, for the World, have him imagine I do not constantly lodge here. The Landlady assured her she would do every Thing as she desired, and gave her to understand she wanted not the Gift of Secrecy.

Every Thing being ordered at this Home for the Security of her Reputation, she repaired to the other, where she easily excused to an unsuspecting Aunt, with whom she boarded, her having been abroad all Night, saying, she went with a Gentleman and his Lady in a Barge, to a little Country Seat of theirs up the River, all of them designing to return the same Evening; but that one of the Bargemen happening to be taken ill on the sudden, and no other Waterman to be got that Night, they were obliged to tarry till Morning. Thus did this Lady's Wit and Vivacity assist her in all, but where it was most needful. – She had Discernment to foresee, and avoid all those Ills which might attend the loss of her *Reputation*, but was wholly blind to those of the Ruin of her *Virtue*; and having managed her Affairs so as to secure the *one*, grew perfectly easy with the Remembrance, she had forfeited the *other*. – The more she reflected on the Merits of *Beauplaisir*, the more she excused herself for what she had done; and the Prospect of that continued Bliss she expected to share with him, took from her all Remorse for having engaged in an Affair which promised her so much Satisfaction, and in which she found not the least Danger of Misfortune. – 'If he is really', said she, to herself, 'the faithful, the constant Lover he has sworn to be, how charming will be our Amour? – And if he should be false, grow satiated, like other Men, I shall but, at the worst, have the private Vexation of knowing I lost him; – the Intrigue being a Secret, my Disgrace will be so too: – I shall hear no Whispers as I pass, – "She is Forsaken": – The odious Word *Forsaken* will never wound my Ears; nor will my Wrongs excite either Mirth or Pity of the talking World: – It will not be even in the Power of my Undoer Himself to triumph over me; and while he laughs at, and perhaps despises the fond, the yielding *Fantomina*, he will revere and esteem the virtuous, the reserved Lady'. – In this Manner did she applaud her own Conduct, and exult with the Imagination that she had more Prudence than all her Sex beside. And it must be confessed, indeed, that she preserved an Economy in the management of this Intrigue, beyond what almost any Woman but herself ever did: In the first Place, by making no Person in the World a Confidant in it; and in the next, in concealing from *Beauplaisir* himself the Knowledge who she was; for though she met him three or four Days in a Week, at the Lodging she had taken for that Purpose, yet as much as he employed her Time and Thoughts, she was never missed from any Assembly she had been accustomed to frequent. – The Business of her Love has engrossed her till Six in the Evening, and before Seven she has been dressed in a different Habit, and in another Place. – Slippers, and a Nightgown loosely flowing, has been the Garb in which he has left the languishing *Fantomina*; – Laced, and adorned with all the Blaze of Jewels, has he, in less than an Hour after, beheld at the Royal Chapel, the Palace Gardens, Drawing-Room, Opera, or Play, the Haughty

Notes

[10] *Broad Piece* seventeenth-century gold coin roughly equivalent to the later guinea or modern pound.

Awe-inspiring Lady – A thousand Times has he stood amazed at the prodigious Likeness between his little Mistress, and this Court Beauty; but was still as far from imagining they were the same, as he was the first Hour he accosted her in the Playhouse, though it is not impossible, but that her Resemblance to this celebrated Lady, might keep his Inclinations alive something longer than otherwise they would have been; and that it was to the Thoughts of this (as he supposed) unenjoyed Charmer, she owed in great measure the Vigour of his latter Caresses.

But he varied not so much from his Sex as to be able to prolong Desire, to any great Length after Possession: The rifled Charms of *Fantomina* soon lost their Poignancy, and grew tasteless and insipid; and when the Season of the Year inviting the Company to the *Bath*, she offered to accompany him, he made an Excuse to go without her. She easily perceived his Coldness, and the Reason why he pretended her going would be inconvenient, and endured as much from the Discovery as any of her Sex could do: She dissembled it, however, before him, and took her Leave of him with the Show of no other Concern than his Absence occasioned: But this she did to take from him all Suspicion of her following him, as she intended, and had already laid a Scheme for. – From her first finding out that he designed to leave her behind, she plainly saw it was for no other Reason, than being tired of her Conversation, he was willing to be at liberty to pursue new Conquests; and wisely considering that Complaints, Tears, Swooning, and all the Extravagancies which Women make use of in such Cases, have little Prevalence over a Heart inclined to rove, and only serve to render those who practise them more contemptible, by robbing them of that Beauty which alone can bring back the fugitive Lover, she resolved to take another Course; and remembering the Height of Transport she enjoyed when the agreeable *Beauplaisir* kneeled at her Feet, imploring her first Favours, she longed to prove the same again. Not but a Woman of her Beauty and Accomplishments might have beheld a Thousand in that Condition *Beauplaisir* had been; but with her Sex's Modesty, she had not also thrown off another Virtue equally valuable, though generally unfortunate, *Constancy*: She loved *Beauplaisir*; it was only he whose Solicitations could give her Pleasure; and had she seen the whole Species despairing, dying for her sake, it might, perhaps, have been a Satisfaction to her Pride, but none to her more tender Inclination. – Her Design was once more to engage him, to hear him sigh, to see him languish, to feel the strenuous Pressures of his eager Arms, to be compelled, to be sweetly forced to what she wished with equal Ardour, was what she wanted, and what she had formed a Stratagem to obtain, in which she promised herself Success.

She no sooner heard he had left the Town, than making a Pretence to her Aunt, that she was going to visit a Relation in the Country, went towards *Bath*, attended but by two Servants, who she found Reasons to quarrel with on the Road and discharged: Clothing herself in a Habit she had brought with her, she forsook the Coach, and went into a Wagon, in which Equipage she arrived at *Bath*. The Dress she was in, was a round-eared Cap, a short Red Petticoat, and a little Jacket of Grey Stuff; all the rest of her Accoutrements were answerable to these, and joined with a broad Country Dialect, a rude unpolished Air, which she, having been bred in these Parts, knew very well how to imitate, with her Hair and Eye-brows blacked, made it impossible for her to be known, or taken for any other than what she seemed. Thus disguised did she offer herself to Service in the House where *Beauplaisir* lodged, having made it her Business to find out immediately where he was. Notwithstanding this Metamorphosis she was still extremely pretty; and the Mistress of the House happening at that Time to want a Maid, was very glad of the Opportunity of taking her. She was presently received into the Family; and had a Post in it (such as she would have chose, had she been left at her Liberty), that of making the Gentlemen's Beds, getting them their

Breakfasts, and waiting on them in their Chambers. Fortune in this Exploit was extremely on her side; there were no others of the Male-Sex in the House, than an old Gentleman, who had lost the Use of his Limbs with the Rheumatism, and had come thither for the Benefit of the Waters, and her beloved *Beauplaisir*; so that she was in no Apprehensions of any Amorous Violence, but where she wished to find it. Nor were her Designs disappointed: He was fired with the first Sight of her; and though he did not presently take any further Notice of her, than giving her two or three hearty Kisses, yet she, who now understood that Language but too well, easily saw they were the Prelude to more substantial Joys. – Coming the next Morning to bring his Chocolate, as he ordered, he catched her by the pretty Leg, which the Shortness of her Petticoat did not in the least oppose; then pulling her gently to him, asked her, how long she had been at Service? – How many Sweethearts she had? If she had ever been in Love? and many other such Questions, befitting one of the Degree she appeared to be: All which she answered with such seeming Innocence, as more inflamed the amorous Heart of him who talked to her. He compelled her to sit in his Lap; and gazing on her blushing Beauties, which, if possible, received Addition from her plain and rural Dress, he soon lost the Power of containing himself. – His wild Desires burst out in all his Words and Actions: he called her little Angel, Cherubim, swore he must enjoy her, though Death were to be the Consequence, devoured her Lips, her Breasts with greedy Kisses, held to his burning Bosom her half-yielding, half-reluctant Body, nor suffered her to get loose, till he had ravaged all, and glutted each rapacious Sense with the sweet Beauties of the pretty *Celia*, for that was the name she bore in this second Expedition. – Generous as Liberality itself to all who gave him Joy this way, he gave her a handsome Sum of Gold, which she durst not now refuse, for fear of creating some Mistrust, and losing the Heart she so lately had regained; therefore taking it with an humble Curtsy, and a well counterfeited Show of Surprise and Joy, cried, 'O Law, Sir! what must I do for all this?' He laughed at her Simplicity, and kissing her again, though less fervently than he had done before, bade her not be out of the Way when he came home at Night. She promised she would not, and very obediently kept her Word.

His Stay at *Bath* exceeded not a Month; but in that Time his supposed Country Lass had persecuted him so much with her Fondness, that in spite of the Eagerness with which he first enjoyed her, he was at last grown more weary of her, than he had been of *Fantomina*; which she perceiving, would not be troublesome, but quitting her Service, remained privately in the Town till she heard he was on his Return; and in that Time provided herself of another Disguise to carry on a third Plot, which her inventing Brain had furnished her with, once more to renew his twice-decayed Ardours. The Dress she had ordered to be made, was such as Widows wear in their first Mourning, which, together with the most afflicted and penitential Countenance that ever was seen, was no small Alteration to her who used to seem all Gaiety. – To add to this, her Hair, which she was accustomed to wear very loose, both when *Fantomina* and *Celia*, was now tied back so straight, and her Pinners[11] coming so very forward, that there was none of it to be seen. In fine, her Habit and her Air were so much changed, that she was not more difficult to be known in the rude Country *Girl*, than she was now in the sorrowful *Widow*.

She knew that *Beauplaisir* came alone in his Chariot to the *Bath*, and in the Time of her being Servant in the House where he lodged, heard nothing of any Body that was

Notes

[11] *Pinners* the long flaps of a coif or headdress worn by women of rank.

to accompany him to *London*, and hoped he would return in the same Manner he had gone: She therefore hired Horses and a Man to attend her to an Inn about ten Miles on this side *Bath*, where having discharged them, she waited till the Chariot should come by; which when it did, and she saw that he was alone in it, she called to him that drove it to stop a Moment, and going to the Door saluted the Master with these Words: 'The Distressed and Wretched, Sir', said she, 'never fail to excite Compassion in a generous Mind; and I hope I am not deceived in my Opinion that yours is such: – You have the Appearance of a Gentleman, and cannot, when you hear my Story, refuse that Assistance which is in your Power to give to an unhappy Woman, who without it, may be rendered the most miserable of all created Beings'.

It would not be very easy to represent the Surprise, so odd an Address created in the Mind of him to whom it was made. – She had not the Appearance of one who wanted Charity; and what other Favour she required he could not conceive: But telling her, she might command any Thing in his Power, gave her Encouragement to declare herself in this Manner: 'You may judge', resumed she, 'by the melancholy Garb I am in, that I have lately lost all that ought to be valuable to Womankind; but it is impossible for you to guess the Greatness of my Misfortune, unless you had known my Husband, who was Master of every Perfection to endear him to a Wife's Affections. – But, notwithstanding, I look on myself as the most unhappy of my Sex in out-living him, I must so far obey the Dictates of my Discretion, as to take care of the little Fortune he left behind him, which being in the hands of a Brother of his in *London*, will be all carried off to *Holland*, where he is going to settle; if I reach not the Town before he leaves it, I am undone for ever. – To which End I left *Bristol*, the Place where we lived, hoping to get a Place in the Stage at *Bath*, but they were all taken up before I came; and being, by a Hurt I got in a Fall, rendered incapable of travelling any long Journey on Horseback, I have no Way to go to *London*, and must be inevitably ruined in the Loss of all I have on Earth, without you have good Nature enough to admit me to take Part of your Chariot'.

Here the feigned Widow ended her sorrowful Tale, which had been several Times interrupted by a Parenthesis of Sighs and Groans; and *Beauplaisir*, with a complaisant and tender Air, assured her of his Readiness to serve her in Things of much greater Consequence than what she desired of him; and told her, it would be an Impossibility of denying a Place in his Chariot to a Lady, who he could not behold without yielding one in his Heart. She answered the Compliments he made her but with Tears, which seemed to stream in such abundance from her Eyes, that she could not keep her handkerchief from her Face one Moment. Being come into the Chariot, *Beauplaisir* said a thousand handsome Things to persuade her from giving way to so violent a Grief, which, he told her, would not only be destructive to her Beauty, but likewise her Health. But all his Endeavours for Consolement appeared ineffectual, and he began to think he should have but a dull Journey in the Company of one who seemed so obstinately devoted to the Memory of her dead Husband, that there was no getting a Word from her on any other Theme: – But bethinking himself of the celebrated Story of the *Ephesian* Matron,[12] it came into his Head to make Trial, she who seemed equally susceptible of *Sorrow*, might not also be so too of *Love*; and having begun a Discourse

Notes

[12] *Ephesian Matron* Petronius (*Satyricon* 111–12) tells the story of a chaste wife who weeps for days at her husband's grave but is seduced by a soldier who courts her and weds her in the tomb; in the end she gives her husband's body to save him from punishment for the theft of the crucified criminal's body that he was supposed to be guarding; the story, which Petronius tells at the expense of women, became a commonplace in the literature of sensibility and she a kind of heroine.

on almost every other Topic, and finding her still incapable of answering, resolved to put it to the Proof, if this would have no more Effect to rouse her sleeping Spirits: – With a gay Air, therefore, though accompanied with the greatest Modesty and Respect, he turned the Conversation, as though without Design, on that Joy-giving Passion, and soon discovered that was indeed the Subject she was best pleased to be entertained with; for on his giving her a Hint to begin upon, never any Tongue run more voluble than hers, on the prodigious Power it had to influence the Souls of those possessed of it, to Actions even the most distant from their Intentions, Principles, or Humours.[13] – From that she passed to a Description of the Happiness of mutual Affection; – the unspeakable Ecstasy of those who meet with equal Ardency; and represented it in Colours so lively, and disclosed by the Gestures with which her Words were accompanied, and the Accent of her Voice so true a Feeling of what she said, that *Beauplaisir*, without being as stupid, as he was really the contrary, could not avoid perceiving there were Seeds of Fire, not yet extinguished, in this fair Widow's Soul, which wanted but the kindling Breath of tender Sighs to light into a Blaze. – He now thought himself as fortunate, as some Moments before he had the Reverse; and doubted not, but, that before they parted, he should find a Way to dry the Tears of this lovely Mourner, to the Satisfaction of them both. He did not, however, offer, as he had done to *Fantomina* and *Celia*, to urge his Passion directly to her, but by a thousand little softening Artifices, which he well knew how to use, gave her leave to guess he was enamoured. When they came to the Inn where they were to lie, he declared himself somewhat more freely, and perceiving she did not resent it past Forgiveness, grew more encroaching still: – He now took the Liberty of kissing away her Tears, and catching the Sighs as they issued from her Lips; telling her if Grief was infectious, he was resolved to have his Share; protesting he would gladly exchange Passions with her, and be content to bear her Load of *Sorrow*, if she would as willingly ease the Burden of his *Love*. – She said little in answer to the strenuous Pressures with which at last he ventured to enfold her, but not thinking it Decent, for the Character she had assumed, to yield so suddenly, and unable to deny both his and her own Inclinations, she counterfeited a fainting, and fell motionless upon his Breast. – He had no great Notion that she was in a real Fit, and the Room they supped in happening to have a Bed in it, he took her in his Arms and laid her on it, believing, that whatever her Distemper was, that was the most proper Place to convey her to. – He laid himself down by her, and endeavoured to bring her to herself; and she was too grateful to her kind Physician at her returning Sense, to remove from the Posture he had put her in, without his Leave.

It may, perhaps, seem strange that *Beauplaisir* should in such near Intimacies continue still deceived: I know there are Men who will swear it is an Impossibility, and that no Disguise could hinder them from knowing a Woman they had once enjoyed. In answer to these Scruples, I can only say, that besides the Alteration which the Change of Dress made in her, she was so admirably skilled in the Art of feigning, that she had the Power of putting on almost what Face she pleased, and knew so exactly how to form her Behaviour to the Character she represented, that all the Comedians at both Playhouses[14] are infinitely short of her Performances: She could vary her very Glances, tune her Voice to Accents the most different imaginable from those in which she spoke when she appeared herself. – These Aids from Nature, joined to the Wiles of Art, and

Notes

[13] *Humour* "General turn or temper of mind" (Johnson).

[14] *both Playhouses* Covent Garden and Drury Lane, the King's Theatre in Haymarket being used for opera.

the Distance between the Places where the imagined *Fantomina* and *Celia* were, might very well prevent his having any Thought that they were the same, or that the fair *Widow* was either of them: It never so much as entered his Head, and though he did fancy he observed in the Face of the latter, Features which were not altogether unknown to him, yet he could not recollect when or where he had known them; – and being told by her, that from her Birth, she had never removed from *Bristol*, a Place where he never was, he rejected the Belief of having seen her, and supposed his Mind had been deluded by an Idea of some other, whom she might have a Resemblance of.

They passed the Time of their Journey in as much Happiness as the most luxurious Gratification of wild Desires could make them; and when they came to the End of it, parted not without a mutual Promise of seeing each other often. – He told her to what Place she should direct a Letter to him; and she assured him she would send to let him know where to come to her, as soon as she was fixed in Lodgings.

She kept her Promise; and charmed with the Continuance of his eager Fondness, went not home, but into private Lodgings, whence she wrote to him to visit her the first Opportunity, and enquire for the Widow *Bloomer*. – She had no sooner dispatched this Billet, than she repaired to the House where she had lodged as *Fantomina*, charging the People if *Beauplaisir* should come there, not to let him know she had been out of Town. From thence she wrote to him, in a different Hand, a long Letter of Complaint, that he had been so cruel in not sending one Letter to her all the Time he had been absent, entreated to see him, and concluded with subscribing herself his unalterably Affectionate *Fantomina*. She received in one Day Answers to both these. The first contained these Lines:

To the Charming Mrs. Bloomer,

It would be impossible, my Angel! for me to express the thousandth Part of that Infinity of Transport, the Sight of your dear Letter gave me. – Never was Woman formed to charm like you: Never did any look like you, – write like you, – bless like you; – nor did ever Man adore as I do. – Since Yesterday we parted, I have seemed a Body without a Soul; and had you not by this inspiring Billet, given me new Life, I know not what by To-morrow I should have been. – I will be with you this Evening about Five: – O, 'tis an Age till then! – But the cursed formalities of Duty oblige me to Dine with my Lord – who never rises from Table till that Hour; – therefore Adieu till then sweet lovely Mistress of the Soul and all the Faculties of

Your most faithful,
BEAUPLAISIR

The other was in this Manner:

To the Lovely Fantomina

If you were half so sensible as you ought of your own Power of charming, you would be assured, that to be unfaithful or unkind to you, would be among the Things that are in their very Natures Impossibilities. – It was my Misfortune, not my Fault, that you were not persecuted every Post with a Declaration of my unchanging Passion; but I had unluckily forgot the Name of the Woman at whose House you are, and knew not how to form a Direction that it might come safe to your Hands. – And, indeed, the Reflection how you might misconstrue my Silence, brought me to Town some Weeks sooner than I intended – If you knew how I have languished to renew those Blessings I am permitted to enjoy in your Society, you would rather pity than condemn.

Your ever faithful,
BEAUPLAISIR

P.S. I fear I cannot see you till To-morrow; some Business has unluckily fallen out that will engross my Hours till then. – Once more, my Dear, *Adieu*.

'TRAITOR!' cried she, as soon as she had read them, ''tis thus our silly, fond, believing Sex are served when they put Faith in Man: So had I been deceived and cheated, had I like the rest believed, and sat down mourning in Absence, and vainly waiting recovered Tenderness. – How do some Women', continued she 'make their Life a Hell, burning in fruitless Expectations, and dreaming out their Days in Hopes and Fears, then wake at last to all the Horror of Despair? – But I have outwitted even the most Subtle of the deceiving Kind, and while he thinks to fool me, is himself the only beguiled Person'.

She made herself, most certainly, extremely happy in the Reflection on the Success of her Stratagems; and while the Knowledge of his Inconstancy and Levity of Nature kept her from having that real Tenderness for him she would else have had, she found the Means of gratifying the Inclination she had for his agreeable Person, in as full a Manner as she could wish. She had all the Sweets of Love, but as yet had tasted none of the Gall, and was in a State of Contentment, which might be envied by the more Delicate.

When the expected Hour arrived, she found that her Lover had lost no part of the Fervency with which he had parted from her; but when the next Day she received him as *Fantomina*, she perceived a prodigious Difference; which led her again into Reflections on the Unaccountableness of Men's Fancies, who still prefer the last Conquest, only because it is the last. – Here was an evident Proof of it; for there could not be a Difference in Merit, because they were the same Person; but the Widow *Bloomer* was a more new Acquaintance than *Fantomina*, and therefore esteemed more valuable. This, indeed, must be said of *Beauplaisir*, that he had a greater Share of good Nature than most of his Sex, who, for the most part, when they are weary of an Intrigue, break it entirely off, without any Regard to the Despair of the abandoned Nymph. Though he retained no more than a bare Pity and Complaisance for *Fantomina*, yet believing she loved him to an Excess, would not entirely forsake her, though the Continuance of his Visits was now become rather a Penance than a Pleasure.

The Widow *Bloomer* triumphed some Time longer over the Heart of this Inconstant, but at length her Sway was at an End, and she sunk in this Character, to the same Degree of Tastelessness, as she had done before in that of *Fantomina* and *Celia*. – She presently perceived it, but bore it as she had always done; it being but what she expected, she had prepared herself for it, and had another Project in *embryo*, which she soon ripened into Action. She did not, indeed, complete it altogether so suddenly as she had done the others, by reason there must be Persons employed in it; and the Aversion she had to any *Confidants* in her Affairs, and the Caution with which she had hitherto acted, and which she was still determined to continue, made it very difficult for her to find a Way without breaking through that Resolution to compass what she wished. – She got over the Difficulty at last, however, by proceeding in a Manner, if possible, more extraordinary than all her former Behaviour: – Muffling herself up in her Hood one Day, she went into the Park about the Hour when there are a great many necessitous Gentlemen, who think themselves above what they call little Things for a Maintenance, walking in the *Mall*,[15] to take a *Chameleon* Treat,[16] and fill their Stomachs with Air instead of Meat. Two of those, who by their Physiognomy she thought most proper for her Purpose, she beckoned to come to her; and taking them into a Walk more remote from Company, began to communicate the Business she had with them in these Words: 'I am sensible, Gentlemen', said she, 'that, through the Blindness of Fortune, and Partiality of the World, Merit frequently goes unrewarded, and that those of the best Pretensions meet with the least Encouragement: – I ask your Pardon', continued she, perceiving they seemed surprised, 'if I am mistaken in the Notion, that you two may, perhaps, be of the Number of those who have Reason to complain of the Injustice of Fate; but if you are such as I take you for, have a Proposal to make you, which may be of some little Advantage to you'. Neither of them made any immediate Answer, but appeared buried in Consideration for some Moments. At length, 'We should, doubtless, Madam', said one of them, 'willingly come into any Measures to oblige you, provided they are such as may bring us into no Danger, either as to our Persons or Reputations'.

'That which I require of you', resumed she, 'has nothing in it criminal: All that I desire is *Secrecy* in what you are entrusted, and to disguise yourselves in such a Manner as you cannot be known, if hereafter seen by the Person on whom you are to impose. – In fine, the Business is only an innocent Frolic, but if blazed abroad, might be taken for too great a Freedom in me: – Therefore, if you resolve to assist me, here are five Pieces to Drink my Health, and assure you, that I have not discoursed you on an Affair, I design not to proceed in; and when it is accomplished fifty more lie ready for your Acceptance'. These Words, and, above all, the Money, which was a Sum which, 'tis probable, they had not seen of a long Time, made them immediately assent to all she desired, and press for the Beginning of their Employment: But things were not yet ripe for Execution; and she told them, that the next Day they should be let into the Secret, charging them to meet her in the same Place at an hour she appointed. 'Tis hard to say, which of these Parties went away best pleased; *they*, that Fortune had sent them so unexpected a Windfall; or *she*, that she had found Persons, who appeared so well qualified to serve her.

Indefatigable in the Pursuit of whatsoever her Humour was bent upon, she had no sooner left her new-engaged Emissaries, than she went in search of a House for the completing her Project. – She pitched on one very large, and magnificently furnished, which she hired by the Week, giving them the Money before-hand, to prevent any Inquiries. The next Day she repaired to the Park, where she met the punctual Squires of low Degree; and ordering them to follow her to the House she had taken, told them they must condescend to appear like Servants, and gave each of them a very rich Livery. Then writing a Letter to *Beauplaisir*, in a Character vastly different from either of those she had made use of, as *Fantomina*, or the fair Widow *Bloomer*, ordered one of them to deliver it into his own Hands, to bring back an Answer, and to be careful that he sifted out nothing of the Truth. – 'I do not fear', said she, 'that you should discover to him who I am, because that is a Secret, of which you yourselves are ignorant; but I would have you be so careful in your Replies, that he may not think the Concealment

Notes

[15] *Mall* a fashionable walk in St. James's Park.

[16] *Chameleon Treat* it was once popularly believed that chameleons subsisted on air.

springs from any other Reasons than your great Integrity to your Trust. – Seem therefore to know my whole Affairs; and let your refusing to make him Partaker in the Secret, appear to be only the Effect of your Zeal for my Interest and Reputation'. Promises of entire Fidelity on the one side, and Reward on the other, being passed, the Messenger made what haste he could to the House of *Beauplaisir*; and being there told where he might find him, performed exactly the Injunction that had been given him. But never Astonishment exceeding that which *Beauplaisir* felt at the reading this Billet, in which he found these Lines:

To the All-conquering Beauplaisir.

I Imagine not that 'tis a new Thing to you, to be told, you are the greatest Charm in Nature to our Sex: I shall therefore, not to fill up my Letter with any impertinent Praises on your Wit or Person, only tell you, that I am infinite in Love with both, and if you have a Heart not too deeply engaged, should think myself the happiest of my Sex in being capable of inspiring it with some Tenderness. – There is but one Thing in my Power to refuse you, which is the Knowledge of my Name, which believing the Sight of my Face will render no Secret, you must not take it ill that I conceal from you. – The Bearer of this is a Person I can trust; send by him your Answer; but endeavour not to dive into the Meaning of this Mystery, which will be impossible to unravel, and at the same Time very much disoblige me: – But that you may be in no Apprehensions of being imposed on by a Woman unworthy of your Regard, I will venture to assure you, the first and greatest Men in the Kingdom, would think themselves blessed to have that Influence over me you have, though unknown to yourself acquired. – But I need not go about to raise your Curiosity, by giving you any Idea of what my Person is; if you think fit to be satisfied, resolve to visit me To-morrow about Three in the afternoon; and though my Face is hid, you shall not want sufficient Demonstration, that she who takes these unusual Measures to commence a Friendship with you, is neither Old, nor Deformed. Till then I am,

Yours,
INCOGNITA

He had scarce come to the Conclusion, before he asked the Person who brought it, from what Place he came; – the Name of the Lady he served; – if she were a Wife, or Widow, and several other Questions directly opposite to the Directions of the Letter; but Silence would have availed him as much as did all those Testimonies of Curiosity: No *Italian Bravo*,[17] employed in a Business of the like Nature, performed his Office with more Artifice; and the impatient Enquirer was convinced that nothing but doing as he was desired, could give him any Light into the Character of the Woman who declared so violent a Passion for him; and little fearing any Consequence which could ensue from such an Encounter, resolved to rest satisfied till he was informed of every Thing from herself, not imagining this *Incognita* varied so much from the Generality of her Sex, as to be able to refuse the Knowledge of any Thing to the Man she loved with that Transcendency of Passion she professed, and which his many Successes with the

Notes

[17] *Bravo* "A man who murders for hire" (Johnson).

Ladies gave him Encouragement enough to believe. He therefore took Pen and Paper, and answered her Letter in terms tender enough for a Man who had never seen the Person to whom he wrote. The Words were as follows:

To the Obliging and Witty
INCOGNITA.

Though to tell me I am happy enough to be liked by a Woman, such, as by your Manner of Writing, I imagine you to be, is an Honour which I can never sufficiently acknowledge, yet I know not how I am able to content myself with admiring the Wonders of your Wit alone: I am certain, a Soul like yours must shine in your Eyes with a Vivacity, which must bless all they look on. – I shall, however, endeavour to restrain myself in those Bounds you are pleased to set me, till by the Knowledge of my inviolable Fidelity, I may be thought worthy of gazing on that Heaven I am now but to enjoy in Contemplation. – You need not doubt my glad Compliance with your obliging Summons: There is a Charm in your Lines, which gives too sweet an Idea of their lovely Author to be resisted. – I am all impatient for the blissful Moment, which is to throw me at your Feet, and give me an Opportunity of convincing you that I am,

Your everlasting Slave,
BEAUPLAISIR

Nothing could be more pleased than she, to whom it was directed, at the Receipt of this Letter; but when she was told how inquisitive he had been concerning her Character and Circumstances, she could not forbear laughing heartily to think of the Tricks she had played him, and applauding her own Strength of Genius, and Force of Resolution, which by such unthought-of Ways could triumph over her Lover's Inconstancy, and render that very Temper, which to other Women is the greatest Curse, a Means to make herself more blessed. – 'Had he been faithful to me', said she, to herself, 'either as *Fantomina*, or *Celia*, or the Widow *Bloomer*, the most violent Passion, if it does not change its Object, in Time will wither: Possession naturally abates the Vigour of Desire, and I should have had, at best, but a cold, insipid, husband-like Lover in my Arms; but by these Arts of passing on him as a new Mistress whenever the Ardour, which alone makes Love a Blessing, begins to diminish, for the former one, I have him always raving, wild, impatient, longing, dying. – O that all neglected Wives, and fond abandoned Nymphs would take this Method! – Men would be caught in their own Snare, and have no Cause to scorn our easy, weeping, wailing Sex!' Thus did she pride herself as if secure she never should have any Reason to repent the present Gaiety of her Humour. The Hour drawing near in which he was to come, she dressed herself in as magnificent a Manner, as if she were to be that Night at a Ball at Court, endeavouring to repair the want of those Beauties which the Vizard[18] should conceal, by setting forth the others with the greatest Care and Exactness. Her fine Shape, and Air, and Neck, appeared to great Advantage; and by that which was to be seen of her, one might believe the rest to be perfectly agreeable. *Beauplaisir* was prodigiously charmed, as well with her Appearance, as with the Manner she entertained him: But though he was wild with Impatience for the Sight of a Face which belonged

Notes

[18] *Vizard* mask.

to so exquisite a Body, yet he would not immediately press for it, believing before he left her he should easily obtain that Satisfaction. – A noble Collation being over, he began to sue for the Performance of her Promise of granting every Thing he could ask, excepting the Sight of her Face, and knowledge of her Name. It would have been a ridiculous Piece of Affection[19] in her to have seemed coy in complying with what she herself had been the first in desiring: She yielded without even a Show of Reluctance: And if there be any true Felicity in an Amour such as theirs, both here enjoyed it to the full. But not in the Height of all their mutual Raptures, could he prevail on her to satisfy his Curiosity with the Sight of her Face: She told him that she hoped he knew so much of her, as might serve to convince him, she was not unworthy of his tenderest Regard; and if he could not content himself with that which she was willing to reveal, and which was the Conditions of their meeting, dear as he was to her, she would rather part with him for ever, than consent to gratify an Inquisitiveness, which, in her Opinion, had no Business with his Love. It was in vain that he endeavoured to make her sensible of her Mistake; and that this Restraint was the greatest Enemy imaginable to the Happiness of them both: She was not to be persuaded, and he was obliged to desist his Solicitations, though determined in his Mind to compass what he so ardently desired, before he left the House. He then turned the Discourse wholly on the Violence of the Passion he had for her; and expressed the greatest Discontent in the World at the Apprehensions of being separated; – swore he could dwell for ever in her Arms, and with such an undeniable Earnestness pressed to be permitted to tarry with her the whole Night, that had she been less charmed with his renewed Eagerness of Desire, she scarce would have had the Power of refusing him; but in granting this Request, she was not without a Thought that he had another Reason for making it besides the Extremity of his Passion, and had it immediately in her Head how to disappoint him.

The Hours of Repose being arrived, he begged she would retire to her Chamber; to which she consented, but obliged him to go to Bed first; which he did not much oppose, because he supposed she would not lie in her Mask, and doubted not but the Morning's Dawn would bring the wished Discovery. – The two imagined Servants ushered him to his new Lodging; where he lay some Moments in all the Perplexity imaginable at the Oddness of this Adventure. But she suffered not these Cogitations to be of any long Continuance: She came, but came in the Dark; which being no more than he expected by the former Part of her Proceedings, he said nothing of; but as much Satisfaction as he found in her Embraces, nothing ever longed for the Approach of Day with more Impatience than he did. At last it came; but how great was his Disappointment, when by the Noises he heard in the Street, the Hurry of the Coaches, and the Cries of Penny-Merchants, he was convinced it was Night no where but with him? He was still in the same Darkness as before; for she had taken care to blind the Windows in such a manner, that not the least Chink was left to let in Day. – He complained of her Behaviour in Terms that she would not have been able to resist yielding to, if she had not been certain it would have been the Ruin of her Passion: – She, therefore, answered him only as she had done before; and getting out of the Bed from him, flew out of the Room with too much Swiftness for him to have overtaken her, if he had attempted it. The Moment she left him, the two Attendants entered the Chamber, and plucking down the Implements which had screened him from the Knowledge of that which he so much desired to find out, restored his Eyes once more to Day: – They

Notes

[19] *affection* affectation.

attended to assist him in Dressing, brought him Tea, and by their Obsequiousness, let him see there was but one Thing which the Mistress of them would not gladly oblige him in. – He was so much out of Humour, however, at the Disappointment of his Curiosity, that he resolved never to make a second Visit. – Finding her in an outer Room, he made no Scruples of expressing the Sense he had of the little Trust she reposed in him, and at last plainly told her, he could not submit to receive Obligations from a Lady, who thought him incapable of keeping a Secret, which she made no Difficulty of letting her Servants into. – He resented, – he once more entreated, – he said all that Man could do, to prevail on her to unfold the Mystery; but all his Adjurations were fruitless; and he went out of the House determined never to re-enter it, till she should pay the Price of his Company with the Discovery of her Face and Circumstances. – She suffered him to go with this Resolution, and doubted not but he would recede from it, when he reflected on the happy Moments they had passed together; but if he did not, she comforted herself with the Design of forming some other Stratagem, with which to impose on him a fourth Time.

She kept the House, and her Gentlemen-Equipage[20] for about a Fortnight, in which Time she continued to write to him as *Fantomina* and the Widow *Bloomer*, and received the Visits he sometimes made to each; but his Behaviour to both was grown so cold, that she began to grow as weary of receiving his now insipid Caresses as he was of offering them: She was beginning to think in what Manner she should drop these two Characters, when the sudden Arrival of her Mother, who had been some Time in a foreign Country, obliged her to put an immediate Stop to the Course of her whimsical Adventures. – That Lady, who was severely virtuous, did not approve of many Things she had been told of the Conduct of her Daughter; and though it was not in the Power of any Person in the World to inform her of the Truth of what she had been guilty of, yet she heard enough to make her keep her afterwards in a Restraint, little agreeable to her Humour, and the Liberties to which she had been accustomed.

But this Confinement was not the greatest Part of the Trouble of this now afflicted Lady: She found the Consequences of her amorous Follies would be, without almost a Miracle, impossible to be concealed: – She was with Child; and though she would easily have found Means to have screened even this from the Knowledge of the World, had she been at liberty to have acted with the same unquestionable Authority over herself, as she did before the coming of her Mother, yet now all her Invention was at a Loss for a Stratagem to impose on a Woman of her Penetration: – By eating little, lacing prodigious strait, and the Advantage of a great Hoop-Petticoat, however, her Bigness was not taken notice of, and, perhaps, she would not have been suspected till the Time of her going into the Country, where her Mother designed to send her, and from whence she intended to make her escape to some Place where she might be delivered with Secrecy, if the Time of it had not happened much sooner than she expected. – A Ball being at Court, the good Old Lady was willing she should partake of the Diversion of it as a Farewell to the Town. – It was there she was seized with those Pangs, which none in her Condition are exempt from: – She could not conceal the sudden Rack which all at once invaded her; or had her Tongue been mute, her wildly rolling Eyes, the Distortion of her Features, and the Convulsions which shook her whole Frame, in spite of her, would have revealed she laboured under some terrible Shock of Nature. – Every Body was surprised, every Body was concerned, but few

Notes

[20] *Equipage* "Attendance, retinue" (Johnson).

guessed at the Occasion. – Her Mother grieved beyond Expression, doubted not but she was struck with the Hand of Death; and ordered her to be carried Home in a Chair, while herself followed in another. – A Physician was immediately sent for: But he presently perceiving what was her Distemper, called the old Lady aside, and told her, it was not a Doctor of his Sex, but one of her own, her Daughter stood in need of. – Never was Astonishment and Horror greater than that which seized the Soul of this afflicted Parent at these Words: She could not for a Time believe the Truth of what she heard; but he insisting on it, and conjuring her to send for a Midwife, she was at length convinced of it. – All the Pity and Tenderness she had been for some Moment before possessed of, now vanished, and were succeeded by an adequate Shame and Indignation: – She flew to the Bed where her Daughter was lying, and telling her what she had been informed of, and which she was now far from doubting, commanded her to reveal the Name of the Person whose Insinuations had drawn her to this Dishonour. – It was a great while before she could be brought to confess any Thing, and much longer before she could be prevailed on to name the Man whom she so fatally had loved; but the Rack of Nature growing more fierce, and the enraged old Lady protesting no Help should be afforded her while she persisted in her Obstinancy, she, with great Difficulty and Hesitation in her Speech, at last pronounced the Name of *Beauplaisir*. She had no sooner satisfied her weeping Mother, than that sorrowful Lady sent Messengers at the same Time, for a Midwife, and for that Gentleman who had occasioned the other's being wanted. – He happened by Accident to be at home, and immediately obeyed the Summons, though prodigiously surprised what Business a Lady so much a Stranger to him could have to impart. – But how much greater was his Amazement, when taking him into her Closet, she there acquainted him with her Daughter's Misfortune, of the Discovery she had made, and how far he was concerned in it? – All the Idea one can form of wild Astonishment, was mean to what he felt: – He assured her, that the young Lady her Daughter was a Person whom he had never, more than at a Distance, admired: – That he had indeed, spoke to her in public Company, but that he never had a Thought which tended to her Dishonour. – His Denials, if possible, added to the Indignation she was before inflamed with: – She had no longer Patience; and carrying him into the Chamber, where she was just delivered of a fine Girl, cried out, I will not be imposed on: The Truth by one of you shall be revealed. ——*Beauplaisir* being brought to the Bed side, was beginning to address himself to the Lady in it, to beg she would clear the Mistake her Mother was involved in; when she, covering herself with the Clothes, and ready to die a second Time with the inward Agitations of her Soul, shrieked out, 'Oh, I am undone! – I cannot live, and bear this Shame!' – But the old Lady believing that now or never was the Time to dive into the Bottom of this Mystery, forcing her to rear her Head, told her, she should not hope to Escape the Scrutiny of a Parent she had dishonoured in such a Manner, and pointing to *Beauplaisir*, 'Is this the Gentleman', said she, 'to whom you owe your Ruin? or have you deceived me by a fictitious Tale?'

'Oh! no', resumed the trembling Creature, 'he is, indeed, the innocent Cause of my Undoing: – Promise me your Pardon', continued she, 'and I will relate the Means'. Here she ceased, expecting what she would reply, which, on hearing *Beauplaisir* cry out, 'What mean you Madam? I your Undoing, who never harboured the least Design on you in my Life', she did in these Words, 'Though the Injury you have done your Family', said she, 'is of a Nature which cannot justly hope Forgiveness, yet be assured, I shall much sooner excuse you when satisfied of the Truth, than while I am kept in a Suspense, if possible, as vexatious as the Crime itself is to me'. Encouraged by this she related the whole Truth. And 'tis difficult to determine, if *Beauplaisir*, or the Lady, were most surprised at what they heard; he, that he should have been blinded so often by her Artifice; or she, that so young a Creature should have the Skill to make use of them. Both sat for some Time in a profound Reverie; till at length she broke it first in these Words: 'Pardon, Sir', said she, 'the Trouble I have given you: I must confess it was with a Design to oblige you to repair the supposed Injury you had done this unfortunate Girl, by marrying her, but now I know not what to say; – The Blame is wholly hers, and I have nothing to request further of you, than that you will not divulge the distracted Folly she has been guilty of'. – He answered her in Terms perfectly polite; but made no Offer of that which, perhaps, she expected, though could not, now informed of her Daughter's Proceedings, demand. He assured her, however, that if she would commit the new-born Lady to his Care, he would discharge it faithfully. But neither of them would consent to that; and he took his Leave, full of Cogitations, more confused than ever he had known in his whole Life. He continued to visit there, to enquire after her Health every Day; but the old Lady perceiving there was nothing likely to ensue from these Civilities, but, perhaps, a Renewing of the Crime, she entreated him to refrain; and as soon as her Daughter was in a Condition, sent her to a Monastery in *France*, the Abbess of which had been her particular Friend. And thus ended an Intrigue, which, considering the Time it lasted, was as full of Variety as any, perhaps, that many Ages has produced.

FINIS

James Thomson (1700–1748)

Like many other poets in the eighteenth century, Thomson left home to seek fame and fortune in London. He arrived from Edinburgh, as Samuel Johnson reports in his biography, in need of a pair of shoes and with no capital except the manuscript of his poem *Winter*. He finally found a publisher willing to take the manuscript for £3, and he published it in 1726 with a dedication to a prospective patron. Through the help of friends, the patron was alerted that his help had been solicited, and Thomson received a "present" of £20. On the heels of this windfall came widespread popular excitement over Thomson's poem. He produced poems on the other seasons, and all four poems together became *The Seasons*, one of the most successful publications of the century, and one of the few that suffered no loss of reputation after the "Romantic revolution" that ushered in the new aesthetic of the nineteenth century. In fact, Thomson has often been seen as a precursor of that revolution in taste.

Thomson wrote several plays, a long historical poem called *Liberty* (1735), and two cantos of a verse romance in the manner of Edmund Spenser called *The Castle of Indolence* (1748), but his reputation rests on *The Seasons*. I have chosen the first part of that poem to be printed and its first edition. It is considerably shorter than Thomson's final revision of the poem, perhaps less carefully connected, and certainly less correct. However, as Johnson said, adopting a metaphor from wine-tasting, the "race" of Thomson's verse, its own unique quality, is most clear in the original version. In choosing blank verse over heroic couplets and in representing the effects on the mind of grand natural events, Thomson sought to ally himself with epic poets, especially "the British Muse," Milton.

The standard edition of *The Seasons* is edited by James Sambrook (Clarendon Press, 1980), who has also written his biography (Clarendon Press, 1991).

Winter. A Poem (1726)

See! Winter comes, to rule the varied Year,
Sullen, and sad; with all his rising Train,[1]
Vapours, and *Clouds*, and *Storms*: Be these my Theme,
These, that exalt the Soul to solemn Thought,
And heavenly musing. Welcome kindred Glooms!
Wished, wintry, Horrors, hail! – With frequent Foot,
Pleased, have I, in my cheerful Morn of Life,
When, nursed by careless *Solitude*, I lived,
And sung of Nature with unceasing Joy,
Pleased, have I wandered through your rough Domains;
Trod the pure, virgin, Snows, my self as pure:
Heard the Winds roar, and the big Torrent burst:
Or seen the deep, fermenting, Tempest brewed,

Notes

WINTER. A POEM
[1] *sad* serious.

British Literature 1640–1789: An Anthology, Fourth Edition. Edited by Robert DeMaria, Jr.

In the red, evening, Sky. – Thus passed the Time,
Till, through the opening Chambers of the South,
Looked out the joyous *Spring*, looked out, and smiled.
   Thee too, Inspirer of the toiling Swain!
Fair AUTUMN, yellow-robed! I'll sing of thee,
Of thy last, tempered, Days, and sunny Calms;
When all the golden *Hours* are on the Wing,[2]
Attending thy Retreat, and round thy Wain,[3]
Slow-rolling, onward to the Southern Sky.
   Behold! the well-poised *Hornet*, hovering, hangs,
With quivering Pinions, in the genial Blaze;[4]
Flies off, in airy Circles: then returns,
And hums, and dances to the beating Ray.
Nor shall the Man, that, musing, walks alone,
And, heedless, strays within his radiant Lists,[5]
Go unchastised away. – Sometimes, a Fleece
Of Clouds, wide-scattering, with a lucid Veil,[6]
Soft, shadow o'er th' unruffled Face of Heaven;
And, through their dewy Sluices, shed the Sun,
With tempered Influence down. Then is the Time,
For those, whom *Wisdom*, and whom *Nature* charm,
To steal themselves from the degenerate Crowd,
And soar above this *little* Scene of Things:
To tread low-thoughted *Vice* beneath their Feet:
To lay their Passions in a gentle Calm,
And woo lone *Quiet*, in her silent *Walks*.
   Now, solitary, and in pensive Guise,
Oft, let me wander o'er the russet Mead,[7]
Or through the pining Grove; where scarce is heard
One dying Strain, to cheer the *Woodman*'s Toil:
Sad *Philomel*,[8] perchance, pours forth her Plaint,
Far, through the withering Copse. Mean while, the Leaves,
That, late, the Forest clad with lively Green,
Nipped by the drizzly Night, and Sallow hued,
Fall, wavering, through the Air; or shower amain,[9]
Urged by the Breeze, that sobs amid the Boughs.
Then list'ning *Hares* forsake the rustling Woods,
And, starting at the frequent Noise, escape
To the rough Stubble, and the rushy Fen.
The *Woodcocks*, o'er the fluctuating Main,
That glimmers to the Glimpses of the Moon,
Stretch their long Voyage to the woodland Glade:[10]
Where, wheeling with uncertain Flight, they mock

Notes

[2] *the golden Hours* the Horae, goddesses of the seasons.
[3] *Wain* wagon; a name for Ursa Major or the Big Dipper.
[4] *genial* "That gives cheerfulness or supports life" (Johnson).
[5] *Lists* borders, but also the enclosed ground on which knights jousted.
[6] *lucid* made of light.
[7] *Mead* meadow.
[8] *Philomel* the nightingale, the bird into which Philomela is transformed when she flees from Tereus, who raped her and cut out her tongue (see Ovid, *Metamorphoses* 6.412–721).
[9] *amain* in full force.
[10] *Stretch* direct, steer.

The nimble *Fowler*'s Aim. – Now *Nature* droops;
Languish the living Herbs, with pale Decay:
And all the *various Family* of Flowers
Their sunny Robes resign. The falling Fruits,
Through the still Night, forsake the Parent-Bough,
That, in the first, grey, Glances of the Dawn,
Looks wild, and wonders at the wintry Waste.
The *Year*, yet pleasing, but declining fast,
Soft, o'er the secret Soul, in gentle Gales,[11]
A philosophic Melancholy breathes,
And bears the swelling Thought aloft to Heaven.
The forming *Fancy* rouses to conceive,
What never mingled with the Vulgar's Dream:[12]
Then wake the tender *Pang*, the pitying *Tear*,
The *Sigh* for suffering Worth, the *Wish* preferred[13]
For Humankind, the *Joy* to see them blessed,
And all the *Social Off-spring* of the Heart!
Oh! bear me then to high, embowering, Shades;
To twilight Groves, and visionary Vales;
To weeping Grottos, and to hoary Caves;
Where Angel-Forms are seen, and Voices heard,
Sighed in low Whispers, that abstract the Soul,
From outward Sense, far into Worlds remote.
Now, when the Western Sun withdraws the Day,
And humid *Evening*, gliding o'er the Sky,
In her chill Progress, checks the straggling Beams,
And robs them of their gathered, vapoury, Prey,
Where Marshes stagnate, and where Rivers wind,
Cluster the rolling *Fogs*, and swim along
The dusky-mantled Lawn: then slow descend,
Once more to mingle with their *Wat'ry Friends*.
The vivid Stars shine out, in radiant Files;
And boundless *Ether* glows, till the fair Moon[14]
Shows her broad Visage, in the crimsoned East;
Now, stooping, seems to kiss the passing Cloud:
Now, o'er the pure *Cerulean*, rides sublime.[15]
Wide the pale Deluge floats, with silver Waves,
O'er the sky'd Mountain, to the low-laid Vale;[16]
From the white Rocks, with dim Reflection, gleams,
And faintly glitters through the waving Shades.
All Night, abundant Dews, unnoted, fall,
And, at Return of Morning, silver o'er
The Face of Mother-Earth; from every Branch
Depending, tremble the translucent Gems,[17]

Notes

11 *Gale* "A wind not tempestuous, yet stronger than a breeze" (Johnson).
12 *Vulgar* common folk.
13 *prefer* "To offer solemnly" (Johnson), as a prayer.
14 *Ether* "The matter of the highest regions above" (Johnson).
15 *Cerulean* the blue of the sky.
16 *sky'd* "Enveloped by the skies. This is unusual and unauthorized" (Johnson, citing this passage).
17 *Depending* hanging.

And, quivering, seem to fall away, yet cling,
And sparkle in the Sun, whose rising Eye,
With Fogs bedimmed, portends a beauteous Day.
   Now, giddy Youth, whom headlong Passions fire,
Rouse the wild Game, and stain the guiltless Grove,
With Violence, and Death; yet call it Sport,
To scatter Ruin through the Realms of *Love*,
And *Peace*, that thinks no Ill: But These, the *Muse*,
Whose Charity, unlimited, extends
As wide as *Nature* works, disdains to sing,
Returning to her nobler Theme in view –
   For, see! where *Winter* comes, himself, confessed,[18]
Striding the gloomy Blast. First Rains obscure
Drive through the mingling Skies, with Tempest foul;
Beat on the Mountain's Brow, and shake the Woods,
That, sounding, wave below. The dreary Plain
Lies overwhelmed, and lost. The bellying Clouds
Combine, and deepening into Night, shut up
The Day's fair Face. The Wanderers of Heaven,[19]
Each to his Home, retire; save those that love
To take their Pastime in the troubled Air,
And, skimming, flutter round the dimply Flood.
The Cattle, from th' untasted Fields, return,
And ask, with Meaning low, their wonted Stalls;[20]
Or ruminate in the contiguous Shade:[21]
Thither, the household, feathery, People crowd,[22]
The crested Cock, with all his female Train,
Pensive, and wet. Mean while, the Cottage-Swain
Hangs o'er th' enlivening Blaze, and taleful, there,
Recounts his simple Frolic: Much he talks,
And much he laughs, nor recks the Storm that blows[23]
Without, and rattles on his humble Roof.
   At last, the muddy Deluge pours along,
Resistless, roaring; dreadful down it comes
From the chapped Mountain, and the mossy Wild,[24]
Tumbling through Rocks abrupt, and sounding far:[25]
Then o'er the sanded Valley, floating, spread,[26]
Calm, sluggish, silent; till again constrained,
Betwixt two meeting Hills, it bursts a Way,
Where Rocks, and Woods o'erhang the turbid Stream.
There gathering triple Force, rapid, and deep,
It boils, and wheels, and foams, and thunders through.

Notes

[18] *confessed* openly appearing.
[19] *Wanderers of Heaven* birds.
[20] *low* bellow of a cow.
[21] *ruminate* chew the cud.
[22] *People* "those who compose a community" (Johnson).
[23] *recks* minds.
[24] *chapped* cleft.
[25] *abrupt* "Broken; craggy" (Johnson).
[26] *sanded* covered with sand or silt.

Nature! great Parent! whose directing Hand
Rolls round the Seasons of the changeful Year,
How mighty! how majestic are thy Works!
With what a pleasing Dread they swell the Soul,
That sees, astonished! and, astonished sings!
You too, ye *Winds*! that now begin to blow,
With boisterous Sweep, I raise my Voice to you.
Where are your Stores, ye viewless *Beings*! say?
Where your aerial Magazines reserved,
Against the Day of Tempest perilous?
In what untravelled Country of the Air, –
Hushed in still Silence, sleep you, when 'tis calm?
Late, in the louring Sky, red, fiery, Streaks[27]
Begin to flush about; the reeling Clouds[28]
Stagger with dizzy Aim, as doubting yet
Which Master to obey: while rising, slow,
Sad, in the Leaden-coloured East, the Moon
Wears a bleak Circle round her sullied Orb.
Then issues forth the Storm, with loud Control,[29]
And the thin Fabric of the pillared Air[30]
O'erturns, at once. Prone, on th' uncertain Main,
Descends th' Ethereal Force, and ploughs its Waves,
With dreadful Rift: from the mid-Deep, appears,
Surge after Surge, the rising, wat'ry, War.
Whitening, the angry Billows roll immense,
And roar their Terrors, through the shuddering Soul
Of feeble Man, amidst their Fury caught,
And, dashed upon his Fate: Then, o'er the Cliff,
Where dwells the *Sea-Mew*, unconfined, they fly,[31]
And, hurrying, swallow up the sterile Shore.
The Mountain growls; and all its sturdy *Sons*[32]
Stoop to the Bottom of the Rocks they shade:
Lone, on its Midnight-Side, and all aghast,
The dark, way-faring, *Stranger*, breathless, toils,
And climbs against the Blast –
Low, waves the rooted Forest, vexed, and sheds
What of its leafy Honours yet remains.
Thus, struggling through the dissipated Grove,
The whirling Tempest raves along the Plain;
And, on the Cottage thatched, or lordly Dome,[33]
Keen-fastening, shakes 'em to the solid Base.
Sleep, frighted, flies; the hollow Chimney howls,
The Windows rattle, and the Hinges creak.
Then, too, they say, through all the burthened Air,
Long Groans are heard, shrill Sounds, and distant Sighs

Notes

27 *louring* "dark, stormy, and gloomy" (Johnson).

28 *flush* "To glow in the skin; to produce a colour in the face" (Johnson).

29 *Control* power.

30 *Fabric* building.

31 *Sea-Mew* "A fowl that frequents the sea" (Johnson).

32 *sturdy Sons* trees.

33 *Dome* "A building; a house; a fabric" (Johnson).

That, murmured by the *Demon* of the Night,
Warn the devoted *Wretch* of Woe, and Death![34]
Wild Uproar lords it wide: the Clouds commixed,
With Stars, swift-gliding, sweep along the Sky.
All Nature reels. – But hark! the *Almighty* speaks:
Instant, the chidden Storm begins to pant,
And dies, at once, into a noiseless Calm.
  As yet, 'tis Midnight's Reign; the weary Clouds
Slow-meeting, mingle into solid Gloom:
Now, while the drowsy World lies lost in Sleep,
Let me associate with the low-browed *Night*,[35]
And *Contemplation*, her sedate Compeer;
Let me shake off th' intrusive Cares of Day,
And lay the meddling Senses all aside.
  And now, ye lying *Vanities* of Life!
You ever-tempting, ever-cheating Train!
Where are you now? and what is your Amount?
Vexation, Disappointment, and Remorse.
Sad, sickening, Thought! and yet, deluded Man,
A Scene of wild, disjointed, Visions past,
And broken Slumbers, rises, still resolved,
With new-flushed Hopes, to run your giddy Round.
  Father of Light, and Life! Thou *Good Supreme*!
O! teach me what is Good! teach me thy self!
Save me from Folly, Vanity and Vice,
From every low Pursuit! and feed my Soul,
With Knowledge, conscious Peace, and Virtue pure,
Sacred, substantial, never-fading Bliss![36]
  Lo! from the livid East, or piercing North,
Thick Clouds ascend, in whose capacious Womb,
A vapoury Deluge lies, to Snow congealed:
Heavy, they roll their fleecy World along;
And the Sky saddens with th' impending Storm.
Through the hushed Air, the whitening Shower descends,
At first, thin-wavering; till, at last, the Flakes
Fall broad, and wide, and fast, dimming the Day,
With a continual Flow. See! sudden, hoared,
The Woods beneath the stainless Burden bow,
Black'ning, along the mazy Stream it melts;
Earth's universal Face, deep-hid, and chill,
Is all one, dazzling, Waste. The Labourer-Ox
Stands covered o'er with Snow, and then demands
The Fruit of all his Toil. The Fowls of Heaven,
Tamed by the cruel Season, crowd around
The winnowing Store, and claim the little Boon,[37]

Notes

[34] *devoted* cursed, doomed to destruction.
[35] *low-browed* louring, gloomy.
[36] *substantial* "Real; actually existing" (Johnson).
[37] *winnowing Store* the stored grain being winnowed by the wind.

That *Providence* allows. The foodless Wilds
Pour forth their brown *Inhabitants*; the Hare,
Though timorous of Heart, and hard beset
By death, in various Forms, dark Snares, and Dogs,
And more unpitying Men, the Garden seeks,
Urged on by *fearless* Want. The bleating Kind
Eye the bleak Heavens, and next, the glistening Earth,
With Looks of dumb Despair; then sad, dispersed,
Dig, for the withered Herb, through Heaps of Snow.
Now, *Shepherds*, to your helpless Charge be kind;
Baffle the raging Year, and fill their Pens
With Food, at will: lodge them below the Blast,
And watch them strict; for from the bellowing East,
In this dire Season, oft the Whirlwind's Wing
Sweeps up the Burthen of whole wintry Plains,
In one fierce Blast, and o'er th' unhappy Flocks,
Lodged in the Hollow of two neighbouring Hills,
The billowy Tempest whelms; till, upwards urged,
The Valley to a shining Mountain swells,
That curls its Wreaths amid the freezing Sky.[38]
Now, all amid the Rigours of the Year,
In the wild Depth of Winter, while without
The ceaseless Winds blow keen, be my Retreat
A rural, sheltered, solitary, Scene;
Where ruddy Fire, and beaming Tapers join
To chase the cheerless Gloom: there let me sit,
And hold high Converse with the mighty Dead.[39]
Sages of ancient Time, as Gods revered,
As Gods beneficent, who blessed Mankind,
With Arts, and Arms, and humanized a World.
Roused at th' inspiring Thought – I throw aside
The long-lived Volume, and, deep-musing, hail[40]
The sacred *Shades*, that, slowly-rising, pass
Before my wondering Eyes – First, *Socrates*,
Truth's early Champion, Martyr for his God:[41]
Solon, the next, who built his Commonweal,[42]
On Equity's firm Base: *Lycurgus*, then,[43]
Severely good, and him of rugged *Rome*,
Numa, who softened *her* rapacious *Sons*.[44]
Cimon sweet-souled, and *Aristides* just.[45]

Notes

38 *Wreaths* Scottish, "snowdrifts."

39 *Converse with the mighty Dead* a conventional description of reading.

40 *long-lived Volume* Plutarch's *Parallel Lives* of Greeks and Romans; Plutarch wrote about all the heroes whom Thomson praises.

41 *Martyr for his God* perhaps Platonic dialogues like *Parmenides* and *Socrates' Apology* were read as showing that Socrates was a monotheist and a prototype of Moses; he is important in Plutarch's life of Alcibiades.

42 *Solon* (639–559 BCE), great Athenian lawmaker.

43 *Lycurgus* legendary Spartan lawgiver.

44 *Numa* Numa Pompilius, legendary second King of Rome.

45 *Cimon* Athenian general and statesman of the fifth century BCE; *Aristides* great Athenian general of the early fifth century BCE.

Unconquered *Cato*, virtuous in Extreme;[46]
With that attempered Hero, mild, and firm,[47]
Who wept the Brother, while the Tyrant bled.
Scipio, the humane Warrior, gently brave,[48]
Fair Learning's Friend; who early sought the Shade,
To dwell, with *Innocence*, and *Truth*, retired.
And, equal to the best, the *Theban*, He[49]
Who, *single*, raised his Country into Fame.
Thousands behind, the Boast of *Greece* and *Rome*,
Whom *Virtue* owns, the Tribute of a Verse
Demand, but who can count the Stars of Heaven?
Who sing their Influence on this lower World?
But see who yonder comes! nor comes alone,
With *sober* State, and of *majestic* Mien,
The Sister-Muses in his Train – 'Tis He!
Maro! the best of Poets, and of Men![50]
Great *Homer* too appears, of *daring* Wing!
Parent of Song! and, *equal*, by his Side,
The *British Muse*, joined Hand in Hand, they walk,[51]
Darkling, nor miss their Way to Fame's Ascent.[52]
  Society divine! Immortal Minds!
Still visit thus my Nights, for *you* reserved,
And mount my soaring Soul to Deeds like yours.
Silence! thou lonely *Power*! the Door be thine:
See, on the hallowed Hour, that none intrude,
Save *Lycidas*, the Friend, with Sense refined,[53]
Learning digested well, exalted Faith,
Unstudied Wit, and Humour ever gay.
  Clear Frost succeeds, and through the blue Serene,
For Sight too fine, th' Ethereal Nitre flies,[54]
To bake the Glebe, and bind the slipp'ry Flood.[55]
This of the wintry Season is the Prime;
Pure are the Days, and lustrous are the Nights,
Brightened with starry Worlds, till then unseen.
Meanwhile, the Orient, darkly red, breathes forth
An Icy Gale, that, in its mid Career,
Arrests the bickering Stream. The nightly Sky,

Notes

[46] *Cato* Cato Uticensis, first-century BCE Roman general and statesman who killed himself rather than submit to the conquering Julius Caesar.

[47] *that attempered Hero* Timoleon [d. 337 BCE] killed his brother when he tried to usurp the government of Corinth; expelled Roman tyrants from the Greek cities of Sicily and ruled well in their stead [Thomson's note].

[48] *Scipio* Scipio Africanus, third-century BCE Roman general who defeated Hannibal; popular support defeated an attempt by political enemies to prosecute him seventeen years later to the day; but after that he retired to his country estate.

[49] *Theban* Pelopidas or Epaminondas, fourth-century BCE friends who expelled the Spartans from Thebes (Thomson changed "Theban, He" to "Theban pair" in later versions of the poem and indicated whom he meant in a footnote; see edition of 1746, l. 479).

[50] *Maro* Virgil's surname.

[51] *British Muse* Milton.

[52] *Darkling* because they were blind.

[53] *Lycidas* the title of Milton's famous elegy (1638); the friend from whom the poet takes inspiration.

[54] *Nitre* a salt thought to be borne by the north wind, impressing coldness on what it touched.

[55] *Glebe* soil.

And all her glowing Constellations pour
Their rigid Influence down: It freezes on[56]
Till Morn, late-rising, o'er the drooping World,
Lifts her pale Eye, unjoyous: then appears
The various Labour of the silent Night,
The pendant Icicle, the Frost-Work fair,
Where thousand Figures rise, the crusted Snow,
Tho' white, made whiter, by the fining North.[57]
On blithesome Frolics bent, the youthful Swains,
While every Work of Man is laid at Rest,
Rush o'er the watry Plains, and, shuddering, view
The fearful Deeps below: or with the Gun,
And faithful Spaniel, range the ravaged Fields,
And, adding to the Ruins of the Year,
Distress the Feathery, or the Footed *Game*.

But hark! the nightly Winds, with hollow Voice,
Blow, blustering, from the South – the Frost subdued,
Gradual, resolves into a weeping Thaw.[58]
Spotted, the Mountains shine: loose Sleet descends,
And floods the Country round: the Rivers swell,
Impatient for the Day. – Those sullen Seas,
That wash th' ungenial Pole, will rest no more,[59]
Beneath the Shackles of the mighty North;
But, rousing all their Waves, resistless heave, –
And hark! – the length'ning Roar, continuous, runs
Athwart the rifted Main; at once, it bursts,
And piles a thousand Mountains to the Clouds!
Ill fares the Bark, the Wretches' last Resort,[60]
That, lost amid the floating Fragments, moors
Beneath the Shelter of an Icy Isle;
While Night o'erwhelms the Sea, and Horror looks
More horrible. Can human Hearts endure
Th' assembled *Mischiefs*, that besiege them round:
Unlist'ning *Hunger*, fainting *Weariness*,
The *Roar* of Winds, and Waves, the *Crush* of Ice,
Now, ceasing, now, renewed, with louder Rage,
And bellowing round the Main: Nations remote,
Shook from their Midnight-Slumbers, deem they hear
Portentous Thunder, in the troubled Sky.
More to embroil the Deep, Leviathan,[61]
And his unwieldy Train, in horrid Sport,
Tempest the loosened Brine; while, through the Gloom,
Far, from the dire, unhospitable Shore,

Notes

[56] *Influence* "Power of celestial aspects operating upon terrestrial bodies and affairs" (Johnson).

[57] *fining* refining.

[58] *resolves* melts.

[59] *ungenial* "Not kind or favourable to nature" (Johnson).

[60] *Bark* a poetic name for a boat; the passage recalls *Paradise Lost* 1.203–8.

[61] *Leviathan* biblical sea-monster, the whale.

The Lion's Rage, the Wolf's sad Howl is heard,
And all the fell Society of Night.[62]
Yet, *Providence*, that ever-waking *Eye*
Looks down, with Pity, on the fruitless Toil
Of Mortals, lost to Hope, and *lights* them safe,
Through all this dreary Labyrinth of Fate.
'Tis done! – Dread WINTER has subdued the Year,
And reigns, tremendous, o'er the desert Plains!
How dead the Vegetable Kingdom lies!
How dumb the Tuneful! *Horror* wide extends
His solitary Empire. – Now, fond *Man*!
Behold thy pictured Life: pass some few Years,
Thy flow'ring SPRING, thy short-lived SUMMER's Strength,
Thy sober AUTUMN, fading into Age,
And pale, concluding, WINTER shuts thy Scene,
And shrouds *Thee* in the Grave – where now, are fled
Those Dreams of Greatness? those unsolid Hopes
Of Happiness? those Longings after Fame?
Those restless Cares? those busy, bustling Days?
Those Nights of secret Guilt? those veering Thoughts,
Flutt'ring 'twixt Good, and Ill, that shared thy Life?
All, now, are vanished! *Virtue*, sole, survives,
Immortal, Mankind's never-failing Friend,
His Guide to Happiness on high – and see!
'Tis come, the Glorious *Morn*! the second Birth
Of Heaven, and Earth! – awakening *Nature* hears
Th' Almighty Trumpet's Voice, and starts to Life,
Renewed, unfading. Now, th' Eternal *Scheme*,
That Dark Perplexity, that Mystic Maze,
Which Sight could never trace, nor Heart conceive,
To *Reason*'s Eye, refined, clears up apace.
Angels, and Men, astonished, pause – and dread
To travel through the Depths of Providence,
Untried, unbounded. Ye vain *Learned*! see,
And, prostrate in the Dust, adore that *Power*,
And *Goodness*, oft arraigned. See now the Cause,
Why conscious *Worth*, oppressed, in secret long
Mourned, unregarded: Why the *Good Man*'s Share
In Life, was Gall, and Bitterness of Soul:
Why the lone *Widow*, and her *Orphans*, pined,
In starving Solitude; while *Luxury*,
In Palaces, lay prompting her low Thought,
To form unreal Wants: why Heaven-born *Faith*,
And *Charity*, prime Grace! wore the *red* Marks
Of *Persecution*'s Scourge: why licensed *Pain*,
That cruel *Spoiler*, that embosomed *Foe*,

Notes

[62] *fell* cruel.

Embittered all our Bliss. Ye Good *Distressed*!
Ye Noble *Few*! that, here, unbending, stand
Beneath Life's Pressures – yet a little while,
And all your Woes are past. *Time* swiftly fleets,
And wished *Eternity*, approaching, brings
Life undecaying, Love without Allay,[63]
Pure flowing Joy, and Happiness sincere.

Notes

[63] *without Allay* undiminished; unstinting.

Stephen Duck (1705–1756)

By age fourteen Duck was a full-time agricultural laborer earning the equivalent in modern money of about £100 or $150 per week. By age twenty-five he was supporting a wife and three children. Around this time he began to teach himself how to read and write poetry. He got hold of Milton, Addison, Shakespeare, and Dryden, and soon he began writing verse himself. His fame spread from his native Wiltshire to Oxford, and then to Queen Caroline, who gave him a salary of about four times what he was making as a laborer. He became the keeper of her library in Richmond, and later was ordained a priest and appointed to a rectory in Surrey. Unfortunately, however, Duck became a victim of depression and drowned himself in a trout stream. He was known to his contemporaries as "the thresher poet" after his most famous poem "The Thresher's Labour." It was the main piece in *Poems on Several Subjects*, which ran to ten editions in a single year, 1730. My text is based on the sixth of these and represents a little over a third of the poem.

from *Poems on Several Subjects* (1730)

from The Thresher's Labour

But now the Field we must no longer range,
And yet, hard Fate! still Work for Work we change.
Back to the Barns again in haste we're sent,
Where lately so much Time we pensive spent:
Not pensive now; we bless the friendly Shade,
And to avoid the parching Sun are glad.
But few Days here we're destined to remain,
Before our Master calls us forth again:
'For Harvest now', says he, 'yourselves prepare,
The ripened Harvest now demands your Care.
Early next Morn I shall disturb your Rest,
Get all things ready, and be quickly dressed'.
Strict to his Word, scarce the next Dawn appears,
Before his hasty Summons fills our Ears.
Obedient to his Call, straight up we get,
And finding soon our Company complete;
With him, our Guide, we to the Wheat-Field go;
He, to appoint, and we, the Work to do.
Ye Reapers, cast your Eyes around the Field,
And view the Scene its different Beauties yield:
Then look again with a more tender Eye,
To think how soon it must in Ruin lie.
For once set in, where-e'er our Blows we deal,
There's no resisting of the well-whet Steel:
But here or there, where-e'er our Course we bend,
Sure Desolation does our Steps attend.
Thus, when *Arabia*'s Sons, in hopes of Prey,

British Literature 1640–1789: An Anthology, Fourth Edition. Edited by Robert DeMaria, Jr.

To some more fertile Country take their way;
How beauteous all things in the Morn appear,
There Villages, and pleasing Cots are here;[1]
So many pleasing Objects meet the Sight,
The ravished Eye could willing gaze till Night:
But long ere then, where'er their Troops have passed,
Those pleasant Prospects lie a gloomy Waste.
The Morning passed, we sweat beneath the Sun,
And but uneasily our Work goes on.
Before us we perplexing Thistles find,
And Corn blown adverse with the ruffling Wind:[2]
Behind our Backs the Female Gleaners wait,
Who sometimes stoop, and sometimes hold a Chat.
Each Morn we early rise, go late to Bed,
And lab'ring hard, a painful Life we lead:
For Toils, scarce ever ceasing, press us now,
Rest never does, but on the Sabbath show,
And barely that, our Master will allow.
Nor, when asleep, are we secure from Pain,
We then perform our Labours o'er again:
Our mimic Fancy always restless seems,
And what we act awake, she acts in Dreams.
Hard Fate! Our Labours ev'n in Sleep don't cease,
Scarce *Hercules* e'er felt such Toils as these.
At length in Rows stands up the well-dried Corn,
A grateful Scene, and ready for the Barn.
Our well-pleased Master views the Sight with joy,
And we for carrying all our Force employ.
Confusion soon o'er all the Field appears,
And stunning Clamours fill the Workmen's Ears;
The Bells, and clashing Whips, alternate sound,
And rattling Waggons thunder o'er the Ground.
The Wheat got in, the Peas, and other Grain,
Share the same Fate, and soon leave bare the Plain:
In noisy Triumph the last Load moves on,
The loud Huzzas proclaim the Harvest done.
Our Master joyful at the welcome Sight,
Invites us all to feast with him at Night.
A Table plentifully spread we find,
And Jugs of humming Beer to cheer the Mind;
Which he, too generous, pushes on so fast,
We think no Toils to come, nor mind the past.
But the next Morning soon reveals the Cheat,
When the same Toils we must again repeat:
To the same Barns again must back return,
To labour there for room for next Year's Corn.

Notes

FROM THE THRESHER'S LABOUR

1 *Cots* cottages.

2 *Corn* unreaped or unthreshed grain in general.

Thus, as the Year's revolving Course goes round,
No respite from our Labour can be found:
Like *Sisyphus*, our Work is never done,[3]
Continually rolls back the restless Stone:
Now growing Labours still succeed the past,
And growing always new, must always last.

Notes

[3] *Sisyphus* a figure in Greek mythology doomed forever to roll a rock unsuccessfully up a steep incline in Hades.

Mary Jones (1707–1778)

Jones lived all her life in Oxford, where late in life she became the postmistress. She had very little money or social standing. Her poverty is a subject in her poetry, but it fuels mostly comic rather than pathetic expressions of her lot in life. She associated with the Oxford professor Thomas Warton, and through him became friends with Samuel Johnson. She published one book, *Miscellanies in Prose and Verse* (1750), the first forty-six pages of which are devoted to listing the names of the subscribers. The following selections come from that lone volume.

from *Miscellanies in Prose and Verse* (1750)

Soliloquy, on an Empty Purse

Alas! my Purse! how lean and low!
My silken Purse! what art thou now!
Once I beheld – but stocks will fall –
When *both* thy ends had *wherewithal*.
When I within thy slender fence
My fortune placed, and confidence;
A poet's fortune! – not immense:
Yet, mixed with keys, and coins among,
Chinked to the melody of song.

Canst thou forget, when, high in air,
I saw thee flutt'ring at a fair?
And took thee, destined to be sold,
My lawful Purse, to *have* and *hold*?
Yet used so oft to disembogue,[1]
No prudence could thy fate prorogue.[2]
Like wax thy silver melted down,
Touch but the brass, and lo! 'twas gone:
And gold would never with thee stay,
For gold had wings, and flew away.

Alas! my Purse! yet still be proud,
For see the *Virtues* round thee crowd!
See, in the room of paltry wealth,[3]
Calm Temp'rance rise, the nurse of Health;

Notes

Soliloquy, on an Empty Purse

[1] *disembogue* to pour out; to flow.

[2] *prorogue* delay or protract.

[3] *room* place.

And Self-denial, slim and spare,
And Fortitude, with look severe;
And Abstinence, to leanness prone,
And Patience, worn to skin and bone:
Prudence and Foresight on thee wait,
And Poverty lies here in state!
Hopeless her spirits to recruit,[4]
For every Virtue is a mute.

Well then, my Purse, thy sabbaths keep;
Now thou art empty, I shall sleep.
No silver sounds shall thee molest,
Nor golden dreams disturb my breast.
Safe shall I walk the streets along,
Amidst temptations thick and strong;
Catched by the eye, no more shall stop
At *Wildey's* toys, or *Pinchbeck's* shop;[5]
Nor cheap'ning *Payne's* ungodly books,[6]
Be drawn aside by pastry cooks:
But fearless now we both may go
Where *Ludgate's* Mercers bow so low;[7]
Beholding all with equal eye,
Nor moved at – 'Madam, what d'ye buy?'
Away, far hence each worldly care!
Nor dun nor pick-purse shalt Thou fear,[8]
Nor flatt'rer base annoy My ear.
Snug shalt thou travel through the mob,
For who a Poet's purse will rob?
And softly sweet in garret high[9]
Will I thy virtues magnify;
Out-soaring flatt'rers' stinking breath,
And gently rhyming rats to death.

After the Small Pox

When skilful traders first set up,
To draw the people to their shop,
They straight hang out some gaudy sign,
Expressive of the goods within.

Notes

4 *recruit* "To repair any thing wasted by new supplies" (Johnson).

5 *toy* "A petty commodity" (Johnson), including makeup, fans, and other trifles for ladies; *Pinchbeck's shop* where clocks designed by Christopher Pinchbeck (1670?–1732) were sold by his son Edward (1713?–66?).

6 *cheap'ning* bargaining for; attempting to buy; *Payne* probably Thomas (1719–99), who succeeded his brother Oliver in 1739; the *Paynes* were among the first booksellers to issue catalogues and sell books at advertised prices, so "cheap'ning" has special emphasis here.

7 *Ludgate's Mercers* tradesmen in an area just west of the City where there was a minimum-security debtors' prison.

8 *dun* one who "claims a debt with vehemence and importunity" (Johnson).

9 *garret* "A room on the highest floor of a house" (Johnson), the cheapest room to rent.

The Vintner has his boy and grapes,
The Haberdasher thread and tapes,
The Shoemaker exposes boots,
And Monmouth Street old tattered suits,

So fares it with the nymph divine;
For what is Beauty but a Sign?
A face hung out, through which is seen
The nature of the goods within.
Thus the coquette her beau ensnares
With studied smiles, and forward airs:
The graver prude hangs out a frown
To strike th' audacious gazer down;
But she alone, whose temperate wit
Each nicer medium can hit,
Is still adorned with every grace,
And wears a sample in her face.

What though some envious folks have said,
That *Stella* now must hide her head,[1]
That all her stock of beauty's gone,
And ev'n the very sign took down;
Yet grieve not at the fatal blow;
For if you break a while, we know,[2]
'Tis bankrupt like, more rich to grow,
A fairer sign you'll soon hang up,
And with fresh credit open shop:
For nature's pencil soon shall trace,
And once more finish off your face,
Which all your neighbours shall outshine,
And of your Mind remain the Sign.

Her Epitaph

(Which the Author hopes will live as long as she does)

Here rests poor *Stella*'s restless part:
A riddle! but I loved her heart.
Through life she rushed a headlong wave,
And never slept, but in her grave.
Some wit, I think, and worth she had:
No saint indeed, nor yet quite mad;
But laughed, built castles, rhymed and sung,

Notes

AFTER THE SMALL POX
[1] *Stella* Jones's poetic name for herself.
[2] *break* "To become bankrupt" (Johnson, sense 7).

'Was everything, but nothing long'.[1]
Some honest truths she would let fall;
But much too wise to tell you all.

From thought to thought incessant hurled,
Her scheme was – but to rule the world.
At morn she won it with her eyes,
At night, when beauty sick'ning sighs,
Like the mad *Macedonian* cried,[2]
'What, no more worlds, ye Gods!' – and died.

Notes

Her Epitaph

[1] *"Was everything ... long"* a general reference to Pope's "Of the Characters of Women."

[2] *mad Macedonian* Alexander the Great.

Samuel Johnson (1709–1784)

Johnson was disfigured by scrofula (a form of tuberculosis), by the wounds made in treating it, by small-pox, and by nervous disorders that resembled Tourette's syndrome, but he was gifted with extraordinary mental powers. Through intellectual achievement he hoped to vault himself out of the confines of his middle-class home and the family business of bookselling in provincial Lichfield. He went to Oxford in 1728, but his financial and emotional resources lasted only thirteen months. After the death of his father in 1731 he realized he would have to make a living on his own. He nevertheless clung for some years to his adolescent dream of becoming a Latin poet-scholar and joining the European community of the learned that knew few boundaries of time or place. He was all his life an admirer of great humanists like Joseph Scaliger, and he hoped to perform in their league. But it was impossible to unite such dreams with the requirement that he earn a living. His failed attempt to publish by subscription an edition of Politian's Latin poetry gave Johnson an early indication of this fact. He turned to teaching, but his personal appearance was against him as much as his own inclination. In 1732 he went to Birmingham and began producing articles for the publisher of a newspaper who then commissioned him to write his first book, a translation of a Jesuit priest's narrative of his travels in Abyssinia.

Johnson's first book came out in 1735, the same year he married and attempted to establish his own boarding school. The academy at Edial was a failure, and Johnson went to London with David Garrick, one of his few pupils, to earn his living as a writer. He carried with him *Irene*, a learned tragedy, but he was unable to produce or publish this work until 1749. Instead, he sought the offices of Edward Cave, publisher of *The Gentleman's Magazine*. First publishing Latin verse in the monthly journal, Johnson went on to be its greatest contributor and virtual editor in the late 1730s. Among other things, he wrote book reviews and imaginative accounts of the debates in Parliament, which were not allowed to be reported at that time. Johnson and his publisher protected themselves from prosecution partly by printing the debates well after they occurred and by thinly disguising them as *Debates in the Senate of Magna Lilliput*. Meanwhile, Johnson also published *London* (1738), an "imitation" or adaptation of Juvenal's third satire, and began to make a name for himself as a learned writer.

Although he had written numerous short biographies and a longer *Life of Richard Savage* (1744), various translations, political pamphlets, a huge catalogue of the Harleian Library, and the specimen of an edition of Shakespeare, Johnson was still struggling in 1746 when he signed a contract with a syndicate of London booksellers to produce *A Dictionary of the English Language*. His advance allowed him to lease a couple of years later a large house in Gough Square. In this location beside Fleet Street Johnson produced the *Dictionary* (1755) as well as the periodical *The Rambler* (1750–2). He also published his most famous and greatest poem at this time, *The Vanity of Human Wishes* (1749). But the *Dictionary* was the turning point in Johnson's career, and in some ways its climax: it made him famous, though only temporarily well-heeled, and it represented an ingenious and satisfying compromise between his wish for traditional scholarly achievement and his need to earn money. The *Dictionary* is a work on a par with

British Literature 1640–1789: An Anthology, Fourth Edition. Edited by Robert DeMaria, Jr.

the great achievements of continental academies of learning and aspires to the greatness of the Latin and Greek dictionaries produced by Johnson's humanist heroes.

Johnson's wife Elizabeth died in 1752, and Johnson lived the rest of his life without an intimate companion. He formed close friendships, however, with many people: the most famous of these is his friendship with James Boswell, which led to the *Life of Samuel Johnson LL.D.* (1791); the closest was his friendship with Hester Thrale, which ended sadly in 1783 when, a few years after the death of her husband, she remarried. About 1755 Johnson courted a woman named Hill Boothby, but her life changed tragically and marriage became impossible. From 1755 to 1762 Johnson was again writing journalism and doing odd literary jobs to make ends meet. He was incensed by the Seven Years War (called the French and Indian War in America), and spoke out against it in *The Literary Magazine* (1756). He wrote *The Idler* (1758–61), an easier series of essays than *The Rambler*, and in 1759 he quickly contracted for and wrote *Rasselas*, to defray the costs of his mother's death.

In 1762, to the amazement and disgust of those who knew his anti-Hanoverian talk and journalism, Johnson received and accepted a pension from King George III. He was now secure with a living of £300 per year. It was a fixed income, however, and especially later in life, he had to augment it by writing for money. Partly from a sense of obligation to his government patrons, Johnson wrote four political pamphlets. His response to the American discontent in 1776, *Taxation no Tyranny*, is the source, along with Boswell's partial accounts, of Johnson being generally and incorrectly seen as a kind of arch-conservative. His politics contain elements of conservatism, but politically, and every other way, Johnson is complex. In 1765 Johnson produced his long-promised edition of *The Plays of William Shakespeare*, which includes both his own commentary and selections from those of earlier editors. Again Johnson brought to the more popular and financially viable project his proclivity for classical scholarship. He revised this work, as well as his *Dictionary*, for republication in 1773, whereupon he took his famous tour of Scotland with Boswell. Johnson published an account of his journey in 1775. His last major work was a series of introductions to a huge collection put together by a group of London publishers. Johnson's *Prefaces Biographical and Critical, to The Works of the English Poets* (1779–81) were collected and published separately as *The Lives of the Most Eminent English Poets*, 4 vols. (1781).

The Yale Edition of the Works of Samuel Johnson (1958–) is the standard, but even when all twenty-three volumes are completed, much that Johnson wrote (including the body of his *Dictionary*) or may have written, will still have to be sought elsewhere. The standard bibliography, the work of a lifetime for the late David Fleeman, has been published in two large volumes (Oxford University Press, 2000). My texts here are based on first editions, but I have benefited from the Yale volumes of the *Poems*, ed. E. L. MacAdam, Jr. (1964), *The Idler and Adventurer*, ed. W. J. Bate, John M. Bullit, and L. F. Powell (1963), *The Rambler*, ed. W. J. Bate and Albrecht Strauss (1969), *Johnson on Shakespeare*, ed. Arthur Sherbo (1968), *Rasselas*, ed. Gwin Kolb (1990), *Johnson on the English Language*, ed. Gwin Kolb and myself (2005), and *The Lives of the Poets*, ed. John H. Middendorf (2010). I have also reveled in the notes to Roger Lonsdale's edition of the *Lives* (Clarendon Press, 2006). There are many fine biographies of Johnson. W. J. Bate's *Samuel Johnson* (1977) is indispensable; despite its flaws, however, and the sometimes obnoxiously invasive personality of its author, Boswell's biography will always be the best. In the edition edited by G. B. Hill, revised by L. F. Powell, 6 vols. (Clarendon Press, 1934–64), there is no more essential reading for students of the eighteenth century.

from *The Life of Mr. Richard Savage, Son of the Earl of Rivers* (1744)[1]

It has been observed in all Ages, that the Advantages of Nature or of Fortune have contributed very little to the Promotion of Happiness; and that those whom the Splendour of their Rank or the Extent of their Capacity, have placed upon the Summits of human Life, have not often given any just Occasion to Envy in those who look up to them from a lower Station. Whether it be that apparent Superiority incites great Designs, and great Designs are naturally liable to fatal Miscarriages; or that the general Lot of Mankind is Misery, and the Misfortunes of those whose Eminence drew upon them an universal Attention have been more carefully recorded, because they were more generally observed, and have in reality been only more conspicuous than those of others, not more frequent, or more severe.

That Affluence and Power, Advantages extrinsic and adventitious, and therefore easily separable from those by whom they are possessed, should very often flatter the Mind with Expectation of Felicity which they cannot give, raises no Astonishment; but it seems rational to hope, that intellectual Greatness should produce better Effects, that Minds qualified for great Attainments should first endeavour their own Benefit; and that they who are most able to teach others the Way to Happiness should with most Certainty follow it themselves.

But this Expectation, however plausible, has been very frequently disappointed. The Heroes of literary as well as civil History have been very often no less remarkable for what they have suffered than for what they have achieved; and Volumes have been written only to enumerate the Miseries of the Learned, and relate their unhappy Lives and untimely Deaths.

To these mournful Narratives I am about to add the Life of *Richard Savage*, a Man whose Writings entitle him to an eminent Rank in the Classes of Learning, and whose Misfortunes claim a Degree of Compassion, not always due to the Unhappy, as they were often the Consequences of the Crimes of others rather than his own ….

He was now advancing in Reputation, and, though frequently involved in very distressful Perplexities, appeared however to be gaining upon Mankind, when both his Fame and his Life were endangered by an event, of which it is not yet determined, whether it ought to be mentioned as a Crime or a Calamity.

On the 20th of November 1727, Mr. *Savage* came from *Richmond*, where he then lodged, that he might pursue his Studies with less Interruption, with an Intent to discharge another Lodging which he had in *Westminster*, and accidentally meeting two Gentlemen, his Acquaintances, whose Names were *Merchant* and *Gregory*, he went in with them to a neighbouring Coffee-house, and sat drinking till it was late, it being in no Time of Mr. *Savage*'s Life any Part of his Character to be the first of the Company that desired to separate. He would willingly have gone to Bed in the same House; but there was not Room for the whole Company, and therefore they agreed to ramble about the Streets, and divert themselves with such Amusements as should offer themselves till Morning.

In their Walk they happened unluckily to discover Light in *Robinson*'s Coffee-house, near *Charing-Cross*, and therefore went in. *Merchant*, with some Rudeness,

Notes

FROM *THE LIFE OF MR. RICHARD SAVAGE*

[1] *Richard Savage* (1697/8–1743), a poet and playwright who claimed he was the illegitimate son of Richard Savage, fourth earl of Rivers and Lady Macclesfield; there is no evidence that his claim was just, but Johnson and many others believed him; see the official account of his trial for the murder of James Sinclair (p. 767 above).

demanded a Room, and was told that there was a good Fire in the next Parlour, which the Company were about to leave, being then paying their Reckoning. *Merchant*, not satisfied with this Answer, rushed into the Room, and was followed by his Companions. He then petulantly placed himself between the Company and the Fire, and soon after kicked down the Table. This produced a Quarrel, Swords were drawn on both Sides, and one Mr. *James Sinclair* was killed. *Savage* having wounded likewise a Maid that held him, forced his Way with *Merchant* out of the House; but being intimidated and confused, without Resolution either to fly or stay, they were taken in a back Court by one of the Company and some Soldiers, whom he had called to his Assistance.

Being secured and guarded that Night, they were in the Morning carried before three Justices, who committed them to the *Gate-house*, from whence, upon the Death of Mr. *Sinclair*, which happened the same Day, they were removed in the Night to *Newgate*, where they were however treated with some Distinction, exempted from the Ignominy of Chains, and confined, not among the common Criminals, but in the *Press-yard*.[2]

When the Day of Trial came, the Court was crowded in a very unusual Manner, and the Public appeared to interest itself as in a Cause of general Concern. The Witnesses against Mr. *Savage* and his Friends were, the Woman who kept the House, which was a House of ill Fame, and her Maid, the Men who were in the Room with Mr. *Sinclair*, and a Woman of the Town, who had been drinking with them, and with whom one of them had been seen in Bed. They swore in general, that *Merchant* gave the Provocation, which *Savage* and *Gregory* drew their Swords to justify; that *Savage* drew first, and that he stabbed *Sinclair* when he was not in a Posture of Defence, or while *Gregory* commanded his Sword; that after he had given the Thrust he turned pale, and would have retired, but that the Maid clung round him, and one of the Company endeavoured to detain him, from whom he broke, by cutting the Maid on the Head, but was afterwards taken in a Court.

There was some Difference in their Depositions; one did not see *Savage* give the Wound, another saw it given when *Sinclair* held his Point towards the Ground; and the Woman of the Town asserted, that she did not see *Sinclair*'s Sword at all: This Difference, however, was very far from amounting to Inconsistency, but it was sufficient to show, that the Hurry of the Quarrel was such, that it was not easy to discover the Truth with relation to particular Circumstances, and that therefore some Deductions were to be made from the Credibility of the Testimonies.

Sinclair had declared several times before his Death, that he received his Wound from *Savage*; nor did *Savage* at his Trial deny the Fact, but endeavoured partly to extenuate it by urging the Suddenness of the whole Action, and the Impossibility of any ill Design, or premeditated Malice, and partly to justify it by the Necessity of Self-Defence, and the Hazard of his own Life, if he had lost that Opportunity of giving the Thrust: He observed that neither Reason nor Law obliged a Man to wait for the Blow which was threatened, and which, if he should suffer it, he might never be able to return; that it was always allowable to prevent an Assault, and to preserve Life by taking away that of the Adversary, by whom it was endangered.

Notes

[2] *Press-yard* a place of confinement outside Newgate Prison, where punishments were inflicted.

With regard to the Violence with which he endeavoured to Escape, he declared, that it was not his Design to fly from Justice, or decline a Trial, but to avoid the Expenses and Severities of a Prison,[3] and that he intended to have appeared at the Bar without Compulsion.

This Defence, which took up more than an Hour, was heard by the Multitude that thronged the Court with the most attentive and respectful Silence: Those who thought he ought not to be acquitted owned that Applause could not be refused him; and those who before pitied his Misfortunes, now reverenced his Abilities.

The Witnesses which appeared against him were proved to be Persons of Characters which did not entitle them to much Credit: a common Strumpet, a Woman by whom Strumpets were entertained, and a Man by whom they were supported; and the Character of *Savage* was by several Persons of Distinction asserted to be that of a modest inoffensive Man, not inclined to Broils,[4] or to Insolence, and who had, to that Time, been only known for his Misfortunes and his Wit.

Had his Audience been his Judges, he had undoubtedly been acquitted; but Mr. *Page*, who was then upon the Bench, treated him with his usual Insolence and Severity, and when he had summed up the Evidence, endeavoured to exasperate the Jury, as Mr. *Savage* used to relate it, with this eloquent Harangue:

'Gentlemen of the Jury, you are to consider that Mr. *Savage* is a very great Man, a much greater Man than you or I, Gentlemen of the Jury; that he wears very fine Clothes, much finer Clothes than you or I, Gentlemen of the Jury; that he has Abundance of Money in his Pocket, much more Money than you or I, Gentlemen of the Jury; but, Gentlemen of the Jury, is it not a very hard Case, Gentlemen of the Jury, that Mr. *Savage* should therefore kill you or me, Gentlemen of the Jury?'

Mr. *Savage* hearing his defence thus misrepresented, and the Men who were to decide his Fate incited against him by invidious Comparisons, resolutely asserted that his Cause was not candidly explained, and began to recapitulate what he had before said with regard to his Condition, and the Necessity of endeavouring to escape the Expenses of Imprisonment; but the Judge, having ordered him to be silent, and repeated his Orders without Effect, commanded that he should be taken from the Bar by Force.

The Jury then heard the Opinion of the Judge, that good Characters were of no Weight against positive Evidence, though they might turn the Scale, where it was doubtful; and that though when two Men attack each other, the Death of either is only Manslaughter; but where one is the Aggressor, as in the Case before them, and, in Pursuance of his first Attack, kills the other, the Law supposes the Action, however sudden, to be malicious. They then deliberated upon their Verdict, and determined that Mr. *Savage* and Mr. *Gregory* were guilty of Murder, and Mr. *Merchant*, who had no Sword, only of Manslaughter. …

Mr. Savage had now no Hopes of Life, but from the Mercy of the Crown, which was very earnestly solicited by his Friends, and which, with whatever Difficulty the Story may obtain Belief, was obstructed only by his Mother.

To prejudice the Queen against him, she made use of an Incident, which was omitted in the order of Time, that it might be mentioned together with the purpose which it was made to serve. Mr. *Savage*, when he had discovered his Birth, had an incessant

Notes

[3] *Expenses … of a Prison* prisoners were expected to pay fees (called a garnish) to their jailers.

[4] *Broils* fights.

Desire to speak to his Mother, who always avoided him in public, and refused him Admission into her House. One Evening walking, as it was his Custom, in the Street that she inhabited, he saw the Door of her House by Accident open; he entered it, and, finding none in the Passage, to hinder him, went up Stairs to salute[5] her. She discovered him before he could enter her Chamber, alarmed the Family with the most distressful Outcries, and when she had by her Screams gathered them about her, ordered them to drive out of the House that Villain, who had forced himself in upon her, and endeavoured to murder her. *Savage*, who had attempted with the most submissive Tenderness to soften her Rage, hearing her utter so detestable an Accusation, thought it prudent to retire, and, I believe, never attempted afterwards to speak to her.

But, shocked as he was with her Falsehood and her Cruelty, he imagined that she intended no other Use of her Lie, than to set herself free from his Embraces and Solicitations, and was very far from suspecting that she would treasure it in her Memory, as an Instrument of future Wickedness, or that she would endeavour for this fictitious Assault to deprive him of his Life.

But when the Queen was solicited for his Pardon, and informed of the severe Treatments which he had suffered from his Judge, she answered, that however unjustifiable might be the Manner of his Trial, or whatever Extenuation the Action for which he was condemned might admit, she could not think that Man a proper Object of the King's Mercy, who had been capable of entering his Mother's House in the Night, with an Intent to murder her.

By whom this atrocious Calumny had been transmitted to the Queen, whether she that invented, had the Front to relate it; whether she found any one weak enough to credit it, or corrupt enough to concur with her in her hateful Design, I know not; but Methods had been taken to persuade the Queen so strongly of the Truth of it, that she for a long Time refused to hear any of those who petitioned for his Life.

Thus had *Savage* perished by the evidence of a Bawd, a Strumpet, and his Mother, had not Justice and Compassion procured him an Advocate of Rank too great to be rejected unheard, and of Virtue too eminent to be heard without being believed. His Merit and his Calamities happened to reach the ear of the Countess of *Hertford*, who engaged in his Support with all the Tenderness that is excited by Pity, and all the Zeal which is kindled by Generosity, and demanding an Audience of the Queen, laid before her the whole Series of his Mother's Cruelty, exposed the Improbability of an Accusation by which he was charged with an Intent to commit a Murder that could produce no Advantage, and soon convinced her how little his former Conduct could deserve to be mentioned as a Reason for extraordinary Severity.

The Interposition of this Lady was so successful, that he was soon after admitted to Bail, and, on the 9th of *March*, 1728, pleaded the King's Pardon.

It is natural to enquire upon what Motives his Mother could persecute him in a Manner so outrageous and implacable; for what Reason she could employ all the Acts of Malice, and all the Snares of Calumny, to take away the Life of her own Son, of a Son who never injured her, who was never supported by her Expense, nor obstructed any Prospect of Pleasure or Advantage; why she should endeavour to destroy him by a Lie – a Lie which could not gain Credit, but must vanish of itself at the first Moment of Examination, and of which only this can be said to make it probable, that it may be

Notes

5 *salute* greet.

observed from her Conduct, that the most execrable Crimes are sometimes committed without apparent Temptation.

This Mother is still alive, and may perhaps even yet, though her Malice was so often defeated, enjoy the Pleasure of reflecting that the Life, which she often endeavoured to destroy, was at least shortened by her maternal Offices; that though she could not transport her Son to the Plantations,[6] bury him in the Shop of a Mechanic,[7] or hasten the Hand of the public Executioner, she has yet had the Satisfaction of embittering all his Hours, and forcing him into Exigencies, that hurried on his Death.

It is by no Means necessary to aggravate the Enormity of this Woman's Conduct, by placing it in Opposition to that of the Countess of *Hertford*; no one can fail to observe how much more amiable it is to relieve, than to oppress, and to rescue Innocence from Destruction than to destroy without an Injury.

Mr. *Savage*, during his Imprisonment, his Trial, and the Time in which he lay under Sentence of Death, behaved with great Firmness and Equality of Mind, and confirmed by his Fortitude the Esteem of those, who before admired him for his Abilities. The peculiar Circumstances of his Life were made more generally known by a short Account, which was then published, and of which several thousands were in a few Weeks dispersed over the Nation; and the Compassion of Mankind operated so powerfully in his Favour, that he was enabled by frequent Presents, not only to support himself, but to assist Mr. *Gregory* in Prison; and when he was pardoned and released, he found the Number of his Friends not lessened.

The Nature of the Act for which he had been tried was in itself doubtful; of the Evidences which appeared against him, the Character of the Man was not unexceptionable, that of the Women notoriously infamous; she whose Testimony chiefly influenced the Jury to condemn him, afterwards retracted her Assertions. He always himself denied that he was drunk, as had been generally reported. Mr. *Gregory*, who is now Collector[8] of *Antigua*, is said to declare him far less criminal than he was imagined, even by some who favoured him: And *Page* himself afterwards confessed that he had treated him with uncommon Rigour. When all these Particulars are rated together, perhaps the Memory of Savage may not be much sullied by his Trial.

Some Time after he had obtained his Liberty he met in the Street the Woman who had sworn with so much malignity against him. She informed him, that she was in Distress, and, with a Degree of Confidence not easily attainable, desired him to relieve her. He, instead of insulting her Misery, and taking Pleasure in the Calamities of one who had brought his Life into Danger, reproved her gently for her Perjury, and changing the only Guinea that he had, divided it equally between her and himself.

This is an Action which in some Ages would have made a Saint, and perhaps in others a Hero, and which, without any hyperbolical Encomiums, must be allowed to be an Instance of uncommon Generosity, an Act of complicated Virtue; by which he at once relieved the Poor, corrected the Vicious, and forgave an Enemy; by which he at once remitted the strongest Provocations, and exercised the most ardent Charity. …

Notes

[6] *transport her Son to the Plantations* transportation to the colonies was a common substitute for execution in capital offenses.

[7] *Mechanic* manual laborer.

[8] *Collector* tax collector.

The Vanity of Human Wishes (1749)

The Tenth Satire of *Juvenal*, Imitated

Let Observation with extensive View,
Survey Mankind, from *China* to *Peru*;
Remark each anxious Toil, each eager Strife,
And watch the busy Scenes of crowded Life;
Then say how Hope and Fear, Desire and Hate,
O'erspread with Snares the clouded Maze of Fate,
Where wav'ring Man, betrayed by vent'rous Pride,
To tread the dreary Paths without a Guide;
As treach'rous Phantoms in the Mist delude,
Shuns fancied Ills, or chases airy Good.
How rarely Reason guides the stubborn Choice,
Rules the bold Hand, or prompts the suppliant Voice,
How Nations sink, by darling Schemes oppressed,
When Vengeance listens to the Fool's Request.
Fate wings with every Wish th' afflictive Dart,[1]
Each Gift of Nature, and each Grace of Art,
With fatal Heat impetuous Courage glows,
With fatal Sweetness Elocution flows,
Impeachment stops the Speaker's pow'rful Breath,
And restless Fire precipitates on Death.[2]
But scarce observed the Knowing and the Bold,
Fall in the gen'ral Massacre of Gold;
Wide-wasting Pest! that rages unconfined,
And crowds with Crimes the Records of Mankind,
For Gold his Sword the hireling Ruffian draws,
For Gold the hireling Judge distorts the Laws;
Wealth heaped on wealth, nor Truth nor Safety buys,[3]
The Dangers gather as the Treasures rise.
Let Hist'ry tell where rival Kings command,
And dubious Title shakes the madded Land,[4]
When Statutes glean the Refuse of the Sword,[5]
How much more safe the Vassal than the Lord,
Low skulks the Hind beneath the Rage of Pow'r,
And leaves the *bonny Traitor* in the *Tow'r*,[6]
Untouched his Cottage, and his Slumbers sound,
Though Confiscation's Vultures clang around.
The needy Traveller, serene and gay,
Walks the wild Heath, and sings his Toil away.
Does Envy seize thee? crush th' upbraiding Joy,

Notes

THE VANITY OF HUMAN WISHES

1 *wing* "To furnish with wings; to enable to fly" (Johnson).

2 *precipitate on* "To hasten without just preparation" (Johnson).

3 *nor … nor* neither… nor.

4 *madded* driven mad.

5 *When Statutes glean the Refuse of the Sword* when taxes take what direct assault leaves behind.

6 *bonny Traitor* four Scottish lords imprisoned and executed after the Jacobite rebellion of 1745; Johnson dropped the allusion in the revision of 1755.

Increase his Riches and his Peace destroy;
Now Fears in dire Vicissitude invade,
The rustling Brake alarms, and quiv'ring Shade,
Nor Light nor Darkness bring his Pain Relief,
One shows the Plunder, and one hides the Thief.
   Yet still one gen'ral Cry the Skies assails,
And Gain and Grandeur load the tainted Gales;[7]
Few know the toiling Statesman's Fear or Care,
Th' insidious Rival and the gaping Heir.
   Once more, Democritus, arise on Earth,[8]
With cheerful Wisdom and instructive Mirth,
See motley Life in modern Trappings dressed,[9]
And feed with varied Fools th' eternal Jest:
Thou who couldst laugh where Want enchained Caprice,
Toil crushed Conceit, and Man was of a Piece;
Where Wealth unloved without a Mourner died,
And scarce a Sycophant was fed by pride;
Where ne'er was known the Form of mock Debate,
Or seen a new-made Mayor's unwieldy State;
Where change of Fav'rites made no Change of Laws,[10]
And Senates heard before they judged a Cause;
How wouldst thou shake at *Britain*'s modish Tribe,
Dart the quick Taunt, and edge the piercing Gibe?
Attentive Truth and Nature to descry,
And pierce each Scene with Philosophic Eye.
To thee were solemn Toys or empty Show,
The Robes of Pleasure and the Veils of Woe:
All aid the Farce, and all thy Mirth maintain,
Whose Joys are causeless, or whose Griefs are vain.
   Such was the Scorn that filled the Sage's Mind,
Renewed at every Glance on Humankind;
How just that Scorn ere yet thy Voice declare,
Search every State, and canvass every Prayer.
   Unnumbered Suppliants crowd Preferment's Gate,
Athirst for Wealth, and burning to be great;
Delusive Fortune hears th' incessant Call,
They mount, they shine, evaporate, and fall.[11]
On every Stage the Foes of Peace attend,[12]
Hate dogs their Flight, and Insult mocks their End.
Love ends with Hope, the sinking Statesman's Door

Notes

7 *Gale* "A wind not tempestuous, yet stronger than a breeze" (Johnson).

8 *Democritus* (fl. fifth century BCE), known as the "laughing philosopher" because of his ideal of cheerfulness, despite recognition of severe human limitation; Robert Burton styled himself Democritus Junior in his *Anatomy of Melancholy* (1628), one of Johnson's favorite books.

9 *motley* the dress of court jesters, or fools.

10 *Change of Laws* in 1746 the Act of 19 George II, *c.* 8 changed the administrative structure of London, giving more power to the Common Council and less to the aldermen as a separate group.

11 *evaporate* "To fly away in vapours or fumes; to waste insensibly as a volatile spirit" (Johnson); the image is of a meteor.

12 *Stage* "Any place where anything public is transacted or performed" (Johnson).

Pours in the Morning Worshipper no more;
For growing Names the weekly Scribbler lies,[13]
To growing Wealth the Dedicator flies,[14]
From every Room descends the painted Face,
That hung the bright *Palladium* of the Place,[15]
And smoked in Kitchens, or in Auctions sold,
To better Features yields the Frame of Gold;
For now no more we trace in every Line
Heroic Worth, Benevolence Divine:
The Form distorted justifies the Fall,
And Detestation rids th' indignant Wall.
　But will not *Britain* hear the last Appeal,
Sign her Foes' Doom, or guard her Favourites' Zeal?
Through Freedom's Sons no more Remonstrance rings,[16]
Degrading Nobles and controlling Kings;
Our supple Tribes repress their Patriot Throats,
And ask no Questions but the Price of Votes;
With Weekly Libels and Septennial Ale,[17]
Their Wish is full to riot and to rail.
　In full-blown dignity, see *Wolsey* stand,[18]
Law in his Voice, and Fortune in his Hand:
To him the Church, the Realm, their Pow'rs consign,
Through him the Rays of regal Bounty shine,
Turned by his Nod the Stream of Honour flows,
His Smile alone Security bestows:
Still to new Heights his restless Wishes tow'r,
Claim leads to Claim, and Pow'r advances Pow'r;
Till Conquest unresisted ceased to please,
And Rights submitted, left him none to seize.
At length his Sovereign frowns – the Train of State
Mark the keen Glance, and watch the Sign to hate.
Where'er he turns he meets a Stranger's Eye,
His Suppliants scorn him, and his Followers fly;
Now drops at once the Pride of awful State,
The golden Canopy, the glitt'ring Plate,
The regal Palace, the luxurious Board,
The liv'ried Army, and the menial Lord.[19]
With Age, with Cares, with Maladies oppressed,

Notes

13 *weekly Scribbler* journalist.

14 *Dedicator* an author writing a dedication of his book or poem to someone important.

15 *Palladium* the sacred image of Pallas Athena sent by Zeus as a symbol of protection to the city of Troy.

16 *Remonstrance* recalling the Grand Remonstrance, a catalog of grievances against the king narrowly passed by the House of Commons in 1641.

17 *Libels* pamphlets for railing (Latin, *libellus*); *Septennial Ale* free alcoholic drink for rioting on election day; parliaments were made seven years long under George I.

18 *Wolsey* Thomas (1475?–1530), cardinal and lord chancellor under Henry VIII, until he lost favor; was indicted in the King's Bench (1529), forfeited his estate, was falsely accused of treason, and soon died.

19 *menial* "Belonging to the retinue or train of servants" (Johnson).

He seeks the Refuge of Monastic Rest.
Grief aids Disease, remembered Folly stings,
And his last Sighs reproach the Faith of Kings.
  Speak thou, whose Thoughts at humble Peace repine,
Shall *Wolsey*'s Wealth, with *Wolsey*'s End be thine?
Or liv'st thou now, with safer Pride content,
The richest Landlord on the Banks of *Trent*?[20]
For why did *Wolsey* by the Steps of Fate,
On weak Foundations raise th' enormous Weight?
Why but to sink beneath Misfortune's Blow,
With louder Ruin to the Gulfs below?
  What gave great *Villiers* to th' Assassin's Knife,[21]
And fixed Disease on *Harley*'s closing Life?[22]
What murdered *Wentworth*, and what exiled *Hyde*,[23]
By Kings protected and to Kings allied?
What but their Wish indulged in Courts to shine,
And Pow'r too great to keep or to resign?
  When first the College Rolls receive his Name,
The young Enthusiast quits his Ease for Fame;[24]
Through all his Veins the Fever of Renown,
Burns from the strong Contagion of the Gown;[25]
O'er *Bodley*'s Dome his future Labours spread,[26]
And *Bacon*'s Mansion trembles o'er his Head;[27]
Are these thy Views? proceed, illustrious Youth,
And virtue guard thee to the Throne of Truth!
Yet should thy Soul indulge the gen'rous Heat,
Till captive Science yields her last Retreat;[28]
Should Reason guide thee with her brightest Ray,
And pour on misty Doubt resistless Day;
Should no false Kindness lure to loose Delight,
Nor Praise relax, nor Difficulty fright;
Should tempting Novelty thy Cell refrain,
And Sloth effuse her Opiate Fumes in vain;
Should Beauty blunt on Fops her fatal Dart,

Notes

20 *Trent* the river goes no further south than the environs of Lichfield, Johnson's home town about 85 miles north of London, the center of wealth and fame; in 1755 Johnson changed "richest landlord" to "wisest justice."

21 *Villiers* George, first duke of Buckingham (1592–1628), court favorite whom the Commons tried to force Charles I to remove; his assassin, a naval lieutenant, believed he was acting on the will of the people.

22 *Harley* Robert (1661–1724), first earl of Oxford, leader of the Tory ministry in 1710, dismissed in 1714, imprisoned in 1715, and impeached after the fact in 1717.

23 *Wentworth* Thomas, first earl of Strafford (1593–1641), Charles I's chief advisor, impeached by the House of Commons and executed in a flurry of rumors and fears of mob violence; *Hyde* Edward, earl of Clarendon (1609–74), lord chancellor in 1660, impeached by the Commons and banished in 1668, died in exile.

24 *Enthusiast* "One of a hot imagination, or violent passions" (Johnson).

25 *Gown* "The long habit of a man dedicated to acts of peace, as divinity, medicine, law" (Johnson).

26 *Dome* building; Sir Thomas Bodley (1545–1613) formed, endowed and gave his name to the Oxford University library.

27 *Bacon's Mansion* the study used by the philosopher Roger Bacon (1214?–94), a gatehouse on Folly Bridge in Oxford; an Oxford tradition said that the study would fall if someone more learned than Bacon walked under the bridge.

28 *Science* knowledge.

Nor claim the Triumph of a lettered Heart;
Should no Disease thy torpid Veins invade,
Nor Melancholy's Phantoms haunt thy Shade;
Yet hope not Life from Grief or Danger free,
Nor think the Doom of Man reversed for thee:
Deign on the passing World to turn thine Eyes,
And pause awhile from Learning, to be wise;
There mark what Ills the Scholar's Life assail,
Toil, Envy, Want, the Patron, and the Jail.[29]
See Nations slowly wise, and meanly just,
To buried Merit raise the tardy Bust.[30]
If Dreams yet flatter, once again attend,
Hear *Lydiat*'s life, and *Galileo*'s end.[31]
  Nor deem, when Learning her last Prize bestows
The glitt'ring Eminence exempt from Foes;
See when the Vulgar 'scape, despised or awed,[32]
Rebellion's vengeful Talons seize on *Laud*.[33]
From meaner Minds, though smaller Fines content
The plundered Palace or sequestered Rent;
Marked out by dangerous Parts he meets the Shock,
And fatal Learning leads him to the Block:
Around his Tomb let Art and Genius weep,
But hear his Death, ye Blockheads, hear and sleep.
  The festal Blazes, the triumphal Show,
The ravished Standard, and the captive Foe,
The Senate's Thanks, the Gázette's pompous Tale,[34]
With Force resistless o'er the Brave prevail.
Such Bribes the rapid *Greek* o'er *Asia* whirled[35]
For such the steady *Romans* shook the World;
For such in distant Lands the *Britons* shine,[36]
And stain with Blood the *Danube* or the *Rhine*;
This Pow'r has Praise, that Virtue scarce can warm,
Till Fame supplies the universal Charm.
Yet Reason frowns on War's unequal Game,
Where wasted Nations raise a single Name,
And mortgaged States their Grandsires Wreaths regret,[37]

Notes

29 *Patron* "Commonly a wretch who supports with insolence, and is paid with flattery" (Johnson); it was "Garret" in the first edition; the change is connected with Johnson's formal repudiation of Chesterfield's tardy patronage of the *Dictionary*, which he effected with a famous letter written about the same time that he revised his poem in 1755.

30 *tardy Bust* the burial monument; see Pope: "Patrons, who sneak from living worth to dead,/Withhold the pension, and set up the head" (*Dunciad* 4.95–6).

31 *Lydiat* Thomas (1572–1646), a famous astronomer in his time; died in poverty and was forgotten; *Galileo* (1564–1642), the great astronomer; forced by the church to deny his Copernican views, lived the last eight years of his life under house arrest.

32 *Vulgar* common, unlearned persons.

33 *Laud* William (1573–1645), Archbishop of Canterbury under Charles I, accused of high treason by Parliament and executed in 1645.

34 *Gazette* the government-run newspaper.

35 *the rapid Greek* Alexander the Great.

36 *the Britons* an allusion to the surprising and ambitious military victory over the French at Blenheim by the brilliant and ambitious John Churchill (1650–1722), first duke of Marlborough.

37 *Wreaths* victory garlands.

From Age to Age in everlasting Debt;
Wreaths which at last the dear-bought Right convey
To rust on Medals, or on Stones decay.
On what Foundation stands the Warrior's Pride?
How just his Hopes let *Swedish Charles* decide;[38]
A Frame of Adamant, a Soul of Fire,
No Dangers fright him, and no Labours tire;
O'er Love, o'er Force, extends his wide Domain,
Unconquered Lord of Pleasure and of Pain;
No Joys to him pacific Sceptres yield,
War sounds the Trump, he rushes to the Field;
Behold surrounding Kings their Pow'r combine,
And One capitulate, and One resign;
Peace courts his Hand, but spreads her Charms in vain;
'Think Nothing gained', he cries, 'till nought remain,
On *Moscow*'s Walls till *Gothic* Standards fly,
And all is Mine beneath the Polar Sky'.
The March begins in Military State,
And Nations on his Eye suspended wait;
Stern Famine guards the solitary Coast,
And Winter barricades the Realms of Frost;
He comes, nor Want nor Cold his Course delay; –
Hide, blushing Glory, hide *Pultowa*'s Day:
The vanquished Hero leaves his broken Bands,
And shows his Miseries in distant Lands;
Condemned a needy Supplicant to wait,
While Ladies interpose, and Slaves debate.
But did not Chance at length her Error mend?
Did no subverted Empire mark his End?
Did rival Monarchs give the fatal Wound?
Or hostile Millions press him to the Ground?
His Fall was destined to a barren Strand,
A petty Fortress, and a dubious Hand;[39]
He left the Name, at which the World grew pale,
To point a Moral, or adorn a Tale.
All Times their Scenes of pompous Woes afford,
From *Persia*'s Tyrant to *Bavaria*'s Lord.[40]
In gay Hostility, and barb'rous Pride,
With half Mankind embattled at his Side,
Great *Xerxes* comes to seize the certain Prey,

Notes

[38] *Swedish Charles* Charles XII of Sweden (1682–1718), a very active general and statesman; pursued the Russian army toward Moscow in 1707; defeated at *Pultowa* (Ukraine) in 1709; sought allies in Turkey, where he was involved in intrigues; sympathized with English Jacobites as a threat to George I and Hanover; began a new military campaign in 1718 but was killed in battle before it was well under way.

[39] *a dubious hand* some say Charles was killed by one of his own soldiers at the siege of Frederikshald (Halden, Norway).

[40] *Persia's Tyrant* Xerxes the Great (519–465 BCE), whose massive invasions of Greece failed; *Bavaria's Lord* Charles Albert (1697–1745), Elector of Bavaria; became Holy Roman Emperor in 1742.

And starves exhausted Regions in his Way;
Attendant Flatt'ry counts his Myriads o'er,
Till counted Myriads soothe his Pride no more;
Fresh Praise is tried till Madness fires his Mind,
The Waves he lashes, and enchains the Wind;[41]
New Pow'rs are claimed, new Pow'rs are still bestowed,
Till rude Resistance lops the spreading God;
The daring *Greeks* deride the Martial Show,
And heap their Valleys with the gaudy Foe;[42]
Th' insulted Sea with humbler Thoughts he gains,
A single Skiff to speed his Flight remains;
Th' incumbered Oar scarce leaves the dreaded Coast
Through purple Billows and a floating Host.
The bold *Bavarian*, in a luckless Hour,
Tries the dread Summits of *Cesarean* Pow'r,
With unexpected Legions bursts away,
And sees defenceless Realms receive his Sway;
Short Sway! fair *Austria* spreads her mournful Charms,[43]
The Queen, the Beauty, sets the World in Arms;
From Hill to Hill the Beacon's rousing Blaze
Spreads wide the Hope of Plunder and of Praise;
The fierce *Croatian*, and the wild *Hussar*,[44]
And all the Sons of Ravage crowd the War;
The baffled Prince in Honour's flatt'ring Bloom
Of hasty Greatness finds the fatal Doom,
His Foes' Derision, and his Subjects' Blame,
And steals to Death from Anguish and from Shame.
Enlarge my Life with Multitude of Days,
In Health, in Sickness, thus the Suppliant prays;
Hides from himself his State, and shuns to know,
That Life protracted is protracted Woe.
Time hovers o'er, impatient to destroy,
And shuts up all the Passages of Joy:
In vain their Gifts the bounteous Seasons pour,
The Fruit Autumnal, and the Vernal Flow'r,
With listless Eyes the Dotard views the Store,
He views, and wonders that they please no more;
Now pall the tasteless Meats, and joyless Wines,
And Luxury with Sighs her Slave resigns.
Approach, ye Minstrels, try the soothing Strain,
And yield the tuneful Lenitives of Pain:
No Sounds alas would touch th' impervious Ear,

Notes

41 *Waves ... Wind* when bad weather hindered his assault, he ordered his men to punish the sea and air (Herodotus 7.35, 54).

42 *Valleys* especially Thermopylae, where Xerxes won a costly victory, before he was defeated at sea near Salamis and had to retreat.

43 *fair Austria* Maria Theresa of Austria, ruler of the Hapsburg dominions; led the attack on Bavaria even as Charles was being crowned emperor.

44 *Hussar* Hungarian cavalryman.

Though dancing Mountains witnessed *Orpheus* near;[45]
Nor Lute nor Lyre his feeble Pow'rs attend,
Nor sweeter Music of a virtuous Friend,
But everlasting Dictates crowd his Tongue,
Perversely grave, or positively wrong.
The still returning Tale, and ling'ring Jest,
Perplex the fawning Niece and pampered Guest,
While growing Hopes scarce awe the gath'ring Sneer,
And scarce a Legacy can bribe to hear;
The watchful Guests still hint the last Offence,
The Daughter's Petulance, the Son's Expense,
Improve his heady Rage with treach'rous Skill,
And mould his Passions till they make his Will.
  Unnumbered Maladies each Joint invade,
Lay Siege to Life and press the dire Blockade;
But unextinguished Av'rice still remains,
And dreaded Losses aggravate his Pains;
He turns, with anxious Heart and crippled Hands,
His Bonds of Debt, and Mortgages of Lands;
Or views his Coffers with suspicious Eyes,
Unlocks his Gold, and counts it till he dies.
  But grant, the Virtues of a temp'rate Prime
Bless with an Age exempt from Scorn or Crime;
An Age that melts in unperceived Decay,
And glides in modest Innocence away;
Whose peaceful Day Benevolence endears,
Whose Night congratulating Conscience cheers;
The gen'ral Fav'rite as the gen'ral Friend:
Such Age there is, and who could wish its End?
  Yet ev'n on this her Load Misfortune flings,
To press the weary Minutes' flagging Wings:
New Sorrow rises as the Day returns,
A Sister sickens, or a Daughter mourns.
Now Kindred Merit fills the sable Bier,
Now lacerated Friendship claims a Tear.
Year chases Year, Decay pursues Decay,
Still drops some Joy from with'ring Life away;
New Forms arise, and diff'rent Views engage,
Superfluous lags the Vet'ran on the Stage
Till pitying Nature signs the last Release,
And bids afflicted Worth retire to Peace.
  But few there are whom Hours like these await,
Who set unclouded in the Gulfs of Fate.
From *Lydia*'s Monarch should the Search descend,[46]

Notes

[45] *Orpheus* legendary pre-Homeric poet whose music could charm beasts and animate rocks.

[46] *Lydia's Monarch* Croesus, the wealthy sixth-century BCE king defeated by Cyrus of Persia.

By *Solon* cautioned to regard his End,[47]
In Life's last Scene what Prodigies surprise,
Fears of the Brave, and Follies of the Wise?
From *Marlborough*'s Eyes the Streams of Dotage flow,
And *Swift* expires a Driv'ler and a Show.[48]
The teeming Mother, anxious for her Race,[49]
Begs for each Birth the Fortune of a Face:
Yet *Vane* could tell what Ills from Beauty spring;[50]
And *Sedley* cursed the Form that pleased a King.[51]
Ye Nymphs of rosy Lips and radiant Eyes,
Whom Pleasure keeps too busy to be wise,
Whom Joys with soft Varieties invite
By Day the Frolic, and the Dance by Night,
Who frown with Vanity, who smile with Art,
And ask the latest Fashion of the Heart,
What Care, what Rules your heedless Charms shall save,
Each Nymph your Rival, and each Youth your Slave?
Against your Fame with Fondness Hate combines,
The Rival batters, and the Lover mines.
With distant Voice neglected Virtue calls,
Less heard, and less the faint Remonstrance falls;
Tir'd with Contempt, she quits the slipp'ry Reign,
And Pride and Prudence take her Seat in vain.
In crowd at once, where none the Pass defend,
The harmless Freedom, and the private Friend.
The Guardians yield, by Force superior plied;
By Int'rest, Prudence; and by Flatt'ry, Pride.
Here Beauty falls betrayed, despised, distressed,
And hissing Infamy proclaims the rest.
Where then shall Hope and Fear their Objects find?
Must dull Suspense corrupt the stagnant Mind?
Must helpless Man, in Ignorance sedate,
Roll darkling down the Current of his Fate?
Must no Dislike alarm, no Wishes rise,
No Cries attempt the Mercies of the Skies?
Enquirer, cease, Petitions yet remain,
Which Heav'n may hear, nor deem Religion vain.
Still raise for Good the supplicating Voice,
But leave to Heav'n the Measure and the Choice.
Safe in his Pow'r, whose Eyes discern afar
The secret Ambush of a specious Pray'r.
Implore his Aid, in his Decisions rest,

Notes

[47] *Solon* the Athenian lawgiver was said to have advised Croesus that fortune, not wealth, determined happiness; Johnson has him repeat a version of the Latin motto to that effect: *respice finem*.

[48] *Swift* at the age of seventy-three, four years before his death, Swift was declared legally incompetent.

[49] *teeming* pregnant.

[50] *Vane* Anne (1705–36), mistress of Frederick, Prince of Wales.

[51] *Sedley* Catherine (1657–1717), mistress of the duke of York (later James II).

Secure whate'er he gives, he gives the best.
Yet when the Sense of sacred Presence fires,
And strong Devotion to the skies aspires,
Pour forth thy Fervours for a healthful Mind,
Obedient Passions, and a Will resigned;
For Love, which scarce collective Man can fill;
For Patience sovereign o'er transmuted Ill;
For Faith, that panting for a happier Seat,
Counts Death kind Nature's Signal of Retreat:
These Goods for Man the Laws of Heav'n ordain,
These Goods he grants, who grants the Pow'r to gain;
With these celestial Wisdom calms the Mind,
And makes the Happiness she does not find.

from the *Rambler*

Number 2
Saturday, 24 March 1750

Stare Loco nescit, pereunt Vestigia mille
Ante Fugam, absentemque ferit gravis Ungula Campum.
Statius, *Thebaid* 6.400–1

Th' impatient courser pants in ev'ry vein,
And pawing seems to beat the distant plain;
Hills, vales, and floods, appear already crossed,
And, ere he starts, a thousand steps are lost.
Pope [*Windsor Forest*, 151–4]

That the Mind of Man is never satisfied with the Objects immediately before it, but is always breaking away from the present Moment, and losing itself in Schemes of future Felicity – that we forget the proper Use of the Time now in our Power, to provide for the Enjoyment of that which, perhaps, may never be granted us – has been frequently remarked; and as this Practice is a commodious Subject of Raillery to the Gay, and of Declamation to the Serious, it has been ridiculed with all the Pleasantry of Wit, and exaggerated with all the Amplifications of Rhetoric. Every Instance, by which its Absurdity might appear most flagrant, has been studiously collected; it has been marked with every Epithet of Contempt, and all the Tropes and Figures have been called forth against it.

Censure is willingly indulged, because it always implies some Superiority. Men please themselves with imagining that they have made a deeper Search, or wider Survey, than others, and detected Faults and Follies, which escaped vulgar Observation; and the Pleasure of wantoning in common Topics is so tempting to a Writer, that he cannot easily resign it. A Train of Sentiments generally received enables him to shine without Labour, and to conquer without a Contest. It is so easy to laugh at the Folly of him who lives only in Idea, refuses immediate Ease for distant Pleasures, and, instead of enjoying the Blessings of Life, lets Life glide away in Preparations to enjoy them; it affords such Opportunities of triumphant Exultations, to exemplify the Uncertainty of the human State, to rouse Mortals from their Dream, and inform them of the silent Celerity of Time, that we may reasonably believe most Authors willing rather to transmit than examine so advantageous a Principle, and more inclined to pursue a Track so smooth and so flowery, than attentively to consider whether it leads to Truth.

This Quality of looking forward into Futurity seems the unavoidable Condition of a Being, whose Motions are gradual, and whose Life is progressive: As his Powers are limited, he must use Means for the Attainment of his Ends, and must intend first what he performs last; as, by continual Advances from his first Stage of Existence, he is perpetually varying the Horizon of his Prospects, he must always discover new Motives of Action, new Excitements of Fear, and Allurements of Desire.

The End, therefore, which, at present, calls forth our Efforts will be found, when it is once gained, to be only one of the Means to some remoter End. The natural Flights of the human Mind are not from Pleasure to Pleasure, but from Hope to Hope.

He that directs his Steps to a certain Point, must frequently turn his Eyes to that Place which he strives to reach; he that undergoes the Fatigue of Labour, must solace his Weariness with the Contemplation of its Reward. In Agriculture, one of the most simple and necessary Employments, no Man turns up the Ground, but because he thinks of the Harvest, that Harvest which Blights may intercept, which Inundations may sweep away, or which Death, or Calamity, may hinder him from reaping.

Yet as few Maxims are widely received, or long retained, but for some Conformity with Truth and Nature, it must be confessed, that this Caution against keeping our View too intent upon remote Advantages is not without its Propriety or Usefulness, though it may have been recited with too much Levity, or enforced with too little Distinction: for, not to speak of that Vehemence of Desire which presses through right and wrong to its Gratification, or that anxious Inquietude which is justly chargeable with Distrust of Heaven, Subjects too solemn for my present Purpose; it frequently happens that, by indulging too early the Raptures of Success, we forget the Measures necessary to secure it; and suffer the Imagination to riot in the Fruition of some possible Good, till the Time of obtaining it has slipped away.

There would however be few Enterprises of great Labour or Hazard, undertaken, if we had not the Power of magnifying the Advantages, which we persuade ourselves to expect from them. When the Knight of *La Mancha*[1] gravely recounts to his Companion the Adventures by which he is to signalize himself in such a manner that he shall be summoned to the Support of Empires, solicited to accept the Heiress of the Crown he has preserved, have Honours and Riches to scatter about him, and an Island to bestow on his worthy Squire, very few Readers, amidst their Mirth or Pity, can deny that they have admitted Visions of the same Kind; though they have not, perhaps, expected Events equally strange, or by Means equally inadequate. When we pity him, we reflect our own Disappointments, and when we laugh, our Hearts inform us that he is not more ridiculous than ourselves, except that he tells what we have only thought.

The Understanding of a Man, naturally sanguine, may, indeed, be easily vitiated by too luxurious an Indulgence of the Pleasures of Hope, however necessary to the Production of every Thing great or excellent, as some Plants are destroyed by a too open Exposure to that Sun which gives Life and Beauty to the vegetable World.

Perhaps no Class of the Human Species requires more to be cautioned against this Anticipation of Happiness, than those that aspire to the Name of Authors. A Man of

Notes

FROM THE *RAMBLER*

[1] *the Knight of La Mancha* the hero of Cervantes' *Don Quixote*.

lively Fancy no sooner finds a Hint moving in his Mind, than he makes momentaneous Excursions to the Press, and to the World; and, with a little Encouragement from Flattery, pushes forward into future Ages, and prognosticates the Honours to be paid him, when Envy is extinct, and Faction forgotten; and those, whom the Partiality of the present Generation suffers to obscure him, shall give way to other Triflers of as short Duration as themselves.

Those, who have proceeded so far as to appeal to the Tribunal of succeeding Times, are not likely to be cured of their Infatuation; but all Endeavours ought to be used for the Prevention of a Disease, for which, when it has attained its Height, perhaps, no Remedy will be found in the Gardens of Philosophy; however she may boast her Physic[2] of the Mind, her Cathartics of Vice, or Lenitives[3] of Passion.

I shall, therefore, while I am yet but lightly touched with the Symptoms of the Writer's Malady,[4] endeavour to fortify myself against the Infection, not without some weak Hope, that my Preservatives may extend their Virtue to others, whose Employment exposes them to the same Danger:

Laudis Amore tumes? Sunt certa Piacula, quæ te
Ter pure lecto poterunt recreare Libello.
Horace, *Epistles* 1.1.36–7

Is fame your passion? Wisdom's pow'rful charm,
If thrice read over, shall its force disarm.
[Philip] Francis [1708–73]

It is the sage Advice of *Epictetus*,[5] that a Man should accustom himself often to think of what is most shocking and terrible, that by such Reflections he may be preserved from too ardent Wishes for seeming Good, and from too much Dejection in real Evil.

There is nothing more dreadful to an Author than Neglect; compared with which Reproach, Hatred, and Opposition, are Names of Happiness: yet this worst, this meanest Fate every Man who dares to write has Reason to fear.

I nunc, et Versus tecum meditare canoros.
Horace, *Epistles* 2.2.76

Go now, and meditate thy tuneful lays.
[James] Elphinstone [1721–1809]

It may not be unfit for him who makes a new Entrance into the lettered World, so far to suspect his own Powers as to believe that he possibly may deserve Neglect; that Nature may not have qualified him much to enlarge or embellish Knowledge, nor sent him forth entitled by indisputable Superiority to regulate the Conduct of the Rest of Mankind; that, though the World must be granted to be yet in Ignorance, he is not destined to dispel the Cloud, nor to shine out as one of the Luminaries of Life: For this Suspicion, every Catalogue of a Library will furnish sufficient Reason; as he will find

Notes

2 *Physic* medical treatment, especially purges.
3 *Lenitive* emollient, soothing agent.
4 *lightly touched … Malady* Johnson is speaking in the character of Mr. Rambler, who has just begun his career as a writer.
5 *Epictetus* Stoic philosopher of the first century CE whose teachings are collected in a manual, *Enchiridion*.

it crowded with Names of Men, who, though now forgotten, were once no less enterprising or confident than himself, equally pleased with their own Productions, equally caressed by their Patrons, and flattered by their Friends.

But, though it should happen that an Author is capable of excelling, yet his Merit may pass without Notice, huddled in the Variety of things, and thrown into the general Miscellany of Life. He that endeavours after Fame, by writing, solicits the Regard of a Multitude fluctuating in Pleasures, or immersed in Business, without Time for intellectual Amusements; he appeals to Judges prepossessed by Passions, or corrupted by Prejudices, which preclude their Approbation of any new Performance. Some are too indolent to read any Thing, till its Reputation is established; others too envious to promote that Fame, which gives them Pain by its Increase. What is new is opposed, because most are unwilling to be taught; and what is known is rejected, because it is not sufficiently considered, that Men more frequently require to be reminded than informed. The Learned are afraid to declare their Opinion early, lest they should put their Reputation in Hazard; the Ignorant always imagine themselves giving some Proof of Delicacy, when they refuse to be pleased: and he that finds his Way to Reputation, through all these Obstructions, must acknowledge that he is indebted to other Causes besides his Industry, his Learning, or his Wit.

Number 28
Saturday, 23 June 1750

Illi mors gravis incubat,
Qui, notus nimis omnibus,
Ignotus moritur sibi.
Seneca, *Thyestes*, ll.401–3.

To him, alas, to him, I fear,
The face of death will terrible appear,
Who in his life, flatt'ring his senseless pride,
By being known to all the world beside,
Does not himself, when he is dying, know,
Nor what he is, nor whither he's to go.
[Abraham] Cowley ["Of Solitude," 1668]

I have shown, in a late essay,[6] to what errors men are hourly betrayed by a mistaken opinion of their own powers, and a negligent inspection of their own character. But as I then confined my observations to common occurrences, and familiar scenes, I think it proper to enquire how far a nearer acquaintance with ourselves is necessary to our preservation from crimes as well as follies, and how much the attentive study of our own minds may contribute to secure to us the approbation of that being, to whom we are accountable for our thoughts and our actions, and whose favour must finally constitute our total happiness.

If it be reasonable to estimate the difficulty of any enterprise by frequent miscarriages, it may justly be concluded that it is not easy for a man to know himself; for

Notes

[6] *Rambler* 24.

wheresoever we turn our view, we shall find almost all with whom we converse so nearly as to judge of their sentiments, indulging more favourable conceptions of their own virtue than they have been able to impress upon others, and congratulating themselves upon degrees of excellence, which their fondest admirers cannot allow them to have attained.

Those representations of imaginary virtue are generally considered as arts of hypocrisy, and as snares laid for confidence and praise. But I believe the suspicion often unjust; those who thus propagate their own reputation, only extend the fraud by which they have been themselves deceived; for this failing is incident to numbers, who seem to live without designs, competitions, or pursuits; it appears on occasions which promise no accession of honour or of profit, and to persons from whom very little is to be hoped or feared. It is, indeed, not easy to tell how far we may be blinded by the love of ourselves, when we reflect how much a secondary passion can cloud our judgment, and how few faults a man, in the first raptures of love, can discover in the person or conduct of his mistress.

To lay open all the sources from which error flows in upon him who contemplates his own character, would require more exact knowledge of the human heart, than, perhaps, the most acute and laborious observers have acquired. And, since falsehood may be diversified without end, it is not unlikely that every man admits an imposture in some respect peculiar to himself, as his views have been accidentally directed, or his ideas particularly combined.

Some fallacies, however, there are, more frequently insidious, which it may, perhaps, not be useless to detect, because though they are gross they may be fatal, and because nothing but attention is necessary to defeat them.

One sophism by which men persuade themselves that they have those virtues which they really want, is formed by the substitution of single acts for habits. A miser who once relieved a friend from the danger of a prison, suffers his imagination to dwell for ever upon his own heroic generosity; he yields his heart up to indignation at those who are blind to merit, or insensible to misery, and who can please themselves with the enjoyment of that wealth, which they never permit others to partake. From any censures of the world, or reproaches of his conscience, he has an appeal to action and to knowledge; and though his whole life is a course of rapacity and avarice, he concludes himself to be tender and liberal, because he has once performed an act of liberality and tenderness.

As a glass which magnifies objects by the approach of one end to the eye, lessens them by the application of the other, so vices are extenuated by the inversion of that fallacy, by which virtues are augmented. Those faults which we cannot conceal from our own notice, are considered, however frequent, not as habitual corruptions, or settled practices, but as casual failures, and single lapses. A man who has, from year to year, set his country to sale, either for the gratification of his ambition or resentment, confesses that the heat of party now and then betrays the severest virtue to measures that cannot be seriously defended. He that spends his days and nights in riot and debauchery, owns that his passions oftentimes overpower his resolutions. But each comforts himself that his faults are not without precedent, for the best and the wisest men have given way to the violence of sudden temptations.

There are men who always confound the praise of goodness with the practice, and who believe themselves mild and moderate, charitable and faithful, because they have exerted their eloquence in commendation of mildness, fidelity, and other virtues. This is an error almost universal among those that converse much with dependants, with such whose fear or interest disposes them to a seeming reverence for any declamation, however enthusiastic, and submission to any boast, however arrogant. Having none to recall their attention to their lives, they rate themselves by the goodness of their opinions, and forget how much more easily men may show their virtue in their talk than in their actions.

The tribe is likewise very numerous of those who regulate their lives, not by the standard of religion, but the measure of other men's virtue; who lull their own remorse with the remembrance of crimes more atrocious than their own, and seem to believe that they are not bad while another can be found worse.

For escaping these and a thousand other deceits, many expedients have been proposed. Some have recommended the frequent consultation of a wise friend, admitted to intimacy, and encouraged to sincerity. But this appears a remedy by no means adapted to general use: for in order to secure the virtue of one, it presupposes more virtue in two than will generally be found. In the first, such a desire of rectitude and amendment, as may incline him to hear his own accusation from the mouth of him whom he esteems, and by whom, therefore, he will always hope that his faults are not discovered; and in the second such zeal and honesty, as will make him content for his friend's advantage to lose his kindness.

A long life may be passed without finding a friend in whose understanding and virtue we can equally confide, and whose opinion we can value at once for its justness and sincerity. A weak man, however honest, is not qualified to judge. A man of the world, however penetrating, is not fit to counsel. Friends are often chosen for similitude of manners, and therefore each palliates the other's failing, because they are his own. Friends are tender and unwilling to give pain, or they are interested, and fearful to offend.

These objections have inclined others to advise, that he who would know himself, should consult his enemies, remember the reproaches that are vented to his face, and listen for the censures that are uttered in private. For his great business is to know his faults, and those malignity will discover, and resentment will reveal. But this precept may be often frustrated; for it seldom happens that rivals or opponents are suffered to come near enough to know our conduct with so much exactness as that conscience should allow and reflect the accusation. The charge of an enemy is often totally false, and commonly so mingled with falsehood, that the mind takes advantage from the failure of one part to discredit the rest, and never suffers any disturbance afterward from such partial reports.

Yet it seems that enemies have been always found by experience the most faithful monitors; for adversity has ever been considered as the state in which a man most easily becomes acquainted with himself, and this effect it must produce by withdrawing flatterers, whose business it is to hide our weaknesses from us, or by giving loose to malice, and licence to reproach; or at least by cutting off those pleasures which called us away from meditation on our conduct, and repressing that pride which too easily persuades us, that we merit whatever we enjoy.

Part of these benefits it is in every man's power to procure to himself, by assigning proper portions of his life to the examination of the rest, and by putting himself frequently in such a situation by retirement and abstraction, as may weaken the influence of external objects. By this practice he may obtain the solitude of adversity without its melancholy, its instructions without its censures, and its sensibility without its perturbations.

The necessity of setting the world at a distance from us, when we are to take a survey of ourselves, has sent many from high stations to the severities of a monastic life; and indeed, every man deeply engaged in business, if all regard to another state be not extinguished, must have the conviction, though, perhaps, not the resolution of

Valdesso,[7] who, when he solicited Charles the Fifth to dismiss him, being asked, whether he retired upon disgust, answered that he laid down his commission for no other reason but because "there ought to be some time for sober reflection between the life of a soldier and his death."

There are few conditions which do not entangle us with sublunary hopes and fears, from which it is necessary to be at intervals disencumbered, that we may place ourselves in his presence who views effects in their causes, and actions in their motives; that we may, as Chillingworth[8] expresses it, consider things as if there were no other beings in the world but God and ourselves; or, to use language yet more awful, "may commune with our own hearts, and be still."[9]

Death, says Seneca, falls heavy upon him who is too much known to others, and too little to himself;[10] and Pontanus, a man celebrated among the early restorers of literature, thought the study of our own hearts of so much importance, that he has recommended it from his tomb. *Sum Joannes Jovianus Pontanus, quem amaverunt bonae musae, suspexerunt viri probi, honestaverunt reges domini; jam scis tenebris nequeo, sed teipsum ut noscas rogo.* "I am Pontanus, beloved by the powers of literature, admired by men of worth, and dignified by the monarchs of the world. Thou knowest now who I am, or more properly who I was. For thee, stranger, I who am in darkness cannot know thee, but I entreat thee to know thyself."[11]

I hope every reader of this paper will consider himself as engaged to the observation of a precept, which the wisdom and virtue of all ages have concurred to enforce, a precept dictated by philosophers, inculcated by poets, and ratified by saints.

Number 207
Tuesday, 10 March 1752

Solve senescentem mature sanus equum, ne
Peccet ad extremum ridendus.
Horace, EPISTLES, 1.1.8–9.

The voice of reason cries with winning force,
Loose from the rapid car your aged horse,
Lest, in the race derided, left behind,
He drag his jaded limbs and burst his wind.
Francis.

Such is the emptiness of human enjoyment, that we are always impatient of the present. Attainment is followed by neglect, and possession by disgust; and the malicious remark of the Greek epigrammatist on marriage may be applied to every other course of life, that its two days of happiness are the first and the last.[12]

Few moments are more pleasing than those in which the mind is concerting measures for a new undertaking. From the first hint that wakens the fancy, till the hour of

Notes

7 Alfonso de Valdés (1490–1532), Spanish humanist and chancellor to Emperor Charles V.

8 William Chillingworth (1602–44).

9 Psalms 4.4.

10 See motto above.

11 Giovanni Gioviano Pontano (1426–1503), Italian poet and humanist. The epitaph has been variously attributed.

12 A two-line poem included in the *Greek Anthology*, a collection of short verse by various known and unknown authors (Book XI, Poem 381).

actual execution, all is improvement and progress, triumph and felicity. Every hour brings additions to the original scheme, suggests some new expedient to secure success, or discovers consequential advantages not hitherto foreseen. While preparations are made, and materials accumulated, day glides after day through elysian[13] prospects, and the heart dances to the song of hope.

Such is the pleasure of projecting, that many content themselves with a succession of visionary schemes, and wear out their allotted time in the calm amusement of contriving what they never attempt or hope to execute.

Others, not able to feast their imagination with pure ideas, advance somewhat nearer to the grossness of action, with great diligence collect whatever is requisite to their design, and, after a thousand researches and consultations, are snatched away by death, as they stand *in procinctu*[14] waiting for a proper opportunity to begin.

If there were no other end of life, than to find some adequate solace for every day, I know not whether any condition could be preferred to that of the man who involves himself in his own thoughts, and never suffers experience to show him the vanity of speculation; for no sooner are notions reduced to practice, than tranquillity and confidence forsake the breast; every day brings its task, and often without bringing abilities to perform it: difficulties embarrass, uncertainty perplexes, opposition retards, censure exasperates, or neglect depresses. We proceed, because we have begun; we complete our design, that the labour already spent may not be vain; but as expectation gradually dies away, the gay smile of alacrity disappears, we are compelled to implore severer powers, and trust the event to patience and constancy.

When once our labour has begun, the comfort that enables us to endure it is the prospect of its end; for though in every long work there are some joyous intervals of self-applause, when the attention is recreated by unexpected facility, and the imagination soothed by incidental excellencies; yet the toil with which performance struggles after idea, is so irksome and disgusting, and so frequent is the necessity of resting below that perfection which we imagined within our reach, that seldom any man obtains more from his endeavours than a painful conviction of his defects, and a continual resuscitation of desires which he feels himself unable to gratify.

So certainly is weariness the concomitant of our undertakings, that every man, in whatever he is engaged, consoles himself with the hope of change; if he has made his way by assiduity to public employment, he talks among his friends of the delight of retreat; if by the necessity of solitary application he is secluded from the world, he listens with a beating heart to distant noises, longs to mingle with living beings, and resolves to take hereafter his fill of diversions, or display his abilities on the universal theatre, and enjoy the pleasure of distinction and applause.

Every desire, however innocent, grows dangerous, as by long indulgence it becomes ascendant in the mind. When we have been much accustomed to consider any thing as capable of giving happiness, it is not easy to restrain our ardour, or forbear some precipitation in our advances, and irregularity in our pursuits. He that has cultivated the tree, watched the swelling bud and opening blossom, and pleased himself with computing how much every sun and shower add to its growth, scarcely stays till the fruit has obtained its maturity, but defeats his own cares by eagerness to reward them. When we have

Notes

13 Pertaining to Elysium, the best place in the classical underworld; hence, pleasant.

14 Girded up.

diligently laboured for any purpose, we are willing to believe that we have attained it, and, because we have already done much, too suddenly conclude that no more is to be done.

All attraction is increased by the approach of the attracting body.[15] We never find ourselves so desirous to finish, as in the latter part of our work, or so impatient of delay, as when we know that delay cannot be long. This unseasonable importunity of discontent may be partly imputed to languor and weariness, which must always oppress those more whose toil has been longer continued; but the greater part usually proceeds from frequent contemplation of that ease which is now considered as within reach, and which, when it has once flattered our hopes, we cannot suffer to be withheld.

In some of the noblest compositions of wit,[16] the conclusion falls below the vigour and spirit of the first books; and as a genius is not to be degraded by the imputation of human failings, the cause of this declension is commonly sought in the structure of the work, and plausible reasons are given why in the defective part less ornament was necessary, or less could be admitted. But, perhaps, the author would have confessed, that his fancy was tired, and his perseverance broken; that he knew his design to be unfinished, but that, when he saw the end so near, he could no longer refuse to be at rest.

Against the instillations of this frigid opiate,[17] the heart should be secured by all the considerations which once concurred to kindle the ardour[18] of enterprise. Whatever motive first incited action, has still greater force to stimulate perseverance; since he that might have lain still at first in blameless obscurity, cannot afterwards desist but with infamy and reproach. He, whom a doubtful promise of distant good, could encourage to set difficulties at defiance, ought not to remit his vigour, when he has almost obtained his recompense. To faint or loiter, when only the last efforts are required, is to steer the ship through tempests, and abandon it to the winds in sight of land; it is to break the ground and scatter the seed, and at last to neglect the harvest.

The masters of rhetoric direct, that the most forcible arguments be produced in the latter part of an oration, lest they should be effaced or perplexed by supervenient[19] images. This precept may be justly extended to the series of life: nothing is ended with honour, which does not conclude better than it begun. It is not sufficient to maintain the first vigour; for excellence loses its effect upon the mind by custom, as light after a time ceases to dazzle. Admiration must be continued by that novelty which first produced it, and how much soever is given, there must always be reason to imagine that more remains.

We not only are most sensible of the last impressions, but such is the unwillingness of mankind to admit transcendent merit, that, though it be difficult to obliterate the reproach of miscarriages by any subsequent achievement, however illustrious, yet the reputation raised by a long train of success, may be finally ruined by a single failure, for weakness or error will be always remembered by that malice and envy which it gratifies.

For the prevention of that disgrace, which lassitude and negligence may bring at last upon the greatest performances, it is necessary to proportion carefully our labour to our strength. If the design comprises many parts, equally essential, and therefore not to

Notes

15 A paraphrase of the law of gravitation, most importantly developed in SJ's time by Isaac Newton.

16 *wit* "Imagination; quickness of fancy" (*Dictionary*, sense 2).

17 *frigid* "Dull; without fire of fancy" (*Dictionary*, sense 4); the "opiate" of the desire to leave off here makes one frigid.

18 *ardour* "Heat" (*Dictionary*, sense 1).

19 *supervenient* "Added; additional" (*Dictionary*). The "masters of rhetoric" are Cicero and Quintilian.

be separated, the only time for caution is before we engage; the powers of the mind must be then impartially estimated, and it must be remembered, that not to complete the plan, is not to have begun it; and, that nothing is done, while any thing is omitted.

But, if the task consists in the repetition of single acts, no one of which derives its efficacy from the rest, it may be attempted with less scruple,[20] because there is always opportunity to retreat with honour. The danger is only lest we expect from the world the indulgence with which most are disposed to treat themselves; and in the hour of listlessness imagine, that the diligence of one day will atone for the idleness of another, and that applause begun by approbation will be continued by habit.

He that is himself weary will soon weary the public. Let him therefore lay down his employment, whatever it be, who can no longer exert his former activity or attention; let him not endeavour to struggle with censure, or obstinately infest the stage till a general hiss commands him to depart.

from the *Idler*

Number 22
Saturday, 9 September 1758[1]

Many naturalists are of opinion, that the animals which we commonly consider as mute, have the power of imparting their thoughts to one another. That they can express general sensations is very certain; every being that can utter sounds, has a different voice for pleasure and for pain. The hound informs his fellows when he scents his game; the hen calls her chickens to their food by her cluck, and drives them from danger by her scream.

Birds have the greatest variety of notes; they have indeed a variety, which seems almost sufficient to make a speech adequate to the purposes of a life which is regulated by instinct, and can admit little change or improvement. To the cries of birds, curiosity or superstition has been always attentive, many have studied the language of the feathered tribes, and some have boasted that they understood it.

The most skilful or most confident interpreters of the sylvan dialogues have been commonly found among the philosophers of the East, in a country where the calmness of the air, and the mildness of the seasons, allow the student to pass a great part of the year in groves and bowers. But what may be done in one place by peculiar opportunities, may be performed in another by peculiar diligence. A shepherd of Bohemia[2] has, by long abode in the forests, enabled himself to understand the voice of birds, at least he relates with great confidence a story of which the credibility may be considered by the learned.

"As I was sitting, (said he) within a hollow rock, and watching my sheep that fed in the valley, I heard two vultures interchangeably crying on the summit of the cliff. Both voices were earnest and deliberate. My curiosity prevailed over my care of the flock; I climbed slowly and silently from crag to crag, concealed among the shrubs, till I found a cavity where I might sit and listen without suffering or giving disturbance.

Notes

[20] *scruple* "Doubt ... perplexity" (*Dictionary*, sense 1).

FROM THE *IDLER*

[1] This essay was the original Idler *22* in the *Universal Chronicle*. Johnson or his publishers, however, decided to exclude it from the collected edition of 1761, which is the basis of all later editions, including the Yale Edition.

[2] *Bohemia* An historical country of central Europe, mainly occupying much of the current Czech Republic.

"I soon perceived, that my labour would be well repaid; for an old vulture was sitting on a naked prominence, with her young about her, whom she was instructing in the arts of a vulture's life, and preparing, by the last lecture, for their final dismission to the mountains and the skies.

"'My children,' said the old vulture, 'you will the less want my instructions because you have had my practice before your eyes; you have seen me snatch from the farm the household fowl, you have seen me seize the leveret[3] in the bush, and the kid in the pasture, you know how to fix your talons, and how to balance your flight when you are laden with your prey. But you remember the taste of more delicious food; I have often regaled you with the flesh of man.' 'Tell us,' said the young vultures, 'where man may be found, and how he may be known; his flesh is surely the natural food of a vulture. Why have you never brought a man in your talons to the nest?' 'He is too bulky,' said the mother; 'when we find a man, we can only tear away his flesh, and leave his bones upon the ground.' 'Since man is so big,' said the young ones, 'how do you kill him. You are afraid of the wolf and of the bear, by what power are vultures superior to man, is man more defenceless than a sheep?' 'We have not the strength of man,' returned the mother, 'and I am sometimes in doubt whether we have the subtlety; and the vultures would seldom feast upon his flesh, had not nature, that devoted him to our uses, infused into him a strange ferocity, which I have never observed in any other being that feeds upon the earth. Two herds of men will often meet and shake the earth with noise, and fill the air with fire. When you hear noise and see fire, which flashes along the ground, hasten to the place with your swiftest wing, for men are surely destroying one another; you will then find the ground smoking with blood and covered with carcasses, of which many are dismembered and mangled for the convenience of the vulture.' 'But when men have killed their prey,' said the pupil, 'why do they not eat it? When the wolf has killed a sheep, he suffers not the vulture to touch it till he has satisfied himself. Is not man another kind of wolf?' 'Man', said the mother, 'is the only beast who kills that which he does not devour, and this quality makes him so much a benefactor to our species.' 'If men kill our prey and lay it in our way,' said the young one, 'what need shall we have of labouring for ourselves.' 'Because man will, sometimes,' replied the mother, 'remain for a long time quiet in his den. The old vultures will tell you when you are to watch his motions. When you see men in great numbers moving close together, like a flight of storks, you may conclude that they are hunting, and that you will soon revel in human blood.' 'But still,' said the young one, 'I would gladly know the reason of this mutual slaughter. I could never kill what I could not eat.' 'My child,' said the mother, 'this is a question which I cannot answer, though I am reckoned the most subtle bird of the mountain. When I was young I used frequently to visit the eyrie of an old vulture who dwelt upon the Carpathian rocks;[4] he had made many observations; he knew the places that afforded prey round his habitation, as far in every direction as the strongest wing can fly between the rising and setting of the summer sun; he had fed year after year on the entrails of men. His opinion was, that men had only the appearance of animal life, being really vegetables with a power of motion; and that as the boughs of an oak are dashed together by the storm, that swine may fatten upon the fallen acorns, so men are by some unaccountable power driven one against another, till they lose their motion, that vultures may be fed. Others think

Notes

[3] *leveret* "A young hare" (*Dictionary*).

[4] A range of mountains running through current Slovakia and Romania.

they have observed something of contrivance and policy among these mischievous beings, and those that hover more closely round them, pretend, that there is, in every herd, one that gives directions to the rest, and seems to be more eminently delighted with a wide carnage. What it is that entitles him to such pre-eminence we know not; he is seldom the biggest or the swiftest, but he shows by his eagerness and diligence that he is, more than any of the others, a friend to vultures.'"

Number 81
Saturday, 3 November 1759

As the English army was passing towards Quebec[5] along a soft savanna[6] between a mountain and a lake, one of the petty chiefs of the inland regions stood upon a rock surrounded by his clan, and from behind the shelter of the bushes contemplated the art and regularity of European war. It was evening, the tents were pitched, he observed the security with which the troops rested in the night, and the order with which the march was renewed in the morning. He continued to pursue them with his eye till they could be seen no longer, and then stood for some time silent and pensive.

Then turning to his followers, "My children, (said he) I have often heard from men hoary with long life, that there was a time when our ancestors were absolute lords of the woods, the meadows and the lakes, wherever the eye can reach or the foot can pass. They fished and hunted, feasted and danced, and when they were weary lay down under the first thicket, without danger and without fear. They changed their habitations as the seasons required, convenience prompted, or curiosity allured them, and sometimes gathered the fruits of the mountain, and sometimes sported in canoes along the coast.

"Many years and ages are supposed to have been thus passed in plenty and security; when at last, a new race of men entered our country from the great ocean. They enclosed themselves in habitations of stone, which our ancestors could neither enter by violence, nor destroy by fire. They issued from those fastnesses, sometimes covered like the armadillo with shells, from which the lance rebounded on the striker, and sometimes carried by mighty beasts which had never been seen in our vales or forests, of such strength and swiftness, that flight and opposition were vain alike.[7] Those invaders ranged over the continent, slaughtering in their rage those that resisted, and those that submitted, in their mirth. Of those that remained, some were buried in caverns, and condemned to dig metals for their masters; some were employed in tilling the ground, of which foreign tyrants devour the produce; and when the sword and the mines have destroyed the natives, they supply their place by human beings of another colour, brought from some distant country to perish here under toil and torture.

"Some there are who boast their humanity, and content themselves to seize our chaces[8] and fisheries, who drive us from every track of ground where fertility and pleasantness invite them to settle, and make no war upon us except when we intrude upon our own lands.

Notes

5 The battle of Québec took place on 13 September 1759; the French capitulated on 18 September; both James Wolfe, the British commanding officer, and the Marquis de Montcalm, the French commander, died in the battle.

6 *savanna* "An open meadow without wood; pasture-ground in America" (*Dictionary*).

7 Spanish conquistadors first introduced horses to North America.

8 *chace* "Open ground stored with such beasts as are hunted" (*Dictionary*, sense 7).

"Others pretend to have purchased a right of residence and tyranny; but surely the insolence of such bargains is more offensive than the avowed and open dominion of force. What reward can induce the possessor of a country to admit a stranger more powerful than himself? Fraud or terror must operate in such contracts; either they promised protection which they never have afforded, or instruction which they never imparted. We hoped to be secured by their favour from some other evil, or to learn the arts of Europe, by which we might be able to secure ourselves. Their power they have never exerted in our defence, and their arts they have studiously concealed from us. Their treaties are only to deceive, and their traffic only to defraud us. They have a written law among them, of which they boast as derived from him who made the earth and sea, and by which they profess to believe that man will be made happy when life shall forsake him. Why is not this law communicated to us? It is concealed because it is violated. For how can they preach it to an Indian nation, when I am told that one of its first precepts forbids them to do to others what they would not that others should do to them.

"But the time, perhaps is now approaching when the pride of usurpation shall be crushed, and the cruelties of invasion shall be revenged. The sons of rapacity have now drawn their swords upon each other, and referred their claims to the decision of war; let us look unconcerned upon the slaughter, and remember that the death of every European delivers the country from a tyrant and a robber; for what is the claim of either nation, but the claim of the vulture to the leveret, of the tiger to the fawn? Let them then continue to dispute their title to regions which they cannot people, to purchase by danger and blood the empty dignity of dominion over mountains which they will never climb, and rivers which they will never pass. Let us endeavour, in the mean time, to learn their discipline, and to forge their weapons; and when they shall be weakened with mutual slaughter, let us rush down upon them, force their remains to take shelter in their ships, and reign once more in our native country."

from the Preface to *A Dictionary of the English Language* (1755)

It is the fate of those who toil at the lower employments of life, to be rather driven by the fear of evil, than attracted by the prospect of good; to be exposed to censure, without hope of praise; to be disgraced by miscarriage, or punished for neglect, where success would have been without applause, and diligence without reward.

Among these unhappy mortals is the writer of dictionaries; whom mankind have considered, not as the pupil, but the slave of science, the pioneer[1] of literature, doomed only to remove rubbish and clear obstructions from the paths through which Learning and Genius press forward to conquest and glory, without bestowing a smile on the humble drudge that facilitates their progress.[2] Every other author may aspire to praise; the lexicographer can only hope to escape reproach, and even this negative recompense has been yet granted to very few.

I have, notwithstanding this discouragement, attempted a dictionary of the *English* language, which, while it was employed in the cultivation of every species of literature,

Notes

FROM THE PREFACE

[1] *pioneer* "One whose business is to level the road, throw up the works, or sink the mines in military operations" (Johnson).

[2] *humble drudge* Johnson defines "lexicographer" in the *Dictionary* as "A harmless drudge, that busies himself in tracing the original, and detailing the signification of words."

has itself been hitherto neglected, suffered to spread, under the direction of chance, into wild exuberance, resigned to the tyranny of time and fashion, and exposed to the corruptions of ignorance, and caprices of innovation.

When I took the first survey of my undertaking, I found our speech copious without order, and energetic without rules: wherever I turned my view, there was perplexity to be disentangled, and confusion to be regulated; choice was to be made out of boundless variety, without any established principle of selection; adulterations were to be detected, without a settled test of purity, and modes of expression to be rejected or received, without the suffrages of any writers of classical reputation or acknowledged authority.

Having therefore no assistance but from general grammar, I applied myself to the perusal of our writers; and noting whatever might be of use to ascertain or illustrate any word or phrase, accumulated in time the materials of a dictionary, which, by degrees, I reduced to method, establishing to myself, in the progress of the work, such rules as experience and analogy suggested to me; experience, which practice and observation were continually increasing; and analogy, which, though in some words obscure, was evident in others.

In adjusting the ORTHOGRAPHY, which has been to this time unsettled and fortuitous, I found it necessary to distinguish those irregularities that are inherent in our tongue, and perhaps coeval with it, from others which the ignorance or negligence of later writers has produced. Every language has its anomalies, which, though inconvenient, and in themselves once unnecessary, must be tolerated among the imperfections of human things, and which require only to be registered, that they may not be increased, and ascertained, that they may not be confounded: but every language has likewise its improprieties and absurdities, which it is the duty of the lexicographer to correct or proscribe.

As language was at its beginning merely oral, all words of necessary or common use were spoken before they were written; and while they were unfixed by any visible signs, must have been spoken with great diversity, as we now observe those who cannot read to catch sounds imperfectly, and utter them negligently. When this wild and barbarous jargon was first reduced to an alphabet, every penman endeavoured to express, as he could, the sounds which he was accustomed to pronounce or to receive, and vitiated in writing such words as were already vitiated in speech. The powers of the letters, when they were applied to a new language, must have been vague and unsettled, and therefore different hands would exhibit the same sound by different combinations.

From this uncertain pronunciation arise in a great part the various dialects of the same country, which will always be observed to grow fewer, and less different, as books are multiplied; and from this arbitrary representation of sounds by letters, proceeds that diversity of spelling observable in the *Saxon* remains, and I suppose in the first books of every nation, which perplexes or destroys analogy, and produces anomalous formations, that, being once incorporated, can never be afterward dismissed or reformed. …

In this part of the work, where caprice has long wantoned without control, and vanity sought praise by petty reformation, I have endeavoured to proceed with a scholar's reverence for antiquity, and a grammarian's regard to the genius of our tongue. I have attempted few alterations, and among those few, perhaps the greater part is from the modern to the ancient practice, and I hope I may be allowed to recommend to those, whose thoughts have been, perhaps, employed too anxiously on verbal singularities, not to disturb, upon narrow views, or for minute propriety, the orthography of their fathers. It has been asserted, that for the law to be *known*, is of more importance than to be *right*.[3] Change, says *Hooker*, is not made without inconvenience, even from worse to better.[4] There is in constancy and stability a general and lasting advantage, which will always overbalance the slow improvements of gradual correction. Much less ought our written language to comply with the corruptions of oral utterance, or copy that which every variation of time or place makes different from itself, and imitate those changes, which will again be changed, while imitation is employed in observing them.

This recommendation of steadiness and uniformity does not proceed from an opinion, that particular combinations of letters have much influence on human happiness; or that truth may not be successfully taught by modes of spelling fanciful and erroneous: I am not yet so lost in lexicography, as to forget that *words are the daughters of earth, and that things are the sons of heaven*.[5] Language is only the instrument of science, and words are but the signs of ideas: I wish, however, that the instrument might be less apt to decay, and that signs might be permanent, like the things which they denote. ...

That part of my work on which I expect malignity most frequently to fasten, is the *Explanation*; in which I cannot hope to satisfy those, who are perhaps not inclined to be pleased, since I have not always been able to satisfy myself. To interpret a language by itself is very difficult; many words cannot be explained by synonyms, because the idea signified by them has not more than one appellation; nor by paraphrase, because simple ideas cannot be described. When the nature of things is unknown, or the notion unsettled and indefinite, and various in various minds, the words by which such notions are conveyed, or such things denoted, will be ambiguous and perplexed. And such is the fate of hapless lexicography, that not only darkness, but light, impedes and distresses it; things may be not only too little, but too much known, to be happily illustrated. To explain, requires the use of terms less abstruse than that which is to be explained, and such terms cannot always be found; for as nothing can be proved but by supposing something intuitively known, and evident without proof, so nothing can be defined but by the use of words too plain to admit a definition.

Other words there are, of which the sense is too subtle and evanescent to be fixed in a paraphrase; such are all those which are by the grammarians termed *expletives*, and, in dead languages, are suffered to pass for empty sounds, of no other use than to fill a verse, or to modulate a period, but which are easily perceived in living tongues to have power and emphasis, though it be sometimes such as no other form of expression can convey.

My labour has likewise been much increased by a class of verbs too frequent in the *English* language, of which the signification is so loose and general, the use so vague and indeterminate, and the senses detorted so widely from the first idea, that it is hard to trace them through the maze of variation, to catch them on the brink of utter inanity, to circumscribe them by any limitations, or interpret them by any words of distinct and settled meaning: such are *bear, break, come, cast, fall, get, give, do, put, set, go, run, make, take, turn, throw*. If of these the whole power is not accurately delivered, it must be remembered, that while our language is yet living, and variable by the caprice of every tongue that speaks it, these words are hourly shifting their relations, and can no

Notes

[3] *It has been asserted ... right* untraced.

[4] *Change ... better* Richard Hooker (1554–1600), *Of the Laws of Ecclesiastical Polity*, 4.14.

[5] *words ... heaven* a paraphrase of an ancient thought.

more be ascertained in a dictionary, than a grove, in the agitation of a storm, can be accurately delineated from its picture in the water. ...

In every word of extensive use, it was requisite to mark the progress of its meaning, and show by what gradations of intermediate sense it has passed from its primitive to its remote and accidental signification; so that every foregoing explanation should tend to that which follows, and the series be regularly concatenated from the first notion to the last.

This is specious, but not always practicable; kindred senses may be so interwoven, that the perplexity cannot be disentangled, nor any reason be assigned why one should be ranged before the other. When the radical idea branches out into parallel ramifications, how can a consecutive series be formed of senses in their nature collateral? The shades of meaning sometimes pass imperceptibly into each other; so that though on one side they apparently differ, yet it is impossible to mark the point of contact. Ideas of the same race, though not exactly alike, are sometimes so little different, that no words can express the dissimilitude, though the mind easily perceives it, when they are exhibited together; and sometimes there is such a confusion of acceptations, that discernment is wearied, and distinction puzzled, and perseverance herself hurries to an end, by crowding together what she cannot separate.

These complaints of difficulty will, by those that have never considered words beyond their popular use, be thought only the jargon of a man willing to magnify his labours, and procure veneration to his studies by involution and obscurity. But every art is obscure to those that have not learned it: this uncertainty of terms, and commixture of ideas, is well known to those who have joined philosophy with grammar; and if I have not expressed them very clearly, it must be remembered that I am speaking of that which words are insufficient to explain. ...

All the interpretations of words are not written with the same skill, or the same happiness: things equally easy in themselves, are not all equally easy to any single mind. Every writer of a long work commits errors, where there appears neither ambiguity to mislead, nor obscurity to confound him; and in a search like this, many felicities of expression will be casually overlooked, many convenient parallels will be forgotten, and many particulars will admit improvement from a mind utterly unequal to the whole performance.

The solution of all difficulties, and the supply of all defects, must be sought in the examples, subjoined to the various senses of each word, and ranged according to the time of their authors.

When first I collected these authorities, I was desirous that every quotation should be useful to some other end than the illustration of a word; I therefore extracted from philosophers principles of science; from historians remarkable facts; from chemists complete processes; from divines striking exhortations; and from poets beautiful descriptions. Such is design, while it is yet at a distance from execution. When the time called upon me to range this accumulation of elegance and wisdom into an alphabetical series, I soon discovered that the bulk of my volumes would fright away the student, and was forced to depart from my scheme of including all that was pleasing or useful in *English* literature, and reduce my transcripts very often to clusters of words, in which scarcely any meaning is retained; thus to the weariness of copying, I was condemned to add the vexation of expunging. Some passages I have yet spared, which may relieve the labour of verbal searches, and intersperse with verdure and flowers the dusty deserts of barren philology.

The examples, thus mutilated, are no longer to be considered as conveying the sentiments or doctrine of their authors; the word for the sake of which they are inserted, with all its appendant clauses, has been carefully preserved; but it may sometimes happen, by hasty detruncation, that the general tendency of the sentence may be changed: the divine may desert his tenets, or the philosopher his system.[6]

Some of the examples have been taken from writers who were never mentioned as masters of elegance or models of style; but words must be sought where they are used; and in what pages, eminent for purity, can terms of manufacture or agriculture be found? Many quotations serve no other purpose, than that of proving the bare existence of words, and are therefore selected with less scrupulousness than those which are to teach their structures and relations.

My purpose was to admit no testimony of living authors, that I might not be misled by partiality, and that none of my contemporaries might have reason to complain; nor have I departed from this resolution, but when some performance of uncommon excellence excited my veneration, when my memory supplied me, from late books, with an example that was wanting, or when my heart, in the tenderness of friendship, solicited admission for a favourite name.[7]

So far have I been from any care to grace my pages with modern decorations, that I have studiously endeavoured to collect examples and authorities from the writers before the restoration, whose works I regard as *the wells of English undefiled*, as the pure sources of genuine diction. Our language, for almost a century, has, by the concurrence of many causes, been gradually departing from its original *Teutonic* character, and deviating towards a *Gallic* structure and phraseology, from which it ought to be our endeavour to recall it, by making our ancient volumes the ground-work of style, admitting among the additions of later times, only such as may supply real deficiencies, such as are readily adopted by the genius of our tongue, and incorporate easily with our native idioms.

But as every language has a time of rudeness antecedent to perfection, as well as of false refinement and declension, I have been cautious lest my zeal for antiquity might drive me into times too remote, and crowd my book with words now no longer understood. I have fixed *Sidney*'s work[8] for the boundary, beyond which I make few excursions. From the authors which rose in the time of *Elizabeth*, a speech might be formed adequate to all the purposes of use and elegance. If the language of theology were extracted from *Hooker* and the translation of the Bible;[9] the terms of natural knowledge from Bacon; the phrases of policy, war, and navigation from *Raleigh*; the dialect of poetry and fiction from *Spenser* and *Sidney*; and the diction of common life from *Shakespeare*, few ideas would be lost to mankind, for want of *English* words, in which they might be expressed. …

There is more danger of censure from the multiplicity than paucity of examples; authorities will sometimes seem to have been accumulated without necessity or use, and perhaps some will be found, which might, without loss, have been omitted. But a work of this kind is not hastily to be charged with superfluities: those quotations which to careless or unskilful perusers appear only to repeat the same sense, will often exhibit, to a more accurate examiner, diversities of signification, or, at least, afford different shades of the same meaning: one will show the word applied to persons, another to things; one will express an ill, another a good, and a third a neutral sense; one will prove the expression genuine from an ancient author; another will

Notes

6 *divine … system* in fact, this rarely happens.

7 *a favourite name* among the living authors whom Johnson cited were David Garrick, Charlotte Lennox, Samuel Richardson, and himself.

8 *Sidney's work* Sir Philip Sidney (1554–86).

9 *Bible* the King James Version (1611).

show it elegant from a modern: a doubtful authority is corroborated by another of more credit; an ambiguous sentence is ascertained by a passage clear and determinate; the word, how often soever repeated, appears with new associates and in different combinations, and every quotation contributes something to the stability or enlargement of the language. …

I have sometimes, though rarely, yielded to the temptation of exhibiting a genealogy of sentiments, by showing how one author copied the thoughts and diction of another: such quotations are indeed little more than repetitions, which might justly be censured, did they not gratify the mind, by affording a kind of intellectual history. …

When first I engaged in this work, I resolved to leave neither words nor things unexamined, and pleased myself with a prospect of the hours which I should revel away in feasts of literature, the obscure recesses of northern learning, which I should enter and ransack, the treasures with which I expected every search into those neglected mines to reward my labour, and the triumph with which I should display my acquisitions to mankind. When I had thus enquired into the original of words, I resolved to show likewise my attention to things; to pierce deep into every science, to enquire the nature of every substance of which I inserted the name, to limit every idea by a definition strictly logical, and exhibit every production of art or nature in an accurate description, that my book might be in place of all other dictionaries whether appellative or technical. But these were the dreams of a poet doomed at last to wake a lexicographer. I soon found that it is too late to look for instruments, when the work calls for execution, and that whatever abilities I had brought to my task, with those I must finally perform it. To deliberate whenever I doubted, to enquire whenever I was ignorant, would have protracted the undertaking without end, and, perhaps, without much improvement; for I did not find by my first experiments, that what I had not of my own was easily to be obtained: I saw that one enquiry only gave occasion to another, that book referred to book, that to search was not always to find, and to find was not always to be informed; and that thus to pursue perfection, was, like the first inhabitants of Arcadia, to chase the sun, which, when they had reached the hill where he seemed to rest, was still beheld at the same distance from them. …

A large work is difficult because it is large, even though all its parts might singly be performed with facility; where there are many things to be done, each must be allowed its share of time and labour, in the proportion only which it bears to the whole; nor can it be expected, that the stones which form the dome of a temple, should be squared and polished like the diamond of a ring.

Of the event[10] of this work, for which, having laboured it with so much application, I cannot but have some degree of parental fondness, it is natural to form conjectures. Those who have been persuaded to think well of my design, will require that it should fix our language, and put a stop to those alterations which time and chance have hitherto been suffered to make in it without opposition. With this consequence I will confess that I flattered myself for a while; but now begin to fear that I have indulged expectation which neither reason nor experience can justify. When we see men grow old and die at a certain time one after another, from century to century, we laugh at the elixir that promises to prolong life to a thousand years; and

Notes

[10] *event* the outcome, the result.

with equal justice may the lexicographer be derided, who being able to produce no example of a nation that has preserved their words and phrases from mutability, shall imagine that his dictionary can embalm his language, and secure it from corruption and decay, that it is in his power to change sublunary nature, and clear the world at once from folly, vanity, and affectation.

With this hope, however, academies have been instituted, to guard the avenues of their languages, to retain fugitives, and repulse intruders; but their vigilance and activity have hitherto been vain; sounds are too volatile and subtle for legal restraints; to enchain syllables, and to lash the wind,[11] are equally the undertakings of pride, unwilling to measure its desires by its strength. …

Total and sudden transformations of a language seldom happen; conquests and migrations are now very rare: but there are other causes of change, which, though slow in their operation, and invisible in their progress, are perhaps as much superior to human resistance, as the revolutions of the sky, or intumescence of the tide. Commerce, however necessary, however lucrative, as it depraves the manners, corrupts the language; they that have frequent intercourse with strangers, to whom they endeavour to accommodate themselves, must in time learn a mingled dialect, like the jargon which serves the traffickers on the *Mediterranean* and *Indian* coasts. This will not always be confined to the exchange, the warehouse, or the port, but will be communicated by degrees to other ranks of the people, and be at last incorporated with the current speech.

There are likewise internal causes equally forcible. The language most likely to continue long without alteration, would be that of a nation raised a little, and but a little, above barbarity, secluded from strangers, and totally employed in procuring the conveniencies of life; either without books, or, like some of the *Mahometan* countries, with very few: men thus busied and unlearned, having only such words as common use requires, would perhaps long continue to express the same notions by the same signs. But no such constancy can be expected in a people polished by arts, and classed by subordination, where one part of the community is sustained and accommodated by the labour of the other. Those who have much leisure to think, will always be enlarging the stock of ideas, and every increase of knowledge, whether real or fancied, will produce new words, or combinations of words. When the mind is unchained from necessity, it will range after convenience; when it is left at large in the fields of speculation, it will shift opinions; as any custom is disused, the words that expressed it must perish with it; as any opinion grows popular, it will innovate speech in the same proportion as it alters practice.

As by the cultivation of various sciences, a language is amplified, it will be more furnished with words deflected from their original sense; the geometrician will talk of a courtier's *zenith*, or the *eccentric* virtue of a wild hero, and the physician of sanguine expectations and phlegmatic delays. Copiousness of speech will give opportunities to capricious choice, by which some words will be preferred, and others degraded; vicissitudes of fashion will enforce the use of new, or extend the signification of known terms. The tropes of poetry will make hourly encroachments, and the metaphorical will become the current sense: pronunciation will be varied by levity or ignorance, and the pen must at length comply with the tongue; illiterate

Notes

11 *to lash the wind* Xerxes' mad attempt (see *The Vanity of Human Wishes*, l. 232).

writers[12] will at one time or other, by public infatuation, rise into renown, who, not knowing the original import of words, will use them with colloquial licentiousness, confound distinction, and forget propriety. As politeness increases, some expressions will be considered as too gross and vulgar for the delicate, others as too formal and ceremonious for the gay and airy; new phrases are therefore adopted, which must, for the same reasons, be in time dismissed. …

If the changes that we fear be thus irresistible, what remains but to acquiesce with silence, as in the other insurmountable distresses of humanity? It remains that we retard what we cannot repel, that we palliate what we cannot cure. Life may be lengthened by care, though death cannot be ultimately defeated: tongues, like governments, have a natural tendency to degeneration; we have long preserved our constitution, let us make some struggles for our language.

In hope of giving longevity to that which its own nature forbids to be immortal, I have devoted this book, the labour of years, to the honour of my country, that we may no longer yield the palm of philology, without a contest, to the nations of the continent.[13] The chief glory of every people arises from its authors: whether I shall add any thing by my own writings to the reputation of *English* literature, must be left to time: much of my life has been lost under the pressures of disease; much has been trifled away; and much has always been spent in provision for the day that was passing over me; but I shall not think my employment useless or ignoble, if by my assistance foreign nations, and distant ages, gain access to the propagators of knowledge, and understand the teachers of truth; if my labours afford light to the repositories of science, and add celebrity to *Bacon*, to *Hooker*, to *Milton*, and to *Boyle*.[14]

When I am animated by this wish, I look with pleasure on my book, however defective, and deliver it to the world with the spirit of a man that has endeavoured well. That it will immediately become popular I have not promised to myself: a few wild blunders, and risible absurdities, from which no work of such multiplicity was ever free, may for a time furnish folly with laughter, and harden ignorance in contempt; but useful diligence will at last prevail, and there never can be wanting some who distinguish desert; who will consider that no dictionary of a living tongue ever can be perfect, since while it is hastening to publication, some words are budding, and some falling away; that a whole life cannot be spent upon syntax and etymology, and that even a whole life would not be sufficient; that he, whose design includes whatever language can express, must often speak of what he does not understand; that a writer will sometimes be hurried by eagerness to the end, and sometimes faint with weariness under a task, which *Scaliger* compares to the labours of the anvil and the mine;[15] that what is obvious is not always known, and what is known is not always present; that sudden fits of inadvertency will surprise vigilance, slight avocations will seduce attention, and casual eclipses of the mind will darken learning; and that the writer shall often in vain trace his memory at the moment of need, for that which yesterday he knew with intuitive readiness, and which will come uncalled into his thoughts to-morrow.

Notes

12 *illiterate writers* who do not know Latin or the history of English.

13 *the nations of the continent* Italy and France had both produced national dictionaries through the work of academies formed for the purpose.

14 *Boyle* Robert (1627–91), chemist and, like the other three, an author whose works are frequently cited in the *Dictionary*.

15 *Scaliger… mine* Joseph Scaliger (1540–1609), one of Johnson's heroes, author of an Arabic–Latin dictionary, so described lexicography in a Latin poem.

In this work, when it shall be found that much is omitted, let it not be forgotten that much likewise is performed; and though no book was ever spared out of tenderness to the author, and the world is little solicitous to know whence proceeded the faults of that which it condemns; yet it may gratify curiosity to inform it, that the *English Dictionary* was written with little assistance of the learned, and without any patronage of the great; not in the soft obscurities of retirement, or under the shelter of academic bowers, but amidst inconvenience and distraction, in sickness and in sorrow. It may repress the triumph of malignant criticism to observe, that if our language is not here fully displayed, I have only failed in an attempt which no human powers have hitherto completed. If the lexicons of ancient tongues, now immutably fixed, and comprised in a few volumes, are yet, after the toil of successive ages, inadequate and delusive; if the aggregated knowledge, and co-operating diligence of the *Italian* academicians, did not secure them from the censure of *Beni*;[16] if the embodied critics of *France*, when fifty years had been spent upon their work, were obliged to change its economy, and give their second edition another form,[17] I may surely be contented without the praise of perfection, which, if I could obtain, in this gloom of solitude, what would it avail me? I have protracted my work till most of those whom I wished to please, have sunk into the grave,[18] and success and miscarriage are empty sounds: I therefore dismiss it with frigid tranquillity, having little to fear or hope from censure or from praise.

The History of Rasselas, Prince of Abyssinia (1759)

Chapter 1
Description of a palace in a valley

Ye who listen with credulity to the whispers of fancy, and pursue with eagerness the phantoms of hope; who expect that age will perform the promises of youth, and that the deficiencies of the present day will be supplied by the morrow; attend to the history of Rasselas prince of Abyssinia.

Rasselas was the fourth son of the mighty emperor, in whose dominions the Father of waters begins his course; whose bounty pours down the streams of plenty, and scatters over half the world the harvests of Egypt.

According to the custom which has descended from age to age among the monarchs of the torrid zone, he was confined in a private palace, with the other sons and daughters of Abyssinian royalty, till the order of succession should call him to the throne.

The place, which the wisdom or policy of antiquity had destined for the residence of the Abyssinian princes, was a spacious valley in the kingdom of Amhara, surrounded on every side by mountains, of which the summits overhang the middle part. The only passage, by which it could be entered, was a cavern that passed under a rock, of which it has long been disputed whether it was the work of nature or of human industry. The outlet of the cavern was concealed by a thick wood, and the mouth which opened into

Notes

16 *Beni* Paolo Beni attacked the first edition of the *Vocabolario della Crusca* (1612).

17 *another form* for the second edition (1718) the editors strengthened the alphabetical ordering of the book by listing many words separately that had first appeared under their root forms.

18 *sunk into the grave* Johnson was thinking especially of his wife Elizabeth, who died in 1752.

the valley was closed with gates of iron, forged by the artificers of ancient days, so massy that no man could, without the help of engines, open or shut them.

From the mountains on every side, rivulets descended that filled all the valley with verdure and fertility, and formed a lake in the middle inhabited by fish of every species, and frequented by every fowl whom nature has taught to dip the wing in water. This lake discharged its superfluities by a stream which entered a dark cleft of the mountain on the northern side, and fell with dreadful noise from precipice to precipice till it was heard no more.

The sides of the mountains were covered with trees, the banks of the brooks were diversified with flowers; every blast shook spices from the rocks, and every month dropped fruits upon the ground. All animals that bite the grass, or browse the shrub, whether wild or tame, wandered in this extensive circuit, secured from beasts of prey by the mountains which confined them. On one part were flocks and herds feeding in the pastures, on another all the beasts of chase frisking in the lawns;[1] the spritely kid was bounding on the rocks, the subtle monkey frolicking in the trees, and the solemn elephant reposing in the shade. All the diversities of the world were brought together, the blessings of nature were collected, and its evils extracted and excluded.

The valley, wide and fruitful, supplied its inhabitants with the necessaries of life, and all delights and superfluities were added at the annual visit which the emperor paid his children, when the iron gate was opened to the sound of music; and during eight days every one that resided in the valley was required to propose whatever might contribute to make seclusion pleasant, to fill up the vacancies of attention, and lessen the tediousness of time. Every desire was immediately granted. All the artificers of pleasure were called to gladden the festivity; the musicians exerted the power of harmony, and the dancers showed their activity before the princes, in hope that they should pass their lives in this blissful captivity, to which those only were admitted whose performance was thought able to add novelty to luxury. Such was the appearance of security and delight which this retirement afforded, that they to whom it was new always desired that it might be perpetual; and as those, on whom the iron gate had once closed, were never suffered to return, the effect of longer experience could not be known. Thus every year produced new schemes of delight, and new competitors for imprisonment.

The palace stood on an eminence raised about thirty paces above the surface of the lake. It was divided into many squares or courts, built with greater or less magnificence according to the rank of those for whom they were designed. The roofs were turned into arches of massy stone joined with a cement that grew harder by time, and the building stood from century to century, deriding the solstitial rains and equinoctial hurricanes, without need of reparation.

This house, which was so large as to be fully known to none but some ancient officers who successively inherited the secrets of the place, was built as if suspicion herself had dictated the plan. To every room there was an open and secret passage, every square had a communication with the rest, either from the upper stories by private galleries, or by subterranean passages from the lower apartments. Many of the columns had unsuspected cavities, in which successive monarchs reposited their

Notes

The History of Rasselas, Prince of Abyssinia

1 *lawn* "An open space between woods" (Johnson).

treasures. They then closed up the opening with marble, which was never to be removed but in the utmost exigencies of the kingdom; and recorded their accumulations in a book which was itself concealed in a tower not entered but by the emperor, attended by the prince who stood next in succession.

Chapter 2
The discontent of Rasselas in the happy valley

Here the sons and daughters of Abyssinia lived only to know the soft vicissitudes of pleasure and repose, attended by all that were skilful to delight, and gratified with whatever the senses can enjoy. They wandered in gardens of fragrance, and slept in the fortresses of security. Every art was practised to make them pleased with their own condition. The sages who instructed them, told them of nothing but the miseries of public life, and described all beyond the mountains as regions of calamity, where discord was always raging, and where man preyed upon man.

To heighten their opinion of their own felicity, they were daily entertained with songs, the subject of which was the *happy valley*. Their appetites were excited by frequent enumerations of different enjoyments, and revelry and merriment was the business of every hour from the dawn of morning to the close of even.

These methods were generally successful; few of the princes had ever wished to enlarge their bounds, but passed their lives in full conviction that they had all within their reach that art or nature could bestow, and pitied those whom fate had excluded from this seat of tranquillity, as the sport of chance, and the slaves of misery.

Thus they rose in the morning, and lay down at night, pleased with each other and with themselves, all but Rasselas, who, in the twenty-sixth year of his age, began to withdraw himself from their pastimes and assemblies, and to delight in solitary walks and silent meditation. He often sat before tables covered with luxury, and forgot to taste the dainties that were placed before him: he rose abruptly in the midst of the song, and hastily retired beyond the sound of music. His attendants observed the change and endeavoured to renew his love of pleasure: he neglected their endeavours, repulsed their invitations, and spent day after day on the banks of rivulets sheltered with trees, where he sometimes listened to the birds in the branches, sometimes observed the fish playing in the stream, and anon cast his eyes upon the pastures and mountains filled with animals, of which some were biting the herbage, and some sleeping among the bushes.

This singularity of his humour made him much observed. One of the Sages, in whose conversation he had formerly delighted, followed him secretly, in hope of discovering the cause of his disquiet. Rasselas, who knew not that any one was near him, having for some time fixed his eyes upon the goats that were browsing among the rocks, began to compare their condition with his own.

'What', said he, 'makes the difference between man and all the rest of the animal creation? Every beast that strays beside me has the same corporal necessities with myself; he is hungry and crops the grass, he is thirsty and drinks the stream, his thirst and hunger are appeased, he is satisfied and sleeps; he rises again and is hungry, he is again fed and is at rest. I am hungry and thirsty like him, but when thirst and hunger cease I am not at rest; I am, like him, pained with want, but am not, like him, satisfied with fullness. The intermediate hours are tedious and gloomy; I long again to be hungry that I may again quicken my attention. The birds peck the berries or the corn, and fly away to the groves where they sit in seeming happiness on the branches, and waste their lives in tuning one unvaried series of sounds. I likewise can call the lutanist and the singer, but the sounds that pleased me yesterday weary me today, and will grow yet more wearisome tomorrow. I can discover within me no power of perception which is not glutted with its proper pleasure, yet I do not feel myself delighted. Man has surely some latent sense for which this place affords no gratification, or he has some desires distinct from sense which must be satisfied before he can be happy'.[2]

After this he lifted up his head, and seeing the moon rising, walked towards the palace. As he passed through the fields, and saw the animals around him, 'Ye', said he, 'are happy, and need not envy me that walk thus among you, burthened with myself; nor do I, ye gentle beings, envy your felicity; for it is not the felicity of man. I have many distresses from which ye are free; I fear pain when I do not feel it; I sometimes shrink at evils recollected, and sometimes start at evils anticipated: surely the equity of providence has balanced peculiar sufferings with peculiar enjoyments'.

With observations like these the prince amused himself as he returned, uttering them with a plaintive voice, yet with a look that discovered him to feel some complacence in his own perspicacity, and to receive some solace of the miseries of life, from consciousness of the delicacy with which he felt, and the eloquence with which he bewailed them. He mingled cheerfully in the diversions of the evening, and all rejoiced to find that his heart was lightened.

Chapter 3
The wants of him that wants nothing

On the next day his old instructor, imagining that he had now made himself acquainted with his disease of mind, was in hope of curing it by counsel, and officiously sought an opportunity of conference, which the prince, having long considered him as one whose intellects were exhausted, was not very willing to afford: 'Why', said he, 'does this man thus intrude upon me; shall I be never suffered to forget those lectures which pleased only while they were new, and to become new again must be forgotten?' He then walked into the wood, and composed himself to his usual meditations; when, before his thoughts had taken any settled form, he perceived his pursuer at his side, and was at first prompted by his impatience to go hastily away; but, being unwilling to offend a man whom he had once reverenced and still loved, he invited him to sit down with him on the bank.

The old man, thus encouraged, began to lament the change which had been lately observed in the prince, and to enquire why he so often retired from the pleasures of the palace, to loneliness and silence. 'I fly from pleasure', said the prince, 'because pleasure has ceased to please; I am lonely because I am miserable, and am unwilling to cloud with my presence the happiness of others'. 'You, Sir', said the sage, 'are the first who has complained of misery in the *happy valley*. I hope to convince you that your complaints have no real cause. You are here in full possession of all that the emperor of Abyssinia can bestow; here is neither labour to be endured nor danger to be dreaded, yet here is all that labour or danger can procure. Look round and tell me which of your wants is without supply: if you want nothing, how are you unhappy?'

Notes

[2] *Man … happy* among many theologians this was a standard argument for the existence of an immortal soul.

'That I want nothing', said the prince, 'or that I know not what I want, is the cause of my complaint; if I had any known want, I should have a certain wish; that wish would excite endeavour, and I should not then repine to see the sun move so slowly towards the western mountain, or lament when the day breaks and sleep will no longer hide me from myself. When I see the kids and the lambs chasing one another, I fancy that I should be happy if I had something to pursue. But, possessing all that I can want, I find one day and one hour exactly like another, except that the latter is still more tedious than the former. Let your experience inform me how the day may now seem as short as in my childhood, while nature was yet fresh, and every moment showed me what I never had observed before. I have already enjoyed too much; give me something to desire'.

The old man was surprised at this new species of affliction, and knew not what to reply, yet was unwilling to be silent. 'Sir', said he, 'if you had seen the miseries of the world, you would know how to value your present state'. 'Now', said the prince, 'you have given me something to desire; I shall long to see the miseries of the world, since the sight of them is necessary to happiness'.

Chapter 4
The prince continues to grieve and muse

At this time the sound of music proclaimed the hour of repast, and the conversation was concluded. The old man went away sufficiently discontented to find that his reasonings had produced the only conclusion which they were intended to prevent. But in the decline of life shame and grief are of short duration; whether it be that we bear easily what we have borne long, or that, finding ourselves in age less regarded, we less regard others; or, that we look with slight regard upon afflictions, to which we know that the hand of death is about to put an end.

The prince, whose views were extended to a wider space, could not speedily quiet his emotions. He had been before terrified at the length of life which nature promised him, because he considered that in a long time much must be endured; he now rejoiced in his youth, because in many years much might be done.

This first beam of hope, that had been ever darted into his mind, rekindled youth in his cheeks, and doubled the lustre of his eyes. He was fired with the desire of doing something, though he knew not yet with distinctness, either end or means.

He was now no longer gloomy and unsocial; but, considering himself as master of a secret stock of happiness, which he could enjoy only by concealing it, he affected to be busy in all schemes of diversion, and endeavoured to make others pleased with the state of which he himself was weary. But pleasures never can be so multiplied or continued, as not to leave much of life unemployed; there were many hours, both of the night and day, which he could spend without suspicion in solitary thought. The load of life was much lightened: he went eagerly into the assemblies, because he supposed the frequency of his presence necessary to the success of his purposes; he retired gladly to privacy, because he had now a subject of thought.

His chief amusement was to picture to himself that world which he had never seen; to place himself in various conditions; to be entangled in imaginary difficulties, and to be engaged in wild adventures: but his benevolence always terminated his projects in the relief of distress, the detection of fraud, the defeat of oppression, and the diffusion of happiness.

Thus passed twenty months of the life of Rasselas. He busied himself so intensely in visionary bustle, that he forgot his real solitude; and, amidst hourly preparations for the various incidents of human affairs, neglected to consider by what means he should mingle with mankind.

One day, as he was sitting on a bank, he feigned to himself an orphan virgin robbed of her little portion[3] by a treacherous lover, and crying after him for restitution and redress. So strongly was the image impressed upon his mind, that he started up in the maid's defence, and ran forward to seize the plunderer with all the eagerness of real pursuit. Fear naturally quickens the flight of guilt. Rasselas could not catch the fugitive with his utmost efforts; but, resolving to weary, by perseverance, him whom he could not surpass in speed, he pressed on till the foot of the mountain stopped his course.

Here he recollected himself, and smiled at his own useless impetuosity. Then raising his eyes to the mountain, 'This', said he, 'is the fatal obstacle that hinders at once the enjoyment of pleasure, and the exercise of virtue. How long is it that my hopes and wishes have flown beyond this boundary of my life, which yet I never have attempted to surmount!'

Struck with this reflection, he sat down to muse, and remembered, that since he first resolved to escape from his confinement, the sun had passed twice over him in his annual course. He now felt a degree of regret with which he had never been before acquainted. He considered how much might have been done in the time which had passed, and left nothing real behind it. He compared twenty months with the life of man. 'In life', said he, 'is not to be counted the ignorance of infancy, or imbecility of age. We are long before we are able to think, and we soon cease from the power of acting. The true period of human existence may be reasonably estimated as forty years, of which I have mused away the four and twentieth part. What I have lost was certain, for I have certainly possessed it; but of twenty months to come who can assure me?'

The consciousness of his own folly pierced him deeply, and he was long before he could be reconciled to himself. 'The rest of my time', said he, 'has been lost by the crime or folly of my ancestors, and the absurd institutions of my country; I remember it with disgust, but without remorse: but the months that have passed since new light darted into my soul, since I formed a scheme of reasonable felicity, have been squandered by my own fault. I have lost that which can never be restored: I have seen the sun rise and set for twenty months, an idle gazer on the light of heaven: In this time the birds have left the nest of their mother, and committed themselves to the woods and to the skies: the kid has forsaken the teat, and learned by degrees to climb the rocks in quest of independent sustenance. I only have made no advances, but am still helpless and ignorant. The moon, by more than twenty changes, admonished me of the flux of life; the stream that rolled before my feet upbraided my inactivity. I sat feasting on intellectual luxury, regardless alike of the examples of the earth, and the instructions of the planets. Twenty months are past, who shall restore them!'

These sorrowful meditations fastened upon his mind; he passed four months in resolving to lose no more time in idle resolves, and was awakened to more vigorous exertion by hearing a maid, who had broken a porcelain cup, remark, that what cannot be repaired is not to be regretted.

This was obvious; and Rasselas reproached himself that he had not discovered it, having not known, or not considered, how many useful hints are obtained by chance, and how often the mind, hurried by her own ardour to distant views, neglects the truths that lie open before her. He, for a few hours, regretted his regret, and from that time bent his whole mind upon the means of escaping from the valley of happiness.

Notes

[3] *portion* inheritance.

Chapter 5
The prince meditates his escape

He now found that it would be very difficult to effect that which it was very easy to suppose effected. When he looked round about him, he saw himself confined by the bars of nature which had never yet been broken, and by the gate, through which none that once had passed it were ever able to return. He was now impatient as an eagle in a grate.[4] He passed week after week in clambering the mountains, to see if there was any aperture which the bushes might conceal, but found all the summits inaccessible by their prominence. The iron gate he despaired to open; for it was not only secured with all the power of art, but was always watched by successive sentinels, and was by its position exposed to the perpetual observation of all the inhabitants.

He then examined the cavern through which the waters of the lake were discharged; and, looking down at a time when the sun shone strongly upon its mouth, he discovered it to be full of broken rocks, which, though they permitted the stream to flow through many narrow passages, would stop any body of solid bulk. He returned discouraged and dejected; but, having now known the blessing of hope, resolved never to despair.

In these fruitless searches he spent ten months. The time, however, passed cheerfully away: in the morning he rose with new hope, in the evening applauded his own diligence, and in the night slept sound after his fatigue. He met a thousand amusements which beguiled his labour, and diversified his thoughts. He discerned the various instincts of animals, and properties of plants, and found the place replete with wonders, of which he purposed to solace himself with the contemplation, if he should never be able to accomplish his flight; rejoicing that his endeavours, though yet unsuccessful, had supplied him with a source of inexhaustible enquiry.

But his original curiosity was not yet abated; he resolved to obtain some knowledge of the ways of men. His wish still continued, but his hope grew less. He ceased to survey any longer the walls of his prison, and spared to search by new toils for interstices which he knew could not be found, yet determined to keep his design always in view, and lay hold on any expedient that time should offer.

Chapter 6
A dissertation on the art of flying

Among the artists that had been allured into the happy valley, to labour for the accommodation and pleasure of its inhabitants, was a man eminent for his knowledge of the mechanic powers, who had contrived many engines both of use and recreation. By a wheel, which the stream turned, he forced the water into a tower, whence it was distributed to all the apartments of the palace. He erected a pavilion in the garden, around which he kept the air always cool by artificial showers. One of the groves, appropriated to the ladies, was ventilated by fans, to which the rivulet that ran through it gave a constant motion; and instruments of soft music were placed at proper distances, of which some played by the impulse of the wind, and some by the power of the stream.

Notes

[4] *grate* prison cell with bars, or a cage.

This artist was sometimes visited by Rasselas, who was pleased with every kind of knowledge, imagining that the time would come when all his acquisitions should be of use to him in the open world. He came one day to amuse himself in his usual manner, and found the master busy in building a sailing chariot: he saw that the design was practicable upon a level surface, and with expressions of great esteem solicited its completion. The workman was pleased to find himself so much regarded by the prince, and resolved to gain yet higher honours. 'Sir', said he, 'you have seen but a small part of what the mechanic[5] sciences can perform. I have been long of opinion, that, instead of the tardy conveyance of ships and chariots, man might use the swifter migration of wings; that the fields of air are open to knowledge, and that only ignorance and idleness need crawl upon the ground'.

This hint rekindled the prince's desire of passing the mountains; and having seen what the mechanist had already performed, he was willing to fancy that he could do more; yet resolved to enquire further before he suffered hope to afflict him by disappointment. 'I am afraid', said he to the artist, 'that your imagination prevails over your skill, and that you now tell me rather what you wish than what you know. Every animal has his element assigned him; the birds have the air, and man and beasts the earth'. 'So', replied the mechanist, 'fishes have the water, in which yet beasts can swim by nature, and men by art. He that can swim needs not despair to fly: to swim is to fly in a grosser fluid, and to fly is to swim in a subtler.[6] We are only to proportion our power of resistance to the different density of the matter through which we are to pass. You will be necessarily upborne by the air, if you can renew any impulse upon it, faster than the air can recede from the pressure'.

'But the exercise of swimming, said the prince, is very laborious; the strongest limbs are soon wearied; I am afraid the act of flying will be yet more violent, and wings will be of no great use, unless we can fly further than we can swim'.

'The labour of rising from the ground', said the artist, 'will be great, as we see it in the heavier domestic fowls; but, as we mount higher, the earth's attraction, and the body's gravity, will be gradually diminished, till we shall arrive at a region where the man will float in the air without any tendency to fall: no care will then be necessary, but to move forwards, which the gentlest impulse will effect. You, Sir, whose curiosity is so extensive, will easily conceive with what pleasure a philosopher, furnished with wings, and hovering in the sky, would see the earth, and all its inhabitants, rolling beneath him, and presenting to him successively, by its diurnal motion, all the countries within the same parallel. How must it amuse the pendent[7] spectator to see the moving scene of land and ocean, cities and deserts! To survey with equal security the marts of trade, and the fields of battle; mountains infested by barbarians, and fruitful regions gladdened by plenty, and lulled by peace! How easily shall we then trace the Nile through all his passage; pass over to distant regions, and examine the face of nature from one extremity of the earth to the other!'

'All this', said the prince, 'is much to be desired, but I am afraid that no man will be able to breathe in these regions of speculation and tranquillity. I have been told, that respiration is difficult upon lofty mountains, yet from these precipices, though so high as to produce great tenuity[8] of the air, it is very easy to fall: therefore I suspect, that from any height, where life can be supported, there may be danger of too quick descent'.

Notes

5 *mechanic* practical or applied.

6 *subtle* "Thin; not dense; not gross" (Johnson).

7 *pendent* suspended, in air.

8 *tenuity* thinness.

'Nothing', replied the artist, 'will ever be attempted, if all possible objections must be first overcome. If you will favour my project I will try the first flight at my own hazard. I have considered the structure of all volant[9] animals, and find the folding continuity of the bat's wings most easily accommodated to the human form. Upon this model I shall begin my task tomorrow, and in a year expect to tower into the air beyond the malice or pursuit of man. But I will work only on this condition, that the art shall not be divulged, and that you shall not require me to make wings for any but ourselves'.

'Why', said Rasselas, 'should you envy others so great an advantage? All skill ought to be exerted for universal good; every man has owed much to others, and ought to repay the kindness that he has received'.

'If men were all virtuous', returned the artist, 'I should with great alacrity teach them all to fly. But what would be the security of the good, if the bad could at pleasure invade them from the sky? Against an army sailing through the cloud neither walls, nor mountains, nor seas, could afford any security. A flight of northern savages might hover in the wind, and light at once with irresistible violence upon the capital of a fruitful region that was rolling under them. Even this valley, the retreat of princes, the abode of happiness, might be violated by the sudden descent of some of the naked nations that swarm on the coast of the southern sea'.

The prince promised secrecy, and waited for the performance, not wholly hopeless of success. He visited the work from time to time, observed its progress, and remarked many ingenious contrivances to facilitate motion, and unite levity with strength. The artist was every day more certain that he should leave vultures and eagles behind him, and the contagion of his confidence seized upon the prince.

In a year the wings were finished, and, on a morning appointed, the maker appeared furnished for flight on a little promontory: he waved his pinions a while to gather air, then leaped from his stand, and in an instant dropped into the lake. His wings, which were of no use in the air, sustained him in the water, and the prince drew him to land, half dead with terror and vexation.

Chapter 7
The prince finds a man of learning

The prince was not much afflicted by this disaster, having suffered himself to hope for a happier event, only because he had no other means of escape in view. He still persisted in his design to leave the happy valley by the first opportunity.

His imagination was now at a stand; he had no prospect of entering into the world; and, notwithstanding all his endeavours to support himself, discontent by degrees preyed upon him, and he began again to lose his thoughts in sadness, when the rainy season, which in these countries is periodical, made it inconvenient to wander in the woods.

The rain continued longer and with more violence than had been ever known: the clouds broke on the surrounding mountains, and the torrents streamed into the plain on every side, till the cavern was too narrow to discharge the water. The lake overflowed its banks, and all the level of the valley was covered with the inundation. The eminence, on which the palace was built, and some other spots of rising ground, were

Notes

[9] *volant* flying (Latinate words, like "tenuity" and "volant," comprised the technical vocabulary of contemporary researchers and inventors).

all that the eye could now discover. The herds and flocks left the pastures, and both the wild beasts and the tame retreated to the mountains.

This inundation confined all the princes to domestic amusements, and the attention of Rasselas was particularly seized by a poem, which Imlac recited, upon the various conditions of humanity. He commanded the poet to attend him in his apartment, and recite his verses a second time; then entering into familiar talk, he thought himself happy in having found a man who knew the world so well, and could so skilfully paint the scenes of life. He asked a thousand questions about things, to which, though common to all other mortals, his confinement from childhood had kept him a stranger. The poet pitied his ignorance, and loved his curiosity, and entertained him from day to day with novelty and instruction, so that the prince regretted the necessity of sleep, and longed till the morning should renew his pleasure.

As they were sitting together, the prince commanded Imlac to relate his history, and to tell by what accident he was forced, or by what motive induced, to close his life in the happy valley. As he was going to begin his narrative, Rasselas was called to a concert, and obliged to restrain his curiosity till the evening.

Chapter 8
The history of Imlac

The close of the day is, in the regions of the torrid zone, the only season of diversion and entertainment, and it was therefore mid-night before the music ceased, and the princesses retired. Rasselas then called for his companion and required him to begin the story of his life.

'Sir', said Imlac, 'my history will not be long: the life that is devoted to knowledge passes silently away, and is very little diversified by events. To talk in public, to think in solitude, to read and to hear, to enquire, and answer enquiries, is the business of a scholar. He wanders about the world without pomp or terror, and is neither known nor valued but by men like himself.

'I was born in the kingdom of Goiama, at no great distance from the fountain of the Nile. My father was a wealthy merchant, who traded between the inland countries of Africa and the ports of the Red Sea. He was honest, frugal and diligent, but of mean sentiments, and narrow comprehension: he desired only to be rich, and to conceal his riches, lest he should be spoiled by the governors of the province'.

'Surely', said the prince, 'my father must be negligent of his charge, if any man in his dominions dares take that which belongs to another. Does he not know that kings are accountable for injustice permitted as well as done? If I were emperor, not the meanest of my subjects should be oppressed with impunity. My blood boils when I am told that a merchant durst not enjoy his honest gains for fear of losing them by the rapacity of power. Name the governor who robbed the people, that I may declare his crimes to the emperor'.

'Sir', said Imlac, 'your ardour is the natural effect of virtue animated by youth: the time will come when you will acquit your father, and perhaps hear with less impatience of the governor. Oppression is, in the Abyssinian dominions, neither frequent nor tolerated; but no form of government has been yet discovered, by which cruelty can be wholly prevented. Subordination supposes power on one part and subjection on the other; and if power be in the hands of men, it will sometimes be abused. The vigilance of the supreme magistrate may do much, but much will still remain undone. He can never know all the crimes that are committed, and can seldom punish all that he knows'.

'This', said the prince, 'I do not understand, but I had rather hear thee than dispute. Continue thy narration'.

'My father', proceeded Imlac, 'originally intended that I should have no other education, than such as might qualify me for commerce; and discovering in me great strength of memory, and quickness of apprehension, often declared his hope that I should be some time the richest man in Abyssinia'.

'Why', said the prince, 'did thy father desire the increase of his wealth, when it was already greater than he durst discover or enjoy? I am unwilling to doubt thy veracity, yet inconsistencies cannot both be true'.

'Inconsistencies', answered Imlac, 'cannot both be right, but, imputed to man, they may both be true. Yet diversity is not inconsistency. My father might expect a time of greater security. However, some desire is necessary to keep life in motion, and he, whose real wants are supplied, must admit those of fancy'.

'This', said the prince, 'I can in some measure conceive. I repent that I interrupted thee'.

'With this hope', proceeded Imlac, 'he sent me to school; but when I had once found the delight of knowledge, and felt the pleasure of intelligence and the pride of invention, I began silently to despise riches, and determined to disappoint the purpose of my father, whose grossness of conception raised my pity. I was twenty years old before his tenderness would expose me to the fatigue of travel, in which time I had been instructed, by successive masters, in all the literature of my native country. As every hour taught me something new, I lived in a continual course of gratifications; but, as I advanced towards manhood, I lost much of the reverence with which I had been used to look on my instructors; because, when the lesson was ended, I did not find them wiser or better than common men.

'At length my father resolved to initiate me in commerce, and, opening one of his subterranean treasuries, counted out ten thousand pieces of gold. "This, young man", said he, "is the stock with which you must negotiate. I began with less than the fifth part, and you see how diligence and parsimony have increased it. This is your own to waste or to improve. If you squander it by negligence or caprice, you must wait for my death before you will be rich: if, in four years, you double your stock, we will thenceforward let subordination cease, and live together as friends and partners; for he shall always be equal with me, who is equally skilled in the art of growing rich" '.

'We laid our money upon camels, concealed in bales of cheap goods, and travelled to the shore of the Red Sea. When I cast my eye on the expanse of waters my heart bounded like that of a prisoner escaped. I felt an unextinguishable curiosity kindle in my mind, and resolved to snatch this opportunity of seeing the manners of other nations, and of learning sciences unknown in Abyssinia.

'I remembered that my father had obliged me to the improvement of my stock, not by a promise which I ought not to violate, but by a penalty which I was at liberty to incur; and therefore determined to gratify my predominant desire, and by drinking at the fountains of knowledge, to quench the thirst of curiosity.

'As I was supposed to trade without connection with my father, it was easy for me to become acquainted with the master of a ship, and procure a passage to some other country. I had no motives of choice to regulate my voyage; it was sufficient for me that, wherever I wandered, I should see a country which I had not seen before. I therefore entered a ship bound for Surat,[10] having left a letter for my father declaring my intention.

Notes

[10] *Surat* a city in India famous for trade.

Chapter 9
The history of Imlac continued

'When I first entered upon the world of waters, and lost sight of land, I looked round about me with pleasing terror, and thinking my soul enlarged by the boundless prospect, imagined that I could gaze round for ever without satiety; but, in a short time, I grew weary of looking on barren uniformity, where I could only see again what I had already seen. I then descended into the ship, and doubted for a while whether all my future pleasures would not end like this in disgust and disappointment. Yet, surely, said I, the ocean and the land are very different; the only variety of water is rest and motion, but the earth has mountains and valleys, deserts and cities: it is inhabited by men of different customs and contrary opinions; and I may hope to find variety in life, though I should miss it in nature.

'With this hope I quieted my mind; and amused myself during the voyage; sometimes by learning from the sailors the art of navigation, which I have never practised, and sometimes by forming schemes for my conduct in different situations, in not one of which I have been ever placed.

'I was almost weary of my naval amusements when we landed safely at Surat. I secured my money, and purchasing some commodities for show, joined myself to a caravan that was passing into the inland country. My companions, for some reason or other, conjecturing that I was rich, and, by my enquiries and admiration, finding that I was ignorant, considered me as a novice whom they had a right to cheat, and who was to learn at the usual expense the art of fraud. They exposed me to the theft of servants, and the exaction of officers, and saw me plundered upon false pretences, without any advantage to themselves, but that of rejoicing in the superiority of their own knowledge'.

'Stop a moment', said the prince. 'Is there such depravity in man, as that he should injure another without benefit to himself? I can easily conceive that all are pleased with superiority; but your ignorance was merely accidental, which, being neither your crime nor your folly, could afford them no reason to applaud themselves; and the knowledge which they had, and which you wanted, they might as effectually have shown by warning, as betraying you'.

'Pride', said Imlac, 'is seldom delicate, it will please itself with very mean advantages; and envy feels not its own happiness, but when it may be compared with the misery of others. They were my enemies because they thought me rich, and my oppressors because they delighted to find me weak'.

'Proceed', said the prince: 'I doubt not of the facts which you relate, but imagine that you impute them to mistaken motives'.

'In this company', said Imlac, 'I arrived at Agra,[11] the capital of Indostan, the city in which the great Mogul commonly resides. I applied myself to the language of the country, and in a few months was able to converse with the learned men; some of whom I found morose and reserved, and others easy and communicative; some were unwilling to teach another what they had with difficulty learned themselves; and some showed that the end of their studies was to gain the dignity of instructing.

Notes

[11] *Agra* city in north central India, the capital of the Islamic Mughal Empire, which controlled the subcontinent from the early sixteenth century until 1761.

'To the tutor of the young princes I recommended myself so much, that I was presented to the emperor as a man of uncommon knowledge. The emperor asked me many questions concerning my country and my travels; and though I cannot now recollect any thing that he uttered above the power of a common man, he dismissed me astonished at his wisdom, and enamoured of his goodness.

'My credit was now so high, that the merchants, with whom I had travelled, applied to me for recommendations to the ladies of the court. I was surprised at their confidence of solicitation, and gently reproached them with their practices on the road. They heard me with cold indifference, and showed no tokens of shame or sorrow.

'They then urged their request with the offer of a bribe; but what I would not do for kindness I would not do for money; and refused them, not because they had injured me, but because I would not enable them to injure others; for I knew they would have made use of my credit to cheat those who should buy their wares.

'Having resided at Agra till there was no more to be learned, I travelled into Persia, where I saw many remains of ancient magnificence, and observed many new accommodations of life. The Persians are a nation eminently social, and their assemblies afforded me daily opportunities of remarking characters and manners, and of tracing human nature through all its variations.

'From Persia I passed into Arabia, where I saw a nation at once pastoral and warlike; who live without any settled habitation; whose only wealth is their flocks and herds; and who have yet carried on, through all ages, an hereditary war with all mankind, though they neither covet nor envy their possessions'.

Chapter 10
Imlac's history continued: A dissertation upon poetry

'Wherever I went, I found that Poetry was considered as the highest learning, and regarded with a veneration somewhat approaching to that which man would pay to the Angelic Nature. And it yet fills me with wonder, that, in almost all countries, the most ancient poets are considered as the best: whether it be that every other kind of knowledge is an acquisition gradually attained, and poetry is a gift conferred at once; or that the first poetry of every nation surprised them as a novelty, and retained the credit by consent which it received by accident at first: or whether the province of poetry is to describe Nature and passion, which are always the same, the first writers took possession of the most striking objects for description, and the most probable occurrences for fiction, and left nothing to those that followed them, but transcription of the same events, and new combinations of the same images. Whatever be the reason, it is commonly observed that the early writers are in possession of nature, and their followers of art: that the first excel in strength and invention, and the latter in elegance and refinement.

'I was desirous to add my name to this illustrious fraternity. I read all the poets of Persia and Arabia, and was able to repeat by memory the volumes that are suspended in the mosque of Mecca. But I soon found that no man was ever great by imitation. My desire of excellence impelled me to transfer my attention to nature and to life. Nature was to be my subject, and men to be my auditors: I could never describe what I had not seen: I could not hope to move those with delight or terror, whose interests and opinions I did not understand.

'Being now resolved to be a poet, I saw every thing with a new purpose; my sphere of attention was suddenly magnified: no kind of knowledge was to be overlooked. I ranged mountains and deserts for images and resemblances, and pictured upon my mind every tree of the forest and flower of the valley. I observed with equal care the crags of the rock and the pinnacles of the palace. Sometimes I wandered along the mazes of the rivulet, and sometimes watched the changes of the summer clouds. To a poet nothing can be useless. Whatever is beautiful, and whatever is dreadful, must be familiar to his imagination: he must be conversant with all that is awfully vast or elegantly little. The plants of the garden, the animals of the wood, the minerals of the earth, and meteors of the sky, must all concur to store his mind with inexhaustible variety: for every idea is useful for the enforcement or decoration of moral or religious truth; and he, who knows most, will have most power of diversifying his scenes, and of gratifying his reader with remote allusions and unexpected instruction.

'All the appearances of nature I was therefore careful to study, and every country which I have surveyed has contributed something to my poetical powers'.

'In so wide a survey', said the prince, 'you must surely have left much unobserved. I have lived, till now, within the circuit of these mountains, and yet cannot walk abroad without the sight of something which I had never beheld before, or never heeded'.

'The business of a poet', said Imlac, 'is to examine, not the individual, but the species; to remark general properties and large appearances: he does not number the streaks of the tulip, or describe the different shades in the verdure of the forest. He is to exhibit in his portraits of nature such prominent and striking features, as recall the original to every mind; and must neglect the minuter discriminations, which one may have remarked, and another have neglected, for those characteristics which are alike obvious to vigilance and carelessness.

'But the knowledge of nature is only half the task of a poet; he must be acquainted likewise with all the modes of life. His character requires that he estimate the happiness and misery of every condition; observe the power of all the passions in all their combinations, and trace the changes of the human mind as they are modified by various institutions and accidental influences of climate or custom, from the spriteliness of infancy to the despondence of decrepitude. He must divest himself of the prejudices of his age or country; he must consider right and wrong in their abstracted and invariable state; he must disregard present laws and opinions, and rise to general and transcendental truths, which will always be the same: he must therefore content himself with the slow progress of his name; contemn the applause of his own time, and commit his claims to the justice of posterity. He must write as the interpreter of nature, and the legislator of mankind, and consider himself as presiding over the thoughts and manners of successive generations; as a being superior to time and place. His labour is not yet at an end: he must know many languages and many sciences; and, that his style may be worthy of his thoughts, must, by incessant practice, familiarize to himself every delicacy of speech and grace of harmony'.

Chapter 11
Imlac's narrative continued: A hint on pilgrimage

Imlac now felt the enthusiastic fit, and was proceeding to aggrandize his own profession, when the prince cried out, 'Enough! Thou hast convinced me, that no human being can ever be a poet. Proceed with thy narration'.

'To be a poet', said Imlac, 'is indeed very difficult'. 'So difficult', returned the prince, 'that I will at present hear no more of his labours. Tell me whither you went when you had seen Persia'.

'From Persia', said the poet, 'I travelled through Syria, and for three years resided in Palestine, where I conversed with great numbers of the northern and western nations of Europe; the nations which are now in possession of all power and all knowledge; whose armies are irresistible, and whose fleets command the remotest parts of the globe. When I compared these men with the natives of our own kingdom, and those that surround us, they appeared almost another order of beings. In their countries it is difficult to wish for any thing that may not be obtained: a thousand arts, of which we never heard, are continually labouring for their convenience and pleasure; and whatever their own climate has denied them is supplied by their commerce'.

'By what means', said the prince, 'are the Europeans thus powerful? or why, since they can so easily visit Asia and Africa for trade or conquest, cannot the Asiatics and Africans invade their coasts, plant colonies in their ports, and give laws to their natural princes? The same wind that carries them back would bring us thither'.

'They are more powerful, Sir, than we', answered Imlac, 'because they are wiser; knowledge will always predominate over ignorance, as man governs the other animals. But why their knowledge is more than ours, I know not what reason can be given, but the unsearchable will of the Supreme Being'.

'When', said the prince with a sigh, 'shall I be able to visit Palestine, and mingle with this mighty confluence of nations? Till that happy moment shall arrive, let me fill up the time with such representations as thou canst give me. I am not ignorant of the motive that assembles such numbers in that place, and cannot but consider it as the centre of wisdom and piety, to which the best and wisest men of every land must be continually resorting'.

'There are some nations', said Imlac, 'that send few visitants to Palestine; for many numerous and learned sects in Europe concur to censure pilgrimage as superstitious, or deride it as ridiculous'.

'You know', said the prince, 'how little my life has made me acquainted with diversity of opinions: it will be too long to hear the arguments on both sides; you, that have considered them, tell me the result'.

'Pilgrimage', said Imlac, 'like many other acts of piety, may be reasonable or superstitious, according to the principles upon which it is performed. Long journeys in search of truth are not commanded. Truth, such as is necessary to the regulation of life, is always found where it is honestly sought. Change of place is no natural cause of the increase of piety, for it inevitably produces dissipation of mind. Yet, since men go every day to view the fields where great actions have been performed, and return with stronger impressions of the event, curiosity of the same kind may naturally dispose us to view that country whence our religion had its beginning; and I believe no man surveys those awful scenes without some confirmation of holy resolutions. That the Supreme Being may be more easily propitiated in one place than in another, is the dream of idle superstition; but that some places may operate upon our own minds in an uncommon manner, is an opinion which hourly experience will justify. He who supposes that his vices may be more successfully combated in Palestine, will, perhaps, find himself mistaken, yet he may go thither without folly: he who thinks they will be more freely pardoned, dishonours at once his reason and religion'.

'These', said the prince, 'are European distinctions. I will consider them another time. What have you found to be the effect of knowledge? Are those nations happier than we?'

'There is so much infelicity', said the poet, 'in the world, that scarce any man has leisure from his own distresses to estimate the comparative happiness of others. Knowledge is certainly one of the means of pleasure, as is confessed by the natural desire which every mind feels of increasing its ideas. Ignorance is mere privation, by which nothing can be produced: it is a vacuity in which the soul sits motionless and torpid for want of attraction; and, without knowing why, we always rejoice when we learn, and grieve when we forget. I am therefore inclined to conclude, that, if nothing counteracts the natural consequence of learning, we grow more happy as our minds take a wider range.

'In enumerating the particular comforts of life we shall find many advantages on the side of the Europeans. They cure wounds and diseases with which we languish and perish. We suffer inclemencies of weather which they can obviate. They have engines for the dispatch of many laborious works, which we must perform by manual industry. There is such communication between distant places, that one friend can hardly be said to be absent from another. Their policy removes all public inconveniencies: they have roads cut through their mountains, and bridges laid upon their rivers. And, if we descend to the privacies of life, their habitations are more commodious, and their possessions are more secure'.

'They are surely happy', said the prince, 'who have all these conveniencies, of which I envy none so much as the facility with which separated friends interchange their thoughts'.

'The Europeans', answered Imlac, 'are less unhappy than we, but they are not happy. Human life is every where a state in which much is to be endured, and little to be enjoyed'.

Chapter 12
The story of Imlac continued

'I am not yet willing', said the prince, 'to suppose that happiness is so parsimoniously distributed to mortals; nor can believe but that, if I had the choice of life, I should be able to fill every day with pleasure. I would injure no man, and should provoke no resentment: I would relieve every distress, and should enjoy the benedictions of gratitude. I would choose my friends among the wise, and my wife among the virtuous; and therefore should be in no danger from treachery, or unkindness. My children should, by my care, be learned and pious, and would repay to my age what their childhood had received. What would dare to molest him who might call on every side to thousands enriched by his bounty, or assisted by his power? And why should not life glide quietly away in the soft reciprocation of protection and reverence? All this may be done without the help of European refinements, which appear by their effects to be rather specious than useful. Let us leave them and pursue our journey'.

'From Palestine', said Imlac, 'I passed through many regions of Asia; in the more civilized kingdoms as a trader, and among the Barbarians of the mountains as a pilgrim. At last I began to long for my native country, that I might repose after my travels, and fatigues, in the places where I had spent my earliest years, and gladden my old companions with the recital of my adventures. Often did I figure to myself those, with whom I had sported away the gay hours of dawning life, sitting round me in its evening, wondering at my tales, and listening to my counsels.

'When this thought had taken possession of my mind, I considered every moment as wasted which did not bring me nearer to Abyssinia. I hastened into Egypt, and, notwithstanding my impatience, was detained ten months in the contemplation of its ancient magnificence, and in enquiries after the remains of its ancient learning. I found in Cairo a mixture of all nations; some brought thither by the love of knowledge, some by the hope of gain, and many by the desire of living after their own manner without observation, and of lying hid in the obscurity of multitudes: for, in a city, populous as Cairo, it is possible to obtain at the same time the gratifications of society, and the secrecy of solitude.

'From Cairo I travelled to Suez, and embarked on the Red Sea, passing along the coast till I arrived at the port from which I had departed twenty years before. Here I joined myself to a caravan and re-entered my native country.

'I now expected the caresses of my kinsmen, and the congratulations of my friends, and was not without hope that my father, whatever value he had set upon riches, would own with gladness and pride a son who was able to add to the felicity and honour of the nation. But I was soon convinced that my thoughts were vain. My father had been dead fourteen years, having divided his wealth among my brothers, who were removed to some other provinces. Of my companions the greater part was in the grave; of the rest some could with difficulty remember me, and some considered me as one corrupted by foreign manners.

'A man used to vicissitudes is not easily dejected. I forgot, after a time, my disappointment, and endeavoured to recommend myself to the nobles of the kingdom: they admitted me to their tables, heard my story, and dismissed me. I opened a school, and was prohibited to teach. I then resolved to sit down in the quiet of domestic life, and addressed a lady that was fond of my conversation, but rejected my suit, because my father was a merchant.

'Wearied at last with solicitation and repulses, I resolved to hide myself for ever from the world, and depend no longer on the opinion or caprice of others. I waited for the time when the gate of the *happy valley* should open, that I might bid farewell to hope and fear: the day came; my performance was distinguished with favour, and I resigned myself with joy to perpetual confinement'.

'Hast thou here found happiness at last?' said Rasselas. 'Tell me without reserve; art thou content with thy condition? or, dost thou wish to be again wandering and enquiring? All the inhabitants of this valley celebrate their lot, and, at the annual visit of the emperor, invite others to partake of their felicity'.

'Great prince', said Imlac, 'I shall speak the truth: I know not one of all your attendants who does not lament the hour when he entered this retreat. I am less unhappy than the rest, because I have a mind replete with images, which I can vary and combine at pleasure. I can amuse my solitude by the renovation of the knowledge which begins to fade from my memory, and by recollection of the accidents of my past life. Yet all this ends in the sorrowful consideration, that my acquirements are now useless, and that none of my pleasures can be again enjoyed. The rest, whose minds have no impression but of the present moment, are either corroded by malignant passions, or sit stupid in the gloom of perpetual vacancy'.

'What passions can infest those', said the prince, 'who have no rivals? We are in a place where impotence precludes malice, and where all envy is repressed by community of enjoyments'.

'There may be community', said Imlac, 'of material possessions, but there can never be community of love or of esteem. It must happen that one will please more than another; he that knows himself despised will always be envious; and still more envious and malevolent, if he is condemned to live in the presence of those who despise him. The invitations, by which they allure others to a state which they feel to be wretched, proceed from the natural malignity of hopeless misery. They are weary of themselves, and of each other, and expect to find relief in new companions. They envy the liberty which their folly has forfeited, and would gladly see all mankind imprisoned like themselves.

'From this crime, however, I am wholly free. No man can say that he is wretched by my persuasion. I look with pity on the crowds who are annually soliciting admission to captivity, and wish that it were lawful for me to warn them of their danger'.

'My dear Imlac', said the prince, 'I will open to thee my whole heart. I have long meditated an escape from the *happy valley*. I have examined the mountains on every side, but find myself insuperably barred: teach me the way to break my prison; thou shalt be the companion of my flight, the guide of my rambles, the partner of my fortune, and my sole director in the choice of life'.

'Sir', answered the poet, 'your escape will be difficult, and, perhaps, you may soon repent your curiosity. The world, which you figure to yourself smooth and quiet as the lake in the valley, you will find a sea foaming with tempests, and boiling with whirlpools: you will be sometimes overwhelmed by the waves of violence, and sometimes dashed against the rocks of treachery. Amidst wrongs and frauds, competitions and anxieties, you will wish a thousand times for these seats of quiet, and willingly quit hope to be free from fear'.

'Do not seek to deter me from my purpose', said the prince: 'I am impatient to see what thou hast seen; and, since thou art thyself weary of the valley, it is evident, that thy former state was better than this. Whatever be the consequence of my experiment, I am resolved to judge with my own eyes of the various conditions of men, and then to make deliberately my *choice of life*'.

'I am afraid', said Imlac, 'you are hindered by stronger restraints than my persuasions; yet, if your determination is fixed, I do not counsel you to despair. Few things are impossible to diligence and skill'.

Chapter 13
Rasselas discovers the means of escape

The prince now dismissed his favourite to rest, but the narrative of wonders and novelties filled his mind with perturbation. He revolved all that he had heard, and prepared innumerable questions for the morning.

Much of his uneasiness was now removed. He had a friend to whom he could impart his thoughts, and whose experience could assist him in his designs. His heart was no longer condemned to swell with silent vexation. He thought that even the *happy valley* might be endured with such a companion, and that, if they could range the world together, he should have nothing further to desire.

In a few days the water was discharged, and the ground dried. The prince and Imlac then walked out together to converse without the notice of the rest. The prince, whose thoughts were always on the wing, as he passed by the gate, said, with a countenance of sorrow, 'Why art thou so strong, and why is man so weak?'

'Man is not weak', answered his companion; 'knowledge is more than equivalent to force. The master of mechanics laughs at strength. I can burst the gate, but cannot do it secretly. Some other expedient must be tried'.

As they were walking on the side of the mountain, they observed that the conies,[12] which the rain had driven from their burrows, had taken shelter among the bushes, and formed holes behind them, tending upwards in an oblique line. 'It has been the opinion of antiquity', said Imlac, 'that human reason borrowed many arts from the instinct of animals; let us, therefore, not think ourselves degraded by learning from the coney. We may escape by piercing the mountain in the same direction. We will begin where the summit hangs over the middle part, and labour upward till we shall issue out beyond the prominence'.

The eyes of the prince, when he heard this proposal, sparkled with joy. The execution was easy, and the success certain.

No time was now lost. They hastened early in the morning to choose a place proper for their mine. They clambered with great fatigue among crags and brambles, and returned without having discovered any part that favoured their design. The second and the third day were spent in the same manner, and with the same

Notes

[12] *conies* rabbits.

frustration. But, on the fourth, they found a small cavern, concealed by a thicket, where they resolved to make their experiment.

Imlac procured instruments proper to hew stone and remove earth, and they fell to their work on the next day with more eagerness than vigour. They were presently exhausted by their efforts, and sat down to pant upon the grass. The prince, for the moment, appeared to be discouraged. 'Sir', said his companion, 'practice will enable us to continue our labour for a longer time; mark, however, how far we have advanced, and you will find that our toil will some time have an end. Great works are performed, not by strength but perseverance: yonder palace was raised by single stones, yet you see its height and spaciousness. He that shall walk with vigour three hours a day will pass in seven years a space equal to the circumference of the globe'.

They returned to their work day after day, and, in a short time, found a fissure in the rock, which enabled them to pass far with very little obstruction. This Rasselas considered as a good omen. 'Do not disturb your mind', said Imlac, 'with other hopes or fears than reason may suggest: if you are pleased with prognostics of good, you will be terrified likewise with tokens of evil, and your whole life will be a prey to superstition. Whatever facilitates our work is more than an omen, it is a cause of success. This is one of those pleasing surprises which often happen to active resolution. Many things difficult to design prove easy in performance'.

Chapter 14
Rasselas and Imlac receive an unexpected visit

They had now wrought their way to the middle, and solaced their labour with the approach of liberty, when the prince, coming down to refresh himself with air, found his sister Nekayah standing before the mouth of the cavity. He started and stood confused, afraid to tell his design, and yet hopeless to conceal it. A few moments determined him to repose on her fidelity, and secure her secrecy by a declaration without reserve.

'Do not imagine', said the princess, 'that I came hither as a spy: I had often observed from my window, that you and Imlac directed your walk every day towards the same point, but I did not suppose you had any better reason for the preference than a cooler shade, or more fragrant bank; nor followed you with any other design than to partake of your conversation. Since then not suspicion but fondness has detected you, let me not lose the advantage of my discovery. I am equally weary of confinement with yourself, and not less desirous of knowing what is done or suffered in the world. Permit me to fly with you from this tasteless tranquillity, which will yet grow more loathsome when you have left me. You may deny me to accompany you, but cannot hinder me from following'.

The prince, who loved Nekayah above his other sisters, had no inclination to refuse her request, and grieved that he had lost an opportunity of showing his confidence by a voluntary communication. It was therefore agreed that she should leave the valley with them; and that, in the mean time, she should watch, lest any other straggler should, by chance or curiosity, follow them to the mountain.

At length their labour was at an end; they saw light beyond the prominence, and, issuing to the top of the mountain, beheld the Nile, yet a narrow current, wandering beneath them.

The prince looked round with rapture, anticipated all the pleasures of travel, and in thought was already transported beyond his father's dominions. Imlac, though very joyful at his escape, had less expectation of pleasure in the world, which he had before tried, and of which he had been weary.

Rasselas was so much delighted with a wider horizon, that he could not soon be persuaded to return into the valley. He informed his sister that the way was open, and that nothing now remained but to prepare for their departure.

Chapter 15
The prince and princess leave the valley, and see many wonders

The prince and princess had jewels sufficient to make them rich whenever they came into a place of commerce, which, by Imlac's direction, they hid in their clothes, and, on the night of the next full moon, all left the valley. The princess was followed only by a single favourite, who did not know whither she was going.

They clambered through the cavity, and began to go down on the other side. The princess and her maid turned their eyes towards every part, and, seeing nothing to bound their prospect, considered themselves as in danger of being lost in a dreary vacuity. They stopped and trembled. 'I am almost afraid', said the princess, 'to begin a journey of which I cannot perceive an end, and to venture into this immense plain where I may be approached on every side by men whom I never saw'. The prince felt nearly the same emotions, though he thought it more manly to conceal them.

Imlac smiled at their terrors, and encouraged them to proceed; but the princess continued irresolute till she had been imperceptibly drawn forward too far to return.

In the morning they found some shepherds in the field, who set milk and fruits before them. The princess wondered that she did not see a palace ready for her reception, and a table spread with delicacies; but, being faint and hungry, she drank the milk and eat[13] the fruits, and thought them of a higher flavour than the products of the valley.

They travelled forward by easy journeys, being all unaccustomed to toil or difficulty, and knowing, that though they might be missed, they could not be pursued. In a few days they came into a more populous region, where Imlac was diverted with the admiration which his companions expressed at the diversity of manners, stations and employments.

Their dress was such as might not bring upon them the suspicion of having any thing to conceal, yet the prince, wherever he came, expected to be obeyed, and the princess was frighted, because those that came into her presence did not prostrate themselves before her. Imlac was forced to observe them with great vigilance, lest they should betray their rank by their unusual behaviour, and detained them several weeks in the first village to accustom them to the sight of common mortals.

By degrees the royal wanderers were taught to understand that they had for a time laid aside their dignity, and were to expect only such regard as liberality and courtesy could procure. And Imlac, having, by many admonitions, prepared them to endure the tumults of a port, and the ruggedness of the commercial race, brought them down to the seacoast.

The prince and his sister, to whom every thing was new, were gratified equally at all places, and therefore remained for some months at the port without any inclination to pass further. Imlac was content with their stay, because he did not think it safe to expose them, unpractised in the world, to the hazards of a foreign country.

Notes

[13] *eat* an acceptable form of the past tense at this time.

At last he began to fear lest they should be discovered, and proposed to fix a day for their departure. They had no pretensions to judge for themselves, and referred the whole scheme to his direction. He therefore took passage in a ship to Suez; and, when the time came, with great difficulty prevailed on the princess to enter the vessel. They had a quick and prosperous voyage, and from Suez travelled by land to Cairo.

Chapter 16
They enter Cairo, and find every man happy

As they approached the city, which filled the strangers with astonishment, 'This', said Imlac to the prince, 'is the place where travellers and merchants assemble from all the corners of the earth. You will here find men of every character, and every occupation. Commerce is here honourable: I will act as a merchant, and you shall live as strangers, who have no other end of travel than curiosity; it will soon be observed that we are rich; our reputation will procure us access to all whom we shall desire to know; you will see all the conditions of humanity, and enable yourself at leisure to make your *choice of life*'.

They now entered the town, stunned by the noise, and offended by the crowds. Instruction had not yet so prevailed over habit but that they wondered to see themselves pass undistinguished along the street, and met by the lowest of the people without reverence or notice. The princess could not at first bear the thought of being levelled with the vulgar, and, for some days, continued in her chamber, where she was served by her favourite as in the palace of the valley.

Imlac, who understood traffic,[14] sold part of the jewels the next day, and hired a house, which he adorned with such magnificence, that he was immediately considered as a merchant of great wealth. His politeness attracted many acquaintances, and his generosity made him courted by many dependants. His table was crowded by men of every nation, who all admired his knowledge, and solicited his favour. His companions, not being able to mix in the conversation, could make no discovery of their ignorance or surprise, and were gradually initiated in the world as they gained knowledge of the language.

The prince had, by frequent lectures, been taught the use and nature of money; but the ladies could not, for a long time, comprehend what the merchants did with small pieces of gold and silver, or why things of so little use should be received as equivalent to the necessaries of life.

They studied the language two years, while Imlac was preparing to set before them the various ranks and conditions of mankind. He grew acquainted with all who had any thing uncommon in their fortune or conduct. He frequented the voluptuous and the frugal, the idle and the busy, the merchants and the men of learning.

The prince, being now able to converse with fluency, and having learned the caution necessary to be observed in his intercourse with strangers, began to accompany Imlac to places of resort, and to enter into all assemblies, that he might make his *choice of life*.

For some time he thought choice needless, because all appeared to him equally happy. Wherever he went he met gaiety and kindness, and heard the song of joy, or the laugh of carelessness. He began to believe that the world overflowed with universal plenty, and that nothing was withheld either from want or merit; that every hand

Notes

[14] *traffic* commerce.

showered liberality, and every heart melted with benevolence: 'and who then', says he, 'will be suffered to be wretched?'

Imlac permitted the pleasing delusion, and was unwilling to crush the hope of inexperience; till one day, having sat a while silent, 'I know not', said the prince, 'what can be the reason that I am more unhappy than any of our friends. I see them perpetually and unalterably cheerful, but feel my own mind restless and uneasy. I am unsatisfied with those pleasures which I seem most to court; I live in the crowds of jollity, not so much to enjoy company as to shun myself, and am only loud and merry to conceal my sadness'.

'Every man', said Imlac, 'may, by examining his own mind, guess what passes in the minds of others: when you feel that your own gaiety is counterfeit, it may justly lead you to suspect that of your companions not to be sincere. Envy is commonly reciprocal. We are long before we are convinced that happiness is never to be found, and each believes it possessed by others, to keep alive the hope of obtaining it for himself. In the assembly, where you passed the last night, there appeared such spriteliness of air, and volatility of fancy as might have suited beings of an higher order, formed to inhabit serener regions inaccessible to care or sorrow: yet, believe me, prince, there was not one who did not dread the moment when solitude should deliver him to the tyranny of reflection'.

'This', said the prince, 'may be true of others, since it is true of me; yet, whatever be the general infelicity of man, one condition is more happy than another, and wisdom surely directs us to take the least evil in the *choice of life*'.

'The causes of good and evil', answered Imlac, 'are so various and uncertain, so often entangled with each other, so diversified by various relations, and so much subject to accidents which cannot be foreseen, that he who would fix his condition upon incontestable reasons of preference, must live and die enquiring and deliberating'.

'But surely', said Rasselas, 'the wise men, to whom we listen with reverence and wonder, chose that mode of life for themselves which they thought most likely to make them happy'.

'Very few', said the poet, 'live by choice. Every man is placed in his present condition by causes which acted without his foresight, and with which he did not always willingly co-operate; and therefore you will rarely meet one who does not think the lot of his neighbour better than his own'.

'I am pleased to think', said the prince, 'that my birth has given me at least one advantage over others, by enabling me to determine for myself. I have here the world before me; I will review it at leisure: surely happiness is somewhere to be found'.

Chapter 17
The prince associates with young men of spirit and gaiety

Rasselas rose next day, and resolved to begin his experiments upon life. 'Youth', cried he, 'is the time of gladness: I will join myself to the young men, whose only business is to gratify their desires, and whose time is all spent in a succession of enjoyments'.

To such societies he was readily admitted, but a few days brought him back weary and disgusted. Their mirth was without images, their laughter without motive; their pleasures were gross and sensual, in which the mind had no part; their conduct was at once wild and mean; they laughed at order and at law, but the frown of power dejected, and the eye of wisdom abashed them.

The prince soon concluded, that he should never be happy in a course of life of which he was ashamed. He thought it unsuitable to a reasonable being to act without a plan, and to be sad or cheerful only by chance. 'Happiness', said he, 'must be something solid and permanent, without fear and without uncertainty'.

But his young companions had gained so much of his regard by their frankness and courtesy, that he could not leave them without warning and remonstrance. 'My friends', said he, 'I have seriously considered our manners and our prospects, and find that we have mistaken our own interest. The first years of man must make provision for the last. He that never thinks never can be wise. Perpetual levity must end in ignorance; and intemperance, though it may fire the spirits for an hour, will make life short or miserable. Let us consider that youth is of no long duration, and that in maturer age, when the enchantments of fancy shall cease, and phantoms of delight dance no more about us, we shall have no comforts but the esteem of wise men, and the means of doing good. Let us, therefore, stop, while to stop is in our power: let us live as men who are sometime to grow old, and to whom it will be the most dreadful of all evils not to count their past years but by follies, and to be reminded of their former luxuriance of health only by the maladies which riot has produced'. They stared a while in silence one upon another, and, at last, drove him away by a general chorus of continued laughter.

The consciousness that his sentiments were just, and his intentions kind, was scarcely sufficient to support him against the horror of derision. But he recovered his tranquillity, and pursued his search.

Chapter 18
The prince finds a wise and happy man

As he was one day walking in the street, he saw a spacious building which all were, by the open doors, invited to enter: he followed the stream of people, and found it a hall or school of declamation, in which professors read lectures to their auditory.[15] He fixed his eye upon a sage raised above the rest, who discoursed with great energy on the government of the passions. His look was venerable, his action graceful, his pronunciation clear, and his diction elegant. He showed, with great strength of sentiment, and variety of illustration, that human nature is degraded and debased, when the lower faculties predominate over the higher; that when fancy, the parent of passion, usurps the dominion of the mind, nothing ensues but the natural effect of unlawful government, perturbation and confusion; that she betrays the fortresses of the intellect to rebels, and excites her children to sedition against reason, their lawful sovereign.[16] He compared reason to the sun, of which the light is constant, uniform, and lasting; and fancy to a meteor, of bright but transitory lustre, irregular in its motion, and delusive in its direction.

He then communicated the various precepts given from time to time for the conquest of passion, and displayed the happiness of those who had obtained the important victory, after which man is no longer the slave of fear, nor the fool of hope; is no more emaciated by envy, inflamed by anger, emasculated by tenderness, or depressed by grief; but walks on calmly through the tumults or the privacies of life, as the sun pursues alike his course through the calm or the stormy sky.

He enumerated many examples of heroes immovable by pain or pleasure, who looked with indifference on those modes or accidents to which the vulgar give the names of

Notes

[15] *auditory* audience.

[16] *He showed ... sovereign* as Johnson's readers would readily have recognized, the "wise and happy man" propounds a version of Stoicism.

good and evil. He exhorted his hearers to lay aside their prejudices, and arm themselves against the shafts of malice or misfortune, by invulnerable patience; concluding, that this state only was happiness, and that this happiness was in every one's power.

Rasselas listened to him with the veneration due to the instructions of a superior being, and, waiting for him at the door, humbly implored the liberty of visiting so great a master of true wisdom. The lecturer hesitated a moment, when Rasselas put a purse of gold into his hand, which he received with a mixture of joy and wonder.

'I have found', said the prince, at his return to Imlac, 'a man who can teach all that is necessary to be known, who, from the unshaken throne of rational fortitude, looks down on the scenes of life changing beneath him.[17] He speaks, and attention watches his lips. He reasons, and conviction closes his periods. This man shall be my future guide: I will learn his doctrines, and imitate his life'.

'Be not too hasty', said Imlac, 'to trust, or to admire, the teachers of morality: they discourse like angels, but they live like men'.

Rasselas, who could not conceive how any man could reason so forcibly without feeling the cogency of his own arguments, paid his visit in a few days, and was denied admission. He had now learned the power of money, and made his way by a piece of gold to the inner apartment, where he found the philosopher in a room half darkened, with his eyes misty, and his face pale. 'Sir', said he, 'you are come at a time when all human friendship is useless; what I suffer cannot be remedied, what I have lost cannot be supplied. My daughter, my only daughter, from whose tenderness I expected all the comforts of my age, died last night of a fever. My views, my purposes, my hopes are at an end: I am now a lonely being disunited from society'.

'Sir', said the prince, 'mortality is an event by which a wise man can never be surprised: we know that death is always near, and it should therefore always be expected'. 'Young man', answered the philosopher, 'you speak like one that has never felt the pangs of separation'. 'Have you then forgot the precepts', said Rasselas, 'which you so powerfully enforced? Has wisdom no strength to arm the heart against calamity? Consider, that external things are naturally variable, but truth and reason are always the same'. 'What comfort', said the mourner, 'can truth and reason afford me? of what effect are they now, but to tell me, that my daughter will not be restored?'

The prince, whose humanity would not suffer him to insult misery with reproof, went away convinced of the emptiness of rhetorical sound, and the inefficacy of polished periods and studied sentences.

Chapter 19
A glimpse of pastoral life

He was still eager upon the same enquiry; and, having heard of a hermit, that lived near the lowest cataract of the Nile, and filled the whole country with the fame of his sanctity, resolved to visit his retreat, and enquire whether that felicity, which public life could not afford, was to be found in solitude; and whether a man, whose age and virtue made him venerable, could teach any peculiar art of shunning evils, or enduring them.

Notes

[17] *from the unshaken throne ... beneath him* one of the most traditional images of Stoicism (e.g., Lucretius, *De Rerum Natura* 2.7–10).

Imlac and the princess agreed to accompany him, and, after the necessary preparations, they began their journey. Their way lay through fields, where shepherds tended their flocks, and the lambs were playing upon the pasture. 'This', said the poet, 'is the life which has been often celebrated for its innocence and quiet: let us pass the heat of the day among the shepherds' tents, and know whether all our searches are not to terminate in pastoral simplicity'.

The proposal pleased them, and they induced the shepherds, by small presents and familiar[18] questions, to tell their opinion of their own state: they were so rude and ignorant, so little able to compare the good with the evil of the occupation, and so indistinct in their narratives and descriptions, that very little could be learned from them. But it was evident that their hearts were cankered with discontent; that they considered themselves as condemned to labour for the luxury of the rich, and looked up with stupid malevolence toward those that were placed above them.

The princess pronounced with vehemence, that she would never suffer these envious savages to be her companions, and that she should not soon be desirous of seeing any more specimens of rustic happiness; but could not believe that all the accounts of primeval pleasures were fabulous, and was yet in doubt whether life had any thing that could be justly preferred to the placid gratifications of fields and woods. She hoped that the time would come, when with a few virtuous and elegant companions, she should gather flowers planted by her own hand, fondle the lambs of her own ewe, and listen, without care, among brooks and breezes, to one of her maidens reading in the shade.

Chapter 20
The danger of prosperity

On the next day they continued their journey, till the heat compelled them to look round for shelter. At a small distance they saw a thick wood, which they no sooner entered than they perceived that they were approaching the habitations of men. The shrubs were diligently cut away to open walks where the shades were darkest; the boughs of opposite trees were artificially interwoven; seats of flowery turf were raised in vacant spaces, and a rivulet, that wantoned along the side of a winding path, had its banks sometimes opened into small basins, and its stream sometimes obstructed by little mounds of stone heaped together to increase its murmurs.

They passed slowly through the wood, delighted with such unexpected accommodations, and entertained each other with conjecturing what, or who, he could be, that, in those rude and unfrequented regions, had leisure and art for such harmless luxury.

As they advanced, they heard the sound of music, and saw youths and virgins dancing in the grove; and, going still further, beheld a stately palace built upon a hill surrounded with woods. The laws of eastern hospitality allowed them to enter, and the master welcomed them like a man liberal and wealthy.

He was skilful enough in appearances soon to discern that they were no common guests, and spread his table with magnificence. The eloquence of Imlac caught his attention, and the lofty courtesy of the princess excited his respect. When they offered to depart he entreated their stay, and was the next day still more unwilling to dismiss

Notes

[18] *familiar* "Affable; not formal; easy in conversation" (Johnson).

them than before. They were easily persuaded to stop, and civility grew up in time to freedom and confidence.

The prince now saw all the domestics cheerful, and all the face of nature smiling round the place, and could not forbear to hope that he should find here what he was seeking; but when he was congratulating the master upon his possessions, he answered with a sigh, 'My condition has indeed the appearance of happiness, but appearances are delusive. My prosperity puts my life in danger; the Bassa[19] of Egypt is my enemy, incensed only by my wealth and popularity. I have been hitherto protected against him by the princes of the country; but, as the favour of the great is uncertain, I know not how soon my defenders may be persuaded to share the plunder with the Bassa. I have sent my treasures into a distant country, and, upon the first alarm, am prepared to follow them. Then will my enemies riot in my mansion, and enjoy the gardens which I have planted'.

They all joined in lamenting his danger, and deprecating his exile; and the princess was so much disturbed with the tumult of grief and indignation, that she retired to her apartment. They continued with their kind inviter a few days longer, and then went forward to find the hermit.

Chapter 21
The happiness of solitude: The hermit's history

They came on the third day, by the direction of the peasants, to the Hermit's cell: it was a cavern in the side of a mountain, over-shadowed with palm-trees; at such a distance from the cataract, that nothing more was heard than a gentle uniform murmur, such as composed the mind to pensive meditation, especially when it was assisted by the wind whistling among the branches. The first rude essay of nature had been so much improved by human labour, that the cave contained several apartments, appropriated to different uses, and often afforded lodging to travellers, whom darkness or tempests happened to overtake.

The hermit sat on a bench at the door, to enjoy the coolness of the evening. On one side lay a book with pens and papers, on the other mechanical instruments of various kinds. As they approached him unregarded, the princess observed that he had not the countenance of a man that had found, or could teach, the way to happiness.

They saluted him with great respect, which he repaid like a man not unaccustomed to the forms of courts, 'My children', said he, 'if you have lost your way, you shall be willingly supplied with such conveniences for the night as this cavern will afford. I have all that nature requires, and you will not expect delicacies in a hermit's cell'.

They thanked him, and entering, were pleased with the neatness and regularity of the place. The hermit set flesh and wine before them, though he fed only upon fruits and water. His discourse was cheerful without levity, and pious without enthusiasm.[20] He soon gained the esteem of his guests, and the princess repented of her hasty censure.

At last Imlac began thus: 'I do not now wonder that your reputation is so far extended; we have heard at Cairo of your wisdom, and came hither to implore your direction for this young man and maiden in the *choice of life*'.

Notes

[19] *Bassa* or "bashaw," "A title of honour and command among the Turks, the viceroy of a province; the general of an army" (Johnson).

[20] *enthusiasm* "A vain belief of private revelation; a vain confidence of divine favour or communication" (Johnson).

'To him that lives well', answered the hermit, 'every form of life is good; nor can I give any other rule for choice, than to remove from all apparent evil'.

'He will remove most certainly from evil', said the prince, 'who shall devote himself to that solitude which you have recommended by your example'.

'I have indeed lived fifteen years in solitude', said the hermit, 'but have no desire that my example should gain any imitators. In my youth I professed arms, and was raised by degrees to the highest military rank. I have traversed wide countries at the head of my troops, and seen many battles and sieges. At last, being disgusted by the preferment of a younger officer, and finding my vigour was beginning to decay, I resolved to close my life in peace, having found the world full of snares, discord, and misery. I had once escaped from the pursuit of the enemy by the shelter of this cavern, and therefore chose it for my final residence. I employed artificers to form it into chambers, and stored it with all that I was likely to want.

'For some time after my retreat, I rejoiced like a tempest-beaten sailor at his entrance into the harbour, being delighted with the sudden change of the noise and hurry of war, to stillness and repose. When the pleasure of novelty went away, I employed my hours in examining the plants which grow in the valley, and the minerals which I collected from the rocks. But that enquiry is now grown tasteless and irksome. I have been for some time unsettled and distracted: my mind is disturbed with a thousand perplexities of doubt, and vanities of imagination, which hourly prevail upon me, because I have no opportunities of relaxation or diversion. I am sometimes ashamed to think that I could not secure myself from vice, but by retiring from the exercise of virtue, and begin to suspect that I was rather impelled by resentment, than led by devotion, into solitude. My fancy riots in scenes of folly, and I lament that I have lost so much, and have gained so little. In solitude, if I escape the example of bad men, I want likewise the counsel and conversation of the good. I have been long comparing the evils with the advantages of society, and resolve to return into the world tomorrow. The life of a solitary man will be certainly miserable, but not certainly devout'.

They heard his resolution with surprise, but, after a short pause, offered to conduct him to Cairo. He dug up a considerable treasure which he had hid among the rocks, and accompanied them to the city, on which, as he approached it, he gazed with rapture.

Chapter 22
The happiness of a life led according to nature

Rasselas went often to an assembly of learned men, who met at stated times to unbend their minds, and compare their opinions. Their manners were somewhat coarse, but their conversation was instructive, and their disputations acute, though sometimes too violent, and often continued till neither controvertist[21] remembered upon what question they began. Some faults were almost general among them: every one was desirous to dictate to the rest, and every one was pleased to hear the genius or knowledge of another depreciated.

In this assembly Rasselas was relating his interview with the hermit, and the wonder with which he heard him censure a course of life which he had so deliberately chosen, and so laudably followed. The sentiments of the hearers were various. Some were of opinion, that the folly of his choice had been justly punished by condemnation to

Notes

[21] *controvertist* disputant.

perpetual perseverance. One of the youngest among them, with great vehemence, pronounced him an hypocrite. Some talked of the right of society to the labour of individuals, and considered retirement as a desertion of duty. Others readily allowed, that there was a time when the claims of the public were satisfied, and when a man might properly sequester himself, to review his life, and purify his heart.

One, who appeared more affected with the narrative than the rest, thought it likely, that the hermit would, in a few years, go back to his retreat, and, perhaps, if shame did not restrain, or death intercept him, return once more from his retreat into the world: 'For the hope of happiness', says he, 'is so strongly impressed, that the longest experience is not able to efface it. Of the present state, whatever it be, we feel, and are forced to confess, the misery, yet, when the same state is again at a distance, imagination paints it as desirable. But the time will surely come, when desire will be no longer our torment, and no man shall be wretched but by his own fault'.

'This', said a philosopher, who had heard him with tokens of great impatience, 'is the present condition of a wise man. The time is already come, when none are wretched but by their own fault. Nothing is more idle, than to enquire after happiness, which nature has kindly placed within our reach. The way to be happy is to live according to nature,[22] in obedience to that universal and unalterable law with which every heart is originally impressed; which is not written on it by precept, but engraven by destiny, not instilled by education but infused at our nativity. He that lives according to nature will suffer nothing from the delusions of hope, or importunities of desire: he will receive and reject with equability of temper; and act or suffer as the reason of things shall alternately prescribe. Other men may amuse themselves with subtle definitions, or intricate ratiocination. Let them learn to be wise by easier means: let them observe the hind of the forest, and the linnet of the grove: let them consider the life of animals, whose motions are regulated by instinct; they obey their guide and are happy. Let us therefore, at length, cease to dispute, and learn to live; throw away the encumbrance of precepts, which they who utter them with so much pride and pomp do not understand, and carry with us this simple and intelligible maxim, That deviation from nature is deviation from happiness'.

When he had spoken, he looked round him with a placid air, and enjoyed the consciousness of his own beneficence. 'Sir', said the prince, with great modesty, 'as I, like all the rest of mankind, am desirous of felicity, my closest attention has been fixed upon your discourse: I doubt not the truth of a position which a man so learned has so confidently advanced. Let me only know what it is to live according to nature'.

'When I find young men so humble and so docile', said the philosopher, 'I can deny them no information which my studies have enabled me to afford. To live according to nature, is to act always with due regard to the fitness arising from the relations and qualities of causes and effects; to concur with the great and unchangeable scheme of universal felicity; to co-operate with the general disposition and tendency of the present system of things'.

The prince soon found that this was one of the sages whom he should understand less as he heard him longer. He therefore bowed and was silent, and the philosopher, supposing him satisfied, and the rest vanquished, rose up and departed with the air of a man that had co-operated with the present system.

Notes

22 *to live according to nature* Johnson is parodying the tenets of Deism or Natural Religion, which were controversial contemporary movements, although they have classical backgrounds.

Chapter 23
The prince and his sister divide between them the work of observation

Rasselas returned home full of reflections, doubtful how to direct his future steps. Of the way to happiness he found the learned and simple equally ignorant; but, as he was yet young, he flattered himself that he had time remaining for more experiments, and further enquiries. He communicated to Imlac his observations and his doubts, but was answered by him with new doubts, and remarks that gave him no comfort. He therefore discoursed more frequently and freely with his sister, who had yet the same hope with himself, and always assisted him to give some reason why, though he had been hitherto frustrated, he might succeed at last.

'We have hitherto', said she, 'known but little of the world: we have never yet been either great or mean. In our own country, though we had royalty, we had no power, and in this we have not yet seen the private recesses of domestic peace. Imlac favours not our search, lest we should in time find him mistaken. We will divide the task between us: you shall try what is to be found in the splendour of courts, and I will range the shades of humbler life. Perhaps command and authority may be the supreme blessings, as they afford most opportunities of doing good: or, perhaps, what this world can give may be found in the modest habitations of middle fortune; too low for great designs, and too high for penury and distress'.

Chapter 24
The prince examines the happiness of high stations

Rasselas applauded the design, and appeared next day with a splendid retinue at the court of the Bassa. He was soon distinguished for his magnificence, and admitted, as a prince whose curiosity had brought him from distant countries, to an intimacy with the great officers, and frequent conversation with the Bassa himself.

He was at first inclined to believe, that the man must be pleased with his own condition, whom all approached with reverence, and heard with obedience, and who had the power to extend his edicts to a whole kingdom. 'There can be no pleasure', said he, 'equal to that of feeling at once the joy of thousands all made happy by wise administration. Yet, since, by the law of subordination, this sublime delight can be in one nation but the lot of one, it is surely reasonable to think that there is some satisfaction more popular and accessible, and that millions can hardly be subjected to the will of a single man, only to fill his particular breast with incommunicable content'.

These thoughts were often in his mind, and he found no solution of the difficulty. But as presents and civilities gained him more familiarity, he found that almost every man who stood high in employment hated all the rest, and was hated by them, and that their lives were a continual succession of plots and detections, stratagems and escapes, faction and treachery. Many of those, who surrounded the Bassa, were sent only to watch and report his conduct; every tongue was muttering censure, and every eye was searching for a fault.

At last the letters of revocation arrived, the Bassa was carried in chains to Constantinople, and his name was mentioned no more.

'What are we now to think of the prerogatives of power', said Rasselas to his sister; 'is it without any efficacy to good? or, is the subordinate degree only dangerous, and the supreme safe and glorious? Is the Sultan the only happy man in his dominions? or, is the Sultan himself subject to the torments of suspicion, and the dread of enemies?'

In a short time the second Bassa was deposed. The Sultan, that had advanced him, was murdered by the Janisaries,[23] and his successor had other views and different favourites.

Chapter 25
The princess pursues her enquiry with more diligence than success

The princess, in the mean time, insinuated herself into many families; for there are few doors, through which liberality, joined with good humour, cannot find its way. The daughters of many houses were airy and cheerful, but Nekayah had been too long accustomed to the conversation of Imlac and her brother to be much pleased with childish levity and prattle which had no meaning. She found their thoughts narrow, their wishes low, and their merriment often artificial. Their pleasures, poor as they were, could not be preserved pure, but were embittered by petty competitions and worthless emulation. They were always jealous of the beauty of each other; of a quality to which solicitude can add nothing, and from which detraction can take nothing away. Many were in love with triflers like themselves, and many fancied that they were in love when in truth they were only idle. Their affection was seldom fixed on sense or virtue, and therefore seldom ended but in vexation. Their grief, however, like their joy, was transient; every thing floated in their mind unconnected with the past or future, so that one desire easily gave way to another, as a second stone cast into the water effaces and confounds the circles of the first.

With these girls she played as with inoffensive animals, and found them proud of her countenance, and weary of her company.

But her purpose was to examine more deeply, and her affability easily persuaded the hearts that were swelling with sorrow to discharge their secrets in her ear: and those whom hope flattered, or prosperity delighted, often courted her to partake their pleasures.

The princess and her brother commonly met in the evening in a private summer-house on the bank of the Nile, and related to each other the occurrences of the day. As they were sitting together, the princess cast her eyes upon the river that flowed before her. 'Answer', said she, 'great father of waters, thou that rollest thy floods through eighty nations, to the invocations of the daughter of thy native king. Tell me if thou waterest, through all thy course, a single habitation from which thou dost not hear the murmurs of complaint?'

'You are then', said Rasselas, 'not more successful in private houses than I have been in courts'. 'I have, since the last partition of our provinces', said the princess, 'enabled myself to enter familiarly into many families, where there was the fairest show of prosperity and peace, and know not one house that is not haunted by some fiend that destroys its quiet.

'I did not seek ease among the poor, because I concluded that there it could not be found. But I saw many poor whom I had supposed to live in affluence. Poverty has, in large cities, very different appearances: it is often concealed in splendour, and often in extravagance. It is the care of a very great part of mankind to conceal their indigence

Notes

[23] *Janisary* "One of the guards of the Turkish king [sultan]" (Johnson).

from the rest: they support themselves by temporary expedients, and every day is lost in contriving for the morrow.

'This, however, was an evil, which, though frequent, I saw with less pain, because I could relieve it. Yet some have refused my bounties; more offended with my quickness to detect their wants, than pleased with my readiness to succour them: and others, whose exigencies compelled them to admit my kindness, have never been able to forgive their benefactress. Many, however, have been sincerely grateful without the ostentation of gratitude, or the hope of other favours'.

Chapter 26[24]
The princess continues her remarks upon private life

Nekayah perceiving her brother's attention fixed, proceeded in her narrative.

'In families, where there is or is not poverty, there is commonly discord: if a kingdom be, as Imlac tells us, a great family, a family likewise is a little kingdom, torn with factions and exposed to revolutions. An unpractised observer expects the love of parents and children to be constant and equal; but this kindness seldom continues beyond the years of infancy: in a short time the children become rivals to their parents. Benefits are allayed by reproaches, and gratitude debased by envy.

'Parents and children seldom act in concert: each child endeavours to appropriate the esteem or fondness of the parents, and the parents, with yet less temptation, betray each other to their children; thus some place their confidence in the father, and some in the mother, and, by degrees, the house is filled with artifices and feuds.

'The opinions of children and parents, of the young and the old, are naturally opposite, by the contrary effects of hope and despondence, of expectation and experience, without crime or folly on either side. The colours of life in youth and age appear different, as the face of nature in spring and winter. And how can children credit the assertions of parents, which their own eyes show them to be false?

'Few parents act in such a manner as much to enforce their maxims by the credit of their lives. The old man trusts wholly to slow contrivance and gradual progression: the youth expects to force his way by genius, vigour, and precipitance. The old man pays regard to riches, and the youth reverences virtue. The old man deifies prudence: the youth commits himself to magnanimity and chance. The young man, who intends no ill, believes that none is intended, and therefore acts with openness and candour: but his father, having suffered the injuries of fraud, is impelled to suspect, and too often allured to practise it. Age looks with anger on the temerity of youth, and youth with contempt on the scrupulosity of age. Thus parents and children, for the greatest part, live on to love less and less: and, if those whom nature has thus closely united are the torments of each other, where shall we look for tenderness and consolation?'

'Surely', said the prince, 'you must have been unfortunate in your choice of acquaintance: I am unwilling to believe, that the most tender of all relations is thus impeded in its effects by natural necessity'.

'Domestic discord', answered she, 'is not inevitably and fatally necessary; but yet is not easily avoided. We seldom see that a whole family is virtuous: the good and evil

Notes

[24] *Chapter 26* this is the beginning of volume 2 in the original edition.

cannot well agree; and the evil can yet less agree with one another: even the virtuous fall sometimes to variance, when their virtues are of different kinds and tending to extremes. In general, those parents have most reverence who most deserve it: for he that lives well cannot be despised.

'Many other evils infest private life. Some are the slaves of servants whom they have trusted with their affairs. Some are kept in continual anxiety to the caprice of rich relations, whom they cannot please, and dare not offend. Some husbands are imperious, and some wives perverse: and, as it is always more easy to do evil than good, though the wisdom or virtue of one can very rarely make many happy, the folly or vice of one may often make many miserable'.

'If such be the general effect of marriage', said the prince, 'I shall, for the future, think it dangerous to connect my interest with that of another, lest I should be unhappy by my partner's fault'.

'I have met', said the princess, 'with many who live single for that reason; but I never found that their prudence ought to raise envy. They dream away their time without friendship, without fondness, and are driven to rid themselves of the day, for which they have no use, by childish amusements, or vicious delights. They act as beings under the constant sense of some known inferiority, that fills their minds with rancour, and their tongues with censure. They are peevish at home, and malevolent abroad; and, as the outlaws of human nature, make it their business and their pleasure to disturb that society which debars them from its privileges. To live without feeling or exciting sympathy, to be fortunate without adding to the felicity of others, or afflicted without tasting the balm of pity, is a state more gloomy than solitude: it is not retreat but exclusion from mankind. Marriage has many pains, but celibacy has no pleasures'.

'What then is to be done?' said Rasselas; 'the more we enquire, the less we can resolve. Surely he is most likely to please himself that has no other inclination to regard'.

Chapter 27
Disquisition upon greatness

The conversation had a short pause. The prince having considered his sister's observations, told her, that she had surveyed life with prejudice, and supposed misery where she did not find it. 'Your narrative', says he, 'throws yet a darker gloom upon the prospects of futurity: the predictions of Imlac were but faint sketches of the evils painted by Nekayah. I have been lately convinced that quiet is not the daughter of grandeur, or of power: that her presence is not to be bought by wealth, nor enforced by conquest. It is evident, that as any man acts in a wider compass, he must be more exposed to opposition from enmity or miscarriage from chance; whoever has many to please or to govern, must use the ministry of many agents, some of whom will be wicked, and some ignorant; by some he will be misled, and by others betrayed. If he gratifies one he will offend another: those that are not favoured will think themselves injured; and, since favours can be conferred but upon few, the greater number will be always discontented'.

'The discontent', said the princess, 'which is thus unreasonable, I hope that I shall always have spirit to despise, and you, power to repress'.

'Discontent', answered Rasselas, 'will not always be without reason under the most just or vigilant administration of public affairs. None however attentive, can always discover that merit which indigence or faction may happen to obscure; and none, however powerful, can always reward it. Yet, he that sees inferior desert advanced above him, will naturally impute that preference to partiality or caprice; and, indeed, it can scarcely be hoped that any man, however magnanimous by nature, or exalted by condition, will be able to persist for ever in fixed and inexorable justice of distribution: he will sometimes indulge his own affections, and sometimes those of his favourites; he will permit some to please him who can never serve him; he will discover in those whom he loves qualities which in reality they do not possess; and to those, from whom he receives pleasure, he will in his turn endeavour to give it. Thus will recommendations sometimes prevail which were purchased by money, or by the more destructive bribery of flattery and servility.

'He that has much to do will do something wrong, and of that wrong must suffer the consequences; and, if it were possible that he should always act rightly, yet when such numbers are to judge of his conduct, the bad will censure and obstruct him by malevolence, and the good sometimes by mistake.

'The highest stations cannot therefore hope to be the abodes of happiness, which I would willingly believe to have fled from thrones and palaces to seats of humble privacy and placid obscurity. For what can hinder the satisfaction, or intercept the expectations, of him whose abilities are adequate to his employments, who sees with his own eyes the whole circuit of his influence, who chooses by his own knowledge all whom he trusts, and whom none are tempted to deceive by hope or fear? Surely he has nothing to do but to love and to be loved, to be virtuous and to be happy'.

'Whether perfect happiness would be procured by perfect goodness', said Nekayah, 'this world will never afford an opportunity of deciding. But this, at least, may be maintained, that we do not always find visible happiness in proportion to visible virtue. All natural and almost all political evils, are incident alike to the bad and good: they are confounded in the misery of a famine, and not much distinguished in the fury of a faction; they sink together in a tempest, and are driven together from their country by invaders. All that virtue can afford is quietness of conscience, a steady prospect of a happier state; this may enable us to endure calamity with patience; but remember that patience must suppose pain'.

Chapter 28
Rasselas and Nekayah continue their conversation

'Dear princess', said Rasselas, 'you fall into the common errors of exaggeratory declamation, by producing, in a familiar disquisition, examples of national calamities, and scenes of extensive misery, which are found in books rather than in the world, and which, as they are horrid, are ordained to be rare. Let us not imagine evils which we do not feel, nor injure life by misrepresentations. I cannot bear that querulous eloquence which threatens every city with a siege like that of Jerusalem,[25] that makes famine attend on every flight of locusts, and suspends pestilence on the wing of every blast that issues from the south.

'On necessary and inevitable evils, which overwhelm kingdoms at once, all disputation is vain: when they happen they must be endured. But it is evident, that these bursts of universal distress are more dreaded than felt: thousands and ten thousands

Notes

[25] *Jerusalem* the city was brutally besieged by the Emperor Titus in 70 CE and by the Christian crusaders in 1099, among others.

flourish in youth, and wither in age, without the knowledge of any other than domestic evils, and share the same pleasures and vexations whether their kings are mild or cruel, whether the armies of their country pursue their enemies, or retreat before them. While courts are disturbed with intestine competitions, and ambassadors are negotiating in foreign countries, the smith still plies his anvil, and the husbandman drives his plough forward; the necessaries of life are required and obtained, and the successive business of the seasons continues to make its wonted[26] revolutions.

'Let us cease to consider what, perhaps, may never happen, and what, when it shall happen, will laugh at human speculation. We will not endeavour to modify the motions of the elements, or to fix the destiny of kingdoms. It is our business to consider what beings like us may perform; each labouring for his own happiness, by promoting within his circle, however narrow, the happiness of others.

'Marriage is evidently the dictate of nature; men and women were made to be companions of each other, and therefore I cannot be persuaded but that marriage is one of the means of happiness'.

'I know not', said the princess, 'whether marriage be more than one of the innumerable modes of human misery. When I see and reckon the various forms of connubial infelicity, the unexpected causes of lasting discord, the diversities of temper, the oppositions of opinion, the rude collisions of contrary desire where both are urged by violent impulses, the obstinate contests of disagreeing virtues, where both are supported by consciousness of good intention, I am sometimes disposed to think with the severer casuists[27] of most nations, that marriage is rather permitted than approved, and that none, but by the instigation of a passion too much indulged, entangle themselves with indissoluble compacts'.

'You seem to forget', replied Rasselas, 'that you have, even now, represented celibacy as less happy than marriage. Both conditions may be bad, but they cannot both be worst. Thus it happens when wrong opinions are entertained, that they mutually destroy each other, and leave the mind open to truth'.

'I did not expect', answered the princess, 'to hear that imputed to falsehood which is the consequence only of frailty. To the mind, as to the eye, it is difficult to compare with exactness objects vast in their extent, and various in their parts. Where we see or conceive the whole at once we readily note the discriminations and decide the preference: but of two systems, of which neither can be surveyed by any human being in its full compass of magnitude and multiplicity of complication, where is the wonder, that judging of the whole by parts, I am alternately affected by one and the other as either presses on my memory or fancy? We differ from ourselves just as we differ from each other, when we see only part of the question, as in the multifarious relations of politics and morality: but when we perceive the whole at once, as in numerical computations, all agree in one judgement, and none ever varies his opinion'.

'Let us not add', said the prince, 'to the other evils of life, the bitterness of controversy, nor endeavour to vie with each other in subtleties of argument. We are employed in a search, of which both are equally to enjoy the success, or suffer by the miscarriage. It is therefore fit that we assist each other. You surely conclude too hastily from the infelicity of marriage against its institution. Will not the misery of life prove equally that life cannot be the gift of heaven? The world must be peopled by marriage, or peopled without it'.

Notes

[26] *wonted* usual, customary.

[27] *casuists* moralists.

'How the world is to be peopled', returned Nekayah, 'is not my care, and needs not be yours. I see no danger that the present generation should omit to leave successors behind them: we are not now enquiring for the world, but for ourselves'.

Chapter 29
The debate on marriage continued

'The good of the whole', says Rasselas, 'is the same with the good of all its parts. If marriage be best for mankind it must be evidently best for individuals, or a permanent and necessary duty must be the cause of evil, and some must be inevitably sacrificed to the convenience of others. In the estimate which you have made of the two states, it appears that the incommodities of a single life are, in a great measure, necessary and certain, but those of the conjugal state accidental and avoidable.

'I cannot forbear to flatter myself that prudence and benevolence will make marriage happy. The general folly of mankind is the cause of general complaint. What can be expected but disappointment and repentance from a choice made in the immaturity of youth, in the ardour of desire, without judgement, without foresight, without an enquiry after conformity of opinions, similarity of manners, rectitude of judgement, or purity of sentiment.

'Such is the common process of marriage. A youth and maiden meeting by chance, or brought together by artifice, exchange glances, reciprocate civilities, go home, and dream of one another. Having little to divert attention, or diversify thought, they find themselves uneasy when they are apart, and therefore conclude that they shall be happy together. They marry, and discover what nothing but voluntary blindness had before concealed; they wear out life in altercations, and charge nature with cruelty.

'From those early marriages proceeds likewise the rivalry of parents and children: the son is eager to enjoy the world before the father is willing to forsake it, and there is hardly room at once for two generations. The daughter begins to bloom before the mother can be content to fade, and neither can forbear to wish for the absence of the other.

'Surely all these evils may be avoided by that deliberation and delay which prudence prescribes to irrevocable choice. In the variety and jollity of youthful pleasures life may be well enough supported without the help of a partner. Longer time will increase experience, and wider views will allow better opportunities of enquiry and selection: one advantage, at least, will be certain; the parents will be visibly older than their children'.

'What reason cannot collect', said Nekayah, 'and what experiment has not yet taught, can be known only from the report of others. I have been told that late marriages are not eminently happy. This is a question too important to be neglected, and I have often proposed it to those, whose accuracy of remark, and comprehensiveness of knowledge, made their suffrages worthy of regard. They have generally determined, that it is dangerous for a man and woman to suspend their fate upon each other, at a time when opinions are fixed, and habits are established; when friendships have been contracted on both sides, when life has been planned into method, and the mind has long enjoyed the contemplation of its own prospects.

'It is scarcely possible that two travelling through the world under the conduct of chance, should have been both directed to the same path, and it will not often happen that either will quit the track which custom has made pleasing. When the desultory levity of youth has settled into regularity, it is soon succeeded by pride ashamed to yield, or obstinacy delighting to contend. And even though mutual esteem produces mutual desire to please, time itself, as it modifies unchangeably the external mien, determines likewise the direction of the passions, and gives an inflexible rigidity to the manners. Long customs are not easily broken: he that attempts to change the course of his own life, very often labours in vain; and how shall we do that for others which we are seldom able to do for ourselves?'

'But surely', interposed the prince, 'you suppose the chief motive of choice forgotten or neglected. Whenever I shall seek a wife, it shall be my first question, whether she be willing to be led by reason?'

'Thus it is', said Nekayah, 'that philosophers are deceived. There are a thousand familiar disputes which reason never can decide; questions that elude investigation, and make logic ridiculous; cases where something must be done, and where little can be said. Consider the state of mankind, and enquire how few can be supposed to act upon any occasions, whether small or great, with all the reasons of action present to their minds. Wretched would be the pair above all names of wretchedness, who should be doomed to adjust by reason every morning all the minute detail of a domestic day.

'Those who marry at an advanced age, will probably escape the encroachments of their children; but, in diminution of this advantage, they will be likely to leave them, ignorant and helpless, to a guardian's mercy: or, if that should not happen, they must at least go out of the world before they see those whom they love best either wise or great.

'From their children, if they have less to fear, they have less also to hope, and they lose, without equivalent, the joys of early love and the convenience of uniting with manners pliant, and minds susceptible of new impressions, which might wear away their dissimilitudes by long cohabitation, as soft bodies, by continual attrition, conform their surfaces to each other.

'I believe it will be found that those who marry late are best pleased with their children, and those who marry early with their partners'.

'The union of these two affections', said Rasselas, 'would produce all that could be wished. Perhaps there is a time when marriage might unite them, a time neither too early for the father, nor too late for the husband'.

'Every hour', answered the princess, 'confirms my prejudice in favour of the position so often uttered by the mouth of Imlac, "That nature sets her gifts on the right hand and on the left". Those conditions, which flatter hope and attract desire, are so constituted, that, as we approach one, we recede from another. There are goods so opposed that we cannot seize both, but, by too much prudence, may pass between them at too great a distance to reach either. This is often the fate of long consideration; he does nothing who endeavours to do more than is allowed to humanity. Flatter not yourself with contrarieties of pleasure. Of the blessings set before you make your choice, and be content. No man can taste the fruits of autumn while he is delighting his scent with the flowers of the spring: no man can, at the same time, fill his cup from the source and from the mouth of the Nile'.

Chapter 30
Imlac enters, and changes the conversation

Here Imlac entered, and interrupted them. His look was clouded with thought. 'Imlac', said Rasselas, 'I have been taking from the princess the dismal history of private life, and am almost discouraged from further search'.

'It seems to me', said Imlac, 'that while you are making the choice of life, you neglect to live. You wander about a single city, which, however large and diversified, can now afford few novelties, and forget that you are in a country, famous among the earliest monarchies for the power and wisdom of its inhabitants; a country where the sciences first dawned that illuminate the world, and beyond which the arts cannot be traced of civil society or domestic life.

'The old Egyptians have left behind them monuments of industry and power before which all European magnificence is confessed to fade away. The ruins of their architecture are the schools of modern builders, and from the wonders which time has spared we may conjecture, though uncertainly, what it has destroyed'.

'My curiosity', said Rasselas, 'does not very strongly lead me to survey piles of stone, or mounds of earth; my business is with man. I came hither not to measure fragments of temples, or trace choked aqueducts, but to look upon the various scenes of the present world'.

'The things that are now before us', said the princess, 'require attention, and deserve it. What have I to do with the heroes or the monuments of ancient times? with times which never can return, and heroes, whose form of life was different from all that the present condition of mankind requires or allows'.

'To know any thing', returned the poet, 'we must know its effects; to see men we must see their works, that we may learn what reason has dictated, or passion has incited, and find what are the most powerful motives of action. To judge rightly of the present we must oppose it to the past; for all judgement is comparative, and of the future nothing can be known. The truth is, that no mind is much employed upon the present: recollection and anticipation fill up almost all our moments. Our passions are joy and grief, love and hatred, hope and fear. Of joy and grief the past is the object, and the future of hope and fear; even love and hatred respect the past, for the cause must have been before the effect.

'The present state of things is the consequence of the former, and it is natural to enquire what were the sources of the good that we enjoy, or of the evil that we suffer. If we act only for ourselves, to neglect the study of history is not prudent: if we are entrusted with the care of others, it is not just. Ignorance, when it is voluntary, is criminal; and he may properly be charged with evil who refused to learn how he might prevent it.

'There is no part of history so generally useful as that which relates the progress of the human mind, the gradual improvement of reason, the successive advances of science, the vicissitudes of learning and ignorance, which are the light and darkness of thinking beings, the extinction and resuscitation of arts, and all the revolutions of the intellectual world. If accounts of battles and invasions are peculiarly the business of princes, the useful or elegant arts are not to be neglected; those who have kingdoms to govern, have understandings to cultivate.

'Example is always more efficacious than precept. A soldier is formed in war, and a painter must copy pictures. In this, contemplative life has the advantage: great actions are seldom seen, but the labours of art are always at hand for those who desire to know what art has been able to perform.

'When the eye or the imagination is struck with any uncommon work the next transition of an active mind is to the means by which it was performed. Here begins the true use of such contemplation; we enlarge our comprehension by new ideas, and perhaps recover some art lost to mankind, or learn what is less perfectly known in our own country. At least we compare our own with former times, and either rejoice at our improvements, or, what is the first motion towards good, discover our defects'.

'I am willing', said the prince, 'to see all that can deserve my search'. 'And I', said the princess, 'shall rejoice to learn something of the manners of antiquity'.

'The most pompous monument of Egyptian greatness, and one of the most bulky works of manual industry', said Imlac, 'are the pyramids; fabrics[28] raised before the time of history, and of which the earliest narratives afford us only uncertain traditions. Of these the greatest is still standing, very little injured by time'.

'Let us visit them tomorrow', said Nekayah. 'I have often heard of the Pyramids, and shall not rest, till I have seen them within and without with my own eyes'.

Chapter 31
They visit the Pyramids

The resolution being thus taken, they set out the next day. They laid tents upon their camels, being resolved to stay among the pyramids till their curiosity was fully satisfied. They travelled gently, turned aside to every thing remarkable, stopped from time to time and conversed with the inhabitants, and observed the various appearances of towns ruined and inhabited, of wild and cultivated nature.

When they came to the Great Pyramid they were astonished at the extent of the base, and the height of the top. Imlac explained to them the principles upon which the pyramidal form was chosen for a fabric intended to co-extend its duration with that of the world: he showed that its gradual diminution gave it such stability, as defeated all the common attacks of the elements, and could scarcely be overthrown by earthquakes themselves, the least resistible of natural violence. A concussion that should shatter the pyramid would threaten the dissolution of the continent.

They measured all its dimensions, and pitched their tents at its foot. Next day they prepared to enter its interior apartments, and having hired the common guides climbed up to the first passage, when the favourite of the princess, looking into the cavity, stepped back and trembled. 'Pekuah', said the princess, 'of what art thou afraid?' 'Of the narrow entrance', answered the lady, 'and of the dreadful gloom. I dare not enter a place which must surely be inhabited by unquiet souls. The original possessors of these dreadful vaults will start up before us, and, perhaps, shut us in for ever'. She spoke, and threw her arms round the neck of her mistress.

'If all your fear be of apparitions', said the prince, 'I will promise you safety: there is no danger from the dead; he that is once buried will be seen no more'.

'That the dead are seen no more', said Imlac, 'I will not undertake to maintain against the concurrent and unvaried testimony of all ages, and of all nations. There is no people, rude or learned, among whom apparitions of the dead are not related and believed. This opinion, which, perhaps, prevails as far as human nature is diffused, could become universal only by its truth: those, that never heard of one another, would not have agreed in a tale which nothing but experience can make credible. That it is doubted by single cavillers can very little weaken the general evidence, and some who deny it with their tongues confess it by their fears.

'Yet I do not mean to add new terrors to those which have already seized upon Pekuah. There can be no reason why spectres should haunt the pyramid more than other places, or why they should have power or will to hurt innocence and purity. Our entrance is no violation of their privileges; we can take nothing from them, how then can we offend them?'

Notes

[28] *fabrics* buildings.

'My dear Pekuah', said the princess, 'I will always go before you, and Imlac shall follow you. Remember that you are the companion of the princess of Abyssinia'.

'If the princess is pleased that her servant should die', returned the lady, 'let her command some death less dreadful than enclosure in this horrid cavern. You know I dare not disobey you: I must go if you command me; but, if I once enter, I never shall come back'.

The princess saw that her fear was too strong for expostulation or reproof, and embracing her, told her that she should stay in the tent till their return. Pekuah was yet not satisfied, but entreated the princess not to pursue so dreadful a purpose, as that of entering the recesses of the pyramid. 'Though I cannot teach courage', said Nekayah, 'I must not learn cowardice; nor leave at last undone what I came hither only to do'.

Chapter 32
They enter the Pyramid

Pekuah descended to the tents and the rest entered the pyramid: they passed through the galleries, surveyed the vaults of marble, and examined the chest in which the body of the founder is supposed to have been reposited. They then sat down in one of the most spacious chambers to rest a while before they attempted to return.

'We have now', said Imlac, 'gratified our minds with an exact view of the greatest work of man, except the wall of China.

'Of the wall it is very easy to assign the motives. It secured a wealthy and timorous nation from the incursions of Barbarians, whose unskilfulness in arts made it easier for them to supply their wants by rapine than by industry, and who from time to time poured in upon the habitations of peaceful commerce, as vultures descend upon domestic fowl. Their celerity and fierceness made the wall necessary, and their ignorance made it efficacious.

'But for the pyramids no reason has ever been given adequate to the cost and labour of the work. The narrowness of the chambers proves that it could afford no retreat from enemies, and treasures might have been reposited at far less expense with equal security. It seems to have been erected only in compliance with that hunger of imagination which preys incessantly upon life, and must be always appeased by some employment. Those who have already all that they can enjoy, must enlarge their desires. He that has built for use, till use is supplied, must begin to build for vanity, and extend his plan to the utmost power of human performance, that he may not be soon reduced to form another wish.

'I consider this mighty structure as a monument of the insufficiency of human enjoyments. A king, whose power is unlimited, and whose treasures surmount all real and imaginary wants, is compelled to solace, by the erection of a pyramid, the satiety of dominion and tastelessness of pleasures, and to amuse the tediousness of declining life, by seeing thousands labouring without end, and one stone, for no purpose, laid upon another. Whoever thou art, that, not content with a moderate condition, imaginest happiness in royal magnificence, and dreamest that command or riches can feed the appetite of novelty with perpetual gratifications, survey the pyramids, and confess thy folly!'

Chapter 33
The princess meets with an unexpected misfortune

They rose up, and returned through the cavity at which they had entered, and the princess prepared for her favourite a long narrative of dark labyrinths, and costly rooms, and of the different impressions which the varieties of the way had made upon her. But, when they came to their train, they found every one silent and dejected: the men discovered shame and fear in their countenances, and the women were weeping in the tents.

What had happened they did not try to conjecture, but immediately enquired. 'You had scarcely entered into the pyramid', said one of the attendants, 'when a troop of Arabs rushed upon us: we were too few to resist them, and too slow to escape. They were about to search the tents, set us on our camels, and drive us along before them, when the approach of some Turkish horsemen put them to flight; but they seized the lady Pekuah with her two maids, and carried them away: the Turks are now pursuing them by our instigation, but I fear they will not be able to overtake them'.

The princess was overpowered with surprise and grief. Rasselas, in the first heat of his resentment, ordered his servants to follow him, and prepared to pursue the robbers with his sabre in his hand. 'Sir', said Imlac, 'what can you hope from violence or valour? the Arabs are mounted on horses trained to battle and retreat; we have only beasts of burthen. By leaving our present station we may lose the princess, but cannot hope to regain Pekuah'.

In a short time the Turks returned, having not been able to reach the enemy. The princess burst out into new lamentations, and Rasselas could scarcely forbear to reproach them with cowardice; but Imlac was of opinion, that the escape of the Arabs was no addition to their misfortune, for, perhaps, they would have killed their captives rather than have resigned them.

Chapter 34
They return to Cairo without Pekuah

There was nothing to be hoped from longer stay. They returned to Cairo repenting of their curiosity, censuring the negligence of the government, lamenting their own rashness which had neglected to procure a guard, imagining many expedients by which the loss of Pekuah might have been prevented, and resolving to do something for her recovery, though none could find any thing proper to be done.

Nekayah retired to her chamber, where her women attempted to comfort her, by telling her that all had their troubles, and that lady Pekuah had enjoyed much happiness in the world for a long time, and might reasonably expect a change of fortune. They hoped that some good would befall her wheresoever she was, and that their mistress would find another friend who might supply her place.

The princess made them no answer, and they continued the form of condolence, not much grieved in their hearts that the favourite was lost.

Next day the prince presented to the Bassa a memorial of the wrong which he had suffered, and a petition for redress. The Bassa threatened to punish the robbers, but did not attempt to catch them, nor, indeed, could any account or description be given by which he might direct the pursuit.

It soon appeared that nothing would be done by authority. Governors, being accustomed to hear of more crimes than they can punish, and more wrongs than they can redress, set themselves at ease by indiscriminate negligence, and presently forget the request when they lose sight of the petitioner.

Imlac then endeavoured to gain some intelligence by private agents. He found many who pretended to an exact knowledge of all the haunts of the Arabs, and to regular correspondence with their chiefs, and who readily undertook the recovery of Pekuah. Of these, some were furnished with money for their journey, and came back no more; some were liberally paid for accounts which a few days discovered to be false. But the princess would not suffer any means, however improbable, to be left untried. While she was doing something she kept her hope alive. As one expedient failed, another was suggested; when one messenger returned unsuccessful, another was dispatched to a different quarter.

Two months had now passed, and of Pekuah nothing had been heard; the hopes which they had endeavoured to raise in each other grew more languid, and the princess, when she saw nothing more to be tried, sunk down inconsolable in hopeless dejection. A thousand times she reproached herself with the easy compliance by which she permitted her favourite to stay behind her. 'Had not my fondness', said she, 'lessened my authority, Pekuah had not dared to talk of her terrors. She ought to have feared me more than spectres. A severe look would have overpowered her; a peremptory command would have compelled obedience. Why did foolish indulgence prevail upon me? Why did I not speak and refuse to hear?'

'Great princess', said Imlac, 'do not reproach yourself for your virtue, or consider that as blameable by which evil has accidentally been caused. Your tenderness for the timidity of Pekuah was generous and kind. When we act according to our duty, we commit the event to him by whose laws our actions are governed, and who will suffer none to be finally punished for obedience. When, in prospect of some good, whether natural or moral, we break the rules prescribed us, we withdraw from the direction of superior wisdom, and take all consequences upon ourselves. Man cannot so far know the connection of causes and events, as that he may venture to do wrong in order to do right. When we pursue our end by lawful means, we may always console our miscarriage by the hope of future recompense. When we consult only our own policy, and attempt to find a nearer way to good, by overleaping the settled boundaries of right and wrong, we cannot be happy even by success, because we cannot escape the consciousness of our fault; but, if we miscarry, the disappointment is irremediably embittered. How comfortless is the sorrow of him; who feels at once the pangs of guilt, and the vexation of calamity which guilt has brought upon him?

'Consider, princess, what would have been your condition, if the lady Pekuah had entreated to accompany you, and, being compelled to stay in the tents, had been carried away; or how would you have borne the thought, if you had forced her into the pyramid, and she had died before you in agonies of terror'.

'Had either happened', said Nekayah, 'I could not have endured life till now: I should have been tortured to madness by the remembrance of such cruelty, or must have pined away in abhorrence of myself'.

'This at least', said Imlac, 'is the present reward of virtuous conduct, that no unlucky consequence can oblige us to repent it'.

Chapter 35
The princess continues to lament Pekuah

Nekayah, being thus reconciled to herself, found that no evil is insupportable but that which is accompanied with consciousness of wrong. She was, from that time, delivered from the violence of tempestuous sorrow, and sunk into silent pensiveness and gloomy tranquillity. She sat from morning to evening recollecting all that had been done or said by her Pekuah, treasured up with care every trifle on which Pekuah had set an accidental value, and which might recall to mind any little incident or careless conversation. The sentiments of her, whom she now expected to see no more, were treasured in her memory as rules of life, and she deliberated to no other end than to conjecture on any occasion what would have been the opinion and counsel of Pekuah.

The women, by whom she was attended, knew nothing of her real condition, and therefore she could not talk to them but with caution and reserve. She began to remit her curiosity, having no great care to collect notions which she had no convenience of uttering. Rasselas endeavoured first to comfort and afterwards to divert her; he hired musicians, to whom she seemed to listen, but did not hear them, and procured masters to instruct her in various arts, whose lectures, when they visited her again, were again to be repeated. She had lost her taste of pleasure and her ambition of excellence. And her mind, though forced into short excursions, always recurred to the image of her friend.

Imlac was every morning earnestly enjoined to renew his enquiries, and was asked every night whether he had yet heard of Pekuah, till not being able to return the princess the answer that she desired, he was less and less willing to come into her presence. She observed his backwardness, and commanded him to attend her. 'You are not', said she, 'to confound impatience with resentment, or to suppose that I charge you with negligence, because I repine at your unsuccessfulness. I do not much wonder at your absence; I know that the unhappy are never pleasing, and that all naturally avoid the contagion of misery. To hear complaints is wearisome alike to the wretched and the happy; for who would cloud by adventitious grief the short gleams of gaiety which life allows us? or who, that is struggling under his own evils, will add to them the miseries of another?

'The time is at hand, when none shall be disturbed any longer by the sighs of Nekayah: my search after happiness is now at an end. I am resolved to retire from the world with all its flatteries and deceits, and will hide myself in solitude, without any other care than to compose my thoughts, and regulate my hours by a constant succession of innocent occupations, till, with a mind purified from all earthly desires, I shall enter into that state, to which all are hastening, and in which I hope again to enjoy the friendship of Pekuah'.

'Do not entangle your mind', said Imlac, 'by irrevocable determinations, nor increase the burden of life by a voluntary accumulation of misery: the weariness of retirement will continue or increase when the loss of Pekuah is forgotten. That you have been deprived of one pleasure is no very good reason for rejection of the rest'.

'Since Pekuah was taken from me', said the princess, 'I have no pleasure to reject or to retain. She that has no one to love or trust has little to hope. She wants the radical principle of happiness. We may, perhaps, allow that what satisfaction this world can afford, must arise from the conjunction of wealth, knowledge and goodness: wealth is nothing but as it is bestowed, and knowledge nothing but as it is communicated: they must therefore be imparted to others, and to whom could I now delight to impart them? Goodness affords the only comfort which can be enjoyed without a partner, and goodness may be practised in retirement'.

'How far solitude may admit goodness, or advance it, I shall not', replied Imlac, 'dispute at present. Remember the confession of the pious hermit. You will wish to return into the world, when the image of your companion has left your thoughts'. 'That time', said Nekayah, 'will never come. The generous frankness, the modest obsequiousness,[29] and the faithful secrecy of my dear Pekuah, will always be more missed, as I shall live longer to see vice and folly'.

Notes

[29] *obsequiousness* "Obedience; compliance" (Johnson).

'The state of a mind oppressed with a sudden calamity', said Imlac, 'is like that of the fabulous inhabitants of the new created earth, who, when the first night came upon them, supposed that day never would return. When the clouds of sorrow gather over us, we see nothing beyond them, nor can imagine how they will be dispelled: yet a new day succeeded to the night, and sorrow is never long without a dawn of ease. But they who restrain themselves from receiving comfort, do as the savages would have done, had they put out their eyes when it was dark. Our minds, like our bodies, are in continual flux; something is hourly lost, and something acquired. To lose much at once is inconvenient to either, but while the vital powers remain uninjured, nature will find the means of reparation. Distance has the same effect on the mind as on the eye, and while we glide along the stream of time, whatever we leave behind us is always lessening, and that which we approach increasing in magnitude. Do not suffer life to stagnate; it will grow muddy for want of motion: commit yourself again to the current of the world; Pekuah will vanish by degrees; you will meet in your way some other favourite, or learn to diffuse yourself in general conversation'.

'At least', said the prince, 'do not despair before all remedies have been tried: the enquiry after the unfortunate lady is still continued, and shall be carried on with yet greater diligence, on condition that you will promise to wait a year for the event, without any unalterable resolution'.

Nekayah thought this a reasonable demand, and made the promise to her brother, who had been advised by Imlac to require it. Imlac had, indeed, no great hope of regaining Pekuah, but he supposed, that if he could secure the interval of a year, the princess would be then in no danger of a cloister.

Chapter 36
Pekuah is still remembered by the princess

Nekayah, seeing that nothing was omitted for the recovery of her favourite, and having, by her promise, set her intention of retirement at a distance, began imperceptibly to return to common cares and common pleasures. She rejoiced without her own consent at the suspension of her sorrows, and sometimes caught herself with indignation in the act of turning away her mind from the remembrance of her, whom yet she resolved never to forget.

She then appointed a certain hour of the day for meditation on the merits and fondness of Pekuah, and for some weeks retired constantly at the time fixed, and returned with her eyes swollen and her countenance clouded. By degrees she grew less scrupulous, and suffered any important and pressing avocation to delay the tribute of daily tears. She then yielded to less occasions; sometimes forgot what she was indeed afraid to remember, and, at last, wholly released herself from the duty of periodical affliction.

Her real love of Pekuah was yet not diminished. A thousand occurrences brought her back to memory, and a thousand wants, which nothing but the confidence of friendship can supply, made her frequently regretted. She, therefore, solicited Imlac never to desist from enquiry, and to leave no art of intelligence untried, that, at least, she might have the comfort of knowing that she did not suffer by negligence or sluggishness. 'Yet what', said she, 'is to be expected from our pursuit of happiness, when we find the state of life to be such, that happiness itself is the cause of misery? Why should we endeavour to attain that, of which the possession cannot be secured? I shall henceforward fear to yield my heart to excellence, however bright, or to fondness, however tender, lest I should lose again what I have lost in Pekuah'.

Chapter 37
The princess hears news of Pekuah

In seven months, one of the messengers, who had been sent away upon the day when the promise was drawn from the princess, returned, after many unsuccessful rambles, from the borders of Nubia,[30] with an account that Pekuah was in the hands of an Arab chief, who possessed a castle or fortress on the extremity of Egypt. The Arab, whose revenue was plunder, was willing to restore her, with her two attendants, for two hundred ounces of gold.

The price was no subject of debate. The princess was in ecstasies when she heard that her favourite was alive, and might so cheaply be ransomed. She could not think of delaying for a moment Pekuah's happiness or her own, but entreated her brother to send back the messenger with the sum required. Imlac, being consulted, was not very confident of the veracity of the relator, and was still more doubtful of the Arab's faith, who might, if he were too liberally trusted, detain at once the money and the captives. He thought it dangerous to put themselves in the power of the Arab, by going into his district, and could not expect that the Rover would so much expose himself as to come into the lower country, where he might be seized by the forces of the Bassa.

It is difficult to negotiate where neither will trust. But Imlac, after some deliberation, directed the messenger to propose that Pekuah should be conducted by ten horsemen to the monastery of St. Anthony, which is situated in the deserts of Upper-Egypt,[31] where she should be met by the same number, and her ransom should be paid.

That no time might be lost, as they expected that the proposal would not be refused, they immediately began their journey to the monastery; and, when they arrived, Imlac went forward with the former messenger to the Arab's fortress. Rasselas was desirous to go with them, but neither his sister nor Imlac would consent. The Arab, according to the custom of his nation, observed the laws of hospitality with great exactness to those who put themselves into his power, and, in a few days, brought Pekuah with her maids, by easy journeys, to their place appointed, where receiving the stipulated price, he restored her with great respect to liberty and her friends, and undertook to conduct them back towards Cairo beyond all danger of robbery or violence.

The princess and her favourite embraced each other with transport too violent to be expressed, and went out together to pour the tears of tenderness in secret, and exchange professions of kindness and gratitude. After a few hours they returned into the refectory of the convent, where, in the presence of the prior and his brethren, the prince required of Pekuah the history of her adventures.

Chapter 38
The adventures of the lady Pekuah

'At what time, and in what manner, I was forced away', said Pekuah, 'your servants have told you. The suddenness of the event struck me with surprise, and I was at first rather stupefied than agitated with any passion of either fear or sorrow. My confusion was increased by the speed and tumult of our flight while we were followed by the

Notes

[30] *Nubia* an ancient region in northeastern Africa, south of Egypt, north of Abyssinia.

[31] *Upper-Egypt* southern, higher Egypt; the monastery was mentioned in books that Johnson knew.

Turks, who, as it seemed, soon despaired to overtake us, or were afraid of those whom they made a show of menacing.

'When the Arabs saw themselves out of danger they slackened their course, and, as I was less harassed by external violence, I began to feel more uneasiness in my mind. After some time we stopped near a spring shaded with trees in a pleasant meadow, where we were set upon the ground, and offered such refreshments as our masters were partaking. I was suffered to sit with my maids apart from the rest, and none attempted to comfort or insult us. Here I first began to feel the full weight of my misery. The girls sat weeping in silence, and from time to time looked on me for succour. I knew not to what condition we were doomed, nor could conjecture where would be the place of our captivity, or whence to draw any hope of deliverance. I was in the hands of robbers and savages, and had no reason to suppose that their pity was more than their justice, or that they would forbear the gratification of any ardour of desire, or caprice of cruelty. I, however, kissed my maids, and endeavoured to pacify them by remarking, that we were yet treated with decency, and that, since we were now carried beyond pursuit, there was no danger of violence to our lives.

'When we were to be set again on horseback, my maids clung round me, and refused to be parted, but I commanded them not to irritate those who had us in their power. We travelled the remaining part of the day through an unfrequented and pathless country, and came by moonlight to the side of a hill, where the rest of the troop was stationed. Their tents were pitched, and their fires kindled, and our chief was welcomed as a man much beloved by his dependants.

'We were received into a large tent, where we found women who had attended their husbands in the expedition. They set before us the supper which they had provided, and I eat it rather to encourage my maids than to comply with any appetite of my own. When the meat was taken away they spread the carpets for repose. I was weary, and hoped to find in sleep that remission of distress which nature seldom denies. Ordering myself therefore to be undressed, I observed that the women looked very earnestly upon me, not expecting, I suppose, to see me so submissively attended. When my upper vest was taken off, they were apparently struck with the splendour of my clothes, and one of them timorously laid her hand upon the embroidery. She then went out, and, in a short time, came back with another woman, who seemed to be of higher rank, and greater authority. She did, at her entrance, the usual act of reverence, and, taking me by the hand, placed me in a smaller tent, spread with finer carpets, where I spent the night quietly with my maids.

'In the morning, as I was sitting on the grass, the chief of the troop came towards me. I rose up to receive him, and he bowed with great respect. "Illustrious lady", said he, "my fortune is better than I had presumed to hope; I am told by my women, that I have a princess in my camp". "Sir", answered I, "your women have deceived themselves and you; I am not a princess, but an unhappy stranger who intended soon to have left this country, in which I am now to be imprisoned for ever".

"Whoever, or whencesoever, you are", returned the Arab, "your dress, and that of your servants, show your rank to be high, and your wealth to be great. Why should you, who can so easily procure your ransom, think yourself in danger of perpetual captivity? The purpose of my incursions is to increase my riches, or more properly to gather tribute. The sons of Ishmael are the natural and hereditary lords of this part of the continent, which is usurped by late invaders, and low-born tyrants, from whom we are compelled to take by the sword what is denied to justice. The violence of war admits no distinction; the lance that is lifted at guilt and power will sometimes fall on innocence and gentleness".

"How little", said I, "did I expect that yesterday it should have fallen upon me".

"Misfortunes", answered the Arab, "should always be expected. If the eye of hostility could learn reverence or pity, excellence like yours had been exempt from injury.

But the angels of affliction spread their toils[32] alike for the virtuous and the wicked, for the mighty and the mean. Do not be disconsolate; I am not one of the lawless and cruel rovers of the desert; I know the rules of civil life: I will fix your ransom, give a passport to your messenger, and perform my stipulation with nice punctuality".

'You will easily believe that I was pleased with his courtesy; and finding that his predominant passion was desire of money, I began now to think my danger less, for I knew that no sum would be thought too great for the release of Pekuah. I told him that he should have no reason to charge me with ingratitude, if I was used with kindness, and that any ransom, which could be expected for a maid of common rank, would be paid, but that he must not persist to rate me as a princess. He said, he would consider what he should demand, and then, smiling, bowed and retired.

'Soon after the women came about me, each contending to be more officious[33] than the other, and my maids themselves were served with reverence. We travelled onward by short journeys. On the fourth day the chief told me, that my ransom must be two hundred ounces of gold, which I not only promised him, but told him, that I would add fifty more, if I and my maids were honourably treated.

'I never knew the power of gold before. From that time I was the leader of the troop. The march of every day was longer or shorter as I commanded, and the tents were pitched where I chose to rest. We now had camels and other conveniencies for travel, my own women were always at my side, and I amused myself with observing the manners of the vagrant nations, and with viewing remains of ancient edifices with which these deserted countries appear to have been, in some distant age, lavishly embellished.

'The chief of the band was a man far from illiterate: he was able to travel by the stars or the compass, and had marked in his erratic expeditions such places as are most worthy the notice of a passenger.[34] He observed to me, that buildings are always best preserved in places little frequented, and difficult of access: for, when once a country declines from its primitive splendour, the more inhabitants are left, the quicker ruin will be made. Walls supply stones more easily than quarries, and palaces and temples will be demolished to make stables of granite, and cottages of porphyry'.

Chapter 39
The adventures of Pekuah continued

'We wandered about in this manner for some weeks, whether, as our chief pretended, for my gratification, or, as I rather suspected, for some convenience of his own. I endeavoured to appear contented where sullenness and resentment would have been of no use, and that endeavour conduced much to the calmness of my mind; but my heart was always with Nekayah, and the troubles of the night much overbalanced the amusements of the day. My women, who threw all their cares upon their mistress, set their minds at ease from the time when they saw me treated with respect, and gave themselves up to the incidental alleviations of our fatigue without solicitude or sorrow. I was pleased with their pleasure, and animated with their confidence. My condition had lost much of its terror, since I found that the Arab ranged the country merely to get riches. Avarice is an uniform and tractable vice: other intellectual distempers are

Notes

32 *toils* traps.
33 *officious* kind.
34 *passenger* traveller.

different in different constitutions of mind; that which soothes the pride of one will offend the pride of another; but to the favour of the covetous there is a ready way, bring money and nothing is denied.

'At last we came to the dwelling of our chief, a strong and spacious house built with stone in an island of the Nile, which lies, as I was told, under the tropic.[35] "Lady", said the Arab, "you shall rest after your journey a few weeks in this place, where you are to consider yourself as sovereign. My occupation is war: I have therefore chosen this obscure residence, from which I can issue unexpected, and to which I can retire unpursued. You may now repose in security: here are few pleasures, but here is no danger". He then led me into the inner apartments, and seating me on the richest couch, bowed to the ground. His women, who considered me as a rival, looked on me with malignity; but being soon informed that I was a great lady detained only for my ransom, they began to vie with each other in obsequiousness and reverence.

'Being again comforted with new assurances of speedy liberty, I was for some days diverted from impatience by the novelty of the place. The turrets overlooked the country to a great distance, and afforded a view of many windings of the stream. In the day I wandered from one place to another as the course of the sun varied the splendour of the prospect, and saw many things which I had never seen before. The crocodiles and river-horses[36] are common in this unpeopled region, and I often looked upon them with terror, though I knew that they could not hurt me. For some time I expected to see mermaids and tritons,[37] which, as Imlac has told me, the European travellers have stationed in the Nile, but no such beings ever appeared, and the Arab, when I enquired after them, laughed at my credulity.

'At night the Arab always attended me to a tower set apart for celestial observations, where he endeavoured to teach me the names and courses of the stars. I had no great inclination to this study, but an appearance of attention was necessary to please my instructor, who valued himself for his skill, and, in a little while, I found some employment requisite to beguile the tediousness of time, which was to be passed always amidst the same objects. I was weary of looking in the morning on things from which I had turned away weary in the evening: I therefore was at last willing to observe the stars rather than do nothing, but could not always compose my thoughts, and was very often thinking on Nekayah when others imagined me contemplating the sky. Soon after the Arab went upon another expedition, and then my only pleasure was to talk with my maids about the accident by which we were carried away, and the happiness that we should all enjoy at the end of our captivity'.

'There were women in your Arab's fortress', said the princess, 'why did you not make them your companions, enjoy their conversation, and partake their diversions? In a place where they found business or amusement, why should you alone sit corroded with idle melancholy? or why should not you bear for a few months that condition to which they were condemned for life?'

'The diversions of the women', answered Pekuah, 'were only childish play, by which the mind accustomed to stronger operations could not be kept busy. I could do all which they delighted in doing by powers merely sensitive,[38] while my intellectual faculties were flown to Cairo. They ran from room to room as a bird hops from wire to wire

Notes

35 *the tropic* latitude 23.5 degrees north.

36 *river-horse* hippopotamus.

37 *tritons* minor sea or river gods.

38 *sensitive* "Having sense or perception, but not reason" (Johnson).

in his cage. They danced for the sake of motion, as lambs frisk in a meadow. One sometimes pretended to be hurt that the rest might be alarmed, or hid herself that another might seek her. Part of their time passed in watching the progress of light bodies that floated on the river, and part in marking the various forms into which clouds broke in the sky.

'Their business was only needlework, in which I and my maids sometimes helped them; but you know that the mind will easily straggle from the fingers, nor will you suspect that captivity and absence from Nekayah could receive solace from silken flowers.

'Nor was much satisfaction to be hoped from their conversation: for of what could they be expected to talk? They had seen nothing; for they had lived from early youth in that narrow spot: of what they had not seen they could have no knowledge, for they could not read. They had no ideas but of the few things that were within their view, and had hardly names for any thing but their clothes and their food. As I bore a superior character, I was often called to terminate their quarrels, which I decided as equitably as I could. If it could have amused me to hear the complaints of each against the rest, I might have been often detained by long stories, but the motives of their animosity were so small that I could not listen without intercepting[39] the tale'.

'How', said Rasselas, 'can the Arab, whom you represented as a man of more than common accomplishments, take any pleasure in his seraglio, when it is filled only with women like these. Are they exquisitely beautiful?'

'They do not', said Pekuah, 'want that unaffecting and ignoble beauty which may subsist without spriteliness or sublimity, without energy of thought or dignity of virtue. But to a man like the Arab such beauty was only a flower casually plucked and carelessly thrown away. Whatever pleasures he might find among them, they were not those of friendship or society. When they were playing about him he looked on them with inattentive superiority: when they vied for his regard he sometimes turned away disgusted. As they had no knowledge, their talk could take nothing from the tediousness of life: as they had no choice, their fondness, or appearance of fondness, excited in him neither pride nor gratitude; he was not exalted in his own esteem by the smiles of a woman who saw no other man, nor was much obliged by that regard, of which he could never know the sincerity, and which he might often perceive to be exerted not so much to delight him as to pain a rival. That which he gave, and they received, as love, was only a careless distribution of superfluous time, such love as man can bestow upon that which he despises, such as has neither hope nor fear, neither joy nor sorrow'.

'You have reason, lady, to think yourself happy', said Imlac, 'that you have been thus easily dismissed. How could a mind, hungry for knowledge, be willing, in an intellectual famine, to lose such a banquet as Pekuah's conversation?'

'I am inclined to believe', answered Pekuah, 'that he was for some time in suspense; notwithstanding his promise, whenever I proposed to dispatch a messenger to Cairo, he found some excuse for delay. While I was detained in his house he made many incursions into the neighbouring countries, and, perhaps, he would have refused to discharge me, had his plunder been equal to his wishes. He returned always courteous, related his adventures, delighted to hear my observations, and endeavoured to advance my acquaintance with the stars. When I importuned him to send away my letters, he

Notes

[39] *intercept* "To stop; to cut off; to stop from being communicated" (Johnson).

soothed me with professions of honour and sincerity; and, when I could be no longer decently denied, put his troop again in motion, and left me to govern in his absence. I was much afflicted by this studied procrastination, and was sometimes afraid that I should be forgotten; that you would leave Cairo, and I must end my days in an island of the Nile.

'I grew at last hopeless and dejected, and cared so little to entertain him, that he for a while more frequently talked with my maids. That he should fall in love with them, or with me, might have been equally fatal, and I was not much pleased with the growing friendship. My anxiety was not long; for, as I recovered some degree of cheerfulness, he returned to me, and I could not forbear to despise my former uneasiness.

'He still delayed to send for my ransom, and would, perhaps, never have determined, had not your agent found his way to him. The gold, which he would not fetch, he could not reject when it was offered. He hastened to prepare for our journey hither, like a man delivered from the pain of an intestine conflict. I took leave of my companions in the house, who dismissed me with cold indifference'.

Nekayah, having heard her favourite's relation, rose and embraced her, and Rasselas gave her an hundred ounces of gold, which she presented to the Arab for the fifty that were promised.

Chapter 40
The history of a man of learning

They returned to Cairo, and were so well pleased at finding themselves together, that none of them went much abroad. The prince began to love learning, and one day declared to Imlac, that he intended to devote himself to science, and pass the rest of his days in literary solitude.

'Before you make your final choice', answered Imlac, 'you ought to examine its hazards, and converse with some of those who are grown old in the company of themselves. I have just left the observatory of one of the most learned astronomers in the world, who has spent forty years in unwearied attention to the motions and appearances of the celestial bodies, and has drawn out his soul in endless calculations. He admits a few friends once a month to hear his deductions and enjoy his discoveries. I was introduced as a man of knowledge worthy of his notice. Men of various ideas and fluent conversation are commonly welcome to those whose thoughts have been long fixed upon a single point, and who find the images of other things stealing away. I delighted him with my remarks, he smiled at the narrative of my travels, and was glad to forget the constellations, and descend for a moment into the lower world.

'On the next day of vacation I renewed my visit, and was so fortunate as to please him again. He relaxed from that time the severity of his rule, and permitted me to enter at my own choice. I found him always busy, and always glad to be relieved. As each knew much which the other was desirous of learning, we exchanged our notions with great delight. I perceived that I had every day more of his confidence, and always found new cause of admiration in the profundity of his mind. His comprehension is vast, his memory capacious and retentive, his discourse is methodical, and his expression clear.

'His integrity and benevolence are equal to his learning. His deepest researches and most favourite studies are willingly interrupted for any opportunity of doing good by his counsel or his riches. To his closest retreat at his most busy moments, all are admitted that want his assistance: "For though I exclude idleness and pleasure I will never", says he, "bar my doors against charity. To man is permitted the contemplation of the skies, but the practice of virtue is commanded" '.

'Surely', said the princess, 'this man is happy'.

'I visited him', said Imlac, 'with more and more frequency and was every time more enamoured of his conversation: he was sublime without haughtiness, courteous without formality, and communicative without ostentation. I was at first, Madam, of your opinion, thought him the happiest of mankind, and often congratulated him on the blessing that he enjoyed. He seemed to hear nothing with indifference but the praises of his condition, to which he always returned a general answer, and diverted the conversation to some other topic.

'Amidst this willingness to be pleased, and labour to please, I had always reason to imagine that some painful sentiment pressed upon his mind. He often looked up earnestly towards the sun, and let his voice fall in the midst of his discourse. He would sometimes, when we were alone, gaze upon me in silence with the air of a man who longed to speak what he was yet resolved to suppress. He would often send for me with vehement injunctions of haste, though, when I came to him, he had nothing extraordinary to say. And sometimes, when I was leaving him, would call me back, pause a few moments and then dismiss me'.

Chapter 41
The astronomer discovers[40] the cause of his uneasiness

'At last the time came when the secret burst his reserve. We were sitting together last night in the turret of his house, watching the emersion[41] of a satellite of Jupiter. A sudden tempest clouded the sky, and disappointed our observation. We sat a while silent in the dark, and then he addressed himself to me in these words: "Imlac, I have long considered thy friendship as the greatest blessing of my life. Integrity without knowledge is weak and useless, and knowledge without integrity is dangerous and dreadful. I have found in thee all the qualities requisite for trust, benevolence, experience, and fortitude. I have long discharged an office which I must soon quit at the call of nature, and shall rejoice in the hour of imbecility and pain to devolve it upon thee".

'I thought myself honoured by this testimony, and protested that whatever could conduce to his happiness would add likewise to mine.

' "Hear, Imlac, what thou wilt not without difficulty credit. I have possessed for five years the regulation of weather, and the distribution of the seasons: the sun has listened to my dictates, and passed from tropic to tropic by my direction; the clouds, at my call, have poured their waters, and the Nile has overflowed at my command; I have restrained the rage of the dog-star,[42] and mitigated the fervours of the crab.[43] The winds alone, of all the elemental powers, have hitherto refused my authority, and multitudes have perished by equinoctial tempests which I found myself unable to prohibit or restrain. I have administered this great office with exact justice, and made to the different nations of the earth an impartial dividend of rain and sunshine. What must have been the misery of half the globe, if I had limited the clouds to particular regions, or confined the sun to either side of the equator?" '

Notes

[40] *discovers* reveals.

[41] *emersion* "The time when a star, having been obscured by its too near approach to the sun, appears again" (Johnson).

[42] *dog-star* Sirius, which rises with the sun in late summer and is blamed for scorching heat and famine.

[43] *crab* a constellation in the zodiac also known as Cancer, in which the sun is at its strongest.

Chapter 42
The astronomer justifies his account of himself

'I suppose he discovered in me, through the obscurity of the room, some tokens of amazement and doubt, for, after a short pause, he proceeded thus:

' "Not to be easily credited will neither surprise nor offend me; for I am, probably, the first of human beings to whom this trust has been imparted. Nor do I know whether to deem this distinction as reward or punishment; since I have possessed it I have been far less happy than before, and nothing but the consciousness of good intention could have enabled me to support the weariness of unremitted vigilance".

' "How long, Sir", said I, "has this great office been in your hands?"

' "About ten years ago", said he, "my daily observations of the changes of the sky led me to consider, whether, if I had the power of the seasons, I could confer greater plenty upon the inhabitants of the earth. This contemplation fastened on my mind, and I sat days and nights in imaginary dominion, pouring upon this country and that the showers of fertility, and seconding every fall of rain with a due proportion of sunshine. I had yet only the will to do good, and did not imagine that I should ever have the power.

' "One day as I was looking on the fields withering with heat, I felt in my mind a sudden wish that I could send rain on the southern mountains, and raise the Nile to an inundation. In the hurry of my imagination I commanded rain to fall, and, by comparing the time of my command, with that of the inundation, I found that the clouds had listened to my lips".

' "Might not some other cause", said I, "produce this concurrence? the Nile does not always rise on the same day".

' "Do not believe", said he with impatience, "that such objections could escape me: I reasoned long against my own conviction, and laboured against truth with the utmost obstinacy. I sometimes suspected myself of madness, and should not have dared to impart this secret but to a man like you, capable of distinguishing the wonderful from the impossible, and the incredible from the false".

' "Why, Sir", said I, "do you call that incredible, which you know, or think you know, to be true?"

' "Because", said he, "I cannot prove it by any external evidence; and I know too well the laws of demonstration to think that my conviction ought to influence another, who cannot, like me, be conscious of its force. I, therefore, shall not attempt to gain credit by disputation. It is sufficient that I feel this power, that I have long possessed, and every day exerted it. But the life of man is short, the infirmities of age increase upon me, and the time will soon come when the regulator of the year must mingle with the dust. The care of appointing a successor has long disturbed me; the night and the day have been spent in comparisons of all the characters which have come to my knowledge, and I have yet found none so worthy as thyself" '.

Chapter 43
The astronomer leaves Imlac his directions

'"Hear therefore, what I shall impart, with attention, such as the welfare of a world requires. If the task of a king be considered as difficult, who has the care only of a few millions, to whom he cannot do much good or harm, what must be the anxiety of him, on whom depend the action of the elements, and the great gifts of light and heat! – Hear me therefore with attention.

'"I have diligently considered the position of the earth and sun, and formed innumerable schemes in which I changed their situation. I have sometimes turned aside the axis of the earth, and sometimes varied the ecliptic of the sun: but I have found it impossible to make a disposition by which the world may be advantaged; what one region gains, another loses by any imaginable alteration, even without considering the distant parts of the solar system with which we are unacquainted. Do not, therefore, in thy administration of the year, indulge thy pride by innovation; do not please thyself with thinking that thou canst make thyself renowned to all future ages, by disordering the seasons. The memory of mischief is no desirable fame. Much less will it become thee to let kindness or interest prevail. Never rob other countries of rain to pour it on thine own. For us the Nile is sufficient".

'I promised that when I possessed the power, I would use it with inflexible integrity, and he dismissed me, pressing my hand. "My heart", said he, "will be now at rest, and my benevolence will no more destroy my quiet: I have found a man of wisdom and virtue, to whom I can cheerfully bequeath the inheritance of the sun" '.

The prince heard this narration with very serious regard, but the princess smiled, and Pekuah convulsed herself with laughter. 'Ladies', said Imlac, 'to mock the heaviest of human afflictions is neither charitable nor wise. Few can attain this man's knowledge, and few practise his virtues; but all may suffer his calamity. Of the uncertainties of our present state, the most dreadful and alarming is the uncertain continuance of reason'.

The princess was recollected, and the favourite was abashed. Rasselas, more deeply affected, enquired of Imlac, whether he thought such maladies of the mind frequent, and how they were contracted.

Chapter 44
The dangerous prevalence of imagination

'Disorders of intellect', answered Imlac, 'happen much more often than superficial observers will easily believe. Perhaps, if we speak with rigorous exactness, no human mind is in its right state. There is no man whose imagination does not sometimes predominate over his reason, who can regulate his attention wholly by his will, and whose ideas will come and go at his command. No man will be found in whose mind airy notions do not sometimes tyrannise, and force him to hope or fear beyond the limits of sober probability. All power of fancy over reason is a degree of insanity; but while this power is such as we can control and repress, it is not visible to others, nor considered as any depravation of the mental faculties: it is not pronounced madness but when it comes ungovernable, and apparently influences speech or action.

'To indulge the power of fiction, and send imagination out upon the wing, is often the sport of those who delight too much in silent speculation. When we are alone we are not always busy; the labour of excogitation is too violent to last long; the ardour of enquiry will sometimes give way to idleness or satiety. He who has nothing external that can divert him, must find pleasure in his own thoughts, and must conceive himself what he is not; for who is pleased with what he is? He then expatiates in boundless futurity, and culls from all imaginable conditions that which for the present moment he should most desire, amuses his desires with impossible enjoyments, and confers upon his pride unattainable dominion. The mind dances from scene to scene, unites all pleasures in all combinations, and riots in delights which nature and fortune, with all their bounty, cannot bestow.

'In time some particular train of ideas fixes the attention, all other intellectual gratifications are rejected, the mind, in weariness or leisure, recurs constantly to the favourite conception, and feasts on the luscious falsehood whenever she is offended with the bitterness of truth. By degrees the reign of fancy is confirmed; she grows first imperious, and in time despotic. Then fictions begin to operate as realities, false opinions fasten upon the mind, and life passes in dreams of rapture or of anguish.

'This, Sir, is one of the dangers of solitude, which the hermit has confessed not always to promote goodness, and the astronomer's misery has proved to be not always propitious to wisdom'.

'I will no more', said the favourite, 'imagine myself the queen of Abyssinia. I have often spent the hours, which the princess gave to my own disposal, in adjusting ceremonies and regulating the court; I have repressed the pride of the powerful, and granted the petitions of the poor; I have built new palaces in more happy situations, planted groves upon the tops of mountains, and have exulted in the beneficence of royalty, till, when the princess entered, I had almost forgotten to bow down before her'.

'And I', said the princess, 'will not allow myself any more to play the shepherdess in my waking dreams. I have often soothed my thoughts with the quiet and innocence of pastoral employments, till I have in my chamber heard the winds whistle, and the sheep bleat; sometimes freed the lamb entangled in the thicket, and sometimes with my crook encountered the wolf. I have a dress like that of the village maids, which I put on to help my imagination, and a pipe on which I play softly, and suppose myself followed by my flocks'.

'I will confess', said the prince, 'an indulgence of fantastic delight more dangerous than yours. I have frequently endeavoured to image the possibility of a perfect government, by which all wrong should be restrained, all vice reformed, and all the subjects preserved in tranquillity and innocence. This thought produced innumerable schemes of reformation, and dictated many useful regulations and salutary edicts. This has been the sport and sometimes the labour of my solitude; and I start, when I think with how little anguish I once supposed the death of my father and my brothers'.

'Such', says Imlac, 'are the effects of visionary schemes: when we first form them we know them to be absurd, but familiarise them by degrees, and in time lose sight of their folly'.

Chapter 45
They discourse with an old man

The evening was now far past, and they rose to return home. As they walked along the bank of the Nile, delighted with the beams of the moon quivering on the water, they saw at a small distance an old man, whom the prince had often heard in the assembly of the sages. 'Yonder', said he, 'is one whose years have calmed his passions, but not clouded his reason: let us close the disquisitions of the night, by enquiring what are his sentiments of his own state, that we may know whether youth alone is to struggle with vexation, and whether any better hope remains for the latter part of life'.

Here the sage approached and saluted them. They invited him to join their walk, and prattled a while as acquaintance that had unexpectedly met one another. The old man was cheerful and talkative, and the way seemed short in his company. He was pleased to find himself not disregarded, accompanied them to their house, and, at the prince's request, entered with them. They placed him in the seat of honour, and set wine and conserves[44] before him.

Notes

[44] *conserve* "A sweetmeat made of the inspissated juices of fruit, boiled with sugar till they will harden and candy" (Johnson).

'Sir', said the princess, 'an evening walk must give to a man of learning, like you, pleasures which ignorance and youth can hardly conceive. You know the qualities and the causes of all that you behold, the laws by which the river flows, the periods in which the planets perform their revolutions. Every thing must supply you with contemplation, and renew the consciousness of your own dignity'.

'Lady', answered he, 'let the gay and the vigorous expect pleasure in their excursions; it is enough that age can obtain ease. To me the world has lost its novelty: I look round, and see what I remember to have seen in happier days. I rest against a tree, and consider, that in the same shade I once disputed upon the annual overflow of the Nile[45] with a friend who is now silent in the grave. I cast my eyes upwards, fix them on the changing moon, and think with pain on the vicissitudes of life. I have ceased to take much delight in physical truth; for what have I to do with those things which I am soon to leave?'

'You may at least recreate yourself', said Imlac, 'with the recollection of an honourable and useful life, and enjoy the praise which all agree to give you'.

'Praise', said the sage, with a sigh, 'is to an old man an empty sound. I have neither mother to be delighted with the reputation of her son, nor wife to partake the honours of her husband. I have outlived my friends and my rivals. Nothing is now of much importance; for I cannot extend my interest beyond myself. Youth is delighted with applause, because it is considered as the earnest of some future good, and because the prospect of life is far extended: but to me, who am now declining to decrepitude, there is little to be feared from the malevolence of men, and yet less to be hoped from their affection or esteem. Something they may yet take away, but they can give me nothing. Riches would now be useless, and high employment would be pain. My retrospect of life recalls to my view many opportunities of good neglected, much time squandered upon trifles, and more lost in idleness and vacancy. I leave many great designs unattempted, and many great attempts unfinished. My mind is burthened with no heavy crime, and therefore I compose myself to tranquillity; endeavour to abstract my thoughts from hopes and cares, which, though reason knows them to be vain, still try to keep their old possession of the heart; expect, with serene humility, that hour which nature cannot long delay; and hope to possess in a better state that happiness which here I could not find, and that virtue which here I have not attained'.

He rose and went away, leaving his audience not much elated with the hope of long life. The prince consoled himself with remarking, that it was not reasonable to be disappointed by this account; for age had never been considered as the season of felicity, and, if it was possible to be easy in decline and weakness, it was likely that the days of vigour and alacrity might be happy: that the moon of life might be bright, if the evening could be calm.

The princess suspected that age was querulous and malignant, and delighted to repress the expectations of those who had newly entered the world. She had seen the possessors of estates look with envy on their heirs, and known many who enjoy pleasure no longer than they can confine it to themselves.

Notes

[45] *the annual overflow of the Nile* like the source of the Nile, an age-old subject of debate, which was still not fully understood in Johnson's time.

Pekuah conjectured, that the man was older than he appeared, and was willing to impute his complaints to delirious dejection; or else supposed that he had been unfortunate, and was therefore discontented: 'For nothing', said she, 'is more common than to call our own condition, the condition of life'.

Imlac, who had no desire to see them depressed, smiled at the comforts which they could so readily procure to themselves, and remembered, that at the same age, he was equally confident of unmingled prosperity, and equally fertile of consolatory expedients. He forbore to force upon them unwelcome knowledge, which time itself would too soon impress. The princess and her lady retired; the madness of the astronomer hung upon their minds, and they desired Imlac to enter upon his office, and delay next morning the rising of the sun.

Chapter 46
The princess and Pekuah visit the astronomer

The princess and Pekuah having talked in private of Imlac's astronomer, thought his character at once so amiable and so strange, that they could not be satisfied without a nearer knowledge, and Imlac was requested to find the means of bringing them together.

This was somewhat difficult; the philosopher had never received any visits from women, though he lived in a city that had in it many Europeans who followed the manners of their own countries, and many from other parts of the world that lived there with European liberty. The ladies would not be refused, and several schemes were proposed for the accomplishment of their design. It was proposed to introduce them as strangers in distress, to whom the sage was always accessible; but, after some deliberation, it appeared, that by this artifice, no acquaintance could be formed, for their conversation would be short, and they could not decently importune him often. 'This', said Rasselas, 'is true; but I have yet a stronger objection against the misrepresentation of your state. I have always considered it as treason against the great republic of human nature, to make any man's virtues the means of deceiving him, whether on great or little occasions. All imposture weakens confidence and chills benevolence. When the sage finds that you are not what you seemed, he will feel the resentment natural to a man who, conscious of great abilities, discovers that he has been tricked by understandings meaner than his own, and, perhaps, the distrust, which he can never afterwards wholly lay aside, may stop the voice of counsel, and close the hand of charity; and where will you find the power of restoring his benefactions to mankind, or his peace to himself?'

To this no reply was attempted, and Imlac began to hope that their curiosity would subside; but, next day, Pekuah told him, she had now found an honest pretence for a visit to the astronomer, for she would solicit permission to continue under him the studies in which she had been initiated by the Arab, and the princess might go with her either as a fellow-student, or because a woman could not decently come alone. 'I am afraid', said Imlac, 'that he will be soon weary of your company: men advanced far in knowledge do not love to repeat the elements of their art, and I am not certain that even of the elements, as he will deliver them connected with inferences, and mingled with reflections, you are a very capable auditress'. 'That', said Pekuah, 'must be my care: I ask of you only to take me thither. My knowledge is, perhaps, more than you imagine it, and by concurring always with his opinions I shall make him think it greater than it is'.

The astronomer, in pursuance of this resolution, was told, that a foreign lady, travelling in search of knowledge, had heard of his reputation, and was desirous to become his scholar.[46] The uncommonness of the proposal raised at once his surprise and curiosity, and when, after a short deliberation, he consented to admit her, he could not stay without impatience till the next day.

The ladies dressed themselves magnificently, and were attended by Imlac to the astronomer, who was pleased to see himself approached with respect by persons of so splendid an appearance. In the exchange of the first civilities he was timorous and bashful; but when the talk became regular, he recollected his powers, and justified the character which Imlac had given. Enquiring of Pekuah what could have turned her inclination towards astronomy, he received from her a history of her adventure at the pyramid, and of the time passed in the Arab's island. She told her tale with ease and elegance, and her conversation took possession of his heart. The discourse was then turned to astronomy: Pekuah displayed what she knew: he looked upon her as a prodigy of genius, and entreated her not to desist from a study which she had so happily begun.

They came again and again, and were every time more welcome than before. The sage endeavoured to amuse them, that they might prolong their visits, for he found his thoughts grow brighter in their company; the clouds of solicitude vanished by degrees, as he forced himself to entertain them, and he grieved when he was left at their departure to his old employment of regulating the seasons.

The princess and her favourite had now watched his lips for several months, and could not catch a single word from which they could judge whether he continued, or not, in the opinion of his preternatural commission. They often contrived to bring him to an open declaration, but he easily eluded all their attacks, and on which side soever they pressed him escaped from them to some other topic.

As their familiarity increased they invited him often to the house of Imlac, where they distinguished him by extraordinary respect. He began gradually to delight in sublunary pleasures. He came early and departed late; laboured to recommend himself by assiduity and compliance; excited their curiosity after new arts, that they might still want his assistance; and when they made any excursion of pleasure or enquiry, entreated to attend them.

By long experience of his integrity and wisdom, the prince and his sister were convinced that he might be trusted without danger; and lest he should draw any false hopes from the civilities which he received, discovered to him their condition with the motives of their journey, and required his opinion on the choice of life.

'Of the various conditions which the world spreads before you, which you shall prefer', said the sage, 'I am not able to instruct you. I can only tell that I have chosen wrong. I have passed my time in study without experience; in the attainment of sciences which can, for the most part, be but remotely useful to mankind. I have purchased knowledge at the expense of all the common comforts of life: I have missed the endearing elegance of female friendship, and the happy commerce of domestic tenderness. If I have obtained any prerogatives above other students, they have been accompanied with fear, disquiet, and scrupulosity; but even of these prerogatives, whatever they were, I have, since my thoughts have been diversified by more intercourse with the world, begun to question the reality. When I have been for a few days lost in pleasing dissipation, I am always tempted to think that my enquiries have ended in error, and that I have suffered much, and suffered it in vain'.

Notes

[46] *scholar*: student.

Imlac was delighted to find that the sage's understanding was breaking through its mists, and resolved to detain him from the planets till he should forget his task of ruling them, and reason should recover its original influence.

From this time the astronomer was received into familiar friendship, and partook of all their projects and pleasures: his respect kept him attentive, and the activity of Rasselas did not leave much time unengaged. Something was always to be done; the day was spent in making observations which furnished talk for the evening, and the evening was closed with a scheme for the morrow.

The sage confessed to Imlac, that since he had mingled in the gay tumults of life, and divided his hours by a succession of amusements, he found the conviction of his authority over the skies fade gradually from his mind, and began to trust less to an opinion which he never could prove to others, and which he now found subject to variation from causes in which reason had no part. 'If I am accidentally left alone for a few hours', said he, 'my inveterate persuasion rushes upon my soul, and my thoughts are chained down by some irresistible violence, but they are soon disentangled by the prince's conversation, and instantaneously released at the entrance of Pekuah. I am like a man habitually afraid of spectres, who is set at ease by a lamp, and wonders at the dread which harassed him in the dark, yet, if his lamp be extinguished, feels again the terrors which he knows that when it is light he shall feel no more. But I am sometimes afraid lest I indulge my quiet by criminal negligence, and voluntarily forget the great charge with which I am entrusted. If I favour myself in a known error, or am determined by my own ease in a doubtful question of this importance, how dreadful is my crime!'

'No disease of the imagination', answered Imlac, 'is so difficult of cure, as that which is complicated with the dread of guilt: fancy and conscience then act interchangeably upon us, and so often shift their places, that the illusions of one are not distinguished from the dictates of the other. If fancy presents images not moral or religious, the mind drives them away when they give it pain, but when melancholic notions take the form of duty, they lay hold on the faculties without opposition, because we are afraid to exclude or banish them. For this reason the superstitious are often melancholy, and the melancholy almost always superstitious.

'But do not let the suggestions of timidity overpower your better reason: the danger of neglect can be but as the probability of the obligation, which when you consider it with freedom, you find very little, and that little growing every day less. Open your heart to the influence of the light which, from time to time, breaks in upon you: when scruples importune you, which you in your lucid moments know to be vain, do not stand to parley, but fly to business or to Pekuah, and keep this thought always prevalent, that you are only one atom of the mass of humanity, and have neither such virtue nor vice, as that you should be singled out for supernatural favours or afflictions'.

Chapter 47
The prince enters and brings a new topic

'All this', said the astronomer, 'I have often thought, but my reason has been so long subjugated by an uncontrollable and overwhelming idea, that it durst not confide in its own decisions. I now see how fatally I betrayed my quiet, by suffering chimeras to prey upon me in secret; but melancholy shrinks from communication, and I never found a man before, to whom I could impart my troubles, though I had been certain of relief. I rejoice to find my own sentiments confirmed by yours, who are not easily deceived, and can have no motive or purpose to deceive. I hope that time and variety will dissipate the gloom that has so long surrounded me, and the latter part of my days will be spent in peace'.

'Your learning and virtue', said Imlac, 'may justly give you hopes'.

Rasselas then entered with the princess and Pekuah, and enquired whether they had contrived any new diversion for the next day. 'Such', said Nekayah, 'is the state of life, that none are happy but by the anticipation of change: the change itself is nothing; when we have made it, the next wish is to change again. The world is not yet exhausted; let me see something tomorrow which I never saw before'.

'Variety', said Rasselas, 'is so necessary to content, that even the *happy valley* disgusted me by the recurrence of its luxuries; yet I could not forbear to reproach myself with impatience, when I saw the monks of St. Anthony support without complaint, a life, not of uniform delight, but uniform hardship'.

'Those men', answered Imlac, 'are less wretched in their silent convent than the Abyssinian princes in their prison of pleasure. Whatever is done by the monks is incited by an adequate and reasonable motive. Their labour supplies them with necessaries; it therefore cannot be omitted, and is certainly rewarded. Their devotion prepares them for another state, and reminds them of its approach, while it fits them for it. Their time is regularly distributed; one duty succeeds another, so that they are not left open to the distraction of unguided choice, nor lost in the shades of listless inactivity. There is a certain task to be performed at an appropriated hour; and their toils are cheerful, because they consider them as acts of piety, by which they are always advancing towards endless felicity'.

'Do you think', said Nekayah, 'that the monastic rule is a more holy and less imperfect state than any other? May not he equally hope for future happiness who converses openly with mankind, who succours the distressed by his charity, instructs the ignorant by his learning, and contributes by his industry to the general system of life; even though he should omit some of the mortifications which are practised in the cloister, and allow himself such harmless delights as his condition may place within his reach?'

'This', said Imlac, 'is a question which has long divided the wise, and perplexed the good. I am afraid to decide on either part. He that lives well in the world is better than he that lives well in a monastery. But, perhaps, every one is not able to stem the temptations of public life; and, if he cannot conquer, he may properly retreat. Some have little power to do good, and have likewise little strength to resist evil. Many are weary of their conflicts with adversity, and are willing to eject those passions which have long busied them in vain. And many are dismissed by age and diseases from the more laborious duties of society. In monasteries the weak and timorous may be happily sheltered, the weary may repose, and the penitent may meditate. Those retreats of prayer and contemplation have something so congenial to the mind of man that, perhaps, there is scarcely one that does not purpose to close his life in pious abstraction with a few associates serious as himself'.

'Such', said Pekuah, 'has often been my wish, and I have heard the princess declare, that she should not willingly die in a crowd'.

'The liberty of using harmless pleasures', proceeded Imlac, 'will not be disputed; but it is still to be examined what pleasures are harmless. The evil of any pleasure that Nekayah can image is not in the act itself, but in its consequences. Pleasure, in itself harmless, may become mischievous, by endearing to us a state which we know to be transient and probatory, and withdrawing our thoughts from that, of which every hour brings us nearer to the beginning, and of which no length of time will bring us to the end. Mortification is not virtuous in itself, nor has any other use, but that it disengages us from the allurements of sense. In the state of future perfection, to which we all aspire, there will be pleasure without danger, and security without restraint'.

The princess was silent, and Rasselas, turning to the astronomer, asked him, whether he could not delay her retreat, by showing her something which she had not seen before.

'Your curiosity', said the sage, 'has been so general, and your pursuit of knowledge so vigorous, that novelties are not now very easily to be found: but what you can no longer procure from the living may be given by the dead. Among the wonders of this country are the catacombs, or the ancient repositories, in which the bodies of the earliest generations were lodged, and where, by the virtue of the gums which embalmed them, they yet remain without corruption'.

'I know not', said Rasselas, 'what pleasure the sight of the catacombs can afford; but, since nothing else is offered, I am resolved to view them, and shall place this with many other things which I have done, because I would do something'.

They hired a guard of horsemen, and the next day visited the catacombs. When they were about to descend into the sepulchral caves, 'Pekuah', said the princess, 'we are now again invading the habitations of the dead; I know that you will stay behind; let me find you safe when I return'. 'No, I will not be left', answered Pekuah; 'I will go down between you and the prince'.

They then all descended, and roved with wonder through the labyrinth of subterraneous passages, where the bodies were laid in rows on either side.

Chapter 48
Imlac discourses on the nature of the soul

'What reason', said the prince, 'can be given, why the Egyptians should thus expensively preserve those carcasses which some nations consume with fire, others lay to mingle with the earth, and all agree to remove from their sight, as soon as decent rites can be performed?'

'The original of ancient customs', said Imlac, 'is commonly unknown; for the practice often continues when the cause has ceased; and concerning superstitious ceremonies it is vain to conjecture; for what reason did not dictate reason cannot explain. I have long believed that the practice of embalming arose only from tenderness to the remains of relations or friends, and to this opinion I am more inclined, because it seems impossible that this care should have been general: had all the dead been embalmed, their repositories must in time have been more spacious than the dwellings of the living. I suppose only the rich or honourable were secured from corruption, and the rest left to the course of nature.

'But it is commonly supposed that the Egyptians believed the soul to live as long as the body continued undissolved and therefore tried this method of eluding death'.

'Could the wise Egyptians', said Nekayah, 'think so grossly of the soul? If the soul could once survive its separation, what could it afterwards receive or suffer from the body?'

'The Egyptians would doubtless think erroneously', said the astronomer, 'in the darkness of heathenism,[47] and the first dawn of philosophy.[48] The nature of the soul is still disputed amidst all our opportunities of clearer knowledge: some yet say that it may be material, who, nevertheless, believe it to be immortal'.

'Some', answered Imlac, 'have indeed said that the soul is material, but I can scarcely believe that any man has thought it, who knew how to think; for all the conclusions of reason enforce the immateriality of mind, and all the notices of sense and investigations of science concur to prove the unconsciousness of matter.

Notes

[47] *heathenism* the religion of those who did not know of or acknowledge the Judeo-Christian God.

[48] *philosophy* particularly Socratic thought, which was regarded as proto-Judeo-Christian.

'It was never supposed that cogitation is inherent in matter, or that every particle is a thinking being. Yet, if any part of matter be devoid of thought, what part can we suppose to think? Matter can differ from matter only in form, density, bulk, motion, and direction of motion: to which of these, however varied or combined, can consciousness be annexed? To be round or square, to be solid or fluid, to be great or little, to be moved slowly or swiftly one way or another, are modes of material existence, all equally alien from the nature of cogitation. If matter be once without thought, it can only be made to think by some new modification, but all the modifications which it can admit are equally unconnected with cogitative powers'.

'But the materialists', said the astronomer, 'urge that matter may have qualities with which we are unacquainted'.

'He who will determine', returned Imlac, 'against that which he knows, because there may be something which he knows not; he that can set hypothetical possibility against acknowledged certainty, is not to be admitted among reasonable beings. All that we know of matter is, that matter is inert, senseless and lifeless; and if this conviction cannot be opposed but by referring us to something that we know not, we have all the evidence that human intellect can admit. If that which is known may be over-ruled by that which is unknown, no being, not omniscient, can arrive at certainty'.

'Yet let us not', said the astronomer, 'too arrogantly limit the Creator's power'.

'It is no limitation of omnipotence', replied the poet, 'to suppose that one thing is not consistent with another, that the same proposition cannot be at once true and false, that the same number cannot be even and odd, that cogitation cannot be conferred on that which is created incapable of cogitation'.

'I know not', said Nekayah, 'any great use of this question. Does that immateriality, which, in my opinion, you have sufficiently proved, necessarily include eternal duration?'

'Of immateriality', said Imlac, 'our ideas are negative, and therefore obscure. Immateriality seems to imply a natural power of perpetual duration as a consequence of exemption from all causes of decay: whatever perishes, is destroyed by the solution of its contexture, and separation of its parts; nor can we conceive how that which has no parts, and therefore admits no solution,[49] can be naturally corrupted or impaired'.

'I know not', said Rasselas, 'how to conceive any thing without extension: what is extended must have parts, and you allow, that whatever has parts may be destroyed'.

'Consider your own conceptions', replied Imlac, 'and the difficulty will be less. You will find substance without extension. An ideal form is no less real than material bulk: yet an ideal form has no extension. It is no less certain, when you think on a pyramid, that your mind possesses the idea of a pyramid, than that the pyramid itself is standing. What space does the idea of a pyramid occupy more than the idea of a grain of corn? or how can either idea suffer laceration? As is the effect such is the cause; as thought is, such is the power that thinks; a power impassive and indiscerptible'.[50]

'But the Being', said Nekayah, 'whom I fear to name, the Being which made the soul, can destroy it'.

'He, surely, can destroy it', answered Imlac, 'since, however unperishable, it receives from a superior nature its power of duration. That it will not perish by any inherent

Notes

[49] *solution* dissolution.

[50] *indiscerptible* "not to be broken or destroyed by dissolution of parts" (Johnson).

cause of decay, or principle of corruption, may be shown by philosophy; but philosophy can tell no more. That it will not be annihilated by him that made it, we must humbly learn from higher authority'.

The whole assembly stood a while silent and collected.[51] 'Let us return', said Rasselas, 'from this scene of mortality. How gloomy would be these mansions of the dead to him who did not know that he shall never die; that what now acts shall continue its agency, and what now thinks shall think on for ever. Those that lie here stretched before us, the wise and the powerful of ancient times, warn us to remember the shortness of our present state; they were, perhaps, snatched away while they were busy, like us, in the choice of life'.

'To me', said the princess, 'the choice of life is become less important; I hope hereafter to think only on the choice of eternity'.

They then hastened out of the caverns, and, under the protection of their guard, returned to Cairo.

Chapter 49
The conclusion, in which nothing is concluded

It was now the time of the inundation of the Nile: a few days after their visit to the catacombs, the river began to rise.

They were confined to their house. The whole region being under water gave them no invitation to any excursions, and, being well supplied with materials for talk, they diverted themselves with comparisons of the different forms of life which they had observed, and with various schemes of happiness which each of them had formed.

Pekuah was never so much charmed with any place as the convent of St. Anthony, where the Arab restored her to the princess, and wished only to fill it with pious maidens, and to be made prioress of the order: she was weary of expectation and disgust, and would gladly be fixed in some unvariable state.

The princess thought, that of all sublunary things, knowledge was the best: She desired first to learn all sciences,[52] and then purposed to found a college of learned women, in which she would preside, that, by conversing with the old, and educating the young, she might divide her time between the acquisition and communication of wisdom, and raise up for the next age models of prudence, and patterns of piety.

The prince desired a little kingdom, in which he might administer justice in his own person, and see all the parts of government with his own eyes; but he could never fix the limits of his dominion, and was always adding to the number of his subjects.

Imlac and the astronomer were contented to be driven along the stream of life without directing their course to any particular port.

Of these wishes that they had formed they well knew that none could be obtained. They deliberated a while what was to be done, and resolved, when the inundation should cease, to return to Abyssinia.

FINIS

Notes

[51] *collected* gained command over their thoughts (see Johnson, sense 5).

[52] *sciences* all fields of knowledge.

from the Preface to *The Plays of William Shakespeare* (1765)

That praises are without reason lavished on the dead, and that the honours due only to excellence are paid to antiquity is a complaint likely to be always continued by those, who, being able to add nothing to truth, hope for eminence from the heresies of paradox; or those, who, being forced by disappointment upon consolatory expedients, are willing to hope from posterity what the present age refuses, and flatter themselves that the regard which is yet denied by envy, will be at last bestowed by time.

Antiquity, like every other quality that attracts the notice of mankind, has undoubtedly votaries that reverence it, not from reason, but from prejudice. Some seem to admire indiscriminately whatever has been long preserved, without considering that time has sometimes co-operated with chance; and perhaps are more willing to honour past than present excellence; and the mind contemplates genius through the shades of age, as the eye surveys the sun through artificial opacity. The great contention of criticism is to find the faults of the moderns, and the beauties of the ancients. While an author is yet living we estimate his powers by his worst performance, and when he is dead we rate them by his best.

To works, however, of which the excellence is not absolute and definite, but gradual and comparative; to works not raised upon principles demonstrative and scientific, but appealing wholly to observation and experience, no other test can be applied than length of duration and continuance of esteem. What mankind have long possessed they have often examined and compared, and if they persist to value the possession, it is because frequent comparisons have confirmed opinion in its favour. As among the works of nature no man can properly call a river deep or mountain high, without the knowledge of many mountains and many rivers; so in the productions of genius, nothing can be styled excellent till it has been compared with other works of the same kind. Demonstration immediately displays its power, and has nothing to hope or fear from the flux of years; but works tentative and experimental must be estimated by their proportion to the general and collective ability of man, as it is discovered in a long succession of endeavours. Of the first building that was raised, it might be with certainty determined that it was round or square, but whether it was spacious or lofty must have been referred to time. The Pythagorean scale of numbers[1] was at once discovered to be perfect; but the poems of Homer we yet know not to transcend the common limits of human intelligence, but by remarking, that nation after nation, and century after century, has been able to do little more than transpose his incidents, new name his characters, and paraphrase his sentiments.

The reverence due to writings that have long subsisted arises therefore not from any credulous confidence in the superior wisdom of past ages, or gloomy persuasion of the degeneracy of mankind, but is the consequence of acknowledged and indubitable positions, that what has been longest known has been most considered, and what is most considered is best understood.

The poet, of whose works I have undertaken the revision, may now begin to assume the dignity of an ancient, and claim the privilege of established fame and prescriptive veneration. He has long outlived his century, the term commonly fixed as the test of

Notes

FROM THE PREFACE

[1] *Pythagorean scale of numbers* the system of ratios in math and music established by the sixth-century BCE philosopher.

literary merit.[2] Whatever advantages he might once derive from personal allusions, local customs, or temporary opinions, have for many years been lost; and every topic of merriment or motive of sorrow, which the modes of artificial life afforded him, now only obscure the scenes which they once illuminated. The effects of favour and competition are at an end; the tradition of his friendships and his enmities has perished; his works support no opinion with arguments, nor supply any faction with invectives; they can neither indulge vanity nor gratify malignity, but are read without any other reason than the desire for pleasure, and are therefore praised only as pleasure is obtained; yet, thus unassisted by interest or passion, they have passed through variations of taste and changes of manners, and, as they developed from one generation to another, have received new honours at every transmission.

But because human judgement, though it be gradually gaining upon certainty, never becomes infallible; and approbation, though long continued, may yet be only the approbation of prejudice and fashion; it is proper to enquire, by what peculiarities of excellence Shakespeare has gained and kept the favour of his countrymen.

Nothing can please many, and please long, but just representations of general nature. Particular manners can be known to few, and therefore few only can judge how nearly they are copied. The irregular combinations of fanciful invention may delight a-while, by that novelty of which the common satiety of life sends us all in quest; but the pleasures of sudden wonder are soon exhausted, and the mind can only repose on the stability of truth.

Shakespeare is above all writers, at least above all modern writers, the poet of nature; the poet that holds up to his readers a faithful mirror of manners and of life. His characters are not modified by the customs of particular places, unpractised by the rest of the world; by the peculiarities of studies or professions, which can operate but upon small numbers; or by the accidents of transient fashions or temporary opinions: they are the genuine progeny of common humanity, such as the world will always supply, and observation will always find. His persons act and speak by the influence of those general persons and principles by which all minds are agitated, and the whole system of life is continued in motion. In the writings of other poets a character is too often an individual; in those of Shakespeare it is commonly a species.

It is from this wide extension of design that so much instruction is derived. It is this which fills the plays of Shakespeare with practical axioms and domestic wisdom. It was said of Euripides, that every verse was a precept; and it may be said of Shakespeare, that from his works may be collected a system of civil and economical[3] prudence. Yet his real power is not shown in the splendour of particular passages, but by the progress of his fable,[4] and the tenor of his dialogue; and that he that tries to recommend him by select quotations, will succeed like the pedant in Hierocles, who, when he offered his house to sale, carried a brick in his pocket as a specimen.[5]

It will not easily be imagined how much Shakespeare excels in accommodating his sentiments to real life, but by comparing him with other authors. It was observed of the ancient schools of declamation, that the more diligently they were frequented, the

Notes

[2] *Century ... merit* "We cannot say that this or that is a custom, except we can justify that it hath continued so one hundred years" (Johnson, citing John Cowell under *custom*, sense 6).

[3] *economical* "Pertaining to the regulation of an household" (Johnson).

[4] *fable* story or plot.

[5] *the pedant in Hierocles ... specimen* in one of the *Ἀστεία* (urbanities or jests) attributed to this Neoplatonic, fifth-century philosopher and included in a commentary on Pythagoras.

more was the student disqualified for the world, because he found nothing there which he should ever meet in any other place. The same remark may be applied to every stage but that of Shakespeare. The theatre, when it is under any other direction, is peopled by such characters as were never seen, conversing in a language which was never heard, upon topics which will never arise in the commerce of mankind. But the dialogue of this author is often so evidently determined by the incident which produces it, and is pursued with so much ease and simplicity, that it seems scarcely to claim the merit of fiction, but to have been gleaned by diligent selection out of common conversation, and common occurrences.

Upon every other stage the universal agent is love, by whose power all good and evil is distributed, and every action quickened or retarded. To bring a lover, a lady and a rival into the fable; to entangle them in contradictory obligations, perplex them with oppositions of interest, and harass them with violence of desires inconsistent with each other; to make them meet in rapture and part in agony; to fill their mouths with hyperbolical joy and outrageous sorrow; to distress them as nothing human ever was distressed; to deliver them as nothing human ever was delivered, is the business of a modern dramatist. For this, probability is violated, life is misrepresented, and language is depraved. But love is only one of many passions, and as it has no great influence upon the sum of life, it has little operation in the dramas of a poet, who caught his ideas from the living world, and exhibited only what he saw before him. He knew, that any other passion, as it was regular or exorbitant, was a cause of happiness or calamity.

Characters thus ample and general were not easily discriminated or preserved, yet perhaps no poet ever kept his personages more distinct from each other. I will not say with Pope, that every speech may be assigned to the proper speaker,[6] because many speeches there are which have nothing characteristical; but perhaps, though some may be equally adapted to every person, it will be difficult to find any that can be properly transferred from the present possessor to another claimant. The choice is right, when there is reason for choice.

Other dramatists can only gain attention by hyperbolical or aggravated characters, by fabulous and unexampled excellence or depravity, as the writers of barbarous romances invigorated the reader by a giant and a dwarf; and he that should form his expectations of human affairs from the play, or from the tale, would be equally deceived. Shakespeare has no heroes; his scenes are occupied only by men, who act and speak as the reader thinks that he should himself have spoken or acted on the same occasion: Even where the agency is supernatural the dialogue is level with life. Other writers disguise the most natural passions and most frequent incidents; so that he who contemplates them in the book will not know them in the world: Shakespeare approximates the remote, and familiarises the wonderful; the event which he represents will not happen, but if it were possible, its effects would probably be such as he assigned; and it may be said, that he has not only shown human nature as it acts in real exigencies, but as it would be found in trials, to which it cannot be exposed.

This therefore is the praise of Shakespeare, that his drama is the mirror of life; that he who has mazed his imagination, in following the phantoms which other writers raise up before him, may here be cured of his delirious ecstasies, by reading human

Notes

[6] *Pope ... proper speaker* he made this remark in the Preface to his edition of Shakespeare (1725).

sentiments in human language; by scenes from which a hermit may estimate the transactions of the world, and a confessor[7] predict the progress of the passions.

His adherence to general nature has exposed him to the censure of critics, who form their judgements upon narrower principles. Dennis and Rymer[8] think his Romans not sufficiently Roman; and Voltaire censures his kings as not completely royal.[9] Dennis is offended, that Menenius, a senator of Rome, should play the buffoon; and Voltaire perhaps thinks decency violated when the Danish usurper[10] is represented as a drunkard. But Shakespeare always makes nature predominate over accident; and if he preserves the essential character, is not very careful of distinctions superinduced and adventitious. His story requires Romans or kings, but he thinks only on men. He knew that Rome, like every other city, had men of all dispositions; and wanting a buffoon, he went into the senate-house for that which the senate-house would certainly have afforded him. He was inclined to show an usurper and a murderer not only odious but despicable; he therefore added drunkenness to his other qualities, knowing that kings love wine like other men, and that wine exerts its natural power upon kings. These are the petty cavils of petty minds; a poet overlooks the casual distinction of country and condition, as a painter, satisfied with the figure, neglects the drapery.

The censure which he has incurred by mixing comic and tragic scenes, as it extends to all his works, deserves more consideration. Let the fact be first stated, and then examined.

Shakespeare's plays are not in the rigorous and critical sense either tragedies or comedies, but compositions of a distinct kind; exhibiting the real state of sublunary nature, which partakes of good and evil, joy and sorrow, mingled with endless variety of proportion and innumerable modes of communication; and expressing the course of the world, in which the loss of one is the gain of another; in which, at the same time, the reveller is hasting to his wine, and the mourner burying his friend; in which the malignity of one is sometimes defeated by the frolic of another; and many mischiefs and many benefits are done and hindered without design.

Out of this chaos of mingled purposes and casualties the ancient poets, according to the laws which custom had prescribed, selected some the crimes of men, and some their absurdities; some the momentous vicissitudes of life, and some the lighter occurrences; some the terrors of distress, and some the gaieties of prosperity. Thus rose the two modes of imitation, known by the names of tragedy and comedy, compositions intended to promote different ends by contrary means, and considered as so little allied, that I do not recollect among the Greeks or Romans a single writer who attempted both.

Shakespeare has united the powers of exciting laughter and sorrow not only in one mind but in one composition. Almost all his plays are divided between serious and ludicrous characters, and, in the successive evolutions of the design, sometimes produce seriousness and sorrow, and sometimes levity and laughter.

That this is a practice contrary to the rules of criticism will be readily allowed; but there is always an appeal open from criticism to nature. The end of writing is to instruct; the end of poetry is to instruct by pleasing. That the mingled drama may convey all the instruction of tragedy or comedy cannot be denied, because it includes both in its alternations[11] of exhibition, and approaches nearer than either to the

Notes

7 *confessor* "He that hears confessions, and prescribes rules and measures of penitence" (Johnson).

8 *Dennis and Rymer* John (1657–1734) and Thomas (1643–1713), leading critics of their day.

9 *Voltaire* see *Appel à toutes les nations de l'Europe* (1761).

10 *Danish usurper* Claudius in *Hamlet*.

11 *alternations* changed from "alterations" by Edmund Malone.

appearance of life, by showing how great machinations and slender designs may promote or obviate one another, and the high and the low co-operate in the general system by unavoidable concatenation.

It is objected, that by this change of scenes the passions are interrupted in their progression, and that the principal event, being not advanced by a due graduation of preparatory incidents, wants at last the power to move, which constitutes the perfection of dramatic poetry. This reasoning is so specious, that it is received as true even by those who in daily experience feel it to be false. The interchanges of mingled scenes seldom fail to produce the intended vicissitudes of passion. Fiction cannot move so much, but that the attention may be easily transferred; and though it must be allowed that pleasing melancholy be sometimes interrupted by unwelcome levity, yet let it be considered likewise, that melancholy is often not pleasing, and that the disturbance of one man may be the relief of another; that different auditors have different habitudes; and that, upon the whole, all pleasure consists in variety.

The players, who in their edition[12] divided our author's works into comedies, histories, and tragedies, seem not to have distinguished the three kinds, by any very exact or definite ideas.

An action which ended happily to the principal persons, however serious or distressful through its intermediate incidents, in their opinion constituted a comedy. This idea of a comedy continued long amongst us, and plays were written, which, by changing the catastrophe, were tragedies to-day and comedies to-morrow.

Tragedy was not in those times a poem of more general dignity or elevation than comedy; it required only a calamitous conclusion, with which the common criticism of that age was satisfied, whatever lighter pleasure it afforded in its progress.

History was a series of actions, with no other than chronological succession, independent on each other, and without any tendency to introduce or regulate the conclusion. It is not always very nicely distinguished from tragedy. There is not much nearer approach to unity of action[13] in the tragedy of *Antony and Cleopatra*, than in the history of *Richard the Second*. But a history might be continued through many plays; as it had no plan, it had no limits.

Through all these denominations of the drama, Shakespeare's mode of composition is the same; an interchange of seriousness and merriment, by which the mind is softened at one time, and exhilarated at another. But whatever be his purpose, whether to gladden or depress, or to conduct the story, without vehemence or emotion, through tracts of easy and familiar dialogue, he never fails to attain his purpose; as he commands us, we laugh or mourn, or sit silent with quiet expectation, in tranquillity without indifference.

When Shakespeare's plan is understood, most of the criticisms of Rymer and Voltaire vanish away. The play of *Hamlet* is opened, without impropriety, by two sentinels; Iago bellows at Brabantio's window,[14] without injury to the scheme of the play, though in terms which a modern audience would not easily endure; the character of Polonius is seasonable and useful; and the Grave-diggers themselves may be heard with applause.[15]

Notes

[12] *their edition* the First Folio, edited by John Heming and Henry Condell (1623).

[13] *unity of action* a neoclassical standard of dramatic criticism derived from Aristotle's *Poetics*.

[14] *Iago bellows at Brabantio's window* *Othello* I.i.

[15] *Grave-diggers … applause* *Hamlet* V.i.

Shakespeare engaged in dramatic poetry with the world open before him; the rules of the ancients were yet known to few; the public judgement was uninformed; he had no example of such fame as might force him upon imitation, nor critics of such authority as might restrain his extravagance: He therefore indulged his natural disposition, and his disposition, as Rymer has remarked, led him to comedy. In tragedy he often writes with great appearance of toil and study, what is written at last with little felicity; but in his comic scenes, he seems to produce without labour, what no labour can improve. In tragedy he is always struggling after some occasion to be comic, but in comedy he seems to repose, or to luxuriate, as in a mode of thinking congenial to his nature. In his tragic scenes there is always something wanting, but his comedy often surpasses expectation or desire. His comedy pleases by the thoughts and the language, and his tragedy for the greater part by incident and action. His tragedy seems to be skill, his comedy to be instinct.

The force of his comic scenes has suffered little diminution from the changes made by a century and a half, in manners or in words. As his personages act upon principles arising from genuine passion, very little modified by particular forms, their pleasures and vexations are communicable to all times and to all places; they are natural, and therefore durable; the adventitious peculiarities of personal habits, are only superficial dyes, bright and pleasing for a little while, yet soon fading to a dim tinct, without any remains of former lustre; but the discriminations of true passion are the colours of nature; they pervade the whole mass, and can only perish with the body that exhibits them. The accidental compositions of heterogeneous modes are dissolved by the chance which combined them; but the uniform simplicity of primitive qualities neither admits increase, nor suffers decay. The sand heaped by one flood is scattered by another, but the rock always continues in its place. The stream of time, which is continually washing the dissoluble fabrics of other poets, passes without injury by the adamant of Shakespeare.

If there be, what I believe there is, in every nation, a style which never becomes obsolete, a certain mode of phraseology so consonant and congenial to the analogy and principles of its respective language as to remain settled and unaltered; this style is to be sought in the common intercourse of life, among those who speak only to be understood, without ambition of elegance. The polite are always catching modish innovations, and the learned depart from established forms of speech, in hope of finding or making better; those who wish for distinction forsake the vulgar, when the vulgar is right; but there is a conversation above grossness and below refinement, where propriety resides, and where this poet seems to have gathered his comic dialogue. He is therefore more agreeable to the ears of the present age than any other author equally remote, and among his other excellencies deserves to be studied as one of the original masters of our language.

These observations are to be considered not as unexceptionably constant, but as containing general and predominant truth. Shakespeare's familiar dialogue is affirmed to be smooth and clear, yet not wholly without ruggedness or difficulty; as a country may be eminently fruitful, though it has spots unfit for cultivation: His characters are praised as natural, though their sentiments are sometimes forced, and their actions improbable; as the earth upon the whole is spherical, though its surface is varied with protuberances and cavities.

Shakespeare with his excellencies has likewise faults, and faults sufficient to obscure and overwhelm any other merit. I shall show them in the proportion in which they appear to me, without envious malignity or superstitious veneration. No question can be more innocently discussed than a dead poet's pretensions to renown; and little regard is due to that bigotry which sets candour[16] higher than truth.

His first defect is that to which may be imputed most of the evil in books or in men. He sacrifices virtue to convenience, and is so much more careful to please than to instruct, that he seems to write without any moral purpose. From his writings indeed a system of social duty may be selected, for he that thinks reasonably must think morally; but his precepts and axioms drop casually from him; he makes no just distribution of good or evil, nor is always careful to show in the virtuous a disapprobation of the wicked; he carries his persons indifferently through right and wrong, and at the close dismisses them without further care, and leaves their examples to operate by chance. This fault the barbarity of his age cannot extenuate; for it is always a writer's duty to make the world better, and justice is a virtue independent on time or place.

The plots are often so loosely formed, that a very slight consideration may improve them, and so carelessly pursued, that he seems not always fully to comprehend his own design. He omits opportunities of instructing or delighting which the train of his story seems to force upon him, and apparently rejects those exhibitions which would be more affecting, for the sake of those which are more easy.

It may be observed, that in many of his plays the latter part is evidently neglected. When he found himself near the end of his work, and in view of his reward, he shortened the labour, to snatch the profit. He therefore remits his efforts where he should most vigorously exert them, and his catastrophe is improbably produced or imperfectly represented.

He had no regard to distinction of time or place, but gives to one age or nation, without scruple, the customs, institutions, and opinions of another, at the expense not only of likelihood, but of possibility. These faults Pope has endeavoured, with more zeal than judgement, to transfer to his imagined interpolators.[17] We need not wonder to find Hector quoting Aristotle,[18] when we see the loves of Theseus and Hippolyta combined with the Gothic mythology of fairies.[19] Shakespeare, indeed, was not the only violator of chronology, for in the same age Sidney,[20] who wanted not the advantage of learning, has, in his *Arcadia*, confounded the pastoral with the feudal times, the days of innocence, quiet and security, with those of turbulence, violence and adventure.

In his comic scenes he is seldom very successful, when he engages his characters in reciprocations of smartness and contests of sarcasm; their jests are commonly gross, and their pleasantry licentious; neither his gentlemen nor his ladies have much delicacy, nor are sufficiently distinguished from his clowns by any appearance of refined manners. Whether he represented the real conversation of his time is not easy to determine; the reign of Elizabeth is commonly supposed to have been a time of stateliness, formality and reserve, yet perhaps the relaxations of that severity were not very elegant. There must, however, have always been some modes of gaiety preferable to others, and a writer ought to choose best.

In tragedy his performance seems constantly to be worse, as his labour is more. The effusions of passion which exigence forces out are for the most part striking and energetic; but whenever he solicits his invention, or strains his faculties, the offspring of his throws is tumour, meanness, tediousness, and obscurity.

Notes

16 *candour* mildness, gentleness.

17 *interpolators* editors who may have added passages to the plays.

18 *Hector quoting Aristotle* *Troilus and Cressida* II.ii.166–7.

19 *mythology of fairies* in *A Midsummer Night's Dream*.

20 *Sidney* Sir Philip (1554–86).

In narration he affects a disproportionate pomp of diction and a wearisome train of circumlocution, and tells the incident imperfectly in many words, which might have been more plainly delivered in few. Narration in dramatic poetry is naturally tedious, as it is unanimated and inactive, and obstructs the progress of the action; it should therefore always be rapid, and enlivened by frequent interruption. Shakespeare found it an encumbrance, and instead of lightening it by brevity, endeavoured to recommend it by dignity and splendour.

His declamations or set speeches are commonly cold and weak, for his power was the power of nature; when he endeavoured, like other tragic writers, to catch opportunities of amplification, and instead of enquiring what the occasion demanded, to show how much his stores of knowledge could supply, he seldom escapes without the pity or resentment of his reader.

It is incident to him to be now and then entangled with an unwieldy sentiment, which he cannot well express, and will not reject; he struggles with it a while, and if it continues stubborn, comprises it in words such as occur, and leaves it to be disentangled and evolved by those who have more leisure to bestow upon it.

Not that always where the language is intricate the thought is subtle, or the image always great where the line is bulky; the equality of words to things is very often neglected, and trivial sentiments and vulgar ideas disappoint the attention, to which they are recommended by sonorous epithets and swelling figures.[21]

But the admirers of this great poet have most reason to complain when he approaches nearest to his highest excellence, and seems fully resolved to sink them in dejection, and mollify them with tender emotions by the fall of greatness, the danger of innocence, or the crosses of love. What he does best, he soon ceases to do. He is not long soft and pathetic without some idle conceit, or contemptible equivocation. He no sooner begins to move, than he counteracts himself; and terror and pity, as they are rising in the mind, are checked and blasted by sudden frigidity.

A quibble is to Shakespeare, what luminous vapours[22] are to the traveller; he follows it at all adventures, it is sure to lead him out of the way, and sure to engulf him in the mire. It has some malignant power over his mind, and its fascinations are irresistible. Whatever be the dignity or profundity of his disquisition, whether he be enlarging knowledge or exalting affection, whether he be amusing attention with incidents, or enchaining it in suspense, let but a quibble spring up before him, and he leaves his work unfinished. A quibble is the golden apple for which he will always turn aside from his career, or stoop from his elevation.[23] A quibble, poor and barren as it is, gave him such delight, that he was content to purchase it, by the sacrifice of reason, propriety and truth. A quibble was to him the fatal Cleopatra for which he lost the world, and was content to lose it. …

Notes

[21] *figures* figures of speech, like metaphor.

[22] *luminous vapours* "*ignis fatuus*, will-o'-the-wisp, or Jack with a lanthorn, marsh gas that travellers take for beacons and, following them, lose their way" (see Johnson, *will*, sense II).

[23] *golden apple … elevation* an allusion to the story of Atalanta, who paused in her race to pick up the golden apples dropped by her opponent and suitor.

David Hume (1711–1776)

Hume's short autobiographical sketch, "My Own Life," makes up the bulk of my minor offering from this major philosopher and supplies sufficient biographical information. The piece was considered offensive by many people at the time, because it stresses Hume's composure in the face of death despite his lack of belief in the Christian dispensation. Hume's atheism, though infamous, was a matter more of personal conviction than public exposition. His works are philosophical, psychological, historical, and social. They do not talk about theology; they just exclude it. The work for which he is now best known was his first and least successful, *A Treatise of Human Nature: Being an Attempt to Introduce the Experimental Method of Reasoning into Moral Subjects* (1739). Book 1 treats the understanding and establishes an epistemology that is even more strictly empirical than Locke's. Book 3 is about morals and largely focuses on the concept of justice. Best of all, however, is the centerpiece of the central book on the passions, the discussion of pride. Pride and humility are simple, unanalyzable passions, for Hume, the causes of which, being constant and uniform through the ages, provide an unmoving sun for his moral Copernican revolution. This surely is a landmark in the emergence of everything, good and ill, that we call modern.

The pieces presented here are from Hume's far more successful and very variously republished essays. "Of the Liberty of the Press" was one of Hume's first attempts; it suggests how very much his career and his approach to the world was that of a writer working in an environment that permitted and even fostered the profession of writing. The text is based on *Essays Moral and Political* (1741; second edition 1742). The autobiographical essay speaks for itself. The text is based on its first publication in *Essays and Treatises on Several Subjects* (1777). For insightful treatments of Hume as a writer, see John Richetti, *Philosophical Writing* (Harvard University Press, 1983) and Adam Potkay, *The Fate of Eloquence in the Age of Hume* (Cornell University Press, 1994).

from *Essays Moral and Political* (1742)

Of the Liberty of the Press

Nothing is more apt to surprise a foreigner, than the extreme liberty, which we enjoy in this country, of communicating whatever we please to the public, and of openly censuring every measure, entered into by the king or his ministers. If the administration resolve upon war, it is affirmed, that, either wilfully or ignorantly, they mistake the interests of the nation, and that peace, in the present situation of affairs, is infinitely preferable. If the passion of the ministers lie towards peace, our political writers breathe nothing but war and devastation, and represent the pacific conduct of the government as mean and pusillanimous. As this liberty is not indulged in any other government, either republican or monarchical; in HOLLAND and VENICE, more than in FRANCE or SPAIN; it may very naturally give occasion to a question, 'How it happens that GREAT BRITAIN alone enjoys this peculiar privilege? And whether the unlimited exercise of this liberty be advantageous or prejudicial to the public?'

British Literature 1640–1789: An Anthology, Fourth Edition. Edited by Robert DeMaria, Jr.

The reason, why the laws indulge us in such a liberty seems to be derived from our mixed form of government, which is neither wholly monarchical, nor wholly republican. It will be found, if I mistake not, a true observation in politics, that the two extremes in government, liberty and slavery, commonly approach nearest to each other; and that, as you depart from the extremes, and mix a little of monarchy with liberty, the government becomes always the more free; and on the other hand, when you mix a little of liberty with monarchy, the yoke becomes always the more grievous and intolerable. In a government, such as that of FRANCE, which is absolute, and where law, custom, and religion concur, all of them, to make people fully satisfied with their condition, the monarch cannot entertain any *jealousy*[1] against his subjects, and therefore is apt to indulge them in great *liberties* both of speech and action. In a government altogether republican, such as that of HOLLAND, where there is no magistrate so eminent as to give *jealousy* to the state, there is no danger in entrusting the magistrates with large discretionary powers; and though many advantages result from such powers, in preserving peace and order, yet they lay a considerable restraint on men's actions, and make every private citizen pay a great respect to the government. Thus it seems evident, that the two extremes of absolute monarchy and of a republic, approach near to each other in some material circumstances. In the *first*, the magistrate has no jealousy of the people: in the *second*, the people have none of the magistrate: Which want of jealousy begets a mutual confidence and trust in both cases, and produces a species of liberty in monarchies, and of arbitrary power in republics.

To justify the other part of the foregoing observation, that, in every government, the means are most wide of each other, and that the mixtures of monarchy and liberty render the yoke more easy or more grievous; I must take notice of a remark in TACITUS with regard to the ROMANS under the emperors, that they neither could bear total slavery nor total liberty, *Nec totam servitutem, nec totam libertatem pati possunt.* This remark a celebrated poet has translated and applied to the ENGLISH, in his lively description of queen ELIZABETH's policy and government,

> Et fit aimer son joug a l'Anglois indompté,
> Qui ne peut ni servir, ni vivre en liberté.
> HENRIADE, *liv.* 1.[2]

According to these remarks, we are to consider the ROMAN government under the emperors as a mixture of despotism and liberty, where the despotism prevailed; and the ENGLISH government as a mixture of the same kind, where the liberty predominates. The consequences are conformable to the foregoing observation; and such as may be expected from those mixed forms of government, which beget a mutual watchfulness and jealousy. The ROMAN emperors were, many of them, the most frightful tyrants that ever disgraced human nature; and it is evident, that their cruelty was chiefly excited by their *jealousy,* and by their observing that all the great men of ROME bore with impatience the dominion of a family, which, but a little before, was no wise superior to their own. On the other hand, as the republican part of the government prevails in ENGLAND, though with a great mixture of monarchy, it is obliged,

Notes

OF THE LIBERTY OF THE PRESS

1 *jealousy* "suspicious fear" (Johnson).

2 *HENRIADE, liv. 1* Voltaire's epic, first published in England (1729) and dedicated to Queen Caroline: "She made her reign agreeable to the untamed English, who could neither serve nor live free."

for its own preservation, to maintain a watchful *jealousy* over the magistrates, to remove all discretionary powers, and to secure every one's life and fortune by general and inflexible laws. No action must be deemed a crime but what the law has plainly determined to be such: No crime must be imputed to a man but from a legal proof before his judges; and even these judges must be his fellow-subjects, who are obliged, by their own interest, to have a watchful eye over the encroachments and violence of the ministers. From these causes it proceeds, that there is as much liberty, and, even, perhaps, licentiousness in GREAT BRITAIN, as there were formerly slavery and tyranny in ROME.

These principles account for the great liberty of the press in these kingdoms, beyond what is indulged in any other government. 'Tis sufficiently known that arbitrary power would steal in upon us, were we not careful to prevent its progress, and were there not an easy method of conveying the alarm from one end of the kingdom to the other. The spirit of the people must frequently be roused, in order to curb the ambition of the court; and the dread of rousing this spirit must be employed to prevent that ambition. Nothing so effectual to this purpose as the liberty of the press, by which all the learning, wit, and genius of the nation may be employed on the side of freedom, and every one be animated to its defence. As long, therefore, as the republican part of our government can maintain itself against the monarchical, it will naturally be careful to keep the press open, as of importance to its own preservation.

Since[3] therefore that liberty is so essential to the support of our mixed government; this sufficiently decides the second question, 'Whether such a liberty be advantageous or prejudicial'; there being nothing of greater importance in every state than the preservation of the ancient government, especially if it be a free one. But I would fain go a step further, and assert, that this liberty is attended with so few inconveniencies, that it may be claimed as the common right of mankind, and ought to be indulged them almost in every government: except the ecclesiastical, to which indeed it would prove fatal. We need not dread from this liberty any such ill consequences as followed from the harangues of the popular demagogues of ATHENS and tribunes of ROME. A man reads a book or pamphlet alone and coolly. There is none present from whom he can catch the passion by contagion. He is not hurried away by the force and energy of action. And should he be wrought up to ever so seditious a humour, there is no violent resolution presented to him, by which he can immediately vent his passion. The liberty of the press, therefore, however abused, can scarce ever excite popular tumults or rebellion. And as to those murmurs or secret discontents it may occasion, 'tis better they should get vent in words, that they may come to the knowledge of the magistrate before it be too late, in order to his providing a remedy against them. Mankind, it is true, have always a greater propension to believe what is said to the disadvantage of their governors, than the contrary; but this inclination is inseparable from them, whether they have liberty or not. A whisper may fly as quick, and be as pernicious as a pamphlet. Nay, it will be more pernicious, where men are not accustomed to think freely, or distinguish between truth and falsehood.

It has also been found, as the experience of mankind increases, that the *people* are no such dangerous monster as they have been represented, and that it is in every respect better to guide them, like rational creatures, than to lead or drive them, like brute beasts.

Notes

[3] *Since* ... Hume omitted the following two paragraphs in his revision of 1770.

Before the United Provinces set the example, toleration was deemed incompatible with good government; and it was thought impossible, that a number of religious sects could live together in harmony and peace, and have all of them an equal affection to their common country, and to each other. ENGLAND has set a like example of civil liberty; and though this liberty seems to occasion some small ferment at present, it has not as yet produced any pernicious effects; and it is to be hoped, that men, being every day more accustomed to the free discussion of public affairs, will improve in the judgement of them, and be with greater difficulty seduced by every idle rumour and popular clamour.

It is a very comfortable reflection to the lovers of liberty, that this peculiar privilege of BRITAIN is of a kind that cannot easily be wrested from us, but must last as long as our government remains, in any degree, free and independent. It is seldom, that liberty of any kind is lost all at once. Slavery has so frightful an aspect to men accustomed to freedom, that it must steal upon them by degrees, and must disguise itself in a thousand shapes, in order to be received. But, if the liberty of the press ever be lost, it must be lost at once. The general laws against sedition and libelling are at present as strong as they possibly can be made. Nothing can impose a further restraint, but either the clapping an IMPRIMATUR[4] upon the press, or the giving to the court very large discretionary powers to punish whatever displeases them. But these concessions would be such a bare-faced violation of liberty, that they will probably be the last efforts of a despotic government. We may conclude, that the liberty of *Britain* is gone for ever when these attempts shall succeed.

from *Essays and Treatises on Several Subjects* (1777)

My Own Life

It is difficult for a man to speak long of himself without vanity; therefore, I shall be short. It may be thought an instance of vanity that I pretend at all to write my life; but this Narrative shall contain little more than the History of my Writings; as, indeed, almost all my life has been spent in literary pursuits and occupations. The first success of most of my writings was not such as to be an object of vanity.

I was born the 26th of April 1711, old style,[1] at Edinburgh. I was of a good family, both by father and mother: my father's family is a branch of the Earl of Home's, or Hume's; and my ancestors had been proprietors of the estate, which my brother possesses, for several generations. My mother was daughter of Sir David Falconer, President of the College of Justice: the title of Lord Halkerton came by succession to her brother.

My family, however, was not rich, and being myself a younger brother, my patrimony, according to the mode of my country, was of course very slender. My father, who passed for a man of parts,[2] died when I was an infant, leaving me, with an elder brother and a sister, under the care of our mother, a woman of singular merit, who, though young and handsome, devoted herself entirely to the rearing

Notes

[4] *IMPRIMATUR* "let it be printed," the indication of papal permission to print, applied to other forms of licensing.

My Own Life

[1] *old style* according to the old Julian calendar, which was eleven days short of the reformed Gregorian calendar.

[2] *a man of parts* a talented, resourceful man.

and educating of her children. I passed through the ordinary course of education with success, and was seized very early with a passion for literature, which has been the ruling passion of my life, and the great source of my enjoyments. My studious disposition, my sobriety, and my industry, gave my family a notion that the law was a proper profession for me; but I found an insurmountable aversion to every thing but the pursuits of philosophy and general learning; and while they fancied I was poring upon Voet and Vinnius,[3] Cicero and Virgil were the authors which I was secretly devouring.

My very slender fortune, however, being unsuitable to this plan of life, and my health being a little broken by my ardent application, I was tempted, or rather forced, to make a very feeble trial for entering into a more active scene of life. In 1734, I went to Bristol, with some recommendations to eminent merchants, but in a few months found that scene totally unsuitable to me. I went over to France, with a view of prosecuting my studies in a country retreat; and I there laid that plan of life, which I have steadily and successfully pursued. I resolved to make a very rigid frugality supply my deficiency of fortune, to maintain unimpaired my independency, and to regard every object as contemptible, except the improvement of my talents in literature.

During my retreat in France, first at Reims, but chiefly at La Fleche, in Anjou, I composed my *Treatise of Human Nature*. After passing three years very agreeably in that country, I came over to London in 1737. In the end of 1738, I published my Treatise, and immediately went down to my mother and my brother, who lived at his country house, and was employing himself very judiciously and successfully in the improvement of his fortune.

Never literary attempt was more unfortunate than my *Treatise of Human Nature*. It fell *dead-born from the press*, without reaching such distinction, as even to excite a murmur among the zealots. But being naturally of a cheerful and sanguine temper, I very soon recovered the blow, and prosecuted with great ardour my studies to the contrary. In 1742 I printed at Edinburgh the first part of my Essays: the work was favourably received, and soon made me entirely forget my former disappointment. I continued with my mother and brother in the country, and in that time recovered the knowledge of the Greek language, which I had too much neglected in my early youth.

In 1745, I received a letter from the Marquis of Annandale, inviting me to come and live with him in England; I found also, that the friends and family of that young nobleman were desirous of putting him under my care and direction, for the state of his mind and health required it. I lived with him a twelvemonth. My appointments during that time made a considerable accession to my small fortune. I then received an invitation from General St. Clair to attend him as a secretary to his expedition, which was at first meant against Canada, but ended in an incursion on the coast of France. Next year, to wit, 1747, I received an invitation from the General to attend him in the same station in his military embassy to the courts of Vienna and Turin. I then wore the uniform of an officer, and was introduced at these courts as aide-de-camp to the general, along with Sir Harry Erskine and Captain Grant, now General Grant. These two years were almost the only interruptions which my studies have received during the course of my life: I passed them agreeably and in good company; and my

Notes

[3] *Voet and Vinnius* the legal writers Voetius Gysbertus (1588–1676) and Arnold Vinnen (Vinnius) (1588–1657).

appointments, with my frugality, had made me reach a fortune, which I called independent, though most of my friends were inclined to smile when I said so; in short, I was now master of near a thousand pounds.

I had always entertained a notion, that my want of success in publishing the *Treatise of Human Nature*, had proceeded more from the manner than the matter, and that I had been guilty of a very usual indiscretion, in going to the press too early. I, therefore, cast the first part of that work anew in the Enquiry concerning Human Understanding, which was published while I was at Turin. But this piece was at first little more successful than the *Treatise of Human Nature*. On my return from Italy, I had the mortification to find all England in a ferment, on account of Dr. Middleton's *Free Enquiry*,[4] while my performance was entirely overlooked and neglected. A new edition, which had been published at London, of my *Essays*, moral and political, met not with a much better reception.

Such is the force of natural temper, that these disappointments made little or no impression on me. I went down in 1749, and lived two years with my brother at his country house, for my mother was now dead. I there composed the second part of my Essays, which I called Political Discourses, and also my Enquiry concerning the Principles of Morals, which is another part of my treatise that I cast anew. Meanwhile, my bookseller, A. Millar, informed me, that my former publications (all but the unfortunate Treatise) were beginning to be the subject of conversation; that the sale of them was gradually increasing, and that new editions were demanded. Answers by Reverends, and Right Reverends, came out two or three in a year; and I found, by Dr. Warburton's railing,[5] that the books were beginning to be esteemed in good company. However, I had fixed a resolution, which I inflexibly maintained, never to reply to anybody; and not being very irascible in my temper, I have easily kept myself clear of all literary squabbles. These symptoms of a rising reputation gave me encouragement, as I was ever more disposed to see the favourable than unfavourable side of things; a turn of mind which it is more happy to possess, than to be born to an estate of ten thousand a year.

In 1751, I removed from the country to the town, the true scene for a man of letters. In 1752, were published at Edinburgh, where I then lived, my Political Discourses, the only work of mine that was successful on the first publication. It was well received abroad and at home. In the same year was published at London, my Enquiry concerning the Principles of Morals; which, in my own opinion (who ought not to judge on that subject), is of all my writings, historical, philosophical, or literary, incomparably the best. It came unnoticed and unobserved into the world.

In 1752, the Faculty of Advocates chose me their Librarian, an office from which I received little or no emolument, but which gave me the command of a large library. I then formed the plan of writing the History of England; but being frightened with the notion of continuing a narrative through a period of 1700 years, I commenced with the accession of the House of Stuart, an epoch when, I thought, the misrepresentations of faction began chiefly to take place. I was, I own, sanguine in my expectation of the success of this work. I thought that I was the only historian, that had at once neglected present power, interest, and authority, and the cry of popular prejudices; and as the

Notes

[4] *Dr. Middleton's Free Enquiry* Conyers Middleton (1683–1750), author of *A Free Inquiry into Miracles* (1748).

[5] *Dr. Warburton* William (1698–1779), later Bishop of Gloucester, editor of Shakespeare and Pope as well as a theological writer.

subject was suited to every capacity, I expected proportional applause. But miserable was my disappointment: I was assailed by one cry of reproach, disapprobation, and even detestation; English, Scotch, and Irish, Whig and Tory, churchman and sectary,[6] free-thinker[7] and religionist, patriot[8] and courtier, united in their rage against the man, who had presumed to shed a generous tear for the fate of Charles I and the Earl of Strafford;[9] and after the first ebullitions of their fury were over, what was still more mortifying, the book seemed to sink into oblivion. Mr. Millar told me, that in a twelvemonth he sold only forty-five copies of it. I scarcely, indeed, heard of one man in the three kingdoms,[10] considerable for rank of letters, that could endure the book. I must only except the primate of England, Dr. Herring, and the primate of Ireland, Dr. Stone, which seem two odd exceptions. These dignified prelates separately sent me messages not to be discouraged.

I was, however, I confess, discouraged; and had not the war been at that time breaking out between France and England,[11] I had certainly retired to some provincial town of the former kingdom, have changed my name, and never more have returned to my native country. But as this scheme was not now practicable, and the subsequent volume was considerably advanced, I resolved to pick up courage and to persevere.

In this interval, I published at London my *Natural History of Religion*, along with some other small pieces: its public entry was rather obscure, except only that Dr. Hurd[12] wrote a pamphlet against it, with all the illiberal petulance, arrogance, and scurrility which distinguish the Warburtonian school. This pamphlet gave me some consolation for the otherwise indifferent reception of my performance.

In 1756, two years after the fall of the first volume, was published the second volume of my *History*, containing the period from the death of Charles I till the Revolution. This performance happened to give less displeasure to the Whigs, and was better received. It not only rose itself, but helped to buoy up its unfortunate brother.

But though I had been taught by experience, that the Whig party were in possession of bestowing all places, both in the state and in literature, I was so little inclined to yield to their senseless clamour, that in about a hundred alterations, which further study, reading, or reflection engaged me to make in the reigns of the first two Stuarts, I have made all of them invariably to the Tory side. It is ridiculous to consider the English constitution before that period as a regular plan of liberty.

In 1759, I published my *History of the House of Tudor*. The clamour against this performance was almost equal to that against the History of the two first Stuarts. The reign of Elizabeth was particularly obnoxious. But I was now callous against the impressions of public folly, and continued very peaceably and contentedly in my retreat at Edinburgh, to finish, in two volumes, the more early part of the *English History*, which I gave to the public in 1761, with tolerable, and but tolerable success.

But, notwithstanding this variety of winds and seasons, to which my writings had been exposed, they had still been making such advances, that the copy-money[13] given me

Notes

6 *sectary* one who belongs to a sect, a different church than the Church of England.

7 *free-thinker* one who stresses reason in theology over faith.

8 *patriot* an opponent of the (Hanoverian) court, its government and its proponents or courtiers.

9 *Earl of Strafford* Thomas Wentworth, executed by Parliament in 1641.

10 *the three kingdoms* England, Scotland, and Ireland.

11 *war... France and England* the Seven Years War, known in America as the French and Indian War.

12 *Dr. Hurd* Richard Hurd (1720–1808), editor of Horace, colleague of Warburton and author of theological, literary, and political essays; later Bishop of Worcester.

13 *copy-money* payment by a publisher to an author for his manuscript or for the copyright.

by the booksellers, much exceeded any thing formerly known in England; I was become not only independent, but opulent. I retired to my native country of Scotland, determined never more to set my foot out of it; and retaining the satisfaction of never having preferred[14] a request to one great man, or even making advances of friendship to any of them. As I was now turned of fifty, I thought of passing all the rest of my life in this philosophical manner, when I received, in 1763, an invitation from the Earl of Hertford, with whom I was not in the least acquainted, to attend him on his embassy to Paris, with a near prospect of being appointed secretary to the embassy; and, in the meanwhile of performing the functions of that office. This offer, however inviting, I at first declined, both because I was reluctant to begin connections with the great, and because I was afraid that the civilities and gay company of Paris, would prove disagreeable to a person of my age and humour: but on his lordship's repeating the invitation, I accepted of it. I have every reason, both of pleasure and interest, to think myself happy in my connections with that nobleman, as well as afterwards with his brother, General Conway.

Those who have not seen the strange effects of modes,[15] will never imagine the reception I met with at Paris, from men and women of all ranks and stations. The more I resiled[16] from their excessive civilities, the more I was loaded with them. There is, however, a real satisfaction in living at Paris, from the great number of sensible, knowing, and polite company with which that city abounds above all places in the universe. I thought once of settling there for life.

I was appointed secretary to the embassy; and in summer 1765, Lord Hertford left me, being appointed Lord Lieutenant of Ireland. I was *chargé d'affaires* till the arrival of the Duke of Richmond, towards the end of the year. In the beginning of 1766, I left Paris, and next summer went to Edinburgh, with the same view as formerly, of burying myself in a philosophical retreat. I returned to that place, not richer, but with much more money, and a much larger income, by means of Lord Hertford's friendship, than I left it; and I was desirous of trying what superfluity could produce, as I had formerly made an experiment of a competency.[17] But in 1767, I received from Mr. Conway an invitation to be Under-secretary; and this invitation, both the character of the person, and my connections with Lord Hertford, prevented me from declining. I returned to Edinburgh in 1769, very opulent (for I possessed a revenue of £1,000 a year), healthy, and though somewhat stricken in years, with the prospect of enjoying long my ease, and of seeing the increase of my reputation.

In spring 1775, I was struck with a disorder in my bowels, which at first gave me no alarm, but has since, as I apprehend it, become mortal and incurable. I now reckon upon a speedy dissolution.[18] I have suffered very little pain from my disorder; and what is more strange, have, notwithstanding the great decline of my person, never suffered a moment's abatement of my spirits; insomuch, that were I to name the period of my life, which I should most choose to pass over again, I might be tempted to point to this latter period. I possess the same ardour as ever in study, and the same gaiety in company. I consider, besides, that a man of sixty-five, by dying, cuts off only a few years of infirmities; and though I see many symptoms of my literary reputation's breaking out at last with additional lustre, I know that I could have but few years to enjoy it. It is difficult to be more detached from life than I am at present.

Notes

14 *prefer* "To offer solemnly; to propose publicly; to exhibit" (Johnson).

15 *mode* "Fashion; custom" (Johnson).

16 *resiled* drew back (a Scottish usage).

17 *competency* "Such a fortune as, without exuberance, is equal to the necessities of life" (Johnson).

18 *dissolution* "Death; the resolution of the body into its constituent elements" (Johnson).

To conclude historically with my own character. I am, or rather was (for that is the style I must now use in speaking of myself, which emboldens me the more to speak my sentiments); I was, I say, a man of mild dispositions, of command of temper, of an open, social, and cheerful humour, capable of attachment, but little susceptible of enmity, and of great moderation in all my passions. Even my love of literary fame, my ruling passion, never soured my temper, notwithstanding my frequent disappointments. My company was not unacceptable to the young and careless, as well as to the studious and literary; and as I took a particular pleasure in the company of modest women, I had no reason to be displeased with the reception I met with from them. In a word, though most men anywise eminent, have found reason to complain of calumny, I never was touched, or even attacked by her baleful tooth: and though, I wantonly exposed myself to the rage of both civil and religious factions, they seemed to be disarmed in my behalf of their wonted[19] fury. My friends never had occasion to vindicate any one circumstance of my character and conduct: not but that the zealots, we may well suppose, would have been glad to invent and propagate any story to my disadvantage, but they could never find any which they thought would wear the face of probability. I cannot say there is no vanity in making this funeral oration of myself, but I hope it is not a misplaced one; and this is a matter of fact which is easily cleared and ascertained.

APRIL 18, 1776.[20]

Notes

[19] *wonted* usual, customary.

[20] *APRIL 18, 1776* Hume died on August 25, 1776.

Jane Collier (1714/15–1755)

Jane Collier was the daughter of Arthur Collier of Wiltshire, an Anglican priest devoted to Berkeleian metaphysics, which he expounded in *Clavis Universalis, or a New Inquiry after Truth, being a demonstration of the non-existence or impossibility of an external world* (1713). Although it is not kind to the memory of Arthur, it is possible to imagine that his daughter's realistic, satirical bent is a response to her father's idealist philosophical position. After their father's death Jane and her sister Margaret lived in London and enjoyed the literary society of both the Fielding family and Samuel Richardson. Jane collaborated with Sarah Fielding (Henry's sister) on a three-volume didactic romance called *The Cry* (1754) at about the same time that she wrote the *Art of Tormenting* (1753). Collier's collaborative novel adopts and projects the view that marriage should solemnize a relationship between candid, consenting, and spiritually equal adults. She must have provided much of the support for her little household because her sister, who had accompanied the Fieldings on their famous trip to Lisbon, was after Jane's death forced by poverty to retreat to the Isle of Wight, then a very cheap place to live. There are extant a few letters exchanged between Richardson and both sisters. Those from Jane show that she was a skillful critic whose comments were valued. Those from her sister show that Jane was sorely missed after she was gone.

There were several editions of the *Art of Tormenting*, including some with aquatints in the early nineteenth century. The following is a series of excerpts from the second edition, revised, 1757. There is a modern edition, edited by Katherine E. Craik (Oxford University Press, 2006).

from *An Essay on the Art of Ingeniously Tormenting; with Proper Rules for the Exercise of that Pleasant Art* (1753)

… England has ever been allowed to excel most other nations in her improvements of arts and sciences, although she seldom claims to herself the merit of invention: to her improvements also are many of her neighbours indebted, for the exercise of some of their most useful arts.

'Tis not the benefit that may arise to the few from any invention, but its general utility, which ought to make such invention of universal estimation. Had the art of navigation gone no higher than to direct the course of a small boat by oars, the Low Countries only could have been the better for it. Again, should the inhabitants of Lapland invent the most convenient method for warming their houses by stoves, bringing them, by their improvements, to the utmost perfection; yet could not those who live within the Tropics receive the least benefits from such their improvements; any more than the Laplanders could, from the invention of fans, umbrellas, and cooling grottoes.

But as the science recommended in this short essay will be liable to no such exceptions; being, we presume, adapted to the circumstances, genius, and capacity, of every nation under heaven, why should I doubt of that deserved fame, generally given to those

British Literature 1640–1789: An Anthology, Fourth Edition. Edited by Robert DeMaria, Jr.

Inventas aut qui vitam excoluere per artes,
Quique sui memores alios fecere merendo?[1]
Virg. [Aeneid] 6.663.

Unless, indeed, I should be told, that mankind are already too great adepts in this art, to need any further instructions.

May I hope that my dear countrymen will pardon me for presuming (by the very publication of these rules) that they are not already absolutely perfect in this our science? Or at least, that they may not always have an ingenious Torment ready at hand to inflict?

By the common run of Servants, it might have been presumed, that Dean Swift's instructions[2] to them were unnecessary: but I dare believe no one ever read over that ingenious work, without finding there some inventions for idleness, carelessness, and ill-behaviour, which had never happened within his own experience.

Although I do not suppose mankind in general to be thorough proficients in this our art; yet wrong not my judgement so much, gentle reader, as to imagine, that I would write *institutes*[3] of any science, to those who are unqualified for its practice, or do not show some genius in themselves towards it. Should you observe in one child a delight of drawing, in another a turn towards music, would you not do your utmost to assist their genius, and to further their attempts? 'Tis the great progress that I have observed to be already made in this our pleasant art, and the various attempts that I daily see towards bringing it to perfection, that encouraged me to offer this my poor assistance.

One requisite for approbation I confess, is wanting in this work; for, alas! I fear it will contain nothing new. But what is wanting in novelty, shall be made up in utility; for, although I may not be able to show one new and untried method of plaguing, teasing, or tormenting; yet will it not be a very great help to any one, to have all the best and most approved methods collected together, in one small pocket volume? Did I promise a new set of rules, then, whatever was not mine, might be claimed by its proper owner; and, like the jay in the fable, I should justly be stripped of my borrowed plumes:[4] but, as I declare myself only an humble collector, I doubt not, but every one, who has practised, or who in writing has described, an ingenious Torment, will thank me for putting it into this my curious collection.

The following instructions are divided into Two Parts. This First Part is addressed to those, who may be said to have an exterior power from visible authority, such as if vested, by law or custom, in matters over their servants; parents over their children; husbands over their wives; and many others. The Second Part will be addressed to those, who have an interior power, arising from the affection of the person on whom they are to work; as in the case of the wife, the friend, &c.

It would be tiresome, and almost endless, to enumerate every connexion under the two foregoing Heads: I have therefore taken only a few of the principal ones in each division; and shall begin with masters and mistresses, as in the following Chapter.

Notes

FROM *AN ESSAY ON THE ART OF INGENIOUSLY TORMENTING*

1 *Inventas ... merendo* "who improved life by means of ingenious arts and made others mindful of them through their own merit."

2 *Dean Swift's instructions Directions to Servants,* an ironic essay by Swift, posthumously published in 1745.

3 *institute* "Precept; maxim; principle" (Johnson).

4 *jay in the fable ... plumes* in Aesop's fable the jay, or jackdaw, dresses himself in the feathers of his competitors in the beauty contest held by Zeus; he is embarrassed when they take their own feathers back again.

Chapter 2

To the Patronesses of an humble Companion

I have often wondered, considering the great number of families there are, whose fortunes are so large, that the addition of one, or even two, would hardly be felt, that they should not more frequently take into their houses, and under their protection, young women who have been well educated; and who, by the misfortune or death of their friends, have been left destitute of all means of subsistence. There are many methods for young men, in the like circumstances, to acquire a genteel maintenance; but for a girl, I know not of one way of support, that does not by the custom of the world, throw her below the rank of a gentlewoman.

There are two motives for taking such young women under protection.

One is, the pleasure which ('tis said) kind and benevolent hearts must take in relieving from distress one of their fellow-creatures; and, for their repeated kindness and indulgence to an unfortunate deserving person, receiving the daily tribute of grateful assiduity, and cheerful looks. For I have been informed, by a friend well versed in human nature, that, however loud the outcry is against ingratitude for real kindness, yet that true and real kindness seldom or never did excite ingratitude: and moreover, that when those violent outcries came to be examined into, the obliged person had, in fact, been guilty of no ingratitude, or the patron had bestowed no real kindness. Nay, further, that, should it be proved, that ungrateful returns are sometimes made for real favours, it would commonly be found, upon inquiry, that the persons conferring such favours had a blind side open to flattery, or some other passion; by which means they had shut their eyes, and plucked a poisonous weed to place in their bosoms, instead of using their power of sight and distinction, in order to gather one of those many grateful flowers, which nature has scattered over the face of the earth: the intoxicating quality of which weed has still kept their eyes closed, till they are roused by some racking pain, which it instils into the inmost recesses of the heart.

But, notwithstanding the before-mentioned outcry against ingratitude, there are some, I must confess, who, from compassion and generosity, have taken the distressed into their protection, and have treated them with the highest kindness and indulgence. Nay, I have known a set of tasteless, silly, people, who are so void of any relish for this our pleasant game, that they would never wish to see a face in sorrow or tears, unless 'twas in their power to dry those tears, and turn that sorrow into cheerful smiles. But to such insipid folks I write not; as I know my rules, to them, would be of little service. I address myself, therefore, in this chapter, only to those who take young women into their houses, as new subjects of their power. …

In the first place, let me advise you to be very careful in the choice of an humble companion; for be it always remembered, that, in every connexion where this art of Teasing and Tormenting is exercised, much depends upon the subject of your power.

In a servant, you have little to look for but diligence and good-nature; but in a dependent there are many more requisites.

Let her be well born, and well educated. The more acquirements she has, the greater field will you have for insolence, and the pleasure of mortifying her. Out of the numberless families in the church and army, that outlive themselves, and come to decay, great will be your choice. Pick out, if possible, one that has lived a happy life, under tender and indulgent parents. Beauty, or deformity; good sense, or the want of it; may any of them, with proper management, so well answer your purpose, that you need not be very curious as to that matter: but on no account take into your house one that has not a tender heart, with a meek and gentle disposition; for if she has spirit enough to despise your insults, and has not tender affections enough to be soothed and melted by your kindness (which must be sparingly bestowed), all your sport is lost; and you might as well shoot your venom at a marble statue in your garden.

Although I have supposed, that beauty or deformity, good sense or folly, in your dependent, are in some measure indifferent, yet I would have you, if possible, mix them thus: take good sense, with plainness or deformity; and beauty, with a very weak capacity.

If your humble companion be handsome, with no great share of understanding, observe the following directions, towards Miss Kitty:

Take care seldom to call her anything but *Beauty, Pretty Idiot, Puppet, Baby-face*; with as many more of such sarcastical epithets as you can invent.

If you can provoke her enough to show any resentment in her countenance, looking at her with a mixture of anger and contempt, you may say, 'I *beseech* you Child to spare your frowns for those who will fear them; and keep your disdainful looks for the footmen, when they make love to you; which, by your flirting airs, I make no doubt they are encouraged to do'.

If by your discourse, you move her tears, you may call her *Weeping beauty*; and ask her, out of what play, or idle romance, she had learnt, that tears were becoming. Then drive her out of the room with these words, 'Begone out of my sight, you blubbering fool – *Handsome indeed*! If I had a dog that looked so frightful, I would hang him'.

Although you may, generally, insult her with her beauty, yet be sure, at times, to say so many mortifying things, as shall make her believe you don't think her in the least handsome. If her complexion is fair, call her *Whey-face*; if she is really an olive beauty, you may tell her, she is as brown as Mahogany: if she is inclinable to pale, tell her she always looks as white as a cloth: and you may add, 'That whatever people may fancy of their own sweet persons, yet, in your opinion, there could be no beauty in a whited wall'. In this case, sometimes, insultingly, the name of *Lily-face*! will come in. If she has a fine bloom, tell her she looks as red-faced, as if she drank brandy; and you have no notion, you may say, of cook-maid beauty. Thus, by right management, every personal perfection may be turned to her reproach. Fine large eyes may be accused of goggling;[5] small ones may be termed unmeaning, and insignificant; and so of every feature besides. But if she has fine, white, even, teeth, you have no resource, but to tell her, whenever you catch her smiling, that she is mighty fond of grinning, to show her white teeth. Then add, 'Pray remember, child, that you can't show your teeth, without showing your folly'. You may likewise declare, that if you had a girl of your own, who showed such a silly vanity, you would flay her alive.

One thing be sure not to omit, altho' it is ever so false; which is, to tell her, and in the plainest and grossest terms, that she has (oh shocking accusation to a fine girl!) sweaty feet, and a nauseous breath.

To a young creature of beauty, and any degree of delicacy, nothing can be more teasing and grating to hear, than this. From the extreme mortification she must feel, 'tis ten to one but she will deny it, with some resentment, or will shed tears of vexation for the charge: these will both equally serve your purpose. If the first, you have many ways to deal with her. Furious scolding and abuse is no bad method, if not too lately practised; but insulting taunts, I think, will do rather better. Such as follows:

'Oh to be sure! you are too delicate a creature to have any human failings? you are all sweetness and perfection! well, heaven defend me from such *sweet* creatures!' Then

Notes

[5] *goggling* squinting or staring.

changing your tone and looks into fierceness, you may proceed: 'I tell you, Madam Impertinence, whatever you may think, and how impudently soever you may dare to contradict me in this manner, that all your nasty odious imperfections have been often taken notice of by many people besides myself, though nobody has enough regard for you, to tell you of such things. – You may toss your head, and look with as much indignation as you please; but these airs, child, will not do long with me. – If you don't like to be told of your faults, you must find some other person to support you. So pray, for the present, walk off to your own apartment; and consider whether you choose to lay aside that pretty, becoming resentment of yours; or be thrown friendless, as I found you, on the wide world again. – You must not be told of your failings, truly, must you! Oh I would not have such a proud heart as thine is in my breast, for the world! Though let me tell you, Mistress Minx, 'twould much better become my station, than yours'.

For fear this kind and gentle speech of yours should have wounded too deeply; and Miss Kitty should really, on consideration, prefer wandering, beggary, or the most menial service, to such life of dependence, and you should thereby lose your game, be sure not to let it be above half an hour before you send your woman up-stairs to her, with some sweet-meats, fruit, or any thing you know she is fond of. Order your woman, if she finds her in a rage, to soften her mind, till she brings her to tears; then to comfort her; and tell her how kindly you had been just then talking of her; and to leave no means untried to coax her down. You must then receive her with the highest good humour; and tell her, you intend for her some new clothes, a pleasant jaunt or any indulgence that you know would please her: continue this good humour so strongly, that she shall not have the least opportunity of telling you, what undoubtedly, she must have resolved above-stairs; namely that she could live with you no longer. And if this fit of kindness be carried into a proper excess, the poor girl will, at last, begin to think herself to blame; and that you are the kindest, best creature to her in the world. Then is she properly prepared for the next Torment you shall think fit to inflict.

Should Miss Kitty, on the mortifying accusation before-mentioned, burst into tears, you must proceed in a contrary method: and, in a soft and gentle accent, you may say to her, 'I cannot imagine, my dear, what should make you cry, when I am only kindly telling you, as a friend, of some misfortunes you cannot possibly help. I am very far from blaming you, my love; for although, I thank heaven, I am myself free from all such shocking and disagreeable things, yet nobody pities people with such imperfections more than I do'. You might here, also, aggravate the misfortune it was, to so young and so pretty a girl, to have such personal defects: for (you may add) that you had often heard the men declare (and you thought 'em very much in the right), that they should prefer the ugliest girl that was ever born, who was sweet in her person, to the greatest beauty upon the earth, with such nauseous, disgustful imperfections. …

So far for a handsome girl. But, if plainness, with a good share of natural parts, should be the lot of this your dependent, whom we will call Miss Fanny, great scope will you have in a different way, for Tormenting, Teasing, and Plaguing her.

You must begin with all sorts of mortifying observations on her person; and frequently declare, that you hate any thing about you that is not agreeable to look at. This, in the beginning, will vex the girl; first, as 'tis not very pleasant to have a mirror perpetually held to our view, where the reflection is so mortifying: and next, as she will be sorry to find herself disagreeable to a person she would wish to please. But in time she will find you out: she will perceive the malice of such reflections; and, if she has good sense, will get above any concern about what you can say of her person. As soon as you perceive this, change your method; and level most of your darts against her understanding. Never let a day pass, without calling her, in that day, a Wit, at least a hundred times.

Begin most requests, or rather commands, with these sort of phrases, 'Will your *Wisdom* please to do so or so, &c. Can a lady of your *fine parts* condescend to darn this apron? Would it not be too great a condescension for a Wit, to submit to look over my housekeeper's accounts?' Whatever answer she makes to these things; whether it be showing a little resentment for such insolent treatment; or saying, with mildness, that she is ready to do any thing you command her; let your reply be – 'I don't hear, child, what you say – However, I presume it was something mighty smart and witty. – But let me give you one piece of advice; which is, to be more sparing of your tongue, and less sparing of your labour, if you expect a continuance of my favour to you –'.

Although your chief mark is her understanding; yet I would not have you quite drop your reflections on the plainness of her person: for, by continual teasing, you may possibly bring her to say something to the following effect: – That she could not help the plainness of her person: – That she endeavoured to be as contented as she could; but, in short, she did not much concern herself about the matter. – Then have you a double road for Teasing her still more on that head.

If she is clean and well dressed, you may put on a malicious sneer; and, looking her over from top to toe, you may noddle your head; and say, 'So Miss, considering you are a Wit, and a lady who despises all personal advantages, I must needs say you have tricked yourself out pretty handsomely to-day'. Then may you add, that you would hold a good wager, she was every day longer prinking[6] in the glass than you was. – But it was always so. – You had ever observed, that the ugliest women were much fonder of their persons, than the most beautiful.

If she fails, in the least particular, of nicety in dress, than have you the old beaten path before you: load her with the names of trollop, slattern, slut, dirty beast, &c. omit not any of those trite observations; that all Wits are slatterns; – that no girl ever delighted in reading, that was not a slut; – that well might the men say they would not for the world marry a Wit; that they had rather have a woman who could make a pudden, than one who could make a poem; – and that it was the ruin of all girls who had not independent fortunes, to have learnt either to read or write. You may tell her also, that she may thank God, that her ugliness will preserve her from being a whore. – Then conclude all these pious reflexions with thanking heaven, that, for your part, you are no Wit; and that you will take care your children shall not be of that stamp.

Part the Second

Chapter 2
To the Wife

The common disposition with which a married couple generally come together (except for mere lucrative motives) is this.

The man, for some qualification, either personal or mental, which he sees, or dreams he sees, in some woman, fixes his affections on that woman: then, instead of endeavouring to fix her affections on himself, he directs all her thoughts, and her enjoyment, on settlements, equipage, fine clothes, and every other gratification of

Notes

[6] *prink* "To prank; to deck for show" (Johnson, citing this passage).

vanity within his power and fortune to give her. He pays so thorough an adoration and submission to her in all respects, that he soon perfects a work before half finished to his hands; namely, the making her completely and immoveably in love with – herself. – This puts her, for the present, into such good spirits, and good humour, that the poor man, from the pleasure he finds in her company, believes her to be in love with him. This thought, joined to his first inclination to her person, creates in him a pretty strong affection towards her, and gives her that power over him, which I would willingly assist her in exerting. This affection, when he becomes her husband, generally shows itself in real kindness. But as soon as all the joy arising from courtship is gone, the wife generally grows uneasy; her husband, being no longer her lover, grows disgustful to her; and, if she be a woman of violent passions, she turns fractious and sour; and a breach soon ensues. The husband may bluster, and rave, and talk of his authority and power, as much as he pleases; but it is very easy to grow into such a perfect disregard of such storms, that, by wrapping one's self up in a proper degree of contempt, they will blow as vainly over our heads, as the wind over our houses. Besides, if there are not emoluments enough in the husband's house, to make it worth while to bear the ill-humours raised by our own frowardness, separation is the word; to which if a husband will not consent, a cause of cruelty against him, in Doctors Commons,[7] I will soon bring him to; for (as I have heard) the husband there, by paying the expenses of both sides, will be obliged, in a manner, to supply his wife with the means of carrying her own point, and will be glad therefore to make any conditions with her. But a woman of prudence will know when she is well; will take no such precipitate steps; but will rejoice in the discovery of her husband's great affection towards her, as a means for pursuing the course of Teasing and Tormenting, which I here recommend.

'Oh the joy it is to have a good servant', cried Sophronia, who had not goodness of heart enough to be kind to any human creature, and whose joy must therefore arise from having a proper subject to torment! But with what ecstasy then, might the artful Livia cry out – 'Oh the joy it is to have a good husband!' …

Besides nourishing in your mind an inveterate hatred against all your husband's relations and acquaintance, you may show the highest dislike to every place he was fond of before he married: but express the highest joy and raptures on the very mention of any place, that you used to live in yourself before your union with him; and be as lavish as possible of your praises of a single life. You may also, if your husband be not of a very jealous temper, hoard up a parcel of your favourite trinkets, as rings, snuffboxes, &c. which were given you before marriage; and let it appear, from your immoderate fondness for those baubles, that the givers of them are still nearest to your heart.

Carefully study your husband's temper, and find out what he likes, in order never to do any one thing that will please him.

If he expresses his approbation of the domestic qualities of a wife; such as family economy, and that old-fashioned female employment, the needle; neglect your family as much as ever his temper will bear; and always have your white gloves on your hand. Tell him, that every woman of spirit ought to hate and despise a man who could insist on his wife's being a family drudge; and declare, that you will not submit to be a cook

Notes

7 *Doctors Commons* Doctors' Commons, a court of law near St. Paul's Cathedral.

and seamstress to any man. But if he loves company, and cheerful parties of pleasure, and would willingly have you always with him, insult him with your great love of needle-work and housewifery. Or should he be a man of genius, and should employ his leisure hours in writing, be sure to show a tasteless indifference to everything he shows you of his own. The same indifference, also, may you put on, if he should be a man who loves reading, and is of so communicative a disposition, as to take delight in reading to you any of our best and most entertaining authors. If, for instance, he desires you to hear one of Shakespeare's plays, you may give him perpetual interruptions, by sometimes going out of the room, sometimes ringing the bell to give orders for what cannot be wanted till the next day; at other times taking notice (if your children are in the room), that Molly's cap is awry, or that Jackey looks pale; and then begin questioning the child, whether he has done any thing to make himself sick. If you have needle-work in your hands, you may be so busy in cutting out, and measuring one part with another, that it will plainly appear to your husband, that you mind not one word he reads. If all this teases him enough to make him call on you for your attention, you may say, that indeed you have other things to mind besides poetry; and if he was uneasy at your taking care of your family and children, and mending *his* shirts, you wished he had a learned wife; and then he would soon see himself in a jail, and his family in rags. Fail not to be as eloquent as possible on this subject, for I could bring you numberless precedents of silly and illiterate wives, who have half talked their husbands to death, in exclaiming against the loquacity of ALL WOMEN, who have any share of understanding or knowledge. ...

If your husband, on observing you particularly fond of something at a friend's table, should desire you to get it for yourself at home, you may say, that you are so little selfish, that you cannot bear to provide any thing for your own eating; and this you may boldly declare, although it should be your common practice to provide some delicacy for yourself every day. It is most likely, that your husband will let this pass, but should he not, you may, on detection, fly to tears, and complaints of his cruelty and barbarity, in upbraiding you with so small an indulgence as that of a chicken, or a tart sometimes, for your own eating, when he knows, that your weak stomach will not give you leave to make the horse-like meals that he does.

If you manage this scene rightly, and sufficiently reiterate in your husband's ears the words *cruel, unkind, barbarous*, &c. he will, it is most likely, forget the true occasion of all this uproar; will begin to think he had been a little hard upon you in taking notice of a daily indulgence, which he himself had not only allowed, but requested you to accept; he will ask your pardon, and confess himself in fault, doubling his diligence for the future, in providing all sorts of rarities to gratify your palate.

Be it observed, that this knack of turning the tables, and forcing the offended person to ask pardon of the first aggressor, is one of the most ingenious strokes of our art, and may be practised in every connexion, where the power is founded in love.

Conclusion of the Essay

... I know that many learned and good men have taken great pains to undermine this our noble art, by laying down rules, and giving exemplars, in order to teach mankind to give no offence to anyone, and instead of being a torment, to be as great a help and comfort to their friends, as it is in their power to be. But with infinite pleasure do I perceive, either that they are not much read, or, at least, that they have not the power of rooting from the human breast, that growing sprig of mischief there implanted with our birth; and generally, as we come to years of discretion, flourishing like a green palm-tree: yet, to show my great candour[8] and generosity to these my mortal (or rather moral) foes, I will endeavour, as far as my poor recommendation will go, to forward the sale of their books, even among my own pupils. For if, my good scholars, you will guard your minds against the doctrines they intend to teach; if you will consider them as mere amusements; you have my leave to peruse them. Or rather, if you will only remember to observe my orders, in acting in direct opposition to all that a Swift, an Addison, a Richardson, a Fielding, or any other good ethical writer intended to teach, you may (by referring sometimes to these my rules, as helps to your memory) become as profound adepts in this Art, as any of the readers of Mr. Hoyle are in the science of whist.[9]

Great are the disputes amongst the learned, whether man, as an animal, be a savage and ferocious, or a gentle and social beast. Swift's picture, in his Yahoos,[10] gives us not a very favourable view of the natural disposition of the animal man; yet I remember not, that he supposes him naturally to delight in tormenting; nor does he make him guilty of any vices, but following his brutish appetites. Must not this love of Tormenting therefore be cultivated and cherished? There are many tastes, as that of the olive, the oyster, with several high sauces, cooked up with assa foetida and the like, which are at first disgustful to the palate, but when once a man has so far depraved his natural taste, as to get a relish for those dainties, there is nothing he is half so fond of.

I can recollect but one kind of brute, that seems to have any notion of this pleasant practice of Tormenting; and that is the cat, when she has got a mouse – She delays the gratification of her hunger, which prompted her to seek for food, and triumphs in her power over her wretched captive – She not only sticks her claws into it, making it feel the sharpness of her teeth (without touching the vitals enough to render it insensible to her tricks), but she tosses it over her head in sport, seems in the highest joy imaginable, and is also, to all appearance, at that very time, the sweetest, best-humoured animal in the world. Yet should anything approach her, that she fears will rob her of her play-thing (holding her prey fast in her teeth), she swears, she growls, and shows all the savage motions of her heart. As soon as her fears are over, she again resumes her sport; and is, in this one instance only, kinder to her victim, than her imitators men, that by death she at lasts puts a final end to the poor wretch's torments.

Was I to rack my invention and memory for ever, I could not find a more adequate picture of the true lovers of Tormenting than this sportive cat: nor will I tire my reader's patience longer, than to add this further precept:

REMEMBER ALWAYS TO DO UNTO EVERY ONE, WHAT YOU WOULD LEAST WISH TO HAVE DONE UNTO YOURSELF; for in this is contained the whole of our excellent SCIENCE.

Notes

[8] *candour* kindness, mildness.

[9] *Hoyle ... whist* Edmond Hoyle (1672–1769), author of treatises on whist and other card games.

[10] *Swift's picture, in his Yahoos Gulliver's Travels*, Book 4.

Thomas Gray (1716–1771)

Gray was the only one of his mother's twelve children to survive infancy, and he himself was somewhat weak and sickly throughout his life. His father was a brutal, abusive husband against whom his mother unsuccessfully sought legal redress. At the age of eleven Gray went to Eton College, where his mother's brother was a master. He formed important relationships there with classmates Richard West and Horace Walpole, who were also interested in cultivating their minds and avoiding physical education. Gray went to Cambridge, toured Europe with Walpole, and returned to Cambridge, where he spent most of his life in quiet retirement and scholarship. He had a circle of friends, but he never married and perhaps never formed an intimate attachment after the death of West in 1742 (though late in life he was briefly infatuated with a young Swiss scholar named Bonstetten). He was evidently shy and somewhat fussy; he was frightened of fire and kept a rope ladder in his rooms at Peterhouse College, Cambridge. The young men of the college once tormented him by pretending there was a fire and had the pleasure of seeing him descend his rope ladder into a tub of cold water, which they had strategically positioned under his window.

The death of West evidently galvanized Gray and got him writing poetry. But his real inclination was for study rather than production, and he only published thirteen poems in his lifetime. One of these was *An Elegy Wrote in a Country Church Yard* (1751). Gray published the poem reluctantly when it was about to be pirated, and he said little about it during the rest of his life. However, the work was an immediate critical and popular success: there were twelve editions in the next twelve years, and it was pirated by numerous magazines all over England. Memorization of the poem was required in many British schools for two centuries, and it is one of the best-known English poems in the world. It is certainly a large part of the reason that Gray was offered the post of poet laureate, which he immediately rejected, even though the government was willing to excuse him from the duty of writing birthday odes for the king. Gray preferred retirement and study. In 1757 he published two poems about which he really cared, a pair of Pindaric odes, "The Progress of Poesy" and "The Bard." These works are even more learned and more highly allusive than Gray's other works, and they did not achieve popularity. From 1759, Gray spent three years doing research at the newly opened British Library, but sent most of his notes on a prospective history of English literature to Thomas Warton, who was a much more productive scholar. Gray left behind many other unfinished projects, and when Samuel Johnson wrote his critical biography in 1781, ten years after Gray's death, the professional writer was contemptuous of the fussy and pampered academic: "As a writer," says Johnson, Gray "had this peculiarity, that he did not write his pieces first rudely, and then correct them, but laboured every line as it arose in the train of his composition; and he had a notion not very peculiar, that he could not write but at certain times, or at happy moments; a fantastic foppery, to which my kindness for a man of learning and virtue wishes him to have been superior." Johnson was not a great admirer of Gray's poetry, much of which he considered inaccessible to the "common reader," but he closed his life of Gray by saying, "The *Church-yard* abounds with images which find a mirror in every mind, and with sentiments to which every bosom returns an echo. The four stanzas beginning 'Yet even these bones' are to me original: I have never

British Literature 1640–1789: An Anthology, Fourth Edition. Edited by Robert DeMaria, Jr.

seen the notions in any other place; yet he that reads them here, persuades himself that he has always felt them. Had Gray written often thus, it had been vain to blame, and useless to praise him."

As the bases of the following texts I have used first editions supplemented by versions in the collection of his works assembled under Gray's direction in 1768. I have benefited from the collations in the edition by H. W. Starr and J. R. Hendrickson (Clarendon Press, 1966). I have also learned a great deal and borrowed some from the extensive commentary of Roger Lonsdale in *The Poems of Gray, Collins, and Goldsmith* (Longman, 1969). The text of Gray's letter to Richard West is based on *The Correspondence of Thomas Gray*, ed. Paget Toynbee and Leonard Whibley, 3 vols. (Clarendon Press, 1933). Robert Mack has published an insightful biography of Gray (Yale University Press, 2000). For an excellent essay on Gray, see George Haggerty, "Lachrymarum Fons," in *British Literature 1640–1789: A Critical Reader* (Blackwell, 1999).

Letter to Richard West[1]

Florence, 21 April 1741

I know not what degree of satisfaction it will give you to be told that we shall set out from hence the 24th of this month, and not stop above a fortnight at any place in our way. This I feel, that you are the principal pleasure I have to hope for in my own country. Try at least to make me imagine myself not indifferent to you; for I must own I have the vanity of desiring to be esteemed by somebody, and would choose that somebody should be one whom I esteem as much as I do you. As I am recommending myself to your love, methinks I ought to send you my picture (for I am no more what I was, some circumstances excepted, which I hope I need not particularize to you); you must add then, to your former idea, two years of age, reasonable quantity of dullness, a great deal of silence, and something that rather resembles, than is, thinking; a confused notion of many strange and fine things that have swum before my eyes for some time, a want of love for general society, indeed an inability to it. On the good side you may add a sensibility for what others feel, and indulgence for their faults or weaknesses, a love of truth, and detestation of every thing else. Then you are to deduct a little impertinence, a little laughter, a great deal of pride, and some spirits. These are all the alterations I know of, you perhaps may find more. Think not that I have been obliged for this reformation of manners to reason or reflection, but to a severer schoolmistress, Experience. One has little merit in learning her lessons, for one cannot well help it; but they are more useful than others, and imprint themselves in the very heart. I find I have been haranguing in the style of the Son of Sirach,[2] so shall finish here, and tell you that our route is settled as follows: First to Bologna for a few days, to hear the Viscontina[3] sing; next to Reggio, where is a Fair. Now, you must know, a Fair here is not a place where one eats gingerbread or rides upon hobby-horses; here are no musical

Notes

Letter to Richard West

[1] *Richard West* Gray's classmate at Eton and close friend; he died on June 1, 1742 at the age of twenty-five; Gray wrote frequently to West during the two years he spent touring the Continent as the guest of another Eton classmate, Horace Walpole; by the time Gray wrote this letter, the two had separated because of irreconcilable differences of style in traveling.

[2] *Son of Sirach* the author of Ecclesiasticus, a book of wisdom in the Apocrypha.

[3] *Viscontina* Caterina Visconti.

clocks, nor tall Leicestershire women; one has nothing but masquing, gaming, and singing. If you love operas, there will be the most splendid in Italy, four tip-top voices, a new theatre, the Duke and Duchess in all their pomps and vanities. Does not this sound magnificent? Yet is the city of Reggio[4] but one step above Old Brentford.[5] Well; next to Venice by the 11th of May, there to see the old Doge wed the Adriatic Whore.[6] Then to Verona, so to Milan, so to Marseilles, so to Lyons, so to Paris, so to West, &c. in sæcula sæculorum.[7] Amen.

Sonnet [on the Death of Mr Richard West][1] (1742)

In vain to me the smiling Mornings shine,
And redd'ning Phoebus lifts his golden Fire:
The Birds in vain their amorous descant join;[2]
Or cheerful Fields resume their green attire:
These ears, alas! for other notes repine,
A different object do these eyes require.
My lonely anguish melts no heart, but mine;
And in my Breast the imperfect joys expire.
Yet Morning smiles the busy race to cheer,
And new-born Pleasure brings to happier Men:
The Fields to all their wonted tribute bear:[3]
To warm their little loves the birds complain:
I fruitless mourn to him, that cannot hear,
And weep the more, because I weep in vain.

Ode on the Death of a Favourite Cat[1] (1748)

I

'Twas on a lofty vase's side,
Where China's gayest art had dyed
  The azure flowers, that blow;
Demurest of the Tabby kind,
The pensive Selima reclined,
  Gazed on the lake below.

Notes

[4] *Reggio* the city where Walpole and Gray quarreled and parted ways.

[5] *Brentford* a proverbially ugly town about ten miles west of London.

[6] *Doge* A ceremonial marriage between the doge (ruler) of Venice and the sea was performed on Ascension day to celebrate Venetian sea-power.

[7] *in sæcula sæculorum* forever and forever.

Sonnet [On the Death of Mr Richard West]

[1] Gray wrote this poem in August 1742 about two months after the death of his close friend; the sonnet was not published in Gray's lifetime, and he evidently did not think highly of it. The text is that of the first printing, in William Mason's edition of Gray's poems (1775).

[2] *amorous descant see Paradise Lost* 4.603.

[3] *wonted* customary.

Ode on the Death of a Favourite Cat

[1] The text is based on that in *A Collection of Poems by Several Hands*, ed. Robert Dodsley, 3 vols (1748), with a few widely accepted changes from later editions.

2

Her conscious tail her joy declared;
The fair round face, the snowy beard,
The velvet of her paws,
The coat that with the tortoise vies,
Her ears of jet, and emerald eyes,
She saw; and purred applause.

3

Still had she gazed: but 'midst the tide
Two angel forms were seen to glide,
The Genii of the stream:[2]
Their scaly armour's Tyrian hue[3]
Through richest purple to the view
Betrayed a golden gleam.

4

The hapless nymph with wonder saw:
A whisker first and then a claw,
With many an ardent wish,
She stretched in vain to reach the prize.
What female heart can gold despise?
What cat's averse to fish?

5

Presumptuous maid! with looks intent
Again she stretched, again she bent,
Nor knew the gulf between;
(Malignant fate sat by and smiled)
The slipp'ry verge her feet beguiled,
She tumbled headlong in.

6

Eight times emerging from the flood
She mewed to every watry God,
Some speedy aid to send.
No Dolphin came, no Nereid stirred:
Nor cruel Tom, nor Harry heard.[4]
A favourite has no friend![5]

Notes

[2] *Genii* plural of *genius*, "The protecting or ruling power of men, places, or things" (Johnson).

[3] *Tyrian* purple, a color produced from shellfish near the eastern Mediterranean city of Tyre.

[4] *Harry* other editions read "Susan"; both are, like Tom, stereotypical servants' names.

[5] *favourite* the meaning includes "One chosen as a companion by his superior; a mean wretch whose whole business is by any means to please" (Johnson, sense 2).

7

From hence, ye beauties, undeceived,
Know, one false step is ne'er retrieved,
And be with caution bold.
Not all that tempts your wand'ring eyes
And heedless hearts, is lawful prize;
Nor all, that glisters, gold.

An Elegy Wrote in a Country Church Yard (1751)

The *Curfew*[1] tolls the Knell of parting Day,
The lowing Herd wind slowly o'er the Lea,
The Plow-man homeward plods his weary Way,
And leaves the World to Darkness, and to me.
Now fades the glimmering Landscape on the Sight,
And all the Air a solemn Stillness holds;
Save where the Beetle wheels his droning Flight,
And drowsy Tinklings lull the distant Folds.[2]
Save that from yonder Ivy-mantled Tow'r
The moping Owl does to the Moon complain
Of such, as wand'ring near her sacred Bower,
Molest her ancient solitary Reign.
Beneath those rugged Elms, that Yew-Tree's Shade,
Where heaves the Turf in many a mould'ring Heap,
Each in his narrow Cell for ever laid,
The rude Forefathers of the Hamlet sleep.
The breezy Call of Incense-breathing Morn,
The Swallow twitt'ring from the Straw-built Shed,
The Cock's shrill Clarion, or the echoing Horn,
No more shall rouse them from their lowly Bed.
For them no more the blazing Hearth shall burn,
Or busy Housewife ply her Evening Care:
No Children run to lisp their Sire's Return,
Or climb his Knees the envied Kiss to share.
Oft did the Harvest to their Sickle yield,
Their Furrow oft the stubborn Glebe has broke;[3]
How jocund did they drive their Team afield!
How bowed the Woods beneath their sturdy Stroke!
Let not Ambition mock their useful Toil,
Their homely Joys and Destiny obscure;
Nor Grandeur hear with a disdainful Smile,

Notes

AN ELEGY WROTE IN A COUNTRY CHURCH YARD

[1] *Curfew* "An evening peal, by which [William] the conqueror willed that every man should rake up his fire, and put out his light; so that in many places at this day where a bell is customarily rung towards bed time, it is said to ring curfew" (Johnson, citing John Cowell, *The Interpreter*, who cites John Stowe).

[2] *Fold* "The ground in which sheep are confined" (Johnson).

[3] *Glebe* soil.

The short and simple Annals of the Poor.
    The boast of Heraldry, the Pomp of Power,
And all that Beauty, all that Wealth e'er gave,
Awaits alike th' inevitable Hour.
The Paths of Glory lead but to the Grave.
    Nor you, ye Proud, impute to these the Fault,
If Mem'ry o'er their Tomb no Trophies raise,
Where through the long-drawn Aisle and fretted Vault[4]
The pealing Anthem swells the Note of Praise.[5]
    Can storied Urn or animated Bust
Back to its Mansion call the fleeting Breath?
Can Honour's Voice provoke the silent Dust,
Or Flatt'ry soothe the dull cold Ear of Death!
    Perhaps in this neglected Spot is laid
Some Heart once pregnant with celestial Fire,
Hands that the Rod of Empire might have swayed,
Or waked to Ecstasy the living Lyre.
    But Knowledge to their Eyes her ample Page
Rich with the Spoils of Time did ne'er unroll;
Chill Penury repressed their noble Rage,
And froze the genial Current of the Soul.
    Full many a Gem of purest Ray serene,[6]
The dark unfathomed Caves of Ocean bear:
Full many a Flower is born to blush unseen,[7]
And waste its Sweetness on the desert Air.
    Some village-*Hampden* that with dauntless Breast[8]
The little Tyrant of his Fields withstood;
Some mute inglorious *Milton* here may rest,
Some *Cromwell* guiltless of his Country's Blood.
    Th' Applause of list'ning Senates to command,
The Threats of Pain and Ruin to despise,
To scatter Plenty o'er a smiling Land,
And read their Hist'ry in a Nation's Eyes,
    Their Lot forbad: nor circumscribed alone
Their growing Virtues, but their Crimes confined;
Forbad to wade through Slaughter to a Throne,
And Shut the Gates of Mercy on Mankind,
    The struggling Pangs of conscious Truth to hide,
To quench the Blushes of ingenuous Shame,
Or heap the Shrine of Luxury and Pride
With Incense, kindled at the Muse's Flame.[9]

Notes

4 *fretted* ornamented.

5 *Anthem* "A holy song" (Johnson).

6 *serene* clear, bright.

7 *Full many a Flower* two verse feet only.

8 *Hampden* John (1594–1643); like Milton and Cromwell, he opposed the "Tyrant" Charles I and urged civil war, in which he died fighting; in one manuscript version of the poem, Gray had Cato, Cicero, and Caesar in place of these English figures.

9 At one stage in its composition the poem may have concluded after line 72 with the following four stanzas in the Eton College manuscript:

> The thoughtless World to Majesty may bow
> Exalt the brave, & idolise Success
> But more to Innocence their Safety owe
> Than Power & Genius e'er conspired to bless
> And thou, who mindful of the unhonoured Dead
> Dost in these Notes their artless Tale relate

Far from the madding Crowd's ignoble Strife,
Their sober Wishes never learned to stray;
Along the cool sequestered Vale of Life
They kept the noiseless Tenor of their Way.[10]
Yet ev'n these Bones from Insult to protect
Some frail Memorial still erected nigh,
With uncouth Rhymes and shapeless Sculpture decked,[11]
Implores the passing Tribute of a Sigh.
Their Name, their Years, spelt by th' unlettered Muse,[12]
The Place of Fame and Elegy supply:
And many a holy Text around she strews,
That teach the rustic Moralist to die.
For who to dumb Forgetfulness a Prey,
This pleasing anxious Being e'er resigned,
Left the warm Precincts of the cheerful Day,
Nor cast one longing ling'ring Look behind![13]
On some fond Breast the parting Soul relies,
Some pious Drops the closing Eye requires;
Ev'n from the Tomb the Voice of Nature cries
Awake, and faithful to her wonted Fires.[14]
For thee, who mindful of th' unhonoured Dead
Dost in these Lines their artless Tale relate;
If chance, by lonely Contemplation led,
Some kindred Spirit shall inquire thy Fate,[15]
Haply some hoary-headed Swain may say,
'Oft have we seen him at the Peep of Dawn
Brushing with hasty Steps the Dews away
To meet the Sun upon the upland Lawn.[16]
'There at the Foot of yonder nodding Beech
That wreathes its old fantastic Roots so high,
His listless Length at Noontide would he stretch,
And pore upon the Brook that babbles by.
'Hard by yon Wood, now frowning as in Scorn,
Mutt'ring his wayward Fancies he would rove,
Now drooping, woeful wan, like one forlorn,
Or crazed with Care, or crossed in hopeless Love.
'One Morn I missed him on the customed Hill,

Notes

By Night & lonely Contemplation led
To linger in the gloomy Walks of Fate
Hark how the sacred Calm, that broods around
Bids every fierce tumultuous Passion cease
In still small Accents whispering from the Ground
A grateful Earnest of eternal Peace
No more with Reason & thyself at Strife;
Give anxious Cares & endless Wishes room
But through the cool sequestered Vale of Life
Pursue the silent Tenor of thy Doom.

10 *Tenor* "Continuity of state" (Johnson).

11 *uncouth* "Odd; strange; unusual" (Johnson).

12 *unlettered* "Unlearned; untaught" (Johnson).

13 *For who… Look behind* compare *Paradise Lost* 2.146–51.

14 *wonted* customary.

15 In the Eton College manuscript this stanza is replaced by the following:

If chance that e'er some pensive Spirit more
By sympathetic Musings here delayed,
With vain, though kind, Inquiry shall explore
Thy once-loved Haunt, this long-deserted Shade.

16 After this line the Eton manuscript has,

Him have we seen the Green-wood Side along,
While o'er the Heath we hied, our Labours done,
Oft as the Woodlark piped her farewell Song
With wistful eyes pursue the setting Sun.

Along the Heath, and near his favourite Tree;
Another came; nor yet beside the Rill,
Nor up the Lawn, nor at the Wood was he.
'The next with Dirges due in sad Array
Slow through the Church-way Path we saw him borne.
Approach and read (for thou can'st read) the Lay,
Graved on the Stone beneath yon aged Thorn.'

The Epitaph

Here rests his Head upon the Lap of Earth
A Youth to Fortune and to Fame unknown:
Fair Science frowned not on his humble Birth,[1]
And Melancholy marked him for her own.[2]
Large was his Bounty, and his Soul sincere,
Heav'n did a Recompense as largely send:
He gave to Misery all he had, a Tear:
He gained from Heav'n ('twas all he wished) a Friend.
No further seek his Merits to disclose,
Or draw his Frailties from their dread Abode,
(There they alike in trembling Hope repose)
The Bosom of his Father and his God.

The Progress of Poesy: A Pindaric Ode[1] (1768)

I.1[2]

AWAKE, Æolian lyre, awake,[3]
And give to rapture all thy trembling strings.
From Helicon's harmonious springs[4]
A thousand rills their mazy progress take:
The laughing flowers, that round them blow,[5]

Notes

The Epitaph

1 *Science* knowledge.

2 *Melancholy* one of the characteristics of those favored by Science; a positive attribute, like sensibility, Lonsdale suggests.

The Progress of Poesy

1 Gray originally published this poem and "The Bard" in *Odes by Mr. Gray* (1757); the text follows the edition in *Poems by Mr. Gray* (1768), to which Gray added the present title and footnotes. The original title was "Ode in the Greek manner." Referring the style to Pindar, the fifth-century BCE praise poet, signaled that the work would be irregular, rapid, and highly allusive, but Gray correctly understood Pindar's prosody as various and complex rather than wild. His divisions indicate three rounds of strophe, antistrophe, and epode, the regular parts of Pindar's odes.

2 *I.1* The subject and the simile, as usual with Pindar, are united. The various sources of poetry, which gives life and lustre to all it touches, are here described; its quiet majestic progress enriching every subject (otherwise dry and barren) with a pomp of diction and luxuriant harmony of numbers; and its more rapid and irresistible course, when swollen and hurried away by the conflict of tumultuous passions [Gray's note].

3 *Æolian lyre* by citing Pindar in a footnote Gray suggests the phrase means lyric poetry of the kind written by Pindar, which originated in the Aeolian islands, especially Lesbos.

4 *Helicon* a mountain inhabited by the muses; its springs inspire those who drink from them.

5 *blow* blossom.

Drink life and fragrance as they flow.
Now the rich stream of music winds along
Deep, majestic, smooth, and strong,
Through verdant vales, and Ceres' golden reign: [6]
Now rolling down the steep amain,
Headlong, impetuous, see it pour:
The rocks and nodding groves rebellow to the roar.

I.2[7]

Oh! Sovereign of the willing soul,
Parent of sweet and solemn-breathing airs,
Enchanting shell! the sullen Cares[8]
And frantic Passions hear thy soft control.
On Thracia's hills the Lord of War,[9]
Has curbed the fury of his car,
And dropped his thirsty lance at thy command.
Perching on the sceptred hand
Of Jove, thy magic lulls the feathered king[10]
With ruffled plumes and flagging wing:
Quenched in dark clouds of slumber lie
The terror of his beak, and lightnings of his eye.

I.3[11]

Thee the voice, the dance, obey,
Tempered to thy warbled lay.
O'er Idalia's velvet-green[12]
The rosy-crownèd Loves are seen
On Cytherea's day[13]
With antic Sports and blue-eyed Pleasures,[14]
Frisking light in frolic measures;
Now pursuing, now retreating,
Now in circling troops they meet:
To brisk notes in cadence beating
Glance their many-twinkling feet.[15]
Slow melting strains their Queen's approach declare:
Where'er she turns the Graces homage pay.[16]

Notes

[6] *Ceres* an Italian goddess of vegetable regeneration associated with the Greek Demeter.

[7] *I.2* Power of harmony to calm the turbulent sallies of the soul. The thoughts are borrowed from the first Pythian of Pindar [especially the first strophe; Gray's note].

[8] *shell* lyre, because the first such instruments are said to have been strung on tortoise shells.

[9] *Thracia* Thrace, the northernmost part of Greece, considered a rough place with rough gods; *Lord of War* Mars.

[10] *feathered king* the eagle ("ruler of birds" in Pythian 1).

[11] *I.3* Power of harmony to produce all the graces of motion in the body [Gray's note].

[12] *Idalia* Aphrodite, after a town on Cyprus, which was sacred to her.

[13] *Cytherea* another name for Aphrodite, derived from an island sacred to her.

[14] *antic* "Odd; ridiculously wild" (Johnson).

[15] *Glance* "To move nimbly" (Johnson); "twinkling" is a translation of a word Homer used to describe the nimble feet of dancers (*Odyssey* 8.265), as Gray noted.

[16] *Graces* the Charities, three goddesses personifying grace and beauty, associated with Aphrodite.

With arms sublime, that float upon the air,
In gliding state she wins her easy way:
O'er her warm cheek and rising bosom move
The bloom of young Desire and purple light of Love.

II.1[17]

Man's feeble race what ills await,
Labour, and Penury, the racks of Pain,
Disease, and Sorrow's weeping train,
And Death, sad refuge from the storms of Fate!
The fond complaint, my song, disprove,
And justify the laws of Jove.[18]
Say, has he giv'n in vain the heav'nly Muse?
Night, and all her sickly dews,
Her spectres wan, and birds of boding cry,
He gives to range the dreary sky:
Till down the eastern cliffs afar
Hyperion's march they spy, and glitt'ring shafts of war.[19]

II.2[20]

In climes beyond the solar road,
Where shaggy forms o'er ice-built mountains roam,
The Muse has broke the twilight-gloom
To cheer the shiv'ring native's dull abode.
And oft, beneath the od'rous shade
Of Chile's boundless forests laid,
She deigns to hear the savage youth repeat
In loose numbers wildly sweet
Their feather-cinctured chiefs, and dusky loves.
Her track, where'er the goddess roves,
Glory pursue, and generous Shame,
Th' unconquerable Mind, and Freedom's holy flame.

II.3[21]

  Woods, that wave o'er Delphi's steep,[22]
Isles, that crown th' Ægean deep,
Fields, that cool Ilissus laves,[23]

Notes

[17] *II.1* To compensate the real and imaginary ills of life, the Muse was given to Mankind by the same Providence that sends the Day by its cheerful presence to dispel the gloom and terrors of the Night [Gray's note].

[18] *And justify the laws of Jove* compare *Paradise Lost* 1.26.

[19] *Hyperion* a Titan identified with the sun.

[20] *II.2* Extensive influence of poetic Genius over the remotest and most uncivilised nations: its connection with liberty, and the virtues that naturally attend on it. (See the Erse, Norwegian, and Welsh Fragments, the Lapland and American songs.) [Gray's note].

[21] *II.3* Progress of Poetry from Greece to Italy, and from Italy to England. Chaucer was not unacquainted with the writings of Dante or of Petrarch. The Earl of Surrey and Sir Thomas Wyatt had travelled in Italy, and formed their taste there; Spenser imitated the Italian writers; Milton improved on them: but this School expired soon after the Restoration, and a new one arose on the French model, which has subsisted ever since [Gray's note].

[22] *Delphi* site of the oracle of Apollo, the god of poetry.

[23] *Ilissus* a stream running past Athens.

Or where Mæander's amber waves[24]
In lingering Lab'rinths creep,
How do your tuneful Echoes languish,
Mute, but to the voice of Anguish?
Where each old poetic Mountain
Inspiration breathed around:
Every shade and hallowed Fountain
Murmured deep a solemn sound:
Till the sad Nine in Greece's evil hour[25]
Left their Parnassus for the Latian plains.[26]
Alike they scorn the pomp of tyrant Power,
And coward Vice, that revels in her chains.
When Latium had her lofty spirit lost,
They sought, O Albion! next thy sea-encircled coast.[27]

III.1

Far from the sun and summer-gale,[28]
In thy green lap was Nature's Darling laid,[29]
What time, where lucid Avon strayed,[30]
To Him the mighty Mother did unveil
Her awful face: the dauntless Child
Stretched forth his little arms, and smiled.
'This pencil take', she said 'whose colours clear
Richly paint the vernal year:
Thine too these golden keys, immortal Boy!
This can unlock the gates of Joy;
Of Horror that, and thrilling Fears,
Or ope the sacred source of sympathetic Tears'.

III.2

Nor second he, that rode sublime[31]
Upon the seraph-wings of Ecstasy,
The secrets of th' Abyss to spy.
He passed the flaming bounds of Place and Time:
The living Throne, the sapphire-blaze,
Where Angels tremble, while they gaze,
He saw; but blasted with excess of light,
Closed his eyes in endless night.[32]
Behold, where Dryden's less presumptuous car,[33]

Notes

[24] *Mæander* a winding river in Asia Minor.

[25] *the sad Nine* the Muses; *Greece's evil hour* when it was conquered by Alexander.

[26] *Parnassus* the mountain above Delphi sacred to the Muses; *Latian* Italian.

[27] *Albion* England, after its white (Latin, *albus*) cliffs.

[28] *gale* "A wind not tempestuous, yet stronger than a breeze" (Johnson).

[29] *Nature's Darling* Shakespeare [Gray's note].

[30] *Avon* the river that flows through Stratford, where Shakespeare was born.

[31] *He* Milton [Gray's note].

[32] *endless night* Milton became totally blind in the winter of 1650–1, well before he began work in earnest on *paradise Lost*.

[33] *car* chariot.

Wide o'er the fields of Glory bear
Two Coursers of ethereal race,[34]
With necks in thunder clothed, and long-resounding pace.

III.3

Hark, his hands the lyre explore![35]
Bright-eyed Fancy hovering o'er
Scatters from her pictured urn
Thoughts that breathe, and words, that burn.
But ah! 'tis heard no more–[36]
O lyre divine, what daring Spirit
Wakes thee now? though he inherit[37]
Nor the pride, nor ample pinion,[38]
That the Theban Eagle bear,[39]
Sailing with supreme dominion
Through the azure deep of air:
Yet oft before his infant eyes would run
Such forms, as glitter in the Muse's ray
With orient hues, unborrowed of the Sun:
Yet shall he mount, and keep his distant way
Beyond the limits of a vulgar fate,
Beneath the Good how far – but far above the Great.

Notes

[34] *Two Coursers of ethereal race* Meant to express the stately march and sounding energy of Dryden's rhymes [i.e., heroic couplets; Gray's note].

[35] *the lyre* lyric poetry, particularly his odes (see the selections from Dryden above).

[36] *'tis heard no more* We have had in our language no other odes of the sublime kind, than that of Dryden on St. Cecilia's day: for Cowley (who had his merit) yet wanted judgement, style, and harmony, for such a task. That of Pope is not worthy of so great a man. … [Gray's note].

[37] *he* Gray.

[38] *nor … nor* neither … nor.

[39] *Theban Eagle* Pindar compares himself to that bird, and his enemies to ravens that croak and clamour in vain below, while it pursues its flight regardless of their noise [Gray's note, citing *Olympian* 2.8].

William Collins (1721–1759)

A brilliant student at Winchester College and highly regarded at Oxford, Collins seemed bound for literary success when he graduated with his Bachelor of Arts degree in 1743. He arrived in London in 1744 and began making ambitious plans to write a *History of the Revival of Learning, 1300–1521*. Later he planned a translation of Aristotle's Poetics with a commentary. He evidently made progress on these projects, or spoke very plausibly about them, because both were publicly described by others as "in press." Nothing appeared, however, and there are reports that Collins spent a good deal of time going to assemblies or masques at Ranelagh and frequenting the playhouses. Collins was not altogether idle: in 1746 he wrote a series of odes published in that year as *Odes on Several Descriptive and Allegoric Subjects* (dated 1747). In the succeeding years he wrote a few more odes. Collins published very little, but his odes make a major contribution to English lyric poetry. They are less learned but more daring than Gray's odes; they link the poetry of the middle of the eighteenth century with the line of imaginative poetry established by Spenser and Milton; and they pave the way for the odes of John Keats. As small a body of work as Collins produced, British literature would be very different without him.

The facts are unclear, but Collins evidently became both physically and mentally ill around 1751. He traveled to Bath and to France for his health, but ended up confined in a madhouse for a while in England in 1754. Johnson visited him in Islington, London around this time, but evidence of his whereabouts and mental state are spotty. There were evidently periods of remission in the course of his disease, but after eight years of suffering what Johnson called "misery and degradation," Collins died at the age of thirty-seven.

The following texts are based on those in *Odes on Several Descriptive and Allegoric Subjects* (1747). The "Ode to Evening," however, was reprinted by Robert Dodsley in the second edition of his *A Collection of Poems by Several Hands* (1748), and I incorporate the changes introduced there. In doing so, I follow Richard Wendorf and Charles Ryskamp, editors of *The Works of William Collins* (Clarendon Press, 1979). I take advantage also of their commentary and that of Roger Lonsdale in his edition of Collins (Longman, 1969).

from *Odes on Several Descriptive and Allegoric Subjects* (1747)

Ode to Fear

Thou, to whom the World unknown
With all its shadowy Shapes is shown;
Who see'st appalled th' unreal Scene
While Fancy lifts the Veil between:
  Ah *Fear*! Ah frantic *Fear*!
  I see, I see Thee near.
I know thy hurried Step, thy haggard Eye!
Like Thee I start, like Thee disordered fly,

British Literature 1640–1789: An Anthology, Fourth Edition. Edited by Robert DeMaria, Jr.

For lo what *Monsters* in thy Train appear!
Danger, whose Limbs of Giant Mould
What mortal Eye can fixed behold?
Who stalks his Round, an hideous Form,
Howling amidst the Midnight Storm,
Or throws him on the ridgy Steep
Of some loose hanging Rock to sleep:
And with him thousand Phantoms joined,
Who prompt to Deeds accursed the Mind:
And those, the Fiends, who near allied,
O'er Nature's Wounds, and Wrecks preside;
Whilst *Vengeance*, in the lurid Air,
Lifts her red Arm, exposed and bare:
On whom that rav'ning Brood of Fate,[1]
Who lap the Blood of Sorrow, wait;
Who, *Fear*, this ghastly Train can see,
And look not madly wild, like Thee?

Epode

In earliest *Greece* to Thee with partial Choice,
The Grief-ful Muse addressed her infant Tongue;
The Maids and Matrons, on her awful Voice,
Silent and pale in wild Amazement hung.

Yet He the Bard who first invoked thy Name,[2]
Disdained in *Marathon* its Pow'r to feel:
For not alone he nursed the Poet's flame,
But reached from Virtue's Hand the Patriot's Steel.

But who is He whom later Garlands grace,[3]
Who left a-while o'er *Hybla*'s Dews to rove,[4]
With trembling Eyes thy dreary Steps to trace,
Where Thou and *Furies* shared the baleful Grove?[5]

Wrapped in thy cloudy Veil th' *Incestuous Queen*[6]
Sighed the sad Call her Son and Husband heared,[7]
When once alone it broke the silent Scene,
And He the Wretch of *Thebes* no more appeared.

Notes

ODE TO FEAR

1 *that rav'ning Brood of Fate* Alluding to the Κυνας αφυκτους [hounds which none can escape – the Furies] of Sophocles. See the *Electra* [l. 1388, where the case and order of words are different; Collins's note].

2 *the Bard* Aeschylus [Greek tragic poet who fought the Persians at the battle of Marathon; Collins's note].

3 *He* Sophocles, Greek tragic poet thirty years younger than Aeschylus.

4 *Hybla* a place in Sicily famous for honey; Sophocles was, like Xenophon, praised as a bee because of his fine style.

5 *Furies* the Eumenides, avenging deities, to whom "the baleful Grove" in Sophocles' *Oedipus at Colonus* is dedicated.

6 *Incestuous Queen* Jocasta [wife and mother of Oedipus, King of Thebes; Collins's note].

7 *the sad Call* Collins quotes *Oedipus at Colonus* ll. 1622–5, although the "call" comes from the heavens, not Jocasta.

O *Fear*, I know Thee by my throbbing Heart,
  Thy with'ring Pow'r inspired each mournful Line,
Though gentle *Pity* claim her mingled Part,[8]
  Yet all the Thunders of the Scene are thine!

Antistrophe

Thou who such weary Lengths hast passed,
Where wilt thou rest, mad Nymph, at last?
Say, wilt thou shroud in haunted Cell,[9]
Where gloomy *Rape* and *Murder* dwell?
Or in some hollowed Seat,
'Gainst which the big Waves beat,
Hear drowning Seamen's Cries in Tempests brought!
Dark Pow'r, with shudd'ring meek submitted Thought
Be mine, to read the Visions old,
Which thy awak'ning Bards have told:[10]
And lest thou meet my blasted View,[11]
Hold each strange tale devoutly true;
Ne'er be I found, by Thee o'erawed,
In that thrice-hallowed Eve abroad,[12]
When Ghosts, as Cottage-Maids believe,
Their pebbled Beds permitted leave,
And *Goblins* haunt from Fire, or Fen,
Or Mine, or Flood, the Walks of Men!
  O Thou whose Spirit most possessed
The sacred Seat of *Shakespeare*'s Breast!
But all that from thy Prophet broke,
In thy Divine Emotions spoke:
Hither again thy Fury deal,
Teach me but once like Him to feel:
His *Cypress Wreath* my Meed decree,[13]
And I, O *Fear*, will dwell with *Thee!*

Ode on the Poetical Character

I

As once, if not with light Regard,[1]
I read aright that gifted Bard[2]

Notes

[8] *Pity* in his *Poetics* Aristotle says tragedy must raise the emotions of fear and pity in the audience.

[9] *shroud* "To harbour; to take shelter" (Johnson).

[10] *awak'ning* exciting.

[11] *blasted* "confounded, struck with terror" (Johnson, sense 5), as though Fear were a Gorgon, blasting or killing those who look on her.

[12] *thrice-hallowed Eve* Hallowe'en, October 31.

[13] *Cypress Wreath* a triumphal crown for a tragic poet, because cypress is a funereal plant; *Meed* "Reward; recompense. Now rarely used" (Johnson).

Ode on the Poetical Character

[1] *Regard* attention.

[2] *Bard* Edmund Spenser, author of *The Faerie Queene*.

(Him whose School above the rest[3]
His Loveliest *Elfin* Queen has blessed),[4]
One, only One, unrivalled Fair,[5]
Might hope the magic Girdle wear,
At solemn Tourney hung on high,
The Wish of each love-darting Eye;
Lo! to each other Nymph in turn applied,
As if, in Air unseen, some hov'ring Hand,
Some chaste and Angel-Friend to Virgin-Fame,
With whispered Spell had burst the starting Band,
It left unblessed her loathed dishonoured Side;
Happier hopeless Fair, if never
Her baffled Hand with vain Endeavour
Had touched that fatal Zone to her denied![6]
Young *Fancy* thus, to me Divinest Name,
To whom, prepared and bathed in Heav'n,
The Cest[7] of amplest Pow'r is giv'n:
To few the God-like Gift assigns,
To gird their blessed prophetic Loins,
And gaze her Visions wild, and feel unmixed her Flame!

2

The Band, as Fairy Legends say,
Was wove on that creating Day,[8]
When He, who called with Thought to Birth
Yon tented Sky, this laughing Earth,
And dressed with Springs, and Forest tall,
And poured the Main engirting all,
Long by the loved *Enthusiast* wooed,[9]
Himself in some Diviner Mood,
Retiring, sate with her alone,
And placed her on his Sapphire Throne,
The whiles, the vaulted Shrine around,
Seraphic Wires were heard to sound,[10]
Now sublimest Triumph swelling,
Now on Love and Mercy dwelling;
And she, from out the veiling Cloud,
Breathed her magic Notes aloud:
And Thou, Thou rich-haired Youth of Morn,[11]

Notes

3 *School* numerous writers followed in Spenser's "school" (or tradition), including Milton (see ll. 55–76).

4 *Elfin Queen* Spenser's Land of Faerie is a place of the imagination, so its queen is a center of poetic inspiration, a muse (although the allegory also has a political dimension, in which the queen is Elizabeth I).

5 *unrivalled Fair* Florimel [Collins's note, with a reference to *The Faerie Queene* (4.5.1–20); a pretend Florimel wins the beauty contest described there, but she cannot don the girdle for the reasons Collins states; the true Florimel gets the girdle back at 5.3.27–8].

6 *Zone* the girdle or belt.

7 *Cest* belt or girdle, particularly the one belonging to Aphrodite, which she loans to Hera (*Iliad*, 14.214–21).

8 *that creating Day* the fourth day of creation; see *Paradise Lost* 7.339–56.

9 *by* beside; *Enthusiast Fancy*, l.17.

10 *Wires* strings of a harp or other instrument.

11 *rich-haired Youth of Morn* the sun and Apollo, god of the sun and of poetry.

And all thy subject Life was born!
The dang'rous Passions kept aloof,
Far from the sainted growing Woof:[12]
But near it sate Ecstatic *Wonder*,
List'ning the deep applauding Thunder:
And *Truth*, in sunny Vest arrayed,
By whose the Tarsel's Eyes were made;[13]
All the shad'wy Tribes of *Mind*,
In braided Dance their Murmurs joined,
And all the bright uncounted *Pow'rs*,
Who feed on Heav'n's ambrosial Flow'rs.[14]
Where is the Bard, whose Soul can now
Its high presuming Hopes avow?
Where He who thinks, with Rapture blind,
This hallowed Work for Him designed?[15]

3

High on some Cliff, to Heav'n up-piled
Of rude Accéss, of Prospect wild,[16]
Where, tangled round the jealous Steep,
Strange Shades o'erbore the Valleys deep,
And holy Genii guard the Rock,[17]
Its Glooms embrown, its Springs unlock,
While on its rich ambitious Head,
An Eden, like his own, lies spread:
I view that Oak, the fancied Glades among,[18]
  By which as Milton lay, His Evening Ear,
From many a Cloud that dropped Ethereal Dew,
  Nigh sphered in Heav'n its native Strains could hear:
On which that ancient Trump he reached was hung;
  Thither oft his Glory greeting,
  From *Waller*'s Myrtle Shades retreating,[19]
With many a Vow from Hope's aspiring Tongue,
My trembling Feet his guiding Steps pursue;
In vain – Such Bliss to One alone,
Of all the Sons of Soul was known,
And Heav'n, and Fancy, *kindred* Pow'rs,
Have now o'erturned th' inspiring Bow'rs,
Or curtained close such Scene from every future View.

Notes

[12] *sainted* "Holy; sacred" (Johnson); *Woof* woven cloth, tapestry.

[13] *By whose* on the model of whose (eyes); *Tarsel* Tercel, or male hawk.

[14] *ambrosial Flow'rs* see *Paradise Lost* 2.245.

[15] *This hallowed Work* the girdle.

[16] *Of rude Accéss* this phrase and the whole description of Mount Parnassus (sacred to Apollo and poetry) recall Milton's descriptions of Eden as it appeared to those, like Satan, who sought entrance from without (*Paradise Lost* 4.132–8; 172–7; 543–50).

[17] *Genii* more than one genius, "The protecting or ruling power of men, places, or things" (Johnson).

[18] *that Oak* a reference to the place where Milton receives poetic inspiration in *Il Penseroso* (l. 60).

[19] *Waller* Edmund (1606–87), a poet whom Dryden (Preface to the *Fables*, 1700) identified as belonging to a different poetic school than Spenser and Milton; *Myrtle* "A fragrant tree sacred to Venus" (Johnson).

from *A Collection of Poems by Several Hands* (1748)

Ode to Evening

If aught of Oaten Stop, or Pastoral Song,[1]
May hope, chaste *Eve*, to soothe thy modest Ear,
Like thy own solemn Springs,
Thy Springs and dying Gales,[2]
O *Nymph* reserved, while now the bright-haired Sun
Sits in yon western Tent, whose cloudy Skirts,
With Brede ethereal wove,[3]
O'erhang his wavy Bed:
Now Air is hushed, save where the weak-eyed Bat,
With short shrill Shriek, flits by on leathern Wing,
Or where the Beetle winds
His small but sullen Horn,
As oft he rises 'midst the twilight Path,
Against the Pilgrim borne in heedless Hum:[4]
Now teach me, *Maid* composed,
To breathe some softened Strain,
Whose Numbers stealing through thy dark'ning Vale[5]
May not unseemly with its Stillness suit,
As musing slow, I hail
Thy genial loved Return!
For when thy folding Star arising shows[6]
His paly Circlet, at his warning Lamp
The fragrant *Hours*, and *Elves*[7]
Who slept in Flow'rs the Day,
And many a *Nymph* who wreathes her Brows with Sedge,
And sheds the fresh'ning Dew, and, lovelier still,
The *Pensive Pleasures* sweet,
Prepare thy shadowy Car.[8]
Then lead, calm *Vot'ress*, where some sheety Lake[9]
Cheers the lone Heath, or some time-hallowed Pile,[10]
Or up-land Fallows grey
Reflect its last cool Gleam.
But when chill blust'ring Winds, or driving Rain,
Forbid my willing Feet, be mine the Hut
That from the Mountain's Side

Notes

Ode to Evening

[1] *Oaten Stop* a finger hole on a rustic flute, and hence the flute itself, which, with the lyre, accompanied the performance of classical odes.

[2] *Gale* "A wind not tempestuous, yet stronger than a breeze" (Johnson).

[3] *Brede* braid, "Applied by the poets to things that show or suggest interweaving of colours, or embroidery" (*OED*).

[4] *Pilgrim* "A traveller; a wanderer" (Johnson).

[5] *Numbers* "Harmony" (Johnson).

[6] *folding Star* an evening star signaling the time for shepherds to fold or pen their sheep.

[7] *Hours* the Horae, minor goddesses of natural order.

[8] *Car* chariot.

[9] *Vot'ress* "A woman devoted to any worship or state" (Johnson).

[10] *Pile* building.

Views Wilds, and swelling Floods,
And Hamlets brown, and dim-discovered Spires,
And hears their simple Bell, and marks o'er all
Thy Dewy Fingers draw
The gradual dusky Veil.
While *Spring* shall pour his Show'rs, as oft he wont,[11]
And bathe thy breathing Tresses, meekest *Eve*!
While *Summer* loves to sport
Beneath thy ling'ring Light;
While sallow *Autumn* fills thy Lap with Leaves;
Or *Winter*, yelling through the troublous Air,
Affrights thy shrinking Train,
And rudely rends thy Robes;
So long, sure-found beneath the Sylvan Shed,
Shall *Fancy, Friendship, Science*, rose-lipp'd *Health*,[12]
Thy gentlest Influence own,
And hymn thy favourite Name!

Notes

[11] *wont* is accustomed to do.
[12] *Science* knowledge.

Mary Leapor (1722–1746)

Leapor's father was a gardener in Northamptonshire, and she worked for a time in the kitchen of an estate near Brackley. Despite discouragement from her mother and other local folk, from an early age Leapor spent her time reading and, much more unusually for a woman, writing. Her poems circulated in manuscript and came to the attention of Bridget Freemantle, daughter of the former rector of Hinton. Freemantle became Leapor's friend, patron, and, after Leapor's very early death, her literary executor. She saw two volumes of Leapor's poems through subscription publication, both called *Poems on Several Occasions* (1748 and 1751). The second volume was printed by Samuel Richardson, who also participated in editing it, with some members of his literary circle. Richardson described Leapor's poems as "sweetly easy." They are easy in that they are not highly allusive or learned, but many of Leapor's poems have a satiric edge as well as a country sweetness. As a versifier, she was an imitator of Alexander Pope, but her sphere is rural and domestic. Her manor poem, "Crumble-Hall," is altogether different in feeling from Pope's great house poem *Windsor Forest*. Her "Epistle to a Lady" incorporates some elements of Pope's poem of the same name, but there is again a sharp contrast in feeling and, quite obviously, in point of view. Like many other women writers of the period, Leapor regularly used poetic names for herself and for friends who appear in her verse: Mira is her name for herself and Artemisia for her patron, Bridget Freemantle.

The texts presented here are based on the first editions. *The Works of Mary Leapor* is edited by Richard Greene and Ann Messenger (Oxford University Press, 2003). For an insightful reading of "Crumble-Hall," see Donna Landry, "Mary Leapor Laughs at the Fathers," in *British Literature 1640–1789: A Critical Reader* (Blackwell, 1999).

from *Poems on Several Occasions* (1748)

The Month of August

Sylvanus, *a Courtier*. Phillis, *a Country Maid*.

SYLVANUS

Hail, *Phillis*, brighter than a Morning Sky,
Joy of my Heart, and Darling of my Eye;
See the kind Year her grateful Tribute yields,
And round-faced Plenty triumphs o'er the Fields.
But to yon Gardens let me lead thy Charms,
Where the curled Vine extends her willing Arms:
Whose purple Clusters lure the longing Eye,
And the ripe Cherries show their scarlet Dye.

PHILLIS

Not all the Sights your bloated Gardens yield,
Are half so lovely as my Father's Field,
Where large Increase has blessed the fruitful Plain,

British Literature 1640–1789: An Anthology, Fourth Edition. Edited by Robert DeMaria, Jr.

And we with Joy behold the swelling Grain,
Whose heavy Ears towards the Earth reclined,
Wave, nod, and tremble to the whisking Wind.

SYLVANUS

But see, to emulate those Cheeks of thine,
On yon fair Tree the blushing Nect'rins shine:
Beneath their Leaves the ruddy Peaches glow,
And the plump Figs compose a gallant Show.
With gaudy Plums see yonder Boughs recline,
And ruddy Pears in yon *Espalier* twine.
There humble Dwarfs in pleasing Order stand,
Whose golden Product seems to court thy Hand.

PHILLIS

In vain you tempt me while our Orchard bears
Long-keeping Russets, lovely Cath'rine Pears,
Pearmains and Codlings, wheaten Plums enough,[1]
And the black Damsons load the bending Bough.
No Pruning-knives our fertile Branches tease,
While yours must grow but as their Masters please.
The grateful Trees our Mercy well repay,
And rain us Bushels at the rising Day.

SYLVANUS

Fair are my Gardens, yet you slight them all;
Then let us haste to yon majestic Hall,
Where the glad Roofs shall to thy Voice Resound,
Thy Voice more sweet than Music's melting Sound:
Now *Órion*'s Beam infests the sultry Sky,[2]
And scorching Fevers through the Welkin fly;
But Art shall teach us to evade his Ray,
And the forced Fountains near the Windows play;
There choice Perfumes shall give a pleasing Gale,[3]
And Orange-flow'rs their od'rous Breath exhale,
While on the Walls the well-wrought Paintings glow,
And dazzling Carpets deck the Floors below:
O tell me, Thou whose careless Beauties charm,
Are these not fairer than a Thresher's Barn?

PHILLIS

Believe me, I can find no Charms at all
In your fine Carpets and your painted Hall.
'Tis true our Parlour has an earthen Floor,

Notes

The Month of August

[1] *Russets ... Pearmains and Codlings* varieties of apple.

[2] *Orion* the constellation in the ascendant at the warmest time of year.

[3] *Gale* breeze.

The Sides of Plaster and of Elm the Door:
Yet the rubbed Chest and Table sweetly shines,
And the spread Mint along the Window climbs:
An agèd Laurel keeps away the Sun,
And two cool Streams across the Garden run.

SYLVANUS

Can Feasts or Music win my lovely maid?
In both those Pleasures be her Taste obeyed.
The ransacked Earth shall all its Dainties send,
Till with its Load her plenteous Tables bend.
Then to the Roofs the swelling Notes shall rise,
Pierce the glad Air and gain upon the Skies,
While Ease and Rapture spreads itself around,
And distant Hills roll back the charming Sound.

PHILLIS

Not this will lure me, for I'd have you know
This Night to feast with *Corydon* I go:
To Night his Reapers bring the gathered Grain,
Home to his Barns, and leave the naked Plain:
Then Beef and Coleworts, Beans and Bacon too,[4]
And the Plum-pudding of delicious Hue,
Sweet-spiced Cake, and Apple-pies good Store,
Deck the brown Board; who can desire more?
His Flute and Tabor too *Amyntor* brings,[5]
And while he plays soft *Amaryllis* sings.
Then strive no more to win a simple maid,
From her loved Cottage and her silent Shade.
Let *Phillis* ne'er, ah never let her rove
From her first Virtue and her humble grove.
Go seek some Nymph that equals your Degree,
And leave Content and *Corydon* for me.

An Epistle to a Lady

In vain, dear Madam, yes, in vain you strive,
Alas! to make your luckless *Mira* thrive,[1]
For *Tycho* and *Copernicus* agree,[2]
No golden Planet bent its Rays on me.[3]

Notes

4 *Coleworts* cabbages.
5 *Tabor* a kind of drum.

An Epistle to a Lady
1 *Mira* Leapor's poetic name for herself.
2 *Tycho* Tycho Brahe (1546–1601), Danish astronomer who rejected Copernican theory.
3 *No golden planet bent its rays on me* her astrological chart is not favorable.

'Tis twenty Winters, if it is no more,
To speak the Truth it may be Twenty four:
As many Springs their 'pointed Space have run,
Since *Mira*'s eyes first opened on the Sun.
'Twas when the Flocks on slabby Hillocks lie,
And the cold Fishes rule the wat'ry sky:[4]
But though these eyes the learnèd page explore,
And turn the pond'rous volumes o'er and o'er,
I find no comfort from their systems flow,
But am dejected more as more I know.
Hope shines a while, but like a vapour flies
(The fate of all the curious and the wise),
For, ah! cold Saturn triumphed on that day,[5]
And frowning Sol denied his golden ray.[6]

You see I'm learnèd, and I show't the more,
That none may wonder when they find me poor.
Yet *Mira* dreams, as slumb'ring poets may,
And rolls in Treasures till the breaking Day,
While Books and Pictures in bright Order rise,
And painted Parlours swim before her Eyes:
Till the shrill Clock impertinently rings,
And the soft Visions move their shining Wings:
Then *Mira* wakes, – her Pictures are no more,
And through her Fingers slides the vanished Ore.
Convinced too soon, her Eye unwilling falls
On the blue Curtains and the dusty Walls:
She wakes, alas! to Business and to Woes,
To sweep her Kitchen, and to mend her Clothes.

But see pale Sickness with her languid Eyes,
At whose Appearance all Delusion flies:
The World recedes, its Vanities decline,
Clorinda's Features seem as faint as mine:
Gay Robes no more the aching Sight admires,
Wit grates the Ear, and melting Music tires.
Its wonted Pleasures with each Sense decay,[7]
Books please no more, and Paintings fade away,
The sliding Joys in misty Vapours end:
Yet let me still, ah! let me grasp a Friend:
And when each Joy, when each loved Object flies,
Be you the last that leaves my closing Eyes.

Notes

[4] *Fishes* the constellation Pisces, a water sign, which "rules" in late winter.

[5] *Saturn* "The remotest planet of the Solar System, supposed by astrologers to impress melancholy, dullness, or severity of temper" (Johnson).

[6] *Sol* the sun.

[7] *wonted* customary.

But how will this dismantled Soul appear,
When stripped of all it lately held so dear,
Forced from its Prison of expiring Clay,
Afraid and shivering at the doubtful Way?

Yet did these Eyes a dying Parent see,
Loosed from all Cares except a Thought for me,
Without a Tear resign her shortening Breath,
And dauntless meet the lingering Stroke of Death.
Then at th' Almighty's Sentence shall I mourn,
'Of Dust thou art, to Dust shalt thou return?'
Or shall I wish to stretch the Line of Fate,
That the dull Years may bear a longer Date,
To share the Follies of succeeding Times
With more Vexations and with deeper Crimes?
Ah no – though Heav'n brings near the final Day,
For such a Life I will not, dare not pray;
But let the Tear for future Mercy flow,
And fall resigned beneath the mighty Blow.
Nor I alone – for through the spacious Ball,
With me will Numbers of all Ages fall:
And the same Day that *Mira* yields her Breath,
Thousands may enter through the Gates of Death.

Mira's Will

IMPRIMIS – My departed Shade I trust[1]
To Heav'n – My Body to the silent Dust;
My Name to public Censure I submit,
To be disposed of as the World thinks fit;
My Vice and Folly let Oblivion close,
The World already is o'erstocked with those;
My Wit I give, as Misers give their Store,
To those who think they had enough before.
Bestow my Patience to compose the Lives
Of slighted Virgins and neglected Wives;
To modish Lovers I resign my Truth,
My cool Reflection to unthinking Youth;
And some Good-nature give ('tis my Desire)
To surly Husbands, as their Needs require;
And first discharge my Funeral – and then
To the small Poets I bequeath my Pen.

Let a small Sprig (true Emblem of my Rhyme)
Of blasted Laurel on my Hearse recline;[2]

Notes

Mira's Will
[1] *IMPRIMIS* in the first place.
[2] *blasted Laurel* bay laurel, symbolic of poetic achievement, withered by weather or the change of seasons.

Let some grave Wight, that struggles for renown
By chanting Dirges through a Market-Town,
With gentle Step precede the solemn Train;
A broken Flute upon his Arm shall lean.[3]
Six comic Poets may the Corse surround,
And All Free-holders, if they can be found:[4]
Then follow the next melancholy Throng,
As shrewd Instructors, who themselves are wrong:
The Virtuoso, rich in Sun-dried Weeds,[5]
The Politician, whom no Mortal heeds,
The silent Lawyer, chambered all the day,
And the stern Soldier that receives no Pay.
But stay – the Mourners should be first our care:
Let the freed 'Prentice lead the Miser's Heir;
Let the young Relict wipe her mournful Eye,[6]
And widowed Husbands o'er their Garlic cry.

All this let my executors fulfil,
And rest assured that this is *Mira*'s will,
Who was, when she these legacies designed,
In body healthy, and composed in mind.

from *Poems on Several Occasions* (1751)

An Essay on Woman

Woman, a pleasing but a short-lived Flow'r,
Too soft for Business and too weak for Pow'r:
A Wife in Bondage, or neglected Maid;
Despised, if ugly; if she's fair, Betrayed.
'Tis Wealth alone inspires every Grace,
And calls the Raptures to her plenteous Face.
What Numbers for those charming Features pine,
If blooming Acres round her Temples twine!
Her Lip the Strawberry, and her Eyes more bright
Than sparkling Venus in a frosty Night;
Pale Lilies fade and, when the Fair appears,
Snow turns a Negro and dissolves in Tears,
And, where the Charmer treads her magic Toe,
On *English* ground *Arabian* odours grow;[1]
Till mighty Hymen lifts his sceptred Rod,[2]
And sinks her Glories with a fatal Nod,
Dissolves her Triumphs, sweeps her Charms away,
And turns the Goddess to her native Clay.

Notes

3 *Flute* symbolic of lyric poetry.

4 *Free-holder* one who owns property or holds it free from seizure for his lifetime.

5 *Virtuoso* natural scientist.

6 *relict* widow.

AN ESSAY ON WOMAN

1 *Arabian odours* Arabia was an old source of aromatic spices and gums.

2 *Hymen* god of marriage.

But, *Artemisia*, let your Servant sing
What small Advantage Wealth and Beauties bring.
Who would be Wise, that knew *Pamphilia*'s fate?
Or who be Fair, and joined to *Sylvia*'s mate?
Sylvia, whose Cheeks are fresh as early Day,
As Evening mild, and sweet as spicy May:
And yet that Face her partial Husband tires,
And those bright Eyes, that all the World admires.
Pamphilia's Wit who does not strive to shun,
Like Death's Infection or a Dog-day's Sun?[3]
The Damsels view her with malignant Eyes,
The Men are vexed to find a Nymph so Wise:
And Wisdom only serves to make her know
The keen Sensation of superior Woe.
The secret Whisper and the list'ning Ear,
The scornful Eyebrow and the hated Sneer,
The giddy Censures of her babbling Kind,
With thousand Ills that grate a gentle Mind,
By her are tasted in the first Degree,
Though overlooked by *Simplicus* and me.
Does thirst of Gold a Virgin's Heart inspire,
Instilled by Nature or a careful Sire?
Then let her quit Extravagance and Play,
The brisk Companion and expensive Tea,
To feast with *Cordia* in her filthy Sty
On stewed Potatoes or on a mouldy Pie;
Whose eager Eyes stare ghastly at the Poor,
And fright the Beggars from her hated Door;
In greasy Clouts she wraps her smoky Chin,[4]
And holds that Pride's a never-pardoned Sin.
If this be Wealth, no matter where it falls;
But save, ye Muses, save your *Mira*'s walls:
Still give me pleasing Indolence and Ease,
A Fire to warm me and a Friend to please.
Since, whether sunk in Avarice or Pride,
A wanton Virgin or a starving Bride,
Or wond'ring Crowds attend her charming Tongue,
Or, deemed an Idiot, ever speaks the Wrong;
Though Nature armed us for the growing Ill
With fraudful Cunning and a headstrong Will;
Yet, with ten thousand Follies to her Charge,
Unhappy Woman's but a Slave at large.

Notes

[3] *Dog-day's* late summer, when Sirius, the Dog Star, is prominent in the sky.

[4] *Clouts* rags.

Crumble-Hall

When Friends or Fortune frown on *Mira*'s Lay,
Or gloomy Vapours hide the Lamp of Day;
With low'ring Forehead, and with aching Limbs,
Oppressed with Head-ache, and eternal Whims,
Sad *Mira* vows to quit the darling Crime:
Yet takes her Farewell, and repents, in Rhyme.

But see (more charming than *Armida*'s Wiles)
The Sun returns, and *Artemisia*[1] smiles:
Then in a trice the Resolutions fly;
And who so frolic as the Muse and I?
We sing once more, obedient to her Call;
Once more we sing; and 'tis of *Crumble-Hall*;[2]
That *Crumble-Hall*, whose hospitable Door
Has fed the Stranger, and relieved the Poor;
Whose *Gothic* Towers, and whose rusty Spires,
Were known of old to Knights, and hungry Squires.
There powdered Beef, and Warden-Pies, were found;[3]
And Pudden dwelt within her spacious Bound:
Pork, Peas, and Bacon (good old *English* Fare!),
With tainted Ven'son, and with hunted Hare:[4]
With humming Beer her Vats were wont to flow,[5]
And ruddy *Nectar* in her Vaults to glow.[6]
Here came the Wights, who battled for Renown,
The sable Friar, and the russet Clown:
The loaded Tables sent a sav'ry Gale,[7]
And the brown bowls were crowned with simp'ring Ale;[8]
While the Guests ravaged on the smoking Store,
Till their stretched Girdles would contain no more.

Of this rude Palace might a Poet sing
From cold *December* to returning Spring;
Tell how the Building spreads on either hand,
And two grim Giants o'er the Portals stand;
Whose grizzled Beards are neither combed nor shorn,[9]
But look severe, and horribly adorn.

Then step within – there stands a goodly Row
Of oaken Pillars – where a gallant Show

Notes

CRUMBLE-HALL

1 *Artemisia* Leapor's poetic name for her patron, Bridget Freemantle.

2 *Crumble-Hall* the model for this was Edgcote House, where Leapor was employed as a kitchen-maid.

3 *powdered* salted or pickled, preserved; *Warden-Pies* warden was a kind of baking pear.

4 *tainted* "Imbued with the scent of an animal (usually a hunted animal)" (*OED*).

5 *humming* strong, as well as frothing; *wont* accustomed.

6 *ruddy Nectar* cider.

7 *gale* a breeze.

8 *simp'ring* simmering.

9 *grilled* helmeted; grills are the bars on a knight's helmet.

Of mimic Pears and carved Pom'granates twine,
With the plump Clusters of the spreading Vine.
Strange Forms above, present themselves to View;
Some mouths that grin, some smile, and some that spew.
Here a soft Maid or Infant seems to cry:
Here stares a Tyrant, with distorted Eye:
The Roof – no *Cyclops* e'er could reach so high:
Not *Polypheme*, though, formed for dreadful Harms,[10]
The Top could measure with extended Arms.
Here the pleased Spider plants her peaceful Loom:
Here weaves secure, nor dreads the hated Broom.
But at the Head (and furbished once a Year)
The Herald's mystic Compliments appear:
Round the fierce Dragon *Honi Soit* twines,[11]
And Royal *Edward* o'er the Chimney shines.

Safely the Mice through yon dark Passage run,
Where the dim Windows ne'er admit the Sun.
Along each Wall the Stranger blindly feels;
And (trembling) dreads a Spectre at his heels.

The sav'ry Kitchen much Attention calls:
Westphalia Hams adorn the sable Walls:
The Fires blaze; the greasy Pavements fry;
And steaming Odours from the Kettles fly.

See! yon brown Parlour on the Left appears,
For nothing famous, but its leathern Chairs,
Whose shining Nails like polished Armour glow,
And the dull Clock beats audible and slow.
But on the Right we spy a Room more fair:
The Form – 'tis neither long, nor round, nor square;
The Walls how lofty, and the Floor how wide,
We leave for learned *Quadrus* to decide.
Gay *China* Bowls o'er the broad Chimney shine,
Whose long Description would be too sublime:
And much might of the Tapestry be sung:
But we're content to say, The Parlour's hung.

We count the Stairs, and to the Right ascend,
Where on the Walls the gorgeous Colours blend.
There doughty *George* bestrides the goodly Steed;[12]
The Dragon's slaughtered, and the Virgin freed:

Notes

10 *Polypheme* the name of the cyclops (a race of one-eyed giants) whom Odysseus outwits.

11 *Honi Soit Honi soit qui mal y pense*, "evil to him who thinks evil," the motto of the Most Noble Order of the Garter, founded by Edward III in 1348.

12 *George* St. George, the patron saint of the Order of the Garter.

And there (but lately rescued from their Fears)
The Nymph and serious *Ptolemy* appears:[13]
Their awkward Limbs unwieldy are displayed;
And, like a Milk-wench, glares the royal Maid.

From hence we turn to more familiar Rooms;
Whose Hangings ne'er were wrought in *Grecian* Looms:[14]
Yet the soft Stools, and eke the lazy Chair,
To sleep invite the Weary, and the Fair.

Shall we proceed? – Yes, if you'll break the Wall:
If not, return, and tread once more the Hall.
Up ten Stone Steps now please to drag your Toes,
And a brick Passage will succeed to those.
Here the strong Doors were aptly framed to hold
Sir *Wary*'s Person, and Sir *Wary*'s Gold.
Here *Biron* sleeps, with Books encircled round;
And him you'd guess a Student most profound,
Not so – in Form the dusty Volumes stand:
There's few that wear the Mark of *Biron*'s Hand.

Would you go further? – Stay a little then:
Back through the Passage – down the Steps again;
Through yon dark Room – Be careful how you tread
Up these steep Stairs – or you may break your Head.
These Rooms are furnished amiably, and full:
Old Shoes, and Sheep-ticks bred in Stacks of Wool;
Grey *Dobbin*'s Gears, and Drenching-Horns enow;[15]
Wheel-spokes – the Irons of a tattered Plough.

No further – Yes, a little higher, pray:
At yon small Door you'll find the Beams of Day,
While the hot Leads return the scorching Ray.[16]
Here a gay Prospect meets the ravished Eye:
Meads, Fields, and Groves, in beauteous Order lie.
From hence the Muse precipitant is hurled,
And drags down *Mira* to the nether World.

Thus far the Palace – Yet there still remain
Unsung the Gardens and the menial Train.
Its Groves anon – its People first we sing:
Hear, *Artemisia*, hear the Song we bring.
Sophronia first in Verse shall learn to chime,
And keep her Station, though in *Mira*'s Rhyme;

Notes

[13] *Ptolemy* first-century CE astronomer, author of the *Almagest*, an encyclopedic work.

[14] *Grecian Looms* synonymous with fine weaving.

[15] *Drenching-Horn* an instrument for administering medicine to a horse.

[16] *Leads* lead roofs.

Sophronia sage! whose learned Knuckles know
To form round Cheese-cakes of the pliant Dough;
To bruise the Curd, and through her Fingers squeeze
Ambrosial Butter with the tempered Cheese:
Sweet Tarts and Pudden, too, her Skill declare;
And the soft Jellies, hid from baneful Air.

O'er the warm Kettles, and the sav'ry Steams,
Grave *Colinettus* of his Oxen dreams:
Then starting, anxious for his new-mown Hay,
Runs headlong out to view the doubtful Day:
But Dinner calls with more prevailing Charms;
And surly *Grusso* in his awkward Arms
Bears the tall Jug, and turns a glaring Eye,
As though he feared some Insurrection nigh
From the fierce Crew, that gaping stand a-dry.

O'er-stuffed with Beef; with Cabbage much too full,
And Dumpling too (fit Emblem of his Skull!)
With Mouth wide open, but with closing Eyes
Unwieldy *Roger* on the Table lies.
His able Lungs discharge a rattling Sound:
Prince barks, *Spot* howls, and the tall Roofs rebound.
Him *Urs'la* views; and, with dejected Eyes,
'Ah! *Roger*, Ah!' the mournful Maiden cries:
Is wretched *Ur'sla* then your Care no more,
That, while I sigh, thus you can sleep and snore?
Ingrateful *Roger*! wilt thou leave me now?
For you these Furrows mark my fading Brow:
For you my Pigs resign their Morning Due:
My hungry Chickens lose their Meat for you:
And, was it not, Ah! was it not for thee,
No goodly Pottage would be dressed by me.
For thee these Hands wind up the whirling Jack,[17]
Or place the Spit across the sloping Rack.
I baste the Mutton with a cheerful Heart,
Because I know my *Roger* will have Part'.

Thus she – But now her Dish-kettle began
To boil and blubber with the foaming Bran.
The greasy Apron round her Hips she ties,
And to each Plate the scalding Clout applies:[18]
The purging Bath each glowing Dish refines,
And once again the polished Pewter shines.

Notes

[17] *Jack* an instrument for turning the *Spit* in cooking over the *Rack*, or grate, of an open fire.

[18] *Clout* "A cloth for any mean use" (Johnson).

Now to those Meads let frolic Fancy rove,[19]
Where o'er yon Waters nods a pendent Grove;[20]
In whose clear Waves the pictured Boughs are seen,
With fairer Blossoms, and a brighter Green.
Soft flow'ry Banks the spreading Lakes divide:
Sharp-pointed Flags adorn each tender Side.
See! the pleased Swans along the Surface play;
Where yon cool Willows meet the scorching Ray,
When fierce *Orion* gives too warm a Day.[21]

But, hark! what Scream the wond'ring Ear invades!
The *Dryads* howling for their threatened Shades:[22]
Round the dear Grove each Nymph distracted flies
(Though not discovered but with Poet's Eyes):
And shall those Shades, where *Philomela*'s Strain[23]
Has oft to Slumber lulled the hapless Swain;
Where Turtles used to clap their silken Wings;[24]
Whose rev'rend Oaks have known a hundred Springs;
Shall these ignobly from their Roots be torn,
And perish shameful, as the abject Thorn;
While the slow Car bears off their aged Limbs,[25]
To clear the Way for Slopes, and modern Whims;
Where banished Nature leaves a barren Gloom,
And awkward Art Supplies the vacant Room?
Yet (or the Muse for Vengeance calls in vain)
The injured Nymphs shall haunt the ravaged Plain:
Strange Sounds and Forms shall tease the gloomy Green;
And Fairy-Elves by *Urs'la* shall be seen:
Their new-built Parlour shall with Echoes ring:
And in their Hall shall doleful Crickets sing.

Then cease, *Diracto*, stay thy desp'rate Hand;
And let the Grove, if not the Parlour, stand.

Man the Monarch

Amazed we read of Nature's early Throes,
How the fair Heav'ns and pond'rous Earth arose;
How blooming Trees unplanted first began;
And Beasts submissive to their Tyrant, Man:
To Man, invested with despotic Sway,
While his mute Brethren tremble and obey;

Notes

19 *Meads* meadows.
20 *pendent* hanging, or weeping, like a willow.
21 *Orion* a constellation in the ascension in midsummer; Sirius, the star representing Orion's dog, brings in the dog-days of late summer.
22 *Dryads* demigoddesses of the forest.
23 *Philomela* the nightingale.
24 *Turtles* turtledoves.
25 *Car* wagon.

Till Heav'n beheld him insolently vain,
And checked the Limits of his haughty Reign.
Then from their Lord the rude Deserters fly,
And grinning back, his fruitless Rage defy;
Pards, Tigers, Wolves to gloomy Shades retire,
And Mountain-Goats in purer Gales respire.[1]
To humble Valleys, where soft Flow'rs blow,
And fatt'ning Streams in crystal mazes flow,
Full of new Life, the untamed coursers run,
And roll and wanton in the cheerful Sun;
Round their gay Hearts in dancing Spirits rise,
And rouse the Lightnings in their rolling Eyes:
To craggy Rocks destructive Serpents glide,
Whose mossy Crannies hide their speckled Pride;
And monstrous Whales on foamy Billows ride.
Then joyful Birds ascend their native Sky:
But where! ah, where shall helpless Woman fly?

Here smiling Nature brought her choicest Stores,
And roseate Beauty on her favourite Pours:
Pleased with her Labour, the officious Dame[2]
Withheld no Grace would deck the rising Frame.
Then viewed her Work, and viewed and smiled again,
And kindly whispered, 'Daughter, live and reign'.
But now the Matron mourns her latest Care,
And sees the Sorrows of her darling Fair;
Beholds a Wretch, whom she designed a Queen,
And weeps that e'er she formed the weak Machine.
In vain she boasts her Lip of scarlet dyes,
Cheeks like the Morning, and far-beaming Eyes;
Her Neck refulgent, fair and feeble Arms –
A Set of useless and neglected Charms.
She suffers Hardship with afflictive Moans:
Small tasks of Labour suit her slender Bones.
Beneath a Load her weary Shoulders yield,
Nor can her Fingers grasp the sounding Shield;
She sees and trembles at approaching Harms,
And Fear and Grief destroy her fading Charms.
Then her pale Lips no pearly Teeth disclose,
And Time's rude sickle cuts the yielding Rose.
Thus wretched woman's short-lived Merit dies:
In vain to Wisdom's sacred Help she flies,
Or sparkling Wit but lends a feeble Aid:
'Tis all Delirium from a wrinkled Maid.

Notes

MAN THE MONARCH

[1] *Gales* breezes; *respire* breathe.

[2] *officious* kind.

A tattling Dame, no matter where or who –
Me it concerns not, and it need not you –
Once told this Story to the list'ning Muse,
Which we, as now it serves our Turn, shall use.

When our Grandsire named the feathered Kind,
Pondering their Natures in his careful Mind,
'Twas then, if on our Author we rely,
He viewed his Consort with an envious Eye;
Greedy of Power, he hugged the tott'ring Throne,
Pleased with the Homage, and would reign alone;
And, better to secure his doubtful Rule,
Rolled his wise Eyeballs, and pronounced her *Fool*.
The regal Blood to distant Ages runs:
Sires, Brothers, Husbands, and commanding Sons,
The Sceptre claim; and every Cottage brings
A long Succession of domestic Kings.

Christopher Smart (1722–1771)

Some time in late 1758 or early 1759, Smart entered a private asylum for the insane near London and remained there for at least four years. He was troubled for a few years before that; it is hard to determine if his illness was primarily physical or psychological, but it clearly rendered him mentally infirm. When he emerged from his disease, his marriage to the stepdaughter of the successful publisher John Newbery was over, and his life was in a shambles. He was arrested numerous times for debt, and, despite the efforts of friends to save him, Smart died in the debtors' prison known as the King's Bench.

Smart distinguished himself in classics at Pembroke College, Cambridge and held a fellowship there until marriage disqualified him for it in 1753. Smart pursued serious poetry, publishing Latin versions of some of Pope's poems and winning the Seatonian prize for the best poem on God's attributes five of the first six years it was offered. In addition, Smart launched himself as a journalist, working mostly for John Newbery but contributing to numerous London periodicals. Samuel Johnson gave Smart some assistance in providing copy for the *Universal Visiter*, which began publication in 1756, about the time that Smart's health began to fail.

For all its strangeness, *Jubilate Agno* comprises the same elements that make up the rest of Smart's works: it expresses devotional themes, and it combines biblical and historical imagery with material of a more personal nature. The "Let ... For" structure of the poem comes from biblical hymns or canticles; the *Song of Solomon*, also known as *Canticles*, begins, "Let him kiss me with the kisses of his mouth: for thy love is better than wine." The Jubilate is a part of the Christian Mass which uses Psalm 100, but Smart indicated that his poem most resembled a similar part of the service called the Magnificat, which relies on the hymn of the Virgin Mary (Luke 1.46–55), beginning "My soul doth magnify the Lord." Considering Smart's elaborate magnification of his cat Jeoffry, many readers will feel Smart may have been chasing a quibble or a pun as well as stating his real intentions when he called his poem a magnificat.

The autograph manuscript of *Jubilate Agno* is in the Houghton Library at Harvard University. The text is clearly incomplete, with some pages missing or perhaps never written. Fragment A is on a sheet of paper numbered "1" and contains only "Let" lines; the corresponding "For" passages and the leaf that would have been numbered "2" are missing. Fragment B contains four pairs of leaves: there are more "For"s than "Let"s in this section, but some pairs on leaves both numbered "3" clearly go together. This correspondence helped the Houghton librarian, William H. Bond, to recognize the pattern of the unfinished poem. The selections here follow Bond's discoveries of 1950, as represented in the edition by Karina Williamson (Clarendon Press, 1980). I follow Williamson in printing the "For" verses in italics, but only when they follow "Let" verses. Both my notes and my introductory remarks here are deeply indebted to Williamson's work.

British Literature 1640–1789: An Anthology, Fourth Edition. Edited by Robert DeMaria, Jr.

from *Jubilate Agno*[1] (c.1758–63)

from Fragment A (c.1758–9)

Rejoice in God, O ye Tongues; give the glory to the Lord,
and the Lamb.
Nations, and languages, and every Creature, in which is the
breath of Life.
Let man and beast appear before him, and magnify his name together.
Let Noah and his company approach the throne of Grace,
and do homage to the Ark of their Salvation.
Let Abraham present a Ram, and worship the God of his Redemption.
Let Isaac, the Bridegroom, kneel with his Camels, and bless
the hope of his pilgrimage.
Let Jacob, and his speckled Drove adore the good Shepherd
of Israel.
Let Esau offer a scape Goat for his seed, and rejoice in the
blessing of God his father.
Let Nimrod, the mighty hunter, bind a Leopard to the altar,
and consecrate his spear to the Lord.
Let Ishmael dedicate a Tiger, and give praise for the liberty,
in which the Lord has set him at large. ... [2]

from Fragment B[3] (1759–60)

Let Elizur rejoice with the Partridge,[4] who is a prisoner of
state and is proud of his keepers.
*For I am not without authority in my jeopardy,[5] which I derive
inevitably from the glory of the name of the Lord.*
Let Shedeur rejoice with Pyrausta,[6] who dwelleth in a
medium of fire, which God hath adapted for him.
*For I bless God whose name is Jealous[7] – and there is a zeal to
deliver us from everlasting burnings.*
Let Shelumiel rejoice with Olor,[8] who is of a godly savour,
and the very look of him harmonizes the mind.

Notes

FROM *JUBILATE AGNO*

[1] *Jubilate Agno* "Rejoice in the Lamb"; Christ is several times referred to as the Lamb of God; particularly in John (e.g., 1.29) and Revelation (e.g., 22.1); the opening lines of the poem suggest Revelation 7.9–17, where the tribes of Israel are "sealed" against destruction in the apocalypse by God; the tribes of all tongues respond by offering "salus," "health" or "salvation," to God and to the Lamb.

[2] All ellipses in the text are mine.

[3] *Fragment B* this section was begun in July 1759 during the Seven Years War (known in America as the French and Indian Wars); the biblical names come from Genesis and Numbers.

[4] *Partridge* see Ecclesiasticus 11.30: "As a decoy partridge in a cage, so is the heart of a proud man."

[5] *jeopardy* captivity.

[6] *Pyrausta* Latin, a fly supposed to live in fire (*pyralis* is the more common Latin word for it).

[7] *Jealous* see Exodus 20.5: "I the Lord thy God am a jealous God" and, for the protective rather than punitive implications of the appellation, see Joel 2.18.

[8] *Olor* Latin, "swan"; the word resembles Latin *oleo*, "to give off a smell," "to savor."

For my existimation[9] is good even amongst the slanderers and my memory shall arise for a sweet savour unto the Lord.
Let Jael[10] rejoice with the Plover, who whistles for his life, and foils the marksmen and their guns.
For I bless the PRINCE of PEACE and pray that all the guns may be nailed up, save such as are for the rejoicing days.
Let Raguel rejoice with the Cock of Portugal[11] – God send good Angels to the allies of England!
For I have abstained from the blood of the grape and that even at the Lord's table.
Let Hobab rejoice with Necydalus,[12] who is the Greek of a Grub.
For I have glorified God in GREEK and LATIN, the consecrated languages spoken by the Lord on earth.
Let Zurishaddai with the Polish Cock rejoice – The Lord restore peace to Europe
For I meditate the peace of Europe amongst family bickerings and domestic jars.
Let Zuar rejoice with the Guinea Hen – The Lord add to his mercies in the WEST![13]
For the HOST is in the WEST – The Lord make us thankful unto salvation.
Let Chesed rejoice with Strepsiceros,[14] whose weapons are the ornaments of his peace.
For I preach the very GOSPEL of CHRIST without comment & with this weapon shall I slay envy. …
For I will consider my Cat Jeoffry.
For he is the servant of the Living God, duly and daily serving him.
For at the first glance of the glory of God in the East he worships in his way.
For is this done by wreathing his body seven times round with elegant quickness.
For then he leaps up to catch the musk, which is the blessing of God upon his prayer.
For he rolls upon prank to work it in.[15]
For having done duty and received blessing he begins to consider himself.
For this he performs in ten degrees.
For first he looks upon his fore-paws to see if they are clean.
For secondly he kicks up behind to clear away there.

Notes

9 *existimation* "Esteem" (Johnson).

10 *Jael* the wife of Heber, who killed Sisera, captain of the Canaanite army, by driving a nail through his temples; this and the nails with which Christ was crucified suggest "nailed up" in the "For" verse. Judges 5.21.

11 *Portugal* a long-standing ally of England.

12 *Necydalus* from Greek, the nymph of the silkworm; the word is related to *νέέκυς*, "corpse."

13 *WEST* the West Indies, where part of the Seven Years War was fought, and some of the enemies of Israel, in biblical terms (e.g., Zechariah 8.7: "Behold, I will save my people from the east country, and from the west country").

14 *Strepsiceros* "A kind of animal with twisted horns" (Lewis and Short, *A Latin Dictionary*).

15 *prank* "A frolic; a wild flight; a ludicrous trick" (Johnson).

For thirdly he works it upon stretch with the fore-paws extended.
For fourthly he sharpens his paws by wood.
For fifthly he washes himself.
For sixthly he rolls upon wash.
For Seventhly he fleas himself,[16] that he may not be interrupted upon the beat.
For Eighthly he rubs himself against a post.
For Ninthly he looks up for his instructions.
For Tenthly he goes in quest of food.
For having considered God and himself he will consider his neighbour.
For if he meets another cat he will kiss her in kindness.
For when he takes his prey he plays with it to give it chance.
For one mouse in seven escapes by his dallying.
For when his day's work is done his business more properly begins.
For he keeps the Lord's watch in the night against the adversary.
For he counteracts the powers of darkness by his electrical skin & glaring eyes.
For he counteracts the Devil, who is death, by brisking about the life.
For in his morning orisons he loves the sun and the sun loves him.[17]
For he is of the tribe of Tiger.
For the Cherub Cat is a term of the Angel Tiger.
For he has the subtlety and hissing of a serpent, which in goodness he suppresses.
For he will not do destruction, if he is well-fed, neither will he spit without provocation.
For he purrs in thankfulness, when God tells him he's a good Cat.
For he is an instrument for the children to learn benevolence upon.
For every house is incomplete without him & a blessing is lacking in the spirit.
For the Lord commanded Moses concerning the cats at the departure of the Children of Israel from Egypt.[18]
For every family had one cat at least in the bag.
For the English Cats are the best in Europe.
For he is the cleanest in the use of his fore-paws of any quadruped.
For the dexterity of his defence is an instance of the love of God to him exceedingly.
For he is the quickest to his mark of any creature.

Notes

[16] *fleas himself* rids himself of fleas.

[17] *orisons* prayers.

[18] *Lord commanded Moses concerning the cats* the Lord says, "Take your flocks and your herds … " (Exodus 12.32); there is no order concerning cats.

For he is tenacious of his point.
For he is a mixture of gravity and waggery.
For he knows that God is his Saviour.
For there is nothing sweeter than his peace when at rest.
For there is nothing brisker than his life when in motion.
For he is of the Lord's poor and so indeed is he called by benevolence perpetually – Poor Jeoffry! poor Jeoffry! the rat has bit thy throat.
For I bless the name of the Lord Jesus that Jeoffry is better.
For the divine spirit comes about his body to sustain it in complete cat.
For his tongue is exceeding pure so that it has in purity what it wants in music.
For he is docile and can learn certain things.
For he can set up with gravity which is patience upon approbation.
For he can fetch and carry, which is patience in employment.
For he can jump over a stick which is patience upon proof positive.
For he can spraggle upon waggle at the word of command.
For he can jump from an eminence into his master's bosom.
For he can catch the cork and toss it again.
For he is hated by the hypocrite and miser.
For the former is afraid of detection.
For the latter refuses his charge.
For he camels his back to bear the first notion of business.
For he is good to think on, if a man would express himself neatly.
For he made a great figure in Europe for his signal services.
For he killed the Ichneumon-rat very pernicious by land.[19]
For his ears are so acute that they sting again.
For from this proceeds the passing quickness of his attention.
For by stroking of him I have found out electricity.
For I perceived God's light about him both wax and fire.
For the Electrical fire is the spiritual substance, which God sends from heaven to sustain the bodies both of man and beast.
For God has blessed him in the variety of his movements.
For, though he cannot fly, he is an excellent clamberer.
For his motions upon the face of the earth are more than any other quadruped.
For he can tread to all the measures upon the music.
For he can swim for life.
For he can creep.

Notes

[19] *Ichneumon-rat* "A small animal that breaks the eggs of the crocodile" (Johnson); it was valued by the Egyptians; Smart means to praise cats for killing rats which carried the fleas that spread bubonic plague.

Samson Occom (1723–1792)

Born near New London, Connecticut, Occom was converted to Christianity at age seventeen by the evangelist James Davenport.[1] Soon thereafter he went to Eleazor Wheelock's Preparatory School; he was appointed to his native Mohegan council, and a few years later became a teacher among the Montauks on the other side of the Long Island Sound. From 1766 to 1768 Occom was in England preaching and raising money for Wheelock's school, much of which went instead toward the foundation of Dartmouth College in New Hampshire. His sermon at the execution of Moses Paul, a fellow Native American, is both learned and passionate. It is British in its heritage, which is easily traced to evangelists such as George Whitefield, whom Occom knew, and even to earlier hellfire and brimstone preachers such as Jeremy Taylor, and yet, of course, it could only have been written by a Native American. Occom's work shows how the archipelago of Britain expanded in the eighteenth century to include the eastern American colonies, even as it was implicitly excluding many of their inhabitants. The Sermon ran into many editions in America and England after its first printing in 1772. The text below is based on a 1772 issue. The selection represents about two-thirds of the whole.

from A SERMON Preached at the EXECUTION of Moses Paul, an INDIAN[2]

The PREFACE.

The world is already full of books; and the people of God are abundantly furnished with excellent books upon divine subjects; and, it seems, that every subject has been written upon over & over again: and the people in very deed have had precept upon precept, line upon line, here a little and there a little; and so in the whole, they have much, yea, very much, they have enough and more than enough. And when I come to consider these things, I am ready to say with myself, "What folly and madness is it in me to suffer anything of mine to appear in print, to expose my ignorance to the world."

It seems altogether unlikely that my performance will do any manner of service in the world, since the most excellent writings of worthy and learned men are disregarded. But there are two or three considerations that have induced me to writing, to suffer my broken hints to appear in the world. One is, that the books that are in the world are written in very high and refined language, and the sermons that are delivered every Sabbath in general, are in a very high and lofty style, so that the common people understand but little of them. But I think they can't help understanding my talk; it is common, plain, everyday talk: little children may understand me. And poor Negroes may plainly and fully understand my meaning, and it may be of service to them. Again, it may in a particular manner be serviceable to my poor kindred, the Indians. Further, as it comes from an uncommon quarter, it may induce people to read it, because it is

Notes

Samson Occom

[1] for biographical information I rely on the *ODNB* entry on Occom by Bernd C. Peyer.

[2] The title continues "Who was executed at *New Haven*, on the Second of September, 1772; for the Murder of Mr. *Moses Cook*, late of *Waterbury*, on the 7th of December, 1771."

British Literature 1640–1789: An Anthology, Fourth Edition. Edited by Robert DeMaria, Jr.

from an Indian. Lastly, God works where and when he pleases, and by what instruments he sees fit, and he can and has used weak and unlikely instruments to bring about his great work. It was a stormy and very uncomfortable day, when the following discourse was delivered, and about one half of it was not delivered, as it was written, and now it is a little altered and enlarged in some places.

INTRODUCTION

BY the melancholy providence of God, and at the earnest desire and invitation of the poor condemned criminal, I am here before this great concourse of people at this time, to give the last discourse to the poor miserable object, who is to be executed this day before your eyes, for the due reward of his folly and madness, and enormous wickedness. It is an unwelcome task to me to speak upon such an occasion; but since it is the desire of the poor man himself, who is to die a shameful death this day, in conscience I cannot deny him; I must endeavor to do the great work the dying man requests.

I conclude that this great concourse of people have come together to see the execution of justice upon this poor Indian; and I suppose the biggest part of you look upon yourselves Christians, and as such I hope you will demean[3] yourselves; and that you will have suitable commiseration towards this poor object. Though you can't in justice pray for his life to be continued in this world, yet you can pray earnestly for the salvation of his poor soul, consistently with the mind of God. Let this be therefore, the fervent exercise of our souls: for this is the last day we have to pray for him. As for you, that don't regard religion, it cannot be expected that you will put up one petition for this miserable creature: yet I would entreat you seriously to consider the frailty of corrupt nature, and behave yourselves as becomes rational creatures.

And in a word, let us all be suitably affected with the melancholy occasion of the day, knowing that we are all dying creatures, and accountable unto God. Though this poor condemned criminal will in a few minutes know more than all of us, either in unutterable joy, or in inconceivable woe, yet we shall certainly know as much as he, in a few days.

SERMON

The sacred words that I have chosen to speak from upon this undesirable occasion, are found written in the epistle of St. Paul to the

ROMANS VI.23.

For the wages of sin is death, but the gift of God is eternal life through Jesus Christ our Lord.

DEATH is called the King of Terrors, and it ought to be the subject of every man and woman's thoughts daily; because it is that unto which they are liable every moment of their lives: and therefore, it cannot be unseasonable to think, speak and hear of it at any time, and especially on this mournful occasion; for we must all come to it, how soon we cannot tell; whether we are prepared or not prepared, ready or not ready, whether death is welcome or not welcome, we must feel the force of it: whether we concern ourselves with death or not, it will concern itself with us. Seeing that this is the case with every one of us, what manner or persons ought we to be in all holy conversation and godliness; how ought men to exert themselves in preparation for

Notes

[3] *Demean* conduct or behave (yourselves as Christians).

death continually; for they know not what a day or an hour may bring forth, with respect to them. But, alas! according to the appearance of mankind in general, death is the least thought of. They go on from day to day, as if they were to live here forever, as if this was the only life. They contrive, rack their inventions, disturb their rest, and even hazard their lives in all manner of dangers, both by sea and land; yea they leave no stone unturned that they may live in the world, and at the same time have little or no contrivance to die well: God and their souls are neglected, and heaven and eternal happiness are disregarded; Christ and his religion are despised—yet most of these very men intend to be happy when they come to die, not considering that there must be great preparation in order to die well. Yea there is not so fit to live as those that are fit to die; those that are not fit to die are not fit to live. Life & death are nearly connected; we generally own that it is a great and solemn thing to die. If this be true, then it is a great and solemn thing to live; for as we live, so we shall die. But I say again, how little do mankind realize these things? They are busy about the things of this world as if there was no death before them. Dr. *Watts*[4] pictures them out to the life in his psalms:

See the vain race of mortals move
Like shadows o'er the plain,
They rage and strive, desire and love,
But all the noise is vain.

Some walk in honor's gaudy show,
Some dig for golden ore,
They toil for heirs they know not who,
And straight are seen no more.

But on the other hand, life is the most precious thing, and ought to be the most desired by all rational creatures. It ought to be prized above all things; yet there is nothing so abused and despised as life, and nothing so neglected: I mean eternal life is shamefully disregarded by men in general, and eternal death is chosen rather than life. ...

But in further speaking upon our text, by divine assistance, I shall consider these two general propositions:

I. That sin is the cause of all the miseries that befall the children of men, both as to their bodies and souls, for time and eternity.
II. That eternal life and happiness is the free gift of God through Jesus Christ our Lord.

In speaking to the first proposition I shall first consider the nature of sin; and secondly shall consider the consequences of sin, or the wages of sin, which is death.

First then, we are to describe the nature of sin.

Sin is the transgression of the law:—This is the scripture definition of sin. Now the law of God being holy, just and good; sin must be altogether unholy, unjust and evil. If I was to define sin, I should call it a contrariety to GOD; and as such it must be the vilest thing in the world; it is full of evil; it is the evil of evils; the only evil, in which

Notes

4 Isaac Watts (see p. 626 above); Watts's translation, *The Psalms of David* (1719), was reprinted hundreds of times in the eighteenth century. Occom quotes Psalm 39, part 2.

dwells no good thing; and is most destructive to God's creation, wherever it takes effect. It was sin that transformed the very angels in heaven, into devils; and it was sin that caused hell to be made. If it had not been for sin, there never would have been such a thing as hell or devil, death or misery.

And if sin is such a thing as we have just described; it must be worse than the devils and hell itself.—Sin is full of deadly poison; it is full of malignity and hatred against God, against all his divine perfections and attributes, against his wisdom, against his power, against his holiness and goodness, against his mercy and justice, against his written law and gospel; yea, against his very being and existence. Were it in the power of sin, it would even dethrone God, and set itself on the throne.

2. I shall endeavor to show the sad consequences or effects of sin upon the children of men.

Sin has poisoned them, & made them distracted or fools. The Psalmist says, "The fool hath said in his heart, there is no God."[5] And Solomon, through his Proverbs, calls ungodly sinners fools; and their sin he calls their folly, and foolishness.[6] The Apostle James says, "But the tongue can no man tame, it is an unruly evil, full of deadly poison."[7] It is the heart that is in the first place full of deadly poison. The tongue is only an interpreter of the heart. Sin has vitiated the whole man, both soul and body; all the powers are corrupted; it has turned the minds of men against all good, towards all evil. So poisoned are they, according to the prophet Isaiah v. 20. "Woe unto them that call evil good, and good evil; that put darkness for light, and light for darkness; that put bitter for sweet, and sweet for bitter." And Christ Jesus saith in John iii. 19, 20. "And this is the condemnation that light is come into the world, and men loved darkness rather than light, because their deeds were evil. For everyone that doth evil hateth the light, neither cometh to the light, lest his deeds should be reproved." Sin has stupefied mankind, they are now ignorant of God their maker; neither do they enquire after him. And they are ignorant of themselves, they know not what is good for them, neither do they understand their danger; and they have no fear of God before their eyes.

Further, sin has blinded their eyes, so that they can't discern spiritual things; neither do they see the way that they should go, and they are deaf as adders, so that they cannot hear the joyful sound of the gospel that brings glad tidings of peace and pardon to sinners of mankind. Neither do they regard the Charmer charming never so wisely.—Not only so, but sin has made man proud, though he has nothing to be proud of; for he has lost all his excellency, his beauty and happiness; he is a bankrupt, and is excommunicated from God; he was turned out of paradise by God himself, and become a vagabond in God's world, and as such he has no right nor title to the least crumb of mercy in the world: yet he is proud, he is haughty, and exalts himself above God, though he is wretched and miserable, and poor, and blind and naked. He glories in his shame. Sin has made him beastly and devilish; yea he is sunk beneath the beasts, and is worse than the ravenous beasts of the wilderness. He is become ill-natured, cruel and murderous; he is contentious and quarrelsome. I said he is worse than the ravenous beasts, for wolves and bears don't devour their own kind, but man does; yea we have numberless instances of women killing their own children; such women I think are worse than she-tigers. …

Notes

[5] Psalms 14.1.

[6] Proverbs 1.7 and 10.14, for example.

[7] James 3.7.

We have given some few hints of the nature of sin, and the effects of sin on mankind. We shall in the next place consider the wages or the reward of sin, which is death.

Sin is the cause of all the miseries that attend poor sinful man, which will finally bring him to death, death temporal and eternal. I shall first consider his temporal death.

His temporal death then begins as soon as he is born. Though it seems to us that he is just beginning to live, yet in fact he is just entered into a state of death: as St. Paul says, "Wherefore, as by one man sin entered into the world, and death by sin; and so death passed upon all men, for that all have sinned."[8] Man is surrounded with ten thousand instruments of death, and is liable to death every moment of his life; a thousand diseases await him on every side continually; the sentence of death is passed upon them as soon as they are born: yea they are struck with death as soon as they breathe. And it seems all the enjoyments of men in this world are also poisoned with sin: for GOD said to Adam after he had sinned, "Cursed is the ground for thy sake, in sorrow shalt thou eat of it all the days of they life."[9] By this we plainly see that everything that grows out of the ground is cursed and all creatures that God hath made for man are cursed also; and whatever God curses is a cursed thing indeed. Thus death and destruction is in all the enjoyments of men in this life, every enjoyment in this world is liable to misfortune in a thousand ways, both by sea and land. …

And secondly, we are to consider man's spiritual death, while he is here in this world. We find it thus written in the word of God. "And the Lord God commanded the man, saying, of every tree of the garden thou mayest freely eat: but of the tree of knowledge of good and evil, thou shalt not eat of it, for in the day that thou eatest thereof thou shalt surely die."[10] And yet he did eat of it, and so he and all his posterity, are but dead men. And St. Paul to the Ephesians saith, "You hath he quickened, who were dead in trespasses and sins."[11]—The great Mr. Henry says in this place, that unregenerate souls are dead in trespasses and sins.[12] All those who are in their sins, are dead in sins; yea, in trespasses and sins; which may signify all sorts of sins, habitual and actual; sins of heart and life. Sin is the death of the soul. Wherever that prevails, there is a privation of all spiritual life. Sinners are dead in state, being destitute of the principles and powers of spiritual life; and cut off from God, the fountain of life: and they are dead in law, as a condemned malefactor is said to be a dead man. …

The next thing I shall consider, is the actual death of the body, or separation between soul and body. At the cessation of natural life, there is an end of all the enjoyments of this life; there is no more joy nor sorrow; no more hope nor fear, as to the body; no more contrivance and carrying on any business; no more merchandizing and trading; no more farming; no more buying and selling; nor more building of any kind, no more contrivance at all to live in the world; no more flatteries nor frowns from the world; no more honor nor reproach; no more praise; no more good report, nor evil report; no more learning of any trades, arts or sciences in the world; no more sinful pleasures, they are all at an end; recreations, visiting, tavern haunting, music and dancing, chambering and carousing, playing at dice and cards, or any game whatsoever; cursing and swearing, and profaning the holy name of God, drunkenness, fighting, debauchery, lying and cheating, in this world, must cease forever. Not only so, they must bid an

Notes

[8] Romans 5.12.

[9] Genesis 3.17.

[10] Genesis 2.16.

[11] Ephesians 2.1.

[12] See Matthew Henry (1662–1714), *Exposition of the Old and New Testament*, a commentary completed after Henry's death (6 vols., 1721) and often reprinted.

eternal farewell to all the world; bid farewell to all their beloved sins and pleasures; and the places and possessions, that knew them once, shall know them no more forever. And further, they must bid adieu to all sacred and divine things. They are obliged to leave the Bible, and all the ordinances thereof; and to bid farewell to preachers, and all sermons and all Christian people, and Christian conversation; they must bid a long farewell to Sabbaths and seasons, and opportunities of worship; yea, an eternal farewell to all mercy, and all hope; an eternal farewell to God the Father, Son and Holy Ghost, and adieu to heaven and all happiness, to saints and all the inhabitants of the upper world. …

On the other hand, the poor departed soul must take up its lodging in sorrow, woe and misery, in the lake that burns with fire and brimstone, where the worm dieth not, and the fire is not quenched; where a multitude of frightful deformed devils dwell, and the damned ghosts of Adam's race; where darkness, horror and despair reigns, where hope never comes, and where poor guilty naked souls will be tormented with exquisite torments, even the wrath of the Almighty poured out-upon their damned souls; the smoke of their torments ascending up forever and ever; their mouths and nostrils streaming forth with living fire; and hellish groans, howlings, cries and shrieks all round them, and merciless devils upbraiding them for their folly and madness, and tormenting them incessantly. …

The next thing that I was to consider is this: That eternal life and happiness is the free gift of God, through Jesus Christ our Lord.

Under this proposition I shall endeavor to show what this life and happiness is.

The life that is mentioned in our text is, a spiritual life: it is the life of the soul, a restoration of the soul from sin, to holiness, from darkness to light, a translation from the kingdom and dominion of Satan, to the kingdom of God's grace. In other words, it is being restored to the image of God, and delivered from the image of Satan. And this life consists in union of the soul to God, and communion with God; a real participation of the divine nature, or in the apostle's words, it is Christ formed within us; I live, says he, yet not I, but Christ liveth in me. And the apostle John saith, "God is love, and he that dwelleth in love, dwelleth in God, and God in him."[13] This is the life of the soul. It is called emphatically life, because it is a life that shall never have a period, a stable, permanent, and unchangeable life, called in the scriptures, everlasting life, or life eternal. And the happiness of this life consists in communion with God, or in the spiritual enjoyment of God. As much as a soul enjoys of God in this life, just so much of life and happiness he enjoys or possesses; yea, just so much of heaven he enjoys. A true Christian, desires no other heaven, but the enjoyment of God, a full and perfect enjoyment of God, is a full and perfect heaven and happiness to a gracious soul.—Further, this life is called eternal life, because God has planted a living principle in the soul; and whereas he was dead before, now he is made alive unto God; there is an active principle within him towards God, he now moves towards God in his religious devotions and exercises; is daily comfortably and sweetly walking with God, in all his ordinances and commands; his delight is in the ways of God; he breathes towards God, a living breath, in praises, prayers, adorations and thanksgivings; his prayers are now heard in the heavens, and his praises delight the ears of the Almighty, and his thanksgivings are accepted. So alive is he now to God, that he is his meat and drink, yea more than his meat and drink, to do the will of his heavenly Father. It is his delight, his happiness and pleasure to serve God. He does not drag himself to his duties now, but he does them out of

Notes

[13] 1 John 4.16.

choice, and with alacrity of soul. Yea, so alive is he to God, that he gives up himself and all that he has entirely to God, to be for him and none other; his whole aim is to glorify God in all things, whether by life or death, all the same to him. …

We proceed in the next place to show, that this life, which we have described, is the free gift of God, through Jesus Christ our Lord.

Sinners have forfeited all mercy into the hand of divine justice, and have merited hell and damnation to themselves; for the wages of sin is everlasting death, but heaven and happiness is a free gift; it comes by favour; and all merit is excluded: and especially if we consider that we are fallen sinful creatures, and there is nothing in us that can recommend us to the favour of God and we can do nothing that is agreeable and acceptable to God; and the mercies we enjoy in this life are altogether from the pure mercy of God; we are unequal to them. Good old Jacob cried out, under a sense of his unworthiness, "I am less than the least of all thy mercies,"[14] and we have nothing to give unto God, if we essay to give all the service that we are capable of, we should give him nothing but what was his own, and when we give up ourselves unto God, both soul and body, we give him nothing; for we were his before; he had right to do with us as he pleased, either to throw us into hell, or save us.—There is nothing that we can call our own, but our sins; and who is he that dares to say, I expect to have heaven for my sins? for our text says, that the wages of sin is death. If we are thus unequal and unworthy of the least mercy in this life, how much more are we unworthy of eternal life? yet God can find it in his heart to give it. And it is altogether unmerited; it is a free gift to undeserving and hell-deserving sinners of mankind: it is altogether of God's sovereign good pleasure to give it. It is of free grace & sovereign mercy, and from the unbounded goodness of God; he was self-moved to it. And it is said that this life is given in and through the Lord Jesus Christ. It could not be given in any other way, but in and through the death and sufferings of the Lord Jesus Christ; Christ himself is the gift, and he is the Christian's life.

I have now gone through what I proposed from my text. And I shall now make some application of the whole.

First to the criminal in particular; and then to the auditory in general.

My poor unhappy brother MOSES;

As it was your own desire that I should preach to you this last discourse, so I shall speak plainly to you.—You are the bone of my bone, and flesh of my flesh.[15] You are an Indian, a despised creature; but you have despised yourself; yea you have despised God more; you have trodden underfoot his authority; you have despised his commands and precepts: and now, as God says, be sure your sins will find you out.[16] And now, poor Moses, your sins have found you out, and they have overtaken you this day; the day of your death is now come; the king of terrors is at hand; you have but a very few moments to breathe in this world.—The just laws of man, and the holy law of Jehovah, call aloud for the destruction of your mortal life; God says, "Whoso sheddeth man's blood, by man shall his blood be shed."[17] This is the ancient decree of heaven, and it is to be executed by man; nor have you the least gleam of hope of escape, for the unalterable sentence is past; the terrible day of execution is come; the unwelcome guard is about you; and the fatal instruments of death are now made ready; your coffin and your grave, your last lodging, are open ready to receive you.

Alas! poor Moses, now you know, by sad, by woeful experience, the living truth of our text, that the wages of sin is death. You have been already dead; yea twice dead: by

Notes

[14] Genesis 32.10.

[15] 2 Samuel 19.12.

[16] Numbers 32.23.

[17] Genesis 9.6.

nature spiritually dead. And since the awful sentence of death has been passed upon you, you have been dead to all the pleasures of this life; or all the pleasures, lawful or unlawful, have been dead to you: And death, which is the wages of sin, is standing even on this side of your grave ready to put a final period to your mortal life; and just beyond the grave, eternal death awaits your poor soul, and the devils are ready to drag your miserable soul down to their bottomless den, where everlasting woe and horror reigns; the place is filled with doleful shrieks, howls and groans of the damned. Oh! to what a miserable, forlorn, and wretched condition have your extravagant folly and wickedness brought you! i.e. if you die in your sins. And O! what manner of repentance ought you to manifest! How ought your heart to bleed for what you have done! How ought you to prostrate your soul before a bleeding God! And under self-condemnation, cry out, "Ah Lord, ah Lord, what have I done!"—Whatever partiality, injustice and error there may be among the judges of the earth, remember that you have deserved a thousand deaths, and a thousand hells, by reason of your sins, at the hands of a holy God. Should God come out against you in strict justice, alas! what could you say for yourself? for you have been brought up under the bright sunshine, and plain, and loud sound of the gospel; and you have had a good education; you can read and write well; and God has given you a good natural understanding: and therefore your sins are so much more aggravated. You have not sinned in such an ignorant manner as others have done; but you have sinned with both your eyes open as it were, under the light, even the glorious light of the gospel of the Lord Jesus Christ.—You have sinned against the light of your own conscience, against your knowledge and understanding; you have sinned against the pure and holy laws of God, and the just laws of men; you have sinned against heaven and earth; you have sinned against all the mercies and goodness of God; you have sinned against the whole Bible, against the Old and New Testament; you have sinned against the blood of Christ, which is the blood of the everlasting covenant. O poor Moses, see what you have done! and now repent, repent, I say again repent; see how the blood you shed cries against you, and the Avenger of Blood is at your heels. O fly, fly to the Blood of the Lamb of God for the pardon of all your aggravated sins.

But let us now turn to a more pleasant theme.—Though you have been a great sinner, a heaven-daring sinner; yet hark and hear the joyful sound from heaven, even from the King of kings, and Lord of lords; that the gift of God is eternal life, through Jesus Christ our lord. It is a free gift, and offered to the greatest sinners, and upon their true repentance towards God and faith in the Lord Jesus Christ, they shall be welcome to the life, which we have spoken of; it is offered upon free terms. He that hath no money may come; he that hath no righteousness, no goodness, may come; the call is to poor undone sinners; the call is not to the righteous, but sinners, calling them to repentance. Hear the voice of the Son of the most high God, Come unto me, all ye that labour and are heavy laden, and I will give you rest.[18] This is a call, a gracious call to you, poor Moses, under your present burdens and distresses. And Christ alone has a right to call sinners to himself. It would be a presumption for a mighty angel to call a poor sinner in this manner; and were it possible for you to apply to all God's creatures, they would with one voice tell you, that it was not in them to help you. Go to all the means of grace, they would prove miserable helps, without Christ himself. Yea, apply to all the ministers of the gospel in the world, they would all say, that it was not in them, but would only prove as indexes,[19] to point out to you, the Lord Jesus Christ, the

Notes

[18] Matthew 11.28.

[19] *index* the forefinger.

only savior of sinners of mankind. Yea, go to all the angels in heaven, they would do the same. Yea, go to God the Father himself, without Christ, he could not help you, to speak after the manner of men, he would also point to the Lord Jesus Christ, & say "This is my beloved Son, in whom I am well pleased, hear ye him."[20] Thus you see, poor Moses, that there is no one in heaven, or on the earth, that can help you, but Christ; he alone has power to save, and to give life.—God the eternal appointed him, chose him, authorized, and fully commissioned him to save sinners. He came down from heaven, into this lower world, and became as one of us, and stood in our room. He was the second Adam. And as God demanded perfect obedience of the first Adam; the second fulfilled it; and as the first sinned, and incurred the wrath and anger of God, the second endured it; he suffered in our room. As he became sin for us, he was a man of sorrows,[21] and acquainted with grief; all our stripes were laid upon him; yea he was finally condemned, because we were under condemnation; and at last was executed and put to death, for our sins; was lifted up between the heaven and the earth, and was crucified on the accursed tree; his blessed hands and feet were fastened there;—there he died a shameful and ignominious death: there he finished the great work of our redemption: there his heart's blood was shed for our cleaning: there he fully satisfied the divine justice of God, for penitent, believing sinners, though they have been the chief of sinners.—O Moses! this is good news to you, in this last day of your life; here is a crucified Saviour at hand for your sins; his blessed hands are outstretched, all in a gore of blood for you. This is the only Saviour, an almighty Saviour, just such as you stand in infinite and perishing need of. O, poor Moses! hear the dying prayer of a gracious Saviour on the accursed tree,—Father forgive them, for they know not what they do. This was a prayer for his enemies and murderers; and it is for you, if you would only repent and believe in him. O why will you die eternally, poor Moses, since Christ has died for sinners? Why will you go to hell from beneath the bleeding Saviour as it were? This is the day of your execution, yet it is the accepted time, it is the day of salvation if you will now believe in the Lord Jesus Christ. Must Christ follow you into the prison by his servants, and there entreat you to accept of eternal life, and will you refuse it? and must he follow you even to the gallows, and there beseech you to accept of him, and will you refuse him? Shall he be crucified hard by your gallows, as it were, and will you regard him not? O, poor Moses, now believe on the Lord Jesus Christ with all your heart, and thou shalt be saved eternally. Come just as you are, with all your sins and abominations, with all your filthiness, with all your blood-guiltiness, with all your condemnation, and lay hold of the hope set before you this day. This is the last day of salvation with your soul; you will be beyond the bounds of mercy in a few minutes more. O, what a joyful day would it be if you would now openly believe in and receive the Lord Jesus Christ; it would be the beginning of heavenly days with your poor soul; instead of a melancholy day, it would be a wedding day to your soul; it would cause the very angels in heaven to rejoice, and saints on earth to be glad; it would cause the angels to come down from the realms above, and wait hovering about your gallows, ready to convey your soul to the heavenly mansions, there to take the possession of eternal glory and happiness, and join the heavenly choirs in singing the songs of Moses and the Lamb: there to set down forever with Abraham, Isaac and Jacob in the kingdom of God's glory; and your shame and guilt shall be forever banished from the place, and all sorrow and fear forever fly away, and tears be wiped

Notes

[20] Matthew 17.5.

[21] *man of sorrows* Isaiah 53.3.

from your face;[22] and there shall you forever admire the astonishing and amazing and infinite mercy of God in Christ Jesus, in pardoning such a monstrous sinner as you have been; there you will claim the highest note of praise, for the riches of free grace in Christ Jesus. But if you will not accept of a Saviour so freely offered to you in the last day of your life, you must this very day bid farewell to God the Father, Son, and Holy Ghost, to heaven and all the saints and angels that are there, and you must bid all the saints in this lower world an eternal farewell, and even the whole world. And so I must leave you in the hands of God; and I must turn to the whole auditory.

Sirs, We may plainly see, from what we have heard, and from the miserable object before us, into what a doleful condition sin has brought mankind, even into a state of death and misery. We are by nature as certainly under sentence of death from God, as this miserable man is, by the just determination of man; and we are all dying creatures, and we are, or ought to be, sensible of it; and this is the dreadful fruit of sin. O! let us then fly from all appearance of sin; let us fight against it with all our might; let us repent and turn to our God, and believe on the Lord Jesus Christ, that we may live forever; let us all prepare for death, for we know not how soon, nor how suddenly we may be called out of the world.

Permit me in particular, reverend Gentlemen and fathers in Israel,[23] to speak a few words to you, though I am well sensible that I need to be taught the first principles of the oracles of God, by the least of you. But since the providence of God has so ordered it, that I must speak here on this occasion, I beg that you would not be offended nor be angry with me.

God has raised you up, from among your brethren, and has qualified, and authorized you to do his great work; and you are the servants of the Most High GOD, and ministers of the Lord Jesus the Son of the living God: you are Christ's ambassadors; you are called Shepherds, watchmen, overseers, or bishops, and you are rulers of the temples of God, or of the assemblies of God's people; you are God's angels, and as such you have nothing to do but to wait upon God, and to do the work the Lord Jesus Christ your blessed Lord and Master has set you about, not fearing the face of any man, nor seeking to please men, but your master. You are to declare the whole counsel of God, and to give a portion to every soul in due season; as a physician gives a portion to his patients, according to their diseases, so you are to give a portion to every soul in due season, according to their spiritual maladies; whether it be agreeable or disagreeable to them, you must give it them; whether they will love you or hate you for it, you must do your work. Your work is to encounter sin and Satan; this was the very end of the coming of Christ into the world, and the end of his death and sufferings; it was to make an end of sin and to destroy the works of the devil. And this is your work still, you are to fight the battles of the Lord. Therefore combine together, and be terrible as an army with banners; attack this monster sin in all its shapes and windings, and lift up your voices as trumpets and not spare, call aloud, call your people to arms against this common enemy of mankind, that sin may not be their ruin. …

I shall now address myself to the Indians, my brethren and kindred according to the flesh.

My poor kindred,

You see the woeful consequences of sin, by seeing this our poor miserable countryman now before us, who is to die this day for his sins and great wickedness. And it was the sin

Notes

22 Isaiah 25.8.

23 *Israel* the chosen people; Christians, in this case, as often.

of drunkenness that has brought this destruction and untimely death upon him. There is a dreadful woe denounced from the Almighty against drunkards and it is this sin, this abominable, this beastly and accursed sin drunkenness, that has stripped us of every desirable comfort in this life; by this we are poor, miserable and wretched; by this sin we have no name nor credit in the world among polite nations; for this sin we are despised in the world, and it is all right and just, for we despise ourselves more; and if we don't regard ourselves, who will regard us? And it is for our sins, and especially for that accursed, that most devilish sin of drunkenness that we suffer every day. For the love of strong drink we spend all that we have, and everything we can get. By this sin we can't have comfortable houses, nor anything comfortable in our houses; neither food nor raiment, nor decent utensils. We are obliged to put up with any sort of shelter just to screen us from the severity of the weather; and we go about with very mean, ragged and dirty clothes, almost naked. And we are half-starved, for the most of the time obliged to pick up anything to eat.—And our poor children are suffering every day for want of the necessaries of life; they are very often crying for want of food, and we have nothing to give them; and in the cold weather they are shivering and crying, being pinched with cold.—All this is for the love of strong drink. And this is not all the misery and evil we bring on ourselves in this world; but when we are intoxicated with strong drink, we drown our rational powers, by which we are distinguished from the brutal creation; we unman ourselves, and bring ourselves not only level with the beasts of the field, but seven degrees beneath them; yea we bring ourselves level with the devils; I don't know but we make ourselves worse than devils, for I never heard of drunken devils.

My poor kindred, do consider what a dreadful abominable sin drunkenness is. God made us men, and we choose to be beasts and devils; God made us rational creatures, and we choose to be fools. Do consider further, and behold a drunkard, and see how he looks, when he has drowned his reason; how deformed and shameful does he appear? He disfigures every part of him, both soul and body, which was made after the image of God. He appears with awful deformity, and his whole visage is disfigured; if he attempts to speak he cannot bring out his words distinct, so as to be understood; if he walks he reels and staggers to and fro, and tumbles down. And see how he behaves, he is now laughing, and then he is crying; he is singing and the next minute he is mourning; and is all love to everyone, and anon he is raging, & for fighting, & killing all before him, even the nearest and dearest relations and friends: Yea nothing is too bad for a drunken man to do. He will do that which he would not do for the world, in his right mind; he may lie with his own sister or daughter as Lot did.[24]

Further, when a person is drunk, he is just good for nothing in the world; he is of no service to himself, to his family, to his neighbours, or his country; and how much more unfit is he to serve God: yet he is just fit for the service of the devil.

Again, a man in drunkenness is in all manner of dangers, he may be killed by his fellow men, by wild beasts, and tame beasts; he may fall into the fire, into the water, or into a ditch; or he may fall down as he walks along, and break his bones or his neck; he may cut himself with edge-tools.—Further, if he has any money or anything valuable, he may lose it all, or may be robbed; or he may make a foolish bargain, and be cheated out of all he has.

I believe you know the truth of what I have just now said, many of you by sad experience; yet you will go on still in your drunkenness. Though you have been cheated

Notes

[24] Genesis 19.36.

over and over again, and you have lost your substance by drunkenness, yet you will venture to go on in this most destructive sin. O fools, when will ye be wise?—We all know the truth of what I have been saying, by what we have seen and heard of drunken deaths. How many have been drowned in our rivers, and how many frozen to death in the winter seasons! yet drunkards go on without fear and consideration: alas, alas! What will become of all such drunkards? Without doubt they must all go to hell, except they truly repent and turn to God. Drunkenness is so common amongst us, that even our young men and young women are not ashamed to get drunk. Our young men will get drunk as soon as they will eat when they are hungry.—It is generally esteemed amongst men, more abominable for a woman to be drunk, than a man; and yet there is nothing more common amongst us than female drunkards. Women ought to be more modest than men; the holy scriptures recommend modesty to women in particular:—but drunken women have no modesty at all. It is more intolerable for a woman to get drunk, if we consider further, that she is in great danger of falling into the hands of the sons of Belial, or wicked men; and being shamefully treated by them.

And here I cannot but observe, we find in sacred writ, a woe denounced against men, who put their bottles to their neighbours' mouth to make them drunk, that they may see their nakedness: and no doubt there are such devilish men now in our day, as there were in the days of old.

And to conclude, consider my poor kindred, you that are drunkards, into what a miserable condition you have brought yourselves. There is a dreadful woe thundering against you every day, and the Lord says, "That drunkards shall not inherit the kingdom of God."[25]

And now let me exhort you all to break off from your drunkenness, by a gospel repentance, and believe on the Lord Jesus and you shall be saved. Take warning by this doleful sight before us, and by all the dreadful judgments that have befallen poor drunkards. O let us all reform our lives, and live as becomes dying creatures, in time to come. Let us be persuaded that we are accountable creatures to God, and we must be called to an account in a few days. You that have been careless all your days, now awake to righteousness, and be concerned for your poor and never dying souls. Fight against all sins, and especially the sin that easily bests you, and behave in time to come as becomes rational creatures; and above all things, receive and believe on the Lord Jesus Christ, and you shall have eternal life; and when you come to die, your souls will be received into heaven, there to be with the Lord Jesus in eternal happiness, with all the saints in glory; which, God of his infinite mercy grant, through Jesus Christ our Lord.

AMEN.

Notes

[25] Corinthians 6.10.

John Newton (1725–1807)

While on a slave-trading mission in Africa in 1749 Newton experienced a deep conversion to evangelical Christianity.[1] When illness forced him to give up merchant sailing, he became acquainted with John Wesley and George Whitefield in London and eventually supported William Wilberforce in his anti-slavery campaign. He studied hard for the ministry and eventually became curate-in-charge at Olney in Buckinghamshire. William Cowper, who suffered from depression, sought out Newton, and the two collaborated on the *Olney Hymns* (1779). The most famous of these is Newton's "Amazing Grace." The fame of this hymn is especially great in America, where it has been recorded thousands of times, including versions by every major twentieth-century folk and blues singer from Mahalia Jackson to Elvis Presley, Sam Cooke, and Aretha Franklin. The text is based on the first edition.

HYMN XLI [Amazing Grace].

1. Amazing grace! (how sweet the sound)
   That saved a wretch like me!
I once was lost, but now am found,
   Was blind, but now I see.

2. 'Twas grace that taught my heart to fear,
   And grace my fears relieved;
How precious did that grace appear,
   The hour I first believed!

3. Through many dangers, toils and snares,
   I have already come;
'Tis grace has brought me safe thus far,
   And grace will lead me home.

4. The Lord has promised good to me,
   His word my hope secures;
He will my shield and portion be,
   As long as life endures.

5. Yes, when this flesh and heart shall fail,
   And mortal life shall cease;
I shall possess, within the veil,
   A life of joy and peace.

Notes

John Newton

[1] For biographical information on Newton I rely on the *ODNB* entry by D. Bruce Hindmarsh.

6. The earth shall soon dissolve like snow,
    The sun forbear to shine;
But God, who called me here below,
    Will be forever mine.

Oliver Goldsmith (1728?–1774)

Known sometimes as *ursa minor*, little bear, to Samuel Johnson's *ursa major*, Goldsmith was as productive a writer as any in his time. Having dropped out once and even sold his books, Goldsmith achieved his Bachelor of Arts degree at Trinity College, Dublin in 1750. He went first to Edinburgh and then to Padua to study medicine, and, having dallied in Europe, he arrived destitute in London in 1756. He tried on and off to establish a medical practice but soon gave all of his considerable energies to writing. Between 1759 and 1774 he published an extraordinary number of works; many were poorly researched and hastily compiled, such as his histories of England, Rome, and Greece, but all display his characteristically easy style.

The Citizen of the World; or, Letters from a Chinese Philosopher, Residing in London, to his Friends in the East (1762) established Goldsmith's reputation, but his most popular work, one of the most popular works in British literary history, is *The Vicar of Wakefield* (1766). Johnson sold the manuscript for Goldsmith for the sum of £63. The work went into nine editions in the next eight years, and there have been over a hundred since. Like the *Vicar*, Goldsmith's *Deserted Village* evokes sympathy and sentiment for country life. Unlike traditional pastoral poetry, Goldsmith's works do not present the country as an Arcadian paradise, but rather as a paradise lost. As he makes clear in his important essay, "The Revolution in Low Life," Goldsmith believed country life was being ruined by British interest in foreign trade and the concentration of capital and land in the hands of a small number of millionaires. He did not live long enough to witness the impact of the Industrial Revolution, which would finish, in some respects, the degradation he deplored.

Goldsmith produced a couple of important plays, *She Stoops to Conquer* and *The Good Natured Man*. His long poem *The Traveller* and his eight-volume *History of the Earth and Animated Nature* are also very worthy of mention. The standard edition of *Goldsmith's Collected Works*, which cannot of course include everything, is edited by Arthur Friedman, 5 vols. (Clarendon Press, 1966). The poems are edited with a complete commentary by Roger Lonsdale (Longman, 1969). My text of *The Deserted Village* is based on the first quarto edition (1770), with variants from the fourth quarto edition (also 1770). The text of "The Revolution in Low Life" comes from *Lloyd's Evening Post*, June 14–16, 1762. I am indebted to Lonsdale's and Friedman's editions for help with my notes.

The Revolution in Low Life

To the Editor of Lloyd's Evening Post (14–16 June 1762)

SIR, I spent part of the last summer in a little village, distant about fifty miles from town, consisting of near an hundred houses. It lay entirely out of the road of commerce, and was inhabited by a race of men who followed the primeval profession of agriculture for several generations. Though strangers to opulence, they were unacquainted with distress; few of them were known either to acquire a fortune or to die in indigence. By a long intercourse and frequent intermarriages they were all become in a manner one family; and, when the work of the day was done, spent the night agreeably

British Literature 1640–1789: An Anthology, Fourth Edition. Edited by Robert DeMaria, Jr.

in visits at each other's houses. Upon those occasions the poor traveller and stranger were always welcome; and they kept up the stated days of festivity with the strictest observance. They were merry at Christmas and mournful in Lent, got drunk on St. George's-day,[1] and religiously cracked nuts on Michaelmas-eve.[2]

Upon my first arrival I felt a secret pleasure in observing this happy community. The cheerfulness of the old, and the blooming beauty of the young, was no disagreeable change to one like me, whose whole life had been spent in cities. But my satisfaction was soon repressed, when I understood that they were shortly to leave this abode of felicity, of which they and their ancestors had been in possession time immemorial, and that they had received orders to seek for a new habitation. I was informed that a Merchant of immense fortune in London, who had lately purchased the estate on which they lived, intended to lay the whole out in a seat of pleasure for himself. I stayed till the day on which they were compelled to remove, and own I never felt so sincere a concern before.

I was grieved to see a generous, virtuous race of men, who should be considered as the strength and the ornament of their country, torn from their little habitations, and driven out to meet poverty and hardship among strangers. No longer to earn and enjoy the fruits of their labour, they were now going to toil as hirelings under some rigid Master, to flatter the opulent for a precarious meal, and to leave their children the inheritance of want and slavery. The modest matron followed her husband in tears, and often looked back at the little mansion[3] where she had passed her life in innocence, and to which she was never more to return; while the beautiful daughter parted for ever from her Lover, who was now become too poor to maintain her as his wife. All the connections of kindred were now irreparably broken; their neat gardens and well cultivated fields were left to desolation.

Strata jacent passim, hominumque boumque labores.[4]

Such was their misery, and I could wish that this were the only instance of such migrations of late. But I am informed that nothing is at present more common than such revolutions. In almost every part of the kingdom the laborious husbandman has been reduced, and the lands are now either occupied by some general undertaker, or turned into enclosures destined for the purposes of amusement or luxury. Wherever the traveller turns, while he sees one part of the inhabitants of the country becoming immensely rich, he sees the other growing miserably poor, and the happy equality of condition now entirely removed.

Let others felicitate their country upon the increase of foreign commerce and the extension of our foreign conquests; but for my part, this new introduction of wealth gives me but very little satisfaction. Foreign commerce, as it can be managed only by a few, tends proportionably to enrich only a few; neither moderate fortunes nor moderate abilities can carry it on; thus it tends rather to the accumulation of immense wealth in the hands of some, than to a diffusion of it among all; it is calculated rather to make individuals rich, than to make the aggregate happy.

Notes

The Revolution in Low Life

[1] *St. George's-day* April 23.

[2] *Michaelmas* the Feast of St. Michael and All Angels, September 29.

[3] *mansion* home.

[4] *Strata ... labores* "the works of men and beasts are strewn all over" (echoing Virgil, *Eclogues* 7.54).

Wherever we turn we shall find those governments that have pursued foreign commerce with too much assiduity at length becoming Aristocratical; and the immense property, thus necessarily acquired by some, has swallowed up the liberties of all. Venice, Genoa, and Holland, are little better at present than retreats for tyrants and prisons for slaves. The Great, indeed, boast of their liberties there, and they have liberty. The poor boast of liberty too; but, alas, they groan under the most rigorous oppression.

A country, thus parcelled out among the rich alone, is of all others the most miserable. The Great, in themselves, perhaps, are not so bad as they are generally represented; but I have almost ever found the dependants and favourites of the Great, strangers to every sentiment of honour and generosity. Wretches, who, by giving up their own dignity to those above them, insolently exact the same tribute from those below. A country, therefore, where the inhabitants are thus divided into the very rich and very poor, is, indeed, of all others the most helpless; without courage and without strength; neither enjoying peace within itself, and, after a time, unable to resist foreign invasion.

I shall conclude this paper with a picture of Italy just before its conquest, by Theodoric the Ostrogoth.[5] 'The whole country was at that time', says the Historian, 'one garden of pleasure; the seats of the great men of Rome covered the face of the whole kingdom; and even their villas were supplied with provisions not of their own growth, but produced in distant countries, where they were more industrious. But in proportion as Italy was then beautiful, and its possessors rich, it was also weak and defenceless. The rough peasant and hardy husbandman had been long obliged to seek for liberty and subsistence in Britain or Gaul; and, by leaving their native country, brought with them all the strength of the nation. There was none now to resist an invading army, but the slaves of the nobility or the effeminate citizens of Rome, the one without motive, the other without strength to make any opposition. They were easily, therefore, overcome, by a people more savage indeed, but far more brave than they'.

The Deserted Village, a Poem (1770)

SWEET Auburn! loveliest village of the plain,[1]
Where health and plenty cheered the labouring swain,
Where smiling spring its earliest visit paid,
And parting summer's lingering blooms delayed:
Dear lovely bowers of innocence and ease,
Seats of my youth, when every sport could please,
How often have I loitered o'er thy green,
Where humble happiness endeared each scene!
How often have I paused on every charm,

Notes

[5] *Theodoric the Ostrogoth* he became King of Italy in 493 and died in 526; among Goldsmith's many rapid productions was a Roman history (1769).

THE DESERTED VILLAGE

[1] *Auburn* Goldsmith uses the name of one or more real villages in rural England, and there are some resemblances between "Auburn" and Lissoy near Kilkenny West, Ireland, where Goldsmith grew up. However, Goldsmith is mostly talking about an abstract place that exemplifies the ills of rural depopulation, which he also discusses in "The Revolution in Low Life" (above).

The sheltered cot, the cultivated farm,
The never-failing brook, the busy mill,
The decent church that topped the neighbouring hill,
The hawthorn bush, with seats beneath the shade,
For talking age and whisp'ring lovers made!
How often have I blessed the coming day,
When toil remitting lent its turn to play,
And all the village train, from labour free,
Led up their sports beneath the spreading tree;
While many a pastime circled in the shade,
The young contending as the old surveyed;
And many a gambol frolicked o'er the ground,
And sleights of art and feats of strength went round;
And still, as each repeated pleasure tired,
Succeeding sports the mirthful band inspired;
The dancing pair that simply sought renown
By holding out to tire each other down:
The swain mistrustless of his smutted face,
While secret laughter tittered round the place;
The bashful virgin's sidelong looks of love,
The matron's glance that would those looks reprove:
These were thy charms, sweet village! sports like these
With sweet succession, taught e'en toil to please:
These round thy bowers their cheerful influence shed,
These were thy charms – but all these charms are fled.
    Sweet smiling village, loveliest of the lawn,
Thy sports are fled, and all thy charms withdrawn;
Amidst thy bowers the tyrant's hand is seen,
And desolation saddens all thy green:
One only master grasps the whole domain,
And half a tillage stints thy smiling plain.[2]
No more thy glassy brook reflects the day,
But, choked with sedges, works its weedy way;
Along thy glades, a solitary guest,
The hollow-sounding bittern guards its nest;[3]
Amidst thy desert walks the lapwing flies,[4]
And tires their echoes with unvaried cries;
Sunk are thy bowers in shapeless ruin all,
And the long grass o'ertops the mould'ring wall;
And trembling, shrinking from the spoiler's hand,
Far, far away, thy children leave the land.
    Ill fares the land, to hastening ills a prey,
Where wealth accumulates, and men decay:
Princes and lords may flourish, or may fade;

Notes

[2] *tillage* plowed land (as opposed to pasturage) which now occupies only half of what it once did.

[3] *bittern* a marsh bird known for its booming sound.

[4] *lapwing* "A clamorous bird with long wings" (Johnson); a kind of plover.

A breath can make them, as a breath has made:
But a bold peasantry, their country's pride,
When once destroyed, can never be supplied.
A time there was, ere England's griefs began,
When every rood of ground maintained its man;[5]
For him light labour spread her wholesome store,
Just gave what life required, but gave no more:
His best companions, innocence and health;
And his best riches, ignorance of wealth.
But times are altered; trade's unfeeling train
Usurp the land and dispossess the swain;
Along the lawn, where scattered hamlets rose,
Unwieldy wealth and cumbrous pomp repose,
And every want to opulence allied,
And every pang that folly pays to pride.
Those gentle hours that plenty bade to bloom,
Those calm desires that asked but little room,
Those healthful sports that graced the peaceful scene,
Lived in each look, and brightened all the green, –
These, far departing, seek a kinder shore,
And rural mirth and manners are no more.
Sweet Auburn! parent of the blissful hour,
Thy glades forlorn confess the tyrant's power.
Here, as I take my solitary rounds,
Amidst thy tangling walks and ruined grounds,
And, many a year elapsed, return to view
Where once the cottage stood, the hawthorn grew,
Remembrance wakes with all her busy train,
Swells at my breast, and turns the past to pain.
In all my wand'rings round this world of care,
In all my griefs – and God has giv'n my share –
I still had hopes, my latest hours to crown,
Amidst these humble bowers to lay me down;
To husband out life's taper at the close,
And keep the flame from wasting by repose:
I still had hopes, for pride attends us still,
Amidst the swains to show my book-learned skill,
Around my fire an evening group to draw,
And tell of all I felt and all I saw;
And as a hare whom hounds and horns pursue,
Pants to the place from whence at first she flew,
I still had hopes, my long vexations past,
Here to return, and die at home at last.
O blessed retirement, friend to life's decline,
Retreats from care, that never must be mine!
How happy he who crowns in shades like these

Notes

[5] *rood* a quarter of an acre.

A youth of labour with an age of ease;
Who quits a world where strong temptations try,
And, since 'tis hard to combat, learns to fly!
For him no wretches, born to work and weep,
Explore the mine, or tempt the dangerous deep;[6]
No surly porter stands in guilty state,
To spurn imploring famine from the gate;
But on he moves to meet his latter end,
Angels around befriending virtue's friend;
Bends to the grave with unperceived decay,
While resignation gently slopes the way;
And, all his prospects bright'ning to the last,
His heav'n commences ere the world be past!
  Sweet was the sound, when oft at evening's close
Up yonder hill the village murmur rose.
There, as I passed with careless steps and slow,
The mingling notes came softened from below;
The swain responsive as the milk-maid sung,
The sober herd that lowed to meet their young,
The noisy geese that gabbled o'er the pool,
The playful children just let loose from school,
The watch-dog's voice that bayed the whisp'ring wind,
And the loud laugh that spoke the vacant mind, –
These all in sweet confusion sought the shade,
And filled each pause the nightingale had made.
But now the sounds of population fail,
No cheerful murmurs fluctuate in the gale,[7]
No busy steps the grass-grown foot-way tread,
For all the bloomy flush of life is fled!
All but yon widowed, solitary thing,
That feebly bends beside the plashy spring:[8]
She, wretched matron, forced in age for bread,
To strip the brook with mantling cresses spread,[9]
To pick her wintry faggot from the thorn,[10]
To seek her nightly shed, and weep till morn;
She only left of all the harmless train,
The sad historian of the pensive plain.
  Near yonder copse, where once the garden smiled,
And still where many a garden flower grows wild;
There, where a few torn shrubs the place disclose,
The village preacher's modest mansion rose.[11]
A man he was to all the country dear,
And passing rich with forty pounds a year;[12]

Notes

[6] *tempt* attempt, try; venture upon.
[7] *gale* breeze.
[8] *plashy* "Watry; filled with puddles" (Johnson).
[9] *cresses* such as watercress, a green used in salads.
[10] *faggot* "A bundle of sticks bound together for the fire" (Johnson).
[11] *village preacher* said to portray Goldsmith's father, the Reverend Charles Goldsmith.
[12] *passing rich* exceedingly rich.

Remote from towns he ran his godly race,
Nor e'er had changed, nor wished to change, his place;
Unpractised he to fawn, or seek for power,
By doctrines fashioned to the varying hour;
Far other aims his heart had learned to prize,
More skilled to raise the wretched than to rise.
His house was known to all the vagrant train;
He chid their wand'rings but relieved their pain;
The long remembered beggar was his guest,
Whose beard descending swept his aged breast;
The ruined spendthrift, now no longer proud,
Claimed kindred there, and had his claims allowed;
The broken soldier, kindly bade to stay,
Sat by his fire, and talked the night away,
Wept o'er his wounds, or, tales of sorrow done,
Shouldered his crutch and showed how fields were won.
Pleased with his guests, the good man learned to glow,
And quite forgot their vices in their woe;
Careless their merits or their faults to scan,
His pity gave ere charity began.
   Thus to relieve the wretched was his pride,
And e'en his failings leaned to virtue's side;
But in his duty prompt at every call,
He watched and wept, he prayed and felt for all;
And, as a bird each fond endearment tries
To tempt its new-fledged offspring to the skies,
He tried each art, reproved each dull delay,
Allured to brighter worlds, and led the way.
   Beside the bed where parting life was laid,
And sorrow, guilt, and pain, by turns dismayed
The rev'rend champion stood. At his control
Despair and anguish fled the struggling soul;
Comfort came down the trembling wretch to raise,
And his last falt'ring accents whispered praise.
   At church, with meek and unaffected grace,
His looks adorned the venerable place;
Truth from his lips prevailed with double sway,
And fools who came to scoff remained to pray.
The service past, around the pious man,
With steady zeal, each honest rustic ran;
E'en children followed with endearing wile,
And plucked his gown to share the good man's smile.
His ready smile a parent's warmth expressed:
Their welfare pleased him, and their cares distressed:
To them his heart, his love, his griefs were given,
But all his serious thoughts had rest in Heaven.
As some tall cliff that lifts its awful form,
Swells from the vale, and midway leaves the storm,
Though round its breast the rolling clouds are spread,
Eternal sunshine settles on its head.
   Beside yon straggling fence that skirts the way,

With blossomed furze unprofitably gay,[13]
There, in his noisy mansion, skilled to rule,
The village master taught his little school.
A man severe he was, and stern to view;
I knew him well, and every truant knew;
Well had the boding tremblers learned to trace[14]
The day's disasters in his morning face;
Full well they laughed with counterfeited glee
At all his jokes, for many a joke had he;
Full well the busy whisper circling round
Conveyed the dismal tidings when he frowned.
Yet he was kind, or, if severe in aught,
The love he bore to learning was in fault;
The village all declared how much he knew;
'Twas certain he could write, and cipher too:[15]
Lands he could measure, terms and tides presage,[16]
And ev'n the story ran that he could gauge.[17]
In arguing, too, the parson owned his skill,
For, ev'n though vanquished, he could argue still;
While words of learned length and thundering sound
Amazed the gazing rustics ranged around;
And still they gazed, and still the wonder grew,
That one small head could carry all he knew.
But past is all his fame. The very spot
Where many a time he triumphed is forgot.
Near yonder thorn, that lifts its head on high,
Where once the sign-post caught the passing eye,
Low lies that house where nut-brown draughts inspired,[18]
Where grey-beard mirth and smiling toil retired,
Where village statesmen talked with looks profound,
And news much older than their ale went round.
Imagination fondly stoops to trace
The parlour splendours of that festive place;
The white-washed wall, the nicely sanded floor,
The varnished clock that clicked behind the door;
The chest contrived a double debt to pay,
A bed by night, a chest of drawers by day;
The pictures placed for ornament and use,
The Twelve Good Rules, the Royal Game of Goose;[19]
The hearth, except when winter chilled the day,
With aspen boughs, and flowers, and fennel gay;

Notes

13 *furze* gorse, a spiny, evergreen shrub.

14 *boding* foreboding, foretelling.

15 *cipher* "To practise arithmetic" (Johnson).

16 *terms and tides* calendar dates for the payment of debts and the celebration of holidays, respectively.

17 *gauge* "Measure with respect to the contents of a vessel" (Johnson); this involved dipping a gauge, or measuring rod, in a barrel containing some liquid and figuring its volume.

18 *nut-brown draughts* ale.

19 *The Twelve Good Rules* short bits of practical advice for living (e.g., "lay no wagers"), supposedly found in Charles I's study after his execution; *Goose* a simple game like Chutes and Ladders (Snakes and Ladders) in which players roll dice and advance their pieces on a board with hazards.

While broken tea-cups, wisely kept for show,
Ranged o'er the chimney, glistened in a row.
 Vain transitory splendours! could not all
Reprieve the tottering mansion from its fall?
Obscure it sinks, nor shall it more impart
An hour's importance to the poor man's heart.
Thither no more the peasant shall repair
To sweet oblivion of his daily care;
No more the farmer's news, the barber's tale,
No more the woodman's ballad shall prevail;
No more the smith his dusky brow shall clear,
Relax his pond'rous strength, and lean to hear;
The host himself no longer shall be found
Careful to see the mantling bliss go round;
Nor the coy maid, half willing to be pressed,
Shall kiss the cup to pass it to the rest.
 Yes! let the rich deride, the proud disdain,
These simple blessings of the lowly train;
To me more dear, congenial to my heart,
One native charm, than all the gloss of art;
Spontaneous joys, where nature has its play,
The soul adopts, and owns their first born sway;
Lightly they frolic o'er the vacant mind,
Unenvied, unmolested, unconfined.
But the long pomp, the midnight masquerade,
With all the freaks of wanton wealth arrayed –
In these, ere triflers half their wish obtain,
The toiling pleasure sickens into pain;
And, e'en while fashion's brightest arts decoy,
The heart distrusting asks if this be joy.
 Ye friends to truth, ye statesmen who survey
The rich man's joys increase, the poor's decay,
'Tis yours to judge, how wide the limits stand
Between a splendid and a happy land.
Proud swells the tide with loads of freighted ore,
And shouting Folly hails them from her shore;
Hoards e'en beyond the miser's wish abound,
And rich men flock from all the world around.
Yet count our gains. This wealth is but a name
That leaves our useful products still the same.
Not so the loss. The man of wealth and pride
Takes up a space that many poor supplied;
Space for his lake, his park's extended bounds,
Space for his horses, equipage, and hounds:
The robe that wraps his limbs in silken sloth
Has robbed the neighb'ring fields of half their growth:
His seat, where solitary sports are seen,
Indignant spurns the cottage from the green:
Around the world each needful product flies,
For all the luxuries the world supplies;
While thus the land adorned for pleasure all,

In barren splendour feebly waits the fall.
As some fair female unadorned and plain,
Secure to please while youth confirms her reign,
Slights every borrowed charm that dress supplies,
Nor shares with art the triumph of her eyes;
But when those charms are past, for charms are frail,
When time advances, and when lovers fail,
She then shines forth, solicitous to bless,
In all the glaring impotence of dress.
Thus fares the land by luxury betrayed:
In nature's simplest charms at first arrayed,
But verging to decline, its splendours rise,
Its vistas strike, its palaces surprise;
While, scourged by famine from the smiling land,
The mournful peasant leads his humble band,
And while he sinks, without one arm to save,
The country blooms – a garden and a grave.
Where then, ah! where, shall poverty reside,
To 'scape the pressure of contiguous pride?
If to some common's fenceless limits strayed[20]
He drives his flock to pick the scanty blade,
Those fenceless fields the sons of wealth divide,
And ev'n the bare-worn common is denied.
If to the city sped – what waits him there?
To see profusion that he must not share;
To see ten thousand baneful arts combined
To pamper luxury, and thin mankind;
To see those joys the sons of pleasure know
Extorted from his fellow-creature's woe.
Here while the courtier glitters in brocade,
There the pale artist plies the sickly trade;
Here while the proud their long-drawn pomps display,
There the black gibbet glooms beside the way.[21]
The dome where pleasure holds her midnight reign[22]
Here, richly decked, admits the gorgeous train:
Tumultuous grandeur crowds the blazing square,
The rattling chariots clash, the torches glare.
Sure scenes like these no troubles e'er annoy!
Sure these denote one universal joy!
Are these thy serious thoughts? – Ah, turn thine eyes
Where the poor houseless shiv'ring female lies.
She once, perhaps, in village plenty blessed,
Has wept at tales of innocence distressed;
Her modest looks the cottage might adorn

Notes

[20] *common* public lands for grazing, which were increasingly "enclosed" or acquired and fenced by the wealthy in the late eighteenth and nineteenth centuries.

[21] *gibbet* gallows.

[22] *dome* grand house.

Sweet as the primrose peeps beneath the thorn:
Now lost to all – her friends, her virtue fled,
Near her betrayer's door she lays her head,
And, pinched with cold, and shrinking from the shower,
With heavy heart deplores that luckless hour,
When idly first, ambitious of the town,
She left her wheel and robes of country brown.[23]
  Do thine, sweet Auburn, thine, the loveliest train –
Do thy fair tribes participate her pain?
Ev'n now, perhaps, by cold and hunger led,
At proud men's doors they ask a little bread!
  Ah, no! To distant climes, a dreary scene,
Where half the convex world intrudes between,
Through torrid tracts with fainting steps they go,
Where wild Altama murmurs to their woe.[24]
Far different there from all that charmed before,
The various terrors of that horrid shore:
Those blazing suns that dart a downward ray,
And fiercely shed intolerable day;
Those matted woods, where birds forget to sing,
But silent bats in drowsy clusters cling;
Those pois'nous fields with rank luxuriance crowned,
Where the dark scorpion gathers death around;
Where at each step the stranger fears to wake
The rattling terrors of the vengeful snake;
Where crouching tigers wait their hapless prey,[25]
And savage men more murd'rous still than they;
While oft in whirls the mad tornado flies,
Mingling the ravaged landscape with the skies.
Far different these from every former scene,
The cooling brook, the grassy-vested green,
The breezy covert of the warbling grove,
That only sheltered thefts of harmless love.
  Good Heaven! what sorrows gloomed that parting day,
That called them from their native walks away;
When the poor exiles, every pleasure past,
Hung round their bowers, and fondly looked their last,
And took a long farewell, and wished in vain
For seats like these beyond the western main,[26]
And shudd'ring still to face the distant deep,
Returned and wept, and still returned to weep!
The good old sire the first prepared to go
To new found worlds, and wept for others' woe;
But for himself, in conscious virtue brave,

Notes

[23] *wheel* spinning wheel.

[24] *Altama* the River Altamaha in southeast Georgia, then a British colony to which many bankrupt or otherwise disgraced persons fled or were sent.

[25] *tigers* naturalists of Goldsmith's day used the name for cougars as well as for other large cats.

[26] *seats* abodes, residences.

He only wished for worlds beyond the grave.
His lovely daughter, lovelier in her tears,
The fond companion of his helpless years,
Silent went next, neglectful of her charms,
And left a lover's for a father's arms.
With louder plaints the mother spoke her woes,
And blessed the cot where every pleasure rose,[27]
And kissed her thoughtless babes with many a tear,
And clasped them close, in sorrow doubly dear,
Whilst her fond husband strove to lend relief
In all the silent manliness of grief.
O luxury! thou cursed by Heaven's decree,
How ill exchanged are things like these for thee!
How do thy potions, with insidious joy,
Diffuse their pleasures only to destroy!
Kingdoms by thee, to sickly greatness grown,
Boast of a florid vigour not their own.
At every draught more large and large they grow,
A bloated mass of rank unwieldy woe;
Till sapped their strength, and every part unsound,
Down, down they sink, and spread a ruin round.
Ev'n now the devastation is begun,
And half the business of destruction done;
Ev'n now, methinks, as pond'ring here I stand,
I see the rural virtues leave the land.
Down where yon anchoring vessel spreads the sail,
That idly waiting flaps with every gale,
Downward they move, a melancholy band,
Pass from the shore, and darken all the strand.
Contented toil, and hospitable care,
And kind connubial tenderness, are there;
And piety, with wishes placed above,
And steady loyalty, and faithful love.
And thou, sweet Poetry, thou loveliest maid,
Still first to fly where sensual joys invade;
Unfit in these degenerate times of shame
To catch the heart, or strike for honest fame;
Dear charming nymph, neglected and decried,
My shame in crowds, my solitary pride;
Thou source of all my bliss, and all my woe,
That found'st me poor at first, and keep'st me so;
Thou guide by which the nobler arts excel,
Thou nurse of every virtue, fare thee well!
Farewell, and oh! where'er thy voice be tried,
On Torno's cliffs, or Pambamarca's side,[28]
Whether where equinoctial fervours glow,

Notes

[27] *cot* cottage.

[28] *Torno* a river in Sweden; *Pambamarca* a mountain in Ecuador.

Or winter wraps the polar world in snow,
Still let thy voice, prevailing over time,
Redress the rigours of th' inclement clime;
Aid slighted truth, with thy persuasive strain
Teach erring man to spurn the rage of gain;
Teach him that states of native strength possessed,
Though very poor, may still be very blessed;
That trade's proud empire hastes to swift decay,
As ocean sweeps the laboured mole away;[29]
While self-dependent power can time defy,
As rocks resist the billows and the sky.[30]

Notes

[29] *mole* a pier or breakwater.

[30] *That trade's … and the sky* these two couplets were written by Samuel Johnson.

Edmund Burke (1729–1797)

In his *Life of Johnson* Boswell reports, "once, when Johnson was ill, and unable to exert himself as much as usual without fatigue, Mr. Burke having been mentioned, he said, 'That fellow calls forth all my powers. Were I to see Burke now, it would kill me.' " Johnson and Burke disagreed on some political and aesthetic issues, but their mutual respect for each other was unshakeable. Burke's powers of speaking were developed during his many years as a very active Member of Parliament. He was a Whig allied to Lord Rockingham, and he made a famous and original defense of party politics, but in all of his opinions and all of his writing there is evidence of the quality that Johnson perceived and even occasionally feared. Political opinions or positions in Burke's work are always rooted not only in a sense of cultural history but also in an appreciation of his participation in the ongoing, long-standing life of culture. He was critical of George III's handling of the American colonies and infuriated by the corruption of the British administration in India, yet he was horrified by the French Revolution and the sympathy it aroused in England. This constellation of opinions used to be looked upon as representative of Burke's growing conservatism, but a deeper appreciation of his thought shows broad areas of consistency throughout his apparently diverse positions. There are principles of civility and compassion, a confidence in the benefits of conversation and compromise, and a hatred of mechanistic or absolutist approaches to human problems that persist throughout his political writings.

In 1790, when Burke published his *Reflections on the Revolution in France*, Mary Wollstonecraft and others in England who thought about the wretched lives of the French people under the old regime would have none of his sympathy for Marie Antoinette and the world of chivalry that seemed to die along with her. It is perhaps even harder today to worry about the loss of chivalry, but like all works with real "mind," Burke's contains a prophetic element, and seems now to have predicted the excesses and tyranny of the new French Republic and its eventual turn to imperialism under Napoleon.

Born in Dublin, educated at Trinity College and then at Middle Temple (law school) in London, Burke did not successfully enter politics until 1765. Before that he wrote some philosophical works, including his very influential *Philosophical Inquiry into the Origin of our Ideas of the Sublime and the Beautiful* (1757). This became an important text for continental writers like Lessing and in the whole movement of Romanticism. Burke also started *The Annual Register*, a review of worldwide political events, in 1758 and continued to make contributions to it throughout his lifetime.

The following extract from Burke's *Philosophical Inquiry* is based on the second edition (1759); the small selection from his *Reflections* comes from the first edition. I have benefited from the Penguin edition of *Reflections on the Revolution in France* edited by Conor Cruise O'Brien. His *Great Melody: a Biography and Commented Anthology of Edmund Burke* (University of Chicago Press, 1993) is impassioned and interesting, but F. P. Lock's new biography, *Edmund Burke* (Clarendon Press, 1998–2006), is definitive. Also essential is David Bromwich's *The Intellectual Life of Edmund Burke* (Harvard University Press, 2014). Volume VIII of *The Writings and Speeches of Edmund Burke*, ed. L. G. Mitchell (Clarendon Press, 1989) provides standard texts of Burke's writings on the French Revolution. Volume I of this series includes his essay on the sublime and the beautiful.

British Literature 1640–1789: An Anthology, Fourth Edition. Edited by Robert DeMaria, Jr.

from *A Philosophical Inquiry into the Origin of our Ideas of the Sublime and the Beautiful* (1757)

Part 2, Section 1, Of the Passion caused by the SUBLIME

The passion caused by the great and sublime in *nature*, when those causes operate most powerfully, is Astonishment; and astonishment is that state of the soul, in which all its motions are suspended, with some degree of horror. In this case the mind is so entirely filled with its object, that it cannot entertain any other, nor by consequence reason on that object which employs it. Hence arises the great power of the sublime, that far from being produced by them, it anticipates our reasonings, and hurries us on by an irresistible force. Astonishment, as I have said, is the effect of the sublime in its highest degree; the inferior effects are admiration, reverence and respect.

Section 2
TERROR

No passion so effectually robs the mind of all its powers of acting and reasoning as fear. For fear being an apprehension of pain or death, it operates in a manner that resembles actual pain. Whatever therefore is terrible, with regard to sight, is sublime too, whether this cause of terror, be endued with greatness of dimensions or not; for it is impossible to look on anything as trifling, or contemptible, that may be dangerous. There are many animals, who though far from being large, are yet capable of raising ideas of the sublime, because they are considered as objects of terror. As serpents and poisonous animals of almost all kinds. And to things of great dimensions, if we annex an adventitious idea of terror, they become without comparison greater. A level plain of a vast extent on land, is certainly no mean idea; the prospect of such a plain may be as extensive as a prospect of the ocean; but can it ever fill the mind with any thing so great as the ocean itself? This is owing to several causes, but it is owing to none more than this, that the ocean is an object of no small terror. Indeed terror is in all cases whatsoever, either more openly or latently the ruling principle of the sublime. Several languages bear a strong testimony to the affinity of these ideas. They frequently use the same word, to signify indifferently the modes of astonishment or admiration and those of terror. θάμβος is in Greek, either fear or wonder; δείνος is terrible or respectable; αἰδέω to reverence or fear. *Vereor* in Latin, is what αἰδέω is in Greek. The Romans used the verb *stupeo*, a term which strongly marks the state of an astonished mind, to express the effect either of simple fear, or of astonishment; the word *attonitus* (thunderstruck) is equally expressive of the alliance of these ideas; and do not the French *étonnement*, and the English *astonishment* and *amazement*, point out as clearly the kindred emotions which attend fear and wonder? They who have a more general knowledge of languages, could produce, I make no doubt, many other and equally striking examples.

Section 3
OBSCURITY

To make anything very terrible, obscurity seems in general to be necessary. When we know the full extent of any danger, when we can accustom our eyes to it, a great deal of the apprehension vanishes. Every one will be sensible of this, who considers how greatly night adds to our dread, in all cases of danger, and how much the notions of ghosts and goblins, of which none can form clear ideas, affect minds, which give credit to the popular tales concerning such sorts of beings. Those despotic governments, which are founded on the passions of men, and principally upon the passion of fear, keep their chief as much as may be from the public eye. The policy has been the same in many cases of religion. Almost all the heathen temples were dark. Even in the barbarous temples of the Americans at this day, they keep their idol in a dark part of the hut, which is consecrated to his worship. For this purpose too the Druids performed all their ceremonies in the bosom of the darkest woods, and in the shade of the oldest and most spreading oaks. No person seems better to have understood the secret of heightening, or of setting terrible things, if I may use the expression, in their strongest light by the force of a judicious obscurity, than Milton. His description of Death in the second book[1] is admirably studied; it is astonishing with what a gloomy pomp, with what a significant and expressive uncertainty of strokes and colouring he has finished the portrait of the king of terrors.

The other shape,
If shape it might be called that shape had none
Distinguishable, in member, joint, or limb;
Or substance might be called that shadow seemed,
For each seemed either; black he stood as night;
Fierce as ten furies; terrible as hell;
And shook a deadly dart. What seemed his head
The likeness of a kingly crown had on.

In this description all is dark, uncertain, confused, terrible, and sublime to the last degree.

Section 4
Of the difference between CLEARNESS and OBSCURITY with regard to the passions

It is one thing to make an idea clear, and another to make it *affecting* to the imagination. If I make a drawing of a palace, or a temple, or a landscape, I present a very clear idea of those objects; but then (allowing for the effect of imitation which is something) my picture can at most affect only as the palace, temple, or landscape would have affected in the reality. On the other hand, the most lively and spirited verbal description I can give, raises a very obscure and imperfect *idea* of such objects; but then it is in my power to raise a stronger *emotion* by the description than I could do by the best painting. This experience constantly evinces. The proper manner of conveying the *affections* of the mind from one to another, is by words; there is a great insufficiency in all other methods of communication; and so far is a clearness of imagery from being absolutely necessary to an influence upon the passions, that they may be considerably operated upon without presenting any image at all, by certain sounds adapted to that purpose;

Notes

FROM *A PHILOSOPHICAL INQUIRY*

[1] *second book Paradise Lost* 2.666–73.

of which we have sufficient proof in the acknowledged and powerful effects of instrumental music. In reality a great clearness helps but little towards affecting the passions, as it is in some sort an enemy to all enthusiasms whatsoever.

Section [5]
The same subject continued

There are two verses in Horace's art of poetry that seem to contradict this opinion, for which reason I shall take a little more pains in clearing it all up. The verses are,

> Segnius irritant animos demissa per aures
> Quam quæ sunt oculis subjecta fidelibus[2]

On this the Abbé du Bos[3] founds a criticism, wherein he gives painting the preference to poetry in the article of moving the passions; principally on account of the greater *clearness* of the idea it represents. I believe this excellent judge was led into this mistake (if it be a mistake) by his system, to which he found it more conformable than I imagine it will be found to experience. I know several who admire and love painting, and yet who regard the objects of their admiration in that art, with coolness enough, in comparison of that warmth with which they are animated by affecting pieces of poetry or rhetoric. Among the common sort of people, I could never perceive that painting had much influence on their passions. It is true that the best sorts of painting, as well as the best sorts of poetry, are not much understood in that sphere. But it is most certain, that their passions are very strongly roused by a fanatic preacher, or by the ballads of Chevy-chase, or the children in the wood, and by other little popular poems and tales that are current in that rank of life. I do not know of any paintings, bad or good, that produce the same effect. So that poetry with all its obscurity, has a more general as well as a more powerful dominion over the passions than the other art. And I think there are reasons in nature why the obscure idea, when properly conveyed, should be more affecting than the clear. It is our ignorance of things that causes all our admiration, and chiefly excites our passions. Knowledge and acquaintance make the most striking causes affect but little. It is thus with the vulgar, and all men are as vulgar in what they do not understand. The ideas of eternity, and infinity, are among the most affecting we have, and yet perhaps there is nothing of which we really understand so little, as of infinity and eternity. We do not anywhere meet a more sublime description than this justly celebrated one of Milton, wherein he gives the portrait of Satan with a dignity so suitable to the subject.

> He above the rest
> In shape and gesture proudly eminent
> Stood like a tower; his form had not yet lost
> All her original brightness, nor appeared
> Less than archangel ruined, and th' excess
> Of glory obscured: as when the sun new ris'n
> Looks through the horizontal misty air

Notes

[2] "[actions] reported in hearing affect the mind more sluggishly than those which are exposed to the faithful eyes" (*Ars Poetica* 180–1).

[3] *Abbé du Bos* Jean-Baptiste Dubos (1670–1742), author of *Réflexions critiques sur la poésie et sur la peinture* (1719; trans. Thomas Nugent, 1748).

Shorn of his beams; or from behind the moon
In dim eclipse disastrous twilight sheds
On half the nations; and with fear of change
Perplexes monarchs. [*Paradise Lost* 1.589–99]

Here is a very noble picture; and in what does this poetical picture consist? in images of a tower, an archangel, the sun rising through the mists, or in an eclipse, the ruin of monarchs, and the revolution of kingdoms. The mind is hurried out of itself, by a crowd of great and confused images; which affect because they are crowded and confused. For separate them, and you lose much of the greatness, and join them, and you infallibly lose the clearness. The images raised by poetry are always of this obscure kind; though in general the effects of poetry, are by no means to be attributed to the images it raises; which point we shall examine more at large hereafter. But painting, when we have allowed for the pleasure of imitation, can only affect simply by the images it presents; and even in painting a judicious obscurity in some things contributes to the effect of the picture; because the images in painting are exactly similar to those in nature; and in nature dark, confused, uncertain images have a greater power on the fancy[4] to form the grander passions than those have which are more clear and determinate. But where and when this observation may be applied to practice, and how far it shall be extended, will be better deduced from the nature of the subject, and from the occasion, than from any rules that can be given.

I am sensible that this idea has met with opposition, and is likely still to be rejected by several. But let it be considered that hardly any thing can strike the mind with its greatness, which does not make some sort of approach towards infinity; which nothing can do whilst we are able to perceive its bounds; but to see an object distinctly, and to perceive its bounds, is one and the same thing. A clear idea is therefore another name for a little idea. There is a passage in the book of Job amazingly sublime, and this sublimity is principally due to the terrible uncertainty of the thing described. 'In thoughts from the visions of the night, when deep sleep falleth upon men, fear came upon me and trembling, which made all my bones to shake. Then a spirit passed before my face. The hair of my flesh stood up. It stood still, but I could not discern the form thereof; an image was before mine eyes; there was silence; and I heard a voice, – Shall mortal man be more just than God?' [4.13–17]. We are first prepared with the utmost solemnity for the vision; we are first terrified, before we are let even into the obscure cause of our emotion; but when this grand cause of terror makes its appearance, what is it? is it not, wrapped up in the shades of its own incomprehensible darkness, more awful, more striking, more terrible, than the liveliest description, than the clearest painting could possibly represent it? When painters have attempted to give us a clear representation of these fanciful and terrible ideas, they have I think almost always failed; insomuch that I have been at a loss, in all the pictures I have seen of hell, whether the painter did not intend something ludicrous. Several painters have handled a subject of this kind, with a view of assembling as many horrid phantoms as their imagination could suggest; but all the designs I have chanced to meet of the temptations of St. Anthony,[5] were rather a sort of odd wild grotesques, than any thing capable of producing a serious passion. In all these subjects poetry is very happy. Its apparitions, its

Notes

[4] *fancy* imagination.

[5] *temptations of St. Anthony* e.g., engraving by Martin Schongauer (c.1480–90; Metropolitan Museum of Art, New York), in which demons of all sorts pull and cudgel him every which way.

chimeras, its harpies, its allegorical figures, are grand and affecting; and though Virgil's Fame, and Homer's Discord, are obscure, they are magnificent figures. These figures in painting would be clear enough, but I fear they might become ridiculous. ...

Section 13
Beautiful objects small

The most obvious point that presents itself to us in examining any object, is its extent or quantity. And what degree of extent prevails in bodies, that are held beautiful, may be gathered from the usual manner of expression concerning it. I am told that in most languages, the objects of love are spoken of under diminutive epithets. It is so in all the languages of which I have any knowledge. In Greek the ιον,[6] and other diminutive terms, are almost always the terms of affection and tenderness. These diminutives were commonly added by the Greeks to the names of persons with whom they conversed on terms of friendship and familiarity. Though the Romans were a people of less quick and delicate feelings, yet they naturally slid into the lessening termination upon the same occasions. Anciently in the English language the diminishing *ling* was added to the names of persons and things that were the objects of love. Some we retain still, as darling (or little dear) and a few others. But to this day in ordinary conversation, it is usual to add the endearing name of *little* to every thing we love; the French and Italians make use of these affectionate diminutives even more than we. In the animal creation, out of our own species, it is the small we are inclined to be fond of; little birds, and some of the smaller kinds of beasts. A great beautiful thing, is a manner of expression scarcely ever used; but that of a great ugly thing, is very common. There is a wide difference between admiration and love. The sublime, which is the cause of the former, always dwells on great objects, and terrible; the latter on small ones, and pleasing; we submit to what we admire, but we love what submits to us; in one case we are forced, in the other we are flattered into compliance. In short, the ideas of the sublime and the beautiful stand on foundations so different, that it is hard, I had almost said impossible, to think of reconciling them in the same subject, without considerably lessening the effect of the one or the other upon the passions. So that attending to their quantity, beautiful objects are comparatively small.

Section 14
SMOOTHNESS

The next property constantly observable in such objects is *Smoothness*. A quality so essential to beauty, that I do not now recollect anything beautiful that is not smooth. In trees and flowers, smooth leaves are beautiful; smooth slopes of earth in gardens; smooth streams in the landscape; smooth coats of birds and beasts in animal beauties; in fine women, smooth skins; and in several sorts of ornamental furniture, smooth and polished surfaces. A very considerable part of the effect of beauty is owing to this quality; indeed the most considerable. For take any beautiful object, and give it a broken and rugged surface, and however well formed it may be in other

Notes

[6] ιον a diminutive suffix.

respects, it pleases no longer. Whereas let it want ever so many of the other constituents, if it wants not this, it becomes more pleasing than almost all the others without it. This seems to me so evident, that I am a good deal surprised, that none who have handled the subject have made any mention of the quality of smoothness in the enumeration of those that go to the forming of beauty. For indeed any ruggedness, any sudden projection, any sharp angle, is in the highest degree contrary to that idea.

Section 15
Gradual VARIATION

But as perfectly beautiful bodies are not composed of angular parts, so their parts never continue long in the same right line. They vary their direction every moment, and they change under the eye by a deviation continually carrying on, but for whose beginning or end you will find it difficult to ascertain a point. The view of a beautiful bird will illustrate this observation. Here we see the head increasing insensibly to the middle, from whence it lessens gradually until it mixes with the neck; the neck loses itself in a larger swell, which continues to the middle of the body, when the whole decreases again to the tail; the tail takes a new direction; but it soon varies its new course; it blends again with the other parts; and the line is perpetually changing, above, below, upon every side. In this description I have before me the idea of a dove; it agrees very well with most of the conditions of beauty. It is smooth and downy; its parts are (to use that expression) melted into one another; you are presented with no sudden protuberance through the whole, and yet the whole is continually changing. Observe that part of a beautiful woman where she is perhaps the most beautiful, about the neck and the breasts; the smoothness; the softness; the easy and insensible swell; the variety of the surface, which is never for the smallest space the same; the deceitful maze, through which the unsteady eye slides giddily, without knowing where to fix, or whither it is carried. Is not this a demonstration of that change of surface continual and yet hardly perceptible at any point which forms one of the great constituents of beauty? It gives me no small pleasure to find that I can strengthen my theory in this point, by the opinion of the very ingenious Mr. Hogarth; whose idea of the line of beauty[7] I take in general to be extremely just. But the idea of variation, without attending so accurately to the *manner* of the variation, has led him to consider angular figures as beautiful; these figures, it is true, vary greatly; yet they vary in a sudden and broken manner; and I do not find any natural object which is angular, and at the same time beautiful. Indeed few natural objects are entirely angular. But I think those which approach the most nearly to it, are the ugliest. I must add too, that, so far as I could observe of nature, though the varied line is that alone in which complete beauty is found, yet there is no particular line which is always found in the most completely beautiful; and which is therefore beautiful in preference to all other lines. At least I never could observe it.

Notes

[7] *Hogarth ... line of beauty* William Hogarth, in his *Analysis of Beauty* (1753), proposes an essential aesthetic standard in his "line of beauty," a serpentine or winding line, combining uniformity and variety in the most pleasing proportion.

Section 16
DELICACY

An air of robustness and strength is very prejudicial to beauty. An appearance of *delicacy*, and even of fragility, is almost essential to it. Whoever examines the vegetable or animal creation, will find this observation to be founded in nature. It is not the oak, the ash, or the elm, or any of the robust trees of the forest, which we consider as beautiful; they are awful and majestic; they inspire a sort of reverence. It is the delicate myrtle, it is the orange, it is the almond, it is the jessamine, it is the vine, which we look on as vegetable beauties. It is the flowery species, so remarkable for its weakness and momentary duration, that gives us the liveliest idea of beauty, and elegance. Among animals; the greyhound is more beautiful than the mastiff; and the delicacy of a jennet,[8] a barb,[9] or an Arabian horse, is much more amiable than the strength and stability of some horses of war or carriage. I need here say little of the fair sex, where I believe the point will be easily allowed me. The beauty of women is considerably owing to their weakness, or delicacy, and is even enhanced by their timidity, a quality of mind analogous to it. I would not here be understood to say, that weakness betraying very bad health has any share in beauty; but the ill effect of this is not because it is weakness, but because the ill state of health which produces such weakness alters the other conditions of beauty; the parts in such a case collapse; the bright colour, the *lumen purpureum juventae*[10] is gone; and the fine variation is lost in wrinkles, sudden breaks, and right lines.

from *Reflections on the Revolution in France, and on the Proceedings in Certain Societies in London Relative to that Event In a Letter Intended to have been sent to a Gentleman In Paris* (1790)

Far am I from denying in theory; full as far is my heart from withholding in practice (if I were of power to give or to withhold) the *real* rights of men.[1] In denying their false claims of right, I do not mean to injure those which are real, and are such as their pretended rights would totally destroy. If civil society be made for the advantage of man, all the advantages for which it is made become his right. It is an institution of beneficence; and law itself is only beneficence acting by a rule. Men have a right to live by that rule; they have a right to do justice; as between their fellows, whether their fellows are in public function or in ordinary occupation. They have a right to the fruits of their industry; and to the means of making their industry fruitful. They have a right to the acquisitions of their parents; to the nourishment and improvement of their offspring; to instruction in life, and to consolation in death. Whatever each man can separately do, without trespassing upon others, he has a right to do for himself; and he has a right to a fair portion of all which society, with all its combinations of skill and force, can do in his favour. But as to the share of power, authority, and direction which each

Notes

[8] *jennet* a small Spanish horse.

[9] *barb* or Barbary, a Moroccan horse noted for speed.

[10] *lumen purpureum juventae* "the beautiful light of youth" (Virgil, *Aeneid* 1.590–1).

FROM *REFLECTIONS*

[1] *rights of men* or the *Rights of Man*, as Thomas Paine would entitle his response to Burke (see the selection below), was a key phrase in the rhetoric of the French Revolution, but it already had a history in seventeenth- and early eighteenth-century political writings (such as John Locke's) with which most commentators in the late eighteenth century agreed.

individual ought to have in the management of the state, that I must deny to be amongst the direct original rights of man in civil society; for I have in my contemplation the civil social man, and no other. It is a thing to be settled by convention.

If civil society be the offspring of convention, that convention must be its law. That convention must limit and modify all the descriptions of constitution which are formed under it. Every sort of legislative, judicial, or executory power are its creatures. They can have no being in any other state of things; and how can any man claim under the conventions of civil society, rights which do not so much as suppose its existence? Rights which are absolutely repugnant to it? One of the first motives to civil society, and which becomes one of its fundamental rules, is, *that no man should be judge in his own cause*. By this each person has at once divested himself of the first fundamental right of uncovenanted man,[2] that is, to judge for himself, and to assert his own cause. He abdicates all right to be his own governor. He inclusively, in a great measure, abandons the right of self-defence, the first law of nature. Men cannot enjoy the rights of an uncivil and of a civil state together. That he may obtain justice he gives up his right of determining what it is in points the most essential to him. That he may secure some liberty, he makes a surrender in trust of the whole of it.

Government is not made in virtue of natural rights, which may and do exist in total independence of it; and exist in much greater clearness, and in a much greater degree of abstract perfection: but their abstract perfection is their practical defect. By having a right to every thing they want[3] every thing. Government is a contrivance of human wisdom to provide for human *wants*. Men have a right that these wants should be provided for by this wisdom. Among these wants is to be reckoned the want, out of civil society, of a sufficient restraint upon their passions. Society requires not only that the passions of individuals should be subjected, but that even in the mass and body as well as in the individuals, the inclinations of men should frequently be thwarted, their will controlled, and their passions brought into subjection. This can only be done *by a power out of themselves*; and not, in the exercise of its function, subject to that will and to those passions which it is its office to bridle and subdue. In this sense the restraints on men, as well as their liberties, are to be reckoned among their rights. But as the liberties and the restrictions vary with times and circumstances, and admit of infinite modifications, they cannot be settled upon any abstract rule; and nothing is so foolish as to discuss them upon that principle.

The moment you abate any thing from the full rights of men, each to govern himself, and suffer any artificial positive limitation upon those rights, from that moment the whole organization of government becomes a consideration of convenience. This it is which makes the constitution of a state, and the due distribution of its powers, a matter of the most delicate and complicated skill. It requires a deep knowledge of human nature and human necessities, and of the things which facilitate or obstruct the various ends which are to be pursued by the mechanism of civil institutions. The state is to have recruits to its strength, and remedies to its distempers. What is the use of discussing a man's abstract right to food or medicine? The question is upon the method of procuring and administering them. In that deliberation I shall always advise to call in the aid of the farmer and the physician, rather than the professor of metaphysics. The science of constructing a commonwealth, or renovating it, or reforming it, is, like every other experimental science, not to be taught *a priori*. Nor is it a short experience that can instruct us in that practical science; because the real effects of moral causes are not always immediate; but that which in

Notes

[2] *uncovenanted man* human beings with no covenant or compact of society; asocial, barbarous humanity.

[3] *want* lack, need.

the first instance is prejudicial may be excellent in its remoter operation; and its excellence may arise even from the ill effects it produces in the beginning. The reverse also happens; and very plausible schemes, with very pleasing commencements, have often shameful and lamentable conclusions. In states there are often some obscure and almost latent causes, things which appear at first view of little moment, on which a very great part of its prosperity or adversity may most essentially depend. The science of government being therefore so practical in itself, and intended for such practical purposes, a matter which requires experience, and even more experience than any person can gain in his whole life, however sagacious and observing he may be, it is with infinite caution that any man ought to venture upon pulling down an edifice which has answered in any tolerable degree for ages the common purposes of society, or on building it up again, without having models and patterns of approved utility before his eyes.

These metaphysic rights entering into common life, like rays of light which pierce into a dense medium, are, by the laws of nature refracted from their straight line. Indeed in the gross and complicated mass of human passions and concerns, the primitive rights of men undergo such a variety of refractions and reflections, that it becomes absurd to talk of them as if they continued in the simplicity of their original direction. The nature of man is intricate; the objects of society are of the greatest possible complexity; and therefore no simple disposition or direction of power can be suitable either to man's nature, or to the quality of his affairs. When I hear the simplicity of contrivance aimed at and boasted of in any new political constitutions, I am at no loss to decide that the artificers are grossly ignorant of their trade, or totally negligent of their duty. The simple governments are fundamentally defective, to say no worse of them. If you were to contemplate society in but one point of view, all these simple modes of polity are infinitely captivating. In effect each would answer its single end much more perfectly than the more complex is able to attain all its complex purposes. But it is better that the whole should be imperfectly and anomalously answered than that, while some parts are provided for with great exactness, others might be totally neglected, or perhaps materially injured, by the over-care of a favourite member.

The pretended rights of these theorists are all extremes; and in proportion as they are metaphysically true, they are morally and politically false. The rights of men are in a sort of *middle*, incapable of definition, but not impossible to be discerned. The rights of men in governments are their advantages; and these are often in balances between differences of good; in compromises sometimes between good and evil, and sometimes between evil and evil. Political reason is a computing principle; adding, subtracting, multiplying, and dividing, morally and not metaphysically or mathematically, true moral denominations.

By these theorists the right of the people is almost always sophistically confounded with their power. The body of the community, whenever it can come to act, can meet with no effectual resistance; but till power and right are the same, the whole body of them has no right inconsistent with virtue, and the first of all virtues, prudence. Men have no right to what is not reasonable, and to what is not for their benefit; for though a pleasant writer said, *Liceat perire poetis* when one of them, in cold blood, is said to have leaped into the flames of a volcanic revolution, *Ardentem frigidus Ætnam insiluit*,[4] I consider such a frolic rather as an unjustifiable poetic licence, than as one of the

Notes

[4] *Ardentem frigidus Ætnam/insiluit ... liceat perire poetis* "[Empedocles] coolly leapt into volcanic Mount Ætna ... let poets have the right to depart from life" (Horace, *Ars Poetica* 465–6); the poet did this in hope of convincing people that he had left the world and become a god; only his bronze sandals were found to indicate his fate.

franchises of Parnassus;[5] and whether he was a poet or divine, or politician that chose to exercise this kind of right, I think that more wise, because more charitable thoughts would urge me rather to save the man, than to preserve his brazen slippers as the monuments of his folly.

The kind of anniversary sermons,[6] to which a great part of what I write refers, if men are not shamed out of their present course, in commemorating the fact, will cheat many out of the principles, and deprive them of the benefits of the Revolution they commemorate. I confess to you, Sir, I never liked this continual talk of resistance and revolution, or the practice of making the extreme medicine of the constitution its daily bread. It renders the habit of society dangerously valetudinary: it is taking periodical doses of mercury sublimate,[7] and swallowing down repeated provocatives of cantharides[8] to our love of liberty.

This distemper of remedy, grown habitual, relaxes and wears out, by a vulgar and prostituted use, the spring of that spirit which is to be exerted on great occasions. It was in the most patient period of Roman servitude that themes of tyrannicide made the ordinary exercise of boys at school – *cum perimit sævos classis numerosa tyrannos*.[9] In the ordinary state of things, it produces in a country like ours the worst effects, even on the cause of that liberty which it abuses with the dissoluteness of an extravagant speculation. Almost all the high-bred republicans[10] of my time have, after a short space, become the most decided, thorough-paced courtiers; they soon left the business of a tedious, moderate, but practical resistance to those of us whom, in the pride and intoxication of their theories, they have slighted, as not much better than tories.[11] Hypocrisy, of course, delights in the most sublime speculations; for, never intending to go beyond speculation, it costs nothing to have it magnificent. But even in cases where rather levity than fraud was to be suspected in these ranting speculations, the issue has been much the same. These professors, finding their extreme principles not applicable to cases which call only for a qualified, or, as I may say, civil and legal resistance, in such cases employ no resistance at all. It is with them a war or a revolution, or it is nothing. Finding their schemes of politics not adapted to the state of the world in which they live, they often come to think lightly of all public principle; and are ready, on their part, to abandon for a very trivial interest what they find of very trivial value. Some indeed are of more steady and persevering natures; but these are eager politicians out of parliament who have little to tempt them to abandon their favourite projects. They have some change in the church or state, or both, constantly in their view. When that is the case, they are always bad citizens, and perfectly unsure connections. For, considering their speculative designs as of infinite value, and the actual arrangement of the state as of no estimation, they are at best indifferent about it. They see no merit in the good, and no fault in the vicious, management of public affairs; they rather rejoice in the latter, as more propitious to revolution. They see no merit or demerit in any man, or any action, or any political principle, any further than as they may forward or retard

Notes

5 *franchises of Parnassus* rights of poets, those inhabiting the mountain sacred to Apollo and the muses.

6 *anniversary sermons* Burke refers to a sermon by Richard Price, a dissenting minister, who celebrated the hundredth anniversary of the Glorious Revolution (1688) and expressed much sympathy for the French Revolution.

7 *mercury sublimate* also called "corrosive sublimate," once a common but admittedly dangerous treatment for many diseases, including syphilis.

8 *cantharides* Spanish fly, used as a stimulant.

9 *cum perimit sævos classis numerosa tyrannos* "when a numerous class slays the wretched tyrant" to fulfill their hackneyed assignment in rhetoric (Juvenal 6.151).

10 *republican* "One who thinks a commonwealth without monarchy the best government" (Johnson, 1773).

11 *tory* "One who adheres to the ancient constitution of the state and the apostolical hierarchy of the church of England; opposed to a *whig*" (Johnson, 1773).

their design of change: they therefore take up, one day, the most violent and stretched prerogative,[12] and another time the wildest democratic ideas of freedom, and pass from one to the other without any sort of regard to cause, to person, or to party.

In France you are now in the crisis of a revolution, and in the transit from one form of government to another – you cannot see that character of men exactly in the same situation in which we see it in this country. With us it is militant; with you it is triumphant; and you know how it can act when its power is commensurate to its will. I would not be supposed to confine those observations to any description of men, or to comprehend all men of any description within them – No! far from it. I am as incapable of that injustice, as I am of keeping terms with those who profess principles of extremes; and who under the name of religion teach little else than wild and dangerous politics. The worst of these politics of revolution is this; they temper and harden the breast, in order to prepare it for the desperate strokes which are sometimes used in extreme occasions. But as these occasions may never arrive, the mind receives a gratuitous taint; and the moral sentiments suffer not a little, when no political purpose is served by the depravation. This sort of people are so taken up with their theories about the rights of man, that they have totally forgotten his nature. Without opening one new avenue to the understanding, they have succeeded in stopping up those that lead to the heart. They have perverted in themselves, and in those that attend to them, all the well-placed sympathies of the human breast.

This famous sermon of the Old Jewry[13] breathes nothing but this spirit through all the political part. Plots, massacres, assassinations seem to some people a trivial price for obtaining a revolution. Cheap, bloodless reformation, a guiltless liberty appear flat and vapid to their taste. There must be a great change of scene; there must be a magnificent stage effect; there must be a grand spectacle to rouse the imagination, grown torpid with the lazy enjoyment of sixty years security, and the still unanimating repose of public prosperity. The Preacher found them all in the French revolution. This inspires a juvenile warmth through his whole frame. His enthusiasm kindles as he advances; and when he arrives at his peroration, it is in a full blaze. Then viewing, from the Pisgah[14] of his pulpit, the free, moral, happy, flourishing and glorious state of France as in a bird-eye landscape of a promised land, he breaks out into the following rapture:

> What an eventful period is this! I am *thankful* that I have lived to it; I could almost say, 'Lord, now lettest thou thy servant depart in peace, for mine eyes have seen thy salvation'. I have lived to see a *diffusion* of knowledge, which has undermined superstition and error. – I have lived to see *the rights of men* better understood than ever; and nations panting for liberty which seemed to have lost the idea of it. – I have lived to see *Thirty Millions of People*, indignant and resolute, spurning at slavery, and demanding liberty with an irresistible voice. *Their King led in triumph, and an arbitrary monarch surrendering himself to his subjects.*

Before I proceed further, I have to remark, that Dr. Price seems rather to over-value the great acquisitions of light which he has obtained and diffused in this age. The last

Notes

[12] *prerogative* the king's right to power.

[13] *Old Jewry* the Dissenters' chapel, where Price gave his sermon.

[14] *Pisgah* the mount from which Moses had a view of the Promised Land.

century appears to me to have been quite as much enlightened. It had, though in a different place, a triumph as memorable as that of Dr. Price; and some of the great preachers of that period partook of it as eagerly as he has done in the triumph of France. On the trial of the Rev. Hugh Peters[15] for high treason, it was deposed, that when King Charles was brought to London for his trial, the Apostle of Liberty in that day conducted the *triumph*. 'I saw', says the witness, 'his majesty in the coach with six horses, and Peters riding before the king *triumphing*'. Dr. Price, when he talks as if he had made a discovery, only follows a precedent; for after the commencement of the king's trial this precursor, the same Dr. Peters, concluding a long prayer at the royal chapel at Whitehall (he had very triumphantly chosen his place) said, 'I have prayed and preached these twenty years; and now I may say with old Simeon, 'Lord, now lettest thou thy servant depart in peace, for mine eyes have seen thy salvation'.[16] Peters had not the fruits of his prayer; for he neither departed so soon as he wished, nor in peace. He became (what I heartily hope none of his followers may be in this country) himself a sacrifice to the triumph which he led as Pontiff. They dealt at the Restoration, perhaps, too hardly with this poor good man. But we owe it to his memory and his sufferings, that he had as much illumination, and as much zeal, and had as effectually undermined all 'the superstition and error' which might impede the great business he was engaged in, as any who follow and repeat after him, in this age, which would assume to itself an exclusive title to the knowledge of the rights of men, and all the glorious consequences of that knowledge.

After this sally of the preacher of the Old Jewry, which differs only in place and time, but agrees perfectly with the spirit and letter of the rapture of 1648, the Revolution Society,[17] the fabricators of governments, the heroic band of *cashierers*[18] of *monarchs*, electors of sovereigns, and leaders of kings in triumph, strutting with a proud consciousness of the diffusion of knowledge, of which every member had obtained so large a share in the donative, were in haste to make a generous diffusion of the knowledge they had thus gratuitously received. To make this bountiful communication, they adjourned from the church in the Old Jewry, to the London Tavern; where the same Dr. Price, in whom the fumes of his oracular tripod[19] were not entirely evaporated, moved and carried the resolution, or address of congratulation, transmitted by Lord Stanhope[20] to the National Assembly of France.

I find a preacher of the gospel profaning the beautiful and prophetic ejaculation, commonly called *nunc dimittis*[21] made on the first presentation of our Saviour in the Temple, and applying it with an inhuman and unnatural rapture, to the most horrid, atrocious, and afflicting spectacle, that perhaps ever was exhibited to the pity and indignation of mankind. This 'leading in triumph', a thing in its best form unmanly and irreligious, which fills our Preacher with such unhallowed transports, must shock, I believe, the moral taste of every well-born mind. Several English were the stupefied and indignant spectators of that triumph. It was (unless we have been strangely

Notes

[15] *Hugh Peters* (1598–1660), independent minister, executed for complicity in the execution of Charles I.

[16] *old Simeon … salvation* the Holy Spirit revealed to Simeon that he would not die until he had seen "the Lord's Christ"; he speaks these words when he sees the baby Jesus (Luke 2.29–30).

[17] *Revolution Societ* founded in 1788 to celebrate the centenary of the Glorious Revolution.

[18] *cashierers* deposers; eliminators.

[19] *oracular tripod* the Pythia at Delphi, inspired by Apollo, sat on a tripod and made oracular pronouncements.

[20] *Lord Stanhope* Charles, third earl Stanhope, leader of the Revolution Society, sent congratulations to the National Assembly.

[21] *nunc dimittis* the Latin version of the first words of old Simeon (above), used in evening masses since the fourth century.

deceived) a spectacle more resembling a procession of American savages, entering into Onondaga,[22] after some of their murders called victories, and leading into hovels hung round with scalps, their captives, overpowered with the scoffs and buffets of women as ferocious as themselves, much more than it resembled the triumphal pomp of a civilized martial nation; – if a civilized nation, or any men who had a sense of generosity, were capable of a personal triumph over the fallen and afflicted.

This, my dear Sir, was not the triumph of France. I must believe that, as a nation, it overwhelmed you with shame and horror. I must believe that the National Assembly find themselves in the state of the greatest humiliation, in not being able to punish the authors of this triumph, or the actors in it; and that they are in a situation in which any inquiry they may make upon the subject, must be destitute even of the appearance of liberty or impartiality. The apology of that Assembly is found in their situation; but when we approve what they *must* bear, it is in us the degenerate choice of a vitiated mind.

With a compelled appearance of deliberation, they vote under the dominion of a stern necessity. They sit in the heart, as it were, of a foreign republic: they have their residence in a city whose constitution has emanated neither from the charter of their king nor from their legislative power. There they are surrounded by an army not raised either by the authority of their crown, or by their command; and which, if they should order to dissolve itself, would instantly dissolve them. There they sit, after a gang of assassins had driven away all the men of moderate minds and moderating authority amongst them, and left them as a sort of dregs and refuse, under the apparent lead of those in whom they do not so much as pretend to have any confidence. There they sit, in mockery of legislation, repeating in resolutions the words of those whom they detest and despise. Captives themselves, they compel a captive king to issue as royal edicts, at third hand, the polluted nonsense of their most licentious and giddy coffee-houses. It is notorious, that all their measures are decided before they are debated. It is beyond doubt, that under the terror of the bayonet, and the lamp-post,[23] and the torch to their houses, they are obliged to adopt all the crude and desperate measures suggested by clubs composed of a monstrous medley of all conditions, tongues, and nations. Among these are found persons, in comparison of whom Catiline[24] would be thought scrupulous, and Cethegus[25] a man of sobriety and moderation. Not is it in these clubs alone that the public measures are deformed into monsters. They undergo a previous distortion in academies, intended as so many seminaries for these clubs, which are set up in all the places of public resort. In these meetings of all sorts, every counsel, in proportion as it is daring, and violent, and perfidious, is taken for the mark of superior genius. Humanity and compassion are ridiculed as the fruits of superstition and ignorance. Tenderness to individuals is considered as treason to the public. Liberty is always to be estimated perfect as property is rendered insecure. Amidst assassination, massacre, and confiscation, perpetrated or meditated, they are forming plans for the good order of future society. Embracing in their arms the carcasses of base criminals, and promoting their relations on the title of their offences, they drive

Notes

[22] *Onondaga* the name of a tribe of Iroquois-speaking Indians, some of whom favored the French in the Seven Years War and migrated to Catholic settlements on the St. Lawrence River called by the name of the tribe.

[23] *lamp-post* where the heads of those decapitated were displayed.

[24] *Catiline* a demagogue and conspirator, successfully prosecuted by Cicero and killed in 62 BCE.

[25] *Cethegus* a corrupt political insider in early first-century BCE Rome; like Catiline, he was active in the bloody purges following the first Roman civil war.

hundreds of virtuous persons to the same end, by forcing them to subsist by beggary or by crime.

The Assembly, their organ, acts before them the farce of deliberation with as little decency as liberty. They act like the comedians of a fair before a riotous audience; they act amidst the tumultuous cries of a mixed mob of ferocious men, and of women lost to shame, who, according to their insolent fancies, direct, control, applaud, explode[26] them; and sometimes mix and take their seats amongst them; domineering over them with a strange mixture of servile petulance and proud, presumptuous authority. As they have inverted order in all things, the gallery is in the place of the house. This Assembly, which overthrows kings and kingdoms, has not even the physiognomy and aspect of a grave legislative body – *nec color imperii, nec frons ulla senatus*.[27] They have a power given to them, like that of the evil principle, to subvert and destroy; but none to construct, except such machines as may be fitted for further subversion and further destruction.

Who is it that admires, and from the heart is attached to national representative assemblies, but must turn with horror and disgust from such a profane burlesque, and abominable perversion of that sacred institute? Lovers of monarchy, lovers of republics must alike abhor it. The members of your Assembly must themselves groan under the tyranny of which they have all the shame, none of the direction, and little of the profit. I am sure many of the members who compose even the majority of that body, must feel as I do, notwithstanding the applauses of the Revolution Society. – Miserable king! miserable Assembly! How must that assembly be silently scandalized with those of their members, who could call a day which seemed to blot the sun out of Heaven, 'un beau jour!'[28] How must they be inwardly indignant at hearing others, who thought fit to declare to them, 'that the vessel of the state would fly forward in her course towards regeneration with more speed than ever', from the stiff gale of treason and murder which preceded our Preacher's triumph! What must they have felt, whilst with outward patience and inward indignation they heard of the slaughter of innocent gentlemen in their houses, that 'the blood spilled was not the most pure'?[29] What must they have felt, when they were besieged by complaints of disorders which shook their country to its foundations, at being compelled coolly to tell the complainants, that they were under the protection of the law, and that they would address the king (the captive king) to cause the laws to be enforced for their protection; when the enslaved ministers of that captive king had formally notified to them, that there were neither law, nor authority, nor power left to protect? What must they have felt at being obliged, as a felicitation on the present new year, to request their captive king to forget the stormy period of the last, on account of the great good which *he* was likely to produce to his people; to the complete attainment of which good they adjourned the practical demonstrations of their loyalty, assuring him of their obedience, when he should no longer possess any authority to command?

Notes

26 *explode* "To drive out disgracefully with some noise of contempt" (Johnson, 1773).

27 *nec color imperii, nec frons ulla senatus* Lucan, *Pharsalia* (9.207), an epic poem about the Roman civil wars; Burke translates in the previous clause.

28 *un beau jour* October 6, 1789 ["a beautiful day"; Burke's note; the date when the King and Queen of France were taken from their palace at Versailles to Paris].

29 *the blood spilled was not the most pure* the quotation has been attributed to Barnave, a member of the National Assembly, upon hearing of further mob lynchings of unpopular beneficiaries of government corruption.

This address was made with much good-nature and affection, to be sure. But among the revolutions in France, must be reckoned a considerable revolution in their ideas of politeness. In England we are said to learn manners at second-hand from your side of the water, and that we dress our behaviour in the frippery of France. If so, we are still in the old cut; and have not so far conformed to the new Parisian mode of good breeding, as to think it quite in the most refined strain of delicate compliment (whether in condolence or congratulation) to say, to the most humiliated creature that crawls upon the earth, that great public benefits are derived from the murder of his servants, the attempted assassination of himself and of his wife, and the mortification, disgrace, and degradation that he has personally suffered. It is a topic of consolation which our ordinary of Newgate[30] would be too humane to use to a criminal at the foot of the gallows. I should have thought that the hangman of Paris, now that he is liberalized by the vote of the National Assembly, and is allowed his rank and arms in the Herald's College of the rights of men, would be too generous, too gallant a man, too full of the sense of his new dignity, to employ that cutting consolation to any of the persons whom the *lese nation*[31] might bring under the administration of his *executive powers*.

A man is fallen indeed, when he is thus flattered. The anodyne draught of oblivion, thus drugged, is well calculated to preserve a galling wakefulness, and to feed the living ulcer of a corroding memory. Thus to administer the opiate potion of amnesty, powdered with all the ingredients of scorn and contempt, is to hold to his lips, instead of 'the balm of hurt minds',[32] the cup of human misery full to the brim and to force him to drink it to the dregs.

Yielding to reasons, at least as forcible as those which were so delicately urged in the compliment on the new year, the king of France will probably endeavour to forget these events, and that compliment. But history, who keeps a durable record of all our acts, and exercises her awful censure over the proceedings of all sorts of sovereigns, will not forget either those events, or the era of this liberal refinement in the intercourse of mankind. History will record, that on the morning of the 6th of October, 1789, the king and queen of France, after a day of confusion, alarm, dismay, and slaughter, lay down, under the pledged security of public faith, to indulge nature in a few hours of respite, and troubled, melancholy repose. From this sleep the queen was first startled by the sentinel at her door, who cried out to her, to save herself by flight – that this was the last proof of fidelity he could give – that they were upon him, and he was dead. Instantly he was cut down. A band of cruel ruffians and assassins, reeking with his blood, rushed into the chamber of the queen, and pierced with a hundred strokes of bayonets and poniards the bed, from whence this persecuted woman had but just time to fly almost naked, and through ways unknown to the murderers, had escaped to seek refuge at the feet of a king and husband, not secure of his own life for a moment.

This king, to say no more of him, and this queen, and their infant children (who once would have been the pride and hope of a great and generous people) were then forced to abandon the sanctuary of the most splendid palace in the world, which they left swimming in blood, polluted by massacre and strewed with scattered limbs and mutilated carcasses. Thence they were conducted into the capital of their kingdom. Two had been selected from the unprovoked, unresisted, promiscuous slaughter, which was

Notes

30 *ordinary of Newgate* the priest assigned to minister to condemned criminals in Newgate Prison.

31 *lese nation* injured nation (formed after *lese majesty*, the anglicized French for high treason).

32 *'the balm of hurt minds' Macbeth* II.ii.39 (said of sleep).

made of the gentlemen of birth and family who composed the king's body guard. These two gentlemen, with all the parade of an execution of justice, were cruelly and publicly dragged to the block, and beheaded in the great court of the palace. Their heads were stuck upon spears and led the procession; whilst the royal captives who followed in the train were slowly moved along, amidst the horrid yells, and shrilling screams, and frantic dances, and infamous contumelies, and all the unutterable abominations of the furies of hell, in the abused shape of the vilest of women. After they had been made to taste, drop by drop, more than the bitterness of death in the slow torture of a journey of twelve miles, protracted to six hours, they were, under a guard, composed of those very soldiers who had thus conducted them through this famous triumph, lodged in one of the old palaces of Paris, now converted into a Bastille for kings.

Is this a triumph to be consecrated at altars? to be commemorated with grateful thanksgiving? to be offered to the divine humanity with fervent prayer and enthusiastic ejaculation?[33] – These Theban and Thracian Orgies,[34] acted in France, and applauded only in the Old Jewry, I assure you, kindle prophetic enthusiasm in the minds but of very few people in this kingdom; although a saint and apostle, who may have revelations of his own, and who has so completely vanquished all the mean superstitions of the heart, may incline to think it pious and decorous to compare it with the entrance into the world of the Prince of Peace, proclaimed in a holy temple by a venerable sage,[35] and not long before not worse announced by the voice of angels to the quiet innocence of shepherds.

At first I was at a loss to account for this fit of unguarded transport. I knew, indeed, that the sufferings of monarchs make a delicious repast to some sort of palates. There were reflections which might serve to keep this appetite within some bounds of temperance. But when I took one circumstance into my consideration, I was obliged to confess, that much allowance ought to be made for the Society, and that the temptation was too strong for common discretion; I mean, the circumstance of the Io Pæan[36] of the triumph, the animating cry which called 'for *all* the BISHOPS to be hanged on the lamp-posts',[37] might well have brought forth a burst of enthusiasm on the foreseen consequences of this happy day. I allow to so much enthusiasm some little deviation from prudence. I allow this prophet to break forth into hymns of joy and thanksgiving on an event which appears like the precursor of the Millennium, and the projected fifth monarchy,[38] in the destruction of all church establishments. There was, however (as in all human affairs there is) in the midst of this joy something to exercise the patience of these worthy gentlemen, and to try the long-suffering of their faith. The actual murder of the king and queen, and their child, was wanting to the other auspicious circumstances of this '*beautiful day*'. The actual murder of the bishops, though called for by so many holy ejaculations, was also wanting. A group of regicide and sacrilegious slaughter, was indeed boldly sketched, but it was only sketched. It unhappily was left unfinished in this great history-piece of the massacre of innocents.[39] What

Notes

[33] *enthusiastic ejaculation* inspired, religious utterance.

[34] *Theban and Thracian Orgies* Bacchic or Dionysian revels.

[35] *venerable sage* old Simeon (above).

[36] *Io Pæan* beginning of a Greek song of triumph, properly addressed to Apollo.

[37] *all the BISHOPS to be hanged on the lamp-posts* "Tous les Evêques à la lanterne" [Burke's note].

[38] *fifth monarchy* the everlasting kingdom described in the prophetic Book of Daniel (2.44) and associated with the Millennium, or thousand-year reign of Christ described in Revelation (20.1–5); there was a radical sect of Protestants called Fifth-Monarchy Men during the English Civil War.

[39] *the massacre of innocents* a common topic of grand historical painting of the high Renaissance, depicting the events described in Matthew 2.16–18.

hardy pencil of a great master, from the school of the rights of man will finish it is to be seen hereafter. The age has not yet the complete benefit of that diffusion of knowledge that has undermined superstition and error; and the king of France wants another object or two, to consign to oblivion, in consideration of all the good which is to arise from his own sufferings, and the patriotic crimes of an enlightened age.

Although this work of our new light and knowledge, did not go to the length, that in all probability it was intended it should be carried; yet I must think, that such treatment of any human creatures must be shocking to any but those who are made for accomplishing Revolutions. But I cannot stop here. Influenced by the inborn feelings of my nature, and not being illuminated by a single ray of this new-sprung modern light, I confess to you, Sir, that the exalted rank of the persons suffering, and particularly the sex, the beauty, and the amiable qualities of the descendant of so many kings and emperors, with the tender age of royal infants, insensible only through infancy and innocence of the cruel outrages to which their parents were exposed, instead of being a subject of exultation, adds not a little to any sensibility on that most melancholy occasion.

I hear that the august person, who was the principal object of our preacher's triumph, though he supported himself, felt much on that shameful occasion. As a man, it became him to feel for his wife and his children, and the faithful guards of his person, that were massacred in cold blood about him; as a prince, it became him to feel for the strange and frightful transformation of his civilised subjects, and to be more grieved for them than solicitous for himself. It derogates little from his fortitude, while it adds infinitely to the honour of his humanity. I am very sorry to say it, very sorry indeed, that such personages are in a situation in which it is not unbecoming in us to praise the virtues of the great.

I hear, and I rejoice to hear, that the great lady, the other object of the triumph, has borne that day (one is interested that beings made for suffering should suffer well) and that she bears all the succeeding days, that she bears the imprisonment of her husband, and her own captivity, and the exile of her friends, and the insulting adulation of addresses, and the whole weight of her accumulated wrongs, with a serene patience, in a manner suited to her rank and race, and becoming the offspring of a sovereign distinguished for her piety and her courage; that like her she has lofty sentiments; that she feels with the dignity of a Roman matron; that in the last extremity she will save herself from the last disgrace, and that, if she must fall, she will fall by no ignoble hand.

It is now sixteen or seventeen years since I saw the queen of France, then the dauphiness, at Versailles; and surely never lighted on this orb, which she hardly seemed to touch, a more delightful vision. I saw her just above the horizon, decorating and cheering the elevated sphere she just began to move in, – glittering like the morning-star, full of life, and splendour and joy. Oh! what a revolution! and what a heart must I have to contemplate without emotion that elevation and that fall! Little did I dream that, when she added titles of veneration to those of enthusiastic, distant, respectful love, that she should ever be obliged to carry the sharp antidote against disgrace concealed in that bosom; little did I dream that I should have lived to see such disasters fallen upon her in a nation of gallant men, in a nation of men of honour and of cavaliers. I thought ten thousand swords must have leaped from their scabbards to avenge even a look that threatened her with insult. – But the age of chivalry is gone. – That of sophisters, economists, and calculators, has succeeded; and the glory of Europe is extinguished for ever. Never, never more, shall we behold that generous loyalty to rank and sex, that proud submission, that dignified obedience, that subordination of the heart which kept alive, even in servitude itself, the spirit of an exalted freedom.

The unbought grace of life, the cheap defence of nations, the nurse of manly sentiment and heroic enterprise, is gone! It is gone, that sensibility of principle, that chastity of honour which felt a stain like a wound, which inspired courage whilst it mitigated ferocity, which ennobled whatever it touched, and under which vice itself lost half its evil, by losing all its grossness.

This mixed system of opinion and sentiment had its origin in the ancient chivalry; and the principle, though varied in its appearance by the varying state of human affairs, subsisted and influenced through a long succession of generations even to the time we live in. If it should ever be totally extinguished, the loss I fear will be great. It is this which has given its character to modern Europe. It is this which has distinguished it under all its forms of government, and distinguished it to its advantage, from the states of Asia, and possibly from those states which flourished in the most brilliant periods of the antique world. It was this, which, without confounding ranks, had produced a noble equality, and handed it down through all the gradations of social life. It was this opinion which mitigated kings into companions, and raised private men to be fellows with kings. Without force, or opposition, it subdued the fierceness of pride and power; it obliged sovereigns to submit to the soft collar of social esteem, compelled stern authority to submit to elegance, and gave domination, a vanquisher of laws,[40] to be subdued by manners.

But now all is to be changed. All the pleasing illusions, which made power gentle, and obedience liberal, which harmonized the different shades of life, and which, by a bland assimilation, incorporated into politics the sentiments which beautify and soften private society, are to be dissolved by this new conquering empire of light and reason. All the decent drapery of life is to be rudely torn off. All the superadded ideas, furnished from the wardrobe of a moral imagination, which the heart owns, and the understanding ratifies, as necessary to cover the defects of our naked shivering nature, and to raise it to dignity in our own estimation, are to be exploded as a ridiculous, absurd, and antiquated fashion.

On this scheme of things, a king is but a man; a queen is but a woman; a woman is but an animal; and an animal not of the highest order. All homage paid to the sex in general as such, and without distinct views, is to be regarded as romance and folly. Regicide, and parricide, and sacrilege, are but fictions of superstition, corrupting jurisprudence by destroying its simplicity. The murder of a king, or a queen, or a bishop, or a father, are only common homicide; and if the people are by any chance, or in any way gainers by it, a sort of homicide much the most pardonable, and into which we ought not to make too severe a scrutiny.

On the scheme of this barbarous philosophy, which is the offspring of cold hearts and muddy understandings, and which is as void of solid wisdom, as it is destitute of all taste and elegance, laws are to be supported only by their own terrors, and by the concern, which each individual may find in them, from his own private speculations, or can spare to them from his own private interests. In the groves of *their* academy, at the end of every visto,[41] you see nothing but the gallows. Nothing is left which engages the affections on the part of the commonwealth. On the principles of this mechanic philosophy, our institutions can never be embodied, if I may use the expression, in persons; so as to create in us love, veneration, admiration, or attachment. But that sort

Notes

[40] *domination, a vanquisher of laws* I have emended this from "a domination vanquisher of laws."

[41] *visto* vista; "View; prospect through an avenue" (Johnson, 1773).

of reason which banishes the affections is incapable of filling their place. These public affections, combined with manners, are required sometimes as supplements, sometimes as correctives, always as aids to law. The precept given by a wise man, as well as a great critic, for the construction of poems, is equally true as to states. *Non satis est pulchra esse poemata, dulcia sunto.*[42] There ought to be a system of manners in every nation which a well-informed mind would be disposed to relish. To make us love our country, our country ought to be lovely.

But power, of some kind or other, will survive the shock in which manners and opinions perish; and it will find other and worse means for its support. The usurpation which, in order to subvert ancient institutions, has destroyed ancient principles, will hold power by arts similar to those by which it has acquired it. When the old feudal and chivalrous spirit of *Fealty*, which, by freeing kings from fear, freed both kings and subjects from the precautions of tyranny, shall be extinct in the minds of men, plots and assassinations will be anticipated by preventive murder and preventive confiscation, and that long roll of grim and bloody maxims, which form the political code of all power, not standing on its own honour, and the honour of those who are to obey it. Kings will be tyrants from policy when subjects are rebels from principle.

When ancient opinions and rules of life are taken away, the loss cannot possibly be estimated. From that moment we have no compass to govern us; nor can we know distinctly to what port we steer. Europe undoubtedly, taken in a mass, was in a flourishing condition the day on which your Revolution was completed. How much of that prosperous state was owing to the spirit of our old manners and opinions is not easy to say; but as such causes cannot be indifferent in their operation, we must presume, that, on the whole, their operation was beneficial.

We are but too apt to consider things in the state in which we find them, without sufficiently adverting to the causes by which they have been produced and possibly may be upheld. Nothing is more certain, than that our manners, our civilization, and all the good things which are connected with manners, and with civilization, have, in this European world of ours, depended for ages upon two principles; and were indeed the result of both combined; I mean the spirit of a gentleman and the spirit of religion. The nobility and the clergy, the one by profession, the other by patronage, kept learning in existence, even in the midst of arms and confusions, and whilst governments were rather in their causes[43] than formed. Learning paid back what it received to nobility and to priesthood; and paid it with usury, by enlarging their ideas and by furnishing their minds. Happy if they had all continued to know their indissoluble union, and their proper place! Happy if learning, not debauched by ambition, had been satisfied to continue the instructor, and not aspired to be the master! Along with its natural protectors and guardians, learning will be cast into the mire and trodden down under the hoofs of a swinish multitude.

If, as I suspect, modern letters owe more than they are always willing to own to ancient manners, so do other interests which we value full as much as they are worth. Even commerce, and trade, and manufacture, the gods of our economical politicians, are themselves perhaps but creatures; are themselves but effects, which, as first causes, we choose to worship. They certainly grew under the same shade in which learning flourished. They too may decay with their natural protecting principles. With you, for

Notes

[42] *Non satis est pulchra esse poemata, dulcia sunto* "It is not enough for poems to be beautiful; they must also be pleasing" (Horace, *Ars Poetica* 99).

[43] *causes* the state or condition that gives rise to something.

the present at least, they all threaten to disappear together. Where trade and manufactures are wanting to a people, and the spirit of nobility and religion remains, sentiment supplies, and not always ill supplies their place; but if commerce and the arts should be lost in an experiment to try how well a state may stand without these old fundamental principles, what sort of a thing must be a nation of gross, stupid, ferocious, and at the same time, poor and sordid barbarians, destitute of religion, honour, or manly pride, possessing nothing at present, and hoping for nothing hereafter?

I wish you may not be going fast, and by the shortest cut, to that horrible and disgustful situation. Already there appears a poverty of conception, a coarseness and a vulgarity in all the proceedings of the assembly and of all their instructors. Their liberty is not liberal. Their science[44] is presumptuous ignorance. Their humanity is savage and brutal.

It is not clear, whether in England we learned those grand and decorous principles, and manners, of which considerable traces yet remain, from you, or whether you took them from us. But to you, I think, we trace them best. You seem to me to be – *gentis incunabula nostræ*.[45] France has always more or less influenced manners in England; and when your fountain is choked up and polluted, the stream will not run long, or not run clear with us or perhaps with any nation. This gives all Europe, in my opinion, but too close and connected a concern in what is done in France. Excuse me, therefore, if I have dwelt too long on the atrocious spectacle of the sixth of October 1789, or have given too much scope to the reflections which have arisen in my mind on occasion of the most important of all revolutions, which may be dated from that day, I mean a revolution in sentiments, manners, and moral opinions. As things now stand, with everything respectable destroyed without us, and an attempt to destroy within us every principle of respect, one is almost forced to apologise for harbouring the common feelings of men.

Why do I feel so differently from the Reverend Dr. Price, and those of his lay flock, who will choose to adopt the sentiments of his discourse? – For this plain reason – because it is *natural* I should; because we are so made as to be affected at such spectacles with melancholy sentiments upon the unstable condition of mortal prosperity, and the tremendous uncertainty of human greatness; because in those natural feelings we learn great lessons; because in events like these our passions instruct our reason; because when kings are hurled from their thrones by the Supreme Director of this great drama, and become the objects of insult to the base, and of pity to the good, we behold such disasters in the moral as we should behold a miracle in the physical order of things. We are alarmed into reflection; our minds (as it has long since been observed) are purified by terror and pity;[46] our weak, unthinking pride is humbled, under the dispensations of a mysterious wisdom. – Some tears might be drawn from me, if such a spectacle were exhibited on the stage. I should be truly ashamed of finding in myself that superficial, theatric sense of painted distress, whilst I could exult over it in real life. With such a perverted mind, I could never venture to show my face at a tragedy. People would think the tears that Garrick[47] formerly, or that Siddons[48] not long since, have extorted from me, were the tears of hypocrisy; I should know them to be the tears of folly.

Notes

44 *science* knowledge.

45 *gentis incunabula nostræ* "the cradle of our race."

46 *our minds … by terror and pity* adapted from Aristotle's *Poetics*.

47 *Garrick* David (1717–79), greatest actor of his age.

48 *Siddons* Sarah Kemble (1755–1831), famous Shakespearean actress.

Indeed the theatre is a better school of moral sentiments than churches, where the feelings of humanity are thus outraged. Poets, who have to deal with an audience not yet graduated in the school of the rights of men, and who must apply themselves to the moral constitution of the heart, would not dare to produce such a triumph as a matter of exultation. There, where men follow their natural impulses, they would not bear the odious maxims of a Machiavellian policy, whether applied to the attainments of monarchical or democratic tyranny. They would reject them on the modern, as they once did on the ancient stage, where they could not bear even the hypothetical proposition of such wickedness in the mouth of a personated tyrant, though suitable to the character he sustained. No theatric audience in Athens would bear what has been borne, in the midst of the real tragedy of this triumphal day; a principal actor weighing, as it were in scales hung in a shop of horrors, – so much actual crime against so much contingent advantage, – and after putting in and out weights, declaring that the balance was on the side of the advantages. They would not bear to see the crimes of new democracy posted as in a ledger against the crimes of old despotism, and the book-keepers of politics finding democracy still in debt, but by no means unable or unwilling to pay the balance. In the theatre, the first intuitive glance, without any elaborate process of reasoning, would show that this method of political computation would justify every extent of crime. They would see, that on these principles, even where the very worst acts were not perpetrated, it was owing rather to the fortune of the conspirators than to their parsimony in the expenditure of treachery and blood. They would soon see, that criminal means once tolerated are soon preferred. They present a shorter cut to the object than through the highway of the moral virtues. Justifying perfidy and murder for public benefit, public benefit would soon become the pretext, and perfidy and murder the end; until rapacity, malice, revenge, and fear more dreadful than revenge could satiate their insatiable appetites. Such must be the consequences of losing in the splendour of these triumphs of the rights of men, all natural sense of wrong and right.

William Cowper (1731–1800)

At the age of thirty-two, Cowper was offered a government sinecure, clerk of the journals of the House of Lords. He had been in the legal profession as a student in Middle Temple, then at the bar and in Inner Temple, for fifteen years; he had done some writing for journals, some translations, and some poetry; he was well-read and literary; he was not particularly ambitious; he was obviously intelligent and came from a distinguished family. In short, he was just the sort of man for whom sinecures were made. However, there was a dispute about the offer, and Cowper was required to appear in court to defend his qualifications for the position. But he found he was unable to do this, and the feelings of self-reproach and self-doubt that surrounded the event plunged Cowper into a depression so severe that he attempted suicide at least three times and wound up in an insane asylum for eighteen months. When he emerged, he was a changed person: no longer a man about town, he embraced evangelical ideas and feelings; he retreated from the town to live in the country; he interested himself in gardening and later in pet animals.

Around 1770 poetry became Cowper's principal means of dealing with depression and his main activity. He lived in a long-term, intimate, but perhaps not fully adult relationship with Mary Unwin, the surviving member of a couple who befriended him and took him in shortly after his departure from the insane asylum. He continued to have serious bouts of depression, and his last five years, after the death of Unwin, were lived in continuous emotional pain, with a fear of personal inadequacy and of impending damnation at the hands of an angry God. But through it all, Cowper produced poetry. His collected poems came out in 1782; *The Task*, a long, autobiographical, immensely popular poem about country household life, came out in 1785; he undertook and eventually finished a new translation of Homer; and many other poems of varying lengths appeared in successive editions of his collected poems that came out frequently before and after his death. The poetry reflects Cowper's painful inner life and his frightening identification of his own troubled state with the lives of caged animals and the victims of disaster or oppression. Yet his acts of identification are not without sympathy for creatures outside of himself and not without an appreciation of other lives than his own.

Cowper's bibliography is complicated. I have indicated the bases of my texts in the footnotes to each poem. Cowper's poetry has been edited by John Baird and Charles Ryskamp in 3 volumes (Clarendon Press, 1980–95); the *Letters and Prose Writings* have been edited by Ryskamp and James King (5 vols., Clarendon Press, 1979–86). I have also benefited from the collations in the edition of the *Poetical Works* by H. S. Milford (corr. Norma Russell, Oxford University Press, 1967). The most recent biography is by James King (Duke University Press, 1986).

British Literature 1640–1789: An Anthology, Fourth Edition. Edited by Robert DeMaria, Jr.

On a Goldfinch Starved to Death in his Cage (1782)[1]

Time was when I was free as air,
The thistle's downy seed my fare,
My drink the morning dew;
I perched at will on every spray,
My form genteel, my plumage gay,
My strains forever new.

But gaudy plumage, sprightly strain,
And form genteel, were all in vain,
And of a transient date;
For, caught and caged, and starved to death,
In dying sighs my little breath
Soon passed the wiry gate.

Thanks, gentle swain, for all my woes,
And thanks for this effectual close
And cure of every ill!
More cruelty could none express;
And I, if you had shown me less,
Had been your pris'ner still.

Epitaph on an Hare (1784)[1]

HERE lies, whom hound did ne'er pursue,
Nor swifter greyhound follow,
Whose foot ne'er tainted morning dew,[2]
Nor ear heard huntsman's halloo,

Tiney, the surliest of his kind,
Who, nursed with tender care,
And to domestic bounds confined,
Was still a wild Jack-hare.

Though duly from my hand he took
His pittance every night,
He did it with a jealous look,
And, when he could, would bite.

His diet was of wheaten bread,
And milk, and oats, and straw;
Thistles, or lettuces instead;
And sand to cleanse his maw.

Notes

On a Goldfinch Starved to Death in his Cage

[1] The text is based on the first printing in *Poems by William Cowper, of the Inner Temple, Esq.* (1782).

Epitaph on an Hare

[1] The text is based on the first printing (*Gentleman's Magazine*, December 1784).

[2] *tainted* gave a scent to.

On twigs of hawthorn he regaled,
  On pippins' russet peel;[3]
And, when his juicier salads failed,
  Sliced carrot pleased him well.

A Turkey carpet was his lawn,
  Whereon he loved to bound,
To skip and gambol like a fawn,
  And swing himself around.[4]

His frisking was at evening hours,
  For then he lost his fear;
But most before approaching showers,
  Or when a storm drew near.

Eight years and five round rolling moons
  He thus saw steal away,
Dozing out all his idle noons,
  And every night at play.

I kept him for old service sake,[5]
  For he would oft beguile
My heart of thoughts that made it ache,
  And force me to a smile.

But now, beneath this walnut shade
  He finds his long, last home,
And waits in snug concealment laid,
  Till gentler Puss shall come.

He, in his turn, must feel the shocks[6]
  From which no care can save,
And, partner once of Tiney's box,
  Be partner of his grave.[7]

To the Immortal Memory of the Halibut on which I Dined this Day[1] (1784)

Where hast thou floated, in what seas pursued
Thy pastime? when wast thou an egg new-spawned,
Lost in th' immensity of ocean's waste?[2]
Roar as they might, the overbearing winds
That rocked the deep, thy cradle, thou wast safe –

Notes

3 *pippin* a kind of apple.
4 *himself* the MS and later editions read "his rump."
5 *old service* later editions have "his humour's."
6 *in his turn* later editions have "still more aged."
7 *Be partner of* the MS and later editions read "Must soon partake."

To the Immortal Memory of the Halibut
1 The text is based on the first publication of the poem in *The Private Correspondence of William Cowper, Esq.*, ed. John Johnson (1824).
2 *waste* "Desolate or uncultivated ground" (Johnson).

And in thy minikin and embryo state,[3]
Attached to the firm leaf of some salt weed,
Didst outlive tempests, such as wrung and racked
The joints of many a stout and gallant bark,[4]
And whelmed them in the unexplored abyss.
Indebted to no magnet and no chart,
Nor under guidance of the polar fire,[5]
Thou wast a voyager on many coasts,
Grazing at large in meadows submarine,
Where flat Batavia just emerging peeps[6]
Above the brine, – where Caledonia's rocks[7]
Beat back the surge, – and where Hibernia shoots[8]
Her wondrous causeway far into the main.[9]
– Wherever thou hast fed, thou little thought'st,
And I not more, that I should feed on thee.
Peace therefore, and good health, and much good fish,
To him who sent thee! and success, as oft
As it descends into the billowy gulf,
To the same drag that caught thee! – Fare thee well![10]
Thy lot thy brethren of the slimy fin
Would envy, could they know that thou wast doomed
To feed a bard, and to be praised in verse.

The Negro's Complaint (1789)[1]

Forced from home, and all its pleasures,
  Afric's coast I left forlorn;
To increase a stranger's treasures,
  O'er the raging billows borne.
Men from England bought and sold me,
  Paid my price in paltry gold;
But, though slave they have enrolled me,
  Minds are never to be sold.

Still in thought as free as ever,
  What are England's rights, I ask,

Notes

[3] *minikin* "Small; diminutive. Used in slight contempt" (Johnson).

[4] *bark* boat.

[5] *polar fire* the Pole Star, used in navigation to determine latitude.

[6] *Batavia* Roman name for the Netherlands.

[7] *Caledonia* Roman name for Scotland.

[8] *Hibernia* Roman name for Ireland

[9] *causeway* the Giant's Causeway, a dramatic volcanic formation on the northeast coast of Ireland, imagined to be a road built by giants walking across the sea from Scotland to Ireland.

[10] *drag* "A net drawn along the bottom of the water" (Johnson).

The Negro's Complaint

[1] First published in *Stuart's Star* in 1789, this poem was often reprinted with many variations; my text is based on *Poems of William Cowper of the Inner Temple* (1815), but with a few variants substituted from later editions.

Me from my delights to sever,
  Me to torture, me to task?
Fleecy locks, and black complexion
  Cannot forfeit Nature's claim;
Skins may differ, but affection
  Dwells in white and black the same.

Why did all-creating Nature
  Make the plant for which we toil?[2]
Sighs must fan it, tears must water,
  Sweat of ours must dress the soil.
Think, ye masters, iron-hearted,
  Lolling at your jovial boards;
Think how many blacks have smarted
  For the sweets your cane affords.

Is there, as ye sometimes tell us,
  Is there one who reigns on high?
Has he bid you buy and sell us,
  Speaking from his throne the sky?
Ask him, if your knotted scourges,
  Fetters, blood-extorting screws,[3]
Are the means which duty urges
  Agents of his will to use?

Hark! he answers – Wild tornadoes,
  Strewing yonder sea with wrecks;
Wasting towns, plantations, meadows,
  Are the voice with which he speaks.
He, foreseeing what vexations
  Afric's sons should undergo,
Fixed their tyrants' habitations
  Where his whirlwinds answer – No.

By our blood in Afric wasted,
  Ere our necks received the chain;
By the mis'ries we have tasted,
  Crossing in your barks the main;[4]
By our suff'rings since ye brought us
  To the man-degrading mart;
All sustained by patience, taught us
  Only by a broken heart:

Notes

[2] *plant* sugar cane, produced with slave labor in the West Indies.

[3] *Fetters* the edition of 1815 and others have "matches," which I do not understand (short for "matchlock," a gun?); *screw* "An instrument of torture … designed to compress the thumbs" (OED, citing this passage).

[4] *barks* ships.

Deem our nation brutes no longer
Till some reason ye shall find
Worthier of regard and stronger
Than the colour of our kind.
Slaves of gold, whose sordid dealings
Tarnish all your boasted pow'rs,
Prove that you have human feelings,
Ere you proudly question ours!

On a Spaniel Called Beau Killing a Young Bird[1] (1793)

A Spaniel, Beau, that fares like you,
Well-fed, and at his ease,
Should wiser be, than to pursue
Each trifle that he sees.

But you have killed a tiny Bird,
Which flew not till to-day,
Against my orders, whom you heard
Forbidding you the prey.

Nor did you kill, that you might eat,
And ease a doggish pain,
For him, though chased with furious heat,
You left where he was slain.

Nor was he of the thievish sort,
Or one whom blood allures,
But innocent was all his sport,
Whom you have torn for yours.

My Dog! what remedy remains,
Since, teach you all I can,
I see you, after all my pains,
So much resemble man!

Beau's Reply

Sir! when I flew to seize the Bird,
In spite of your command,
A louder voice than yours I heard,
And harder to withstand:

Notes

On a Spaniel Called Beau Killing a Young Bird

1 The text of this pair of poems is based on the first printing in William Hayley, *The Life and Posthumous Writings, William Cowper, Esqr.*, 3 vols. (1803–4).

You cried – 'Forbear! – but in my breast
A mightier cried – 'Proceed!'
'Twas Nature, Sir, whose strong behest
Impelled me to the deed.

Yet much as Nature I respect,
I ventured once to break
(As you perhaps may recollect)
Her precept, for your sake:

And when your Linnet on a day,
Passing his prison door,
Had fluttered all his strength away,
And panting pressed the floor,

Well knowing him a sacred thing,
Not destined to my tooth,
I only kissed his ruffled wing,
And licked his feathers smooth.

Let my obedience then excuse
My disobedience now!
Nor some reproof yourself refuse
From your aggrieved Bow-wow!

If killing Birds be such a crime,
(Which I can hardly see)
What think you, Sir, of killing Time
With verse addressed to me?

On the Ice Islands Seen floating in the German Ocean[1] (1799)

What portents, from what distant region, ride,
Unseen till now in ours, th' astonished tide?[2]
In ages past, old Proteus, with his droves[3]
Of sea-calves, sought the mountains and the groves:
But now, descending whence of late they stood,
Themselves the mountains seem to rove the flood.
Dire times were they, full-charged with human woes;
And these, scarce less calamitous than those.
What view we now? More wondrous still! Behold!
Like burnished brass they shine, or beaten gold;

Notes

On The Ice Islands

[1] The text is based on the first printing in William Hayley, *The Life and Posthumous Writings, William Cowper, Esqr.*, 3 vols. (1803–4); Cowper first composed a Latin version of this poem, which he wrote in his last illness, in response to an incident recorded in the newspapers.

[2] *tide* sea.

[3] *Proteus* the shape-shifting, prophetic old man of the sea; a subject of the god Poseidon, he tended his flocks of seals and slept with them on land at midday.

And all around the pearl's pure splendour show,
And all around the ruby's fiery glow.
Come they from India? where the burning earth,
All-bounteous, gives her richest treasures birth;
And where the costly gems, that beam around
The brows of mighty potentates, are found?
No. Never such a countless dazzling store
Had left unseen the Ganges' peopled shore.
Rapacious hands, and ever-watchful eyes,
Should sooner far have marked and seized the prize.
Whence sprang they then? Ejected have they come
From Ves'vius', or from Ætna's burning womb?[4]
Thus shine they self-illumed, or but display
The borrowed splendours of a cloudless day?
With borrowed beams they shine. The gales that breathe[5]
Now landward, and the current's force beneath,
Have borne them nearer: and the nearer sight,
Advantaged more, contemplates them aright.
Their lofty summits, crested high, they show,
With mingled sleet and long-incumbent snow.
The rest is ice. Far hence, where, most severe,
Bleak winter well-nigh saddens all the year,
Their infant growth began. He bade arise
Their uncouth forms, portentous in our eyes.
Oft as, dissolved by transient suns, the snow
Left the tall cliff, to join the flood below,
He caught and curdled, with a freezing blast,
The current, ere it reached the boundless waste.
By slow degrees uprose the wondrous pile,
And long-successive ages rolled the while;
Till, ceaseless in its growth, it claimed to stand
Tall as its rival mountains on the land.
Thus stood – and, unremovable by skill
Or force of man, had stood the structure still;
But that, though firmly fixed, supplanted yet
By pressure of its own enormous weight,
It left the shelving beach – and, with a sound[6]
That shook the bellowing waves and rocks around,
Self-launched, and swiftly, to the briny wave,
As if instinct with strong desire to lave,
Down went the pond'rous mass. So Bards of old,
How Delos swam th' Ægean deep, have told.[7]
But not of ice was Delos; Delos bore
Herb, fruit, and flow'r. She, crowned with laurel, wore,

Notes

[4] *Ves[u]vius … Ætna* volcanoes in Italy.

[5] *gale* "A wind not tempestuous, yet stronger than a breeze" (Johnson).

[6] *shelving* "Sloping; inclining; having declivity" (Johnson).

[7] *Delos* smallest of the Cyclades, it was a floating isle until Zeus chained it to the bottom of the sea to make a secure place for Leto to give birth to Apollo and Artemis.

E'en under wintry skies, a summer smile;
And Delos was Apollo's favourite isle.
But, horrid wand'rers of the deep, to you
He deems Cimmerian darkness only due.[8]
Your hated birth he deigned not to survey,
But, scornful, turned his glorious eyes away.
Hence! Seek your home; no longer rashly dare
The darts of Phoebus, and a softer air;[9]
Lest ye regret, too late, your native coast,
In no congenial gulf for ever lost!

The Castaway[1] (1799)

Obscurest night involved the sky,
  Th' Atlantic billows roared,
When such a destined wretch as I,
  Washed headlong from on board,
Of friends, of hope, of all bereft,
His floating home for ever left.

No braver chief could Albion boast[2]
  Than he with whom he went,
Nor ever ship left Albion's coast,
  With warmer wishes sent.
He loved them both, but both in vain,
Nor him beheld, nor her again.

Not long beneath the whelming brine,
  Expert to swim, he lay;
Nor soon he felt his strength decline,
  Or courage die away;
But waged with death a lasting strife,
Supported by despair of life.

He shouted: nor his friends had failed
  To check the vessel's course,
But so the furious blast prevailed,
  That, pitiless perforce,
They left their outcast mate behind,
And scudded still before the wind.

Notes

[8] *Cimmeria* a mythical land of mists and darkness (also a real place near the Caspian Sea).

[9] *Phoebus* Apollo, the sun.

THE CASTAWAY

[1] The text is from the first printing, in Hayley. The poem, Cowper's last, is based on an account of a sailor swept overboard, which Hayley says the poet read many years before in Richard Walter's *A Voyage Round the World, by George Anson* (1748).

[2] *Albion* England (a Latin name, after its white cliffs).

Some succour yet they could afford;
And, such as storms allow,
The cask, the coop, the floated cord,[3]
Delayed not to bestow.
But he (they knew) nor ship, nor shore,
Whate'er they gave, should visit more.

Nor, cruel as it seemed, could he
Their haste himself condemn,
Aware that flight, in such a sea,
Alone could rescue them;
Yet bitter felt it still to die
Deserted, and his friends so nigh.

He long survives, who lives an hour
In ocean, self-upheld:
And so long he, with unspent pow'r,
His destiny repelled;
And ever, as the minutes flew,
Entreated help, or cried – 'Adieu!'

At length, his transient respite past,
His comrades, who before
Had heard his voice in every blast,
Could catch the sound no more.
For then, by toil subdued, he drank
The stifling wave, and then he sank.

No poet wept him: but the page
Of narrative sincere,
That tells his name, his worth, his age,
Is wet with Anson's tear.
And tears by bards or heroes shed
Alike immortalize the dead.

I therefore purpose not, or dream,
Descanting on his fate,
To give the melancholy theme
A more enduring date:
But misery still delights to trace
Its semblance in another's case.

No voice divine the storm allayed,
No light propitious shone;
When, snatched from all effectual aid,
We perished, each alone:
But I beneath a rougher sea,
And whelmed in deeper gulfs than he.

Notes

[3] *coop* barrel.

James Macpherson (1736–1796)

The debate about Macpherson continues today. No one now, and relatively few educated people in the eighteenth century, believed for long that Macpherson's poems were, as he claimed, translations of long-lost Gaelic epics. At first, Burke was taken in; Hume thought a fragment or two might be genuine; Johnson would have none of it, and the literary community soon followed his sound judgment. But Macpherson's "poems" (most of them really prose poems) were immensely popular and made the author a small fortune. And it should mitigate Johnson's blanket rejection that many of the characters and tales that Macpherson wrote up do exist in Gaelic (Irish and Scottish) folk stories, some in writing (especially in Old Irish). In reviving these traditional tales and embodying them in a kind of feverish prose, Macpherson appealed to the emerging spirit of Romanticism, especially in Germany, where the movement was deeply involved with the rediscovery of folk tales and popular, national cultural life. Macpherson actually sent Johnson a challenge, demanding his retraction (before publication) of his damaging critique in the *Journey to the Western Isles of Scotland* (1775). Johnson's response was to arm himself with a large oak stick. Macpherson's dishonesty in itself appalled Johnson, but it seems likely that the nationalistic, Romantic love of folk traditions to which Macpherson appealed, and their popularity, added to Johnson's hostility to the work.

The following fragment comes from *Fingal, an Ancient Epic Poem in Six Books, together with Several other Poems composed by Ossian, the Son of Fingal, translated from the Gaelic Language* (1762). There is a modern edition by Howard Gaskill (Edinburgh University Press, 1996).

from *Fingal*, *an Ancient Epic Poem in Six Books*, *together with Several other Poems composed by Ossian*, *the Son of Fingal*, *translated from the Gaelic Language* (1762)

from Book IV[1]

Who comes with her songs from the mountain, like the bow of the showery Lena? It is the maid of the voice of love. The white-armed daughter of Toscar. Often hast thou heard my song, and given the tear of beauty. Dost thou come to the wars of thy people, to hear the actions of Oscar? When shall I cease to mourn by the streams of echoing Cona? My years have passed away in battle, and my age is darkened with sorrow.

Notes

FROM *FINGAL*

[1] Fingal being asleep, and the action suspended by night, the poet introduces the story of his courtship of Everallin the daughter of Branno. The episode is necessary to clear up several passages that follow in the poem; at the same time that it naturally brings on the action of the book, which may be supposed to begin about the middle of the third night from the opening of the poem. – This book, as many of Ossian's other compositions, is addressed to the beautiful Malvina the daughter of Toscar. She appears to have been in love with Oscar, and to have affected the company of the father after the death of the son [Macpherson's note].

Daughter of the hand of snow! I was not so mournful and blind; I was not so dark and forlorn when Everallin loved me. Everallin with the dark-brown hair, the white-bosomed love of Cormac. A thousand heroes sought the maid, she denied her love to a thousand; the sons of the sword were despised: for graceful in her eyes was Ossian.

I went in suit of the maid to Lego's sable surge; twelve of my people were there, the sons of the streamy Morven. We came to Branno friend of strangers: Branno of the sounding mail. – 'From whence', he said, 'are the arms of steel? Not easy to win is the maid that has denied the blue-eyed sons of Erin. But blessed be thou, O son of Fingal, happy is the maid that waits thee! Though twelve daughters of beauty were mine, thine were the choice, thou son of fame!' – Then he opened the hall of the maid, the dark-haired Everallin. Joy kindled in our breasts of steel and blessed the maid of Branno.

Above us on the hill appeared the people of stately Cormac. Eight were the heroes of the chief; and the heath flamed with their arms. There Colla, Durra of the wounds, there mighty Toscar, and Tago, there Frestal the victorious stood; Dairo of the happy deeds, and Dala the battle's bulwark in the narrow way. – The sword flamed in the hand of Cormac, and graceful was the look of the hero.

Eight were the heroes of Ossian; Ullin stormy son of war; Mullo of the generous deeds; the noble, the graceful Scelacha; Oglan, and Cerdal the wrathful, and Dumariccan's brows of death. And why should Ogar be the last, so wide renowned on the hills of Ardven?

Ogar met Dala the strong, face to face, on the field of heroes. The battle of the chiefs was like the wind on ocean's foamy waves. The dagger is remembered by Ogar; the weapon which he loved; nine times he drowned it in Dala's side. The stormy battle turned. Three times I broke on Cormac's shield: three times he broke his spear. But, unhappy youth of love! I cut his head away. – Five times I shook it by the lock. The friends of Cormac fled.

Whoever would have told me, lovely maid, when then I strove in battle, that blind, forsaken, and forlorn, I now should pass the night, firm ought his mail to have been, and unmatched his arm in battle.

Now on Lena's[2] gloomy heath, the voice of music died away. The unconstant blast blew hard, and the high oak shook its leaves around me; of Everallin were my thoughts, when she, in all the light of beauty, and her blue eyes rolling in tears, stood on a cloud before my sight, and spoke with feeble voice.

'O Ossian, rise and save my son; save Oscar, prince of men, near the red oak of Lubar's stream, he fights with Lochlin's sons'. – She sunk into her cloud again. I clothed me with my steel. My spear supported my steps, and my rattling armour rung. I hummed, as I was wont in danger, the songs of heroes of old. Like distant thunder[3] Lochlin heard; they fled; my son pursued.

Notes

[2] The poet returns to his subject. If one could fix the time of year in which the action of the poem happened, from the scene described here, I should be tempted to place it in autumn. – The trees shed their leaves, and the winds are variable, both which circumstances agree with that season of the year [Macpherson's note].

[3] Ossian gives the reader a high idea of himself. His very song frightens the enemy. This passage resembles one in the eighteenth Iliad, where the voice of Achilles frightens the Trojans from the body of Patroclus.

> Forth marched the chief, and distant from the crowd
> High on the rampart raised his voice aloud ...
> So high his brazen voice the hero reared,
> Hosts drop their arms and trembled as they feared.

POPE [Macpherson's note; Pope's *Iliad* 18.255–6, 263–4]

I called him like a distant stream. 'My son return over Lena. No further pursue the foe, though Ossian is behind thee'. – He came; and lovely in my ear was Oscar's sounding steel. 'Why didst thou stop my hand', he said, 'till death had covered all? For dark and dreadful by the stream they met thy son and Fillan. They watched the terrors of the night. Our swords have conquered some. But as the winds of night pour the ocean over the white sands of Mora, so dark advance the sons of Lochlin over Lena's rustling heath. The ghosts of night shriek afar; I have seen the meteors of death. Let me awake the king of Morven, he that smiles in danger; for he is like the sun of heaven that rises in a storm'. …

Thomas Paine (1737–1809)

At the age of thirty-seven Paine met Benjamin Franklin in London. He had been a staymaker and a tax-collector – an exciseman, whose job was to search for smuggled goods and assess taxes on tobacco and alcohol. He had tried to raise the rate at which excisemen were paid and lost his job in a climate decidedly unfavorable to job actions of any kind. Franklin gave him a letter of recommendation and packed him off to Philadelphia. He took work as a contributor and then as editor of the *Pennsylvania Magazine or American Museum*. Paine wrote editorials against slavery and the oppression of women before addressing the topic of American independence. Fighting broke out in April 1775, and in October Paine published an article urging a declaration of independence. He expanded his arguments into a pamphlet called *Common Sense*, which came out in January of 1776. By April 120,000 copies were sold, and the work certainly helped ripen the times for the Declaration of Independence, which was signed on July 4 (see p. 1040 below).

Paine served briefly in the continental army before beginning work on his series of *Crises*; the first of the eight in the series came out in December 1776 and begins with one of the most famous sentences in journalistic history: "These are the times that try men's souls." The pamphlet sold half a million copies and must be credited with helping to bind the revolutionary nation together.

After the war Paine was out of work. The State of New York gave him a farm in New Rochelle, but by 1787 he was back in England trying to raise money for a bridge-building scheme. There he read Burke's *Reflections on the Revolution in France* and was incensed. He answered in print with *The Rights of Man* (1791), perhaps the most important of the many angry responses to Burke. So well received was the work in France that Paine was elected to a seat in the National Assembly. Unfortunately, the Assembly was finally controlled by the extremists, and Paine, who argued against the execution of Louis, was imprisoned. While in jail he wrote one of the defining statements of his time, *The Age of Reason* (1794). However, this work branded him as an atheist and earned him derision; the age was not yet willing to confess the drift of its own assumptions.

After more than a decade in France, Paine went back to America, where his reputation was just as tarnished as it was in England and France. Paine lived in poverty until 1809 when he died and was buried on his farm in New Rochelle. The great liberal politician and journalist William Cobbett tried unsuccessfully to have Paine's bones moved to England for burial at a more conspicuous site. In the end the bones were lost, and no one knows in which country the physical any more than the literary remains of Paine truly belong. Indeed, he is one of many authors who cannot be seen as belonging exclusively either to America or to Britain, and even France can make some claim to his spirit. The Library of America edition of Paine, *Collected Writings*, is edited by Eric Foner (1995).

British Literature 1640–1789: An Anthology, Fourth Edition. Edited by Robert DeMaria, Jr.

from *Common Sense* (1776)

Of the Origin and Design of Government in General, with Concise Remarks on the English Constitution

Some writers have so confounded society with government, as to leave little or no distinction between them; whereas they are not only different, but have different origins. Society is produced by our wants, and government by our wickedness; the former promotes our happiness *positively* by uniting our affections, the latter *negatively* by restraining our vices. The one encourages intercourse, the other creates distinctions. The first is a patron, the last a punisher.

Society in every state is a blessing, but Government even in its best state is but a necessary evil; in its worst state an intolerable one: for when we suffer, or are exposed to the same miseries *by a Government*, which we might expect in a country *without Government*, our calamity is heightened by reflecting that we furnish the means by which we suffer. Government like dress is the badge of lost innocence; the palaces of kings are built on the ruins of the bowers of paradise. For were the impulses of conscience clear, uniform, and irresistibly obeyed, man would need no other lawgiver; but that not being the case, he finds it necessary to surrender up a part of his property to furnish means for the protection of the rest; and this he is induced to do, by the same prudence which in every other case advises him, out of two evils to choose the least. Wherefore, security being the true design and end of government, it unanswerably follows, that whatever form thereof appears most likely to ensure it to us, with the least expense and greatest benefit, is preferable to all others.

In order to gain a clear and just idea of the design and end of government, let us suppose a small number of persons settled in some sequestered part of the earth, unconnected with the rest; they will then represent the first peopling of any country; or of the world. In this state of natural liberty, society will be their first thought. A thousand motives will excite them thereto, the strength of one man is so unequal to his wants, and his mind so unfitted for perpetual solitude, that he is soon obliged to seek assistance and relief of another, who in his turn requires the same. Four or five united would be able to raise a tolerable dwelling in the midst of a wilderness, but one man might labour out the common period of life without accomplishing any thing; when he had felled his timber he could not remove it, nor erect it after it was removed; hunger in the mean time would urge him from his work, and every different want call him a different way. Disease, nay even misfortune would be death; for though neither might be mortal, yet either would disable him from living, and reduce him to a state in which he might rather be said to perish, than to die.

Thus necessity like a gravitating power would soon form our newly arrived emigrants into society, the reciprocal blessings of which, would supersede, and render the obligations of law and government unnecessary while they remained perfectly just to each other: but as nothing but Heaven is impregnable to vice, it will unavoidably happen that in proportion as they surmount the first difficulties of emigration, which bound them together in common cause, they will begin to relax in their duty and attachment to each other: and this remissness, will point out the necessity of establishing some form of government to supply the defect of moral virtue.

Some convenient tree will afford them a State House, under the branches of which the whole Colony may assemble to deliberate on public matters. It is more than probable that their first laws will have the title only of REGULATIONS and be enforced by no other penalty than public disesteem. In this first parliament every man by natural right will have a seat.

But as the Colony increases, the public concerns will increase likewise, and the distance at which the members may be separated, will render it too inconvenient for all of them to meet on every occasion as at first, when their number was small, their habitations near, and the public concerns few and trifling. This will point out the convenience of their consenting to leave the legislative part to be managed by a select number chosen from the whole body, who are supposed to have the same concerns at stake which those have who appointed them, and who will act in the same manner as the whole body would act were they present. If the colony continues increasing, it will become necessary to augment the number of the representatives, and that the interest of every part of the colony may be attended to, it will be found best to divide the whole into convenient parts, each part sending its proper number: and that the *elected* might never form to themselves an interest separate from the electors, prudence will point out the propriety of having elections often: because as the elected might by that means return and mix again with the general body of the electors in a few months, their fidelity to the public will be secured by the prudent reflection of not making a rod for themselves. And as this frequent interchange will establish a common interest with every part of the community, they will mutually and naturally support each other, and on this (not on the unmeaning name of king) depends the *strength of government; and the happiness of the governed.*

Here then is the origin and rise of government; namely, a mode rendered necessary by the inability of moral virtue to govern the world; here too is the design and end of government, viz. Freedom and security. And however our eyes may be dazzled with snow, or our ears deceived by sound; however prejudice may warp our wills, or interest darken our understanding, the simple voice of nature and of reason will say, ''tis right'.

I draw my idea of the form of government from a principle in nature which no art can overturn, viz. That the more simple any thing is, the less liable it is to be disordered, and the easier repaired when disordered; and with this maxim in view I offer a few remarks on the so much boasted constitution of England. That it was noble for the dark and slavish times in which it was erected, is granted. When the world was overrun with tyranny the least remove therefrom was a glorious rescue. But that it is imperfect, subject to convulsions, and incapable of producing what it seems to promise, is easily demonstrated.

Absolute governments (though the disgrace of human nature) have this advantage with them, that they are simple; if the people suffer, they know the head from which their suffering springs; know likewise the remedy; and are not bewildered by a variety of causes and cures. But the constitution of England is so exceedingly complex, that the nation may suffer for years together without being able to discover in which part the fault lies, some will say in one and some in another, and every political physician will advise a different medicine.

I know it is difficult to get over local or long standing prejudices, yet if we will suffer ourselves to examine the component parts of the English constitution, we shall find them to be the base remains of two ancient tyrannies, compounded with some new Republican materials.

First. – The remains of Monarchical tyranny in the person of the King.

Secondly. – The remains of Aristocratical tyranny in the persons of the Peers.

Thirdly. – The new Republican materials, in the persons of the Commons, on whose virtue depends the freedom of England.

The two first by being hereditary are independent of the People; wherefore in a *constitutional sense* they contribute nothing towards the freedom of the State.

To say that the constitution of England is an *union* of three powers reciprocally *checking* each other, is farcical: either the words have no meaning or they are flat contradictions.

To say that the Commons are a check upon the King, presupposes two things.

First. – That the King is not to be trusted without being looked after; or in other words, that a thirst for absolute power is the natural disease of Monarchy.

Secondly. – That the Commons, by being appointed for that purpose, are either wiser or more worthy of confidence than the Crown.

But as the same constitution which gives the Commons a power to check the King by with-holding the supplies, gives afterwards the King a power to check the Commons by empowering him to reject their other bills; it again supposes that the King is wiser than those whom it has already supposed to be wiser than him. A mere absurdity!

There is something exceedingly ridiculous in the composition of Monarchy; it first excludes a man from the means of information, yet empowers him to act in cases where the highest judgement is required. – The state of a king shuts him from the world, yet the business of a king requires him to know it thoroughly: wherefore, the different parts by unnaturally opposing and destroying each other, prove the whole character to be absurd and useless.

Some writers have explained the English constitution thus; the King, say they, is one, the people another; the Peers are an house in behalf of the King; the Commons in behalf of the people; but this hath all the distinctions of an house divided against itself;[1] and though the expressions be pleasantly arranged, yet when examined they appear idle and ambiguous: and it will always happen, that the nicest construction that words are capable of, when applied to the description of something which either cannot exist, or is too incomprehensible to be within the compass of description, will be words of sound only, and though they may amuse the ear, they cannot inform the mind: for this explanation includes a previous question, viz. *how came the King by a power which the people are afraid to trust and always obliged to check?* Such a power could not be the gift of a wise people; neither can any power *which needs checking* be from God: yet the provision which the constitution makes, supposes such a power to exist.

But the provision is unequal to the task, the means either cannot or will not accomplish the end, and the whole affair is *Felo de se*:[2] for as the greater weight will always carry up the less, and as all the wheels of a machine are put in motion by one, it only remains to know which power in the constitution has the most weight, for that will govern: and though the others, or a part of them, may clog, or check the rapidity of its motion, yet so long as they cannot stop it, their endeavours will be ineffectual: The first moving power will at last have its way, and what it wants in speed will be supplied by time.

That the crown is this overbearing part in the English constitution needs not be mentioned, and that it derives its whole consequence merely from being the giver of places and pensions is self-evident, wherefore, though we have been wise enough to shut and lock a door against absolute Monarchy, we at the same time have been foolish enough to put the Crown in possession of the key.

The prejudice of Englishmen in favour of their own government by King, Lords, and Commons, arises as much or more from national pride than reason. Individuals

Notes

FROM *COMMON SENSE*

[1] *an house divided against itself* a reference to the saying of Jesus that such a house or such a nation cannot stand (Matthew 12.25).

[2] *Felo de se* legal term for the felony of suicide.

are undoubtedly safer in England than in some other countries: but the will of the King is as much the law of the land in Britain as in France with this difference, that instead of proceeding directly from his mouth, it is handed to the people under the more formidable shape of an act of parliament. For the fate of Charles the First,[3] hath only made kings more subtle – not more just.

Wherefore laying aside all national pride and prejudice in favour of modes and forms, the plain truth is, that *it is wholly owing to the constitution of the people, and not to the constitution of the government* that the crown is not as oppressive in England as in Turkey.

An inquiry into the *constitutional errors* in the English form of government, is at this time highly necessary; for as we are never in a proper condition of doing justice to others, while we continue under the influence of some leading partiality, so neither are we capable of doing it to ourselves while we remain fettered by any obstinate prejudice. And as a man who is attached to a prostitute is unfitted to choose or judge of a wife, so any prepossession in favour of a rotten constitution of government will disable us from discerning a good one.

from *The American Crisis* (1777)

Number I

By the Author of *Common Sense*

These are the times that try men's souls: The summer soldier and the sunshine patriot will, in this crisis, shrink from the service of his country, but he that stands it NOW, deserves the love and thanks of man and woman. Tyranny, like hell, is not easily conquered; yet we have this consolation with us, that the harder the conflict, the more glorious the triumph. What we obtain too cheap, we esteem too lightly: – 'Tis dearness only that gives every thing its value. Heaven knows how to set a proper price upon its goods; and it would be strange indeed, if so celestial an article as FREEDOM should not be highly rated. Britain, with an army to enforce her tyranny, has declared, that she has a right (*not only to* TAX) but '*to* BIND *us in* ALL CASES WHATSOEVER', and if being *bound in that manner* is not slavery, then is there not such a thing as slavery upon earth. Even the expression is impious, for so unlimited a power can belong only to GOD.

Whether the Independence of the Continent was declared too soon, or delayed too long, I will not now enter into as an argument; my own simple opinion is, that had it been eight months earlier, it would have been much better. We did not make a proper use of last winter, neither could we, while we were in a dependent state. However, the fault, if it were one, was all our own; we have none to blame but ourselves. But no great deal is lost yet; all that Howe[1] has been doing for this month past is rather a ravage than a conquest, which the spirit of the Jerseys[2] a year ago would have quickly repulsed, and which time and a little resolution will soon recover.

Notes

[3] *Charles the First* executed by Parliament in 1649.

FROM *THE AMERICAN CRISIS*

[1] *Howe* Sir William (1729–1814), commander of British forces in America; defeated American forces in and around New York City several times in 1776; beat Washington at Brandywine at the head of the Chesapeake Bay and drove the Continental Congress from its headquarters in Philadelphia in September 1777; resigned his command in 1778.

[2] *the Jersies* recalling Washington's Christmas night attack on the Hessian troops at Trenton in 1776.

I have as little superstition in me as any man living, but my secret opinion has ever been, and still is, that GOD almighty will not give up a people to military destruction, or leave them unsupported to perish, who had so earnestly and so repeatedly sought to avoid the calamities of war, by every decent method which wisdom could invent. Neither have I so much of the infidel in me, as to suppose, that HE has relinquished the government of the world, and given us up to the care of devils; and as I do not, I cannot see on what grounds the king of Britain can look up to heaven for help against us: A common murderer, a highwayman, or a housebreaker, has as good a pretence as he.

from *The Rights of Man: being an Answer to Mr. Burke's Attack on the French Revolution* (1791)

... Mr. Burke does not attend to the distinction between *men* and *principles*, and, therefore, he does not see that a revolt may take place against the despotism of the latter, while there lies no charge of despotism against the former.

The natural moderation of Louis XVI contributed nothing to alter the hereditary despotism of the monarchy. All the tyrannies of former reigns, acted under that hereditary despotism, were still liable to be revived in the hands of a successor. It was not the respite of a reign that would satisfy France, enlightened as she was then become. A casual discontinuance of the *practice* of despotism, is not a discontinuance of its *principles*; the former depends on the virtue of the individual who is in immediate possession of the power; the latter, on the virtue and fortitude of the nation. In the case of Charles I and James II of England, the revolt was against the personal despotism of the men; whereas in France, it was against the hereditary despotism of the established government. – But men who can consign over the rights of posterity for ever on the authority of a mouldy parchment, like Mr. Burke, are not qualified to judge of this Revolution. It takes in a field too vast for their views to explore, and proceeds with a mightiness of reason they cannot keep pace with.

But there are many points of view in which this revolution may be considered. When despotism has established itself for ages in a country, as in France, it is not in the person of the King only that it resides. It has the appearance of being so in show, and in nominal authority; but it is not so in practice and in fact. It has its standard every where. Every office and department has its despotism, founded upon custom and usage. Every place has its Bastille, and every Bastille its despot. The original hereditary despotism resident in the person of the King, divides and subdivides itself into a thousand shapes and forms, till at last the whole of it is acted by deputation. This was the case in France; and against this species of despotism, proceeding on through an endless labyrinth of office till the source of it is scarcely perceptible, there is no mode of redress. It strengthens itself by assuming the appearance of duty, and tyrannises under the pretence of obeying.

When a man reflects on the condition which France was in from the nature of her government, he will see other causes for revolt than those which immediately connect themselves with the person or character of Louis XVI. There were, if I may so express it, a thousand despotisms to be reformed in France, which had grown up under the hereditary despotism of the monarchy, and became so rooted as to be in a great measure independent of it. Between the Monarchy, the Parliament, and the Church there was a *rivalship* of despotism; besides the feudal despotism operating locally, and the ministerial despotism operating every where. But Mr. Burke, by considering the King as the only possible object of a revolt, speaks as if France was a village, in which every thing that passed must be known to its commanding officer, and no oppression could be acted but what he could immediately control. Mr. Burke might have been in the Bastille his whole life, as well under Louis XVI as Louis XIV, and neither the one nor the other have known that such a man as Mr. Burke existed. The despotic principles of the government were the same in both reigns, though the dispositions of the men were as remote as tyranny and benevolence.

What Mr. Burke considers as a reproach to the French revolution (that of bringing it forward under a reign more mild than the preceding ones) is one of its highest honours. The revolutions that have taken place in other European countries, have been excited by personal hatred. The rage was against the man, and he became the victim. But, in the instance of France we see a Revolution generated in the rational contemplation of the rights of man, and distinguishing from the beginning between persons and principles.

But Mr. Burke appears to have no idea of principles, when he is contemplating governments. 'Ten years ago', says he, 'I could have felicitated France on her having a government, without inquiring what the nature of that Government was, or how it was administered'. Is this the language of a rational man? Is it the language of a heart feeling as it ought to feel for the rights and happiness of the human race? On this ground Mr. Burke must compliment every government in the world, while the victims who suffer under them, whether sold into slavery, or tortured out of existence, are wholly forgotten. It is power, and not principles, that Mr. Burke venerates; and under this abominable depravity he is disqualified to judge between them. – Thus much for his opinion as to the occasions of the French Revolution. I now proceed to other considerations.

I know a place in America called Point-no-Point, because as you proceed along the shore, gay and flowery as Mr. Burke's language, it continually recedes and presents itself at a distance ahead; and when you have got as far as you can go, there is no point at all. Just thus it is with Mr. Burke's three hundred and fifty-six pages. It is therefore difficult to reply to him. But as the points he wishes to establish may be inferred from what he abuses, it is in his paradoxes that we must look for his arguments.

As to the tragic paintings by which Mr. Burke has outraged his own imagination, and seeks to work upon that of his readers, they are very well calculated for theatrical representation where facts are manufactured for the sake of show, and accommodated to produce, through the weakness of sympathy, a weeping effect. But Mr. Burke should recollect that he is writing history, and not *Plays*; and that his readers will expect truth, and not the spouting rant of high-toned exclamation.

When we see a man dramatically lamenting in a publication intended to be believed, that 'The age of chivalry is gone!' that 'The glory of Europe is extinguished for ever!' that 'The unbought grace of life' (if anyone knows what it is), 'the cheap defence of nations, the nurse of manly sentiment and heroic enterprise is gone!' and all this because the Quixote age of chivalry nonsense is gone, what opinion can we form of his judgement, or what regard can we pay to his facts? In the rhapsody of his imagination, he has discovered a world of wind mills, and his sorrows are, that there are no Quixotes to attack them. But if the age of aristocracy, like that of chivalry, should fall, and they had originally some connection, Mr. Burke, the trumpeter of the Order, may continue his parody to the end, and finish with exclaiming – 'Othello's occupation's gone!'[1]

Notes

FROM *THE RIGHTS OF MAN*

[1] *Othello's occupation's gone!* Shakespeare, Othello III.iii.357: Othello's lament for his loss of honor and purpose when he foolishly believes Desdemona unfaithful.

Notwithstanding Mr. Burke's horrid paintings, when the French Revolution is compared with that of other countries, the astonishment will be that it is marked with so few sacrifices; but this astonishment will cease when we reflect that it was *principles*, and not persons, that were the meditated objects of destruction. The mind of the nation was acted upon by a higher stimulus than what the consideration of persons could inspire, and sought a higher conquest than could be produced by the downfall of an enemy. Among the few who fell there do not appear to be any that were intentionally singled out. They all of them had their fate in the circumstances of the moment, and were not pursued with that long, cold-blooded, unabated revenge which pursued the unfortunate Scotch in the affair of 1745.[2]

Through the whole of Mr. Burke's book I do not observe that the Bastille is mentioned more than once, and that with a kind of implication as if he were sorry it was pulled down, and wished it were built up again. 'We have rebuilt Newgate', says he 'and tenanted the mansion; and we have prisons almost as strong as the Bastille for those who dare to libel the Queens of France'. As to what a madman, like the person called Lord George Gordon,[3] might say, and to whom Newgate is rather a bedlam than a prison, it is unworthy a rational consideration. It was a madman that libelled – and that is sufficient apology; and it afforded an opportunity for confining him, which was the thing that was wished for. But certain it is that Mr. Burke, who does not call himself a madman (whatever other people may do), has libelled, in the most unprovoked manner, and in the grossest style of the most vulgar abuse, the whole representative authority of France; and yet Mr. Burke takes his seat in the British House of Commons! From his violence and his grief, his silence on some points and his excess on others, it is difficult not to believe that Mr. Burke is sorry, extremely sorry, that arbitrary power, the power of the Pope, and the Bastille, are pulled down.

Not one glance of compassion, not one commiserating reflection that I can find throughout his book, has he bestowed on those who lingered out the most wretched of lives, a life without hope, in the most miserable of prisons. It is painful to behold a man employing his talents to corrupt himself. Nature has been kinder to Mr. Burke than he is to her. He is not affected by the reality of distress touching upon his heart, but by the showy resemblance of it striking his imagination. He pities the plumage, but forgets the dying bird. Accustomed to kiss the aristocratical hand that hath purloined him from himself, he degenerates into a composition of art, and the genuine soul of nature forsakes him. His hero or heroine must be a tragedy victim expiring in show, and not the real prisoner of misery, sliding into death in the silence of a dungeon. …

Notes

2 *the affair of 1745* the last attempt by Jacobites to restore the House of Stuart to power, crushed at Culloden (1746) and severely recriminated thereafter.

3 *Lord George Gordon* instigator of the anti-Catholic Gordon riots of 1780 in which many buildings were burned in London and 300 people killed.

The American Declaration of Independence (1776)

Thomas Jefferson (1743–1826) composed a draft of this important document in Philadelphia in June of 1776. He sent his draft for comments and corrections to Benjamin Franklin and John Adams, two members of a committee of five assigned the task of producing the document. The corrections appear on Jefferson's draft (now in the Library of Congress) along with his notes concerning changes made by Congress before the committee of five had the document printed as a broadside on a single, unfolded sheet of paper.[1]

In CONGRESS,[2] July 4, 1776.

A DECLARATION

By the REPRESENTATIVES of the

UNITED STATES OF AMERICA,

In GENERAL CONGRESS ASSEMBLED.

WHEN in the Course of human Events, it becomes necessary for one People to dissolve the Political Bands which have connected them with another, and to assume among the Powers of the Earth, the separate and equal Station to which the Laws of Nature and of Nature's God entitle them, a decent Respect to the Opinions of Mankind requires that they should declare the Causes which impel them to the Separation.

We hold these Truths to be self evident, that all Men are created equal, that they are endowed by their Creator with certain unalienable Rights, that among these are Life, Liberty and the Pursuit of Happiness.—That to secure these Rights, Governments are instituted among Men, deriving their just Powers from the Consent of the Governed, that whenever any Form of Government becomes destructive of these Ends, it is the Right of the People to alter or to abolish it, and to institute new Government, laying its Foundation on such Principles, and organizing its Powers in such Form, as to them shall seem most likely to effect their Safety and Happiness. Prudence, indeed, will dictate that Governments long established should not be changed for light and transient Causes; and accordingly all Experience hath shown, that Mankind are more disposed to suffer, while Evils are sufferable, than to right themselves by abolishing the Forms to which they are accustomed. But when a long Train of Abuses and Usurpations, pursuing invariably the same Object, evinces a Design to reduce them under absolute

Notes

THE AMERICAN DECLARATION OF INDEPENDENCE

[1] For information on the text of the Declaration, I rely on the readily accessible website of the U.S. National Archives (www.archives.gov/exhibits/charters/declaration.html).

[2] The Second Continental Congress, first convened May 1775.

Despotism, it is their Right, it is their Duty, to throw off such Government, and to provide new Guards for their future Security. Such has been the patient Sufferance of these Colonies; and such is now the Necessity which constrains them to alter their former System of Government. The History of the present King of Great Britain is a History of repeated Injuries and Usurpations, all having in direct Object the Establishment of an absolute Tyranny over these States. To prove this, let Facts be submitted to a candid[3] World.

He has refused his Assent to Laws, the most wholesome and necessary for the public Good.[4]

He has forbidden his Governors to pass Laws of immediate and presiding Importance, unless suspended in their Operation till his Assent should be obtained; and when so suspended, he has utterly neglected to attend to them.

He has refused to pass other Laws for the Accommodation of large Districts of People, unless those People would relinquish the Right of Representation in the Legislature, a Right inestimable to them, and formidable to Tyrants only.

He has called together Legislative Bodies at Places unusual, uncomfortable, and distant from the Depository of their public Records, for the sole Purpose of fatiguing them into Compliance with his Measures.

He has dissolved Representative Houses repeatedly, for opposing with manly Firmness his Invasions on the Rights of the People.

He has refused for a long Time, after such Dissolutions, to cause others to be elected; whereby the Legislative Powers, incapable of Annihilation, have returned to the People at large for their exercise; the State remaining in the Meantime exposed to all the Dangers of Invasion from without, and Convulsions within.

He has endeavoured to prevent the Population of these States; for that Purpose obstructing the Laws for Naturalization of Foreigners; refusing to pass others to encourage their Migrations hither, and raising the Conditions of new Appropriations of Lands.

He has obstructed the Administration of Justice, by refusing his Assent to Laws for establishing Judiciary Powers.

He has made Judges dependent on his Will alone, for the Tenure of their Offices, and the Amount and Payment of their Salaries.

He has erected a Multitude of new Offices, and sent hither Swarms of Officers to harass our People, and eat out their Substance.

He has kept among us, in Times of Peace, Standing Armies, without the Consent of our Legislatures.

He has affected to render the Military independent of and superior to the Civil Power.

He has combined with others to subject us to a Jurisdiction foreign to our Constitution, and unacknowledged by our Laws; given his Assent to their Acts of pretended Legislation:

For quartering large Bodies of armed Troops among us:

For protecting them, by a mock Trial, from Punishment for any Murders which they should commit on the Inhabitants of these States:

For cutting off our Trade with all Parts of the World:

Notes

[3] *Candid* fair; unbiased.

[4] Stephen E. Lucas points out that the vagueness (or ambiguity) of the charges against King George III is part of the rhetorical strategy of the document ("The Stylistic Artistry of the Declaration of Independence," National Archives Website, www.archives.gov/exhibits/charters/declaration_style.html).

For imposing Taxes on us without our Consent:

For depriving us in many Cases, of the Benefits of Trial by Jury:

For transporting us beyond Seas to be tried for pretended Offences:

For abolishing the free System of English Laws in a neighbouring Province, establishing therein an arbitrary Government, and enlarging its Boundaries, so as to render it at once an Example and fit Instrument for introducing the same absolute Rule into these Colonies:

For taking away our Charters, abolishing our most valuable Laws, and altering fundamentally the Forms of our Governments:

For suspending our own Legislatures, and declaring themselves invested with Power to legislate for us in all Cases whatsoever:

He has abdicated Government here, by declaring us out of his Protection and waging War against us.

He has plundered our Seas, ravaged our Coasts, burnt our Towns, and destroyed the Lives of our People.

He is, at this Time, transporting large Armies of foreign Mercenaries to complete the Works of Death, Desolation and Tyranny, already begun with Circumstances of Cruelty and Perfidy, scarcely paralleled in the most barbarous Ages, and totally unworthy the Head of a civilized Nation.

He has constrained our fellow Citizens taken Captive on the high Seas to bear Arms against their Country, to become the Executioners of their Friends and Brethren, or to fall themselves by their Hands.

He has excited Domestic Insurrections amongst us, and has endeavoured to bring on the Inhabitants of our Frontiers, the merciless Indian Savages, whose known Rule of Warfare, is an undistinguished Destruction, of all Ages, Sexes and Conditions:

In every Stage of these Oppressions we have petitioned for Redress, in the most humble Terms: Our repeated Petitions have been answered only by repeated Injury. A Prince, whose Character is thus marked by every Act which may define a Tyrant, is unfit to be the Ruler of a free People.

Nor have we been wanting in Attentions to our British Brethren. We have warned them from Time to Time of Attempts by their Legislature to extend an unwarrantable Jurisdiction over us. We have reminded them of the Circumstances of our Emigration and Settlement here. We have appealed to their native Justice and Magnanimity, and we have conjured them by the Ties of our common Kindred to disavow these Usurpations, which would inevitably interrupt our Connections and Correspondence. They too have been deaf to the Voice of Justice and Consanguinity. We must, therefore, acquiesce in the Necessity which denounces[5] our Separation, and hold them, as we hold the rest of Mankind, Enemies in War, in Peace, Friends.

We, therefore, the Representatives of the UNITED STATES OF AMERICA, in GENERAL CONGRESS assembled, appealing to the Supreme Judge of the World for the Rectitude of our Intentions, do in the Name and by the Authority of the good People of these Colonies, solemnly Publish and Declare, That these United Colonies are, and of Right ought to be FREE AND INDEPENDENT STATES; that they are absolved from all Allegiance to the British Crown, and that all political Connection between them and the State of Great Britain, is and ought to be totally dissolved; and that as FREE AND INDEPENDENT STATES, they have full power to levy War, conclude Peace, contract Alliances, establish Commerce, and to do all other Acts and

Notes

[5] *Denounce* declare; publish.

Things which INDEPENDENT STATES may of right do. And for the Support of this Declaration, with a firm Reliance on the Protection of divine Providence we mutually pledge to each other our Lives, our Fortunes, and our sacred Honor.

Signed by ORDER *and in* BEHALF *of the* CONGRESS,
JOHN HANCOCK, President.
ATTEST.
CHARLES THOMSON, Secretary.

James Boswell (1740–1795)

Scholars specializing in the study of Samuel Johnson have spent a good part of the last two generations trying to reconstruct the "real" Johnson concealed by Boswell's brilliant and captivating biography. Difficult as it has proved to picture Johnson without Boswell, it would be even harder to imagine Boswell without Johnson. It was a part of Boswell's nature to attach himself to great men, to relish describing himself in their company, and to re-create the feeling of being in their presence for future generations. Boswell certainly did not wish to keep himself out of the picture, as more "objective" biographers have attempted to do, and he has been criticized and even ridiculed for this from the beginning. He competed with Hester Thrale for Johnson's intimacy; he resented Goldsmith for attempting "to shine" in company and thus hindering the full blaze of Johnson's talents, which it was always his hope to evoke. Burke evidently did not like to speak in front of Boswell because it was known that he used social occasions as a mine for his literary projects. Reading about his fawning and self-regarding behavior, even in his own books, one is likely to feel that Boswell, as someone in Johnson's circle said bluntly, was "an ass." Yet the appeal of his *Life of Johnson* is undeniable. One could argue that he cheapened literature by turning the interest of readers from literature to mere anecdote and that Johnson in particular has suffered because more readers know him through Boswell's account than through his own writing. But this is an argument for academics, and the world of readers must always be grateful to Boswell.

In his notebooks and journals, which are gradually emerging from the immense archive known as the Boswell Papers at Yale University, Boswell often writes more directly about himself. These works provide the richest extant account of life in eighteenth-century Britain. Boswell himself seems to have felt that the unrecorded experience was barely worth having. In this way he is curiously modern: he seems willing to admit that his identity is a sort of fiction or a composition, and he is full of anxiety that can arguably be called existential.

The late director of the Boswell Papers, Frank Brady, completed a fine biography of Boswell, begun by his predecessor Frederick Pottle. *The Life of Johnson* exists in a magnificent six-volume set, edited by G. B. Hill, and revised by L. F. Powell (Clarendon Press, 1934–64). Although my text comes from the first edition of 1791, I have relied on Hill and Powell in annotating my selection from the *Life*. The original manuscript of the *Life* is also gradually coming out as part of the Boswell Papers. Volume 3 of 4 came out in 2012 (Yale University Press and Edinburgh University Press).

from *The Life of Dr Samuel Johnson, LL.D.* (1791)

At last, on Monday the 16th of May [1763], when I was sitting in Mr. Davies's[1] back-parlour, after having drunk tea with him and Mrs. Davies, Johnson unexpectedly came into the shop; and Mr. Davies having perceived him through the glass door in the room in which we were sitting, advancing towards us, – he announced his awful approach to

Notes

FROM *THE LIFE OF DR SAMUEL JOHNSON*

[1] *Mr. Davies* Thomas (1712?–85), bookseller, actor, and author.

British Literature 1640–1789: An Anthology, Fourth Edition. Edited by Robert DeMaria, Jr.

me, somewhat in the manner of an actor in the part of Horatio, when he addresses Hamlet on the appearance of his father's ghost, 'Look, my Lord, it comes'. I found that I had a very perfect idea of Johnson's figure, from the portrait of him painted by Sir Joshua Reynolds soon after he had published his *Dictionary*, in the attitude of sitting in his easy chair in deep meditation, which was the first picture his friend did for him, which Sir Joshua has very kindly presented to me, and from which an engraving has been made for this work.[2] Mr. Davies mentioned my name, and respectfully introduced me to him. I was much agitated; and recollecting his prejudice against the Scotch, of which I had heard much, I said to Davies, 'Don't tell him where I come from'. – 'From Scotland', cried Davies roguishly. 'Mr. Johnson', said I, 'I do indeed come from Scotland, but I cannot help it'. I am willing to flatter myself that I meant this as light pleasantry to soothe and conciliate him, and not as an humiliating abasement at the expense of my country. But however that might be, this speech was somewhat unlucky; for with that quickness of wit for which he was so remarkable, he seized the expression 'come from Scotland', which I used in the sense of being of that country, and as if I had said that I had come away from it or left it, retorted, 'That, Sir, I find, is what a very great many of your countrymen cannot help'. This stroke stunned me a good deal; and when he had sat down, I felt myself not a little embarrassed, and apprehensive of what might come next. He then addressed himself to Davies: 'What do you think of Garrick?[3] He has refused me an order for the play for Miss Williams,[4] because he knows the house will be full, and that an order would be worth three shillings'. Eager to take any opening to get into conversation with him, I ventured to say, 'O, Sir, I cannot think Mr. Garrick would grudge such a trifle to you'. 'Sir', said he, with a stern look, 'I have known David Garrick longer than you have done; and I know no right you have to talk to me on the subject'. Perhaps I deserved this check; for it was rather presumptuous in me, an entire stranger, to express any doubt of the justice of his animadversion upon his old acquaintance and pupil. I now felt myself much mortified, and began to think that the hope which I had long indulged of obtaining his acquaintance was blasted. And, in truth, had not my ardour been uncommonly strong, and my resolution uncommonly persevering, so rough a reception might have deterred me for ever from making any further attempts. Fortunately, however, I remained upon the field not wholly discomfited; and was soon rewarded by hearing some of his conversation, of which I preserved the following short minute, without marking the questions and observations by which it was produced.

'People', he remarked, 'may be taken in once, who imagine that an author is greater in private life than other men. Uncommon parts require uncommon opportunities for their exertion.

'In barbarous society, superiority of parts is of real consequence. Great strength or great wisdom is of much value to an individual. But in more polished times there are people to do every thing for money, and then there are a number of other superiorities, such as those of birth and fortune, and rank, that dissipate men's attention, and leave no extraordinary share of respect for personal and intellectual superiority. This is wisely ordered by Providence, to preserve some equality among mankind. ...'

Speaking of one[5] who with more than ordinary boldness attacked public measures and the royal family, he said, 'I think he is safe from the law, but he is an abusive scoun-

Notes

[2] *portrait of him ... for this work* engraved by James Heath (1757–1834) and inserted by Boswell as a frontispiece in his *Life of Johnson*.

[3] *Garrick* David (1717–79), greatest actor of his age and then co-manager of the Drury Lane Theatre.

[4] *Miss Williams* Anna (1706–83), a blind, sometime writer, a close friend and a boarder for many years in Johnson's house.

[5] *one* John Wilkes (1727–97), famous advocate of "Liberty," author in 1763 of the notorious Number 45 of the *North Briton*.

drel; and instead of applying to my Lord Chief Justice to punish him, I would send half a dozen footmen and have him well ducked.

'The notion of liberty amuses the people of England, and helps to keep off the *tædium vitæ*.[6] When a butcher tells you that his heart bleeds for his country, he has, in fact, no uneasy feeling. …'

I was highly pleased with the extraordinary vigour of his conversation, and regretted that I was drawn away from it by an engagement at another place. I had, for a part of the evening, been left alone with him, and had ventured to make an observation now and then, which he received very civilly; so that I was satisfied that though there was a roughness in his manner, there was no ill-nature in his disposition. Davies followed me to the door, and when I complained to him a little of the hard blows which the great man had given me, he kindly took upon him to console me by saying, 'Don't be uneasy. I can see he likes you very well'.

A few days afterwards I called on Davies, and asked him if he thought I might take the liberty of waiting on Mr. Johnson at his Chambers in the Temple. He said I certainly might, and that Mr. Johnson would take it as a compliment. So upon Tuesday the 24th of May, after having been enlivened by the witty sallies of Messieurs Thornton, Wilkes, Churchill and Lloyd,[7] with whom I had passed the morning, I boldly repaired to Johnson. His Chambers were on the first floor of No. 1, Inner Temple-lane, and I entered them with an impression given me by the Reverend Dr. Blair,[8] of Edinburgh, who had been introduced to him not long before, and described his having 'found the Giant in his den'; an expression, which, when I came to be pretty well acquainted with Johnson, I repeated to him, and he was diverted at this picturesque account of himself. Dr. Blair had been presented to him by Dr. James Fordyce.[9] At this time the controversy concerning the pieces published by Mr. James Macpherson,[10] as translations of Ossian, was at its height. Johnson had all along denied their authenticity; and, what was still more provoking to their admirers, maintained that they had no merit. The subject having been introduced by Dr. Fordyce, Dr. Blair, relying on the internal evidence of their antiquity, asked Dr. Johnson whether he thought any man of a modern age could have written such poems? Johnson replied, 'Yes, Sir, many men, many women, and many children'. Johnson, at this time, did not know that Dr. Blair had just published a Dissertation, not only defending their authenticity, but seriously ranking them with the poems of Homer and Virgil; and when he was afterwards informed of this circumstance, he expressed some displeasure at Dr. Fordyce's having suggested the topic, and said, 'I am not sorry that they got thus much for their pains. Sir, it was like leading one to talk of a book, when the author is concealed behind the door'.

He received me very courteously; but, it must be confessed, that his apartment, and furniture, and morning dress, were sufficiently uncouth. His brown suit of clothes looked very rusty; he had on a little old shrivelled unpowdered wig, which was too small for his head; his shirt-neck and knees of his breeches were loose; his black worsted stockings ill drawn up; and he had a pair of unbuckled shoes by way of slippers. But all these slovenly particularities were forgotten the moment that he began to talk. Some gentlemen, whom I do not recollect, were sitting with him; and when they went away, I also rose; but he said to me, 'Nay, don't go'. 'Sir', said I, 'I am afraid that I intrude upon you. It is benevolent to allow me to sit and hear you'. He seemed pleased with this

Notes

[6] *tædium vitæ* boredom, ennui.

[7] *Thornton, Wilkes, Churchill and Lloyd* Bonnell Thornton (1724–68), writer; John Wilkes; Charles Churchill (1731–64), poet and dramatist; Robert Lloyd (1733–64), writer.

[8] *Dr. Blair* Hugh (1718–1800), divine and critic, author of an important work on rhetoric.

[9] *James Fordyce* (1720–96), Presbyterian divine.

[10] *James Macpherson* see the selection from Macpherson, p. 1029 above.

compliment, which I sincerely paid him, and answered, 'Sir, I am obliged to any man who visits me'. I have preserved the following short minute of what passed this day.

'Madness frequently discovers itself merely by unnecessary deviation from the usual modes of the world. My poor friend Smart[11] showed the disturbance of his mind, by falling upon his knees, and saying his prayers in the street, or in any other unusual place. Now although, rationally speaking, it is greater madness not to pray at all, than to pray as Smart did, I am afraid there are so many who do not pray, that their understanding is not called in question'.

Concerning this unfortunate poet, Christopher Smart, who was confined in a madhouse, he had, at another time the following conversation with Dr. Burney. JOHNSON. 'It seems as if his mind had ceased to struggle with the disease; for he grows fat upon it'. BURNEY. 'Perhaps, Sir, that may be from want of exercise'. JOHNSON. 'No, Sir; he has partly as much exercise as he used to have, for he digs in the garden. Indeed, before his confinement, he used for exercise to walk to the alehouse; but he was *carried* back again. I did not think he ought to be shut up. His infirmities were not noxious to society. He insisted on people praying with him; and I'd as lief pray with Kit Smart as any one else. Another charge was, that he did not love clean linen; and I have no passion for it.

'Mankind have a great aversion to intellectual labour; but even supposing knowledge to be easily attainable, more people would be content to to be ignorant than would take even a little trouble to acquire it.

'The morality of an action depends on the motive from which we act. If I fling half a crown to a beggar with intention to break his head, and he picks it up and buys victuals with it, the physical effect is good; but, with respect to me, the action is very wrong. So, religious exercises, if not performed with an intention to please GOD, avail us nothing. As our Saviour says of those who perform them from other motives, "Verily they have their own reward".'...

Talking of Garrick, he said, 'He is the first man in the world for sprightly conversation'.

When I rose a second time he again pressed me to stay, which I did.

He told me, that he generally went abroad at four in the afternoon, and seldom came home till two in the morning. I took the liberty to ask if he did not think it wrong to live thus, and not make more use of his great talents. He owned it was a bad habit. On reviewing, at the distance of many years, my journal of this period, I wonder how, at my first visit, I ventured to talk to him so freely, and that he bore it with so much indulgence.

Before we parted, he was so good as to promise to favour me with his company one evening at my lodgings; and, as I took my leave, shook me cordially by the hand. It is almost needless to add, that I felt no little elation at having now so happily established an acquaintance of which I had been so long ambitious.

My readers will, I trust, excuse me for being thus minutely circumstantial, when it is considered that the acquaintance of Dr. Johnson was to me a most valuable acquisition, and laid the foundation of whatever instruction and entertainment they may receive from my collections concerning the great subject of the work which they are now perusing. ...

A revolution of some importance in my plan of life had just taken place; for instead of procuring a commission in the foot-guards, which was my own inclination, I had, in compliance with my father's wishes, agreed to study the law; and was soon to set out for Utrecht, to hear the lectures of an excellent Civilian[12] in that University, and then to proceed on my travels. Though very desirous of obtaining Dr. Johnson's advice and

Notes

[11] *Smart* Christopher; see the selection from his works, p. 965 above.

[12] *Civilian* "One that possesses the knowledge of the old Roman law, and of general equity" (Johnson); an expert on civil law.

instructions on the mode of pursuing my studies, I was at this time so occupied, shall I call it? or so dissipated, by the amusements of London, that our next meeting was not till Saturday, June 25, when happening to dine at Clifton's eating-house, in Butcher-row, I was surprised to perceive Johnson come in and take his seat at another table. The mode of dining, or rather being fed, at such houses in London, is well known to many to be particularly unsocial, as there is no Ordinary, or united company, but each person has his own mess, and is under no obligation to hold any intercourse with any one. A liberal and full-minded man, however, who loves to talk, will break through this churlish and unsocial restraint. Johnson and an Irish gentleman got into a dispute concerning the cause of some part of mankind being black. 'Why, Sir', said Johnson, 'it has been accounted for in three ways: either by supposing that they are the posterity of Ham, who was cursed; or that GOD at first created two kinds of men, one black and another white; or that by the heat of the sun the skin is scorched, and so acquires a sooty hue. This matter has been much canvassed among naturalists, but has never been brought to any certain issue'. What the Irishman said is totally obliterated from my mind; but I remember that he became very warm and intemperate in his expressions; upon which Johnson rose, and quietly walked away. When he had retired, his antagonist took his revenge, as he thought, by saying, 'He has a most ungainly figure, and an affectation of pomposity unworthy of a man of genius'.

Johnson had not observed that I was in the room. I followed him, however, and he agreed to meet me in the evening at the Mitre.[13] I called on him, and we went thither at nine. We had a good supper, and port wine, of which he then sometimes drank a bottle. The orthodox high-church sound of the Mitre, the figure and manner of the celebrated Samuel Johnson, the extraordinary power and precision of his conversation, and the pride arising from finding myself admitted as his companion, produced a variety of sensations, and a pleasing elevation of mind beyond what I had ever before experienced. I find in my journal the following minute of our conversation, which, though it will give but a very faint notion of what passed, is, in some degree, a valuable record; and it will be curious in this view, as showing how habitual to his mind were some opinions which appear in his works. …

'Sir, I do not think Gray a first-rate poet. He has not a bold imagination, nor much command of words. The obscurity in which he has involved himself will not persuade us that he is sublime. His Elegy in a church-yard has a happy selection of images, but I don't like what are called his great things. His Ode which begins

> Ruin seize thee, ruthless King,
> Confusion on thy banner wait![14]

has been celebrated for its abruptness, and plunging into the subject all at once. But such arts as these have no merit, unless when they are original. We admire them only once; and this abruptness has nothing new in it. We have had it often before. Nay, we have it in the old song of Johnny Armstrong:

> 'Is there ever a man in all Scotland
> From the highest estate to the lowest degree, &c.'.

And then, Sir,

> Yes, there is a man in Westmoreland,
> And Johnny Armstrong they do him call.

Notes

[13] *Mitre* a tavern in Fleet Street.

[14] *Ruin … wait* the opening of "The Bard."

There, now, you plunge at once into the subject. You have no previous narration to lead you to it. – The two next lines in that Ode are, I think, very good:

> Though fanned by conquest's crimson wing,
> They mock the air with idle state.

Here let it be observed, that although his opinion of Gray's poetry was widely different from mine, and I believe from that of most men of taste, by whom it is with justice highly admired, there is certainly much absurdity in the clamour which has been raised, as if he had been culpably injurious to the merit of that bard, and had been actuated by envy. Alas! ye little short-sighted critics, could Johnson be envious of the talents of any of his contemporaries? That his opinion on this subject was what in private and in public he uniformly expressed, regardless of what others might think, we may wonder, and perhaps regret; but it is shallow and unjust to charge him with expressing what he did not think.

Finding him in a placid humour, and wishing to avail myself of the opportunity which I fortunately had of consulting a sage, to hear whose wisdom, I conceived in the ardour of youthful imagination, that men filled with a noble enthusiasm for intellectual improvement would gladly have resorted from distant lands; I opened my mind to him ingenuously, and gave him a little sketch of my life, to which he was pleased to listen with great attention.

I acknowledged, that though educated very strictly in the principles of religion, I had for some time been misled into a certain degree of infidelity; but that I was come now to a better way of thinking, and was fully satisfied of the truth of the Christian revelation, though I was not clear as to every point considered to be orthodox. Being at all times a curious examiner of the human mind, and pleased with an undisguised display of what had passed in it, he called to me with warmth, 'Give me your hand; I have taken a liking to you'. He then began to descant upon the force of testimony, and the little we could know of final causes; so that the objections of, why was it so? or why was it not so? ought not to disturb us: adding, that he himself had at one period been guilty of a temporary neglect of religion, but that it was not the result of argument, but mere absence of thought.

After having given credit to reports of his bigotry, I was agreeably surprised when he expressed the following very liberal sentiment, which has the additional value of obviating an objection to our holy religion, founded upon the discordant tenets of Christians themselves: 'For my part, Sir, I think all Christians, whether Papists or Protestants, agree in the essential articles, and that their differences are trivial, and rather political than religious'.

We talked of belief in ghosts. He said, 'Sir, I make a distinction between what a man may experience by the mere strength of his imagination, and what imagination cannot possibly produce. Thus, suppose I should think that I saw a form, and heard a voice cry "Johnson, you are a very wicked fellow, and unless you repent you will certainly be punished"; my own unworthiness is so deeply impressed upon my mind, that I might *imagine* I thus saw and heard, and therefore I should not believe that an external communication had been made to me. But if a form should appear, and a voice should tell me that a particular man had died at a particular place, and a particular hour, a fact which I had no apprehension of, nor any means of knowing, and this fact, with all its circumstances should afterwards be unquestionably proved, I should, in that case be persuaded that I had supernatural intelligence imparted to me'. ...

He proceeded: 'Your going abroad, Sir, and breaking off with idle habits, may be of great importance to you. I would go where there are courts and learned men. There is a good deal of Spain that has not been perambulated. I would have you go thither. A man of inferior talents to yours may furnish us with useful observations upon that country'. His supposing me, at that period of life, capable of writing an account of my travels that would deserve to be read, elated me not a little.

I appeal to every impartial reader whether this faithful detail of his frankness, complacency,[15] and kindness to a young man, a stranger and a Scotchman, does not refute the unjust opinion of the harshness of his general demeanour. His occasional reproofs of folly, impudence, or impiety, and even the sudden sallies of his constitutional irritability of temper, which have been preserved for the poignancy of their wit, have produced that opinion among those who have not considered that such instances, though collected by Mrs. Piozzi into a small volume,[16] and read over in a few hours, were, in fact, scattered through a long series of years; years, in which his time was chiefly spent in instructing and delighting mankind by his writings and conversation, in acts of piety to GOD, and good-will to men.

I complained to him that I had not yet acquired much knowledge, and asked his advice as to my studies. He said, 'Don't talk of study now. I will give you a plan; but it will require some time to consider of it'. 'It is very good in you, Mr. Johnson', I replied, 'to allow me to be with you thus. Had it been foretold to me some years ago that I should pass an evening with the author of The RAMBLER, how should I have exulted!' What I then expressed was sincerely from the heart. He was satisfied that it was, and cordially answered, 'Sir, I am glad we have met. I hope we shall pass many evenings and mornings too, together'. We finished a couple of bottles of port, and sat till between one and two in the morning. …

He recommended to me to keep a journal of my life, full and unreserved. He said it would be a very good exercise, and would yield me great satisfaction when the particulars were faded from my remembrance. I was uncommonly fortunate in having had a previous coincidence of opinion with him upon this subject, for I had kept such a journal for some time;[17] and it was no small pleasure to me to have this to tell him, and to receive his approbation. He counselled me to keep it private, and said I might surely have a friend who would burn it in case of my death. From this habit I have been enabled to give the world so many anecdotes, which would otherwise have been lost to posterity. I mentioned that I was afraid I put into my journal too many little incidents. JOHNSON. 'There is nothing, Sir, too little for so little a creature as man. It is by studying little things that we attain the great art of having as little misery and as much happiness as possible'…

Mr. Levet[18] this day showed me Dr. Johnson's library, which was contained in two garrets over his Chambers, where Lintot,[19] son of the celebrated bookseller of that name, had formerly his printing-house. I found a number of good books, but very dusty and in great confusion. The floor was strewed with manuscript leaves, in Johnson's own handwriting, which I beheld with a degree of veneration, supposing they might contain portions of The Rambler, or of Rasselas. I observed an apparatus for chemical experiments, of which Johnson was all his life very fond. The place seemed to be very favourable for retirement and meditation. Johnson told me, that he went up thither without mentioning it to his servant, when he wanted to study, secure from interruption; for he would not allow his servant to say he was not at home when he really was. 'A servant's strict regard for truth', said he 'must be weakened by such a practice. A philosopher may know that it is merely a form of denial; but few servants are such nice distinguishers. If I accustom a servant to tell a lie for *me*, have I not reason

Notes

[15] *complacency* "Civility; complaisance; softness of manners" (Johnson).

[16] *Mrs. Piozzi … volume* Hester Lynch Thrale Piozzi (1741–1821) published her *Anecdotes of the Late Samuel Johnson* in 1786; see the selection from her letters below.

[17] *I had kept such a journal for some time* Boswell kept voluminous and "unreserved" journals; he preserved them all, and the work of publishing them and his various notebooks and manuscripts has occupied teams of scholars for three generations.

[18] *Mr. Levet* a physician without university training, who ministered to the poor and lived for many years as a boarder in Johnson's house.

[19] *Lintot* Henry (1709–58), son of Bernard (1675–1736), proprietor of the lucrative copyright for Pope's *Iliad*.

to apprehend that he will tell many lies for *himself*?' I am, however, satisfied that every servant, of any degree of intelligence, understands saying his master is not at home, not at all as the affirmation of a fact, but as customary words, intimating that his master wishes not to be seen; so that there can be no bad effect from it.

Mr. Temple, now vicar of St Gluvias, Cornwall, who had been my intimate friend for many years, had at this time chambers in Farrar's-buildings, at the bottom of Inner Temple-lane, which he kindly lent me upon my quitting my lodgings, he being to return to Trinity Hall, Cambridge. I found them particularly convenient for me, as they were so near Dr. Johnson's.

On Wednesday, July 20, Dr. Johnson, Mr. Dempster,[20] and my uncle Dr. Boswell, who happened to be now in London, supped with me at these Chambers. JOHNSON. 'Pity is not natural to man. Children are always cruel. Savages are always cruel. Pity is acquired and improved by the cultivation of reason. We may have uneasy sensations from seeing a creature in distress, without pity; for we have not pity unless we wish to relieve them. When I am on my way to dine with a friend, and finding it late, have bid the coachman make haste, if I happen to attend when he whips his horses, I may feel unpleasantly that the animals are put to pain, but I do not wish him to desist. No, Sir, I wish him to drive on'.

Mr. Alexander Donaldson, bookseller of Edinburgh, had for some time opened a shop in London, and sold his cheap editions of the most popular English books, in defiance of the supposed common-law right of *Literary Property*. Johnson, though he concurred in the opinion which was afterwards sanctioned by a decree from the House of Lords, that there was no such right, was at this time very angry that the booksellers of London, for whom he uniformly professed much regard, should suffer from an invasion of what they had ever considered to be secure: and he was loud and violent against Mr. Donaldson.[21] 'He is a fellow who takes advantage of the law to injure his brethren; for, notwithstanding that the statute[22] secures only fourteen years of exclusive right, it has always been understood by the trade, that he, who buys the copy-right of a book from the author, obtains a perpetual property; and upon that belief, numberless bargains are made to transfer that property after the expiration of the statutory term. Now Donaldson, I say, takes advantage here, of people who have really an equitable title from usage; and if we consider how few of the books, of which they buy the property, succeed so well as to bring profit, we should be of opinion that the term of fourteen years is too short; it should be sixty years'. DEMPSTER. 'Donaldson, Sir, is anxious for the encouragement of literature. He reduces the price of books, so that poor students may buy them'. JOHNSON, (laughing) 'Well, Sir, allowing that to be his motive, he is no better than Robin Hood, who robbed the rich in order to give to the poor'.

It is remarkable, that when the great question concerning Literary Property came to be ultimately tried before the supreme tribunal of this country,[23] in consequence of the very spirited exertions of Mr. Donaldson, Dr. Johnson was zealous against a perpetuity; but he thought that the term of the exclusive right of authors should be considerably enlarged. He was then for granting a hundred years.[24]

Notes

20 *Mr. Dempster* Scottish Member of Parliament and agriculturist.

21 *Mr. Donaldson* several actions were brought against him by London booksellers, but they all failed or were overturned; Boswell acted as his attorney in one suit in 1773.

22 *statute* "A Bill for the Encouragement of Learning by Vesting the Copies of Printed Books in the Authors, or Purchasers, of such Copies during the Times therein Mentioned"; a second fourteen-year term was allowed to authors still living after the expiration of the first term; the bill became law in 1710.

23 *the supreme tribunal of this country* the House of Lords, which determined in 1774 that copyright should be limited.

24 *a hundred years* Johnson gave his opinion in a letter to William Strahan on March 7, 1774; fifty years is the term he settles on.

The conversation now turned upon Mr. David Hume's style. JOHNSON. 'Why, Sir, his style is not English; the structure of his sentences is French. Now the French structure and the English structure may, in the nature of things, be equally good. But if you allow that the English language is established, he is wrong. My name might originally have been Nicholson, as well as Johnson; but were you to call me Nicholson now, you would call me very absurdly'.

Rousseau's treatise on the inequality of mankind[25] was at this time a fashionable topic. It gave rise to an observation by Mr. Dempster, that the advantages of fortune and rank were nothing to a wise man, who ought to value only merit. JOHNSON. 'If man were a savage, living in the woods by himself, this might be true; but in civilised society we all depend on each other, and our happiness is very much owing to the good opinion of mankind. Now, Sir, in civilised society, external advantages make us more respected. A man with a good coat upon his back meets with a better reception than he who has a bad one. Sir, you may analyse this, and say what is there in it? But that will avail you nothing, for it is a part of a general system. Pound St Paul's Church into atoms, and consider any single atom; it is, to be sure, good for nothing: but, put all these atoms together, and you have St Paul's Church. So it is with human felicity, which is made up of many ingredients, each of which may be shown to be very insignificant. In civilised society, personal merit will not serve you so much as money will. Sir, you may make the experiment. Go into the street, and give one man a lecture on morality, and another a shilling, and see which will respect you most. If you wish only to support nature, Sir William Petty[26] fixes your allowance at three pounds a year; but as times are much altered, let us call it six pounds. This sum will fill your belly, shelter you from the weather, and even get you a strong lasting coat, supposing it be made of good bull's hide. Now, Sir, all beyond this is artificial, and is desired in order to obtain a greater degree of respect from our fellow-creatures. And, Sir, if six hundred pounds a year procure a man more consequence, and, of course, more happiness than six pounds a year, the same proportion will hold as to six thousand, and so on as far as opulence can be carried. Perhaps he who has a large fortune may not be so happy as he who has a small one; but that must proceed from other causes than from his having the large fortune: for, *cæteris paribus*,[27] he who is rich in a civilised society, must be happier than he who is poor; as riches, if properly used (and it is a man's own fault if they are not) must be productive of the highest advantages. Money, to be sure, of itself is no use; for its only use is to part with it. Rousseau, and all those who deal in paradoxes, are led away by a childish desire of novelty. When I was a boy, I used always to choose the wrong side of a debate, because most ingenious things, that is to say, most new things, could be said upon it. Sir, there is nothing for which you may not muster up more plausible arguments, than those which are urged against wealth and other external advantages. Why, now, there is stealing; why should it be thought a crime? When we consider by what unjust methods property has been often acquired, and that what was unjustly got it must be unjust to keep, where is the harm in one man's taking the property of another from him? Besides, Sir, when we consider the bad use that many people make of their property, and how much better use the thief may make of it, it may be defended as a very allowable practice. Yet, Sir, the experience of mankind has discovered stealing to be so very bad a thing, that they make no scruple to hang a man for it. When I was running about this town a very poor fellow, I was a great arguer for the advantages of poverty; but I was, at the same time, very sorry to be poor. Sir, all the arguments which are brought to represent poverty as no

Notes

[25] *Rousseau's treatise on the inequality of mankind* *Discours sur l'origine et les fondements de l'inégalité parmi les hommes* (1755).

[26] *Sir William Petty* (1623–87), political economist; he also estimated the mean annual per capita expenditure at £7.

[27] *cæteris paribus* other things being equal.

evil, show it to be evidently a great evil. You never find people labouring to convince you that you may live very happily upon a plentiful fortune. – So you hear people talking how miserable a king must be; and yet they all wish to be in his place'. ...

At night Mr. Johnson and I supped in a private room at the Turk's Head coffee-house, in the Strand. 'I encourage this house' said he, 'for the mistress is a good civil woman, and has not much business.

'Sir, I love the acquaintance of young people; because, in the first place, I don't like to think myself growing old. In the next place, young acquaintances must last longest, if they do last; and then, Sir, young men have more virtue than old men; they have more generous sentiments in every respect. I love the young dogs of this age: they have more wit and humour and knowledge of life than we had; but then the dogs are not so good scholars. Sir, in my early years I read very hard. It is a sad reflection, but a true one, that I knew almost as much at eighteen as I do now. My judgement, to be sure, was not so good; but, I had all the facts. I remember very well, when I was at Oxford, an old gentleman said to me, "Young man, ply your book diligently now, and acquire a stock of knowledge; for when years come upon you, you will find that poring upon books will be but an irksome task". ...'

He mentioned to me now, for the first time, that he had been distressed by melancholy, and for that reason had been obliged to fly from study and meditation, to the dissipating variety of life. Against melancholy he recommended constant occupation of mind, a great deal of exercise, moderation in eating and drinking, and especially to shun drinking at night. He said melancholy people were apt to fly to intemperance for relief, but that it sunk them much deeper in misery. He observed, that labouring men who work hard, and live sparingly, are seldom or never troubled with low spirits. ...

He maintained, that a boy at school was the happiest of human beings. I supported a different opinion, from which I have never yet varied, that a man is happier; and I enlarged upon the anxiety and sufferings which are endured at school. JOHNSON. 'Ah! Sir, a boy's being flogged is not so severe as a man's having the hiss of the world against him. Men have a solicitude about fame; and the greater share they have of it, the more afraid they are of losing it'. I silently asked myself, 'Is it possible that the great Samuel Johnson really entertains any such apprehension, and is not confident that his exalted fame is established upon a foundation never to be shaken?'...

On Tuesday, July 26, I found Mr. Johnson alone. It was a very wet day, and I again complained of the disagreeable effects of such weather. JOHNSON. 'Sir, this is all imagination, which physicians encourage; for man lives in air, as a fish lives in water; so that if the atmosphere press heavy from above, there is an equal resistance from below. To be sure, bad weather is hard upon people who are obliged to be abroad; and men cannot labour so well in the open air in bad weather, as in good: but, Sir, a smith or a tailor, whose work is within doors, will surely do as much in rainy weather as in fair. Some very delicate frames, indeed, may be affected by wet weather, but not common constitutions'.

We talked of the education of children; and I asked him what he thought was best to teach them first. JOHNSON. 'Sir, it is no matter what you teach them first, any more than what leg you shall put into your breeches first. Sir, you may stand disputing which is best to put in first, but in the mean time your breech is bare. Sir, while you are considering which of two things you should teach your child first, another boy has learnt them both'.

On Thursday, July 28, we again supped in private at the Turk's Head coffee-house. JOHNSON. 'Swift has a higher reputation than he deserves. His excellence is strong sense; for his humour, though very well, is not remarkably good. I doubt whether the 'Tale of a Tub' be his; for he never owned it, and it is much above his usual manner.

'Thomson, I think, had as much of the poet about him as most writers. Every thing appeared to him through the medium of his favourite pursuit. He could not have viewed those two candles burning but with a poetical eye'. ...

The conversation then took a philosophical turn. JOHNSON. 'Human experience, which is constantly contradicting theory, is the great test of truth. A system, built upon the discoveries of a great many minds, is always of more strength, than what is produced by the mere workings of any one mind, which, of itself, can do little. There is not so poor a book in the world that would not be a prodigious effort were it wrought out entirely by a single mind, without the aid of prior investigators. The French writers are superficial, because they are not scholars, and so proceed upon the mere power of their own minds; and we see how very little power they have.

'As to the Christian religion, Sir, besides the strong evidence which we have for it, there is a balance in its favour from the number of great men who have been convinced of its truth, after a serious consideration of the question. Grotius[28] was an acute man, a lawyer, a man accustomed to examine evidence, and he was convinced. Grotius was not a recluse, but a man of the world, who certainly had no bias on the side of religion. Sir Isaac Newton set out an infidel, and came to be a very firm believer'.

He this evening again recommended to me to perambulate Spain. I said it would amuse him to get a letter from me dated at Salamancha. JOHNSON. 'I love the University of Salamancha; for when the Spaniards were in doubt as to the lawfulness of their conquering of America, the University of Salamancha gave it as their opinion that it was not lawful'. He spoke this with great emotion ....

I again begged his advice as to my method of study at Utrecht. 'Come', said he, 'let us make a day of it. Let us go down to Greenwich and dine, and talk of it there'. The following Saturday was fixed for this excursion.

As we walked along the Strand to-night, arm in arm, a woman of the town accosted us, in the usual enticing manner. 'No, no, my girl', said Johnson, 'it won't do'. He, however, did not treat her with harshness, and we talked of the wretched life of such women; and agreed, that much more misery than happiness, upon the whole, is produced by illicit commerce between the sexes.[29]

On Saturday, July 30, Dr. Johnson and I took a sculler at the Temple-stairs, and set out for Greenwich.[30] I asked him if he really thought a knowledge of the Greek and Latin languages an essential requisite to a good education. JOHNSON. 'Most certainly, Sir; for those who know them have a very great advantage over those who do not. Nay, Sir, it is wonderful what a difference learning makes upon people even in the common intercourse of life, which does not appear to be much connected with it'. 'And yet', said I, 'people go through the world very well, and carry on the business of life to good advantage, without learning'. JOHNSON. 'Why, Sir, that may be true in cases where learning cannot possibly be any use; for instance, this boy rows as well without learning, as if he could sing the song of Orpheus to the Argonauts, who were the first sailors'. He then called to the boy, 'What would you give, my lad, to know about the Argonauts?' 'Sir', said the boy, 'I would give what I have'. Johnson was much pleased with his answer, and we gave him a double fare. Mr. Johnson then turning to me, 'Sir', said he 'a desire of knowledge is the natural feeling of mankind; and every human being, whose mind is not debauched, will be willing to give all that he has to get knowledge.'...

We stayed so long at Greenwich, that our sail up the river, in our return to London, was by no means so pleasant as in the morning; for the night air was so cold that it made

Notes

[28] *Grotius* Hugo (1583–1645), legal scholar and author of a fundamental religious handbook, *De veritate religionis*.

[29] *illicit commerce between the sexes* Boswell, however, records his very frequent use of such commerce in his journals.

[30] *Greenwich* they are traveling down the Thames in a small hired boat.

me shiver. I was the more sensible of it from having sat up all the night before, recollecting and writing in my journal what I thought worthy of preservation; an exertion, which, during the first part of my acquaintance with Johnson, I frequently made. I remember having sat up four nights in one week, without being much incommoded in the day time.

Johnson, whose robust frame was not in the least affected by the cold, scolded me, as if my shivering had been a paltry effeminacy, saying, 'Why do you shiver?' Sir William Scott, of the Commons, told me, that when he complained of a head-ache in the post-chaise, as they were travelling together to Scotland, Johnson treated him in the same manner: 'At your age, Sir, I had no head-ache'. It is not easy to make allowance for sensations in others, which ourselves have not at the time. We must all have experienced how very differently we are affected by the complaints of our neighbours, when we are well and when we are ill. In full health, we can scarcely believe that they suffer much; so faint is the image of pain upon our imagination: when softened by sickness, we readily sympathise with the sufferings of others. …

After we had again talked of my setting out for Holland, he said, 'I must see thee out of England: I will accompany you to Harwich'. I could not find words to express what I felt upon this unexpected and very great mark of his affectionate regard. …

On Friday, August 5, we set out early in the morning in the Harwich stage coach. A fat elderly gentlewoman, and a young Dutchman, seemed the most inclined among us to conversation. At the inn where we dined, the gentlewoman said that she had done her best to educate her children; and particularly, that she had never suffered them to be a moment idle. JOHNSON. 'I wish, madam, you would educate me too; for I have been an idle fellow all my life'. 'I am sure, Sir', said she 'you have not been idle'. JOHNSON. 'Nay, Madam, it is very true; and that gentleman there (pointing to me), has been idle. He was idle at Edinburgh. His father sent him to Glasgow, where he continued to be idle. He then came to London, where he has been very idle; and now he is going to Utrecht, where he will be as idle as ever'. I asked him privately how he could expose me so. JOHNSON. 'Poh, poh!' said he, 'they knew nothing about you, and will think of it no more'. In the afternoon the gentlewoman talked violently against the Roman Catholics, and of the horrors of the Inquisition. To the utter astonishment of all the passengers but myself, who knew that he could talk upon any side of a question, he defended the Inquisition, and maintained, 'that false doctrine should be checked on its first appearance; that the civil power should unite with the church in punishing those who dared to attack the established religion, and that such only were punished by the Inquisition.' …

Having stopped a night at Colchester, Johnson talked of that town with veneration, for having stood a siege for Charles the First. The Dutchman alone now remained with us. He spoke English tolerably well; and thinking to recommend himself to us by expatiating on the superiority of the criminal jurisprudence of this country over that of Holland, he inveighed against the barbarity of putting an accused person to the torture, in order to force a confession. But Johnson was as ready for this, as for the Inquisition. 'Why, Sir, you do not, I find, understand the law of your own country. The torture in Holland is considered as a favour to an accused person; for no man is put to the torture there, unless there is as much evidence against him as would amount to a conviction in England. An accused person among you, therefore, has one chance more to escape punishment, than those who are tried among us'.

At supper this night he talked of good eating with uncommon satisfaction. 'Some people', said he, 'have a foolish way of not minding, or pretending not to mind, what they eat. For my part, I mind my belly very studiously, and very carefully; for I look upon it, that he who does not mind his belly will hardly mind anything else'. He now appeared to me *Jean Bull philosophe*,[31] and he was, for the moment, not only serious but vehement. Yet I have heard him, upon other occasions, talk with great contempt of people who were anxious to gratify their palates; and the 206th number of his Rambler is a masterly essay against gulosity. His practice, indeed, I must acknowledge, may be considered as casting the balance of his different opinions upon this subject; for I never knew any man who relished good eating more than he did. When at table, he was totally absorbed in the business of the moment; his looks seemed riveted to his plate; nor would he, unless when in very high company, say one word, or even pay the least attention to what was said by others, till he had satisfied his appetite, which was so fierce, and indulged with such intenseness, that while in the act of eating, the veins of his forehead swelled, and generally a strong perspiration was visible. To those whose sensations were delicate, this could not but be disgusting; and it was doubtless not very suitable to the character of a philosopher, who should be distinguished by self-command. But it must be owned, that Johnson, though he could be rigidly *abstemious*, was not a *temperate* man either in eating or drinking. He could refrain, but he could not use moderately. He told me, that he had fasted two days without inconvenience, and that he had never been hungry but once. They who beheld with wonder how much he eat[32] upon all occasions when his dinner was to his taste, could not easily conceive what he must have meant by hunger; and not only was he remarkable for the extraordinary quantity which he eat, but he was, or affected to be, a man of very nice discernment in the science of cookery. He used to descant critically on the dishes which had been at table where he had dined or supped, and to recollect very minutely what he had liked. I remember, when he was in Scotland, his praising '*Gordon's palates*', (a dish of palates[33] at the Honourable Alexander Gordon's) with a warmth of expression which might have done honour to more important subjects. ... He about the same time was so much displeased with the performances of a nobleman's French cook, that he exclaimed with vehemence, 'I'd throw such a rascal into the river'; and he then proceeded to alarm a lady at whose house he was to sup, by the following manifesto of his skill: 'I, Madam, who live at a variety of good tables, am a much better judge of cookery, than any person who has a very tolerable cook, but lives much at home; for his palate is gradually adapted to the taste of his cook; whereas, Madam, in trying by a wider range, I can more exquisitely judge'. When invited to dine, even with an intimate friend, he was not pleased if something better than a plain dinner was not prepared for him. I have heard him say on such an occasion, 'This was a good dinner enough, to be sure; but it was not a dinner to *ask* a man to'. On the other hand, he was wont to express, with great glee, his satisfaction when he had been entertained quite to his mind. One day when we had dined with his neighbour and landlord in Bolt-court, Mr. Allen,[34] the printer, whose old housekeeper had studied his taste in every thing, he pronounced this eulogy, 'Sir, we could not have had a better dinner had there been a *Synod of Cooks*'.

While we were left by ourselves, after the Dutchman had gone to bed, Dr. Johnson talked of that studied behaviour which many have recommended and practised. He disapproved of it; and said, 'I never considered whether I should be a grave man, or a merry man, but just let inclination, for the time, have its course'....

Notes

[31] *Jean Bull philosophe* John Bull was a caricature of an Englishman invented by John Arbuthnot; Boswell turns the phrase to suggest a caricature of a French *philosophe*, like Voltaire.

[32] *eat* an acceptable form of the past tense at this time.

[33] *palates* fricasseed ox palates made a fancy dish in the eighteenth century.

[34] *Mr. Allen* Edmund (d. 1780).

I teased him with fanciful apprehensions of unhappiness. A moth having fluttered round the candle, and burnt itself, he laid hold of this little incident to admonish me; saying, with a sly look, and in a solemn but quiet tone, 'That creature was its own tormentor, and I believe his name was BOSWELL'.

Next day we got to Harwich to dinner; and my passage in the packet-boat to Helvoetsluys being secured, and my baggage put on board, we dined at our inn by ourselves. I happened to say it would be terrible if he should not find a speedy opportunity of returning to London, and be confined to so dull a place. JOHNSON. 'Don't, Sir, accustom yourself to use big words for little matters. It would *not* be *terrible*, though I *were* to be detained some time here'. The practice of using words of disproportionate magnitude, is, no doubt, too frequent every where; but, I think, most remarkable among the French, of which, all who have travelled in France must have been struck with innumerable instances.

We went and looked at the church, and having gone into it and walked up to the altar, Johnson, whose piety was constant and fervent, sent me to my knees, saying, 'Now that you are going to leave your native country, recommend yourself to the protection of your Creator and Redeemer'.

After we came out of the church, we stood talking for some time together of Bishop Berkeley's[35] ingenious sophistry to prove the non-existence of matter, and that everything in the universe is merely ideal. I observed, that though we are satisfied his doctrine is not true, it is impossible to refute it. I never shall forget the alacrity with which Johnson answered, striking his foot with mighty force against a large stone, till he rebounded from it, 'I refute it *thus*'. …

My revered friend walked down with me to the beach, where we embraced and parted with tenderness, and engaged to correspond by letters. I said, 'I hope, Sir, you will not forget me in my absence'. JOHNSON. 'Nay, Sir, it is more likely you should forget me, than that I should forget you'. As the vessel put out to sea, I kept my eyes upon him for a considerable time, while he remained rolling his majestic frame in his usual manner; and at last I perceived him walk back into the town, and he disappeared.

Notes

[35] *Bishop Berkeley* George (1685–1753), author of several treatises showing that what we call material reality is merely subjective sense-impressions.

Hester Lynch Thrale Piozzi (1741–1821)

In 1763 Johnson met both Boswell and Hester Thrale for the first time. Although the meeting with Boswell has meant more to literary history, the meeting with Hester Thrale meant more to Johnson personally. She was his closest friend for most of the next twenty years; her house in greater London (Streatham) was often home to Johnson; he had his own room there, with a bed made to the full length of his unusually large frame (5ft. 11in.), and even a little gazebo in the garden for writing on pleasant days. Henry Thrale's father had made a small fortune in brewing, and his son was enjoying a life on the edges of the upper class. He served in Parliament, and he and his beautiful wife knew some of the most interesting people in London. Johnson was in some respects a prize acquisition, but they gave him as much as they received from his friendship. The precise nature of his friendship with Hester will probably never be known. It did involve flirtation of a kind, however, and certainly personal revelations. Johnson evidently told her, as he told her almost everything, something about his vigorous imagination, which occasionally ran to sexual fantasy. There is a long-standing debate in Johnsonian circles about a letter in French that Johnson wrote to Hester Thrale that seems to suggest that he submitted to some sort of sexual bondage in their relationship. (There is a rare echo of that famous letter in the first selection offered here.) This is probably just wishful thinking, and the relationship, in reality, was probably much more decorous. Johnson did depend on this much younger woman in many respects, however, and he submitted to her rules for domestic life in the most elaborately courteous and sometimes suggestive ways.

After the death of Henry Thrale, Johnson's relationship with Hester was diminished. Their friendship flourished in the context of her successful, if not perfect, marriage, and fell apart afterward. She married Piozzi, a music teacher and an Italian, both features unforgivable in the spouse of a woman with pretensions to high society. This was virtually the end of her friendship with Johnson, though there was something of a reconciliation at last. She lived nearly forty years as Mrs. Piozzi and was a productive writer much of the time. She had always enjoyed scribbling in the margins of her books, and, partly at Johnson's suggestion, she became an avid diarist. Some of the materials she collected in her "Thraliana" (as she called her notebooks) went to make up her *Anecdotes of the Late Samuel Johnson, LL.D.* My selection from the conclusion is based on the first edition (1786). From Thrale's many letters to Samuel Johnson, I select one that concerns his supposed bondage to her, and another that speaks about the tragic death of one of her children. She lost nine of her twelve offspring, several through a most painful disease of the brain. I reprint the letters from R. W. Chapman's edition of *The Letters of Samuel Johnson* (Clarendon Press, 1952). Thrale's correspondence has been edited by Edward and Lillian Bloom (University of Delaware Press, 1989–2002).

from *Anecdotes of the Late Samuel Johnson, LL.D. during the Last Twenty Years of his Life* (1786)

With regard to common occurrences, Mr. Johnson had, when I first knew him, looked on the still-shifting scenes of life till he was weary; for as a mind slow in its own nature, or unenlivened by information, will contentedly read in the same book for twenty

British Literature 1640–1789: An Anthology, Fourth Edition. Edited by Robert DeMaria, Jr.

times perhaps, the very act of reading it, being more than half the business, and every period[1] being at every reading better understood; while a mind more active or more skilful to comprehend its meaning is made sincerely sick at the second perusal; so a soul like his, acute to discern the truth, vigorous to embrace, and powerful to retain it, soon sees enough of the world's dull prospect, which at first, like that of the sea, pleases by its extent, but soon, like that too, fatigues from its uniformity; a calm and a storm being the only variations that the nature of either will admit.

Of Mr. Johnson's erudition the world has been the judge, and we who produce each a score of his sayings, as proofs of that wit which in him was inexhaustible, resemble travellers who having visited Delhi or Golconda, bring home each a handful of Oriental pearl to evince the riches of the Great Mogul.[2] May the Public condescend to accept my *ill-strung* selection with patience at least, remembering only that they are relics of him who was great on all occasions, and, like a cube in architecture, you beheld him on each side, and his size still appeared undiminished.

As his purse was ever open to almsgiving, so was his heart tender to those who wanted relief, and his soul susceptible of gratitude, and of every kind impression: yet though he had refined his sensibility, he had not endangered his quiet, by encouraging in himself a solicitude about trifles, which he treated with the contempt they deserve.

It was well enough known before these sheets were published, that Mr. Johnson had a roughness in his manner which subdued the saucy, and terrified the meek: this was, when I knew him, the prominent part of a character which few durst venture to approach so nearly; and which was for that reason in many respects grossly and frequently mistaken, and it was perhaps peculiar to him, that the lofty consciousness of his own superiority, which animated his looks, and raised his voice in conversation, cast likewise an impenetrable veil over him when he said nothing. His talk therefore had commonly the complexion of arrogance, his silence of superciliousness. He was however seldom inclined to be silent when any moral or literary question was started: and it was on such occasions, that, like the sage in *Rasselas*,[3] he spoke and attention watched his lips; he reasoned, and conviction closed his periods: if poetry was talked of, his quotations were the readiest; and had he not been eminent for more solid and brilliant qualities, mankind would have united to extol his extraordinary memory. His manner of repeating deserves to be described, though at the same time it defeats all power of description; but whoever once heard him repeat an ode of Horace, would be long before they could endure to hear it repeated by another.

His equity in giving the character of living acquaintance ought not undoubtedly to be omitted in his own, whence partiality and prejudice were totally excluded, and truth alone presided in his tongue: a steadiness of conduct the more to be commended, as no man had stronger liking or aversions. His veracity was indeed, from the most trivial to the most solemn occasions, strict, even to severity; he scorned to embellish a story with fictitious circumstances, which (he used to say) took off from its real value. 'A story', says Johnson, 'should be a specimen of life and manners, but if the surrounding circumstances are false, as it is no more a representation of reality, it is no longer worthy our attention'.

Notes

FROM *ANECDOTES OF THE LATE SAMUEL JOHNSON*

1 *period* sentence.

2 *the Great Mogul* meaning Akbhar the Great, seventeenth-century ruler of the Mogul empire; at *Golconda*, a place in southern India where the country's largest diamond (787 carats) was found.

3 *the sage in Rasselas* see Johnson, *Rasselas*, chapter 18, p. 867 above.

For the rest – That beneficence which during his life increased the comforts of so many, may after his death be perhaps ungratefully forgotten; but that piety which dictated the serious papers in the *Rambler*, will be for ever remembered; for ever, I think, revered. That ample repository of religious truth, moral wisdom, and accurate criticism, breathes indeed the genuine emanations of its great Author's mind, expressed too in a style so natural to him, and so much like his common mode of conversing, that I was myself but little astonished when he told me, that he had scarcely read over one of those inimitable essays before they went to the press.

I will add one or two peculiarities more, before I lay down my pen.——Though at an immeasurable distance from content in the contemplation of his own uncouth form and figure, he did not like another man much the less for being a coxcomb. I mentioned two friends who were particularly fond of looking at themselves in a glass – 'They do not surprise me at all by so doing' said Johnson, 'they see, reflected in that glass, men who have risen from almost the lowest situations in life; one to enormous riches, the other to every thing this world can give – rank, fame, and fortune. They see likewise, men who have merited their advancement by the exertion and improvement of those talents which God had given them; and I see not why they should avoid the mirror'.

The other singularity I promised to record, is this: That though a man of obscure birth himself, his partiality to people of family was visible on every occasion; his zeal for subordination warm even to bigotry; his hatred to innovation, and reverence for the old feudal times, apparent, whenever any possible manner of showing them occurred. I have spoken of his piety, his charity, and his truth, the enlargement of his heart, and the delicacy of his sentiments; and when I search for shadow to my portrait, none can I find but what was formed by pride, differently modified as different occasions showed it; yet never was pride so purified as Johnson's, at once from meanness and from vanity. The mind of this man was indeed expanded beyond the common limits of human nature, and stored with such variety of knowledge, that I used to think it resembled a royal pleasure-ground, where every plant, of every name and nation, flourished in the full perfection of their powers, and where, though lofty woods and falling cataracts first caught the eye, and fixed the earliest attention of beholders, yet neither the trim parterre nor the pleasing shrubbery, nor even the antiquated evergreens, were denied a place in some fit corner of the happy valley.

from *Correspondence with Samuel Johnson* (1773–5)

Saturday 29 May '73
from Johnson

Madam

My eye is yet so dark that I could not read your note. I have had a poor darkling week. But the dear Lady[1] is worse. My eye is easier and bears light better, but sees little. I wish you could fetch me on Wednesday. I long to be in my own room. Have you got your key? I hope I shall not add much to your trouble, and will wish at least to give you some little solace or amusement. I long to be under your care.

I am, Madam, your most &c.
Sam: Johnson

Streatham.[2]

Notes

FROM *CORRESPONDENCE WITH SAMUEL JOHNSON*

1 *dear Lady* Hester Thrale's mother.

2 *Streatham* where the Thrales lived, in suburban London.

What care can I promise my dear Mr. Johnson that I have not already taken? what Tenderness that he has not already experienced? yet is it a very gloomy reflection that so much of bad prevails in our best enjoyments, and embitters the purest friendship. You were saying but on Sunday that of all the unhappy you was the happiest, in consequence of my Attention to your Complaint; and to day I have been reproached by you for neglect, and by myself for exciting that generous Confidence which prompts you to repose all Care on me, and tempts you to neglect yourself, and brood in secret upon an Idea hateful in itself, but which your kind partiality to me has unhappily rendered pleasing. If it be possible, shake off these uneasy Weights, heavier to the Mind by far than Fetters to the body. Let not your fancy dwell thus upon Confinement and Severity. I am sorry you are obliged to be so much alone; I foresaw some ill Consequences of your being here while my Mother was dying thus; yet could not resist the temptation of having you near me, but if you find this irksome and dangerous Idea fasten upon your fancy, leave me to struggle with the loss of one Friend, and let me not put to hazard what I esteem beyond Kingdoms, and value beyond the possession of them.

If we go on together your Confinement shall be as strict as possible except when Company comes in, which I shall more willingly endure on your Account.

Dissipation is to you a glorious Medicine, and I believe Mr. Boswell[3] will be at last your best Physician, for the rest you really are well enough now if you will keep so; and not suffer the noblest of human Minds to be tortured with fantastic notions which rob it of all its Quiet. I will detain you no longer, so farewell and be good; and do not quarrel with your Governess for not using the Rod enough. – H:L:T.

8 July 1775

My Dear Sir

This poor unfortunate Child[4] will die at last. The Matter which discharged from his Ear was it seems a temporary Relief, but that was all over when I came down & the Stupor was returned in a most alarming Manner: he has however violent fits of rage – proceeding from Pain I guess – just as Lucy & Miss Anna[5] had – Kipping[6] says the Brain is oppressed of which I have no doubt. What shall I do? What can I do? has the flattery of my Friends made me too proud of my own Brains? & must these poor Children suffer for my Crime? I can neither go on with this Subject nor quit it. – I have heard no more of Mr. Thrale's Intentions about my Estate &c. & you know I am not inquisitive. He spends whole Hours with Scrase[7] engaged in some Business – he does not tell me what. I opened the Ball last Night – tonight I go to the Play: Oh that there was a Play or a Ball for every hour of the four & twenty.

Adieu! my head & my heart are so full I forgot to say how glad I shall be to see you. as I am with the truest Regard

Sir Your most faithful Servant H: L: Thrale

Streatham Saturday 9 July [1775]

Notes

3 *Boswell* Johnson and Boswell were about to take their celebrated trip to Scotland.

4 *Child* Ralph, the Thrales' two-year-old.

5 *Lucy & Miss Anna* Lucy died earlier in the year, at the age of four; Anna died at the age of two in 1770.

6 *Kipping* Henry (1726–85), a surgeon and apothecary in Brighton, near the Thrales' estate in Brighthelmstone.

7 *Scrase* Charles (1707–92), family lawyer; he was working out the details so that Hester would have the clear, personal disposal of her family's Welsh estate.

Dear Sir

I came home very late last Night and found your sweet Letters all three lying on the Table: I would not have come home at all but Mr. Thrale insisted on it – so I have left this poor Child to die at Brighthelmstone. Doctor Pepys says he will write every Post & Kipping too. What signifies their writing? What signifies anything? the Child will die & I fear in sad Torments too – he is now exactly as Lucy was. The discharge at the Ear stopping on a sudden, they bathed him exactly as you would have bid them yourself – by Bromfield's advice indeed but all to no purpose: they are now blistering away about the Ear, Head & Neck, & if he should give them time to do all they intend he will have a Fontanelle cut in his Arm.[8]

Now it is not the Death of this Boy that affects me so; he is very young, & had he lived would probably have been a greater Misfortune to me: but it is the horrible Apprehension of losing the others by the same cruel Disease that haunts my affrighted Imagination & makes me look upon them with an Anxiety scarce to be endured. If Hetty tells me that her Head aches, I am more shocked than if I heard She had broken her Leg.

Poor old Captain Conway is dead. Carter[9] is dolorous still: the Horse is in Weston's Possession at present, nobody would bid above five pounds for him, so Mr. Weston was forced to take him back: as he is now at the Expense of keeping him I will not buy him to ease Weston's Pocket & empty my own, but whenever he is going to be parted with I shall step in & save him for Carter. …

When we came home last Night here to Streatham, the first Man I saw was Perkins;[10] my Spirits were already low, & I feared there was some sad News from London; but it was only a Story about that Crossby who broke[11] in our Debt last Winter, & who has some concerns at Derby – you may remember Avis saying he was struck dumb or stupid or something about it. I warrant you recollect his Expression which I have forgotten. Pray tell me if your Relation Mr. Flint has all his Children alive? there was a sweet little Girl among them very like my poor Lucy – & afflicted with Headaches: do enquire whether She be living or no: I took an Interest in her from the Resemblance, & was not without many Apprehensions for her Life. I have forgotten her name if it was not Lucy – I think it was.

I am ever Sir Your most faithful Servant H L T

Notes

[8] *Fontanelle* a surgically imposed discharge of fluid from the body; Ralph and several other of the Thrales' children seem to have had some kind of congenital hydrocephalus.

[9] *Carter* Charles, Hester Thrale's riding master.

[10] *Perkins* John, chief clerk of the Thrale brewery.

[11] *broke* went bankrupt.

Anna Laetitia Aiken Barbauld (1743–1825)

Barbauld learned to read so quickly and mastered French so easily that her father reluctantly agreed to let her go on to Latin and Greek. In the company of her father's pupils and colleagues at a college for dissenters at Warrington, Barbauld grew learned and began writing poetry. She published her first volume in 1773. The next year she married and helped her husband establish a boys' school for dissenters. After her husband's death in 1808, she became much more active as a writer and as an editor. One of her projects was an edition of *The British Novelists* in fifty volumes. Another was an anthology of passages of English literature for women called *The Female Speaker*. She also edited the letters of Richardson, prepared several books for children's reading, and wrote more poems, including an epistle to the great abolitionist William Wilberforce. "The Mouse's Petition" and "Verses Written in an Alcove" are based on the versions published in *Poems* (1792). "Washing-Day" comes from the *Monthly Magazine*, December 1797. There is a recent edition of Barbauld's poems, edited by William McCarthy and Elizabeth Kraft (University of Georgia Press, 1994). McCarthy has written an important study, *Anna Laetitia Barbauld: Voice of the Enlightenment* (Johns Hopkins University Press, 2008).

from *Poems* (1792)

The Mouse's Petition[1]

Parcere subjectis, & debellare superbos.
VIRGIL[2]

Oh! hear a pensive prisoner's prayer,
For liberty that sighs;
And never let thine heart be shut
Against the wretch's cries.

For here forlorn and sad I sit,
Within the wiry grate;[3]
And tremble at th' approaching morn,
Which brings impending fate.

Notes

THE MOUSE'S PETITION

1 *The Mouse's Petition* Found in the trap where he had been confined all night by Dr. [Joseph] Priestley, for the sake of making experiments with different kinds of air [Barbauld's note].

2 *Parcere ... Virgil* "to spare the downtrodden and do battle with the proud" (*Aeneid* 8.653).

3 *grate* barred walls of a prison.

British Literature 1640–1789: An Anthology, Fourth Edition. Edited by Robert DeMaria, Jr.

If e'er thy breast with freedom glowed,
And spurned a tyrant's chain,
Let not thy strong oppressive force
A free-born mouse detain.

Oh! do not stain with guiltless blood
Thy hospitable hearth;
Nor triumph that thy wiles betrayed
A prize so little worth.

The scattered gleanings of a feast
My frugal meals supply;
But if thine unrelenting heart
That slender boon deny,

The cheerful light, the vital air,
Are blessings widely given;
Let nature's commoners enjoy
The common gifts of heaven.

The well-taught philosophic mind
To all compassion gives;
Casts round the world an equal eye,
And feels for all that lives.

If mind, as ancient sages taught,
A never dying flame,
Still shifts through matter's varying forms,
In every form the same,

Beware, lest in the worm you crush
A brother's soul you find;
And tremble lest thy luckless hand
Dislodge a kindred mind.

Or, if this transient gleam of day
Be *all* of life we share,
Let pity plead within thy breast
That little *all* to spare.

So may thy hospitable board
With health and peace be crowned;
And every charm of heartfelt ease
Beneath thy roof be found.

So, when destruction lurks unseen,
Which men, like mice, may share,
May some kind angel clear thy path,
And break the hidden snare.

Verses Written in an Alcove

Jam Cytherea choros ducit Venus imminente Luna.
HORAT.[1]

Now the moon-beam's trembling lustre
Silvers o'er the dewy green,
And in lost and shadowy colours
Sweetly paints the chequered scene.

Here between the opening branches
Streams a flood of softened light,
There the thick and twisted foliage
Spreads the browner gloom of night.

This is sure the haunt of fairies,
In yon cool alcove they play;
Care can never cross the threshold,
Care was only made for day.

Far from hence be noisy clamour,
Sick disgust and anxious fear;
Pining grief and wasting anguish
Never keep their vigils here.

Tell no tales of sheeted spectres
Rising from the quiet tomb;
Fairer forms this cell shall visit,
Brighter visions gild the gloom.

Choral songs and sprightly voices
Echo from her cell shall call;
Sweeter, sweeter than the murmur
Of the distant water-fall.

Every ruder gust of passion
Lulled with music dies away,
Till within the charmèd bosom
None but soft affections play:

Soft, as when the evening breezes
Gently stir the poplar grove;
Brighter than the smile of summer,
Sweeter than the breath of love.

Notes

VERSES WRITTEN IN AN ALCOVE

[1] *Jam Cytherea … Horat.* "Already Cytherean Venus leads her chorus beneath the neighbouring Moon" (Horace, *Odes* 1.4.5).

Thee, th' enchanted Muse shall follow,
LISSY! to the rustic cell,
And each careless note repeating
Tune them to her charming shell.[2]

Not the Muse who wreathed with laurel[3]
Solemn stalks with tragic gait,
And in clear and lofty vision
Sees the future births of fate;

Not the maid who crowned with cypress[4]
Sweeps along in sceptred pall,
And in sad and solemn accents
Mourns the crested hero's fall;

But that other smiling sister,[5]
With the blue and laughing eye,
Singing, in a lighter measure,
Strains of woodland harmony:

All unknown to fame and glory,
Easy, blithe and debonair,
Crowned with flowers, her careless tresses
Loosely floating on the air.

Then, when next the star of evening
Softly sheds the silent dew,
Let me in this rustic temple,
LISSY! meet the Muse and you.

from the *Monthly Magazine* (1797)

Washing-Day

——— and their voice,
Turning again towards childish treble, pipes
And whistles in its sound. –[1]

The Muses are turned gossips; they have lost
Their buskined step, and clear high-sounding phrase,[2]
Language of gods. Come, then, domestic Muse,
In slip-shod measure loosely prattling on
Of farm and orchard, pleasant curds and cream,

Notes

[2] *shell* a poetic name for the lyre, an instrument originally strung on tortoise shells.

[3] *Muse ... laurel* perhaps Calliope, muse of epic poetry, or one of the three graces.

[4] *maid ... cypress* perhaps Melpomene, the muse of tragedy.

[5] *smiling sister* perhaps Erato, muse of lyric and love poetry.

WASHING-DAY

[1] *and their voice ... sound* Shakespeare, *As You Like It*, II. vi.161–3, with some changes.

[2] *buskined* shod in the elevated sandals worn in performances of classical Greek tragedy to indicate the great stature of the characters.

Or drowning flies, or shoe lost in the mire
By little whimpering boy, with rueful face;
Come, Muse, and sing the dreaded *Washing-Day*.
– Ye who beneath the yoke of wedlock bend,
With bowèd soul, full well ye ken the day
Which week, smooth sliding after week, brings on
Too soon; for to that day nor peace belongs
Nor comfort; ere the first grey streak of dawn,[3]
The red-armed washers come and chase repose.
Nor pleasant smile, nor quaint device of mirth,
E'er visited that day; the very cat,
From the wet kitchen scared, and reeking hearth,[4]
Visits the parlour, an unwonted guest.
The silent breakfast-meal is soon dispatched
Uninterrupted, save by anxious looks
Cast at the lowering sky, if sky should lower,
From that last evil, oh preserve us, heavens!
For should the skies pour down, adieu to all
Remains of quiet; then expect to hear
Of sad disasters – dirt and gravel stains
Hard to efface, and loaded lines at once
Snapped short – and linen-horse by dog thrown down,
And all the petty miseries of life.
Saints have been calm while stretched upon the rack,
And Montezuma smil'd on burning coals;[5]
But never yet did housewife notable
Greet with a smile a rainy washing-day.
– But grant the welkin fair, require not thou
Who call'st thyself perchance the master there,
Or study swept, or nicely dusted coat,[6]
Or usual 'tendance; ask not, indiscreet,
Thy stockings mended, though the yawning rents
Gape wide as Erebus, nor hope to find[7]
Some snug recess impervious; should'st thou try
The customed garden walks, thine eye shall rue
The budding fragrance of thy tender shrubs,
Myrtle or rose, all crushed beneath the weight
Of coarse checked apron, with impatient hand
Twitched off when showers impend: or crossing lines
Shall mar thy musings, as the wet cold sheet
Flaps in thy face abrupt. Woe to the friend
Whose evil stars have urged him forth to claim
On such a day the hospitable rites;
Looks, blank at best, and stinted courtesy,

Notes

[3] *nor … nor* neither … nor.
[4] *reeking* smoking.
[5] *Montezuma* in later editions, corrected to Guatimozin, a name for Cuauhtémoc, who became the last emperor of the Aztecs in 1520 on the death of Montezuma II's successor; he stoically resisted the tortures imposed on him by Cortés, the conqueror of his people.
[6] *Or … or* either … or.
[7] *Erebus* a place of darkness forming a passage from earth to Hades in classical mythology.

Shall he receive; vainly he feeds his hopes
With dinner of roast chicken, savoury pie,
Or tart or pudding: – pudding he nor tart
That day shall eat; nor, though the husband try,
Mending what can't be helped, to kindle mirth
From cheer deficient, shall his consort's brow
Clear up propitious; the unlucky guest
In silence dines, and early slinks away.
   I well remember, when a child, the awe
This day struck into me; for then the maids,
I scarce knew why, looked cross, and drove me from them;
Nor soft caress could I obtain, nor hope
Usual indulgencies; jelly or creams,
Relic of costly suppers, and set by
For me their petted one; or buttered toast,
When butter was forbid; or thrilling tale
Of ghost, or witch, or murder – so I went
And sheltered me beside the parlour fire,
There my dear grandmother, eldest of forms,
Tended the little ones, and watched from harm,
Anxiously fond, though oft her spectacles
With elfin cunning hid, and oft the pins
Drawn from her ravelled stockings, might have soured
One less indulgent –
At intervals my mother's voice was heard,
Urging dispatch; briskly the work went on,
All hands employed to wash, to rinse, to wring,
To fold, and starch, and clap, and iron, and plait.
Then would I sit me down, and ponder much
Why washings were. Sometimes through hollow bowl
Of pipe amused we blew, and sent aloft
The floating bubbles, little dreaming then
To see, Mongolfier, thy silken ball[8]
Ride buoyant through the clouds – so near approach
The sports of children and the toils of men.
Earth, air, and sky, and ocean, hath its bubbles,[9]
And verse is one of them – this most of all.

Notes

[8] *Mon[t]golfier* Joseph-Michel (1740–1810) and his brother Jacques-Étienne (1745–99), inventors of manned balloon flight.

[9] *bubbles* echoes Shakespeare's *Macbeth* I.iii.79, where Banquo describes the weird sisters as bubbles from the earth, but also means anything worthless or insubstantial.

Olaudah Equiano (1745?–1797)

Sold into slavery and taken from his native Nigerian home at the age of twelve, Equiano became one of the most widely travelled men of his time. After very brief stays in Virginia and the West Indies, he was sold to the owner of a trading ship who named him Gustavus Vassa. The name, which belonged to the sixteenth-century liberator of the Swedes, may have been meant as an ironical comment on Equiano's color, but it came to be somewhat prophetic because Equiano became one of the most powerful eighteenth-century spokesmen for the abolition of slavery. He first went to England in 1757 and was baptized there in 1759. Throughout the Seven Years War (1756–63) he served in the navy and saw action in the Mediterranean and North America. In 1763 he went to the West Indies in the possession of a Quaker plantation owner. Partly through this man's protection, he was able to save the money required to buy his freedom (£40), and he became a free man in 1766. He then signed on for voyages to Turkey and the West Indies, and one to the Arctic.

In 1779 Equiano settled in London, where he spent most of the rest of his life. He held various posts including commissary of provisions for those going to the new free colony in Sierra Leone, established for blacks discharged from the army after the Revolutionary War and former slaves who had sought asylum in England. Equiano published his autobiography in 1789, and it was successful enough to run to eight editions in his lifetime (seven in England and one in America). The book indicts slavery for its cruelty, its inhumanity, its sinfulness, and also its impracticality. Equiano is not only interested in what is fair but also in what will work for the economy of his adopted country and his people. He also anchors his arguments in an intellectual and literary tradition that includes classical aphorisms, the Bible, Hobbes, and Milton. Equiano is very far from rejecting Western tradition in his arguments against slavery; in fact, he warmly embraces many liberal elements of that tradition. He styled himself an African in presenting a petition to the Queen "on behalf of his brethren," but England (where he finally married in 1792) was his home.

The text presented here is based on the first American edition (W. Durell, 1791) with some minor corrections from other editions. The whole work is available in a Penguin Books volume, edited by Vincent Carretta, who is also the author of a recent biography (University of Georgia Press, 2005).

from *The Interesting Narrative of the Life of Olaudah Equiano, or Gustavus Vassa, the African* (1789)

Chapter 5

The author's reflections on his situation – Is deceived by a promise of being delivered – His despair at sailing for the West-Indies – Arrives at Montserrat, where he is sold to Mr. King – Various interesting instances of oppression, cruelty, and extortion, which the author saw practised upon the slaves in the West-Indies during his captivity, from the year 1763 to 1766 – Address on it to the Planters.

British Literature 1640–1789: An Anthology, Fourth Edition. Edited by Robert DeMaria, Jr.

Thus, at the moment I expected all my toils to end, was I plunged, as I supposed, in a new slavery;[1] in comparison of which all my service hitherto had been perfect freedom; and whose horrors, always present to my mind, now rushed on it with tenfold aggravation. I wept very bitterly for some time; and began to think that I must have done something to displease the Lord, that he thus punished me so severely. This filled me with painful reflections on my past conduct. I recollected that, on the morning of our arrival at Deptford, I had very rashly sworn that as soon as we reached London, I would spend the day in rambling and sport. My conscience smote me for this unguarded expression: I felt that the Lord was able to disappoint me in all things, and immediately considered my present situation as a judgement of Heaven, on account of my presumption in swearing. I therefore, with contrition of heart, acknowledged my transgression to God, and poured out my soul before Him with unfeigned repentance, and with earnest supplications I besought Him not to abandon me in my distress, nor cast me from his mercy for ever. In a little time my grief, spent with its own violence, began to subside; and after the first confusion of my thoughts was over, I reflected with more calmness on my present condition. I considered that trials and disappointments are sometimes for our good; and I thought God might perhaps have permitted this, in order to teach me wisdom and resignation. For he had hitherto shadowed me with the wings of his mercy and by his invisible, but powerful hand, had brought me the way I knew not. These reflections gave me a little comfort, and I arose at last from the deck with dejection and sorrow in my countenance, yet mixed with some faint hope that the *Lord would appear* for my deliverance.

Soon afterwards, as my new master was going on shore, he called me to him, and told me to behave myself well, and do the business of the ship the same as any of the rest of the boys, and that I should fare the better for it; but I made him no answer. I was then asked if I could swim, and I said, 'No'. However, I was made to go under the deck, and was carefully watched. The next tide the ship got under way, and soon arrived at the Mother Bank, Portsmouth; where she waited a few days for some of the West-India convoy. While here I tried every means I could devise amongst the people of the ship to get me a boat from the shore, as there was none suffered to come alongside of the ship; and their own, whenever it was used, was hoisted in again immediately. A sailor on board took a guinea from me, on pretence of getting me a boat; and promised me, time after time, that it was hourly to come off. When he had the watch upon deck I watched also, and looked long enough, but all in vain; I could never see either the boat or my guinea again. And, what I thought was still the worst of all, the fellow gave information, as I afterwards found, all the while to the mates of my intention to go off if possible; but, rogue-like, he never told them he had got a guinea from me to procure my escape. However, after we had sailed, and his trick was made known to the ship's crew, I had some satisfaction in seeing him detested and despised by them all for his behaviour to me.

I was still in hopes that my old shipmates would not forget their promise to come for me to Portsmouth; and, indeed, at last, but not till the day before we sailed, some of them did come there, and sent me off some oranges, and other tokens of their regard. They also sent me word they would come off to me themselves the next day,

Notes

FROM *THE INTERESTING NARRATIVE*

[1] *at the moment ... a new slavery* after returning to England from fighting, as a slave, in the Mediterranean theater of the Seven Years War, Equiano had hoped to disembark and escape in London with the help of his shipmates, but he was sold again and taken off to Portsmouth by a new master.

or the day after: and a lady also who lived in Gosport, wrote to me that she would come and take me out of the ship at the same time. This lady had been once very intimate with my former master. I used to sell and take care of a great deal of property for her, in different ships; and in return she always showed great friendship for me, and used to tell my master she would take me away to live with her. But, unfortunately for me, a disagreement soon afterwards took place between them; and she was succeeded in my master's good graces by another lady, who appeared sole mistress of the Ætna, and mostly lodged on board. I was not so great a favourite with this lady as with the former; she had conceived a pique against me, on some occasion when she was on board, and she did not fail to instigate my master to treat me in the manner he did.[2]

However, the next morning, the 30th of December, the wind being brisk and easterly, the Æolus frigate, which was to escort the convoy, made a signal for sailing. All the ships then got up their anchors; and before any of my friends had an opportunity to come off to my relief, to my inexpressible anguish, our ship had got under way. What tumultuous emotions agitated my soul when the convoy got under sail, and I a prisoner on board, now without hope! I kept my swimming eyes upon the land in a state of unutterable grief; not knowing what to do, and despairing how to help myself. While my mind was in this situation, the fleet sailed on, and in one day's time I lost sight of the wished-for land. In the first expressions of my grief, I reproached my fate, and wished I had never been born. I was ready to curse the tide that bore us; the gale[3] that wafted my prison, and even the ship that conducted us; and, in the despair of the moment, I called on death to relieve me from the horrors I felt and dreaded, that I might be in that place –

> Where slaves are free, and men oppress no more.
> Fool that I was, inured so long to pain,
> To trust to hope, or dream of joy again!
>
> * * * * * * *
>
> Now dragged once more beyond the western main
> To groan beneath some dastard planter's chain;
> Where my poor countrymen in bondage wait
> The long enfranchisement of ling'ring fate:
> Hard ling'ring fate! while, ere the dawn of day,
> Roused by the lash they go their cheerless way;
> And as their souls with shame and anguish burn,
> Salute with groans unwelcome morn's return,
> And, chiding every hour the slow-paced sun,
> Pursue their toils till all his race is run.
> No eye to mark their suff'rings with a tear;
> No friend to comfort, and no hope to cheer:
> Then, like the dull unpitied brutes, repair

Notes

2 *she did not fail to instigate my master to treat me in the manner he did* Thus was I sacrificed to the envy and resentment of this woman, for knowing that the other lady designed to take me into her service; which, had I once got on shore, she would not have been able to prevent. She felt her pride alarmed at the superiority of her rival in being attended by a black servant: it was not less to prevent this, than to be revenged on me, that she caused the captain to treat me thus cruelly [Equiano's note].

3 *gale* "A wind not tempestuous, but stronger than a breeze" (Johnson).

To stalls as wretched, and as coarse a fare;
Thank heaven one day of mis'ry was o'er,
Then sink to sleep, and wish to wake no more.[4]

The turbulence of my emotions, however, naturally gave way to calmer thoughts, and I soon perceived what fate had decreed no mortal on earth could prevent. The convoy sailed on without any accident, with a pleasant gale and smooth sea, for six weeks, till February, when one morning the Æolus ran down a brig, one of the convoy, and she instantly went down and was engulfed in the dark recesses of the ocean. The convoy was immediately thrown into great confusion till it was day-light; and the Æolus illuminated with lights to prevent further mischief. On the 13th of February 1763, from the mast-head, we descried our destined island, Montserrat,[5] and soon after I beheld those

Regions of sorrow, doleful shades, where peace
And rest can rarely dwell. Hope never comes
That comes to all; but torture without end
Still urges ...[6]

At the sight of this land of bondage, a fresh horror ran through all my frame, and chilled me to the heart. My former slavery now rose in dreadful review to my mind, and displayed nothing but misery, stripes, and chains; and in the first paroxysm of my grief, I called upon God's thunder, and his avenging power, to direct the stroke of death to me, rather than permit me to become a slave, and to be sold from lord to lord.

In this state of my mind our ship came to an anchor, and soon after discharged her cargo. I now knew what it was to work hard; I was made to help to unload and load the ship. And to comfort me in my distress, at that time two of the sailors robbed me of all my money, and ran away from the ship. I had been so long used to an European climate, that at first I felt the scorching West-India sun very painful, while the dashing surf would toss the boat and the people in it, frequently above high-water mark. Sometimes our limbs were broken with this, or even attended with instant death, and I was day by day mangled and torn.

About the middle of May, when the ship was got ready to sail for England, I all the time believing that fate's blackest clouds were gathering over my head, and expecting that their bursting would mix me with the dead, Captain Doran sent for me on shore one morning; and I was told by the messenger that my fate was determined. With trembling steps and a fluttering heart I came to the captain, and found with him one Mr. Robert King, a quaker, and the first merchant in the place. The captain then told me my former master had sent me there to be sold; but that he desired him to get me the best master he could, as he told him I was a very deserving boy, which Captain Doran said he found to be true, and if he were to stay in the West-Indies he would be glad to keep me himself; but he could not

Notes

4 *Where slaves are free ... wake no more* "The Dying Negro," a poem originally published in 1773. Published anonymously but written by Thomas Day and John Bicknall. Perhaps it may not be deemed impertinent here to add, that this elegant and pathetic little poem, was occasioned by the following incident, as appears from the advertisement prefixed to it: – "A black who, a few days before, had run away from his master, and got himself christened, with intent to marry a white woman, his fellow-servant, being taken and sent on board a ship in the Thames, took an opportunity of shooting himself through the head." [Equiano's note].

5 *Montserrat* in the West Indies, near Antigua.

6 *Regions of sorrow ... urges Paradise Lost* 1.65–8 imperfectly recalled.

venture to take me to London, for he was very sure that when I came there, I would leave him. I at that instant burst out a crying, and begged much of him to take me with him to England, but all to no purpose. He told me he had got me the very best master in the whole island, with whom I should be as happy as if I were in England, and for that reason he chose to let him have me, though he could sell me to his own brother-in-law for a great deal more money than what he got from that gentleman. My new master, Mr. King, then made a reply, and said that the reason he had bought me was on account of my good character; and, as I understood something of the rules of arithmetic, when we got there he would put me to school, and fit me for a clerk. This conversation relieved my mind a little, and I left those gentlemen considerably more at ease in myself than when I came to them; and I was very thankful to Captain Doran, and even to my old master, for the character[7] they had given me; a character which I afterwards found of infinite service to me.

I went on board again, and took leave of all my shipmates, and the next day the ship sailed. When she weighed anchor I went to the waterside, and looked at her with a very wishful and aching heart, following her with my eyes until she was totally out of sight. I was so bowed down with grief, that I could not hold up my head for many months; and if my new master had not been kind to me, I believe I should have died under it at last. And indeed I soon found that he fully deserved the good character which Capt. Doran had given me of him; for he possessed a most amiable disposition and temper, and was very charitable and humane. If any of his slaves behaved amiss, he did not beat them or use them ill, but parted with them. This made them afraid of disobliging him; and as he treated his slaves better than any other man on the island, so he was better and more faithfully served by them in return. By this kind treatment I did at last endeavour to compose myself; and with fortitude, though moneyless, determined to face whatever fate had decreed for me. Mr. King soon asked me what I could do; and at the same time said he did not mean to treat me as a common slave. I told him I knew something of seamanship, and could shave and dress hair pretty well; I could refine wines, which I had learned on shipboard, where I had often done it; and that I could write, and understood arithmetic tolerably well as far as the Rule of Three.[8] He then asked me if I knew any thing of gauging;[9] and, on my answering that I did not, he said one of his clerks should teach me to gauge.

Mr. King dealt in all manner of merchandize, and kept from one to six clerks. He loaded many vessels in a year, particularly to Philadelphia, where he was born, and was connected with a great mercantile house in that city. He had besides many vessels and doggers,[10] of different sizes, which used to go about the island; and others to collect rum, sugar, and other goods. I understood pulling[11] and managing those boats very well; and this hard work, which was the first that he set me to, in the sugar seasons used to be my constant employment. I have rowed the boat and slaved at the oars, from one hour to sixteen in the twenty-four; during which I had fifteen pence sterling per day to live on, though sometimes only ten pence. However, this was much more

Notes

[7] *character* "A representation of any man as to his personal qualities" (Johnson).

[8] *Rule of Three* a method of finding a fourth number when three numbers are known, and the first two are in a proportion equal to that between the third known and the unknown number.

[9] *gauging* measuring the contents of barrels and other containers.

[10] *dogger* "A small ship with one mast" (Johnson).

[11] *pulling* rowing.

than was allowed to other slaves that used to work often with me, and belonged to other gentlemen on the island: these poor souls had never more than ninepence a day, and seldom more than sixpence, from their masters or owners, though they earned them three or four pisterines.[12] For it is a common practice in the West-Indies for men to purchase slaves, though they have not plantations themselves, in order to let them out to planters and merchants, at so much a piece by the day, and they give what they choose, out of this produce of their daily work, to their slaves for subsistence. This allowance is often very scanty.

My master often gave the owners of these slaves two and a half of these pieces per day, and found the poor fellows in victuals[13] himself, because he thought their owners did not feed them well enough, according to the work they did. The slaves used to like this very well; and, as they knew my master to be a man of feeling,[14] they were always glad to work for him in preference to any other gentleman; some of whom, after they had been paid for these poor people's labours, would not give them their allowance out of it. Many times have I seen these unfortunate wretches beaten for asking for their pay; and often severely flogged by their owners, if they did not bring them their daily or weekly money exactly to the time; though the poor creatures were obliged to wait on the gentlemen they had worked for, sometimes more than half the day before they could get their pay, and this generally on Sundays, when they wanted the time for themselves. In particular, I knew a countryman of mine, who once did not bring the weekly money directly that it was earned; and though he brought it the same day to his master, yet he was staked to the ground for his pretended negligence, and was just going to receive a hundred lashes, but for a gentleman who begged him off[15] fifty.

This poor man was very industrious, and by his frugality had saved so much money, by working on shipboard, that he had got a white man to buy him a boat, unknown to his master. Some time after he had this little estate, the governor wanted a boat to bring his sugar from different parts of the island; and, knowing this to be a negro-man's boat, he seized upon it for himself, and would not pay the owner a farthing. The man on this went to his master, and complained to him of this act of the governor; but the only satisfaction he received was to be damned very heartily by his master, who asked him how dared any of his negroes to have a boat. If the justly-merited ruin of the governor's fortune could be any gratification to the poor man he had thus robbed, he was not without consolation. Extortion and rapine are poor providers; and some time after this, the governor died in the King's Bench,[16] in England, as I was told, in great poverty. The last war favoured this poor negro-man, and he found some means to escape from his Christian master: he came to England, where I saw him afterwards several times. Such treatment as this often drives these miserable wretches to despair, and they run away from their masters at the hazard of their lives. Many of them, in this place, unable to get their pay when they have earned it, and fearing to be flogged, as usual, if they return home without it, run away where they can for shelter, and a reward is often offered to bring them in dead or alive. My master used sometimes, in these cases, to agree with their owners, and to settle with them himself; and thereby he saved many of them a flogging.

Notes

[12] *pisterines* These pisterines are of the value of a shilling [Equiano's note].

[13] *found … in victuals* supplied them with food (*OED, find*, sense 19).

[14] *a man of feeling* a sensitive person.

[15] *begged him off* successfully pleaded for a reduced sentence.

[16] *King's Bench* a debtors' prison in London.

Once, for a few days, I was let out to fit a vessel, and I had no victuals allowed me by either party; at last I told my master of this treatment, and he took me away from it. In many of the estates, on the different islands where I used to be sent for rum or sugar, they would not deliver it to me, or to any other negro; he was therefore obliged to send a white man along with me to those places; and then he used to pay him from six to ten pisterines a day. From being thus employed, during the time I served Mr. King, in going about the different estates on the island, I had all the opportunity I could wish for to see the dreadful usage of the poor men – usage that reconciled me to my situation, and made me bless God for the hands into which I had fallen.

I had the good fortune to please my master in every department in which he employed me; and there was scarcely any part of his business, or household affairs, in which I was not occasionally engaged. I often supplied the place of a clerk, in receiving and delivering cargoes to the ships, in tending stores, and delivering goods; and, besides this, I used to shave and dress my master, when convenient, and take care of his horse; and when it was necessary, which was very often, I worked likewise on board of his different vessels. By these means I became very useful to my master, and saved him, as he used to acknowledge, above a hundred pounds a year. Nor did he scruple to say I was of more advantage to him than any of his clerks; though their usual wages in the West-Indies are from sixty to a hundred pounds current[17] in a year.

I have sometimes heard it asserted that a negro cannot earn his master the first cost; but nothing can be further from the truth. I suppose nine tenths of the mechanics[18] throughout the West-Indies are negro slaves; and I well know the coopers[19] among them earn two dollars a-day; the carpenters the same, and oftentimes more; also the masons, smiths, and fishermen, &c. and I have known many slaves whose masters would not take a thousand pounds current for them. But surely this assertion refutes itself: for, if it be true, why do the planters and merchants pay such a price for slaves? And, above all, why do those, who make this assertion, exclaim the most loudly against the abolition of the slave trade? So much are men blinded, and to such inconsistent arguments are they driven by mistaken interest! I grant, indeed, that slaves are sometimes, by half-feeding, half-clothing, over-working, and stripes, reduced so low, that they are turned out as unfit for service, and left to perish in the woods, or to expire on a dunghill.

My master was several times offered by different gentlemen one hundred guineas for me; but he always told them he would not sell me, to my great joy: and I used to double my diligence and care for fear of getting into the hands of these men, who did not allow a valuable slave the common support of life. Many of them used to find fault with my master for feeding his slaves so well as he did; although I often went hungry, and an Englishman might think my fare very indifferent: but he used to tell them he always would do it, because the slaves thereby looked better and did more work.

While I was thus employed by my master, I was often a witness to cruelties of every kind, which were exercised on my unhappy fellow slaves. I used frequently to have different cargoes of new negroes in my care for sale; and it was almost a constant practice with our clerks, and other whites, to commit violent depradations on the chastity of the female slaves; and to these atrocities I was, though with reluctance, obliged to submit at all times, being unable to help them. When we have had some of these slaves on

Notes

17 *current* in currency, cash.

18 *mechanic* "a low workman" (Johnson).

19 *cooper* barrel maker.

board my master's vessels to carry them to other islands, or to America, I have known our mates commit these acts most shamefully, to the disgrace not of Christians only, but of men. I have even known them gratify their brutal passions with females not ten years old; and these abominations some of them practised to such a scandalous excess, that one of our captains discharged the mate and others on that account. And yet in Montserrat I have seen a negro-man staked to the ground, and cut most shockingly, and then his ears cut off, bit by bit, because he had been connected with a white woman, who was a common prostitute! As if it were no crime in the whites to rob an innocent African girl of her virtue; but most heinous in a black man only to gratify a passion of nature, where the temptation was offered by one of a different colour, though the most abandoned woman of her species.

One Mr. D——, told me he had sold 41,000 negroes, and he once cut off a negro-man's leg for running away. I asked him if the man had died in the operation, how he, as a Christian, could answer, for the horrid act, before God. And he told me, answering was a thing of another world; what he thought and did were policy. I told him that the Christian doctrine taught us 'to do unto others as we would that others should do unto us'. He then said that his scheme had the desired effect – it cured that man and some others of running away.

Another negro-man was half-hanged, and then burnt, for attempting to poison a cruel overseer. Thus, by repeated cruelties, are the wretched first urged to despair, and then murdered, because they still retain so much of human nature about them as to wish to put an end to their misery, and to retaliate on their tyrants! These overseers are, indeed, for the most part, persons of the worst character of any denomination of men in the West-Indies. Unfortunately, many humane gentlemen, by not residing on their estates, are obliged to leave the management of them in the hands of these human butchers, who cut and mangle the slaves in a shocking manner, on the most trivial occasions, and altogether treat them, in every respect, like brutes. They pay no regard to the situation of pregnant women, nor the least attention to the lodging of the field negroes. Their huts, which ought to be well covered, and the place where they take their short repose, are often open sheds, built in damp places; so that, when the poor creatures return tired from the toils of the field, they contract many disorders, from being exposed to the damp air in this uncomfortable state, while they are heated, and their pores are open.

The neglect certainly conspires with many others to cause a decrease in the births, as well as in the lives of the grown negroes. I can quote many instances of gentlemen who reside on their own estates in the West-Indies, and then the scene is quite changed; the negroes are treated with lenity and proper care, by which their lives are prolonged, and their masters profited. To the honour of humanity, I know several gentlemen who managed their estates in this manner, and found that benevolence was their true interest. And, among many[20] I could mention in Montserrat, whose slaves looked remarkably well, and never needed any fresh supplies of negroes (and there are many other estates, especially in Barbadoes, which, from such judicious treatment, need no fresh stock of negroes at any time) I have the honour of knowing a most worthy and humane gentleman,[21] who is

Notes

[20] *many* Mr. Dubury and many others, in Montserrat [Equiano's note].

[21] *humane gentleman* Sir Philip Gibbes, Bart. Barbadoes [Equiano's note].

a native of Barbadoes, and has estates there. This gentleman has written a treatise on the usage of his own slaves. He allows them two hours for refreshment at mid-day, and many other indulgences and comforts, particularly in their lying [in]; and besides this, he raises more provisions on his estate than they can destroy; so that by these attentions he saves the lives of his negroes, and keeps them healthy, and as happy as the condition of slavery can admit. I myself, as shall appear in the sequel, managed an estate, where, by such attentions, the negroes were uncommonly cheerful and healthy, and did more work by half than by the common mode of treatment they usually do. For want, therefore, of such care and attention to the poor negroes, and otherwise oppressed as they are, it is no wonder that the decrease should require 20,000 new negroes annually to fill up the vacant places of the dead.

Even in Barbadoes, notwithstanding those humane exceptions which I have mentioned and others with which I am acquainted that justly make it quoted as a place where slaves meet with the best treatment, and need fewest recruits of any in the West-Indies; yet this island requires 1,000 negroes annually to keep up the original stock, which is only 80,000. So that the whole term of a negro's life may be said to be there, but sixteen years! And yet the climate here is in every respect the same as that from which they are taken, except in being more wholesome. Do the British colonies decrease in this manner? And yet what a prodigious difference is there between an English and West-India climate?

While I was in Montserrat I knew a negro-man, one Emanuel Sankey, who endeavoured to escape from his miserable bondage, by concealing himself on board of a London ship. But fate did not favour the poor oppressed man; for, being discovered when the vessel was under sail, he was delivered up again to his master. This *Christian master* immediately pinned the wretch to the ground, at each wrist and ankle, and then took some sticks of sealing wax, lighted them, and dropped it all over his back. There was another master noted for cruelty: – I believe he had not a slave but had been cut, and pieces fairly taken out of the flesh: and after they had been punished thus, he used to make them get into a long wooden box, or case, he had for that purpose, and shut them up during pleasure. It was just about the height and breadth of a man; and the poor wretches had no room when in the case to move.

It was very common in several of the islands, particularly in St. Kitt's, for the slaves to be branded with the initial letters of their master's name, and a load of heavy iron hooks hung about their necks. Indeed on the most trivial occasions they were loaded with chains, and often instruments of torture were added. The iron muzzle, thumb-screws, &c. are so well known as not to need a description, and were sometimes applied for the slightest faults. I have seen a negro beaten till some of his bones were broken, for only letting a pot boil over. It is not uncommon, after a flogging, to make slaves go on their knees and thank their owners, and pray, or rather say, 'God bless you'. I have often asked many of the men slaves (who used to go several miles to their wives, and late in the night, after having been wearied with a hard day's labour) why they went so far for wives, and did not take them of their own master's negro-women, and particularly those who lived together as household slaves. Their answers have ever been – 'Because when the master or mistress choose to punish the women, they make the husbands flog their own wives, and that we could not bear to do'. Is it surprising such usage should drive the poor creatures to despair, and make them seek a refuge in death, from those evils which render their lives intolerable – while

With shudd'ring horror pale, and eyes aghast,
They view their lamentable lot, and find
No rest?[22]

This they frequently do. A negro-man, on board a vessel of my master's, while I belonged to her, having been put in irons for some trifling misdemeanour, and kept in that state some days, being weary of life, took an opportunity of jumping overboard into the sea; however, he was picked up without being drowned. Another, whose life was also a burden to him, resolved to starve himself to death, and refused to eat any victuals; this procured him a severe flogging; and he also on the first occasion that offered, jumped overboard at Charles Town, but was saved.

Nor is there any greater regard shown to the little property than there is to the persons and lives of the negroes. I have already related an instance or two of particular oppression, out of many which I have witnessed; but the following is frequent in all the islands: – The wretched field-slaves, after toiling all the day for an unfeeling owner, who gives them but little victuals, steal sometimes a few moments from rest or refreshment to gather some small portion of grass, according as their time will admit. This they commonly tie up in a parcel; either a bit's worth (sixpence) or half a bit's worth, and bring it to town, or to the market to sell. Nothing is more common than for the white people, on this occasion, to take the grass from them without paying for it; and not only so, but too often also, to my knowledge, our clerks and many others, at the same time have committed acts of violence on the poor, wretched, and helpless females; whom I have seen for hours stand crying to no purpose, and get no redress or pay of any kind. Is not this one common and crying sin enough to bring down God's judgement upon the islands? He tells us the oppressor and the oppressed are both in his hands; and if these are not the poor, the broken-hearted, the blind, the captive, and the bruised,[23] of which our Saviour speaks, who are they?

One of these depredators once, in St. Eustasia, came on board of our vessel, and bought some fowls and pigs of me; and a whole day after his departure with the things, he returned and wanted his money back: – I refused to give it; and, he not seeing my captain on board, began the common pranks with me; and swore he would even break open my chest and take my money. I therefore expected, as my captain was absent, that he would be as good as his word: and he was just proceeding to strike me, when fortunately a British seaman on board, whose heart had not been debauched by a West-India climate, interposed and prevented him. But had the cruel man struck me, I certainly should have defended myself, at the hazard of my life. For what is life to a man thus oppressed? He went away, however, swearing; and threatened that whenever he caught me a-shore he would shoot me, and pay for me afterwards.

The small account, in which the life of a negro is held in the West-Indies, is so universally known, that it might seem impertinent to quote the following extract, if some people had not been hardy enough of late to assert, that negroes are on the same footing in that respect as Europeans. By the 329th Act, page 125, of the Assembly of Barbadoes, it is enacted 'That if any negro, or other slave, under punishment by his

Notes

[22] *With shudd'ring ... No rest? Paradise Lost* 2. 616–18 imperfectly recalled.

[23] *the poor ... bruised* Luke 4.18.

master, or his order, for running away, or any other crime or misdemeanour towards his said master, unfortunately shall suffer in life or member, no person whatsoever shall be liable to a fine; but if any man out of *wantonness, or only of bloody-mindedness, or cruel intention, wilfully kill a negro, or other slave, of his own, he shall pay into the public treasury £15. sterling*'. And it is the same in most, if not all, of the West-India islands. Is not this one of the many acts of the islands which call loudly for redress? And do not the Assembly, which enacted it, deserve the appellation of savages and brutes rather than of Christians and men? It is an act at once unmerciful, unjust, and unwise; which for cruelty would disgrace an assembly of those who are called barbarians; and for its injustice and insanity would shock the morality and common sense of a Sama[n]ide[24] or Hottentot.[25]

Shocking as this and many other acts of the bloody West-India code at first view appear, how is the iniquity of it heightened when we consider to whom it may be extended! Mr. James Tobin, a zealous labourer in the vineyard of slavery, gives an account[26] of a French planter, of his acquaintance, who showed him many mulattoes working in the fields like beasts of burden; and he told Mr. Tobin these *were all products of his own loins*! And I myself have known similar instances. Pray, reader, are these sons and daughters of the French planter less his children by being begotten on black women? And what must be the virtue of those legislators, and the feelings of those fathers, who estimate the lives of their sons, however begotten, at no more than fifteen pounds; though they should be murdered, as the act says, *out of wantonness and bloody-mindedness*? But is not the slave-trade entirely a war with the heart of man? And surely that which is begun by breaking down the barriers of virtue, involves in its continuance destruction to every principle, and buries all sentiments in ruin!

I have often seen slaves, particularly those who were meagre, in different islands, put into scales and weighed; and then sold from three-pence to six-pence or nine-pence a pound. My master, however, whose humanity was shocked at this mode, used to sell such by the lump. And at or after a sale, even those negroes born in the island it is not uncommon to see taken from their wives, wives from their husbands, and children from their parents, and sent off to other islands, and wherever else their merciless lords choose; and, probably, never more, during life, see each other! Oftentimes my heart has bled at these partings; when the friends of the departed have been at the water-side, and, with sighs and tears, have kept their eyes fixed on the vessel till it went out of sight.

A poor Creole negro I know well, who, after having been thus transported from island to island, at last resided in Montserrat. This man used to tell me many melancholy tales of himself. Generally, after he had done working for his master, he used to employ his few leisure moments to go a fishing. When he had caught any fish, his master would frequently take them from him without paying him; and at other times some other white people would serve him in the same manner. One day he said to me very movingly, 'Sometimes when a white man take away my fish I go to my maser, and he get me my right; and when my maser, by strength, take away my fishes, what me must do? I can't go to any body to be righted; then', said the poor

Notes

[24] *Sama[n]ide* member of an Islamic Persian dynasty begun in the ninth century.

[25] *Hottentot* one of the native people of southern Africa.

[26] *account* In his *Cursory Remarks* [Bristol, 1785; Equiano's note].

man, looking up above, 'I must look up to God Mighty in the top for right'. This artless tale moved me much, and I could not help feeling the just cause Moses had in redressing his brother against the Egyptian.[27] I exhorted the man to look up still to the God in the top, since there was no redress below. Though I little thought then that I myself should more than once experience such imposition, and need the same exhortation hereafter, in my own transactions in the islands; and that even this poor man and I should some time after, suffer together in the same manner, as shall be related hereafter.

Nor was such usage as this confined to particular places or individuals; for, in all the different islands in which I have been (and I have visited no less than fifteen) the treatment of the slaves was nearly the same; so nearly, indeed, that the history of an island, or even a plantation, with a few such exceptions as I have mentioned, might serve for a history of the whole. Such a tendency has the slave-trade to debauch men's minds, and harden them to every feeling of humanity! For I will not suppose that the dealers in slaves are born worse than other men. No; it is the fatality of this mistaken avarice, that it corrupts the milk of human kindness and turns it into gall. And, had the pursuits of those men been different, they might have been as generous, as tender-hearted, and just, as they are unfeeling, rapacious and cruel. Surely this traffic cannot be good, which spreads like a pestilence, and taints what it touches! Which violates that first natural right of mankind, equality, and independency; and gives one man a dominion over his fellows which God could never intend! For it raises the owner to a state as far above man as it depresses the slave below it; and, with all the presumption of human pride, sets distinction between them, immeasurable in extent, and endless in duration! Yet how mistaken is the avarice even of the planters. Are slaves more useful by being thus humbled to the condition of brutes, than they would be if suffered to enjoy the privileges of men? The freedom which diffuses health and prosperity throughout Britain answers you – 'No'. When you make men slaves, you deprive them of half their virtue,[28] and you set them, in your own conduct, an example of fraud, rapine, and cruelty, and compel them to live with you in a state of war;[29] and yet you complain that they are not honest or faithful! You stupefy them with stripes, and think it necessary to keep them in a state of ignorance; and yet you assert that they are incapable of learning; that their minds are such a barren soil or moor that culture would be lost on them; and that they came from a climate, where nature, though prodigal of her bounties in a degree unknown to yourselves, has left man alone scant and unfinished, and incapable of enjoying the treasures she has poured out for him! – An assertion at once impious and absurd. Why do you use those instruments of torture? Are they fit to be applied by one rational being to another? And are ye not struck with shame and mortification, to see the partakers of your nature reduced so low? But, above all, are there no dangers attending this mode of treatment? Are you not hourly in dread of an insurrection? Nor would it be surprising: for when

Notes

[27] *Moses ... Egyptian* While still in Egypt, Moses killed an Egyptian for striking his fellow Hebrew (Exodus 2.11–12).

[28] *When you make men slaves, you deprive them of half their virtue* translation of a classical aphorism attributed to Homer (see Johnson's *Dictionary*, s.v. *caitiff*).

[29] *a state of war* a reference to Hobbes's *Leviathan*; see p. 10 above.

No peace is given
To us enslaved, but custody severe;
And stripes and arbitrary punishment
Inflicted – What peace can we return?
But to our power, hostility and hate,
Untamed reluctance, and revenge, though slow.
Yet ever plotting how the conqueror least
May reap his conquest, and may least rejoice
In doing what we most in suff'ring feel? MILTON.[30]

But by changing your conduct, and treating your slaves as men, every cause of fear would be banished. They would be faithful, honest, intelligent and vigorous; and peace, prosperity, and happiness, would attend you.

Notes

[30] *MILTON Paradise Lost* 2.332–40 (*mutatis*).

Hannah More (1745–1833)

Hannah More lived through two distinct literary periods. She was a friend of Johnson, Garrick, Burke, Reynolds, and Walpole, but she outlived them all by forty years. Unfortunately, More did not enjoy the favor in the new regime that she had in the old. She was popular, however, and is said to have earned £30,000 from her writings over her lifetime. She started as a playwright, but soon began writing works with explicit social, moral, and religious purposes. She wrote and campaigned in other ways for the abolition of slavery, for women's rights (especially for women's right to education), and for humane treatment of children and the poor. She was not romantic about her causes in any way. Unlike romantics, she was horrified by the French Revolution and wrote fifty of her *Cheap Repository Tracts* in opposition to the French turmoil and in support of old-fashioned English village politics. More was a Tory with a strong evangelical streak; Johnson recognized her warmly right away, and she was loved by common readers.

Sensibility was first published in 1782 in More's collection of Bible stories, *Sacred Dramas. The Slave Trade* was first published independently as *Slavery, a Poem* but took its present title in later collections of More. The following texts are based on those in *The Works of Hannah More* (1813). An important recent study is *Hannah More, the First Victorian* by Anne Stott (Oxford University Press, 2003).

from *Sensibility* (1782)

… Sweet Sensibility! thou secret power
Who shedd'st thy gifts upon the natal hour,
Like fairy favours; art can never seize,
Nor affectation catch thy power to please:
Thy subtle essence still eludes the chains
Of definition, and defeats her pains.
Sweet Sensibility! thou keen delight!
Unprompted moral! sudden sense of right!
Perception exquisite! fair virtue's seed!
Thou quick precursor of the liberal deed!
Thou hasty conscience! reason's blushing morn!
Instinctive kindness ere reflection's born!
Prompt sense of equity! to thee belongs
The swift redress of unexamined wrongs!
Eager to serve, the cause perhaps untried,
But always apt to choose the suff'ring side!
To those who know thee not, no words can paint,
And those who know thee, know all words are faint!
  She does not feel thy pow'r who boasts thy flame
And rounds her every period with thy name;
Nor she who vents her disproportioned sighs
With pining Lesbia when her sparrow dies:

British Literature 1640–1789: An Anthology, Fourth Edition. Edited by Robert DeMaria, Jr.

Nor she who melts when hapless Shore expires,[1]
While real mis'ry unrelieved retires!
Who thinks feigned sorrows all her tears deserve,
And weeps o'er Werter while her children starve.[2]
  As words are but th' external marks to tell
The fair ideas in the mind that dwell;
And only are of things the outward sign,
And not the things themselves they but define;
So exclamations, tender tones, fond tears,
And all the graceful drapery feeling wears;
These are her garb, not her, they but express
Her form, her semblance, her appropriate dress;
And these fair marks, reluctant I relate,
These lovely symbols may be counterfeit.
There are, who fill with brilliant plaints the page,
If a poor linnet meet the gunner's rage;
There are, who for a dying fawn deplore,
As if friend, parent, country were no more;
Who boast quick rapture trembling in their eye,
If from the spider's snare they snatch a fly;
There are, who well-sung plaints each breast inflame,
And break all hearts – but his from whom they came!
He, scorning life's low duties to attend,
Writes odes on friendship, while he cheats his friend.
Of jails and punishments he grieves to hear,
And pensions 'prisoned virtue with a tear;
While unpaid bills his creditor presents,
And ruined innocence his crime laments.
Not so the tender moralist of Tweed,[3]
His gen'rous Man of Feeling feels indeed.
  O love divine! sole source of charity!
More dear one genuine deed performed for thee,
Than all the periods feeling e'er could turn,[4]
Than all thy touching page, perverted Sterne![5]
Not that by deeds alone this love's expressed,
If so the affluent only were the blessed;
One silent wish, one prayer, one soothing word,
The page of mercy shall, well pleased, record;
One soul-felt sigh by pow'rless pity given,
Accepted incense! shall ascend to heav'n.

Notes

FROM *SENSIBILITY*

[1] *Shore* Jane, a commoner, the mistress of Edward IV, later accused of sorcery by Richard III; died in poverty; her rise and fall are the subject of some sad ballads and a play by Nicholas Rowe (1714).

[2] *Werter* the hero of Goethe's novel *The Sorrows of Young Werther* (1774).

[3] *the tender moralist of Tweed* Henry Mackenzie, author of *The Man of Feeling* (1771).

[4] *periods* sentences.

[5] *Sterne* Laurence, author of *Tristram Shandy* (1759–67); More is thinking of Sterne's infidelity to his wife.

from *The Slave Trade* (1790)

... Whene'er to Afric's shores I turn my eyes,
Horrors of deepest, deadliest guilt arise;
I see, by more than fancy's mirror shown,
The burning village and the blazing town:
See the dire victim torn from social life,
The shrieking babe, the agonizing wife;
She, wretch forlorn! is dragged by hostile hands,
To distant tyrants sold, in distant lands!
Transmitted miseries, and successive chains,
The sole sad heritage her child obtains!
E'en this last wretched boon their foes deny,
To weep together, or together die.
By felon hands, by one relentless stroke,
See the fond links of feeling nature broke!
The fibres twisting round a parent's heart,
Torn from their grasp, and bleeding as they part.
    Hold, murderers, hold! nor aggravate distress;
Respect the passions you yourselves possess:
E'en you, of ruffian heart and ruthless hand,
Love your own offspring, love your native land:
E'en you, with fond impatient feelings burn,
Though free as air, though certain of return.
Then, if to you, who voluntary roam,
So dear the memory of your distant home,
O think how absence the loved scene endears
To him, whose food is groans, whose drink is tears;
Think on the wretch, whose aggravated pains,
To exile misery adds, to misery chains.
If warm your heart, to British feelings true,
As dear his land to him, as yours to you;
And liberty, in you a hallowed flame,
Burns unextinguished, in his breast the same.
Then leave him holy freedom's cheering smile,
The heav'n-taught fondness for the parent soil;
In every nature, every clime the same;
In all, these feelings equal sway maintain;
In all, the love of home and freedom reign:
And Tempe's vale, and parched Angola's sand,[1]
One equal fondness of their sons command.
Th' unconquered savage laughs at pain and toil,
Basking in freedom's beams which gild his native soil.
    Does thirst of empire, does desire of fame,
(For these are specious crimes) our rage inflame?
No: sordid lust of gold their fate controls,

Notes

FROM *THE SLAVE TRADE*

[1] *Tempe's vale* a valley in Thessaly near Mount Olympus.

The basest appetite of basest souls:
Gold, better gained by what their ripening sky,
Their fertile fields, their arts and mines supply.[2]
    What wrongs, what injuries does oppression plead,
To smooth the crime and sanctify the deed?
What strange offence, what aggravated sin?
They stand convicted – of a darker skin!
Barbarians, hold! th' opprobrious commerce spare,
Though dark and savage, ignorant and blind,
They claim the common privilege of kind;
Let malice strip them of each other plea,
They still are men, and men should still be free.
Insulted reason loathes th' inverted trade –
Loathes, as she views the human purchase made;
The outraged goddess, with abhorrent eyes,
Sees man the traffic, souls the merchandise!
Man, whom fair commerce taught with judging eye,
And liberal hand, to barter or to buy,
Indignant Nature blushes to behold
Degraded man himself trucked, bartered, sold:[3]
Of every native privilege bereft,
Yet cursed with every wounded feeling left.
Hard lot! each brutal suff'ring to sustain,
Yet keep the sense acute of human pain.
Plead not, in reason's palpable abuse,
Their sense of feeling callous and obtuse:[4]
From heads to hearts lies nature's plain appeal,
Though few can reason, all mankind can feel.
Though wit may boast a livelier dread of shame;
A loftier sense of wrong, refinement claim;
Though polished manners may fresh wants invent,
And nice distinctions nicer souls torment;
Though these on finer spirits heavier fall,
Yet natural evils are the same to all.
Though wounds there are which reason's force may heal,
There needs no logic sure to make us feel.
The nerve, howe'er untutored, can sustain
A sharp, unutterable sense of pain;
As exquisitely fashioned in a slave,
As where unequal fate a sceptre gave.
Sense is as keen where Gambia's waters glide,[5]
As where proud Tiber rolls his classic tide.
Though voice or rhetoric point the feeling line,

Notes

[2] *arts* Besides many valuable productions of the soil, cloths and carpets of exquisite manufacture are brought from the coast of Guinea [More's note].

[2] *trucked* exchanged, bartered.

[4] *feeling* Nothing is more frequent than this cruel and stupid argument, that they do not feel the miseries inflicted on them as Europeans would do [More's note].

[5] *Gambia* a river in West Africa.

They do not whet sensation, but define.
Did ever wretch less feel the galling chain,
When Zeno proved there was no ill in pain?[6]
In vain the sage to smooth its horror tries;
Spartans and Helots see with different eyes;[7]
Their miseries philosophic quirks deride,[8]
Slaves groan in pangs disowned by Stoic pride.
When the fierce sun darts vertical his beams,
And thirst and hunger mix their wild extremes;
When the sharp iron wounds his inmost soul,[9]
And his strained eyes in burning anguish roll;
Will the parched negro own, ere he expire,
No pain in hunger, and no heat in fire?
For him, when agony his frame destroys,
What hope of present fame or future joys?
For *that* have heroes shortened nature's date;
For *this* have martyrs gladly met their fate;
But him, forlorn, no hero's pride sustains,
No martyr's blissful visions soothe his pains;
Sullen, he mingles with his kindred dust,
For he has learned to dread the Christian's trust;
To him what mercy can that God display,
Whose servants murder, and whose sons betray?
Savage! thy venial error I deplore,[10]
They are *not* Christians who infest thy shore.
O thou sad spirit, whose preposterous yoke
The great deliverer death, at length, has broke!
Released from misery, and escaped from care,
Go, meet that mercy man denied thee here.
In thy dark home, sure refuge of th' oppressed,
The wicked vex not, and the weary rest.
And if some notions, vague and undefined,
Of future terrors have assailed thy mind;
If such thy masters have presumed to teach,
As terrors only they are prone to preach;
(For should they paint eternal mercy's reign,
Where were th' oppressor's rod, the captive's chain?)
If, then, thy troubled soul has learned to dread
The dark unknown thy trembling footsteps tread;
On Him, who made thee what thou art, depend;

Notes

6 *Zeno* of Citium, Cyprus (335–263 BCE), founder of Stoicism.

7 *Helots* an underclass in Sparta, kept in servile positions, yet slightly above true slaves.

8 *quirk* "Subtlety; nicety; artful distinction" (Johnson).

9 *iron ... soul* [an expression taken from Psalm 105.18, meaning to feel the pain of captivity (*OED, iron*, 7b)]. This is not said figuratively. The writer of these lines has seen a complete set of chains, fitted to every separate limb of these unhappy innocent men; together with instruments for wrenching open the jaws, contrived with such ingenious cruelty as would gratify the tender mercies of an inquisitor [More's note].

10 *venial* permitted, allowed.

He, who withholds the means, accepts the end.
Thy mental night thy Saviour will not blame,
He died for those who never heard his name.
Not *thine* the reckoning dire of light abused,
Knowledge disgraced, and liberty misused;
On *thee* no awful judge incensed shall sit
For parts perverted, and dishonoured wit.
Where ignorance will be found the safest plea,
How many learned and wise shall envy *thee*!

Richard Brinsley Sheridan (1751–1816)

The son of an actor, who was also an expert on pronunciation, and a playwright, who was also a novelist, Richard Sheridan was born into the literary and theatrical worlds of London. At the age of thirteen, however, he was left on his own at Harrow, an upperclass boarding school, as his parents fled creditors and settled for a time in France. His mother died during this period of four years, but Richard was reunited with his father, first in London (where he continued his education) and then in Bath, where he began publishing poetry and entered into the first of many spectacular romances. After fighting two duels with a married man who was in pursuit of his beloved, and enduring the disapprobation of his own father and hers, Sheridan married Eliza Linley in 1773. Marriage, however, did not dampen Sheridan's passion for women, and he eventually drove his wife to other men. After Eliza's death, Sheridan, at forty-four, married the nineteen-year-old Hester Jan Ogle, but continued to pursue affairs begun in his first marriage.

Sheridan's theatrical career was almost as volatile as his private life. Early in 1775, *The Rivals*, the first of his two great comedies, was performed at Covent Garden. Soon thereafter Sheridan gained controlling interest of the Drury Lane Theatre, which reopened under his management in the autumn of 1776. In the spring of 1777 he produced his second great comedy, *The School for Scandal*. In succeeding years, he financed his extravagant living through mortgages of the theater until it burned down in 1807 and was taken over by Samuel Whitbred.

Given the tempestuousness of his private and theatrical lives, it is amazing that the principal occupation of Sheridan's life was politics. He served in Parliament from 1780 to 1812 and was deeply embroiled in the turbulence of party politics from the time of the Gordon riots through the illness of George III, the appointment of the Regent, the French Revolution, and the Napoleonic wars. He was closely allied with Pitt and Fox, the most important Whig politicians of the time, and served as treasurer of the navy and a member of the privy council. He was also sympathetic to the movement for Irish independence and opposed excessive British oppression in Ireland just as he supported the impeachment of Warren Hastings for his massive thefts while governor general of Bengal.

Cecil Price has edited Sheridan's plays with painstaking attention to the many manuscripts that exceed the authority of the printed versions (Clarendon Press, 1973). I have used the earliest printed version (Dublin, 1780) as a copy-text and made emendations, often consulting Price's edition, where the Dublin text is unclear. (I am also indebted to Price in many of my footnotes.) I have no doubt that Price's edition comes closer to what Sheridan wrote and authorized, but the printed versions that first reached readers in the eighteenth century have their own kind of authenticity, and Sheridan's quick wit and resourcefulness are abundantly present in every version of the play.

The School for Scandal (1777)

Dramatis Personae.

Men.

Sir Peter Teazle,
Sir Oliver Surface,

British Literature 1640–1789: An Anthology, Fourth Edition. Edited by Robert DeMaria, Jr.

Joseph Surface,
Charles,
Rowley,
Sir Benjamin Backbite,
Crabtree,
Moses,
Snake,
Trip,
Sir Toby Bumper,
Gentlemen,
Servant to Joseph Surface,
Servant to Lady Sneerwell.

Women

Lady Teazle,
Maria,
Lady Sneerwell,
Mrs. Candour,
Maid to Lady Teazle.

Act I.

SCENE Lady Sneerwell's House.

Lady Sneerwell *and* Snake *discovered at a tea table.*

L. SNEERWELL. The paragraphs, you say, Mr. Snake, were all inserted.

SNAKE. They were, Madam; and as I copied them myself in a feigned hand, there can be no suspicion from whence they came.

L. SNEERWELL. Did you circulate the report of lady Brittle's intrigue with captain Boastall?

SNAKE. That's in as fine a train as your Ladyship could wish; in the common course of things, I think it must reach Mrs. Clacket's ears within twenty-four hours, and then the business, you know, is as good as done.

L. SNEERWELL. Why, yes, Mrs. Clacket has talents, and a great deal of industry.

SNAKE. True, Madam, and has been tolerably successful in her day; to my knowledge she has been the cause of six matches being broken off, and three sons disinherited; of four forced elopements, as many close confinements, nine desperate maintenances, and two divorces; – nay, I have more than once traced her causing a *tête a tête* in the *Town and Country Magazine*[1] when the parties never saw one another before in the whole course of their lives.

L. SNEERWELL. Why yes, she has genius, but her manner is too gross.

SNAKE. True, Madam; she has a fine tongue, and a bold invention; but then, her colouring is too dark, and the outlines rather too extravagant; she wants that delicacy of hint, and mellowness of sneer, which distinguishes your Ladyship's scandal.

Notes

THE SCHOOL FOR SCANDAL

[1] *Town and Country Magazine* this gossipy publication began in January 1769 and ran through 1796.

L. SNEERWELL. You are partial, Snake.

SNAKE. Not in the least; everybody will allow that Lady Sneerwell can do more with a word or look, than many others with the most laboured detail, even though they accidentally happen to have a little truth on their side to support it.

L. SNEERWELL. Yes, my dear Snake, and I'll not deny the pleasure I feel at the success of my schemes; *(both rise)* wounded myself, in the early part of my life, by the envenomed tongue of slander, I confess nothing can give me greater satisfaction, than reducing others to the level of my own injured reputation.

SNAKE. Nothing can be more natural – But, Lady Sneerwell, there is one affair, in which you have lately employed me, wherein, I confess, I am at a loss to guess at your motives.

L. SNEERWELL. I presume you mean with regard to my friend Sir Peter Teazle, and his family.

SNAKE. I do; here are two young men, to whom Sir Peter has acted as guardian since their father's death; the eldest possessing the most amiable character, and universally well spoken of; the youngest the most dissipated, wild, extravagant young fellow in the world; the former an avowed admirer of your Ladyship, and apparently your favourite; the latter attached to Maria, Sir Peter's ward, and confessedly admired by her: Now, on the face of these circumstances, it is utterly unaccountable to me, why you, the widow of a city knight, with a large fortune, should not immediately close with the passion of a man of such character and expectation as Mr. Surface; and more so, why you are so uncommonly earnest to destroy the mutual attachment subsisting between his brother Charles and Maria.

L. SNEERWELL. Then at once, to unravel this mystery, I must inform you, that love has no share whatever in the intercourse between Mr. Surface and me.

SNAKE. No! –

L. SNEERWELL. No! his real views are to Maria, or her fortune, while in his brother he finds a favoured rival; he is, therefore, obliged to mask his real intentions, and profit by my assistance.

SNAKE. Yet still I am more puzzled why you should interest yourself for his success.

L. SNEERWELL. Heavens! how dull you are! can't you surmise a weakness I have hitherto, through shame, concealed even from you? Must I confess it that Charles, that profligate, that libertine, that bankrupt in fortune and reputation, that he it is for whom I am thus anxious and malicious; and to gain whom I would sacrifice everything.

SNAKE. Now, indeed, your conduct appears consistent; but pray how come you and Mr. Surface so confidential?

L. SNEERWELL. For our mutual interest; he pretends to, and recommends sentiment and liberality, but I know him to be artful, close and malicious. In short, a sentimental[2] knave, while with Sir Peter, and indeed with most of his acquaintance, he passes for a youthful miracle of virtue, good sense, and benevolence.

SNAKE. Yes, I know Sir Peter vows he has not his fellow in England, and has praised him as a man of character and sentiment.

Notes

[2] *sentimental* a word in vogue in the second half of the eighteenth century and used in so many different senses that it was hackneyed by 1777. It means, among other things, "expressive of moral sentiments" and "given to feeling emotions strongly," but it is also a worn-out and therefore ironic term of approbation.

L. Sneerwell. Yes; and with the appearance of being sentimental, he has brought Sir Peter to favour his addresses to Maria, while poor Charles has no friend in the house, though I fear he has a powerful one in Maria's heart, against whom we must direct our schemes.

Enter Servant.

Servant. Mr. Surface, Madam.

L. Sneerwell. Show him up; *(Exit Servant)* he generally calls about this hour – I don't wonder at people's giving him to me for a lover.

Enter Joseph Surface.

Joseph. Lady Sneerwell, good morning to you – Mr. Snake, your most obedient.

L. Sneerwell. Snake has just been rallying me upon our attachment, but I have told him our real views; I need not tell you how useful he has been to us, and believe me, our confidence has not been ill placed.

Joseph. Oh, Madam, 'tis impossible for me to suspect a man of Mr. Snake's merit and accomplishments.

L. Sneerwell. Oh, no compliments; but tell me when you saw Maria, or what's more material to us, your brother.

Joseph. I have not seen either since I left you, but I can tell you they never meet; some of your stories have had a good effect in that quarter.

L. Sneerwell. The merit of this, my dear Snake, belongs to you; but do your brother's distresses increase?

Joseph. Every hour! I am told he had another execution[3] in his house yesterday – In short, his dissipation and extravagance exceeds anything I ever heard.

L. Sneerwell. Poor Charles!

Joseph. Aye, poor Charles indeed! notwithstanding his extravagance one cannot help pitying him; I wish it was in my power to be of any essential service to him; for the man who does not feel for the distresses of a brother, even though merited by his own misconduct, deserves to be –

L. Sneerwell. Now you are going to be moral, and forget you are among friends.

Joseph. Gad, so I was, ha! ha! I'll keep that sentiment till I see Sir Peter, ha! ha! however, it would certainly be a generous act in you to rescue Maria from such a libertine, who, if he is to be reclaimed at all, can only be so by a person of your superior accomplishments and understanding.

Snake. I believe Lady Sneerwell hears company coming; I'll go and copy the letter I mentioned to your Ladyship. Mr. Surface, your most obedient. [*Exit Snake.*]

Joseph. Mr. Snake, your most obedient. I wonder, Lady Sneerwell, you would put any confidence in that fellow.

L. Sneerwell. Why so?

Joseph. I have discovered he has of late had several conferences with old *Rowley*, who was formerly my father's steward; he has never, you know, been a friend of mine.

L. Sneerwell. And do you think he would betray us?

Joseph. Not unlikely; and take my word for it, Lady *Sneerwell*, that fellow has not virtue enough to be faithful to his own villainies.

Notes

[3] *execution* "the seizure of the goods … of a debtor in default of payment" (*OED*, 7a).

Enter Maria.

L. Sneerwell. Ah, Maria, my dear, how do you do? What's the matter?

Maria. Nothing, Madam, only this odious lover of mine, Sir Benjamin Backbite, and his uncle Crabtree, just called in at my guardian's; but I took the first opportunity to slip out, and run away to your Ladyship.

L. Sneerwell. Is that all?

Joseph. Had my brother Charles been of the party you would not have been so much alarmed.

L. Sneerwell. Nay, now you are too severe; for I dare say the truth of the matter is, Maria heard you was here, and therefore came; but pray, *Maria,* what particular objection have you to Sir Benjamin that you avoid him so?

Maria. Oh, madam, he has done nothing; But his whole conversation is a perpetual libel upon all his acquaintance.

Joseph. Yes, and the worst of it is, there is no advantage in not knowing him, for he would abuse a stranger as soon as his best friend, and his uncle is as bad.

Maria. For my part, I own wit loses its respect with me, when I see it in company with malice; – what think you, Mr. Surface?

Joseph. To be sure, Madam, – to smile at a jest that plants a thorn in the breast of another, is to become a principal in the mischief.

L. Sneerwell. Pshaw – there is no possibility of being witty without a little ill nature; the malice in a good thing is the barb that makes it stick – What is your *real* opinion, Mr. Surface?

Joseph. Why my opinion is, that where the spirit of raillery is suppressed, the conversation must be naturally insipid.

Maria. Well, I will not argue how far slander may be allowed, but in a man, I am sure it is despicable. – We have pride, envy, rivalship, and a thousand motives to depreciate each other; but the male slanderer, must have the cowardice of a woman, before he can traduce one.

Enter Servant.

Servant. Mrs. Candour, Madam, if you are at leisure, will leave her carriage.

L. Sneerwell. Desire her to walk up. *(Exit Servant.)* Now, Maria, here's a character to your taste; though Mrs. Candour is a little talkative, yet everybody allows she is the best natured sort of woman in the world.

Maria. Yes – with the very gross affectation of good nature, she does more mischief, than the direct malice of old Crabtree.

Joseph. Faith it's very true; and whenever I hear the current of abuse running hard against the characters of my best friends, I never think them in such danger, as when Candour undertakes their defence.

L. Sneerwell. Hush! Hush! here she is.

Enter Mrs. Candour.

Mrs. Candour. Oh! my dear Lady Sneerwell; well, how do you do? Mr. Surface, your most obedient – Is there any news abroad? No! nothing good I suppose – No! nothing but scandal! – nothing but scandal!

Joseph. Just so indeed, Madam.

Mrs. Candour. Nothing but scandal! – Ah, Maria, how do you do child; what, is everything at an end between you and Charles? What, he is too extravagant. – Aye! the town talks of nothing else.

Maria. I am sorry, Madam, the town is so ill employed.

MRS. CANDOUR. Aye, so am I child – but what can one do? we can't stop people's tongues: – They hint too, that your guardian and his Lady don't live so agreeably together as they did.

MARIA. I am sure such reports are without foundation.

MRS. CANDOUR. Aye, so these things generally are: – It's like Mrs. Fashion's affair with Colonel Coterie; though, indeed, that affair was never rightly cleared up; and it was but yesterday Miss Prim assured me, that Mr. and Mrs. Honeymoon are now become mere man and wife, like the rest of their acquaintance. She likewise hinted, that a certain widow in the next street, had got rid of her dropsy, and recovered her shape in a most surprising manner.

JOSEPH. The licence of invention, some people give themselves, is astonishing.

MRS. CANDOUR. 'Tis so – but how will you stop people's tongues? 'Twas but yesterday Mrs. Clacket informed me, that our old friend, Miss Prudely, was going to elope, and that her guardian caught her just stepping into the York Diligence,[4] with her dancing-master. I was informed too, that Lord Flimsy caught his wife at a house of no extraordinary fame, and that Tom Saunter and Sir Harry Idle, were to measure swords on a similar occasion. – But I dare say there is no truth in the story, and I would not circulate such a report for the world.

JOSEPH. You? report? No, no, no.

MRS. CANDOUR. No, no, – talebearers are just as bad as the tale-makers.

Enter Servant.

SERVANT. Sir Benjamin Backbite and Mr. Crabtree. [*Exit Servant.*]

CRABTREE. Lady Sneerwell, your most obedient humble servant. Mrs. Candour, I believe you don't know my nephew, Sir Benjamin Backbite; he has a very pretty taste for poetry, and shall make a rebus or a charade[5] with any one.

SIR BENJAMIN. Oh fie! uncle.

CRABTREE. In faith he will: did you ever hear the lines he made at Lady Ponto's rout,[6] on Mrs. Frizzle's feathers catching fire; and the rebuses – his first is the name of a fish; the next, a great naval commander, and –

SIR BENJAMIN. Uncle, now prithee.

L. SNEERWELL. I wonder, Sir Benjamin, you never publish anything.

SIR BENJAMIN. Why, to say the truth, 'tis very vulgar to print – and as my little productions are chiefly satires, and lampoons on particular persons, I find they circulate better by giving copies in confidence to the friends of the parties; – however, I have some love elegies, which, when favoured by this Lady's smiles, (*to Maria*) I mean to give to the public.

CRABTREE. 'Foregad, Madam, they'll immortalize you, (*to Maria*) you will be handed down to posterity, like Petrarch's Laura, or Waller's Sacharissa.[7]

SIR BENJAMIN. Yes, Madam, I think you'll like them, (*to Maria*) when you shall see them on a beautiful quarto page, where a neat rivulet of text shall murmur through a meadow of margin; – 'foregad they'll be the most elegant things of their kind.

CRABTREE. But, odso,[8] Ladies, did you hear the news?

Notes

4 *Diligence* a public stage-coach.

5 *charade* like a *rebus*, a word guessing game in which the clues were not necessarily acted out as they are now, but written or sketched.

6 *rout* a large fashionable gathering.

7 *Laura* [Laura de Noves] and *Saccharissa* [Lady Dorothy Sidney] the objects, respectively, of Petrarch's (1304–74) and Edmund Waller's (1606–87) love poems.

8 *odso* a fashionable form of "Godso," an expression of surprise.

Mrs. Candour. What – do you mean the report of –

Crabtree. No, Madam, that's not it – Miss Nicely going to be married to her own footman.

Mrs. Candour. Impossible!

Sir Benjamin. 'Tis very true, indeed Madam; everything is fixed, and the wedding liveries bespoke.

Crabtree. Yes, and they do say there were very pressing reasons for it.

Mrs. Candour. I heard something of this before.

L. Sneerwell. Oh! It cannot be; and I wonder they'd report such a thing of so prudent a Lady.

Sir Benjamin. Oh! but Madam, that is the very reason that it was believed at once; for she has always been so very cautious and reserved, that everybody was sure there was some reason for it at bottom.

Mrs. Candour. It is true, there is a sort of puny, sickly reputation, that would outlive the robuster character of an hundred prudes.

Sir Benjamin. True, Madam; there are Valetudinarians in reputation as well as in constitution, who being conscious of their weak part, avoid the least breath of air, and supply their want of stamina by care and circumspection.

Mrs. Candour. I believe this may be some mistake; you know, Sir Benjamin, very trifling circumstances have often given rise to the most ingenious tales.

Crabtree. Very true; – but odso, Ladies, did you hear of Miss Laetitia Piper's losing her lover and her character at Scarborough. Sir Benjamin, you remember it.

Sir Benjamin. Oh, to be sure, the most whimsical circumstance!

L. Sneerwell. Pray let us hear it.

Crabtree. Why, one evening, at Lady Spadille's assembly, the conversation happened to turn upon the difficulty of breeding Nova Scotia sheep in this country; no, says a lady present, I have seen an instance of it, for a cousin of mine, Miss Laetitia Piper, had one that produced twins. 'What, what', says old Lady Dandizzy, (whom we know is as deaf as a post) 'has Miss Laetitia Piper had twins?' – This, you may easily imagine, set the company in a loud laugh; and the next morning it was everywhere reported, and believed, that Miss Laetitia Piper had actually been brought to bed of a fine boy and girl.

Omnes. Ha, ha, ha, ha.

Crabtree. 'Tis true, upon my honour – Oh, Mr. Surface, how do you do; I hear your uncle, Sir Oliver, is expected in town; sad news upon his arrival, to hear how your brother has gone on.

Joseph. I hope no busy people have already prejudiced his uncle against him – he may reform.

Sir Benjamin. True, he may; for my part, I never thought him so utterly void of principle as people say – and though he has lost all his friends, I am told nobody is better spoken of amongst the Jews.[9]

Crabtree. 'Foregad if the Old Jewry[10] was a ward, Charles would be an Alderman, for he pays as many annuities as the Irish Tontine;[11] and when he is sick, they have prayers for his recovery in all the Synagogues.

Notes

[9] *Jews* an opprobrious name for money-lenders.

[10] *Old Jewry* a district in the City of London best known at this time for the dissenters' chapel of the same name.

[11] *Tontine* an annuities lottery, named after its Italian inventor, in which survivors inherit the contributions of their late co-investors. The Irish government ran such a scheme in the eighteenth century.

SIR BENJAMIN. Yet no man lives in greater splendour. – They tell me, when he entertains his friends, he can sit down to dinner with a dozen of his own securities,[12] have a score of tradesmen waiting in the antechamber, and an officer behind every guest's chair.

JOSEPH. This may be entertaining to you, Gentlemen; – but you pay very little regard to the feelings of a brother.

MARIA. Their malice is intolerable. *(Aside.)* Lady Sneerwell, I must wish you a good morning; I'm not very well. [*Exit Maria.*]

MRS. CANDOUR. She changes colour.

L. SNEERWELL. Do, Mrs. Candour, follow her.

MRS. CANDOUR. To be sure I will; – poor dear girl, who knows what her situation may be? [*Mrs. Candour follows her.*]

L. SNEERWELL. 'Twas nothing, but that she could not bear to hear Charles reflected on, notwithstanding their difference.

SIR BENJAMIN. The young Lady's penchant is obvious.

CRABTREE. Come, don't let this dishearten you – follow her, and repeat some of your odes to her, and I'll assist you.

SIR BENJAMIN. Mr. Surface, I did not come to hurt you, but depend on't your brother is utterly undone.

CRABTREE. Oh! undone as ever man was – can't raise a guinea.

SIR BENJAMIN. Everything is sold, I am told, that was moveable.

CRABTREE. Not a moveable left, except some old bottles, and some pictures, and they seem to be framed in the wainscot, egad.

SIR BENJAMIN. I am sorry to hear also some bad stories of him.

CRABTREE. Oh! he has done many mean things, that's certain.

SIR BENJAMIN. But, however, he's your brother.

CRABTREE. Aye! as he's your brother – we'll tell you more another opportunity. [*Exeunt Crabtree and Sir Benjamin.*]

L. SNEERWELL. 'Tis very hard for them, indeed, to leave a subject they have not quite run down.

JOSEPH. And I fancy, their abuse was no more acceptable to your Ladyship, than to Maria.

L. SNEERWELL. I doubt[13] her affections are further engaged than we imagine; – but the family are to be here this afternoon, so you may as well dine where you are; we shall have an opportunity of observing her further; – in the meantime I'll go and plot mischief, and you shall study. [*Exeunt.*]

SCENE Sir Peter Teazle's House.

SIR PETER. When an old bachelor marries a young wife, what is he to expect? – 'Tis now above six months since my Lady Teazle made me the happiest of men – and I have been the most miserable dog ever since. – We tifted[14] a little going to church, and fairly quarrelled before the bells were done ringing. I was more than once nearly choked with gall during the honeymoon, and had lost every satisfaction in life, before my friends had done wishing me joy. – And yet, I chose with caution a girl bred wholly in the country, who had never known luxury, beyond one silk gown, or

Notes

[12] *securities* persons who have pledged themselves to him as financial security.

[13] *doubt* believe.

[14] *tifted* had a tiff or petty fight.

dissipation beyond the annual gala of a race ball[15] – Yet now, she plays her part in all the extravagant fopperies of the town, with as good a grace as if she had never seen a bush, or a grass plot out of Grosvenor Square.[16] – I am sneered at by all my acquaintance – paragraphed in the newspapers – she dissipates my fortune, and contradicts all my humours. – And yet, the worst of it is, I doubt I love her, or I should never bear all this – but I am determined never to be weak enough to let her know it – No! no! no!

Enter Rowley.

Rowley. Sir Peter, your servant, how do you find yourself to day?

Sir Peter. Very bad, master Rowley, very bad indeed.

Rowley. I'm sorry to hear that – what has happened to make you uneasy since yesterday?

Sir Peter. A pretty question truly to a married man.

Rowley. Sure my Lady is not the cause!

Sir Peter. Why! has any one told you she was dead?

Rowley. Come, come, Sir Peter, notwithstanding you sometimes dispute and disagree, I am sure you love her.

Sir Peter. Aye, master Rowley; but the worst of it is, that in all our disputes and quarrels, she is ever in the wrong, and continues to thwart and vex me; – I am myself the sweetest tempered man in the world, and so I tell her an hundred times a day.

Rowley. Indeed, Sir Peter!

Sir Peter. Yes – and then there's Lady Sneerwell, and the set she meets at her house, encourage her to disobedience; and Maria, my ward, she too presumes to have a will of her own, and refused the man I propose for her; designing, I suppose, to bestow herself and fortune upon that profligate his brother.

Rowley. You know, Sir Peter, I have often taken the liberty to differ in opinion with you, in regard to these two young men; for Charles, my life on't, will retrieve all one day or other. – Their worthy father, my once honoured master, at his years, was full as wild and extravagant as Charles now is; but at his death he did not leave a more benevolent heart to lament his loss.

Sir Peter. You are wrong, master Rowley, you are very wrong; – by their father's will, you know, I became guardian to these young men, which gave me an opportunity of knowing their different dispositions; but their uncle's Eastern liberality soon took them out of my power, by giving them an early independence. – But for Charles, whatever good qualities he might have inherited, they are long since squandered away with the rest of his fortune; – Joseph, indeed, is a pattern for the young men of the age – a youth of the noblest sentiments, and acts up to the sentiments he professes.

Rowley. Well, well, Sir Peter, I shan't oppose your opinion at present, though I am sorry you are prejudiced against Charles, as this may probably be the most critical period of his life, for his uncle, Sir Oliver, is arrived, and now in town.

Sir Peter. What! my old friend, Sir Oliver, is he arrived? I thought you had not expected him this month.

Notes

[15] *race ball* a party associated with an annual horse race.

[16] *Grosvenor Square* one of the grandest residential areas of the time.

ROWLEY. No more we did, Sir, but his passage has been remarkably quick.

SIR PETER. I shall be heartily glad to see him – 'tis sixteen years since old Nol and I met – But does he still enjoin us to keep his arrival a secret from his nephews?

ROWLEY. He does, Sir; and is determined, under a feigned character, to make trial of their different dispositions.

SIR PETER. Ah! there is no need of it, for Joseph, I am sure, is the man. – But hark ye, *Rowley*, does Sir Oliver know that I am married?

ROWLEY. He does, Sir, and intends shortly to wish you joy.

SIR PETER. What, as we wish health to a friend in a consumption. – But I must have him at my house – do you conduct him, *Rowley*, I'll go and give orders for his reception (*going*). We used to rail at matrimony together – he has stood firm to his text. – But Rowley, don't give him the least hint that my wife and I disagree, for I would have him think (Heaven forgive me) that we are a very happy couple.

ROWLEY. Then you must be careful not to quarrel whilst he is here.

SIR PETER. And so we must – but that will be impossible! – Zounds, Rowley, when an old bachelor marries a young wife, he deserves – aye, he deserves – no – the crime carries the punishment along with it.

End of the First Act.

Act II.

SCENE Sir Peter Teazle's House.

Enter Sir Peter *and Lady* Teazle.

SIR PETER. Lady *Teazle*, Lady *Teazle*, I won't bear it.

L. TEAZLE. Very well, Sir *Peter*, you may bear it or not, just as you please; but I know I ought to have my own way in everything, and what's more, I will.

SIR PETER. What, Madam! is there no respect due to the authority of a husband?

L. TEAZLE. Why, don't I know that no woman of fashion does as she is bid after her marriage. – Though I was bred in the country, I'm no stranger to that: if you wanted me to be obedient, you should have adopted me, and not married me – I'm sure you were old enough.

SIR PETER. Aye, there it is – Oons,[17] Madam, what right have you to run me into all this extravagance?

L. TEAZLE. I'm sure I am not more extravagant than a woman of quality ought to be.

SIR PETER. 'Slife,[18] Madam, I'll have no more sums squandered away upon such unmeaning luxuries; you have as many flowers in your dressing room, as would turn the Pantheon[19] into a green house; or make a Fête Champêtre at Christmas.

L. TEAZLE. Lord, Sir *Peter*, am I to blame that flowers don't blow in cold weather; you must blame the climate, and not me – I'm sure, for my part, I wish it was Spring all the year round, and that roses grew under our feet.

SIR PETER. Zounds, Madam, I should not wonder at your extravagance if you had been bred to it – Had you any of these things before you married me?

L. TEAZLE. Lord, Sir *Peter*, how can you be angry at those little elegant expenses?

Notes

[17] *Oons* like *zounds*, a socially acceptable version of "God's wounds," a mild imprecation.

[18] *'Slife* short for "God's life."

[19] *Pantheon* a fashionable London ballroom.

Sir Peter. Had you any of those little elegant expenses when you married me?

L. Teazle. For my part, I think you ought to be pleased your wife should be thought a woman of taste.

Sir Peter. Zounds, Madam, you had no taste when you married me.

L. Teazle. Very true, indeed; and after having married you, I never should pretend to taste again.

Sir Peter. Very well, very well, Madam; you have entirely forgot what your situation was when first I saw you.

L. Teazle. No, no, I have not; a very disagreeable situation it was, or I'm sure I never should have married you.

Sir Peter. You forget the humble state I took you from – the daughter of a poor country Squire – when I came to your father's, I found you sitting at your tambour,[20] in a linen gown, a bunch of keys to your side, and your hair combed smoothly over a roll.

L. Teazle. Yes, I remember very well; – my daily occupations were to overlook the dairy, superintend the poultry, make extracts from the family receipt book, and comb my aunt Deborah's lap dog.

Sir Peter. Oh! I am glad to find you have so good a recollection.

L. Teazle. My evening employments were to draw patterns for ruffles, which I had not materials to make up; play at Pope Joan[21] with the curate; read a sermon to my aunt Deborah, or perhaps be stuck up at an old spinet to strum my father to sleep after a fox-chase.

Sir Peter. Then you was glad to take a ride out behind the butler, upon the old docked coach horse.

L. Teazle. No, no, I deny the butler and the coach horse.

Sir Peter. I say you did. This was your situation – Now, Madam, you must have your coach, vis-à-vis,[22] and three powdered footmen to walk before your chair;[23] and in summer, two white cats[24] to draw you to Kensington Gardens; and instead of your living in that hole in the country, I have brought you home here, made a woman of fortune of you, a woman of quality – in short, Madam, I have made you my wife.

L. Teazle. Well, and there is but one thing more you can now do to add to the obligation, and that is –

Sir Peter. To make you my widow, I suppose.

L. Teazle. Hem! –

Sir Peter. Very well, madam, very well; I am much obliged to you for the hint.

L. Teazle. Why then will you force me to say shocking things to you. But now we have finished our morning conversation, I presume I may go to my engagement at Lady *Sneerwell*'s.

Sir Peter. Lady *Sneerwell*! – a precious acquaintance you have made with her too, and the set that frequent her house. – Such a set, mercy on us! – Many a wretch who has been drawn upon a hurdle,[25] has done less mischief than those barterers of forged lies, coiners of scandal, and clippers of reputation.

L. Teazle. How can you be so severe; I'm sure they are all people of fashion, and very tenacious of reputation.

Notes

20 *tambour* an embroidering hoop.

21 *Pope Joan* a card game named after a fictional female pope.

22 *vis-à-vis* a light carriage in which two people could sit facing each other.

23 *chair* a sedan chair, borne by footmen.

24 *cats* perhaps horses of some description.

25 *drawn upon a hurdle* as a form of torture imposed on convicted criminals.

SIR PETER. Yes, so tenacious of it, they'll not allow it to any but themselves.

L. TEAZLE. I vow, Sir Peter, when I say an ill-natured thing I mean no harm by it, for I take it for granted they'd do the same by me.

SIR PETER. They've made you as bad as any of them.

L. TEAZLE. Yes – I think I bear my part with a tolerable grace –

SIR PETER. Grace! indeed –

L. TEAZLE. Well, but Sir Peter, you know you promised to come.

SIR PETER. Well, I shall just call in to look after my own character.

L. TEAZLE. Then, upon my word, you must make haste after me, or you'll be too late. [*Exit Lady Teazle.*]

SIR PETER. I have got much by my intended expostulation – What a charming air she has! – what a neck, and how pleasingly she shows her contempt of my authority! – Well, though I can't make her love me, 'tis some pleasure to tease her a little, and I think she never appears to such advantage, as when she is doing everything to vex and plague me.

SCENE Lady Sneerwell's House.

Enter Lady *Sneerwell, Crabtree,* Sir *Benjamin, Joseph,* Mrs. *Candour,* and *Maria.*

LADY SNEERWELL. Nay, positively we'll have it.

JOSEPH. Aye, aye, the epigram by all means.

SIR BENJAMIN. Oh! plague on it, it's mere nonsense.

CRABTREE. Faith, Ladies, 'twas excellent for an extempore.

SIR BENJAMIN. But, Ladies, you should be acquainted with the circumstances – You must know that one day last week, as Lady Bab Curricle was taking the dust in Hyde Park, in a sort of duodecimo phaeton,[26] she desires me to write some verses on her ponies; upon which I took out my pocket book, and in a moment produced the following:

> Sure never were seen two such beautiful ponies,
> Other horses are clowns, and these macaronis;[27]
> To give them this title I'm sure can't be wrong,
> Their legs are so slim, and their tails are so long.

CRABTREE. There, Ladies, – done in the crack of a whip – and on horseback too!

JOSEPH. Oh! a very Phoebus mounted –

MRS. CANDOUR. I must have a copy.

Enter Lady Teazle.

L. SNEERWELL. Lady *Teazle*, how do you do, – I hope we shall see Sir Peter.

L. TEAZLE. I believe he will wait on your Ladyship presently.

L. SNEERWELL. Maria, my love, you look grave; come, you shall sit down to piquet with Mr. Surface.

MARIA. I take very little pleasure in cards – but I'll do as your Ladyship pleases.

L. TEAZLE. I wonder he should sit down to cards with Maria – I thought he would have taken an opportunity of speaking to me before Sir Peter came. [*Aside.*]

MRS. CANDOUR. Well, now I'll forswear his society. [*Aside.*]

L. TEAZLE. What's the matter, Mrs. Candour?

Notes

[26] *duodecimo phaeton* a small chariot (after the name for a book printed in a small format).

[27] *macaronis* fashionably and extravagantly dressed gallants.

Mrs. Candour. Why, they are so censorious they won't allow our friend, Miss Vermilion, to be handsome.

L. Sneerwell. Oh, surely she's a pretty woman.

Crabtree. I'm glad you think so.

Mrs. Candour. She has a charming fresh colour.

L. Teazle. Yes, when it is fresh put on.

Mrs. Candour. Well, I'll swear its natural, for I've seen it come and go.

L. Teazle. Yes, it comes at night, and goes again in the morning.

Sir Benjamin. True, Madam, it not only goes and comes, but what's more, egad, her maid can fetch and carry it.

Mrs. Candour. Well, – and what do you think of her sister?

Crabtree. What, Mrs. Evergreen – 'foregad, she's six and fifty if she's a day.

Mrs. Candour. Nay, I'll swear two or three and sixty is the outside – I don't think she looks more.

Sir Benjamin. Oh, there's no judging by her looks, unless we could see her face.

L. Sneerwell. Well, if Mrs. Evergreen does take some pains to repair the ravages of time, she certainly effects it with great ingenuity, and surely that's better than the careless manner in which the widow Oaker chalks her wrinkles.

Sir Benjamin. Nay, now my Lady Sneerwell, you are too severe upon the widow – Come, it is not that she paints so ill, but when she has finished her face, she joins it so badly to her neck, that she looks like a mended statue, in which the connoisseur may see at once, that the head is modern, though the trunk's antique.

Crabtree. What do you think of Miss Simper?

Sir Benjamin. Why she has pretty teeth.

L. Teazle. Yes, and upon that account never shuts her mouth, but keeps it always ajar, as it were, this (*shows her teeth*).

Omnes. Ha, ha, ha, ha.

L. Teazle. And yet, I vow that's better than the pains Mrs. Prim takes to conceal her losses in front; – she draws her mouth till it resembles the aperture of a poor box, and all her words appear to slide out edgeways as it were, thus – 'How do you do madam? – Yes, madam.'

L. Sneerwell. Ha, ha, ha; very well, Lady Teazle – I vow you appear to be a little severe.

L. Teazle. In defence of a friend, you know, it is but just. – But here comes Sir Peter to spoil our pleasantry.

Enter Sir Peter.

Sir Peter. Ladies your servant – mercy upon me! – The whole set – a character dead at every sentence.

Mrs. Candour. They won't allow good qualities to anyone – not even good nature to our friend Mrs. Pursey.

Crabtree. What! the old fat dowager that was at Mrs. Quadrille's last night?

Mrs. Candour. Her bulk is her misfortune; and when she takes such pains to get rid of it, you ought not to reflect on her.

L. Sneerwell. That's very true, indeed.

L. Teazle. Yes, – I'm told she absolutely lives upon acids[28] and small whey, laces herself with pulleys; – often in the hottest day in Summer, you shall see her on a little squat

Notes

[28] *acids* sharp seasonings, such as salt and vinegar.

pony, with her hair plaited and turned up like a drummer's, and away she goes puffing round the ring in a full trot.

SIR PETER. Mercy on me! this is her own relation; a person they dine with twice a week. *(Aside.)*

MRS. CANDOUR. I vow you shan't be so severe upon the dowager; for let me tell you, great allowances are to be made for a woman who strives to pass for a flirt at six and thirty.

L. SNEERWELL. Though surely she's handsome still; and for the weakness in her eyes, considering how much she reads by candlelight, 'tis not to be wondered at.

MRS. CANDOUR. Very true; and for her manner, I think it very graceful, considering she never had any education; for her mother, you know, was a Welsh milliner, and her father a sugar baker at Bristol.

SIR BENJAMIN. Aye, you are both of ye too good-natured.

MRS. CANDOUR. Well, I never will join in the ridicule of a friend; so I tell my cousin Ogle, and ye all know what pretensions she has to beauty.

CRABTREE. She has the oddest countenance – a collection of features from all corners of the globe.

SIR BENJAMIN. She has, indeed, an Irish front.

CRABTREE. Caledonian locks.

SIR BENJAMIN. Dutch nose.

CRABTREE. Austrian lips.

SIR BENJAMIN. The complexion of a Spaniard.

CRABTREE. And teeth à la Chinoise.

SIR BENJAMIN. In short, her face resembles a table d'hôte at Spaw,[29] where no two guests are of a nation.

CRABTREE. Or a Congress at the close of a general war, where every member seems to have a different interest, and the nose and chin are the only parties likely to join issue.

SIR BENJAMIN. Ha, ha, ha.

L. SNEERWELL. Ha, ha, – Well, I vow you are a couple of provoking toads.

MRS. CANDOUR. Well, I vow you shan't carry the laugh so – let me tell you that, Mrs. Ogle.

SIR PETER. Madam, madam, 'tis impossible to stop those good gentlemen's tongues; but when I tell you, Mrs. Candour, that the lady they are speaking of is a particular friend of mine, I hope you will be so good as not to undertake her defence.

L. SNEERWELL. Well said, Sir Peter; but you are a cruel creature, too phlegmatic yourself for a wit, and too peevish to allow it to others.

SIR PETER. True wit, Madam, is more nearly allied to good nature than you are aware of.

L. TEAZLE. True, Sir *Peter*; I believe they are so near a kin that they can never be united.

SIR BENJAMIN. Or rather, Madam, suppose them to be man and wife, one so seldom sees them together.[30]

L. TEAZLE. But Sir *Peter* is such an enemy to scandal, I believe he would have it put down by Parliament.

SIR PETER. 'Foregad, Madam, if they considered the sporting with reputations of as much consequence as poaching on manors, and passed an act for the preservation of fame, they would find many would thank them for the bill.

Notes

[29] *Spaw* Spa, a place in Belgium famous for its curative waters.

[30] This exchange echoes Pope, "Essays on Criticism," 82–3 (p. 681 above).

L. Sneerwell. Oh lud! – Sir Peter would deprive us of our *privileges*.

Sir Peter. Yes, Madam; and none should then have the liberty to kill characters, and run down reputations, but *privileged* old maids, and *disappointed* widows.

L. Sneerwell. Go, you monster!

Mrs. Candour. But surely you would not be so severe on those who only report what they hear?

Sir Peter. Yes, madam, I would have law for them too; and wherever the drawer of the lie was not to be found, the injured party should have a right to come on any of the endorsers.

Crabtree. Well, I verily believe there never was a scandalous story without some foundation.

Sir Peter. Nine out of ten are formed on some malicious invention, or idle representation.

L. Sneerwell. Come, Ladies, shall we sit down to cards in the next room?

Enter a Servant, *who whispers Sir* Peter.

Sir Peter. I'll come directly – I'll steal away unperceived. [*Aside.*]

L. Sneerwell. Sir *Peter*, you're not leaving us.

Sir Peter. beg pardon, Ladies, 'tis particular business, and I must – But I leave my character behind me. [*Exit Sir Peter.*]

Sir Benjamin. Well, certainly Lady Teazle, that Lord of yours is a strange being; I could tell you some stories of him would make you laugh heartily, if he was not your husband.

L. Teazle. Oh, never mind that – This way. [*They walk up and exeunt.*]

Joseph. You take no pleasure in this society.

Maria. How can I? If to raise a malicious smile at the misfortunes and infirmities of those who are unhappy, be a proof of wit and humour, Heaven grant me a double portion of dullness.

Joseph. And yet, they have no malice in their hearts.

Maria. Then it is the more inexcusable, since nothing but an ungovernable depravity of heart, could tempt them to such a practice.

Joseph. And is it possible, Maria, that you can thus feel for others, and yet be cruel to me alone? – Is hope to be denied the tenderest passion?

Maria. Why will you persist to persecute me on a subject on which you have long since known my sentiments.

Joseph. Oh, Maria, you would not be this deaf to me, but that Charles, that libertine, is still a favoured rival.

Maria. Ungenerously urged; but whatever my sentiments are, with regard to that unfortunate young man, be assured I shall not consider myself more bound to give him up, because his misfortunes have lost him the regards – even of a brother – [*Going out.*]

Joseph. Nay, Maria, you shall not leave me with a frown; by all that's honest I swear – (*Kneels, and sees Lady Teazle entering behind*) Ah! Lady Teazle, ah! you shall not stir – (*To Maria*) I have the greatest regard in the world for Lady Teazle, but if Sir Peter was once to suspect –

Maria. Lady Teazle! –

L. Teazle. What is all this, child? You are wanted in the next room. [*Exit Maria*] – What is the meaning of all this? – What! did you take her for me?

Joseph. Why, you must know – Maria – by some means suspecting – the – great regard I entertain for your Ladyship – was – was – threatening – if I did not desist, to acquaint Sir Peter – and I – I – was just reasoning with her –

L. TEAZLE. You seem to have adopted a very tender method of reasoning – pray, do you usually argue on your knees?

JOSEPH. Why, you know, she's but a child, and I thought a little bombast might be useful to keep her silent. – But, my dear Lady Teazle, when will you come and give me your opinion of my library.

L. TEAZLE. Why, I really begin to think it not so proper, and you know I admit you as a lover no farther than fashion dictates.

JOSEPH. Oh, no more; – a mere platonic Cicisbeo,[31] that every Lady is entitled to.

L. TEAZLE. No further – and though Sir Peter's treatment may make me uneasy, it shall never provoke me –

JOSEPH. To the only revenge in your power.

L. TEAZLE. Go, you insinuating wretch – but we shall be missed, let us join the company.

JOSEPH. I'll follow your Ladyship.

L. TEAZLE. Don't stay long, for I promise you Maria shan't come to hear any more of your reasoning. [*Exit Lady Teazle.*]

JOSEPH. A pretty situation I am in – by gaining the wife I shall lose the heiress. – I at first intended to make her Ladyship only the instrument in my designs on Maria, but, – I don't know how it is – I am become her serious admirer. I begin now to wish I had not made a point of gaining so very good a character, for it has brought me into so many confounded rogueries, that I fear I shall be exposed at last. [*Exit Joseph.*]

SCENE Sir Peter Teazle's House.

Enter Sir Oliver *and* Rowley.

SIR OLIVER. Ha, ha, and so my old friend is married at last, eh Rowley, – and to a young wife out of the country, ha, ha, ha. That he should buff[32] to old bachelors so long, and sink into a husband at last.

ROWLEY. But let me beg of you, Sir, not to rally him upon the subject, for he cannot bear it, though he has been married these seven months.

SIR OLIVER. Then he has been just half a year on the stool of repentance. Poor Sir Peter! – But you say he has entirely given up Charles – never sees him, eh.

ROWLEY. His prejudice against him is astonishing, and I believe is greatly aggravated by a suspicion of a connection between Charles and Lady Teazle, and such a report I know has been circulated and kept up, by means of Lady Sneerwell, and a scandalous party who associate at her house; where, as I am convinced, if there is any partiality in the case, that Joseph is the favourite.

SIR OLIVER. Ay, ay, – I know there are a set of mischievous prating gossips, both male and female, who murder characters to kill time, and rob a young fellow of his good name, before he has sense enough to know the value of it: – but I am not to be prejudiced against me nephew by any such, I promise you – No, no, if Charles has done nothing false or mean, I shall compound for[33] his extravagance.

ROWLEY. I rejoice, sir, to hear you say so; and am happy to find the son of my old master has one friend left however.

Notes

[31] *Cicisbeo* the lover or gallant of a married woman.

[32] *buff* swear to; be firm in.

[33] *compound for* settle; come to terms with; condone.

Sir Oliver. What! shall I forget, Master Rowley, when I was at his years myself; – egad, neither my brother or I were very prudent youths, and yet, I believe, you have not seen many better men than your old master was.

Rowley. 'Tis that reflection I build my hopes on – and, my life on't! Charles will prove deserving of your kindness – But here comes Sir Peter.

Enter Sir Peter.

Sir Peter. Where is he? where is Sir Oliver? – Ah, my dear friend, I rejoice to see you! – You are welcome, – indeed you are welcome – you are welcome to England a thousand, – and a thousand times! –

Sir Oliver. Thank you, thank you, Sir Peter – and I am glad to find you so well, believe me.

Sir Peter. Ah, Sir Oliver! – It's sixteen years since last we saw each other – many a bout we have had together in our time!

Sir Oliver. Aye! I have had my share – But what, I find you are married – hey old boy! – Well, well, it can't be helped, and so I wish you joy with all my heart.

Sir Peter. Thank you, thank you – yes, Sir Oliver, I have entered into that happy state – but we won't talk of that now.

Sir Oliver. That's true, Sir Peter, old friends should not begin upon grievances at their first meeting, no, no, no.

Rowley. (*Aside to Sir Oliver.*) Have a care, Sir; – don't touch upon that subject.

Sir Oliver. Well, – so, one of my nephews, I find, is a wild young rogue.

Sir Peter. Oh, my dear friend, I grieve at your disappointment there – Charles is, indeed, a sad libertine – but no matter, Joseph will make you ample amends – everybody speaks well of him.

Sir Oliver. I am very sorry to hear it; he has too good a character to be an honest fellow – everybody speaks well of him! – pshaw – then he has bowed as low to knaves and fools, as to the honest dignity of genius and virtue.

Sir Peter. What the plague! are you angry with Joseph for not making enemies?

Sir Oliver. Why not, if he has merit enough to deserve them.

Sir Peter. Well, well, see him, and you'll be convinced how worthy he is – He's a pattern for all the young men of the age – He's a man of the noblest sentiments.

Sir Oliver. Oh! plague of his sentiments – If he salutes me with a scrap of morality in his mouth I shall be sick directly – but don't however mistake me, Sir Peter, I don't mean to defend Charles's errors; but before I form my judgment of either of them, I intend to make a trial of their hearts, and my friend Rowley and I have planned something for that purpose.

Sir Peter. My life on Joseph's honour.

Sir Oliver. Well, well, give us a bottle of good wine, and we'll drink your Lady's health, and tell you all our schemes.

Sir Peter. *Allons*[34] then.

Sir Oliver. And don't, Sir Peter, be too severe against your old friend's son; – Odds my life, I am not sorry he has run a little out of the course – for my part, I hate to see prudence clinging to the green suckers of youth; 'tis like ivy round the sapling, and spoils the growth of the tree. [*Exeunt omnes.*]

Notes

[34] *Allons* let's go.

Act III.

SCENE Sir Peter's House.

Enter Sir Peter, *Sir* Oliver, *and* Rowley.

SIR PETER. Well, well, we'll see this man first, and then have our wine afterwards. – But Rowley, I don't see the jet[35] of your scheme.

ROWLEY. Why, Sir, this Mr. Stanley was a near relation of their mother's, and formerly an eminent merchant in Dublin – he failed in trade, and is greatly reduced; he has applied by letter to Mr. Surface and Charles for assistance – from the former of whom he has received nothing but fair promises; while Charles, in the midst of his own distresses, is at present endeavouring to raise a sum of money, part of which I know he intends for the use of Mr. Stanley.

SIR OLIVER. Aye – he's my brother's son.

ROWLEY. Now, Sir, we propose, that Sir Oliver shall visit them both, in the character of Mr. Stanley; as I have informed them he has obtained leave of his creditors to wait on his friends in person – and in the younger, believe me, you'll find one, who, in the midst of dissipation and extravagance, has still, as our immortal Bard expresses it, 'a tear for pity, and a hand open as day for melting charity'.[36]

SIR PETER. What signifies his open hand and purse, if he has nothing to give? But where is this person you were speaking of ?

ROWLEY. Below, Sir, waiting your commands – you must know, Sir Oliver, this is a friendly Jew; one who, to do him justice, has done everything in his power to assist Charles – Who waits – (*Enter a Servant*) desire Mr. Moses to walk up. [*Exit Servant.*]

SIR PETER. But how are you sure he'll speak truth?

ROWLEY. Why, Sir, I have persuaded him, there's no prospect of his being paid several sums of money he has advanced for Charles, but through the bounty of Sir Oliver, who he knows is in town; therefore you may depend on his being faithful to his interest – Oh! here comes the honest Israelite –

Enter Moses.

Sir Oliver, this is Mr. *Moses*. – Mr. Moses, this is Sir Oliver.

SIR OLIVER. I understand you have lately had great dealings with my nephew *Charles*.

MOSES. Yes, Sir Oliver – I have done all I could for him – but he was ruined before he came to me for assistance.

SIR OLIVER. That was unlucky truly, for you had no opportunity of showing your talent.

MOSES. None at all; I had not the pleasure of knowing his distresses, till he was some thousands worse than nothing.

SIR OLIVER. Unfortunate indeed! But I suppose you have done all in your power for him.

MOSES. Yes, he knows that – This very evening I was to have brought him a gentleman from the city, who does not know him, and will advance him some monies.

SIR PETER. What! a person that Charles has never borrowed money of before, lend him any in his present circumstances.

Notes

[35] *jet* gist.

[36] 'A tear ... charity' Shakespeare, *2 Henry IV* IV.iv.31–2 (modern editors emend *melting* to *meting* – i.e. giving out).

MOSES. Yes –

SIR OLIVER. What is the gentleman's name?

MOSES. Mr. Premium, of Crutched Friars,[37] formerly a broker.

SIR PETER. Does he know Mr. Premium?

MOSES. Not at all.

SIR PETER. A thought strikes me – suppose, Sir Oliver, you was to visit him in that character; 'twill be much better than the romantic one of an old relation; you will then have an opportunity of seeing Charles in all his glory.

SIR OLIVER. Egad, I like that idea better than the other, and then I may visit Joseph afterwards as old Stanley.

ROWLEY. Gentlemen, this is taking Charles rather unawares; but Moses, you understand Sir Oliver, and I dare say will be faithful.

MOSES. You may depend upon me. – This is very near the time I was to have gone.

SIR OLIVER. I'll accompany you as soon as you please, Moses, but hold – I had forgot one thing – how the plague shall I be able to pass for a Jew?

MOSES. There is no need – the principal is a Christian.

SIR OLIVER. Is he? I am very sorry for it – but then again, am I not too smartly dressed to look like a moneylender?

SIR PETER. Not at all – it would not be out of character if you went in your own chariot; would it Moses?

MOSES. Not in the least.

SIR OLIVER. Well, but how must I talk? There's certainly some cant of usury, or mode of treating; that I ought to know.

SIR PETER. As I take it Sir Oliver, the great point is to be exorbitant in your demands – Eh! Moses?

MOSES. Yes, that's a very great point.

SIR OLIVER. I'll answer for't, I'll not be wanting in that – eight or ten per cent on the loan at least.

MOSES. Oh! if you ask him no more than that, you'll be discovered immediately.

SIR OLIVER. Hey, what the plague – how much then?

MOSES. That depends upon the circumstances – if he appears not very anxious for the supply, you should require only forty or fifty per cent, but if you find him in great distress, and he wants money very bad – you must ask double.

SIR PETER. Upon my word, Sir Oliver, – Mr. Premium I mean – it's a very pretty trade you're learning.

SIR OLIVER. Truly I think so; and not unprofitable.

MOSES. Then you know – you have not the money yourself, but are forced to borrow it of a friend.

SIR OLIVER. Oh! I borrow it for him of a friend – do I?

MOSES. Yes, and your friend's an unconscionable dog – but you can't help that.

SIR OLIVER. Oh! my friend's an unconscionable dog – is he?

MOSES. And then he himself has not the monies by him, but is forced to sell stock at a great loss.

SIR OLIVER. He's forced to sell stock at a great loss, – well, really, that's very kind of him.

Notes

[37] *Crutched Friars* a continuation of Jewry Street (Price).

Sir Peter. But hark'ye, Moses, if Sir Oliver was to rail a little at the annuity bill,[38] don't you think it would have a good effect?

Moses. Very much.

Rowley. And lament that a young man must now come to years of discretion, before he has it in his power to ruin himself.

Moses. Aye! a great pity.

Sir Peter. Yes, and abuse the public for allowing merit to a bill, whose only object was to ruin youth and inexperience, from the rapacious grip of usury, and to give the young heir an opportunity of enjoying his fortune, without being ruined by coming into possession.

Sir Oliver. So, – so, – *Moses* shall give me further instructions as we go together.

Sir Peter. You'll scarce have time to learn your trade, for Charles lives but hard by.

Sir Oliver. Oh! never fear – my tutor appears so able, that though *Charles* lived in the next street, it must be my own fault if I am not a complete rogue before I have turned the corner. [*Exeunt Sir Oliver & Moses.*]

Sir Peter. So Rowley, you would have been partial, and given Charles notice of our plot.

Rowley. No indeed, Sir Peter.

Sir Peter. Well, I see Maria coming, I want to have some talk with her. [*Exit Rowley.*]

Enter Maria

So Maria, What, is Mr. Surface come home with you?

Maria. No, Sir, he was engaged.

Sir Peter. Maria, I wish you were more sensible to his excellent qualities, – does not every time you are in his company convince you of the merit of that amiable young man?

Maria. You know, Sir Peter, I have often told you, that of all the men who have paid me a particular attention, there is not one I would not sooner prefer, than Mr. Surface.

Sir Peter. Aye, aye, this blindness to his merit proceeds from your attachment to that profligate brother of his.

Maria. This is unkind; you know, at your request, I have forborne to see or correspond with him, as I have long been convinced he is unworthy my regard; but while my reason condemns his vices, my heart suggests some pity for his misfortunes.

Sir Peter. Ah! you had best resolve to think of him no more, but give your heart and hand to a worthier object.

Maria. Never to his brother.

Sir Peter. Have a care, Maria, I have not yet made you know what the authority of a guardian is – don't force me to exert it.

Maria. I know, that for a short time I am to obey you as my father, – but must cease to think you so, when you would compel me to be miserable. [*Exit in tears.*]

Sir Peter. Sure never man was plagued as I am; I had not been married above three weeks, before her father, a hale, hearty man, died, – on purpose, I believe, to plague

Notes

[38] *annuity bill* a law passed in May 1777 limiting the interest that could be charged on annuities and voiding contracts made with persons under the age of twenty-one (Price, 301).

me with the care of his daughter: but here comes my helpmate, she seems in mighty good humour; I wish I could tease her into loving me a little.

Enter Lady Teazle.

L. Teazle. What's the matter, Sir Peter? What have you done to Maria? It is not fair to quarrel and I not by.

Sir Peter. Ah! Lady Teazle, it is in your power to put me into good humour at any time.

L. Teazle. Is it? I am glad of it – for I want you to be in a monstrous good humour now; come, do be good humoured, and let me have two hundred pounds.

Sir Peter. What the plague! Can't I be in a good humour without paying for it? – but look always thus, and you shall want for nothing. *(Pulls out a pocketbook.)* There, there's two hundred pounds for you *(going to kiss)* – now seal me a bond for the repayment.

L. Teazle. No, my note of hand will do as well. [*Giving her hand.*]

Sir Peter. Well, well, I must be satisfied with that – you shan't much longer reproach me for not having made you a proper settlement – I intend shortly to surprise you.

L. Teazle. Do you? You can't think, Sir Peter, how good humour becomes you; now you look just as you did before I married you.

Sir Peter. Do I indeed?

L. Teazle. Don't you remember when you used to walk with me under the elms, and tell me stories of what a gallant you were in your youth, and asked me if I could like an old fellow, who could deny me nothing.

Sir Peter. Aye, and you were so attentive and obliging to me then.

L. Teazle. Aye, to be sure I was, and used to take your part against all my acquaintances, and when my cousin Sophy used to laugh at me, for thinking of marrying a man old enough to be my father, and call you an ugly, stiff, formal old bachelor, I contradicted her, and said I did not think you so ugly by any means, and that I dared say, you would make a good sort of a husband.

Sir Peter. That was very kind of you – Well, and you were not mistaken; you have found it so, have not you? – But shall we always live thus happy?

L. Teazle. With all my heart; – I'm – I don't care how soon we leave off quarrelling – provided you will own you are tired first.

Sir Peter. With all my heart.

L. Teazle. Then we shall be as happy as the day is long, and never, never, – never quarrel more.

Sir Peter. Never – never – never – and, let our future contest be, who shall be most obliging.

L. Teazle. Aye! –

Sir Peter. But, my dear Lady Teazle – my love – indeed you must keep a strict watch over your temper – for, you know, my dear, that in all our disputes and quarrels, you always begin first.

L. Teazle. No, no, Sir *Peter*, my dear, 'tis always you that begins.

Sir Peter. No, no, – no such thing.

L. Teazle. Have a care, this is not the way to live happy if you fly out thus.

Sir Peter. No, no, – 'tis you.

L. Teazle. No – 'tis you.

Sir Peter. Zounds! – I say 'tis you.

L. Teazle. Lord! I never saw such a man in my life – just what my cousin Sophy told me.

Sir Peter. Your cousin Sophy is a forward, saucy, impertinent minx.

L. Teazle. You are a very great bear, I am sure, to abuse my relations.

Sir Peter. But I am well enough served for marrying you – a pert, forward, rural coquette; who had refused half the honest squires in the country.

L. Teazle. I am sure I was a great fool for marrying you – a stiff, cropped, dangling old bachelor, who was unmarried at fifty, because nobody would have him.

Sir Peter. You was very glad to have me – you never had such an offer before.

L. Teazle. Oh, yes I had – there was Sir Tivey Terrier, who everybody said would be a better match; for his estate was full as good as yours, and – he has broke his neck since we were married.

Sir Peter. Very – very well, Madam – you're an ungrateful woman; and may plagues light on me, if I ever try to be friends with you again. – You shall have a separate maintenance.

L. Teazle. By all means a separate maintenance.

Sir Peter. Very well, Madam – Oh, very well. Aye, Madam, and I believe the stories of you and *Charles* – of you and *Charles*, Madam, – were not without foundation.

L. Teazle. Take care, Sir *Peter*; take care what you say, for I won't be suspected without a cause, I promise you.

Sir Peter. A divorce!

L. Teazle. Aye, a divorce.

Sir Peter. Aye, zounds! I'll make an example of myself for the benefit of all old bachelors.

L. Teazle. Well, Sir *Peter*, I see you are going to be in a passion, so I'll leave you, and when you come properly to your temper, we shall be the happiest couple in the world; and never – never – quarrel more. Ha, ha, ha. [*Exit.*]

Sir Peter. What the Devil! can't I make her angry neither. – I'll after her – zounds – she must not presume to keep her temper. – No, no, – she may break my heart – but damn it – I'm determined she shan't keep her temper. [*Exit.*]

Scene Charles's House.

Enter Trip, *Sir* Oliver *and* Moses.

Trip. This way, Gentlemen, this way. – *Moses*, what's the gentleman's name?

Sir Oliver. Mr. *Moses*, what's my name?

Moses. Mr. Premium –

Trip. Oh, Mr. Premium, – very well. [*Exit.*]

Sir Oliver. To judge by the servant, one would not imagine the master was ruined. – Sure this was my brother's house.

Moses. Yes, Sir, – Mr. *Charles* bought it of Mr. *Joseph*, with furniture, pictures, etc. just as the old gentleman left it. – Sir *Peter* thought it a great piece of extravagance in him.

Sir Oliver. In my mind, the other's economy in selling it to him, was more reprehensible by half.

Enter Trip.

Trip. Gentlemen, my master is very sorry he has company at present, and cannot see you.

Sir Oliver. If he knew who it was that wanted to see him, perhaps he would not have sent such a message.

Trip. Oh! yes, I told him who it was – I did not forget my little Premium, no, no.

Sir Oliver. Very well, Sir; and pray what may your name be?

Trip. *Trip*, Sir; *Trip* at your service.

Sir Oliver. Very well, Mr. *Trip*, – you have a pleasant sort of a place here, I guess.

TRIP. Pretty well – There are four of us, who pass our time agreeably enough – Our wages, indeed, are but small, and sometimes a little in arrear – We have but fifty guineas a year, and find our own bags and bouquets.

SIR OLIVER. Bags and bouquets! – halters and bastinadoes!

TRIP. Oh, *Moses*, hark'ye – did you get that little bill discounted for me?

SIR OLIVER. Wants to raise money too! – Mercy on me! – He has distresses, I warrant, like a Lord, and affects creditors and duns. [*Aside.*]

MOSES. 'Twas not to be done, indeed, Mr. *Trip*. [*Gives the note.*]

TRIP. No! why I thought when my friend Brush had set his mark on it, it was as good as cash.

MOSES. No, indeed, it would not do.

TRIP. Perhaps you could get it done by way of annuity.

SIR OLIVER. An annuity! – A footman raise money by annuity! – Well said, Luxury, egad. [*Aside.*]

MOSES. Well, but you must insure your place.

TRIP. Oh! I'll insure my life if you please.

SIR OLIVER. That's more than I would your neck. [*Aside.*]

TRIP. Well, but I should like to have it done before this damned registry[39] takes place; one would not wish to have one's name made public.

MOSES. No, certainly – but is there nothing you could deposit?

TRIP. Why, there's none of my master's clothes will fall very soon, I believe; but I can give a mortgage on some of his winter suits, with equity of redemption before Christmas – or a *post obit* [40] on his blue[41] and silver. Now these, with a few pair of point ruffles, by way of security, *(bell rings)* coming, coming. Gentlemen, if you'll walk this way, perhaps I may introduce you now. – *Moses*, don't forget the annuity – I'll insure my place, my little fellow.

SIR OLIVER. If the man is the shadow of the master, this is the temple of dissipation indeed. [*Exeunt Trip, Sir Oliver and Moses.*]

Charles, Careless, *Sir* Toby, *and Gentlemen, discovered drinking.*

CHARLES. Ha, ha, ha, – 'Fore Heaven you are in the right – the degeneracy of the age is astonishing; there are many of our acquaintance who are men of wit, genius, and spirit, but then they won't drink.

CARELESS. True, Charles; they sink into the more substantial luxuries of the table, and quite neglect the bottle.

CHARLES. Right – besides, society suffers by it; for, instead of the mirth and humour that used to mantle over a bottle of Burgundy, their conversation is become as insipid as the Spa water they drink, which has all the pertness of Champagne, without its spirit or flavour.

SIR TOBY. But what will you say to those who prefer play to the bottle? – There's Harry, Dick, and Careless himself, who are under a hazard regimen.

CHARLES. Pshaw! no such thing – What, would you train a horse for the course by keeping him from corn? – Let me throw upon a bottle of Burgundy and I never lose; at least I never feel my loss, and that's the same thing.

Notes

39 The annuities bill (see n. 36 above) also required registration of all grants for life annuities (Price, 301).

40 *post obit* a bond to be paid after the death of person from whom the lender has an expectation of inheritance.

41 *blue* an expensive kind of clothing.

1ST GENT. True; besides, 'tis wine that determines if a man be really in love.

CHARLES. So it is – Fill up a dozen bumpers to a dozen beauties, and she that floats at the top, is the girl that has bewitched you.

CARELESS. But come, Charles, you have not given us your real favourite.

CHARLES. Faith I have withheld her only in compassion to you, for if I give her, you must toast a round of her peers, which is impossible *(sighs)* on earth.

CARELESS. We'll toast some heathen deity, or celestial goddess to match her.

CHARLES. Why then bumpers – bumpers all round – here's Maria – Maria. – *(Sighs.)*

1ST GENT. Maria – Pshaw – give us her surname.

CHARLES. Pshaw – hang her surname, that's too formal to be registered on love's calendar.

1ST GENT. Maria, then – Here's Maria.

SIR TOBY. Maria – come, here's Maria.

CHARLES. Come, Sir *Toby*, have a care; you must give a beauty superlative.

SIR TOBY. Then I'll give you – Here's –

CARELESS. Nay, never hesitate – But Sir Toby has got a song that will excuse him.

OMNES. The song – The song.

Song.

Here's to the maiden of blushing fifteen,
Now to the widow of fifty;
Here's to the flaunting, extravagant quean,
And then to the housewife that's thrifty.
Let the toast pass, drink to the lass,
I warrant she'll find an excuse for the glass.

Here's to the charmer whose dimples we prize,
Now to the damsel with none sir;
Here's to the maid with her pair of blue eyes,
And now to the nymph with but one sir.
Let the toast pass, etc.

Here's to the maid with her bosom of snow,
Now to her that's as brown as a berry;
Here's to the wife with her face full of woe,
And now to the damsel that's merry.
Let the toast pass, etc.

For let them be clumsy, or let then be slim,
Young or ancient I care not a tether;
So fill us a bumper quite up to the brim,
And e'en let us toast them together.
Let the toast pass, etc.

Trip *enters and whispers* Charles.

CHARLES. Gentlemen, I must beg your pardon; *(rising)* I must leave you upon business – Careless, take the chair.

CARELESS. What, this is some wench – but we won't lose you for her.

CHARLES. No, upon my honour – It is only a Jew and a broker that are come by appointment.

CARELESS. A Jew and a broker! we'll have 'em in.

CHARLES. Then desire Mr. Moses to walk in.

TRIP. And little Premium too, Sir.

CARELESS. Aye, Moses and Premium. *(Exit Trip.)* Charles, we'll give the rascals some generous Burgundy.

CHARLES. No, hang it – wine but draws forth the natural qualities of a man's heart, and to make them drink, would only be to whet their knavery.

Enter Sir Oliver *and* Moses.

Walk in, Gentlemen, walk in; Trip give chairs; sit down Mr. Premium, sit down.

MOSES. Glasses, Trip; come, Moses, I'll give you a sentiment. *'Here's success to usury'*. Moses, fill the gentleman a bumper.

MOSES. 'Here's success to usury'.

CARELESS. True, Charles; usury is industry, and deserves to succeed.

SIR OLIVER. Then here's 'All the success it deserves.'

CARELESS. Oh, damn me, Sir, that won't do; you demur to[42] the toast, and shall drink it in a pint bumper at least.

MOSES. Oh, pray Sir, consider Mr. Premium is a gentleman.

CHARLES. And therefore loves good wine, and I'll see justice done to the bottle. – Fill, Moses, a quart.

CHARLES. Pray, consider Gentlemen, Mr. Premium is a stranger.

SIR OLIVER. I wish I was out of their company *(aside)*.

CARELESS. Come along, my boys, if they won't drink with us, we'll not stay with them; the dice are in the next room – You'll settle your business, Charles, and come to us.

CHARLES. Aye, Aye – but Careless, you must be ready, perhaps I may have occasion for you.

CARELESS. Aye, Aye, bill, bond, or annuity, 'tis all the same to me. [*Exit with the rest.*]

MOSES. Mr. Premium is a gentleman of the strictest honour and secrecy, and always performs what he undertakes. – Mr. Premium, this is – *(formally)*.

CHARLES. Pshaw! Hold your tongue – my friend Moses, Sir, is a very honest fellow, but a little slow at expression – I shall cut the matter very short; – I'm an extravagant young fellow that wants to borrow money: and you, as I take it, are a prudent old fellow who has got money to lend – I am such a fool as to give fifty per cent rather than go without it; and you I suppose, are rogue enough to take an hundred if you can get it. And now we understand one another, and may proceed to business without further ceremony.

SIR OLIVER. Exceeding frank, upon my word; I see you are not a man of compliments.

CHARLES. No, Sir.

SIR OLIVER. Sir, I like you the better for it – However, you are mistaken in one thing; I have no money to lend, but I believe I could procure you some from a friend; but then he's a damned unconscionable dog; is he not, Moses?

MOSES. Yes, but you can't help that.

SIR OLIVER. And then, he has not the money by him, but must sell stock at a great loss, must not he, Moses?

MOSES. Yes, indeed – you know I always speak the truth, and scorn to tell a lie.

Notes

[42] *demur to* hesitate over or raise objections to.

CHARLES. Aye, those who speak truth usually do – And Sir, I must pay the difference, I suppose – Why look ye, Mr. Premium, I know that money is not to be had without paying for it.

SIR OLIVER. Well – but what security could you give – you have not any land I suppose.

CHARLES. Not a molehill, nor a twig but what grows in beau-pots[43] out at the windows.

SIR OLIVER. Nor any stock, I presume.

CHARLES. None but livestock, and they are only a few pointers and ponies. – But pray, Sir, are you acquainted with any of my connections?

SIR OLIVER. To say the truth I am.

CHARLES. Then you must have heard that I have a rich old uncle in India, Sir Oliver Surface, from whom I have the greatest expectations.

SIR OLIVER. That you have a wealthy uncle I have heard; but how your expectations will turn out is more, I believe, than you can tell.

CHARLES. Oh yes, I'm told I am a monstrous favourite; and that he intends leaving me everything.

SIR OLIVER. Indeed! this is the first I have heard of it.

CHARLES. Yes, yes, he intends making me his heir – Does he not, Moses?

MOSES. Oh yes, I'll take my oath of that.

SIR OLIVER. Egad they'll persuade me presently that I'm at Bengal. *(Aside.)*

CHARLES. Now, what I propose, Mr. Premium, is to give you a *post obit* on my uncle's life. Though indeed my uncle Oliver has been very kind to me, and upon my soul, I shall be sincerely sorry to hear anything has happened to him.

SIR OLIVER. Not more than I should, I assure you. But the bond you mention happens to be the worst security you could offer me, for I might live to be an hundred, and never recover the principal.

CHARLES. Oh, yes you would, for the moment he dies, you come upon me for the money.

SIR OLIVER. Then I believe I should be the most unwelcome dun you ever had in your life.

CHARLES. What, you are afraid, my little Premium, that my uncle is too good a life.

SIR OLIVER. No, indeed I am not; though I have heard he's as hale, and as hearty, as any man of his years in Christendom.

CHARLES. Oh, there you are misinformed. No – no, poor uncle Oliver! he breaks apace. The climate, Sir, has hurt his constitution, and I'm told he's so much altered of late, that his nearest relations don't know him.

SIR OLIVER. No! ha, ha, ha; so much altered of late, that his nearest relations would not know him. Ha, ha, ha, that's droll egad.

CHARLES. What, you are pleased to hear he is on the decline, my little Premium.

SIR OLIVER. No, I am not, – no, no, no.

CHARLES. Yes you are, for it mends your chance.

SIR OLIVER. But I am told Sir Oliver is coming over, – nay, some say he is actually arrived.

CHARLES. Oh, there you are misinformed again – No – no such thing – he is this moment at Bengal. What! I must certainly know better than you.

Notes

43 *beau-pots* large ornamental vases.

Sir Oliver. Very true, as you say, you must know better than I; though I have it from very good authority – Have I not, Moses?

Moses. Most undoubtedly.

Sir Oliver. But, Sir, as I understand you want a few hundreds immediately; is there nothing that you would dispose of ?

Charles. How do you mean?

Sir Oliver. For instance, now; I have heard your father left behind him a great quantity of massy old plate.

Charles. Yes, but that is gone long ago – Moses can inform you how better than I can.

Sir Oliver. Good lack! all the family race cups, and corporation bowls gone! *(Aside.)* It was also supposed, that his library was one of the most valuable and complete.

Charles. Much too large and valuable for a private gentleman: for my part, I was always of a communicative disposition, and thought it a pity to keep so much knowledge to myself.

Sir Oliver. Mercy on me! knowledge that has run in the family, like an heirloom. *(Aside.)* And pray how may they have been disposed of ?

Charles. O, You must ask the Auctioneer that – I don't believe even Moses can direct you there.

Moses. No – I never meddle with books.

Sir Oliver. The profligate! *(Aside.)* And is there nothing you can dispose of ?

Charles. Nothing – unless you have a taste for old family pictures. I have a whole room full of ancestors above stairs.

Sir Oliver. Why sure you would not sell your relations!

Charles. Every soul of them to the best bidder.

Sir Oliver. Not your great uncles and aunts.

Charles. Ay, and my grandfathers and grandmothers.

Sir Oliver. I'll never forgive him this. *(Aside.)* Why – what – Do you take me for Shylock in the play,[44] to raise money from me on your own flesh and blood.

Charles. Nay, don't be in a passion my little Premium; what is it to you, if you have your money's worth?

Sir Oliver. That's very true, as you say – Well, well, I believe I can dispose of the family canvas. I'll never forgive him this. [*Aside.*]

Enter Careless.

Careless. Come, Charles, what the devil are you doing so long with the broker – we are waiting for you.

Charles. Oh! Careless, you are just come in time, we are to have a sale above stairs – I am going to sell all my ancestors to little Premium.

Careless. Burn your Ancestors.

Charles. No, no, he may do that afterwards if he will. But Careless, you shall be auctioneer.

Careless. With all my heart, I handle a hammer as well as a dice-box – a going – a going.

Charles. Bravo! – And Moses, you shall be appraiser, if we want one.

Moses. Yes, I'll be the appraiser.

Notes

[44] In Shakespeare's *Merchant of Venice* Shylock the money-lender takes a pound of flesh for his surety.

SIR OLIVER. Oh the profligate! [*Aside.*]

CHARLES. But what's the matter, my little Premium? You don't seem to relish this business.

SIR OLIVER. *(Affecting to laugh)* Oh, yes I do, vastly; ha, ha, ha, I – Oh the prodigal! [*Aside.*]

CHARLES. Very true; for when a man wants money, who the devil can he make free with if he can't with his own relations. [*Exit.*]

SIR OLIVER. *(Following)* I'll never forgive him.

Act IV.

Enter Charles, *Sir* Oliver, Careless, *and* Moses.

CHARLES. Walk in, gentlemen, walk in; here they are – the family of the Surfaces up to the Conquest.

SIR OLIVER. And, in my opinion, a goodly collection.

CHARLES. Aye, there they are, done in the true spirit and style of portrait painting, and not like your modern Raphaels, who will make your picture independent of yourself; – no, the great merit of these are, the inveterate likeness they bear to the originals. All stiff and awkward as they were, and like nothing in human nature besides.

SIR OLIVER. Oh, we shall never see such figures of men again.

CHARLES. I hope not – You see, Mr. Premium, what a domestic man I am; here I sit of an evening surrounded by my ancestors – But come, let us proceed to business – To your pulpit, Mr. Auctioneer – Oh, here's a great chair of my father's that seems fit for nothing else.

CARELESS. The very thing – but what shall I do for a hammer, Charles? An Auctioneer is nothing without a hammer.

CHARLES. A hammer! *(looking round)* let's see, what have we here – Sir Richard, heir to Robert – a genealogy in full, egad – Here, Careless, you shall have no common bit of mahogany, here's the family tree, and now you may knock down my ancestors with their own pedigree.

SIR OLIVER. What an unnatural rogue he is! – An ex post facto parricide.[45] *(Aside)*

CARELESS. Gad, Charles, this is lucky, for it will not only serve for a hammer, but a catalogue too if we should want it.

CHARLES. True – Come, here's my great uncle Sir Richard Ravelin, a marvellous good general in his day, – he served in all the Duke of Marlborough's wars, and got that cut over his eye at the battle of Malplaquet[46] – He is not dressed out in feathers like our modern captains, but enveloped in wig and regimentals, as a general should be. – What say you Mr. Premium?

MOSES. Mr. Premium would have you speak.

CHARLES. Why, you shall have him for ten pounds, and I'm sure that's cheap enough for a staff officer.

Notes

[45] *ex post facto parricide* a witticism meaning one who kills a near relative after his death.

[46] *Malplaquet* a battle fought against France on September 11, 1709, in the War of the Spanish Succession; here John Churchill, first Duke of Marlborough (1650–1722), the greatest English general of his time, lost 24,000 thousand troops in an indecisive day of fighting.

SIR OLIVER. Heaven deliver me! his great uncle Sir Richard going for ten pounds – *(Aside)* – Well, Sir, I take him at that price.

CHARLES. Careless, knock down my uncle Richard.

CARELESS. Going, going – a-going – gone.

CHARLES. This is a maiden sister of his, my great aunt Deborah, done by Kneller,[47] thought to be one of his best pictures, and esteemed a very formidable likeness. There she sits, as a shepherdess feeding her flock. – You shall have her for five pounds ten – I'm sure the sheep are worth the money.

SIR OLIVER. Ah, poor aunt Deborah! A woman that set such a value on herself, going for five pounds ten – *(Aside)* – Well, sir, she's mine.

CHARLES. Knock down my aunt Deborah, Careless.

CARELESS. Gone.

CHARLES. Here are two cousins of theirs – Moses, these pictures were done when beaux wore periwigs, and Ladies their own hair.

SIR OLIVER. Yes, truly – head-dresses seem to have been somewhat lower in those days.

CHARLES. Here's a grandfather of my mother's, a judge well known on the western circuit. What would you give for him?

MOSES. Four guineas.

CHARLES. Four guineas! why you don't bid the price of his wig. Premium, you have more respect for the Wool Sack;[48] do let me knock him down at fifteen.

SIR OLIVER. By all means.

CARELESS. Gone.

CHARLES. Here are two brothers, William and Walter Blunt, Esqrs. both members of Parliament, and great speakers; and what's very extraordinary, I believe this is the first time they were ever bought or sold.

SIR OLIVER. That's very extraordinary, indeed! – I'll take them at your own price, for the honour of Parliament.

CHARLES. Well said, Premium.

CARELESS. I'll knock 'em down at forty pounds – Going – going – gone.

CHARLES. Here's a jolly, portly fellow; I don't know what relation he is to the family, but he was formerly mayor of Norwich,[49] let's knock him down at eight pounds.

SIR OLIVER. No. I think six is enough for a mayor.

CHARLES. Come, come, make it guineas, and I'll throw you the two aldermen into the bargain.

SIR OLIVER. They are mine.

CHARLES. Careless, knock down the mayor and the aldermen.

CARELESS. Gone.

CHARLES. But hang it, we shall be all day at this rate; come, come, give me three hundred pounds, and take all on this side the room in a lump. – That will be the best way.

SIR OLIVER. Well, well, anything to accommodate you; they are mine. – But there's one portrait you have always passed over.

CARELESS. What, that little ill-looking fellow over the settee.

Notes

47 *Kneller* Godfrey Kneller (1646–1723), greatest portrait painter of his time.

48 *Wool Sack* the ceremonial seat of judges summoned to the House of Lords; figuratively, the office of judge.

49 *Norwich* the name of the town was varied to suit the place of performance (Price).

Sir Oliver. Yes, sir, 'tis that I mean – but I don't think him so ill-looking a fellow by any means.

Charles. That's the picture of my uncle Oliver – before he went abroad it was done, and is esteemed a very great likeness.

Careless. That's your uncle Oliver! Then in my opinion you will never be friends, for he is one of the most stern looking rogues I ever beheld; he has an unforgiving eye, and a damned disinheriting countenance. Don't you think so, little Premium?

Sir Oliver. Upon my soul I do not, sir; I think it as honest a looking face as any in the room, dead or alive. – But I suppose your uncle Oliver goes with the rest of the lumber.

Charles. No, hang it, the old gentleman has been very good to me, and I'll keep his picture as long as I have a room to put it in.

Sir Oliver. The rogue's my nephew after all – I forgive him everything. *(Aside)* But sir, I have somehow taken a fancy to that picture.

Charles. I am sorry for it, master broker, for you certainly won't have it – What the devil, have you not got enough of the family?

Sir Oliver. I forgive him everything. *(Aside)* Look, sir, I am a strange sort of a fellow, and when I take a whim in my head I don't value money: I'll give you as much for that as for all the rest.

Charles. Prithee don't be troublesome – I tell you I won't part with it, and there's an end on it.

Sir Oliver. How like his father the dog is – I did not perceive it before, but I think I never saw so strong a resemblance. *(Aside)* Well, sir, here's a draft for your sum. *(giving a bill.)*

Charles. Why this bill is for eight hundred pounds.

Sir Oliver. You'll not let Sir Oliver go, then.

Charles. No, I tell you, once for all.

Sir Oliver. Then never mind the difference, we'll balance that some other time – but give me your hand, *(presses it)* you are a damned honest fellow, Charles – O lord! I beg pardon, Sir, for being so free – come along Moses.

Charles. But hark'ye, Premium, you'll provide good lodgings for these gentlemen. *(Going.)*

Sir Oliver. I'll send for 'em in a day or two.

Charles. And pray let it be a genteel conveyance, for I assure you most of 'em have been used to ride in their own carriages.

Sir Oliver. I will for all but Oliver.

Charles. For all but the honest little Nabob.

Sir Oliver. You are fixed on that.

Charles. Peremptorily.

Sir Oliver. Ah the dear extravagant dog! *(Aside)* Good day, Sir. Come, Moses. – Now let me see who dares call him profligate. [*Exit with Moses.*]

Careless. Why, Charles, this is the very prince of Brokers.

Charles. I wonder where Moses got acquainted with so honest a fellow. – But, Careless, step into the company; I'll wait on you presently, I see old Rowley coming.

Careless. But hark'ye, Charles, don't let that fellow make you part with any of that money to discharge musty old debts. Tradesmen, you know, are the most impertinent people in the world.

Charles. True, and paying them would only be encouraging them.

Careless. Well, settle your business, and make what haste you can. [*Exit.*]

Charles. Eight hundred pounds! Two thirds of this are mine by right – five hundred and thirty odd pounds! – Gad, I never knew till now, that my ancestors were such valuable acquaintance. – Kind ladies and gentlemen, I am your very much obliged, most grateful humble servant. *(Bowing to the pictures.)*

Enter Rowley.

Ah! old Rowley, you are just come in time to take leave of your old acquaintance.

Rowley. Yes, sir; I heard they were going – But how can you support such spirits under all your misfortunes?

Charles. That's the cause, Master *Rowley*; my misfortunes are so many, that I can't afford to part with my spirits.

Rowley. And can you really take leave of your ancestors with so much unconcern.

Charles. Unconcern! what, I suppose you are surprised that I am not more sorrowful at losing the company of so many worthy friends. It is very distressing to be sure; but you see, they never move a muscle, then why the Devil should I?

Rowley. Ah, dear Charles! –

Charles. But come, I have no time for trifling; – here, take this bill and get it changed, and carry an hundred pounds to poor Stanley, or we shall have somebody call that has a better right to it.

Rowley. Ah, Sir, I wish you would remember the proverb –

Charles. 'Be just before you are generous.' – Why so I would if I could, but justice is an old, lame, hobbling beldam, and I can't get her to keep pace with generosity for the soul of me.

Rowley. Do, dear Sir, reflect.

Charles. That's very true, as you say – but *Rowley*, while I have, by Heavens I'll give – so damn your morality, and away to old Stanley with the money. [*Exeunt.*]

Enter Sir Oliver *and* Moses.

Moses. Well, Sir, I think, as Sir Peter said, you have seen Mr. Charles in all his glory – 'tis great pity he's so extravagant.

Sir Oliver. True – but he would not sell my picture. –

Moses. And loves wine and women so much.

Sir Oliver. But he would not sell my picture. –

Moses. And games so deep.

Sir Oliver. But he would not sell my picture. – Oh, here comes Rowley.

Enter Rowley.

Rowley. Well, Sir, I find you have made a purchase.

Sir Oliver. Yes, our young rake has parted with his ancestors like old tapestry.

Rowley. And he has commissioned me to return you an hundred pounds of the purchase money, but under your fictitious character of old Stanley. I saw a tailor and two hosiers dancing attendance, who, I know, will go unpaid, and the hundred pounds would just satisfy them.

Sir Oliver. Well, well, I'll pay his debts and his benevolence too. – But now, I'm no more a broker, and you shall introduce me to the elder brother as old Stanley.

Enter Trip.

Trip. Gentlemen, I'm sorry I was not in the way to show out. Hark'ye Moses. [*Exit with Moses.*]

Sir Oliver. There's a fellow, now – Will you believe it, that puppy intercepted the Jew on our coming, and wanted to raise money before he got to his master.

Rowley. Indeed!

SIR OLIVER. And they are now planning an annuity business – Oh, Master Rowley, in my time servants were content with the follies of their masters, when they were worn a little threadbare; but now they have their vices, like their birthday clothes,[50] with the gloss on. [*Exeunt.*]

SCENE the Apartments of Joseph Surface.

Enter Joseph *and a* Servant.

JOSEPH. No letter from Lady Teazle.

SERVANT. No, Sir.

JOSEPH. I wonder she did not write if she could not come – I hope Sir Peter does not suspect me – but Charles's dissipation and extravagance are great points in my favour *(Knocking at the door)* – See if it is her.

SERVANT. 'Tis Lady Teazle, Sir; but she always orders her chair to the milliner's in the next street.

JOSEPH. Then draw that screen – my opposite neighbour is a maiden lady of so curious a temper – you need not wait. *(Exit Servant.)* – My Lady Teazle, I'm afraid, begins to suspect my attachment to Maria; but she must not be acquainted with that secret till I have her more in my power.

Enter Lady Teazle.

L. TEAZLE. What, sentiment in soliloquy! – Have you been very impatient now? Nay, you look so grave, – I assure you I came as soon as I could.

JOSEPH. Oh, Madam, punctuality is a species of constancy – a very unfashionable custom among ladies.

L. TEAZLE. Nay, now you wrong me; I'm sure you'd pity me if you knew my situation – *(both sit)* – Sir Peter really grows so peevish, and so ill-natured, there's no enduring him; and then, to suspect me with Charles. –

JOSEPH. I'm glad my scandalous friends keep up that report. *(Aside.)*

L. TEAZLE. For my part, I wish Sir Peter to let Maria marry him – Wouldn't you, Mr. Surface?

JOSEPH. *(Aside.)* Indeed I would not. – Oh, to be sure; and then my dear Lady Teazle would be convinced how groundless her suspicions were, of my having any thoughts of the silly girl.

L. TEAZLE. Then, there's my friend Lady Sneerwell has propagated malicious stories about me – and what's very provoking, all too without the least foundation.

JOSEPH. Ah! there's the mischief; – for when a scandalous story is believed against me, there's no comfort like the consciousness of having deserved it.

L. TEAZLE. And to be continually censured and suspected, when I know the integrity of my own heart – it would almost prompt me to give him some grounds for it.

JOSEPH. Certainly, – for when a husband grows suspicious, and withdraws his confidence from his wife, it then becomes a part of her duty to endeavour to outwit him. – You owe it to the natural privilege of your sex.

L. TEAZLE. Indeed!

JOSEPH. Oh yes; for your husband should never be deceived in you, and you ought to be frail in compliment to his discernment.

Notes

[50] *birthday clothes* fancy attire for display on the birthday of the King.

L. Teazle. This is the newest doctrine.

Joseph. Very wholesome, believe me.

L. Teazle. So, the only way to prevent his suspicions, is to give him cause for them.

Joseph. Certainly.

L. Teazle. But then, the consciousness of my innocence. –

Joseph. Ah, my dear Lady Teazle, 'tis that consciousness of your innocence that ruins you. – What is it that makes you imprudent in your conduct, and careless of the censures of the world? The consciousness of your innocence. – What is it makes you so regardless of forms, and inattentive to your husband's peace? – Why, the consciousness of your innocence – Now, my dear Lady Teazle, if you could only be prevailed upon to make a trifling *faux-pas*, you can't imagine how circumspect you would grow.

L. Teazle. Do you think so?

Joseph. Depend upon it. – Your case at present, my dear Lady Teazle, resembles that of a person in a plethora[51] – you are absolutely dying of too much health.

L. Teazle. Why, indeed, if my understanding could be convinced.

Joseph. Your understanding! – Oh yes, your understanding *should* be convinced. Heaven forbid that I should persuade you to anything you thought wrong. No, no, I have too much honour for that.

L. Teazle. Don't you think you may as well leave honour out of the question? *(Both rise.)*

Joseph. Ah, I see, Lady Teazle, the effects of your country education still remain.

L. Teazle. They do, indeed, and I begin to find myself imprudent; and if I should be brought to act wrong, it would be sooner from Sir Peter's ill treatment of me, than from your honourable logic, I assure you.

Joseph. Then by this hand, which is unworthy of – *(kneeling, a Servant enters.)* – What do you want, you scoundrel?

Servant. I beg pardon, sir – I thought you would not choose Sir Peter should come up.

Joseph. Sir Peter!

L. Teazle. Sir Peter! Oh, I'm undone! – What shall I do? Hide me somewhere, good Mr. Logic.

Joseph. Here, here, behind this screen, *(She runs behind the screen)* and now reach me a book. *(Sits down and reads.)*

Enter Sir Peter.

Sir Peter. Aye, there he is, ever improving himself – Mr. Surface, Mr. Surface.

Joseph. *(Affecting to gape.)* Oh, Sir Peter! – I rejoice to see you – I was got over a sleepy book here – I am vastly glad to see you – I thank you for this call – I believe you have not been here since I finished my library – Books, books you know, are the only thing I am a coxcomb in.

Sir Peter. Very pretty, indeed, – why even your screen is a source of knowledge – hung round with maps I see.

Joseph. Yes, I find great use in that screen.

Sir Peter. Yes, yes, so you must when you want to find anything in a hurry.

Joseph. Yes, or to hide anything in a hurry. [*Aside.*]

Sir Peter. But, my dear friend, I want to have some private talk with you.

Notes

51 *plethora* an overabundance of blood.

JOSEPH. You need not wait. [*Exit Servant.*]

SIR PETER. Pray sit down – *(both sit)* – My dear friend, I want to impart to you some of my distresses. – In short, Lady Teazle's behaviour of late has given me very great uneasiness. She not only dissipates and destroys my fortune, but I have strong reasons to believe she has formed an attachment elsewhere.

JOSEPH. I am unhappy to hear it.

SIR PETER. Yes, and between you and me, I believe I have discovered the person.

JOSEPH. You alarm me exceedingly.

SIR PETER. I knew you would sympathize with me.

JOSEPH. Believe me, Sir Peter, such a discovery would affect me – just as much as it does you.

SIR PETER. What a happiness to have a friend we can trust, even with our family secrets – Can't you guess who it is?

JOSEPH. I haven't the most distant idea. – It can't be Sir Benjamin Backbite.

SIR PETER. No, no, – What do you think of Charles?

JOSEPH. My brother! impossible! – I can't think he would be capable of such baseness and ingratitude.

SIR PETER. Ah, the goodness of your own mind makes you slow to believe such villainy.

JOSEPH. Very true, Sir Peter. – The man who is conscious of the integrity of his own heart, is ever slow to credit another's baseness.

SIR PETER. And yet, that the son of my old friend should practise against the honour of my family.

JOSEPH. Aye, there's the case, Sir Peter, – when ingratitude barbs the dart of injury, the wound feels double smart.

SIR PETER. What noble sentiments! – He never used a sentiment, ungrateful boy! that I acted as guardian to, and who was brought up under my eye; and I never in my life refused him – my advice.

JOSEPH. I don't know, Sir Peter, – he may be such a man – if it be so, he is no longer a brother of mine; I renounce him. I disclaim him. – For the man who can break through the laws of hospitality, and seduce the wife or daughter of his friend, deserves to be branded as a pest to society.

SIR PETER. And yet, Joseph, if I was to make it public, I should only be sneered and laughed at.

JOSEPH. Why, that's very true – No, no, you must not make it public; people would talk. –

SIR PETER. Talk, – they'd say it was all my own fault; an old doting bachelor, to marry a young giddy girl. They'd paragraph me in the newspapers, and make ballads on me.

JOSEPH. And yet, Sir Peter, I can't think that my Lady Teazle's honour –

SIR PETER. Ah, my dear friend, what's her honour, opposed against the flattery of a handsome young fellow. – But Joseph, she has been upbraiding me of late, that I have not made her a settlement and I think, in our last quarrel, she told me she should not be very sorry if I was dead. Now, I have brought drafts of two deeds for your perusal, and she shall find, if I was to die, that I have not been unattentive to her welfare while living. By the one, she will enjoy eight hundred pounds a year during my life; and by the other, the bulk of my fortune after my death.

JOSEPH. This conduct is truly generous. – I wish it mayn't corrupt my pupil. [*Aside.*]

SIR PETER. But I would not have her as yet acquainted with the least mark of my affection.

JOSEPH. Nor I – if I could help it. [*Aside.*]

SIR PETER. And now I have unburdened myself to you, let us talk over your affair with Maria.

JOSEPH. Not a syllable upon the subject now. *(alarmed)* – Some other time; I am too much affected by your affairs, to think of my own. For, the man who can think of his own happiness, while his friend is in distress, deserves to be hunted as a monster to society.

SIR PETER. I am sure of your affection for her.

JOSEPH. Let me entreat you, Sir Peter. –

SIR PETER. And though you are so averse to Lady Teazle's knowing it, I assure you she is not your enemy, and I am sensibly chagrined you have made no further progress.

JOSEPH. Sir *Peter*, I must not hear you – The man who – *(Enter Servant)* What do you want sirrah?

SERVANT. Your brother, Sir, is at the door talking to a gentleman; he says he knows you are at home, that Sir Peter is with you, and he must see you.

JOSEPH. I'm not at home.

SIR PETER. Yes, yes, you shall be at home.

JOSEPH. *(After some hesitation)* Very well, let him come up. [*Exit Servant.*]

SIR PETER. Now, *Joseph*, I'll hide myself, and do you tax him about the affair with my Lady Teazle, and so draw the secret from him.

JOSEPH. O fie! Sir Peter, – what, join in a plot to trepan[52] my brother!

SIR PETER. Oh aye, so serve your friend; – besides, if he is innocent, as you say he is, it will give him an opportunity to clear himself, and make me very happy. Hark, I hear him coming – Where shall I go? – Behind this screen – What the devil! here has been one listener already, for I'll swear I saw a petticoat.

JOSEPH. *(Affecting to laugh)* It's very ridiculous – ha! ha! ha! – a ridiculous affair, indeed – ha! ha! ha! – Hark ye, Sir Peter *(pulling him aside)* though I hold a man of intrigue to be a most despicable character, yet you know it does not follow, that one is to be an absolute Joseph[53] either. Hark ye, 'tis a little French Milliner, who calls upon me sometimes, and hearing you were coming, and having some character to lose, she slipped behind the screen.

SIR PETER. A French Milliner! *(smiling)* cunning rogue! Joseph – Sly rogue – But zounds, she has overheard everything that has passed about my wife.

JOSEPH. Oh, never fear – Take my word it will never go farther for her.

SIR PETER. Won't it?

JOSEPH. No, depend upon it.

SIR PETER. Well, well, if it will go no further – but – where shall I hide myself?

JOSEPH. Here, here, slip into this closet, and you may overhear every word.

L. TEAZLE. Can I steal away. *(Peeping.)*

JOSEPH. Hush! hush! don't stir.

SIR PETER. Joseph, tax him home. *(Peeping.)*

JOSEPH. In, in my dear Sir Peter.

L. TEAZLE. Can't you lock the closet door?

JOSEPH. Not a word – you'll be discovered.

SIR PETER. Joseph, don't spare him.

JOSEPH. For heaven's sake lie close – A pretty situation I am in, to part man and wife in this manner. [*Aside.*]

SIR PETER. You're sure the little French Milliner won't blab?

Notes

[52] *trepan* entrap.

[53] *Joseph* the biblical personage who refuses his master's wife's invitation to adultery (Genesis 39).

Enter Charles.

CHARLES. Why, how now, brother, your fellow denied you; they said you were not at home. – What, have you had a Jew or a wench with you?

JOSEPH. Neither, brother, neither.

CHARLES. But where's Sir Peter? I thought he was with you.

JOSEPH. He was, brother; but hearing you was coming, he left the house.

CHARLES. What, was the old fellow afraid I wanted to borrow money of him?

JOSEPH. Borrow! no brother; but I am sorry to hear you have given that worthy man cause for great uneasiness.

CHARLES. Yes, I am told I do that to a great many worthy men – But how do you mean, brother?

JOSEPH. Why, he thinks you have endeavoured to alienate the affections of Lady Teazle.

CHARLES. Who, I alienate the affections of Lady Teazle! – Upon my word he accuses me very unjustly. What? has the old gentleman found out that he has got a young wife, or what is worse, has the Lady found out she has got an old husband?

JOSEPH. For shame, brother.

CHARLES. 'Tis true, I did once suspect her Ladyship had a partiality for me, but upon my soul I never gave her the least encouragement, for you know my attachment was to Maria.

JOSEPH. This will make Sir Peter extremely happy – But if she had a partiality for you, sure you would not have been base enough –

CHARLES. Why, look ye, Joseph, I hope I shall never deliberately do a dishonourable action; but if a pretty woman should purposely throw herself in my way, and that pretty woman should happen to be married to a man old enough to be her father. –

JOSEPH. What then?

CHARLES. Why then, I believe I should – have occasion to borrow a little of your morality, brother.

JOSEPH. Oh fie, brother – The man who can jest –

CHARLES. Oh, that's very true, as you were going to observe. – But *Joseph*, do you know that I am surprised at your suspecting me with Lady *Teazle*, I thought you was always the favourite there.

JOSEPH. Me!

CHARLES. Why yes, I have seen you exchange such significant glances.

JOSEPH. Pshaw!

CHARLES. Yes I have; and don't you remember when I came here, and caught you and her at –

JOSEPH. I must stop him *(Aside.) (Stops his mouth)* Sir Peter has overheard every word that you have said.

CHARLES. Sir Peter! where is he? – What? in the closet – 'Foregad I'll have him out.

JOSEPH. No, no. *(Stopping him)*

CHARLES. I will – Sir *Peter* Teazle, come into court. *(Enter Sir Peter)* What, my old guardian turn inquisitor, and take evidence incog.[54]

Notes

[54] *incog* incognito; concealed.

Sir Peter. Give me your hand, – I won, my dear boy; I have suspected you wrongfully, but you must not be angry with Joseph; it was all my plot, and I shall think of you as long as I live for what I overheard.

Charles. Then 'tis well you did not hear more. Is it not, Joseph?

Sir Peter. What? you would have retorted on Joseph, would you?

Charles. And yet you might as well have suspected him as me. Might not he, Joseph?

Enter Servant.

Servant. *(Whispering Joseph)* – Lady Sneerwell, Sir, is just coming up, and says she must see you.

Joseph. Gentlemen, I must beg your pardon, I have company waiting for me, give me leave to conduct you downstairs.

Charles. No, no, speak to 'em in another room; I have not seen Sir Peter a great while, and I want to talk with him.

Joseph. Well, I'll send away the person and return immediately. Sir Peter, not a word of the little French Milliner. [*Exit.*]

Sir Peter. Ah, Charles, what a pity it is you don't associate more with your brother; we might then have some hopes of your reformation; he's a young man of such sentiments. – Ah, there's nothing in the world so noble as a man of sentiment.

Charles. Oh, he's too moral by half, and so apprehensive of his good name, that, I dare say, he would as soon let a priest into his house as a wench.

Sir Peter. No, no, you accuse him wrongfully – Though *Joseph* is not a rake, he is no saint.

Charles. Oh! a perfect anchorite – a young hermit.

Sir Peter. Hush, hush; don't abuse him, or he may chance to hear of it again.

Charles. Why, you won't tell him, will you?

Sir Peter. No, no, but – I have a great mind to tell him *(Aside)* – *(Seems to hesitate)* – Hark'ye, Charles, have you a mind for a laugh at Joseph?

Charles. I should like it of all things – let's have it.

Sir Peter. Gad I'll tell him – I'll be even with Joseph for discovering me in the closet. – *(Aside)* – Hark'ye, Charles, he had a girl with him when I called.

Charles. Who, Joseph? impossible!

Sir Peter. Yes, a little French Milliner *(takes him to the front)* and the best of the joke is, she is now in the room.

Charles. The devil she is – Where?

Sir Peter. Hush, hush – behind the screen.

Charles. I'll have her out.

Sir Peter. No, no, no, no.

Charles. Yes.

Sir Peter. No.

Charles. By the Lord I will – So now for it. *Both run up to the screen – screen falls, at the same time Joseph enters*

Charles. Lady Teazle, by all that's wonderful!

Sir Peter. Lady Teazle, by all that's horrible!

Charles. Sir Peter, this is the smartest little French Milliner I ever saw. – But pray what's the meaning of all this? You seem to have been playing at hide and seek here, and for my part, I don't know who's in or who's out of the secret. – Madam, will you please to explain? – Not a word! – Brother, is it your pleasure to illustrate?[55] – Morality dumb too! – Well, though I can make nothing of it, I suppose you perfectly understand one another, good folks, and so I'll leave you. Brother, I am sorry you have given that worthy man so much cause for uneasiness – Sir Peter, there's nothing in the world so noble as a man of sentiment. – Ha, ha, ha! [*Exit.*]

JOSEPH. Sir Peter, notwithstanding appearances are against me if – if you'll give me leave – I'll explain everything to your satisfaction.

SIR PETER. If you please, Sir.

JOSEPH. Lady *Teazle* knowing my – Lady Teazle – I say – knowing my pretensions – to your ward – Maria – and – Lady Teazle – I say – knowing the jealousy of my – your temper – she called in here – in order that she – that I – might explain – what these pretensions were – And – hearing you were coming – and – as I said before – knowing the jealousy of your temper – she – my Lady Teazle – I say – went behind the screen – and – This is a full and clear account of the whole affair.

SIR PETER. A very clear account truly! and I dare say the Lady will vouch for the truth of every word of it.

LADY TEAZLE. *(Advancing)* For not one syllable, Sir Peter.

SIR PETER. What the devil! don't you think it worth your while to agree in the lie.

LADY TEAZLE. There's not one word of truth in what that gentleman has been saying.

JOSEPH. Zounds, Madam, you won't ruin me?

LADY TEAZLE. Stand out of the way, Mr. Hypocrite. I'll speak for myself.

SIR PETER. Aye, aye, – let her alone – she'll make a better story of it than you did.

LADY TEAZLE. I came here with no intention of listening to his addresses to Maria, and even ignorant of his pretensions; but seduced by his insidious arts, at least to listen to his addresses, if not to sacrifice your honour, as well as my own, to his unwarrantable desires.

SIR PETER. Now I believe the truth is coming indeed.

JOSEPH. What? is the woman mad?

LADY TEAZLE. No, sir, she has recovered her senses. Sir Peter, I cannot expect you will credit me; but the tenderness you expressed for me, when I am certain you did not know I was within hearing, has penetrated so deep into my soul, that could I have escaped the mortification of this discovery, my future life should have convinced you of my sincere repentance. As for that smooth-tongued hypocrite, who would have seduced the wife of his too-credulous friend, while he pretended an honourable passion for his ward, I now view him in so despicable a light, that I shall never again respect myself for having listened to his addresses. [*Exit.*]

JOSEPH. Sir Peter – Notwithstanding all this, Heaven is my witness –

SIR PETER. That you are a villain – and so I'll leave you to your meditations –

JOSEPH. Nay, Sir Peter, you must not leave me – The man who shuts his ears against conviction –[56]

SIR PETER. Oh, damn your sentiments – damn your sentiments – [*Exit. Joseph following.*]

Notes

[55] *illustrate* explain; explicate.

[56] *The man who shuts his ears against conviction* a hackneyed phrase from the language of sermons.

Act V.

SCENE Joseph Surface's Apartments.

Enter Joseph *and a* Servant.

JOSEPH. Mr. Stanley! – why should you think I would see Mr. Stanley; you know well enough he comes entreating for something.

SERVANT. They let him in before I knew of it; and old Rowley is with him.

JOSEPH. Pshaw, you blockhead; I am so distracted with my own misfortunes, I am not in a humour to speak to anyone – but show the fellow up. [*Exit Servant.*] Sure fortune never played a man of my policy such a trick before – My character ruined with Sir *Peter* – my hopes of *Maria* lost – I'm in a pretty humour to listen to poor relations truly. – I shan't be able to bestow even a benevolent sentiment on old Stanley. Oh, here he comes; I'll retire, and endeavour to put a little charity in my face however. [*Exit.*]

Enter Sir Oliver *and* Rowley.

SIR OLIVER. What, does he avoid us? That was him, was it not?

ROWLEY. Yes, Sir; but his nerves are too weak to bear the fight of a poor relation, I should have come first to break the matter to him.

SIR OLIVER. A plague of his nerves – yet this is he whom Sir Peter extols as a man of a most benevolent way of thinking.

ROWLEY. Yes – he has as much speculative benevolence as any man in the kingdom, though he is not so sensual as to indulge himself in the exercise of it.

SIR OLIVER. Yet he has a string of sentiments, I suppose, at his fingers' ends.

ROWLEY. And his favourite one is, 'That charity begins at home'.

SIR OLIVER. And his, I presume, is of that domestic sort, which never stirs abroad at all.

ROWLEY. Well, Sir, I'll leave you to introduce yourself, as old Stanley; I must be here again to announce you in your real character.

SIR OLIVER. True – and you'll afterwards meet me at Sir *Peter*'s.

ROWLEY. Without losing a moment. [*Exit Rowley.*]

SIR OLIVER. Here he comes – I don't like the complaisance of his features.

Enter Joseph.

JOSEPH. Sir, your most obedient; I beg pardon for keeping you a moment – Mr. Stanley, I presume.

SIR OLIVER. At your service, Sir.

JOSEPH. Pray be seated, Mr. Stanley, I entreat you, Sir.

SIR OLIVER. Dear Sir, there's no occasion. Too ceremonious by half. [*Aside.*]

JOSEPH. Though I have not the pleasure of your acquaintance, I am very glad to see you look so well. – I think, Mr. Stanley, you was nearly related to my mother.

SIR OLIVER. I was, Sir; so nearly, that my present poverty I fear may do discredit to her wealthy children; else I would not presume to trouble you now.

JOSEPH. Ah, Sir, don't mention that – For the man who is in distress has ever a right to claim kindred with the wealthy; I am sure I wish I was of that number, or that it was in my power to afford you even a small relief.

SIR OLIVER. If your uncle Sir Oliver was here, I should have a friend.

JOSEPH. I wish he was, Sir, you should not want an advocate with him, believe me.

SIR OLIVER. I should not need one. My distresses would recommend me. But I imagined his bounty had enabled you to be the agent of his charities.

JOSEPH. Ah, Sir, you are mistaken; avarice, avarice, Mr. Stanley, is the vice of age; to be sure it has been spread abroad that he has been very bountiful to me, but without the least provocation, though I never choose to contradict the report.

SIR OLIVER. And has he never remitted you bullion, rupees, or pagodas?

JOSEPH. Oh, dear Sir, no such thing. I have indeed received some trifling presents from him, such as shawls, avadavats,[57] and Indian crackers; nothing more, Sir.

SIR OLIVER. There's gratitude for twelve thousand pounds! *(Aside)* Shawls, avadavats, and Indian crackers!

JOSEPH. Then there's my brother, Mr. Stanley; one would scarce believe what I have done for that unfortunate young man.

SIR OLIVER. Not I for one. *(Aside.)*

JOSEPH. Oh, the sums I have lent him! – Well, 'twas an amiable weakness – I must own I can't defend it, though it appears more blameable at present, as it prevents me from serving you, Mr. Stanley, as my heart directs.

SIR OLIVER. Dissembler – *(Aside)*– Then you cannot assist me.

JOSEPH. I am very unhappy to say it's not in my power at present; but you may depend upon hearing from me when I can be of any service to you.

SIR OLIVER. Sweet Sir, you are too good.

JOSEPH. Not at all, Sir; to pity without the power to relieve, is still more painful, than to ask and be denied. Indeed, Mr. Stanley, you have me deeply affected. Sir, your most devoted; I wish you health and spirits.

SIR OLIVER. Your ever grateful and perpetual *(bowing low)* humble servant.

JOSEPH. I am extremely sorry, Sir, for your misfortunes – Here, open the door – Mr. Stanley your most devoted.

SIR OLIVER. Your most obliged servant. Charles, you are my heir. *(Aside, and exit.)*

JOSEPH. This is another of the evils that attend a man's having so good a character. – It subjects him to the importunity of the necessitous – the pure and sterling ore of charity is a very expensive article in the catalogue of a man's virtues, whereas the sentimental French Plate[58] I use answers the purpose full as well, and pays no tax. *(Going.)*

Enter Rowley.

ROWLEY. Mr. Surface, your most obedient; I wait on you from your uncle who is just arrived. *(Gives him a note.)*

JOSEPH. How! Sir Oliver arrived! – Here, Mr. – call back Mr. Stanley.

ROWLEY. It's too late, Sir, I met him going out of the house.

JOSEPH. Was ever anything so unfortunate! *(Aside)* – I hope my uncle has enjoyed good health and spirits.

ROWLEY. Oh, very good, Sir; he bid me inform you he'll wait on you within this half hour.

JOSEPH. Present him my kind love and duty, and assure him I'm quite impatient to see him. *(Bowing.)*

ROWLEY. I shall, Sir. [*Exit Rowley.*]

JOSEPH. Pray do, Sir *(bows)* – This was the most cursed piece of ill luck. [*Exit Joseph.*]

Notes

[57] *avadavats* Indian song birds.

[58] *Plate* an inferior metal with gold or silver plating.

SCENE Sir Peter Teazle's House

Enter Mrs. Candour *and* Maid.

Maid. Indeed, Madam, my Lady will see no one at present.

MRS. CANDOUR. Did you tell her it was her friend Mrs. Candour?

MAID. I did, Madam, and she begs to be excused.

MRS. CANDOUR. Go again, for I am sure she must be greatly distressed. *(Exit Maid.)* How provoking to be kept waiting – I am not mistress of half the circumstances: – I shall have the whole affair in the newspapers, with the parties' names at full length, before I have dropped the story at a dozen houses.

Enter Sir Benjamin Backbite.

MRS. CANDOUR. Oh, Sir Benjamin, I am glad you are come; have you heard of Lady Teazle's affair? Well, I never was so surprised – and I am so distressed for the parties.

SIR BENJAMIN. Nay, I can't say I pity Sir Peter; he was always so partial to Mr. Surface.

MRS. CANDOUR. Mr. Surface! Why it was Charles.

SIR BENJAMIN. Oh, no, madam, Mr. Surface was the gallant.

MRS. CANDOUR. No, Charles was the lover; and Mr. Surface, to do him justice, was the cause of the discovery; he brought Sir Peter; and –

SIR BENJAMIN. Oh, my dear Madam, no such thing; for I have it from one –

MRS. CANDOUR. Yes, and I had it from one, that had it from one that knew –

SIR BENJAMIN. And I had it from one –

MRS. CANDOUR. No such thing – But here comes my Lady Sneerwell, and perhaps she may have heard the particulars.

Enter Lady Sneerwell.

L. SNEERWELL. Oh, dear Mrs. Candour, here is a sad affair about out friend Lady Teazle.

MRS. CANDOUR. Why, to be sure, poor thing, I am much concerned for her.

L. SNEERWELL. I protest so am I – though I must confess she was always too lively for me.

MRS. CANDOUR. But she had a great deal of good nature.

SIR BENJAMIN. And had a very ready wit.

MRS. CANDOUR. But do you know all the particulars? *(To Lady Sneerwell.)*

SIR BENJAMIN. Yes who could have suspected Mr. Surface?

MRS. CANDOUR. Charles you mean.

SIR BENJAMIN. No, Mr. Surface.

MRS. CANDOUR. Oh, 'twas Charles.

SIR BENJAMIN. I'll not pretend to dispute with you, Mrs. Candour; but be it as it may, I hope Sir Peter's wounds won't prove mortal.

MRS. CANDOUR. Sir Peter's wounds! what! did they fight! I never heard a word of that.

SIR BENJAMIN. No! –

MRS. CANDOUR. No! –

L. SNEERWELL. Nor I, a syllable: Do, dear Sir Benjamin, tell us.

SIR BENJAMIN. Oh, my dear madam, then you don't know half the affair – Why – why – I'll tell you – Sir Peter, you must know, had a long time suspected Lady Teazle's visits to Mr. Surface.

MRS. CANDOUR. To Charles you mean.

SIR BENJAMIN. No, Mr. Surface – and upon going to his house, and finding Lady Teazle there, 'Sir', says Sir Peter, 'you are a very ungrateful fellow'.

MRS. CANDOUR. Aye, that was Charles.

Sir Benjamin. Mr. Surface. – 'And old as I am', says he, 'I demand immediate satisfaction': upon this, they both drew their swords, and to it they fell.

Mrs. Candour. That must be Charles, for it is very unlikely that Mr. Surface should fight him in his own house.

Sir Benjamin. 'Sdeath,[59] madam, not at all. Lady Teazle, upon seeing Sir Peter in such danger, ran out of the room in strong hysterics, and was followed by Charles, calling out for hartshorn[60] and water. They fought, and Sir Peter received a wound in his right side by the thrust of a small sword.

Enter Crabtree.

Crabtree. Pistols! pistols! Nephew.

Mrs. Candour. Oh, Mr. Crabtree, I am glad you are come; now we shall have the whole affair.

Sir Benjamin. No, no, it was a small sword, uncle.

Crabtree. Zounds, nephew, I say it was a pistol.

Sir Benjamin. A thrust in seconde[61] through the small guts.

Crabtree. A bullet lodged in the thorax.

Sir Benjamin. But give me leave, dear uncle, it was a small sword.

Crabtree. I tell you it was a pistol – Won't you suffer anybody to know anything but yourself. – It was a pistol, and Charles –

Mrs. Candour. Aye! I knew it was Charles.

Sir Benjamin. Mr. Surface, uncle.

Crabtree. Why 'swounds, I say it was Charles, must nobody speak but yourself? I'll tell you how the whole affair was.

L. Sneerwell and Mrs. Candour. Ah do, pray tell us.

Sir Benjamin. I see my uncle knows nothing at all about the matter.

Crabtree. Mr. Surface you must know, Ladies, came late from Salt-hill, where he had been the Evening before with a particular friend of his, who has a son at Eton; his pistols were left on the bureau, and unfortunately loaded, and on Sir Peter's taxing Charles –

Sir Benjamin. Mr. Surface you mean.

Crabtree. Do, pray, Nephew, hold your tongue, and let me speak sometimes – I say, Ladies, upon his taking Charles to account, and taxing him with the basest ingratitude –

Sir Benjamin. Aye, Ladies, I told you Sir Peter taxed him with ingratitude.

Crabtree. They agreed each to take a pistol – They fired at the same instant – Charles's ball took place, and lodged in the thorax. Sir Peter's missed, and what is very extraordinary, the ball grazed against a little bronze Shakespeare that stood over the chimney, flew off through the window, at right angles, and wounded the postman, who was just come to the door with a double letter from Northamptonshire.

Sir Benjamin. I heard nothing of all this! I must own, Ladies, my uncle's account is more circumstantial, though I believe mine is the true one.

L. Sneerwell. I am more interested in this affair than they imagine, and must have better information. [*Aside, and exit.*]

Notes

59 *'Sdeath* short for *God's death*, a mild imprecation.

60 *hartshorn* an ammonia solution used to revive one who has fainted.

61 *thrust in seconde* a hit in fencing delivered beneath the opponent's sword (Price).

Sir Benjamin. Lady Sneerwell's alarm is very easily accounted for.

Crabtree. Why yes; they do say – but that's neither here nor there.

Mrs. Candour. But pray where is Sir Peter now? I hope his wound won't prove mortal.

Crabtree. He was carried home immediately, and has given positive orders to be denied to everybody.

Sir Benjamin. And I believe Lady Teazle is attending him.

Mrs. Candour. I do believe so too.

Crabtree. Certainly – I met one of the faculty[62] as I came in.

Sir Benjamin. Gad so! and here he comes.

Crabtree. Yes, yes, that's the Doctor.

Mrs. Candour. That certainly must be the physician – Now we shall get information.

Enter Sir Oliver Surface.

Dear Doctor, how is your patient?

Sir Benjamin. I hope his wounds are not mortal.

Crabtree. Is he in a fair way of recovery?

Sir Benjamin. Pray, Doctor, was he not wounded by a thrust of a sword through the small guts?

Crabtree. Was it not by a bullet that lodged in the thorax?

Sir Benjamin. Nay, pray answer me?

Crabtree. Dear, dear Doctor speak. *(All pulling him.)*

Sir Oliver. Hey, hey, good people, are you all mad? – Why what the devil is the matter? – a sword through the small guts, and a bullet lodged in the thorax! What would you all be at?

Sir Benjamin. Then perhaps, Sir, you are not a Doctor.

Sir Oliver. If I am, Sir, I am to thank you for my degree.

Crabtree. Only a particular friend, I suppose.

Sir Oliver. Nothing more, Sir.

Sir Benjamin. Then I suppose, as you are a friend, you can be better able to give us some account of his wounds.

Sir Oliver. Wounds!

Mrs. Candour. What! haven't you heard he was wounded – The saddest accident.

Sir Benjamin. A thrust with a sword through the small guts.

Crabtree. A bullet in the thorax.

Sir Oliver. Good people, speak one at a time, I beseech you – You both agree, that Sir Peter is dangerously wounded.

Crabtree and Sir Benjamin. Ay, ay, we both agree in that.

Sir Oliver. Then I will be bold to say, Sir Peter is one of the most imprudent men in the world, for here he comes walking as if nothing had happened.

Enter Sir Peter.

My good friend, you are certainly mad to walk about in this condition; you should go to bed, you that have had a sword through your small guts, and a bullet lodged in your thorax.

Sir Peter. A sword through my small guts, and a bullet lodged in my thorax!

Notes

[62] *faculty* the members of the medical profession.

Sir Oliver. Yes, these worthy people would have killed you without law or physic, and wanted to dub me a Doctor, in order to make me an accomplice.
Sir Peter. What is all this!
Sir Benjamin. Sir Peter, we are all very glad to find the story of the duel is not true.
Crabtree. And exceedingly sorry for your other misfortunes.
Sir Peter. So, so, all over the town already. *(Aside.)*
Mrs. Candour. Though, as Sir Peter was so good a husband, I pity him sincerely.
Sir Peter. Plague of your pity.
Crabtree. As you continued so long a bachelor, you was certainly to blame to marry at all.
Sir Peter. Sir, I desire you'll consider this is my own house.
Sir Benjamin. However, you must not be offended at the jests you'll meet on this occasion.
Crabtree. It is no uncommon case, that's one thing.
Sir Peter. I insist upon being master here; in plain terms I desire you'll leave my house immediately.
Mrs. Candour. Well, well, Sir, we are going, and you may depend upon it, we shall make the best of the story. [*Exit.*]
Sir Benjamin. And tell how badly you have been treated.
Sir Peter. Leave my house directly. [*Exit Sir Benjamin.*]
Crabtree. And how patiently you bear it. [*Exit Crabtree.*]
Sir Peter. Leave my house, I say – Fiends, furies, there is no bearing it!

Enter Rowley.

Sir Oliver. Well, Sir Peter, I have seen my Nephews.
Rowley. And Sir Oliver is convinced, your judgement is right after all.
Sir Oliver. Aye, Joseph is the man.
Rowley. Such sentiments.
Sir Oliver. And acts up to the sentiments he professes.
Rowley. Oh, 'tis edification to hear him talk.
Sir Oliver. He is a pattern for the young men of the age. – But how comes it Sir Peter, that you don't join in his praises?
Sir Peter. Sir Oliver we live in a damned wicked world, and the fewer we praise the better.
Sir Oliver. Right, right, my old friend – But was you always so moderate in your judgement?
Rowley. Do you say so, Sir Peter, you who was never mistaken in your life.
Sir Peter. Oh, plague of your jokes – I suppose you are acquainted with the whole affair.
Rowley. I am indeed, Sir. – I met Lady Teazle returning from Mr. Surface's, so humbled, that she deigned to beg even me to become her advocate.
Sir Peter. What! does Sir Oliver know it too?
Sir Oliver. Aye, aye, every circumstance.
Sir Peter. What! about the closet and the screen.
Sir Oliver. Yes, and the little French milliner too. I never laughed more in my life.
Sir Peter. And a very pleasant jest it was.
Sir Oliver. This is your man of sentiment, Sir Peter.
Sir Peter. Oh, damn his sentiments.
Sir Oliver. You must have made a pretty appearance when Charles dragged you out of the closet.
Sir Peter. Yes, yes, that was very diverting.

SIR OLIVER. And, egad Sir Peter, I should like to have seen your face when the screen was thrown down.

SIR PETER. My face when the screen was thrown down! oh yes! – There's no bearing this. [*Aside.*]

SIR OLIVER. Come, come, my old friend, don't be vexed, for I can't help laughing for the soul of me. Ha! ha! ha!

SIR PETER. Oh laugh on – I am not vexed – no, no, it is the pleasantest thing in the world. To be the standing jest of all one's acquaintance – 'tis the happiest situation imaginable.

ROWLEY. See, Sir, yonder's my Lady Teazle coming this way, and in tears, let me beg of you to be reconciled.

SIR OLIVER. Well, well, I'll leave Rowley to mediate between you, and take my leave; but you must make haste after me to Mr. Surface's, where I must go, if not to reclaim a libertine, at least to expose hypocrisy. [*Exit.*]

SIR PETER. I'll be with you at the discovery; I should like to see it, though it is a vile unlucky place for discoveries. Rowley, *(looking out)* she is not coming this way.

ROWLEY. No, Sir, but she has left the room door open, and waits your coming.

SIR PETER. Well, certainly mortification is very becoming in a wife. – Don't you think I had best let her pine a little longer?

ROWLEY. Oh, sir, that's being too severe.

SIR PETER. I don't think so; the letter I found from Charles was evidently intended for her.

ROWLEY. Indeed, Sir Peter, you are much mistaken.

SIR PETER. If I was convinced of that – see, Master Rowley, she looks this way – what a remarkable elegant turn of the head she has – I have a good mind to go to her.

ROWLEY. Do, dear Sir.

SIR PETER. But when it is known that we are reconciled, I shall be laughed at more than ever.

ROWLEY. Let them laugh on, and retort their malice upon themselves, by showing them you can be happy in spite of their slander.

SIR PETER. Faith and so I will, master Rowley, and my Lady Teazle and I may still be the happiest couple in the country.

ROWLEY. O fie, Sir Peter, he that lays aside suspicion –

SIR PETER. My dear Rowley, if you have any regard for me never let me hear you utter anything like a sentiment again; I have had enough of that to last me the remainder of my life. [*Exeunt.*]

SCENE Joseph's Library.

Enter Joseph *and Lady* Sneerwell.

L. SNEERWELL. Impossible! will not Sir Peter be immediately reconciled to Charles, and no longer oppose his union with Maria.

JOSEPH. Can passion mend it?

L. SNEERWELL. No, not cunning neither. I was a fool to league with such a blunderer.

JOSEPH. Sure, my Lady *Sneerwell*, I am the greatest sufferer in this affair, and yet, you see, I bear it with calmness.

L. SNEERWELL. Because the disappointment does not reach your heart; your interest only was concerned. Had you felt for Maria, what I do for that unfortunate libertine, your brother, you would not be dissuaded from taking every revenge in your power.

JOSEPH. Why will you rail at me for the disappointment?

L. SNEERWELL. Are you not the cause? Had you not a sufficient field for your roguery in imposing upon Sir Peter, and supplanting your brother, but you must endeavour to seduce his wife? I hate such an avarice of crimes; 'tis an unfair monopoly, and never prospers.

JOSEPH. Well, I own I am to blame – I have deviated from the direct rule of wrong. Yet, I cannot think circumstances are so bad as your Ladyship apprehends.

L. SNEERWELL. No!

JOSEPH. You tell me you have made another trial of Snake, that he still proves steady to our interest, and that he is ready, if occasion requires, to swear to a contract having passed between Charles and your Ladyship.

L. SNEERWELL. And what then?

JOSEPH. Why, the letters which have been so carefully circulated, will corroborate his evidence, and prove the truth of the assertion. But I expect my uncle every moment, and must beg your Ladyship to retire into the next room.

L. SNEERWELL. But if he should find you out?

JOSEPH. I have no fear of that – Sir Peter won't tell for his own sake, and I shall soon find out Sir Oliver's weak side.

L. SNEERWELL. Nay, I have no doubt of your abilities; only be constant to one villainy at a time.

JOSEPH. Well, I will, I will, – (*Exit Lady Sneerwell*) – It is confounded hard, though, to be baited by one's confederates in wickedness – (*knocking*) – Who have we got here? My uncle Oliver, I suppose – Oh, old Stanley again! How came he here? He must not stay –

Enter Sir Oliver.

I told you already, Mr. Stanley, that it was not in my power to relieve you.

SIR OLIVER. But I hear, Sir, that Sir Oliver is arrived, and perhaps he might.

JOSEPH. Well, Sir, you cannot stay now, Sir; but any other time, Sir, you shall certainly be relieved.

SIR OLIVER. Oh, Sir Oliver and I must be acquainted.

JOSEPH. I must insist upon your going. Indeed, Mr. Stanley, you can't stay.

SIR OLIVER. Positively I must see Sir Oliver.

JOSEPH. Then positively you shan't stay. [*Pushing him out.*]

Enter Charles.

CHARLES. Hey day! what's the matter? Why, who the devil have we got here? What, my little Premium. Oh, brother, you must not hurt my little broker. But hark'ye, Joseph, what, have you been borrowing money too?

JOSEPH. Borrowing money! no brother – We expect my uncle Oliver here every minute, and Mr. Stanley insists upon seeing him.

CHARLES. Stanley! Why his name is Premium.

JOSEPH. No, no! I tell you his name is Stanley.

CHARLES. But I tell you again his name is Premium.

JOSEPH. It don't signify what his name is.

CHARLES. No more it don't, as you say, brother, for I suppose he goes by half a hundred names, besides A. B. at the coffeehouses. But old Oliver must not come and catch my little broker here neither.

JOSEPH. Mr. Stanley, I beg –

CHARLES. And I beg, Mr. Premium –

JOSEPH. You must go indeed, Mr. Stanley.

CHARLES. Aye, you must go, Mr. Premium. *(Both pushing him.)*

Enter Sir Peter, *Lady* Teazle, Maria *and* Rowley.

SIR PETER. What? my old friend Sir *Oliver*! what's the matter? – In the name of wonder, were there ever two such ungracious nephews, to assault their uncle at his first visit.

L. Teazle. On my word, Sir, it was well we came to your rescue.

Joseph. Charles!

Charles. Joseph!

Joseph. Now our ruin is complete.

Charles. Very!

Sir Peter. You find, Sir Oliver, your necessitous character of old Stanley could not protect you.

Sir Oliver. No! nor Premium neither. The necessities of the former could not extract a shilling from that benevolent gentleman there; and with the other I stood a worse chance than my ancestors, and had like to have been knocked down without being bid for. Sir Peter, my friend, and Rowley, look upon that elder nephew of mine; you both know what I have done for him, and how gladly I would have looked upon half my fortune as held only in trust for him. Judge then, of my surprise and disappointment at finding him destitute of truth, charity, and gratitude.

Sir Peter. Sir Oliver, I should be as much surprised as you, if I did not already know him to be artful, selfish, and hypocritical.

L. Teazle. And if he pleads not guilty to all this, let him call on me to finish his character.

Sir Peter. Then I believe we need not add more, for if he knows himself, it will be a sufficient punishment for him that he is known by the world.

Charles. If they talk this way so honestly, what will they say to me by and by. [*Aside.*]

Sir Oliver. As for that profligate there – *(pointing to Charles.)*

Charles. Ay, now comes my turn; the damned family pictures will ruin me. [*Aside.*]

Joseph. Sir Oliver, will you honour me with a hearing?

Charles. Now if Joseph would make one of his long speeches, I should have time to recollect myself. [*Aside.*]

Sir Peter. I suppose you would undertake to justify yourself entirely.

Joseph. In truth, I could, sir.

Sir Oliver. Pshaw; *(turns away from him)* and I suppose you could justify yourself too. *(To Charles.)*

Charles. Not that I know of, Sir.

Sir Oliver. What, my little Premium was let too much into the secret!

Charles. Why yes, Sir; but they were family secrets, and should go no further.

Rowley. Come, come, Sir Oliver, I am sure, cannot look upon Charles's follies with anger.

Sir Oliver. No, nor with gravity neither. – Do you know, Sir Peter, the young rogue has been selling me his ancestors: I have bought judges and staff-officers by the foot, and maiden aunts as cheap as old china. *(During his speech, Charles laughs behind his hat.)*

Charles. Why, that I have made free with the family canvas is true; my ancestors may rise in judgement against me; there's no denying it; but believe me when I tell you (and upon my soul I would not say it, if it was not so) if I don't appear mortified at the exposure of my follies, it is, because I feel at this moment the warmest satisfaction, at seeing you, my liberal benefactor. *(Embraces him.)*

Sir Oliver. Charles, I forgive you; give me your hand again, the little ill-looking fellow over the settee has made your peace for you.

Charles. Then, sir, my gratitude to the original is still increased.

L. Teazle. Sir Oliver, here is another, with whom I dare say Charles is no less anxious to be reconciled.

Sir Oliver. I have heard of that attachment before, and with the lady's leave – if I construe right, that blush –

Sir Peter. Well, child, speak for yourself.

MARIA. I have little more to say, than that I wish him happy, and for any influence I might once have had over his affections, I most willingly resign them to one who has a better claim to them.

SIR PETER. Hey! what's the matter now? While he was a rake and a profligate, you would hear of nobody else; and now that he is likely to reform, you won't have him. What's the meaning of all this?

MARIA. His own heart, and Lady Sneerwell, can best inform you.

CHARLES. Lady Sneerwell!

JOSEPH. I am very sorry, brother, I am obliged to speak to this point, but justice demands it from me; and Lady Sneerwell's wrongs can no longer be concealed.

Enter Lady Sneerwell.

SIR PETER. Another French milliner! – I believe he has one in every room in the house.

L. SNEERWELL. Ungrateful Charles! well you may seem confounded and surprised, at the indelicate situation to which your perfidy has reduced me.

CHARLES. Pray uncle, is this another of your plots? for, as I live, this is the first I ever heard of it.

JOSEPH. There is but one witness, I believe, necessary to the business.

SIR PETER. And that witness is Mr. Snake – you were perfectly in the right in bringing him with you. Let him appear.

ROWLEY. Desire Mr. Snake to walk in. – It is rather unlucky, Madam, that he should be brought to confront, and not support your Ladyship.

Enter Snake.

L. SNEERWELL. I am surprised! What? speak villain! have you too conspired against me?

SNAKE. I beg your Ladyship ten thousand pardons; I must own you paid me very liberally for the lying questions, but I have unfortunately been offered double for speaking the truth.

SIR PETER. Plot and counter-plot – I give your Ladyship much joy of your negotiation.

L. SNEERWELL. May the torments of despair and disappointment light upon you all. *(Going.)*

L. TEAZLE. Hold, Lady Sneerwell; before you go, give me leave to return you thanks, for the trouble you and this gentleman took, in writing letters in my name to Charles, and answering them yourself; – and, at the same time, I must beg you will present my compliments to the scandalous college, of which you are president, and inform them, that Lady Teazle, licentiate, returns the diploma they granted her, as she leaves off practice, and kills characters no longer.

L. SNEERWELL. You too, madam! Provoking Insolent! may your husband live these fifty years. [*Exit.*]

L. TEAZLE. Oh lord – what a malicious creature it is!

SIR PETER. Not for her last wish, I hope.

L. TEAZLE. Oh, no, no, no.

SIR PETER. Well, Sir – what have you to say for yourself? *(to Joseph)*

JOSEPH. Sir, I am so confounded that Lady Sneerwell should impose upon us all, by suborning Mr. Snake, that I know not what to say – but – lest her malice should prompt her to injure my brother – I had better follow her. [*Exit.*]

SIR PETER. Moral to the last.

SIR OLIVER. Marry her, Joseph, marry her if you can – Oil and Vinegar – you'll do very well together.

ROWLEY. Mr. Snake, I believe, we have no further occasion for you.

SNAKE. Before I go, I must beg pardon of these good ladies and gentlemen, for whatever trouble I have been the humble instrument of causing.

SIR PETER. You have made amends by your open confession.

SNAKE. But I must beg it as a favour that it may never be spoke of.

SIR PETER. What! are you ashamed of having done one good action in your life?

SNAKE. Sir, I request you to consider that I live by the badness of my character, and if it was once known that I had been betrayed into an honest action, I should lose every friend I have in the world. [*Exit.*]

SIR OLIVER. Never fear, we shan't traduce you by saying anything in your praise.

SIR PETER. There's a specious rogue for you.

L. TEAZLE. You see, Sir Oliver, it needed no great persuasion to reconcile your nephew and Maria.

SIR OLIVER. So much the better, I'll have the wedding tomorrow morning.

SIR PETER. What, before you ask the girl's consent.

CHARLES. I have done that a long time since – above a minute ago – and she looked –

MARIA. O fie, Charles – I protest, Sir Peter, there has not been a word said.

SIR OLIVER. Well, well, the less the better (*joining their hands*) there – and may your love never know abatement.

SIR PETER. And may you live as happily together, as Lady Teazle and I – intend to do.

CHARLES. I suspect, Rowley, I owe much to you.

SIR OLIVER. You do indeed.

ROWLEY. Sir, if I had failed in my endeavours to serve you, you would have been indebted to me for the attempt. But deserve to be happy, and you overpay me.

SIR PETER. Ay, honest Rowley always said you would reform.

CHARLES. Look ye, Sir Peter, as to reforming, I shall make no promises, and that I take to be the strongest proof that I intend setting about it. But here shall be my monitor, my gentle guide – can I leave the virtuous path those eyes illumine?

Though thou, dear maid, shou'd'st weave thy beauty's sway,
Thou still must rule, because I will obey;
An humble fugitive from folly view,
No sanctuary near but love – and you.

[*to the audience*]

You can, indeed, each anxious fear remove,
For even scandal dies – if you approve.

Thomas Chatterton (1752–1770)

Chatterton's poems have merited a two-volume Clarendon Press edition (1971), and there have been a large number of biographical and critical studies including a novelistic treatment by Peter Ackroyd (1987). In 1994, Routledge published a six-volume set entitled *Thomas Chatterton: Early Sources and Responses.* What makes all of this remarkable is that Chatterton died at the age of seventeen. His most spectacular literary achievement was the creation of a body of poetry purportedly by a fifteenth-century Bristol poet named Thomas Rowley. Some were taken in by the deception, but, as in the case of Macpherson's Ossian poems, more learned readers soon got it all straightened out. Horace Walpole was one of the most indignant, and his hostility to Chatterton has often been identified as a source of the young poet's despair. It was long believed that Chatterton committed suicide, but now it appears that he died of an accidental overdose of opium and arsenic, which he was taking for venereal disease. The romantic myth about "the marvellous boy," as Wordsworth called him, was paramount in conceptions of Chatterton's life and works for a long time; he was seen as the archetypal Romantic poet – sensitive, spurned by conservative society, and a tragic early suicide. More recently, critics have drawn attention to the ways in which Chatterton's poetry, for all its trumped-up medievalism, adheres to many conventional eighteenth-century poetic standards (see the essay on Chatterton by Claude Rawson in *British Literature 1640–1789: A Critical Reader*). "An Excelente Balade of Charitie" has been read romantically as a *cri de coeur* and a suicide note, but it is also a moral fable about charity, the story and theme of which would not be out of place in the works of Isaac Watts, Hannah More, or even Samuel Johnson.

Because the spelling and punctuation are so important to the medieval deception, I suspend my regular procedure of conservative modernization and present this poem *literatim*, just as it appeared the first time it was printed.

from *Poems, Supposed to have been Written at Bristol, By Thomas Rowley, and Others, in the Fifteenth Century* (1777)

An Excelente Balade of Charitie:

As wroten bie the gode Prieste Thomas Rowley, 1464[1]

In Virgyne the sweltrie sun gan sheene,
And hotte upon the mees did caste his raie;[2]
The apple rodded from its palie greene,[3]
And the mole peare did bende the leafy spraie;[4]

Notes

An Excelente Balade of Charitie

[1] Rowley Thomas Rowley, the author, was born at Norton Mal-reward in Somersetshire, educated at the Convent of St. Kenna at Keynesham, and died at Westbury in Gloucestershire [Chatterton's note].

[2] *mees* meads [meadows; Chatterton's note].

[3] *rodded* reddened, ripened [Chatterton's note].

[4] *mole* soft [Chatterton's note].

The peede chelandri sunge the livelong daie;[5]
'Twas nowe the pride, the manhode of the yeare,
And eke the ground was dighte in its most defte aumere.[6]

The sun was glemeing in the midde of daie,
Deadde still the aire, and eke the welkin blue,[7]
When from the sea arist in drear arraie[8]
A hepe of cloudes of sable sullen hue,
The which full fast unto the woodlande drewe,
Hiltring attenes the sunnis fetive face,[9]
And the blacke tempeste swolne and gatherd up apace.

Beneath an holme, faste by a pathwaie side,[10]
Which dide unto Seyncte Godwine's covent lede,[11]
A hapless pilgrim moneynge did abide,[12]
Pore in his viewe, ungentle in his weede,[13]
Longe bretful of the miseries of neede.[14]
Where from the hail-stone coulde the almer flie?[15]
He had no housen theere, ne anie covent nie.

Look in his glommed face, his sprighte there scanne;[16]
Howe woe-be-gone, how withered, forwynd, deade![17]
Haste to thie church-glebe-house, ashrewed manne![18]
Haste to thie kiste, thie onlie dortoure bedde.[19]
Cale as the claie whiche will gre on thie hedde,[20]
Is Charitie and Love aminge highe elves;
Knightis and Barons live for pleasure and themselves.

The gatherd storme is rype; the bigge drops falle,
The forswat meadowes smethe, and drenche the raine;[21]
The comyng ghastness doth the cattle pall,[22]
And the full flockes are drivynge ore the plaine;
Dashde from the cloudes, the waters flott againe;[23]

Notes

[5] *peede chelandri* pied goldfinch [Chatterton's note].

[6] *dighte* dressed, arrayed; *defte* neat, ornamental; *aumere* a loose robe or mantle [Chatterton's notes].

[7] *welkin* the sky, the atmosphere [Chatterton's note].

[8] *arist* arose [Chatterton's note].

[9] *Hiltring* hiding, shrouding; *attenes* at once; *fetive* beautiful [Chatterton's notes].

[10] *holme* holly tree.

[11] *covent* It would have been *charitable*, if the author had not pointed at personal characters in this Ballad of Charity. The Abbot of St. Godwin's at the time of the writing of this was Ralph de Bellomont, a great stickler for the Lancastrian family. Rowley was a Yorkist [Chatterton's note].

[12] *moneynge* moaning.

[13] *ungentle* beggarly [Chatterton's note]; *weede* clothing.

[14] *bretful* filled with [Chatterton's note].

[15] *almer* beggar.

[16] *glommed* cloudy, dejected. A person of some note in the literary world is of opinion, that *glum* and *glom* are modern cant words; and from this circumstance doubts the authenticity of Rowley's Manuscripts. *Glum-mong* in the Saxon signifies twilight, a dark or dubious light; and the modern word *gloomy* is derived from the Saxon *glum* [Chatterton's note].

[17] *forwynd* dry, sapless [Chatterton's note].

[18] *church-glebe-house* the grave; *ashrewed* accursed, unfortunate [Chatterton's notes].

[19] *kiste* coffin; *dortoure* a sleeping room [Chatterton's notes].

[20] *Cale* cold; *gre* grow.

[21] *forswat* sun-burnt; *smethe* smoke; *drenche* drink [Chatterton's notes].

[22] *pall* a contraction from appal, to fright [Chatterton's note].

[23] *flott* fly [Chatterton's note].

The welkin opes; the yellow levynne flies,[24]
And the hot fierie smothe in the wide lowings dies.[25]

List! now the thunder's rattling clymmynge sound[26]
Cheves slowlie on, and then embollen clangs,[27]
Shakes the hie spyre, and losst, dispended, drown'd,
Still on the gallard eaer of terroure hanges;[28]
The windes are up; the lofty elmen swanges;
Again the levynne, and the thunder poures,
And the full cloudes are braste attenes in stonen showers.[29]

Spurreynge his palfrie oere the watrie plaine,
The Abbote of Seyncte Godwynes convente came;
His chapournette was drented with the reine,[30]
And his pencte gyrdle met with mickle shame;[31]
He aynewarde told his bederoll at the same;[32]
The storme encreasen, and he drew aside,
With the mist almes craver neere to the holme to bide.[33]

His cope was all of Lyncolne clothe so fyne,[34]
With a gold button fasten'd neere his chynne;
His autremete was edged with golden twynne,[35]
And his shoone pyke a loverds mighte have binne;[36]
Full well it shewn he thoughten coste no sinne:
The trammels of his palfrye pleasde his sighte,
For the horse-millanare his head with roses dighte.[37]
An almes, sir prieste! the droppynge pilgrim saide,

Oh! let me waite within your covente-dore,
Till the sunne sheneth hie above our heade,
And the loude tempeste of the aire is oer;
Helpless and ould am I alas! and poor;
No house, ne friend, ne moneie in my pouche,
All yatte I call my owne is this my silver crouche.[38]

Varlet! replyd the Abbatte, cease your dinne;
This is no season almes and prayers to give,
Mie porter never lets a faitour in;[39]

Notes

24 *levynne* lightning [Chatterton's note].

25 *smothe* steam, or vapours; *lowings* flames [Chatterton's notes].

26 *clymmynge* noisy [Chatterton's note].

27 *Cheves* moves; *embollen* swelled, strengthened [Chatterton's note].

28 *gallard* frighted [Chatterton's note].

29 *braste* burst [Chatterton's note].

30 *chapournette* a small round hat, not unlike the shapournette in heraldry, fomerly worn by Ecclesiastics and Lawyers [Chatterton's note].

31 *pencte* painted [Chatterton's note].

32 *aynewarde told his bederoll* told his beads backwards [Chatterton's note].

33 *mist* poor, needy [Chatterton's note].

34 *cope* a cloak [Chatterton's note].

35 *autremete* a loose white robe, worn by Priests [Chatterton's note].

36 *shoone pyke* shoes with pointed, upturned toes, popular in the fourteenth century; *loverd* a lord [Chatterton's note].

37 *horse-millanare* I believe this trade is still in being, though but seldom employed [Chatterton's note].

38 *yatte* that; *crouche* cross.

39 *faitour* beggar [Chatterton's note].

None touch mie ring who not in honour live.
And now the sonne with the blacke cloudes did stryve,
And shettynge on the ground his glairie raie:
The Abbatte spurrde his steede, and eftsoones roadde awaie.

Once moe the skie was blacke, the thounder rolde;
Faste reyneyng oer the plaine a prieste was seen;
Not dight full proude, ne buttoned up in golde;
His cope and jape were graie, and eke were clene;[40]
A Limitoure he was of order seene;
And from the pathwaie side then turned hee,
Where the pore almer laie binethe the holmen tree.

An almes, sir priest! the droppynge pilgrim sayde,
For sweete Seyncte Marie and your order sake.
The Limitour then loosen'd his pouche threade,
And did thereoute a groate of silver take;
The mister pilgrim dyd for halline shake.[41]
Here take this silver, it maie eathe thie care;[42]
We are Goddes stewards all, nete of oure owne we bare.[43]

But ah! unhailie pilgrim, lerne of me,[44]
Scathe anie give a renttrolle to their Lorde;[45]
Here, take my semecope, thou arte bare, I see;[46]
'Tis thyne; the Seynctes will give me mie rewarde.
He left the pilgrim, and his waie aborde.[47]
Virgynne and hallie Seyncte, who sitte yn gloure,[48]
Or give the mittee will, or give the gode man power[49]

Notes

40 *jape* a short surplice, worn by Friars of an inferior class, and secular priests [Chatterton's note].

41 *halline* joy [Chatterton's note].

42 *eathe* ease [Chatterton's note].

43 *nete* nought.

44 *unhailie* unhappy [Chatterton's note].

45 *renttrolle* rent-roll, financial statement.

46 *semecope* a short under-cloak [Chatterton's note].

47 *aborde* went on.

48 *gloure* glory [Chatterton's note].

49 *mittee* mighty, rich; *or*... *or* either ... or.

Frances Burney (later d'Arblay) (1752–1840)

At a very early age Frances Burney moved in exalted literary circles, prized and praised by Samuel Johnson, Hester Thrale, and the rest of the "Streatham" circle. She also knew the world of musicians and composers in which her father constantly moved. Charles Burney was an organist and music-master, who became famous as the author of the most important history of music written in English in his time or before. It was, of course, not his musicianship but rather his humanity that made Burney attractive to Johnson. The two were good friends to start with, and the emergence of his literary, highly good-humored daughter "Fanny" increased the warmth and affection between them. Frances delighted her friends and the world with her first novel, *Evelina*, published when she was only twenty-six. *Cecilia* (1782) was also admired, but then Burney's world began to change: she became estranged from Hester Thrale after her second marriage (1783); Samuel Johnson died (1784); she lost an old family friend whom she called "Daddy Crisp." She was presented to King George III and held an unsatisfactory post in the royal service for a time. She married in 1793 and eventually went to France with her husband to reclaim property he had lost during the Revolution. There were two more novels, the third a mixed success and the fourth a failure. But through it all, from the time she was a teenager in her father's house, through her decade in France and after her return to England during the Napoleonic Wars, Burney kept her diaries and journals. These provide some of the best accounts of what it was like to be in the company of Samuel Johnson and many other luminaries of the period. The view is strikingly different from that found in Boswell's more self-centered accounts. In addition to writing about her friends and family, her principal interest, Burney also conveys a vivid sense of many of her private and domestic experiences – none more vivid and striking than her account of her mastectomy in Paris in 1811 before the advent of anesthesia.

The *Journals and Letters* from 1791 on have been produced in twelve volumes by the Clarendon Press (1972–82); the *Court Journals and Letters* are in progress (2011–), as are the *Additional Journals and Letters* (2015–). The *Early Journals and Letters* have come out from McGill University Press (1988–94). Margaret Doody has written a rich critical biography (Rutgers University Press, 1988). My texts are based on those in volume two of the McGill production, edited by Lars Troide, and in volume six of the Clarendon Press edition of the *Journals*, edited by Joyce Hemlow. I am indebted to these scholars for their commentary as well their texts.

British Literature 1640–1789: An Anthology, Fourth Edition. Edited by Robert DeMaria, Jr.

27–8 March 1777

Mrs. & Miss Thrale,[1] Miss Owen[2] & Mr. Seward[3] came long before *Lexiphanes*;[4] – Mrs. Thrale is a very pretty woman still, she is extremely lively and chatty, – has no supercilious or pedantic airs, & is really gay and agreeable. Her Daughter is about 12 years old, &, I believe, not altogether so amiable as her mother. Miss Owen, who is a Relation, is good humoured & sensible *enough*; she is a sort of *Butt*, & as such, a general favourite: for those sort of characters are prodigiously useful in drawing out the Wit & pleasantry of others: Mr. Seward is a very polite, agreeable young man:

My sister was invited to meet, & play, to them.

The Conversation was supported with a good deal of vivacity – (N.B. my Father being at Home) for about half an Hour, & then Hetty, & *Suzette*, for the first time *in public*, played a Duet, &, in the midst of this performance, Dr. Johnson was announced.

He is, indeed, very ill favoured, – he is tall & stout, but stoops terribly, – he is almost bent double. His mouth is in perpetual motion, as if he was chewing; – he has a strange method of frequently twirling his Fingers, & twisting his Hands; – his Body is in continual agitation, *see sawing* up & down; his Feet are never a moment quiet, – &, in short, his whole person is in perpetual motion:

His Dress, too, considering the Times, & that he had meant to put on his best becomes,[5] being engaged to Dine in a large Company, was as much out of the common Road as his Figure: he had a large Wig, snuff colour coat, & Gold Buttons; but no Ruffles to his Wrist, & Black Worsted Stockings – so, you see, there is another *Worsted Stocking Knave*, besides me, – that's my comfort.

He is shockingly near sighted, & did not, till she held out her Hand to him, even know Mrs. Thrale. He *poked his Nose* over the keys of the Harpsichord, till the Duet was finished, & then, my Father introduced Hetty to him, as an old acquaintance,[6] & he instantly kissed her.

His attention, however, was not to be diverted five minutes from the Books, as we were in the Library; he pored over them, almost brushing the Backs of them, with his Eyelashes, as he read their Titles; at last, having fixed upon one, he began, without further ceremony, to Read, all the time standing at a distance from the Company. We were very much provoked, as we perfectly languished to hear him talk; but, it seems, he is the most silent creature, when not particularly drawn out, in the World.

My sister then played another Duet, with my Father: but Dr. Johnson was so deep in the Encyclopédie, that, as he is very deaf, I question if he ever knew what was going forward. When this was over, Mrs. Thrale, in a laughing manner, said, 'Pray, Dr. Burney, can you tell me what that song was, & whose, which Savoi sung last night at

Notes

FROM *JOURNALS AND LETTERS*

1 *Mrs. & Miss Thrale* Hester Lynch Thrale (1741–1821), perhaps Johnson's closest friend until the death of her husband and her subsequent marriage to Gabriel Piozzi (see the selection from her correspondence above) and her daughter Hester Maria (Queeney).

2 *Miss Owen* Margaret (1743–1816).

3 *Mr. Seward* William (1747–99), compiler of *Anecdotes of Some Distinguished Persons* (1795–7).

4 *Lexiphanes* a name taken from a Roman satire by Lucian and applied to Samuel Johnson by James Callender (1758–1803).

5 *best becomes* most attractive clothes.

6 *Hetty* Hester Maria Thrale, Johnson's god-daughter and much more than a mere acquaintance.

Bach's[7] Concert, & which you did not hear?' My Father confessed himself by no means a good Diviner, not having Time to consult the stars, though in the House of Sir Isaac Newton.[8] However, wishing to draw Dr. Johnson in some Conversation, he told him the Question. The Doctor, seeing his drift, good naturedly put away his Book, & said very drolly 'And pray, Sir – *Who is Bach*? – is he a Piper?' – Many exclamations of surprise, you will believe, followed this Question. 'Why you have Read his name often in the papers', said Mrs. Thrale; & then gave him some account of his Concert, & the number of fine performances she had heard at it.

'Pray', said he, 'Madam, what is the Expense?'

'O', answered she, 'much trouble & solicitation to get a subscriber's Ticket; – or else half a Guinea'.[9]

'Trouble and solicitation', said he, 'I will have nothing to do with; – but I would be willing to give Eighteen Pence'.

Chocolate being then brought, we adjourned to the Dining Room. And here, Dr. Johnson, being taken from the Books, entered freely & most cleverly into conversation: though it is remarkable, that he never speaks at all, but when spoken to; nor does he ever *start*, though he so admirably supports any *subject*.

The whole party was engaged to Dine at Mrs. Montague's:[10] Dr. Johnson said he had received the most flattering note he had ever read, or anybody else had ever Read, by way of invitation. 'Well, so have, I, too', cried Mrs. Thrale, 'so if a note from Mrs. Montague is to be boasted of, I beg mine may not be forgot'.

'Your note', cried Dr. Johnson, 'can bear no comparison with *mine*; – I am *at the Head of Philosophers*; she says'.

'And I', cried Mrs. Thrale, '*have all the muses in my Train*!'

'A fair Battle', said my Father; 'come, Compliment for Compliment, & see who will hold out longest'.

'O, I am afraid for Mrs. Thrale!' cried Mr. Seward, 'for I know Mrs. Montague exerts all her forces when she attacks Dr. Johnson'.

'O yes', said Mrs. Thrale, 'she has often, I know, flattered *him* till he has been ready to Faint'.

'Well, Ladies', said my Father, 'You must get him between you to Day, & see which can lay on the paint thickest, Mrs. Thrale or Mrs. Montague'.

'I had rather', cried the Doctor, 'go to Bach's Concert!'

After this, they talked of Mr. Garrick,[11] & his late Exhibition before the King, to whom, & the Queen & Royal Family, he read Lethe,[12] *in character, c'est á dire*,[13] in different Voices, & Theatrically. Mr. Seward gave us an account of a Fable, which Mr. Garrick had written, by way of Prologue, or Introduction, upon the occasion: In this, he says, that a Black Bird, grown old & feeble, droops his Wings, &c, &c, & gives up singing; but, being called upon by the Eagle, his Voice recovers its powers, his spirits revive, he sets age at defiance, & sings better than ever. The application is obvious.

'There is not', said Dr. Johnson, 'much of the spirit of *Fabulosity* in this Fable; for the call of an *Eagle* never yet had much tendency to restore the voice of a *Black Bird*! 'Tis

Notes

[7] *Bach* Johann Christian (1735–82), the "London Bach," son of the great Johann Sebastian Bach.

[8] *Newton* The Burneys lived in the house in St. Martin's Street where Isaac Newton lived and died.

[9] *Guinea* twenty-one shillings, £1.05; half a guinea at this time would be worth about £100 or $180 now.

[10] *Mrs. Montague* Elizabeth (1720–1800), author and socialite.

[11] *Garrick* David (1717–79), greatest actor of his time and one of Johnson's oldest friends.

[12] *Lethe* (1740), a one-act farce by Garrick himself.

[13] *in character, c'est á dire* "in character, that is to say…"

true, the Fabulists frequently make the *Wolves* converse with the *Lambs*, – but, when the conversation is over, the *Lambs* are sure to be Eaten! – & so, the *Eagle* may entertain the *Black Bird*, – but the entertainment always ends in a *Feast* for the Eagles!'

'They say', cried Mrs. Thrale, 'that Garrick was extremely hurt by the coolness of the King's applause, & did not find his reception such as he expected'.

'He has been so long accustomed', said Mr. Seward, 'to the Thundering approbation of the Theatre, that a mere *very well*, must necessarily & naturally disappoint him'.

'Sir', said Dr. Johnson, 'he should not, in a Royal apartment, expect the hallooing & clamour of the one shilling gallery. The King, I doubt not, gave him as much applause as was rationally his due: &, indeed, great & uncommon as is the merit of Mr. Garrick, no man will be bold enough to assert that he has not his just proportion both of Fame & Profit: he has long reigned the unequalled favourite of the public, – & therefore, nobody will mourn his hard fate, if the King, & the Royal Family, were not transported into rapture, upon hearing him Read Lethe. Yet, Mr. Garrick will complain to his Friends, & his Friends will lament the King's want of feeling & taste; – then, Mr. Garrick will *excuse* the King! he will say that he might be thinking of something else; – that the affairs of America might occur to him, – or some subject of more importance than Lethe; – but though he will say this himself, he will not forgive his Friends, if they do not contradict him!'

But now, that I have written this *satire*, it is but just both to Mr. Garrick, & Dr. Johnson, to tell you what he said of him afterwards, when he discriminated his character with equal candour & humour.

'Garrick', said he, 'is accused of vanity; – but few men would have borne such unremitting prosperity with greater, if with equal moderation: he is accused, too, of avarice, – but, were he not, he would be accused of just the contrary, for he now lives rather as a *prince*, than as an Actor: but the frugality he practised when he first appeared in the World, & which, even then, was perhaps beyond his necessity, has marked his character ever since; & now, though his Table, his Equipage, & manner of Living, are all the most expensive, and equal to those of a Nobleman, yet the original stain still blots his name, – though, had he not fixed upon himself the charge of Avarice, he would, long since, have been reproached with *luxury*, & with living beyond his station in magnificence & splendour'.

Another Time, he said of him, 'Garrick never enters a Room, but he regards himself as the object of general attention, & from whom the Entertainment of the Company is expected, & true it is, that he seldom disappoints them; for he has infinite humour, a very just proportion of Wit, & more convivial pleasantry than almost any other man.

But then, off, as well as *on* the stage, he is always an Actor! for he thinks it so incumbent upon him to be supportive, that his gaiety becomes mechanical, as it is habitual, & [he] can exert his spirits at all Times alike, without consulting his real Disposition to hilarity'. . . .

22 March 1812

To Esther Burney[14]

Separated as I have now so long – long been from my dearest Father – BROTHERS – SISTERS – NIECES, & NATIVE FRIENDS, I would spare, at least, their kind hearts any grief for me but what they must inevitably feel in reflecting upon the sorrow of

Notes

[14] *Esther Burney* (1749–1832), Frances's sister.

such an absence to one so tenderly attached to all her first and for-ever so dear & regretted ties – nevertheless, if they should hear that I have been dangerously ill from any hand but my own, they might have doubts of my perfect recovery which my own alone can obviate. And how can I hope they will escape hearing what has reached Seville to the South, and Constantinople to the East? from both I have had messages – yet nothing could urge me to this communication till I heard that M. de Boinville had written it to his Wife, without any precaution, because in ignorance of my plan of silence. Still I must hope it may never travel to my dearest Father – But to You, my beloved Esther, who, living more in the World, will surely hear it ere long, to you I will write the whole history, certain that, from the moment you know any evil has befallen me your kind kind heart will be constantly anxious to learn its extent, & its circumstances, as well as its termination.

About August, in the year 1810, I began to be annoyed by a small pain in my breast, which went on augmenting from week to week, yet, being rather heavy than acute, without causing me any uneasiness with respect to consequences: Alas, '*what was the ignorance?*' The most sympathising of Partners, however, was more disturbed: not a start, not a wry face, not a movement that indicated pain was unobserved, & he early conceived apprehensions to which I was a stranger. He pressed me to see some Surgeon; I revolted from the idea, & hoped, by care & warmth, to make all succour unnecessary. Thus passed some months, during which Madame de Maisonneuve, my particularly intimate friend, joined with M. d'Arblay[15] to press me to consent to an examination. I thought their fears groundless, and could not make so great a conquest over my repugnance. I relate this false confidence, now, as a warning to my dear Esther – my Sisters & Nieces, should any similar sensations excite similar alarm. M. d'A. now revealed his uneasiness to another of our kind friends, Mad. de Tracy, who wrote to me a long & eloquent Letter upon the subject, that began to awaken very unpleasant surmises; & a conference with her ensued, in which her urgency & representations, aided by her long experience of disease, & most miserable existence by art, subdued me, and, most painfully & reluctantly, I ceased to object, & M. d'A. summoned a physician – 'M. Bourdois?' Maria will cry; – No, my dear Maria, I would not give your beau frere that trouble; not him, but Dr. Jouart, the physician of Miss Potts. Thinking but slightly of my statement, he gave me some directions that produced no fruit – on the contrary, I grew worse, & M. d'A. now would take no denial to my consulting M. Dubois, who had already attended and cured me in an abscess of which Maria, my dearest Esther, can give you the history. M. Dubois, the most celebrated surgeon of France, was then appointed accoucheur[16] to the Empress, & already lodged in the Tuileries,[17] & in constant attendance: but nothing could slacken the ardour of M. d'A. to obtain the first advice. Fortunately for his kind wishes, M. Dubois had retained a partial regard for me from the time of his former attendance, &, when applied to through a third person, he took the first moment of liberty, granted by a *promenade* taken by the Empress, to come to me. It was now I began to perceive my real danger, M. Dubois gave me a prescription to be pursued for a month, during which time he could not undertake to see me again, & pronounced nothing – but uttered so many charges to me to be tranquil, & to suffer no uneasiness, that I could not but suspect there was room for terrible inquietude. My alarm was increased by the non-appearance of M. d'A. after his departure. They had

Notes

[15] *M. d'Arblay* Alexandre-Jean-Baptiste Piochard d'Arblay (1754–1818), Burney's husband.

[16] *accoucheur* male midwife, obstetrician.

[17] *Tuileries* French royal palace adjacent to the Louvre in Paris.

remained together some time in the Book room, & M. d'A. did not return – till, unable to bear the suspense, I begged him to come back. He, also, sought then to tranquillize me – but in words only; his looks were shocking! his features, his whole face displayed the bitterest woe. I had not, therefore, much difficulty in telling myself what he endeavoured not to tell me – that a small operation would be necessary to avert evil consequences! – Ah, my dearest Esther, for this I felt no courage – my dread and repugnance, from a thousand reasons *besides* the pain, almost shook all my faculties, &, for some time, I was rather confounded & stupefied than affrighted. – Direful, however, was the effect of this interview; the pains became quicker & more violent, & the hardness of the spot affected increased. I took, but vainly, my prescription, & every symptom grew more serious. At this time, M. de Narbonne spoke to M. d'A. of a Surgeon of great eminence, M. Larrey, who had cured a *polonaise*[18] lady of his acquaintance of a similar malady; & as my horror of an operation was insuperable, M. de N. strongly recommended that I should have recourse to M. Larrey. I thankfully caught at any hope; & another friend of M. d'A. gave the same counsel at the same instant, which other, M. Barbier Neuville, has an influence irresistible over this M. Larrey, to whom he wrote the most earnest injunction that he would use every exertion to rescue me from what I so much dreaded. M. Larrey came, though very unwillingly, & full of scruples concerning M. Dubois; nor would he give me his services till I wrote myself to state my affright at the delay of attendance occasioned by the present high office & royal confinement of M. Dubois, & requesting that I might be made over to M. Larrey. An answer such as might be expected arrived, & I was now put upon a new *regime*, & animated by the fairest hopes. – M. Larrey has proved one of the worthiest, most disinterested, & singularly excellent of men, endowed with real Genius in his profession, though with an ignorance of the World & its usages that induces a *naiveté* that leads those who do not see him thoroughly to think him not alone simple, but weak. They are mistaken; but his attention and thoughts having exclusively turned one way, he is hardly awake any other. His directions seemed all to succeed, for though I had still cruel seizures of terrible pain, the fits were shorter & more rare, & my spirits revived, & I went out almost daily, & quite daily received in my Apartment some friend or intimate acquaintance, contrarily to my usual mode of *sauvagerie*[19] – and what friends I have found! what kind, consoling, zealous friends during all this painful period! In fine,[20] I was much better, & every symptom of alarm abated. My good M. Larrey was enchanted, yet so anxious, that he forced me to see le Docteur Ribe, the first anatomist, he said, in France, from his own fear lest he was under any delusion, from the excess of his desire to save me. I was as rebellious to the first visit of this famous anatomist as Maria will tell you I had been to that of M. Dubois, so odious to me was this sort of process: however, I was obliged to submit: & M. Ribe confirmed our best hopes – – Here, my dearest Esther, I must grow brief, for my theme becomes less pleasant – Sundry circumstances, too long to detail, combined to counter-act all my flattering expectations, & all the skill, & all the cares of my assiduous & excellent Surgeon. The principal of these evils were – the death, broke to me by a newspaper! of the lovely & loved P[rincess] Amelia – the illness of her venerated Father – & the sudden loss of my nearly adored – my Susan's nearly worshipped Mr. Locke[21] – which terrible calamity reached me in *a few lines* from Fanny Waddington, when I knew not of any illness or fear! – Oh my Esther, I must indeed here be brief, for I am not yet strong enough for sorrow. – The good M. Larrey, when he came to me next

Notes

[18] *polonaise* Polish.

[19] *sauvagerie* wildness, incivility.

[20] *In fine* in brief,

[21] *Mr. Locke* William (1732–1810), a close friend of the family.

after the last of these trials, was quite thrown into a consternation, so changed he found all for the worse – 'Et qu'est il donc arrivé?'[22] he cried, & presently, sadly announced his hope of dissolving the hardness were nearly extinguished. M. Ribe was now again called in – but he only corroborated the terrible judgement: yet they allowed to my pleadings some further essays,[23] & the more easily as the weather was not propitious to any operation. My Exercise, at this time, though always useful & cheering occasioned me great suffering in its conclusion, from mounting up three pair of stairs: my tenderest Partner, therefore, removed me to La Rue de Mirmenil, where I began my Paris residence nearly 10 years ago! – *quite* 10 next Month! Here we are! *au premier*[24] – but alas – to no effect! once only have I yet descended the short flight of steps from which I had entertained new hopes. A Physician was now called in, Dr. Moreau, to hear if he could suggest any new means: but Dr. Larrey had left him no resources untried. A formal consultation now was held, of Larrey, Ribe, & Moreau – &, in fine, I was formally condemned to an operation by all Three. I was as much astonished as disappointed – for the poor breast was no where discoloured, & not much larger than its healthy neighbour. Yet I felt the evil to be deep, so deep, that I often thought if it could not be dissolved, it could only with life be extirpated. I called up, however, all the reason I possessed, or could assume, & told them – that if they saw no other alternative, I would not resist their opinion & experience: – the good Dr. Larrey, who, during his long attendance had conceived for me the warmest friendship, had now tears in his Eyes; from my dread he had expected resistance. He proposed again calling in M. Dubois. No, I told him, if I could not by himself be saved, I had no sort of hope elsewhere, &, if it must be, what I wanted in courage should be supplied by his Confidence. The good man was now dissatisfied with himself, and declared I ought to have the First and most eminent advice his Country could afford; '*Vous êtes si considerée, Madame*', said he, '*ici que le public même sera mécontent si vous n'avez pas tout le secours que nous avons à vous offrir*'.[25] – Yet this modest man is premier chirugien de la Garde Imperiale, & had been lately created a Baron for his eminent services! – M. Dubois, he added, from his super-skill & experience, might yet, perhaps, suggest some cure. This conquered me quickly, ah – Send for him! Send for him! I cried – & Dr. Moreau received the commission to consult with him. – What an interval was this! Yet my poor M. d'A. was more to be pitied than myself, though he knew not the terrible idea I had internally annexed to the trial – but Oh what he suffered! – & with what exquisite tenderness he solaced all I had to bear! My poor Alex[26] I kept as much as possible, and as long, ignorant of my situation. – M. Dubois behaved extremely well, no pique intervened with the interest he had professed in my well-doing, & his conduct was manly & generous. It was difficult still to see him, but he appointed the earliest day in his power for a general & final consultation. I was informed of it only on the Same day, to avoid useless agitation. He met here Drs. Larrey, Ribe, & Moreau. The case, I saw, offered uncommon difficulties, or presented eminent danger, but, the examination over, they desired to consult together. I left them – what an half hour I passed alone! – M. d'A. was at his office. Dr. Larrey then came to summon me. He did not speak, but looked very like my dear Brother James, to whom he has a personal resemblance that has struck M. d'A. as well as myself. I came back, & took my seat, with what calmness I was able. All were silent, & Dr. Larrey, I saw, hid himself nearly behind my Sofa. My

Notes

22 *Et qu'est il donc arrivé?* "And what's happened here?"
23 *essays* attempts, efforts.
24 *au premier* on the first floor, one flight above the ground floor.
25 *Vous êtes ... offrir* "You are so highly regarded, Madame, that here even the public will be displeased if you do not have all the assistance that we can offer you."
26 *Alex* her seventeen-year-old son.

heart beat fast: I saw all hope was over. I called upon them to speak. M. Dubois then, after a long & unintelligible harangue, from his own disturbance, pronounced my doom. I now saw it was inevitable, and abstained from any further effort. They received my formal consent, & retired to fix a day.

All hope of escaping this evil being now at an end, I could only console or employ my Mind in considering how to render it less dreadful to M. d'A. M. Dubois had pronounced *'il faut s'attendre à souffrir; Je ne veux pas vous trompez – Vous Souffrirez – vous souffrirez beaucoup!'*[27] – M. Ribe had *charged* me to cry! to withhold or restrain myself might have seriously bad consequences, he said. M. Moreau, in echoing this injunction, enquired whether I had cried or screamed at the birth of Alexander – Alas, I told him, it had not been possible to do otherwise; Oh then, he answered, there is no fear! – What terrible inferences were here to be drawn! I desired, therefore, that M. d'A. might be kept in ignorance of the day till the operation should be over. To this they agreed, except M. Larrey, with high approbation: M. Larrey looked dissentient, but was silent. M. Dubois protested he would not undertake to act, after what he had seen of the agitated spirits of M. d'A. if he were present: nor would he suffer me to know the time myself over night; I obtained with difficulty a promise of 4 hours' warning, which were essential to me for sundry regulations.

From this time, I assumed the best spirits in my power, *to meet the coming blow*; – & support my too sympathising Partner. They would let me make no preparations, refusing to inform me what would be necessary; I have known, since, that Mad. de Tessé, an admirable old friend of M. d'A., now mine, equally, & one of the first of her sex, in any country, for uncommon abilities, & nearly universal knowledge, had insisted upon sending all that might be necessary, & of keeping me in ignorance. M. d'A. filled a Closet with Charpie,[28] compresses, & bandages – All that to *me* was owned, as wanting, was an arm Chair & some Towels. – Many things, however, joined to the depth of my pains, assured me the business was not without danger. I therefore made my Will – unknown, to this moment, to M. d'A., & entrusted it privately to M. La Tour Maubourg, without even letting my friend his Sister, Mad. de Maisonneuve, share the secret. M. de M. conveyed it for me to Maria's excellent M. Gillet, from whom M. de M. brought me directions. As soon as I am able to go out I shall reveal this clandestine affair to M. d'A. – till then, it might still affect him. Mad. de Maisonneuve desired to be present at the operation; but I would not inflict such pain. M. de Chastel belle sœur to Mad. de Boinville, would also have sustained the shock; but I secured two Guards, one of whom is known to my two dear Charlottes, Ma. Soubiren, portière to l'Hotel Marengo: a very good Creature, who often amuses me by repeating *'ver. vell, Mawm;'* which she tells me she learnt of Charlotte the younger whom she never names but with rapture. The other is a workwoman whom I have often employed. The kindness I received at this period would have made me for-ever love France, had I hitherto been hard enough of heart to hate it – but Mad. d'Henin – the tenderness she showed me surpasses all description. Twice she came to Paris from the Country, to see, watch & sit with me; there is nothing that can be suggested of use or comfort that she omitted. She loves me not only from her kind heart, but also from her love of Mrs. Locke, often, often exclaiming 'Ah! si votre angelique amie étoit ici!–'[29] But I must force myself from these episodes, though my dearest Esther will not think them *de trop*.[30]

Notes

[27] *il faut … beaucoup* "you must expect pain; I do not wish to deceive you – you will suffer – you will suffer a great deal."

[28] *Charpie* unravelled linen.

[29] *si votre angelique amie étoit ici*! "If only your angelic friend were here!"

[30] *de trop* too much, excessive.

After sentence thus passed, I was in hourly expectation of a summons to execution; judge, then, my surprise to be suffered to go on full 3 Weeks in the same state! M. Larrey from time to time visited me, but pronounced nothing, & was always melancholy. At length, M. d'A. was told that he waited himself for a Summons! & that, a formal one, & in writing! *I* could not give one. A *consent* was my utmost effort. But poor M. d'A. wrote a desire that the operation, if necessary, might take place without further delay. In my own mind, I had all this time been persuaded there were hopes of a cure: why else, I thought, let me know my doom thus long? But here I must account for this apparently useless, & therefore cruel measure, though I only learnt it myself 2 months afterward. M. Dubois had given his opinion that the evil was too far advanced for any remedy; that the cancer was already internally declared; that I was inevitably destined to that most frightful of deaths, & that an operation would but accelerate my dissolution. Poor M. Larrey was so deeply affected by this sentence, that – as he has lately told me, – he regretted to his Soul ever having known me, & was upon the point of demanding a commission to the furthest end of France in order to force me into other hands. I had said, however, he remembered, once, that I would far rather suffer a quick end without, than a lingering life with this dreadfullest of maladies: he finally, therefore, considered it might be possible to save me by the trial, but that without it my case was desperate, & resolved to make the attempt. Nevertheless, the responsibility was too great to rest upon his own head entirely; & therefore he waited for the formal summons. – In fine, One morning – the last of September, 1811, while I was still in Bed, & M. d'A. was arranging some papers for his office, I received a letter written by M. de Lally to a Journalist, in vindication of the honoured memory of his Father against the assertions of Mad. du Deffand. I read it aloud to My Alexanders, with tears of admiration and sympathy, & then sent it by Alex: to its excellent Author, as I had promised the preceding evening. I then dressed, aided, as usual for many months, by my maid, my right arm being condemned to total inaction; but not yet was the grand business over, when another Letter was delivered to me – another, indeed! – 'twas from M. Larrey, to acquaint me that at 10 o'clock he should be with me, properly accompanied, & to exhort me to rely as much upon his sensibility & his prudence, as upon his dexterity & his experience; he charged to secure the absence of M. d'A.: & told me that the young Physician who would deliver me this *annonce*, would prepare for the operation, in which he must lend his aid: & also that it had been the decision of the consultation to allow me but two hours' notice. – Judge, my Esther, if I read this unmoved! – yet I had to disguise my sensations & intentions from M. d'A.! – Dr. Aumont, the Messenger & terrible Herald, was in waiting; M. d'A. stood by my bed side; I affected to be long reading the Note, to gain time for forming some plan, & such was my terror of involving M. d'A. in the unavailing wretchedness of witnessing what I must go through, that it conquered every other, & gave me the force to act as if I were directing some third person. The detail would be too *Wordy*, as James[31] says, but *wholesale* is – I called Alex to my Bed side, & sent him to inform M. Barbier Neuville, chef du division du Bureau de M. d'A. that *the moment was come*, & entreated him to write a summons upon urgent business for M. d'A. & to detain him till all should be over. Speechless & appalled, off went Alex, &, as I have since heard, was forced to sit down & sob in executing his commission. I then, by the Maid, sent word to the young Dr. Aumont that I could not be ready till one o'clock: and finished my breakfast, & not with much appetite, you will

Notes

[31] *James* her brother (1750–1821), a rear admiral in the Navy.

believe! forced down a crust of bread, & hurried off, under various pretences, M. d'A. He was scarcely gone, when M. Dubois arrived: I renewed my request for one o'clock: the rest came; all were fain to consent to the delay, for I had an apartment to prepare for my banished Mate. The arrangement, & those for myself, occupied me completely. Two engaged nurses were out of the way – I had a bed, Curtains, & heaven knows what to prepare – but business was good for my nerves, I was obliged to quit my room to have it put in order: – Dr. Aumont would not leave the house; he remained in the Salon, folding linen! – He had demanded 4 or 5 old & fine left off under Garments – I glided to our Book Cabinet: sundry necessary works and orders filled up my time entirely till One O'clock, When all was ready – – but Dr. Moreau then arrived, with news that M. Dubois could not attend till three. Dr. Aumont went away & the Coast was clear. This indeed, was a dreadful interval. I had no longer any thing to do – I had only to think – TWO HOURS thus spent seemed never-ending. I would fain have written to my dearest Father – to You, my Esther – to Charlotte James Charles – Amelia Locke – but my arm prohibited me: I strolled to the Salon – I saw it fitted with preparations, & I recoiled – But I soon returned; to what effect disguise from myself what I must so soon know? – yet the sight of the immense quantity of bandages, compresses, sponges, Lint – – Made me a little sick: – I walked backwards & forwards till I quieted all emotion, & became, by degrees, nearly stupid – torpid, without sentiment or consciousness; – & thus I remained till the Clock struck three. A sudden spirit of exertion then returned, – I defied my poor arm, no longer worth sparing, & took my long banished pen to write a few words to M. d'A. – & a few more for Alex, in case of a fatal result. These short billets I could only deposit safely, when the Cabriolets[32] – one – two – three – four – succeeded rapidly to each other in stopping at the door. Dr. Moreau instantly entered my room, to see if I were alive. He gave me a wine cordial, & went to the Salon. I rang for my maid & Nurses, – but before I could speak to them, my room, without previous message, was entered by 7 Men in black, Dr. Larry, M. Dubois, Dr. Moreau, Dr. Aumont, Dr. Ribe, & a pupil of Dr. Larry, & another of M. Dubois. I was now awakened from my stupor – & by sort of indignation – Why so many? & without leave? – But I could not utter a syllable. M. Dubois acted as Commander in Chief. Dr. Larry kept out of sight; M. Dubois ordered a Bed stead into the middle of the room. Astonished, I turned to Dr. Larry, who had promised that an Arm Chair would suffice; but he hung his head, & would not look at me. Two *old mattrasses* M. Dubois then demanded, & an old Sheet. I now began to tremble violently, more with distaste & horror of the preparations even than of the pain. These arranged to his liking, he desired me to mount the Bed stead. I stood suspended, for a moment, whether I should not abruptly escape – I looked at the door, the windows – I felt desperate – but it was only for a moment, my reason then took command, & my fears & feelings struggled vainly against it. I called to my maid – she was crying, & the two Nurses stood, transfixed, at the door. Let those women all go! cried M. Dubois. This order recovered me my Voice – No, I cried, let them stay! *qu'elles restent*! This occasioned a little dispute, that re-animated me – The Maid, however, & one of the nurses ran off – I chid the other to approach, & she obeyed. M. Dubois now tried to issue his commands *en militaire*, but I resisted all that were resistible – I was compelled, however, to submit to taking off my robe de Chambre, which I had meant to retain – Ah, then, how did I think of My Sisters! – not one, at so dreadful an instant, at hand, to

Notes

[32] *Cabriolets* carriages.

protect – adjust – guard me – I regretted that I had refused Madam de Maisonneuve – Madam Chastel – no one upon whom I could rely – my departed Angel! – how did I think of her! – how did I long – long for my Esther – my Charlotte! – My distress was, I suppose, apparent, though not my Wishes, for M. Dubois himself now softened, & spoke soothing. 'Can *You*', I cried, 'feel for an operation that, to *You* must seem so trivial?' – 'Trivial?' he repeated – taking up a bit of paper, which he tore, unconsciously, into a million pieces, *'oui – c'est peu de chose – mais –'*[33] he stammered, & could not go on. No one else attempted to speak, but I was softened myself, when I saw even M. Dubois grow agitated, while Dr. Larrey kept always aloof, yet a glance showed me he was pale as ashes. I knew not, positively, then, the immediate danger, but every thing convinced me danger was hovering about me, & that this experiment could alone save me from its jaws. I mounted, therefore, unbidden, the Bed stead – & M. Dubois placed me upon the Mattress, & spread a cambric handkerchief upon my face. It was transparent, however, & I saw, through it, that the Bed stead was instantly surrounded by the 7 men & my nurse. I refused to be held; but when, Bright through the cambric, I saw the glitter of polished Steel – I closed my Eyes. I would not trust to convulsive fear the sight of the terrible incision. A silence the most profound ensued, which lasted for some minutes, during which, I imagine, they took their orders by signs, & made their examination – Oh what a horrible suspension! – I did not breathe – & M. Dubois tried vainly to find any pulse. This pause, at length, was broken by Dr. Larry, who in a voice of solemn melancholy, said *'Qui me tiendra ce sein? –'*[34]

No one answered; at least not verbally; but this aroused me from my passively submissive state, for I feared they imagined the whole breast infected – feared it too justly, – for, again through the Cambric, I saw the hand of M. Dubois held up, while his fore finger first described a straight line from the top to bottom of the breast, secondly a Cross, & thirdly a circle; intimating that the WHOLE was to be taken off. Excited by this idea, I started up, threw off my veil, &, in answer to the demand *'Qui me tiendra ce sein'*? cried *'C'est moi, Monsieur!'* & I held My hand under it, & explained the nature of my sufferings, which all sprang from one point, though they darted into every part. I was heard attentively, but in utter silence, & M. Dubois then re-placed me as before, &, as before, spread my veil over my face. How vain, alas, my representation! immediately again I saw the fatal finger describe the Cross – & the circle – Hopeless, then, desperate, & self-given up, I closed once more my Eyes, relinquishing all watching, all resistance, all interference, & sadly resolute to be wholly resigned.

My dearest Esther, – & all my dears to whom she communicates this doleful ditty, will rejoice to hear that this resolution once taken, was firmly adhered to, in defiance of a terror that surpasses all description, & the most torturing pain. Yet – when the dreadful steel was plunged into the breast – cutting through veins – arteries – flesh – nerves – I needed no injunctions not to restrain my cries. I began a scream that lasted unintermittingly during the whole time of the incision – & I almost marvel that it rings not in my Ears still! so excruciating was the agony. When the wound was made, & the instrument was withdrawn, the pain seemed undiminished, for the air that suddenly rushed into those delicate parts felt like a mass of minute but sharp & forked poniards, that were tearing the edges of the wound – but when again I felt the instrument – describing a curve – cutting against the grain, if I may so say, while the flesh resisted in a manner so forcible to change from the right to the left – then, indeed, I thought

Notes

[33] *oui – c'est peu de chose – mais* – "Yes, it is a little thing, but . . . "

[34] *Qui me tiendra ce sein?* "Who will take this breast for me?"

I must have expired. I attempted no more to open my Eyes, – they felt as if hermetically shut, & so firmly closed, that the Eyelids seemed indented into the Cheeks. The instrument this second time withdrawn, I concluded the operation over – Oh no! presently the terrible cutting was renewed – & worse than ever, to separate the bottom, the foundation of this dreadful gland from the parts to which it adhered – Again all description would be baffled – yet again all was not over, – Dr. Larrey rested but his own hand, & – Oh Heaven! – I then felt the Knife rackling against the breast bone – scraping it! – This performed, while I yet remained in utterly speechless torture, I heard the Voice of Mr. Larrey, – (all others guarded a dead silence) in a tone nearly tragic, desire every one present to pronounce if any thing more remained to be done; The general voice was Yes, – but the finger of Mr. Dubois – which I literally *felt* elevated over the wound, though I saw nothing, & though he touched nothing, so indescribably sensitive was the spot – pointed to some further requisition – & again began the scraping! – and, after this, Dr. Moreau thought he discerned a peccant atom – My dearest Esther, not for days, not for Weeks, but for Months I could not speak of this terrible business without nearly again going through it! I could not *think* of it with impunity! I was sick, I was disordered by a single question – even now, 9 months after it is over, I have a head ache from going on with the account! & this miserable account, which I began 3 Months ago, at least, I dare not revise, nor read, the recollection is still so painful.

To conclude, the evil was so profound, the case so delicate, & the precautions necessary for preventing a return so numerous, that the operation, including the treatment & dressing, lasted 20 minutes! a time, for sufferings so acute, that was hardly supportable – However, I bore it with all the courage I could exert, & never moved, nor stopped them, nor resisted, nor remonstrated, nor spoke – except once or twice, during the dressings, to say '*Ah Messieurs! que je vous plains*! –'[35] for indeed I was sensible to the feeling concern with which they all saw what I endured, though my speech was principally – *very* principally meant for Dr. Larrey. Except this, I uttered not a syllable, save, when they so often recommenced, calling out '*Avertissez moi, Messieurs! avertissez moi*! –'[36] Twice, I believe, I fainted; at least, I have two total chasms in my memory of this transaction, that impede my tying together what passed. When all was done, & they lifted me up that I might be put to bed, my strength was so totally annihilated, that I was obliged to be carried, & could not even sustain my hands & arms, which hung as if I had been lifeless; while my face, as the Nurse has told me, was utterly colourless. This removal made me open my Eyes – & I then saw my good Dr. Larrey, pale nearly as myself, his face streaked with blood, & its expression depicting grief, apprehension, & almost horror.

When I was in bed, – my poor M. d'Arblay – who ought to write you himself his own history of this Morning – was called to me – & afterwards our Alex. –

[d'Arblay's addition follows]

No! No my dearest & ever more dear friends, I shall not make a fruitless attempt. No language could convey what I felt in the deadly course of these seven hours. Nevertheless, every one *of you, my dearest dearest friends*, can guess must even know it. Alexandre had no less feeling, but showed more fortitude. He, perhaps, will be more able to describe you, nearly at least, the torturing state of my poor heart and soul. Besides, I must own, to you, that these details which were, till just now, quite unknown

Notes

[35] *que je vous plains*! "how I pity you!"

[36] *Avertissez moi, Messieurs! avertissez moi*! "Warn me, good sirs! Warn me!"

to me, have almost killed me, & I am only able to thank God that this more than half Angel has had the sublime courage to deny herself the comfort I might have offered her, to spare me, not the sharing of her excruciating pains, that was impossible, but the witnessing so terrific a scene, & perhaps the remorse to have rendered it more tragic. For I don't flatter my self I could have gotten through it – I must confess it.

Thank Heaven! She is now surprisingly well, & in good spirits, & we hope to have many still happy days. May that of peace soon arrive, and enable me to embrace better than with my pen beloved & ever ever more dear friends of the town & country. Amen. Amen!

[Burney proceeds]

God bless my dearest Esther – I fear this is all written confusedly, but I cannot read it – & I can write it no more, therefore I entreat you to let all my dear Brethren male & female take a perusal – and that you will lend it also to my tender & most beloved Mrs. Angerstein, who will pardon, I well know, my sparing myself – which is sparing her, a separate letter upon such a theme. My dearest Father & my dearest Mrs. Locke live so little in the world, that I flatter myself they will never hear of this adventure. I earnestly desire it may never reach them. My kind Miss Cambridge & Miss Baker, also, may easily escape it. I leave all others, & all else, to your own decision.

I ought to have mentioned Sarah[37] when I regretted & sighed for my Sisters, for I am sure she would gladly & affectionately have nursed me had she been at hand: but at that critical moment I only thought of those who had already – & so often – had opportunity as well as Soul to demonstrate their tenderness. – and She who is gone[38] is ever, & on all occasions, still present to me. Adieu, adieu, my beloved Esther –

P.S. I have promised my dearest Esther a Volume – & here it is: I am at this moment quite Well – So are my Alexanders. Read, therefore, this Narrative at your leisure, & without emotion – for all has ended happily. I will send the rest by the very first opportunity: I seize this present with eagerness oh let none – none pass by that may bring me a return! – I have no more yet written.

Enquire means to write to me, my Esther, and All my dears, in pity.

I have not had a Word since the noble packet of M. Wurst!

Notes

[37] *Sarah* Burney's half-sister.

[38] *She who is gone* Burney's mother, Esther, died in 1762.

Ann Cromartie Yearsley (1753–1806)

Married to a poor laborer in Bristol, Yearsley was a genuinely poor milkmaid when she was "discovered" by Hannah More. Like Stephen Duck, "the thresher poet," a few generations before, Yearsley, "a milkwoman of Bristol," rose to instant fame. More groomed her work and financed the publication of her *Poems on Several Occasions* (1785), to which 1,000 purchasers subscribed. Unfortunately, the kind of regular clerical living into which his patrons thrust Duck was unavailable to Yearsley, and More, with the help of Elizabeth Montagu, cobbled together a financial arrangement that seemed to Yearsley a form of perpetual dependency. She broke with More, got control of the money from the publication, and later opened a circulating library. She eventually secured another patron and published two more volumes of poetry, a play, and a four-volume novel, as well as several occasional poems.

Yearsley's work displays a curious combination of the overblown and the conventional melting into a language of romantic self-expression. She certainly lacks the polish and sophistication of many "transitional" poets, yet there is a fierce personal pride and a vigor in her self-expression that a better sense of poetic tradition might have suppressed. All of Yearsley's poems are available through the Brown University Women Writers Project. There is a study of Yearsley by Mary Waldron called *Lactilla, Milkwoman of Clifton* (University of Georgia Press, 1996). My text of "On Mrs. Montagu" is based on *Poems on Several Occasions* (1785), and I take the other two pieces from *Poems on Various Subjects* (1787). The *Collected Works* have been edited by Kerri Andrews (3 vols., Pickering and Chatto, 2014).

from *Poems on Several Occasions* (1785)

On Mrs. Montagu[1]

Why boast, O arrogant, imperious man,
Perfection so exclusive? are thy powers
Nearer approaching Deity? can'st thou solve
Questions which high Infinity propounds,
Soar nobler flights, or dare immortal deeds,
Unknown to woman, if she greatly dares
To use the powers assigned her? Active strength,
The boast of animals, is clearly thine;
By this upheld, thou think'st the lesson rare
That female virtues teach; and poor the height
Which female wit obtains. The theme unfolds
Its ample maze, for MONTAGU befriends

Notes

ON MRS. MONTAGU

[1] *Mrs. Montagu* Elizabeth (1720–1800), writer, socialite, and patron of many women writers; she and Hannah More were Yearsley's patrons.

The puzzled thought, and, blazing in the eye
Of boldest Opposition, straight presents
The soul's best energies, her keenest powers,
Clear, vigorous, enlightened; with firm wing
Swift she o'ertakes *his* Muse, which spread afar
Its brightest glories in the days of yore;
Lo! where she, mounting, spurns the steadfast earth,
And, sailing on the cloud of science, bears[2]
The banner of Perfection. –
Ask GALLIA's mimic sons how strong her powers,
Whom, flushed with plunder from her SHAKESPEARE's page,[3]
She swift detects amid their dark retreats;
(Horrid as CACUS in their thievish dens)[4]
Regains the trophies, bears in triumph back
The pilfered glories to a wond'ring world.
So STELLA boasts, from her tale I learned;[5]
With pride she told it, I with rapture heard.
O, MONTAGU! forgive me, if I sing
Thy wisdom tempered with the milder ray
Of soft humanity, and kindness bland:
So wide its influence, that the bright beams
Reach the low vale where mists of ignorance lodge,
Strike on the innate spark which lay immersed,
Thick clogged, and almost quenched in total night –
On me it fell, and cheered my joyless heart.
Unwelcome is the first bright dawn of light
To that dark soul; impatient, she rejects,
And fain would push the heavenly stranger back;
She loathes the cranny which admits the day;
Confused, afraid of the intruding guest;
Disturbed, unwilling to receive the beam,
Which to herself the native darkness shows.
The effort rude to quench the cheering flame
Was mine, and e'en on STELLA could I gaze
With sullen envy, and admiring pride,
Till, doubly roused by MONTAGU, the pair
Conspire to clear my dull, imprisoned sense,
And chase the mists which dimmed my visual beam.
Oft as I trod my native wilds alone,
Strong gusts of thought would rise, but rise to die;
The portals of the swelling soul ne'er oped
By liberal converse, rude ideas strove
Awhile for vent, but found it not, and died.
Thus rust the Mind's best powers. Yon starry orbs,

Notes

2 *science* knowledge.

3 *her SHAKESPEARE's page* Montagu wrote *An Essay on the Writings and Genius of Shakespeare* (1769), in which she defended the bard from the criticisms of Voltaire and argued his superiority to Gallic (i.e., French) writers.

4 *CACUS* a fire-breathing monster who dragged some of Hercules' cattle into his cave; Hercules recovered the cattle and killed the beast.

5 *STELLA* Hannah More (1745–1833); Yearsley's most important patron, who also helped her improve her writing (see selection above).

Majestic ocean, flowery vales, gay groves,
Eye-wasting lawns, and Heaven-attempting hills,
Which bound th' horizons, and which curb the view;
All those, with beauteous imagery, awaked
My ravished soul to ecstasy untaught,
To all the transport the rapt sense can bear;
But all expired, for want of powers to speak;
All perished in the mind as soon as born,
Erased more quick than ciphers on the shore,
O'er which the cruel waves, unheedful, roll.
Such timid rapture as young EDWIN seized,[6]
When his lone footsteps on the Sage obtrude,
Whose noble precept charmed his wondering[7]
Such rapture filled Lactilla's vacant soul,
When the bright Moralist, in softness dressed,[8]
Opes all the glories of the mental world,
Deigns to direct the infant thought, to prune
The budding sentiment, uprear the stalk
Of feeble fancy, bid idea live,
Woo the abstracted spirit from its cares,
And gently guide her to the scenes of peace.
Mine was that balm, and mine the grateful heart,
Which breathes its thanks in rough, but timid strains.

from *Poems on Various Subjects* (1787)

To Indifference

INDIFFERENCE come! thy torpid juices shed
On my keen sense: plunge deep my wounded heart,
In thickest apathy, till it congeal,
Or mix with thee incorp'rate. Come, thou foe
To sharp sensation, in thy cold embrace
A death-like slumber shall a respite give
To my long restless soul, tossed on extreme,
From bliss to pointed woe. Oh, gentle Pow'r,
Dear substitute of Patience! thou canst ease
The Soldier's toil, the gloomy Captive's chain,
The Lover's anguish, and the Miser's fear.
Proud Beauty will not own thee! *her* loud boast
Is VIRTUE – while thy chilling breath alone
Blows o'er her soul, bidding her passions sleep.
Mistaken *Cause*, the frozen Fair denies
Thy saving influence. VIRTUE never lives,
But in thy bosom, struggling with its wound:

Notes

[6] *young EDWIN* see *The Minstrel* [(1771–4) by James Beattie; Yearsley's note].

[7] *Lactilla* Yearsley's poetical name for herself, based on the Latin word for milk, because she was a milkmaid.

[8] *bright Moralist* More.

There she supports the conflict, *there* augments
The pang of *hopeless Love*, the senseless stab
Of gaudy Ign'rance, and more deeply drives
The poisoned dart, hurled by the long-loved friend;
Then pants with painful Victory. Bear me hence,
Thou antidote to pain! thy real worth
Mortals can never know. What's the vain boast
Of Sensibility but to be wretched?
In *her* best transports lives a latent sting,
Which wounds as they expire. On her high heights
Our souls can never sit; the point so nice,
We quick fly off – secure, but in descent.
To SENSIBILITY, what is not bliss
Is woe. No placid medium's ever held
Beneath her torrid line, when straining high
The fibres of the soul. Of Pain, or Joy,
She gives too large a share; but thou, more kind,
Wrapp'st up the heart from both, and bidd'st it rest
In ever-wished-for ease. By all the pow'rs
Which move within the mind for different ends,
I'd rather lose myself with *thee*, and share
Thine happy indolence, for one short hour,
Than live of Sensibility the tool
For endless ages. Oh! her points have pierced
My soul, till, like a sponge, it drinks up woe.
Then leave me, Sensibility! be gone,
Thou chequered angel! Seek the soul refined:
I hate thee! and thy long progressive brood
Of joys and mis'ries. Soft Indifference, come!
In this low cottage thou shalt be my guest,
Till Death shuts out the hour: here down I'll sink
With thee upon my couch of homely rush,
Which fading forms of Friendship, Love, or Hope,
Must ne'er approach. Ah! – quickly hide, thou pow'r,
Those dear intruding images! Oh, seal
The lids of mental sight, lest I abjure
My freezing supplication.– All is still.
IDEA, smothered, leaves my mind a waste,
Where SENSIBILITY must lose her prey.

To those who accuse the Author of Ingratitude[1]

You, who through optics dim, so falsely view
This wondrous maze of things, and rend a part
From the well-ordered whole, to fit your sense

Notes

TO THOSE WHO ACCUSE THE AUTHOR

1 *Ingratitude* written after Yearsley broke with More, who had invested some £350 in her; Yearsley was widely and angrily denounced.

Low, grovelling, and confined; say from what source
Spring your all-wise opinions? Can you dare
Pronounce from proof, who ne'er pursued event
To its minutest cause? Yet further soar,
In swift gradation, to the verge of space;
Where, wrapped in worlds, Time's origin exists:
There breathe your question; there the cause explore,
Why dark afflictions, borne upon the wing
Of Love invisible, light on the wretch
Inured and patient in the pangs of woe?
Or Wisdom infinite with Pride arraign;
Rebuke the Deity, and madly ask,
Why Man's sad hour of anguish ever ends?
What are your boasts, ye incapacious souls,
Who would confine, within your narrow orbs,
Th' extensive All? Can sense, like yours, discern
An object, wand'ring from her destined course,
Quitting the purer path, where spirit roves,
To sip Mortality's soul-clogging dews,
And feast on Craft's poor dregs? What though she owned
An office, would have borne her to the stars
While list'ning Angels had the plaudit hailed,
And blessed her force of soul, unequal proved
Her strongest pow'rs, to top fair Virtue's height,
Or, on the act, to fix the stamp of *Merit*.
What's noosed opinion but a creeping curse,
That leads the Idiot through yon beaten track,
When keener spirits ask it? Which of you
Dare, on the wing of Candour, stretch afar
To seize the bright sublimity of Truth?
A wish to share the false, though public din,
In which the popular, not virtuous, live;
A fear of being singular, which claims
A fortitude of mind you ne'er could boast;
A love of base detraction, when the charm
Sits on a flowing tongue, and willing moves
Upon its darling topic. These are yours.
But were the steadfast adamantine pow'rs
Of Principle unmoved? Fantastic group!
Spread wide your arms and turn yon flaming Sun
From his most fair direction; dash the stars
With Earth's poor pebbles, and ask the World's great Sire,
Why, in Creation's system, HE dare fix
More orbs than your weak sense shall e'er discern?
Then scan the feelings of Lactilla's soul.

William Blake (1757–1827)

Blake is one of the figures in British literary history who tend to reveal the inadequacy of academic categories. He was more an artist than a poet, but he blended the two in ways that make it impossible to separate his contributions to the two fields; he was startlingly original and yet an immense amount of his work consists in the designs and engravings he produced to illustrate works by others; his political views were radical and he celebrated the French Revolution, but he was devout, inspired, and anti-rationalistic in religion; his work is obscure and apparently dependent on his own personal system of thought, and yet one of the greatest critics of the twentieth century, Northrop Frye, spent the better part of a lifetime showing how profoundly conventional Blake is. Given these larger paradoxes, it is not surprising that it is difficult to locate Blake in one or another of the intellectual currents that were crossing each other at the end of the eighteenth century. He is certainly an important Romantic poet, but his romanticism harks back to Milton and certain kinds of Protestant radicalism that flourished during the interregnum. As E. P. Thompson has shown, Blake was a Muggletonian, a follower of a man who proclaimed himself a prophet in 1651 and preached a radical form of Arianism: he believed God to be completely unitary, even in body, and he believed in a great multiplicity of prophets. Blake himself had visions and regarded his prophetic leanings almost casually, although he could be vociferous in his criticism of those whom he accused of stifling prophecy or the holy imagination. He led a life of continuous, imaginative productivity; the large amount of work that survives is only a fraction of what Blake produced.

Blake's poetry has been edited by David Erdman in one large volume (1965; rev. University of California Press, 1981) and by G. E. Bentley in two volumes, one for the engraved and etched writings and one for those in conventional typography (Clarendon Press, 1978). In addition there are numerous wonderful reprints of his engraved works. *Songs of Innocence* was his first entirely homemade book. He drew the poems and their surrounding illustrations on copper plates, from which he printed his colored pages; his wife assisted him in printing, tinting, and binding the books. A few years later the two produced the companion book *Songs of Experience*. Blake's notion is that these are parallel aspects of life that must be passed through on the way to revelation. But, like so much of Blake's work, the *Songs* have an appeal that goes beyond their place in Blake's or anyone else's explanatory system. The texts here are based on editions made in the first year of printing, though I have been a little freer than usual in adding useful punctuation. The poems should be appreciated in their pictorial context in one or more of the numerous facsimiles that have been produced or on the website blakearchive.org.

from *Songs of Innocence* (1789)

Introduction

Piping down the valleys wild
Piping songs of pleasant glee
On a cloud I saw a child.
And he laughing said to me.

British Literature 1640–1789: An Anthology, Fourth Edition. Edited by Robert DeMaria, Jr.

'Pipe a song about a Lamb!'
So I piped with merry cheer,
'Piper pipe that song again' –
So I piped, he wept to hear.

'Drop thy pipe thy happy pipe;
Sing thy songs of happy cheer',
So I sung the same again
While he wept with joy to hear.

'Piper sit thee down and write
In a book, that all may read' –
So he vanished from my sight,
And I plucked a hollow reed.

And I made a rural pen,
And I stained the water clear,
And I wrote my happy songs,
Every child may joy to hear.

The Lamb

Little Lamb who made thee?
Dost thou know who made thee,
Gave thee life & bid thee feed,
By the stream & o'er the mead;
Gave thee clothing of delight,
Softest clothing woolly bright;
Gave thee such a tender voice,
Making all the vales rejoice?
Little Lamb, who made thee?
Dost thou know who made thee?
Little Lamb I'll tell thee
Little Lamb I'll tell thee;
He is callèd by thy name,[1]
For he calls himself a Lamb:
He is meek & he is mild,
He became a little child:
I a child & thou a lamb,
We are called by his name.
Little Lamb, God bless thee,
Little Lamb, God bless thee.

Notes

FROM *SONGS OF INNOCENCE*

[1] *He* Christ, called the Lamb of God (John 1.29).

The Little Black Boy

My mother bore me in the southern wild,
And I am black, but O! my soul is white,
White as an angel is the English child:
But I am black as if bereaved of light.

My mother taught me underneath a tree
And sitting down before the heat of day,
She took me on her lap and kissèd me,
And pointing to the east, began to say,

'Look on the rising sun: there God does live
And gives his light, and gives his heat away
And flowers and trees and beasts and men receive
Comfort in morning joy in the noon day.

'And we are put on earth a little space,
That we may learn to bear the beams of love.
And these black bodies and this sun-burnt face
Is but a cloud, and like a shady grove.

'For when our souls have learned the heat to bear,
The cloud will vanish, we shall hear his voice,
Saying: "Come out from the grove my love & care,
And round my golden tent like lambs rejoice" '

Thus did my mother say and kissèd me,
And thus I say to little English boy.
When I from black and he from white cloud free,
And round the tent of God like lambs we joy:

I'll shade him from the heat till he can bear,
To lean in joy upon our father's knee.
And then I'll stand and stroke his silver hair,
And be like him and he will then love me.

The Chimney Sweeper

When my mother died I was very young,
And my father sold me while yet my tongue,
Could scarcely cry 'weep weep weep weep'.
So your chimneys I sweep & in soot I sleep.

There's little Tom Dacre, who cried when his head
That curled like a lamb's back, was shaved, so I said,
'Hush Tom never mind it, for when your head's bare,
You know that the soot cannot spoil your white hair'.

And so he was quiet, & that very night,
As Tom was a sleeping, he had such a sight,

That thousands of sweepers Dick, Joe, Ned & Jack
Were all of them locked up in coffins of black,

And by came an Angel who had a bright key,
And he opened the coffins & set them all free.
Then down a green plain leaping laughing they run
And wash in a river, and shine in the Sun.

Then naked and white, all their bags left behind,
They rise upon clouds, and sport in the wind.
And the Angel told Tom, if he'd be a good boy,
He'd have God for his father & never want joy.

And so Tom awoke and we rose in the dark,
And got with our bags & our brushes to work.
Though the morning was cold, Tom was happy & warm;
So if all do their duty, they need not fear harm.

Holy Thursday

'Twas on a Holy Thursday their innocent faces clean
The children walking two & two in red & blue & green;
Grey headed beadles walked before with wands as white as snow[2]
Till into the high dome of Paul's they like Thames' waters flow.[3]

O what a multitude they seemed these flowers of London town;
Seated in companies they sit with radiance all their own;
The hum of multitudes was there but multitudes of lambs,
Thousands of little boys & girls raising their innocent hands.

Now like a mighty wind they raise to heaven the voice of song
Or like harmonious thunderings the seats of heaven among;
Beneath them sit the aged men, wise guardians of the poor;
Then cherish pity; lest you drive an angel from your door.

Infant Joy

'I have no name
I am but two days old'. –
What shall I call thee?
'I happy am
Joy is my name', –
Sweet joy befall thee!

Notes

[2] *beadles* ceremonial church officers.
[3] *Paul's* St. Paul's Cathedral, London.

Pretty joy!
Sweet joy but two days old.
Sweet joy I call thee:
Thou dost smile.
I sing the while
Sweet joy befall thee.

from *Songs of Experience* (1794)

Introduction

Hear the voice of the Bard!
Who Present, Past, and Future, sees
Whose ears have heard,
The Holy Word,
That walked among the ancient trees.

Calling the lapsèd Soul
And weeping in the evening dew:
That might control
The starry pole:[1]
And fallen fallen light renew!

O Earth, O Earth return!
Arise from out the dewy grass;
Night is worn,
And the morn
Rises from the slumberous mass.

Turn away no more:
Why wilt thou turn away?
The starry floor
The wat'ry shore
Is giv'n thee till the break of day.

Holy Thursday

Is this a holy thing to see,
In a rich and fruitful land,
Babes reduced to misery,
Fed with cold and usurous hand?

Is that trembling cry a song?
Can it be a song of joy?

Notes

FROM *SONGS OF EXPERIENCE*
[1] *pole* sky.

And so many children poor?
It is a land of poverty!

And their sun does never shine.
And their fields are bleak & bare,
And their ways are filled with thorns
It is eternal winter there.

For where-e'er the sun does shine,
And where-e'er the rain does fall:
Babe can never hunger there,
Nor poverty the mind appal.

The Chimney Sweeper

A little black thing among the snow:
Crying weep! weep! in notes of woe!
Where are thy father & mother? say?
They are both gone up to the church to pray.

Because I was happy upon the heath,
And smiled among the winter's snow:
They clothed me in the clothes of death,
And taught me to sing the notes of woe.

And because I am happy, & dance & sing,
They think they have done me no injury:
And are gone to praise God & his Priest & King,
Who make up a heaven of our misery.

The Tyger

Tyger, Tyger, burning bright,
In the forests of the night;
What immortal hand or eye,
Could frame thy fearful symmetry?

In what distant deeps or skies,
Burnt the fire of thine eyes?
On what wings dare he aspire?
What the hand dare seize the fire?

And what shoulder, & what art,
Could twist the sinews of thy heart?
And when thy heart began to beat,
What dread hand? & what dread feet?
What the hammer? what the chain?
In what furnace was thy brain?

What the anvil? what dread grasp,
Dare its deadly terrors clasp?

When the stars threw down their spears
And watered heaven with their tears:
Did he smile his work to see?
Did he who made the Lamb make thee?

Tyger, Tyger, burning bright
In the forests of the night:
What immortal hand or eye,
Dare frame thy fearful symmetry?

Ah! Sun-Flower

Ah, Sun-flower! weary of time,
Who countest the steps of the Sun:
Seeking after that sweet golden clime,
Where the traveller's journey is done.

Where the Youth pined away with desire,
And the pale Virgin shrouded in snow:
Arise from their graves and aspire,
Where my Sun-flower wishes to go.

Robert Burns (1759–1796)

There were certainly earlier poets who wrote successfully in the Scottish dialect of English. Allan Ramsay in the early eighteenth century was important (see selection above), and there had been a real flowering around 1500 with Robert Henryson, Gavin Douglas, and William Dunbar all writing at the same time. Robert Fergusson's (1750–74) poems in vernacular Scots were a key influence. But despite his meager education and his struggles with poverty, whisky, and women, Burns surpassed them all. He hit the perfect medium between repetition and revision of the traditional songs and stories of his native land. He had a reputation for poetry and wild living as a youth and in his early days as a farmer in Ayrshire. Having had an illegitimate child with one woman, he attempted to marry another, Jean Armour, who was also pregnant by him. Her parents blocked him, and Burns was set to go to Jamaica for a fresh start. To fund the expedition, he published *Poems, Chiefly in the Scottish Dialect* in 1786. The work was such a success that Burns decided to stay home. He was lionized in Edinburgh, and there were several subsequent, expanded editions of his *Poems*. He also wrote poetry in standard, southern English, but this effort did not amount to much. Most of his best work had been written by 1787, and after that he spent a good deal of time traveling around Scotland collecting and somewhat creatively transcribing folk songs and tales for a large publishing project called *The Scots Musical Museum* (1787–1803).

To pay the bills, Burns, like Thomas Paine, worked as an excise man, gauging the volume of barrels of liquor and assessing a tax. This ran somewhat counter to his naturally rebellious tendencies; he publicly suppressed his enthusiasm for the French Revolution, but he could not control the opportunities to drink attendant upon his duties. Burns died in poverty at the age of thirty-seven from rheumatic fever.

The Poems and Songs of Robert Burns, edited by James Kinsley, 3 vols. (Clarendon Press, 1968), includes a glossary of Scottish words to which my notes to the following poems are deeply indebted. I take my texts from the edition of 1787, which came to hand; they vary only slightly from the first edition of 1786, which is preferable as a copy-text.

from *Poems, Chiefly in the Scottish Dialect* (1786)

Epistle to Davie, A Brother Poet[1]

January—

I

While winds frae off *Ben-Lomond* blaw,[2]
And bar the doors wi' driving snaw,
  And hing us owre the ingle,[3]

Notes

Epistle to Davie

[1] *Davie* David Sillar (1760–1830), author of *Poems* (1789).

[2] *Ben-Lomond* a mountain over 3,000 feet high in the central highlands of Scotland.

[3] *hing* make us hang; *ingle* fire in the hearth.

British Literature 1640–1789: An Anthology, Fourth Edition. Edited by Robert DeMaria, Jr.

I set me down, to pass the time,
And spin a verse or twa o' rhyme,
In hamely, *westlin* jingle.[4]
While frosty winds blaw in the drift,
Ben to the chimla lug,[5]
I grudge a wee the Great-folk's gift,
That live sae bien an' snug:[6]
I tent less, and want less[7]
Their roomy fire-side;
But hanker, and canker,[8]
To see their cursèd pride.

2

It's hardly in a body's pow'r,
To keep, at times, frae being sour,
To see how things are shared;
How best o' chiels are whyles in want,[9]
While Coofs on countless thousands rant,[10]
And ken na how to wair't:[11]
But *Davie*, lad, ne'er fash your head,[12]
Though we hae little gear,
We're fit to win our daily bread,
As lang's we're hale and fier:[13]
'Mair spier na, nor fear na',[14]
Auld age ne'er mind a feg;
The last o't, the warst o't,
Is only but to beg.

3

To lie in kilns and barns at e'en,[15]
When banes are crazed, and bluid is thin,
Is, doubtless, great distress!
Yet then content could make us blessed;
Ev'n then, sometimes we'd snatch a taste
Of truest happiness.
The honest heart that's free frae a'
Intended fraud or guile,
However Fortune kick the ba',
Has ay some cause to smile:
And mind still, you'll find still,

Notes

[4] *westlin* of the west lands.
[5] *Ben* within; *chimla lug* chimney corner.
[6] *bien* comfortable.
[7] *tent* care; mind.
[8] *hanker, and canker* mope and become peevish.
[9] *chiels* lads; *whyles* sometimes.
[10] *Coofs* louts, fools; *rant* make merry.
[11] *ken* know; *wair* spend.
[12] *fash* trouble.
[13] *fier* hearty.
[14] *'Mair spier na, nor fear na'* [Allan] Ramsay [Burns's note]; *spier* ask for, require.
[15] *kilns* places for drying grain.

A comfort this nae sma';
Nae mair then, we'll care then,
Nae farther we can fa'.

4

What though, like Commoners of air,[16]
We wander out, we know not where,
But either house or hal'?[17]
Yet Nature's charms, the hills and woods,
The sweeping vales, and foaming floods,
Are free alike to all.
In days when Daisies deck the ground,
And Blackbirds whistle clear,
With honest joy our hearts will bound,
To see the coming year:
On braes when we please, then,[18]
We'll sit and sowth a tune;[19]
Syne *rhyme* till't, we'll time till't,[20]
And sing't when we hae done.

5

It's no in titles nor in rank;
It's no in wealth like Lon'on Bank,
To purchase peace and rest;
It's no in makin muckle, *mair*:[21]
It's no in books, it's no in lear,[22]
To make us truly blessed:
If Happiness hae not her seat
And centre in the breast,
We may be wise, or rich, or great,
But never can be blessed:
Nae treasure nor pleasures
Could make us happy lang;
The *heart* ay's the part ay
That makes us right or wrang.

6

Think ye, that sic as you and I,
Wha drudge and drive through wet and dry,
Wi' never-ceasing toil;
Think ye, are we less blessed than they,
Wha scarcely tent us in their way,

Notes

[16] *Commoner* "One who has a joint right in the common ground" (Johnson, 1773).

[17] *But* without; *hal'* home.

[18] *braes* hillsides.

[19] *sowth* attempt to carry a tune with a low whistle.

[20] *Syne* then; *till 't* to it.

[21] *muckle* much, a great amount.

[22] *lear* learning.

As hardly worth their while?
Alas! how aft, in haughty mood,
GOD's creatures they oppress!
Or else, neglecting a' that's guid,
They riot in excess!
Baith careless and fearless
Of either Heaven or Hell;
Esteeming, and deeming
It's a' an idle tale!

7

Then let us cheerfu' acquiesce,
Nor make our scanty Pleasures less,
By pining at our state:
And, ev'n should Misfortunes come,
I here wha sit has met wi' some,
An's thankfu' for them yet.
They gie the wit of Age to Youth;
They let us ken oursel';
They make us see the naked truth,
The *real* guid and ill.
Though losses and crosses
Be lessons right severe,
There's wit there, ye'll get there,
Ye'll find nae other where.

8

But tent me, *Davie*, Ace o' Hearts!
(To say aught less wad wrang the cartes,[23]
And flatt'ry I detest)
This life has joys for you and I,
And joys that riches ne'er could buy,
And joys the very best.
There's a' the *Pleasures o' the Heart*,
The Lover an' the Frien';
Ye hae your *Meg*, your dearest part,
And I my darling *Jean*!
It warms me, it charms me,
To mention but her *name*:
It heats me, it beets me,[24]
And sets me a' on flame!

Notes

[23] *cartes* cards.

[24] *beets* kindles.

9

O all you Pow'rs who rule above!
O *Thou*, whose very self art *love!*
Thou know'st my words sincere!
The life-blood streaming through my heart,
Or my more dear Immortal part,
Is not more fondly dear!
When heart-corroding care and grief
Deprive my soul of rest,
Her dear idea brings relief,
And solace to my breast.
Thou *Being*, All-seeing,
O hear my fervent prayer!
Still take her, and make her
Thy most peculiar care!

10

All hail! ye tender feelings dear!
The smile of love, the friendly tear,
The sympathetic glow!
Long since, this world's thorny ways
Had numbered out my weary days,
Had it not been for you!
Fate still has blessed me with a friend,
In every care and ill;
And oft a more endearing band,
A tie more tender still.
It lightens, it brightens,
The tenebrific scene,[25]
To meet with, and greet with
My *Davie*, or my *Jean*!

11

O, how that *name* inspires my style!
The words come skelpin, rank and file,[26]
Amaist before I ken!
The ready measure rins as fine,
As Phœbus and the famous Nine[27]
Were glowrin owre my pen.[28]
My spaviet *Pegasus* will limp,[29]
Till ance he's fairly het;[30]

Notes

[25] *tenebrific* dark and gloomy.
[26] *skelpin* beating, striking.
[27] *Phœbus and the famous Nine* Apollo, god of poetry, and the muses.
[28] *glowrin* looking intently.
[29] *spaviet* spavined, stricken with an inflammation of the hock; *Pegasus* the winged horse inhabiting Mount Helicon, sacred to the muses; a symbol of the literary imagination.
[30] *het* heated up.

And then he'll hilch, and stilt, and jimp,[31]
And rin an unco fit:[32]
But least then the beast then[33]
Should rue this hasty ride,
I'll light now, and dight now[34]
His swaety, wizen'd hide.

To a Mouse, On turning her up in her Nest, with the Plough, November 1785

Wee, sleekit, cowrin, tim'rous beastie,[1]
O, what a panic's in thy breastie!
Thou need na start awa sae hasty,
Wi' bickering brattle![2]
I wad be laith to rin an' chase thee,
Wi' murd'ring *pattle*![3]

I'm truly sorry Man's dominion
Has broken Nature's social union,
An' justifies that ill opinion,
Which makes thee startle,
At me, thy poor, earth-born companion,
An' *fellow-mortal*!

I doubt na, whyles, but thou may thieve;[4]
What then? poor beastie, thou maun live![5]
A *daimen-icker* in a *thrave*[6]
'S a sma' request;
I'll get a blessin wi' the lave,[7]
An' never miss't!

Thy wee-bit *housie*, too, in ruin
Its silly wa's the win's are strewin![8]
An' naething, now, to big a new ane,[9]
O' foggage green![10]
An' bleak December's winds ensuin,
Baith snell an' keen![11]

Notes

[31] *hilch, and stilt, and jimp* lurch, and prance, and jump.
[32] *unco* strange.
[33] *least* lest.
[34] *dight* rub down.

To A Mouse
[1] *sleekit* sleek, glossy.
[2] *bickering* hurrying; *brattle* the sound of scampering feet.
[3] *pattle* a tool like a spade for removing earth from the plow.
[4] *whyles* sometimes.
[5] *maun* must.
[6] *daimen-icker in a thrave* an occasional ear of corn in two stooks of corn.
[7] *lave* the remainder.
[8] *silly wa's* weak walls.
[9] *big* build.
[10] *foggage* rank grass.
[11] *snell* bitter.

Thou saw the fields laid bare an' waste,
An' weary Winter comin fast,
An' cozie here, beneath the blast,
Thou thought to dwell,
Till crash! the cruel *coulter* passed[12]
Out through thy cell.

That wee-bit heap o' leaves an' stibble,
Has cost thee monie a weary nibble!
Now thou's turned out, for a' thy trouble,
But house or hald,[13]
To thole the Winter's sleety dribble,[14]
An cranreuch cauld![15]

But, Mousie, thou art no thy lane,[16]
In proving *foresight* may be vain:
The best-laid schemes o' *Mice* an' *Men*
Gang aft a-gley,[17]
An' lea'e us nought but grief an' pain,
For promised joy!

Still thou art blessed, compared wi' *me*!
The present only toucheth thee:
But, Och! I backward cast my e'e
On prospects drear!
An' forward, though I canna *see*,
I *guess* an' *fear*!

Address to the Deil

O Prince! O Chief of many thronèd Pow'rs,
That led th' embattled Seraphim to war—
MILTON[1]

O Thou! whatever title suit thee,
Auld Hornie, Satan, Nick, or Clootie,[2]
Wha in yon cavern grim an' sootie,
Closed under hatches,
Spairges about the brunstane cootie,[3]
To scaud poor wretches![4]

Notes

[12] *coulter* the vertical cutting blade of the plow.
[13] *But* without; *hald* home.
[14] *thole* endure.
[15] *cranreuch* hoarfrost.
[16] *thy lane* on your own.
[17] *a-gley* astray.

Address to the Deil
[1] *MILTON Paradise Lost* I.128–9.
[2] *Clootie* cloven-hoofed.
[3] *Spairges* sprinkles; *brunstane cootie* brimstone tub.
[4] *scaud* scald.

Hear me, auld *Hangie*, for a wee,[5]
An' let poor damnèd bodies be;
I'm sure sma' pleasures it can gie,
Ev'n to a *deil*,
To skelp an' scaud poor dogs like me,[6]
An' hear us squeel!

Great is thy pow'r, an' great thy fame;
Far kend an' rioted is thy name;[7]
An' though yon lowin heugh's thy hame,[8]
Thou travels far;
An' faith! thou's neither lag nor lame,
Nor blate nor scaur.[9]

Whyles, ranging like a roaring lion,[10]
For prey, a' holes an' corners tryin;
Whyles, on the strong-winged Tempest flyin,
Tirlin the kirks;[11]
Whyles, in the human bosom pryin,
Unseen thou lurks.

I've heard my reverend *Graunie* say,
In lanely glens ye like to stray;
Or where auld, ruined castles, grey,
Nod to the moon,
Ye fright the nightly wand'rer's way,
Wi' eldritch croon.[12]

When twilight did my *Graunie* summon,
To say her pray'rs, douce, honest woman![13]
Aft yont the dyke she's heard you bummin,[14]
Wi' eerie drone;
Or, rustlin, through the boortries comin,[15]
Wi' heavy groan.

Ae dreary, windy, winter night,[16]
The stars shot down wi' sklentin light,[17]
Wi' you, mysel, I gat a fright,
Ayont the lough;[18]
Ye, like a rash-buss, stood in sight,[19]
Wi' waving sugh.[20]

Notes

5 *Hangie* hangman.
6 *skelp* strike.
7 *kend* renowned.
8 *lowin heugh* flaming crag.
9 *blate* bashful; *scaur* frightened.
10 *Whyles* sometimes.
11 *Tirlin* stripping or rattling; *kirks* churches.
12 *eldritch croon* unearthly moan.
13 *douce* kindly, prudent.
14 *yont* beyond; *dyke* low dry-stone wall; *bumming* humming.
15 *boortries* the elders, a flowering shrub.
16 *Ae* one.
17 *sklentin* slanting, oblique.
18 *Ayont* beyond.
19 *rash-buss* clump of rushes.
20 *sugh* the rushing sound of wind.

The cudgel in my nieve did shake,[21]
Each bristled hair stood like a stake,
When wi' an eldritch, stoor quaick, quaick,[22]
Amang the springs,
Awa ye squattered like a drake,
On whistling wings.

Let *warlocks* grim, an' wither'd *hags*,
Tell how wi' you on ragweed nags,
They skim the muirs an' dizzy crages,[23]
Wi' wicked speed;
And in kirk-yards renew their leagues,
Ower howkit dead.[24]

Thence, countra wives, wi' toil an' pain,
May plunge an' plunge the kirn in vain;[25]
For, O! the yellow treasure's taen
By witching skill;
An' dawtit, twal-pint *Hawkie*'s gaen[26]
As yell's the Bill.[27]

Thence, mystic knots mak great abuse,
On young Guidmen, fond, keen, an' crouse;[28]
When the best wark-lume i' the house,[29]
By cantrip wit,[30]
Is instant made no worth a louse,
Just at the bit.[31]

When thowes dissolve the snawy hoord,
An' float the jinglin icy-boord,[32]
Then, *Water-kelpies* haunt the foord,[33]
By your direction,
An' nighted Trav'llers are allured
To their destruction.

An' aft your moss-traversing *Spunkies*[34]
Decoy the wight that late an' drunk is:
The bleezin, curst, mischievous monkies
Delude his eyes,
Till in some miry slough he sunk is,
Ne'er mair to rise.

Notes

21 *nieve* fist.
22 *stoor* harsh, hoarse.
23 *muirs* moors, bogs.
24 *howkit* exhumed.
25 *kirn* butter churn.
26 *dawtit* spoiled; *Hawkie* pet name for a cow.
27 *Bill* bull.
28 *crouse* self-confident.
29 *wark-lume* tool; penis.
30 *cantrip* witching.
31 *bit* crisis.
32 *icy-boord* sheet of ice.
33 *kelpies* demons.
34 *Spunkies* will o' the wisp, *ignis fatuus*, glowing marsh gas.

When *Masons'* mystic *word* an' *grip*,
In storms an' tempests raise you up,
Some cock or cat your rage maun stop,
Or, strange to tell!
The youngest Brother ye wad whip
Aff straught to h-ll.

Lang syne, in *Eden*'s bonny yard,[35]
When youthfu' lovers first were paired,
An' all the Soul of Love they shared,
The raptured hour,
Sweet on the fragrant, flow'ry swaird,
In shady bow'r:

Then you, ye auld, snick-drawing dog![36]
Ye cam to Paradise incog.[37]
An' played on man a cursed brogue,[38]
(Black be your fa'!)
An gied the infant warld a shog,[39]
Maist ruin'd a'.[40]

D'ye mind that day, when in a bizz,[41]
Wi' reekit duds, and reestit gizz,[42]
Ye did present your smoutie phiz,[43]
'Mang better folk,
An' sklented on the *man of Uz*[44]
Your spitefu' joke?

An' how ye gat him i' your thrall,
An' brak him out o' house an' hal',
While scabs an' botches did him gall,
Wi' bitter claw,
An' lowsed his ill-tongued, wicked Scawl,[45]
Was warst ava?[46]

But a' your doings to rehearse,
Your wily snares an' fechtin fierce,[47]
Sin' that day *Michael* did you pierce,[48]
Down to this time,
Wad ding a' Lallan tongue, or Erse,[49]
In prose or rhyme.

Notes

35 *syne* ago.
36 *snick-drawing* crafty.
37 *incog* incognito, in disguise.
38 *brogue* trick.
39 *shog* shock.
40 *Maist* almost.
41 *bizz* flurry.
42 *reekit* smoky; *duds* rags; *reestit* smoke-dried; *gizz* wig.
43 *phiz* face.
44 *man of Uz* Job.
45 *Scawl* scold, abusive woman.
46 *ava* of all.
47 *fechtin* fighting.
48 *Michael* stabs Satan in the war in Heaven (*Paradise Lost* 6.320–34).
49 *ding* tire out; *Lallan* Lowland Scots; *Erse* Highland Scots, Gaelic.

An' now, auld *Cloots*, I ken ye're thinkin,
A certain Bardie's rantin, drinkin,
Some luckless hour will send him linkin,[50]
To your black pit;
But, faith! he'll turn a corner jinkin,[51]
An' cheat you yet.

But, fare you weel, auld *Nickie-ben*!
O wad ye tak a thought an' men'!
Ye aiblins might – I dinna ken –[52]
Still hae a *stake* –
I'm wae to think upo' yon den,[53]
Ev'n for your sake!

Notes

[50] *linkin* skipping.
[51] *jinkin* dodging.
[52] *aiblins* perhaps.
[53] *wae* sad.

Mary Wollstonecraft (1759–1797)

With his drunken habits, his bullying, and his favoritism for his eldest son, Wollstonecraft's father sensitized his eldest daughter to the unequal place of women in British society. After the death of their mother in 1780, Mary took a great deal of responsibility for the support of her two sisters. She rescued the younger of the two from a hasty and apparently brutal marriage, and with a long-time friend the three started a school in Newington Green, site of the dissenters' academy which Defoe had attended and center of a community of progressive thinkers which included Richard Price, the minister whose sympathetic sermon had stimulated Burke to write his *Reflections on the Revolution in France*. After a couple of years of teaching, Wollstonecraft published a treatise called *Thoughts on the Education of Daughters*, published by Joseph Johnson in 1787. She then went to work for the London publisher. She wrote reviews, translated books, wrote some books for children, and compiled *The Female Reader*, an anthology for the education of women. She also wrote *A Vindication of the Rights of Men* (1790), the first of many replies to Burke's *Reflections*. She followed that with *A Vindication of the Rights of Woman* (1792), which is one of the most important documents in the history of feminist thought. She tried herself to live a life liberated from the ordinary restrictions placed on women. She was unlucky in love, however, falling first for the married artist Fuseli and then for a man named Imlay whose infidelities drove her to attempt suicide. Later she found intimacy with William Godwin, another progressive thinker, and though neither of them believed in the institution, they married in expectation of their daughter. Wollstonecraft died from complications in the birth of her child Mary, who later became Mary Shelley, the author of *Frankenstein*.

Wollstonecraft later went to France and was horrified by the excesses of the Revolution. Like Thomas Paine, she became a moderate among the French revolutionaries, but she was always decisive in her rejection of the old regime and the older romantic view of women that tended to miniaturize them spiritually and intellectually even when it placed them on pedestals of admiration. Wollstonecraft's works have been edited by Janet Todd and Marilyn Butler in seven volumes (New York University Press, 1989). The following excerpt from Wollstonecraft's first *Vindication* is based on the first edition.

from *A Vindication of the Rights of Men, in a Letter to the Right Honourable Edmund Burke; occasioned by his* Reflections on the Revolution in France (1790)

The only security of property that nature authorises and reason sanctions is, the right a man has to enjoy the acquisitions which his talents or industry have acquired; and happy would it be for the world if there was no other road to wealth or honour; if pride, in the shape of parental affection, did not absorb the man. Luxury and effeminacy would not then introduce so much idiotism into the noble families which form one of the pillars of our state. The ground would not lie fallow, nor would their activity of mind spread the contagion of idleness, and its concomitant vices, through the whole mass of society.

British Literature 1640–1789: An Anthology, Fourth Edition. Edited by Robert DeMaria, Jr.

Instead of gaming they might nourish a virtuous ambition, and love might take the place of the gallantry which you,[1] with knightly fealty, venerate. Women would then act like mothers, and the fine lady, become a rational woman, might superintend her family and suckle her children, in order to fulfil her part of the social compact. The unnatural vices, produced in the hot-bed of wealth, would then give place to natural affections, instead 'of losing half their evil by losing all their grossness.' – What a sentiment to come from a moral pen!

A surgeon would tell you that by skinning over a wound you spread disease through the whole frame; and, surely, they indirectly aim at destroying all purity of morals, who poison the very source of virtue, by smearing a sentimental varnish over vice to hide its natural deformity. Stealing, whoring, and drunkenness are gross vices, I presume, though they may not obliterate every moral sentiment, and have a vulgar brand that makes them appear with all their native deformity; but overreaching, adultery, and coquetry, are venial offences, though they reduce virtue to an empty name, and make wisdom consist in saving appearances.

'On this scheme of things[2] a king *is* but a man; a queen *is* but a woman; and woman is but an animal, and an animal not of the highest order.' – All true, Sir; if she is not more attentive to the duties of humanity than fashionable ladies and queens are in general. I will still further accede to the opinion you have so justly conceived of the spirit which begins to animate this age. – 'All homage paid to the sex in general, as such, and without distinct views, is to be regarded as *romance* and folly'. Undoubtedly; because such homage vitiates them, prevents their endeavouring to obtain solid personal merit; and, in short, makes those beings vain inconsiderate dolls, who ought to be prudent mothers and useful members of society. 'Regicide and sacrilege are but fictions of superstition corrupting jurisprudence, by destroying its simplicity. The murder of a king, or a queen, or a bishop, are only common homicide'. – Again I agree with you; but perceive, Sir, that by leaving out the word *father*, I think the comparison invidious. …

But it is not very extraordinary that *you* should, for throughout your letter you frequently advert to a sentimental jargon, which has long been current in conversation, and even in books of morals, though it never received the *regal* stamp of reason. A kind of mysterious instinct is *supposed* to reside in the soul, that instantaneously discerns truth, without the tedious labour of ratiocination. This instinct, for I know not what other name to give it, has been termed *common sense*, and more frequently *sensibility*; and, by a kind of *indefeasible* right, it has been *supposed*, for rights of this kind are not easily proved, to reign paramount over the other faculties of the mind, and to be an authority from which there is no appeal.

This subtle magnetic fluid, that runs around the whole circle of society, is not subject to any known rule, or, to use an obnoxious phrase, in spite of the sneers of mock humility, or the timid fears of well-meaning Christians, who shrink from any freedom of thought, lest they should rouse the old serpent, to the *eternal fitness of things*. It dips, we know not why, granting it to be an infallible instinct, and, though supposed always to the point to truth, its pole-star; the point is always shifting, and seldom stands due north. …

Notes

FROM A VINDICATION OF THE RIGHTS OF MEN

[1] *you* Edmund Burke, to whom the essay is addressed, in answer to his *Reflections on the Revolution in France* (see the selection above [p. 1004] for Wollstonecraft's citations of Burke's essay).

[2] *"On this scheme of things…"* As you ironically observe [Wollstonecraft's note].

Where is the dignity, the infallibility of sensibility, in the fair ladies, whom, if the voice of rumour is to be credited, the captive negroes curse in all agony of bodily pain, for the unheard of tortures they invent? It is probable that some of them, after a flagellation, compose their ruffled spirits and exercise their tender feelings by the perusal of the last new novel. – How true these tears are to nature, I leave you to determine. But these ladies may have read your Enquiries concerning the origin of the Sublime and the Beautiful,[3] and, convinced by your arguments, have laboured to be pretty, by counterfeiting weakness.

You may have convinced them that *littleness* and weakness are the very essence of beauty; and that the Supreme Being, in giving women beauty in the most supereminent degree, seemed to command them, by the powerful voice of Nature, not to cultivate the moral virtues that might chance to excite respect, and interfere with the pleasing sensations they were created to inspire. Confining thus truth, fortitude, and humanity, within the rigid pale of manly morals, they might justly argue, that to be loved, woman's high end and great distinction! they should 'learn to lisp, to totter in the walk', and nick-name God's creatures.[4] Never, they might repeat after you, was any man, much less a woman, rendered amiable by the force of those exalted qualities, fortitude, justice, wisdom, and truth; and thus forewarned of the sacrifice they must make to those austere, unnatural virtues, they would be authorised to turn all their attention to their persons, systematically neglecting morals to secure beauty. …

Notes

[3] *Enquiries concerning the origin of the Sublime and the Beautiful* see above, p. 998.

[4] Cf. Hamlet to Ophelia, III.i.145–7: "You jig and amble, and you lisp; you nickname God's creatures and make your wantonness your ignorance."

Index of Titles and First Lines

British Literature 1640–1789: An Anthology, Fourth Edition. Edited by Robert DeMaria, Jr.

Index to the Introductions and Footnotes

British Literature 1640–1789: An Anthology, Fourth Edition. Edited by Robert DeMaria, Jr.

Printed in the USA/Agawam, MA
August 5, 2022
796561.002